BRITISH WOMEN ARTISTS

A Biographical Dictionary of 1,000 Women Artists in the British Decorative Arts

Dr Sara Gray

DARK
RIVER

An imprint of Bennion Kearny

Published by Dark River, an imprint of Bennion Kearny Limited

6 Woodside, Churnet View Road,

Oakamoor,

ST10 3AE

United Kingdom

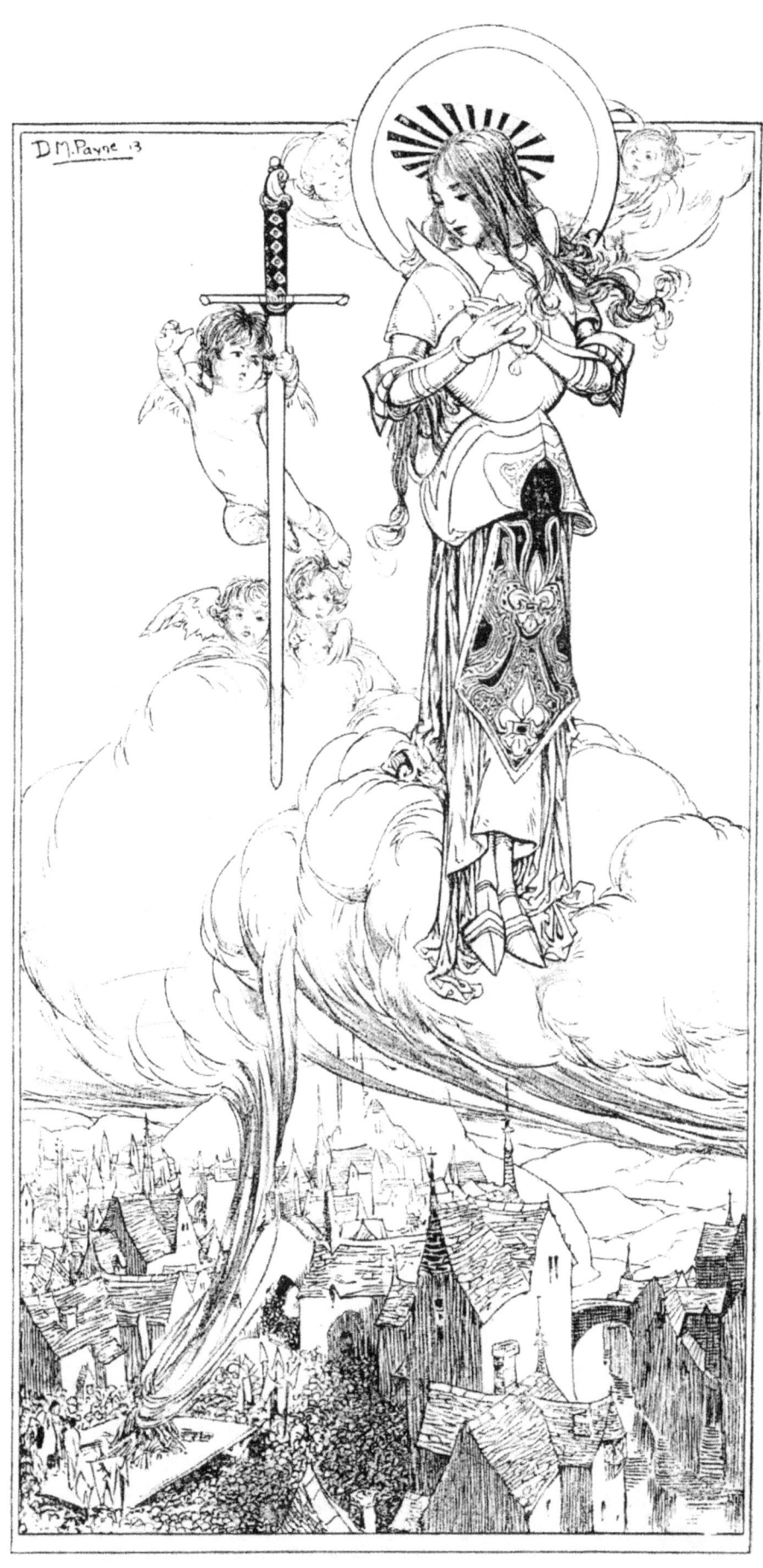

Joan of Arc by Dorothy M. Payne

PREFACE

Charting the history of women in the British decorative arts is akin to attempting an enormous and complex jigsaw. Some of the pieces are lost, irretrievable; some are still missing; some are only recently rediscovered; and some have long been known about. Creating an overall picture that makes clear sense is, therefore, a considerable task.

In the past, some attempts have been made to record something of the history of British women artists and decorative artists, most notably by Mrs Ellet in her *Women Artists of All Ages and Countries* (London, Bentley, 1859), and by Ellen C. Clayton in her *English Female Artists* (London, Tinsley, 1876). Although Ellet discusses women from around the world, she makes some effort to include some of the earliest British active women such as Mary Beale, Anne Killigrew and Diana Beauclerk. She also refers to the then recently founded Society of Female Artists (later the Society of Lady Artists, then the Society of Women Artists), and lists some of its earliest members. Some of those earliest members included Elizabeth Murray who published *Sixteen Years of an Artist's Life*. Ellet concluded that, up to 1859, it was extremely rare for a woman to make the conscious decision to be an artist – of any sort – for a living.

By 1876, some 17 years later, considerable changes had taken place in British art and design. Now, there were noticeably more women actively studying art and the decorative arts, with more art schools and formal tuition available, and more women exhibiting their work at home and abroad. Clayton gives what was possibly the first comprehensive written account of English women artists as a whole, beginning with the very earliest in the seventeenth century, concluding with some of the then very latest such as Ellen Vernon, Linnie Watt, Marie Spartali and Lucy Madox Brown. Clayton similarly draws attention to the Society of Lady Artists, and includes a number of sculptors and decorative artists as well as painters. Over two volumes, she reaffirms the significant contributions made by women to British art over several centuries, concluding that their general omission from the history books was due, in part, to a lack of effort on the part of historians.

In 1904, Clara Erskine Clement's volume *Women in the Fine Arts* (New York, The Riverside Press) was published in America, in which she followed Ellet's example, discussing women from around the world. Some of the featured artists were British, such as Jane Dealy, Helen Allingham, Louise Jopling and Elizabeth Stanhope Forbes. The significance of Clement's work, however, lies in the fact that she also chose to include more British women active in the broader decorative arts. Beginning with Hester Inglis, who decorated manuscripts at the turn of the seventeenth century, Clement moved on to modern sculptors and decorative artists such as Ellen Rope, Ruby Levick and Mary Grant. Evidently, as the twentieth century dawned, there was increasing recognition that women in Britain were making more positive contributions to art, but also to the broader decorative arts.

That was only reaffirmed further with the publication of Walter Shaw Sparrow's volume *Women Painters of the World* (London, Hodder & Stoughton) in 1905. Sparrow devoted one chapter to early British women artists, and another to modern. Like Clement, he included women who, by 1905, did not fit comfortably under the title of 'sculptor' or 'painter', such as Ann Macbeth, Kate Greenaway and Christine Angus, such was their artistic diversity. Sparrow was possibly the first male to write so extensively on the subject of British women artists, and contributed articles on the subject to *The Studio* magazine (founded 1893) at around the same time. In May 1900, for example, he contributed an illustrated article on Evelyn De Morgan to The Studio (pp.220-232). Sparrow's volume was also one of the earliest to include a range of illustrations of works by women artists, and decorative artists, in a written study published in Britain.

Despite the swelling numbers of women involved in British art and the decorative arts since 1905, few attempts have been made to record their overall progress or contributions on a significant scale. In 1979, Anthea Callen exhumed some of those women in her volume *Angel in the Studio: Women in the Arts and Crafts Movement 1870-1914* (Astragal Books), though she clearly concentrated on a specific movement, and only hinted at who else and what else lay undisturbed. Shortly after, in 1988, Virago published Patricia Jaffe's *Women Engravers*, one of the first books to offer a significant number of engravings by a selection of women associated with that particular art.

Some inspired thinking has also seen the staging of a number of critically important exhibitions which have reintroduced a number of women artists and decorative artists to the outside world. In 1979, for example, coincidentally the same year that Callen's book was published, the Museum of Oxford staged an exhibition devoted to women engravers – *Shall We Join the Ladies?* Shortly after, in 1985-86 (just prior to the publication of Jaffe's book), the William Morris Gallery, London, held an exhibition devoted to Women Stained Glass Artists of the Arts and Crafts Movement, possibly the first of its kind. More recently, in 2007, the Walker Art Gallery, Liverpool, staged an exhibition titled *Doves and Dreams*, devoted to the decorative art of Frances Macdonald and James Herbert MacNair. Otherwise, much remains lost, unrecovered or unrecorded.

This book, therefore, strives to improve matters to some degree by offering details of 1,000 women active in Britain in the fields of illustration, illumination, embroidery, metalwork, decorative jewellery, engraving, sculpture, ceramics, woodcarving, lace making, stained glass, bookbinding and decoration, textiles, lithography and design, as well as the occasional painter, and to put the human back into them. Where possible, their backgrounds and origins, their colleagues, their husbands and children, their work, their careers and their individuality are discussed. Some, such as Kate Button and Amy Singer, have rarely, if ever, been written about since their deaths. Others, such as Ella Naper, have been included in the occasional smaller exhibition; and some, such as Barbara Hepworth and Elisabeth Frink, are still popular today, decades after their deaths.

Although some of these women can be traced back to the 1600s, such as embroideress Damaris Pearse, the majority were active in the nineteenth and twentieth centuries. The reasons for this are many and varied, but include, as indicated already, greater access to schools of art. Women artists also benefitted from the spread of the women's rights movement, with some, such as Margaret Bartels, Mabel Esplin and Mary Lowndes, becoming actively involved in the suffragette movement. Other factors included the establishing of many more schools of art across the country, the increasing diversity of subjects available for study, more women tutors, an increased interest in traditionally female crafts such as embroidery and lace making, and the open support of a number of key male figures in British art and design at that time.

At the Glasgow School of Art, for example, Francis H. Newbery, supported by his artistically-talented wife Jessie Rowat, took great pains to encourage women to study the broader decorative arts (rather than just painting and drawing) in order to increase their chances of finding employment once they left the School. Newbery also encouraged some, such as Ann Macbeth, to take up teaching. In the very early 1900s, the Birmingham School of Art established a School of Jewellery and Silversmithing, supervised in the early years by Arthur Gaskin, husband of craftswoman Georgina. It too encouraged women to take up crafts which might lead to more regular employment. The spread of the female-friendly Arts and Crafts movement, which awarded new respect to crafts such as embroidery, and of the Home Arts and Industries Association (founded in 1884), also encouraged women to become skilled not merely as artists, but as decorative artists, on both amateur and professional levels.

Some of the women discussed here were considered amateurs in their day, and some were professional. Some, such as Mary Watts and Mabel De Grey, founded classes and workshops which offered men and women of all levels of society the opportunity to express individual creativity. Some of their pupils even forged new careers as a result, such as bookbinder Alice Shepherd of Leighton Buzzard.

All 1,000 women, without exception, made important contributions to British art and design. Some took no payment for their work; some had paid employment throughout their careers. Some received little or no acknowledgement during their lifetime; some are still lauded today. Some have proved exceedingly difficult to trace, others remarkably easy. Some never married and dedicated their lives to their work, others gave up promising careers upon marrying. Some managed to conduct extensive and successful careers whilst having husbands and children.

Some, such as Edith Dawson, Georgina Gaskin and Mary Crane, worked with their husbands, or with other male contemporaries. Many, such as Jessie Bayes and Catherine Cockerell, came from artistic backgrounds, with strong evidence of inherited talent. Others came from seemingly the most unlikely backgrounds; from poor, working-class families or, contrastingly, from aristocratic backgrounds. Sculptor Jessie Riding, for example, was the daughter of a bricklayer. Mabel De Grey was the daughter of a Baron. Some were encouraged in their choice of art; some were not. No clear pattern, therefore, has emerged from this research. There is no such thing as a typical female artist, any more than there is a typical male artist. No one set of circumstances or conditions promoted artistic creativity in these women, and all produced highly distinctive work. Sadly, too few completed autobiographies, or have been the subject of biographies.

During this research, it also came to light that, collectively, both women artists and women decorative artists have taken a leading role in creating their own opportunities, founding their own schools and societies. For example, in the very early 1840s (c.1842), the Female School of Design was founded in London, specifically to train women, and only women. Unusually for the times, the students were taught by women too. Initially run by artist Mrs Fanny McIan (1814-97), the School taught a variety of crafts such as pottery, bookbinding, embroidery and wood engraving. Such was demand, women were also eventually able to study art.

Ellen Clayton refers to the School in her two volumes on English Women Artists, noting that painter Eliza Turck attended the School's figure class in 1852, though women were then only able to draw from casts of the human figure and not from life models. Although successful in many respects, the School (later known as the Female School of Art) eventually amalgamated with the Central School of Arts and Crafts. Early on, financial support was given by Angela Burdett-Coutts, who also founded the Art Students' Home for Women in London. Somewhat radically for the times, and against prevailing attitudes, the *Art Journal* (1839-1911) reported on the School and its progress from time to time.

In the mid-1850s, the Society of Women Artists was founded, with the express intention of offering women additional opportunities to exhibit their work. Suffragette campaigner Harriet Grote was one of its key supporters. Exhibits from the 1850s up to the present day have included not only paintings, drawings and sculptures, but a wide variety of handcrafts and decorative works. Many of the 1,000 women discussed here exhibited regularly with the Society as well as elsewhere, and were often elected associates or members. Some women exhibited exclusively with the Society; some never exhibited there. Interestingly, records of the Society's exhibitions give a very clear indication of just how many women have worked as professional artists in Britain over the last 160 years. Records also reveal what they were producing, how much their works sold for, where they were living, and sometimes which studios they were using. Sadly, the Society has never been made 'Royal'.

Similarly, in 1877 the Working Ladies' Guild was founded in London to assist women in need of employment. The Guild became widely known for its embroideries and painted vellum bindings. Later, in 1904, the Home Work Co-operative Society was founded with the objective of selling needlework and decorative work executed by women in their own homes. Its first exhibition was held at Clifford's Inn Hall, Fleet Street, London. Some societies and schools, such as the Red Spider Association (active late 1890s) and the Women Metal Workers' Company, have virtually disappeared without trace. The latter involved women who worked as architectural metalworkers or wrought iron workers. Their history, like that of women who worked in the British coal industry in the late nineteenth and early twentieth centuries, has been poorly documented.

Some schools and societies, such as the Royal School of Art Needlework, have always been highly regarded. Founded in the early 1870s in Sloane Street, London, the School's President was Princess Christian Schleswig-Holstein who was also President of the similarly important Decorative Art Needlework Society, with which Elizabeth Gemmell was associated. The School initially aimed to provide suitable employment for middle-class women, and to restore needlework to its rightful place in the decorative arts. In 1875, it moved to Exhibition Road. In rooms above the School was the School of Art Woodcarving which offered tuition, and took on female students as well as female tutors. One of its earliest teachers was Mr W.H. Grimwood. Another was Maria Reeks.

Of similar significance was the Church Crafts League, founded in 1899 at The Church House, Dean's Yard, Westminster. The League aimed to restore falling standards in church art. Although by no means an exclusively female society, by 1920 as many women as men were involved. At that point, some 73 professional artists, craftsmen and craftswomen were working in association with the League, including Jessie Bayes, Evelyn Barrow, Ellen Rope and Emily Ford; they were involved in areas such as embroidery, illumination, metalwork, painting, sculpture and stained glass.

Away from London, other workshops, schools and societies have thrived under the direct influence of women. Those have included the Compton terracotta industry at Surrey run by Mary Watts. Also, The Spinnery textiles industry run by Annie Garnett in Windermere, and the Leighton Buzzard handcraft class run by Mary Ann Bassett, to list but a few. All produced, sold and exhibited their own decorative work, proving to be not only financially viable but artistically important too. Again, some involved male and female pupils, staff and teachers. Many such ventures were noted and discussed in leading arts journals of the day, particularly in the *Art Journal*, *The Studio* and the *Art Workers' Quarterly* (1902-06), all of which have provided additional information used in this book.

The *Art Journal* was one of the earliest magazines to report on women artists, and on design in Britain, though it closed in 1911, just as many more women were becoming better known as decorative artists. However, *The Studio* ably took over, regularly reporting on exhibitions held by the Society of Women Artists, the Women's International Art Club, the Scottish Society of Women Artists, the Glasgow Society of Lady Artists' Club, and other such bodies. It also included articles about individual women artists, articles written by women, illustrations of works by women artists, and the names of promising female students and their contributions to national exhibitions. The Year's Art, in particular, has provided important detail on such things as exhibitions held, and awards given to female as well as male exhibitors. In 1896, the journal even offered a critically important series of photographs of women artists including Lily Blatherwick, Anna Lea Merritt, Louisa Starr Canziani and Annie Swynnerton.

Records of other exhibitions have provided further insight into the history of women in art and the decorative arts in Britain. Some of the very earliest British exhibitions, such as those staged by the Society of Artists and the Free Society of Artists in the 1700s, did include a variety of crafts by women, as well as some paintings. But those were primarily fashionable works executed in human hair, cut paper or shells, or embroideries. In their day, however, such exhibitions were not highly regarded or regulated, and included mostly female amateurs. Generally, they did not give women a high profile as serious, professional artists, and few rules existed to ensure that works were of a recognised standard. When larger exhibitions were established, such as those held by the Royal Academy and the Royal Scottish Academy, women exhibited paintings and sculptures predominantly. But some crafts have been included through the centuries, such as embroideries by Caroline, Countess of Ailesbury in the late eighteenth century.

Catalogues for other exhibitions have given some useful information too, giving extra clues as to the extent of the exhibiting careers of some of the women discussed here. Catalogues for some of the major exhibitions held by, for example, the Northern Art Workers' Guild, the Home Arts and Industries Association and the Arts and Crafts Exhibition Society reveal that, from at least the 1880s, women have often made up at least half of exhibitors, though that information seems lost today. Where more personal details are concerned, national census recordings have offered greater insight into the backgrounds of many of the women included in this study, and have even inadvertently thrown up names of women artists entirely forgotten today, such as May Heatherington Barker. In many instances, the personal backgrounds of those women included here have proved as interesting as their careers. Some of the earlier census recordings, for example, offer personal details of such things like a lost eye or deafness, or even who lived in suffragette houses.

References are also made here to books which featured women artists and decorative artists during their lifetime, reaffirming that their contributions to art and design were valued by their contemporaries, and their talents acknowledged in their own lifetime. Those include Norna Labouchere's *Ladies' Book-Plates* (London, G. Bell, 1895); M.H. Spielmann's *British Sculpture and Sculptors of Today* (London, Cassell & Co., 1901); R.E.D. Sketchley's *English Book Illustration of Today* (London, Kegan Paul, 1903); Malcolm Salaman's *Modern Book Illustrators and Their Work* (London, The Studio, 1914) and Frank L. Emanuel's *Etching and Etchings* (London, Pitman & Sons, 1930).

Although this book is firmly centred on British art and design, it is important to note that it is by no means a limited subject. Many of the 1,000 women discussed here trained abroad as well as in Britain. Some were born elsewhere, such as Australia, America, India or France, and came to Britain to study, or to work. Some stayed permanently; some moved elsewhere. Some, such as Ethel Reed and Jean Hadaway, came to Britain to work for a comparatively short time, yet still made a considerable impact. Others were born and educated in Britain, but later chose to move abroad, continuing and concluding their careers elsewhere. Many exhibited their work overseas as well as in Britain, and many carried out commissions far and wide. So rich is British art and design history that it cannot be seen only in terms of what happened in Britain. No country is an artistic island.

Whilst many paintings and sculptures have been preserved in museum and gallery collections across the country, and abroad, the very nature of the decorative arts – but in particular of handcrafts such as decorative embroidery and metalwork – means that much remains in private hands or has been lost altogether. However, enough survives today as evidence of the existence of its creators, forgotten or otherwise.

For a small number of women, such as Lily Day, no surviving examples of their work have been identified to date. For others, details of work produced by their pupils or workers have been given, such as those by the Keswick School of Industrial Arts under Edith Rawnsley, or those by the Ruskin Linen Industry under Marian Twelves. Ultimately, this book strives to show that more research needs to be carried out on women in the decorative arts as well as those active as painters, so that a fair, accurate, balanced picture of their contributions to British art and design can finally be drawn.

BIBLIOGRAPHY

Armitage, E. Liddall, Stained Glass, 1960

Barbara Hepworth Centenary, Tate Publishing, 2003, Exhibition Catalogue

Barrow-in-Furness Ecclesiastical Art Exhibition Catalogue, 1906

Billington, Dora, The Art of the Potter, London, Oxford University Press, 1937

Blamires, Hyde & Jaffe, Margaret Pilkington 1891-1974, Buxton, Hermit Press, c.1995

Bliss, Douglas Percy, A History of Wood-Engraving, London, Spring Books, 1928

Bradfield, John, Ella and Charles Naper, Samson & Co., Penlee House Art Gallery, 2003

Bradshaw, Maurice (ed.), Royal Society of British Artists, Members Exhibiting, Vols 1-3, Leigh-on-Sea, F. Lewis, 1975

Brooke, Xanthe, Catalogue of Embroideries, Lady Lever Art Gallery, Stroud, Alan Sutton, 1992

Callen, Anthea, Angel in the Studio: Women in the Arts and Crafts Movement 1870-1914, Astragal Books, 1979

Carruthers, Annette & Greensted, Mary (eds), Simplicity or Splendour: Objects From the Cheltenham Collections, Cheltenham Art Gallery & Museums, Lund Humphries, 1999

Catalogue of the Arts, Crafts & Loan Exhibition, Kendal, 1891, Kendal Library

Catalogue of the Coniston Exhibition, 1900-1919, Ruskin Museum, Coniston

Catalogue of the Exhibition of Pictures & Decorative Art, Kendal, 1899, Kendal Library

Catalogue of the Cumberland and Westmorland Society of Arts and Crafts, 1903, 1914

Chancellor, E. Beresford, The Lives of the British Sculptors, London, Chapman & Hall, 1911

Clark, Betty, Shall We Join the Ladies? Wood Engravings by Women Artists of the Twentieth Century, Oxford, Studio One Gallery, 1979

Clayton, Ellen C., English Female Artists, 2 vols, London, Tinsley, 1876

Clement, C.E., Women in the Fine Arts, New York, The Riverside Press, 1904

Coatts, Margot, A Weaver's Life, Ethel Mairet 1872-1952, Crafts Council, 1983

Dallaway, James, Anecdotes of the Arts in England, n.d.

de Laperriere, Charles Baile (ed.), Royal Scottish Academy Exhibitors, Wiltshire, Hilmarton Manor Press, 1991

de Laperriere, Charles Baile (ed.), The Society of Women Artists Exhibitors 1855-1996, Wiltshire, Hilmarton Manor Press, 1996

Dictionary of Irish Artists, 1913

Dodgson, Campbell, Contemporary Woodcuts, London, Duckworth & Co., 1922

Egerton, Diane Allwood, Artist and Aristocrat: The Life and Work of Lady Mabel Annesley, 2010

Ellet, Mrs, Women Artists in All Ages and Countries, London, Bentley, 1859

Emanuel, Frank L., Etching and Etchings, London, Pitman & Sons, 1930

Erskine, Mrs Steuart, Lady Diana Beauclerk: Her Life and Work, London, T. Fisher Unwin, 1903.

Ewan, Innes & Reynolds (eds), The Biographical Dictionary of Scottish Women, Edinburgh University, 2006

Furst, Herbert, The Modern Woodcut, London, John Lane, 1924

Furst, Herbert, The Art of Still-Life Painting, London, Chapman & Hall, 1927

Garnett, Annie, Notes on Hand Spinning, 1896

Garnett, Annie, Spinnery Notes, 1912

Gleichen, Edward, London's Open-Air Statuary, Bath, Cedric Chivers, 1928

Graves, Algernon, The Society of Artists of Great Britain 1760-1791, The Free Society of Artists 1761-1783, London, G. Bell, 1907

Graves, Algernon, The British Institution 1806-67, London, G. Bell, 1908

Graves, Algernon, Royal Academy Exhibitors 1769-1904

Greensted, Mary, Gimson and the Barnsleys, Alan Sutton, 1991

Hammerton, J.A., Humorists of the Pencil, London, Hurst & Blackett Ltd, 1905

Haslam, Sara E., John Ruskin and the Lakeland Arts Revival, Cardiff, Merton Priory Press, 2004

Jaffe, Patricia, Women Engravers, London, Virago, 1988

Joel, David, The Adventure of British Furniture 1851-1951, London, Ernest Benn Ltd, 1953

Johnson, Jane (ed.), The Royal Society of British Artists 1824-1893 and the New English Art Club 1888-1917, Suffolk, Antique Collectors' Club, 1975

Labouchere, Norna, Ladies' Book-Plates, London, G. Bell, 1895

The Lady Lever Art Gallery, National Museums Liverpool, The Blue Coat Press, n.d.

Laver, James, Vera Willoughby, Illustrator of Books, J. & E. Bumpus, 1929

McLeish, Minnie, Beginnings: Teaching Art to Children, London, Studio Publications, 1941

Macbeth, Ann & Spence, May, School and Fireside Crafts, London, Methuen & Co., 1920

Macbeth, Ann, The Country Woman's Rug Book, Dryad Press, 1929

Macbeth, Ann, The Playwork Book, London, Methuen & Co., 1918

Mahony, Latimer & Folmsbee, Illustrators of Children's Books 1744-1945, Boston, The Horn Book Inc., 1947

Northern Art Workers' Guild Exhibition Catalogue, 1903, Collection of Manchester Central Library

Oil Paintings in the Ownership in the Imperial War Museum, London, The Public Catalogue Foundation, 2006

Peterson, William S., The Beautiful Poster Lady, Oak Knoll Press, 2013

S.T. Prideaux, An Historical Sketch of Bookbinding, London, Lawrence & Bullen, 1893

S.T. Prideaux, Bookbinders and Their Craft, London, Zaehnsdorf, 1903

S.T. Prideaux, Modern Bookbindings: Their Design and Decoration, London, Archibald Constable & Co., 1906

S.T. Prideaux, Aquatint Engraving: A Chapter in the History of Book Illustration, London, Duckworth & Co., 1909

Rinder, Frank & McKay, W. Darling, The Royal Scottish Academy 1826-1916, Glasgow, Rinder & McKay, 1917

Rose Muriel, Artist Potters in England, London, Faber & Faber, 1955/1970

Rowe, Eleanor, French Wood Carvings From The National Museum, London, B.T. Batsford, 1896

Royal Academy Exhibitors 1905-70, Wakefield, E.P. Publishing, 1977

Royal Glasgow Institute Exhibitors, Glasgow

Salaman, Malcolm C., Modern Book Illustrators and Their Work, London, The Studio, 1914

Schoeser, Mary, English Church Embroidery 1833-1953, London, Watts, 1998

Schofield, Anne, The Australian Dictionary of Biography, 1990

Sketching Grounds, London, The Studio, 1909

Sketchley, R.E.D., English Book Illustrators of To-day, London, Kegan Paul, 1903

Sleigh, Bernard, Wood Engraving Since 1890, London, Pitman, 1932

Smith, Janet Adam, Children's Illustrated Books, London, Collins, 1948

Sparrow, Walter Shaw, Women Painters of the World, London, Hodder & Stoughton, 1905

Spielmann, M.H., British Sculpture and Sculptors of To-day, London, Cassell & Co., 1901

Stewart, Ann M. (ed.), Royal Hibernian Academy Index of Exhibitors and Their Work 1826-1979, Dublin, Manton, 1985

Thorpe, James, Illustration: The Nineties, 1935

Tidcombe, Marianne, Women Bookbinders 1880-1920, Oak Knoll Press/The British Library, 1996

Walke, Bernard, Twenty Years at St Hilary, London, Methuen, 1935

The Walker Art Gallery, National Museums Liverpool, 1994

Warner, H.H., Songs of the Spindle & Legends of the Loom, London, N.J. Powell & Co., 1889

Who's Who in Art, Hampshire, The Trade Press, 1927, 1934, 1948, 1952

Women Stained Glass Artists of the Arts and Crafts Movement, William Morris Gallery, London, 1985-86, Exhibition Catalogue

JOURNALS/MAGAZINES

Apollo

Architectural Review

Artist, The

Art Journal, The

Art Workers' Quarterly, The (1902-06)

Colour

English Illustrated Magazine, The

Journal of the British Society of Master Glass-Painters

Magazine of Art, The

Matthews New Bristol Directory

Rural Industries Bureau Magazine

Studio, The (1893-1975)

Studio Year Book, The

Windsor Magazine, The

Year's Art, The

A

ABLETT, JANE (1856-1937)

Artist. Born in Woodmansey, Yorkshire in late 1856. The daughter of Robert Crump and Jane, both of whom originated from Yorkshire. One of at least 10 children (Robert, Mary, Margaret, Jane, Elizabeth, Thomas, Sarah, Annie, Harriet and Kate). Her father changed occupation a number of times but remained in Yorkshire. In the 1860s, he was the owner of houses and land. By the 1880s he was a farmer of some 69 acres, and at some point was the owner of iron foundries and timber yards. He was also a Freeman of Beverley, Yorkshire. The children were taught by a governess. Jane went on to study art at South Kensington, London and in Paris. She was elected a Member of the Croydon Art Society and a Member of the Council of the Royal Drawing Society. Also Vice-President of the League of Mercy and a Member of the Primrose League. In 1880 she married painter Thomas Robert Ablett (1848-1945) in Skirlaugh, Yorkshire. Ablett, the son of Thomas Ablett, a porter, and Elizabeth, was born in London. He was the founder and Art Director of the Royal Drawing Society. Prior to his marriage, he was a teacher in Bideford, Devon. Later, he was art master at the Bradford Grammar School. The couple had at least one son, Charles Anthony, who was born in Ilkley in the early 1880s. He became an engineer. The Abletts lived mainly in London and, latterly, at Addiscombe, Surrey. Jane died at Addiscombe in September 1937. Thomas died in Surrey in mid-1945, aged 96.

ACHESON, ANNE CRAWFORD (1882-1962)

Sculptor. A highly gifted and successful sculptor who exhibited widely in Britain, Ireland and abroad. Born at Portadown, Co. Armagh, Northern Ireland. The daughter of John Acheson (1846-1914), a manufacturer, and Harriet Glasgow (1852-1914). Educated at the Victoria College, Belfast and the Belfast School of Art. Also studied at the Royal College of Art, London under Professor Edouard Lanteri. Awarded a B.A. degree by the Royal University, Ireland. Elected an Associate of the Royal College of Art in 1910. A contemporary of Jessie Mutter Lawson, with whom she shared digs in Kensington along with art students Mary Chambers (from Co. Donegal), Nora Simmons (from Plymouth) and Grace Barber (from Manchester). On completion of her studies, Anne

became a teacher of art at a secondary school under London County Council. She lived primarily in London during her lengthy career, but also latterly in Co. Antrim, where she died. Elected C.B.E. in around 1919. In 1938 she was awarded the distinguished Gleichen Memorial Award. Elected an Associate of the Royal Society of British Sculptors in 1924, and later elected a Fellow.

Acheson produced garden figures, portrait busts, portrait masks, motor mascots, pottery figures, plaster groups, porcelain figures, earthenware, fountain designs and designs for calendars. Worked in a variety of materials including lead, bronze, wood earthenware, plaster and ivory. Had a studio in King's Road, London for a time. Exhibited her work, including at the Royal Scottish Academy (1944), the Royal Hibernian Academy (1910-14), the Royal Glasgow Institute (1923-38) and the Royal Academy (29 works, 1911-49). Exhibited regularly with the Society of Women Artists (86 works, 1915-57). Elected a Member of the Society from 1923 to 1961, and acted as Secretary between 1926 and 1933. Also exhibited at the Paris Salon (from at least 1914), and in Rome, Stockholm, Brussels, New Zealand, America and Toronto as well as with the Royal Society of Portrait Painters and at the Walker Art Gallery, Liverpool. Other works were exhibited with the Ridley Art Club, London. In 1930, for example, she showed a lead garden figure titled Harriet Emily.

Examples of Acheson's pottery were shown at the United Society of Artists (formerly the New Society of Artists) exhibition held at the Suffolk Street Galleries. She was also a Member of the Forum Club. Exhibited works included: Echo Mocking, The Imp (lead garden figure), Tangles (lead statuette), Mrs Cecil Rowntree and a portrait bust for the Gertrude Bell memorial. Other subjects included Harriet Glasgow Acheson, Sir James Acheson, C.I.E., Janet Acheson and Nell Gwynne. Commissions were many and varied and included a garden figure for King's School, Worcester. Works illustrated in the Studio Yearbook. Living at the same address for a time was Harriet E. Acheson, a painter who exhibited at the Society of Women Artists in 1950.

ADAMS, CECILIA CHESTER MARY (1875-1954)

Craftworker in Enamels. Born in London. The daughter of Maurice Bingham Adams and Emily Ellen Louisa. Her father, who originated from Brighton, was an architect. Her mother originated from London. One of at least six children (Cecilia, Winifred, Gladys, Sophia, Etheldreda and Maurice). Her brother, Maurice Chester Rowe Adams, also became an architect. Cecilia was raised in London and became an art student there. Produced enamels, particularly for decorative jewellery. Exhibited her work, including at the Society of Women Artists (1908-17) and at the Royal Academy (1913-16). Exhibited jewellery at the 1916 Arts and Crafts Exhibition Society exhibition in London. One of her exhibits on that occasion was a highly decorative necklace which consisted of rectangular panels of green and white enamel on chains of beads, with a pendant of gold, pearls and rubies. On the pendant was an oblong centrepiece, on both sides of which were figures of Pavlova and Nijinska. The necklace, titled Bacchanale, designed and executed by Adams, was illustrated in The Studio, Vol.70, 1917, p.21. Other works exhibited by Adams included King James II as a Child (enamel, after Van Dyck) and The Kneeling Madonna (enamel, after Botticelli). Adams was based at Marlborough Crescent, London during her exhibiting career. She died in London, aged 79.

ADAMS, HILDA MARGARET (b.1912)

Book Decorator. Known as Margaret. Born in Bridgnorth, Shropshire. Studied at the Birmingham College of Art. A pupil of Harry Adams and Daisy Alcock. Her principal work was for Stanbrook Abbey, Worcestershire. She hand decorated and gilded the fine printing of this press. One of her most successful works was for Siegfried Sassoon's The Path of Peace (1959) printed by Stanbrook Abbey. Executed numerous commissions, including the gilding of the two Books of Consecration for the new Coventry Cathedral. Elected to the Society of Scribes and Illuminators in 1955.

ADAMS, KATHARINE (1862-1952)

Bookbinder / Book Decorator. Born at Bracknell, Berkshire. The second daughter of the Rev. William Fulford Adams. He originated from Bowden, Devon and was curate at Bromsgrove before moving to Easthampstead near Wokingham, Berkshire in 1861. Her mother's name was Horton. Katharine had a sister, Margaret, who died in 1890. Her brother, William Dacre Adams (1864-1951), became a painter and Member of the Art Workers' Guild. The Rev. Adams was later based at Little Faringdon near Lechlade in Gloucestershire, close to Kelmscott Manor and William Morris. Katharine knew the Morris girls, May and Jenny. William Fulford

Adams had been at Marlborough and Oxford with Morris, and in 1896 officiated at Morris's funeral.

Katharine showed an early interest in book decoration but took it up seriously only in her 30s. In 1897 she spent three months with professional bookbinder Sarah Treverbian Prideaux. This was followed by one month with Douglas Cockerell who taught bookbinding at his workshop in Denmark Street, Charing Cross Road, and taught the subject at the L.C.C. Central School of Arts and Crafts. Since she could not afford any further tuition, she spent a year teaching herself in a room at Lechlade. Her first commission came from Mrs William Morris. Adams later took on two pupils. In May 1898 she won first prize in Amateur Bookbinding at the Oxford Arts and Crafts Exhibition held in the Town Hall. In May 1901 she exhibited 56 bindings at Worcester House, Oxford, home of the Daniel Press. Some of those bindings were owned by eminent collectors such as Emery Walker.

Later in 1901, her father became Rector of Weston-sub-Edge in Gloucestershire. Katharine lived at the vicarage but took a small cottage at Broadway where she established the Eadburgha Bindery. The Bindery ran from around 1909 to 1915. In 1907 she commissioned designer / architect Ernest Barnsley to carry out alterations to her Cotswold stone cottage, then known as York House. Adams was part of an artistic circle active in the Cotswolds which included Ernest and Sidney Barnsley and Ernest Gimson. Adams had two assistants, Jessie Gregory who did sewing and needlework, and Georgina Hampshire who assisted with the forwarding. Adams produced new bindings to her own designs, but also repaired and restored old books, mending and cleaning valuable illuminated manuscripts. She was commissioned by numerous important individuals including Sydney Cockerell, with whom she corresponded for many years. Adams also gave lessons to the nuns of Stanbrook Abbey near Worcester.

In 1912 Katharine's father died, and in 1913 she married Edmund James Webb, a graduate of Christ Church, Oxford. Adams continued with her work since Webb appeared to have no income. During the First World War, the couple moved to the old vicarage at Otmoor near Islip in Oxfordshire. Katharine continued to work and give occasional lessons. In the 1930s they lived at St Briavels near Lydney, Gloucestershire. Most of her bindings were not expensive, but she occasionally produced special pieces. For example, a volume of Dante sold for £60, and a volume of Morte d'Arthur sold for £100. In 1935 Adams became President of the Women's Guild of Art, following May Morris, who had retired. In

1938 she was offered a fellowship of the Royal Society of Arts. Edmund Webb died in 1945. Adams died seven years later.

One of her last bindings was the two-volume Ashendene Press Don Quixote, now in the British Library. Adams bound several hundred books during her career. Some were executed for the Kelmscott Press. Cockerell owned around 100. She also executed work for Fairfax Murray, St John Hornby (of the Ashendene Press) and Emery Walker among others. Some of her works are in the British Library and in the Bodleian Library. Hornby mentions Adams in his Anthology of Appreciations (London, 1946). With Sarah Prideaux, Adams produced A Catalogue of Books Bound by S.T. Prideaux Between 1890 and 1900, with 26 illustrations, printed by Prideaux and Adams in 1900.

Adams exhibited consistently throughout her lengthy career. She showed regularly at the major Arts and Crafts Exhibition Society exhibitions from 1899 until around 1930. One of her exhibits in 1906 was a binding for the Holy Bible which was illustrated in The Studio, Vol.37, April 1906, p.228. In 1910 she showed Faust in black leather and silver, and Dante, with a detachable outer cover of richly embroidered silk. Another of her bindings, shown at the 1913 Exhibition held at the Grosvenor Gallery, was Pseudoxia Epidemica. Adams also contributed to the 1902 Bristol "Art Work" Exhibition, the fifth held by the Bristol and Clifton Arts and Crafts Society. There, she was awarded a certificate for a binding of Tennyson's Maud. Some of her work appeared at the New Gallery summer exhibition for 1908 along with work by May Morris, Ethel Virtue and Kate Button among others.

In 1905 Adams and May Morris held a joint exhibition which included jewellery, embroidery and bookbindings in Mayfair, London. In February 1906 she exhibited with her brother, artist William Dacre Adams, at W.B. Paterson's in Old Bond Street, London. She contributed 36 bindings. Adams also contributed to the 1914 Exposition des Arts Decoratifs in Paris where she showed a binding for Tutte Le Opere di Dante Alighieri (1899). One of her bindings, for the writings of William Morris, News From Nowhere, was illustrated in Sarah Prideaux's Modern Bookbindings: Their Design and Decoration (London, Archibald Constable & Co., 1906). Her two bindings for Paradise Lost and Paradise Found were illustrated in the Art Journal, 1907, p.339. Both volumes, worked in gold tooling, were produced for the Dove's Press. For St John Hornby's Ashendene Press, in 1903 Adams completed 25 vellum copies of Fysshinge With An Angle. Other works were exhibited in Dresden, Brussels, Ghent, Leipzig and Cape Town. Adams won numerous awards over the years, including a gold medal in Brussels in 1910. On Sarah Prideaux's death, Adams wrote an obituary for The Times (March 1933). She also wrote a tribute to Prideaux which was printed in a limited edition of 25 copies with the title Sarah Prideaux, A Pupil's Tribute (Bancroft Library Press).

ADAMS, MINNIE WALTERS - SEE ANSON, M.W.

ADENEY, ELAINE THERESE - SEE LESSORE, E.T.

ADENEY, NOEL GILFORD (1891-1978)
Painter / Textile Designer. Was Margaret Noel, known as Noel. Born in Surrey. The daughter of landowner William Gilford and Elizabeth. One of a large family. Given the considerable age gap between her parents, and between some of the children, it appears likely that her father had been married previously. When Noel was born, he was 63. She was educated in Darlington. All the siblings were well educated. One of her sisters, Alice, trained to be a vet. Another, Grace, became a drawing teacher. Her brother Hubert became an architect. Noel studied at the Slade School, London. In early 1921 she married (William) Bernard Adeney (b.1878) in Middlesex. They had at least one son and one daughter. Bernard Adeney had also studied at the Slade School, but also at the Royal Academy schools. He subsequently became Head of the Design School (school of textiles) at the London County Council Central School of Arts and Crafts. Both became members of the London Group, and he acted as President of the Group from 1918 until 1923. Noel exhibited with the Group, and with the National Society. The couple were based at Haverstock Hill, London and at West Wittering, Sussex for a time, and at Crooms Hill, Greenwich. Noel died in Greenwich, aged 87.

AGNEW, ETHEL P. (active 1900s to 1930s)
Craftswoman. Possibly Ethel Patricia Agnew, born in Liverpool in January 1873. The daughter of Thomas F.A. Agnew, a cotton merchant and later a bank manager, and Julia Thomas. Her father originated from London. Her mother was born in India. Their first child, Henrietta, was also born in India. A further seven children (Douglas, Marion, Geraldine, Ernest, Ethel, Percy and Harold) were born in Liverpool. The family remained in Liverpool. If this is the correct Ethel Agnew, she died in the West Indies in 1965.

Ethel P. Agnew was active in London from the early 1900s until at least 1930. In 1930 she is listed in London directories as a jeweller and enameller. In 1906 she opened a class in enamelling and jewellery with May Hart at the Cathcart Studios, Redcliffe Road, London. However, she came to prominence at the 1908 New Gallery exhibition where she showed examples of her decorative jewellery, some of which, made in silver and decorated with various stones, was illustrated in The Studio, Vol.44, p.62. Also in 1908, she contributed to the Sir John Cass Arts and Crafts Society exhibition held at the Walker's Gallery, New Bond Street, London. On that occasion, she was commended for her use of colour and arrangement of jewels. Earlier in 1908, The Studio had already illustrated her gold lace-pin, two pendants and a brooch (Vol.43, March, p.165). Exhibited at the Sir John Cass Arts and Crafts Society exhibition in 1911. The Society was made up of students and staff of the School of Art. Harold Stabler taught at the Sir John Cass School of Art. The 1911 fifth exhibition was held in Sloane Street. Agnew may have been a student of the School.

AILESBURY, CAROLINE, COUNTESS OF (d.1803)

Embroideress. Exhibited one work at the Society of Artists in 1768, A Piece of Flowers in needlework. Also exhibited one work at the Royal Academy in 1770, A Heron and a Dog in needlework. Some confusion exists over this lady's identity. She is listed as Susanna for both the above exhibits. However, she is presumed to be Caroline, Dowager Countess of Ailesbury, widow of the third Earl of the first creation since, in 1770, Susanna (to whom Graves attributes the above needlework) was the Hon. Mrs Bruce according to Walpole. He calls her Caroline, not Susanna, and praised her 'masterly' needlework. Caroline, Countess of Ailesbury, was the wife of the Hon. Henry Seymour Conway and mother of sculptor Anne Seymour Conway (Mrs Damer), their only child. Caroline is mentioned in E. Beresford Chancellor's volume The Lives of the British Sculptors (London, Chapman & Hall, 1911) as a 'cultivated and artistic lady'. Caroline was the daughter of Colonel Campbell of Mamore. She first married Lord Bruce, afterwards third Earl of Ailesbury, whose title she retained after her second marriage to General Seymour Conway. Anne was born in 1748 and died in 1828. Anne executed a bust of her mother. Caroline died some eight years after her second husband. SEE: DAMER, ANNE

AITKEN, PAULINE (1893-1958)

Sculptor. Born in Accrington, Lancashire in June 1893. The daughter of Arthur Henry Aitken, town clerk and solicitor for the Corporation of Accrington. He originated from Edenfield, Lancashire. Her mother, Maud, originated from Clitheroe, Lancashire. Had an older brother, Arthur Eastham Aitken, who became a solicitor. While Pauline was still young, the family moved to Huncoat, Lancashire. By the age of 17, she was a student, living at the family home in Clitheroe. She studied at the Manchester School of Art, then at the Chelsea Polytechnic, and at the Royal Academy schools, London. Lived and worked mainly in London, using a studio in Upper Cheyne Row, Chelsea for much of her career. Produced statuettes. Worked mainly in bronze. Exhibited at the Paris Salon and at various provincial galleries. Also exhibited at the Royal Academy (1918-32), the Royal Scottish Academy (1928-32), the Society of Women Artists (21 works, 1924-39) and the Walker Art Gallery, Liverpool. Exhibited works included: Nocturne (statuette, bronze), Salome (statuette, bronze), Undine (statuette, bronze) and Down the Fairway (statuette). Produced the design for the Issota Fraschini mascot. Elected a Member of the Faculty of Art. Died in Surrey in late 1958, aged 65.

ALDERTON, DOROTHY EILEEN - SEE ANDREWS, D.E.

ALEXANDER, MARGARET (1902-97)

Illuminator / Calligrapher. Born at Hampstead in June 1902. The daughter of Philip Frederick Alexander, a metalworker, and Frances Emma. Both parents originated from Hampstead. Her father was associated with the handcraft classes in woodcarving and metalwork which ran in Southwold, Suffolk between 1882 and 1914. Some examples of decorative metalwork by him are kept in the Southwold Museum. The family were certainly in Suffolk, in Walberswick, in 1911 at the time of the national census. Margaret had at least one sibling, Catharine, who was born in Norfolk in 1904. Margaret was educated at the St Felix School, Southwold and at the Bedales School. She subsequently went to London to study at the Slade School, and at the L.C.C. Central School of Arts and Crafts. She became a teacher of illumination and calligraphy at the Slade School between 1928 and 1957. Also acted as calligrapher to the House of Lords between 1926 and 1963. Elected a Member of the Society of Scribes and Illuminators (founded 1921). Acted as Honorary Secretary of the Society

(1934-36). An example of her work, an opening page from The Book of Proverbs written out and illuminated for A.D. Power, Esq., was given in The Studio, Vol.138, July 1949, pp.1-5 in an article by fellow Society member Claire Evans. Exhibited at the Arts and Crafts Exhibitions, at Burlington House, the Victoria & Albert Museum, London and in Berlin and Copenhagen. Works included a war memorial volume for London University. Also, an address to the late George Moore, and an address to Professor Legouis. Based for part of her career at Pembroke Road, London. Active from at least the 1920s until at least the 1960s. Died in Henley, Oxfordshire, aged 95.

ALLAN, GRISELDA NORMA (1905-87)
Artist / Lithographer. Born and raised in Sunderland. The daughter of Walter Beattie Allan, B.A., B.D., and Christian Gray. One of at least three children. Her father, a shipowner, originated from Sunderland. Her mother originated from Lockerbie, Dumfries. Educated at the Church High School, Sunderland and at the St Felix School, Southwold, Suffolk. Studied art in Sunderland under Richard Archibald Ray, A.R.C.A. and at various schools in France and Germany. Also studied at the Ruskin School of Drawing under Albert Rutherston (1935-39). Taught at the Slade School, London and the Ruskin School of Drawing between 1941 and 1945. Then taught only at the Ruskin School from 1946. Produced paintings in oils and watercolours and lithographs. Did not appear to exhibit a great deal. In 1949 she married Karl E.A.T. Buddeberg in Sunderland. Official purchasers of her work included the War Artists' Committee in 1943. Based at Holywell Street, Oxford for a time. Latterly based in Sunderland. Died in Sunderland, aged 81.

ALLCOTT, MAUD B.S. - SEE BIRD, M.B.S.

ALLEN, ALICE - SEE PATTINSON, A.

ALLEN, EVELINE M. - SEE WATTS, E.M.

ALLEN, OLIVE (b.1879)
Artist / Illustrator. Born in Ormskirk, Lancashire. The daughter of George Allen and Mary. One of at least five children (Margaret, Dorothea, George, Edward and Olive). Margaret became a school teacher. Olive studied at the Liverpool School of Art. As a student, she entered several of The Studio competitions. For example, in 1900 she won an Honourable Mention for a card / calendar design, and a Second Prize of half a

guinea for a design for a title page, shown under the name 'Malvolio'. Also won a Second Prize in 1900 for a 'Design Symbolic of Winter'. The prize was, again, half a guinea. That particular design was illustrated in The Studio, Vol.19, 1900, p.214. Allen became a painter and book illustrator. Exhibited her work at the Walker Art Gallery, Liverpool. Rewrote and illustrated several of the titles in the Grandmother's Favourites series of children's books published by T.C. & E.C. Jack. Also illustrated, for example, Effie Johnson, Facts and Fables (London, Chapman & Hall, 1901, price 6s), Lewis Carroll, Alice's Adventures in Wonderland (1910) and J.A. Henderson, Gardens Shown to the Children (1911). Spent the early part of her career in Liverpool, but subsequently moved to Launceston, Cornwall, living with an aunt, and then with her sister Margaret.

AMOORE, BETH (1862-1944)
Enameller / Jewellery Maker / Engraver / Painter / Metalworker. Was Elizabeth Anne, known as Beth. Born in Hastings, Sussex. Her father, Joseph Figgis Amoore, was a grocer and tea dealer employing several people in the family business. Her mother was Mary. Both parents originated from Sussex. Beth was one of at least seven children (five boys and two girls), all born and raised in Hastings. The Amoores were sufficiently well off to afford several servants. By the age of 16, Beth was acting as a daily governess whilst living at home. By this time, Joseph Amoore had died, and Mary had taken over running the family business with her second eldest son, Ernest. Subsequently, Beth moved to London to study art, at the South Kensington School, at Westminster and at the Slade School. She was awarded an Art Masters' Teaching Certificate and spent many years teaching art, including at the Sydenham High School for Girls.
Amoore was a talented and diverse artist who produced jewellery and enamels, engravings, pencil drawings, decorative metalwork, bookplates, designs for advertisements and cards, black & white sketches, wallpaper designs and watercolour paintings of landscapes, figures and portraits. She spent much of her life in and around London, dying in Lambeth in 1944 at the age of 81, never witnessing the end of the Second World War or its full consequences. In 1891, aged 29, Beth is listed as living in the same flats in Chelsea's Oakley Crescent as artists Mary B. Downing, Edith Downing and Elizabeth Piper. By 1901, aged 39, she was sharing a house in Wandsworth with Mary Downing along with barrister Edward Laws. By 1911, aged 49, she

was still in Wandsworth but living with her youngest brother, Alfred, a journalist who, like Beth, was unmarried. Beth is also listed as an employer in 1911, which would indicate that she employed staff to assist in her work.

Amoore exhibited her work over a period of more than 50 years, still contributing to exhibitions at the age of at least 77. Exhibited at the Royal West of England Academy, the Royal Cambrian Academy and the Dudley Watercolour Society. At the Society of Women Artists, she showed well over 100 works of various sorts between 1891 and 1940 including Portrait Study (watercolour), A Fresh Morning (watercolour), My Studio Outlook and Street Corner in Montreuil. One of her final exhibits during her lengthy career was her study of The Farm's Untidy Corner, exhibited in 1940. Amoore was elected an Associate of the Society of Women Artists in 1915, and a Member between 1916 and 1940. She acted as Secretary between 1922 and 1925. Her work appeared elsewhere, including, for example, at an Arts and Crafts Exhibition held in late 1905 at the Bruton Galleries. There, she showed a beaten brass fire screen that was noted in the Art Workers' Quarterly for 1905. Her subjects for engravings and paintings suggest that Amoore travelled widely, producing studies of Wales, Sussex, Dorset, Norfolk, Kent, the Cotswolds, Essex, Wells and Glastonbury and, further afield, France and Bruges. In 1929 sculptor Irene M. Brown exhibited a stoneware portrait of Amoore.

ANDERSON, KAY (1902-74)

Painter / Etcher / Engraver / Lithographer. Was Kathleen, known as Kay. Born in Chingford, Essex. The daughter of the Rev. Alfred William Anderson, a congregational minister, and Agnes (d.1941). Her parents originated from Ireland, her father from Omagh, her mother from Antrim. The eldest of at least four children (Kay, John, Maurice and Alice). Initially raised in Kent, then Newport, Monmouthshire. Taught by a governess, then attended the Newport High School, followed by the Merchant Taylors', Crosby, Liverpool. Studied at the Liverpool School of Fine Arts under etcher / painter George Marples. Also, at the Royal College of Art, London under Professor William Rothenstein. Awarded a student scholarship in 1922 and 1924. Awarded an Art Teachers' Certificate. Elected an Associate of the Royal College of Art in 1927. Produced paintings in oils and watercolours, etchings, engravings and lithographs, various subjects. Exhibited in London and the provinces. Also, in Paris, Chicago and Canada. Exhibited at the Royal Academy (1931-49). Exhibited works included The Blind Beggar Healed at the Pool of Siloam (etching), Sussex Farmyard and Cafe Scene (etching). In late 1933 she married artist Thomas Collingwood Clough (1903-79) in Godstone, Surrey. He originated from Conway, and studied at the Slade School and at the Royal College of Art. He exhibited at the Royal Academy, the New English Art Club and with the London Group. His father, Thomas Clough (1867-1943), was also an artist. Thomas and Kay remained in Surrey, where she died, aged 71. Previously based in Redcliffe Road, London. Works reproduced in The Studio.

ANDRAS, CATHERINE (c.1775-1860)

Wax Modeller. A self-taught artist in wax, linked to the Historic Gallery, Pall Mall, London. Active from around the turn of the nineteenth century. Listed in the Matthews New Bristol Directory for 1795 as resident at 16, St Augustine's Back, Bristol, which was also the site of Andras & Co., a perfume and toy warehouse. Andras is supposed to have been orphaned and adopted by miniature painter Robert Bowyer and his wife, Mary. Andras was awarded the Larger Silver Pallet by the Society for the Encouragement of the Arts, Manufactures and Commerce. She exhibited 22 works at the Royal Academy from 1799 until 1824, then living in London. Exhibits included a model of Princess Charlotte (Victoria & Albert Museum), another of Lord Wellington, and one of Lady Charlemont. Evidently, given her list of subjects, a society modeller and highly regarded. Andras also exhibited at the British Institution between 1806 and 1820. Listed in contemporary records as 'modeller in wax to Her Majesty'. Executed a mould of William Pitt (1759-1806). Modelled Nelson, and after his death in 1805 Andras was commissioned to produce a life-size effigy for Westminster Abbey, London. Based mainly in London. Believed to have worked until around 1855. Did mostly small-scale works, mainly people, but also animals. Sometimes incorporated real hair and fur into her creations. The Victoria & Albert Museum, London has a number of her moulds and reliefs. Died in London.

ANDREWS, DOROTHY EILEEN (1897-1991)

Painter / Craftworker. Born in May 1897 at West Bridgford, Nottinghamshire. The daughter of Arthur James Alderton and Lilian. Her father was a commercial traveller, initially in sugar and fruit, then soap. He originated from Ipswich, Suffolk, her mother from Dublin, Ireland. The eldest of at least three children (Dorothy Eileen, Constance Lilian and Francis Arthur). Her siblings were also born in West Bridgford. Raised in Nottinghamshire and at Abington, Northamptonshire. Educated in Northamptonshire. Studied at the Northampton School of Art under Oswald Crompton, A.R.C.A., between 1916 and 1921. Also, at the Royal College of Art, London under Professor William Rothenstein between 1921 and 1923. Elected an Associate of the Royal College of Art. Awarded an Art Teachers' Diploma and became an art mistress. Acted as senior assistant at the Leyton School of Art between 1923 and 1938. Also on the visiting staff of the Borough Polytechnic School of Art between 1924 and 1938. Senior assistant at the S.W. Essex Technical College School of Art from 1938. Produced paintings in oils and watercolours and various craftwork. Exhibited at the Royal Institute of Painters in Watercolours, the Royal College of Art, the Essex Sketch Club and with the Northampton Town and Country Art Society. Possibly exhibited two works at the Society of Women Artists in 1970 and 1971 (Mrs Eileen Andrews, no address). In 1945 she married Leonard Gordon Andrews (b.1885) in Essex. He originated from Sussex and was a carpet designer, art master, artist and designer. He taught at the Kidderminster and Leyton Schools of Art, and at the S.W. Essex Technical College School of Art. Based for much of their careers in Essex. Dorothy died in Redbridge, Essex, aged 93.

ANDREWS, EDITH ALICE - SEE CUBITT, E.A.

ANDREWS, EDITH LOVELL (1886-1979)
Decorative Artist / Painter. Born in Newport, Monmouthshire in late 1886. The daughter of William Kingsland Andrews, Senior Superintendent Inspector of H.M. Customs and Excise. Her mother was Anna. Spent her childhood in Monmouthshire. Had an older sister, Margaret. Educated at the Forest Gate Collegiate School. By 1901, the two sisters were living in West Ham, London with their mother. Edith subsequently studied art, first at the Worcester School of Art under J.J. Brownsword (1903-07). Then studied at the Glasgow School of Art under Francis Newbery and Ann Macbeth (1908-10), followed by three years at Heatherley's in London under Gerald Massey (1911-14). By 1911, Edith was already undertaking work as an artist, and is recorded in that year as a 'designer of art work such as Christmas cards'. By that time, William, Anna and their two daughters were resident in London, and Margaret was employed as a literary

contributor to newspapers and magazines. As a student, Edith had designed and drawn a presentation address which was given to Francis Newbery by the students of the Glasgow School of Art in connection with the inauguration of an extension. The address was illustrated in black & white in The Studio, Vol.49, April 1910, p.248.

Edith produced a variety of decorative work throughout her career, including decorative lettering and ballads, and scrolls on vellum. Some of her works were reproduced in The Studio in 1912 and 1913. She also produced scraperboard images, landscape paintings in watercolours and posters in tempera. Her work was exhibited in Glasgow (1911), Toronto (1912), at the Canadian National Exhibition (1913, 1914), at Helsingfors and Stockholm (1912), Turin (1913), Kensington (1918) and St Ives, Cornwall from 1949. Latterly, Andrews lived in Cornwall, including at Bellair Terrace, St Ives. She was elected a Member of the St Ives Society of Artists (1949-78), and acted on the Society's Council from 1955 as well as acting as Secretary of the Fabric Fund to purchase the freehold of the new gallery. Elected Honorary Vice President of the Society in 1977. Also joined the St Ives Arts Club. Early in her career, she acted as curator of Derry and Toms, Kensington Art Gallery (1918-20). Works also reproduced in the Studio Year Book (1913) and the Christian Science Monitor (1920-25). Works acquired for collections in Australia and at the British Museum. Andrews died in Camborne, Cornwall, aged 92.

ANDREWS, EMILY JANE - SEE HARDING, E.J.

ANDREWS, LILIAN (1878-c.1962)
Artist / Designer. Born and raised in Brighton, Sussex. The daughter of Stephen Rusbridge and Emily, both of whom originated from Sussex. One of at least seven children, four girls and three boys. One of her brothers became an upholsterer. Another was apprenticed to a brass finisher. Her father was an engineer at a laundry for a time, then went into confectionery. Later, two of her sisters, Ida and Margaret, worked with their father. Lilian, however, showed artistic talent and became a student at the Brighton School of Art. There, she won a bronze medal for design. Awarded an Art Masters' Teaching Certificate. By the age of 22, she was living at home in Brighton and working as an art teacher. Became a painter of landscapes and animals, and a designer. For a time, taught design and animal drawing at the Brighton School of Art. In 1910

she married Douglas S. Andrews in Steyning, Sussex. They had one daughter.

Lilian had an extensive career as an artist, exhibiting her work for over 50 years. Exhibited widely, including at the Royal Scottish Academy (1954-55), the Royal Glasgow Institute (1952) and the Royal Academy (39 works, 1912-60). Also exhibited in Leeds, Bradford, Newcastle, Bournemouth and Brighton. And with the International Society of Sculptors, Painters and Gravers, and at the London Arts and Crafts Exhibitions. Exhibited works included: The Nanny Goat, Chinese Geese and A Wren. Three of her works, Yew Berries, A Silver Carp and A'Brambling, were published in The Studio in 1928. Spent time in Brighton, but also in Bath, Sheffield, Leeds and London. Later concentrated on watercolours of birds and animals. The Nottingham Art Gallery purchased her Peahen and Chick.

ANDREWS, MARY FRANCES - SEE CRANE, M.F.

ANGLE, BEATRICE (1859-1915)
Sculptor. Was Eva Beatrice, sometimes Beatrice. Born in Hornsey. Raised in Islington, where she lived for several decades. The daughter of John Angle, a job master, and Susan. One of at least 11 children. Latterly based at Egerton Studios, Yeoman's Row, Kensington and at The Hut, Sandwich, Kent. Lived for a time with one of her sisters, Edith Florence Angle (1858-1950), also known as Florence. Beatrice specialised in small busts, heads and groups. Worked in terracotta and bronze. Exhibited in Liverpool, and at the Paris Salon where, in 1892, she showed a figure of A Young Venetian. Also exhibited at the Royal Academy (16 works, 1885-99). Showed two works at the Society of Women Artists in 1890, In the Springtime (bust) and Sabina (bust). Other exhibited works included: Ada (terracotta), Poetry (bust) and A Bacchante (bust, terracotta). Died in Kent, aged 55.

ANGUS, CHRISTINE DRUMMOND (1877-1920)
Artist / Illustrator / Embroideress. A promising talent in illustration and embroidery who died prematurely. Born in Liverpool. The daughter of John Henry Angus (1846-1930) and Andrina Agnes (1853-1930). Her father, a hide and leather merchant, originated from Durham. Her mother originated from Scotland. One of at least nine children (Lizzie, Christine, Archibald, Moray, Minnie, Harold, Andrina, Marion and Joan), all born between 1875 and 1896. All were raised in

Liverpool. Her parents, John and Andrina, died within a few months of each other, and her father left a substantial estate. Sometime in the late 1890s Christine began studying at the Liverpool School of Art, completing her studies by around 1900. As a student, she won a number of prizes, including a Second Prize in The Studio competition for 1900 with an illustration for Paradise Lost. In the same year, she won an Honourable Mention in The Studio competition for a Christmas card design, and won a First Prize of one guinea for a 'Design Symbolic of Winter'. The latter was illustrated in The Studio, Vol.19, 1900, p.214 under the pseudonym 'Meliagaunce'.

Christine became an illustrator of children's books and an expert embroideress. Occasionally exhibited at the Walker Art Gallery, Liverpool. In 1916 exhibited an embroidered dalmatic of blue brocade at the Needlecraft Exhibition held at the Glasgow School of Art. The dalmatic (a loose vestment, wide-sleeved, open at the sides and worn by deacons and bishops and by monarchs at their coronation) had a border and medallion of linen and was designed and executed by Christine. The dalmatic was illustrated in The Studio, Vol.67, May 1916, p.264 with details on p.265. The embroidery was very fine, time-consuming work. After completing her studies, Christine spent some time in Torquay, Devon in around 1901. At some unspecified date, she met and married painter Walter Richard Sickert (1860-1942). The marriage may have taken place abroad. Sickert had first married Ellen M.A. Cobden in 1885, but the union had ended in divorce. Angus was his second wife but died young in Dieppe in October 1920, where Sickert had spent time painting. In 1918 they were listed as living in Camden, London, but were evidently in France soon after. Sickert went on to marry for a third time, to artist Therese Lessore in 1926. He died in Bath, Somerset in January 1942.

ANNESLEY, MABEL MARGUERITE (1881-1959)
Wood Engraver. Lady Mabel Annesley. Born in London. The daughter of Hugh, fifth Earl of Annesley of Castlewellan, Co. Down. Married Gerald Sowerby in 1904 and had a son. She inherited the impoverished family estate in Ireland from her father and brother, and took on its management and the farming. Lost her husband in 1913. At some point, when she was around 40, she was able to study wood engraving at the London County Council Central School of Arts and Crafts under Noel Rooke. From 1912, Rooke taught a number of women who went on to achieve considerable success as engravers in

the 1920s and 1930s, including Vivien Gribble, Millicent Jackson and Margaret Pilkington. Annesley produced distinct, small-scale wood engravings with a strong contrast in black and white. She initially had some art training at Frank Calderon's School of Painting in 1895. But she remains best known for her wood engravings and woodcuts. Illustrated a number of books during her career, including a limited edition of Songs From Robert Burns (ed. by A.E. Coppard, 1925) for the Golden Cockerel Press. Also illustrated Richard Rowley's County Down Songs (1924) and Apollo in Mourne (1926). Based mainly in Ireland. Later travelled abroad to Egypt, New Zealand and Australia. She emigrated to New Zealand in 1945.

Annesley exhibited her work, including with the Society of Wood Engravers. Her A Country Road was shown there in 1931 and was mentioned in Apollo (January 1931, p.67). At the 1934 exhibition of the Society of Wood Engravers, she showed Moel Siabod which was illustrated in Apollo (Vol.19, January 1934). Annesley was an early member of the Society. Fellow exhibitors included Gwen Raverat, Douglas Percy Bliss, Frank Medworth and Muriel Jackson. Annesley was also a member of the Belfast Art Society. She exhibited in Belfast at her studio in Lombard Street. Also exhibited in Dublin with the Watercolour Society of Ireland (certainly in 1923). Held a one-woman exhibition at the Batsford Gallery, London in 1933. Held other one-woman shows in Dublin, and in Wellington, New Zealand. Some of her engravings were included in an exhibition held in Manchester in 1960 after her death. Works also included in an exhibition of women wood engravers, Shall We Join the Ladies?, held at the Museum of Oxford in October 1979. The exhibition consisted of the work of 27 women. Works acquired by the British Museum and by the Ulster Museum. Her woodcut Slieve-na-Slat was included in Campbell Dodgson's volume Contemporary Woodcuts (London, Duckworth & Co., 1922). Annesley was one of only a small number of engravers chosen by Dodgson to represent the very best in modern woodcuts. Noted in Douglas Percy Bliss, A History of Wood-Engraving (London, Spring Books, 1928). Annesley was elected a Member of the Society of Wood Engravers. She died in England, in Suffolk. SEE: Diane Allwood Egerton, Artist and Aristocrat: The Life and Work of Lady Mabel Annesley, 2010.

ANSELL, NORAH MARJORIE (1906-90)

Modeller / Sculptor. Born in Wiltshire in July 1906. The daughter of W.H.G. Ansell. Studied at the Birmingham College of Arts and Crafts in the evenings under William Bloye. Remained in Birmingham throughout her career, at York Road, Edgbaston. A modeller in clay for bronze and a sculptor. Produced portrait and figure works in plaster, alabaster, bronze, ivory and wood (including French walnut and Kapur hardwood). Exhibited at the Royal Glasgow Institute (1945), the Royal Academy (1945-47) and the Society of Women Artists (1951-55). Appears to have begun exhibiting her work later in her career, or to have taken up sculpture later in life. Exhibited works included: Gillian Growing Her Hair (head, plaster), Kindlein (head), Virgin From the Congo (French walnut) and Sleeping Girl (ivory). Works sold for between £25 and £262. Her Little Bather (ivory) was exhibited at the International Ivory Sculpture Competition and Exhibition held at the Carlebach Gallery, New York in 1953. The sculpture was illustrated in The Studio, Vol.146, December 1953, p.190. This was the first exhibition of its kind held at the gallery and Ansell won a $100 prize. Dr S.A. Schneidman of Queens Village, Long Island sponsored the competition along with his wife. He was a collector of Oriental ivory sculptures. In 1951 he had purchased a wood sculpture by Ansell and persuaded her to try working in ivory. Her Little Bather was her first work in that material. In 1955 Ansell visited New York. She died in Birmingham, aged 84.

ANSON, MINNIE WALTERS (1875-1959)

Painter / Illustrator. Born in London in February 1875. The daughter of Edwin Alexander Anson, a timber merchant, and Harriet. One of at least four children (Arthur, Minnie, Maude and Harold). Raised in London. Educated privately. Studied at the Lambeth School of Art where she won seven medals, including two gold for flower painting. Became a miniature, portrait, landscape and flower painter. Based mainly in London, including at a studio in Streatham, but latterly moved to Parkstone, Dorset. Exhibited her work, including at the Royal Academy (1902-51), the Paris Salon, the Walker Art Gallery, Liverpool, with the Royal Society of Miniature Painters and in Manchester, Bradford, Guildford and Toronto. Exhibited works included: The Pink Dress, A Breton Peasant, Peaceful Eventide and Christopher Adams, R.M.S. Other sitters of note included W. Thomas, F.R.P.S. and Marcus Adams, F.R.P.S. Elected an Associate of the Royal Society of Miniature Painters. Occasionally produced illustrations, including for Colour Planning of the Garden for Messrs Jack.

In 1943 she married Arthur Christopher Adams in Poole, Dorset. She died in Dorset, aged 84.

ANTRIM, ANGELA CHRISTINA, COUNTESS OF (1911-84)

Sculptor / Artist. Born in Malton, Yorkshire in September 1911. The daughter of Sir Mark Sykes, Bt., of Sledmere, Malton. Educated privately. Her father, who produced caricatures, died when she was only 10. She had a brother, Christopher. Studied art at Brussels between 1927 and 1932 under Professor M. d'Haveloose, and at the British School in Rome. Produced murals, cartoons in black ink and sculptures in bronze, stone and terracotta. Worked in a studio near Regent's Park for a while. In 1934 she married the Earl of Antrim and had two sons and a daughter. At the onset of the Second World War, she moved to Glenarm Castle, Co. Antrim in Ireland. Spent a considerable part of her time there. Held strong political views, anti-fascist. One of her most significant works was a study of a starved mother and child, Mother and Child, made at Belsen towards the end of the war. At that time she was in the Low Countries. Exhibited throughout her lengthy career. Exhibited at the Royal Hibernian Academy (1948-49) and at the Royal Academy (1929-32). Also exhibited at the Irish Exhibition of Living Art, at the Ulster Academy and at the Whitechapel Art Gallery. Held one-woman shows at the Beaux Art Gallery (1937) and the Belfast Art Gallery (1950). Exhibited works included: Alexander (head, bronze), The Descent From the Cross and The Comtesse Beatrice de Liedekerke (head, bronze). Executed a number of commissions in Ireland, including for St Joseph's Church, Ballygally, Larne, Co. Antrim. Elected to the Ulster Academy of Fine Arts (1950). Works reproduced in Tatler, Sketch, Country Life, La Revue Moderne and other journals.

ANTROBUS, MARY - SEE SYMONDS, M.

ANTROBUS, PHYLLIS MARY (b.1905)

Painter / Craftswoman / Pen & Ink Artist. Born in Great Malvern, Worcestershire in October 1905. The daughter of Edmund Antrobus, M.D. Educated at the Belvedere School, Liverpool. Awarded a First Class Teacher Artist Certificate. Produced paintings in watercolours, pen & ink drawings and was involved in various crafts. Based in Aigburth, Liverpool during her career. Exhibited at the Walker Art Gallery, Liverpool and the Basnett Gallery, Liverpool. Works included: Day Dreams, The Garden, The Fairy Wood and Sea Elves. Possibly married Henry G.

Topham in Liverpool in 1939, and died in Staffordshire in 1983.

ARCHIBALD, PHYLLIS MURIEL COWAN (1880-1947)

Sculptor. Born in Tonbridge, Kent. The daughter of Edmund Douglas Archibald (1851-1913) and Janet Helen Finlay (b.1849). Her father, who originated from Hampstead, London was a meteorologist, a Professor of Mathematics in the Bengal Educational Department and a military tutor. Her mother originated from Glasgow. The couple married in India in 1876, then returned to live in Tonbridge after the birth of their first child, Constance. Phyllis was born two years after Constance, followed by Robert and Elizabeth. By at least 1891, Janet Archibald was living in Lanarkshire, Scotland with her four children and remained there for over 10 years. Phyllis was educated at the Park School, Glasgow. She then studied at the Glasgow School of Art from at least 1901. Became a sculptor of a variety of subjects including animals, figures and portraits. Worked in various materials including plaster, wood, bronze, marble, stone, lead, chromium-plated bronze and silver-plated bronze.

Exhibited her work, including at the Royal Scottish Academy (1908-33), the Royal Glasgow Institute (1902-37), the Royal Academy (1913-30) and the Society of Women Artists (12 works, 1927-37). Also, at the Paris Salon, the British Empire Exhibition, Stockholm, London, Leipzig and the British Institute of Industrial Art. Works carried out included a figure for the choir stall in Congregational Church, Whitchurch, a bronze relief of Lady Archibald, David Dancing Before the Ark, Charity for Trinity Church Convalescent Home and Daughters of Great Zeus (statuette group, bronze). Works illustrated in the Architectural Review (The Moon, silver-plated bronze). Initially worked in Glasgow, and spent time in Paris. In late 1911 she married journalist Charles Clay (1856-1941) who was 25 years her senior. He originated from Wakefield, Yorkshire. The couple lived at Hampstead, London initially. Latterly lived at Thyme Cottage, Bletchingley, Surrey, and at Grasmere in Westmorland. Phyllis died in Westmorland in March 1947, aged 66. Left a sizeable estate of just over £24,000 to her sister, Constance.

ARMFIELD, CONSTANCE (1876-1941)

Embroideress / Writer. Was Annie Constance, known as Constance. Born in Birmingham in June 1876. The daughter of William Thomas Smedley (1851-1934), a chartered accountant. Her mother, Annie Elizabeth (1851-1923), was the daughter of a Birmingham coffee merchant. Constance was educated at home and at the King Edward VI High School for Girls. Showed natural artistic talent and had her first illustration published in the Pall Mall Magazine at the age of 16. She was affected by a childhood illness which left her disabled. However, she was able to study at the Birmingham School of Art. The family moved to London, where Constance mixed with leading artistic figures of the day, including Alice Meynell and Gertrude Hudson. She experimented in various areas of the decorative arts but was perhaps best known for her embroidery. An example of her work was illustrated in The Studio, Vol.90, September 1925, p.184. Another of her embroideries was Damsels in a Wood (1916), a lunette of linen worked with silks and wools.

In 1909 Constance married painter / writer / designer and illustrator Maxwell Ashby Armfield (1881-1972), also a former student of the Birmingham School of Art. The exact nature of the marriage, given that he was homosexual and she was an invalid, is unclear. But they worked together successfully for many years. For a while, they lived at Minchinhampton in Gloucestershire. At the onset of war in 1914, they moved to Glebe Place, Chelsea. Together, they formed the Greenleaf Theatre for the study and practise of drama. They visited America to teach dance and theatre. Constance wrote plays that were performed on stage, and wrote novels. Her first novel was An April Princess. The couple wrote and illustrated books together. For example, Tales From Timbuktu (1923). Her autobiography, Crusaders, was published in 1929. Constance founded the International Lyceum Clubs for women artists and writers. Clubs were established in London, Amsterdam, Berlin, Paris and Florence in the early 1900s. She acted as Honorary Secretary. She and her mother were ardent supporters of women's rights. Constance was also associated with the New Forest Group, formed in around 1924. She acted as Organising Secretary for the Group. She contributed embroideries to the Group's first exhibition held in 1925 at the Mansard Galleries. In 1923 Maxwell Armfield exhibited a portrait of Mrs Smedley in tempera at the Royal Academy. Constance died in West Wycombe.

ARMOUR, HAZEL RUTHVEN (1894-1985)

Sculptor. Born in Edinburgh. Studied at the Edinburgh College of Art and in Paris. Won numerous scholarships, bursaries, diplomas and travelling scholarships. Spent time in London, but based mainly in Edinburgh, including at Moray Place, and a studio in Bedford Road, Edinburgh. Enjoyed an extensive career as an exhibiting sculptor. Worked in bronze, plaster, terracotta, lead, silver, brass and gold. Produced sketches, waxes, busts and medals. Concentrated on portrait works, but also produced other subjects. Exhibited at the Royal Scottish Academy (1914-61), the Royal Glasgow Institute (1917-39), the Royal Academy (1916-38) and the Society of Women Artists (1938). Also, at the Paris Salon, elsewhere in London and in Liverpool and Helsingfors. Works included a bronze medal for the Scottish Women's Hospital, a silver medal for Pollok House Auxiliary Hospital, and a number of medals for the Glasgow School of Architecture. Produced a panel in the Scottish National War Memorial. Also produced a gold medal for Moral Philosophy at the Edinburgh University, and an equestrian statuette made in collaboration with sculptor Phyllis Bone (who specialised in animals) for the Rt Hon. the Earl of Home. Exhibited works included portrait works of Dame Edith Evans, Henry J. Lintott, R.S.A., artist Anne Redpath and Nairne (Armour's sister). Exhibited through six decades. Married John Gould Kennedy. Visited South Africa. Armour died in Suffolk, aged 90.

ASKEW, FELICITY KATHERINE SARAH (b.1894)

Painter / Sculptor / Black & White Artist. Born in Chelsea. The daughter of John Bertram Askew and Frederica. A pupil of Max Kruse, Frank Calderon and Ernest Bazzaro. Specialised in equestrian subjects. Spent seven years in horse training stables and several seasons in hunting. Exhibited at the Paris Salon, the Permanente in Milan, the Goupil Gallery, the Grosse Berliner Kunstausstellung, the Walker Art Gallery, Liverpool, the Society of Scottish Artists and elsewhere in Europe. Worked in bronze. Works included: Working Partners (bronze). Particularly known for her Companions of Labour (1926), another bronze of horses. Also produced rodeo and racing subjects. Based in Newmarket during her career and, later, Berwick-on-Tweed. Possibly the same artist is Mrs Felicity Kourmoiaroff-Askew, also of Berwick-on-Tweed. She exhibited two works at the Society of Women Artists, Pav Espagnol and Haute Ecole, in 1931.

ASPDEN, RUTH SPENCER (1909-2004)

Etcher / Painter / Camouflage Designer. Born in October 1909 in Blackburn, Lancashire. The daughter of William Edward Aspden and Alice. Her father, a timber merchant, originated from

Blackburn, as did her mother. One of at least five children, and appears to have been a twin with Joan Spencer Aspden. Her siblings were also born in Blackburn, but the family spent time at Lytham on the Lancashire coast. Ruth was educated at the St Anne's School, Windermere. Subsequently studied at the Blackburn School of Art between 1927 and 1933 under Arthur Jackson and G.A.N. Reed. Then attended the Royal College of Art, London between 1933 and 1937, studying under Sir William Rothenstein and Percy Hague Jowett. Elected an Associate of the Royal College of Art in 1936. Produced etchings and oil paintings. During the Second World War, between 1941 and 1943, she worked as a camouflage designer. In June 1942 she married Robert Walker Rutter (1909-55) in Warwickshire. The son of a builder, Rutter was also a painter and Associate of the Royal College of Art. They had one daughter. Ruth exhibited her work at the Royal Academy (1936-46), the Royal Society of Painter-Etchers and Engravers and at various provincial galleries in Britain, Canada and America. Exhibited works included: The Kitchen (etching), The Theatre (etching), The Big Skirt (etching) and Girl Reading. Based mainly in London. Purchasers of her work included the Blackburn Art Gallery. Works reproduced in The Artist. Elected an Associate of the Royal Society of Painter-Etchers and Engravers in 1937. Died in Leamington Spa, Warwickshire, aged 95.

ASTON, EVELIN WINIFRED (1891-1975)

Painter / Black & White Artist / Woodcut Artist / Modeller / Sculptor. A multi-talented artist who produced paintings in oils, woodcuts, black & white drawings, models and figure sculptures in stone, wood, alabaster and other materials. Born in Birmingham. The daughter of Walter Edward Aston, a house builder, and Emily. Her father originated from Warwickshire, her mother from Birmingham. One of at least four children (Walter, Harold, Evelin and Horace). Raised in Erdington, Birmingham. Remained in Birmingham, dying there aged 84. Educated privately. Studied at the School of Arts and Crafts at the Birmingham College of Art under William Bloye. Also studied under Bernard Fleetwood Walker, A.R.A. Remained active into the 1950s. Exhibited at the Paris Salon, the Royal Scottish Academy (1934), the Society of Women Artists (1934-39) and with the Royal Birmingham Society of Artists. Exhibited works included: The Adoration (walnut), Virgin and Child (alabaster), The Comforter (alabaster) and Decorative Cock. Elected a Member of the Birmingham Art Circle. In the 1920s she was a teacher of modelling to

boys at the Royal Institute for the Blind in Birmingham. Her The Adoration was reproduced in Revue Moderne, in Revue du Vrai et du Beau and in the Paris Salon illustrated catalogue.

ATKINSON, AMY BEATRICE (1859-1916)

Painter / Illustrator. Born in Fakenham, Norfolk. The daughter of Michael A. Atkinson, Rector of Fakenham, and Amelia Eliza. One of at least three children (Stuart, Amy and Ethel). Spent much of her early life in Fakenham, living there until at least the late 1880s. By the early 1900s, she was living in Looe, Cornwall, working as an artist. Soon after, she moved to Kensington, London, living in a neighbourhood filled with artists and writers. There, she shared lodgings with author Ann Macdonnell who originated from Aberdeen. They lived together for at least 10 years. Amy also spent time in York and Paris. She died in Tonbridge, Kent, though her address was then Cheyne Walk, Chelsea. She may have studied under a local artist in Norfolk. Produced paintings of various subjects including portraits and landscapes in oils and watercolours, and book illustrations. Exhibited her work over a period of more than 25 years. Exhibited widely, including at the Royal Academy (1892-1910), the Society of Women Artists (1884-1905), the Royal Glasgow Institute (1892-96) and the Royal Hibernian Academy (1910). Also, at the New English Art Club (1892-98) and the Royal Society of British Artists (1893 / 4). In 1909 she contributed to an exhibition of pictures of children held at the Baillie Gallery. Other exhibitors on that occasion included Eva Roos and Clare Atwood. Exhibited with the Women's International Art Club, including in 1909. Produced colour illustrations for Ann Macdonnell's Touraine and Its Story (London, Dent, 1907) which was highly praised in The Studio, Vol.39, 1907, pp.364-365. Works included: School's Over!, The Lamp, Cinderella and Low Tide, Whitby Harbour (watercolour).

ATTWELL, MABEL LUCIE (1879-1964)

Artist / Illustrator / Writer. Born in Mile End, London. The daughter of Augustus Attwell, a butcher, and Emily Ann. One of a large family, six of whom were Emily, Ernest, Mabel, Jesse, Augustus and Norman. Raised in Mile End. Educated at the Cooper's Company School. Then studied at the Regent Street Polytechnic School of Art and at the Heatherley's School of Art, but completed neither course. However, she became a prolific and busy artist and illustrator who worked up until her death. Designed postcards for Valentines of Dundee from 1911. Designed advertisements, posters, bed linen, calendars, figurines and wall plaques. Contributed to annuals and gift books including Father Tuck's Annual, Little Folks, Pearson's Magazine and Cassell's Children's Annual. Worked mainly in watercolours and pen & ink. Produced illustrations for books by Charles Kingsley, Hans Andersen, Grimm, Lewis Carroll and J.M. Barrie among others. Illustrated books for publishers including W. & R. Chambers and Raphael Tuck. For the latter, she illustrated some of their Raphael Tuck Library of Gift Books edited by Captain Edric Vredenburg including Mother Goose (1910) and The Water Babies (1915). Also worked on her own Mabel Lucie Attwell annuals from 1922 until her death. Also produced work for Hodder & Stoughton. Attwell was highly successful commercially. Exhibited her work occasionally, including at the Society of Women Artists where she showed two works in 1924, One of the Fairies Stole a Baby and There are Fairies at the Bottom of Our Garden. Elected a Member of the Society (1924-31). In 1908 she married artist Harold Cecil Earnshaw (1886-1937) who originated from Essex. He belonged to the London Sketch Club. The couple lived in Coulsdon, Surrey. They had at least one child, Marjorie. Latterly, Attwell lived at Fowey, Cornwall, where she died. Emily Attwell, Mabel's sister, also studied art.

AULTON, MARGARET (active 1930s)

Etcher / Illustrator / Drypoint Artist. Born in Littlebridge, Herefordshire. Educated privately. Based in Birmingham and Vowchurch, Herefordshire during her career. Produced etchings and drypoint, and illustrations in chalk and pencil. Exhibited her work with the Royal Birmingham Society of Artists and in Southport. A number of her works were reproduced by Alfred Bell & Co. and others. Produced 13 copperplates and 80 pencil drawings for Fair Touraine (Bodley Head).

AUMONIER, LOUISA (1846-1901)

Painter / Artist / Designer. Born in Barnet, Middlesex. The daughter of Henry Collingwood Aumonier, a jeweller, and Nancy Frances. One of a large family. Her brother William (1840-1914) became an eminent architectural carver. Another brother, James, became a painter. Louisa spent time living with James, and with another brother, Frederick. Louisa became a designer and a painter of various subjects including landscapes and flowers. Exhibited her work widely, including at the Royal Academy (1885-1900), the Royal Society of British Artists (from 1868), the

Royal Hibernian Academy (1885-95), the Royal Glasgow Institute (1888-92) and the Society of Women Artists (1870-86). Exhibited works included Hollyhocks at Kew Gardens, Love's Message, Buttercups and An Italian Home, Spoleto, Umbria. In 1898 Louisa married widower Alfred Edward Warner (b.1844) in St Pancras, London. Formerly married to Ellen Ravaison, Warner was a seal engraver. Louisa continued to paint and was active until her untimely death in London in October 1901, aged 55. One of A.E. Warner's daughters by his first marriage, Rosa, became an art student. Three of Louisa's nieces, the daughters of William Aumonier, became involved in art and the decorative arts. Her nephew, John Stacy Aumonier, the son of James Aumonier, married Emmeline Bayes, sister of, and assistant to, decorative artist Jessie Bayes. Based largely in London. SEE: AUMONIER, MINNIE & EDITH & ANNE LOUISE

AUMONIER, MINNIE & EDITH & ANNE LOUISE

Designers / Artists. The artist daughters of eminent architectural carver William Aumonier (1840-1914) and Annie (b.1838). He originated from London, his wife from Essex. Aumonier was a brother to painters James and Louisa. William had at least five children, all born in London. The eldest son, also William (1870-1943), also became an architectural carver. Another child, Minnie (1865-1952), became a costume designer and painter. She exhibited her work at the Royal Academy (1920) and the Society of Women Artists (10 works, 1918-32). Exhibited works included: The Scented Silence and Lilies and Lavender. She died in London, aged 87. Another daughter, Edith (1868-1953), became an art needlework designer, working for an ecclesiastical furnisher. Edith lived with Minnie, latterly at Temple-Fortune Lane, London. Neither married, Edith died in London soon after Minnie, aged 85. A third daughter, Anne Louise (1873-1962), became an art student but appears not to have taken up art as a career. In 1899 she married author / journalist Henry Theodore Stahel Farmer. They had at least three children. Anne died, aged 89, having spent her later years as a widow, living with Minnie and Edith. SEE: AUMONIER, LOUISA

AWDRY, MARGARET JANE (1854-1939)

Repoussé Worker / Jewellery Maker / Watercolour Painter. Born in Brockton, Shropshire. The daughter of the Rev. Walter Herbert Awdry and Mary. The eldest of at least eight children (four boys and four girls). As a small child, she lived in Shropshire. Subsequently moved to Ramsey on the Isle of Man. As a young adult, she lived in Edgbaston, Warwickshire. She was still living with her widowed mother and four of her siblings at the age of 26. One of her brothers became a civil engineer, another a bank clerk and another a solicitor. Her sister Laura became a music teacher. It was whilst living in Warwickshire that Margaret attended the Birmingham Municipal School of Art. A promising student, she won national book prizes and medal certificates for jewellery exhibited at various exhibitions. Subsequently concentrated on producing jewellery, decorative metalwork and watercolour paintings. She remained in Warwickshire with her widowed mother until at least the early 1900s but later lived with her brother Walter and another sister Mary in Moseley, Worcestershire. She spent her final years in Clevedon, Somerset where she died in September 1939, aged 84. Left her small estate to another sister, Lydia.

For over 28 years, Awdry taught at the School for Jewellers and Silversmiths, Birmingham, and taught art at a number of private schools. Exhibited her work in Britain and abroad. Had a close affinity with the Arts and Crafts Exhibition Society. At the Society's 1906 exhibition, one of her exhibits was a brooch / pendant with a setting based on Signs of the Ionian Islands which was illustrated in the Art Journal, 1906, p.125. The piece is typical of the neat, meticulous, detailed jewellery which she produced. Another of her exhibits on that occasion was a pendant with decorative chain titled Briar Rose which Awdry had executed to a design by William Morris. It was illustrated in The Studio, Vol.37, March 1906, p.139. In The Studio it was described as 'one of the most purely beautiful things amongst the jewellery, the workmanship is exquisite and sensitive '. Awdry also exhibited at the Arts and Crafts exhibitions staged by the Royal Birmingham Society of Artists, including in 1909 when she showed 19 pieces of jewellery. Also exhibited in Liverpool, Ghent, Paris. America, Canada, New Zealand, Wembley and elsewhere. Exhibited four works at the Society of Women Artists (1910-25). A contemporary of jewellery makers Kate Eadie, the Dawsons and the Gaskins, all of whom had similar connections with Birmingham. Awdry may have exhibited in Cornwall in 1911 at the St Ives Show Day (details not specific).

AYERS, LOTTIE MARY PIMM (1882-1951)
Sculptor. Born and raised in London. The daughter of Joseph Ayers, a butcher, and Georgina. Her parents originated from Eynsham, Oxfordshire. One of at least three children. As a child, she attended the Oxford Gardens School, Kensington. Her brothers Percival and George went into the family business. Lottie, however, became a student at the St Martin's School of Art, Westminster. In 1911, aged 28, she is listed as an art student and designer, indicating that she either studied for a considerable number of years, or took up art only in her late 20s. At that stage, she was still living with her parents at Blenheim Crescent, North Kensington. As a student, she won gold, silver and bronze medals for modelling. In the 1910 National Competition of Schools of Art, she won a gold medal for a study of a man tugging on a rope. Received three London County Council scholarships. Awarded an Art Class Teachers' Certificate. Became a modeller from life, a wax-work artist and finisher. Early in her career, she was a decorative modeller in clay and colour, a lampshade painter, an embroideress and an art teacher. She still had a studio at Blenheim Crescent, the site of the family home, in 1934. Exhibited occasionally, including at the Royal Academy where she showed two works in 1924: The Lazy Boy (statuette) and Portrait of a Lady (relief). Also exhibited in Doncaster and Plymouth. Other works included: Ophelia (head in relief) and The Wrecker (figure in the round). Died in London, aged 68.

B

BACH, MADELEINE (active 1910s)
Painter / Pottery Worker. Born in London. Studied in London at the Royal Female School of Art and the Royal College of Art. Produced miniature paintings, mostly portraits, and painted landscapes on porcelain. Based in London. Elected a Member of the Emerson Club. Exhibited her work, including at the Society of Women Artists (1917), the Royal Society of Miniature Painters, the Society of Miniaturists and in Liverpool, Birmingham and Manchester. Exhibited works included: Beatrice and A Portrait.

BACON, MARJORIE MAY (1902-88)
Painter / Engraver. Born in Ipswich in January 1902. The daughter of Arthur Bacon, a pastry cook, and Mary Emily Humm. Her father originated from Great Yarmouth, her mother from Colchester, Essex. Raised in Great

Yarmouth. Had at least one sibling, Audrey. Studied at the Norwich School of Art and the Royal College of Art, London. Elected an Associate of the Royal College of Art. Produced etchings, aquatints, mezzotints, works in sepia and paintings in oils. Various subjects including animals, still life and buildings. Based at Great Yarmouth, Newbury in Berkshire, London and Dedham, Essex during her career. Exhibited at the Royal Academy (1927-44) and the New English Art Club. Exhibited works included: The Black Jug (oil), A Corner of Old Norfolk (aquatint), Ichabod - Thy Glory Hath Departed (sepia) and 'Felstead', Winner of the Derby, 1928 (etching). In 1936 she married Henry Macbeth-Raeburn in Kensington. He died in 1947. Marjorie died in Great Yarmouth, aged 86.

BAILEY, RUBY W. - SEE LEVICK, R.W.

BAKER, ANNIE (1840-1901)

Craftswoman. Also Anne or Anna. For a period of around 10 years, Annie Baker ran the Porlock Weir, Somerset handcraft class, which produced embossed and gilded leatherwork in the 1890s and early 1900s. The class ran from at least 1892 under her guidance, and on her death in Porlock Weir in late 1901 her sister, Sophia Agnes Cunninghame (1838-1916), took it over. Like Yattendon, Compton, Fivemiletown and other similar handcraft classes of the period, Porlock Weir ran in conjunction with the Home Arts and Industries Association, showing work at its annual exhibition in London. The class, strictly for amateurs, was mostly made up of local fishermen. It appears to have been a smaller venture than its contemporaries, though it too caused a stir nationally for a short time. Designs were provided by Miss Baker, but the work was mostly executed by the class. Porlock Weir exhibited at the Home Arts exhibitions from at least 1897 until at least 1906, on one occasion showing several large embossed panels for a hall, and a travelling writing case with a decoration of flying seagulls and the inscription 'As cold water to a thirsty soul, so is good news from a far land'. All were to Miss Baker's designs. Those associated with the class included Philip Burgess (1863-1936). Born at Porlock Weir, the son of a labourer, Burgess was initially a stonemason. By the time of the 1911 census, however, he is listed as an embossed leatherworker. He spent much of his life at Sea Breeze Cottage in West Porlock, dying there in December 1936. He was married to Caroline Saville but had no children. How long he was active as a leatherworker remains unclear, but he doubtless studied at the Porlock Weir class.

Porlock Weir was noted in The Studio magazine for making bold experiments in decorative leatherwork, and was particularly noted for its highly decorative and attractive applique panels. In 1900 The Studio (Vol.20, July, p.78) illustrated a book cover shown at that year's Home Arts exhibition, executed for the St George the Martyr Public Library. The cover bore a design of St George and the Dragon, and was executed by Philip Burgess and Miss Baker. Although considered an amateur, like its contemporaries, Porlock Weir produced exceptional work which deserves reassessment, as does Miss Baker's role in its success. Very little has so far come to light about Annie Baker. She was born in Gibraltar but spent much of her life in Somerset. The family spent some time in Bristol, at Westbury-on-Trym, but moved to Porlock Weir sometime in the 1880s. Although Sophia married in 1874, she was widowed soon after and lived with Annie. She too died in Porlock Weir, at Chapel Knap. They were the daughters of Thomas Baker, a magistrate and one-time major in the army. Sophia was born in Ireland. They had at least one sister, Charlotte. Since Sophia died in 1916, it can be presumed that, like Mrs Waterhouse's Yattendon class, what remained of Porlock Weir after Annie's death would have come to an end as the First World War started, if not before.

BAKER, ETHELWYN MARY (1899-1988)

Sculptor / Painter / Commercial Artist. Born in Belfast, Ireland. The daughter of artist Alfred Rawlings Baker and Hannah. Had one elder sibling, Alfreda Helen. Studied at the Slade School, London under Professor Henry Tonks and George Havard Thomas. Also, at the Royal Academy schools. Produced sculptures in stone, wood and clay and paintings in watercolours. Produced decorative work, including decorative figure designs for the Royal Worcester Porcelain Company, two examples of which were illustrated in The Studio, Vol.102, December 1931, p.367 in an article British Pottery of To-day (pp.366-377). Exhibited at the Royal Academy (1932-35), the Royal Society of British Sculptors, the American Institute of Architecture, the Cooling Galleries and the Walker Art Gallery, Liverpool. Exhibited works included: Vulture (carved pear wood) and Indra Roy (head). Elected a Member of the Society of Industrial Artists. In the 1930s worked at the Cockloft Studios, St John's Wood. Subsequently, in the 1950s, based at a studio at Portman Close, Portman Square, London. Other works reproduced in Designers in Britain and Graphis. In 1943 she married composer Robert F. Cox in Paddington, London.

BAKER, FRANCES CAUTLEY - SEE FARRELL, F.C.

BAKER, GLADYS MARGUERITE (1889-1974)

Pencil Artist / Portrait Painter / Decorator. Born in St Pancras, London in October 1889. The daughter of Joseph Samson Baker and Sarah Jane Rudman. Early on, her father was a warehouseman. She was one of at least nine children (Alice, Emily, Dorothy, James, Joseph, Stuart, Howard, Gladys and Kathleen). By the early 1890s her father, who originated from Bristol but lived in St Pancras, London, had become a clothing manufacturer. Despite coming from such a large family, Gladys was well educated, at Queen's College, London. Evidently a promising student, she went on to study art at the St John's Wood School of Art, London, followed by the prestigious Royal Academy schools. As a student aged 21 she lived at home, but by that time her mother had died. Her father was then still involved in the clothing trade. A promising scholar, she won the Graphic Prize, and a Royal Academy silver medal for 'composition in colour'.

Gladys remained in and around London throughout her life and career. She died in Barnet, aged 84. Spent some of her time living and working in Tavistock Square and Finchley. Produced landscapes, still life and portraits in oils and watercolours, pencil studies, and carried out decorative work. Exhibited at the Royal Academy (1916-47), the Royal Institute of Painters in Watercolours, the International Society of Sculptors, Painters and Gravers, the Society of Women Artists (103 works, 1917-69), the National Portrait Society and in Stockholm, Liverpool, Hull and Oldham as well as the Academy of Design, New York. Exhibited works included: Old Glass, Sussex Downs From Pulborough, Miss Buchan-Smith, Founder & Past Principal of Northwood College, Middlesex and Les Sylphides No.2 (oil). Elected an Associate of the Society of Women Artists (1929-30) and a Member (1931-75).

BAKER, MARY (b.1897)

Book Illustrator / Black & White Artist / Painter. Born in Runcorn, Cheshire in July 1897. The daughter of Harry Baker and Mary. Her father, a work's chemist involved in the manufacture of caustic soda and bleaching powder, originated from Hackney, London. Her mother originated from Blackburn, Lancashire. The third of at least four children (Margaret, Henry, Mary and Wilson). Raised in Runcorn. Educated privately.

Encouraged in art. In her late teens, she sold some of her pictures to magazines. Then took a correspondence course in illustration with the Press Art School. This included silhouette drawing which she used to illustrate her sister Margaret's story The Black Cats and the Tinker's Wife which was published in 1923. This became the first of a series of books produced jointly by the Baker sisters, which eventually numbered more than 17 by 1948. Others included The Girl Who Curtsied (1925), Pixies and the Silver Crown (1927), The Best of Health (1930) and Mrs Bobbity's Crust (1937). Mary also spent time studying at the Chester School of Art. Although principally an illustrator, she produced landscapes in watercolours, and was an amateur naturalist. When her father retired, the family moved to Leominster, Herefordshire. After his death, the remaining family moved to Sutton under Brailes, Warwickshire. Exhibited her work occasionally, including at the Walker Art Gallery, Liverpool, The Mound, Edinburgh, and at an exhibition of children's illustrated books held at the Victoria & Albert Museum, London. Still active as an illustrator in 1948. Noted in Mahony, Latimer & Folmsbee, Illustrators of Children's Books 1744-1945, Boston, The Horn Book Inc., 1947.

BALL, MAUDE MARY & ETHEL (active 1910s-1940s)

The artist daughters of Valentine Ball, C.B., L.L.D., F.R.S. Maude was born in Dublin in April 1883, and was educated privately. She studied at the Royal Hibernian Academy schools and at the Dublin Metropolitan School of Art. Maude became an oil painter and miniaturist based in Waterloo Road, Dublin. Concentrated on figures and portraits. Exhibited at the Royal Hibernian Academy (54 works, 1910-35). Exhibited works included: In the Big Armchair, Girl With a Blue Chain, Mrs Valentine Ball, Sir Thomas Moffett, Late President of Queen's College, Galway and Saluting the Colours - Boys of the Royal Hibernian Military School, Phoenix Park, 1922. Also executed a portrait of Cornish-based artist Adrian Stokes (1854-1935), indicating that the Ball sisters were familiar with leading artists of the day in both Ireland and England.

Ethel Ball became a sculptor, also based at Waterloo Road, Dublin. Worked in bronze, marble and plaster, specialising in animal subjects. Like Maude, she exhibited at the Royal Hibernian Academy (58 works, 1917-40). Exhibited works included: Chimpanzee and Her Baby (bronze & marble), Arabian Baboon (plaster model), Shetland Pony and Sketch -

Young Donkey Foal. Ethel also exhibited further afield at the Royal Scottish Academy (1940), the Royal Academy (1928) and the Society of Women Artists (1939). Both sisters enjoyed long and productive careers, both ceasing to exhibit at around the same time.

BANISTER, BARBARA GILLIAN (1895-1984)

Jewellery Designer & Maker / Enameller / Silversmith. Born in Epsom in October 1895. The daughter of Frederick Jonas Banister (1856-1927), an architect and surveyor, and Annie Rita Barrow (1865-1953). Had at least one sibling, Dorothy. Raised in Epsom. Educated at the Worcester Park School, Westgate-on-Sea, Kent. Studied art privately, and at the Royal College of Art, London. Based in Epsom. Died in Uckfield, Sussex. For a time she acted as a draughtswoman in the Hydrographic Department of the Admiralty. Designed and made decorative jewellery, working mostly in silver and enamels. Exhibited her work occasionally, including at the Society of Women Artists (1930), at the London Arts and Crafts Exhibitions and the British Industries Fair. Awarded a gold cross at the Home Arts and Industries Association exhibition. Photographs of some of her work appeared in Queen and La Revue Moderne.

BANKART, EVELYN MABEL (1869-1953)

Embroideress. Born in India. Was Evelyn M. Fosberry. In 1894 she married George Percy Bankart (1866-1929) in Yorkshire. The couple lived in London and had at least two sons, Hugh and George. Bankart was a successful architect, surveyor, decorative artist and manufacturer who originated from Leicester. He was elected a Member of the Art Workers' Guild. He was particularly known for his decorative plasterwork, modelling and metalwork. He collaborated with designer Ernest Gimson (1864-1919) on several decorative plasterwork projects. Gimson was also an expert on plasterwork, but also produced embroidery designs, some of which were executed by Evelyn, who was a skilled needlewoman. Influenced by nature, Gimson's embroidery designs, executed by Evelyn, included those worked in white silk thread on white linen in the early 1900s. Evelyn died in Somerset, aged 84.

BANKS, VIOLET (b.1896)

Painter / Pottery Decorator. Born near Kinghorn, Fife in March 1896. The daughter of James Banks and Christina. Had at least one sibling, James. Educated at Craigmount, Edinburgh. Studied at

the Edinburgh College of Art where she was awarded a diploma. Became senior art mistress at St Oran's School, Edinburgh. Also a painter of still life, figures and landscapes in oils and watercolours, and a decorator of pottery. Also had an interest in photography. Exhibited her work, including at the Royal Scottish Academy (1918-28), the Royal Glasgow Institute (1924), with the Society of Scottish Artists, the Royal Scottish Watercolour Society, the Scottish Society of Women Artists, at the Liverpool Institute and in Aberdeen. Exhibited works included: The Red Chart, Staffa From Iona, Tea in the Studio and Dancer Resting. Based in Fife and Edinburgh during her career. Used The Blue Studio in Kirkcaldy, Fife.

BANNER, JOSEPHINA - SEE VASCONCELLOS, J. DE

BANNIN, KATE MARY (b.c.1862-post-1915)

Sculptor. Born in Clerkenwell, London. The daughter of Mary Bannin who originated from Ireland. Raised in Clerkenwell. Lived elsewhere in London, for part of the time with her mother. Studied at the Royal Academy schools, London. In 1885 she was awarded the Landseer Scholarship of £10 for two years. Produced heads and busts in bronze. Exhibited at the Royal Academy (1889-90), the Royal Society of British Artists (1887-89), the Society of Women Artists (1888-90) and the Walker Art Gallery, Liverpool. Exhibited works included: Head of an Old Man, She Was the Daughter of a Cottager, An Albanian and A Monk (bust). Dates of Kate's birth vary on records, from 1857, to 1862, to 1866. No death can be traced, suggesting she may have died abroad.

BARBER, FLORENCE G. - SEE RICHTER, F.G.

BARHAM, SYBIL (1877-1950)

Painter / Illustrator. Born in Birmingham. The daughter of Francis Foster Barham, a bank manager, and Sibella. They were a literary family. Her uncle, William, was a poet. Another uncle, Francis, was a journalist and writer. Sybil was one of at least six children (also Margaret, Harold, Charles, Muriel and Gertrude). From 1899 she studied at the Herkomer School at Bushey, Hertfordshire. Spent three years there, meeting Kate Cowderoy who also became a painter and illustrator. After leaving Bushey, she lived at The Priest's House at Grafton Manor near Bromsgrove. From around 1905 she worked for C.W. Faulkner, designing colourful postcards.

Her designs were also used as prints, greetings cards and calendars. Also illustrated children's books, annuals and magazines for Harrap, Darton and others. Barham had an extensive career in illustration, working mainly for Faulkner but also Reinthal & Newman. Latterly, she lived in Hampshire, her death registered in Petersfield, aged 73. In her later years, she lived with another friend from Bushey, Elizabeth Maynard. Books illustrated by Barham included: The Story of Angelina Wacks (Clayton, Palmer, Darton, 1913), The Elf of the Orchard (with E. Peacock, Darton, n.d.), Stories From Browning (Turnbull, Harrap, 1914) and Peter Pan Postcard Painting Book (C.W. Faulkner, c.1920). Occasionally exhibited her work in and around Birmingham.

BARKER, MAY HEATHERINGTON (1857-1912)

Artist / Sculptor. Born in Spelsbury, Oxfordshire. The daughter of Thomas Barker and Margaret. Her father, who was the vicar of Spelsbury, originated from Yorkshire, her mother from Berkshire. The eldest of at least seven children (May, Edward, Charlotte, Helen, Edith, Alice and Rayner). By at least 1881 May was a student in London, living in Cavendish Square. Became an artist, decorative sculptor and medallist. Produced pencil studies, portrait medals, plaster reliefs, paintings and silverpoint. Remained in London for the rest of her life and career, dying there in August 1912. Also worked as an art teacher in London. Latterly, shared accommodation with decorative sculptors Ellen and Dorothy Rope in Marylebone Road. Exhibited her work occasionally, including at the Royal Academy (1891-1907) and the Royal Society of British Artists (1890). Exhibited works included: Medal: St Martin, An Old Salt, Study in Silverpoint and Passage du Chateau Gisors.

BARNETT, ALICE MAY - SEE COOK, A.M.

BARNSLEY, GRACE (1896-1975)

Designer / Ceramic Decorator. Was Emily Grace, known as Grace. Born near Cirencester, Gloucestershire in late 1896 in the village of Duntisbourne Rouse. The daughter and first child of Sidney Howard Barnsley (1865-1926) and Lucy Evelyn Morley (b.1865). Her father originated from Birmingham, her mother from Lincoln. Raised in Duntisbourne Rouse as a child, but in her teens was living in Sapperton, Gloucestershire. Had a younger brother, William Edward (b.1900), who went on to study at the London County Council Central School of Arts

and Crafts, and who became a furniture designer. Sidney Barnsley was a highly respected architect and designer who was part of the Cotswolds circle which included his brother Ernest (1863-1926) and architect Ernest Gimson (1864-1919). Gimson and the Barnsley brothers began their careers in London but deliberately moved to the Cotswolds in 1893 to work. They adhered to Arts and Crafts principles. Bookbinder Katharine Adams was also based in the Cotswolds, at nearby Broadway. Grace was, therefore, exposed to various artistic influences from an early age.

Grace attended the Birmingham School of Art in around 1914. She then trained in London as a decorator of pottery with Alfred and Louise Powell, friends of her father. She then returned to the Cotswolds to work. Decorated in natural motifs, mainly flowers and plants. Worked freelance for Wedgwood. Also worked in collaboration with F.L.M. Griggs and with Oscar C. Davies whom she married in early 1926 in Gloucestershire. In around 1934 the couple moved to Rainham, Kent and subsequently established the Roeinga Pottery, producing decorated pottery. Grace appears to have done little after the onset of the Second World War. She died in early 1975 in Broxbourne, Hertfordshire, aged 78.

BARR, ROBINA (active 1910s-1950s)

Sculptor / Modeller. Born in Glasgow. The daughter of Robert Barr. Educated at the Hutcheson's Grammar School. Studied at the Glasgow School of Art and at the Glasgow University. Produced heads, plaques and reliefs in various materials including plaster. Exhibited at the Royal Glasgow Institute (29 works, 1919-53) and in Liverpool. Exhibited works included: The Mite (head, plaster), A Movie Fan (relief, plaster), The Lass With the Delicate Air (relief, plaster) and Our Mr Churchill (plaque, plaster). Based in Glasgow and Milngavie during her career.

BARRON, GLADYS CAROLINE (b.c.1885-1966)

Sculptor / Modeller / Painter. Born in India. The daughter of Maxwell Beckett Logan, a banker, and Ismay Bellew Adams. Spent part of her childhood in St Albans, Hertfordshire. Studied under Mrs Gilbert Bayes at the St John's Wood School of Art. Produced various subjects including portrait works in materials including bronze and plaster. Had numerous distinguished sitters. Exhibited at the Royal Scottish Academy (34 works, 1925-64), the Royal Glasgow Institute (1946-53), the Royal Academy (1912-59) and in

Liverpool. Exhibited works included: The Wind Sprite (statuette), Sir Alexander M. MacEwan (bust, bronze), Lady Hermione Roberts (plaster) and Polish Partisan (head, bronze). Initially based in London, then later Inverness and Morayshire. A Member of the Overseas Club and of the Inverness Golf Club. Married Evan M. Barron. Works illustrated included portrait busts of Sir Murdoch Macdonald, K.C.M.G., M.P., and Mackintosh of Mackintosh in the Scotsman.

BARROW, EVELYN (1871-1945)

Embroideress. Was Mary Evelyn, known as Evelyn. Born in Surbiton, Surrey. The daughter of Robert Knapp Barrow, an officer, and Elizabeth. By at least the age of 19, Evelyn was an apprentice embroideress with the Sisters of Mercy, Convent of St John the Baptist at 72 Gower Street, London. Assistant Head of the Convent was Katharine Lungley of the Ladies' Ecclesiastical Embroidery Teaching Guild of Great Britain and Ireland. A number of women at the convent were involved in needlework or embroidery, some apprentices, including Mary Eliza Negus. Barrow subsequently worked as an ecclesiastical embroideress, and by at least 1911 was teaching the subject at St Peter's Home and Sisterhood at Mortimer Road, Kilburn. Evelyn was a member of the Church Crafts League, one of its embroiderers. Others included Mary Symonds and Helen Stebbing. The London-based League had considerable influence on the decoration of churches from the time of its founding in 1899. By 1920, some 73 artists, craftsmen and craftswomen were working in association with the League. Evelyn died in Surrey, aged 73

BARTELS, MARGARET (1887-1932)

Painter / Illuminator. Born in Surbiton, Surrey in April 1887. The daughter of William Alfred Bartels and Marion. Her father, a merchant, died whilst Margaret was still a child. Her mother originated from Ireland. One of at least four children (Margaret, Olive, Ruth and Wilfred). Raised in Farnborough (Gt. London). Her widowed mother had independent means and educated her children well. As an adult, Margaret lived in Camberwell, and at Acacia Grove, Dulwich where she died, aged 45. Lived with her mother and adult siblings for part of the time. The Bartels are noted on the 1911 national census with the note 'prominent suffragettes schedule filled up by order of the Registrar General'. This would indicate that the Bartels ladies may have had some involvement with the suffragette movement, and were marked out as such.

Margaret probably studied in London and became a painter and illuminator. Exhibited her work at the Society of Women Artists (1917). Exhibited works included: Illumination, Design for Bookplates and The Inner Beauty. Elected a Member of the Society of Scribes and Illuminators. Left her estate to her mother, who outlived her.

BASE, IRENE ESTHER MURIEL (1896-1982)

Illuminator / Calligrapher / Scribe. Born in Norwich, Norfolk in May 1896. The daughter of George William Base (1872-1935) and Esther Elizabeth Brown (1871-1963). Her father, a manager for the Anglo American Oil Co. Ltd, originated from Norwich, her mother from Blickling, Norfolk. Had a younger brother, George Cecil Base (1899-1959), also born in Norwich. Raised in Norwich initially, then moved to Lowestoft, Suffolk. Educated at private schools. Subsequently studied at the Norwich School of Art and the Chelsea School of Art, London. Won the Christopher Head Scholarship. At Chelsea, she studied calligraphy under Mervyn C. Oliver. Chose to concentrate on illumination and lettering. Based in Shirehampton, Bristol for much of her life and career. Worked for over 45 years. Taught at the West of England College of Art between 1945 and 1970. Did some work for St Mary's, Shirehampton, Bristol, including an altar book and memorial books. Also executed the Slough Book of Remembrance.

Base was elected a Member of the Society of Scribes and Illuminators (founded 1921). An example of her work, a written quotation taken from John Donne's Sermons, was illustrated in an article about the Society of Scribes and Illuminators written by fellow member Claire Evans in The Studio, Vol.138, July 1949, pp.1-5. In 1959 Base founded the Bristol Manuscript Club. In 1965 she was elected a Member of the prestigious Art Workers' Guild. Exhibited her work occasionally, including at Wembley (1924-25), with the Arts and Crafts Exhibition Society, at the International Exhibitions in Vienna and Dunedin, with the Royal West of England Academy and the Society of Women Artists (1930-31). Exhibited works included: The Grasshopper and the Cricket (illuminated sonnet), the Arms of Bristol University, the Arms of King's College, Cambridge and the Arms of Eton College. Died in Bristol in March 1982, aged 85.

BASS, IRENE - SEE WELLINGTON, I.

BASSETT, MARY ANN (1854-1948)

Craftswoman. Founder and instructor of the Leighton Buzzard handcraft class in Bedfordshire. Mary Ann was born in Leighton Buzzard, the daughter of Francis Bassett (1820-99) and Ellen Harris (1820-1903). Her father was a banker and magistrate who originated from Leighton Buzzard. Her mother originated from Middlesex. One of at least seven children (Ellen Mary, Thomas, Frederick, Isabella, Mary Ann, Louisa and Katharine). Frederick also went into banking. The family lived at The Heath, a large house in Leighton Buzzard, and employed several servants. Mary Ann and Louisa were still living at the house in 1901 at the ages of 47 and 45. But soon after, probably after their mother's death in 1903, Mary Ann was living alone in Billington Road, Leighton Buzzard with three servants. She never married. Died in Chelsea in November 1948, aged 95. Left a substantial estate of some £23,110.

Sometime between 1892 and 1893, Mary Ann founded a leatherwork class at Leighton Buzzard, originally to give instruction and employment to a local cripple child. It would appear that Mary Ann was an expert leatherworker who produced her own designs, and taught the class. By 1897, she had at least six or seven cripples working regularly at binding and leatherwork. They were paid by the hour according to the standard of their work. The class adopted a method of tooling the leather used in German bindings, and developed a speciality of tinting and gilding the leather after it was embossed. The class also developed a style of beaten leatherwork similar in method to repoussé metalwork. Various items were made and sold, including stationery and letter cases, leather boxes, bookbindings and folding photograph screens.

Early on, in 1897, the class was noted and praised in the Art Journal in an article Art Workers at Home (pp.14-17). The article included illustrations of three leather bindings by Miss Bassett. As with other similar handcraft ventures of the period, including Marian Twelves and her Langdale Linen Industry, a high standard of workmanship was carefully maintained and the end results were considered to be individual works of art as well as functional items. From at least 1894, when the class first began to expand, Leighton Buzzard contributed to the annual exhibition of the Home Arts and Industries Association, held in London. The Association was founded in 1884 with the purpose of reviving traditional handcrafts and offering alternative employment to the working class. Classes were established across the country where crafts such as spinning, weaving, lace making, metalwork and woodcarving were taught. Workers were encouraged to contribute to its annual exhibition, the first of which was held in 1885. The Association's central offices and studios were at the Royal Albert Hall, London, where other classes were also held. Mary Ann's leatherwork class clearly had strong ties with the Home Arts and Industries Association, and contributed regularly to its annual exhibition until at least 1907.

Many of the Home Arts classes flourished and produced excellent craftsmen and craftswomen, as at Leighton Buzzard. In particular, Arthur Smallbones (1876-1941), the son of a local miller, proved gifted and deft under Miss Bassett's guidance. He exhibited regularly at the Home Arts exhibition. In 1899, for example, he showed a leather-covered chest which was illustrated in The Studio, Vol.17, July 1899, p.100. Smallbones also exhibited leather caskets and leather bookbindings. At the 1900 Home Arts exhibition, he showed a decorative book cover adapted by a Miss Willis. It would appear that Smallbones, like other craftworkers linked to the Home Arts, mainly executed the designs of others, particularly those by Mary Ann. Herbert Metcalf and J. Mercy also flourished at Leighton Buzzard.

The class also produced a number of successful craftswomen. Another of Mary Ann's pupils, Minnie King, firmly established herself as a skilled craftworker. She worked on a number of important projects at Leighton Buzzard, including a binding for Spenser's The Shepheardes Calender which was designed by Mary Ann and exhibited at the 1899 Home Arts exhibition. Minnie King also executed a copy of a leather casket kept at the South Kensington Museum, London which was highly praised. Ada Coster, also of the Leighton Buzzard class, made similar caskets, as did Arthur Smallbones. King had ties with the short-lived Guild of Women Binders, as did Mary Ann. King's associations with Leighton Buzzard continued into the early 1900s. At the 1905 Home Arts exhibition, she showed a guest book in embossed leather designed by Alys M. Hawkins and illustrated in the Art Journal, 1905, p216. In 1900 and 1902 Minnie King exhibited with the Society of Women Artists, showing various 'handicrafts'.

Mary Ann Bassett also taught Alice Shepherd who, such were her talents and successes, is dealt with as a separate entry. She also exhibited at the Home Arts annual exhibition. Shepherd, however, later worked for bookbinder Cedric

Chivers of Bath. Fannie Brown, another of Mary Ann's pupils, exhibited handicrafts at the Society of Women Artists in 1902. Mary Ann revealed herself to be an equally talented craftswoman, but also a designer, who exhibited her work along with that of her pupils. Her many and varied projects included a small leather handbag with steel fittings and ornamentation by Arthur Smallbones which was designed by Mary Ann and Alice Shepherd and exhibited at the Home Arts exhibition for 1900. Mary Ann's designs were used by other classes, including a woodwork class at Ascott, Warwickshire where leatherwork was used in items such as chairs. Mary Ann exhibited some of her own work at the Society of Women Artists in 1903. Perhaps the pinnacle of the Leighton Buzzard class was reached in 1907. Then, a reredos was donated to the local Parish Church by a local resident, on the understanding that the work was carried out by local craftsmen. The reredos was designed by architect G.F. Bodley, and he supervised the woodcarving and embossing in leather of four angels for adornment. This was possibly one of the earliest uses of leather in ecclesiastical decoration of this type. The woodcarving was executed by H. Wibberley and the leatherwork by Minnie King and Arthur Smallbones. The reredos was illustrated in The Studio, Vol.41, June 1907, p.65. It remains difficult to assess exactly how long the Leighton Buzzard class survived. But in 1911 Arthur Smallbones is listed in census recordings as a bookbinder attached to 'handicraft classes'. This was, presumably, Mary Ann's class. The start of war in 1914 saw the demise of many such classes, however.

BATESON, EDITH HONORA (1867-1938)

Sculptor / Painter. Born in Cambridge in early 1867. The daughter of the Rev. William Henry Bateson, D.D, Master of St John's College, Cambridge, and Anna. Her father, who was some 17 years older than her mother, originated from Liverpool, as did her mother. Edith was the fifth of at least six children (two sons and four daughters), all of whom were raised at St John's College Lodge, Cambridge. By 1881, Anna is listed as a widow, but was still living at the Lodge with her six children, and is listed as being an 'assistant'. William, the eldest son, was an undergraduate at Cambridge at that time, and Edith was still only 14 years of age. Another of Edith's brothers, Edward, also distinguished himself, becoming a university scholar and subsequently a barrister. Among his many accomplishments, he became Stipendiary Magistrate of Mauritius (1901-03), Attorney-General of St Lucia (1903-06) and Judge of Egyptian native tribunals (1907-12) as well as editor of A History of Northumberland.

Edith forged a successful career as a sculptor and painter, producing busts and heads in bronze and marble and bright, vivid watercolour landscapes. Initially, she was educated at the Perse School, Cambridge. Then studied at the Royal Academy schools, London where she won the First and Second Silver Medals for 'Busts From Life', and a First Silver Medal for a 'Model From the Antique'. By at least 1911 she was working as a professional artist in Singers Lane at Robin Hood's Bay, Yorkshire. Also acted as Honorary Secretary of the N.D.P Ridings Federation in Women's Suffrage at that time, sharing her home with visitor Marie Belter, a private teacher, and one servant. Her mother, by then 81 years of age, was still alive. Bateson was also friends with sculptor Anna Maria Gayton, with whom she lived in the last years of Gayton's life at Bushey, Hertfordshire.

By the 1920s and 1930s, Edith was based at Nightingale Corner in Bushey, which was still something of an artists' colony and once the site of Hubert von Herkomer's School of Art (later run by Lucy Kemp-Welch). Herkomer's school had produced a considerable number of women artists. Edith died in Storrington, Sussex in January 1938, aged 70. She left her £15,888 estate to her brother, Edward (then a retired judge), and to Catherine Constance Cooper. Had a distinguished career, covering most of her adult life.

Edith exhibited her work from at least the 1890s until at least the 1920s. Exhibited at the Paris Salon, the Royal Academy (1891-1912), the Royal Society of British Artists (from 1892), the Royal Glasgow Institute (1912), the New Gallery and the New English Art Club. Also, at the International Society of Sculptors, Painters & Gravers, the Liverpool Art Gallery and the Society of Women Artists (1916-25). Exhibited works included: Edward Bateson, Esq. (bust), Mrs Bateson (bust), Angelique (head), Swaledale (watercolour) and Prometheus (bronze & marble). Official purchasers of her work included the Chemical Laboratory, Cambridge, for whom she executed a bronze bust of Professor Liveing, F.R.S. Also executed a marble bust for Newnham College, Cambridge. Her The Dead Highlander was illustrated in at least one national newspaper, while her Everlasting Arms was illustrated in Architectural Review. A group executed for a monument was illustrated in the Builder. One of her marble groups was owned by Lady Margaret Hall, Oxford. Elected a Member of the Lyceum Club. SEE: GAYTON, ANNA MARIA

BATTEN, MARY EMMELINE (1874-1952)

Carver / Gilder. Born in Aveley, Essex. The daughter of Charles Glen Bott, a medical practitioner, and Kate (Catherine Cecilia Maria). They married in 1868 in Oxfordshire. Her father originated from Chelsea, London, her mother from Oxford. One of at least five children (Cecilia, Louisa, Mary, Walter and Hugh). Some time between 1877 and 1881 her father died, and the family moved to London, to Tottenham, followed by Kensington, then Fulham. Cecilia initially worked as a typist, and Walter became a draughtsman. Eventually, Kate Bott returned to Essex, dying in Rochford in 1915, aged 67. Mary became a woodcarver and gilder, though it remains unclear where she studied. Certainly, by 1901, aged 27, she is listed as earning a living in those two arts, and is living in Fulham with her mother, Cecilia (now a hospital nurse) and Hugh (now a bookkeeper). In July 1903 Mary married painter and illustrator John Dickinson Batten (1860-1932) in Kensington, London. He originated from Plymouth, Devon. Initially, they lived in Kensington, then Richmond, Surrey. Had one son, Leonard John Batten, born in 1904. John D. Batten died in Surrey in August 1932. Mary later lived at Horsham, Sussex where she died, aged 78. Mary is perhaps best known today for a triptych at the Church of St Martin, Kensal Rise, London, which was carved and gilded by her and painted in tempera by her husband. The triptych was illustrated in The Studio, Vol.49, 1910, and in Vol.62, August 1914, p.181 in an article on the Society of Mural Decorators and Painters in Tempera (pp.173-182). The Battens presumably had connections with the Society. John Batten was also a member of the Art Workers' Guild Committee and Honorary Secretary.

BAUERLE, AMELIA MATHILDA (1873-1916)

Etcher / Painter / Illustrator. Born in London in November 1873. The daughter of Carl Bauerle, an historic painter, and Matilda. Both her parents originated from Germany, and two of their seven children (three boys and four girls) were born there. The remaining five were born in Kent, London and Sussex. Amelia was the third child. She adopted the spelling Bowerley sometime after 1901. Studied in London at South Kensington under Frank Short, and at the Slade School. Remained in London, living mainly in Willesden, but travelled abroad. Became a book illustrator, etcher, painter and decorative artist. Contributed to The Yellow Book (Vol.XIII, April 1897) and to The English Illustrated Magazine (1895-97). Illustrated a number of books including Ismay Thorn, Happy-go-Lucky (Innes, 1894), W.E. Cule, Sir Constant: Knight of the Great King (London, Melrose, 1899) and W. Farrar, Allegories (Longmans Green, 1902). Illustrated Alfred Tennyson's poem The Day Dream (Lane, 1901). Noted for her book illustration in R.E.D. Sketchley, English Book Illustration of To-Day (London, Kegan Paul, 1903). Also produced portrait and flower paintings.

Amelia was a proficient etcher, praised in The Studio, Vol.23, 1901, p.270 for her The Goblin Market and When the World Was Young. Two of her etchings were reproduced in Walter Shaw Sparrow's volume Women Painters of the World (London, Hodder & Stoughton, 1905, p.132), A Song of the Sea and Fauns. One of her illustrations, The Minstrel, was given in The Studio, Vol.39, October 1906, p.59. Exhibited her work in Liverpool, at the Royal Society of Painter-Etchers & Engravers, the Royal Institute of Painters in Watercolours, the Royal Academy (1897-1915) and the Society of Women Artists (1899-1900). An exhibition of her watercolours and etchings, titled When the World Was Young, was held at the Dowdeswell Galleries, London in 1908. Also exhibited in Paris and America. Exhibited works included: The Maids of Elfin-Mere, The Little Princess, The Wood, Full Fathoms Five and an illustration to Scott's Songs. Elected an Associate of the Royal Society of Painter-Etchers & Engravers. Amelia died at the age of only 43 in the Westminster Hospital, Middlesex in March 1916. She left her small estate of some £280 to her youngest brother, Andrew, a lance-corporal in the 7th London Regiment.

Amelia's younger sister, Marta Caroline Bauerle (1880-1945), also became a successful artist. She produced paintings on silk, illustrations, illuminations on vellum, paintings on vellum and illuminations on parchment. Also produced designs for embroidery, some of which were illustrated in the Art Workers' Quarterly in October 1903 (an embroidered square) and April 1904 (two embroidered panels). She too was based in London, in Hampstead and Clapham Common. Marta exhibited at the Society of Women Artists (1900, 1921-38) and was elected an Associate of the Society (1921-24). Also exhibited at Wembley and the Paris International Exhibition. Exhibited works included: In Praise of Love, Lilies Sacred and Profane (painting on silk) and The Song of Brother Sun (illumination on vellum). She was elected a Member of the Society of Scribes and Illuminators. Marta died in London, aged 65. Also used the surname Bowerley.

BAUMANN, PAULINE (1899-1977)

Engraver / Painter / Etcher. Was Constance Amy Pauline, known as Pauline. Born in London in January 1899. The daughter of Carl Ernst Gottlieb Baumann and Annie. Her father, a journeyman tailor, originated from Prussia, her mother from London. One of at least six children (Carl, Margaret, William, Annie, Albert and Constance). Raised in London. Educated at the Wimbledon County and Secondary Schools. Studied under Frank Jones, A.R.C.A. at the St Martin's School of Art, London. Also, under William Rothenstein at the Royal College of Art between 1923 and 1927. Awarded a Diploma of the Royal College of Art. Elected an Associate of the Royal College of Art. Based in London thereafter. Died there, aged 78. Became a teacher of art. Produced paintings in oils and watercolours, lithographs, wood engravings and etchings. Exhibited at the Royal Academy (1929-68), the Art Institute of Chicago, the Society of Wood Engravers, the Senefelder Club and the International Artists' Association. Exhibited works included: The Fortune-Teller (wood engraving), Barber's Shop (etching), A London Street (lithograph) and The Tree (lithograph). Works reproduced in The Studio. Works purchased by the Museums Group, Hertford Council and Cambridge Council.

BAYES, GERTRUDE (1870-1952)

Sculptor / Decorative Artist. The daughter of William Smith (b.1829) and Sarah. Her father, who originated from Leamington Spa, Warwickshire was a chemist and druggist in London. Her mother originated from Coventry. One of at least eight children (Elizabeth, Alice, Gertrude, Gilbert, Ellen, Catherine, William and Charlotte), all born in Paddington, London between 1863 and 1880. All were raised in Paddington. Catherine became a painter and teacher of drawing, design and painting. She exhibited her work at the Royal Academy (1898-1900). Gertrude studied sculpture in the 1890s, probably in London and abroad. Produced medallions, busts, groups and statuettes in marble and bronze. Also produced enamel plaques, usually set into panels. Initially shared a house in Rathbone Place with her sister Catherine and with a painter named Ernest Smith who exhibited at the Royal Academy (1869-90). He was presumably a member of the same family.

In 1906 Gertrude married sculptor Gilbert William Bayes (1872-1953) in Farnham, Surrey. Bayes came from a family of artists which included his father, painter Alfred Walter Bayes (1831-1909), his sister Jessie (1876-1970), who was a decorative artist, and his brother Walter (1869-1956), also a painter. Gilbert taught for a while at the Sir John Cass Technical Institute in London. Gertrude taught at the St John's Wood School of Art. One of her pupils was Gladys Barron. The couple lived in Boundary Road, St John's Wood, and later at Greville Place. They had two children, Eleanor Jean Gilbert Bayes (1908-98) and Geoffrey Gilbert Bayes (1912-2001). Gilbert, who also worked in marble, exhibited his work extensively, including at the Royal Academy (1905-52). Gertrude exhibited less regularly.

Prior to her marriage, she showed a portrait bust at the Society of Women Artists in 1897. Also exhibited three works, A Slave (statuette), Mrs R. Davies (medallion, bronze) and A Water-Nymph (bust), at the Royal Academy between 1899 and 1905. Exhibited a panel with enamel plaque at the 1901 Glasgow International Exhibition which was illustrated in The Studio, Vol.23, 1901, p.237. In 1906, at the time of her marriage, she contributed an enamel plaque, Twilight, to that year's Arts and Crafts Exhibition Society exhibition. She showed a further four works at the Royal Academy between 1911 and 1913, including A Child (bust), The Birds of Venus (group, bronze) and Whilst I'm Still Four (bust, marble). Gertrude's sister, Charlotte Smith, a teacher, stayed with the Bayes family at Boundary Road for a time. Gertrude died at Greville Place in April 1952. Gilbert died there shortly after, in July 1953. Their son Geoffrey became an electrical engineer.
SEE - SMITH, CATHERINE

BAYES, JESSIE (1876-1970)

Designer / Artist / Illuminator / Woodcarver / Gesso Worker. Born in London in November 1876. One of at least four surviving children of oil painter Alfred Walter Bayes (1831-1909) and Emily Ann Fielden (1837-1924). Her father originated from York, her mother from Todmorden, Lancashire. Jessie was raised in Hampstead, London. Her three siblings were Emmeline (1867-1957), Walter John (1869-1956) and Gilbert William (1872-1953). Walter Bayes became an artist and Member of the Camden Town Group. He was also Headmaster at the Westminster School of Art and art master at Camberwell. Gilbert became a sculptor who taught for a while at the Sir John Cass Technical Institute with Harold Stabler. He married sculptor Gertrude Smith. Initially, Jessie attended evening classes at the London County Council School of Arts and Crafts, studying gilding on wood and calligraphy. But she was clearly equally influenced by her artistic family and studied under her brother Walter at Finsbury. For two years she was able to work in the engraving house of Messrs Walker and Cockerell. This she found of particular value, finding additional inspiration in early Tuscan and Florentine pictures and old French romances. She travelled to Belgium, Italy, France and Germany during her career, finding her visits to Florence and Siena particularly useful, and visited America at least once. Spent much of her career in London.

Jessie became a talented and productive craftswoman involved in various key areas of the decorative arts, including woodcarving, gesso work, gilding, calligraphy, illumination and tempera painting. Much of her work was inspired by fantasy, fiction, ancient myths and legend, giving it a distinctly 'other-worldly' feel. She particularly excelled in the art of illumination. Her first work in lettering and illumination was a series of poems by W. Garth Wilkinson. That was followed by a collection of poems by Rossetti and a portion of William Morris's Defence of Guinevere. She also worked on transcriptions and illuminations of Psalms I-XXV, and a small booklet by herself titled Melrose, 1886. Tennyson's In Memoriam, Browning's Saul and Elizabeth Barrett Browning's Sonnets From the Portuguese also received her meticulous attention. Bayes produced an illuminated manuscript of Shelley's Night and The Lady of Shalott, while Lapo Gianni's A Madrigal, translated by Rossetti, was written and illuminated on vellum by her. She also delivered lectures on ancient illuminated manuscripts to, for example, the Junior Art Workers' Guild, to other artists, and on one occasion to an audience at a gallery in Bond Street, London. Elected a Member of the Arts and Crafts Exhibition Society. An admirer of William Morris and his philosophies, Bayes contributed to several of the Arts and Crafts exhibitions, certainly from 1906. At the 1912, tenth exhibition, she showed a painted and gilded cabinet, in the execution of which she was assisted by her sister, Emmeline, Kathleen Figgis and Mr F. Stuttig. Also showed her illumination of Rossetti's Ave. At the 1916, eleventh exhibition she showed a large altar in blue and gold. Also exhibited regularly at Mr John Baillie's Annual Arts and Crafts Exhibition held in London. Contributed to the National Competition of Schools of Art until at least 1906.

Bayes was associated with the short-lived Guild of Women Binders. Formed in around 1898, the Guild disbanded after only a few years. It aimed to promote the work of women bookbinders and book decorators. At its second exhibition, held in Charing Cross Road in late 1898 / early 1899, she

showed among other works her Elizabeth Barrett Browning's Sonnets From the Portuguese. Also elected a Member of the Royal Society of Miniature Painters in 1904, and a Member of the Society of Mural Decorators and Painters in Tempera. Other members of the latter Society included Marianne Stokes, Sir Charles Holroyd and Robert Anning Bell. Bayes not only produced paintings in tempera, but designed and decorated the frames for those works. One of her paintings, The Dayspring From on High, was in Lord Beauchamp's collection. Also executed tempera paintings on silk. Produced interior design schemes, including a frieze for a bedroom at Hornton Lodge, Kensington, and a design for a boudoir decoration intended for a house in Vienna (c.1914). Bayes worked from her own studio, assisted by Emmeline Bayes, Kathleen Figgis and Mr F. Stuttig. The London studio was set up specifically for the production of decorative work for the interiors of chapels and houses. She became a Member of the Church Crafts League (founded 1899) which aimed to restore standards in church art. In the League's papers, Bayes is listed as an illuminator.

Jessie exhibited her work further afield, in New York, Chicago, Detroit, Cleveland, Toronto, Paris, Rome and Ghent. Won popularity abroad. At the Royal Academy, she showed 14 works between 1905 and 1935, including several works in tempera such as Tobias and the Angel and Flowers and Brocade. Elsewhere, exhibited at the Royal Scottish Academy (1927), the Society of Women Artists (1923) and with the Society of Scottish Artists. Contributed to other, smaller exhibitions, including an exhibition of arts and crafts held at the Old Monastery, Rye. Works reproduced in The Studio on several occasions. For example, in November 1913, p.141 (The Road to Elfland, a decorative panel). The subject of an article in The Studio, Vol.61, May 1914, The Art of Jessie Bayes, Painter and Craftswoman by J. Quigley.

Jessie died in Paddington, London in June 1970, aged 93. Emmeline Bayes, although involved in Jessie's art work, was a dressmaker by profession. In 1912 she married John Stacy Aumonier (1874-1963), a commercial clerk. He was the son of artist James Aumonier and the nephew of renowned architectural carver William Aumonier. Most of the Aumonier family were involved in art in some way, and it is probable that Jessie knew, and even worked with, the Aumoniers at some point in her career. Jessie was certainly friends with bookbinders Ellen and Sofita Woolrich who were active in the early 1900s.

BEALE, AILEEN MARY - SEE ELLIOTT, A.M.

BEALE, EVELYN (1870-1944)

Sculptor / Maker of Decorative Pottery. Studied at the Slade School, London. Subsequently based in Edinburgh, North Shields, the Isle of Bute and, latterly, at a studio in Woodside Place Lane, Glasgow. Produced various subjects including decorative panels, bas-reliefs and statuettes. Worked in plaster, terracotta and porcelain. Works included: The Call of the Coalman (plaster), The Angel of Prayer (bas-relief), A Glasgow Worker (statuette, porcelain) and Hospitality (design for a porch panel). Commissions included a panel The Young St Bride for St Bride's School, Helensburgh. Also, a three-panelled memorial for Lansdowne Church, Glasgow. Executed work for Christ Church, Glasgow, Old St Paul's Church, Edinburgh and St Michael's Church, Retford, Nottinghamshire. A number of her works related to young children, executed for junior schools and nurseries, and to work and workers. Associated with the Glasgow Society of Lady Artists' Club. Exhibited at the Royal Scottish Academy (18 works, 1904-31) and the Royal Glasgow Institute (36 works, 1904-38). Exhibited works included: The Embroideress, In Remembrance of a Little Child and A Little Maid (statuette).

BEAUCLERK, LADY DIANA (1734-1808)

Artist / Designer. The subject of a book, Lady Diana Beauclerk: Her Life and Work, by Mrs Steuart Erskine (London, T. Fisher Unwin, 1903). The book was dedicated to Walter Shaw Sparrow. Sparrow then included Beauclerk in his volume Women Painters of the World (London, Hodder & Stoughton, 1905). Beauclerk's work, Erskine notes, was still largely unappreciated in 1903 when her volume was published, and the situation remains much unchanged today. Erskine reproduced some of Diana's published and unpublished work. Since Beauclerk left no notebooks or diaries, and appears to have destroyed her letters, Erskine used other sources. Lady Diana Spencer, as Beauclerk was, was the eldest daughter of Charles, Fifth Earl of Sunderland and Third Duke of Marlborough. She was also the great-granddaughter of Sarah, Duchess of Marlborough. She spent her childhood at Blenheim Palace. Showed artistic talent from an early age and always drew and painted. Initially took to copying the old masters, as was typical of the day, there being no schools of art. She certainly studied Rubens since she executed a copy, aged 11. Beauclerk, Erskine

notes, was tall, slim and beautiful. One of five children (Diana, Elizabeth (b.1737), George (b.1738), Charles (b.1740) and Robert (b.1747)). All were captured in a family portrait by Hudson which hung over the staircase at Blenheim.

In 1757, Diana became engaged to Frederick, Second Viscount Bolingbroke. The marriage was unsuccessful. In 1758 her father died, and in 1761 she gave birth to a son, George Richard. She was then chosen for the Queen's household. Also in 1761, her mother died. In 1762 she had a daughter, Charlotte, who died very young. In 1765 she had a second son, Frederick. She eventually left her husband for Topham Beauclerk. They married in 1768. He was the son of Lord Sidney Beauclerk and the great-grandson of Charles II and Nell Gwynn. This marriage too was unsuccessful. Diana had at least three other children, Charles, Mary and Elizabeth. Later in her life, her work became more important to her. This included a series of illustrations for Horace Walpole's The Mysterious Mother. She also decorated entire rooms at one of her homes, Little Marble Hill. Also executed many pastel portraits. Produced designs for Wedgwood, drawings for the engraver Bartolozzi, and watercolour drawings. She particularly loved drawing children, Cupids, baby Pans, little goats and bacchanals. She completed a considerable amount of work in her lifetime.

Diana painted and sketched many people, including Charles James Fox and the Duchess of Devonshire, and executed a caricature of Edward Gibbon. Drew her own children, friends and relatives. Her portrait of her cousin, the Duchess of Devonshire, drawn in 1778, was engraved by Bartolozzi. He also engraved one of her drawings of her two daughters in 1780. Reynolds may have had some influence on her work since he dined with her and Topham. She was essentially a designer and used colour sparingly. The design and composition were always more important to her than colour. Preferred pen & ink to colour. Although she studied the old masters, nature was also an inspiration. Sketched glades, including Richmond Park. Studied village life too. Her The Gipsies, painted in 1792, was acquired for the South Kensington Museum.

The Beauclerks were married for 12 years. In 1766 they rented a house at Cookham Ferry and lived elsewhere including Little Marble Hill. Walpole noted of Diana that she never made preliminary sketches, but painted quickly and directly. But in using watercolours in her interior decoration, little survived. In 1780 Topham Beauclerk died. Diana eventually settled at Devonshire Cottage in Richmond. Her daughter Elizabeth married the son of Lord and Lady

Pembroke in 1787. In the spring of 1780, Elizabeth had sat for Reynolds's picture Una and the Lion which was exhibited at the Royal Academy. After Topham's death, Diana continued with her work. Some of her designs were used on furniture. For example, a spindle-legged cabinet was decorated with Wedgwood plaques to her design. Wedgwood used her designs of bacchanals most successfully. Some Wedgwood jars were also after her designs. Her first connection with Wedgwood was in around 1785. Her designs for the firm, however, were unsigned. There is no comprehensive, complete record of all her work and no record of which works were used by Wedgwood or Bartolozzi.

Diana illustrated at least three publications during her career other than for Walpole, Dryden's Fables, Spenser's Faerie Queene and Bhurger's Leonore (1796), a ballad translated by W.R. Spencer. Blake worked on a version of Leonore around the same time. But hers, with engravings by Bartolozzi, was more popular. After a slow decline in her health, Diana died in August 1808, aged 73. She is buried in Richmond Parish Church. There is no monument to her. A list of her known works is given in Erskine's biography. They include a self-portrait, a portrait of the Hon. George St John as a boy, and a portrait of Mary and Elizabeth Beauclerk with doves. Also decorated a book cover for a copy of Virgil, printed by Baskerville, and produced numerous watercolours such as Hawking Party, Landscape With Figures and Nymphs and Fauns in a Glade. Other furniture decorated with her designs included an ebony cabinet with bas-reliefs by Wedgwood, with 17 of her drawings as decoration. Also, a Sheraton cabinet with three Wedgwood plaques after her designs, and a two-leaved screen of Manchester velvet with heads of a satyr and a nymph (1788). A large terracotta vase with black cameo figures of a young Bacchus and fauns, taken from her designs, by the Victoria & Albert Museum, London.

Erskine's volume includes illustrations of other works by Diana, such as designs for ceilings and some of her watercolour drawings such as Infant Pan, some of Bartolozzi's engravings and some of her Wedgwood designs. One of those, Boys as Bacchanals with Trophies, had already appeared in Miss Meteyard's volume Wedgwood and His Work (Bell & Daldy), published a short time before Erskine's biography. Erskine also includes a photograph of a tea-set painted by Diana. She was included in Mrs Ellet's Women Artists in All Ages and Countries, London, Bentley, 1859. Ellet notes Beauclerk was an amateur rather than a professional, and that Walpole built a hexagonal tower in 1776 which he called 'Beauclerk Closet',

constructed to house seven of her drawings depicting scenes from his The Mysterious Mother. Walter Shaw Sparrow included two illustrations of her work in his 1905 volume, the caricature of Edward Gibbon, historian in the Print Room of the British Museum, and Cupids, engraved by Bartolozzi.

BEECHEY, RUTH - SEE LATTER, R.

BELL, EDITH ANNA (b.c.1870)
Sculptor. Born in Dublin, Ireland. Presumed to have studied in Dublin. Moved to England sometime just prior to 1896 to teach modelling at the London County Council Central School of Arts and Crafts. Whilst in England, spent most of her time living in London but also spent time in Reading. Spent at least 15 years in England, living with her companion, Alice Emily Crawford. Produced medallions in silver and bronze and statuettes in bronze. Exhibited her work at the Royal Academy, showing 10 works between 1896 and 1912 including Idleness (statuette), Eros (statuette, bronze) and Francis Bate, Esq. (medallion, bronze). Also exhibited at the Walker Art Gallery, Liverpool. Since no death can be traced, it has been presumed Bell left England sometime after 1912.

BELL, EDITH M. - SEE UNDERWOOD, E.M.

BELL, ERNESTINE E. - SEE MILLS, E.E.

BELL, JEANNE (1888-1978)
Sculptor. Was Dorothy Jeanne Bell. Born in Hampstead. The daughter of John Clement Bell (1860-1944) and Mary Matilda Jessie Wahn (b.1861). Her father was a stained glass and ecclesiastical artist, and a senior partner in Clayton & Bell, Clifford Street, London. Jeanne had one brother, Reginald (b.1886). Raised in Hampstead, living at The Pryors into the 1930s with her parents. Latterly, she lived at Dinton near Aylesbury, Buckinghamshire, where she died, aged 90. Possibly studied in London. Produced statuettes in ivory, oak, alabaster, terracotta and bronze, and animal studies in glazed earthenware, marble and limewood. Exhibited her work, including at the Royal Academy (37 works, 1927-66), the Royal Glasgow Institute (1938-41) and the Society of Women Artists (1925-38). Exhibited works included Naiad (statuette, ivory), Tortoise (pottery statuette), Minstrel (glazed earthenware) and Conversation (statuette group, terracotta).

Her career covered five decades, and she was still active in her 70s.

BELL, MARY ELIZABETH - SEE DAWSON, M.E.

BELL, OPHELIA GORDON (1915-75)

Sculptor / Painter. Was Joan Ophelia Gordon Bell, known as Ophelia. Born in July 1915 in Kensington, London. The daughter of etcher F. Lawrence Bell and animal painter Winifred Gordon Bell. Educated at home. Evidently inherited her artistic abilities from her parents. Studied sculpture at the Regent Street Polytechnic, London under Harold Brownsword, F.R.B.S., Charlotte E. Gibson, A.R.B.S. and Geoffrey H. Deeley between 1932 and 1936. Produced reliefs, busts and statuettes in plaster, stone, terracotta and other materials, and paintings in watercolours. Exhibited at the Royal Scottish Academy (1936-39), the Royal Glasgow Institute (1938) and the Royal Academy (1935-39, 1957). Also, at the Glasgow Empire Exhibition and with the Lake Artists' Society. Exhibited works included: The Ride of the Valkyries (relief), Lakeland Dalesman (equestrian statuette), Agnus Dei (relief, anhydrite) and Elizabeth, Daughter of Arthur and Cynthia Goodland (head, bronze). Initially based in London. In 1940 she married Lakeland artist William Heaton Cooper (1903-95), the son of landscape painter Alfred Heaton Cooper. The couple lived in the Lake District, mainly in Grasmere where the Heaton Cooper studio was built. They had four children, one of whom, Julian, became an artist. Ophelia died in Grasmere.

BENNETT, NOREEN FRANCES (b.1923)

Designer / Textile Designer. Born in London in July 1923. The daughter of Francis H. Bennett, a company director, and Ethel James. Educated in Epsom, Surrey. Studied at the Wimbledon School of Art under Gerald Cooper and Margaret Simeon between 1939 and 1942. Also, at the Royal College of Art under Ernest William Tristram and Percy Hague Jowett between 1942 and 1945. An Exhibition Scholar at the Royal College of Art. Elected an Associate of the Royal College of Art in 1945. Became a designer in various areas of the decorative arts, but concentrating on textiles. Elected to the Society of Industrial Artists in 1946. Elected a Fellow of the Royal Society of Arts in 1951. Lectured in design and crafts at the Lincoln Training College between 1945 and 1947. Lectured in textiles and calligraphy at the Cheltenham College of Art from 1948, living at

Coombe Hill near Gloucester for a while. Exhibited her work, including at the Guildhall, the Victoria & Albert Museum, London, the Cotton Board, Manchester, the Royal Society of British Artists, the Britain Can Make It Exhibition, the Royal College of Art and the British Industries Fair. Her works were reproduced numerous times, including in Architectural Design (1946), Furnishing (1947), Cabinet Maker and Complete House Furnisher (1947), Designers in Britain (1947), Art and Industry (1948), Designers in Britain 2 (1949), Country Life (1949), British Furnishing (1949), Ideal Home (1949), Furnishings From Britain (1949, 1950), International Textiles (1950), Ambassador (1950), Decorative Art (1950, 1951) and Designers in Britain 3 (1951).

BENSON, EVA ELLENOR (1875-1949)

Sculptor. Although born in Australia, and died there, Benson spent time studying and exhibiting in England. She initially trained in Perth but came to London in around 1911 to study at the Regent Street Polytechnic. There, she won various awards. Also studied at the City & Guilds London Institute under sculptor R.B.S. Stephenson. She remained in London until around 1920, when she returned to Australia. Produced medallions, portrait works and figure studies. Worked in plaster, bronze and marble. In London, she used the Clifton Hill Studios at St John's Wood. Exhibited her work in England and Scotland at the Royal Scottish Academy (1918), the Royal Glasgow Institute (1917-18), the Royal Academy (1915-20) and the Society of Women Artists (1916-18). Exhibited works included: Persephone (bronze), Psyche (statuette), The Hon. Sir J. Winthrop Hackett (bust, marble) and A Bacchante (bronze).

BENSON, MARY KATE (1842-1921)

Artist / Book Decorator. The daughter of Dr Charles Benson (1797-1886) of Fitzwilliam Square, Dublin, and Maria Andrews. Her father was a celebrated surgeon and President of the Royal College of Surgeons, Dublin. Her mother was the daughter of Maunsell Andrews of Rathenny, King's County. One of her brothers was Sir J. Hawtrey Benson (d.1931). Her sister, Charlotte E. Benson (1846-93), also became an artist. Mary studied under Hubert von Herkomer at the Bushey School, Hertfordshire. Also, under Frank Calderon and in Paris under Lazare. She spent time in London in the 1870s, in Hertfordshire in the early 1880s, and at South Parade, Bath in the early 1900s. Evidently returned to Dublin, where she died in mid-1921, aged 79. She spent time touring Britain, visiting Cumberland and Cornwall, and travelled abroad to France, Belgium and Switzerland to paint. Produced a variety of subjects including landscapes, flowers, figures, portraits and interiors.

Benson exhibited her work, including at the Society of Women Artists (1877-90), the Royal Academy (1884), the Royal Society of British Artists (1880-84) and the Royal Scottish Academy (1888). Also, with the Amateur Art Society and the Nineteenth Century Art Society. Exhibited 120 works at the Royal Hibernian Academy between 1873 and 1906. Exhibited works included: Snowdrops, A Seaweed Gatherer, Belgian Interior and A Normandy Shrimper. Worked in oils, watercolours and pastels. Possibly drew a headpiece for The Quarto in 1896. A Katherine Benson, a student at the Female School of Art, Queen Square, London in 1879, won a National Gold Medal for her Fighting Gladiator, against 144 schools of art that were competing for it. Charlotte Benson studied for two years at the Dublin Society school, where she won three prizes and a medal for still life drawing in the National Competition. She produced landscapes and other subjects. Exhibited at the Royal Hibernian Academy between 1873 and 1893, including Harvest in Borrowdale, The Twelve Pins, Connemara and In the Ardennes, Belgium. Her paintings, and the dates that they were completed, suggest that Charlotte travelled with Mary until her early death, aged around 47. Charlotte also visited one of her brothers in India, where she painted. Charlotte is listed in A Dictionary of Irish Artists (1913).

BERESFORD, DAISY RADCLIFFE (1879-1939)

Painter / Decorative Artist. Born in London. The daughter of William L. Clague, a school inspector, and Emma. One of at least three children (Cyril, Muriel and Daisy). Cyril became a teacher. Raised in London. Daisy studied in London, at the Heatherley's School of Art and the Royal Academy schools. As a student, she was awarded three silver and two bronze medals. A young talent, she was awarded an Art Class Teachers' Certificate at the age of 13, and an Art Mistress Certificate at the age of 16. Became a painter of portraits, landscapes, buildings and interiors, of miniatures and of decorative panels. Based in London for much of her career. Exhibited her work occasionally, including at the Royal Academy (1907-38) and the Society of Women Artists (1904-17). Exhibited works included: An Inspiration, St Bartholomew the Great, Her Majesty the Queen (miniature) and Sir Cecil Levita, L.C.C. Elected a Member of the New Society of Artists and of the Hampshire Society of Artists. In 1910 Daisy married artist Frank Ernest Beresford (1881-1967) who originated from Derby. He too was a young talent, studying at the Derby School of Art from the age of 14. He then went on to study in London, at the St John's Wood School of Art and the Royal Academy schools. They had two daughters. Daisy remained active until her death.

BESS OF HARDWICK (1527-1608)

Born at Hardwick, Chesterfield, Elizabeth (Bess) Hardwick lost her father in 1528, and by the early 1540s had gone into service at nearby Codnor Castle. In around 1543 she married her cousin, Robert Barlow. It was her second marriage to Sir William Cavendish in 1547, however, which brought her increased status, Bess proving herself to be a shrewd and practical businesswoman. Her third marriage to Sir William St Loe in 1559 saw her wealth and status increase yet further, and in 1567 she benefitted further from her marriage to George Talbot, Sixth Earl of Shrewsbury. Around the time of the Earl's death in 1590, Bess began to build a new Hardwick Hall in Derbyshire, having bought the old family estate from her brother in 1583. She spent until around 1599 building and furnishing the new Hall entirely to her own schemes, using her initials as exterior decor and her coat of arms as interior decor. Hardwick was by no means her only building project and, in some respects, she might be classified as one of Britain's earliest female designers. But Hardwick was certainly her most vociferous statement of her power and wealth, accumulated through careful choice of husbands. A surviving testament to Elizabethan design, with its expression of symmetry and prolific use of glass, Hardwick is now in the care of the National Trust (given in 1959). Bess is also believed to have been an expert needlewoman. Given her talent for design, she was probably responsible for some of the smaller tapestries and embroideries which still survive at Hardwick. A small number of petit point panels, copied from Faerno's Book of Fables, are currently accepted as her own needlework. A depiction of Diana and Actaeon, worked in tent stitch by Bess and her ladies, is kept at Hardwick. In the 1890s, George S. Elgood painted Hardwick and its gardens.

BETHUNE, EVELYN ISABEL (1855-1930)

Sculptor / Craftswoman. Born in Marylebone, London. The daughter of Aaron Goldsmid (d.1875) and Sophia (d.1895). Her father originated from Surrey, her mother from London. Appears to have been an only child. In 1886 Evelyn married Charles Congalton Bethune (1849-1923) in Marylebone. But only three years later, in 1889, Evelyn instigated a divorce and returned to live with her widowed mother at Bryanston Square. Prior to her marriage, Evelyn worked as a sculptor, and as Evelyn Goldsmid exhibited one work, Girl's Head (bust, marble), at the Royal Academy in 1886. After separating from Bethune, she worked in metalwork, enamels and decorative jewellery for at least eight years (1902-09). In 1902 she contributed jewellery to the Cork Exhibition in Ireland, which organised a special section devoted to women in the decorative arts. One of her pendants, exhibited at Cork, was illustrated in The Studio, Vols.24-25, 1902, p.299. In 1903 she contributed to the Clarion Guild of Handicrafts exhibition in Chester, organised by Julia Dawson. The Chester exhibition was made up of around 900 exhibits. In 1907 a seal with agate handle and turquoise and enamel, designed and executed by Evelyn, was illustrated in the Art Journal, p.175 in an article Metal-Work and Jewellery by R.E.D. Sketchley. In 1908 Evelyn contributed jewellery to an exhibition held at the New Gallery, and in 1909 contributed to the Autumn Exhibition at the Walker Art Gallery, Liverpool. She also exhibited regularly at the Society of Women Artists (1902-08). She remained in London, at Bryanston Square, after her mother's death. Died in Marylebone, aged 73. She kept the name Bethune until her death.

BETTS, GERTRUDE E. - SEE MORGAN, G.E.

BIDDER, MURIEL JOYCE (1906-99)
Sculptor. Born in Wimbledon. The daughter of Frederick William Bidder, a civil engineer, and Annie. Had at least one sibling, Edward. Raised in Wimbledon. Had a studio in Wimbledon initially. Then based in a studio at Spencer Hill Road, London. Died in London, aged 93. Had an extensive career as a sculptor, covering at least five decades. Produced statuettes, groups and other works. Worked in a variety of materials including green slate, marble, walnut, Spanish chestnut, mahogany, terracotta, ebony, oak, glazed earthenware, plaster and birch. Exhibited at the Royal Academy (1931-57) and the Society of Women Artists (65 works, 1933-71). Exhibited works included: The Enchanted Unicorn (panel, carved mahogany), St Jerome, St Hubert, St Francis (triptych, earthenware), St Christopher

(statuette group, birch) and Dryad (oak). Elected an Associate of the Society of Women Artists (1949-51) and a Member (1951-81).

BILLING, CLARA ELLEN (1881-1963)
Sculptor / Painter. The daughter of George Billing and Emily Clara. Her father, a surgeon's assistant and later a physician and surgeon, originated from Longsight, Manchester, her mother from Gorton, Manchester. One of at least four children (Elizabeth Emily, John Henry, Clara Ellen and May (1883-1939)). All were born and raised in Blackpool, Lancashire. John Henry Billing later became a surgeon's assistant, like his father. Clara studied at the Manchester School of Art, followed by the Royal College of Art, London. Also spent time studying in Paris. Won a Lancashire County Council Scholarship. Produced medallions and portrait works in a variety of materials including cement and concrete. Also produced landscape, portrait and still life paintings. Exhibited at the Royal Academy (1923 & 1957), the Society of Women Artists (18 works, 1924-39), the Royal Institute of Oil Painters, the Women's International Art Club, the International Society of Sculptors, Painters and Gravers and with the London Group. Exhibited works included: Jeunesse (head, cement), Portrait of a Little Foreigner, Dahlias, A Sunny Window and Betty (concrete). Elected an Associate of the Society of Women Artists (1925-34). Works illustrated in Colour.

Clara's sister, May, became a craftworker, also exhibiting at the Society of Women Artists (1927-32). She too was elected an Associate of the Society (1926-33). For a while, certainly into the early 1920s, Clara was based at Paulton Square, London. But by 1925 she had moved to Blewbury, nr. Didcot, Oxfordshire, where May was already living. May had moved to Blewbury by at least 1911, living alone at Eastbrook Cottage where she was listed as a poultry farmer and market gardener. Evidently also took up some form of craftwork at Blewbury, since she later exhibited examples in London with the Society of Women Artists. May died at Eastbrook Cottage, aged 54. In early 1929, Clara married painter / engraver / sculptor (of medals and small statuettes) Sydney Langford Jones in Fulham, London. Born in Chelsea in 1888, he was the son of a lecturer in chemistry and photography at the Imperial College of Science and Technology, London. Langford Jones had also been a student at the Royal College of Art. For much of their marriage, they lived at Blewbury. Clara died a widow in an Oxfordshire Infirmary in August

1963, aged 82. Her address at the time of her death was Gatehouse Studio, Blewbury.

BILLINGTON, DORA MAY (1890-1968)

Potter / Designer. Born in Tunstall, Staffordshire, in the heart of the Potteries. The daughter of Henry Billington, a commercial traveller, and Mary Eliza Shirley. Raised in Tunstall and in Stoke-on-Trent, Staffordshire, living for some of the time with grandparents, presumably because her father worked away. Initially, Dora studied locally, at the Tunstall and Hanley Schools of Art until 1913. Then went to London to study at the Royal College of Art, where she later taught ceramics. In her volume Artist Potters in England (London, Faber & Faber, 1955 / 1970), Muriel Rose notes that Billington arrived at the Royal College of Art with John Adams and other students from the Potteries. Dora was already experienced in clay when she arrived there. Billington and her contemporaries continued to work at the College even when there was no tutor or tuition, following Richard Lunn's death. Lunn had been appointed instructor in pottery at the College in 1903. When a pottery department was subsequently established, it was run under Dora's direction. She also subsequently taught at the L.C.C. Central School of Arts and Crafts, with an assistant from Doulton's.

Dora became President of the Arts and Crafts Exhibition Society. She also worked at the Bernard Moore Pottery, which had been established in Stoke-on-Trent in 1905. Moore was a glaze chemist. There, her colleagues included Hilda Lindop. During her career, Billington taught, among others, Kathleen Pleydell-Bouverie and Norah Braden, both of whom made significant contributions to British studio pottery in the 1920s and 1930s. Billington was the author of The Art of the Potter (London, Oxford University Press, 1937). She exhibited her work only occasionally, including at the Society of Women Artists (1929). She was the author of an article The Young English Potters in The Studio, Vol.145, 1953, in which she referred to Lucie Rie and Eleanor Whittall. Contributed other articles to The Studio. For example, in 1955 she was the author of Contemporary Needlework Pictures (Vol.50, September) in which she discussed the embroidery of Constance Howard. Latterly, Billington lived in Surbiton, Surrey. She died in London, aged 78.

BINDER, PEARL (1904-90)

Artist / Illustrator. Born in June 1904 in Broughton, Manchester. The daughter of Morris Binder and Janet. Her father, a tailor, originated from Russia, her mother from Cheetham, Manchester. One of at least three children (Mark, Annie and Pearl). Her siblings were also born in Broughton. Raised in Hanley, Staffordshire for a while. Pearl returned to Lancashire and studied at the Manchester School of Art. Already a talented caricaturist as a student, Binder developed a strong sense of humour and wit in her drawings, ridiculing aspects of British social life. In 1925 she moved to London to improve her career prospects. In 1926 she spent a year in Paris, drawing for Le Rire to supplement her income. Returned to London in 1927 and began to draw for The Sketch and other magazines. Also took up lithography around this time. From around the late 1920s, she began to illustrate books too. One of the earliest was an edition of Jane Austen's Persuasion (Gerald Howe, 1928). In 1933 illustrated Philip Godfrey's Back Stage (Harrap, price 10s 6d) which contained lithographs and drawings by Binder who, by this time, was already well known for a series of lithographs of East end life. Produced a number of studies of the South Wales mines which were published in New Masses.

In around 1935 Binder's first book, Odd Jobs, was published. Perhaps influenced by her father's background, Binder visited Moscow in 1933, 1934 and 1935. Held a large exhibition of her lithographs there, some of which were purchased by the Moscow Museum of Modern Western Art. She contributed to numerous other books during her lengthy career, both by herself and by others. Those included: Everyday Life in Russia (compiled by B. Malnick, 1938), Muffs and Morals (by Binder, 1953), Harriet and Her Harmonium (by Alan Lomax, 1955), Pocahontas (by K. Goell, 1963) and Magic Symbols of the World (by Binder, 1972). In 1937 Binder married Frederick Elwyn Jones in London. He was a barrister, an Army Major and a political writer. They had at least one daughter, Josephine, who was born in early 1938 in London. Later, Binder was one of the first artists to draw for television. Works illustrated in The Studio, Vol.89, April 1925, p.221. Noted in Mahony, Latimer & Folmsbee, Illustrators of Children's Books 1744-1945, Boston, The Horn Book Inc., 1947. Also, in Janet Adam Smith, Children's Illustrated Books, London, Collins, 1948. Died in Brighton, Sussex in early 1990, aged 85.

BINYON, HELEN FRANCESCA MARY (1904-79)

Illustrator / Engraver / Painter / Lithographer. Born in London in December 1904. The daughter of Laurence Binyon (1869-1943) and Cicely

Powell, who married in 1904. One of at least three daughters. Her father, who was Robert Laurence, was the son of the Rev. F. Binyon. He was a poet, member of the Art Workers' Guild and Deputy Keeper in the British Museum in charge of oriental prints and drawings. Helen was educated at the St Paul's Girls' School. Subsequently studied design and illustration at the Royal College of Art between 1922 and 1926 under Ernest William Tristram and Paul Nash. Awarded a Royal College of Art Diploma and elected as Associate of the College. Also studied in Paris for a year (1927), at the Academie de la Grand Chaumiere Studio. In 1928 she studied engraving at the London County Council Central School of Arts and Crafts under William Palmer Robins. Produced lithographs, watercolour paintings, wood and line engravings and book illustrations. Also developed a strong interest in puppets and puppetry. Worked as a teacher at the Eastbourne College of Art, the North London Collegiate School, the Willesden School of Art and the Bath Academy of Art (1950-65). Ran a travelling puppet theatre with her twin sister Margaret. Acted as artist to the College of Arms.

In 1940 Binyon moved from London to Bath to draw charts for the Hydrographic Department of the Royal Navy, and subsequently worked in the exhibitions section of the Ministry of Information, London (1942-45). Later worked for the Arts Council and the Central School of Speech and Drama in relation to puppetry. She illustrated a number of books during her career, including The Street of Queer Houses (Vernon Knowles, 1925) for Wells, Gardner Darton Ltd, Sophro the Wise (Laurence Binyon, 1926) for Benn, and Brief Candles (six engravings, Laurence Binyon, 1938) for the Golden Cockerel Press. Illustrated her own books too, including The Children Next Door (1949), An Everyday Alphabet (1952) and Puppetry Today (Studio Vista, 1965). Produced some books in conjunction with Margaret Binyon including A Day at Sea (1940), Christmas Eve (1942), Polly Goes to School (1944) and The Railway Journey (1949). Exhibited her work, including with the New English Art Club, the English Wood-Engraving Society and the Society of Wood Engravers. Elected to the last of those. One of her illustrations, from Pride and Prejudice (Penguin), was given in The Studio, Vol.117, February 1939, p.50 in an article Wood Engraving of To-day by Gwen Raverat. Another of Binyon's works was illustrated in The Studio, Vol.119, May 1940, p.161. Works included in an exhibition of women wood engravers titled Shall We Join the Ladies? held at the Museum of Oxford in October 1979. Binyon was one of 27 women represented.

BIRD, MARY HOLDEN (1890-1978)

Etcher / Painter. Born in Cambridge in the district of Chesterton in early 1890. The daughter of William Hay Caldwell and Margaret. Her father originated from Scotland, her mother from New South Wales. Her father had independent wealth and was recorded as a gentleman. The family employed seven servants when Mary was a child. She had at least one sister, older, Margaret. Mary studied at the Heatherley's School of Art in London. Produced etchings and landscape paintings in oils and watercolours. Had an extensive career as an artist, covering six decades, from the 1920s into the 1970s. Exhibited her work up to, and just beyond, her death. Based in London, in Lewes, Sussex and Invernesshire, spending her last days at Forres, Morayshire. Exhibited throughout her career, including at the Royal Scottish Academy (1927-31), the Royal Academy (1926-34), the Royal Scottish Watercolour Society, the Society of Scottish Artists, the Royal Institute of Painters in Watercolours, the Royal Society of Painters in Watercolours, the Royal Society of British Artists and the Paris Salon.

Mary held one-woman shows at the Fine Art Society, including in 1924 and 1926, and at Messrs Reid & Lefevre in Glasgow (1926). Exhibited most prolifically at the Society of Women Artists, showing 90 works there between 1950 and 1978. Exhibited works included: December Stillness, Hebridean June, The Black Rocks and Poole Harbour. Elected a Member of the Society of Women Artists (1952-77). Elected Honorary Treasurer of the Society (1959-64). Some of her works were reproduced by the Medici Society. In September 1914 Mary married Cyril Kenneth Bird (1888-1965) in Bayswater, London. Bird was the son of a wine merchant. He was a poster and press artist who worked under the name Fougasse, and published at least three books of his drawings. He was also Art Editor of Punch magazine from 1937, and Editor from 1949, as well as a Member of the Art Workers' Guild.

BIRD, MAUD BEATRICE STEDMAN (1878-1952)

Bookbinder. Born in Aston, Warwickshire. The daughter of Herbert Henry Bird, a wine merchant, and Mary. One of at least five children (Maud, Ethel, Ida, Herbert and Frank). Raised in Birmingham. Studied at the Birmingham School of Art, Margaret Street. As a student, she showed a book cover for British Ballads at the 1909 National Competition of Schools of Art. She became associated with Frank G. Garrett, a pupil of Douglas Cockerell. Garrett was linked to the Birmingham Guild of Handicrafts. Maud had a studio in Newhall Street, Birmingham. She showed some of her work at the 1912 Arts and Crafts Exhibition Society exhibition. In 1911 she had already shown bookbindings at the Second Exhibition of Arts and Crafts in connection with the Annual Autumn Exhibition of the Society of Artists. Some of her work was included later, in 1924, in an exhibition of arts and crafts held at Chipping Campden, Gloucestershire. Other exhibitors included Arthur and Georgina Gaskin. All exhibits on that occasion were by artists and craftworkers living and working in the area. In 1913 Maud married Walter H. Allcott in Warwickshire. He was a wholesale confectioner who was born in Birmingham in 1880. Maud died in Haslemere, Surrey, aged 74.

BIRKENRUTH, JOHANNA (1853-1929)

Bookbinder. Born in South Africa. The daughter of Nathan Birkenruth and Rosa. Both were born abroad, her mother in Prussia. Her father was initially an importer of goods, then later a diamond broker. Johanna was one of at least five children (also Helen, Edward, William and Adolphus). William became a stockbroker, Adolphus an artist. The family lived in London from at least the early 1870s. Johanna died there, aged 76. After their father's death, Johanna, Helen and William lived with their mother into their late 50s. Johanna became a bookbinder and decorator, active from at least the late 1880s until at least 1918. She probably trained in London. Had a bindery at 89 Cromwell Road, Kensington. There, she also gave classes, not only in bookbinding but in the art of making decorative frames, miniature cases, caskets and boxes for lace and fans. Her work was highly regarded and was illustrated in a number of arts journals of the period. For example, one of her more decorative bindings was illustrated in an article Women Workers in the Art Crafts in the Art Journal, 1896, pp.116-118. In 1897 the same journal illustrated two of her bindings in an article The Arts and Industries Today, p.380. Those were a pale green morocco binding for a volume of Keats and a brown morocco binding for Vailima Letters. For the latter, a small panel with an embossed figure let into the cover was modelled by Charpentier in saddler's leather.

Other bindings by Birkenruth were illustrated in The Studio, Vol.13, March 1898, pp.113-115. Also, in The Studio, Vol.18, Special No. 1899-1900 in an article British Tooled Bookbindings and Their Designers (pp.41-43). In 1899, the Art Journal again illustrated two of her designs in a

short article Recent Bookbinding (p.317). Although her designs could be highly complex, often incorporating figures, flowers or leaves, they could also have a simple reliance on line decoration. At other times she produced highly decorative jewelled bindings. For example, for a cover of a copy of Omar Khayyam's Rubaiyat she used amethysts and moonstones. Her work was noted for its striking colour too. For a volume of Thomas a Kempis she worked in purple leather, tooled and gilded, the lining of which (also in leather) was inlaid with a design of lilies in white and green. Another of her designs, for a copy of The Little Mermaid, incorporated a leather panel with a mermaid design executed by Mary G. Houston, for which Birkenruth tooled the binding.

Birkenruth exhibited her work over a period of some 29 years. In 1889 she contributed to the Arts and Crafts Exhibition Society's exhibition. In 1893 she sent work to the Columbian Exposition in Chicago. In 1898 she exhibited at the Goupil Gallery, and between 1896 and 1918 exhibited with the Society of Women Artists. She also sent to the 1901 Glasgow Exhibition. In 1897 / 98 she exhibited with a number of other women binders at an exhibition organised by Frank Karslake, from which the Guild of Women Binders originated. The Guild, however, was short-lived and Birkenruth never joined officially. In 1898 she contributed to an Exhibition of Artistic Bookbinding held at the Howard Gallery, Sheffield. Other exhibitors included T.J. Cobden-Sanderson. At least one of her bindings is in the collection of the British Library.

BISHOP, DOROTHY L. - SEE MAHONEY, D.L.

BISHOP, GWEN (active early 1900s)

Craftswoman. Made jewellery to the designs of Charles Ricketts. He worked in theatre design, among other things, after 1906. He designed jewellery for a stage production of Attila in 1907 at Her Majesty's Theatre executed by Mrs Bishop. Made of relatively cheap materials such as brass, copper and gilded leather. She made some 130 pieces to Ricketts's designs.

BLACKLOCK, NELLIE (1889-1956)

Flower Painter. Was Ellen Eliza Richardson, known as Nellie. Born in London. In 1909 she married Sunderland-born artist William Kirkbride (sometimes Kay) Blacklock (1870-1924) in Chelsea. He was an Associate of the Royal College of Art, and during his career is listed as of the School of Art, Royal Institution,

Edinburgh. They had at least one daughter, Eleanor. The couple lived in Chelsea, but also in Walberswick, Suffolk, and Leicester. They later moved to Cornwall, where William died. Nellie married again, in 1924, to Edward Sewell, in London. They lived in Cornwall, where Nellie died. She produced flower paintings in watercolours. In 1924 she was elected a Fellow of the Royal Horticultural Society. In 1926 she was awarded the Royal Horticultural Society Silver Grenfell Medal for floral painting. Exhibited some of her work at the Royal Academy (1915-28), including Cornflowers and Sweet Williams.

BLACKMAN, AUDREY BABETTE (1907-90)

Sculptor / Ceramicist / Painter. Born in London in July 1907. The daughter of Dr Richard Seligman, P.P., Institute of Metals, and Hilda Mary McDowell. Her father, who originated from Clapham, was a chemist and chemical engineer. Her mother, who originated from Blackburn, Lancashire, was a sculptor. Had at least one sibling, Adrian. Raised in Leatherhead, Surrey. Educated at the Wimbledon High School. Studied at the Kunstgewerbe Schule, Graz under Professor Gosser between 1924 and 1926. Also, at the Goldsmiths' College, London between 1926 and 1930, followed by Reading University under Albert Clarence Carter and Anthony Betts between 1931 and 1935. Became a sculptor in bronze, then turned to working in clay also. Produced small, decorative, attractive ceramic figures and groups. Worked consistently, exhibiting most prolifically from the late 1930s to the early 1970s.

Audrey initially exhibited her bronze sculptures at the major London galleries until 1939. Then became involved in war work. It was this which lead to a change in direction for Blackman. Now, she aimed to produce something smaller and relatively inexpensive for the modern home, similar to Chelsea porcelain but with a modern twist. Began to work in terracotta and stoneware and to create ceramic character figures. For example, an actress on stage, a ballet dancer with exaggerated limbs, a woman stood at a bar, a woman sat reading poetry, a girl in evening dress gazing into a mirror, a child holding wool as the mother winds it. She adopted a method of using thin ribbons of clay and delicate coloured glazes. Often had no faces to her figures, no detailed realism. Yet she was able to put across most adeptly what she wished to express through her work. She was noted in her day as a good-humoured observer.

Latterly, Blackman also moved into abstract and experimental works in gouache and watercolours. Based in London initially, then Hinksey Hill Top, Oxford and, latterly, Wimbledon Common. Exhibited widely, including at the Royal Academy (17 works, 1938-60), the Royal Glasgow Institute (1951), the Society of Women Artists (48 works, 1939-71) and with the National Society. Also, at the Mayor Gallery, the Berkeley Gallery, the Haslett Gallery, the Museum of Fine Arts, Houston, Texas and the Lefevre Gallery. Exhibited works included: The Three Graces (statuette group, terracotta), A Day by the Sea (statuette group, terracotta), The Common Interest (statuette group, bronze), La Vie (statuette group, terracotta) and Vultures For Culture No.1 (stoneware). Elected an Associate of the Society of Women Artists (1952-60) and a Member (1961-74). Also a Member of the Art Workers' Guild from 1970. Works reproduced in various journals including The Builder, Homes and Gardens and Pictures on Exhibit (U.S.A., 1951). The subject of an article in The Studio, Vol.141, June 1951, pp.168-169, The Ceramic Figurines of Audrey Blackman, written by anthropologist and admirer C.A. Burland. The article included illustrations of her The Poetry Reading, Ride a Cock Horse, Pas de Deux, Home and Dearie. In 1931 Audrey married Geoffrey E. Blackman (b.1903) in Fulham, London. He became Professor of Agriculture at Oxford University. During her career, she visited New York in 1947 and 1959. She died in Abingdon, Oxfordshire in mid-1990, aged 83.
SEE - SELIGMAN, HILDA

BLAKE, EILEEN MARY (1878-1957)

Painter / Black & White Artist. Born in Moseley, Birmingham in December 1878. The daughter of Frederick William Blake, a leather merchant, and May. One of at least three children (also Nora and Percy). Raised in Birmingham. Lived in Cotton Lane, Moseley and Elmfield Crescent, Moseley for much of her life and career. Died in Birmingham, aged 78. Educated at the King Edward VI High School, Birmingham. Studied at the Birmingham School of Art where she won a bronze medal and book prizes. Produced watercolour paintings of landscapes, seascapes, interiors, children and figures. Also a black & white artist of wild and cultivated flowers. Produced Christmas card designs for Alex Baird & Sons. Active for several decades, from at least the 1920s until shortly before her death. Exhibited her work, including with the Royal Birmingham Society of Artists, at Wembley, at the Faculty of Arts Galleries, with the Royal

Cambrian Academy and the Society of Women Artists (1932-39). Also, with the Royal Institute of Painters in Watercolours, with the Coventry Society of Artists, the Warwickshire Society of Artists and the Birmingham Watercolour Society. Works included: A Waterside Posy, An Ancient Dairy, Japanese Guelder Rose and Madam Will You Walk With Me. Elected a Member of the Faculty of Arts in 1924. Elected an Associate of the Royal Birmingham Society of Artists. Elected a Member of the Birmingham Watercolour Society Club and of the Royal Birmingham Society of Artists Club.

BLENCOWE, AGNES (1818-96)
Art Embroideress. Co-founder of the Ladies' Ecclesiastical Embroidery Society in 1854 with Mary Ann Street, sister to architect George Street (1824-81). The principal purpose of the Society was to supply altar cloths of ecclesiastical design, reproducing old examples, or by working under the supervision of an architect. In 1848, some six years previously, the Ecclesiological Society (whose Secretary was Benjamin Webb) had published Ecclesiastical Embroidery: Working Patterns of Flowers, of the Full Size, From Ancient Examples, a volume of 12 plates of working patterns of flowers drawn from medieval vestments and furnishings. The volume was devised by Agnes Blencowe, and she provided the drawings. Also in 1848, Blencowe had exhibited some of her work in an exhibition of ancient and modern embroideries, organised by the Cambridge Camden Society. The Ladies' Ecclesiastical Embroidery Society did not aim to provide employment for women; rather, it concentrated on producing high-quality art embroideries carried out by women free of charge. The churches for whom the embroideries were executed were then charged only for materials. The Society executed some designs by George Street. In 1863 the Society amalgamated with the Wantage Church Needlework Association. This was perhaps under Blencowe's influence since she joined the Sisters of Mercy at St Mary's House, Wantage, Berkshire, around that time. Head of the House was Harriet Day. Blencowe remained there until her death in March 1896, aged 78. Embroidery continued at Wantage after Blencowe's death, and a banner made for the Church of St Barnabas, Oxford by the Sisters of Wantage was illustrated in The Studio, Vol.36, p.316 in 1905.

Religion was clearly an intrinsic part of Blencowe's life. Prior to joining the Sisters of Wantage, she acted as housekeeper to her elder brother, Edward E. Blencowe (1807-96), who was Rector of the Parish Church of St Mary the Virgin, West Walton, Norfolk. The church owned three pieces of embroidery by Blencowe, a white altar frontal, a red stole, and a green stole. Comparatively little is known about either Agnes Blencowe or Mary Ann Street. Records suggest that Blencowe was born in King's Lynn, Norfolk, part of a large family of Blencowes which also included John (b.1801), Henrietta (b.1810), Walter (b.1815), Margaret (b.1819) and Ellen (b.1821). Records do not indicate if these were immediate family or distant relatives. Most were born in King's Lynn also, and remained in Norfolk. Agnes clearly came from a family with money since she is listed in her lifetime as having no regular employment and as living off property and an annuity. She left her small estate to Margaret Blencowe, who died in 1898. Agnes Blencowe knew designer Philip Webb (1831-1915) and appears to have encountered George Street through her brother, Edward.

BLOXAM, JOAN MARY (1884-1948)
Artist / Lithographer. Born in Kensington, London. The daughter of Francis Richard Turner Bloxam and Katharine. Her father was a solicitor and Taxing Master of the Supreme Court. Joan had at least one sister, Dorothy Kate. Raised in Ealing. Educated at the Princess Helena College, Ealing. Studied in London at the Cope and Nicol Schools of Art, John Hassall's School of Art and at the L.C.C. Central School of Arts and Crafts. Awarded four medals for drawing and painting. Produced lithographs, pencil drawings, portraits in miniature and landscapes, working in oils and watercolours. Also worked as an art teacher. Based mainly in London during her career, using the Bolton Studios, Redcliffe Road for a time. Died in London. Exhibited her work, including at the Royal Hibernian Academy (1934-38), the Royal Academy (1913-31), the Society of Women Artists (1936-37), the Walker Art Gallery, Liverpool and with the Royal Birmingham Society of Artists. Exhibited works included: Malines Cathedral (lithograph), Seven Dials (watercolour), Trinity College, Dublin and Mrs J.C. Medlicott Vereker. Elected a Member of the Senefelder Club and of the Women's International Art Club. Purchasers of her work included the libraries of Bermondsey and Kensington, who acquired some of her drawings of London. Some of her lithographs and drawings were illustrated in St Martin's Review. Produced illustrated articles for the same journal. Worked on a series of articles titled Little-Noticed London for the Town Crier.

BLUNDELL, JOAN - SEE WARDLEY, J.

BLUNDELL, MARGARET LEAH (1907-96)
Wood Engraver / Mural Painter / Commercial Artist / Decorator. Born in July 1907 in Wallasey, Wirral. The daughter of Thomas Webster Blundell, a cotton broker. Educated at the Cheltenham Ladies' College. Studied at the Cheltenham School of Art, and the Liverpool School of Art (from 1925) under George Marples and Frederick Carter. Became a highly proficient and expert mural decorator, wood engraver, commercial artist and interior decorator. Carried out numerous commissions during her career including wall decoration for Lewis's Manchester cafeteria and The Crown Hotel restaurant in Liverpool. Executed murals for L.M.S. hotels, the Blackpool Pleasure Beach Co., Messrs Daniel Neal's shops, The Dolphin Square Nurseries, Messrs Heal & Son Ltd, the Cunard White Star liner S.S. Caronia, the Western Command Recruiting Room and others. Executed commercial art work for L.M.S., the Radio Times and W.H. Smith among others.

Blundell's commercial work also included front covers on catalogues for Barker's, Lewis's, W.H. Smith, the Radio Times and L.M.S. Poster. Exhibited her work throughout her career, including at the Royal Society of British Artists, the Society of Wood Engravers, the Walker Art Gallery, Liverpool, the Royal Cambrian Academy, the Manchester Academy and the Aid to China Exhibition. Elected an Associate of the Royal Cambrian Academy. Elected a Member of the Three Arts Club, Marylebone Road, London. Works illustrated in The Decorator. Other work reproduced in Architect, Building News, Shelf Appeal, Decoration, Design for Today, the Architect's Journal and various women's magazines (mainly murals). In 1939 she married Major Robert Jaggar, J.P., in Bangor, Wales. They had at least two children. Lived in Wales latterly. Died in Bangor in March 1996, aged 88.

BLUNT, SYBIL ALLAN (1880-1952)
Painter / Etcher / Designer / Artist. Born in Dorchester, Oxfordshire in October 1880. The daughter of Col. Arthur Blunt (1829-1904), Royal Artillery, and Frances Jemima Roper (1839-1910). Her father originated from Kensington, London; her mother from Yorkshire. Sybil had a twin brother, Allan St John Blunt (d.1931). One of at least seven children (Arthur, Helen, Dorothy, Hugh, Marjory, Allan and Sybil). Raised in Dorchester, Oxfordshire at the local manor house. Educated privately. Studied at the Byam Shaw School of Art, London and the

Edinburgh School of Art. Based in Edinburgh for a short while, then moved to The Old Cottage, Kingsgate Street, Winchester. Remained in Winchester, at various addresses, for the rest of her life and career. Travelled abroad, visiting Portugal, Japan and elsewhere in 1939. Produced paintings in watercolours, etchings, pen & ink drawings and designs, various subjects including landscapes.

Exhibited her work, including at the Royal Scottish Academy (1911-25), the Royal Academy (1924-33), the New English Art Club and the Paris Salon (certainly in 1924, 1926 and 1929), where she won an Honourable Mention in 1929. Exhibited works included: The Grassmarket, Evening, Domme, The Old Windmill and Royal Oak Passage, Winchester. Elected a Member of the Old Watercolour Society, and of the Societe Internationale d'Aquarellistes. Contributed to the first exhibition of the New Forest Group held in 1925, which had the theme of 'Art in Libraries'. Artists from the New Forest area, including Winchester, were invited to contribute. Also a Member of the Winchester Art Club. The Club held its first exhibition in the early 1920s. Initially, the Club was made up of amateurs as well as professionals, but quickly acquired a reputation for excellence, with artists from London and elsewhere submitting their work. Blunt was also elected designer to the Winchester Cathedral Broderers. In 1925 The Studio, Vol.90, p.384 illustrated her watercolour The Memorial Cloisters, Winchester. Blunt died in a Winchester nursing home in October 1952, aged 71.

BOGER, MARGARET A. - SEE WALLACE, M.A.

BOLTON, ELIZABETH E. - SEE HOUGHTON, E.E.

BOND, IDA - SEE NELSON, I.

BONE, PHYLLIS MARY (1893-1972)
Sculptor / Modeller. Born in Hornby, Lancashire in November 1893. The daughter of Douglas John Mayhew Bone (d.1931) and Mary Campbell Bone. Her father was a doctor. She had at least one brother, Wilfred Mayhew Bone. Her mother died in Surrey in 1907, and her father married again in 1909 and had other children. The family had relatives in Scotland and spent time there. Phyllis was educated at the St George's High School for Girls, Edinburgh. She then studied at the Edinburgh College of Art, receiving a sculpture diploma. Then studied in Italy, and in Paris under animal sculptor Edouard Navellier.

Returned to Scotland and spent much of her career in Edinburgh and Kirkcudbright. Produced mainly small animal sculptures during her extensive career, but produced garden sculptures and some larger architectural works too. Worked in bronze, oak, lead and plaster. Carried out numerous commissions during a career which lasted more than 60 years. Those included working on the entrance to the Scottish National War Memorial for Edinburgh, which consisted of a lion and a unicorn. Also produced animal sculptures for Inchcape Monument, Glenapp (granite), and carvings for the interior of St Wilfred's Church, Welbeck. One of her garden sculptures went to Capheaton Hall, Northumberland.

Bone had a successful exhibiting career which stretched over seven decades, from the 1910s to the 1970s. At the Royal Scottish Academy, she showed a considerable 179 works between 1915 and 1973, one of which was sub-divided into seven architectural sculptures. At the Royal Glasgow Institute, she showed an equally considerable 101 works between 1919 and 1967. Exhibited at the Royal Academy between 1920 and 1931. Contributed to the Art Competitions of the 1948 London Summer Games. Also exhibited at the Paris Salon, the British Empire Exhibition at Wembley and the Walker Art Gallery, Liverpool. Exhibited works included: Ebenezer the Goat, The Tawny Owl, King Penguin (owned by the Rt Hon. Lord Salvesen), The Barnyard Cockerel and Belgian Hare. Elected an Associate of the Royal Scottish Academy in 1939 and a Member in 1944. Worked with sculptor Hazel R. Armour on one of her commissions.

During the First World War, Bone served as a driver in the Women's Legion attached to the A.S.C. She was a Member of the Women's United Services Club, and of the Ladies' Caledonian Club, Edinburgh. Her works, including her carvings for the Scottish National War Memorial, were reproduced in various publications during her lifetime, including Builder, Architectural Review and Country Life. Two of her bronzes were acquired for the Aberdeen permanent collection, Shere Khan the Tiger and The Kid. The Glasgow permanent collection acquired her bronze Mallard Drying. Published work included Animal and Heraldic Sculpture and Animals Which Served in the War (Country Life).

BOREEL, WENDELA (1895-c.1985)
Painter / Etcher / Engraver / Lithographer. Born in Pau, Basses Pyrenees, France. The daughter of Robert John Ralph Boreel. Educated privately. Studied at the Slade School, London, the Westminster School of Art, the L.C.C. Central School of Arts and Crafts and under Walter Sickert. Produced paintings in oils and watercolours, etchings, engravings, lithographs and aquatints. Subjects included figures and landscapes. Exhibited her work, including at the Royal Academy (1923-38), the Society of Women Artists (1927), with the Royal Society of Painter-Etchers and Engravers, the National Society, the Salon des Beaux Arts and the New English Art Club. Held one-woman shows in London and abroad. For example, in 1932 she exhibited landscapes and figures in watercolours at the Brook Street Art Galleries, including The Little Pink Villa and Blue Bus. Other exhibited works included: A Girl Dressing (aquatint), Lincoln's Inn Fields (aquatint) and In Lodgings. Elected an Associate of the Royal Society of Painter-Etchers and Engravers. Elected a Member of the National Society and of the Societe Internationale de Philologie, Sciences et Beaux-Arts. Based in Chelsea, Bray-on-Thames and France during her career. Noted in Frank L. Emanuel's Etching and Etchings, London, Pitman & Sons, 1930. Her works were acquired by the Victoria & Albert Museum, London and the Metropolitan Museum, New York. Boreel married Leslie G. Wilde. They had at least one son.

BORNE, DAISY THERESA (1906-98)
Sculptor / Decorative Artist. Born in London. The daughter of William Borne. Educated in London and America. Became a teacher of sculpture. Produced figures, reliefs, statuettes and garden ornaments including fountains. Worked in a variety of materials including plaster, bronze, marble, South African wonderstone, walnut, terracotta, glazed earthenware, teak, glazed pottery, oak, wych elm and Westmorland stone. Exhibited mainly at the Royal Academy (1932-62) and the Society of Women Artists (78 works, 1933-71). Exhibited works included: Madonna of the Adoring Angels (Palombino marble), St Francis of Assisi (relief, walnut), Tom Thumb (glazed earthenware) and The Flute Player (glazed earthenware). Based in London during her career, using a studio in Wimbledon from the 1940s until at least the 1970s. Elected an Associate of the Society of Women Artists (1949-51) and a Member (1952-80). Elected a Member of the Alpha Club. Works illustrated in the Evening Standard.

BOTT, MARY EMMELINE - SEE BATTEN, M.E.

BOURNE, MURIEL - SEE WHEELER, M.

BOWDON, ERICA M. - SEE HASTINGS-GRAY, E.M.

BOWER, ETHEL ALICE CHIVERS (1867-1933)

Medallist / Painter. Born at Wadworth, Doncaster. The daughter of Edward Chivers Bower, J.P., D.L., a magistrate, and Amelia. Raised in Wadworth and in Scarborough. One of at least 10 children (George, Edmund, Arthur, Mary, Ethel, Cecily, Beatrice, Francis, Augusta and Amy). In the early 1900s, Ethel lived in London with her brother, George, a barrister, and her sisters Amy and Cecily. She studied at the Royal College of Art, London. As a student, won bronze and silver medals in the National Competition of Schools of Art. Became a successful society portrait medallist in silver and bronze, and a painter. Based mainly in London during her career, but also spent time in Sussex after her marriage. Exhibited her work at the Royal Academy (36 works, 1893-1922) and at Wembley. Exhibited works included: The Dean of Westminster (medallion), John Roddam Spencer Stanhope, Esq. (medallion), Sir Wilmot Fawkes, G.C.B., K.C.V.O. (medal) and Sir Charles Nicholson, Bt, M.P. (medal). Some of her works were illustrated in Portrait Medals of a Generation (Spink & Son). A Member of the Ladies' V.A.D. Club. In 1908 she married barrister Sir Henry Percy Harris, K.B.E., D.L. She then became Lady Harris. Her death, in Middlesex, was recorded as a possible suicide.

BOWERLEY, AMELIA MATHILDA - SEE BAUERLE, A.M.

BOWERS, GEORGINA HARRIET (1835-1912)

Artist / Illustrator. One of the few women artists of her generation to produce humorous illustrations for nineteenth-century journals and magazines. Born in London in October 1835. The daughter of George Hull Bowers and Harriet Agnes Addington. Her father was Rector of St Paul's, Covent Garden, London, and later Dean of Manchester. Had at least one brother, George. Georgina attended school in Ashbourne, Derbyshire. Her mother died young, and her father married again, to Isabella. With little formal training, Georgina took up art, and had a particular love of animals and sport. She rejected

society life, and worked at the Manchester School of Art. In around 1866 she began to draw for Punch, and continued to do so until 1876, producing mostly hunting sketches. During her career, she also contributed to the Graphic, Once a Week, London Society and the Illustrated Sport and Dramatic News. She also illustrated, for example, Canters in Crampshire, Mr Crop's Harriers, A Month in the Midlands, Notes From a Hunting Box (Not) in the Shires and Across Country by Wanderer, all published in around the early 1880s. Also produced designs for Christmas cards. Exhibited her work at the Society of Women Artists (1868-88). Exhibited works included: Tally-ho!, Hunting Studies, Doubts and Fears and Left Behind. Noted in Ellen C. Clayton, English Female Artists, London, Tinsley, 1876. In 1871 Bowers married Henry Edwards in London. He was a vet who originated from St Albans, Hertfordshire. They lived in St Albans. She died in Hertfordshire.

BOXSIUS, DAISY (1885-1967)

Illuminator / Painter. Born in Islington, London in late 1885. The daughter of Arthur Francis Tuff and Emma. Her father was a law journalist, clerk and barrister, and later sub-editor of a newspaper. Daisy was one of at least four children (Emmie, May, Daisy and Eva). Raised in London. Educated at the Dame Owen's School. Studied at the Camden School of Art and the London County Council Central School of Arts and Crafts. Produced illuminations and paintings in watercolours, including landscapes. Also taught design and lettering at the London County Council School of Photo-Engraving and Lithography. Exhibited at the Royal Academy (1932-54), the Society of Women Artists (1933-50), the Royal Society of British Artists and various provincial galleries. Exhibited works included: By the River at Rye, Sherborne Abbey, St Mawes, Cornwall and Looe in August. Based mainly in London. In July 1917 Daisy married Sylvan George Boxsius (b.1878) in Muswell Hill, London. She was then 31 years of age and listed as a teacher. Boxsius, who was born in London, was also a student of the Camden School of Art, but also of the Royal College of Art. He too taught at the School of Photo-Engraving and Lithography. An illustrator, painter and engraver, he exhibited at the Royal Academy (1913-36) and elsewhere. Daisy continued with her work and was still exhibiting into the 1950s. She died in Hertford, aged 81.

BOYCE, EDITH - SEE LLOYD, E.

BRABY, DOROTHEA (1909-87)

Wood Engraver / Painter / Book Illustrator / Commercial Artist. Born in Putney, London in October 1909. The daughter of Percy Braby, a solicitor and commissioner for oaths for England and 21 colonies, and Maud Churton Braby, an author and journalist. Her father originated from London. Her mother was born in Shanghai, China. One of at least three children (Cedric, Marigold and Dorothea). Educated at the St Felix School, Southwold, Suffolk where illuminator and calligrapher Margaret Alexander was taught. Studied at the Heatherley's School of Art, London under Frederick Whiting. Also, in Florence under Mafori-Savini, at La Grand Chaumiere, Paris and at the L.C.C. Central School of Arts and Crafts under John Farleigh, W. Roberts and Noel Rooke.

Braby became a highly respected wood engraver, portrait and composition painter, illustrator and commercial artist. Designed book jackets for, among other publishers, Bodley Head and Hutchinson. Executed advertising for most newspapers. Produced book illustrations in pen & ink or as wood engravings. Illustrated a number of books during her lengthy career, the majority for limited editions by specialist publishers, particularly during the 1940s and 1950s. For the Golden Cockerel Press, she worked on several time-consuming projects. Those included Mabinogion, a collection of Welsh legends which contained 20 large and intricate wood engravings by Braby, of around 50 square inches. Those took her around 18 months to complete. Also worked on The Ninety-First Psalm, The Labyrinth and V.G. Calderon, The Lottery Ticket (1945) for the Golden Cockerel Press. Worked on editions of Keats's Poems (1950), Emily Eden, Semi-Attached Couple (1955) and Oscar Wilde, Lord Arthur Savile's Crime (1954) for The Folio Society. She edited and illustrated The Commandments (1946) for publisher F.G. Lewis. Also illustrated, among other works, Ida Clarke, Men Who Wouldn't Stay Dead (1936), which was one of her earliest projects in illustration, and Gwyn Jones, The Saga of Llywarch the Old (1955), one of her later projects.

A commercially successful artist, Braby was known as a perfectionist. The author of The Way of Wood Engraving (Studio How-To-Do-It Series, 1953). The subject of an article in The Studio, Vol.133, January 1947, pp.28-29 by Christopher Sandford which included several examples of her work. Sandford, director of the Golden Cockerel Press, notes her as possessing a restless energy and creative fire, but also describes her as a dark, beautiful woman who could have been an artist's model, with an additional interest in philosophy. Exhibited her work occasionally, including at the Beaux Art Gallery, with the Hampstead Artists, the Society of Wood Engravers and at the Arts Council Exhibition. Exhibited two wood engravings at the Society of Women Artists in 1955, Lord Arthur Savile's Crime and Sir Gawain and the Green Giant (from a book with six full-page engravings, 360 copies printed).

Her works were reproduced countless times, including in The Studio, the Radio Times, The Times Literary Supplement and the Observer. A member of the Arts Theatre Club. Elected to the Society of Wood Engravers. Based in London for much of her career. In 1979 her work was included in an exhibition Shall We Join the Ladies? held at the Museum of Oxford in October of that year. Braby was one of 27 women artists included in the exhibition. Braby also contributed an essay on Background to Wood Engraving to a book of the exhibition compiled by Betty Clark titled Shall We Join the Ladies? Wood Engravings by Women Artists of the Twentieth Century, Oxford, Studio One Gallery. The essay was an edited version of a paper read before the Society of Typographical Designers. Braby wrote the introduction to Albert Garrett's British Wood Engraving of the Twentieth Century. In early 1934, Braby married Rupert Douglas Paul (1908-80) in Hampstead, London. They had at least one son and one daughter. Braby died in Camden, London in early February 1987, aged 77.

BRADEN, DOROTHY KATHLEEN NORAH (1901-2001)

Pottery Artist. Known as Norah. Born in Margate, Kent in July 1901. The daughter of John Templeton Braden and Jessie. One of at least three children (Perth, Ronald and Dorothy). Perth became a decorative artist. Raised in Kent and in Tilehurst, Berkshire. Studied at the London County Council Central School of Arts and Crafts, and at the Royal College of Art. A pupil of Dora Billington. Awarded a diploma at the Royal College of Art, and was elected an Associate of the College in 1924. Produced mainly stoneware pots and bowls. In 1928 Braden joined Kathleen Pleydell-Bouverie, and together they worked for eight years at Coleshill in Wiltshire, at a pottery founded by Pleydell-Bouverie in 1925. Braden had also studied under Bernard Leach at St Ives, Cornwall, as had Pleydell-Bouverie. Prior to St Ives, Braden had spent three years at the Royal College of Art studying mainly drawing, but had produced little pottery there. The Coleshill pottery concentrated on unglazed pots and bowls for plants but did not produce tableware. Braden concentrated on brush decoration in a discreet and restrained manner, whilst Pleydell-Bouverie's decoration relied on tones and colours rather than pattern.

Braden left Coleshill in 1936 and virtually ceased to work in pottery. She exhibited her work at the International Exhibition of Industrial Art, held in Paris and New Zealand, and the British Institute of Industrial Art. In 1930 she and Pleydell-Bouverie held an exhibition of stoneware at Paterson's Gallery. Purchasers of Braden's pottery included the Manchester Corporation, the Contemporary Art Society, the Edinburgh Museum, the Aberystwyth Museum and the Victoria & Albert Museum, London. Braden was noted in Muriel Rose's volume Artist Potters in England, London, Faber & Faber, 1955 / 1970. Rose offers four examples of Braden's work, three stoneware jars and a stoneware bowl (all dated between 1933 and 1936). Two of those were in the Victoria & Albert Museum collection and one in the Worcester Art Museum, Massachusetts. Braden was the subject of an article, N. Braden and K. Pleydell-Bouverie, English Stoneware Pottery by W.A. Thorpe in Artwork 6, No.24, 1930. Also the subject of an article K. Pleydell-Bouverie and D.K.N. Braden, Studio Potters of Coleshill, Wiltshire by Ernest Marsh in Apollo, 38, December 1943. Braden died in Chichester. SEE: PLEYDELL-BOUVERIE, KATHLEEN

BRADLEY, GERTRUDE MAY (b.1869)

Illustrator / Painter / Engraver. Born in Richmond, Yorkshire. The daughter of schoolmaster John W. Bradley and Elizabeth. One of at least seven children (Katherine, Gertrude, Lucy, Dora, Bernard, Frederick and Arthur). Raised in Yorkshire, Ealing in London and Edgbaston, Birmingham. Whilst living in Edgbaston with her widowed father and several adult siblings, Gertrude studied at the Birmingham School of Art. In 1895 she contributed to the National Competition of Schools of Art, showing a decorative panel. Subsequently became an illustrator of children's books, a painter and an engraver. Also designed covers and inside decoration for children's books. Later based in London. Worked most prolifically in the 1890s, from at least 1893 until at least 1901. In 1900 she contributed to an exhibition of the Sketch Club of the Birmingham School of Art Union held in the Municipal School of Art. Other exhibitors included Celia Levetus and Sidney Meteyard. Bradley was part of a group which was known informally as the Birmingham School of Book Illustration.

Books illustrated by Bradley included The Red Hen and Other Tales (1893), Dollie Radford, Songs for Somebody (London, David Nutt, 1893), New Pictures in Old Frames (1894), Hamish Henry, Just Forty Winks (Blackie, 1897) and Pillow Stories (Grant Richards, 1901). Exhibited her work occasionally, including at the Royal Academy (1898-1900) and the Society of Women Artists (1897). Exhibited works included: The Cat-witch, Merry Hearts Make Light Feet (watercolour) and The Last Hope of Naumberg (design for a cartoon in tempera). Noted in Mahony, Latimer & Folmsbee, Illustrators of Children's Books 1744-1945, Boston, The Horn Book Inc., 1947. Also in R.E.D. Sketchley, English Book Illustration of To-day, London, Kegan Paul, 1903. Sketchley notes that Bradley had an element of humour to her work.

BRADSHAW, CONSTANCE HELEN (1873-1961)

Painter / Decorative Artist. Born in Manchester. The daughter of William Henry Bradshaw, M.A., and Catharina. Had at least one sibling, Florence. Raised in Brighton, Sussex and in Bickley, Kent. Studied at the Spenlove School of Art, London. Otherwise, spent virtually all her life and career at Rostherne in Bickley, living with her mother for part of the time. Constance died at Rostherne, aged 89. Produced paintings in oils and watercolours, and decorative hand-coloured prints, mainly landscapes and flowers. Travelled extensively to paint, around France, Norway, Italy, Ireland, Portugal, Scotland, Wales and England. Exhibited her work, including at the Royal Academy (1928-45), the Royal Glasgow Institute (1927-44), the Royal Institute of Oil Painters, the Paris Salon, the Royal Society of British Artists and the Society of Women Artists (170 works, 1899-1962). Also, in Stockholm, Canada, New Zealand and the provinces. Exhibited works included: The Spotted Jug, Fishermen's Homes, On Norfolk Coast (oil) and In St Tropez. Elected an Associate of the Society of Women Artists (1912-14) and a Member (1915-61). Was Acting President of the Society (1937-39) with President Dame Laura Knight. Elected a Member of the Royal Society of British Artists (1920) and of the Royal Institute of Oil Painters (1933). Elected a Member of the Forum Club, and of the St Ives Society of Artists (1936-44), with whom she exhibited. Works in the collection of the Salford Art Gallery.

BRADSHAW, GRACE E. - SEE ROGERS, G.E.

BRAUN, MARION W. - SEE STANFIELD, M.W.

BRAY-BAKER, MAY (1887-1975)
Period Embroideress / Tooled Leatherworker / Painter. Born in Acton, Middlesex in March 1887. The daughter of Harry Bray-Baker, director of a public company, and Matilda Ann. One of at least three children (Lilly, Percy and May). Raised in Middlesex and in Bromley, Kent. Spent much of her career in London. Died in Surrey, aged 88. Educated at the Brentford Collegiate School. Studied at the Tottenham Polytechnic, the Beckenham School of Art and the Royal College of Art, London. Also spent some time studying in the Victoria & Albert Museum, London. Awarded an Art Masters' Teaching Certificate in 1909. Won book prizes at the National Competition of Schools of Art, and awarded bronze medals as a student. An expert period embroideress, she also produced tooled leatherwork and paintings of landscapes, flowers and gardens. Acted as assistant art mistress at the Beckenham School of Art. Then took the post of art mistress at the Battersea Continuation School. Also taught crafts under the auspices of the London County Council. During the war, she was a draughtsman in the Munitions and Inventions Department of the War Office and in the Thames Conservancy. Exhibited her work occasionally. In 1928 she exhibited Port Isaac Bay at the Society of Women Artists. Some of her flower paintings were exhibited at the Horticultural Exhibition of 1916. Also exhibited at the galleries of Brighton, Lincoln and Oxford.

BRENNAND, JANET M.G. - SEE MARSH, J.M.G.

BRETT, MOLLY (1902-90)
Illustrator / Painter. Was Mary Elizabeth, known as Molly. Born in Croydon, Surrey. The daughter of John Vaughan Brett, an insurance official, and Mary. Raised in Croydon and in Maybury near Woking, Surrey. Spent virtually all her life in Surrey, dying there aged 88. Educated at Maybury House, Woking and at Crofton Grange, Orpington. Studied book illustration at Percy Venner Bradshaw's Press Art School (founded 1905) in 1921. Bradshaw was an illustrator and writer on art. Brett became an illustrator and artist in watercolours, pen and pencil. Her career lasted over 50 years. She specialised in animals, children and fairies. She kept pets and studied at

zoos and at the Natural History Museum. Produced mainly greetings cards, postcards and children's book illustrations. Worked for, among others, the Medici Society, the Brockhampton Press, the Sonjoy Studio, the Fine Arts Publishing Company, the Amalgamated Press, the Laurence Holman Advertising Service, Messrs William Collins & Sons, Blackie & Co., Raphael Tuck, Frederick Warne, C.W. Faulkner and Robert Gibson & Sons Ltd. Books illustrated by Brett included The Little Garden, Story of a Toy Car, Follow Me Round the Farm, Through the Magic Mirror (Warne, 1940) and A Surprise For Dumpy (Medici, 1964). Illustrated books by Enid Blyton. Wrote her own books as well as illustrating for other writers, including The Molly Brett Picture Book (Medici, 1979). Elected a Member of the Woking Art Society and of the Guildford Art Society.

BRIDGE, VERA E.C. - SEE OSBORNE, V.E.C.

BRIER, ELIZABETH - SEE SCOTT-MOORE, E.

BRIGHT, BEATRICE (1861-1940)
Painter. Was Annie Beatrice, known as Beatrice. Born in Bayswater, London in January 1861. One of at least five children (John, Mary, Agnes, Harrison, Annie Beatrice and Charles), all born between 1854 and 1862. Her father, Charles Tilston Bright (1832-88), originated from Essex and became an eminent figure in engineering. He was appointed engineer to the Magnetic Telegraph Company, travelled abroad with his work, and became the Liberal Member of Parliament for Greenwich. His son, Charles, also became a noted cable engineer. Charles Tilston Bright was knighted for his work. Beatrice's mother, Hannah Barrick Bright (1833-1914), later Lady Bright, originated from Hull. The Bright children were raised and educated in London, living at No.20 Bolton Gardens, Kensington in the 1880s. The family of Beatrix Potter lived at No.2 Bolton Gardens at that time.

Beatrice studied art under portrait and landscape painter Sir Arthur Stockdale Cope, R.A., and became a painter of portraits, figures, landscapes, seascapes and flowers. Began to exhibit her work more seriously in the early 1890s. Exhibited at the Royal Academy (23 works, 1896-1928), the Society of Women Artists (65 works, 1891-1919), the Royal Glasgow Institute (1914), the Paris Salon and with the New Society of Artists (certainly at their seventh annual exhibition, held in 1927). Exhibited works included: The Late Lady Bright, In the Old Armchair, A Yorkshire

Moor, The Orange Seller and War Gardener. Elected an Associate of the Society of Women Artists (1897-1920). Also a Member of the Lyceum Club. Her career lasted for over 37 years. She completed a number of important portrait commissions, including William H. Preece, President of the Institute of Civil Engineers; Fred Dempster Smith as 'Richelieu'; the Hon. Justice Avory; Sir John Denison Pender and Princess Marie Louise of Schleswig-Holstein. Based in London for most of her career. Visited St Ives, Cornwall in 1911. Died in Kensington in May 1940, aged 79. Left a considerable estate of some £33,700 to her nephew, Charles Mervyn King, a Captain in the army, and the Rt Hon. John Denison Pender.

BRIGHTWELL, HELEN (1876-1967)

Painter / Enameller / Jewellery Maker. Known as Nellie. Born in Colchester, Essex in August 1876. The second child of William Brightwell and Miriam. Her father, a schoolmaster, originated from Suffolk, her mother from Colchester. One of at least five children (Beatrice, Helen, Dora, Winifred and William). Her siblings were also born in Colchester. Her father taught at Linton House School in Colchester whilst Helen was a small child. She was educated at the Girls' High School, Colchester. Her father died young, and the remaining family moved to Edgbaston, Birmingham. Helen remained in Birmingham for the rest of her life, dying there in early 1967, aged 90. In the late 1890s, she studied at the Birmingham School of Art, winning three silver national medals, a Queen's Prize and the John Henry Chamberlain Bronze Medal for figure design. She became a miniature painter, enameller and metalworker, also producing works in gesso. Brightwell specialised in making decorative caskets and exhibited some of those at the 1897 annual exhibition of works by students of the Birmingham School of Art. She also exhibited with the Royal Birmingham Society of Artists during her career. She appeared to live at the family home until her mother's death. Education was clearly important to the Brightwells. Dora became a cookery teacher. Winifred, who also remained at the family home, became a violin teacher.

BROADHEAD, MARION ELLEN (1876-1950)

Painter / Etcher. Born in Macclesfield, Cheshire in July 1876. The daughter of John Broadhead (1840-1905) and Ellen Walker (1840-1915). Her father was a coal merchant. Both parents originated from Macclesfield. Marion had a step-sister, Annie. Raised in Macclesfield and Manchester. Studied at the London School of Art and in Paris. Produced portrait paintings in oils, miniatures, etchings and drypoint. Based in Manchester, Harrow, Macclesfield and London at various times during her career. Died in Macclesfield, aged 74. Exhibited her work, including at the Royal Academy (29 works, 1907-37), the Society of Women Artists (1923) and the Paris Salon. Exhibited works included: The Artist's Mother, Mrs Malcolm Gillies, The Artist, H.S.H. Princess Mary Lieven, A Polish Artist and The Rev. G.E. Robson. Elected a Member of the Society of Graphic Art. Noted and illustrated in Frank L. Emanuel's volume Etching and Etchings, London, Pitman & Sons, 1930. Of Miss Broadhead, Emanuel says: 'This portrait was rapidly needled direct on to the plate. Miss Broadhead is most successful with such likenesses in needlework - on copper - be it understood' (p.273).

BROCK, CHARLOTTE (active 1900s-1910s)

Embroideress. A highly accomplished and expert needlewoman who produced various embroideries, but particularly church embroideries, in the early years of the twentieth century. Three examples of her work were illustrated in the Art Journal, 1911-12, pp.85-87. One of those was a large festival altar cloth executed by Miss Brock for St Albans. The design was by Luther Hooper. Also illustrated was a violet burse and veil with gold couched embroidery.

BROMET, MARY (1862-1937)

Sculptor. Born in Leigh, Lancashire. The daughter of James Pownall and Mary Swanwick. Her father, who originated from Manchester, was a silk manufacturer. Her mother originated from Prestbury, Cheshire. Mary had at least three siblings, Ellen, Lucy and Frank. Frank became a West African merchant. Mary spent her early years in Cheshire. She was still there with her parents in 1891, just prior to beginning her studies in sculpture. Studied in Frankfurt for a year, in Paris for six years (in the late 1890s) and in Rome for four years. Believed to have been a pupil of Rodin. On her return to England, in the early 1900s (c.1903), she married barrister Alfred Bromet (b.1866). He originated from Tadcaster, Yorkshire and was a student of Magdalen College, Oxford. The couple had no children. They lived at Lime Lodge, Oxhey, Hertfordshire. Mary remained there until her death in February 1937. Alfred Bromet outlived her. She continued to work and to exhibit until shortly before her death.

Bromet produced figures, busts, statues and groups. Worked in marble, plaster and bronze. She was highly regarded in her lifetime. Exhibited her work over a period of more than 35 years, including at the Royal Academy (27 works, 1897-1932), the Royal Glasgow Institute (1923-31, possibly in 1901 also) and the Society of Women Artists (24 works, 1907-22). Also, at the Paris Salon, where she won an Honourable Mention in 1899, the International Exhibition at Rome, White City, Wembley and with the Royal Birmingham Society of Artists. Exhibited at the Walker Art Gallery, Liverpool. For example, in 1909 she showed The Kiss, a bronze group which was illustrated in The Studio, Vol.48, January 1910, p.314 and exhibited at the Society of Women Artists in 1912. Exhibited at the Leeds and Manchester City Art Galleries. Exhibited works included: Mercury (bust, marble), A Bolshevik Commissar (bronze), Politics (group, bronze), The Flood (group) and Ragamuffin (bronze). Other works included Spirit of War, a memorial which was eventually placed next to Watford Town Hall. Works sold for up to £750, then a considerable sum. Elected a Member of the Society of Women Artists (1909-24), and was President of the Society (1913-15). Listed in the Society's papers as Patroness of the British Academy of Arts, Rome. Elected an Associate of the Royal Society of British Sculptors.

The Glasgow Museum and Art Galleries, Scotland acquired Bromet's The Harpy Celaeno which was first exhibited in Rome in 1902. Works illustrated in The Studio, The Year's Art and the Art Journal. Other significant works by her included Sir George Makin's Presentation Portrait Bust for the Royal College of Surgeons, Lincoln's Inn Fields. Also, a memorial for St Thomas's Hospital, and The Intruder which was purchased by H.M. Queen Mary. In 2010 one of Bromet's sculptures was sold in France - a brown patina bronze proof representing a nude woman brandishing a man's head in her hand while clasping a dummy. It stood on a trapezoid socle decorated in bas-relief with the four allegories of Arts. Dated 1904, it stood just over 31" in height. Some of Bromet's works, and her avid support for the Society of Women Artists, suggest that she quietly supported female independence. She later signed her works Mary Pownall Bromet.

BROOKE, IRIS E.M. - SEE GIFFARD, E.M.

BROOKS, IRENE G. - SEE HEATH, I.G.

BROWN, GERTRUDE - SEE DALE, G.

BROWN, MILDRED MARY M. (1898-1979)
Artist / Designer. Born in Preston, Lancashire in June 1898. The daughter of Charles Robert Brown and Mary Winifred. Her father, a brick manufacturer in Preston, originated from Preston, as did her mother. The third of at least four children. Educated in Preston, Blackburn, Liverpool and Manchester. In 1911 she is listed as a student at the Collegiate School Convent, Convent Lodge, Blackburn. Became a painter in oils and watercolours, and a designer of decorative fans. Exhibited her work occasionally, including at Wembley (1925), the Walker Art Gallery, Liverpool (1921-28), the Manchester Academy of Fine Arts (1926-28) and at Dunedin (1925-26). Elected a Member of the Faculty of Arts. Also a Member of the Manchester Attic Club and of the Salon Club. Elected an Associate of the Manchester Academy of Fine Arts. Based mainly in the north of England, including in Marple and Cheadle, Cheshire. Died in Stockport, aged 81.

BROWN, NELLIE GERTRUDE (1887-1969)
Painter / Black & White Artist. Born in Wolverhampton. The daughter of William Lyes Brown and Adelaide. Her mother died young. Her father was an ecclesiastical carver and, later, the founder of the printing firm W. Brown & Sons, Wolverhampton. One of at least four children (Leonard, William, Nellie and Arthur). Educated privately, and at the Higher Grade School, Wolverhampton. Raised in Wolverhampton, but also in Penn, Staffordshire where she died, aged 82. Studied at the Wolverhampton School of Art under A. Scoope and Robert Jackson Emerson. Produced landscapes in oils and watercolours, and black & white drawings. Exhibited only occasionally, including at the Royal Academy (1939-49). Exhibited works included: A South Staffordshire Lane, An Autumn Day and Down the Chine to the Sea.

BROWN, VIOLET MARY - SEE COPESTICK, V.M.

BROWNE, FAITH ISABEL KENWORTHY (1882-1973)
Painter / Poster Artist / Etcher. Born in Bournemouth in October 1882. The daughter of the Rev. Elliott Kenworthy Browne and Katharine Alice.

Her father was Rector at North Stoneham in Southampton. One of at least three children (Dorothy, Faith and Bernard). Educated at home and abroad. Studied at Cope's School of Art and at the London School of Art. As a student, she lodged in Wimbledon with other female art students including Florence Bevan, Lillian Griffiths, Edith Whitchurch, Mabel Wilkinson and Lucy Roe. The girls were supervised there by artist and Lady President Edith Finlinson. Faith was a bronze medallist and a gold medallist at the Calcutta Exhibition. Produced portrait, flower, interior, still life and landscape paintings in oils and watercolours, etchings and poster designs. For a time, early in her career, she taught art at the St Albans College, Prince Albert, Saskatchewan, Canada. Otherwise, based in London and Dorset. Had an extensive career covering at least five decades, and worked until shortly before her death. Died in Surrey, aged 90. Exhibited her work, including at the Royal Academy (1924 & 1958), the Society of Women Artists (1923-69), the Royal Institute of Oil Painters, the Royal Society of British Artists, the Paris Salon, in Calcutta, Delhi and Canada. Exhibited works included: Wind in the Trees (etching), Zinnias (watercolour), Trovaso Canal, Venice (oil) and The Letter. Her portrait of Field Marshal Sir Claud Jacob was acquired for the Masonic Hall, Quetta, India. Elected a Member of the Campden Hill Club and of the Ex-Service Women's Club.

BROWNE, IRENE MARY F.C. (1881-1977)

Sculptor / Potter. Born in Fulham, London in September 1881. Her mother was Mary M. Browne. A modelling pupil at the Chelsea Polytechnic School of Art. Based in Surrey, London and Sussex during her career. Died in Sussex, aged 95. Produced statuettes in bronze, pottery medallions, pottery statuettes, stoneware groups and unglazed stoneware. Exhibited her work, including at the Royal Hibernian Academy (1913), the Royal Glasgow Institute (1911), the Royal Academy (1908-32) and the Society of Women Artists (1924-30). Exhibited works included: Protected (statuette, bronze), Young Things (statuette group, bronze), Singalese Potter (statuette, stoneware) and Everyday Life (hard-fired stoneware group). Elected an Associate of the Royal Society of Miniature Painters. Elected an Associate of the Society of Women Artists (1926-30) and a Member (1930-51). Her stoneware statuettes were acquired by the Victoria & Albert Museum, London, the Manchester Art Gallery, the Hanley Museum, Staffordshire and the Aberystwyth Museum.

BROWNING, AMY KATHERINE (1881-1978)

Artist / Illustrator. Born in March 1881 at Little Bramingham, Bedfordshire. The daughter of James Day Browning (1857-1933) and Katherine Lucy Saunderson (1858-1956). Her father ran a farm of some 615 acres in Bedfordshire, employing several workers. Amy was one of at least seven children (Ethel, Amy, James, Ursula, Cecil, Dorothy and Agnes). Raised in Bedfordshire. Educated privately and abroad. Studied at the Royal College of Art, London on a scholarship between 1899 and 1904, working under Gerald Moira. Also studied in Paris. Elected an Associate of the Royal College of Art in 1905. Became an artist in oils, watercolours, tempera, pencil and chalk. Subjects included portraits, landscapes, interiors and flowers. Did some illustration work. Worked plein air.

After completing her studies, Browning remained largely in London, working at various locations including the Albert Studios, Albert Bridge Road, in Battersea, and at the Cedar Studios, Chelsea. Also spent time at the family home, Kitchen End, Pulloxhill in Ampthill, Bedfordshire. Evidently maintained ties with her family, and with the county of her birth. Also based in Iken, Suffolk and Derbyshire for a while. Exhibited extensively, including at the Royal Hibernian Academy (1913), the Royal Glasgow Institute (1926-53), the Royal Academy (116 works, 1906-70) and the Society of Women Artists (79 works, 1915-64). Also exhibited at the Royal Institute of Oil Painters, the New English Art Club, the Royal Photographic Society and in Pittsburgh, Vienna, Paris, Wellington, New Zealand and Sydney, Australia. Exhibited at numerous smaller galleries too. For example, she showed The Lime Tree Shade at the annual Southport exhibition in 1926. In The Studio, Vol.92, July 1926, p.50 it was described as 'a most compellingly interesting picture'. Other exhibited works included: Studio Supper, Bee Master, The Hammock-Swing, Lady Phipps and Wash Day. Browning was awarded the Medaille d'Argent (1912) and the Medaille d'Or Paris Salon (1922). Elected a Member of the Royal Institute of Oil Painters (1912). Elected a Member of the Society of Women Artists (1921-35, 1952-58). Elected Vice President of the Society of Women Artists (1931-33). A Member of the Forum Club.

Purchasers of Browning's work included Glasgow, Manchester, Wolverhampton, Wellington in New Zealand, the National Gallery, the French Government for the Luxembourg galleries and Vienna. Her works were reproduced in numerous magazines and journals including The Studio and The Artist. She held feminist views, contributing illustrations to the suffragette magazine The Women's Dreadnought in 1917. In 1916 she married Thomas Cantrell Dugdale in Kensington. Dugdale, the son of an engineer, was born in 1880 and was also a student at the Royal College of Art and in Paris. He became a successful painter, decorator and designer, sharing studios with Amy at times. In early 1957, Browning visited New York, then aged 76 and still listed as an artist. She continued to work and to exhibit until at least 1970, at the age of 89. Evidently a busy, determined, intelligent and resolute woman of considerable talent. She died in Hertfordshire in early 1978, aged 97.

BUCKTON, EVELEEN (1872-1962)

Sculptor / Painter / Etcher. Born in Haslemere, Surrey. The daughter of George R. Buckton, F.R.S., and Mary. Her father was a scientific author. Raised in Haslemere and Chiddingfold, Surrey. One of at least six children (Alice, Jessie, Maud, Florence, Eileen and William). Studied art in London in the early 1900s, when she was in her late 20s. Remained mainly in London, dying there, aged 90, but also spent some time in Salisbury. Produced etchings, drypoint, statuettes in bronze and marble and landscape paintings. Exhibited at the New English Art Club (from 1900), the Royal Scottish Academy (1936), the Royal Glasgow Institute (1934) and the Royal Academy (36 works, 1917-59). Exhibited works included: Nymph (statuette, bronze), The Little Wood, Avening (drypoint), The Old Willow Tree (etching) and Before Rain, Suffolk. Her exhibiting career stretched over some 59 years. Noted in Frank L. Emanuel's Etching and Etchings, London, Pitman & Sons, 1930.

BUDD, BARBARA NELLIE (1895-1949)

Illuminator / Embroideress / Designer. Born in Dulwich, London in November 1895. The daughter of Charles Budd and Ellen Huggett. Her father, a head cashier and clerk in a city warehouse, originated from Sussex, as did her mother. Barbara was one of at least four children (Archibald, John, Phyllis and Barbara). Raised in London. Educated at the Forest Hill County Secondary School. Then studied at the Camberwell School of Arts and Crafts, where she was awarded a college diploma. Subsequently studied at the Royal College of Art, London. Elected an Associate of the Royal College of Art in 1924. Taught crafts for a while. Exhibited at the 1926 Arts and Crafts Exhibition at the Royal Academy. Produced work of a varied nature. For example, she assisted in illuminating the Rolls of Honour for the House of Commons and for Liverpool city. Executed an illuminated map of Sussex and an illuminated title page. Designed and executed a sign for The Three Black Crows Inn. Her embroideries included a panel titled The Seasons. Produced stained glass designs, including one based on Guy Fawkes. Also involved in pottery design, one of her works being a Net of Fish vase. Elected a Member of the Society of Scribes and Illuminators (1926) and of the Embroiderers' Guild. Also a Member of the South London Group. Some of her works were reproduced by the Prager Press and in La Revue Moderne. Budd died in Camberwell, aged 53.

BUDDEBERG, GRISELDA - SEE ALLAN, G.

BULLEY, GEORGINA EMILY (1853-1927)

Sculptor / Painter. Born in Chelsea, London. The daughter of artist Ashburnham Henry Bulley (1815-88) and Frances Ellen (d.1886). Her father was a painter of animals. Georgina had at least three siblings (William, Henry and Charles). She was raised in London. Possibly studied under her father. Sometime shortly before the death of her parents, she began living with her elder unmarried brother, William, a solicitor, in Chelsea. The siblings spent well over two decades sharing a house. Georgina died in Kensington, aged 73. Produced busts in terracotta and paintings in oils and watercolours, of portraits, landscapes and flowers. Exhibited her work, including at the Royal Academy (1880-1920) and the Society of Women Artists (1890-1903). Exhibited works included: At Sunrise (watercolour), St Elizabeth of Hungary (bust, terracotta), Ragwort and One of Her Majesty's Subjects.

BULLICK, ESME (active 1930s)

Embroideress. Produced silk embroidered pictures. Educated at the Cheltenham Ladies' College. Won a First Prize for her work at the Manchester School of Embroidery, and at the Schools of Shrewsbury, Oxford and elsewhere. Exhibited at the Royal Cambrian Academy and the Walker Art Gallery, Liverpool. One of her embroidered portieres was illustrated in the Manchester School of Art Magazine. Based in Bath in the 1930s. Records suggest this may have been Merriell Esme H. Bullick (1909-2003), born in London and raised in Bournemouth. Possibly the daughter of Herbert Charles Bullick, a bank accountant, and Beatrice Esme. Records are not conclusive.

BUNN, FANNY (1870-1950)

Decorative Artist. Born in West Bromwich, Staffordshire. The daughter of Levi Bunn and Emma. Her father, who had financial independence, originated from West Bromwich. Fanny had at least one elder sibling, Rebecca. Raised in West Bromwich, and lived there for much of her life and career, dying in Staffordshire. Listed as an art student from at least 1891. Was a student at the Birmingham School of Art in the early 1900s. In 1904 she won a gold medal at the National Competition of Schools of Art for a decorative panel. Produced panels and plaques in enamel. Exhibited her work occasionally, including at the Royal Academy (1904-05) and with the Royal Birmingham Society of Artists. Exhibited works included: Gloria in Excelsis (plaque, enamel), The Three Seasons (panel, enamel) and The Victor (panel, enamel).

BURFORD, STELLA ANDRIA (1902-75)

Painter in Oils / Mural Decorator / Illuminator / Stained Glass and Lettering Artist. Born and raised in Shepshed, Leicestershire. The daughter of William Wilkinson, a bootmaker and dealer, and Alice. Had at least one sibling, Nellie Alicia. Studied at the Leicester School of Art. Exhibited at the Daily Express Young Artists' Exhibition, at the New English Art Club, in Belfast, and under the Duveen Scheme. In 1927 she married Roger d'Este Burford in Kensington. Based in Chelsea for a time. Died in Yorkshire, aged 73.

BURGESS, ELIZA MARY (1878-1961)

Painter / Designer. Born in March 1878. The daughter of William Weston Burgess and Martha Chignell. Her father, a florist and gardener, originated from Frimley, Surrey. Her mother was a dressmaker who originated from Middlesex. One of at least seven children, five girls and two boys, which included twin girls, Maria and Emma. All the children were born in Walthamstow. Eliza was educated at Elementary School, and at Pembroke College, Walthamstow under W. Milnes. From there, in 1897 she gained a National Gilchrist Scholarship tenable at the Royal Female School of Art, London, under the direction of Miss Wilson. Won the Queen's Gold Medal for figure drawing, two National Silver Medals for flower painting, four National Bronze Medals for design, flower painting and still life, a Queen's Scholarship, a Clothworkers' Scholarship and a National Scholarship of £50 a year for two years.

In 1901 Eliza is listed as still living at home in Walthamstow, where her brother Cornelius was now a metalworker, and her sister Elizabeth was now a dressmaker. Eliza is listed as a colour artist at this time, apparently the only one in the family. Remained living and working in Walthamstow into the late 1920s. Then moved to London, remaining there into the 1950s. She died in late 1961 in Bristol, aged 84. Became a productive artist whose exhibiting career covered more than 50 years. Produced designs, portraits, particularly of children, miniatures and children's subject pictures. Also, some flower and garden studies. Worked mainly in watercolours and tempera. Spent some time painting Scottish Society in Scotland. Exhibited extensively, including at the Royal Academy (1900-51), the Royal Scottish Academy (1920-43), the Royal Hibernian Academy (1912), the Royal West of England Academy and the Royal Society of Miniature Painters. Also, in Bristol, Manchester, Liverpool, Birmingham, Edinburgh and Ireland. Showed 45 works at the Society of Women Artists between 1900 and 1951.

Further afield, Eliza exhibited at the Paris Salon, in Philadelphia, Toronto and Australia. Showed work at some smaller exhibitions too. For example, she showed drawings at the tenth annual exhibition of the Essex Grosvenor Sketch Club at the Court House, Walthamstow in November 1905. Exhibited works included: Design For a Ceiling Paper, The Young Philosopher, Hollyhocks, The Age of Innocence and The Daughter of a Soldier. Elected an Associate of the Royal West of England Academy (1910) and a Member of the Royal Society of Miniature Painters (1912). Purchasers of her work included the Walker Art Gallery, Liverpool who acquired her The Daisy Hat (miniature, 1915). Sheffield Art Gallery purchased her Snowdrops (watercolour, 1941). Queen Victoria purchased one of her watercolours, and Queen Alexandra purchased four of her paintings. Works requested for the Queen's Doll's House. The Victoria & Albert Museum, London acquired her So Tired.

BURGESS, ETHEL KATE (1876-1953)

Painter / Illustrator. Born in Lambeth, London. The daughter of Charles Burgess and Martha. Her father, a stone carver and mason, originated from Southwark, her mother from Camberwell. Ethel was one of at least five children (Amy, Ethel, Hilda, Arthur and Mabel). Mabel Burgess also became an artist. Ethel remained in London throughout her life, dying in Wandsworth, aged 77. She was a student at the Lambeth School of Art. In 1897 she won a scholarship offered by the London County Council. In November 1899, she won a first prize for figure composition at the

Gilbert Sketching Club. Produced illustrations, black & white drawings, bookplates and figure paintings. Influenced by Nico Jungmann. However, she was never an imitator. Rather, she was known for her distinct style, her industry, for her use of colour and for her observation, vigour and humour.

Early in her career, Ethel spent time in Yorkshire drawing fisher boys, men and women. Some of those drawings were illustrated in The Studio, Vol.20, 1900, pp.190-192. Selwyn Image owned her A Yorkshire Fisher Boy. In 1908 Burgess won an Honourable Mention at the exhibition of the Lambeth School of Art Club, which was made up of past and present students of the Lambeth School. Exhibited her work elsewhere, including at the Royal Academy (1901-07) and with the Women's International Art Club (including in 1901). Exhibited works included: The Story of a Mother - Hans Andersen, On the Sands, Age and Toil and The Beggars. Burgess also studied chromo-xylography, producing chromo-xylographs. She exhibited her designs for chromo-xylographs, and one was reproduced in The Studio, Vol.21, November 1900, p.103 in an article about the subject. One of her bookplates was also illustrated in The Studio, Vol.10, 1897, p.113.

BURLISON, FRANCES BESSIE (1875-1974)
Sculptor / Decorative Artist. Born in St Pancras, London. The daughter of John Burlison, an artist, and Elizabeth Sarah. Educated at home. Studied at the Slade School, London. Produced statuettes and groups in bronze. Also, the occasional triptych and decorative panel in plaster. Exhibited at the Royal Academy (1899-1917), the International Society of Sculptors, Painters & Gravers, the Paris Salon and the Society of Women Artists (1898-1900). Also exhibited at the Walker Art Gallery, Liverpool. For example, in 1907 she showed a small group, The Gossips, at the Gallery's Autumn Exhibition. Exhibited works included: Mother and Child (statuette, bronze), The Annunciation (panel in plaster), Gloria in Excelsis Deo (triptych) and The Boy and the Tortoise (group, bronze). One of her bronze groups was acquired by the Preston Museum. Produced works for churches at Walthamstow and Nottingham. Executed figures for the Beaumont College, Liverpool and various war memorials. Based in London, using the Primrose Hill Studios for a time. Died in Hampstead, aged 98.

BURNE, WINIFRED (1877-c.1946)
Painter / Decorative Artist. Born in Tranmere, Cheshire in October 1877. The daughter of Joseph Burne (1820-88), an actuary, and Martha Louisa Elvis (1844-1919). Her parents married in Wirral, Cheshire in 1863. Winifred was one of at least nine children. She was raised in Tranmere and, after her father's death, in Llandudno, Wales. She returned to Cheshire to study at the Birkenhead School of Art and the Liverpool University School of Architecture. Also studied at the Munich Kunstlerinnen Verein. Studied Applied Art under Hermann Groeber at Munich. Her sister Mary was also a student at the Liverpool University. Her brother Benjamin (b.1876) gained a Ph.D. Winifred subsequently produced paintings in oils and watercolours, lithographs and block prints. Began to exhibit her work in around 1899, whilst still a student. Exhibited at the International Society of Sculptors, Painters & Gravers, in Munich, Bristol, Liverpool, Hull, Derby, Plymouth and elsewhere. In Plymouth, she exhibited with the Cornish Artists at the annual exhibition held at Harris & Sons in 1923. Moved to Cornwall in around 1914, to Carbis Bay. In the 1920s she was based at The Alison Studio at St Ives. In the 1930s she was based at Sunset, Porthmeor, St Ives. A founder member of the St Ives Society of Artists. Also a Member of the Faculty of Arts. Praised in La Revue Moderne. Wrote an article on hanging at exhibitions for Drawing and Design. Possibly the same Winifred Burne who died in Bangor, Wales in early 1946, aged 68.

BURNEY, GLADYS D.F. - SEE MELLIAR, G.D.F.

BURNS, JEAN DOUGLAS (b.1903)
Painter / Engraver. Born in Cumbernauld in June 1903. The daughter of Captain Alan Burns, Advocate. Educated at Northlands. Studied at the Glasgow School of Art and in Edinburgh. Awarded a Diploma of the Edinburgh College of Art in 1927. Produced paintings and engravings on wood and metal. Exhibited at the Royal Scottish Academy (1926-42), the Royal Glasgow Institute (1930-32), the Society of Women Artists (1930-38) and in Liverpool. Also exhibited with the Society of Artist-Printers in Glasgow. For example, at their sixth exhibition in 1927 she exhibited The Horseman. Other exhibited works included The Cossacks (woodcut), The River (wood engraving), The Show (wood engraving) and Equatorial America. Based at Cumbernauld for much of her career.

BURNS, MARGARET ALICE DELISLE (1888-1974)

Artist. Born in London in July 1888. The daughter of A. Arnold Hanray. Studied at the Slade School, London just before the First World War. Won a prize there for figure drawing in 1910. Produced portraits in oils and pastels, and drawings in ink with watercolour. Exhibited her work occasionally, including at the New English Art Club (from 1914), the Royal Glasgow Institute (1929), the Royal Academy (1957) and the Society of Women Artists (1927). Also, at the Goupil Gallery and with the International Society of Sculptors, Painters & Gravers. Exhibited works included: Old Houses, Assisi, Rue St Catherine, A View of Hampstead From Upper Terrace and Medici Chapel, Florence. Based mainly in London. Died in Surrey, aged 86. However, she also spent time working in France, Italy and the United States, drawing some of their most important buildings. Executed some architectural drawings in Dieppe, which established her style and technique.

In Italy, Burns worked in Siena, Arezzo, Cortona, Perugia, Assisi and Florence. Most of her drawings were done in Indian ink with a watercolour body-colour on brown paper. In December 1915, The Studio published her drawing Philadelphia on a Wet Day. In 1925, The Studio (Vol.89, February, pp.81-85) offered an article Old Buildings. Drawings by Margaret Delisle Burns with four illustrations, two of Rapallo and two of Hampstead houses, one of which was the home of Mrs Siddons. In Hampstead, she also executed drawings of the fair on the Heath on bank holidays. Elsewhere in England, she drew, for example, Paycocks House at Coggeshall which was given to the National Trust. Also, the Manor House at West Hoathly which was exhibited at the Goupil Gallery. In Southwold, Suffolk she drew the local church, and drew Poplars, a Suffolk farmhouse. In Cambridge, she drew the Gate of Honour of Caius College.

BURRAS, CAROLINE AGNES (1890-1967)

Illuminator / Metalworker / Painter. Born in Headingley, Leeds in August 1890. The daughter of William C. Burras (1854-1929) and Jenny Eliza Clark. Her father was a manufacturers' agent. Caroline was one of at least six children (Kate, Charles, Caroline, Guy, Mabel and Elsie). Educated at the Central High School, Leeds. Studied at the Leeds School of Art. Awarded various scholarships, prizes and bronze medals. Awarded a teaching certificate for teachers of art in 1924. Produced illuminations, metalwork and paintings in oils and watercolours, mainly landscapes, miniatures and portraits. Initially based in Leeds during her career, but later moved to Southampton. Died in Kensington, London, aged 76. In the 1920s acted as assistant art mistress at the Leeds School of Art. In the 1930s acted as art mistress at various grammar schools, and at the Elland Secondary School.

Exhibited her work at the Royal Academy (1918-27), the Royal Miniature Society, the Paris Salon, the Walker Art Gallery, Liverpool, the Leeds Art Gallery and the Bradford Art Gallery. Exhibited works included: An Old Fisherman, Miss Maud Flint and Portrait Study in Uniform. Elected a Member of the Yorkshire Society of Artists, and of the National Society of Art Masters. Some of her illuminated pages were reproduced in a special The Studio number, Arts and Crafts, in 1916. Her Portrait of the Artist was reproduced in Les Artistes d'Aujourd hui. Her Portrait of a Fisherman was reproduced in Revue du Vrai et du Beau. Her illuminated addresses were purchased by Leeds University, the Leeds and West Yorkshire Architectural Society, the Leeds College of Art and the churches of Cottingley, Horsforth and Folkestone.

BURRELL, NAOMI (1832-78)

Sculptor. Records suggest that Burrell was born in London, the daughter of Thomas Burrell, a veterinary surgeon, and Ruth Rolf. One of at least seven children. Lived and worked in London. Died there, aged 45. Became a teacher at the Female School of Art, Queen Square, London. Produced mainly figure and portrait works. Exhibited at the Society of Women Artists (1857-62). Exhibited works included: Rev. W. Garrett Lewis (bust), Factory Girls, Portrait Statue of Boy Fishing and Miss Palmer (bust). Elected an early Member of the Society of Women Artists (1859-70).

BURROUGHES, DOROTHY MARY B. (1883-1963)

Decorative Artist / Book Illustrator. Born in St Pancras, London. The daughter of James Samuel Burroughes (1841-1912) and Rosabel K. Buttery (1842-91). Her father, a billiard table manufacturer, was not without money. Her mother came from a similar background, and was the daughter of artist and art restorer Charles Buttery. He worked on a number of highly important restoration projects, and for a time worked for the National Gallery, London. Rosabel's brother, Horace Buttery, also became a noted picture restorer. Dorothy was one of at least five children (Rosabel, Faith, Ida, Laurence and

Dorothy), all raised in London where the family business was based. Dorothy opted for art and studied in London at the Slade School and at the Heatherley's School of Art. She also spent time studying in Germany.

Dorothy produced paintings, posters, linocuts and illustrations for children's books. Also produced miniatures, pencil drawings, chalk drawings and watercolours. Subjects included animals, figures, portraits, birds, fish, flowers and other still life. Illustrated books until at least 1949, including The Heart of the Ancient Wood (Dent), Hans Britterman and the Silver Skates (Dent) and Queer Birds and Queer Beasts (Allan & Unwin). Illustrated Rose Fyleman, Fifty-One New Nursery Rhymes (1931). Her posters were visually striking, using brilliant colours and simple shapes. At least one of her posters was illustrated in Colour magazine in 1923. Designed a Monkey poster and a zoo poster for the Underground Railways. Exhibited her work, including with the Royal Society of British Artists at the Suffolk Street Galleries, in Brighton and Hull, and at the Dorien Leigh Gallery. At the last of those she showed, for example, Lynx in 1926. At the Fine Art Society, she exhibited, for example, Gluck and At the Races, which were illustrated in Colour magazine in April 1926.

Dorothy exhibited extensively with the Society of Women Artists, showing 77 works between 1924 and 1962, the last of those just prior to her death. Exhibited works included: The Old Rose Roof, Elizabeth Scott at the Microphone, Angel Fish (watercolour), Creation of the Daisy (watercolour) and Early Morning Mist (watercolour). Elected an Associate of the Society of Women Artists (1923-24) and a Member (1934-64). Elected a Member of the Royal Society of British Artists. Also a Member of the New Autumn Group and exhibited with them, including in 1925 at the Gieves Gallery. Works purchased by the Victoria & Albert Museum, London. Other works illustrated in the Illustrated London News, Bystander, Sketch, John O'London, Drawing and Design and Commercial Art. Initially based in central London, then at Stanmore, at Hampshire and, latterly at Henley-on-Thames, Oxfordshire. She died at Henley, aged 79.

BURROWES, MARGARET ELEANORE BERESFORD (1866-1936)

Organised and ran the North Bucks Lace Association from the family home, the Manor House at Maids Moreton in Buckinghamshire. Although Margaret was born in Ontario, Canada, she spent virtually her whole life in England,

dying at The Old House in the village of Maids Moreton. Her father was Arnold Burrowes (d.1907), a wealthy timber dealer who originated from Derbyshire. Her mother was Jane Elizabeth Clarke. Margaret was the eldest of at least seven children (Margaret, Kathleen, Richard, Mary, Agatha, Gilbert and Alice). The family spent time living in Morecambe, Lancashire, Portsea, Hampshire and Grendon, Buckinghamshire before settling in Maids Moreton some time after 1891. In 1893 the North Bucks Lace Association was founded with the aim of reviving the craft of Bucks pillow lace, which had virtually died out. Eventually, the industry had over 50 workers, though many were the older women of the community. North Bucks was just one of numerous handcraft industries to flourish in late nineteenth- and early twentieth-century Britain, influenced by the founding of the Home Arts and Industries Association in 1884. The Association promoted a return to regional handcrafts. Margaret Burrowes provided workers with materials and patterns, enabling the women to work in their own homes.

As with the lace industries of Devon, Northants and Bedfordshire, the North Bucks venture thrived for a number of years. There are indications that Audrey Trevelyan and Mrs Bruce Clark not only taught at the Devon, Northants and Bedfordshire classes, but had some influence at North Bucks too. All four industries exhibited regularly at the annual Home Arts and Industries Association exhibition. In 1896, all four contributed to a large display which won them, collectively, six gold and 15 blue awards. By 1900, North Bucks was winning recognition further afield. In America, the industry won a gold medal at the 1904 St Louis Exhibition. They also contributed to the Society of Artists at Work Exhibition held at the Grafton Galleries in October 1906. The Society was organised by Mrs Charles Muller in order to help promote and sell handicrafts. North Bucks also exhibited at the Exposition des Arts Decoratifs de Grande-Bretagne et d'Irlande, Paris in 1914. At its peak, North Bucks had the patronage of four duchesses. However, they were no doubt affected by the First World War, as were many other similar handcraft industries across Britain. Its success, however, indicates that North Bucks should be acknowledged and remembered today, not least because of the tireless work of Margaret Burrowes. She was also the author of Buckingham Lace (n.d.), and contributed an article, Buckinghamshire Lace, to the Art Workers' Quarterly, January 1904, p.15. The article contained illustrations. It can be presumed, given that she founded and ran the North Bucks industry, that Burrowes herself was a lace maker.

BUSH, PHYLLIS MADELEINE HYLIE (1896-1943)

Etcher / Artist. Born in Bristol in September 1896. The daughter of Reginald Edgar James Bush (1869-1956) and Flora Hyland (1870-1940). Her father originated from Cardiff, Wales, her mother from Bethersden, Kent. Both parents were artists. Her father, a painter and etcher, was a teacher at the Royal College of Art, London until 1894, a Member of the Royal Society of Painter-Etchers & Engravers and of the Royal West of England Academy, and became Principal of the Bristol Municipal School of Art. Her mother, a watercolour painter (mainly of flowers), was a silver medal winner at the Royal College of Art and a painting mistress at the Bristol Municipal School of Art. Reginald Bush's brother, Frederick, was also a painter.

Phyllis was the eldest of at least four children (Phyllis, James, Doris and Reginald), all raised in Bristol. She was educated at the Redland High School in Bristol. Then attended the Bristol Municipal School of Art, followed by the Royal West of England Academy School of Architecture. She won a local silver medal for life drawing. Unusually for the time, Phyllis became an etcher and artist in architectural perspective, and became assistant to architect Cyril Arthur Farey, A.R.I.B.A. (b.1888), who was based in London. In the 1920s she was living at Westbourne Terrace, London. She exhibited her work at the Royal West of England Academy. Otherwise, not a prolific exhibitor. Elected a Member of the Faculty of Arts. Also a Member of the Architectural Association. Still active into the 1930s. In 1930 she married James MacGregor (b.c.1890) in Bristol. Subsequently based in Cambridge. MacGregor was Director of a School of Architecture there. Phyllis died in Cambridge in late 1943, aged only 47. MacGregor died there in 1953. Her mother exhibited her work at the Royal Academy (1929).

BUTCHER, ENID CONSTANCE (1902-c.97)

Engraver / Illustrator. Born in London. Records suggest that Enid was the daughter of Thomas Everard Butler, a dairyman, and Flora. Had at least one sister, Flora. Studied in London at the Chelsea School of Art and the Royal College of Art. Elected an Associate of the Royal College of Art in 1927. Produced line engravings and etchings, various subjects including figures. Exhibited her work, including at the Royal Academy (1927-33), the Royal Glasgow Institute

(1932-33) and in the provinces. Exhibited works included: A Knife Grinder (line engraving), The Sawyers (etching), A Farm Kitchen (line engraving) and Girl Driving Pigs (line engraving). Based at Kingswood, Surrey for part of her career. Works illustrated in Fine Prints of the Year. Her line engraving Swiss Peasants was illustrated in Colour magazine in August 1930 and was exhibited at the Twenty-One Gallery, London. Her engraving Breton Washerwomen was illustrated in Colour magazine in September 1931, p.8.

BUTLER, BERENICE (1902-65)

Illustrator. Born in Dunedin, New Zealand in September 1902. The daughter of George Edmund Butler (b.1872) and Jane. Her parents originated from Southampton. Her father was a painter / etcher and a Member of the Royal West of England Academy. He was Official Artist in the New Zealand Expeditionary Force. Berenice had a younger brother, Joseph. She grew up mainly in Westbury-on-Trym, Bristol. Later in her career (in the 1930s), she was based in Ipswich, Suffolk. Presumably studied under her father. Became an illustrator of children's books. Worked for publishers including Nelson & Sons and Ward Lock Co. Exhibited her work occasionally, including at the Royal Society of Arts. In 1936 she married Guy Richard Bisby in Middlesex. He was a teacher. She died in Buckinghamshire in December 1965, aged 64.

BUTLER, CLEHOROW CAROLINE (1851-93)

Sculptor. Born in Marylebone, London. The daughter of Timothy Butler (b.c.1806), a sculptor who originated from Oxford. Her younger brother, Timothy (b.c.1855), also born in Marylebone, became an illustrative draughtsman. Clehorow spent much of her life and career in London, but died in Kingston, Surrey, aged only 42. Produced portrait works and medallions in marble and terracotta. Exhibited occasionally, including at the Royal Academy (1881-83) and the Society of Women Artists (1888). Works included: The Late Timothy Butler, Sculptor (medallion, terracotta), Kenneth, Youngest Son of the Late Dr Murchison, F.R.S. (medallion, marble) and Rev. W.E. Oliver, LL.D.

BUTTON, KATE (1856-1946)

Embroideress. Was Katherine, known as Kate. Born in Clevedon, Somerset. The daughter of Eustace Button (b.1830), a schoolmaster, and Sarah Maria (b.1826). One of at least eight children (Arthur, Kate, Ellen, Florence, Eustace,

Henry, Marion and Ethel). Kate was a twin with Ellen. All her siblings were also born in Clevedon. All were raised there. In the early 1870s, Kate and Ellen attended a private school in London, but eventually returned to Clevedon. Ellen subsequently married and had four children, but Kate never married. She remained at the family home and was still with her father in 1911, when he was 81, and she was 55. In the early 1880s, Kate is listed as a teacher of drawing and was an exhibiting artist. In 1881 she exhibited one painting, Snowdrops, at the Royal Society of British Artists.

It remains unclear what, if any, formal art tuition Kate Button had. She was still listed as an artist in 1911. Although Somerset appears a considerable distance from London, it is evident that Button mixed with the artistic elite of the day, and had strong ties with the influential Arts and Crafts Exhibition Society. But not as a painter. Rather, as an art embroideress. And it was her embroidery that won her widespread recognition during her lifetime. She produced very fine, highly detailed work, making considerable efforts in needlework to execute landscape pictures effectively. She worked directly from nature, matching her tones as a painter would with paint. This gave her works the quality of being a painting. She used wool or silks and concentrated mainly on landscapes. In the early 1900s, art critics remained sceptical about the artistic merit of decorative needlework. But Button proved to be a leading talent which The Studio, in particular, could not easily fault. Indeed, she was considered as highly skilled. In 1906, The Studio, Vol.38, September, p.344, illustrated two of her needlework panels, The Village on the Hill and The Sandpit.

Button showed her work, including at the Arts and Crafts Exhibition Society exhibitions of 1903 (at the New Gallery), 1906 (at the Grafton Galleries) and 1910. There, she exhibited needlework pictures and needlework panels. In 1905 she contributed to an exhibition of Arts and Crafts held at the Lyceum Club, again showing a needlework landscape. In 1908 she contributed needlework to the New Gallery summer exhibition. Fellow exhibitors on that occasion included Ethel Virtue, May Morris, Georgina Gaskin and other leading craftsmen and craftswomen of the day. She also exhibited locally, including at the 1903 Somerset Home Arts and Crafts Exhibition held in Clevedon by the Somerset Arts and Crafts Association. There, she showed decorative silk panels. Her exhibiting career dwindled after 1911. She died in Portishead, Somerset in December 1946, leaving her small estate to Ellen's two unmarried daughters. Today, Button remains largely forgotten and unknown.

BUZZARD, MARY CONSTANCE (1876-1953)

Sculptor. Born in Brentford, Middlesex. The daughter of architect and surveyor Alfred Lindsey Buzzard and Adelaide Corney. Her father originated from Surrey, her mother from Greenwich. Had at least one elder sister, Margaret. Raised in Middlesex. Studied sculpture in London in the late 1890s and early 1900s. Boarded at Alexander House, Kensington Gore whilst a student, along with a considerable number of other women students of music and art. Those included Nina Oliver, Gertrude Lindsay and Frances Darlington. Buzzard produced reliefs, groups, statuettes, plaquettes, busts and heads. Worked in various materials including bronze and silvered bronze.

She began exhibiting her work in around 1897, and continued to do so until at least 1926. Exhibited at the Royal Academy (1897-1926), the Royal Glasgow Institute (1914) and the Society of Women Artists (1898-1902). Exhibited works included: Pelham Cobbett, Esq. (bust), The Four Evangelists (relief, silvered bronze), Regeneration (group) and A Pilgrim Father (statuette, bronze). Possibly the same M. Buzzard who exhibited embroidery at the 1905 Clarion Guild of Handicraft second annual exhibition at Clifford's Inn. Although based in London during her career, Buzzard also spent time in Surrey, including at Ashtead and Reigate Hill. In 1914 she married sculptor Alfred Bertram Pegram (1873-1941) in London. He originated from London, part of a large family. His sister, Amy Alice Pegram, was an artist, and his brother, Arthur Alfred Pegram, became a cabinet maker. Mary and Alfred Pegram had two children, Mary Lois in 1918 and Edwin Hugh in 1919. Alfred died in London, aged 67. Mary died in Hendon, Middlesex in June 1953, aged 76.

BYFIELD, MARY (1795-1871)

Wood Engraver. Born in Middlesex. Lived with various family members including, in 1841, her widowed sister-in-law, Elizabeth Byfield. In the 1860s she lived with another relative, Louis Byfield. Based throughout her career in Islington. Another relative, Ann Byfield, also worked as a wood engraver. Mary worked for much of her career for the Chiswick Press (founded 1810) in London. Executed some of their best decoration and frontispieces based on sixteenth-century originals. Those included page illustrations to the Pickering 1853 edition of Queen Elizabeth's

Prayer Book and Nicolas's History of the Orders of Knighthood (1842). Died in Islington.

C

CALDER, FANNY DOVE HAMEL (1864-1954)

Book Illustrator / Designer. Born in Seaforth, Liverpool in August 1864. The daughter of James Lister, a cotton broker, and Fanny. One of at least four children (James, Fanny, Joseph and Edith). Raised in Seaforth. Had a comfortable home life in a house with servants. Educated at the Cheltenham Ladies' College. Studied at the Liverpool School of Architecture and Applied Art under Robert Anning Bell, Augustus John and David Muirhead. Remained in and around Liverpool for much of her early career, still living with her elderly widowed father several years after her marriage. Latterly, based in Bath, Somerset where she died, aged 89. In 1908, and now in her mid-40s, she married James Calder (b.1861) in Kendal, Westmorland. Calder, a solicitor, was the son of James Mitchell Calder of Liverpool and South Carolina.

During her career, Fanny produced book illustrations and designs for stained glass, bookplates and decorative friezes. Exhibited her work at the Walker Art Gallery, Liverpool, with the Lake Artists' Society, at the Lyceum Club, with the Bath Society of Artists and at the Sandon Studios in Liverpool. In the early 1900s, the Sandon Studios Society offered prominent local artists an opportunity to display their work. Other Members of the Society included Mary McCrossan, Hamilton Hay, Henry Carr and Gerald Chowne. Fanny Calder was elected Vice President of the Society. Also elected a Member of the Lyceum Club, of the Three Arts Club, of the Bath Society of Artists and of the Lake Artists' Society. Works included wall decorations for the Children's Convalescent Home, West Derby, and for the Seamen's Mission in Liverpool. Some of her illustrations were published in Inheritance of the Saints and Adelicia of Louvaine (Longmans Green & Co.). James Calder died in Bath in 1944, aged 83, some ten years before Fanny.

CALDWELL, MARY H. - SEE BIRD, M.H.

CALLCOTT, FLORENCE - SEE NEWMAN, F.

CALVERT, EDITH LAURA (1865-1938)

Illustrator / Painter / Decorative Artist. Born in Middlesex. The daughter of Charles Anthony Calvert, Secretary to the Colonial Bank, and Mary Ann. Her mother originated from Somerset. Edith was one of at least four children (Alice, Edith, Lucy and Charles). By the early 1890s, the family was based in Islington, by which time Edith was a painter. Lucy became an actress, and Charles became a clerk. Edith spent much of her life and career in London, at various addresses including Camden Town and Tufnell Park. She probably studied in London. Began exhibiting her work in the late 1880s. Exhibited at the Society of Women Artists (1886-98) and the Royal Society of British Artists (1893-94). Produced flowers, landscapes and other subjects in watercolours, book illustrations and decorative works. May have produced decorative bookbindings that were exhibited in 1903. Exhibited works included: An Autumn Idyll (watercolour), Roses, The Spinet and Ships Loading. Her painted panel St Cecilia was illustrated in The Studio, Vol.13, April 1898, p.186. Calvert was active as a book illustrator mainly in the 1890s and early 1900s. Illustrated, among others, A. Stow, Baby's Lays (1897) and More Baby's Lays (1898), and Dorothea Gore, Sweetbriar (1905). Some of her work was published by Elkin Mathews. Contributed to The Quarto (1898).

In July 1896 Edith married Charles Elkin Mathews (b.1851), of the publishing firm Elkin Mathews, in Islington. He was then 45 years of age; she was 31. In 1897 they had a daughter, Nest Calvert Elkin Mathews, who was born in Brentford, Middlesex. Nest died in East Sussex in 1994, aged 97, unmarried. Edith evidently continued to work and to exhibit after her marriage and the birth of her daughter, but appears to have largely given up her career by the early 1900s. Charles Elkin Mathews died in late 1921, aged 70, in Watford, Hertfordshire. He and Edith were then living at Chorleywood, Hertfordshire and Cook Street, Middlesex. Edith died in Hendon, Middlesex in June 1938, aged 74. Noted in R.E.D. Sketchley, English Book Illustration of To-day, London, Kegan Paul, 1903. Noted in Mahony, Latimer & Folmsbee, Illustrators of Children's Books 1744-1945, Boston, The Horn Book Inc., 1947. Possibly of the same family were Ada and Alice Elkin Mathews, both of whom exhibited handicrafts at the Society of Women Artists between 1906 and 1913.

CAMERON, SISTER M. GERTRUDE (active 1930s)

Miniaturist / Embroideress / Illuminator. The daughter of William Cameron, a Fellow of the

Royal Geographical Society. Studied illuminating at the British Museum. Exhibited at the Royal Institute of Painters in Watercolours. Became a Franciscan nun. Based at the Franciscan Convent, Bocking, Braintree, Essex.

CAMM, FLORENCE (1874-1960)

Stained Glass Artist. Born in Smethwick, Staffordshire. The daughter of Thomas William Camm (1839-1912) and Charlotte Middleton (1840-1909). Her father ran a successful stained glass studio and workshop in Smethwick. Florence was one of at least eight children (Adeline, Charlotte, Alice, Florence, Louisa, Robert, Walter and Mabel). Florence was educated at the local Summer Hill Grammar School. In the 1890s and early 1900s, she studied at the Birmingham Municipal School of Art, initially taking pottery, enamelling and metalwork. In 1898 she exhibited a set of watercolour studies of turkeys at the annual Birmingham School of Art exhibition. In 1901 she also began classes in stained glass. As a student, Camm won numerous prizes for her work, including a silver medal for stained glass designs submitted to the 1903 National Competition of Schools of Art held at South Kensington. Also as a student, she designed with Evelyn Holden a silver casket with enamel and repoussé decoration, to contain the Freedom of the City of Birmingham and to be presented to local J.P. J. Thackeray Bunce. The casket was exhibited at the Royal Birmingham Society of Artists exhibition in 1901.

After completing her studies, Camm joined her two brothers, Robert (1878-1954) and Walter (1881-1967), in their father's studio. For a short time, she also worked part-time as an art teacher in Smethwick. When Thomas Camm died in 1912, the studio was taken over by the three Camm siblings, and the business continued to thrive. Over the following decades, the studio carried out numerous stained glass commissions. All three Camms were active designers as well as overseeing the actual execution of the stained glass in their workshop, occasionally producing joint designs. During her lengthy career, Florence's designs included a two-lancet window for St Mary's Church, Bearswood, Warwickshire (1910) and a stained glass screen for Edstone Hall, Wootton Wawen, Warwickshire (c.1943).

Florence Camm exhibited her designs during her career, including at the 1901 Glasgow Exhibition and in Liverpool, Paris, Berlin and Turin. At the Royal Scottish Academy, she showed four designs in 1919, one for a stained glass window on the staircase of the offices of a

steel and iron company, the others for windows based on St Etheldreda, Sintram and His Mother and St Lucan's Vision. At the Royal Glasgow Institute, she showed a portion of a design for staircase windows for the Bradford Town Hall, incorporating the history of Bradford. At the Royal Academy, she showed a more substantial 48 works between 1905 and 1953. Those suitably reflected the diversity of her work, and included designs for private houses, public buildings, churches, war memorials, hospitals, schools, town halls and offices, in Britain and abroad. Outside of Britain, works can be found in Princeton University and Cleveland Museum in America, in New York, in Bilbao, Spain and South Africa. One window was a memorial to engineer and inventor James Watt. Another was a memorial to a local potter for Denbigh Church. In 1911 Florence won the Grand Prix Turin. Thomas, Robert and Walter Camm also exhibited their designs. Florence remained active until a short time before her death. Works were included in an exhibition Women Stained Glass Artists of the Arts and Crafts Movement, held at the William Morris Gallery, London, 1985-86. At the time of her death, Florence was living at Harborne Road, Oldbury, Worcestershire, sharing a home with Robert, Adeline, Mabel and Louisa until their deaths.

CAMPBELL, FELICITY (b.1909)

Illustrator / Commercial Artist / Painter. Born in Sussex in August 1909. The daughter of Vere Douglas Graice Campbell. Educated at home. Studied art in London, Paris and Rome, and at The Hague. Studied illustration and lithography under Edmund J. Sullivan. Worked as a book illustrator, a commercial artist, a painter of miniatures and an artist in black & white, watercolours, pencil and pastels. Exhibited her work with the International Society, at the Walker's Gallery and at the Royal Academy (1960-61). Works included portraits of Sir Anthony Hills, Bt. (miniature), Biddy Newsome, the children of Brig.-Gen. Tilney and Toby Archer. Illustrated books including Elliott O'Donnell, Haunted Houses of Britain (1930) and Marjorie Bowen, The Pond, The Rosemary Book (1949) and Back of the North Wind (c.1952). A Member of the Vermin Club. Based at Guestling, Sussex for part of her career. Active for at least four decades, from the 1930s through to the 1960s.

CAMWELL, ALICE MABEL (1880-1946)

Jeweller / Enameller. Born in Walsall, Staffordshire in June 1880. The daughter of Charles

Camwell, a mining engineer who originated from Coventry, and Mary Jane who originated from Walsall. One of at least five daughters (Edith, Alice, Maud, Helen and Florence). Raised in Staffordshire, and remained there for most of her life. Studied at the Birmingham Central School of Art. Won one gold and four silver medals for designs for jewellery in the National Competition of Schools of Art as a student. Worked in gold, silver and enamels. Based at Walsall and, latterly, Birmingham. Lived with her mother and three of her sisters until at least 1911, by which time her father had died. Camwell continued to work into the 1930s. Taught metalwork and jewellery at various schools of art. Contributed to the Arts and Crafts exhibitions of the Royal Birmingham Society of Artists. In 1925 won a silver medal for jewellery at the International Exhibition of Decorative Art in Paris. Exhibited two works at the Society of Women Artists in 1930. Also exhibited with the Arts and Crafts Exhibition Society, at the British Empire Exhibition and elsewhere. Works illustrated in The Studio. Died in Birmingham.

CANN, ANNIE MARY (1866-1954)

Artist / Embroideress. Born in Liverpool in July 1866 and raised there. The daughter of John Cann (b.1831) and Flora Estella Squire (1840-1923). Her father was a commission agent in sugar and fruit who originated from Devon. Her mother originated from London. One of at least three children (Annie, William and Kathleen). Her siblings were also born in Liverpool. William became a cashier in shipping. All three siblings were still living at the family home in Liverpool in 1901. Annie studied at Blackburne House, Edgehill Training College in Liverpool and became a school teacher in her 20s. At some point, however, she also studied at the Wallasey School of Art, possibly in the early 1890s when local girl and art student Caroline E.E. Frances was a boarder at the family home in Wallasey. In the 1880s their neighbours in West Derby had included watercolour painter James Pelham and his brother, the lithographic draughtsman Frederick Pelham. It is entirely feasible that they had some influence over the young Annie in matters of art. Aside from teaching, she produced watercolour paintings and works in pastel as well as embroideries. She lectured on travel, painting and needlecraft. Exhibited only occasionally, mainly at the Walker Art Gallery, Liverpool. Works included: An Old World Corner, Church Road, Ledbury (pastel) and The Mill by the Loggerheads (petit point). Remained in Wallasey, Cheshire until her death, aged 87.

CANNING, MARY BELLA - SEE HOUSTON, MARY G.

CANTON, SUSAN RUTH (1849-1932)

Sculptor / Painter. Known as Ruth. Born in Middlesex. The eldest child of Crucifix Canton and Eliza. Had a sister, Katherine, two years younger. Her father, a dentist, originated from Middlesex, as did her mother. She lived at the family home in London for many years, then spent the remainder of her life as a boarder in various shared houses in London. Had some tuition in sculpture at the Royal Academy schools in the early 1880s. Subsequently taught at the Royal Female School of Art, London along with (in 1909) Rose Welby, Isobel Gloag, Isabel Farler and others. Held a class in black & white. A highly competent and gifted sculptor, modeller and painter, Canton only began exhibiting her work seriously in her 30s. Exhibited over a period of more than 37 years, including at the Society of Women Artists (1895-1909), the Royal Academy (1880-1917), the Royal Society of British Artists (from 1882), the Walker Art Gallery, Liverpool and Nottingham's Castle Museum (1881). Exhibited works included: The Light of Asia (statuette, bronze), The Star of Fate (group, from Lytton's Pilgrims of the Rhine), The Death of the First Born (group, plaster) and Washing Lettuces: Marburg (bas-relief, terracotta). Worked in coloured wax, bronze, marble, clay, plaster and terracotta. Produced reliefs, silvered bas-reliefs, statuettes, groups and medals. Medal designs were executed for the Hygienic Medal (1882), for a medal commemorating the Jubilee Year of Queen Victoria's reign (1887) and the Huxley Memorial Medal (1897). Two of her silver statuettes were illustrated in The Studio, Vol.8, 1896, p.168. One of those, Skirt Dancer, was exhibited at the Society of Women Artists in 1895. One of her marble figures, Hebe, then owned by the Art Union of London, was illustrated in The Studio, Vol.10, p.130 in 1897. Her sculptures were often graceful and visually beautiful, with an attractive fragility. Her watercolour studies included Left and Abandoned of His Velvet Friends. Canton died in Middlesex in late 1932, aged 84. Left a small estate of some £285 on her death.

CARPENTER, HON. MRS
(active 1890s-1900s)

The instigator and organiser of the Bolton-on-Swale woodcarving class in Yorkshire. Mrs Carpenter may have been part of the Carpenter family of Kiplin Hall in the Parish of Bolton-on-Swale. The class ran in the later 1890s, into the early 1900s. At that time, Kiplin Hall was occupied by the Hon. Walter C. Carpenter and his wife, Beatrice. The class had strong connections with the Home Arts and Industries Association, much like other similar handcraft classes of the period, including those at Yattendon, Compton and Leighton Buzzard. Although essentially amateur, the Bolton-on-Swale class similarly succeeded in surpassing its original aims, producing inlaid woodwork and woodcarving of admirable quality in both design and workmanship. Wares were sold locally, and through the annual exhibitions of the Home Arts and Industries Association in London.

All manner of mainly domestic items were made and sold, including stationery cases, cupboards, settles, chairs, benches, letter boxes, bookcases, cabinets and even decorated caskets. All were worked to the designs of Mrs Carpenter, revealing a degree of creativity on her part. For example, a letterbox was decorated with a design of turkeys. A casket was inlaid with a design titled Reflection, based on cattle crossing a stream. And a stationery case was decorated with a design based on a row of school children. Some pieces were illustrated in The Studio magazine, for example in 1895 (Vol.5, August, p.172), in 1897 (Vol.11, July, p.109) and in 1901 (Vol.23, July, p.109). Those associated with the Bolton-on-Swale handcraft class, all local men, included Edmond and Nathan Fawell, Herbert Hurwood, A. and W. Spooner, Walter Smailes, Arthur Toyer, George Butler and Frank Clarkson. The class also produced a small amount of decorative metalwork. It thrived for at least nine years (1895-1903). It is possible that Mrs Carpenter employed a teacher from elsewhere to instruct the class, which she then supervised and provided with designs.

CARR, EDITH MARY (1865-1949)

Painter / Decorative Artist. Born in Croydon, Surrey. The daughter of Henry Carr and Ada. Her father, a commercial traveller and merchant, originated from Kent, her mother from Sussex. One of a large family, of at least 10 children. Despite the size of the family, the Carrs were able to afford servants, and the children were all well educated. Her sister Alice became a Professor of Music; another sister, Anna, became a teacher. Edith, possibly the eldest, was raised in Croydon and remained there for much of her life. She was still living with her widowed mother in 1911 at the age of 46. She never married and worked for many years as an artist. Studied at the Croydon School of Art under Walter Wallis, and at the Academie Delecluse in Paris under M. Callot.

Worked on church decoration, produced murals, and executed miniatures and portraits in oils and watercolours. Occasionally produced landscape paintings too. Exhibited her work, including at the Royal Academy (1907-43), the Walker Art Gallery, Liverpool, the Paris Salon and the Society of Women Artists (1902-48). Exhibited works included: The Pink Frock, Moonrise in Lyonesse, Portrait of an Invalid, Shot Silk and Dr H.F. Carr, C.B.E. (miniature). Elected an Associate of the Society of Women Artists (1929-32) and a Member (1933-48). Other works included The Nativity and The Ascension for the Cathedral Church, Lebombo. Executed a number of portraits of distinguished sitters including the Bishop of Croydon and Albert Hovenden. Carr died in Croydon, aged 83.

CARR, GERALDINE (1866-1954)

Metalworker / Enameller. Was Margaret Geraldine, known as Geraldine. Born at Wellow House, Rufford, Nottinghamshire. The daughter of Lucius Henry Spooner (1816-74) and Margaret Skottowe Parker (1828-1918). Her father was a land agent. One of a large family, of at least eight children. Raised in Nottinghamshire. Attended school in Hastings, Sussex. In 1890 she married Herbert Wildon Carr (1857-1931), a stockbroker, in London. The couple lived in Sussex and London. They had at least three daughters, Ursula, Joan and Teresa. Later in their lives, the couple spent time in America, including in Los Angeles. Geraldine died in Sussex. She worked as a metalworker and enameller from at least 1901 until at least 1916. Produced mainly decorative jewellery, but also larger pieces, usually with enamel decoration. Exhibited some of her work at the Royal Academy (1901-16), including St Elizabeth, a study in silver and enamel, a portrait work of her daughter, Ursula, and a casket in silver and enamel. In 1903 she showed a small triptych in bronze and enamel at that year's Arts and Crafts Exhibition Society exhibition. The triptych was decorated with panels by W. Dacre Adams. In 1905 she contributed to the Exhibition of Arts and Crafts held at the Lyceum Club, showing a silver and enamel casket and a triptych in copper and enamel which bore three enamelled panels based on the history of Cinderella. Both were illustrated in The Studio, Vol.36, October 1905, pp.72 & 75. A brooch in enamel and wrought metal, set with stones, designed and executed by Mrs Carr, was illustrated in The Studio, Vol.41, August 1907, p.227 along with a blotting book cover and an enamel picture in a silver frame with elaborate doors either side. Mrs Carr was known for using the rose in her design work.

CARR, M. ELLA (active 1900s)

Lace Worker. Produced lace by hand in the early 1900s. Technically an amateur, but was undoubtedly an expert in Lacis work, a little-known craft. Exhibited at the Home Arts and Industries Association exhibitions, including in 1903. There, she exhibited a Lacis work border to a chair-back which was illustrated in the Art Workers' Quarterly, July 1903, p.119.

CARRE, JEAN L. - SEE HADAWAY, J.L.

CARSLAKE, MARY (1904-94)

Illuminator / Lettering Artist / Woodcut Artist. Born in Edgbaston, Birmingham. The daughter of Hugh Barham Carslake, a solicitor, and Florence. One of at least three children (Mary, Joan and John). Raised in Birmingham. Educated at the Edgbaston Church of England College. Studied at the Birmingham School of Art. Remained in the area, later living at nearby Alvechurch, Worcestershire. Produced decorative lettering, illuminations and colour woodcuts. Exhibited with the Royal Society of Painter-Etchers & Engravers, the Royal Birmingham Society of Artists, in Leeds and Manchester, under the Duveen scheme and with the Central Club of Coloured Wood Engravers, Birmingham. Exhibited two works at the Society of Women Artists in 1930, Full Fathom Fire and The Rude Wind of March. Elected a Member of the Central Club of Coloured Wood Engravers, Birmingham. Records suggest that Carslake married Alfred R. Morcom in Bromsgrove in 1938. She died in Worcestershire, aged 90.

CARTER, ELIZABETH ELLIN (1865-1958)

Decorative Leatherworker. More frequently listed as E. Ellin Carter. Born in Sheffield, Yorkshire. The daughter of Robert Carter (b.1838), an agent, and Elizabeth Ann (1841-1923). Her father originated from Sheffield, her mother from Lincolnshire. One of at least four children (Gertrude, Elizabeth, Robert and Fanny). Raised in North Ormesby, Yorkshire. Sometime prior to 1901, Carter moved to Brighton, Sussex with her mother, her sister Gertrude and two other relatives. In Brighton, she worked as a decorative artist in leather. She remained there until 1911, then moved to London. In London, she had a studio in Red Lion Square, then in Stratford Court off Oxford Street and, latterly, from 1926, in Crawford Street off Baker Street. She had a studio in the city until at least 1927. She was an expert

decorative or art leatherworker, though it remains unclear where she studied. She designed, executed and sold various items including caskets, covers, cases, bags and blotters. Some were complex and labour intensive in design, and were visually appealing as well as beautifully executed. Many of her designs were based on nature, in the Arts and Crafts tradition. Carter specialised in the Mexican style of decorative leatherwork. The decoration was all on the surface of the leather, with no padding, the design being raised by carving and modelling. This enabled her to produce carefully detailed, fine work, marked with her own monogram.

From at least 1911 until at least 1927, Carter advertised her work regularly in The Studio magazine, opening her studio to the public on Thursday afternoons initially, and then on Tuesdays, Wednesdays and Thursdays. By the 1920s she was also offering lessons to willing pupils. She was awarded gold and silver medals in the London exhibitions of 1908-1909, including a gold medal at the Shepherd's Bush Exhibition of 1909. Her work also appeared at the Paris Salon and at the Society of Women Artists (1908-23). She was elected an Associate of the British Colonial Society of Artists. Occasionally, her work was illustrated in leading arts journals of the day. For example, two of her decorative blotters were illustrated in The Studio, Vol.51, November 1910, p.145. Carter produced at least two small books on her craft, Artistic Leatherwork: A Handbook on the Art of Decorative Leather (1912) and Designs for Artistic Leatherwork (1922). She died in Sussex, aged 92, having lived latterly at Lancing.

CARTWRIGHT, ENID M.M. - SEE PEATE, E.M.M.

CASELLA, ELLA (1858-1946) & NELIA (1859-1950)

Craftswomen. The daughters of Alexander Casella and Marie. Their father, a member of the Stock Exchange, originated from France, their mother from Switzerland. They had at least one older sibling, Marie. Ella was born Bertha Gabriella, and Nelia was Louisa Cornelia. Both were born in London, lived there and died there. Both studied under Alphonse Legros at the Slade School, London in the late 1870s and early 1880s. They were exceptionally talented and excelled in their chosen fields. They were unusual in that they were active in some areas of the decorative arts not normally associated with women artists. Ella was a sculptor in wax and bas-relief for a period of at least 25 years. Nelia also worked in wax, but also in leather and plaster, and became a recognised talent in the ancient art of enamelling on glass. Nelia's career was still flourishing in 1929, lasting over 45 years. The sisters appear to have worked and lived together from at least 1884, but also worked independently. Early on, they also produced book illustrations for Dreams, Dances and Disappointments (1881) and for Gertrude Konstam's The Maypole (1882). Initially, they were based at Wetherby Road, but Nelia later lived at Queen's Elm Square, Chelsea. The Casella sisters produced wax portrait medallions which were often used to cast in bronze. Sometimes, the medallions were decorated with jewels or semi-precious stones. Some of those were exhibited at the Royal Academy from 1884. Together, they exhibited at the Royal Academy virtually every year up to 1904 (Ella missed in 1894). Early exhibits included: A Venetian Lady of the Sixteenth Century (Ella), Constance, Elder Daughter of C. Crews, Esq. (Ella), Mephistopheles (Nelia) and Luna (Nelia). Ella exhibited at the Royal Academy alone between 1905 and 1909, and at the Society of Women Artists between 1889 and 1897, showing wax medallions and bas-reliefs. Nelia was evidently more active and productive, exhibiting her work more widely and over a longer period of time. She too exhibited alone at the Royal Academy between 1905 and 1929, and exhibited at the Society of Women Artists between 1888 and 1929. But she also showed work at the 1899 Arts and Crafts Exhibition Society exhibition, including some of her embossed leather boxes. At the 1903 Arts and Crafts exhibition, she showed some of her modelled leather bindings. Also in 1903, she showed examples of her enamelled glass at the Brighton Arts and Crafts Exhibition. Other exhibitors on that occasion included Effie Stillman. In the same year, The Studio, Vol.30, pp.255-257 offered illustrations of her work, an enamelled glass jar, tumbler and bottle and a coloured wax medallion of a young boy with real pearls for buttons, all designed and executed by Nelia.

In 1906 Nelia Casella showed more of her decorative leather bookbindings and a leather box at that year's Arts and Crafts exhibition. In 1908 both sisters showed examples of their work (enamelling on glass and modelling in leather, wax and plaster) at that year's New Gallery exhibition, but were criticised by the Press for not developing their scope and ideas. At the 1910 Arts and Crafts exhibition, Nelia showed a leather book cover, enamelled glass vessels and a bronze weight. In the same year, Nelia exhibited at the Royal Society of Miniature Painters. Further

afield, in 1914 Nelia exhibited a glass flower vase with ornamental motto designed and executed by her at the Exposition des Arts Decoratifs in Paris. In her glass, her designs were inspired by such things as fish, seaweed, leaves and flowers. The design would be carried out in colours on the surface of the glass and then fired. Pieces measured between 5" and 10" in height. In 1901 the Art Journal (p.328) illustrated one of her enamelled glass decanters, which was shown at that year's Glasgow Exhibition. The journal reported that 'it is pleasant to find a lady practising an art so neglected, and doing such good work in it' (p.330). Through her leatherwork, Nelia also had some ties with the short-lived Guild of Women Binders. Works can be found in the Victoria & Albert Museum, London.

CASTLE, FLORENCE ELIZABETH (1867-1959)

Painter / Illustrator. Born in London in January 1867. The daughter of James Henry Castle, a commercial traveller, and Elizabeth. Had an older brother, William, who studied music. Raised in London. Educated at the Croydon High School. Studied at the Lambeth School of Art under Sir William Llewellyn. Also studied in Paris. Remained in London for much of her career, dying in Hampstead in late 1959, aged 92. Used the Magravine Studios in West Kensington for a time. Worked through seven decades, from the 1890s until the 1950s. Produced portraits, landscapes and still life in oils and pastels and illustrations. Exhibited her work, including with the Royal Society of British Artists (from 1891), the Royal Academy (1892-1904), the Pastel Society, the New English Art Club, the Society of Women Artists (1905-50) and in the provinces. Exhibited works included: Little Girl with Chinese Sunshade which was shown at the Pastel Society in 1947. Also, The Vale on the Heath, Listening and Tulips and Narcissus. Elected a Member of the Pastel Society.

CAVE, JESSICA MARIA (1865-1934)

Craftswoman. Known as Jessie. Born in Canada. The daughter of Hugh Cochrane, gentleman. In June 1892 Jessie married architect / designer Walter Frederick Cave (1863-1939) in St Marylebone Parish, London. He was the son of Sir Charles Daniel Cave (b.1833), a banker and magistrate, and Edith Harriet Symonds (1835-1912). Born in Clifton, Bristol, Walter Cave, F.R.I.B.A., was regarded in his day as the equal of Voysey. The couple had at least one son, Richard (1901-80). They lived primarily in

London. Prior to her marriage, Jessie had already had an interest in the arts, and had exhibited two watercolours at the Society of Women Artists in 1887 and 1889, Over the Garden Wall and St Brelades, whilst living in London and Paris. She appeared not to exhibit her watercolour paintings again, but later exhibited decorative panels which were paintings on wood.

Walter Cave acted as Secretary to the Art Workers' Guild (1898-1905), and had close ties with those at the heart of the Arts and Crafts movement. As a result, Jessie contributed to the Arts and Crafts Exhibition Society exhibitions. At the fourth, held in 1893, she showed at least two of her decorative panels. In 1896 The Studio, Vol.9, October, pp.134-135, illustrated six panels for a Walter Cave settle, executed by Jessie, which were shown at that year's Arts and Crafts exhibition. At the Society's 1899 (sixth) exhibition she showed other decorative panels, including one titled Peacock Garden which was illustrated in The Studio, Vol.18, 1899, p.179. The ornamental panel was part of a painted decorative scheme for a piano case designed by Walter Cave and painted by Jessie for Messrs Bechstein. Walter and Jessie also became involved in other decorative work. They jointly designed a frontal in applique for the Parish Church of Sidbury, Devon which was executed by the village workers of Sidbury for their own church, displaying the white doe and forest emblems of their patron, St Giles. Jessie also painted ornamental panels for the church. She died in Chelsea, aged 70, some four years before her husband.

Like many architects of the day, Walter Crane became involved in artistic needlework. He produced the designs, and others actually executed those designs. There are indications that some of his embroidery designs were executed by his mother, or by Jessie, or both. At the third Arts and Crafts exhibition, held in 1890 (prior to his marriage), May Morris showed an embroidered binding for A Study of Dante, designed by herself and worked by Mrs Cave. Since Jessie was still Miss Cochrane at that stage, it can be presumed that this was Cave's mother or another family member. Elsewhere, his embroideries are occasionally listed as executed by Lady Cave. However, others are listed as executed by Mrs Cave after his marriage to Jessie. In 1899 The Studio magazine noted that 'Mrs Cave' was always a free spirit in her own embroidery designs. She did not mark them out beforehand, but let the work evolve. The magazine describes an 18" square embroidery then underway which represented a rose bush with interlacing branches and other flowering plants in which the design

was allowed to evolve as the piece was worked. This may have been Jessie. In 1903, Walter Cave contributed a mirror frame to the seventh Arts and Crafts exhibition. The frame was decorated with an embroidered border designed by Walter Cave and May Morris, but worked by Mrs Cave. The border was illustrated in the Art Workers' Quarterly, 1903, p.65 and described (on p.58) as composed of 'leafy scrolls of chain-stitch' and worked in two shades of green silk, and flowers in soft reds, white and pale yellow done in various stitches. In the same year, Mrs Cave won an Honourable Mention for an embroidered panel designed by the firm of Morris & Co. and shown at the 1903 'Art Work' exhibition, staged in Bristol and organised by the Bristol and Clifton Arts and Crafts Society, their fifth exhibition to date. Again, this could have been Jessie or Edith Cave.

CHADBURN, GRACE - SEE CHRISTIE, G.

CHALLONER, SUSANNAH MARY (1900-91)
Jewellery Worker / Silversmith / Enameller. Born in Newcastle-on-Tyne in October 1900. The daughter of John Dixon Challoner, a stockbroker, and Susan Lydia Lovibond. Had at least one sister, Phyllis. Studied at the School of Art, Armstrong College, Newcastle, and at the London County Council Central School of Arts and Crafts. Produced decorative jewellery, silver and enamels. Based mainly in Newcastle during her career. Died in Northumberland. Exhibited her work at the Palace of Art, Wembley and with the Arts and Crafts Society, London.

CHALMERS, GLADYS - SEE MacCABE, G.

CHAMPION, ELLA L.C.S. - SEE NAPER, E.L.C.S.

CHANTRELL, MARY E. - SEE DEAR, M.E.

CHAPLIN, ALICE MARY (1848-1921)
Sculptor. Born in Sudbury, Suffolk. The daughter of James Chaplin and Eliza Hales. One of at least three children (Alice, Florence and Ernest). Raised in Essex. Ernest Chaplin (1852-1948) emigrated to Australia and died there. Florence (1850-1936) became a portrait painter who exhibited her work at the Royal Society of British Artists. She married stained glass artist Christopher Whall. Alice studied sculpture, probably in London, given that she was living in Chelsea from at least the very early 1870s with her mother, Florence and Ernest. She remained in London for the rest of her life, dying in Fulham,

aged 73. Produced mainly statuettes and groups in bronze and terracotta. Exhibited her work, including at the Royal Academy (18 works, 1880-96). At the 1903 Arts and Crafts Exhibition Society exhibition, held at the New Gallery, she showed A Puma (statuette) and a stained glass cartoon.

Evidently a reputable sculptor, Chaplin executed several notable works, including Two Spanish Bullocks which belonged to the Queen, and Flora, a study of a collie belonging to the Queen, executed for her in bronze. Other works by Chaplin included Study of an Elephant (statuette, terracotta), A Little Too Much of a Joke (group, terracotta) and Kassasseen, a model for a silver cup to be presented to the First Life Guards. She was still active in 1911, at the age of 63. She appears to have remained unmarried. But census recordings show that she was responsible for the welfare of four children, Guy (b.1872), Edward (b.1881), Rhoda (b.1886) and Reginald (b.1888), all of whom used the surnames Chaplin and Garnet at various times. Chaplin is sometimes listed as their mother, and is listed as both married and single at various times in her life, though no husband or marriage can be traced so far. Rhoda, Edward and Reginald were still living with Chaplin in 1911. Rhoda became an artist, designing Christmas cards. Edward became a meter inspector and Reginald became a violinist. It is feasible that Chaplin acted as guardian to the four children, or possibly adopted them. Florence's daughter, Veronica Whall, became a stained glass artist.

CHAPMAN, ELIZABETH MARIA (b.1901)
Painter / Lithographer. Born in Chorlton, Lancashire. The daughter of J.T. Chapman. Studied at the Manchester School of Art and privately. Produced paintings in oils and watercolours and lithographs. Various subjects including portraits. Exhibited in Manchester, London, Liverpool, Southport, Newcastle-on-Tyne and Ipswich. Exhibited one work at the Society of Women Artists, Head of a Young Girl (lithograph) , in 1925. Based in Manchester. Elected Honorary Treasurer of the Manchester Academy of Fine Arts. Also Honorary Secretary and Honorary Treasurer of the Attic Club and of the Manchester Society of Women Artists (1918-26).

CHARD, ELSIE ADAH (b.1890)
Sculptor. Born in Paddington, London. The daughter of Richard James Chard, a butcher, and Milly. Had at least one brother, Alexander. Raised in London. Studied in London in the early

1910s. Became a sculptor of medals, heads and statuettes in bronze. Based in London until at least 1933. Exhibited her work, including at the Royal Academy (1914-27) and the Society of Women Artists (21 works, 1915-27). Exhibited works included: The Sea Hath its Pearls (bronze), Stranded (plaster designed for bronze), The Mermaid (bronze) and Meditation (statuette). Elected an Associate of the Society of Women Artists (1920-33).

CHILTON, MABEL B. - SEE LOW, M.B.

CHILTON, MARGARET ISOBEL (1875-1962)
Painter / Stained Glass Designer. Born in early 1875 in Clifton, Bristol. The daughter of George Horace David Chilton, a solicitor, and Isabella. Her father originated from London, her mother from Oundle. One of at least six children. Raised in Gloucestershire. All the children were well educated. One of her brothers studied law; another became a surgeon while another became a solicitor's clerk. Margaret won a national scholarship, and a Royal College of Art scholarship. At the Royal College of Art, London, she was taught the art of stained glass by Christopher Whall (1849-1924), one of the most influential figures of the period, and Alfred J. Drury who, with Mary Lowndes, also ran the Lowndes & Drury stained glass workshop at the Glass House in Fulham, London. Chilton was elected an Associate of the Royal College of Art in 1909. She returned to Bristol and established her own stained glass workshop. One of her earliest projects was the east window for Pilton Church, Somerset (1907). Occasionally, she worked in association with Lowndes & Drury, producing, among others, a window for Croydon Parish Church (1918). Also gave private tuition in stained glass.

In 1918 Chilton moved to Glasgow to work as a designer at the Abbey Studio. There, she met Marjorie Boyce Kemp, a former student of the Glasgow School of Art. In 1922 they formed a partnership, establishing the Chilton & Kemp studio in Edinburgh which was still running into the 1940s. Chilton acted as senior partner in the business. Many of their windows, always designed independently but executed jointly, can be found in Scotland. For example, a two-light window in St Margaret's Episcopal Church, Leven, Fife (1945, designed by Chilton). Chilton's commissions outside Scotland included a series designed for St Andrew's Church, Leytonstone (1922-46) and the east window for the chapel, Hostel of Resurrection, Leeds (1931).

In 1910 Chilton was elected an Associate of the Royal West of England Academy, and in 1913 was made a full Member. Also a Member of the Church Crafts League, a body of artists, designers and craftworkers dedicated to the preserving of standards in church art. Elected to the Society of Scottish Artists in 1922. Elected a Fellow of the British Society of Master Glass Painters.

Chilton exhibited widely throughout her career, which spanned more than five decades, including at the Royal Scottish Academy (35 works, 1923-57), the Royal Glasgow Institute (1955) and the Royal Academy (1909-53). She was still exhibiting her work when she was in her 80s. Exhibited works included stained glass designs for The Swashbuckler (panel), The Wayfarers (panel), The Hudson Smith Memorial Window, Clifton Down Congregational Church, and for The Founders' Window, Bristol University (a competitive design). Other examples of her work can be found in Leith, Bute, Glasgow, Eastbourne, Angus, Edinburgh, St Andrews, Bedfordshire, Leeds and the Colonies. Chilton was a member of staff at the Edinburgh College of Art (1927-33). Included in an exhibition Women Stained Glass Artists of the Arts and Crafts Movement held at the William Morris Gallery, London, 1985-86.

CHILTON, PHYLLIS I. - SEE OSBORNE, P.I.

CHIRM, HILDA MARY (1904-89)
Decorative Artist / Illuminator / Linocut Artist. Born in Edgbaston, Birmingham in September 1904. The daughter of John Richard Chirm and Emma. Her father was a timber merchant but also the publisher of Chirm's Rent Books. Hilda had at least one sibling, John, also born in Birmingham. She was educated at the Edgbaston High School. Then studied at the Birmingham Municipal School of Art. She was awarded the Treglown Memorial Scholarship in 1925. Became a designer of postcards, showcards, lettering and illumination and a linocut artist. Exhibited her work with the Royal Birmingham Society of Artists. Based in Birmingham for much of her life and career. In 1937 she married Eric Scott in Birmingham. Hilda died in Leicestershire, aged 85.

CHRISTIE, GRACE (1872-1953)
Embroideress / Embroidery Teacher / Author. Was Anna Grace Ida, known as Grace. Born in Poplar, London. The daughter of James Chadburn, a Congregational Minister, and Grace. Her father originated from Blackburn,

Lancashire, her mother from Bradford, Yorkshire. One of at least three children (Maud, George and Anna Grace). Raised in London and Surrey. All the children were intelligent and well educated. Maud became a medical student. George became an art student. It remains unclear if Grace underwent any formal tuition. In 1900, with no profession listed on census recordings, Grace married architect Archibald Haswell Christie (1870-1945) in Marylebone, London. He originated from Marylebone. The couple spent most of their marriage living in Surrey, initially at Ewell. At the time of his death, Archibald Christie was living in East Runton, Norfolk. Grace died in February 1953 in Cheam, Surrey. By 1911 Archibald was working as an Inspector of Schools for the County Council. The couple had one son, Robert Noel, born in around 1904.

Records indicate that, after her marriage, Grace Christie became seriously and successfully involved in art embroidery, mixing with those at the forefront of developments in art and design in Britain. This may have been due in part to Christie's influence. If Grace had any formal tuition in embroidery remains unclear. But she was skilled enough to become a needlework instructor at the Royal College of Art sometime after her marriage. In 1908, she is recorded as giving a prize for embroidery at the College, suggesting that she was staff at that time. She held the post until 1921, when she was replaced by Kathleen M. Turner. From at least 1906 she wrote a number of books on her subject, including Embroidery and Tapestry Weaving (Pitman, 1906, priced 6s.), one of the Artistic Crafts Series of Technical Handbooks. The book was edited by W.R. Lethaby (a leading Arts and Crafts figure) and advertised in The Studio in 1910. Other books by Mrs Christie included Samplers and Stitches (Batsford, 1920) and English Medieval Embroidery (1938). The latter was described in its day as the definitive book on the subject, and is considered by some to hold that place still.

The Christies evidently had close ties with the Arts and Crafts Exhibition Society from at least 1903. In that year Grace showed various items at the Society's exhibition, including a stool cushion in heraldic design along with embroidered doyleys. At the Society's 1912 exhibition, by which time she was being described in national arts journals as an experienced teacher and worker, she exhibited several items including a wall panel along with embroidered table linen executed in conjunction with Fraulein Toni Kipping and Fraulein Mussner, along with a cross-stitch sampler by herself. Fraulein Kipping, who originated from Germany, had already spent time visiting the Christies in 1911. At the

Society's 1916 exhibition Grace and Archibald jointly designed a small bedroom along with F.W. Troup. In 1923 an embroidered panel designed by Grace and executed by her and a Miss Ohlsson was shown in an exhibition of decorative art held at the Royal Academy. The panel, with a design based on animals, was illustrated in The Studio, Vol.85, 1923, p.137. Other works by Mrs Christie were illustrated in The Studio. In 1910 an embroidered panel designed by Ann Macbeth, another leading design figure of the day, and worked by Mrs Christie was illustrated in an article The Glasgow School of Embroidery in The Studio, Vol.50, July 1910, p.127. In the same year, the Art Journal, p.252 illustrated an ornament for a mirror head and a tapestry woven in silks and gold threads designed and worked by Mrs Christie. That particular journal also illustrated a number of her textiles over the years, offering a muslin curtain embroidered in white linen thread, designed and partly executed by her, in the same 1910 issue (p.216). It appears that, like many art embroiderers of the period, Mrs Christie worked her own designs, but also those of others. Robert Christie became an accountant. Some of Archibald Christie's work was exhibited at the Royal Scottish Academy (1887-90, 1982).

CHRISTIE, VERA - SEE WILLOUGHBY, V.

CHUBB, JOAN KATHERINE - SEE DUMMETT, J.K.

CLAGUE, DAISY RADCLIFFE - SEE BERESFORD, D.R.

CLARK, CHRISTINE M. - SEE SELLER, C.M.

CLARKE, BETHIA MARY (1867-1959)
Painter / Craftworker. Born in Blackheath, London. The daughter of William H. Clarke (an annuitant) and Bethia Elizabeth Barlow. Her father originated from Berkshire, her mother from Tonbridge, Kent. They married in Lewisham in 1866. Bethia Mary Clarke was raised in London, and spent some time in Hastings, Sussex as a child. Had a younger sister, Margaret. Studied at Westminster, in Paris and Etaples. Taught by M.A. Bohm. Became a painter of portraits, figures and landscapes, and is occasionally listed as a sculptor. Also produced various handicrafts. Worked in oils, watercolours and pastels, and produced drawings. During her career, she was based mainly in London, living with her mother and sister. But also spent time in Eastbourne and Kent. The subjects of her paintings suggest that she travelled abroad. Began to exhibit her work more seriously from 1892, and continued to do so until at least 1953, so she was active through seven decades. Exhibited her work, including at the Royal Academy (1894-1932), the Royal Glasgow Institute (1897-1910), the Royal Society of British Artists (from 1892), with the Ridley Club and the Pastel Society, and at the Paris Salon. Also exhibited at the Society of Women Artists (48 works, 1893-1953), showing various handicrafts (not specified), drawings, paintings and pastel studies. Exhibited with the Women's International Art Club, including in 1907 and 1908. Exhibited works included: A Girl Shelling Peas (watercolour), The Red Hat (watercolour), The Orange Stall and The Scribe (drawing). Produced other works of a more diverse nature including The W.V.S. at Work, Mrs Buckeldee, Painter & Decorator and Making a Carpet in the Wilton Factory. Won an Honorary Mention at the Paris Salon. Elected a Member of the Forum Club and of the Pastel Society. Elected an Associate of the Society of Women Artists (1935-49) and a Member (1950-56). A friend of painter / etcher Gertrude H. Keeling. Clarke died in Kensington in March 1959, aged 91.

CLARKE, DORA THACHER (1895-1989)
Sculptor / Artist. Born in Harrow, Greater London in February 1895. The daughter of Joseph Thacher Clarke (1856-1920) and Agnes Paulina Marie Amalie von Helferich (1861-1935). Her father originated from America and is listed as having several interests including architecture and archaeology, though appears to have had no specific occupation. In 1881 he co-lead an archaeological expedition to Assos, Turkey. He died in France. Dora was one of at least three children (also Rebecca (1886-1979) and Eric (1890-1968)). Raised in and around London. Evidently a young talent, by the age of at least 16 she was living in Kensington with her sister Rebecca, a musician, and was already an art student. She studied on a scholarship at the Slade School under George Havard Thomas and Henry Tonks. She remained largely in London thereafter, working at the Clifton Hill Studios, St John's Wood in the 1920s and 1930s, prior to her marriage.

Clarke produced mainly busts, heads and figures, and some graphic designs. As a sculptor, worked in a wide variety of materials including ebony, whale's tooth, wood (including oak and teak), ivory, stone, bronze, alabaster, Hoptonwood stone and aluminium. Did chiefly direct carving. Highly regarded during her lengthy career, which eventually covered five decades. She began exhibiting at the New English Art Club from at least 1916, and continued to do so fairly regularly until at least 1959. Exhibited elsewhere, including at the Royal Academy (1923-59), the Royal Glasgow Institute (1924-30), the Society of Women Artists (1931-54), the Paris Salon and the French Gallery (certainly in 1936 with a one-woman show). Also, with the Women's International Art Club, the London Group, at the Goupil Gallery, with the New Autumn Group, with the Architectural League (New York), with the Museums Association and at Wembley. In 1932 woodcarvings by various artists, including Dora Clarke, were exhibited at the Wertheim Gallery, Burlington Gardens, London. Clarke exhibited East African Woman. Also in 1932, she held an exhibition of her sculptures at the Beaux Art Gallery. In mentioning the exhibition, The Studio, Vol.103, January 1932, p.49 illustrated her The African. Other exhibited works included: The Artist's Mother (bust, wood), Miss Diana White (medallion, bronze), Elegy (statuette, ebony) and Torso (alabaster). A Member of the New Autumn Group. The Group (founded c.1924) initially consisted of 21 members, all centred around St John's Wood.

In the 1920s Clarke travelled to East Africa, which inspired her work considerably, resulting in a series of studies including Old Kikuyu Woman (head, bronze) and Young Kikuyu Girl (bronze). Produced a portrait study of Joseph Conrad. She travelled abroad again in the 1930s. Evidently at the forefront of modern developments in art and design throughout her career, and highly successful as a sculptor and an exhibiting sculptor. Works illustrated and / or noted in various journals. For example, in 1925 The Studio, Vol.90, December, p.351 illustrated her Scheherezade (gilded wood) which was shown at that year's New Autumn Group exhibition. In 1932 Apollo (p.141) gave a review of the Women's International Art Club exhibition and noted Clarke to be one of the few outstanding exhibitors of that year. In 1936 Apollo (p.232) again praised her talents as a 'sculptress of exceptional talent'. In 1923 sculptor May Creamer exhibited a head of Dora Clarke at the Royal Academy. In 1936 Orovida Pissarro executed a portrait painting of Clarke. In mid-1938 Clarke married Admiral Gervase Boswell Middleton in Marylebone, London. She died in Brent, Middlesex, aged 94.

CLARKE, EFFIE BRUCE (1852-1909)

Along with Miss Audrey Trevelyan, Effie Bruce Clarke instigated a significant revival in regional lace making in key areas of late nineteenth and early twentieth century Britain.

Effie Clarke was born in Newton, Cambridgeshire, the daughter of the Rev. James Berryman and Annie. Her father was rector at Emneth, Norfolk, where she grew up as Annie Euphemia Berryman, one of at least five children. In 1881 she married William Bruce Clarke in Bath, Somerset. He became an eminent surgeon in Harley Street, London, where Effie spent much of the rest of her life. She died in London, aged 56. Where she developed her passion for lace remains unclear. Nor is it clear if she actually made lace herself. However, her tireless supporter, Audrey Trevelyan, was an expert lace maker. Regardless, Mrs Clarke revealed her deep interest in the subject in an illustrated article English Lace in 1896, written for the Art Journal, 1896, pp.297-302.

Between them, Miss Trevelyan and Mrs Clarke took charge of, and revitalised, lace classes in the counties of Bedfordshire, Northamptonshire, Buckinghamshire and Devonshire. Mrs Clarke wished to see a London Lace League start up, to oversee the work of her classes, to select threads and to deliver them to the workers. She particularly valued the home arts and their ability to earn income in dire times in the countryside. She wanted to emulate the Italians in that respect, and like them wanted a Lace League for both sexes. The two main aims of her work were, to create employment for women in reduced circumstances, and to stimulate interest in a vanishing tradition. Audrey Trevelyan not only supervised classes, but continued with her own lace work, showing examples at the 1893 Chicago Exhibition. She also contributed lace to the 1903 Dress Designers' Exhibition Society exhibition, and to the exhibitions held by the Worshipful Company of Broderers in London. From 1894, the Company held open exhibitions to encourage good workmanship and artistic excellence, with prizes offered. Other exhibitors included Mary Symonds, Edith Munn and Constance Hole.

Miss Trevelyan was particularly active in Beer and Seaton in Devon, and introduced Italian and French designs into local lace making. One of the most successful lace makers active in Devon was Edith Mason, who designed and made traditional Honiton lace and who won a Gold Medal at the 1903 St Louis Exhibition. Edith Mason wrote an article on Honiton lace for the Art Workers' Quarterly, 1903, pp.144-146. It is not clear if Mrs Mason was directly involved with Audrey Trevelyan. The Clarke and Trevelyan classes had particularly strong ties with the Home Arts and Industries Association. Formed in around 1884, the Association's headquarters was in London. It had a profound effect across the country, with numerous handcraft classes setting up and thriving, with the chief aims of reviving lost handcrafts in an age of mass mechanisation, and of providing additional income to those in need. The success of the Home Arts movement doubtless only encouraged Mrs Clarke in her work, and her lace workers contributed regularly to the Association's annual exhibition in London from at least 1896.

Audrey Trevelyan showed her own work at the Home Arts exhibitions, including in 1905. On one occasion, in 1896, the lace classes won six gold and 15 blue awards. A photograph of their stall at the 1896 exhibition was shown in the Art Journal, 1896, p.256. Devonshire lace exhibited by Miss Trevelyan at the 1903 Home Arts exhibition was illustrated in the Art Workers' Quarterly, July 1903, p.117. The Clarke / Trevelyan classes also exhibited at the Society of Women Artists in 1896 and 1898 under the title English Lace Makers and under Mrs Clarke's Harley Street, London address. Regional laces drew the attention of a number of eminent designers. A Honiton lace strip, designed by Walter Cave, was executed by the lace workers of the village of Sidbury, Devon for the Communion table of the Parish Church. An altar frontal in applique, the joint design of Mr and Mrs Cave, was made for the same church, displaying the white doe and forest emblems of their patron, St Giles. This may have been done in connection with the Clarke / Trevelyan classes.

In her 1896 article for the Art Journal, Mrs Clarke notes that, five years previously, lace making had been dying out in various regions of Britain. Together, she and Audrey Trevelyan had resolved to revive the type of lace made by hand some 40 years previously by Audrey's great aunt in Devonshire. They had the shared objective of reproducing all the best traditional patterns, but reviving them in a way to create modern textiles. They also used new designs. For example, Colonel Jemmitt Browne produced a design Iris which was illustrated in Mrs Clarke's article, and which won a blue and a gold award at the Home Arts exhibition. Certain laces, she notes, such as the Torchon and the Maltese were not encouraged because they could be made equally well and cheaper abroad, so there was no British market for them. The classes proved most successful for a number of years, but were brought to a decline by Mrs Clarke's death in 1909. Audrey Trevelyan may have been linked to other Trevelyans in Devonshire, including Sarah Ann Trevelyan, a lace maker of Burlescombe and her daughter, Henrietta, a lace-mender. SEE: FOWLER, ANN

CLARKE, IDA M.W. - SEE HARDY, EVELYN

CLAUSEN, MAY SOPHIA - SEE CREAMER, M.S.

CLAY, PHYLLIS M.C. - SEE ARCHIBALD, P.M.C.

CLAYTON, ETHEL WILLIAMSON (1893-1965)

Metalworker / Embroideress. Born in Lancaster, Lancashire in August 1893. The daughter of William Wyatt, a pharmaceutical chemist, and Sophia Gertrude. Her parents originated from Nottingham. One of at least three children (also Nora and Agnes). Raised in Lancaster initially, then Newcastle-upon-Tyne, Northumberland. Educated at the Whalley Range High School, Manchester and the Newcastle-upon-Tyne High School. Studied at the Manchester Municipal School of Art. As a student, won the Lady Whitworth Scholarship, the Primrose Silver Medal and the Proctor Travelling Scholarship. Awarded City & Guilds Diplomas in jewellery and embroidery. Elected an Associate of the Manchester Municipal School of Art in 1920. Was art mistress for the Ministry of Education, Egypt. Also acted as instructor in metalwork and embroidery at the Oldham School of Art. Occasionally exhibited her work at handcraft exhibitions. Married Patrick Clayton (d.1962). Had a son, Peter H. Clayton, in 1928 whilst in Croydon. Latterly, lived in Hove, Sussex. She died in Sussex in December 1965, aged 72.

CLOUGH, KAY - SEE ANDERSON, K.

CLUTTON BROCK, EVELYN ALICE (1876-1964)

Painter / Mural Decorator. Born in Limpsfield, Surrey. The daughter of Leveson F. Vernon Harcourt, a civil engineer and Professor, and Alice. Had at least three siblings, Violet, Leveson and Archibald. Raised in Walton-on-Thames, Surrey. Studied in London, at the Slade School and the Chelsea Polytechnic. Became a portrait, landscape and flower painter and a mural decorator. Based in Surrey during her marriage and career, but also later in Chelsea, Colchester and elsewhere in London. Evelyn died in Cheltenham, aged 87, though at the time her address was Moreton-in-Marsh, Gloucestershire. In 1903 she married Arthur Clutton Brock (1868-1924) in Surrey. He was a journalist for The Times. They had at least three sons. Evelyn exhibited her work, particularly later in her career, after her husband's death, presumably having to work to support herself and her sons. Exhibited at the New English Art Club, the Royal Academy (1935-58), the Society of Women Artists (1932-33), with the London Group and the Women's International Art Club. Exhibited works included: Shirley Poppies, A Sunny Window, The Dresden Vase and Nayland Cornfields.

COATES, DORA (1869-1955)

Painter / Illustrator / Decorator. Born in Melbourne, Australia. The daughter of John Thomas Meeson and Amelia. Her father, a barrister, originated from Lancaster. Her mother originated from London. One of at least four children (Dora, Amy, Ruth and Gertrude). Raised mainly in London. Educated at home. Then studied art at the Melbourne National Gallery under Professor Bernard Hall. Also, at the Slade School, London under Professor Henry Tonks, and at the Academie Julian, Paris under Jean Paul Laurens and Benjamin Constant. Became a painter of landscapes and portraits in oils and watercolours, an illustrator and a decorator in tempera. Illustrated, for example, A History of the World and Sunshine Farm. Produced decorative tempera panels for, among others, St Anne's Church, Limehouse. Exhibited her work with the Society of Painters in Tempera and Mural Decorators. One of her decorative panels, Spring, was reproduced in The Studio, Vol.62, August 1914, p.176 in an article about the Society (pp.173-182).

Coates exhibited elsewhere during her lengthy career, including at the Royal Academy (1916-46), the Royal Scottish Academy (1932), the Royal Hibernian Academy (1939), the Society of Women Artists (1929-51), the Royal Institute of Oil Painters and the Women's International Art Club. Also, at the Paris Salon, with the International Society of Sculptors, Painters & Gravers, at the Royal Cambrian Academy, the Royal West of England Academy, with the Royal Photographic Society, at the Goupil Gallery and the Walker Art Gallery, Liverpool. Exhibited works included: Daisies and Buttercups (tempera), A Glimpse of Melbourne, The King's Barge at London Bridge Peace Celebrations, 1919 and The Last Chapter. Elected a Member of the Women's International Art Club, of the Royal Institute of Oil Painters and of the Society of Painters in Tempera and Mural Decorators. Won an Honourable Mention at the Paris Salon of 1923. Her Sunset From Tower Bridge was illustrated in Colour. Coates spent some time in London during her early career, but also in Sussex with her sister, Ruth. In 1903 Dora married artist George James Coates in London. They remained in London thereafter. Dora died in Chelsea, aged 85. She was the author of The Life and Work of George Coates. Purchasers of her work included H.R.H. Princess Louise, the National Galleries of Melbourne, Sydney, Adelaide, Brisbane, Perth, Hobart, Ballarat and Bendigo, the British and Australian War Museums and the Greenwich Maritime Museum.

COATON, HELEN MARY (1911-2005)

Sculptor. Born in Leicester. The daughter of John Thomas Coaton and Annie. Her father was a tramway motorman. Raised in Leicester and maintained ties with the city for much of her life. She was educated at the Wyggeston School for Girls, Leicester. Attended Bristol University. Awarded a B.A. (Hons Hist.) degree. Then studied at the Leicester College of Art under Percy Brown, A.R.C.A. between 1937 and 1942. Became a sculptor in wood and stone. Exhibited her work occasionally, including at the Leicester Museum and Art Gallery and with the Leicester Society of Artists. Awarded the Hinton Prize of the Leicester Society of Artists in 1942, and was elected a Member. Also a Member of the Artists' International Association. Based in Leicester early in her career. In 1941 she married Edward Kenneth Wilde in Leicestershire. They had at least one son and one daughter. The couple lived in Chelmsford and in Surrey. Helen died in Surrey, aged 94.

COATS, ALICE MARGARET (1905-78)

Illustrator / Painter / Mural Decorator / Woodcut Artist. Born in Handsworth, Staffordshire in June 1905. The daughter of Robert Hay Coats, M.A., B.D., and Margaret. Her father, who originated from Paisley, was a Baptist minister and a university lecturer. Her mother originated from Glasgow. Alice had at least one sibling, Arthur Robertson Coats. Raised in Birmingham. Educated at the Edgbaston High School for Girls. Studied at the Birmingham Central School of Art, and at the Slade School, London. Spent much of her life and career in Handsworth, but died in Bath, Somerset. Produced colour woodcuts, landscape paintings in oils and watercolours, flower paintings on silk, mural decorations, linocuts and book illustrations. The first book she illustrated was The Story of Horace (Faber, 1937), which she also wrote. Exhibited her work, including at the Royal Scottish Academy (1935-37), the Royal Glasgow Institute (1931), the Society of Women Artists (1929-31) and elsewhere in London and Birmingham. Also had close ties with the Birmingham Group of artists.

Exhibited works included: Willow Tree (wood-block print), Datura (plant study on silk / watercolour), The Signpost (colour woodcut) and Cottage Garden (wood-block print). Elected a Member of the Central Club of Wood-Engravers in Colour. Also, of the Women's International Art Club and of the Birmingham Group. Noted in Mahony, Latimer & Folmsbee, Illustrators of Children's Books 1744-1945, Boston, The Horn Book Inc., 1947.

COATS, MARY (b.1868)

Artist / Ceramic Painter. Born in Paisley, Scotland. The daughter of Jervis Coats (1823-76) and Elizabeth Lyle (1840-1929). Her father was an artist and engraver on stone, but also owned a drapery business in Paisley. Her mother was a teacher. One of at least five children (Elizabeth, Mary, George, Maggie and Gervase). Raised in Paisley. Educated at the John Neilston Institute in Paisley and at the Free Church Training College in Glasgow. Studied at the Paisley School of Art, and at the Glasgow School of Art, also studying china painting in America. Awarded William Barbour Art Scholarships whilst at the Paisley School of Art. Also as a student, won prizes for drawing and painting from life the full figure. Produced paintings in oils and watercolours and painted on china. Known for her landscapes and seascapes with figures and animals. Painted across parts of Arran, Clyde and Aviemore. Executed mainly flower and fruit studies on china. Exhibited her work, including at the Royal Glasgow Institute (1899), the Paisley Art Institute, with the Paisley Art Club and at the Stirling Art Institute. Exhibited works included Irises. Based in Paisley for much of her life and career. Acted as Head of the West Public School, Paisley.

COBB, CATHERINE ANNE - SEE COCKERELL, C.A.

COBB, RUTH (1878-1950)

Artist / Illustrator. Born in London. The daughter of Thomas Cobb and Emily. Thomas Cobb was, initially, a master tailor employing a considerable number of men in the 1880s. Later, he became a novelist and author, though it is unclear if his works were published. Thomas and Emily both originated from London. Ruth was one of at least three children, all of whom were raised mainly in London. Her younger brother, Geoffrey, began his career in publishing. Ruth studied art in a private studio, but also studied at the Brighton and Blackheath Schools of Art. She became an artist and illustrator. Her work was published in various children's annuals including The Chatterbox and The Wonderland Annual. Also, in humorous papers such as Punch, in architectural papers and children's books. Books illustrated by her included Baby Ballads (1911), The Golden Thread (1937), This Happy Home (1944) and A Sussex Highway (1946). By the 1930s she was living in Frognal, Hampstead. She died in Lewes, Sussex in 1950, aged 72. Exhibited with the Society of Graphic Art. A Member of the Writer's Club. Noted in Sketching Grounds, a 5s volume published by The Studio in 1909, with contributions by leading artists of the day.

COBBETT, HILARY DULCIE (1885-1976)

Etcher / Painter. Born in Richmond, Surrey in early 1885. The daughter of William V.H. Cobbett, a solicitor. One of at least six children. Their mother died whilst the children were still young. All were raised in Richmond, in a house with servants. Educated privately. Studied at the Richmond School of Art on two separate occasions, between 1903 and 1905, and between 1924 and 1927. Produced etchings, illustrations, paintings in oils and watercolours and miniatures. Concentrated on seascapes, landscapes and flowers. Evidently travelled and painted on her travels, including in France. Exhibited widely, including at the Royal Academy (1937-47), the Society of Women Artists (60 works, 1928-65), the Royal Society of British Artists, the Royal Photographic Society, the Royal Institute of Oil Painters, the Royal Institute of Painters in Watercolours and the Society of Miniaturists. Exhibited works included: Fishing for Tunny, Concarneau, Evening Glow, Brixham, White Phlox and The Mussel Sellers, Dieppe. Elected a Member of the Society of Miniaturists. A Member of the Forum Club. Elected an Associate of the Society of Women Artists (1935-60) and a Member (1961-73). Was a teacher between 1927 and 1933. Produced six illustrations for Heine's Italian Travel Sketches (Emslie & Co.). Based largely in Richmond, Surrey. Died in Sutton, Gt. London, aged 91.

COCHRANE, JESSIE - SEE CAVE, JESSICA MARIA

COCKERELL, CATHERINE ANNE (1903-95)

Jeweller / Silversmith. Known as 'Casty'. Born in London in March 1903. The daughter of Douglas Bennett Cockerell (1870-1945) and Florence Margaret Drew Arundel. The granddaughter of a coal merchant. Had at least two brothers, Sydney and Oliver. Raised at Letchworth, Hertfordshire.

Her mother was a decorative jeweller who contributed to the 1906 Arts and Crafts Exhibition Society exhibition. Some of her mother's work was illustrated in the Art Journal in 1906, p.125. Florence died whilst Catherine was still young. Douglas Cockerell was a bookbinder and teacher of bookbinding at the London County Council Central School of Arts and Crafts. His brother, Sydney Carlyle Cockerell, was Director of the Fitzwilliam Museum, Cambridge, and married decorative artist Florence Kate Kingsford. Douglas and Sydney had a sister, Olive, who became a book illustrator, but who also died young. Catherine, therefore, grew up amidst a strongly artistic family. Her brother Sydney had the middle name of Morris, no doubt after William Morris, a leading Arts and Crafts figure known to the Cockerells. Catherine was educated at the Sidcot School. She then went on to study at the Cambridge School of Art, and at the L.C.C. Central School of Arts and Crafts. Gained a City & Guilds First Class Certificate.

Like her mother, Catherine produced decorative jewellery and metalwork. She also exhibited her work, including at an Arts and Crafts Exhibition held at Burlington House, at Wembley, at the British Industries Fair and the Walker Art Gallery, Liverpool. Exhibited one work at the Society of Women Artists in 1936. Also exhibited jewellery at the 1901 Glasgow Exhibition. Her necklaces were described as 'dainty' in reports of the Glasgow Exhibition. She made silver clasps and bosses for a number of books bound by her father, including a lectern Bible. Another of her works was a key for the Mond Laboratory, Cambridge. She was based in Letchworth with her father until the late 1920s. By the 1930s she was living at Mecklenburgh Square, London. Catherine was also a puppeteer along with friend and former fellow student Joyce Clissold. In the 1930s they toured their Punch and Judy along the south coast and Buckinghamshire. In 1937, Catherine married Arthur R. Cobb in London. During the Second World War, the couple moved to Cambridge where she taught drawing and design and jewellery at the Cambridge Technical College. She was still teaching in some capacity beyond the age of 90, at her workshop near Cambridge. Elected a Member of the distinguished Art Workers' Guild in 1970. In the Guild's papers, she is listed as a jewellery and ivory worker. SEE: COCKERELL, OLIVE JULIET

COCKERELL, OLIVE JULIET (1869-1910)
Artist / Illustrator. Born in Dulwich. The daughter of Sydney John Cockerell (1842-77), a coal merchant, and Alice Elizabeth Bennett (1845-1900). Her brother, Douglas Bennett Cockerell (1870-1945), studied bookbinding under T.J. Cobden-Sanderson (1840-1922) and subsequently wrote about the craft. Douglas became a bookbinder and taught the subject at the London County Council Central School of Arts and Crafts. Douglas's daughter, Catherine, became a decorative jeweller and metalworker, and his wife, Florence Arundel, was also involved in decorative jewellery. Another brother, Sydney Carlyle Cockerell (1867-1962), became Director and curator of the Fitzwilliam Museum, Cambridge. Sydney married decorative artist Florence Kingsford. Olive shared the family's artistic interests and became a student of art in her early 20s. She became a black & white artist and illustrated a number of books including A. Pickering, Queen of the Goblins (1892). She was influenced to some degree by John Ruskin, with whom she is believed to have corresponded. Sydney and Olive visited the Lake District in 1887 and visited Brantwood, Ruskin's home. In 1888 Sydney and Olive visited Ruskin at Sandgate. Ruskin took them to supper and read from the manuscript of his Praeterita. Octavia Hill, also an associate of Ruskin, was Olive's godmother.

Olive Cockerell spent some time in America, from around the age of 24, but returned to England. With her friend Helen Nussey, she compiled A French Garden in England (London, Stead's Publishing House) which was published in 1909. The book was written by Helen and illustrated by Olive, and chronicled their experiences in establishing a garden. Shortly after the book was published, Olive died. Her ashes were scattered at Coniston Water in the Lake District by Douglas and Sydney, using Ruskin's boat. Active around the same time (the early 1900s) was bookbinder Patience Cockerell. She exhibited bookbindings at the Sixth Annual Exhibition of the Sussex Branch of the Royal Amateur Art Society in 1906 in Brighton. She exhibited her work alongside that of Douglas Cockerell, but was not related to the family. SEE: COCKERELL, CATHERINE ANNE

COCKLE, AGNES F.E. - SEE VYSE, A.F.E.

COHEN, ELLEN GERTRUDE (b.1862)
Sculptor / Painter. Born in London. The daughter of Barnet Solomon Cohen and Eliza. Her father, a pencil manufacturer, originated from London, her mother from Chelmsford. One of at least seven children (Wolf, Emily, Rachel, Julia, Ellen, Cohen and Edith). Raised in London. Edith and

Julia became teachers. Ellen studied in Paris under Benjamin Constant, J.P. Laurens and R. Collin. Produced portrait sculptures and figure paintings in oils and watercolours. Exhibited her work, including at the Royal Academy (1884-1905), the Royal Society of British Artists (1884-94), the Royal Glasgow Institute (1903) and the Society of Women Artists (1883-93). Exhibited works included: The Gambler, A Sly Taste, Dr B.W. Richardson (sculpture) and Russian Refugees at the Shelter in Leman Street (watercolour). Based in London for part of her career, and in Haslemere for a short time. May have lived abroad latterly, possibly dying in a convent in Rome in 1946, but this needs absolute clarification. Also possibly exhibited at the New Watercolour Society and the Salon des Artistes Francais (1897-1939). This also needs clarification.

COHN, OLA (b.1892)
Sculptor / Author. Born in Bendigo, Australia in April 1892. Educated at Girton College, Bendigo. Studied at the Bendigo School of Mines under A.T. Woodward and W. Bowbottom, and at the Swinburne Technical College under Trintham Fryer. Also studied at the Royal College of Art, London under Ernest Cole, Gilbert Ledward, Henry Moore and Richard Garbe. Elected an Associate of the Royal College of Art. Although essentially an Australian artist, and later returned to live in East Melbourne, Cohn spent some time working and exhibiting in London. Produced sculptures in bronze, marble, stone, wood, alabaster, ebony, terracotta and plaster. Exhibited at the Paris Salon, with the London Group, the Women's International Art Club, the Royal Society of British Artists, the Society of Women Artists (1929), at the Leicester Galleries, the Redfern Gallery and with the Contemporary Group, Melbourne. Exhibited works included: Head of a Virgin and Comedy. Elected a Member of the Lyceum Club (Melbourne) and of the Overseas Club. Her works were purchased for the permanent collections of the Melbourne Art Gallery, the Adelaide Art Gallery, the Queensland National Gallery and the Bendigo Art Gallery. Also author of Fairies Tree, More About Fairies Tree and Castles in the Air.

COKE, DOROTHY JOSEPHINE (1897-1979)
Painter / Wood Engraver. Born at Southend in April 1897. The only daughter of Joseph Charles Coke (b.1868) and Edith Mary Price (b.1869). Her father was a tea expert who originated from Stepney, London. Her mother originated from Billericay, Essex. Raised in Wanstead, then Leytonstone, Gt. London. Studied at the Slade School, London between 1914 and 1918 under Henry Tonks and Fred Brown. Won the Melville Nettleship Prize for figure composition. Her art studies covered the period of the First World War. She remained in London into the 1930s. But by at least the 1940s she had become an art teacher at the Brighton College of Art, living in nearby Rottingdean. Remained at the College until her retirement in 1963. Died in Brighton in late 1979, aged 82. Produced paintings in oils and watercolours, and wood engravings, various subjects including still life, portrait, figures and landscapes. Exhibited her work, including with the New English Art Club, the Royal Glasgow Institute (1942), the Royal Academy (1933-41), the Society of Women Artists (1934), the Grosvenor Gallery and the Royal Society of Painters in Watercolours. Exhibited works included: Young Girl Asleep, The Doctor's House, Miss Eliot Listening-In and Great Hemsted Farm. Her engravings included: Badgeworthy Valley, Near Folkestone and Old Barns. Elected a Member of the New English Art Club in 1919. Elected an Associate (1935) and Member (1943) of the Royal Society of Painters in Watercolours. Her painting Aero-Engine Accessories Girls (1941) was presented to the Brighton Museum & Art Gallery. The War Museum purchased her Allotments and Wounded Soldiers at Duppashill, Croydon. Works illustrated in The Studio, Vol.88, September 1924, p.158 and Vol.111, 1936. One of her pupils was painter and stained glass designer Marjorie M. Incledon.

COLE, ETHEL KATHLEEN (1892-1976)
Painter / Black& White Artist / Lithographer / Illustrator / Decorator / Theatre and Poster Artist. Born in Beccles, Suffolk in May 1892. The daughter of William Hammond Cole, M.A. and Josephine Harriet. Her father, a Fellow of the Royal Geographical Society, spent time in India. Ethel was one of at least three daughters (Josephine, Frances and Ethel). Educated at the Croydon High School and at Roedean School. Initially studied at the East Grinstead College of Art in her teens. Then studied at the Slade School, London where she was awarded a scholarship and a First Prize for drawing and a First Class Certificate for drawing, painting and perspective. Based mainly in London thereafter, but died in Lewes, Sussex, aged 84. Produced landscape paintings in oils and watercolours, black & white drawings, lithographs, illustrations, poster designs, decorative and theatre designs.

Exhibited her work, including at the Grosvenor Gallery, the New English Art Club (1916), the Royal Academy (1931-35), the Redfern Gallery and with the Friday Club. Exhibited works included: The Silver Birch, Rocks at Cadgwith (chalk), Cedar of Lebanon and Avignon. Her Rocks at Looe was reproduced in Colour magazine. Other works were reproduced in various French magazines. Also taught art. Works acquired by the Government of New South Wales for the Gallery at Sydney.

COLE, MARGUERITE - SEE KIRMSE, M.

COLEBORN, FREDA M. (1911-66)
Designer / Painter. Was Freda Milward. Born in India in February 1911. Educated at the Leeds High School. Studied at the Royal College of Art, London. Elected an Associate of the College in 1936. Produced designs for glass and embroidery, and paintings in oils and gouache. Also worked as an art teacher. Exhibited her designs for glass at most of the major international exhibitions. Official purchasers included H.M. the Queen. Works reproduced in The Studio, Art and Industry, Pottery and Glass and elsewhere. Based in Kent for much of her career. Died in Kent. In 1935 she married artist Edwin Keith Coleborn (1909-2005) in Kensington. He was also an Associate of the Royal College of Art, and acted as Principal of several art schools. They had at least three children.

COLEY, HILDA MAUD (1884-1950)
Botanical and Flower Painter. Born in Bristol, Somerset. The daughter of the Rev. Samuel Birt Coley, a Wesleyan Methodist Minister, and Mary Walker. One of at least three children (Edith, Samuel and Hilda). Raised in Bristol, Warwick and Sleaford, Lincolnshire. Educated at the Warwick and Lincoln High Schools. Studied art in Liverpool. Remained living with her parents and Edith for some years, spending time in Dover, Surrey and, latterly, Dorset. Produced botanical and flower paintings and black & white drawings for a number of publishers. For example, executed coloured and black & white illustrations of flowers for Harmsworth's Children's Encyclopedia. Medici published 12 of her postcards titled The Herb Garden. Coley produced illustrations for Wild Flower Preservation by May Colley for Allan publishers. She was the author and illustrator of Wild Flowers Round the Year (Howe), and produced paintings of cacti, some of which were purchased by the British Museum. Also specialised in flower portraits of orchids. Coley was awarded the silver Flora and Grenfell bronze medals of the Royal Horticultural Society. Exhibited her work, including at the Faculty of Arts, in Venice, at the Walker Art Gallery, Liverpool and with the Royal Birmingham Society of Arts. A Member of the Holmesdale Natural History Club and of the Holmesdale Fine Arts Club. Also an embroideress. Coley died in Langton Matravers, Dorset, aged 65. Left her small estate to her brother, Samuel Ernest Coley, also a Methodist Minister. Her sister Edith (1880-1929) became a writer. Edith died in Surrey.

COLLINGWOOD, MARY ETHEL - SEE WHILE, M.E.

COLLYER, KATE W. - SEE WALKER, K.W.

COLVIN, BRENDA GWYNETH STEWART (1897-1981)
Garden Designer / Landscape Architect. Born and raised in Simla, India. Studied garden design under Madeleine Agar at the Swanley Horticultural College. Initially worked for Agar, but established her own garden design practice in London. Considered to be a recognised professional in her field. Worked for part of her career with Hal Moggridge. With Agar, she became a founder member of the Institute of Landscape Architects in 1929, and was its first woman President from 1951 to 1953. In 1949 she also became a founder member of the International Federation of Landscape Architects. Between the wars, she visited America and there encountered landscape architect Thomas Adams, who introduced Colvin to the design work of Frederick Law Olmsted and his sons. Their influence can be seen in some of her later landscaping projects for industrial sites, power stations and coal mining sites, including in Yorkshire. Her garden commissions included Okeover Hall, Derbyshire and Sutton Courtenay Manor, Oxfordshire. Also, a pond garden for Major Swann at Steeple Manor, Dorset, and a water garden at Haslemere for Lady Bellew. Both were mentioned in The Studio, Vol.93, January 1927, pp.30-33. With her concentration on landscape and architectural qualities, Colvin became a pioneer of landscape architecture in Britain, following on from the likes of Thomas H. Mawson (1861-1933) who aimed to give the subject a more positive identity. In 1954 she bought Little Peacocks at Filkins, Oxfordshire where she developed her own garden. It became her permanent home in the 1960s. Made C.B.E. The author of Trees for Town and Country (1947)

and Land and Landscape (1948). Died at Witney, Oxfordshire, aged 83.

CONNELL, CHRISTINE (1863-1938)

Metalworker / Designer / Enameller. Was Mary Christine, known as Christine or M. Christine. Born in London. The daughter of William G. Connell and Anna. Her father was involved in the jewellery trade. One of a large family. Raised in London. In the early 1880s, she was an art student in London. Produced decorative metalwork, usually with enamelling, and paintings of figure subjects. Contributed to the English Illustrated Magazine and to The Sketch in the 1890s. Had a studio in London and taught her own metalwork pupils. Two of those were Bertha and Blanche Goff who subsequently acted as Connell's assistants. Some of her metalwork was illustrated in The Studio. In 1904, for example, Vol.31, April, p.348 the magazine illustrated two silver candlesticks and a silver bowl designed and executed by Connell. The candlesticks were set with peacock blue enamel decoration and glass candle rings. The bowl was set with turquoise matrix. In 1905, The Studio, Vol.36, November, p.161 illustrated a silver panel set with mother-of-pearl and enamel decoration. The design incorporated figures representing the sea and the heavens.

Connell also produced portrait medallions in bronze, and occasionally designed posters. She exhibited her work, including at the Royal Academy (1885-1907), the Royal Society of British Artists (1886-91) and the Society of Women Artists (1906). Contributed to the 1905 Exhibition of Arts and Crafts held at the Lyceum Club. Exhibited works included: The Mandolinist, She Sees All Past Things Pass, The Sea Hath its Pearls (panel, silver and enamel) and The Late Christopher Mease, Esq. (medallion, bronze). Connell also acted as an art critic. Another member of the family, Janet Connell, was a miniature painter who exhibited at the Royal Academy (1890-1908). Janet and Christine Connell lived together for a while. In 1908 Connell married John Arthur Mease Lomas (1862-1950) in London. He was an artist and designer who originated from Jarrow, Durham. Christine continued with her career after her marriage. Initially, the couple lived in London. Christine died first, in Exmoor, aged 75. SEE: GOFF, BERTHA & BLANCHE

CONSTABLE, ELLEN RAWSON (1866-1952)

Decorative Metalworker / Embroideress. Born in Cirencester, Gloucestershire. The daughter of John Constable and Emily. Her father, who originated from Scotland, was Rector of Marston Bigott in Somerset, where Ellen was raised. Her mother originated from Leeds. Ellen was one of at least five daughters (Charlotte, Emily, Martha, Ellen and Margaret). Sometime between 1892 and 1901 the family moved to Evelyn Gardens in Kensington, London, after John Constable's death. Ellen remained at Evelyn Gardens for the rest of her life. She designed and made jewellery and produced embroidered pictures, having presumably studied either in Somerset or London, or both. Since she began exhibiting her work in around 1901, indications are that she studied in London. One of her embroideries was illustrated in the Art Journal in 1901, p.329. She exhibited at the 1901 Glasgow Exhibition. In 1931 she exhibited one work at the Society of Women Artists, a study of Lady Berkeley. In 1938 she visited Egypt.

CONWAY, ANNE SEYMOUR - SEE DAMER, A.S.

COODE, HELEN HOPPNER (1834-1915)

Painter / Illustrator. Born in Lambeth, London. The daughter of George Coode, a barrister, and Helen. One of at least four children. Her mother owned land, and looked after her family when George died. In the 1860s they lived in Putney, but by the 1870s were in Kent, and later in Surrey. Latterly, Helen lived with two of her sisters, Rose and Violet, in Silver Street, Lyme Regis, Dorset. She died in Dorset in November 1915, aged 84. Helen worked as an illustrator and painter in watercolours, specialising in figures. She was one of the earliest women artists to work for Punch magazine, and contributed to Once a Week. She exhibited her work over a period of at least 22 years, including at the Royal Academy (1865-67), the Royal Society of British Artists (1876-81), the British Institution (1859-66) and the Society of Women Artists (1864-72). Exhibited works included: The Sermon Rehearsed, The Lady of Shalott, Crochet and The Gipsy Fortune Teller. Elected a Member of the Society of Women Artists (1868-72). Coode was still listed as an artist at the age of 77, but also a writer.

COOK, ALICE MAY (1876-1960)

Painter / Illustrator. Known as May. Born in Paddington, London. Raised in London. The daughter of Royal Academician of Music John Francis Barnett and Alice. Her father, a pianist, composer and teacher of music, originated from London. One of at least four children. By 1891, aged 14, Alice was already an art student. She studied at the St John's Wood School of Art, followed by the Royal Academy schools. Produced book illustrations, paintings and miniatures in watercolours. Concentrated on portraits, but some other subjects too. In 1899, she married Walter Frank Cook, a clerk, in Marylebone, London. By 1900 she had already had the first of seven children (five sons and two daughters) and was living in Middlesex. Despite her considerable domestic commitments, May managed to have a long and successful career as an artist, exhibiting her work widely over a period of more than 54 years. Interestingly, her exhibiting career took off only after her marriage. Exhibited at the Royal Academy (51 works, 1907-60), the Royal Scottish Academy (1937-51), the Society of Women Artists (1949), at the Arlington Gallery and in Toronto and Capetown. Exhibited works included: Rt Rev. William Cecil, Lord Bishop of Exeter, The Artist, In the Window and A Fish-Wife. One of her works was a silver triptych set with watercolour miniatures. Elected to the Royal Society of Miniature Painters. Elected a Fellow of the Zoological Society. Elected to the American Institute of Architecture. Illustrated a number of children's books. Her A Kiss was illustrated in The Studio, Vol.75, November 1918, p.39. Based mainly in London during her career and in Edinburgh. May died in Colchester, Essex, aged 82.

COOK, KATHLEEN MARY CARWARDINE (1884-1977)

Painter / Linocut Artist / Embroideress. Born in Lympley Stoke, Somerset in February 1884. The daughter of John Cook (1855-1930) and Charlotte Emily Carwardine Francis (b.1859). Her father had no profession. Kathleen had at least one brother, Cyril. Raised in Weston-super-Mare, Somerset and spent part of her career there. Died in Oxfordshire, aged 93. Educated at Quantock House, Weston-super-Mare. Studied under Cornish artist William H.Y. Titcomb and at the Weston-super-Mare School of Science and Art. Produced paintings in watercolours, linocuts and embroideries. Exhibited her work occasionally, including at the Royal West of England Academy.

COOK, MARGARET M.E. - SEE FITTON, M.M.E.

COOKESLEY, MARGARET MURRAY (1843-1927)

Painter. Was Margaret Deborah Garland. Born at Langton Matravers near Swanage, Dorset. The daughter of John Bingley Garland (d.1875), a landowner and magistrate, and Fanny Maria. Her parents originated from Dorset. One of at least six children (Amy, Marie, Elizabeth, Frances, Margaret and John). Raised in Kensington, London. Studied in Brussels under Leroy and Gallais, and spent a year at South Kensington studying anatomy. Became a painter of portraits, figures, animals and other subjects in oils and watercolours. Commanded reasonable sums for her works, up to £150 each in the early 1900s. Spent some time living in Newfoundland and San Francisco during her career. Also visited elsewhere, including Constantinople, where she was commissioned to paint a portrait of the son of the Sultan of Turkey, executed almost entirely from a photograph. The Sultan then decorated Cookesley with the Order of the Chefakat, and with the Medaille des Beaux Arts. The Sultan invited her to execute portraits of some of his wives. Cookesley declined the commission.

Cookesley executed some (then, for women) unusual subjects on her travels, including a study of an Arab cafe in the slums of Cairo which was exhibited at the Royal Academy in 1895. Other studies included Drinking Fountain, Cairo, Pottery Seller, Egypt, Corner in the Fruit Market, Gibraltar and Entrance to the Old Mosque, Damascus. Executed portraits of notables, including Miss Calhoun as Salome which was purchased for the Haymarket Theatre. Also, a study of Miss Ellen Terry as Imogen which was purchased for a private collection. Her A Priestess of Isis remained in Cairo. Her Death of the First-Born was in a collection in Russia. Won a medal for her Lion Tamers in the Time of Nero. Exhibited her work over a period of more than 50 years. Exhibited at the Society of Women Artists (1868-1909), the Royal Academy (1884-1920) and the Royal Scottish Academy (1871-85). Elected an Associate of the Society of Women Artists (1899-1901). Spent time living in Glasgow and in Kensington, London. In 1866 she married Edward Murray Cookesley in Wimborne, Dorset. He originated from Norfolk, and was a Captain in the Army. This was presumably why Margaret spent so much time abroad. Apparently had no children. Latterly, they moved to Bath, Somerset where Margaret died in February 1927, a widow. A Member of the Empress Club. Noted in C.E. Clement, Women in the Fine Arts, New York, Riverside Press, 1904.

COOKSEY, MAY LOUISE GREVILLE (1878-1943)

Painter / Etcher / Ecclesiastical Artist. Born in Birmingham in November 1878. The daughter of

Harry S. Cooksey and Catherine. Her father originated from Southampton, her mother from Gloucestershire. Her father was initially a manager for Mansell Beer, but was later listed as an architect. May was one of at least five children (May, Edith, Oteline, Max and Alice). Her siblings were also born in Birmingham, and all were raised there. May attended a private school in Leamington. Then studied at the Leamington School of Art, Warwickshire. Subsequently studied at the Mount Street School of Art, Liverpool under Fred V. Burridge. Awarded a travelling scholarship from the Liverpool City Council which enabled her to spend time in Italy, but particularly Florence. There, she spent a year studying the ecclesiastical art of the early Italian masters, which evidently influenced her own work. She won several other prizes as a student, including £30 a year plus free admission to day classes in 1900, again awarded by the Liverpool City Council. May contributed to the National Competition of Schools of Art, including in 1900 when she showed a design for a stained glass window which was illustrated in The Studio, Vol.20, September 1900, p.263. The same journal had already reproduced her illustration for As You Like It in Vol.19, 1900, p.131 along with her design for bellows in brass repoussé which incorporated the figure of a woman in a cape (p.134). Cooksey won silver and bronze medals in the National Competition. Also contributed to the annual exhibition of student work held at the Liverpool School, including in 1901. There, she exhibited a page decoration which was also illustrated in The Studio, Vol.21, January 1901, p.265, and a design for a church banner. Also exhibited a highly praised decorative panel Girlhood of the Virgin, designed for the altar of St Anne's Church, Edge Hill, Liverpool.

After completing her studies, Cooksey remained in Liverpool, using St Luke's Chambers at No.1 Bold Street before moving (sometime after 1912) to St Luke's Studio, Church Path, Freshfield, Lancashire, closer to the coast, near Formby. She apparently lived alone. She remained in that area until her death at nearby Crosby, aged 65. She became a highly regarded and widely respected artist, producing etchings, paintings in oils and watercolours of various subjects including figures and landscapes, and decorative ecclesiastical work. But she also acted as art mistress at South Kensington for a short while. Much of her work was executed for churches in and around Liverpool. Undoubtedly her largest ecclesiastical commission was a series of 14 Stations of the Cross for the Church of St Francis of Assisi at Garston, Lancashire, completed in around 1908. Some of those, along with other

pictures and sketches, the result of several years of hard work, were exhibited in October 1908 in an exhibition of her work held at the church. The exhibition concentrated on sacred subjects and themes, all of which were evidently of great significance to the artist. Also included were sketches of Italy and Bruges, including her sketch of The Corpus Domini Procession of Perugia.

Cooksey's work was exquisitely detailed, highly decorative and visually pleasing with a definite hint of the old masters she so admired, but combined with the modern. Another of her projects was a series of five pictures of biblical subjects executed for the Church of Our Lady Star of the Sea, Seaforth, Lancashire. In 1908, The Studio, Vol.45, November 1908, pp.144-146 illustrated three of those, including The Finding in the Temple. The works were to occupy five panels over the high altar. The Seaforth commission also took Cooksey some considerable time to complete. One of the panels, The Annunciation, was included in a studio exhibition held by Cooksey in 1903, that being intended for the eastern apse above the reredos. The panel was illustrated in The Studio, Vol.30, 1903, p.67. The commission fulfilled Liverpool's aim to employ its up and coming artists and designers to decorate its public buildings.

Some of Cooksey's works were reproduced by the Fine Art Society of London, some by Philomena of Liverpool and some by the Art Book Co. of London. She exhibited her work elsewhere. Showed one work, O Thou Child of Many Prayers, at the Royal Glasgow Institute in 1912. Exhibited eight works at the Royal Academy between 1909 and 1925, including Maria Virgo, The Passing of Vanity and The Marriage of St Catherine. The last of those was illustrated in The Studio, Vol.28, 1903, p.208. Exhibited at the Walker Art Gallery, Liverpool, including in 1906 when she showed The House of Bethany at its Autumn Exhibition. The study, which was rich in colour, was also illustrated in The Studio, Vol.39, November 1906, p.170. Purchasers of her work included the Liverpool Art Gallery (St Catherine of Alexandra). Works also in the collections of the Birkenhead Art Gallery and the Bournemouth Art Gallery.

COOPER, MARY A. (b.c.1845)
Sculptor. Born in Chelsea. The wife of Cuthbert Cooper (b.c.1842), annuitant. Had at least one son, Claude. Based in London during her marriage, at Kilburn and St John's Wood. Worked as a sculptor, but remains elusive in research and largely unknown today. Produced busts and statuettes in marble and terracotta. Exhibited at

the Royal Academy as Mrs Cooper, eight works between 1880 and 1884. Those included: Somebody's Darling (terracotta), Cuthbert Cooper, Esq. (bust, terracotta), La Surprise (statuette, marble) and Mrs Edwin Cox (bust, terracotta).

COOPER, OPHELIA GORDON - SEE BELL, O.G.

COPEMAN, CONSTANCE GERTRUDE (1864-1953)

Painter / Etcher / Illustrator / Poster Designer. Born in Liverpool in February 1864. The daughter of Charles Richard Copeman (1836-95), a solicitor and journalist, and Jane Beggs (1836-1917). Her father originated from Kingston upon Hull, her mother from London. Had a sister, Mabel Marie Adeline (b.1870). Raised in Liverpool and spent much of her life and career there. Died in Liverpool in late 1953, aged 89. Educated privately in Liverpool and London. Mabel subsequently became a music teacher, following in the footsteps of two of her aunts. Constance chose art. Studied at the Liverpool School of Art under John Finnie, R.E., between 1891 and 1900. Also, in Cornwall under Julius Olsson. In 1902 she won the Queen's Prize for Figure Design and a silver medal. Worked as an art teacher for a while. Produced paintings in oils and watercolours, pastel studies, etchings, book illustrations and poster designs. Remained living with her mother, at various addresses including Cook Street, Rotunda Buildings and, latterly, Parliament Street. Since she is listed as still active in 1952, it can be presumed that she worked up until her death. Exhibited her work, but not extensively. Showed at the Royal Academy (1894-1910), the Royal Glasgow Institute (1897), the Royal Society of Painter-Etchers & Engravers, the Walker Art Gallery, Liverpool and in the provinces. Exhibited works included: Last Gleam, A Canal in Bruges, Saturday Morning and Going to School, Trichur, S.W. India. Elected an Associate of the Royal Society of Painter-Etchers & Engravers (1894) and a Member (1897). Works in the collections of Liverpool and Preston.

COPESTICK, VIOLET MARY (1890-1947)

Miniature Painter / Embroideress / Leatherworker. Born in Plymouth. The daughter of John William Brown, a Captain in the Royal Navy, and Mary Facy. Raised in Devon. Educated at Moorfield, Plymouth. Studied at the Plymouth Central School of Arts and Crafts. Remained in Devon thereafter, dying in Plymouth, aged 57.

Produced flower paintings in miniature, leatherwork and embroideries. Exhibited occasionally, including at the Society of Women Artists (12 works, 1927-33), the Toronto Arts and Crafts Exhibition, the Oxford Arts and Crafts Exhibition and the Old Dudley Art Gallery. Exhibited works included: January in a Devon Garden, Apple Blossom and From a Cottage Garden. In 1921 she married Ernest James Copestick, an art master, in Devon.

CORRY, EMILY D. (1873-1942)

Painter / Lithographer / Poster Artist. Born in Belfast, Ireland. The daughter of Robert Workman, D.D., a clergyman. Educated in Belfast and Germany. Became a painter of figures, flowers and landscapes in oils and watercolours, produced lithographs, pen & ink drawings and pencil studies as well as poster designs. Married James W. Corry and had two sons and a daughter. Continued to work after her marriage, exhibiting her work almost until her death. Spent much of her career at Red Roofs, Breda, Belfast. Exhibited her work, including at the Paris Salon, the Royal Hibernian Academy (1920-37), the Royal Scottish Academy (1935-37), the Royal Academy (1931) and the Society of Women Artists (1938). Also, at Wembley, with the Faculty of Arts and at the Municipal Art Gallery, Dublin. Exhibited locally too. Elected a Member of the Faculty of Arts, of the Watercolour Society of Ireland, of the Belfast Art Society and of the Ulster Society of Painters. Works included: Influenza Dreams, Goblin Market, Flowers From a June Garden (oil) and Rocks. Works reproduced in L'Art Contemporain and La Revue Moderne.

COWELL, EVELYN NORMA (1895-1977)

Landscape Architect. Born in Newton Heath, Manchester in July 1895. The daughter of Hudson Newton Cowell (1862-1921) and Edith Dumaresq Fletcher (1865-1957). Her father, a brewer, originated from Bury St Edmunds, Suffolk, her mother from Guildford, Surrey. Had an older sister, Phyllis Dumaresq Cowell. Raised in Newton Heath and Chorlton, Manchester. Neither of the Cowell sisters married. Evelyn was educated on a scholarship from preparatory school. Attended the Withington Girls' School. Then studied at the Manchester University. Awarded a B.Sc. in 1915. Awarded an Honours for Botany. Subsequently took a two-year course at Swanley Horticultural College, aiming at garden design. Awarded a diploma in horticulture in 1917 at Swanley. Became proficient in all branches of garden design. Early in her career (sometime prior to 1927) she was a member of the design and planting staff at T.H. Mawson & Sons, Landscape Architects and Town Planners. The firm had its offices initially in Windermere, Cumbria, but subsequently had offices in London and Lancaster. Evelyn presumably worked at the Lancaster office, depending on the exact dates that she worked for the firm.

Cowell completed numerous garden and landscaping schemes during her career. For example, she laid out gardens on meadowland for A. Garnham and Hugh Dent at Reigate, Surrey. Designed a garden for E.A. Milliken Smith at Edgbaston, Birmingham. Designed alterations to a garden and formation of a wild garden for a Mrs Fox at Fownhope near Hereford. Designed a rock garden with pools for a Miss Dillon of Longworth Hall, Hereford. Designed a rock and rose garden for A. Haigh near Leek. Also replanned the approach and old cattle pond at Lapworth. Some of her schemes were published in journals and magazines. Photographs of some of her finished gardens appeared in Homes and Gardens in May 1926 (garden of Sir Gilbert Barling). Also, in Modern Gardens published by The Studio in 1926 (formal garden for A.W. Heaton). Occasionally exhibited some of her designs, including at the Royal Horticultural Society Autumn Exhibition of 1926 (garden plan in watercolours). In 1929 she exhibited at the Southport Flower Show, winning a Gold Medal. Also exhibited at the Chelsea Flower Show. Later in her career, from at least the 1920s to at least the 1940s, she was based at Sutton Coldfield. Latterly, she lived at Winchester with her sister, Phyllis. Evelyn died in Winchester in mid-1977, aged 81. Phyllis died in 1965.

COWELL, LILIAN (b.1901)

Painter / Modeller / Embroideress. Born in Birkenhead in January 1901. The daughter of Harold Cowell, a foreman baker, and Louisa. Both her parents originated from the Isle of Man, but spent most of their lives in the north of England. There, they had at least seven children (Louisa, Annie, Frances, Catherine, Richard, Margery and Lilian). Lilian was raised at Frankby, Cheshire and was still living and working there into the 1930s. She was educated at Upton in Birkenhead. Studied at the Laird School of Art, Birkenhead. Produced decorative embroideries, landscape paintings in oils and watercolours, and worked as a modeller. Works included: Frankby Hall (watercolour) and St Agnes (embroidered panel). Exhibited at the Walker Art Gallery, Liverpool.

COWLMAN, EMMA LOUISA (1873-1961)

Painter / Poster Artist. Born in Eton, Buckinghamshire. The daughter of William James Cowlman, a house painter and decorator, and Eliza. Had at least one brother, John (1875-1944). Raised in Slough, Buckinghamshire. Educated at the Women's Day College, Chelsea. Studied at the Regent Street Polytechnic, London. Won a national award at the South Kensington National Competition of Schools of Art. Returned to Slough, where she worked as a landscape painter, a pastel artist and a poster designer. Also worked as an art teacher in Slough. For much of her life, she lived with her brother, John, who was also an artist and art teacher. Both were listed as Licentiate Incorporated Faculty of Arts. Emma exhibited her work with the International Society of Sculptors, Painters & Gravers, the Society of Women Artists, the Women's International Art Club, at the Walker Art Gallery, Liverpool, at the Maddox Street Galleries and at Wembley. Emma was elected a Member of the Women's International Art Club. Both Emma and John Cowell died in Eton, Buckinghamshire; she was aged 89, he was 68.

COX, DOROTHY - SEE LEWIS, D.

COX, ETHELWYN M. - SEE BAKER, E.M.

COX, HEBE (1908-93)

Embroideress / Designer / Interior Designer. Born in January 1908 in Knutsford, Cheshire. The daughter of Samuel James Cox and Ethel Neill. Her father was a chemist, involved in making photographic emulsion paper and in coating photographic paper and film. He originated from Manchester, her mother from London. Spent her early years in Knutsford. Educated at a French convent. Before taking up further study, Cox travelled abroad, visiting India, Burma and Ceylon, Australia, New Zealand, Canada and the United States. On her return, in 1931 she began studying at the London County Council Central School of Arts and Crafts, remaining there until 1935. The Principal was then H.G. Murphy, who encouraged her. She specialised in textile and furniture design, interior decoration and embroidery. Awarded a First Class pass in the Advanced Embroidery examination of the City and Guilds of London. Worked for a time on the staff of the Royal School of Needlework, South Kensington, and worked for a while in a textile studio. In 1937, Cox spent several months in Europe, sailing down the Danube and touring Roumania, finding inspiration in their embroidery. In 1940 she married George Ronald

W. Portway (1904-96) in Westminster, London. They had one son, Nicholas W. Portway (b.1942). By that time, the couple had already moved to Suffolk. They would remain there until their deaths at the ages of 85 and 92.

In 1948, Hebe was the subject of an illustrated article in The Studio, Vol.136, August, pp.88-90 titled Hebe Cox: Embroideress and Designer by Ronald Grierson. Grierson notes that her work was exhibited in Europe and America. Also, that she lived in a house named Cricketers at Stowmarket, Suffolk which was originally half pub and half butcher's shop. The house was described as full of her embroideries, including bell-pulls, cushions, chair seats, table mats, teacosies, napkins and nightdress cases. She was not keen on embroidered pictures, however, because the effect was lost behind glass. But she executed embroidered panels, including one titled Pan, on canvas. This was worked in a variety of colours and in 11 different stitches. Others included Pineapple, also on canvas in various colours, and Fantasy, which was white work on stretched organdie. She also executed drawn thread work. Often did personal embroideries for people, incorporating their interests, such as golf, fishing or photography. She did not develop a particular style, but preferred to be artistically flexible. During her career, Cox also worked on carpet designs.

Her work appeared in various London galleries, and in Manchester, Stockholm and America. Also wrote on her subject. Contributed a chapter on embroidery to Fifteen Craftsmen and Their Craft. Also the author of Simple Embroidery Design (1948), Canvas Embroidery (1960) and Embroidery Technique and Design (1964). Became a Member of the handicrafts sub-committee of the National Federation of Women's Institutes, which brought her into contact with women from all across Britain. Also a Council Member of the Arts and Crafts Exhibition Society, and of the Craft Centre of Great Britain. Works in the permanent collections of the Needlework Development Scheme, Scotland and of various county councils.

COXON, EDNA (1902-2000)
Painter / Interior Decorator. Born in Leeds in February 1902. The daughter of Samuel Ginesi, a tax collector, and Ellen. One of at least six children (Irene, Samuel, John, Edna, Harold and Edward). Raised in Leeds. Educated privately and at the Pembroke House School, Leeds. Studied at the Leeds College of Art and at the Royal College of Art, London. Awarded the West Riding Travelling Scholarship and a painting

diploma. Elected an Associate of the Royal College of Art in 1923. Produced paintings in oils, various subjects, and carried out interior design. Initially based in London, but later in Sussex. She died in Sussex, aged 98. Exhibited her work, including at the Royal Academy (1953-70), in Leeds and America, and at various smaller provincial galleries. Contributed to other exhibitions in London. For example, in 1931 she took part in Seventeen Artists, a Second Exhibition held at the Zwemmer Gallery which also included the work of Sine MacKinnon, Barbara Hepworth and others. Exhibited with the London Group, including in 1933 at their thirty-first exhibition at the New Burlington Galleries. Works included: The Garden Cafe, The Wedding, The Bore and Big Fish No.2. In 1926 Ginesi married Raymond James Coxon (b.1896), also a student of Leeds and of the Royal College of Art. He was a painter and mural decorator, and a Member of the Art Workers' Guild, who originated from Stoke-on-Trent. The couple shared No.2, The Grove Studios in Hammersmith for a time. Edna was elected a Member of the London Group and of the Chiswick Group. Works in the collections of the Tate Gallery and the Galleries of Leeds, Wakefield and Manchester.

COXON, ELIZABETH - SEE GOULD, E.

CRANE, MARY FRANCES (1848-1914)
Embroideress / Author. The daughter of Thomas Andrews, a gentleman farmer, and Sarah. One of at least six children (Thomas, Annie, William, Mary, John and Alice). All the family were born in Essex. Raised on her father's farm in Hempstead, Essex, where 21 men and six boys were employed to work 316 acres. Whilst Mary was still a child, her father died, and her mother continued to run the farm. Within a few years, Sarah had given up the farm and had moved to Hastings, Sussex with William, Annie and Mary. In September 1871 Mary married artist / designer Walter Crane (1845-1915) in Westminster, London. Crane, who was born in Liverpool, was the son of artist Thomas Crane, and brother to artist Thomas Crane and artist / writer Lucy Crane. He spent much of his time in London at the centre of artistic developments, and the couple spent much of their marriage living in Hammersmith and Kensington. Between 1873 and 1880 they had three children, Beatrice (born in Rome) and Lionel and Lancelot (born in London). Lionel subsequently became an architect.

It remains unclear what, if any, education Mary had. But during her marriage she proved to be an expert and gifted embroideress, often executing her husband's designs. The majority of her work appears to have been executed in the 1890s and early 1900s, but she was still active as an embroideress and author in 1911. The census for that year notes that Mary (then 63) and Walter (then 65) worked from a shared office at their home. Her work was so highly regarded that it appeared in the exhibitions of the Arts and Crafts Exhibition Society, to which stringent standards were applied. Her work was also illustrated in leading journals of the day. Her work in linen and flax thread, and cotton, was particularly noted in The Catalogue of Works Exhibited by Members of the Northern Art Workers' Guild at the Manchester Art Gallery in 1898. Walter Crane had strong ties with the Guild.

Mary's work appeared in several of the Arts and Crafts Exhibitions, including those held in 1893, 1896, 1899 and 1903 (at least). At the 1893 exhibition, she showed a needlework panel The Vision of Dante, worked in flax thread and filoselle on tinted linen, designed by Walter Crane. The panel was illustrated in The Studio, Vol.2, October 1893, p.12. At the Society's next exhibition, held in 1896, she showed an embroidered cushion with a design of deer and trees, and an embroidered book cover for a copy of The First Book of the Faerie Queene with a lion design, both designed by Walter Crane. Both were illustrated in The Studio, Vol.9, October 1896, p.58. Mary Crane also exhibited embroidered panels for a settle at the 1896 Exhibition. At the next exhibition, held in 1899, she showed a portiere designed by Walter Crane and illustrated in The Studio, Vol.18, November 1899, p.117. The portiere, with its design of figures, was executed by Mary in silks, cotton and gold and silver thread on blue linen, and was divided into three sections, Luna, Mother Earth and the Chariot of the Sun. The portiere had been created by the Cranes for their own home. At the 1903 exhibition, she showed another portiere, of heraldic design. Although she worked large pieces, one of Mrs Crane's specialities was smaller embroidered bindings and book covers, some designed by herself, some by Walter. Others were copies of original designs. One of those was an embroidered binding for the Kelmscott Press edition of Florus and the Fair Jehane, designed by Walter and worked by Mary on flax canvas. In 1894, The Studio, Vol.2, March, pp.211-212 illustrated two of her covers in an article English Embroidered Book-Covers. One was Flora's Head. Exhibited her work twice at the Society of Women Artists, in 1898 (two

handicrafts) and 1906 (three handicrafts). Mary Crane died in Kent, aged 68. Walter Crane died soon after.

CRAWFORD, SUSAN FLETCHER (1863-1918)

Painter / Engraver. Born and raised in Glasgow. The daughter of James Crawford and Janet Hardie. A student of the Glasgow School of Art. Remained in Glasgow thereafter, working at West George Street and Renfield Street over a period of some 32 years. Worked and exhibited up until her death. Produced etchings, studies in black & white and paintings in oils and watercolours. Specialised in old buildings, particularly in Scotland, but also in Paris, Antwerp, Jersey, Ireland, Spain and London. Painted figure subjects. Exhibited her work extensively, including at the Royal Scottish Academy (50 works, 1886-1918), the Royal Hibernian Academy (1902), the Royal Glasgow Institute (61 works, 1887-1918), the Royal Academy (1907-09) and the Society of Women Artists (1904). Also exhibited with the Glasgow Society of Lady Artists, including in 1903 and 1908, and showed prints and designs at the Glasgow School of Art annual exhibition. Exhibited works included: In a Forge (etching), Interior of Central Station, Glasgow (etching), Catedral de Seville (etching) and Thinning Turnips (watercolour). In 1908, The Studio, Vol.42, January, p.316, illustrated her etching of Old Drummond Castle, Stirlingshire. It was noted that Crawford favoured old Scottish architecture and had contributed to many leading exhibitions. In 1910, The Studio, Vol.51, November, pp.151-152, illustrated her etchings of Lambeth Palace and the Tower of London, two in a series of metropolitan studies by Crawford. Some of her works were exhibited posthumously in 1918.

CRAWSHAW, FRANCES (1876-1968)

Painter / Botanical Artist. Born in Manchester in September 1876. The daughter of Robert Fisher, Vicar of Sewerby-cum-Marton, Yorkshire and Canon Of York, and Charlotte. Had at least one brother, John. Raised in Sewerby, near the coast. Studied at the Westminster School of Art, London, at the Scarborough School of Art, Yorkshire, in Milan under Signora Fulria Bisi, and in Paris and Edinburgh. Produced paintings in oils and watercolours, including flowers and landscapes, and botanical drawings. Based in Whitby, Yorkshire, in Edinburgh, at Droitwich near Birmingham and at Newton Abbot, Devon during her career. Exhibited her work, including at the Royal Academy (1933), the Royal Scottish

Academy (1933-37), the Society of Women Artists (1934-37), with the Royal Scottish Watercolour Society and the New English Art Club. Also, with the Royal Institute of Oil Painters, in Leeds and Sheffield, with the Royal Birmingham Society of Artists, the Royal Society of British Artists, the Women's International Art Club and at the Royal Glasgow Institute (1931-33). Exhibited works included: Vase of Garden Flowers, Hell For Leather, Shirley Poppies and Skating, Edinburgh, 1933. Elected a Member of the Ridley Art Club and of the York Art Society. Elected an Associate of the Royal Birmingham Society of Artists. Also a Member of the Overseas League. Produced illustrations for Flowers of Grass by Robert Fisher. Designed the jacket for English Names of Our Common Wild Flowers by Robert Fisher. In 1900 Frances married stockbroker Herbert Anastasius Kettlewell and had one son, Robert. Herbert died in 1903, aged only 33. She subsequently married again, to artist Lionel Townsend Crawshaw (1864-1949). Crawshaw, a widower, had been married to Juliette Menut and had one son. Lionel died in Devon, as did Frances at the age of 91.

CREAMER, MAY SOPHIA (1893-1989)

Painter / Sculptor. Born in London. The daughter of Horatio Isaac Creamer and Julia Magnus (1872-1930). Her father, who originated from Birmingham, was a fur manufacturer in London. Her mother, who was born in London, was an artist. Julia was the daughter of Henry Magnus, a shoe and boot manufacturer, and Rosena. Julia was a Member of the United Arts Club in the early 1900s, and exhibited her work at the New English Art Club (1915-17) and the Royal Academy (1906). May had at least one sibling, Effie. Horatio Creamer apparently did not object to women taking up art since Julia's career appeared to take off after her marriage in 1892, and May was able to study painting and sculpture, presumably in London. May produced figure paintings, reliefs, groups and heads in stone. May also exhibited her work at the New English Art Club (1916-17) and at the Royal Academy (1923-24). Exhibited works included: Dora Clarke (head), Belgians, A Picnic and Portrait (relief, stone). In 1922 May married Hugh Clausen, a civil servant, in Hampstead. May effectively ceased to exhibit some two years after her marriage. Spent much of her life in London. Died in Middlesex, aged 96.

CROCKER, BARBARA FANNY (1910-95)

Painter / Illustrator / Lithographer. Born in London in February 1910. The daughter of

George Ashcombe Crocker, a dealer, and Rosa Anna Francis. One of at least five children (Francis, Phyllis, Joan, Eric and Barbara). Educated at the Putney High School. Studied at the Slade School, London under Professor Henry Tonks and P. Wilson Steer between 1927 and 1930, and in Paris. Produced paintings in oils and watercolours, including landscapes, and lithographs. Produced illustrations for books including Jean Queval, L'Air de Londres (Paris), Eric Whelpton, Book of Dublin and The Intimate Charm of Kensington. Exhibited her work occasionally, including at the Suffolk Street Galleries and the Burlington Galleries. Exhibited three works at the Society of Women Artists between 1932 and 1950, Landscape, White Elms (watercolour) and Place Monge, Paris (oil). In 1943 she married George Eric Whelpton in London. Based in London during her career. Died in East Sussex, aged 85.

CROCKFORD, GERTRUDE (1845-97)

Sculptor. Born in London. The daughter of Joshua Crockford, a manager, and Susanna. One of at least five children. Gertrude was the only one to remain living with her parents well into adulthood, until she was 41. Studied sculpture, probably in London. Produced busts, groups and reliefs in clay and terracotta. Exhibited her work, including at the Royal Academy (1882), the Royal Society of British Artists (19 works, 1877-86) and at the Walker Art Gallery, Liverpool. Exhibited works included: Fidget (bust, clay), A Great Secret (group, terracotta), Shy or Sly (bust, terracotta) and Miss Lingard is "Called Back" (bust, terracotta). Produced designs for decorative pieces, including for interior decoration. In 1886, Gertrude married Joseph Sinclair Fairfax, a patent agent, in London. She appears to have given up her professional career at that point. Initially, the couple lived in London. Gertrude died in Sussex, aged 51, some 11 years after her marriage.

CROFTS, STELLA REBECCA (1898-1964)

Potter / Sculptor / Painter. Born in Nottingham in January 1898. The daughter of Herbert Ludlow Crofts and Dora Maria Victoria Hubbert. Her father was an insurance official. Both her parents originated from Derbyshire, where they were married in 1889. They had three daughters. Stella, the youngest, was raised in Ilford, Essex. She suffered health problems as a child after contracting tuberculosis, and, as a result, was taught at home. But she was later able to study at the London County Council Central School of Arts and Crafts between 1916 and 1922. There, she developed an interest in modelling in clay. She then spent a year (1922-23) at the Royal College of Art, studying pottery and sculpture. Returned to the family home in Ilford and set up her own studio with a kiln. Remained in Essex for much of the rest of her life, active until shortly before her death in Essex, aged 66.

Active through five decades, Crofts developed an acute interest in sculpting animals, wild, domestic, native and foreign. Had a particular interest in birds, but also painted portraits of animals and humans. Was an avid bird watcher, but also studied at the Natural History Museum and the London Zoo. Did portrait models of various dogs in pottery. Also produced studies of, for example, avocets, elephants, giraffes, penguins, monkeys, foxes, herons and badgers. Preferred to represent animals in naturalistic groups. Modelled all her own pieces, then glazed and fired them in her own kiln, which her father had initially helped to set up. Worked in modelled pottery, modelled glazed pottery, matt celadon glaze, vellum matt glaze, semi-matt glaze, biscuit stoneware, satin matt glaze, semi-porcelain, earthenware, glazed stoneware, terracotta, bone china and watercolours. Produced panels in relief, groups, portraits, bookends, statuettes and ashtrays.

By the 1930s, Crofts was based in Billericay, Essex, at the Deerbank Studio, where she remained for over three decades. She exhibited her work successfully for around 40 years. She showed over 210 works at the Society of Women Artists between 1923 and 1963. Those included: Giraffe Family (modelled glazed pottery), Barbary Sheep (vellum matt glaze), Penguin Panel (stoneware) and Purple Heron Group (pottery). Elected an Associate of the Society in 1924, and a Member between 1925 and 1963. Works sold there for between £1 and £16 each. Exhibited other works at the Royal Academy in 1925 and in 1952-62, in the first and the final years of her career. In 1926 she held a small exhibition of ceramic pieces at the Redfern Gallery. Also exhibited with the Royal Society of Miniature Painters, including in 1926 when she showed glazed pottery animals at the Arlington Gallery. In 1927, Crofts held an exhibition of pottery animals along with watercolours by Kate Wilcox at the Chester Gallery, Eaton Square, London.

Elsewhere, Crofts exhibited at the Women's International Art Club, with the Arts and Crafts Exhibition Society, at the Craft Centre of Great Britain and in Paris, Milan, Toronto, Dunedin and Venice. Awarded bronze and silver medals in Paris in 1925. Elected an Associate of the Royal Society of Miniature Painters. Her Pelicans, a

pottery group, was illustrated in Apollo in the late 1920s. Other works were illustrated in, for example, The Queen (Goose and Pelicans, 1951) and Decorative Art. Executed a study of the Princesses Elizabeth and Margaret Rose with their dogs, in pottery, which was also illustrated in The Queen magazine. Official purchasers of her work included the Museum of Decorative Art, Milan (one work), the Manchester Art Gallery (two works) and the Hanley Museum, Stoke-on-Trent (two works). Works purchased and presented to the Victoria & Albert Museum, London.

CROWLE, EILEEN (1903-60)

Modeller / Book Illustrator / Poster Artist. Born in Cork, Ireland. The daughter of Captain Joseph N. Crowle, an engineer commander in the Royal Navy, and Beatrice. Her father originated from Cornwall, her mother from Australia. Had at least one brother, Bedford. Raised in Cork and in Devonport, Devon. Educated at the La Retraite Convent, Weston-super-Mare and in Switzerland and Germany. Studied at the Bath School of Art and at the Lausanne School of Art. Awarded Royal Drawing Society Honours Certificates. Exhibited her work at the Royal Drawing Society and with the Bath Society of Artists. Held a one-woman show at the Pump Room, Bath. Her Morning, Afternoon and Evening was illustrated in La Revue du Vrai et du Beau. Produced other decorative work, including The Days of the Week (decorations). Illustrated various children's verses and stories and Songs for Michael for Heath Cranton Ltd. Elected a Member of the Forum Club and of the Bath and County Ladies' Club. Based in Bath for part of her career. Died in Kensington, London aged 56.

CRUMP, JANE - SEE ABLETT, J.

CUBITT, EDITH ALICE (1873-1958)

Painter / Illustrator. Born and raised in Deptford, London. The daughter of Herbert C. Cubitt and Kate. Her father, who originated from Norfolk, was a clerk to the Colonial Brothers. Her mother originated from Surrey. One of at least four children (Percy, Herbert, Archibald and Edith). Studied at the Goldsmiths' College of Art, London. Awarded bronze and silver medals in the National Competition of Schools of Art, South Kensington, and prizes in the W. Lee Hankey Exhibition and at the Royal Institute of Oil Painters. During her career, she was based at Brockley, Waverley, High Wycombe and Pembury, Kent. Died at Pembury, aged 85. Produced book illustrations, flower paintings, portraits and miniatures. Illustrated for publishers including Blackie, Ernest Nister, Cassell and the Oxford University Press. Queen Mary purchased her painting The Old Rose Bush. Exhibited her work, including at the Royal Academy (1905-54), the Society of Women Artists (1915-29), the Royal Institute of Oil Painters, the Royal Institute of Painters in Watercolours, the Paris Salon and in Liverpool and Birmingham. Exhibited works included: Edward, My Son, Robert in the Looking Glass, Spring is Here and Madonna Lilies. In 1912 she married George Frow Andrews in London. A Professor of Music, he was 40 at that time, she was 38. They had at least one son. Works in the Victoria & Albert Museum, London.

CUNDELL, HELENA ALICE (1891-1975)

Sculptor. Born in Norwich, Norfolk in July 1891. The daughter of William Harding Scott (b.1862) and Eliza Alice Liggett (b.1861). Educated at Polham Hall. Studied at the Slade School, London. Initially worked in St John's Wood, London. Produced portrait works in bronze. Exhibited at the Royal Academy (1929-62). Exhibited works included: Jane Huxley (head, bronze), Denis (head, bronze) and Katherine, Daughter of Lt Col. J.W. Saunders (head, bronze). In 1920 she married musician Henry Edric Arnold Cundell (1893-1961). He originated from London and died in Hertfordshire. They had one son, Norman Scott Cundell, who became an engineer. Helena died in Suffolk, aged 84. Also sometimes Alice Helena.

CURREY, ESME (active 1910s-1950s)

Painter / Etcher. Born in Kensington, London. Educated privately, and in London and Dresden. Studied at the Slade School, London. Also, in Melbourne, Australia under Max Meldrum, and at the Goldsmiths' College of Art, London under Stanley Anderson, R.A. Based mainly in London during her career, including at the Duke of Sussex Studios in Uxbridge Road. Became an artist in pencil, an etcher and a painter in tempera. Subjects included landscapes and buildings. Exhibited at the Royal Hibernian Academy (1940), the Royal Academy (1910-49), the Society of Women Artists (1949-50), the Royal Society of British Artists and the Royal Society of Painter-Etchers & Engravers. Also, with the Senefelder Club, with the United Artists and elsewhere. Exhibited works included: Evening, Alfriston (etching), The Haunted Barn (etching), Old Junk Shop, Chelsea (etching) and St Nicholas, Cole Abbey (etching). Elected an Associate of the Royal Society of Painter-Etchers

& Engravers (1937). Elected a Member of the Ridley Art Club and of the Campden Hill Club. Possibly Esme Mary E. Currey who was born in March 1881, and died in Kensington in June 1973, aged 92. Records are inconclusive.

CURTOIS, ELLA ROSE (1860-1944)

Sculptor. Born in Branston, Lincolnshire. The daughter of Atwell Curtois and Anne Henrietta. Her father was the rector at Branston, but died in 1868 when Ella was still a child. Her mother, who originated from Herefordshire, raised at least 10 children (Margaret, Lisle, Florence, Daniel, Ella, Huntley, Louise, Algernon, Mathilde and Mary) in Bedford. She is listed as a landowner so evidently had money of her own. All the children were well educated. Lisle became a mechanical engineer, Huntley became a clerk in holy orders. Ella became a sculptor, and Mary (Henrietta Dering Curtois, d.1929) became a painter. Mary exhibited at the Royal Academy (1887-92) and the Society of Women Artists (1887-1928). Ella produced portrait and genre works in marble and terracotta. She exhibited at the Royal Academy (1885-97) and the Paris Salon. Exhibited works included: Prayer (statue, terracotta), Bust of a Lady and Child Playing at Marbles (statue, marble). During her early career, Ella was based at Washingborough Manor near Lincoln, but died in Paris.

CUST, EMMELINE MARY ELIZABETH (1867-1955)

Sculptor. Born at Denton Hall, Denton, Lincolnshire in August 1867. The daughter of Sir William E. Welby Gregory and Victoria Stuart Wortley. In 1893 she married Henry John Cockayne Cust (1862-1917) in London. He was editor of the Pall Mall Gazette. The marriage was reputed to be an unhappy one for Cust, though Emmeline was always devoted to her husband. After his death, she edited a small volume of his poems. Emmeline studied sculpture, possibly in London. Produced busts, memorials and monuments in marble, wood, bronze and silvered bronze. Exhibited her work, including at the Royal Academy (1906 & 1927), in Birmingham, Liverpool and Manchester, and in Paris. Exhibited works included: Joan, Daughter of Sir Charles Welby, Bt. (bust). Produced a memorial to her husband, a portion of which was exhibited at the Royal Academy in 1927. The 'recumbent effigy' was part of the original model for the marble monument which was sited at Belton in Lincolnshire. Other works included a memorial tablet to Adelbert, Earl Brownlow in coloured marbles, and a memorial in gilded wood to

Victoria, Lady Welby. Based at Hyde Park Gate, London during her career. Died in London. Signed herself Nina Cust or Mrs Henry Cust.

CUTNER, EFFIE S. - SEE SMITH, E.S.

D

DABIS, ANNA (1847-1927)

Sculptor. Although born in Germany, Dabis spent a considerable part of her life (more than 45 years) in England. She moved to England sometime before 1881 and worked as a teacher. However, she also studied sculpture at the Royal College of Art, London under Eduoard Lanteri. She spent part of her career in London but later lived at South Fleet, Kent, where she died, aged 80. She was evidently a strong, independent woman who lived mostly alone and supported the suffragettes. Her sister, Therese, was a Classics scholar at Newnham College, Cambridge in the early 1880s and later worked as a lecturer. Dabis produced statuettes, medals, busts and heads in bronze. Exhibited 10 works at the Royal Academy (1888-95), including Ecco la Principessa (statuette), Sweet Seventeen (bust, bronze), Emperor Frederick (medal) and Treasure Trove (statuette). Other works included a head of Lanteri. Dabis was still active in 1911, aged 64.

DALE, GERTRUDE (1851-1927)

Sculptor / Engraver. Born in Norwood, Surrey. Raised in Surrey, Cheshire and Watford. The daughter of John B. Brown, a shipbroker and traveller, and Maria. One of at least seven children, possibly the eldest. By 1871 she was already acting as a governess. In mid-1875 she married Robert Dale (b.1844), who also originated from Surrey. He was a Secretary. The couple had at least four sons and two daughters, born between 1872 and 1884, the last born in the same year that Robert Dale died. The dates of birth of the children suggest that either Dale had been married previously and already had children, or that the couple had some children before they married. Robert Dale died in 1884, aged 40. After his death, Gertrude lived in various places, including Islington, Hampstead and Melplash, Dorset. Interestingly, it is only after Dale's death that Gertrude describes herself on census recordings as an artist in mezzotint and engraver. Possibly exhibited at the Society of Women Artists in 1875, showing Left by the Wind (price £10). Certainly exhibited at the Society of Women Artists in 1898, showing Kitty (price £10). Also exhibited a small number of works at the Royal Academy (1892-1910). Contributed bronze figures to the 1910 Arts and Crafts Exhibition Society exhibition. Other exhibited works included: Lead, Kindly Light (after A.E. Emslie), Awakened Memories (after G. Sheridan Knowles) and Dawn: Design for a Castle Fountain (statuette, bronze). Gertrude died in Middlesex, aged 76.

DAMER, THE HON. MRS ANNE SEYMOUR (1748-1828)

Sculptor. Anne Seymour Conway. One of Britain's most successful and accomplished female sculptors, and one of its earliest. Awarded a sizeable space in Mrs Ellet's Women Artists in All Ages and Countries, London, Richard Bentley, 1859, and in E. Beresford Chancellor's The Lives of the British Sculptors, London, Chapman & Hall, 1911. Both note that Mrs Damer was the only child of the Hon. Henry Seymour Conway, who became a General and later a Field-Marshal, and Caroline, Countess of Ailesbury. Caroline was a cultivated and artistic lady who was the daughter of Colonel Campbell of Mamore. Anne was born at Coomb Bank, Tunbridge, Kent, in whose church she would be buried. Lived with relatives for much of her early childhood because her father was constantly away. Lived for part of the time with her godfather and cousin, Horace Walpole. Took an early interest in sculpture, and began producing crude works whilst still young. Beresford Chancellor expresses the opinion that it was her class and wealth that then enabled her to be taught, and if she had been of lower class, she would not have progressed. She received formal tuition between 1765 and 1767. Also studied under sculptor Guiseppe Cerrachi who was based in England from 1773, and studied sculpting in marble under Bacon. In 1767 she married the Hon. John Damer, eldest son of the first Lord Milton. It was a childless and unhappy marriage which ended after nine years, when Damer shot himself in 1776, deep in debt. However, Anne began to produce works of note seven years into the marriage.

After her husband's death, Anne began to travel, to Europe, renewing her studies in sculpture, studying the European greats. She also became keen on politics, joining the Whig party. Produced busts of her friends and groups of animals. Executed studies of Lady Elizabeth Foster, later Duchess of Devonshire (in the collection of the Duke of Devonshire) and Viscountess Melbourne (in the possession of Earl Cowper). Of those two busts, Erasmus Darwin of Botanical Garden fame wrote:

Long with soft touch shall Damer's chisel charm;
With grace delight us and with beauty warm;
Foster's fine form shall hearts unborn engage
And Melbourne's smile enchant another age.
Damer also executed studies of Miss Farren, later Lady Derby, another of her friends, and of Sir Joseph Banks (in the British Museum). Also, one of Nelson, one of Fox, one of Napoleon, and one of her father, General Conway. Walpole particularly admired her Osprey Eagle. Mrs Damer presented Walpole with her two kittens in marble. Also executed two masks on Henley Bridge representing The Thame and the Isis. Beresford Chancellor notes, however, that some of her works were less successful, such as her George III in the Register Office of Scotland at Edinburgh.

Other works by Damer included a bust of Paris in marble, and a bust of Miss Farren as Thalia. Also, a bust of Mrs Siddons as The Tragic Muse. A bust of Nelson (one of at least three made) in bronze was sent by her, at the suggestion of Sir Alexander Johnston, to the King of Tanjore. Mrs Ellet considered Damer's best work to be done after 1780 in marble and terracotta. For the Duke of Richmond, husband of her half-sister, she executed a group of sleeping dogs in marble, with another for Queen Charlotte. Damer presented a bust of herself to the Florentine Gallery in 1778. During her lifetime, Mrs Damer was accused of receiving help in her work from Cerrachi, but that was always denied. Beresford Chancellor also dismisses the suggestion, describing her as a 'brilliant amateur' (p.210) whose work easily equalled that of her forebears. Chancellor adds that neither Cerrachi nor Bacon were available to assist Mrs Damer at the time of the accusations, so could not have done so. There is a suggestion that Damer was treated unkindly by some because she was a woman. Women sculptors were still a rarity at that time, and were open to prejudices no longer tolerated today. Damer exhibited 32 of her works at the Royal Academy (as an Honorary Exhibitor) between 1784 and 1818. Those included her bust of Charles James Fox.

When Walpole died in 1797, he left his home, Strawberry Hill, to Mrs Damer for her lifetime. She lived and entertained there until 10 years before her own death, upon which it was to be given over to Lord Waldegrave. She then bought York House as a summer residence, the birthplace of Queen Anne. She also had a winter house in Park Lane, London. Damer, in turn, sat for Sir Joshua Reynolds (in 1762 and 1773). Angelica Kauffman painted her portrait, part of which was engraved and published by R. Cooper in 1810. Richard Cosway painted a miniature of her in 1794, and a full-length. Cerrachi sculpted Damer as The Muse of Sculpture, which was given to the British Museum. Damer died in May 1828, aged 79. She was buried with her apron and tools. Her small sculpture of two dogs intertwined is kept at Goodwood House, near Chichester, Sussex.

DARLINGTON, FRANCES TAPLIN (1880-1940)

Sculptor. Born in Headingley, Leeds in February 1880. Was originally named Fanny, but subsequently called herself Frances. The daughter of Latimer John De Vere Darlington and Ellen Emma. Her father, a solicitor, originated from Shipley, Yorkshire. Her mother originated from Paddington, London. She had at least one older brother, Hugh, also born in Headingley. Raised in Yorkshire, in Ilkley for part of the time. Studied in London, at the Slade School and at the Royal College of Art, South Kensington. As a student, in the early 1900s, Frances lodged at Alexander House, Kensington Gore with a considerable number of other women students of art and music, including Nina Oliver, Mary Buzzard and Gertrude Lindsay. She worked in London thereafter, using The Garden Studio at Edith Villas, Kensington for part of the time. But also spent time in Yorkshire, at Ilkley and Harrogate. Died in Oxted, Surrey in September 1940, leaving a small estate.

Darlington produced statuettes, groups, medallions, garden statues, busts and decorative panels. Worked in various materials including bronze and copper. Exhibited her work, including at the Royal Academy (1901-09), the Society of Women Artists (1900 & 1928), the Paris Salon, the New Gallery, with the Arts and Crafts Society, at the Leeds City Art Gallery, the Walker Art Gallery, Liverpool and in New Zealand and America. Exhibited works included: Confidences (medallion, copper), The Unforeseen (group), Isis (bust) and Sir Perceval and The Vision of the Holy Grail (panel). Her life-size statue Little Sea Maiden was acquired by the Leeds City Art Gallery. She worked on various important projects during her career, which covered at least four decades, from the early 1900s into the 1930s. Executed 15 large and impressive panels for St Wilfrid's Church, Harrogate as well as various private and war memorials. Also executed a 70-feet frieze for the Opera House, Harrogate, and a number of bronze busts of celebrities for public buildings. Executed a bronze statue of Yorkshireman and writer Joseph Priestley. One of her earliest works was a portrait medallion of Maud Palmer, Superintendent of Alexander

House. Works illustrated in Colour and the Illustrated London News. In November 2003 a rare showing of some of her work took place at the Mercer Gallery, Harrogate.

DARNELL, JANET - SEE LEACH, J.

DARRY, DOROTHY HELEN
(1899-post-1972)
Jeweller / Metalworker / Embroideress / Designer. Born in Liverpool in January 1899. The daughter of William Minto Darry (d.1939) and Sarah Ellen P. Harris, both of whom originated from Liverpool. Possibly their only child. Her father was a commercial traveller in timber. Dorothy was raised in Liverpool and remained there for much of her life and career. Had a private education. Exhibited her work at the Walker Art Gallery, Liverpool, at Southport and at the British Empire Exhibition of 1924.

DARWIN, ELINOR MARY (1879-1954)
Painter / Decorative Artist / Book Illustrator / Woodcut Artist. Born in Co. Limerick, Ireland. The daughter of W.T. Monsell, a Resident Magistrate. Spent her childhood in Ireland. Taught by a governess. Her cousin was artist Charles Furse, who recognised her early talent and offered criticism of her sketchbooks. He encouraged her to study the work of Charles Keene in old volumes of Punch, and Randolph Caldecott's children's books. In 1896, aged 17, she was awarded the Slade Scholarship, which brought her to London to study at the Slade School. Became a painter in oils and watercolours, including of portraits, figures and landscapes, a painter on silk and of fans, a woodcut artist and a book illustrator. Initially based in London. Began exhibiting her work from at least 1899. Exhibited at the New English Art Club (from 1899), the International Society of Sculptors, Painters & Gravers, the Beaux Art Gallery, the Royal Hibernian Academy (1924-25), the Royal Academy (1907), the Women's International Art Club and the Royal Scottish Academy (1899). Exhibited works included: Hair Brushing, A Girl Sleeping - Study, Death and the Woman and Nuns in Contemplation.

In 1906 Elinor married Bernard Richard Meirion Darwin (1876-1961) in Chelsea. He was a barrister and writer who originated from Downe, Kent, and was related to the eminent Charles Darwin. The couple lived in Chelsea, but also in Cambridge and, latterly, at Downe. Elinor died at Downe, aged 75. They had at least two children, Ursula and Robert. Elinor continued to work. Books illustrated by her included: Alice

M.C. Smith, Tom Tug and Others (1898), Walter de la Mare, The Three Mulla Mulgars (1910), Bernard R.M. Darwin, The Tale of Mr Tootleoo (1925) and Every Idle Dream (1948). She also contributed to periodicals including The Dome, The Venture and The Quarto. She was responsible for designing the cover of the handbills and publications of the Irish Literary Society. Works also appeared in Drawing and Design (May and June 1921) and in Country Life (April 1921). A Member of the English Speaking Union. Noted in Herbert Furst's The Modern Woodcut, London, John Lane, 1924). Furst includes a reproduction of her engraving The Bath, which he describes as 'well designed and well cut' (p.133). Furst also notes that Mrs Darwin first instructed Gwen Raverat, a relation. Also noted in Mahony, Latimer & Folmsbee, Illustrators of Children's Books 1744-1945, Boston, The Horn Book Inc., 1947 and in Janet Adam Smith, Children's Illustrated Books, London, Collins, 1948.

DAVEY, EDITH MARY (1867-1953)
Mural Decorator / Painter / Sculptor / Black & White Artist. Born in Chapel St Leonards, Lincolnshire. The daughter of Alfred James Davey, a farmer and landowner, and Frances Mary. One of at least seven children (Edith, Frank, Kate, Fanny, Percy, Adeline and Ethel), all raised in Lincolnshire. Kate became a buyer of drapery, Ethel became an assistant in a fur store, and Adeline became an art teacher. Edith studied at the Lincoln School of Art under A.G. Webster. During that time, she acted as governess to a local family. She then studied at the Royal College of Art, London under a studentship-in-training won in 1898, tenable for four years. During those four years, she studied mural decoration and portrait painting under Professor Gerald Moira. As a student in London, she won a silver medal for figure drawing and other prizes. Elected an Associate of the Royal College of Art in 1903. Remained in London thereafter, dying at Barnes. Became a mural decorator, produced portrait and flower studies in oils, watercolours and chalk, including miniatures, the occasional sculpture in bronze and black & white drawings. Acted as a part-time special teacher of art under the London County Council between 1904 and 1932. Exhibited her work, including at the Royal Academy (1910-37), the Society of Women Artists (1918), the Paris Salon, the Royal Institute of Painters in Watercolours, the Royal Society of Miniature Painters and the Women's International Art Club. Exhibited works included: Paperweight (bronze), The Pageant Dress, His Eminence the

Late Cardinal Bourne and Vice Admiral Arthur O.B. Bromley. Elected an Associate of the Royal Society of Miniature Painters. Produced illustrations for a book published in New York.

DAVEY, ELSIE M. - SEE LINDSLEY-SIMS, E.M.

DAVIES, EMILY GRACE - SEE BARNSLEY, E.G.

DAVISON, MINNIE D. - SEE SPOONER, M.D.

DAWSON, EDITH BREAREY (1864-1929)
Painter / Craftswoman. Better known as the wife and co-worker of craftsman Nelson Ethelred Dawson (1859-1941). Was, however, an outstanding painter and craftworker in her own right. Whilst Nelson Dawson remains comparatively well known today, Edith has all but vanished. She was Edith Brearey Robinson, born in Croydon, Surrey. Her mother was Mary A. Robinson who originated from Dewsbury, Yorkshire. Records do not confirm who her father was, and she appears to have been raised by someone other than family in Yorkshire. By the age of 18, she is listed as living with her mother, a teacher, at West Bank, Scarborough in Yorkshire, and her two sisters, Marian (or Mary) and Ellen (or Nellie). Evidently had artistic leanings, and possibly some art tuition since she began to exhibit at the Royal Academy in 1890 whilst still Miss Robinson of West Bank, Scarborough. Eventually showed nine works there between 1890 and 1896, and a further six works between 1911 and 1919, mostly flower and landscape paintings such as Evening on a Welsh Estuary, A Garden by the River and Orange Lilies.

In 1893 Edith married painter and craftsman Nelson Dawson in Scarborough and subsequently moved to London. Under his direct influence, Edith learnt the art of enamelling. Dawson was the son of baker and confectioner Edwin Dawson (1830-90) and Emma Annie Harris (1837-88). In the early 1880s, Nelson spent time living in Scarborough, acting as shop assistant to Haydn Hare, a fine art publisher (and possibly a relation). Hare, like Dawson, originated from Stamford, Lincolnshire. Dawson initially studied architecture, but in the mid-1880s studied painting at the South Kensington school. However, by the early 1890s, he had begun to study metalwork and enamelling under Alexander Fisher (1864-1936). On their marriage, Edith and Nelson formed a design partnership producing decorative metalwork,

enamelling and jewellery. At their Chelsea home, Mulberry House, they each had a studio. A photograph of the Dawsons stood in one of their studios appeared in the Architectural Review in 1897.

Since Edith exhibited at the Royal Academy as late as 1919, she evidently kept up her painting, using the Wentworth Studios in London, though much of her time was clearly spent on craftwork. She also exhibited her art work at the New English Art Club (1890-94) and the Royal Society of British Artists (1889-91). With Nelson, she exhibited an additional two works at the Royal Academy in 1917, by which time they were based at Staithes House, Chiswick Mall. They also used Swan House, Chiswick Mall and St Peter's Square, Hammersmith as addresses during their careers. Although Nelson was elected a Member of the New English Art Club, Edith apparently was not.

Whilst most of Edith's early exhibits were paintings, from at least 1894 she began to exhibit metalwork and enamels, sometimes under her own name, but also jointly with Nelson, so closely did they work. Over a period of at least 23 years (1894-1917), the Dawsons contributed to a wide variety of exhibitions and executed a considerable number of commissions. Some of their earlier projects included a casket (c.1896) in silver and enamel for the Plumber's Company, executed with architect W.D. Caroe. Also, a silver and enamel casket which was presented by the City of Oxford to the Prince of Wales in 1897. They also executed the arms of Trinity College, Cambridge in bronze and champleve enamel (c.1917). One of their most significant commissions was for a silver and enamel trowel which was used by Queen Victoria in laying the foundation stone of the Victoria & Albert Museum, South Kensington in 1899. The trowel was illustrated in The Studio, Vol.22, April 1901, p.173. One of their larger caskets, made of bronze, silver, enamel and precious stones, was presented by the Corporation of Capetown to Major-General R.S.S. Baden-Powell. Perhaps surprisingly, given the exceptionally high standard of their work, a casket executed jointly by the Dawsons, to be presented to the Speaker by the Corporation of Carlisle, was rejected for exhibition at the Royal Academy. Some of their work, however, was acquired by the South Kensington Museum.

Despite their evidently demanding commitments, and their widespread artistic success, the Dawsons found time to contribute to numerous exhibitions. For example, Edith contributed to the 1901 Glasgow Exhibition along with other leading craftsmen and women of the day including Jessie Newbery and Ann Macbeth. The Dawsons also jointly contributed to the Arts and Crafts Exhibition Society exhibitions, including in 1896 and 1903. In 1900, some of their jewellery was shown at the Fine Art Society galleries in New Bond Street, London, including a gold necklace set with green and blue enamels titled Forget-Me-Not. In late 1905 they held an exhibition of jewellery, enamel and metalwork at the Goupil Gallery Annexe. Other work appeared at the Royal Scottish Academy (1902), at the Grosvenor Gallery, the Leeds City Art Gallery and at the exhibitions of the International Society of Sculptors, Painters & Gravers.

The design and production of jewellery proved highly successful for the Dawsons, with every piece entirely unique and created jointly. There are indications that Ellen C. Woodward was influenced by, and possibly taught by, the Dawsons. Numerous examples of their work appeared in The Studio, including their jewellery, from at least 1896. Those included a triptych in enamel, silver and iron, in which they were assisted by C. Craig, C. Moxey and W. Spencer, shown in Vol. 28, 1903, p.124. In 1895 The Studio offered an entire article, A Chat with Mr and Mrs Nelson Dawson (Vol.6, pp.173-178). At that time, they were still at Mulberry House, and the correspondent gave a detailed description of the interior, with its copper ornamentation, decorative firescreens, oil paintings and work studios. Flowers and animals were noted as a chief source of design inspiration. In 1901, The Studio gave a follow-up article, Some Recent Work by Nelson and Edith Dawson, by Edward F. Strange (Vol.22, April, pp.169-175). Work being carried out at that point included jewellery set with semi-precious stones, enamel buttons, boxes with steel and silver fittings and a copper altar plate.

Edith's career in enamelling, however, drew to a halt in around 1917, largely due to overwork and the noxious fumes she had inhaled over more than two decades. But she was able to carry on with her painting until at least 1919. She also found time to develop her interest in colour-printing. She studied at the School of Colour-Printing in St Peter's Square, Hammersmith in around 1912 under Nelson Dawson and William Lee Hankey. Nelson Dawson first made his name as an oil and watercolour painter before taking up the decorative arts. With Lee Hankey, he ran the Hammersmith school with considerable success. One of Edith's prints, On the Suffolk Coast, was illustrated in The Studio, Vol.70, 1917, p.108 in an article The Art of Colour-Printing by Malcolm C. Salaman. After 1919, Edith began to retreat

from public view and died 10 years later, aged 64. Nelson Dawson lived another 12 years, dying at Staithes House in October 1941, aged 82. The Dawsons had two daughters, Rhoda Nelson Dawson (1897-1992) and Mary Edith Nelson Dawson (1899-1980). Rhoda became a painter and exhibited at the Royal Academy (1924-61). Edith's sister, Nellie, also had some success as an artist, exhibiting her work at the Royal Academy and the New English Art Club in the 1880s and 1890s. The Dawsons were noted in M.H. Spielmann's British Sculpture and Sculptors of To-day (London, Cassell & Co. Ltd) in 1901. Nelson Dawson was elected a Member of the Art Workers' Guild from 1891. Examples of their work can be found in the Cheltenham Collections.

DAWSON, GEORGINA F. - SEE MURE, G.F.

DAWSON, GLADYS (1909-93)
Artist / Illustrator / Designer. Born in Castleton, Rochdale. The daughter of Ernest Jacques Dawson, a bootmaker, and Emily. Educated at the Castleton Villa High School, Rochdale. Studied at the Heatherley's School of Art, London under Ronald Ossory Dunlop, Frederick Whiting and Paul Drury. Became an artist in watercolours, pastels and black & white. Also a children's author and illustrator. Produced designs for textiles and greetings cards. Subjects included flowers, birds, animals and landscapes. Active for over 53 years. Travelled at home and abroad to paint. Exhibited her work, including at the Royal College of Art, the Royal West of England Academy, with the Lancashire Artists, Preston, at the Walker Art Gallery, Liverpool and with the Royal Institute of Painters in Watercolours. Also exhibited with the Society of Women Artists, showing 159 works between 1939 and 1992. Those included: The Open Lock, Pansies (watercolour), Elephant Crossing Kenya (watercolour) and The Wood Urchin (watercolour). Elected an Associate of the Society of Women Artists (1953-55) and a Member (1956-93). Acted as Honorary Treasurer of the Society (1973-76), as Vice President (1977-82) and as President (1983-85). Elected an Associate of the Royal College of Art in 1943 and a Member in 1946. Elected a Fellow of the Royal Society of Arts. Spent some time in London, Denbighshire and Surrey during her career. Died in Surrey, aged 84. Records suggest that Dawson became Mrs Woodruff, possibly marrying a Ronald Woodruff in 1962 in Bromley, Kent.

DAWSON, MARY ELIZABETH (1870-1945)

Painter / Decorative Artist / Embroideress. Born in Skipton, Yorkshire. The daughter of John Bell. Educated at the Salts School and at the Girls' High School, both Shipley, Yorkshire. In 1892 she married Charles Frederick Dawson (1864-1949) in Yorkshire. He was a designer and craftworker who originated from Rillington, Yorkshire. He was also Headmaster of the Schools of Art of Bingley, Nelson and Accrington. Mary may have been taught by Dawson. For much of their marriage, the couple lived at Eaton Bank, Accrington, Lancashire. Mary produced paintings in watercolours and gouache, embroideries and worked as a decorative artist on wood. She was awarded silver and bronze medals for her work, including an international bronze medal. Exhibited her work, including at the Royal Academy (1916-32), the Society of Women Artists (1928-30), in Manchester, Liverpool, Leeds and Bradford, at the Victoria & Albert Museum, London, in Stockholm, at The Hague, in New Zealand and in Canada. Exhibited works included: Book-Keeper's Corner, The White Corridor, An Old Maid's Garden and Old Windows. Charles Dawson also exhibited at the Royal Academy. Purchasers of Mary's work included the Manchester City Art Gallery. One of her embroidered bedspreads and a painted bowl were illustrated in The Studio. Other works were illustrated in The Studio Year Book. Examples of her painted bowls and platters were illustrated in La Revue Moderne. Mary was elected a Member of the Bradford Arts Club and of the Attic Club, Manchester. Mary died in Lancashire, aged 75. Possibly of the same family was artist Robert Arthur Dawson, born in Bingley, Yorkshire.

DAY, LILY (1870-1957)

Metalworker / Painter. Records suggest that Lily Day was Jane Elizabeth Day. She appears to have called herself Lily on one British census, but calls herself Jane Elizabeth on the others. She was, apparently, born in Liverpool and was the daughter of William Day and Margaret, both of whom originated from Liverpool. Her father was the manager of the Loan and Discount Insurance Company. One of at least five children, all raised in Liverpool. As a young child, Lily went to live with her uncle and aunt, Robert and Mary Day who were based in West Derby. Robert Day was a bank cashier and later a bank manager, and appeared to have no children of his own. Lily remained with the couple until she was at least 40 years of age and working as an independent artist and designer. Sometime between 1891 and 1901 Lily studied at the Liverpool School of Applied Arts Art Sheds, and later at the Mount Street School of Art. She specialised in metalwork and enamelling, and became a teacher of both at the Art Sheds. One of her enamelling students was Frances Macdonald.

Day appears to have been predominantly active before 1910. She died in Liverpool in early 1957, aged 86. Latterly, she lived with her sister, Edna Mary (d.1954) who, like Lily, never married. No surviving examples of her work have been found to date. Her work, though not of any quantity, was certainly well received in the early 1900s. In 1902, The Studio, Vol.24, p.256 illustrated examples of her enamelling, and she contributed items in silver to the First International Studio Exhibition of 1901 / 02. Also in 1902, she contributed a case of enamels to the Turin Exhibition as part of the 'Scottish Section' which was overseen by Frances Newbery (of the Glasgow School of Art) and Charles Rennie Mackintosh. In 1903, Lily contributed silver and enamel work to the Walker Art Gallery, Liverpool annual exhibition, and did so on other occasions, including in 1907 along with Elinor Halle, Annie Steen and others. In 1906, The Studio, Vol.38, p.251 illustrated a necklace designed and executed by Day.

DEALY, JANE MARY (b.1856)

Painter / Illustrator. Born in West Derby, Lancashire. The daughter of John Richard Dealy (1828-93) and Jane Anderson (1830-1911). Her father was a bank manager who, like her mother, originated from Ireland. One of at least seven children (Jane, Mary, Alice, Ellen, Maud, John and Edith). Spent much of her life and career in London. Studied in London at the Slade School and at the Royal Academy schools. Won a silver medal at the Royal Academy schools and a prize for the best drawing of the year. Subsequently lived with her parents, working as an artist, until she married Walter Llewellyn Lewis in 1887. Remained in London after her marriage, working as a painter and illustrator. Illustrated a number of books for children, including Sixes and Sevens, The Land of Little People, Children's Prayers and Children's Hymns. In 1901 her picture A Dutch Bargain was etched and engraved. Her Hush-a-Bye-Baby and Good-by Summer were published by Messrs De la Rue et Cie. Exhibited her work until at least the early 1900s, including at the Royal Academy (21 works, 1881-1903), the Royal Society of British Artists (1879-86) and the Royal Institute of Painters in Watercolours. Exhibited works included: Left Behind, Waiting for Somebody, The Last of the Roses, and There is a Change and I am Poor. Elected a Member of the Royal Institute of Painters in Watercolours.

DEAR, MARY E. (b.1833)

Painter / Illustrator. Born in London. The daughter of John Dear and Mary Hannah. In 1867 she married architect Robert Dennis Chantrell in London. He was some 40 years older than Mary, and died in 1872 in Surrey, after only around four years of marriage. They had one daughter, Marian, and lived for a time in Rottingdean, Sussex. Mary worked as an artist from at least 1848 and was still active in her 50s, in the 1880s. After her husband's death, she returned to London. Produced portrait and genre paintings. Also illustrated books, including Nathaniel Hawthorne, The Scarlet Letter (1859). Contributed to the Illustrated Times (1855, Christmas) and the Art Journal . Exhibited her work through Messrs Colnaghi, Pall Mall East. Also exhibited at the Royal Academy (1848-59) and the Royal Society of British Artists (1859-67). Exhibited works included: The Sisters, Playfellows, Early Impressions and Thinking. A Portrait. Completed at least one portrait of Chantrell (c.1859). Later, in 1881, Mary is also listed as an author.

DEARMER, JESSIE MABEL PRICHARD (1872-1915)

Writer / Illustrator / Dramatist. Known as Mabel. Born in Caernarvon, Wales. The daughter of Surgeon-Major William White and Selina. Studied at the Herkomer School at Bushey, Hertfordshire. In May 1892 she married Percy Dearmer (1867-1936) in Richmond, Yorkshire. They had two sons, Geoffrey (1893-1996) and Christopher (1894-1915), both born in Lambeth, London. Both Mabel and Percy Dearmer lead busy, active and successful lives. Percy was a student of Christ Church, Oxford and became a Church of England clergyman. Between 1901 and 1916 he acted as vicar of St Mary the Virgin, Primrose Hill, London. During the First World War, he served as Chaplain to the British Red Cross in Serbia. Mabel accompanied him and was attached to the Stobart Hospital Mission. She died of enteric fever in Serbia in July 1915.

Percy Dearmer had many interests and was Professor of Ecclesiastical Art at King's College, London. He was interested in church art and history in particular, but also wrote a number of books and pamphlets including The Parson's Handbook (published by Grant Richards, priced 3s 6d) and Body and Soul. In 1931 he edited Songs of Praise. Also devised The English Hymnal with contributions from Gustav Holst and Ralph Vaughan Williams. He lectured in India, and wrote for the short-lived Art Workers' Quarterly on such matters as church architecture and church vestments. In 1905 he delivered a paper on the representations of Christ in Art to the Church Crafts League at their annual meeting at Clifford's Inn, London. In 1916 Dearmer went on to marry Nancy Knowles (1889-1979) and had three more children, Gillian (b.1917), Anthony (b.1920) and Imogen (b.1923). Christopher Dearmer, a language student at Christ Church, Oxford, died of wounds during the First World War, in October 1915, shortly after the death of his mother, Mabel.

Although much has been written about Percy Dearmer, Mabel remains less well known, partly because of her early death. A diverse and talented artist, she illustrated children's books and produced bookplates and posters. She also wrote her own books for children, illustrating those in black & white and colour. Books illustrated by her included Roundabout Rhymes (London, Blackie & Son, 1898) which was advertised in The Studio magazine at a cost of 2s 6d. She was a friend of Laurence Housman, who noted her in his The Unexpected Years (1937). Mabel illustrated Housman's The Seven Young Goslings in 1899. Mabel worked on other literary endeavours, including Evelyn Sharp, Wymps (1897) and All the Way to Fairyland (1898). Also, The Noah's Ark Geography (1900), A Comedy of Tears (1904), A Child's Life of Christ (1906), NonPilgrim: a Play (1909) and The Dreamer: a Poetic Drama (1912). One of the very last books she worked on was Letters From a Field Hospital (1915). Contributed to the Yellow Book in 1896 and 1897. Works illustrated in The Studio, Vol.11, 1897, p.264. Noted in R.E.D. Sketchley, English Book Illustration of To-day, London, Kegan Paul & Co., 1903. Two of her bookplates were illustrated in Norna Labouchere, Ladies' Book-Plates, London, George Bell, 1895.

DE GREY, THE HON. MABEL (1855-1942)

Craftswoman. Mabel De Grey ran at least two successful woodcarving classes in London in the late nineteenth and early twentieth centuries, at St Saviour's, Pimlico and at Stepney. The classes were affiliated to the then successful Home Arts and Industries Association (founded 1884), and showed regularly at its annual exhibition, held at the Royal Albert Hall, London. The Association had the dual purpose of offering the working class man and woman the opportunity for creativity, and to offer a means of earning additional income. Although strictly amateur, like many other handcraft classes and industries of the period, Pimlico and Stepney thrived and flourished, achieving much during their lifetime. Mabel De Grey was responsible for the designs, which were then executed by her pupils. The classes adhered to a high standard of workmanship, producing highly decorative inlay work of a professional standard.

Mabel De Grey was born at St George Hanover Square, London into a privileged family. Her father was Thomas De Grey, fourth Baron Walsingham (1804-70), who was also a magistrate. Her mother was Emily Elizabeth Julia Thellusson (d.1879), the daughter of John Thellusson, second Baron Rendlesham. Mabel was one of at least eight children (Thomas, John, Emily, Beatrice, Mabel, Arnold, Robert and Elizabeth Odeyne (1862-1947, known as Odeyne)). The family lived in London, but also had a home, The Hall, at Merton Watton in Norfolk, where Mabel died during the Second World War. Exactly what training Mabel had in woodcarving is unclear. But by at least 1894 she was running the Pimlico and Stepney classes and was exhibiting their work at that year's Home Arts exhibition. Her sister Odeyne also produced designs for the classes, and in The Studio for July 1897 there are suggestions that more than one of Mabel's sisters was involved in woodcarving and assisted in the local classes. Emily and Beatrice De Grey, therefore, may also have been involved in local arts and crafts.

Mabel, however, was the driving force behind Pimlico and Stepney, though she never listed her work on any census recordings, presumably because she took no fee for her efforts, and because her high social status made working for money unacceptable. The classes did, however, offer her the opportunity to show her natural artistic talents. The Pimlico class had several leading craftsmen and women, including Edward Ford and John Reason, who became expert in the art of wood inlay. At Stepney, leading workers included Alfred Porter, William Beer, David Lord, Mary Ellice, H. Shaw and Charlotte Campion. The two classes exhibited regularly at the Home Arts exhibitions until at least 1903, and their work was reported regularly in The Studio magazine over a period of at least 10 years. Exhibits for 1894 included two carved settles with inlay decoration by Arthur Shaw and John Reason, which were illustrated in The Studio, Vol.3, August 1894, p.150. Also, a walnut tray with inlay decoration by T. Bray, worked to the design of Odeyne De Grey, illustrated in the same journal (p.151). Also, a walnut chest with inlay decoration, designed by Mabel and worked by Reason with a design of fungi and the words 'what God hath made, that call not thou unclean'.

The following year, in 1895, the Pimlico class showed a medicine cupboard designed by Mabel and inlaid with coloured woods by Reason. The cupboard, which won a gold cross at the Home Arts exhibition, was illustrated in The Studio, Vol.5, August 1895, p.171. At the 1896 Home Arts exhibition, the classes showed a writing table designed by the Countess of Lovelace (Mary Stuart Wortley) and decorated by Mabel. The table was also illustrated in The Studio, Vol.8, July 1896, p.100 along with at least five other designs by Mabel, executed by either Pimlico or Stepney. A shelf inlaid with a tree design, also shown at the 1896 Home Arts exhibition, worked by William Beer of Stepney, won a gold cross.

In her designs, Mabel De Grey took inspiration from a wide variety of sources, including animals, birds, figures, buildings, landscapes, townscapes, waves, clouds, fungi, flowers and trees. On one occasion, a seat was inlaid with a design based on an industrial landscape complete with tall chimneys belching out smoke. Two bookcases, illustrated in The Studio, Vol.26, July 1902, p.131, were decorated with designs based on Shakespeare and Walter Scott. All manner of wood items were decorated by the Pimlico and Stepney classes, including small boxes, frames, tables, seats, shelves, bookcases, settles, trays, chests, cupboards, children's furniture, panels and caskets. Occasionally, silver, copper and mother-of-pearl were incorporated into the design. In 1903, some of Mabel's designs were executed by a basket maker of Saxmundham, based on those in use in Normandy and Rome. One of Mabel's inlaid wood panels was illustrated in colour in The Studio, Vol.23, 1901, p.277, created to show the natural variations in the different woods used. Another of her designs, used to decorate an oak chest, was titled Scandal and showed a group of women sending gossip by birds. The chest was executed by John Reason and was shown at the 1899 Home Arts exhibition. A small cupboard, shown at the 1901 Home Arts exhibition, incorporated a design based on waves and clouds, whilst a casket, also shown at the 1901 exhibition, had a design based on poplar trees, as seen from the terrace of an Elizabethan manor house at Brympton in Somerset. Mabel's designs, and the work of the Pimlico and Stepney classes, were frequently praised in arts journals of the day. Whilst Mabel never married, Odeyne De Grey married a clergyman, Francis Henry Hodgson, and had children.

DELAHUNT, JENNIE H. (1877-post-1934)
Modeller / Sculptor. Born in Hanley, Staffordshire in April 1887, in the heart of pottery country. The daughter of Charles Delahunt, of the Inland Revenue, and Jane. One of at least six children (Reginald, Mary, Alice, Jane, Daisy and Charles). Raised in Hanley, Stockport and Prestwich, Lancashire. Studied at the Manchester Municipal School of Art. A gold and silver medallist in the National Competition of Schools of Art. Also awarded a Premier Princess of Wales Scholarship, the Lady Whitworth Scholarship and the Travelling Proctor Scholarship. Produced memorial tablets, busts and statuettes in bronze. Spent much of her career in Lancaster. Was art teacher at the Lancaster Municipal School of Art and at the local Girls' Grammar School. Exhibited her work occasionally, including at the Royal Academy (1908-19), in Liverpool and at the Manchester Art Gallery. Works included: The Captive (statuette), Whispers and Sea Breezes. Other works included a war memorial in bronze for Westfield at the disabled soldiers' memorial village which was unveiled by Earl Haig in 1926. Also, a bust of H.L. Storey. Her The Captive was illustrated in Academy. Works also illustrated in the Art Workers' Quarterly (Special Edition) and in the Ladies' Field. Elected an Associate of the Manchester Academy of Fine Arts. Still active into the 1930s.

DE LA MARE, CATHERINE – SEE DONALDSON, C.

D'ELBOUX, ELISE (1870-1956)
Painter / Illustrator. Born in Southampton in December 1870. The daughter of Walter D'Elboux (1839-96) and Mary Jane (1846-1907). Her father originated from Islington, her mother from Salisbury. Her father was an artist and engraver who worked for a time in an Ordnance Survey Office. Elise had at least one sibling, Emilia. Raised in Southampton, but later lived and worked in London. Died in Southend-on-Sea, Essex, aged 85, though her address at the time of her death was still Cromwell Road, London. Educated privately in Southampton. Studied at the Hartley School of Art, Southampton, in Paris and at the Regent Street Polytechnic School of Art, London. Awarded a Royal College of Art Training Scholarship (1896-99). A silver medallist and awarded other national awards. Produced paintings in oils and watercolours, studies in pastels and black & white drawings. Acted as teacher of drawing for the London County Council from 1908 to 1935. Also an assistant teacher at the Royal College of Art.

Experienced a long and productive career, and is listed as still active into the 1950s. Executed black & white illustrations for Girl's Realm, Century, Young Folks, Young England and others. Exhibited her work, including at the Royal College of Art Exhibition (1949), at the Renaissance Gallery, with Portsmouth and Hampshire Art Society, with Southampton Art Society and the Haslemere Art Society. Works in the Budapest Museum.

DEWAR, DE COURCEY LEWTHWAITE (1878-1959)
Painter / Engraver / Craftswoman. Born in Kandy, Ceylon. The daughter of John Lewthwaite Dewar, a tea planter, and Amelia Cochrane. In some records, her father is later listed as a pastor. One of at least three children (De Courcey, Margaret and Katie). Appears to have moved to Britain in 1891. Lived in Glasgow thereafter. Educated privately, and at the Girls' High School, Glasgow. Subsequently studied at the Glasgow School of Art and at the Central School of Arts and Crafts, London. Awarded a Diploma at the Glasgow School of Art. Became a talented and diverse artist. Produced paintings in watercolours and tempera, enamels and metalwork, lithographs, illuminations, illustrations and engravings. Established a studio in Glasgow producing metalwork and enamels, for which she became widely known and respected. Taught enamelling and metalwork at the Glasgow School for over 20 years. Based mainly in Hope Street and Woodside Place, Glasgow during her career. Distinctly Arts and Crafts in style and approach, her work reflected broader developments across Britain, but was also representative of what was being produced at the Glasgow School under its Principal, Francis Newbery. On a number of occasions, Dewar worked with silversmith P. Wylie Davidson (1870-1963) who had a studio close to hers.

Dewar's work was illustrated in leading journals of the day, including The Studio. For example, in January 1899 (Vol.15, p.280) the journal showed a lead mirror frame which she had exhibited at that year's annual exhibition of the Glasgow School of Art Club, held at the Glasgow Fine Art Institute. In 1900 (Vol.19, p.238 & p.241) The Studio illustrated two of her contributions to that year's Art Club exhibition, a jewel casket and a candle sconce. The School of Art Club was run by past and present students of the Glasgow School and competitions were held. In 1916 the same journal (Vol.66, January, p.287) illustrated a trophy cup and a casket which were shown at the 1915 Autumn Exhibition of the Walker Art

Gallery, Liverpool. In 1923 a Challenge Cup, for a girl's school hockey club in Boston, U.S.A, was illustrated in The Studio, Vol.86, September, p.161, designed and executed by Dewar. She was still, at that time, teaching at the Glasgow School. The Challenge Cup was one of her finest pieces, made in silver, set with moonstones and the school's crest in cloisonne enamels on each handle. The entire piece was made by hand. The Art Journal also illustrated her work on occasions. For example, in 1907 a casket in enamel and copper, made for the Scottish Guild of Handicraft by Dewar, was included in an article Scottish Arts and Crafts II (p.316).

Dewar exhibited extensively throughout her lengthy career, including with the Glasgow Society of Lady Artists' Club. In 1907, for example, she showed examples of her bookplates, yet another side to her talent. Some of those were illustrated in The Studio, Vol.42, January, p.317, in 1908. Exhibited at the 1902 Turin Exhibition in the Scottish Section. Exhibited at the 1925 Paris International Decorative Art exhibition, at Wembley, at the Toronto Annual Exhibition and with the Society of Scottish Artists. Dewar showed 10 works at the Royal Scottish Academy between 1903 and 1929, including a presentation casket in zinc, silver and enamel, a lithograph titled The Eternal Saki and an illuminated parchment titled Venite Adoremus. She showed 19 works at the Royal Glasgow Institute between 1901 and 1944 including Praise (enamel panel), Women Foresters at Work (black & white) and A Somerset Cottage (watercolour). Her folio of work included sketches of Ceylon. Contributed to the First International Studio Exhibition in 1901, showing two small tea caddies in copper and enamels. There was sometimes a noticeably Celtic edge to some of her work. Assisted fellow artist Dorothy Carleton Smyth in executing a quaich, or Scottish drinking bowl, for presentation by the Glasgow School to Sir Henry Craik on his retirement as Secretary of the Scottish Education Department. The quaich was illustrated in The Studio and the Art Journal in 1905.

Dewar travelled extensively throughout her life, and is recorded as visiting, among other places, New York (several times), Vermont, the Canary Islands, Boston and Montreal, Canada. Travelled from at least 1909, one of her last visits abroad taking place in 1935 when she was 75 years of age. During her career, she took on various roles of responsibility, some reflecting her interest in women's issues and her support for women in the arts. Elected executive of the National Council of Women, London and was President of the Glasgow branch. Elected President of the Soroptimist Club, Glasgow (1932-33). Was an Artist Member of the Central Committee for the Training and Employment of Women (Scottish branch). Also a Member and President of the Glasgow Society of Lady Artists' Club, a Member of the Literary Club, of the Century Club (Glasgow) and of the English Speaking Union, London. A Member of the Scottish Guild of Handicraft. Her history of the Glasgow Society of Lady Artists' Club was published in 1950. Other works of note by Dewar included enamel panels for the war memorial in St Cuthbert's Chapel, Edinburgh, along with cloisonne enamels executed for other war memorials. Possibly of the same family was artist Miss Margaret D. Dewar of Edinburgh, who exhibited one work at the Royal Scottish Academy in 1933.

DIBDIN, SARA BEATRICE (1874-1963)

Artist / Metalworker. Born in Edinburgh. The daughter of William Guthrie, LL.D., Sheriff Principal of Lanarkshire, and Charlotte. One of at least seven children. Educated in Glasgow and Carlisle. Studied at the Glasgow School of Art and at the Kunst Gewerbe Schule, Munich. Produced oil and watercolour paintings and repoussé metalwork. In 1901 she is listed as a teacher in music and painting. Later based in London and Liverpool. Began exhibiting her work in the 1890s. Exhibited one work, Malt Burn, St Monance (watercolour), at the Royal Glasgow Institute in 1897. Also, one work at the Royal Scottish Academy in 1898, and one work, November Sunshine, Kensington, at the Royal Academy in 1937. Exhibited handicrafts at the Society of Women Artists in 1924. Exhibited at the Walker Art Gallery, including at their 1906 Autumn Exhibition, showing a copper silver-plated cross and items of jewellery. At their 1914 exhibition, she showed a white-metal plaque. Guthrie married artist, writer, lecturer and art expert Edward Rimbault Dibdin (1853-1941). Dibdin's first wife was Charlotte Elizabeth Blott, with whom he had four children. After her death, he married Guthrie and they had one son. Edward Dibdin was responsible for several publications on art and artists. Subjects of his writings included Frank Dicksee, Liverpool art and artists, G.F. Watts and Thomas Gainsborough. He also acted as second curator at the Walker Art Gallery, Liverpool between 1904 and 1920. Guthrie was a Council Member of the Women's International Art Club. A copper gilt necklace with enamelled pendant by her was illustrated in the Art Journal, 1907, p.317. Guthrie evidently travelled. At the age of 58, in 1932, she is listed as returning by ship to London from Yokohama, Japan. She died in Runcorn, Cheshire, aged 88.

DICK, DOROTHEA JANE (1880-1961)

Sculptor. Born in Wallington, Surrey. The daughter of Charles Groom, a ship and insurance agent, and Annie. Had at least one sister, Hilda. Raised in Surrey. Studied sculpture, presumably in London. Produced reliefs, heads and busts in bronze and plaster. Exhibited her work, including at the Royal Academy (1911-20), the Royal Scottish Academy (1913), the Royal Glasgow Institute (1911) and the Society of Women Artists (1913-19). Exhibited works included: The Indian Doll (colour bas-relief), King Edward VII (bas-relief in bronze), Motherhood (coloured relief) and Volendam Peasant Woman (bas-relief). Spent much of her career in London, using Kensington Gardens Studio for a time, and the Alma Studio, Stratford Road. Died in Kent, aged 81. In 1909 she married Stewart Dick (1874-1944) in London. He was initially a bank clerk, but was later an author and a painter who exhibited his work at the Royal Academy in 1914. He too died in Kent.

DICK, EDITH ALICE (1863-1946)

Craftswoman. Born in France. Records suggest that Edith was the daughter of William Laker, a coachman, and Charlotte. Possibly one of seven children (William, Edith, Harry, Frederick, Charlotte, Alfred and Ernest). Raised in London. Remained there after her marriage to Louis H.M. Dick (1859-1928) sometime between 1881 and 1891. He was born in Mauritius, and was an insurance clerk, and later a stockbroker's clerk. He died in Liverpool. Edith died in Surrey, aged 84. The couple had at least two children, Roger and Joyce. In census recordings for 1901, Edith is listed as a music society composer. But in the early 1900s, she was also active as a designer and maker of artistic jewellery, a horn worker and a decorative metalworker. She was possibly a pupil of Gaillard, or studied his work. Edith exhibited her work from at least 1903, when she contributed to that year's Arts and Crafts Exhibition Society exhibition, held at the New Gallery, London. In 1905 / 06 she contributed jewellery to the Second Exhibition of Arts and Crafts held at the Lyceum Club. In October 1906 she showed decorative horn work at the Artists at Work Exhibition held at the Grafton Gallery, London, one of 120 craftsmen and women to contribute. In 1908 she showed coloured horn work, a silver hand mirror of intertwined figures, and an opium smoker's outfit in silver and enamel, all designed and executed by her, at the New Gallery exhibition.

She also exhibited at the Society of Women Artists (1905-12). Examples of her work were illustrated in The Studio, Vol.44, 1908, p.60.

DICKINS, DOROTHY G. - SEE PELTON, D.G.

DICKINSON, ANNIE JOSEPHINE (1863-1953)

Artistic Furniture Maker / Painter. Born in Painswick, Gloucestershire. The daughter of Sebastian Stewart Dickinson and Frances Stephens. Her father, a barrister and M.P., was born in East India. Her mother originated from Gloucestershire. Annie had at least one sibling, Frances Mary. Raised in Painswick. Studied in Paris under Rolshoven, and in England under Ridley. Produced decorative furniture and paintings of various subjects including flowers and landscapes. Spent some time in London, from at least the mid-1880s. But by the early 1910s, she was back in Painswick, where she died. In London, she studied at the University College. Also whilst there, she shared lodgings for a time with artist Gertrude Buckely. In Painswick, she encountered Ernest Gimson (1864-1919) who was in the Cotswolds area from 1893. He produced furniture in the area with the Barnsley brothers from 1894. Dickinson exhibited her work, including at the Royal Academy (1890-97) and the Society of Women Artists (1885-1904). Exhibited works included: A Corner of the Greenhouse, Dutch Spinning Wheels, After a Day's Rain and Sandy Solitudes. For a time, Dickinson worked as head of a crafts school in Yugoslavia. Acted as Secretary of the Ridley Art Club. Elected a Member of the Lyceum Club. During the First World War, she worked as a V.A.D. in the Red Cross in Serbia. She was imprisoned and repatriated. Also founded an orphanage as well as a school of woodwork. In the 1930s her address was given as Painswick, but also Belgrade.

DIGBY, GRACE (1895-1964)

Painter / Designer / Craftswoman. Born in Scarborough, Yorkshire. Educated at the Brussels Academie and Conservatoire. Studied watercolour painting in Brussels under Uytterschaut. Also studied under George Bernier, and studied oil painting at the Blanc Garin Atelier. Produced landscape paintings in oils and watercolours, designed posters, designed and made jewellery in gold and silver and worked in silk and leather. Was also an accomplished violinist. A gold, silver and bronze medallist at Brussels and Tournai. Exhibited her work, including at the Royal Academy (1920), the Society of Women Artists (1948-64), in Brussels, New York, Sydney, Adelaide, and at various provincial and Scottish galleries. Locally, exhibited with the Royal Birmingham Society of Artists and with the Birmingham Art Circle. An exhibition of her hand-dyed silks and leatherwork was held at the Queen's College, Birmingham in 1925. Also in 1925, she exhibited posters and pictures with the Birmingham Craftsmen's Group. Exhibited paintings included: Interior of Vise Church, Belgium, After the German Bombardment, 1914. Another of her paintings, After the Shelling, Louvain (oil, 1914), is in the collection of the Imperial War Museum. Elected a Member of the Scottish Society of Women Artists. Elected an Associate of the Society of Women Artists (1957-60) and a Member (1961-65). One of her silk scarves in batik, with a design of ferns and mushrooms, was illustrated in The Studio, Vol.89, May 1925, p.282. Spent her early career in Shillingford, Oxfordshire, but later lived and worked in Birmingham. Died in Birmingham, aged 68. Married Francis Wilkes and had two daughters. Active until her death.

DIGGLE, JANE CHADDERTON (1882-1977)

Painter / Poster Artist / Illuminator. Born in London in May 1882. The daughter of Joseph Robert Diggle and Jane. Her father, a Church of England clergyman and member of the local County Council, originated from Pendleton, Lancashire. Her mother originated from Cheshire. One of at least three children (Joseph, Annie and Jane), all raised in London. Her brother Joseph was an Oxford undergraduate. Jane was educated at the Baker Street High School, London and in Paris. She then studied at the Heatherley's School of Art, London and at the L.C.C. Central School of Arts and Crafts. Also studied at the Lindsay School under Arthur Lindsay. Produced paintings of various subjects in tempera and watercolour, poster designs, illumination work and character and humorous drawings. In 1911, whilst living in a house with several students in London, she is listed as a fashion artist. Works reproduced in Daily Sketch and Sphere. She was the author of Miss Jemima at a Private View (1933), a tale of two elderly spinsters visiting an art exhibition. Diggle also provided the illustrations. Exhibited her work, including at the Royal Academy (1931), the Society of Women Artists (21 works, 1920-51), the Royal Institute of Painters in Watercolours, the Walker Art Gallery, Liverpool, the Women's International Art Club, with the United Artists,

the National Society and at the Paris Salon. Exhibited works included: St Francis's Canticle to the Sun, Seeing the Galleries of Europe, The Wandering Minstrel and Revels (watercolour). Elected a Member of the Forum Club, and of the Lyceum Club. Spent much of her career in London, but was later based at Tenterden, Kent. Died in Elstree, Hertfordshire.

DIMELOW, AMY BEATRICE CAROLINE (1877-1964)

Sculptor / Painter / Studio Worker. Born in Chorlton, Manchester. The daughter of John Gartside Dimelow and Annie. One of at least three children (Amy, Annie and Marie). Raised in Chorlton and in Withington, Lancashire. Educated in Manchester. Studied at the Manchester School of Art. Won a national silver medal and a Royal Free Studentship. Initially worked in Manchester, but subsequently worked in Surrey. Died in Sutton, Surrey. Produced heads, busts, statuettes and reliefs. Exhibited her work, including at the Walker Art Gallery, Liverpool, at the Manchester Corporation Art Gallery, with the Women's International Art Club and at the Allied Artists' Exhibition, London. Exhibited works included: Henry Watson, Mus. Doc (bust), The Pool (statuette), Head of a Boy and Portrait (miniature relief in silver). Elected a Member of the English Speaking Union, and of the Manchester Academy of Fine Arts. Articles by Dimelow, as well as illustrations of her work, were published by Revue du Vrai et du Beau and in Hippodrome (by request).

DIMMOCK, MARTHA A. - SEE ONIONS, M.A.

DOBBIN, ETHEL MAY (1869-1955)

Etcher / Black & White Artist / Designer. Born in Ruddington, Nottinghamshire. The daughter of the Rev. Abraham J.L. Dobbin and Mary. Her father originated from Ireland, her mother from Oldham, Lancashire. One of at least four children (Lucy, Ernest, Ethel and Charles). Raised in Ruddington, where her father was curate of the local church. Later, he became vicar of Cropwell Bishop, Nottinghamshire. Ethel was educated privately. By at least 1891 she was a student at the Nottingham School of Art. As a student, she won a medal for book illustration at the National Competition of Schools of Art at South Kensington. Worked as an etcher, an illustrator in black & white and a designer of Christmas cards and other cards. Some of her black & white drawings were reproduced in the Art Journal, 1896, pp.244-245. Exhibited her work, including at the Royal West of England Academy, Bristol, with the Ex Libris Society in London, at the Walker Art Gallery, Liverpool, at the Derby Art Gallery and at the Nottingham Castle Art Gallery. Elected a Member of the Nottingham Society of Artists. Still active in the 1930s. Spent much of her life and career in Ruddington and in Nottingham. Died in Stockport, Cheshire, aged 85.

DOBELL, JOAN KEVAN - SEE GREENHALGH, J.K.

DODD, AGNES - SEE SHUTER, A.

DONALDSON, CATHERINE (1901-68)

Engraver / Painter / Etcher. Was Amy Catherine, but always known as Catherine or Katta. She was born in London on 25 November 1901, the eldest child of the Rev. Stuart Alexander Donaldson (1855-1915) and Albinia Frederica Hampden. She had a sister Mary and a brother John. Her father was born into an English family in Sydney, Australia where Catherine's grandfather was Colonial Secretary for New South Wales. Stuart A. Donaldson studied at Trinity College, Cambridge and became a clerk in holy orders as well as Master of Magdalene College, Cambridge (1904-15).

Catherine was educated at the Francis Holland School in Graham Street, London. Although she spent some time living and working in London during her lifetime, she also lived at No.9 The Lodge, Magdalene College in Cambridge, and spent time at the family holiday home, the Old Mill at East Runton near Cromer in north Norfolk. In the early 1920s, Catherine studied art at the Slade School and at the Chelsea Polytechnic in London, winning Slade certificates for drawing and painting. She studied under Graham Sutherland who, at that time, was influenced by the work of Samuel Palmer, which, in turn, was reflected in some of her work. She elected to concentrate on wash drawings, colour lithographs, etchings and engravings of various subjects, but particularly of Norfolk and its scenery.

Catherine began to exhibit her work from at least the mid-1920s. In July 1926 she showed two works at the Norwich Art Circle's 74th exhibition held at Stuart Hall in Norwich. In August 1928 she exhibited 24 wood engravings, etchings and lithographs in the Assembly Rooms, Holway Road in Sheringham, Norfolk which included studies of Cromer From Cliffs, Felbrigg Hall, Wells-next-the-Sea, Heydon Hall, Norfolk, The Hanging Wood and Farm Buildings, East Runton. Catherine also found inspiration elsewhere,

including on her travels, producing other works such as Rome From the Pincio, Piazza Navona, Rome and Barges, Chelsea.

Elsewhere, she exhibited her work with the Society of Wood Engravers and the Women's International Art Club. In 1925, for example, she contributed to the 6th annual exhibition of the Society of Wood Engravers, and contributed to its 7th held the following year at the Redfern Gallery, London. Fellow exhibitors included Gwen Raverat, Eric Ravilious, Eric Gill and David Jones, which indicates the high standard Donaldson reached during her career. Four of her works were reproduced in the London Mercury, and her Talloires was reproduced in The Studio magazine.

Donaldson was active as an artist until at least the mid-1930s. In 1928, she executed 12 wood engravings for Thomas Malory's The Death of King Arthur (Macmillan) which was limited to 525 copies. She also produced drawings and a jacket for Herbert Read's The Innocent Eye published by Faber in 1933. She also executed a number of engravings based on Chaucer's Canterbury Tales.

In June 1930, Catherine married Richard Herbert Ingpen de la Mare (1901-86) in Chelsea. Born in Kent, he was one of four children of writer Walter de la Mare and Elfrida. Richard was a publisher and Principal Director of Faber. The couple lived in London for a time, including at Sloane Gardens in the 1930s. Donaldson then began to sign her work Catherine de la Mare. They had four children, Richard, Ben, Albinia and Giles. Giles also became a publisher. Perhaps opting to concentrate on her marriage and family life, Catherine eventually gave up her career. She died in Hertfordshire on 31 August 1968, aged 66. Richard de la Mare died in Oxfordshire in March 1986. Papers and works relating to Catherine can be found in the care of the Bodleian Library.

DONALDSON, ISOBEL (1881-1954)

Sculptor. Born and raised in Chiswick, London. The daughter of John Donaldson and Frances Sarah. Her father, a civil engineer, originated from Scotland. Her mother originated from Middlesex. One of at least 11 children (Mary, Alyce, Isobel, Thornycroft, Frances, Helen, Norman, Gabel, Malcolm, Alastair and Eric). By the early 1900s, the family had moved to Pangbourne, Berkshire, where Isobel subsequently died, aged 73. However, the family also spent time in Kensington, London, where Isobel worked as a sculptor. She may have studied under Sir Hamo Thornycroft, given that she exhibited a bust of him at the Royal Academy in 1922. Isobel worked in London between (at least) the 1910s to the 1930s, producing heads and busts in marble and bronze. Exhibited her work, including at the Royal Academy (1916-32) and the Society of Women Artists (1930-36). Exhibited works included: Ian (head, bronze), Head of a Baby (marble), Miss Violet Edwardes (bust) and Annabel (head). Elected an Associate of the Royal Society of British Sculptors in 1926. Works in the National Portrait Gallery. Her brother, Thornycroft, possibly named after the dynasty of sculptors, became a student of mechanical engineering. Her sister Mary (1874-1953) became a portrait painter and lived with Isobel for a time. Mary died in London, aged 79. Mary exhibited her work too, including at the Royal Academy (1905-43) and the Society of Women Artists (1952-53). Mary's work included a portrait of Hamo Thornycroft, exhibited at the Royal Academy in 1912. Examples of her work can be found at the Pallant House Gallery, Chichester.

DONGWORTH, WINIFRED CECILE (1893-1975)

Painter / Miniaturist / Decorator. Born in Richmond, Surrey. The daughter of Henry (Harry) C. Dongworth (1866-1948) and Alice (b.1870). Her father, who originated from Derbyshire, initially worked as a fishmonger's manager, but is later listed as a company director. Her mother originated from Berkshire. Raised in Brighton, Sussex. Educated at the Powis School, Brighton. Studied at the Brighton Municipal School of Art, the Putney School of Art and the Royal Academy schools, London. She was subsequently based in London, dying in Lambeth at the age of 82. Became a watercolour artist, a painter of portraits in miniature, an interior decorator, a colour scheme artist and a film set decorator. Also acted as a buyer of fine art and decorations and as a confidential secretary to art trade buyers. Exhibited her work, including at the Royal Academy (1914-40), with the Royal Society of Miniature Painters, at the Brighton Art Gallery, the Worthing Art Gallery, at Wembley, at the British Empire Exhibition and in Buenos Aires. Exhibited works included: Asta, Steve Donoghue (in the colours of Mr James White), Maria Mindszenti and Bette Davis. Other works included portraits of Mr Baldwin, Lord Thomson, the Rt Hon. J. Ramsay Macdonald and Viscount Snowdon. Some of her portraits were reproduced in Sketch. Some of her portraits are in the collection of the National Portrait Gallery.

DONINGTON, MARY (b.1909)

Sculptor. Born in London in April 1909. Possibly died in Hampshire in February 1987 (records are unclear). Educated at the Mary Datchelor School. Studied at the Royal Academy of Music. Published Music for Children. Also studied sculpture under Frank Dobson between 1945 and 1946. Otherwise, a self-taught artist. Produced mainly portrait works in bronze, plaster and terracotta. Based at Furze Hill Road, Headley Down, Hampshire during her career. Exhibited her work, including at the National Society, the Women's International Art Club, the Royal Glasgow Institute (1948), the Royal Academy (1948-49) and the Society of Women Artists (1951-52). Exhibited works included: Daughter of Ludwig (bronze), Father Hogan (plaster), Head of a Blind Man (bronze) and Rosemary Cowper (head, bronze).

DOWNING, MARY MARIA BELLMAN (1854-1939)

Painter / Designer / Craftworker. One of four children (Mary, Caroline, Edith and Edward), all born and raised in Cardiff. Their father, Edward C. Downing, was a merchant and Belgian Consul. He originated from Cornwall. Their mother was Mary Ann Sarah. Edith Downing became a noted sculptor and painter. Mary and Edith studied in London, both living at Oakley Flats, Chelsea as students. Mary produced watercolour paintings of landscapes and flowers, designs for textiles, curtains, wallpaper, wallpaper friezes and fabrics, decorative bookbindings and leatherwork. She became associated with the Chiswick School of Arts and Crafts. Also associated with the short-lived Guild of Women Binders (active late 1890s). One of her bindings was for an edition of Robert Browning's Poems (London, 1897), executed in brown goatskin with gold tooling, now in the Willis Collection, Duke University Library. Mary showed some of her bindings at an exhibition of Arts and Crafts held at the Bruton Galleries in November 1905. Exhibited some of her leatherwork and bookbindings at the 1901 Glasgow Exhibition. Also exhibited leatherwork at the 1904 City of Bradford exhibition, which had a section devoted to artistic handcrafts practised by women. Showed over 30 examples of her work at the Society of Women Artists between 1893 and 1906. Those included: Thistledown, Geese Feeding, The Old Smack and The Usual Fog (all watercolours). In the early 1900s, Mary shared lodgings with artist / craftworker Beth Amoore. Mary died in Surrey. Still active in 1911, according to census recordings, aged 57. SEE: AMOORE, BETH

DOYLE, HONOR CAMILLA (1888-1944)

Artist / Furniture Painter. Born in Cathedral Close, Norwich in June 1888. The only child of Charles William Doyle and Emma. Her mother originated from Willesden. Honor was raised in Cathedral Close, and died there. Spent part of her career in London, at the Alma Studios in Kensington, but also at Rickmansworth, Hertfordshire. Studied at the Slade School, London. Awarded a first-class certificate for figure drawing and a prize for a head drawing. Decorated furniture, including corner cabinets. Executed portrait and landscape paintings such as Mill End and Stocker's Farm. Exhibited her work, including at the New English Art Club, the British Institute of Industrial Art, with the Friday Club and with the Arts League of Service. Also a published poet, she produced Poems (Basil Blackwell, 1923) and Poems (Ernest Benn, 1927). The author of an article, The Vanishing Arts of a Peasantry, for the Burlington Magazine, published in 1926.

DRESCHFELD, VIOLET JENNIE (b.1890)

Sculptor. Born in Chorlton, Manchester. The daughter of Julius Dreschfeld, a physician, and Selina. One of at least three children (Violet, Victor and Stanley), all raised in Manchester. Victor became an engineering student. Violet studied sculpture, possibly in London since she was based in Hampstead in the early 1910s. Produced portrait works. Still active in 1918, but effectively disappears after that date.

DREW, JOAN HARVEY (1875-1961)

Embroideress / Designer. Born in Streatham, London in July 1875. The daughter of Richard William Drew, M.A., an architect, and Anne Bletchley. Her father originated from Westminster, her mother from Stoke Newington, London. Had at least four older sisters, Mary, Sophia, Dorothy and Kathleen, and a younger brother, Geoffrey. Her siblings were also born in Streatham, between 1865 and 1878. The family spent time living in Devon in the 1880s, and by the 1890s were living at Bletchingley, Surrey, by which time her father was widowed. All the Drew children, except Kathleen, were still living at the family home in the early 1900s. Joan remained in Surrey, living at Bletchingley House, Bletchingley and, later, at Heathfield, Albury Heath. She died at the age of 86. Joan studied at the Westminster School of Art. Became a decorative embroideress and a watercolour painter. She became a recognised expert in needlework, and was one of the first to revive embroidery in villages in the early days of the Women's Institute movement.

Joan exhibited her work occasionally, including at various arts and crafts exhibitions in London. For example, she contributed to an Exhibition of Arts and Crafts held at the Lyceum Club in 1905. There, one of her exhibits was a needlework picture The Rose Bower which was illustrated in The Studio, Vol.38, September 1906, p.345. At the Society of Women Artists, she showed four watercolours, including Field Labour, Evening at Bedford and In the Lower Church, Assisi, and two handicrafts between 1898 and 1901. Works illustrated in other journals and magazines. The Art Workers' Quarterly illustrated an embroidered border and an embroidered cushion square, both designed by her, in its January 1903 issue. In October 1903, the same journal illustrated a design for an embroidered border. In 1907, the Art Journal, p.55, illustrated an embroidered casket by her, shown at the Baillie Gallery, London in that year. Drew published several books on embroidery and design. Elected a Member of the Forum Club.

DRING, LILIAN MARGERY (1908-98)

Painter / Needleworker / Embroideress / Designer. Born in Surbiton, Surrey in March 1908. Died in Surrey, aged 90. The daughter of George Robert Welch and Lily Eliza. Her father was a master plumber. Her mother worked in the office of a laundry for a time. One of at least three children (Alice, Lilian and Daisy). Daisy is listed as a music teacher, aged 15. Lilian was raised in Kingston, Surrey. Educated at elementary school. Studied at the Kingston School of Art under Alfred James Collister between 1922 and 1926. Also studied at the Royal College of Art, London under Professor Ernest William Tristram and Reco Capey between 1926 and 1929. Elected an Associate of the Royal College of Art in 1929. Based in Teddington, Middlesex for part of her career. Became a painter in watercolours, an embroideress and a designer of, among other things, posters. Also worked on developing machine-stitched applique.

Lilian exhibited her work, including with the Arts and Crafts Exhibition Society, with the Embroiderers' Guild, at the Whitworth Art Gallery in Manchester, at the British Council Exhibitions in America (1942-45) and at the Royal College of Art Associates' exhibitions. Elected a Member of the Arts and Crafts Exhibition Society, and of the Craft Centre of Great Britain. Some of her work was in the permanent collection of the Scottish Needlework Development Scheme (three pieces). Other works were in the collection of the Victoria & Albert Museum, London, including various cushion covers and scarves designed and executed by Dring during the 1930s, 1940s and 1950s. Some of her work was purchased by the Board of Trade. Dring designed posters for London Transport in the 1930s. Examples can be found in the London Transport Museum. Works illustrated in Vogue, Lady and other journals and magazines. She was also the author of Nursery Verseries, The Milky Way, A Slice of Bread, Cycle of Seasons, Rhyme of Time, Rhyme of the Mine and Days of the Week. Contributed to publications on art and craft education. In 1931 she married Cyril James Dring (d.1985) in Surrey. They had at least one son.

DRUCKER, AMY JULIA (1873-1951)

Lithographer / Painter / Wood Engraver / Colour Printer / Etcher / Woodcut Artist. Born in Hampstead, London to Jewish parents. The daughter of Charles Drucker and Louise, both of whom originated from Germany. Her father was a wine and spirit merchant. Based in London throughout much of her career, dying there, aged 78. One of at least three children (Amy, Ella and Lucy). Ella became a health inspector. Amy was educated at the South Hampstead High School. Studied at the St John's Wood School of Art, at the Lambeth School of Art and at Colarossi's in Paris. Became a diverse artist. Produced works in oils, watercolours and pastels, miniature paintings, colour woodcuts, wood engravings, colour prints, etchings and lithographs. Described in arts journals of the 1920s as specialising at that time in drawing and recording local peasants, including Irish, French, German, Jewish, Arabic, Indian, Chinese and Dutch, and of the South American tribes. Made extensive records of London's coster life. Became a teacher of painting in various schools and taught the Japanese method of colour printing to Indians in Calcutta, at the Jerusalem School of Art and to private pupils in London.

Drucker travelled extensively during her lifetime, recording her surroundings. Also exhibited her work far and wide over a period of more than 47 years, including at the Royal Academy (1899-1946), the Royal Hibernian Academy (1936), the Royal Glasgow Institute (1907) and the Society of Women Artists (1908-30). Also, at the Paris Salon, with the International Society of Sculptors, Painters & Gravers, the Royal Institute of Oil Painters, the Pastel Society and the Royal Society of Portrait Painters. Held one-woman shows in Jerusalem, Shanghai, Peking, London, Buenos Aires, Lima,

Peru and Panama. Exhibited works included: Hop Pickers at Breakfast, Going Home (lithograph), A Wet Night (lithograph) and The Dutch Boy (watercolour). Her The Fruit Shop was hung on the line at the Royal Academy. One of her portraits, of Prince Henry of Wales, was owned by the Queen. Elected a Member of the Cartwright Gardens Club and of the Bloomsbury House Club. Her works were acquired by numerous collections and galleries in, for example, London, Palestine, Shanghai, Peking, Monte Video, Buenos Aires and Malaya. Works reproduced in Sphere, Sketch and various children's newspapers. Produced a frontispiece for a book by Tschiffely. Commissioned to paint a portrait of H.M. Haile Selassie, Emperor of Abyssinia.

DRUMMOND, KATHERINE RUSSELL (1895-1989)

Painter / Bookbinder / Leatherworker / Craftworker. Born in Ceylon. The daughter of Dr R.J. Drummond. Educated at the Morrison's Academy, Crieff, Perthshire and at the St Anne's High School, St Anne's, Lancashire. Studied at the Edinburgh College of Art and at the London County Council Central School of Arts and Crafts. Produced watercolour paintings, bookbindings, decorative leatherwork and other craftwork including enamelled plaques. Also an amateur photographer. Exhibited her work, including at the Society of Women Artists (1916-17), at the Arts and Crafts Exhibitions in London, at Wembley and at the Royal National Eisteddfod, Wales. One of her enamelled plaques was illustrated in The Studio. Wrote a series of articles on leatherwork and design in the Arts and Crafts Quarterly (1925). A Member of the Writer's Club. Based in London during her career, but died in Somerset, aged 94. During the First World War, she worked for the Serbian Red Cross in London.

DRUMMOND, VIOLET HILDA (1911-2000)

Illustrator / Artist / Lithographer. Born in London in July 1911. The daughter of David Robert Drummond, a banker, and Hilda Margaret Harris. Her father was killed in action in 1914, during the First World War. Her mother married again, in 1936, becoming Hilda Gunning. Violet had at least one sister, Joan Cecile. Raised in London. Educated at The Links, Eastbourne. Studied at the St Martin's School of Art, London (1930). Became an illustrator and author of children's books, an artist in pen & ink and an illustrator of humorous books for adults. Also produced colour lithographs. Produced cartoon films for the

B.B.C. based on the Little Laura books. Was the winner of the Kate Greenaway Award for illustrations to Mrs Easter and the Storks (1957). Other books illustrated by Drummond included J.K. Stanford, The Twelfth (1944), Thomas A. Powell, Here and There a Lusty Trout (1947), Arnold Silcock, Verse and Worse (1952), Angela Jean, The Kingdom of the Winds (1957) and Helen Cresswell, The Piemakers (1967). Worked for a number of publishers during her career including Faber & Faber, Penguin Books and Houghton Mifflin. Her own books included Phewtus the Squirrel (1939), Miss Anna Truly (1945), The Mountain That Laughed (1947), The Flying Postman (1948) and I'll Never be Asked Again (1979). Elected to the Society of Industrial Artists. In 1948 she married Anthony Clement Swetenham (1911-2001) in Chelsea. Had at least one son. Based in London for much of her career. Violet died in Essex, aged 88.

DUCKWORTH, RUTH (1919-2009)

Sculptor / Potter. Born in Hamburg in April 1919. The daughter of E. Windmuller, a lawyer. One of five children. Educated at the Kreusler Schule, Hamburg. Came to England in 1936. Studied painting and sculpture at the Liverpool School of Art between 1936 and 1940, but failed to establish herself as a sculptor. Then took up pottery, studying at the Hammersmith School of Art and at the London County Council Central School of Arts and Crafts. Had a studio at Stile Hall Gardens, London. Produced heads, statuettes and pottery. Worked in stone, lead, terracotta, wood and bronze. Exhibited her work, including at the Royal Academy (1950-51), the Manchester Academy of Fine Arts and the Women's International Art Exhibition held at the Lambeth Palace in 1951. Exhibited with the Society of Portrait Sculptors (founded 1953). For example, at their Second Exhibition, in 1955, she showed Aidron Duckworth (head, terracotta) which was illustrated in The Studio, Vol.149, April 1955, p.141. Other works included Mother and Child (statuette group, sycamore). Duckworth was elected a Member of the Society of Portrait Sculptors. Other members included Reg Butler, Charles Wheeler and Louise Hutchinson. Elected an Associate of the Royal Society of British Sculptors in 1951.

In her pottery, Duckworth gradually changed her style, moving away from coiled pieces with strong decoration to more primitive pieces in unglazed stoneware. One of her coiled stoneware pots was illustrated in The Studio, Vol.159, June 1960, p.197. In 1964 she was invited to become artist in residence at the Midway Studio of the University of Chicago, where she remained for two years. She was commissioned to produce a large ceramic mural for the University. In 1949 she married Harry A. Duckworth in Kensington. They divorced in 1967. Noted in Muriel Rose, Artist Potters in England, London, Faber & Faber, 1970 (first edition 1955). Rose illustrates her stoneware bottle (1961) and a porcelain bowl on stem (c.1965). One of her vases was included in an exhibition The New Look, held at the Manchester Art Gallery, 1991-92.

DUGDALE, AMY K. - SEE BROWNING, A.K.

DUGGAN, IRENE SOPHIA (1879-1959)

Embroideress / Craftswoman / Designer / Engraver / Woodcut Artist. Born and raised in Huddersfield, Yorkshire. The daughter of Henry George Duggan and Annie. Her father was a wool merchant and exporter. One of at least six children (Annie, Marie, Henry, Edwin, May and Irene). Irene was educated at Upton Hall, Birkenhead. Then studied at the Huddersfield School of Art, and at the Bradford College of Arts and Crafts, both Yorkshire. Elected an Associate of the Bradford College of Arts and Crafts. Remained in Huddersfield and died there. During her career, she acted as art teacher at the Holmfirth County Secondary School and at the Holmfirth Art Class. Also acted as head of the women's craft department at the Batley School of Art, Yorkshire. Acted as craft teacher under the West Riding County Council. Exhibited her work locally, with the Huddersfield Art Society. Works included a handbook cover and poster for the Bradford Education Week. Still active into the 1930s.

DUMMETT, JOAN KATHERINE (1905-2005)

Sculptor / Artist. Born in Crouch End, Middlesex in January 1905. The daughter of Robert Ernest Dummett, a barrister and Metropolitan Police Magistrate, and Emma Amelia Welton. One of at least four children (Robert, Helen, Joan and Ruth). Raised in Edmonton, Middlesex. Educated at the Monmouth High School. Studied art under Jules Van Biesbroeck. Produced busts, heads and statuettes in bronze, and works in pastels. Exhibited her work, including at the Walker Art Gallery, Liverpool, under the Duveen Scheme and at the Royal Academy (1929-31). Exhibited works included: The Rt Hon. Sir Edward Clarke, K.C. (bust, bronze), Study From Nature (statuette, bronze), Italian Peasant Woman (bust, bronze) and R.E. Dummett, Esq., Metropolitan

Police Court Magistrate (head, bronze). Based in London and Reading during her career. Died in Bristol, aged 100. In 1930 she married Thomas A. Chubb in Middlesex.

DUNKLEY, EDITH E. - SEE MARTIN, E.E.

DUNN, CONSTANCE EDITH (1904-76)
Potter. Born in Wootton, Surrey in March 1904. The daughter of Alfred Mark Wade and Eliza. Her father, a university lodging housekeeper, originated from Hampshire, her mother from Westmorland. Constance was raised in Cambridge. Had at least one brother, Alfred Holme Wade. She studied at the Cambridge School of Art. Also, at the Royal College of Art, London under Professor Ernest William Tristram and William Staite Murray between 1924 and 1928. Elected an Associate of the Royal College of Art. Became a potter, working independently. Also a pottery teacher, at the Constantine College, Middlesbrough between 1929 and 1931. Exhibited her work at the National Society, in Monza, Florence, Prague and America, at the Brygos Gallery in London, at the Walker Art Gallery, Liverpool, the Laing Art Gallery, Newcastle, at the Arts and Crafts Exhibition Society exhibitions and at the Craft Centre, London. Works purchased by the Victoria & Albert Museum, London and the Contemporary Art Society. Works reproduced in the Studio Year Book, the North Eastern Gazette and by the Billingham Press. In 1928 she married John S. Dunn, M.A., Ph.D., A.R.I.C., in Cambridge. They had at least one daughter. Based for a time at Billingham-on-Tees, Middlesbrough. Constance died in Kent, aged 72.

DUNN, FRANCES CECILIA TROYTE (1878-1968)
Ecclesiastical Artist / Black & White Artist / Modeller. Born in Clifton, Bristol in June 1878. The daughter of the Rev. James Dunn, Vicar of St John the Baptist, Bath, Somerset, and Angelina Ann. Her father originated from Hampshire, but spent much of his life in Bath, as a clergyman. Her mother originated from Dorset. Frances spent much of her life in Bath, her death registered in Somerset, aged 90. One of at least six children (Joanna, Frances, Mary, Stephen, William and Robert). She was educated in Brondesbury. Studied at the Byam Shaw and Vicat Cole School of Art, London. Became an ecclesiastical artist, an artist in black & white and a modeller. Works included a bas-relief for St Denys in Warminster, and a decorative altar for Retreat House, Chiswick. Also, a decorative altar for St

Andrew's, Pau, France, and a decoration based on the Stations of the Cross for St Michael's, Teignmouth. Exhibited her work occasionally, including with the Royal Birmingham Society of Artists. Had a studio at Darlington Street, Bath for part of her career.

DURANT, SUSAN D. (1827-73)
Sculptor. Born at Stamford Hill, Middlesex. The daughter of George Durant, a silk broker, and Mary. Both her parents originated from Devon. Susan was raised in London. Studied sculpture in Paris under Baron Henri de Triqueti. In 1869 she had a son secretly by Triqueti. Worked in London and Paris. Enjoyed a successful career despite her premature death in Paris. Produced portrait busts, medallions and figure subjects in marble. One of Queen Victoria's favourite sculptors. Executed numerous busts and medallions of the royal family. Princess Louise was her pupil. In 1856-57 she worked with Baron de Triqueti on a monument to Leopold, King of the Belgians. At the 1851 Great Exhibition, Durant showed two figures, The Chief Mourner and Belisarius. Her statuette of Robin Hood was shown at the Art Treasures Exhibition in Manchester in 1857. Her The Faithful Shepherdess was shown at the Mansion House in 1863. She also exhibited at the Royal Academy (38 works, 1847-73), the Society of Women Artists (1858) and the British Institute (1860). Portrait subjects included Senor Don Adolfo Bayo, Daniel Whittle Harvey, Lady Killeen, the Queen, Princess Louise, Prince Alfred, Princess Beatrice, Princess Helena, Harriet Beecher Stowe (1857) and the Prince of Wales. One of her commissions, a study of the Princess of Wales, was used to decorate Wolsey's Chapel, whilst a study of the Queen was intended for the Inner Temple. Durant also executed self-portraits. Her works commanded respectable sums. Her study of The Negligent Watchboy of the Vineyard Catching Locusts (1858, marble) was priced at 250 guineas.

DUTTON, CONSTANCE - SEE THOMPSON, C.

DYAS, ELLA - SEE HALLWARD, E.

E

EADIE, KATE MURIEL M. (1878-1945)
Designer / Metalworker. A diverse and talented artist and craftswoman who was born in Harborne, Staffordshire. The daughter of Richard W. Eadie and Fanny. Her father originated from

Birmingham, her mother from Warwickshire. Richard Eadie was an engraver who was able to employ six staff in the 1880s and a general servant at home. Kate was one of at least eight children, and possibly the eldest. In the 1880s the family lived in Harborne. But by the 1890s they were based in Handsworth, Birmingham, and by the early 1900s had moved again, to Sparkhill, Warwickshire. This meant that, in the early 1900s, Kate was able to study at the Birmingham School of Art whilst living at home. She attended the new School of Jewellery and Silversmithing which was set up in 1900 in response to the new interest in decorative metalwork and artistic jewellery at that time. From 1902, head of the new school was Arthur Gaskin. As a student, Eadie contributed to the annual exhibition of students' work, certainly in 1901 when it was held at the local Society of Arts rooms. One of her exhibits in 1901 was a plaster model to be executed in lead. Her work also appeared in the National Competition of Schools of Art, in which promising students from across the country vied for attention and awards. Eadie certainly exhibited there in 1903 and 1904.

From at least 1905, Eadie was based more permanently at Moseley, Birmingham where she probably had a separate studio. She spent much of her life in and around Birmingham, and became an integral part of what was known as the Birmingham Group. The Group, which was made up of a number of artists and craftworkers, was originally formed under the influence of E.R.Taylor of the Birmingham School of Art. Members included Arthur and Georgina Gaskin, Edith Payne, Mary Newill and Sidney H. Meteyard. Like her female contemporaries, Eadie became a good, general all-round designer and craftworker as well as a painter. During her career, she designed and executed decorative jewellery, produced modelled leather bookbindings, worked in gesso and enamelling, and designed and executed decorative metalwork such as a silver tea caddy which was shown at the Walker Art Gallery, Liverpool in 1915 and illustrated in The Studio, Vol.66, January 1916. As a student, she also produced designs for stained glass, one of which was shown at the National Competition of Schools of Art, South Kensington, and which was illustrated in The Studio, Vol.23, 1901, p.268.

Eadie's work regularly caught the attention of the press, even as a student. In 1904, for example, The Studio, Vol.32, September, p.325, illustrated two enamelled panels by her. Also in 1904, the Art Workers' Quarterly, January, pp.12-15, published an article by Kate on Gesso Work. In 1913, The Studio, Vol.57, January, p.290,

illustrated two pieces of jewellery, a silver pendant set with pearl blisters and turquoise, and a silver necklet set with opals, both of which had been shown at the 1913 Arts and Crafts Exhibition Society exhibition. Her jewellery was highly intricate and delicate, not dissimilar to that produced by the Gaskins. In 1916, four of her pendants were shown at that year's Arts and Crafts Exhibition Society exhibition and illustrated in The Studio, Vol.70, February 1917.

Eadie exhibited her work elsewhere too. At the Royal Academy, she showed seven works between 1905 and 1915 which included an enamel panel The Staff and Scrip, another panel The Sailing of the Sword in Limoges enamel, a study of St Catherine, and a copper and silver Processional Cross. Other works were shown at the Walker Art Gallery, Liverpool. The Gallery held regular exhibitions of craftwork in the late nineteenth and early twentieth centuries. In 1909, for example, Eadie showed jewellery and metalwork at their Autumn Exhibition. She was elected a Member of the Royal Society of Miniature Painters, and an Associate of the Royal Birmingham Society of Artists, where she also exhibited. At the Society of Women Artists, she showed work in 1912 and 1913.

In 1940, aged 62, Eadie married artist Sidney Harold Meteyard, who was some ten years her senior. The reasons for such a late marriage, when she had known Meteyard for much of her working life, would be purely speculative. Eadie died only five years later, aged 67. Meteyard died two years later, in 1947, aged 78. Meteyard, a painter in tempera and a stained glass painter, had also been a student of the Birmingham School of Art, and was also based in Birmingham for much of his life. Both Eadie and Meteyard died in Alcester, Warwickshire, where they lived latterly.

EARNSHAW, MABEL LUCIE - SEE ATTWELL, M.L.

EDEN, ELIZABETH - SEE FIELD, E.

EDMUNDS, NELLIE MARY HEPBURN (1870-1953)

Painter / Miniature Painter. Was Ellen, known as Nellie. Born at Norwood, Surrey. The daughter of Henry Chase Edmunds (b.1840) and Mary Caroline Hepburn (1845-1921). Her father, who originated from Sussex, was a merchant, dealing in sugar and other goods. Her mother, who originated from Middlesex, was a Professor of Music and Singing. Nellie had an older sister, Catherine Sophia (1868-1938). A third child, Francis (b.1873), died young. Raised in Norwood. Studied at the Slade School, London under Professor Fred Brown. Also studied at the University College, London and at the Westminster School of Art under Mouat Loudan. Became a highly respected portrait painter (life-size) in oils, and a painter of portraits in miniature. She experienced a long and productive career which spanned seven decades, from the 1890s into the 1950s. Worked up until her death in February 1953. Based at Streatham Hill, London for part of her career. Latterly based at Woodside Cottage, Little Heath Lane, Cobham, Surrey.

Edmunds exhibited her work extensively, including at the Royal Academy (102 works, 1896-1952), the Society of Women Artists (11 works, 1898-1932), the Royal Society of Miniature Painters, the Palace of Art, Wembley, the Pall Mall Gallery, the Arlington Gallery in Bond Street, London, the Modern Gallery, Bond Street (until it closed) and the Grafton Galleries. Also, at the Walker Art Gallery, Liverpool and the Royal Institute of Painters in Watercolours. Further afield, she exhibited at the International Exhibition in Brussels and Ghent by special invitation, the Canadian Exhibition at Toronto, in Sweden, South Africa and Washington. Exhibited works included: The Jade Necklace, The Village Artist, Robert Dresses Up and Concentration.

Edmunds painted numerous society figures, including Lady Violet Astor, Alice, Countess of Chichester, Lady Dorothy Macmillan and the Countess of Minto. Other notable sitters included the Rt Rev. the Lord Bishop of Kingston (later Bishop of Blackburn). Contributed works to the Queen's Doll's House. Works in the permanent collection of the Victoria & Albert Museum, London. She also contributed to a Diploma Exhibition of the Royal Society of Miniature Painters held at the Museum. Works reproduced on numerous occasions, including in journals and newspapers such as Connoisseur, The Studio, Royal Academy Illustrated, Sketch, Bystander, Sphere, Graphic, Illustrated London News, the London Evening News, Eve, The Gentlewoman, Lady's Pictorial, the Daily Mirror, Daily Sketch, Cassell's Pictures of the Year and Black and White (until it closed). In the 1920s, Edmunds was included in a book on miniatures by C.M. Williamson and Percy Buckman.

Edmunds was praised in The Studio magazine on a number of occasions. For example, in 1908, Vol.44, p.179, the magazine illustrated two of her miniatures in colour in an article Modern Miniature Painting, which also included references to Mrs Emslie, Marion Llewellyn, Gertrude Massey and Lionel Heath. In 1918, Vol.75, November, p.40, the same magazine

illustrated four of her miniatures in a short article on modern miniatures, including The Lavender Gown. Edmunds had the honour of being the only living miniature painter to have a work in the Permanent Collection at South Kensington (up to 1927), and the only one of the twentieth century to have one in that collection (also up to 1927). Also acted as Honorary Treasurer for the Royal Society of Miniature Painters for four years. Acted as Member of the Council for the Society for some years before being elected Vice President in 1911, a post for which she was re-elected at least 10 times (it being a two-year office). Edmunds died in Bexhill-on-Sea, Sussex, in the county where her father was born.

EDWARDS, GEORGINA H. - SEE BOWERS, G.H.

ELBORNE, JESSIE (1861-1952)

Sculptor. Born in Grantham, Lincolnshire. The daughter of Sydney Lipscomb and Harriet. Her father, a colliery agent, originated from High Wycombe, Buckinghamshire, her mother from Grantham. Jessie was an only child. Whilst she was still young, the family moved to Peterborough, where she remained for much of the rest of her life. Died in Peterborough in January 1952, aged 90. Studied sculpture at the Royal College of Art, South Kensington (then the National Training School), and in Paris. Studied under Edouard Lanteri and Auguste Rodin. Won the Queen's Prize in 1882, and was a national silver medallist in 1883. Produced mainly figures and heads in terracotta and bronze. Specialised in portrait busts. Exhibited at the Royal Academy (1885-87), showing three works: Portrait Study (terracotta), Day-dreams (bust, terracotta) and Study of a Head (bronze). At that point, she was living with her parents at Wootton House, Peterborough. Also exhibited at the Paris Salon. Other works included portrait busts of Alderman Redhead, J.P., W. Elborne Snr, Henry Wootton and Camille Claudel. She did not exhibit a great deal. In 1887 Jessie married William Elborne, M.A., a former Trinity, Cambridge undergraduate, in London. They lived with her widowed mother at Wootton House. The couple had four children (Ellen, Sydney, William and John). In 1947 the couple celebrated their diamond wedding. William Elborne died eight days after Jessie, in January 1952 at Wootton House. Jessie was still active as a sculptor into the 1930s.

ELDRIDGE, MILDRED ELSIE (1909-91)

Artist / Book Illustrator / Designer. Born in Wimbledon in August 1909. The daughter of Frederick Charles Eldridge and Mildred Mary Chevalier. Her father initially worked as manager of a pawnbroker's, then as a jeweller. Raised in Wimbledon. Had at least one brother, Frederick. Studied at the Wimbledon School of Art, the Royal College of Art, London and the British School at Rome. Produced paintings of various subjects in oils and watercolours, including portraits, flowers, figures and landscapes, book illustrations, designs for stained glass and altar cloths, and murals. Illustrated, for example, Walter de la Mare, Three Royal Monkeys (1946) and The Three Mulla Mulgars (1970), Hilda W.W. Leyel, Compassionate Herbs (1946), Henry Williamson, The Star-Born (1948) and her own story Gwenno the Goat (1957). Between 1953 and 1958 she executed a mural for the nurses' canteen at the Robert Jones Agnes Hunt Orthopaedic Hospital, Gobowen, Shropshire. Noted in Janet Adam Smith, Children's Illustrated Books, London, Collins, 1948. Exhibited her work, including at the Royal Academy (1934-53), the Royal Scottish Academy (1935-38), the Royal Hibernian Academy (1940), the Society of Women Artists (1938), the Royal Cambrian Academy, the Royal Society of Painters in Watercolours and the Beaux Art Gallery. Exhibited works included: Singing Magpies, Potato Harvest, Poggio Gherardo, Women and White Goats and The Living Garment. Elected an Associate of the Royal College of Art and an Associate of the Royal Society of Painters in Watercolours. Listed in Who's Who in Art for 1952 as 'recording Wales for Pilgrim Trust (1944-46)'. In 1940 she married poet and curator Ronald S. Thomas (1909-2000) in Wales. Produced the cover for her husband's poems Stories of the Field (1947). Based in Leatherhead, Surrey initially, then Chirk and Montgomery, Wales. Died in Wales, aged 81. Works in the permanent collection of the Victoria & Albert Museum, London and in the corporation galleries of Oldham, Sheffield and Birmingham.

ELLIOTT, AILEEN MARY (1896-1966)

Etcher / Painter. Born in Southampton in December 1896. The daughter of Walter Pearson Elliott (1857-1935), a timber merchant and Managing Director of Elliott Bros Ltd, and Jean Alexander Brown (1864-1944). Her father originated from Southampton, her mother from Hampshire. The eldest of at least three daughters (also Rosie and Ruth), all raised in Southampton. Educated in Eastbourne. Spent time in London in the 1920s, possibly studying there. Latterly, lived in Berkshire. Also spent some time in Lee-on-the-Solent, Hampshire. In 1931 she married Arthur Hugh Lansdowne Beale (1887-1958) in Kensington, London. Died in Windsor, Berkshire in late 1966, aged 69. An artist truly inspired by, and affected by, her surroundings. Produced etchings and watercolour paintings, particularly of boats and the sea. Travelled abroad to paint. Exhibited her work, including at the Royal Academy (1922-40), the Royal Scottish Academy (1927-39), the Society of Women Artists (1924-34), the Walker Art Gallery, Liverpool and with the Winchester Art Club. Exhibited works included: Coaling at Night, Port Said, Discharging Grain, Hull Docks, Thames Barges and The 'Archibald Russell' in London Docks. Produced an etching of the well-known 'Cutty Sark'. Her etching of 'The Majestic' in Southampton Dock, shown at the 1925 Winchester Art Club exhibition, was illustrated in The Studio, Vol.90, 1925, p.384. When Elliott first began to exhibit with the Club in the early 1920s, it was considered to be largely amateur. However, she doubtless played a part in elevating the Club's status, and by the mid to late-1920s numerous artists from London and elsewhere were contributing work. Elliott was noted in Frank L. Emanuel's volume Etching and Etchings, London, Pitman & Sons, 1930. Of Miss Elliott, Emanuel says 'Miss Elliott's marvellous knowledge and draughtsmanship of every kind of craft from the dumpy to the Titanic liner has sent her with a bound into the front rank of marine etchers' (p.264). Emanuel included an illustration of her etching Cement Barges on the Medway. Elected a Member of the Society of Graphic Art, and of the Winchester Art Club. Some of her etchings were reproduced by publisher Arthur Greatorex Ltd.

ELLIOTT, GLADYS - SEE GRIMSHAW, G.

ELLIS, ELEANOR JOAN (1904-89)

Painter / Engraver. Better known as E. Joan. Born in Putney, London in November 1904. The daughter of Henry William Ellis, a wine merchant, and Eleanor Dorothy. One of at least four children (Henry, Dorothy, Eleanor and Janet). Raised in Wimbledon. Educated at the Abbey School, Malvern Wells. Studied at Leon Underwood's School of Art. Produced paintings in oils and watercolours and wood engravings. Exhibited her work, including with the New English Art Club, at the Daily Express Exhibition, with the English Wood Engravers Society, at the Gieves Art Gallery, the Royal

Hibernian Academy (1927) and with the Society of Wood Engravers. Elected a Member of the St Ives Society of Artists (c.1930), exhibiting woodcuts and other works with the Society in the 1930s. Works included: The Alster, Hamburg, shown at the Society of Wood Engravers exhibition, held at the Redfern Gallery in 1933 and illustrated in The Studio, Vol.105, March 1933, p.185. Her Sails and Bathers appeared in an article British Wood Engraving of the Present Day by Maximilien Vox in The Studio, Vol.99, March 1930, pp.155-167. Her Sailors and Seagulls, exhibited with the Society of Wood Engravers at the Redfern Gallery in 1931, was illustrated in The Studio, Vol.101, March 1931. Other works included The Dancers. Her work reflected the 1930s and Art Deco with its simplistic, bold style. Her work would have made equally good posters for advertisements. In 1933 Ellis married Peter Francis White (1899-1994) in Wimbledon. He was a Captain in the Royal Engineers. Ellis spent much of her career in London. She died in Surrey, aged 84.

ELLIS, HILDA M. - SEE LITTLER, H.M.

ELLIS, IVY ANNE (1897-1984)

Wood Engraver. Born in Birmingham in April 1897. The daughter of Ralph Ellis and Emily Jane Price. Her father, a public house manager and later a waiter at a university, originated from Birmingham. Her mother, a dressmaker, originated from Hereford. Ivy had at least two siblings, Cathleen and Ralph. Raised in Birmingham and lived there initially, but later moved to the Cotswolds, Gloucestershire, where she died, aged 86. Studied at the Birmingham School of Arts and Crafts. Illustrated a number of books during her career including The Book of Ruth (1930), Havelock Ellis, XII Sonnets (1930) and Rose S. Dugdale, A Wreath of Flower Legends (1950). Exhibited her work locally with the Royal Birmingham Society of Artists. Works included: Gold Fish and Sea Horses. Works purchased by the British Museum. Her Free Vistas, New York was illustrated in The Serpentine Worker. Two of her works, Smollett's House, Edinburgh and Washing-Day, Whitby, were illustrated in Bernard Sleigh, Wood Engraving Since 1890, London, Pitman, 1932. Sleigh says, 'Miss Ellis should go far, having found by long experience the "graver language" best suited to her temperament' (p.82). Ellis was probably one of Sleigh's pupils. Although married with two children, Sleigh left his small estate to Ellis on his death.

ELMORE, EDITH CONSTANCE - SEE LAW ADAM, E.C.

ELPHINSTONE, MARY H. - SEE McCLINTOCK, M.H.

ELVERY, BEATRICE MOSS - SEE GLENAVY, B.M.

ELWIN, AMY M. - SEE SINGER, A.M.

EMMERSON, GLADYS E. - SEE PETO, G.E.

EMONET, AUBREY PAULINA (1905-93)

Painter / Wood Engraver / Poster Artist / Illuminator. Born in Bath, Somerset in August 1905. Died in Bath, aged 87. The daughter of William Henry Phippen (1861-1941) and Adeline Nott (1874-1955). Her father, who originated from Somerset, was a Professor of Music. Her mother, who originated from Devon, was a private school teacher. Raised in Bath. Possibly an only child. Educated privately. Studied at the Bath School of Art and at the Royal College of Art, London. Elected an Associate of the Royal College of Art in 1932. Worked in Bath as a painter in oils and watercolours, a wood engraver, a poster designer and an illuminator. Exhibited her work, including at the Royal West of England Academy and with the Bath Society of Artists. Works included: Snow (watercolour), Roofs (oil) and Pedigree of the Pinckneys, an illuminated lineage from 1068AD. In 1932 she married Albert Maurice Emonet (1894-1987) in London.

ENGLAND, NORA (1887-1970)

Painter / Designer / Illustrator. Born in London in April 1887. The daughter of Edwin Arthur Ward and Katherine House. Her father was a portrait painter who originated from Bradford. Her mother originated from Middlesex. Raised in London. One of at least six children (Margaret, Peter, Nora, Francis, Libusa and Katherine). Educated privately. Studied at the Kensington and Westminster Schools of Art, London, and with Sir James Shannon, R.A. Became a portrait and figure painter in oils and watercolours, a painter / designer of dresses for the stage, screen and fashion, an interior decorator and an illustrator. Exhibited her work, including at the Royal Academy (1920-28), the Society of Women Artists (1920-23), the Royal Institute of Painters in Watercolours, the Royal Society of British Artists, the Royal Society of Portrait Painters and the International Society of Sculptors, Painters & Gravers. Exhibited works included: A Summer's Day, The Sofa, Sisters and

Getting Ready for the Fancy Dress Ball. Elected a Member of the Royal Society of British Artists (1920-30) and a Member of the Society of Women Artists (1921-22). Produced illustrations for, for example, Songs and Ballads of Robert Burns (Hodder & Stoughton). Some of her illustrations also appeared in journals and magazines including Queen and Sphere. Based largely in London during her career. in 1915 she married Frank De Fontayne England in London. They had at least two children. Nora was still active into the 1950s. She died in Hampshire, aged 83.

ENGLEFIELD, CICELY (1893-1970)

Artist / Illustrator. Born in Lee, London. The daughter of Frederick W. Englefield and Frances Maud. Her father was a solicitor and Registrar of the County Courts. One of at least five children (William, Frederick, Cicely, Rupert and Anita). Spent her childhood in West Malling, Kent. Educated in London, at the Maidstone Grammar School and at the Blackheath High School. Studied at the St Martin's School of Art, London and the London County Council Central School of Arts and Crafts. At that time, the family had returned to London. She began by selling illustrations to various children's annuals. Then began to write and illustrate her own children's books and articles. Produced wood engravings, pen & ink drawings, watercolours and lithographs. Most of her books were published by John Murray. Those included: George and Angela (1932), Katie the Caterpillar (1933), A House for a Mouse (1936), Bessie Black Lamb (1938), Connie the Cow (1939), Bert the Sparrow (1941) and The Tale of a Tadpole (1945). Based in London. Died in Poole, Dorset. Noted in Mahony, Latimer & Folmsbee, Illustrators of Children's Books 1744-1945, Boston, The Horn Book Inc., 1947.

ENTWISTLE, GLADYS - SEE LINES, G.

ERICHSEN, NELLIE (1863-1918)

Painter / Illustrator. Born in Newcastle-upon-Tyne. Remained there for a short time. The family subsequently moved to Tooting, London where Nellie remained into adulthood. She spent most of the rest of her life in London, living at various addresses, but died in Bagni di Lucca, Italy, aged 55. She was one of at least five children. The daughter of Hermann G. Erichsen, who originated from Copenhagen, and Anna. Her father is listed in census recordings as a Telegraph Director. By at least 1881, at the age of 18, Nellie was a student of the Royal Academy

schools and living in Streatham, London. Became a painter of various subjects and an illustrator for books and magazines. Contributed to The English Illustrated Magazine. Books illustrated by her included Henrik Pontoppidan, The Promised Land (1896), Edmund Gardner, The Story of Florence (45 illustrations, 20 by Nellie), Lina Duff Gordon, The Story of Assisi (1900) and A.J. Lawley, The Story of Verona (1902). One of the last books she illustrated was Edward Hutton, Highways and Byways in Wiltshire (1917).

Erichsen exhibited her work, including at the Society of Women Artists (1883-88), the Royal Academy (1884-97), the Royal Society of British Artists (1883-88), the Royal Institute of Oil Painters and in Liverpool. Exhibited works included: After the Sun is Set, A Weedy Corner, Margot, The Street End and The Emperor's New Clothes. Since she is recorded as visiting publisher Alexander Macmillan in 1891, Nellie probably worked for Macmillan among others, and knew him personally. Erichsen was also a translator and editor of contemporary drama. Edited the Duckworth Modern Plays series (1895-1901) with R. Brimley Johnson. She was the first translator into English of August Strindberg's The Father (1899). Noted in R.E.D. Sketchley's English Book Illustration of To-day, London, Kegan Paul, 1903. Sketchley notes that Erichsen and Helen James were both much in demand as illustrators of travel books such as Dent's Mediaeval Towns. The two women collaborated on books about Italian towns. But Nellie did work other than architectural. She also illustrated Florentine Villas by Mrs Ross, and The Story of Rome. Also, The Novels of Susan Edmonstone Ferrier, introduced by R. Brimley Johnson, Dent, 1894, six volumes.

ESPLIN, MABEL (1874-1921)

Stained Glass Designer. Born at Chorlton, Manchester. The daughter of Richard M. Esplin and Sarah Jane. Her father was a furniture manufacturer. One of at least four children (Mabel, Hilda, Mildred and Harold). Harold became an art student. In her youth, Esplin attended a school at Birkdale, Sefton. She subsequently studied at the Slade School, London, followed by a period at the London County Council Central School of Arts and Crafts (1906-10). There, like Mary Lowndes, she fell under the influence of Christopher Whall (1849-1924), Karl Parsons and Alfred J. Drury, three leading figures in British stained glass. As a student, Esplin exhibited stained glass cartoons at the National Competition of Schools of Art, certainly in 1906 and 1907. Also like Lowndes,

Esplin was involved with the women's suffrage movement, and took part in the 1909 International Woman Suffrage Alliance Congress in London. After completing her studies, she set up her own stained glass workshop in Hampstead, at Heath Studios, and in December 1911 held an exhibition of her work there. All her stained glass was actually made in association with Lowndes and Drury at the Glass House, Fulham (where Mary Lowndes was based).

Some of Esplin's early work appeared in the Art Journal (in 1906, pp.276-284, in 1907, pp.265-274). Some of her later work appeared in The Studio, for example, Vol.82, September 1921, pp.114-115. In 1912 she showed work at the Women's Guild of Arts exhibition in London. Became a Member of the Church Crafts League (founded 1899), there listed as a stained glass worker. Commissions included stained glass for St John the Divine, Richmond (1912) and for St Anne's Church, Lewes (1914). She also won a competition for a decorative scheme for the interior of St Jude's Church, Hampstead Garden Suburb by Lutyens. One of her largest commissions was an extensive glazing scheme for All Saints' Cathedral at Khartoum in the Sudan. The building was designed by Robert Weir Schultz in 1909. The commission occupied much of her career. Other design work carried out by Esplin included mural decorations for Christ Church, Spitalfields and for St Andrew's Church, Thornton Heath, Surrey. In 1912 she designed and made a number of small stained glass panels based on subjects from Chaucer, Spenser and Shakespeare for a house on the Clyde, Scotland.

Following a serious mental breakdown in 1916, Esplin was unable to work again, aged only 42. But she did exhibit five of her cartoons at the Society of Women Artists in 1917, including a memorial panel St Michael and a domestic panel Piers the Ploughman. The Khartoum commission was finished by her former assistant Joan Fulleylove in the 1920s. Indications are that Esplin's mother suffered similar mental health problems, and in the early 1900s was living in a clinic near Denbigh. Her mother died in December 1920, her father shortly after in January 1921. Esplin died very soon after her father in 1921, in a nursing home near Manchester, aged only 47. Some of her work was included in an exhibition Women Stained Glass Artists of the Arts and Crafts Movement, held at the William Morris Gallery, London in 1985 / 86.

ETHERINGTON, LILIAN M. - SEE REYNOLDS, L.M.

EVA, SOPHIE FREDERIKA (1872-1964)

Enameller. Also Frederika Sophie. Born in Oxford. The daughter of Oliver Prust Martin (1847-1922) and Elizabeth Frederica Uhlenbeck (1847-1913). Her father originated from Northamptonshire. Her mother was born in Java, in the Dutch East Indies. Initially, her father was a wholesale jeweller and watch manufacturer in Birmingham, but later worked as an upholsterer's clerk in Bath, Somerset. Sophie was one of at least eight children (Sophie, Martha, Charles, Marion, Edith, Christina, Oliver and Margaret). Raised in Oxford, in Edgbaston, Birmingham and in Bath. By at least the age of 18, Sophie was working as an art teacher in a government school in Bath. At some point, she studied enamelling. In 1898 she married Charles Andrew Eva (1867-1945) in Kensington, London. He originated from Penzance, Cornwall, the son of a local auctioneer. He became headmaster of the London County Council School of Art, Hackney Institute and at the L.C.C. Hammersmith School of Arts and Crafts. His brother, artist and poster designer Herbert Edward Eva, lived with them for a number of years. The couple lived mainly in Chiswick, London, but both died at Sherborne, Dorset. They had two daughters, Ursula (b.1900) and Marjorie (b.1904). Sophie continued to work after her marriage. She exhibited five examples of her work at the Royal Academy between 1914 and 1923, including Homeward Bound (cloisonne enamel), Tutankhamen (cloisonne enamel), Marjorie (enamel) and Beatrice d'Este - after da Vinci.

EVANS, CLAIRE GLADYS MARY (c.1893-1965)

Illuminator. Also Gladys Mary. A founder member of the London-based Society of Scribes and Illuminators (founded 1921). She was present at the very first meetings held. Acted as Honorary Secretary of the Society from 1942 to 1946. The Society was devoted to excellence in lettering, writing and illumination. Other early members included Graily Hewitt, Louisa Puller and H. Lawrence Christie. Evans wrote an article on the Society which was published in The Studio, Vol.138, July 1949, pp.1-5. The article included an example of her own work - a pattern for a birth brief. Exhibited one example of her work at the Society of Women Artists in 1930, Herrick's 'Night Piece to Julia'. Based in London. Died at Herstmonceux, East Sussex, aged 72.

EVANS, ELLEN M. - SEE SHENTON, E.M.

EVANS, GWENDOLINE EDITH MARION (b.1898)

Illustrator / Painter / Artist / Wood Engraver. Born in London in February 1898. The daughter of William Evans and Frances. Her father, a County Court Judge, originated from Wales. Had at least one brother, Powys A.L. Evans. Educated privately. Studied at the Slade School, London and at the Westminster Technical Institute. A pupil of Walter Sickert and Sylvia Gosse. Produced illustrations, paintings of animals, pencil portraits and wood engravings. Exhibited her work, including at the Royal Academy (1922-31), the New English Art Club, the Goupil Gallery and with the International Society of Sculptors, Painters & Gravers. Exhibited works included: Hurdled Sheep, In the Library (pencil) and The Tockey Act. Based in London until at least 1934. In 1934 she travelled to Singapore. Powys Evans also studied under Sylvia Gosse, and worked as an artist in London.

EVE, ESME FRANCES OLIVE (1920-2001)

Illustrator / Painter / Designer. Born in Sydenham in September 1920. The daughter of Frank A. Eve and Gertrude Parsons. Educated at the Wallington County School. Studied in London, at the Croydon School of Arts and Crafts between 1937 and 1941, and at the Royal College of Art between 1941 and 1944. Elected an Associate of the Royal College of Art. Became a book illustrator, a commercial and industrial designer of greetings cards, book jackets and fabrics, and a painter in watercolours. Illustrated, for example, The Little Red Steamer, Water of Delight, The Little Lame Prince and Mother Goose Nursery Rhymes (Grosset & Dunlop, 1958). Exhibited some of her work at the Royal College of Art exhibitions and at Burlington House. Based at Wallington, Surrey for part of her career. Later lived at Seaford, Sussex. Died in Sussex, aged 80.

EVERETT, ETHEL FANNY (1878-1951)

Painter / Illustrator. Born and raised in London. The daughter of James Everett and Fanny. One of at least three children (Percy, Ethel and Albert). Educated at the Mary Datchelor School. Studied at the Royal Academy schools, London. Produced portrait paintings, including of children, and illustrated children's books. Books illustrated by her included Charles Kingsley, The Water Babies (1910), M. Dowson, Elizabeth Ann's Delight (1922), Enid Blyton, Silver and Gold (1927), Rose Fyleman, Old-Fashioned Girls (1928) and L.G. Eady, Elizabeth's Book (1928).

Her work also appeared in Graphic, the Daily Telegraph, the Daily Chronicle, Aunt Judy's Magazine and The Jolly Book. A colour print of her Once in Royal David's City was produced by the Burlington Art Publishers. Exhibited her work, including at the Royal Academy (1911-36). Exhibited works included: My Treasures, Tiny Tim and Granny, a Dear Little Old Workhouse Woman. Died in Saffron Walden, Essex, aged 73.

EVERETT, ROBERTA ALICE GORDON (1906-79)

Sculptor. Born in Surrey in May 1906. The daughter of Robert Henry Hatcher and Alice Eliza. An only child, her father died young, and she was raised by her mother in Surrey. Educated at the Wallington County School. Studied at the Goldsmiths' School of Art, London and at the London Art School. Awarded an Art Teachers' Diploma. Became a sculptor of busts, heads and figures, working in clay, plaster, bronze and stone. Exhibited her work, including at the Royal Glasgow Institute (1935), the Royal Academy (1928-49), the Bradford City Art Gallery and the Paris Salon. Exhibited works included: Torso (bronzed plaster), Frances (head, bronze), Torso (Portland stone) and The Artist's Mother (head). Worked as a craft lecturer at the Shoreditch Training College. Also acted as senior art mistress at the Coborn School for Girls, Bow (1948-50). Based in Hornchurch, Essex during much of her career. Works reproduced in, for example, The Schoolmistress, Architect, Builder and Nursery World. Works purchased by the Lancashire Educational Committee. In 1929 she married John Garwood Everett, B.Sc., Ph.D., F.R.I.C., M.I.Ch.E., in Epsom, Surrey. They had at least three children. Roberta died in Middlesex.

EVERSHED, ADA - SEE GELL, A.

EVERSHED, KATHERINE MARY FRANCES (1891-1965)

Sculptor / Pottery Worker. Also known as Kitty. Born and raised in Kendal, Westmorland. The daughter of Wallis Evershed (1864-1911) and Eleanor. Her father was an analytical chemist and later managing director and analyst for a local brewery. One of at least four children (Wallis, Katherine, Eleanor and Joyce). Probably studied in London. Produced mainly animals and figures in glazed earthenware, glazed pottery and terracotta. Based for much of her career in London, certainly from the 1920s. Died in Surrey, aged 74, but was still living in London at the time of her death. Exhibited her work, including at the Royal Scottish Academy (1931), the Royal

Hibernian Academy (1931-36) and the Royal Glasgow Institute (1931). Exhibited 90 works at the Society of Women Artists between 1927 and 1962. Exhibited works included: The Little Milliner (glazed earthenware and enamel), Aurora (glazed earthenware), Dancing Fawn (glazed earthenware) and Serenade (decorative figure, coloured in underglaze). Elected an Associate of the Society of Women Artists (1932) and a Member (1933-64).

EYRE, MAUREEN P. - SEE PROUDMAN, M.P.

F

FAIRFAX, GERTRUDE - SEE CROCKFORD, G.

FARHALL, HILDA M. - SEE SARE, H.M.

FARMILOE, EDITH CAROLINE (1870-1921)

Artist / Illustrator. Born in Chatham, Kent. Died in Bury St Edmunds, Suffolk. The daughter of Arthur Parnell (1841-1914), a Major in the Royal Engineers, and Mary Ann Dunn (d.1920). Her mother was the daughter of a wool merchant. Her father was the son of Henry Parnell, also listed in records as Lord Congleton. Edith was one of at least 10 children. Raised in Kent. In the 1880s she and her sister Winifred lived with their grandparents, the Dunns, whilst at school. In the very early 1890s, the sisters were living with their other grandparents, the Parnells, in London. In 1891 Edith married the Rev. William Thomas Farmiloe. During his career, he acted as vicar of a church at Colchester, of St Augustine's, Victoria Park, and of St Peter's, Soho. Edith worked as an artist and book illustrator. Worked on, for example, V. Lucas, All the World Over (1898) and W. Parnell, Rag, Tag and Bobtail (1899). Illustrated her own books, including 'Chousers' and Other Stories (1898), Chapel Street Children (1900), Piccalilli (1900), Little Citizens (1901), Young George (1901), One Day (1903) and Elizabeth-Over-the-Way (1905). Edith used the young children of her husband's poor London parish as models for her work. She also contributed to periodicals including Little Folks, The Children's Pictorial and Pearson's Magazine. She was still active as a professional artist in 1911, but is no longer listed as such on the national census.

Edith exhibited her work occasionally, including at the Society of Women Artists (36

works, 1893, 1904-09). Contributed to the Second Exhibition of Arts and Crafts held at the Lyceum Club, 1905-06. According to The Studio, Vol.36, January 1906, p.356, at that particular exhibition there was 'quite a large exhibit of the vivacious and clever pen-drawings of Miss Edith Farmiloe' which 'added greatly to the attractiveness of the Exhibition'. Works included: Children of the Rich, Gutter Snipes, A Quiet Smoke and Unemployed. Elected an Associate of the Society of Women Artists (1905) and a Member (1906-11). Noted in R.E.D. Sketchley, English Book Illustration of To-day, London, Kegan Paul, 1903. Her The Children of the Poor was purchased by the Queen. Works illustrated in The Studio, Vol.18, December 1899, p.179. Edith's sister, Gwendolen Parnell, also became an artist. SEE: PARNELL, GWENDOLEN

FARQUHAR, ELIZABETH B. - SEE VIVIAN, E.B.

FARRELL, FRANCES CAUTLEY (b.1902)

Weaver / Dyer. Born in Pulborough, Sussex in November 1902. The daughter of Cecil Cautley Baker, a land surveyor. Educated at the Bedales school. Studied at the Denis Baker School of Weaving in Shottery, Stratford-upon-Avon. Became a decorative hand-loom weaver and dyer. Early in her career, she spent some time teaching pattern and decorative weaving in Switzerland. In 1930 she married Michael Farrell (1899-1962). Moved to Ireland and established The Crock of Gold textile workshop, acting as proprietor and manager. Exhibited her work, including at the Arts and Crafts Exhibitions in London, with the Red Rose Guild in Manchester, at the Dublin Horse Show and at the Foire de Paris. A bronze and gold medallist at the Tailteann Games, Ireland.

FAULKNER, AILEEN M. - SEE HUMPHREYS, A.M.

FAULKNER, KATE (1841-98)

Designer / Decorative Artist. Also listed as Katherine or Catherine on national census recordings. Born and raised in Birmingham. The daughter of Benjamin Faulkner, a maltster and brewer, and Ann. Had at least six siblings (Benjamin, Charles, Hubert, Ann, Lucy and Frank), also born in Birmingham. Charles (1833-92) was a Fellow of University College, Oxford, and by at least 1861 was based in Queen Square, London with his mother and Kate. He subsequently worked as a teacher of mathematics. But he also became involved in the decorative arts, and was a founding partner in the firm of Morris, Marshall, Faulkner & Co. (or Morris & Co.) which began in 1861. In London, Kate also became involved in the decorative arts, joined by Lucy (1839-1910). Kate spent the rest of her life in London, living with Charles until his death. In 1870 Lucy married wood engraver Harvey Orrin Smith who worked for Burn & Co. Kate and Lucy painted tiles for Morris & Co. which were used chiefly in the decoration of entrance porches and fireplaces. Blank tiles were imported from Holland specifically for that purpose. However, when Morris began to work with William De Morgan, he gradually took over much of the tile production. Kate also designed some of the Morris & Co. wallpapers, including 'Blossom' (c.1885).

The Faulkners were part of a close-knit artistic group surrounding Morris, and Kate executed gesso decorations to the designs of Philip Webb, another member of the group. Some of her gesso decorations, worked to Webb's designs, appeared in the 1888 first Arts and Crafts Exhibition Society exhibition held in London. Kate carried out freelance work for ceramic firms including Pinder, Bourne & Co., Burslem, and for other wallpaper firms including Jeffrey & Co. who also exhibited at the London Arts and Crafts exhibitions. Lucy Faulkner was similarly talented and was involved in design, embroidery, china painting and wood engraving. She was also the author of The Drawing Room, its Decoration and Furniture (Macmillan, 1878). In 1868 she engraved a woodblock illustration of Cupid Leaving Psyche for Morris's The Earthly Paradise. Kate Faulkner had a particularly close friendship with Georgiana Burne-Jones, wife of artist Edward. In her Memorials of Edward Burne-Jones (two volumes, first published in 1904), Georgiana refers to Kate as having a 'gentle nature, sympathetic understanding and keen sense of humour' (Volume I). In Volume II she notes that Kate had a 'talent for designing ornament and skill in its execution' which was 'remarkable'. Kate died in London, aged 56.

FAWCETT, EMILY ADDIS (1852-1947)
Sculptor. Born in London. The daughter of Walter T. Fawcett, a member of the stock exchange, and Frances. One of a large family, of at least 10 children, including one set of twins (Frances, Mary, Walter, Blanche, Emily, Mabel, Sybil, Ada, Linda and Arthur). Raised in London. Studied in London and Paris. Based in London thereafter, and died there, aged 96. The family had money, and she left a considerable estate on her death. Worked as a sculptor of statuettes,

heads and busts in plaster, bronze and terracotta for at least 25 years, from at least the early 1880s into the 1900s. Based at Cheniston Gardens Studios for a time. Exhibited her work, including at the Royal Hibernian Academy (1885), the Society of Women Artists (1895-1908), the Royal Academy (1883-96), at the Walker Art Gallery, Liverpool and in Paris. Exhibited works included: Dear Lady Disdain (bust), In Trouble (statuette, bronze), Rustic Music (statue) and Defiance (head, terracotta). Executed at least one study of her sister, Mabel.

FELLOWS, CATHERINE ALLISON (1830-1912)
Sculptor. Also sometimes Fellowes. One of Britain's earliest and more unusual female professional sculptors. Born and raised in Wolverhampton and possibly studied there. Spent much of her life and career at Tettenhall Road, Wolverhampton, and died there, aged 83. The daughter of Isaac Fellows, a Superintendent Registrar, who originated from Staffordshire. In the early 1850s, Catherine was working as a governess in Leicester, but returned to Wolverhampton. By at least the 1860s she was working as a sculptor, and by the early 1870s is listed on census recordings as such. However, she is also listed as having 'lost one eye', which makes her profession only more remarkable, particularly when added to the fact that she was female, and was apparently not based in London, the main centre of artistic activity at that time. Catherine later lived with her brother, Charles Fellows, a manufacturing stationer. She was active predominantly in the 1860s and 1870s, producing portrait medallions and busts in marble, particularly of society figures and dignitaries. She exhibited 15 works at the Royal Academy between 1867 and 1872, and exhibited at the Walker Art Gallery, Liverpool. Subjects included Sir Rowland Hill, K.C.B.; Elihu Burritt, American Consul at Birmingham; Sir John Morris, Mayor of Wolverhampton; the Rev. J.B. Owen; A.M. Skinner, Q.C., Recorder of Windsor; the Rt Hon. William Frank; the Prince Consort as a Child and A Hindy Reformer. Her study of John Henry Robinson, R.A. is at Petworth, Sussex.

FELLS, MARGARET (1905-81)
Jewellery Worker / Enameller. Born in Catford, Kent in December 1905. The daughter of Ernest Fells and Christina Donald. Her father was involved in iron and steel in an ordnance works. Margaret was raised in Charlton, London. Educated at the St Joseph's Convent, Abbey Wood. Studied at the London County Council

Central School of Arts and Crafts. Awarded a London County Council Senior Art Scholarship in 1926. Later based at Plumstead. Exhibited her work occasionally, including at the Arts and Crafts exhibitions in London, and at the Arts and Crafts exhibitions held in Detroit, U.S.A. In 1932 she married Edward G.E. Turner (1906-93) in Woolwich. She died in Crawley, Sussex, aged 75. He died in Crawley some 12 years later.

FENWICK, SYBIL N. - SEE PRINGLE, S.N.

FIDDIAN, DOROTHY EILEEN (1891-1979)
Bookbinder. Born near Calcutta, India in April 1891. The daughter of William Fiddian and Alice Ann. Her father worked for the Indian Civil Service. One of at least five children (Kenneth, Cedric, Alice, Gladys and Dorothy). By at least 1901 the family had returned to England, to Ealing. Dorothy subsequently studied at the Acton and Chiswick Polytechnic. Awarded a First Class Certificate in forwarding and finishing, City & Guilds of London Institute, with silver and bronze medals. Worked mainly in London. Exhibited her work, including at the London Arts and Crafts Exhibitions, at the Walker Art Gallery, Liverpool and at the Society of Women Artists (1918-29). For a time, she had a workshop on Hammersmith Road, London. Fiddian died in St Albans, Hertfordshire, aged 88.

FIELD, ELIZABETH (1902-97)
Painter / Wood Engraver. Born in Birmingham in July 1902. The daughter of Henry Cromwell Field (1853-1929) and Ruth. Her father, an export merchant, originated from New York and died in Birmingham. Educated at the Edgbaston High School and at Crofton Grange, Kent. Studied at the Birmingham Central School of Arts and Crafts and at the Slade School, London. Based in Birmingham during her early career, living with her parents. Later based in Harpenden, Hertfordshire. Died in Hertfordshire, aged 94. In 1932 she married architect William Arthur Eden, A.R.I.B.A. in Birmingham. Produced paintings in watercolours and woodcuts. Various subjects including flowers and landscapes. Remained active until at least the 1960s. Exhibited her work, including with the New English Art Club, the Royal Society of British Artists, the International Print Makers, Los Angeles, the Society of Graver Printers and the Royal Birmingham Society of Artists. Exhibited seven works at the Society of Women Artists (1929-31, 1961-63), including Cotswolds in Snow, Wood Anemones (woodcut) and The Garden in Winter (watercolour). Elected a Member of the Central Club of Colour Wood-

Block Engravers and of the Society of Graver Printers, Birmingham. Also a Member of the Soroptimist Club. Birmingham Art Gallery purchased her Bredon Hill. Possibly the author of Colour Printing From Wood Blocks (Dryad). During the early 1930s, her address was the Queen's College, Birmingham, indicating some ties with the College.

FIELD, MARJORIE V.M. - SEE RHOADES, M.V.M.

FIELDEN, CONSTANCE M. - SEE VILLIERS-STUART, C.M.

FINNEMORE, SYBIL - SEE PARSONS, S.

FIRTH, SUSANNAH (1873-c.1955)
Black & White Artist / Leatherworker / Designer / Decorative Artist. Born in Heckmondwike, Yorkshire. The daughter of John Thomas Firth and Jane. One of at least five children (Frances, Susannah, George, Ellen and Sydney). Initially, the family lived at Dewsbury, Yorkshire where John Firth was, for a time, an unemployed iron moulder. But by at least 1891 the family had moved to Kirkby Lonsdale in Westmorland where John was employed as a gardener and Susannah was an art leatherworker. At some point, Susannah studied art in Liverpool, but also appears to have studied leatherwork at handcraft classes in Kirkby Lonsdale. The classes had been established by the Harris family in the mid-1880s. Head of the family was Alfred Harris of Bradford who, in 1869, bought the 40-acre Lunefield estate in Kirkby Lonsdale. His wife and daughters established classes in pottery, drawing, spinning, woodcarving, repoussé and leatherwork. Other members of the Firth family became involved in the classes, with John, Sydney and Ellen making pottery which was shown at the annual Home Arts and Industries Association exhibition under the Kirkby Lonsdale title. Ellen Firth also studied leatherwork locally. Susannah exhibited some of her leatherwork at the 1891 Arts, Crafts & Loan Exhibition held in Kendal, including a blotter embossed by her and coloured by Mrs Harris. This would indicate that Susannah had ties with the Kirkby Lonsdale classes from at least 1891.

By at least 1901 the family had moved again, to Church Street, Morley in Yorkshire. There, John was now employed as a potter's foreman, Sydney was a potter's thrower, Frances was a dressmaker and Susannah was a teacher of leather embossing. By at least 1911, Susannah had moved to Liverpool with Frances, and was working as an art handicrafts teacher. She appears to have remained in Liverpool, dying in the city. As part of the Kirkby Lonsdale classes, Susannah exhibited her work at the 1898 exhibition held at the Liverpool Royal Institute, showing a photo frame. Ellen Firth showed a decorative blotter case at the same exhibition. Susannah also exhibited her work at the Walker Art Gallery, Liverpool, including in 1909. Also, at the Society of Women Artists (1896), at the Paris Salon and in Canada and America. She had some ties with the short-lived Guild of Women Binders, formed in the late 1890s. Susannah additionally executed a number of bookplates for well-known authors and scientists as well as leather presentation covers for illuminated addresses for royalty, including Princess Louise and Princess Beatrice. Produced decorative jewellery too, to her own designs. A Member of the Sandon Studios Society Club. Works in the collection of the South Kensington Museum.

FISHER, FRANCES - SEE CRAWSHAW, F.

FISHER, KATE / KATIE (active early 1900s)
Metalworker. A student of the Mount Street School of Art, Liverpool in the late 1890s and early 1900s, under Fred V. Burridge. In 1900 she won a prize for her work and a Free Evening Studentship. Won other prizes as a student. Exhibited at the National Competition of Schools of Art, South Kensington, including in 1903. There, she showed a decorative altar panel in coloured relief which was illustrated in The Studio, Vol.30, 1903, p.46. Produced intricate and delicate work. Evidently highly talented. Early in her studies, in 1898, she exhibited decorative panels at the Walker Art Gallery, Liverpool Spring Exhibition of Arts and Crafts. Other works were illustrated in The Studio. For example, in Vol.19, 1900, pp.131-132, The Studio illustrated a brooch in silver and enamel, and three designs for other jewellery and for a girdle in gold and enamel. In 1901, the same journal, Vol.21, January, p.264, illustrated a processional cross in silver and enamel. Also exhibited at the Liverpool School of Art exhibition held in connection with the annual prize distribution. On one occasion she showed a door knocker. Otherwise, remains untraced after 1903. On one occasion, Kate was stated to be the daughter of metalworker Alexander Fisher (1864-1936), but no evidence has been found to date to support this.

FISHER, MAUD CHARLTON (1859-1942)
Painter / Etcher / Pen & Ink Artist / Designer / Illustrator / Textile Artist. Born in Bristol. The daughter of Edward Fisher and Susanna. Her father, a Freeman of Bristol, was involved in the new and second-hand clothing trade. Maud was one of at least four children (Kathleen, Sarah, Maud and Hugh). Kathleen and Sarah took up their father's profession in Bristol. Maud was educated at private school. Then studied at the Bristol School of Art, where she won a bronze medal, the Queen's Prize and a scholarship. Produced paintings in oils and watercolours, etchings, pen & ink drawings, miniature paintings, designs, book illustrations and textile designs, and was a linen stainer for church decoration. She spent much of her career in Bristol, living with Kathleen and Sarah for a number of years, and died there, aged 82. But she also spent some time in London, working as an art mistress at the South Kensington schools. Became head teacher at the Branch Class of the Bristol School of Art, and art mistress in a private school. In 1900 she won an Honourable Mention in a The Studio competition for a design for a Christmas card under the name 'Owl'. By invitation, she contributed to the library of the Queen's Doll's House. Exhibited her work, including at the Royal Academy (1906) and with the Royal West of England Academy. Exhibited works included: The Lady Chapel, St Mary Redcliffe, Bristol. Elected an Associate of the Royal West of England Academy (1911). Some of her work appeared in the Girl's Own Paper.

FITCHEW, EVANGELINE ESTHER MAY (1887-1958)
Craftswoman / Painter / Decorative Designer / Lettering and Illumination Artist. Born in Brighton, Sussex. Spent part of her career in Brighton, but later moved to Bristol. Died in Teignmouth, Devon, aged 71. The daughter of architect and surveyor George T. Fitchew and Ella. One of at least three children (also Rupert and Frederick). Studied in Brighton, at the South Kensington schools, London and in Manchester. Won bronze and silver medals at national level. Awarded City & Guilds prizes for embroidery and bookbinding. Also, two King's Prizes. Awarded an Art Masters' Teaching Certificate. Acted as art teaching assistant in Brighton in the early 1910s. Subsequently became art mistress at the Redland High School, Bristol. Exhibited her work, including at the Royal West of England Academy, in Brighton, and with the Society of Women Artists (1919). Elected an Associate of the Royal West of England Academy. Some of her illumination work was illustrated in The Studio. Produced illustrations for Environment, a Natural Geography. Executed Rolls of Honour and illuminated addresses during her career.

FITTON, MARGARET MARY ELIZABETH (1902-88)

Painter / Sculptor / Illustrator / Lithographer. Born in London in November 1902. The daughter of Walter Frank Cook, a civil service clerk, and Alice Mary. Raised in Willesden. One of at least three children. Educated privately. Studied art in London. Produced paintings of various subjects, lithographs, sculptures and book illustrations. Between 1925 and 1928 she worked as an illustrator in a publishing house. Based mainly in London during her career. Died in Camberwell, aged 85. Exhibited her work, including at the Royal Academy (1931-57), the Society of Women Artists (16 works, 1939-40), with the London Group, the New English Art Club, the Senefelder Club and at the Chicago Institute of Fine Art. In 1931 she showed one work at the Seventeen Artists exhibition, held at the Zwemmer Gallery (Second Exhibition). Other exhibitors included Barbara Hepworth, Sine McKinnon and Edna Ginesi. Exhibited works included: Ironing and Airing, Room With a View, Glasshouse and Child Drawing. In 1928 she married James Fitton in Hampstead.

FLETCHER, EDITH - SEE RAWNSLEY, E.

FLETCHER, ROSAMUND MARY BEATRICE (1908-93)

Sculptor. Born in Dorking, Surrey in August 1908. The daughter of exhibiting artist William Tenlow Blandford Fletcher (1858-1937) and Norah Beatrice Emmeline. Had at least one sister, Christine. Raised in Dorking. Educated at the St Joseph's Priory, Dorking. Studied at the Ruskin School, Oxford between 1935 and 1937 under Albert Rutherston. Then, at the Slade School, London between 1937 and 1939 under Professor Randolph Schwabe and Gerrard. Spent much of her career based at Woodstock Road, Oxford. Died in Essex, aged 84. Produced figures, groups, reliefs, panels and fountains, many inspired by nature and religion. Worked in bronze, stone, plaster and marble. Produced a number of works for churches. In 1948 she won the Feodora Gleichen Award. Exhibited her work, including at the Royal Society of British Artists, the Paris Salon, with the London Group, and in Bournemouth, Cardiff, Leicester, Northampton and Sheffield. Also, at the Royal Academy (1938-65), the Royal Glasgow Institute (1949-51), the Royal Scottish Academy (1950-61) and the Society of Women Artists (1937-50). In 1948 won an Olympic bronze medal for her work. Exhibited works included: Geese (panel, Hoptonwood stone), Anne and Judy (group, bronze), St Joseph the Worker and the Holy Child (relief, Hoptonwood stone) and The Battle of the Seagulls (relief, Portland stone). Elected an Associate and a Fellow of the Royal Society of British Sculptors. Elected a Member of the Guild of Lettering Craftsmen. Also a Member of the Council of the Royal Society of British Sculptors.

FORD, EMILY SUSAN (1851-1930)

Painter / Designer / Stained Glass Artist. Born in Leeds, Yorkshire. The daughter of Robert Lawson Ford, a solicitor, and Hannah Pease. Her father originated from Lancashire. Her mother, who originated from Leeds, was an active campaigner, including for women's rights. The family were Quakers. Emily was one of at least seven children (Mary, Catherine, John, Thomas, Elizabeth, Emily and Isabella). All were raised in Adel cum Eccup, Yorkshire. Isabella became an active socialist and supporter of women's rights. Emily studied at the Slade School, London in the mid-1870s, but was back living in Leeds by at least the early 1880s. Later, in the early 1900s, she was working as an artist in Chelsea, living alone. However, she died in Leeds. Like her mother, Emily became a Member of the Ladies' National Association, and was Vice President of the Leeds Suffrage Society, designing its membership card. She also became interested in socialism.

A successful artist, Ford became a Member of the Women's International Art Club, and of the Church Crafts League. For the latter, she acted on the Committee, and is listed in the League's papers as a stained glass artist and a painter. Whilst at Leeds, she exhibited two works at the Royal Academy in 1894: All the Earth Doth Worship Thee and To Thee All Angels Cry Aloud. She also exhibited four works at the Society of Women Artists between 1880 and 1901 including: On a Yorkshire Moor, Snow and February. Ford was a close friend of painter Evelyn de Morgan. In around 1919, Ford collaborated on a project with fellow stained glass artist Mary Lowndes (1857-1929). In 1908 she contributed to the Liverpool Crafts Exhibition held at the Old Bluecoat School, showing designs in black chalk for mural decoration and stained glass. Works in the Stanley & Audrey Burton Gallery, University of Leeds.

FORRESTER, ANNA HARDIE (1875-1967)

Painter / Designer. Born in Bowdon, Cheshire in March 1875. Raised in Cheshire and in Salford, Lancashire. Spent some time in Manchester later in her career, but died in Cheshire, aged 92. The daughter of Stephen Petrie MacFarlane Forrester, an underwriter, and Anna Hardie. One of at least five children (William, Stephen, Margaret, Agnes and Anna). Probably studied in Manchester. Became a painter of miniatures, portraits and outdoor subjects in oils and watercolours, and worked as a designer for cotton and silk printing. Exhibited her work occasionally, including at the Royal Academy (1912), in Manchester and at the Manchester Academy of Fine Arts. Exhibited works included: Barbara Allen. Elected a Member of the Manchester Society of Miniature Painters, and was the Society's Vice President for a time. Also a Member of the Attic Club, of which she was Secretary in the 1930s.

FORSYTH, MOIRA (1905-c.91)

Stained Glass Artist / Studio Potter. Born in Cresswell, Staffordshire in May 1905. The daughter of Gordon Mitchell Forsyth (b.1879) and Elizabeth Lamont Aiken (b.1879). Her parents originated from Aberdeenshire. Her father was, for a number of years, Principal of the Stoke-on-Trent Schools of Art, in the heart of pottery production. He was also the author of Art & Craft of the Potter (Chapman Hall) and Twentieth Century Ceramics (Studio Ltd), and was latterly based at Crewe, Cheshire. Early in Moira's life, the family also spent time in Salford, Lancashire where her father worked as a designer for a pottery manufacturer. Moira had one brother, John Mitchell Gordon Forsyth. She studied at the Burslem School of Art in Staffordshire, then at the Royal College of Art, London. Elected an Associate of the Royal College of Art in 1930. Subsequently based in Fulham, London at the St Oswald's Studios. Possibly died in Surrey, aged 86.

Stained glass designs by Moira included several windows for Guildford Cathedral, including a rose window and a design for the High Sheriff's window. Other designs included, for example, The Annunciation for Bickleigh Church, Tiverton, Devon. Also, a mosaic panel for Loscoe Church, Derbyshire. And, windows for St John's College, Oxford, for King Edward's School, Birmingham and for St Stephen's Church, Dulwich. Doubtless due in part to her father's influence, Moira also became a pottery artist, particularly of earthenware figures. She practised two old Staffordshire techniques, though her figures were contemporary and naturalistic, with distinct faces and sometimes a sense of humour. One of her pieces was The Ugly Duchess, one of a set of Lewis Carroll subjects taken from Alice in Wonderland. Forsyth created the designs, and the figures were produced by Messrs A.G. Richardson of Burslem. They were illustrated in

The Studio, Vol.103, May 1932, p.283 in an article Art Schools & Industry, ii. Stoke-on-Trent.

Another of Moira's figures, in a glaze of grey olive and pale green, was illustrated in The Studio, Vol.110, November 1935, p.264 in an article Figurines in Pottery. She was the subject of an article, The Ceramic Figures of Moira Forsyth, in The Studio, Vol.143, April 1952, pp.112-113. Three of her pieces, The Cello Player, April and The Cage, were illustrated, all produced in coloured glazes. Forsyth occasionally exhibited her work, including at the Royal Academy (18 works, 1929-52). Exhibited works included: Winter, Chelsea, Taking in the Nets, Polperro and North Light (gouache). Elected a Member of the Art Workers' Guild in 1964. Some of her watercolours were in the museums of Bristol and Stoke-on-Trent. Some of her pottery figures were acquired by Stoke-on-Trent, Brussels and the Museo Internazionale delle Ceramiche, Faenza. Works also reproduced in the Pottery and Glass Record.

FOSBERRY, EVELYN MABEL - SEE BANKART, E.M.

FOSTER, MARCIA LANE - SEE JARRETT, M.L.

FOWLER, ANN (1839-1929)

Lace Maker. Ann Fowler was born in Honiton, Devon, spent much of her life there, and died there, aged 90. She was the daughter of Benjamin Ward, a coachbuilder, and Elizabeth. One of at least seven children. In 1876 she married William Fowler in Honiton. He originated from Somerset. He was initially a lace manufacturer, and later a draper. In the early 1860s, prior to her marriage, Ann spent a short time working as a draper's assistant in Yeovil. But by the very early 1870s, she is listed as a lace maker back in Honiton. In 1871 she submitted a banner screen to the Bath and West of England Agricultural Society Honiton lace competition, but did not receive a prize because it was so well executed the judges decided it had been made elsewhere. She was later awarded a prize, but refused to accept it. Honiton has a long and complex history in lace making, and Ann's sister, Elizabeth, was also involved, along with Ann's neighbour, Priscilla Stevens, and other local women. Ann's involvement continued well into the early 1900s, though by 1911, aged 71, she is no longer listed as a professional lace maker on census recordings. As Mrs Fowler, Ann was granted a royal warrant as lace maker to Queen Victoria, Queen Alexandra and the Princess of Wales. She rediscovered the technique of handmade ground-net lace. Won a number of awards and medals for her lace in Europe and America, exhibiting Honiton lace at the 1904 St Louis Exhibition and elsewhere. Mrs Fowler not only directed other Honiton lace makers, but ran a small school in the town in the 1890s, and a lace shop in High Street, Honiton which sold new lace and offered cleaning and alterations to existing lace. Some examples of her work can be found in the Allhallows Museum, Honiton, Devon. As Mrs Fowler's career came to a close, lace maker Audrey Trevelyan and London-based Effie Bruce Clarke instigated a revival in lace making in Devon, which ran in conjunction with the Home Arts and Industries Association. SEE: CLARKE, EFFIE BRUCE

FOWLER, MARY L. - SEE WALLER, M.L.

FRANCE, GEORGINA E.C. - SEE GASKIN, G.E.C.

FRANCIS, CARRIE (active 1910s-1920s)
Jewellery Designer / Enameller / Painter. Possibly Caroline Francis. A colonial artist, Miss Francis spent a number of years in Europe, studying and working in London. Awarded a South Kensington diploma and silver medals as a student. Based at Edith Road, West Kensington for a time. Produced jewellery and other decorative work designed and executed by her in the early twentieth century. Also a landscape and portrait painter in oils and watercolours. A triptych and two necklaces by her were illustrated in The Studio, Vol.89, June 1925, pp.328-329. The triptych was in silver with dark blue enamel set with jewels and plaited silver wire. The triptych had a centrepiece of a Madonna in Limoges. She also made jewelled pyx boxes for the Sacrament, clasps, silver dishes and Limoges enamel panels. Exhibited at the Royal Academy (1914), the Royal Colonial Institute and the Paris Salon. Effectively disappears from British records in the late 1920s.

FRANCIS, MARY (1812-95)
Sculptor. Born at Thornham, Norfolk. The daughter of sculptor John Francis (1780-1861). A child prodigy, she studied under her father. In 1840 she married sculptor Thomas Thornycroft (1817-85) in London. He originated from Gawsworth, Cheshire. He was a pupil of, and assistant to, her father. Between 1842 and 1843, Mary worked in Rome. Otherwise, she lived and worked in London. There, the Thornycrofts were affluent enough to employ several servants, including a studio sweeper. Mary worked in

plaster, bronze and marble, producing mainly figures and portrait works, but particularly of royalty. Queen Victoria commissioned her several times along with other dignitaries. Produced works of the Prince of Wales, Prince Alfred, Queen Victoria, Princess Beatrice and Princess Louise. Exhibited at the Royal Academy (1835-77), the British Institute (1840-64) and the Society of Women Artists (1857-67). Elected a Member of the Society of Women Artists (1857-64). Exhibited works included: Winter (statuette, bronze), A Head of Psyche (marble), The Skipping Girl and The Flower-Girl (marble). Works illustrated in the Art Journal, including in 1864.

Records are unclear, but suggest that Mary Thornycroft had five children: Mary Alyce (in 1845), Frances (in 1847), Helen (in 1848), William (in 1850) and Theresa Georgiana (in 1853). The children changed their names from time to time, adding to the confusion. Mary Alyce became a painter / sculptor, as did Theresa and Helen. Helen was an Associate and Member of the Society of Women Artists. William Hamo Thornycroft became a sculptor, and his daughter Rosalind became an artist. Mary Francis Thornycroft was noted in M.H. Spielmann's volume British Sculpture and Sculptors of To-day, London, Cassell & Co. Ltd, 1901. Spielmann notes that she had virtually no rivals in her day, being one of the first women sculptors in Britain. But she did live to see the numbers rise during her later years, including her own daughters. Her marble monument to Sarah, Baroness Braye, can be found in the church of St Nicholas at Stanford on Avon, Northamptonshire. SEE: THORNYCROFT, HELEN, MARY ALYCE & ROSALIND

FRANKLIN, DULCIE F. - SEE SASSOON, D.F.

FREEDMAN, BEATRICE CLAUDIA (1904-82)
Artist / Illustrator. Born in Formby, Liverpool in October 1904. The daughter of Vincenzo Guercio of Palermo, Sicily. Studied at the Liverpool School of Art under Frederick Carter. Also, at the Royal College of Art, London under Malcolm Osborne and Sir William Rothenstein. Married artist Barnett Freedman (b.1901). Also a student of the Royal College of Art, he acted as Admiralty war artist and official war artist. They had at least one son. Beatrice worked under the names Guercio and Freedman. She and Barnett executed much design and illustration work, both working for Shell Mex. Beatrice executed black

& white pen work for reproduction. Also executed work for the G.P.O., Faber & Faber, Colman, Prentis & Varley, the Baynard Press, the Curwen Press, the B.B.C., the Medici Society, Fortnum & Mason, W. Collins and George Bell & Son among others. Was a visiting art instructor. Worked for the Rycotewood Trust (1942-45). Worked on a number of publications, including Parables of Our Lord (Faber & Faber), Claudia Freedman, My Toy Cupboard (Transatlantic Arts), Gardener's Diary (Hulton Press), Review of Reviews (Cochrane, 1930), Elroy Flecker's Letters to Frank Savory (Cyril Beaumont), Walter de la Mare, A Snowdrop (1929) and Eleanor Graham (ed.), The Puffin Book of Verse (1953). One of her illustrations, to De Quincey's German Tales and Legends (John Lane, The Bodley Head Ltd), was given in The Studio, Vol.89, May 1925, p.282. Beatrice died in Leeds, Yorkshire, aged 77. Works acquired by the Victoria & Albert Museum, London.

FRENCH, HONORAH MAIDA (1901-92)

Potter. Born in Dulwich in March 1901. The daughter of Frederick W. French, an insurance clerk, and Clarissa. Her parents originated from London. Honorah spent much of her career in London, but died in Kent, aged 91. Educated at the Mary Datchelor School. Studied at the Camberwell School of Arts and Crafts. Exhibited at the Arts and Crafts Exhibitions in London, with the Design and Industries Association and the South London Group. Held a one-woman show at Mrs Summerday's Gallery on Oxford Street, London. Works illustrated in the Studio Year Book.

FREWEN, CLARE C. - SEE SHERIDAN, C.C.

FRINK, ELISABETH JEAN (1930-93)

Sculptor. Born at Thurlow, Suffolk in November 1930. As a child, she went on hunting trips with her father across the Suffolk landscape. This gave her a feeling for the animals and birds she would later sculpt. Studied at the Guildford School of Art between 1946 and 1949, under Willi Soukop. Then, at the Chelsea School of Art between 1949 and 1953, under Bernard Meadows. Produced sculptures, but also etchings and lithographs. Admired Rodin early in her career. Later an admirer of Giacometti, Marini, Henry Moore and Francis Bacon. Had a studio in Chelsea. Spent some time in France between 1967 and 1970. Latterly based at Woolland, Dorset, where she died, aged 62. As a sculptor, produced studies of dogs, boars, fish, birds, cats and horses. Also

known for her bird-men, warriors and sentinels. From 1956 developed a theme in her work where extreme danger and extreme quiet blended together: two things of apparent contrast. Drew crashed men, possibly inspired by then developments in space travel and flying. The subject of an article in The Studio, Vol.162, October 1961, pp.131-134. The article included photographs of Frink in her studio and illustrations of five of her works: Warrior (concrete, 1957), Sentinel (bronze, 1961), Cock (bronze, 1961), Fallen Bird Man (bronze, 1960-61) and Falling Man (bronze, 1961). Her figures were often stick-thin and elongated with a bird-like quality.

Frink also executed portrait works, including a bronze of Sir William Walton (1976), later owned by the Oldham Art Gallery. Other works included Blind Man and Dog (1957) executed in bronze for the Bethnal Green Housing Scheme, which was partly vandalised. Executed a series of Harbinger Birds, depicting almost deformed birds. Produced a copper relief of leaf patterns for the facade of the Carlton Tower Hotel. Her Walking Madonna can be found at Chatsworth House, Derbyshire. Her Sheep and Shepherd was in Paternoster Square, London. Her sculpture of St Edmund can be found outside the Abbey at Bury St Edmunds. Her Crucifixion can be found inside Bury St Edmunds Cathedral. In 1952 The Tate Gallery acquired one of her smaller bird sculptures. Frink exhibited her work throughout her career, holding her first exhibition in London in 1952. Also exhibited at the Royal Academy (1954) and the Royal Scottish Academy (1977-79). Exhibited works included: Gogglehead (bronze), Running Man (pen & watercolour, 1976) and Praecursor (bronze, 1975).

Frink contributed to numerous other exhibitions, including two one-woman shows held at the Waddington Galleries in the late 1950s, reflecting her bird motifs. Exhibited at the Galleries again in 1963, showing Judas (bronze), which was illustrated in The Studio, 1963, p.84. Contributed to a British Sculpture Today exhibition held at Farnham, Surrey in 1962, one of 23 artists, also including Barbara Hepworth and Gertrude Hermes. In 1963 she contributed to the London Triennial exhibition of sculpture at Battersea Park. Other exhibitors included Barbara Hepworth and Lynn Chadwick. In 1964 Frink contributed to the Pittsburgh International Exhibition of Contemporary Painting and Sculpture, again joined by Hepworth. There, Frink showed Carapace II (1963) which was illustrated in The Studio, Vol.168, 1964, p.236. More recently, her portrait work of William Walton was included in an exhibition of portrait works held at the Atkinson Art Gallery, Southport in 2008. Frink was elected an Honorary Member of the Society of Women Artists (1986-93), although apparently did not contribute to the Society's annual exhibition. Also made a D.B.E. (Dame Commander of the Order of the British Empire). Frink married three times, to Michel Jammett in 1955, to Edward Pool in 1969, and to Alexander Csaky in 1974.

FROST, BERTHA (1877-post-1934)

Modeller / Colour Print Artist. Born in Rochdale, Lancashire in December 1877. The daughter of Richard Glazier, A.R.I.B.A., and Eleanor. Her father, who originated from Lincolnshire, was a decorative artist and art master at the Manchester Technical School. Her mother originated from Rochdale. One of at least three children (Bertha, Annie and Mary). Raised in Rochdale and Urmston. Educated at the Manchester High School for Girls. Studied at the Manchester School of Art and at Halifax and Rochdale. A silver medallist as a student. By at least 1901, Bertha was working as an art teacher. Produced colour woodcuts and was involved in modelling work. Exhibited her work, including at the Society of Women Artists (1932-34), the Walker Art Gallery, Liverpool, with the Colour Woodcut Society, the Thames Valley Art Club, and in Shanghai, where she appears to have spent time. Exhibited works included: Junks, Hong Kong (colour print), A Busy Waterway, Wusih (colour print), Chinese Actor (colour print) and The Temple by the Bridge, Wusih (colour print). Elected a Member of the Colour Woodcut Society and of the Thames Valley Art Club. Also a Member of the Committee of the Colour Woodcut Society as well as Chairman of the Art Section of the British Women's Association, Shanghai. Spent part of her career in Barnes, London. Married J. Frost and had two sons and two daughters.

FRY, CAROLINE (1846-87)

Sculptor / Painter. Born and raised in Streatham, London. Died in London, aged only 40. The daughter of Charles Nottidge and Sarah. Her father was, for many years, Secretary to the Deaf & Dumb Asylum, London. One of at least seven children (Sarah, Arthur, Caroline, Frances, Charles, Charlotte and Margaretta). In the very early 1870s, Caroline studied sculpture at the Royal Academy schools, London. In 1873 she was awarded the silver medal of the Royal Academy for her A Restoration of the Venus de Milo, which was exhibited at the Society of Women Artists the following year. Produced portrait works, including medallions. Exhibited her work, including at the Royal Academy (22 works, 1867-83), the Royal Hibernian Academy (1881) and the Society of Women Artists (1874-81). Exhibited works included: A Venetian Senator, James Henry, M.D. (medallion), Rev. A.C. Tarbutt and Inclined to be Obstinate. In 1879 she married sculptor Samuel Fry (1843-1918) in London. He also exhibited at the Royal Academy (1877-1901) and elsewhere. The couple lived in London. Some three years after the marriage, Caroline gave birth to a daughter, Elizabeth Ursula Nottidge Fry. Caroline died only a few years later. Elizabeth lived with her father until his death. He never remarried.

FRYETT, WINIFRED E. - SEE WALKER, W.E.

FULLEYLOVE, JOAN ELIZABETH ANNE (1886-1947)

Stained Glass Artist. Born in London. The daughter of topographical artist John Fulleylove, R.I. (1847-1908) and Elizabeth Sarah Elgood. Her father, who originated from Leicester, exhibited at the Royal Academy and elsewhere. In the 1901 census recordings, her mother, who also originated from Leicester, is listed as a painter in watercolours. Joan had at least one sibling, John. Between 1907 and 1909, Joan studied at the Slade School, London. She then enrolled at the London County Council Central School of Arts and Crafts where Mabel Esplin, Lilian Pocock, Caroline Townshend and Margaret Aldrich Rope also studied at various times. There, she studied book production under Noel Rooke and John Henry Mason, and stained glass under Karl Parsons (a former pupil of Christopher Whall) and Alfred J. Drury (of Lowndes & Drury). In the early 1900s, Fulleylove met Mabel Esplin and assisted on some of her stained glass commissions. The two women shared a strong interest in the women's suffrage movement. In 1907, Joan designed a propaganda postcard for the movement, and in 1909 took part in the International Woman Suffrage Alliance Congress in London. In 1916 Esplin became seriously ill, and in 1919 Fulleylove was asked to complete the scheme of windows Esplin had begun for All Saints' Cathedral at Khartoum. Fulleylove's only complete window up until that point had been a war memorial window for Hampstead Parish Church (1918).

Regardless, by 1930 Joan had successfully completed the Khartoum windows, most to Esplin's original designs. The windows were made in collaboration with Lowndes & Drury, one of the most successful stained glass workshops in London at that time. Fulleylove painted the glass in her studio in Hampstead and Lowndes & Drury fired and leaded it. Fulleylove made a number of other windows for churches in Britain. For example, in the early 1920s, she produced a set of windows for St Peter's Church, Bushey Heath which show the influence of the Khartoum designs. In 1925 she produced a window for Holy Trinity Church, Tooting, and in 1926 designed Adoration of the Magi for St Mary's Church, Pulham, Norfolk. In 1932 she produced a window for Narberth Church, Pembrokeshire. Exhibited her designs occasionally. For example, at the 1923 Decorative Arts Exhibition held at the Royal Academy. Between 1916 and 1930 she showed nine works at the Royal Academy, including a sketch for a proposed window in Christchurch Cathedral, Victoria, and for St Michael's Church, Tenterden, Kent. Joan spent much of her career in Hampstead, using the Holly Bush Studio for part of that time. In the 1930s she retired to Sussex. She died of pneumonia in Clarens Montreux, Switzerland whilst on a visit. Some of her works were included in a more recent exhibition Women Stained Glass Artists of the Arts and Crafts Movement held at the William Morris Gallery, London, 1985-86.

FULTON, MRS (active 1840s-1850s)

Sculptor. Possibly Irish. Produced figures, busts and groups. Worked in marble. Exhibited at the Royal Hibernian Academy (1840-58). Exhibited works included: Muse (a figure in marble in the manner of the Antique) and Relievo, Evening (after Raphael, to be executed in marble for a spandrel of a four-centred arch). Also, Bust of Dr Fulton.

FYFE, ELIZABETH (1899-post-1934)

Etcher / Engraver. Born in Sydney, Australia in August 1899. The daughter of Andrew Fyfe, a bank manager, and Lili. Her father originated from Midlothian, Scotland, her mother from Switzerland. One of at least three children. Had a brother, Alfred (b.1894), and a sister, Agnes (b.1898), also born in Australia. By at least 1911, the family had moved to Britain, to Newport in Monmouthshire where Elizabeth attended the local High School. Then studied in London, at the Slade School and at the L.C.C. Central School of Arts and Crafts. Reached the Prix de Rome finals in engraving. Became an etcher and engraver on copper and wood, of various subjects including figures and buildings. Acted as visiting art

mistress at the Streatham Secondary School for Girls. However, her career was affected by ill-health, and she appears to have largely vanished after 1934. Until that point, she received considerable praise for her work.

Fyfe exhibited her work, including with the New English Art Club, at Wembley, in the International Exhibition of Engravings in Florence, at New York's Brooklyn Museum and the Royal Scottish Academy (1924). Works included: La Poste du Douane. Also, Tower of Babel which was illustrated in the Bookman's Journal and in Graphic. Both were purchased by the Newport Museum and Art Gallery. Her Childhood of Moses and The Gossips were reproduced in Fine Prints of the Year. Other works included: Dance of Miriam, Attic Studio and Middleham Castle. Based mainly in London. Most of her work was dealt with by P.&D. Colnaghi, who acted as her publisher. Noted in Frank L. Emanuel's Etching and Etchings, London, Pitman & Sons, 1930 along with a reproduction of her Tower of Babel. Emanuel says: 'It is nothing short of a tragedy that the brilliant young artist who has produced this and many other plates of surpassing interest and beauty, should for several years have been in such weak health as to temporarily preclude work. Much of her work is far less austere than is the example here given (by kind permission of the Publisher, Messrs P.&D. Colnaghi & Co., New Bond St, London), but in every case, there is great originality' (p.264). In Apollo magazine, Vol.11, 1930, p.69, it is noted that an exhibition of her etchings, woodcuts and drawings, held at a private house in Hampstead, had been organised by friends of Elizabeth Fyfe in order to raise funds for medical attention and nursing care, which Fyfe still required after ill-health. She is described by Apollo as 'one of our most original and accomplished younger etchers'.

G

GAHAGAN, SALLY / SARAH (1801-66)

Sculptor. Born in London. Died in Bath, Somerset. Part of the talented Gahagan dynasty of sculptors who originated from Ireland. Records indicate that she was the daughter of Lucius Gahagan (1773-1855) and Sarah Proudman (1762-1843). Her father was a sculptor, as was her grandfather, Lawrence, and her two uncles, Vincent and Sebastian. She spent some years on her own in Bristol, having studied under her father. Whilst in Bristol, she exhibited her only work at the Royal Academy, Bust of a Child in

1817. Later, she lived with her brother Lucius in Bath. He too was a sculptor. He died in the same year. An S. Gahagan, possibly Sarah, exhibited one work, Prayer, at the Royal Society of British Artists in 1832. She appears to have had at least two sisters, Phoebe and Helen.

GARDINER, LILIAN A. - SEE LANCASTER, L.A.

GARDNER, IVY H. (1894-1975)

Sculptor. Based mainly in Glasgow. Produced animals, garden ornaments, portrait works and figures. Worked in wood, cement, marble, alabaster, bronze, plaster and lead. Exhibited her work extensively over a period of more than 50 years. Exhibited at the Royal Scottish Academy (48 works, 1927-57), the Royal Glasgow Institute (120 works, 1920-70), the Royal Academy (1937), the Society of Women Artists (1939) and elsewhere. Exhibited works included: An Old Mariner (wood), The Midden Raker (plaster), An Artist (head, plaster) and Squirrel (statuette, oak). In 1955 she married sculptor Alexander Proudfoot (1878-1957). Gardner acted as his assistant for some years. He was active until the time of his death. She was still active into the 1970s.

GARDNER, JESSIE M. - SEE RIDING, J.M.

GARDNER, PHYLLIS & DELPHIS
(1890-1939) & (b.1900)

Artists / Decorative Artists. The daughters of Ernest Arthur Gardner (1862-1939) and Mary Wilson (1862-1936). Their father was a Professor of Archaeology at the University of London, a writer on the history of art and an Honorary Member of the Art Workers' Guild. The girls had at least one brother, Christopher. The children were raised in Surrey. The Gardner sisters spent much of their lives together, until Phyllis died in 1939. They lived in London, Tadworth in Surrey and in Maidenhead, where Phyllis died, aged 48.

Phyllis Gardner was born in Cambridge in October 1890. She was educated at the St Felix School, Southwold, Suffolk. Studied at the Slade School, London as well as studying Celtic ornament at the British Museum. Also studied at Frank Calderon's School of Animal Painting. Produced a wide variety of works including wood engravings, carvings, sculptures and paintings in tempera as well as working as a printer. With Delphis, she owned and ran the Asphodel Press. They collaborated on the illustration of a number of books including The Tale of Troy (with woodcuts, 1924-25), The Gospel According to St

Luke (with woodcuts), The Ballad of Alice Brand and Latin Writings of St Patrick (translated by Delphis, illustrated by Phyllis). Phyllis also illustrated, for example, S. Cassan, Rupert Brooke and Skyros (1921), May Cannan, The House of Hope (1923) and Antonio Cippico, Carme Umanistico (1923). Executed wood engravings for Lyke Wake Dirge, A Desert in the Ocean, and illustrated Mary Gardner's book of poems Plain Themes (Dent). Phyllis exhibited her work, including at the Arts and Crafts Exhibitions in London, with the New English Art Club (1913-15), the Royal Society of Miniature Painters, in the New Zealand and South Seas International Exhibition (won a first award diploma for woodcarving), the North-East Coast Exhibition (first award for wood engraving) and the Women's International Art Club.

At the Society of Women Artists Phyllis showed more than 48 individual works between 1917 and 1935. Exhibited a wide variety of arts and crafts during her career, including decorative screens, wood engravings, bas-reliefs in mahogany, woodcuts, coloured reliefs in wood and alabaster, sculptures in wood, works in ivory, boxwood, sycamore, bronze and oak, linocuts, brush drawings and paintings in tempera. Exhibited works included: A Funeral Procession (tempera), Two Horses (bas-relief in mahogany), St Christopher (bronze) and A Young Irish Wolfhound (brush drawing). Her decorative screens included one painted on the obverse with a landscape and on the reverse with Nine Horses. Other decorative works included a chess set for Brasenose College, Oxford, executed with Delphis. Also, a set of chess sets based on famous battles in history (also with Delphis) which was exported to the U.S.A. At the Society of Women Artists, the Queen purchased a carving of flowers by Phyllis. Acted as a Committee Member of the Women's International Art Club. Also a Committee Member and Honorary Secretary of the Women's Guild of Arts. Elected an Associate of the Society of Women Artists (1918-39). One of her chess sets (with Delphis) was illustrated in The Studio. Contributed an illustrated article to Drawing and Design.

Delphis Gardner was born in Tadworth, Surrey in December 1900. She was also educated at the St Felix School, Southwold. Studied at the University College, London. Awarded a B.A. degree in 1924. Then studied at the Slade School, London. Also worked as a wood engraver, carver, sculptor and printer. Worked in collaboration with Phyllis, but also produced her own work. Exhibited at the Arts and Crafts Exhibitions in London, with the Women's International Art Club, at the Canadian National Exhibition in

Toronto and at the Society of Women Artists (1920-34). Exhibited works included: Persephone (woodcut), Doe and Fawn (ivory carving), The Jaws of Hell (woodcut) and The Sun Eloping with Mount Kanchenjunga (woodcut). Elected a Member of the Women's International Art Club. In 1918, Phyllis exhibited a drawing of Delphis at the Society of Women Artists.

GARLAND, MARGARET - SEE COOKESLEY, M.M.

GARNETT, ANNIE (1864-1942)

Textile Designer / Craftswoman. Born in Bowness-on-Windermere, Westmorland. The second of six children. The family home was Fairfield, the dower house to The Crown Hotel, and her father is listed in local directories as a 'house-agent'. Annie remained at Fairfield for the rest of her life. Her three brothers all went to university, but she was entirely self-taught, becoming a proficient artist and embroideress. Cello playing was another of her talents. In 1889 she visited a small but successful spinning and weaving workshop in nearby Elterwater which had been established in 1883 by Albert Fleming and Marian Twelves, two devotees of John Ruskin's teachings. The workshop ran entirely along traditional lines, and rejected all forms of mechanisation relating to the production of linen and other fabrics as well as embroidery and lace making. Annie Garnett immediately began hand spinning lessons at the workshop, and by 1891 had established similar classes in Bowness.

The Bowness classes soon developed into The Spinnery, an equally successful textile industry with over one hundred workers, who used only traditional Westmorland spinning wheels and hand looms. So successful had the industry become by the late 1890s that Miss Garnett was able to support herself financially. The Spinnery produced mainly silks, samites, throwans, tweeds, woollens and brocades, one of which was specially woven for Queen Alexandra, but also embroideries. Fabric and embroidery designs were usually inspired by nature, as Ruskin taught. Textiles were exhibited extensively locally, nationally and internationally, including at the Arts and Crafts Exhibitions, the annual Home Arts and Industries Association exhibition, the Bristol and Clifton Arts and Crafts Society exhibition, the '91 Art Club Exhibition, the 1893 World's Columbian Exposition held in Chicago, the 1904 St Louis Exhibition and the 1909 Deutsch Kunst und Dekoration in Berlin. Also, at the Artists at Work exhibition, held at the Grafton Galleries in 1906, at an Exhibition of Arts and Crafts held at the Lyceum Club in 1905-06, and at the Society of Women Artists (1902-07). Garnett was elected an Associate of the Society of Women Artists (1905-08).

Annie Garnett also had a keen interest in women's issues. Over the years she was associated with the Lancashire Federation of Women's Institutes, the Women's Advisory Committee, the Home Work Co-operative Society and the Westmorland Women's Liberal Association, of which she was Vice President. The Home Work Co-operative Society had a particular interest in helping women to increase their incomes. She was also a Member of the Dress Designers' Exhibition Society, of which Walter Crane was President. During the First World War, Garnett became Honorary Secretary of the Windermere War Hospital Supply Depot, and a Member of the Westmorland Red Cross Demobilization Committee. In July 1919 she was invited to a Buckingham Palace garden party. The Spinnery ran until the 1930s, when her health finally gave way. She died in a Carlisle nursing home in 1942. In 1952 examples of her work were shown in the Decorative Arts Exhibition held at the Victoria & Albert Museum, London. Samples of her fabrics and embroideries can be found at the Abbot Hall Museum, Kendal, Cumbria. Garnett was the author of Notes on Hand-Spinning (1896) and Spinnery Notes (1912). The Spinnery was the subject of an article, Windermere Industry at The Spinnery, Fairfield, Windermere, in the Art Workers' Quarterly, April 1905, pp.56-69. A corner of an embroidered square in white silk with a gold outline, worked on a line ground, designed and executed by her, had been illustrated in the Art Workers' Quarterly, p.119, two years previously, in 1903.

GARNETT, EVE CYNTHIA RUTH (1900-91)

Illustrator / Artist. Born in Worcestershire in January 1900. Died in Lewes, Sussex, aged 91. The daughter of Lt.-Col. Frederick Herbert Garnett and Mary. One of at least three children (Ruby, Beryl and Eve). Raised in Worcestershire and in Bideford, Devon. Studied in London, at the Chelsea Polytechnic School of Art and at the Royal Academy schools. Studied landscape painting under Alexander Jamieson. She studied at the Royal Academy schools on a five-year studentship, but due to ill-health completed only two years. However, she showed such promise that she was awarded the Creswick Prize and a silver medal during that time. Initially intended to concentrate on landscape painting and mural decoration. But whilst still at the Royal Academy schools, she was commissioned by John Lane to illustrate The London Child by Evelyn Sharp (Mrs H.W. Nevinson). As a result, she developed a strong social conscience and went on to illustrate other books with a strong message, including her own The Family From One End Street (1937, foreword by Walter de la Mare, published by Frederick Muller). Also, Is It Well With The Child? (1938) and Further Adventures From One End Street (1956), which she also wrote herself.

During her career, Garnett worked for several publishers, including Penguin, John Lane and the Open University Press. Other books written and illustrated by her included In and Out & Roundabout (1948), A Book of the Seasons (1952), Holiday at the Dew Drop Inn (1962) and Lost and Found: Four Stories (1974). Also illustrated R.L. Stevenson, A Child's Garden of Verse (1948) and James Reeves (ed.), A Golden Land (with others, 1958). Garnett also produced landscape paintings in oils and watercolours and mural decorations as well as working in pencil, pen and ink. Her mural decorations included a 40 ft. work for The Children's House, Bow, London. Some of her work was reproduced in The Times Literary Supplement and in the Collins Magazine. She was awarded the Carnegie Gold Medal for her work in 1938. Exhibited her work occasionally, including at the Society of Women Artists (1924), the Goupil Gallery, the Royal Institute of Oil Painters, the Tate Gallery (photographs of her mural decorations), with the New English Art Club and at the Lefevre Gallery. Exhibited works included: Allotments. Spent her earlier career in London, but later spent time in Sussex. Noted in Mahony, Latimer & Folmsbee, Illustrators of Children's Books 1744-1945, Boston, The Horn Book Inc., 1947.

GARRETT, RHODA & AGNES (1841-82) & (1845-1935)

Decorative Artists. The daughters of the Rev. John Fisher Garrett and Elizabeth. Their father originated from Suffolk. Their mother died young, and John Garrett married again, to Mary. There were several siblings and half-siblings. Neither Rhoda nor Agnes ever married. Rhoda was born in Elton, Derbyshire, where her father was Rector of the local church. Agnes was born in Aldeburgh, Suffolk. Both girls were raised in Elton. It remains unclear exactly what education the sisters had. But by 1871 Rhoda is listed as living in London, and working as editor of a newspaper and a private secretary. In 1876,

however, Rhoda and Agnes published a volume, Suggestions for House Decoration in Painting, Woodwork and Furniture, one of the Art at Home series for Macmillan. By 1881, the sisters are listed as living together in Gower Street, London, and working together as house decorators. However, Rhoda died in London the following year, aged only 40. Agnes continued to work as a house decorator, and by the early 1890s was working in Rustington, West Sussex. She subsequently returned to London, living with another sister, Millicent, a writer, joined by their niece, Phillipa, a maths tutor. By the early 1910s, Agnes is listed as a 'retired house decorator'. She died in London, still at the Gower Street address, aged 89. Although largely forgotten today, the Garrett sisters were highly unusual in their day, earning a living in an area still in its infancy. Agnes was evidently particularly successful, and enjoyed a career which covered more than 30 years.

GARTHWAITE, ANNA MARIA (1688-1763)

Textile Designer. The daughter of a Lincolnshire parson, the Rev. Ephraim Garthwaite, and Rejoyce Housted. Her father was Rector of Harston, Leicestershire at the time of her birth. Garthwaite is one of a small number of identifiable women directly involved in British design in the eighteenth century. She worked as a silk designer in Spitalfields, London from the 1720s. She moved there in 1728 with her twice-widowed sister, Mary, living in a house in Princes Street. She is believed to have produced around 80 designs a year, some of which were influenced by Jean Revel (1684-1751) of Lyon. Revel was known for his naturalistic interpretation of flowers in silk. Garthwaite is presumed to be the author of an essay on designing flowered silks which appeared in G. Smith's volume Laboratory, or School of Arts (1756). Noted in an article Silk Weaving in Spitalfields by Luther Hooper in the Art Journal, 1909, pp.79-82. Hooper notes that some of her designs are marked 'before I came to London' and 'when I was in Yorkshire', which indicates that she moved around the country, and that she was already designing prior to the move to London. Her earlier designs are noticeably less complex. Later, her designs become noticeably stronger and bolder. That would indicate that the move to London had some considerable impact on her artistically. Five of Garthwaite's designs are illustrated in Hooper's article, all inspired by nature. Garthwaite was still designing into the 1750s. The Victoria & Albert Museum, London has a large collection of Garthwaite's watercolour designs, covering the period from the 1720s into the 1750s. Her name also appears in a pattern book belonging to the Museum. Garthwaite died in Princes Street, Spitalfields, aged 75. She did not live to see the decline of the Spitalfields silk trade, or the march of mass-mechanisation in the 1800s.

GASKIN, GEORGINA EVELYN CAVE (1867-1934)

Designer / Metalworker / Artist / Illustrator. Known as Georgie. Born in Shrewsbury, Shropshire. The daughter of William Hammer France and Frances Emily. Her father, who originated from Shropshire, was initially a farmer of some 292 acres in Warwickshire, but was later a manager of a charity institute. Her mother originated from Derbyshire. She had at least two siblings, Emily and James. Emily became a student at Cambridge University. Georgina became a student in silversmithing at the Birmingham Municipal School of Art. There, she met fellow student Arthur Joseph Gaskin (1862-1928). Born in Birmingham, he was the son of Henry Gaskin, a portrait painter and later a japanner. In 1894 they married in Birmingham, and took a house at Acock's Green in the city, which became an artistic hub. Together, they began designing and making gold and silver jewellery, often with enamel decoration. Both became an active part of the Birmingham Group of artists and craftworkers who had a shared objective of raising standards in jewellery design, the mass production of jewellery being a feature of the city. The Group, founded in the 1890s, consisted of the Gaskins, Edith and Henry Payne, Mary Newill, Sidney Meteyard, Bernard Sleigh, Charles and Margaret Gere and Joseph Southall, all of whom, except for Southall, had come under the influence of E.R. Taylor at the Birmingham School. The Gaskins also had ties with the Birmingham Guild of Handicraft.

Influenced by the East and eastern craftsmen, the Gaskins began to use inexpensive stones set into handwrought metals, often of complex form. With the strong emphasis on jewellery making throughout the Arts and Crafts period, many jewellers were trained at Birmingham in the latter part of the nineteenth century, and in around 1900 a new School of Jewellery and Silversmithing was begun at the Birmingham School. In 1902 Arthur Gaskin, who was already working as an art master, became its head. Two of the most successful female students to come out of the Birmingham School during Gaskin's time there were Kate Eadie and May Hart. Although Arthur Gaskin taught metalwork and enamelling until 1924, he and Georgina also continued to design

and make their own jewellery, and won widespread praise for their work. They frequently contributed to national exhibitions, including the 1901 Glasgow Exhibition, and the 1903 Bristol and Clifton Arts and Crafts Society Fifth Exhibition, where they showed some 20 exhibits including lace pins set with moonstones, chrysoprase and almandines, a silver and turquoise necklace, and a silver necklace with pearls, chrysoprase and turquoise which won first and second certificates. Some of their work was also sold through shops.

Other work appeared at the Arts and Crafts Exhibitions in London. In 1903, for example, exhibits included hat pins and lace pins set with precious stones. In the same year, 31 examples of their work were included in the Cumberland and Westmorland Society of Arts and Crafts exhibition held at Tullie House, Carlisle. At the 1916 Arts and Crafts Exhibition, they showed a silver enamelled necklace which was illustrated in The Studio, Vol.70, February 1917, p.18. In 1908 the Gaskins contributed jewellery to the New Gallery Exhibition, and in 1909 contributed to Mr John Baillie's Annual Arts and Crafts Exhibition. They also exhibited their work locally. For example, in 1909 they contributed 53 items of jewellery to an Arts and Crafts Exhibition held by the Royal Birmingham Society of Artists. In 1914, The Studio, Vol.61, May, pp.293-301, offered an article The Jewellery of Mr and Mrs Arthur Gaskin by Arthur S. Wainwright. A number of illustrations were given, showing that the couple had successfully turned decorative jewellery into pieces of art, each one unique, with jewels carefully chosen according to their colour and symbolic meaning rather than their intrinsic value. Wainwright makes it clear that the Gaskins worked together and equally, though Georgina produced many of the designs. In 1909 one of their necklaces, a chain and pendant in gold and decorated with sapphires, emeralds, pearls, pink topaz and diamonds, was presented to the King and Queen on their visit to Birmingham. The necklace was illustrated in The Studio, Vol.47, September 1909. In 1922, the couple exhibited their work under the auspices of the British Institute of Industrial Art.

In 1924, as Arthur Gaskin's health began to deteriorate, the Gaskins left Birmingham and moved to nearby Chipping Campden, Gloucestershire, where Charles R. Ashbee had been active. They continued to work, though it is unclear if they actually continued making jewellery rather than designing it. They contributed to local exhibitions, showing their paintings and drawings. For example, in 1927 they contributed to the fourth annual Chipping Campden exhibition. There, Arthur showed portraits in tempera and crayon and some of his woodcuts, but also a case of jewellery, executed with Georgina, which was noted in reviews as popular with the purchasing public. Other exhibitors included Alec Miller (of Ashbee's Guild), F.L. Griggs and Paul Woodroffe.

Although they spent much of their careers in the designing and making of artistic jewellery, the Gaskins were also gifted artists. Arthur was a successful painter and illustrator who, for example, produced 100 illustrations for Stories by Hans Christian Andersen (two volumes, London, George Allen, 1893). He also produced illustrations for Shepherd's Callendar, printed and published by the Kelmscott Press. He was elected a Member of the Royal Society of Painter-Etchers & Engravers. Georgina was equally productive in other areas of the arts. As a student, she won prizes at the National Competition of Schools of Art as well as awards from the Birmingham School. She continued to win awards after that, including in a competition for an illustrated Calendar of the Seasons in 1896. That was followed by illustrations for Holy Christmas (1896), a book of hymns and carols. One of the illustrations was used as a Christmas card and illustrated in the Art Journal. Another of her Christmas card designs was reproduced in The Studio, Vol.2, 1893 / 94, p.96.

Mrs Gaskin also illustrated children's books during her career, including ABC (56 pictures by her, Elkin Mathews, 1896). Also, Divine and Moral Songs for Children (by Isaac Watts, 14 pictures by her, Elkin Mathews), Horn-Book Jingles (70 pictures by her, Leadenhall Press, 1897), Little Girls and Little Boys (27 pictures by her, 1898) and The Travellers and Other Stories (by Mrs A.G. Bowden, 61 pictures by her, 1898). Her illustration work was noted in R.E.D. Sketchley, English Book Illustration of To-day, London, Kegan Paul, 1903. Also noted in Mahony, Latimer & Folmsbee, Illustrators of Children's Books 1744-1945, Boston, The Horn Book Inc., 1947. One of her bookplates was reproduced in Norna Labouchere's volume Ladies' Book-Plates, London, George Bell & Sons, 1895. Some of her book illustrations were shown at the exhibitions held at the Birmingham School of Art by the Sketch Club of the Birmingham School of Art Union. Mrs Gaskin also contributed to Quest, a magazine produced by the Birmingham Guild of Handicraft, and to the Yellow Book. During her career, she additionally exhibited with the Society of Women Artists (1912-24), and was elected an Associate of the Society (1923-24).

In a minor way, she was also involved in decorative leatherwork. In 1896 she executed a design by Arthur Gaskin for a leather binding which was presented to J. Thackeray Bunce, a retiring member of the Committee of the Birmingham School of Art. Aside from their artistic commitments, the Gaskins found time to raise two daughters, Jocelyne Verney (1903-93) and Margaret Cary (b.1907). Jocelyne was born in Worcestershire, Margaret in Gloucestershire. Jocelyne married Charles Turner in Birmingham in 1924, and died in Kent. Margaret became an actress, spending time in Stratford-upon-Avon and later in Chelsea. Arthur Gaskin died in Birmingham, his address at that time being The Little House, Chipping Campden. Georgina died at The White Cottage, West Malling, Kent, aged 67. Emily Wilmer Cave France (b.1868), Georgina's sister, became a noted academic in Greek. She studied abroad after leaving Cambridge University, and worked in America. Examples of work by the Gaskins can be found in the Cheltenham Collections.

GAY, LYDIA ANN (1855-1949)

Sculptor / Medallist. Born in North Wootton, Norfolk in August 1855. The daughter of Richard Gay, a farmer, merchant and salesman, and Mary. One of at least six children (Mary, Thomas, Louisa, Matilda, Lydia and Agnes). Raised in Norfolk. Possibly studied in London, since she spent her early career there. Also subsequently spent time in Solihull, Birmingham, at Ightham in Kent, and in Letchworth, Hertfordshire. Died in Hertfordshire, aged 94. Produced medals and bas-reliefs in bronze. Exhibited at the Royal Academy (27 works, 1887-1903). Exhibited works included: Rev. B.H. Alford (medal, obverse - allegory representing Virtue and Vice), Sigurd Consulting Brynhilda, Pan (bas-relief) and James Leslie (medal).

GAYTON, ANNA MARIA (1858-1924)

Sculptor / Painter. Born in June 1858 in Much Hadham, Hertfordshire. The daughter of George Gayton, an attorney and solicitor, and Sarah Ann. One of at least six children (three boys, three girls). Raised in Hertfordshire. Died in Bushey, Hertfordshire in early 1924, aged 63. In the 1880s, she was based at The Bolton Studios, Redcliffe Road, London. But by the early 1890s was back with her family at Much Hadham. Produced paintings and sculptures. It is unclear if she had any formal tuition. Exhibited her work, including at the Royal Society of British Artists (1888-92) and the Royal Academy (1890-99). Exhibited works included: Hare and Hounds (relief), Silas Marner (sculpture), Rest, The Greenfield Sleeps in the Sun and The Rev. R.C. Bacon. Gayton was friends with sculptor / painter Edith Bateson. She lived with Bateson at Nightingale Corner in Bushey, Hertfordshire in the final years of her life. Gayton left Bateson part of her small estate on her death. SEE: BATESON, EDITH H.

GEAR, MABEL (b.1898)
Decorative Painter. Born at Ashby Rectory, Suffolk in March 1898. The daughter of Lucas George Gear and Annie Margaret. Her father, who lists his profession as 'gentleman', originated from London, her mother from Norfolk. One of at least three children (Muriel, Dorothy and Mabel). Raised at Ashby, Suffolk and in Colchester, Essex. Studied at the Colchester School of Art, and under Septimus Power at Bushey, Hertfordshire. She used the Meadow Studios at Bushey for some years, but also worked at Babbacombe, Devon and at Tadley, Hampshire. Produced decorative paintings of birds and animals. Always expressed an interest in natural history, animal and insect life. Her Fine Feathers was bought by George Cross and reproduced by Raphael Tuck & Sons. Exhibited her work, including at the Royal Scottish Academy (1928), the Royal Academy (1921-28), the Society of Women Artists (1927-28), the Royal Institute of Painters in Watercolours, the Royal Institute of Oil Painters and the Royal Society of British Artists. Also, at the Goupil Gallery, the Walker's Gallery and in Paris and Sweden. Works included: The Shed, Painted Ladies, Birds of a Feather and The Harlequin Cock. Elected a Member of the Royal Institute of Oil Painters (1925) and of the Royal Institute of Painters in Watercolours (1927). Her Shadows, exhibited at the Royal Institute of Oil Painters in 1923, was illustrated in The Studio, Vol.85, 1923, p.42. Her The Intruders was illustrated in The Studio, Vol.92, November 1926, p.354.

GEARE, MARJORY VIOLET (1881-1969)
Painter / Poster Artist. Born in Wandsworth, London. The daughter of James Henry Watherston, a goldsmith, and Florence. Her sister, Evelyn, also became an artist. Raised in London and spent much of her life there, dying in Merton, Greater London, aged 87. Educated at the South Hampstead High School. Studied in Paris and at the Royal Academy schools. A silver medallist for a portrait head and a silver medallist for figure painting. Awarded a British Institute Scholarship and an extension. Became a painter of still life, portraits, figures, interiors, landscapes and historical subjects in oils, watercolours and pastels; a poster artist and a painter of decorative panels. A prolific artist, Geare worked and exhibited for over 60 years, right up until her death. Worked through two World Wars.

Geare exhibited her work extensively, including at the Royal Academy (1905-63), the Royal Scottish Academy (1936-37), the Society of Women Artists (58 works, 1906-69), the Paris Salon and the Royal Institute of Painters in Watercolours. Also, with the Royal Society of Portrait Painters, the Royal Institute of Oil Painters, the Pastel Society, at the Walker Art Gallery, Liverpool, Walker's Gallery and the Arlington Gallery. Exhibited works included: The Late Violet, Duchess of Rutland in her Drawing Room at Chapel Street (oil), Fruit and Old Silver, Procession of the Most Hon. Order of the Bath, in Westminster Abbey and At the Washtub. Her decorative panels included The Dawn of Bannockburn and Peace. A Member of the Hampstead Society of Artists. Elected an Associate of the Society of Women Artists (1955-57) and a Member (1958-68). Also an Honorary Member of the Paris Salon (1947). Some of her works were illustrated in Connoisseur (The Dug Out), Sporting & Dramatic News (The Centre Court, Wimbledon), the Times Supplement, Academy Illustrated and the Illustrated London News. One of her works, The Dispatch: The Captain's Daughter (oil, 1917), is in the collection of the Imperial War Museum. In 1916 she married Henry Leslie Geare in Hampstead. They had two children. Her The Defence of the Barrier of the 21st Fusiliers, Battle of Inkerman, 1854 was painted for the Royal Scots Fusiliers.

GEDDES, NORAH - SEE MEARS, N.G.

GEDDES, WILHELMINA MARGARET (1887-1955)
Stained Glass Artist / Black & White Artist / Linocut and Woodcut Artist / Watercolour Painter / Needlework Designer. Born in Drumreilly, Co. Leitrim, Ireland. Her father owned a building business. She was raised in Belfast, and was educated at the Methodist College there. In the early 1900s, she studied life drawing, book illustration and graphic design at the Belfast School of Art. In 1911 she won a bronze medal at the National Competition of Schools of Art, South Kensington, London for her first ever stained glass design. In the same year, some of her book illustrations were exhibited in Dublin, where they caught the attention of artist / designer Sarah Purser. Purser encouraged Geddes to move to Dublin and study at the city's

Municipal School of Art. Purser was the founder of An Tur Gloine (The Tower of Glass), a co-operative stained glass studio and workshop (f.c.1903) in Dublin.

At the Dublin School, Geddes studied stained glass under Alfred E. Child, a former pupil of Christopher Whall and Manager of An Tur Gloine. In 1912, Geddes joined Purser and associates and quickly became a highly competent and successful stained glass designer who carried out a number of important commissions. Those included two windows for Karori Crematorium Chapel, Wellington, New Zealand (1914); a window for the Presbyterian Assembly Hall, Belfast (1916); and a memorial window commissioned by the Duke of Connaught for St Bartholomew's Church, Ottawa, Canada (1919) which was first exhibited in London. In 1925, Geddes declined an invitation to take over the running of An Tur Gloine and, instead, moved to London. There, she rented a studio in Lowndes & Drury's Glass House in Lettice Street, Fulham, where she made all her later windows. She would remain in London until her death, aged 68.

One of her first commissions at her new studio was a stained glass window, St Christopher, designed and made for All Saints' Church, Laleham, Middlesex (1926) which was illustrated in The Studio, Vol.93, 1927, p.198. The window was a memorial to the late Percy Goldwin Balfour and incorporated his interests of music, sport and the Thames into its design. Later commissions included a three-light window for Northchapel Parish Church, Sussex (1930), and Te Deum for St Martin's Cathedral, Ypres, Belgium (1938). Also, a window for St David's Church, Lampeter, Cardiganshire (1937, completed in 1944). An admirer of writer Charles Lamb, Geddes designed several glass panels which illustrated aspects of Lamb's essays. Other commissions included The Crucifixion for St Luke's Church, Wallsend-on-Tyne, where the design relied largely on the leading. One of her windows was destroyed in the Belfast bombing of 1941.

Geddes proved to be a gifted stained glass designer, but was also a talented painter and decorative artist, producing black & white drawings, linocuts, woodcuts, bookplates and needlework designs. Her work was widely reported during her lifetime and, despite health problems, she was able to enjoy a full and active career. In 1922, The Studio, Vol.84, October, pp.208-213, offered an illustrated article The Art of Miss W.M. Geddes by Stephen Gwynn. Gwynn praises the simplicity of her designs, and notes this to be the key to her success in all aspects of her work, but also notes the influence of the medieval in her stained glass designs. He also notes her insistence on choosing every piece of glass herself rather than leaving it to others.

Her work was praised in other journals of the day, including Connoisseur, the Illustrated London News and Architecture. She appeared most frequently, however, in The Studio. Even before her move to London, the journal was already noting her promise. In 1917, for example, it reproduced one of her cartoons (Vol.72, October, p.17) and one of her book illustrations (p.221), following her appearance at the fifth Exhibition of the Arts and Crafts Society of Ireland, held in Dublin in 1917. The exhibition went on to Belfast and Cork. In 1929, The Studio, Vol.98, September, pp.682-683, offered an article Stained Glass Windows by Miss W.M. Geddes, which included illustrations of two large windows for the Rosemary Street Presbyterian Church, Belfast based on Moses With the Tables of the Law and Christ Blessing the Little Children. Geddes was also noted in a number of books published before and after her death. Those included E. Liddell Armitage, Stained Glass (1960) and James White and Michael Wynne, Irish Stained Glass (Dublin, 1963).

Geddes exhibited her work widely, including in Paris, Boston, Leipzig, Dublin, Edinburgh, Belfast and Wembley (1924). Exhibited at the Royal Hibernian Academy (1913-30), with the Society of Scottish Artists and at the Ulster Academy. Elected an Academician of the Ulster Academy. In 1914, Geddes showed three panels illustrating the life of St Colman MacDuagh at the Exposition des Arts Decoratifs in Paris, one of her first works after joining Purser in Dublin and commissioned by Purser. In 1924 Geddes held a joint exhibition of works with painter / sculptor Rosamund Praeger in Belfast. Praeger showed sculptures in metal, marble, clay and bronze, Geddes showed drawings, linocuts and stained glass designs. Examples of her work were included in an exhibition Women Stained Glass Artists of the Arts and Crafts Movement held at the William Morris Gallery, London, 1985-86. A centenary exhibition of her work was held in 1987 by the Arts Council of Northern Ireland.

GELL, ADA (1849-1929)

Sculptor. Born in Brighton, Sussex. The daughter of Ewen Evershed, a solicitor, and Elizabeth. Her father originated from Wisborough Green, her mother from Middlesex. The youngest of at least three girls (Louisa, Ellen and Ada). Raised in Brighton. Studied sculpture, possibly in Sussex or London. Worked in bronze and marble. Produced statues, statuettes and bas-reliefs. Began exhibiting her work in the late 1880s, at which time she was still living in Brighton. In 1869 she married Alfred Freeman Gell (1844-1911), a solicitor, in Steyning, Sussex. He originated from Eastbourne, Sussex. They had one son, Ewen. By the late 1890s, the family had moved to London, where Ada continued to work. Exhibited at the Royal Academy (20 works, 1887-1916), the Royal Society of British Artists (1888) and the Royal Glasgow Institute (1898-1908). Also, in Manchester and Leeds, and at the Walker Art Gallery, Liverpool. Exhibited works included: Grief (statuette, bronze), Man's First Disobedience (group), Will O'the Wisp (statue, bronze), Victory (statuette, bronze) and Feeding Pigeons (bas-relief). Her Bird of Peace (marble) sold for a respectable £126 in 1888. Latterly, she used a studio in Adelaide Road, London. Died in Brighton, aged 79.

GEMMELL, ELIZABETH & MARION & MARY (1839-1923) & (1838-1916) & (1845-1904)

Decorative Artists / Artists. The daughters of William Gemmell and Elizabeth. Their father was a merchant. Both parents originated from Scotland. The sisters were three of at least six children (also Thomas (1834-1909), Williamina (b.1843) and Charles (1851-1929)). All were born in Scotland. At some point prior to 1871, the family moved to London and remained in the city until their deaths, living at various addresses. At least five of the siblings never married. Elizabeth, Marion and Mary initially lived with their parents. Later, Thomas, an engineer, returned to live at the family home. After his death, Charles, also a merchant, returned to live with his three sisters. Marion Gemmell became a portrait painter in watercolours. She exhibited her work at the Royal Glasgow Institute (1901). Mary became a painter but also a sculptor, designer and engraver. She produced watercolours, etchings, engravings, sculptures, flower, landscape, portrait and animal studies and numerous designs for such things as wallpaper friezes. She exhibited more extensively than Marion. For example, showed 22 works at the Society of Women Artists (1871-1900), including Roman Peasant (pen & ink etching), The Reader (watercolour), A Penny For Me (watercolour) and Peacocks (wood). Also exhibited at the Royal Academy (1883-94), the Royal Society of British Artists (1892 / 93), the New English Art Club (1890) and the Royal Glasgow Institute (1885-89). Mary died comparatively young, but Marion was still working as a portrait painter in 1911, aged 73.

Elizabeth Gemmell chose a different path into the decorative arts. She became involved in decorative embroidery and took the post of Director of the Decorative Art Needlework Society, which was based at 17 Sloane Street, London. It can be presumed that all three Gemmell sisters underwent some formal tuition, possibly in Scotland, since all three became professionals in their field rather than amateurs. Elizabeth was evidently experienced enough, and competent enough, to act as Director of the Society. Records do not confirm exactly how long she held the post. But census recordings for 1901 and 1911 clearly state her position. In 1911 she would have been 72 years of age, indicating a particularly strong attachment to her position, but also perhaps a financial necessity. The Decorative Art Needlework Society was highly regarded in its day, and received frequent praise from leading arts journals including the Art Workers' Quarterly and The Studio. Begun in the late 1870s (c.1879) by Lady Welby Gregory on a small capital, the Society was formed for the production of high-class needlework for church and decorative purposes. It also carried out needlework restoration, made copies of antique embroideries, executed cross-stitch and petit point work, and specialised in reproducing architects' designs. They repaired old tapestries, some of high value. Its patron was Queen Alexandra. President was Princess Christian Schleswig-Holstein who was also President of the Royal School of Art Needlework. Lady Welby Gregory was also one of the founders of the Royal School of Art Needlework.

The Decorative Art Needlework Society trained its own staff, and lessons were given free to amateurs. As with the Royal School, women became members only when a vacancy arose. The Society exhibited its work. For example, it contributed to the 1901 Glasgow Exhibition. In 1906, textiles were shown at the Barrow-in-Furness Ecclesiastical Art Exhibition; in the same year, they contributed to the Artists at Work exhibition, an extensive display of craftwork held at the Grafton Galleries in London. On that occasion, they exhibited a new loom. In 1900 the Society, under the heading of 'Gemmell', showed four handicrafts at the Society of Women Artists, and showed another six in 1901. It is feasible that Mary Gemmell provided designs for the Society. It also worked designs by the Rev. E. Geldart, two of which were illustrated in The Studio, Vol.12, 1897, p.120. As early as 1880 the Society was noted in the Magazine of Art, whilst other designs executed by them were illustrated in the Art Workers' Quarterly in April 1904. Work by the Society was on show at its Sloane Street depot.

GEORGE, RHODA - SEE WAGER, R.

GERRARD, DORIS MAY (1905-95)

Sculptor. Born in Plymouth, Devon in August 1905. The daughter of Frederick Charles Warne and Alice Elizabeth. Both parents originated from Devon. Raised in Plymouth. Had at least one sister, Kathleen. Studied painting and sculpture in Paris and Florence. Travelled to India and was influenced by Indian carvings and bronzes on their original sites. Inspired to concentrate on form. Visited the cave or rock carvings in the caves of Elephanta, an island off Bombay. Modelled heads whilst in India, from all walks of life. Spent time in Hyderabad studying all the different peoples. There, she worked on busts of the Prime Minister, of Princess Niloufer, the Turkish wife of the second son of H.E.H. the Nizam, and the niece of the late Sultan of Turkey, in white Italian marble. Other works by Gerrard included Arab From Muscat, Nepalese Princess (head, bronze) and Study of Salome (bronze). Produced busts, heads and full-length studies. Did carved and modelled sculptures. Later in her career, she was based at Denham, Buckinghamshire. Died in Buckinghamshire, aged 89. Exhibited her work, including at the Royal Academy (1947-56) and the Royal Glasgow Institute (1948-49). Exhibited works included: Mrs Mirte Berko (head, bronze), Blonde Venus (head, bronze) and Rosetta (head, bronze). Elected to the Royal Society of British Artists. In 1924 she married Charles Robert Gerrard (1892-1964) in Devon. Born in Belgium, he was a painter and Director of the Sir J.J. School of Art in Bombay, India between 1935 and 1946, after which he and Doris settled in Buckinghamshire. Doris was the subject of an article in The Studio, Vol.135, May 1948, pp.152-155. The illustrated article included a portrait photograph.

GIBBONS, ANGELA – SEE LATHAM, A.

GIBBS, CHARLOTTE I. - SEE NEWMAN, C.I.

GIBBS, EVELYN ERIE EVELINA MAY (1905-91)

Painter / Etcher / Engraver / Mural Artist. Born in Liverpool in May 1905. The daughter of Horace Edward Gibbs, a marine engineer, and Euphimia. Her father originated from Sussex, her mother from Edinburgh. Had at least one sister, Marion. Educated at the Queen Mary High School, Liverpool. Studied at the Liverpool School of Art under Frederick Carter between 1922 and 1926, at the Royal College of Art, London under Professor Malcolm Osborne between 1926 and 1929, and at the British School in Rome between 1929 and 1931. Elected an Associate of the Royal College of Art. Produced paintings in oils and gouache, etchings, engravings, aquatints, pen & chalk studies and mural paintings. Worked as a lecturer of art at the Goldsmiths' College, London between 1934 and 1946, and at the Goldsmiths' School of Art between 1946 and 1949. In 1945 she married Robert Hugh Willatt in Nottingham. She spent time in Nottingham and in London, dying in London, aged 85. During her time in Nottingham, she became part of the Midland Group of artists from 1943. In 1946 Gibbs, assisted by Claude Price, painted two murals inside the church of St Martin of Tours at Bilborough, Nottinghamshire, on either side of the east window in the chancel. Depicting The Annunciation, the paintings were commissioned by the then rector, Father Marshall. Since she had studied in Italy, the murals were in the style of the medieval Italian tradition. More recently, the murals have undergone restoration.

In 1934, Gibbs wrote and had published The Teaching of Art in Schools (Williams & Norgate). In 1941 artist Minnie McLeish, in her volume Beginnings: Teaching Art to Children (London, Studio Publications), illustrated work by children from the Holland Street P.D. School in Kensington, London, whose teacher at that time was Miss Evelyn Gibbs. Evidently, Gibbs taught children too. She exhibited her work during her career, including at the Royal Academy (1929-65), the New English Art Club, the American Institute of Architecture, the Leicester Galleries, the Whitechapel Art Gallery and in Liverpool and Bradford. Exhibited works included: Child Knitting (chalk), Persian Women Walking (etching & aquatint), Fisherwomen Mending Nets (pen & chalk) and Sheep-dipping in Yorkshire (wood engraving). Her oil painting Women's Voluntary Services Clothing Exchange (1943) is in the collection of the Imperial War Museum. Other works were acquired by the Castle Art Gallery, Nottingham and the British Museum Print Room. Also, by the county collections of Leicester, Derbyshire, Hertfordshire and Cambridge.

GIBSON, CHARLOTTE E. - SEE OSBORNE, C.E.

GIBSON, MARY GWENLLIAN (1888-1966)

Craftswoman. Born in Wolverhampton and spent much of her life there. Died in Devon, aged 77. The daughter of Frederick John Gibson, a pharmacist, and Gwenllian Bertha. One of at least six children (Mary, Ivor, Charles, Harold, Kathleen and Ida). Educated at the St Anne's School, Abbots Bromley, Staffordshire. Studied at the Wolverhampton School of Art, and studied bookbinding at the Birmingham School of Art. Won several bronze and silver medals as a student, a Royal Society of Arts prize in 1923 and a National Eisteddfod prize in 1926. Specialised in leatherwork and bookbinding. Taught leatherwork and design and bookbinding at the Wolverhampton School of Art. Also a painter of various subjects. Works included a leather altar frontal in modelled, coloured and gilded leather for St Margaret's Church, Birmingham. Also, an altar book for St Peter's Church, Wolverhampton. Executed a decorated book which was presented to the Pope, according to the Who's Who in Art for 1934. Some of her modelled leather bindings were exhibited in 1914. Other works were exhibited at the Royal Birmingham Society of Artists, at two Decorative Arts Exhibitions held at the Royal Academy in 1922 and 1925, at a Paris Exhibition held at the Louvre in 1914 and at the British Arts and Crafts Exhibition. Also, at an exhibition of Contemporary Decorative Art held in Manchester and a Beaux Arts Exhibition held in Cairo. Exhibited eight works at the Royal Academy (1931-57), including: Gwynneth, Spring Morning, The Little Harbour and A White Lily. Elected an Associate of the Royal Birmingham Society of Artists.

GIFFARD, IRIS EVELINA MARGERY (1905-post-1967)

Painter / Author / Book Illustrator. Born at Ryde, Isle of Wight in January 1905. The daughter of Isaac Brooke and Emily Evelina (d.1947). Her father, who had private means, died young. Iris was one of at least four children (also Silvia, Alphonse and Veronica). All were raised on the Isle of Wight. Iris was educated at the Bruntsfield High School, Isle of Wight. Moved to the mainland to study at the Croydon School of Art under Oswald Crompton and Gilroy between 1923 and 1926. Also studied at the Royal College of Art, London under Randolph Schwabe, Ernest W. Tristram and Sir William Rothenstein between 1926 and 1929. Elected an Associate of the Royal College of Art in 1929. Produced portraits in oils and chalk. Also worked as a book illustrator, of her own books and those of others. Contributed to periodicals. Had a particular interest in historical costume. Illustrated, for example, James Laver, English Costume of the Nineteenth Century (1929) and English Costume of the Eighteenth Century (1931), C.M. Matthews

& C.E. Carrington, A Pageant of Kings and Queens (1937) and Susan Knowles, Arpies and Sirens (1942). Her own illustrated books included English Children's Costume Since 1775 (1930), English Costume of the Seventeenth Century (1934), English Costume of the Late Middle Ages (1935), English Costume 1900-50 (1951), Four Walls Adorned (1952) and Medieval Theatre Costume (1967). Elected a Member of the Women's Press Club. In 1944 she married William Hugh Giffard in London. Subsequently based near Honiton, Devon.

GILFORD, NOEL - SEE ADENEY, N.

GILMOUR, MARGARET (1860-1942)

Painter / Craftswoman. Born in Glasgow. The daughter of John Gilmour, a muslin manufacturer, and Jane. Her parents originated from Paisley, Scotland. One of a large family, of at least 11 children. By 1881, she is already listed as an artist. Her sister Mary (1872-1938) also became a painter / craftswoman. With Mary, Margaret founded a teaching craft studio in around 1893 in West George Street, Glasgow, known as the Gilmour Studio. It ran successfully for over 50 years with another sister, Agnes, doing the accounts. At the studio, the Gilmour sisters taught and produced a variety of crafts including decorative metalwork, embroidery, painting, leatherwork, woodcarving and ceramic decoration. Items produced were mainly domestic such as clocks, mirror surrounds, desk sets and paper knives. Their work was heavily reminiscent of that popular at the Glasgow School of Art at that time, promoted by, for example, the Macdonald sisters. Margaret was principal designer at the studio. She also produced watercolour paintings, mainly landscapes and flowers. Some of those were exhibited at the Royal Scottish Academy (1889) and the Royal Glasgow Institute (11 works, 1880-1907). Exhibited works included: Thistle, A Quiet Spot, Poppies and Light and Shade. Also exhibited at the 1901 Glasgow Exhibition. Mary exhibited some of her watercolour paintings, including flower and figure studies, at the Royal Glasgow Institute (1896-1906). Although the Gilmours were essentially Glasgow artists, Margaret did advertise her teaching skills in The Studio magazine in 1906, perhaps attempting to appeal to a wider audience.

GINESI, EDNA - SEE COXON, E.

GLAZIER, BERTHA - SEE FROST, B.

GLAZIER, LOUISE MARIAN (b.1870)
Illustrator / Woodcut Artist. Born in London. The daughter of Frederick W. Glazier, an auctioneer, and Louisa. One of at least five children (Ethel, Lillian, Louise, Frederick and Irene). Raised in London, and by at least 1891 she was an art student in the city. By the early 1900s, she was based in Mitcham, Surrey with her widowed father and sisters, Ethel and Irene. Produced pen & ink drawings, woodcuts and bookplates. Contributed to periodicals including The Dome and The Venture. Illustrated a small number of books including Helumac's Australian Wonderland (1899), G.F. Edwards, Old Time Paris (1908), Animals' Tags and Taits (1910), A Book of Babes (1911) and The Field Flowers Lore (1912). Her own A Book of Thirty Woodcuts was published in 1903. Exhibited some of her colour-print designs at the 1904 Leicester Arts and Crafts Exhibition. One of her woodcuts was illustrated in the Art Workers' Quarterly, April 1906, p.50. She may have moved abroad later in her career.

GLEESON, EVELYN - SEE YEATS, LILY

GLEICHEN, COUNTESS FEODORA MAUD (1861-1922)
Sculptor / Painter. Born in London. The daughter of Admiral Prince Victor of Hohenlohe-Langenburg, the son of Queen Victoria's half-sister, after whom Feodora was named. The sister of artist Helena Gleichen, of professional singer Lady Valda Gleichen and of Lord Edward Gleichen. Her father was a gifted sculptor who exhibited at the Royal Academy. Her brother was the author of London's Open-Air Statuary (Bath, Cedric Chivers) published in 1928. Feodora initially trained under her father, a pupil of Theed. Also attended the Slade School, London, then studied under Professor Alphonse Legros before completing her studies in Rome. She learnt much from her father's head man, Karl Muller, who worked in the studios and workshops built in the grounds of St James's Palace by permission of the Queen. Her father died in 1891. In his memory, Feodora designed a memorial for Sunningdale Church near Windsor.

One of the most outstanding sculptors of her generation, Feodora Gleichen produced mainly figures and portrait works in marble and bronze. She also painted. Along with Helena, she lived mainly at St James's Palace, and never married.

Her career began to take off in the 1890s when she began to exhibit more widely. Exhibited 40 works at the Royal Academy (1892-1922), many of distinguished figures including Queen Victoria. She also exhibited at the Royal Glasgow Institute (1903), the New Gallery and the Grosvenor Gallery. Exhibited watercolours at the Royal Institute of Painters in Watercolours where her father also exhibited. Elected an Honorary Member of the Institute and of the Royal Society of Painter-Etchers & Engravers. Exhibited elsewhere, including in Chicago in 1893 and at the Society of Women Artists in 1896. In 1900 she won a medal at the Paris Exposition for a hand mirror designed in jade and bronze, originally exhibited at the Royal Academy. Other works were exhibited with the Sir John Cass Arts and Crafts Society at the Walker's Gallery. Exhibited works included a marble bust of her father, a bust of Queen Victoria, another of Arthur Strong, Librarian to the House of Lords, and one of Lady Henry Bentinck which was shown at the New Gallery in 1895.

Other works included portrait studies of Madame Calve, Mrs Walter Palmer and Sir Henry Ponsonby with figures in armour as supporters. Also, a half-length figure of violinist Herr Kubelik, and a silver statue of a Madonna in an agate and mosaic shrine. Her Satan, a dramatic, strange and winged creature, caused a considerable stir when exhibited at the Royal Academy in 1894. Also exhibited with the Church Crafts League (founded 1899), including in 1902 when she showed several works including a plaster cast of a tombstone in memory of Mrs Graham which was illustrated in the Art Workers' Quarterly, July 1902. Other works were illustrated in The Studio. For example, her memorial to Lord Newton was illustrated in Vol.66, December 1915, p.190 in an article Wall Tablets and Memorials. The Art Journal, 1899, p.184 illustrated her Peace (statuette, bronze and iron).

Feodora worked on numerous commissions and projects during her lengthy career. One of her busts of Queen Victoria was later to be found at the Cheltenham Ladies' College. The Queen gave sittings for that particular bust shortly before her death. A life-size figure of the Queen was executed for a fountain for the Jubilee Hospital, Canada in 1895. The fountain was eventually placed in London's Hyde Park. Executed a bust of Queen Alexandra when Princess of Wales (exhibited at the Royal Academy in 1895), later owned by the Constitutional Club, London. Her memorial at Monchy-le-Preux won her the Legion of Honour from the French Government. Gleichen was noted in M.H. Spielmann's volume

British Sculpture and Sculptors of To-day (London, Cassell & Co.) published in 1901. Also mentioned in her brother's volume London's Open-Air Statuary which he dedicated to her. The volume included an illustration of her Diana fountain at Rotten Row (p.65).

After her death, Feodora was elected a Member of the Royal Society of British Sculptors, one of its earlier women members. Shortly after her death, the Cotswold Gallery held an exhibition of watercolour and tempera paintings by Feodora. In her honour, the Feodora Gleichen Award was established, for promising young sculptors. One of its recipients was Christine Gregory who became instructor of modelling at the Hammersmith School of Arts and Crafts from 1918. In 1911, artist Dorothea Landau exhibited a portrait work of Gleichen at the Royal Academy. In 1914, sculptor Elinor Halle exhibited a medal in wax, a portrait of Countess Gleichen, at the Royal Academy.

GLENAVY, LADY BEATRICE MOSS (1883-1970)

Stained Glass Artist / Modeller / Painter / Illustrator. Born in Dublin, Ireland in April 1883. The daughter of William Elvery, a shopkeeper of 'Elephant House'. She studied at the Metropolitan School of Art, Dublin. There, studied sculpture under John Hughes. Also studied stained glass under A.E. Child. As a student, in 1900 she won the Queen's Prize for drawing from the life. One of the School's most promising students, she won the Taylor Scholarship three times. Also won bronze and silver medals, including a bronze for a design for a modelled tobacco jar. Contributed to the National Competition of Schools of Art held at South Kensington, London. Whilst still at the Dublin School, her modelled design for a chimney decoration, a large ornate and heavy piece with figures, was illustrated in The Artist, 1901, p.68. In the same year, The Studio, Vol.22, February 1901, p.46, illustrated her statuette Bacchus, for which she was a prize winner in the Taylor Art Competition.

In the early 1900s, Glenavy went to study in Paris for a short time. Then returned to Ireland to work for Sarah Purser's An Tur Gloine (The Tower of Glass), a stained glass workshop established in Dublin in around 1903. She remained there for several years, producing stained glass, mainly for Ireland. Subsequently moved to London to study at the Slade School under Henry Tonks and Philip Wilson Steer. Returned to Ireland, living mainly in Dublin. Acted as a teacher at the Dublin School of Art. Worked in various fields during her busy career.

Executed oil and watercolour paintings, sculptures and modelling work, black & white drawings, and worked in stained glass. Produced work for the Cuala Press for calendars and Christmas cards. Illustrated books, including Violet Russell, Heroes of the Dawn (Maunsel & Co., 1913) and K.F. Purdon, Candle and Crib (1920). Other works included a bronze memorial for Clonmel Barrack Yard. In 1912 she married barrister Charles Henry Gordon Campbell, later Lord Glenavy, and had three children, two sons and a daughter. The couple spent some time living in London, but eventually returned to Dublin. Beatrice worked both before and after her marriage.

Glenavy exhibited her work from at least 1902, with the Young Irish Artists. From at least 1904, she contributed to the Irish Arts and Crafts Society exhibitions in Dublin, for example, showing small statuettes and a panel in relief in 1904. One of her panels, The Mother, was illustrated in The Studio, Vol.33, January 1905, p.361, shortly after. In 1910 she contributed oil and watercolour paintings to the first exhibition held at the Dublin School of Art, of work by past and present students over the previous 10 years. Other exhibitors on that occasion included Ethel Rhind, William Orpen and Kathleen Fox. Held her first one-woman show in 1934 at No.7 St Stephen's Green, Dublin. Exhibited at the Royal Academy (1933-48), the Royal Scottish Academy (1948), the Royal Cambrian Academy, the Royal Hibernian Academy (1902-69) and the Society of Women Artists (1940). Exhibited works included: The Intruder, The Apple and Country Life. Elected an Associate of the Royal Hibernian Academy (1932) and a Royal Hibernian Academician (1934). A Member of the United Arts Club, Dublin. Author of Today We Will Only Gossip (1964), on her life in Dublin, Paris and London. Noted in Malcolm C. Salaman, Modern Book Illustrators and Their Work, London, The Studio Ltd, 1914.

GOFF, BLANCHE CECILIA & BERTHA LILIAN (1874-1965) & (1876-1971)

Decorative Metalworkers / Sculptor / Bookbinder. The Goff sisters became successful and celebrated decorative metalworkers in the late 1890s through to at least the early 1910s, with Bertha also working as a portrait and figure sculptor and a decorative bookbinder. Bertha was the more productive of the sisters, though neither listed themselves as active in any profession on census recordings. That may have been because neither considered themselves to be employed on any professional, full-time level, or because neither made a living out of their work. The sisters were the daughters of William Goff, a timber merchant, and Annie. The family was sufficiently wealthy to employ servants. There were at least two younger siblings, Ethel and Reginald. Both girls were born in Reading, Berkshire, and were raised there initially. Sometime between 1891 and 1901 the family moved to London, living at The Avenue, Lee for most of the time. The sisters were still living with their widowed father in Lee in 1911. Blanche died in Sevenoaks, Kent, aged 89. Bertha died in Newbury, Berkshire, aged 94. Neither ever married.

The Goff sisters were pupils of Christine Connell, who ran a decorative metalwork studio in London. They became Connell's assistants in around 1904, but also designed and executed their own work. From at least 1900 to at least 1904, Bertha also appears to have studied at Holloway. She exhibited her work at the National Competition of Schools of Art, South Kensington between those years, showing examples of her decorative jewellery at the 1904 Competition. The sisters exhibited their work jointly and separately. Jointly, they exhibited jewellery at the Society of Women Artists between 1903 and 1907. Their jewellery was highly ornate and decorative. For example, they designed and executed a Three Rabbit choker made of silver and turquoise, with a design of three rabbits as its central feature, worked in silver. Their Winged Aphrodite necklace was, again, a heavily decorative, typically Arts and Crafts piece. In 1903 the sisters jointly showed jewellery at the Arts and Crafts Exhibition Society's exhibition, held at the New Gallery.

Bertha Goff exhibited elsewhere. For example, she showed statuettes, busts and portrait medallions at the Royal Academy between 1899 and 1905. Those included portrait busts of her mother and father, Child With a Cat (statuette) and Scenes From the Life of a Horse. Some of her bookbindings were exhibited in London in 1906. In 1908 she contributed to an exhibition staged by members of the Sir John Cass Arts and Crafts Society at the Walker's Gallery in London. Other exhibitors on that occasion included Phoebe Stabler, Violet Ramsay and Ethel Agnew, indicating that Bertha Goff, in particular, was easily equal to her contemporaries in terms of design and workmanship. She also contributed to the exhibitions of the Women's International Art Club, including that held in 1910 at the Grafton Galleries. In 1910 a Colonel Goff, possibly of the same family, contributed to the exhibition of the Royal Society of Painter-Etchers & Engravers. SEE: CONNELL, CHRISTINE

GOGGS, EVELYN D. - SEE JOCE, E.D.

GOLDEN, GRACE LYDIA (1904-93)
Poster Artist / Painter / Wood Engraver / Black & White Artist. Born in Merton, London in April 1904. The daughter of Henry F. Golden, a housekeeper, and Grace. Raised in London. Educated at the City of London School for Girls. Studied at the Chelsea School of Art under John Daniel Revel. Also, at the Royal College of Art, London under Sir William Rothenstein. Elected an Associate of the Royal College of Art in 1926. Became a freelance artist in poster design, a painter of various subjects in oils and watercolours, a black & white artist and a wood engraver. Produced posters for, for example, the R.S.P.C.A., the G.P.O. and for Government propaganda. Based in London throughout much of her career. Died in Camden, aged 89. Exhibited her work, including at the Royal Academy (1936-40), the Leicester Galleries, the Fine Art Society, the Redfern Gallery with the Society of Wood Engravers, the Beaux Art Gallery, the Suffolk Gallery and various provincial galleries. Exhibited works included: Catching the Five-Fifteen, The Doctor's House, Westminster Pier and Prelude to Cadenza. Her oil painting An Emergency Food Office (1941) is in the collection of the Imperial War Museum. Works also acquired by the Tate Gallery. The Chantrey Bequest purchased her Summer Evening, Embankment Garden (in 1937) and her Free Speech (in 1940), both of which were exhibited at the Royal Academy. Her works were reproduced in The Studio, Apollo, Tatler, the Art Review, The Artist and the Illustrated London News. Some of her designs were illustrated in The Studio, Vol.94, 1927, along with those of Molly Bateman, Priscilla Ellingford and Vera K. Wheeler.

GOLDSMID, EVELYN ISABEL - SEE BETHUNE, E.I.

GOLDSMITH, BETTY (active 1920s-1930s)
Illuminator / Lettering Artist. Based in New Barnet, London. Elected a Member of the Society of Scribes and Illuminators. In 1925, The Studio, Vol.89, May, p.278, illustrated three pages from the Eighteenth Division Roll of Honour (1914-18), written and illuminated by her. Four examples of her work were exhibited at the Society of Women Artists in 1939.

GOODWIN, EDITH CHESTER (1879-1969)
Illuminator. Born in Handsworth, Staffordshire in September 1879. The daughter of Felix Goodwin,

a general merchant and later a dealer in lamps and lanterns for the motor industry, and Mary. One of at least three children (Ernest, Alice and Edith). Raised in Birmingham. Remained there and died there, aged 89. Exhibited her work at the Royal Academy arts and crafts exhibition, at Wembley and locally in Birmingham. The Victoria & Albert Museum, London acquired three examples of her work, including Whosoever Thou Art for their travelling collection.

GOODWIN, ELISABETH NANCIE (1905-49)

Sculptor / Illustrator / Black & White Artist. Born in Meols, Cheshire in January 1905. The daughter of Richard H.D. Goodwin, a timber merchant and later a West African merchant, and Sarah. Had at least one sibling, Richard. Educated at home with a governess, then at Leatherhead Court, Leatherhead, Surrey. Spent much of her life in Birkenhead. From 1923 she studied art at Miss A.H. Wright's Limner Lee Studios in Liverpool. Exhibited her work locally, at the Walker Art Gallery, Liverpool (1924-26), the Atkinson Gallery, Southport and at the Liverpool Civic Week Exhibition. Died prematurely in Liverpool, aged 44.

GORDINE, DORA (1906-91)

Sculptor. Born in Russia. Became a British citizen. Studied sculpture in Paris, under M. Aristide Maillol. On his advice, she took a studio and worked alone. She was influenced by Maillol, but also by her travels to India, China, Ceylon and Java. Produced heads, life-size figures occasionally and smaller figures. Used colour in her work, and occasionally painted. Worked mainly in bronze and sometimes plaster. In 1936 she married the Hon. Richard Hare in Chelsea. Spent much of her life and career in London. Their London home, Dorich House, was later made into a museum of her work. Her first major commission was for decorative bronzes for the Singapore Town Hall (1930-33). In 1947 she visited Hollywood and designed film sets and lectured on art. Exhibited her work, including at the Paris Salon, the Royal Scottish Academy (1927-51), the Royal Glasgow Institute (1938-61), the Royal Academy (1937-60) and the Society of Women Artists (1939-55). Contributed to the Art Competitions of the 1948 London Summer Games. In 1933 she held an exhibition of her work at the Leicester Galleries which was praised in Apollo, 1933, p.125. Exhibits on that occasion included the torso of a Dyak head-hunter, Diana (a Greek head), Cingalese Girl and Iran (armless, full-length of a girl). Another of

those exhibits, Head of a Girl, was illustrated in Apollo, 1933, p.54. Other exhibited works included: Reclining Girl (bronze), Silent Bride (statuette, bronze) and Sir Kenneth Clark, K.C.B. (head, bronze). Elected a Member of the Society of Women Artists (1955). Elected an Associate of the Royal Society of British Sculptors (1938) and a Fellow (1949). Gordine died in Surrey, aged 85. The subject of a book, Dora Gordine, Sculptor, Artist, Designer by Jonathan Black & Brenda Martin (Philip Wilson, 2008).

GORDON, ROSE G. - SEE HOLT, R.G.

GORST, HESTER GASKELL (1887-1992)

Sculptor. Born in Liverpool in September 1887. Raised in West Derby. The daughter of Walter Holland, a ship owner, and Alice. One of at least seven children (Catherine, Walter, Robert, Franklin, Hester, Alice and Leonard). Studied sculpture at the Slade School, London (1904-06) under Professor Henry Tonks, then in Brussels. Based mainly in London thereafter, dying there at the age of 105. Produced sculptures, but also paintings. Exhibited her work at the Salon des Artistes Francais and other galleries in Paris, in Brussels and in London. Exhibited one work, Spring, at the Society of Women Artists in 1932. In 1914 she married Elliot Marcet Gorst (1885-1973) in Liverpool. He was a law student, and later died in Kent.

GOUDIE, ISOBEL TURNER MAXWELL (b.1903)

Stained Glass Artist / Potter. Born in Stirling, Scotland in March 1903. The daughter of Andrew H. Goudie, a borough engineer. Educated at the High School, Stirling. Studied at the Glasgow School of Art. Awarded a diploma and two scholarships. Produced stained glass designs and pottery. Had a studio in Stirling for a time, but later worked at Queen Street, Edinburgh. Exhibited her work, mainly in Scotland, including at the Royal Scottish Academy (11 works, 1928-46), the Royal Glasgow Institute (1934-40) and with the Society of Scottish Artists. Also contributed to exhibitions of ecclesiastical art. Her stained glass designs included a heraldic window for Dunfermline Abbey, and windows in Nessbank Church, Inverness Church, the Church of Holy Rood, Carnoustie and Rockvilla Church, Glasgow. Also, for the Dalziel High Church, Motherwell, St Leonard's Church, Kinghorn and the church at Fern, Angus. Produced secular designs as well, including The Seasons for a hall window.

GOULD, ELIZABETH (1804-41).

Ornithological Painter. Born in Ramsgate. The daughter of a sea captain named Coxon. In 1829 she married John Gould, F.R.S. (1804-81), author of Gould's Birds. She worked with a young Edward Lear in executing watercolours as guides to the finished illustrated works. Gould was to publish 41 volumes of birds, with almost 3000 illustrations. Elizabeth assisted with The Birds of Europe and A Century of Birds From the Himalayan Mountains. She accompanied Gould to Australia for his Birds of Australia (1838-40). Her work was frequently attributed to her husband. Mrs Gould was noted by Ellen C. Clayton in her volume English Female Artists (Vol.1, London, Tinsley, 1876). Clayton notes that Elizabeth died in August 1841, aged 37, giving birth to her sixth child, a daughter.

GOW, DOROTHY ERMYNTRUDE (1890-1956)

Potter / Modeller / Sculptor. Born in London. The daughter of William Willett, the originator of 'Daylight Saving', afterwards known as 'Summer Time'. Educated in Eastbourne and Paris. Studied at the London County Council Central School of Arts and Crafts. Executed heads in bronze, and worked in pottery and modelling. Exhibited her work, including at the Society of Women Artists (1925-50), the Royal Society of British Artists, the Walker Art Gallery, Liverpool, the Royal Institute of Painters in Watercolours (1925-28), at the International Exhibition of Decorative Art, Paris, the London Arts and Crafts Exhibitions, with the Scottish Society of Women Artists and with the Societe Nationale des Beaux-Arts, Paris. Elected an Associate of the Society of Women Artists (1927-52). Based mainly in London. In 1917 she married Colin C. Gow in London. They had at least one daughter. Dorothy died in Kensington, aged 66.

GOYDER, ALICE KIRKBY (1875-1964)

Painter / Etcher / Drypoint Artist / Woodcarver. Born in Bradford, Yorkshire in December 1875. The daughter of David Goyder (1822-1920) and Anne Eliza (b.1845). Her father, a physician, originated from Lancashire. Her mother originated from Ripon, Yorkshire. One of at least four children (Alice, Mabel, Arnold and Francis), all raised in Bradford. Alice was educated privately. Her brother Francis became a consultant surgeon. Alice studied at the Bradford School of Art and in London. Subsequently lived in Bradford, then moved to Faversham, Kent, latterly living in Orford, Suffolk. Died in Suffolk. Produced paintings in oils and watercolours,

including landscapes and figures. Also, etchings, drypoint and woodcarvings. Had a long and productive career. Exhibited her work, including at the Royal Academy (1899-1939), the Society of Women Artists (1900 & 1955) and at various provincial galleries. A silver medallist at the 1897 Women's Exhibition. Exhibited works included: Shere Khan - The Jungle Book, Hostilities, The Mill Girl and Walberswick Marshes. Elected a Member of the Bradford Arts Club, of the East Kent Art Society and of the Ipswich Art Club. Works illustrated in Colour and the Christian Science Monitor.

GRANT, DOROTHY MARION (1912-88)

Stained Glass Artist. Known as Marion. Born in Bromley, Kent in June 1912. The daughter of Frederick Percy Grant (1884-1945), a company director. Educated at the Kinnaird Park School, Bromley, Kent. Studied at the London County Council Central School of Arts and Crafts between 1931 and 1935. Subsequently became an apprentice to stained glass designer Francis Spear, and used a studio at Lowndes & Drury, London. During the Second World War, she worked for the Air Ministry designing camouflage. Based in Chelsea and elsewhere in London during her career. Died in London, aged 76. Exhibited one of her sketch designs, for a stained glass window in the south aisle of All Saints' Church, Bradbourne, Derbyshire, at the Royal Academy in 1940. Other designs by Grant included for St George the Martyr, Southwark, for the Lady Chapel at Exeter Cathedral and for St Benedict in Sunderland city centre. Elected a Fellow of the British Society of Master Glass Painters. Also served on the Society's Council. Some of her papers and designs are in the collection of the Victoria & Albert Museum, London.

GRANT, MARY (1830-1908)

Sculptor. Born in Scotland. Based at Kilgraston House, Perthshire initially, but by at least the very early 1870s she and some of her family were living in London. Mary remained in London for the rest of her life, dying in Chelsea, aged 77. She was the daughter of John Grant and the Hon. Lady Lucy. Her father was the owner of the Kilgraston and Okaithley Estates in Scotland and a J.P. Records suggest that Mary came from a large family, possibly of up to 13 children (records are not clear). Her background was one of wealth and privilege, but also artistic. Her aunt, Mary Ann Grant, was a portrait and landscape painter. Her uncle, Sir Francis Grant, was a portrait painter and President of the Royal

Academy. Mary executed a portrait study of Francis Grant which was exhibited at the Royal Academy in 1866, her first exhibit there. She studied in Paris under Michel Mercier, in Florence under Odoardo Fantachiotti, in Rome under John Gibson and with portrait sculptor John Henry Foley, R.A. (1818-74). She became a highly successful portrait sculptor in marble and bronze, popular with royalty and other dignitaries.

Mary's career lasted for more than 28 years. She exhibited her work, including at the Royal Academy (42 works, 1866-92) and the Royal Scottish Academy (1864-89). Subjects included Irish politician Charles Parnell (bust, bronze), Viscount Canning, Queen Victoria, Queen Margaret of Scotland, the Very Rev. E.B.K. Fortescue, Provost of St Ninian's, the Dean of Westminster and Lady Augusta Stanley. Other works included a marble bust of her brother, Alan. Also, The Tired Musicians (group, marble), Arthur Saltmarshe, Esq. (bust, marble) for Ridley College, Cambridge, Lady Macbeth and a bas-relief of John the Baptist Preaching in the Wilderness. Her study of Henry Fawcett (1833-84) was unveiled in 1886 at the Women's Memorial at Victoria Embankment Gardens, and was noted in Lord Edward Gleichen's volume London's Open-Air Statuary, Bath, Cedric Chivers, 1928.

In his volume British Sculpture and Sculptors of To-day (London, Cassell & Co. Ltd, 1901), M.H. Spielmann describes Mary Grant as 'one of the busiest lady sculptors', and lists a number of her works including a study of Mr Gladstone, completed in 1901 but not publicly shown at that point. He also notes that she executed a number of decorative figures for the west front and porch of Lichfield Cathedral, a screen for Winchester Cathedral, a marble reredos for Edinburgh Cathedral and a relief of Dean Stanley for the Royal Private Chapel at Windsor Castle. Mary was also noted in C.E. Clement, Women in the Fine Arts (The Riverside Press, 1904). In 1881 the Art Journal, p.284, illustrated an engraving by G.J. Stodart from the statue of St Margaret and the Dragon by Grant. The statue was exhibited at the English Fine Art Galleries in the Paris Exhibition of 1878, and was, the journal notes, 'well received'. Somewhat less flatteringly, the same journal notes it as a subject 'suitable for female handling'. Works in the National Portrait Gallery.

GRANT, NAN (active 1920s-1950s)
Sculptor. Born in Birmingham. Educated at the Hampstead High School. Studied in London and

Paris. Produced statuettes and heads in bronze and plaster. Based mainly in London during her career. Exhibited her work, including at the Royal Academy (1922-54), the Society of Women Artists (1921), the Royal Society of Portrait Painters and the International Society of Sculptors, Painters & Gravers. Also, at the Grafton Galleries and the Grosvenor Gallery. An exhibition of her work was held at the Ruskin Galleries in 1930. Exhibited works included: The Reader (plaster bust), The Pagan (statuette, bronze), The Mirror (statuette) and A Dancer (statuette, bronze).

GRASSETT, KATE (active 1890s-1930s)
Craftswoman. Katherine, known as Kate. A professional tapestry and brocade weaver, and founder of the London School of Weaving in 1890. She studied at the School of Art and Handicraft, Vienna, and possibly in Stockholm. In its early days, the London School of Weaving was based in Davies Street, Berkeley Square, London. Its aim was to give lessons in spinning, weaving, lace making and Italian embroidery. It specialised in metal weaving in gold and aluminium threads, and sold assorted hand-woven silks, linens and woollens for embroidery. The School was highly successful, and from early on won numerous awards for its work, including various gold medals, bronze medals and awards of merit at London, Wembley, Paris, Brussels and Milan. Exhibited its work extensively, including at Burlington House, London and the International Exhibitions of Paris, Brussels, Vienna, Milan and Leipzig (gold medal in London). Also contributed to the Artists at Work Exhibition held at the Grafton Galleries in October 1906, a large exhibition consisting of work by 120 craftworkers. The exhibition aimed to help women in reduced circumstances.

Kate Grassett was a gifted craftswoman in her own right, and exhibited at the Society of Women Artists under her own name between 1906 and 1936, showing various handicrafts (not specified). The School, which was occasionally also called The London School of Tapestry Weaving or The British Spinning and Weaving School, also exhibited various handicrafts at the Society of Women Artists between 1908 and 1925. Grassett was elected a Member of the Society of Women Artists (1933-37). She also belonged to the Church Crafts League, listed as its only weaver, and was on its Committee. The League was formed in December 1899 in Westminster with the primary objective of infusing new life into the building, decoration and furnishing of churches.

By 1920, at which time Grassett was still listed in the Church Crafts League papers, some 73 artists, craftsmen and craftswomen were working in association with the League. Those included Margaret Chilton, Mabel Esplin, Emily Ford and Henry Holiday. Grassett was also a Member of the Arts and Crafts Exhibition Society. Was a Member and Councillor of the Home Arts and Industries Association, which promoted a return to regional crafts and the establishing of classes for the working man and woman. The School of Weaving exhibited at the annual Home Arts and Industries Association exhibition, including in 1897, showing fabrics. Grassett was also a Member and Councillor of the Women's Guild of Arts, and a Member of the Faculty of Arts and of the Forum Club.

The School of Weaving moved premises a number of times and was also based in Blenheim Street, then Old Cavendish Street (from 1925), Bryanston Street, Holly Gardens, Church Street and Bedford Gardens (into the 1930s). Latterly, it was linked to the Kensington Weavers' Association. Artist Isobel Gloag designed a poster for the School. Some works by Grassett and the School were illustrated in The Studio and in an art book produced for Wembley and Paris. Grassett was the author of The Complete Guide to Hand Spinning (London School of Weaving, n.d.). In 1936, the School and the Kensington Weavers' Association jointly advertised in Rural Industries, a quarterly published by the Rural Industries Bureau (Winter, No.45, priced two pence). They were then still offering daily classes in weaving and spinning, and hand-woven materials of all types to order. The School was then in Church Street, Kensington. Grassett's personal life remains unclear. Her death remains, so far, untraced, and she appears not to be listed on national census recordings. She effectively disappears in the later 1930s.

GRAY, MILLICENT ETHELDREDA (1873-post-1938)

Painter / Illustrator. Born in London in September 1873. The daughter of Col. Horace William Gray (V.D., J.P., Political Agent, b.1843) of the Civil Service, and Julia (b.1843). The third of at least seven daughters (Hilda, Monica, Millicent, Naomi, Agatha, Annie and Marjory), all born between 1870 and 1889. All were raised in London. Records indicate that at least four of the Gray sisters, Monica, Millicent, Naomi and Agatha, took up art to varying degrees. Another sister, Annie, became a teacher. Five of the girls, including Millicent, were still living at the family home in 1911, all unmarried, aged between 22

and 40. At that point, Monica and Millicent are listed as painters. Millicent studied at the Cope & Nichols School of Art, London, winning a bronze medal there. Then studied at the Royal Academy schools, London (Proxime Accessit for the Creswick Prize). She remained in London, using a studio at Napier Road, then at Holland Park Road, Kensington. Produced oil paintings and watercolour illustrations. Subjects included landscapes, portraits, figures and flowers. Illustrated a number of books during her career, including Princess Mary's Gift Book (with others, c.1915), The Queen's Gift Book (with others, c.1915), Mabel and Lilian Quiller-Couch (eds), A Book of Children's Verse (1920) and Louisa M. Alcott, Little Women (1922).

Millicent executed a number of significant portrait commissions during her career. Subjects included the Mayor of Kensington for Kensington Town Hall, the Town Clerk of Paddington for Paddington Town Hall, the Vice Chairman of West London Hospital and the High Sheriff of Durham. Also executed portraits of her sister, Marjory, of her father and of Col. Sir Howard Vincent, K.C.M.G., M.P. Other paintings by Gray included The Treasure, an oil painting exhibited at the Royal Academy and reproduced by Forman & Sons, who also reproduced her painting I Remember, I Remember, also exhibited at the Royal Academy. Bemrose Ltd reproduced Her Swan, which was exhibited in Glasgow in 1926. Exhibited her work regularly, including at the Royal Academy (29 works, 1899-1938), the Royal Glasgow Institute (1926-35), the Society of Women Artists (1899-1937), the Walker Art Gallery, Liverpool and the Royal Society of Portrait Painters. Also, at the Royal Institute of Oil Painters, the Leicester Galleries, the Carnegie Institute, Pittsburgh and the Paris Salon where she won an Honourable Mention. Provided a picture for the Queen's Doll's House. Mentioned in Walter Shaw Sparrow's volume Women Painters of the World, London, Hodder & Stoughton, 1905. Sparrow describes her as an up and coming artist of note, but spells her first name incorrectly. Millicent was a Member of the Camden Hill Club, and of the Ridley Art Club. Monica Gray exhibited at the Royal Academy (1900-18) and at the Society of Women Artists (1898-1905). Naomi Gray exhibited handicrafts at the Society of Women Artists in 1900. It remains unclear if Agatha Gray exhibited her work.

GRAZEBROOK, ELLEN LUCY (1859-1949)

Decorative Artist. Born in Hagley, Worcestershire. Died in Worcestershire. The daughter of

John P. Grazebrook, a colliery owner, and Harriet. Raised in Worcestershire. One of at least three children (Tom, Ellen and Alice). Studied drawing for three years under Professor Alphonse Legros at the Slade School, London. Also studied abroad under Norman Garstin at one of his sketching classes. She also took up goldpoint. Held at least one exhibition of her drawings and other decorative works at the Walker's Gallery, London. Some of her works, including her chalk and charcoal sketch The Vegetable Market, were illustrated in The Studio in the early 1900s.

GREEN, LEONORA KATHLEEN (1901-66)

Painter / Textile Designer. Born in Battersea, London in June 1901. The daughter of James Brand Silver and Amelia. Her father was a musician and a pianoforte tuner and repairer. One of at least four children (Roland, Leonora, Millicent and Eveline). Raised in London. Educated at the L.C.C. Lavender Hill Girls' School. Studied at the Camberwell School of Arts and Crafts, London. Awarded several prizes by the Royal Society of Arts. Produced oil paintings and textile designs. Spent much of her career in London. Exhibited her work occasionally, including at the Royal Academy (1931-41). Hung on the line there. Exhibited works included The Cross Roads From My Window, A Three Power Intervention and Charleston and Blackbottom, 1927. At least two of her works were in the collection of the Imperial War Museum: Coupons Required (oil, 1941) and Lest We Forget (oil, 1945). In 1929 she married James E. Green in Wandsworth, London. Died in Surrey, aged 65. Works also in Wandsworth Museum.

GREEN, WINIFRED (1871-1940)

Artist / Illustrator. Born in Birmingham. Lived and worked in and around the city for much of her life, and died there. The daughter of Thomas H. Smith, a stationer and printer, and Jeanie. One of at least six children (Edith, Winifred, Hester, Dora, Mary and Jessie). Edith became a teacher, Dora became a music teacher. Winifred was an art student by at least 1891. She studied at the Birmingham Municipal School of Art. Contributed to at least one exhibition of work held there, in 1900, by the School's Sketch Club. In 1897 she married Charles Stevenson Green (1868-1959) in Worcestershire. They had at least two sons, Stevenson and Michael. Charles was a manufacturing silversmith who used some of Winifred's designs. She was also a successful book illustrator, and continued to work after her marriage. Illustrated, for example, Charles and Mary Lamb, Lamb's Poetry For Children (Dent,

1898), their Mrs Leicester's School (Dent, 1899) and their Stories For Children (Dent, 1903). Exhibited her work occasionally, including at the Society of Women Artists (1914). Noted in R.E.D. Sketchley, English Book Illustration, London, Kegan Paul, 1903. Also, in Mahony, Latimer & Folmsbee, Illustrators of Children's Books 1744-1945, Boston, The Horn Book Inc., 1947.

GREENHALGH, JOAN KEVAN (1906-99)

Painter / Illustrator / Poster Artist / Modeller. Born in Cheshire in April 1906. The daughter of John Kevan Greenhalgh. He was an accountant and deputy director of a soap factory. Joan was raised in Birkenhead by her father. She was taught by a governess, but was also educated at the Dudley Bank School, Cheshire. Won the Ablett's Chairman's Prize at the age of 18, and several gold and silver medals from the same society. She was also awarded a full art teacher's certificate by them. Awarded a scholarship for tuition at Miss Wright's Studios in Liverpool for two years. Later, in the early 1930s, she studied oil painting under Will C. Penn and modelling under Charles John Allen at the Liverpool School of Art. At that time, she worked to the theory that, ideally, art, religion and music should be combined more closely.

Greenhalgh spent her earlier career in Cheshire. In 1930 she married Reginald J. Dobell in Cheshire. In the late 1930s, she spent time in London. She died in New Forest, Hampshire, aged 92. Produced poster designs, paintings in oils and watercolours, pastel studies, statuettes and book illustrations. Received congratulations from H.R.H. the Prince of Wales for a poster exhibited at a children's exhibition held at the Guildhall, London. Produced illustrations for, for example, The Bells of the Old Church Tower, a children's book by the Rev. A. Lownes Moir published in 1925. Exhibited her work occasionally, including at the Walker Art Gallery, Liverpool. Her small statuette Blind was purchased by Lord Leverhulme and was in the collection of the Lady Lever Art Gallery. Her statuette Fantasy was purchased by the succeeding Lord Leverhulme.

GREENWOOD, EILEEN CONSTANCE (1915-2008)

Artist / Craftswoman. Born in Finchley. The daughter of Harold Ernest Messenger (d.1963), an insurance clerk, and Nellie Spackman. Educated at the Frances Mary Buss Camden School (1925-34). Studied at the London County Council Central School of Arts and Crafts, and at the Royal College of Art, London (School of Design) under Professor Ernest W. Tristram. Elected an Associate of the Royal College of Art. Awarded an Art Teachers' Diploma (1937-38). Elected a Member of the Society for Education in Art. Became a lecturer on art at the L.C.C. Battersea Training College. Based in Otford, Kent for part of her career. Produced works in, for example, gouache, pastel, wood and clay. In 1939 she married artist Ernest Greenwood (b.1913) in Middlesex. They had at least one daughter. Ernest was also a student and Associate of the Royal College of Art as well as a Member of the Society for Education in Art. He was a painter in oils and watercolours, a draughtsman and a lecturer on art. His father, Owen Charles Greenwood, was also a painter. Eileen exhibited widely, including at the Royal Society of British Artists, the Royal Institute of Painters in Watercolours, with the London Group, at the Kensington Salon and with the Royal Society. At the Royal Academy, she showed one work, Arum, in 1952. At the Society of Women Artists, she showed one work, Lilies (pastel), in 1950. Held a joint exhibition with Ernest at the Kensington Gallery in 1951. Published Leathercraft (2 vols, E. & F.N. Spon), illustrated by Ernest, indicating an interest in leatherwork. Works reproduced in Revue Moderne (1950) and The Studio (1951). Official purchases made by the Middlesex Education Committee and other educational bodies.

GREGORY, CHRISTINE (1880-1963)

Sculptor / Potter. Born in Middlesex. Raised in London. Confirmed at the St John's Church, Hammersmith in 1896. The daughter of James R. Gregory (b.1833), a mineralogist, and Cassandra Elizabeth Law (b.1838). Her father originated from London, her mother from Berkshire. One of at least seven children, all well educated. One of her sisters, Denise, became a governess. Her brother, Victor, became a structural engineer. Another brother, Leolin, became an architect. In 1899 her father died, and by at least 1901 Christine was an art student in London. She became a sculptor and potter. Won the Feodora Gleichen Award. Also a national gold medallist twice, and won various bronze and silver medals. Produced busts and statuettes in bronze, plaster, lead and terracotta as well as plaquettes and glazed and unglazed earthenware.

Gregory exhibited widely, including at the Royal Academy (37 works, 1900-49), the Royal Glasgow Institute (1916 & 1945), the Royal Scottish Academy (1916) and the Society of Women Artists (24 works, 1909-25). Also, at the Paris Salon, in Toronto and Belfast, at the Decorative Art Exhibition, Wembley, at the Royal West of England Academy, the Walker Art Gallery, Liverpool, in Burnley, at the Leicester Galleries, the Grosvenor Gallery and the International Society of Sculptors, Painters & Gravers. Exhibited works included: The Spirit of Mischief (priced £21), To the Happy Land of Nod (bronze, priced £45), Dolores (pottery statuette, priced £4) and The Problem (pottery statuette, priced £4).

Other works by Gregory included a portrait statuette of Madame Aage Ernst, a bronze panel for Wallington War Memorial and a plaquette of Joseph Kendrick, Esq. Elected an Associate of the Society of Women Artists (1918-22) and a Member (1923-26). Elected an Associate and a Fellow of the Royal Society of British Sculptors. Works illustrated in The Studio, the Architectural Review, Apollo, Builder, Architect, Sphere and Connoisseur. Gregory acted as instructor of life modelling and design at the Hammersmith School of Arts and Crafts from 1918 until 1937. Exhibited her work for around 50 years. In 1911, she was still living with her mother, the only one of the seven Gregory children remaining at home. Latterly, she was based in Hampstead, working at the Lynstone Studio in Glenilla Road. She died in Hampstead in early 1963, aged 83. Works purchased by the Manchester Corporation and the Hanley Museum, Stoke-on-Trent. The Belfast Art Gallery acquired her bronze statuette Circle of Spring.

GRIBBLE, ELEANOR MARY (1883-1960)

Decorative Painter / Designer / Book Illustrator / Interior and Furniture Decorator / Embroideress. Born in London in September 1883. The daughter of Alfred Henry Woolmer (1854-1933), a warehouseman, and Mary Louise Ensor (1861-1926). Her father originated from Norfolk, her mother from Middlesex. The eldest of at least eight children, six of whom survived into adulthood. In the late 1880s, the family moved to Ipswich in Suffolk, where her father worked as a woollen draper's assistant. The family remained in Suffolk, initially living at Elizabeth Cottages in Ipswich, an area inhabited by builders, confectioners, dressmakers and clothing warehouse workers. Eleanor was initially educated at the St Mary's Convent School in Ipswich. By the age of at least 17, Eleanor too was working as a woollen draper's assistant. But over the next few years, her father became a travelling photographer, and Eleanor took up teaching and, certainly by 1911, had become an art student. She studied at the Ipswich School of Art. She later studied at the Royal College of Art, South

Kensington, London, also spending time at the British Museum, observing and drawing. As a student, she was a bronze medallist for painted silk, book illustration and an illuminated casket.

Although her career in art did not truly take off until she was in her late 20s and early 30s, Eleanor became a diverse and talented artist involved in various areas of art and the decorative arts, with wide-ranging talents and interests. Unlike many art students, she did not remain in London, however, and returned to Ipswich, where she remained for much of the rest of her life. She had a private studio there with pupils, and became teacher of interior decoration and decoration of furniture at the Ipswich School of Art between 1917 and 1922. Between 1913 and 1922 she was also head designer, craftswoman and teacher at the Department of Decoration at Messrs Tibbenhams, Ipswich. She was elected Honorary Secretary of the Ipswich Art Club. Queen Mary purchased her pen & ink drawing The First Christmas Morning. Produced children's illustrations for several publishers including William Collins. Also carried out church and book decoration, and other black & white illustrations. Spent time sketching in the country and old churches. Studied medieval ecclesiastical decoration in particular.

One of Eleanor's printed silk fans was illustrated in The Studio. Exhibited her work throughout her career, including at a Graphic Arts exhibition held in 1916. Also, in Belgium in 1914, at an Arts and Crafts exhibition held in London in 1915, and at the Paris International in 1925. One of the earliest exhibitions she contributed to was the Paris Franco-British exhibition of 1913. At the Society of Women Artists, she showed five works between 1925 and 1930, all designs for Christmas cards. In 1918 Eleanor married Ernest Robert Gribble in Suffolk. They had two sons. She died in Suffolk, aged 77, and was buried at St Mary's Church, Little Blakenham, Suffolk.

GRIBBLE, VIVIEN MASSIE (1888-1932)

Wood Engraver / Book Illustrator. Born in Chelsea. Raised in Andover and Bedfordshire. Died in Higham, Suffolk, aged only 43. The daughter of George James Gribble, a merchant and general warehouseman, and Norah. One of at least six children (Vivien, Philip, Julian, Phyllis, Norah and Leslie). Julian also died young, and Vivien designed a memorial window to mark his death. She studied in Munich, and at the Slade School, London. Also studied under Noel Rooke at the London County Council Central School of Arts and Crafts. Produced wood engravings of various subjects. Illustrated and decorated a

number of books, including J. Hilton & J. Thorp, Change, The Beginning of a Chapter (with others, 1919), John Keats, Odes (1923), Alfred, Lord Tennyson, Three Psalms (1912), Songs From 'The Princess' (1924), Sixe Idillia of Theocritus (1922) and Lucius Apuleius, Cupid and Psyche. Contributed to periodicals including Change, Country Life, the London Mercury and The Golden Hind.

Gribble exhibited her work, including with the Society of Wood Engravers. Included in Campbell Dodgson's volume Contemporary Woodcuts, (London, Duckworth & Co., 1922). Dodgson included two of her woodcuts, Rabbits in the Corn and Milking. Gribble also designed the cover for the book. Dodgson notes that Gribble and Margaret Pilkington were among a number of women artists 'who practised wood engraving with zeal and success'. Mentioned in Herbert Furst's volume The Modern Woodcut (London, John Lane, 1924). Furst refers to her decoration of Sixe Idillia of Theocritus published by Duckworth, gives a reproduction of its decorated title page, and refers to her Milking. Also noted in Douglas Percy Bliss, A History of Wood-Engraving (London, Spring Books, 1928). Works illustrated in Bernard Sleigh, Wood Engraving Since 1890, London, Pitman, 1932. In 1919, Gribble married Douglas Doyle Jones, a barrister, in London. Her premature death curtailed a promising career.

GRIFFITH, EMILY (b.1853)

Sculptor. Born and raised in Broadway, Worcestershire. The daughter of Charles Witts and Selina. One of at least seven children (Arabella, Elizabeth, Louisa, Frederick, Fanny, Sarah and Emily). In 1879 she married sculptor James Milo Ap. Griffith (1844-97) in London. Shortly after, they were based in Pembrokeshire, Wales, but by the late 1880s were back in London, where both worked as sculptors. Emily probably studied under her husband. The couple appears to have had no children. James died in Chelsea. Emily produced busts, reliefs and medallions in terracotta and marble. Exhibited four works at the Royal Academy between 1886 and 1892, including Dawn (relief, marble), Little Queen of the May (bust, terracotta) and She Wore a Wreath of Roses (bust, terracotta).

GRIFFITH, LILLIAN ELIZABETH (1881-1972)

Sculptor. Born in Monmouth. Studied at the Wimbledon College of Art in the early 1900s. Studied under Alfred Gilbert and Alfred Drury. Fellow students at that time included Florence

Bevan, Mabel Wilkinson, Edith Whitchurch and Faith Browne. Lillian became a sculptor of medallions, plaques, reliefs, busts and statuettes in marble and bronze. After completing her studies, she returned to Wales, living at Maesteg, Pentre and Hengoed. Died in Monmouthshire, aged 91. Worked and exhibited for at least 57 years. Exhibited at the Royal Academy (22 works, 1902-59). Also, at the Salon des Artistes Francais (1911) and various provincial galleries. Exhibited locally with the South Wales Art Society, at their annual exhibition between at least 1927 and 1936. Exhibited works included: Jack (relief), Griselda (relief, bronze), My Father (plaque, bronze) and Galatea (relief, marble). Dates of her birth and death vary.

GRIMLEY, EDITH M. - SEE LINNELL, E.M.

GRIMSHAW, GLADYS (1908-94)

Sculptor / Potter. Born in Nelson in November 1908. The daughter of Harry Elliot, a master printer, and Clara Annie Holmes. Had at least one sister, Gwendoline. Raised in Nelson and educated at the Nelson Grammar School. Studied at the Liverpool School of Art under George Marples between 1928 and 1931. Also, at the Royal College of Art under Sir William Rothenstein and William Staite Murray between 1931 and 1934. Elected an Associate of the Royal College of Art in 1934. Became a potter and sculptor of statuettes and groups in terracotta. Became instructor of pottery at the Oxford School of Art. In 1937 she married Reginald Grimshaw (1910-94) in Chelsea. He became Head of the Oxford School of Art, and had been a student at the Royal College of Art at the same time as Gladys. They had at least one son. Both Gladys and Reginald died in Oxfordshire, Gladys at the age of 85. She exhibited her work, including at the Royal Academy (14 works, 1944-66), the Royal Glasgow Institute (1945), the Society of Women Artists (1954-58) and the Royal Society of British Artists. Also, at the Paris Salon and with the Women's International Art Club. Exhibited works included: The New Hat (terracotta), Festival Visitor (statuette, terracotta), Winter (statuette group, glazed terracotta) and Trio (statuette group, terracotta). Reginald also exhibited his work at the Royal Academy (1947-60).

GROOM, DOROTHEA JANE - SEE DIBDIN, D.J.

GUERCIO, BEATRICE C. – SEE FREEDMAN, B.C.

GUINNESS, ELIZABETH SARAH (1846-1927)

Painter / Illustrator. Born in Ireland. Spent much of her life living and working in London. Died in Eastbourne, Sussex, aged 81. In London, Guinness shared digs for a while with decorative artist Augusta M. Read. Principally a figure and portrait painter in oils and watercolours. Particularly active in the 1870s and 1880s. Appears to have illustrated books, including an edition of Grimm's Fairy Tales. Exhibited her work, including at the Royal Academy (1874-87), the Royal Society of British Artists (1875-83), the Royal Hibernian Academy (1882-89) and the Society of Women Artists (1875-85). Exhibited works included: The Gold-Spinner (watercolour), Spinsters in Brittany, Little Maid Marion (watercolour) and The First Time (watercolour). One of her portraits was of Lydia Becker of Girton College, Cambridge.

H

HADAWAY, JEAN LOUISE (b.c.1865)

Craftswoman / Artist. Was Jean Louise Carre. Born in Canada. Later became a British subject. A black & white artist initially. Met enameller and metalworker William Snelling Hadaway (b.1872) who originated from Massachusetts, America. The couple came to London in around 1897 and married in the city in late 1904. They had two children, Jean (also Jack) and Lesley Anne, prior to their marriage. Both were born in London. Another child, Hilda, was born in Hertfordshire in 1905. The Hadaways initially lived in London. But by at least 1900 they had established themselves in Bushey, Hertfordshire, amidst an artistic community dominated by the Herkomer School of Art. William Hadaway remained there until around 1908, when he moved to India to become Superintendent of the Madras Government School of Arts, a post he held until 1927. It appears that, under her husband's influence, Mrs Hadaway became involved in jewellery and metalwork, and exhibited in her own right as well as jointly with William. Mrs Hadaway remained in Bushey until at least 1911.

Although only resident together in Bushey for a few years, the Hadaways jointly produced a considerable amount of decorative metalwork and jewellery, some of which was included in leading arts exhibitions of the day. They first began to exhibit in around 1900, when William showed enamels at the Leeds Arts and Crafts Exhibition. William then exhibited enamels again, at the 1903 Chester Exhibition which was organised by Julia Dawson of the Clarion Guild of Handicraft. In the same year, he exhibited enamels at the Arts and Crafts Exhibition Society's seventh exhibition. In May 1905, however, the Hadaways began to exhibit jointly, holding an exhibition of silver and jewellery at the Bruton Galleries, London, the first clear indication that they were, in fact, working together. William exhibited objects of everyday use, such as bowls and spoons. Jean exhibited necklaces, rings and brooches in silver with precious stones. Some of those were illustrated in the Art Workers' Quarterly, July 1905, pp.121-125.

In the winter of 1905 / 06, Jean exhibited jewellery at the Lyceum Club, in its permanent Exhibition of Artistic Handicrafts. In 1906 she also contributed jewellery to the eighth Arts and Crafts Exhibition Society exhibition, held at the Grafton Galleries, London. Two of her exhibits, a silver pendant with sapphires and opals, and another with pink tourmalines and pearls, were illustrated in the Art Workers' Quarterly, April 1906, p.62. She also exhibited silver jewellery at the 1906 Society of Artists at Work exhibition, also held in London. The Society was organised by Mrs Charles Muller to encourage sales of handcrafts. Other exhibitors on that occasion included Fred Partridge, Annie Garnett and Ellen Sparks. In the same year, the Hadaways contributed to the Sixth Annual Exhibition of the Sussex Branch of the Royal Amateur Art Society, held in Brighton.

William Hadaway's last appearance of note, before his move to India, was in the Art Journal in 1907 (p.176) when some of his metalwork was illustrated in an article Metal-Work and Jewellery by R.E.D. Sketchley. Although William left Britain, Jean remained, and continued to contribute to art exhibitions into 1908. In 1908 she contributed jewellery to Mr John Baillie's Annual Arts and Crafts Exhibition, also contributing to the 1908 New Gallery exhibition, showing jewellery in its craft section. Reviews of the exhibition state that Jean Hadaway designed and executed her own jewellery, some of which was illustrated in The Studio, Vol.44, 1908, pp.61-62. Exhibits on that occasion included brooches in silver with opals or turquoise, a pendant in silver and enamel and a silver bowl with enamel. As with the Dawsons and the

Gaskins, much of what the Hadaways produced was of an artistic, less costly nature. For example, decorative stones were used in place of diamonds or rubies, and silver was used in place of gold. The emphasis in artistic jewellery was on the design, and the significance of the stones chosen, rather than on monetary value.

Latterly in 1908, Jean exhibited at the ninth annual Women's International Art Club exhibition. During her time at Bushey, she also exhibited with the Society of Women Artists, showing 'handicrafts' (not specified) every year between 1902 and 1907. During those years, she was based at Penrhyn Cottage and then at The White Cottage, Bushey. Jean was reunited with Hadaway sometime after 1911 and appears to have died abroad in 1939, possibly in France, where William subsequently spent time. She also appears to have largely given up exhibiting her work in Britain after 1908. Nonetheless, the Hadaways made an important contribution to British art and design for a few years, jointly and independently. Some of their papers, dated 1900-35, are kept in the Victoria & Albert Museum, London.

HAGUE, SHEILA (1920-80)
Cartoonist / Illustrator. Born in Wimbledon in July 1920. The daughter of Charles Hoardon Hague (1886-1965) and Ida Johanna Jackson (1888-1966). Studied at the Wimbledon School of Art under R.H. Barnes, G.A. Cooper and E. Sullivan. Also, at the Royal College of Art, London under G. Spencer and P. Horton. Elected an Associate of the Royal College of Art in 1943. Produced cartoons and illustrations in black and white and oils. Some of her work was reproduced by the Central Press. Exhibited occasionally, including at Burlington House and the American Institute of Architecture. Based in London for part of her career. Died in Redhills, Surrey, aged 59.

HAIG, JANET (1883-1951)
Sculptor. Was Helen Janet, known as Janet. Born in Lee, London. The daughter of Alexander Haig and Gertrude Mary. Both parents originated from Scotland. Her father was a physician. Raised in London. Had at least one sibling, Kenneth George, an Oxford graduate who became a doctor. Janet probably studied in London. Became a sculptor of busts, masks and statuettes in various materials including French walnut, bronze and plaster. In 1913 she married James Byers Scott in London. The couple lived in London. Although active as a sculptor before her marriage, Haig exhibited more prolifically after.

Showed work at the Royal Academy (1932-43), the Royal Glasgow Institute (1943), the Society of Women Artists (1933-37) and elsewhere. Exhibited works included: Apollo (statuette, plaster), Meditation (statuette, plated bronze), Lt.-Col. H.C. Stevens (bust, plaster) and Nude (unfinished) (statuette, French walnut). She died in Cheltenham, Gloucestershire, aged 67.

HALL, LILIAN M.B. - SEE ROWLES, L.M.B.

HALLE, ELINOR JESSIE MARIE (1855-1926)

Decorative Sculptor / Craftswoman. Born in Chorlton, Lancashire. The daughter of highly eminent and influential musician and Professor of Music Charles Frederick Halle (d.1895). He was knighted for his work, and his presence is still most keenly felt through the Manchester-based Halle Orchestra. He originated from Prussia, but was a British subject. Elinor's mother, Marie, originated from America. She died young, in 1866, having had at least nine children between 1845 and 1859. The rest of the Halle children were born in France, Manchester or Middlesex. Initially, Elinor was raised in Manchester, but in around 1860 the family moved to Westminster, London. There, they had a fairly affluent lifestyle, employing six servants, though her father left a comparatively small estate on his death. Elinor remained in London for the rest of her life, dying there in May 1926. In London, she studied sculpture at the Slade School under Alphonse Legros (1837-1911), and was stylistically influenced by him. She appears to have shared a studio for a time with fellow student Ellen Mary Rope, also a decorative sculptor. In the 1880s, she lived in Marylebone with her sisters Marie and Mathilda along with several servants. By the early 1890s she was living in Chelsea, alone, and working as a professional sculptor. But by the early 1900s, she is listed as living with her unmarried brother, Charles Emile Halle, in Chelsea. Charles was a painter.

Although primarily a sculptor, producing bas-reliefs and portrait medals in bronze and wax, Elinor also turned to decorative jewellery and metalwork. She was always highly regarded as a medallist, and her numerous eminent subjects included Cardinal Manning, Cardinal Newman, Countess Feodora Gleichen, artist G.F. Watts, Sir Henry M. Stanley and her father, Sir Charles Halle. It was her bas-relief Music, however, which first drew attention when it was exhibited at the Grosvenor Gallery in 1884. That particular piece was one of her earliest exhibits, and marked her as a sculptor of note. Her decorative design work also drew attention, however, and was illustrated in leading journals of the day. For example, in 1905 the Art Journal (pp.61-62) illustrated a comb in silver and gold with enamel and moonstones, a pendant in silver with enamel decoration, sapphires, rubies and pearls, and a stomacher in enamels and silver with garnets with a gold net chain, all designed and executed by Halle.

Elinor went on to exhibit until at least 1914, indicating that her career lasted some 30 years or more. She exhibited a number of times at the Grosvenor Gallery, but also at the Royal Academy (1886-1914), the Walker Art Gallery, Liverpool, at the Salon de la Societe Nationale des Beaux-Arts in Paris (1898-1905) and with the Society of Medallists. Exhibited a number of times at the New Gallery. For example, at the Gallery's twentieth exhibition in 1907, she exhibited alongside the Gaskins and others of note. Contributed to the Gallery's 1908 exhibition, showing a small agate cup and an ivory casket decorated with silver and enamels. Other contributors on that occasion included Harold Stabler, May Morris and Selwyn Image. Also contributed to the Artists at Work exhibition held at the Grafton Galleries in late 1906, one of 120 craftworkers to exhibit. Noted in M.H. Spielmann, British Sculpture and Sculptors of To-day, London, Cassell & Co., 1901. Awarded the C.B.E. for work carried out during the war, designing appliances for disabled soldiers.

HALLWARD, ADELAIDE CAROLINE (1861-1925)

Artist / Illustrator. Born in Ryde, Isle of Wight. The daughter of Robert William Bloxam and Henrietta Louisa Ann Jeanette. Her father died young. Henrietta, who was widowed sometime before 1881, was born in India and had income from land. Adelaide was the fifth of at least eight children (Helen, Katherine, Henrietta, Edith, Adelaide, Arthur, Alice and Louisa). In adulthood, the Bloxam children are listed as having income from houses, dividends and mortgages, except for Adelaide, who is listed as an art student from at least 1881. At that time, the family lived in Guildford, Surrey. Adelaide was the only one of the Bloxam family to take up art and become a professional artist and illustrator. In 1886 she married stained glass artist, painter, sculptor, designer and illustrator Reginald F. Hallward (1858-1948) in Guildford. He originated from Sandown, Isle of Wight and trained at the Slade School, London. His sister, Ella Hallward, was also an artist. Initially, the couple lived in Hammersmith, London. They had at least six children (Michael, Reginald, Christopher, Faith, Patience and Priscilla). Reginald and Patience also became artists. By at least 1901, the family had moved to Shorne, Kent, where they employed a governess and several servants. Later, they were based in Middlesex. Adelaide continued to work after her marriage and was still active in 1922. She died in Brentford, Middlesex, aged 64.

Adelaide produced work for The Children's Pictorial magazine which was published by the Society for the Promotion of Christian Knowledge from 1887. She also produced book illustrations. Exhibited her work rarely, but did show two works at the New English Art Club, an illustration to The Discontented Dolls in 1891 and an illustration Dark Days for The Children's Pictorial in 1892. Reginald Hallward also exhibited at the New English Art Club. Adelaide showed The Angels Adoring at the Arts and Crafts Exhibition Society's 1893 exhibition. Reginald contributed to the Society's 1903 exhibition at the New Gallery, showing a cartoon for St Paul's Church, Bury, Lancashire. In 1896 Reginald exhibited handicrafts at the Society of Women Artists under the name Edith Bloxam of Kensington, possibly Adelaide's sister. Possibly of the same family was Miss Ethel Bloxam who embroidered a book cover for Kingsley's Water Babies, designed by Reginald Hallward and illustrated in The Studio, Vol.2, March 1894, p.121 in an article English Embroidered Book-Covers. The cover was one of a series of modern bindings specially commissioned by a Mr Tregaskis and exhibited at the Caxton Head, Holborn in 1891. This may also have been Edith rather than Ethel.

Patience Mary Hallward (1892-1981), Adelaide's daughter, produced paintings and coloured lithographs. She exhibited her work, including at the Royal Academy (1940) and the Society of Women Artists (1968-69). Exhibited works included: April Morning (coloured lithograph), Midsummer Eve and Ebb Tide. She spent some time in Ealing.

HALLWARD, ELLA (1866-1948)

Artist. Eleanor Frances Graeme Hallward, known as Ella. Born in Bognor Regis, Sussex. Raised in Mitcham, Surrey and in Kensington, London. The family had money, and employed several servants, including a footman. Her father, Charles Burness Hallward, a solicitor and attorney, originated from Kent, as did her mother, Elizabeth. One of at least seven children (Charles, Evelyn, Eleanor, Lillian, William, Reginald and

Arthur). Reginald became a successful artist / designer who married artist Adelaide Bloxam. By at least 1891, Ella is listed as an artist, living in Kensington with her sister Lillian, then a student of music. The sisters were still living together in 1901. Ella presumably studied in London. In 1902 she married James Ridgway Dyas in Kensington. He was a military man born in India, and of poor means. He died in Surrey in 1933, aged 71. Ella died in Surrey, 15 years later, aged 82. She appears to have largely given up her career after her marriage. Rarely exhibited her work. But did contribute to the Arts and Crafts Exhibition Society's 1896 exhibition. A child's bookplate by Ella was included in the 1899 Exhibition of Pictures & Decorative Art held in Kendal, Westmorland. One of her exhibits was illustrated in The Studio, Vol.9, 1897, p.283. One of her bookplates, The Raven, was illustrated in an article Modern Bookplates and Their Designers in The Studio, Vol.15, 1899, pp.3-78 (illustration on p.6).

HALSE, EMMELINE (1853-1930)

Sculptor / Decorative Artist. Born in Kensington, London. The daughter of George Frederick Halse and Matilda, both of whom originated from London. The third of four children (William, Katherine, Emmeline and Edward), born between 1850 and 1855. Raised in Kensington and Chelsea. George F. Halse was a highly respected sculptor who exhibited at the Royal Academy (1855-88), the Royal Glasgow Institute (1861-93) and elsewhere. But he retained his job of bank clerk and later bank manager. Emmeline evidently inherited his artistic nature and studied under Frederick Leighton at the Royal Academy schools, where she won two silver medals. Also studied in Paris at the Ecole des Beaux-Arts. Presumably also studied under her father. She remained living with her parents, spending some time in Margate in the 1890s, but was based for much of her career in London. Active as a sculptor and decorative artist for over 40 years. Died in Amersham, Buckinghamshire in February 1930, aged 74.

Emmeline produced mainly figure and portrait works, but also decorative pieces for churches, friezes and terracotta tiles. Also produced medallions, reliefs and groups. Worked in wax, plaster, marble, bronze and terracotta. Exhibited her work throughout her career, including at the Royal Academy (33 works, 1878-1920), the Royal Glasgow Institute (22 works, 1881-1910), the Walker Art Gallery, Liverpool and in Manchester. Exhibited works included: Blind Man's Buff (tiles in terracotta), Wild Rose (bust, terracotta), A Victim to Art and Earthward Bound (relief). Commissions included a terracotta decoration (reredos) The Call of St John for St John's Church, Notting Hill. In 1891 Halse exhibited a bust of her father at the Royal Academy. She was a friend of artist Helen Trevor. Halse edited her letters as The Ramblings of an Artist: Selections from the Letters of H.M. Trevor to E.H, London, Gay & Bird, 1901.

HAMILTON, LILIAN (1865-1939)

Sculptor / Medallist. Born in Mitcham, Surrey. The daughter of Edwin Newcombe Swainson, Assistant Secretary to the Admiralty, and Helen (or Ellen) Charlotte Swainson. Her father originated from St Albans, her mother from Bristol. One of at least seven children (Mary, Arthur, Lilian, Annie, Margaret, Charles and Esther). Raised in Mitcham, Surrey then London. Taught by a governess. By at least 1881, both Mary and Lilian are listed as art students. Lilian was then still only 15 years of age, and Mary was 18. Evidently developed an early interest in art. Initially educated at the University College, London. Then studied at the Slade School, London on a scholarship from 1884. Studied sculpture under Alphonse Legros (1837-1911). Also possibly influenced by French medallist M. Charpentier. Produced medals, figures, plaques and reliefs in bronze and plaster. In 1886 she married painter Vereker Monteith Hamilton (1856-1931) who originated from Argyllshire. They had four children (Ian, Elizabeth, Marjorie and Janet), born between 1891 and 1898. Lilian continued with her career after her marriage. Based in Netherhampton, Wiltshire during her early marriage, then based in London, and latterly Cowden, Kent. She died in May 1939, some eight years after her husband.

Lilian exhibited her work, including at the Royal Academy (24 works, 1889-1927), the Royal Glasgow Institute (1894), the Paris Salon, with the New York Numismatic Society and at White City, Wembley. Exhibited works included: Les Innocents (bronze plaque), Fatma (relief, bronze) and General Sir Ian Hamilton, K.C.B. (bronze plaque). Elected a Member of the Imperial Arts League. Also elected an Associate of the Royal Society of Painter-Etchers & Engravers and of the Royal Society of Miniature Painters. Other works included a bronze memorial tablet for the South Wales Circuit, a bronze figure of St Augustine for the Church Hall, Aylesham, Kent, and a memorial for the Northern Counties Club, Newcastle. Also, a bronze figure of St George for a war memorial at Chawton, Hampshire, and portrait medals of a number of dignitaries,

including Lord Roberts, Viscount Gort and Sir Donald Stewart. Her portrait medal of the Maharajah of Kapurthala was purchased by the Luxembourg Museum. Other works were acquired by the Victoria & Albert Museum, London and by Dresden. A silver centrepiece for presentation was owned by a club in Warsaw. The Imperial War Museum, London acquired her coloured plaster group Lacing Up An Airship. Other works were acquired by the British Museum.

Notable commissions included the Norman Gold Medal awarded at Sandhurst, the Queen Alexandra Cup Medal, the Daily Mail Trophy Medal and the Society of Miniature Rifle Clubs' Medal (bronze). Some of Hamilton's works were illustrated in the Magazine of Art, Ferrer's Dictionary of Medallists and Spinks' Numismatic Circular. Also noted in M.H. Spielmann, British Sculpture and Sculptors of Today, London, Cassell & Co., 1901. Spielmann offers an illustration of both sides of her portrait medallion of the Maharajah of Kapurthala, and notes her to be 'extremely clever'.

Mary Swainson (1862-1932) also became a successful sculptor, based at the Ladies' College, Cheltenham, in Paris and in Chelsea. She too produced medallions in bronze, but also marble busts. Exhibited her work, including at the Royal Academy (1891-1913). Her subjects included writer Hilaire Belloc (bust, marble), Madame Belloc (medallion, bronze) and the Rev. F. Woolryche Whitmore (medal). Mary died in France, but also had an address in Kent.

HAMILTON, MARY ELIZABETH (1875-1956)

Painter / Bookplate Artist / Designer / Linocut Artist. Born at Skene, Aberdeenshire. The daughter of George Hamilton and Anne Elizabeth. Her mother was born in India. Mary was one of at least six children (Annette, Helen, Florence, John, Margaret and Mary). Raised in Skene. However, the family had connections with England. Margaret Hamilton was born in Wavertree, Lancashire. Mary moved to London to study at the Byam Shaw School of Art. And in 1911, Margaret, Mary and the widowed Anne are listed as living at Henfield, Sussex and subsequently in Kensington, London. Mary later returned to Skene, also living in Murtle, Aberdeenshire. She died in Scotland. Mary produced landscape paintings in oils and watercolours, bookplates, linocuts and various other designs. Exhibited her work, including at the Royal Academy (1914-28), the Royal Glasgow Institute (1906), the Royal Scottish

Academy (1901 & 1927) and the Society of Women Artists (1906-09). Also, in Liverpool, Birmingham and elsewhere. Exhibited works included: Reaping the Oats, While Daylight Lasts, The Edge of the Cotswolds and The Dell of Princes (from Dante's Purgatoria). Elected a Member of the New Century Club. One of her hobbies was bee-keeping.

HAMILTON, RUTH SARGEANT (b.1900)

Craftswoman. Born in Strandtown, Belfast. The daughter of August Warren Hamilton, an engineer, and Annie Sargeant. Had at least one sister, Mary. Raised in Belfast and spent much of her career there. Educated at the Ashleigh House School. Studied at the Belfast School of Art. Produced various craftwork and decorative jewellery. Inspired by Celtic design. Exhibited her work occasionally, including at the Walker Art Gallery, Liverpool and the August Horse Show in Dublin.

HAMMOND, GERTRUDE ELLEN DEMAIN & CHRISTINE MARY DEMAIN (1862-1952) & (1860-1900)

Artists / Illustrators. The daughters of Horatio Demain Hammond, a bank clerk, and Eliza Mary. Both parents originated from Surrey. Gertrude and Christine were born in Lambeth and were raised in London. They had at least one brother, Percy E.D. Hammond (b.1866) who became a noted painter and stained glass artist. Both sisters contributed to periodicals and journals, and illustrated books. Christine's career was cut short by her premature death, aged only 39.

Gertrude Hammond studied at the Lambeth School of Art and the Royal Academy schools. She was considered to be a stronger draughtsman than her sister. She lived with Percy and Christine until around 1898, when she married Henry George McMurdie in West Kensington, London. She was then 36; he was 31. McMurdie worked on the railways. For part of her career, Gertrude was based at St Paul's Studios, West Kensington, surrounded by other artists. Neighbours included a French painter and his wife, artist Herbert Sidney and his family, art student Dorothea Williams and artist Lilian Etherington Reynolds. Later, in the 1920s, she moved to Stow-on-the-Wold, Gloucestershire. She died in Sussex, aged 90. Had a long, productive and successful career as an artist / illustrator. Produced watercolours, chalk drawings, pencil sketches, wash drawings and black & white drawings. Contributed to numerous periodicals and journals during her career including Black and White, The Idler, The Lady's Pictorial, The Ludgate Monthly, Madame,

The Minster, Pick-Me-Up, The Queen, The Quiver, The Yellow Book and St Paul's Magazine.

Gertrude also illustrated numerous books, including Annie E. Armstrong, Mona St Clair and My Ladies Three (Frederick Warne), M. Corbet Seymour, Nicola (Blackie & Son), J.K. Denny, The Clever Miss Follett and Francis Armstrong, A Fair Claimant (both 1898). Also, Katharine Tynan, The Handsome Brandons (1898), E.D. Adams, A Girl of To-day (1898) and Rose Mulholland, Cynthia's Bonnet Shop (1900). Most of her book illustrations were wash, but she also did colour drawings, including for school books for Blackie & Son. Produced colour drawings for, for example, John Bunyan's Pilgrim's Progress which had eight full-page colour drawings. One of the last books she illustrated was The Works of William Shakespeare in 1922. Her work has been praised in several volumes over the years, including Mahony, Latimer & Folmsbee, Illustrators of Children's Books 1744-1945, Boston, The Horn Book Inc., 1947. Both the sisters were also noted in James Thorpe, English Illustration: The Nineties, 1935. The Hammond sisters were the only women included by Thorpe. Gertrude also had an extensive career as an exhibiting artist, beginning in around 1886 and continuing until at least 1928. Exhibited at the Royal Academy (22 works, 1886-1928), the Royal Hibernian Academy (1898) and the Royal Society of British Artists (1887-89). Exhibited works included: The Veil, Miss Florence Burgess, Baffled and All About It. Percy Hammond also exhibited at the Royal Academy, from 1896.

Christine Hammond was actually Christiana, but was known as Christine or Chris. Possibly studied in London, like Gertrude. Contributed to periodicals and journals including The Illustrated London News, The Pall Mall Budget, The Ludgate Monthly, The Idler, The English Illustrated Magazine, The Sphere, St Paul's Magazine, The Quiver, Madame, Good Words, The Temple, Pearson's Magazine, Cassell's Family Magazine and Pick-Me-Up. Some of her drawings were reproduced in black and red. Along with Gertrude, Chris Hammond was one of the principal artistic contributors to St Paul's, a monthly paper begun in March 1894. Chris was also one of the first artists to contribute to Pearson's Magazine and to The Ludgate Monthly. Her contributions to The English Illustrated Magazine included illustrations for The Sisters in Vol.12 Also, like Gertrude, she illustrated books for various publishers. Those included Maria Edgeworth, Popular Tales (1895), The Absentee (1895), Helen (1896), Belinda, Castle Rackrent and The Parents' Assistant (1897), all in Macmillan's series of Illustrated Standard Novels.

For George Allen publishers, Chris illustrated J.R. Richardson's Sir Charles Grandison (1895), Jane Austen, Emma and Sense and Sensibility (both 1898) and Oliver Goldsmith, Comedies. Did some illustrations for The Charm and Other Drawing-Room Plays by Besant and Pollock (Chatto & Windus, 1896). For Nisbet's English Illustrated Library she produced drawings for Thackeray's The History of Henry Esmond (1896), Lord Lytton's The Caxtons (1897) and Mrs Craik's John Halifax, Gentleman (1898). Also exhibited her work, including at the Royal Academy (1886-94) and the Royal Society of British Artists (1886-90). Exhibited works included: A Blue Stocking, A Challenge and The Last Straw (watercolour).

HARBUTT, OLIVE CAMBRIDGE (1878-1965)

Sculptor / Modeller. Born in Bath, Somerset. Raised there, and died there, aged 86. The daughter of William Harbutt and Elizabeth Cambridge (1848-1930). Her father was the inventor and manufacturer of plasticine. He was also formerly an artist and art teacher who originated from Northumberland. Her mother, who was born in Wimpole, Cambridgeshire, was the daughter of Owen and Sarah Cambridge. In the early 1870s, Elizabeth was a student of art pottery in London, and later became a miniature painter of portraits on ivory. She exhibited her work at the Royal Academy (1883-95) and at the Royal Society of British Artists (1888 / 89). Olive was one of at least six children (Olive, Beryl, Enid, Owen, Eric and Noel). Beryl became a plasticine modeller and demonstrator in schools. Enid became a plasticine photographer and a miniature painter. Owen became an electrical engineer. Olive became a sculptor and modeller in plasticine. Exhibited one of her modelled bas-relief panels, The White Wild Horses, at the Society of Women Artists in 1919. She also lectured on the subject of plasticine in schools.

HARCOURT, EVELYN ALICE - SEE CLUTTON BROCK, E.A.

HARD, DEBORAH N. - SEE HARDING, D.N.

HARDING, DEBORAH NEILD (1903-92)

Potter. Born in Sheffield in August 1903. The daughter of Henry Becket Harding, a research chemist. Educated at the Pinehurst School near Tunbridge Wells. Studied in London at the L.C.C.

Central School of Arts and Crafts and the Royal College of Art, and in Holland. Produced decorative pottery, including bowls and jugs. Based in Letchworth, Hertfordshire early in her career, where she had a studio at The Wynd. Worked as a pottery teacher at the St Christopher School and other local schools. Exhibited her work occasionally, including at the London Arts and Crafts exhibitions. Held a one-woman show at the Three Shields Gallery, Kensington. The South Wales Museum acquired one of her pots and three of her bowls. The University of Wales acquired one of her pots. Some of her work was illustrated in The Studio and in the local newspapers. In 1935 she married John F. Hard in Hitchin, Hertfordshire. Remained in the county, dying in Stevenage, Hertfordshire, aged 88.

HARDING, EMILY JANE (1850-post-1911)

Illustrator / Painter. Born in Clifton, Bristol. The daughter of Thomas Giles Harding, a travelling salesman, and Rosa. One of at least five children (Emily, Rosa, Gertrude, Thomas and George). Raised in Bristol. Married painter Edward William Andrews. Based in London for much of her life and career. Latterly, she boarded alone in a London house along with, among others, violinist Mary Louisa Barber and singer Frances McCullock. Harding produced studies in watercolours, miniatures, black & white drawings and book illustrations. Also translated texts. Books illustrated by her included Alice Weber, An Affair of Honour (Farran, 1892), Ellinor Davenport Adams, The Disagreeable Duke (George Allen, 1894), Lullabies of Many Lands, collected by Alma Strettell, with 77 illustrations by Harding (George Allen, 1895), Fairy Tales of the Slav Peasants and Herdsmen (transl. by Emily Harding, with 56 illustrations, George Allen, 1896) and John Milton, Hymn on the Morning of Christ's Nativity (George Allen, 1897, with T. Heath Robinson). Exhibited her work occasionally, including at the Royal Academy (1877-98), the Society of Women Artists (1876-78) and the Royal Society of Miniature Painters. Exhibited works included: The Very Rev. the Dean of Westminster (Arthur Penrhyn Stanley), Phyllis, Female Head (watercolour) and Archbishop of Canterbury (black & white). Noted in R.E.D. Sketchley, English Book Illustration of To-day (London, Kegan Paul, 1903). Still active as an artist in 1911, aged 61.

HARDMAN, WINIFRED ELIZABETH BEATRICE (1890-post-1962)

Painter / Mural Decorator. Born and raised in Rawtenstall, Lancashire. The daughter of George Hardman and Annie E. Catterall. Her father, a woollen and cotton manufacturer, originated from Edenfield, Lancashire. Her mother originated from Broughton, Lancashire. One of at least five children (George, Richard, William, Victoria and Winifred). Studied in London, at the St John's Wood School of Art and the Royal Academy schools. Awarded the Armitage bronze medal and silver medal for perspective at the Royal Academy schools. Produced paintings in oils and tempera, including flowers, portraits and buildings. Exhibited her work, including at the Royal Academy (1923-59), the Royal Scottish Academy (1924), the Society of Women Artists (1962), at the Venice International Exhibition and in Manchester, Liverpool and Leeds. Also, at the London International Exhibition and with the New English Art Club. She was an early Member of the New Autumn Group, which had 21 members including Dora Clarke and Claude Flight. Hardman exhibited with the Group, including in 1925 when she showed a study of the Assisi Amphitheatre which was illustrated in The Studio, Vol.90, December 1925, p.348. Other exhibited works included: Tulips (tempera), Florence From the Window of the Uffizi and The Zulu Baby (tempera). Along with artist A. Dorothy Cohen, she completed two large murals for St Peter's Church, Hammersmith in the early 1930s. Her study of Vorarlberg was illustrated in Drawing & Design. Based in London for part of her career. Later based in Cambridge and in Bosham, Sussex.

HARDY, EVELYN (1866-1935)

Illustrator / Black & White Artist. Was Beatrice Evelyn Elizabeth, known as Evelyn. Born and raised in Bristol. The daughter of artist David Hardy and landscape painter Emily Hardy. One of at least four children (David Paul, or Paul, Norman, Evelyn and Mabel). Norman became an artist. Paul (1862-1942) became an illustrator, painter and metalworker. In 1888 Paul married sculptor Ida Mary Wilton Clarke (1867-1955). They lived in Bexley Heath, Cobham in Surrey and Wiltshire. Ida produced statuettes, groups and animals in bronze and wax. Ida exhibited her work at the Royal Academy (1884-99). Evelyn became an illustrator of children's books and a black & white artist of military subjects. Illustrated, for example, Brothers Grimm, Fairy Tales (with others, 1898), E. Stuart Hardy, Happy Times (1900), Laugh and Play (1900) and Merry

Folk (1903), Lucy Weedon, Nursery Tales (1903) and Hans Christian Andersen, Fairy Tales (1904). Also contributed to periodicals including Cassell's Children's Annual, Little Folks, Our Jabberwock, The Sporting and Dramatic News, The Gentlewoman, The Penny Magazine, Chums and the St James's Budget. Contributed a military drawing to the Illustrated London News in 1889. Evelyn died in Cuckfield, Sussex, aged 68.

HARE, DORA - SEE GORDINE, D.

HARGRAVE, ELIZABETH C. - SEE JAMES, E.C.

HARPER, IVY EMILY (1880-1932)

Illuminator. Born in Birmingham. The daughter of Edward Samuel Harper and Emily Ann Steel (b.1854). Her father, a jeweller, originated from Staffordshire, her mother from Birmingham. One of at least five children (Edward Steel, Ivy, Wilfred, Hal and Guy). Raised in Birmingham. Her father was also an art instructor for the Birmingham City Council. Guy Harper became an art student, as did Edward Steel. Ivy also became an art student, at the Birmingham School of Art. Whilst there, she contributed to the National Competition of Schools of Art, held at South Kensington, London. In the 1906 exhibition, she showed part of an illuminated book, The Litany, which was illustrated in the Art Journal, 1906. One of her illuminated addresses on vellum was illustrated in an article in The Studio, Vol.56, June 1912, pp.45-58. Ivy taught at the Birmingham School of Art for around 30 years. She died in Birmingham, aged 52.

HARRIS, ETHEL A.C. - SEE BOWER, E.A.C.

HARRISON, EMMA FLORENCE (1858-1932)

Illustrator / Painter. Better known as Florence. The daughter of Richard Harrison, a manufacturer, and Elizabeth. One of at least seven children (Elizabeth, Lavinia, Fanny, Albert, Rosaline, Emma and Blanche). All were born and raised in Redditch, Worcestershire. By at least 1881, Emma was based in London. Later in her career, in 1911, she is listed as based in Weymouth, Dorset. She died in Edenbridge, Kent. Worked as an illustrator of children's and adult's books for over 30 years. Adapted her style over the years. Illustrated her own books for children, including Rhymes and Reasons (1905), The Rhyme of a Faun and Other Verses (1907), In the Fairy Ring (1908), Elfin Song (1912),

Tales in Rhyme and Colour (1916) and The Pixy Book (1918). Also illustrated, for example, Christina Rossetti, Poems (intro. by Alice Meynell, 1910), Alfred, Lord Tennyson, Guinevere and Other Poems (1911), William Morris, Early Poems (1914), Agnes G. Herbertson, Tinkler Johnny (1916), Netta Syrett, Godmother's Garden (1918) and My Fairy Tale Book (Blackie, c.1919). Also contributed to periodicals, including The Girl's Budget. Later in her career, she worked for Dent publishers. Exhibited three works at the Royal Academy, Bank's Alley, Tewkesbury (in 1887), Where Now Should Such a Child be Sought (in 1890) and Bahdie (in 1891).

HARRISON, ISABELLA MAUDE (1853-1945)

Founder of the Paulerspury Lace Industry in Northamptonshire in the 1880s. Isabella, also known as Ella, was born in Jersey, the daughter of Barwick John Sams and Susan Luisa. One of at least six children (George, Charles, Joanna, Mary, John and Isabella). The family lived in Grafton Regis, Northamptonshire where Barwick Sams was rector of the parishes of Grafton and Alderton. In 1883, Ella married John Butler Harrison, Rector of Paulerspury. He was some 16 years older than Ella. They had one daughter, Rosamund, born in Paulerspury in 1883. In an attempt to provide suitable employment for the local women, Ella established a lace making industry. The laces were sold through the Ladies' Work Society in Sloane Street, London. The Work Society won the support of Princess Louise, Marchioness of Lorne. Some of the Society's designs were the work of the Princess. Lace from Paulerspury was purchased by Princess Louise and Princess Christian, the daughters of Queen Victoria, both of whom supported the move to provide respectable art training and employment for women. How long the Paulerspury industry ran for is not clear; but Ella remained in Paulerspury until 1910, when John Harrison died. She then moved to Newport Pagnell to live with her brother, George, also a clergyman. Latterly, she lived in Nottinghamshire, but died in Bedfordshire.

HART, ALICE MARION (1848-1931)

Founder of the Donegal Industrial Fund in Ireland in 1883, and founder of local textile workshops under the guise of the fund from around 1884. Alice Hart was born in Surrey, the daughter of Alexander William Rowland, a merchant, and Henrietta. Raised in Surrey and London. In 1872 she married widower and surgeon Ernest Abraham Hart (1835-98) in London. He was the son of Abraham Hart, a dentist. Initially, the couple lived at Wimpole Street, London, but later lived at Totteridge, Hertfordshire. Ernest Hart was also a reformer, and Alice shared his interests. Sometime in the very early 1880s, the Harts visited Ireland. In response to the famine which had hit the area at that time, in 1883 Alice set up the Donegal Industrial Fund to raise money for those affected. Under the guise of the Fund, Mrs Hart also instigated the revival of local textile industries. The local weaving industries and the production of hand-woven Irish tweeds and knitted goods were re-established. Yarns were spun and hand dyed with plant and vegetable extracts. Local girls were also taught to embroider.

As a result of Mrs Hart's efforts, a type of embroidery, known as Kells Embroidery, developed, based on Celtic illuminated manuscripts. Galway flannel or linen, hand spun and hand dyed, formed the basis of the embroidery, which was worked in waxed threads of linen, which gave a shine to the finished textiles. The embroidery thrived under Mrs Hart's direction, and local women became proficient enough to make large curtains and portieres with designs based on Celtic scrolls and animals. The Donegal Industrial Fund industries made curtains for Windsor Castle and for the Associated Artists, a New York organisation founded in 1879 which involved American designers Candace Wheeler (1827-1923) and Louis C. Tiffany (1848-1933).

In 1887, at which time the Harts were still in Ireland, the Fund was awarded a government grant of £1000 for teaching purposes, administered by a committee which included Lord Leitrim. In order to increase sales, a shop was opened in New Cavendish Street, London. Textiles by the Fund appeared in the 1888 Arts and Crafts Exhibition Society exhibition, the first held by the Society. The Harts appear to have left Ireland sometime in the mid-1890s, after which the Donegal workshops went into a slow decline again. The Harts then lived in Totteridge. Ernest died in Hove, Sussex, though his address at that time was Hertfordshire. By 1901, Alice was still in Totteridge, and is listed as an artist / author and a manufacturer of woollens and linens. That may indicate that she still had ties with the Donegal Fund at that stage, and that she may have had some form of art training. Living with her was sculptor / designer Maud Rowland (b.c.1871). By 1911 Alice had returned to London, to Westminster, and had become a manufacturer of waterproofed fabrics and an employer. At that stage, she lived alone, with one servant. Alice Hart was evidently a resourceful, independent and strong character who was still working aged 63 and probably beyond. She died in Middlesex.

HART, ELIZABETH V. - SEE POLUNIN, E.V.

HART, MAY - SEE PARTRIDGE, M.

HARTNELL, KATHERINE GRANT (1886-1970)

Painter / Etcher. Born in Bristol. The daughter of William Jefferies, a solicitor, and Mary. Her father originated from Somerset, her mother from Bristol. The youngest of six children (Mary, Jane, John, Bertha, Hilda and Katherine). Raised in Bristol. Educated at the Guelph College, Clifton, Bristol, and at the Redland High School, Bristol. Studied at the Royal College of Music, London and initially worked as a music teacher in Bristol. Then studied at the Slade School, London under Professor Henry Tonks, Philip Wilson Steer and Sir W. Russell. Awarded a First Prize for figure painting and figure composition. Became a painter of various subjects in oils and watercolours and an etcher. Early in her career as an artist, she was based in Bristol. In 1917 she married Archibald Philip Hartnell in Bristol, and soon after the couple moved to London. Later, they were based at Downshire Hall, Hampstead. Katherine died at Hampstead, aged 83.

Exhibited her work, including at the Royal Academy (1914-64), the Royal Scottish Academy (1947), the Royal Hibernian Academy (1913), the New English Art Club and the Walker Art Gallery, Liverpool. Also, with the Society of Graphic Art and at the Royal West of England Academy, with the London Group, at the Beaux Art Gallery, the Leicester Galleries and with the Women's International Art Club. Exhibited works included: Still Life With Red Chair, Bristol Docks, Waltham Abbey, Essex (drypoint) and Interior With Figure. Elected a Member of the Women's International Art Club and of the Society of Graphic Art. Noted in Frank L. Emanuel's Etching and Etchings, London, Pitman & Sons, 1930. Emanuel gives her etching of Boston Stump, of which he notes 'Daintiness of line, able composition, and wise simplification are combined to make this charming Whistlerian plate' (p.265). Etchings also reproduced in The Bookman's Journal. Works acquired by the Aberdeen Art Gallery. Katherine's brother, John, became a solicitor, like their father. Hilda and Bertha studied art. Hilda exhibited some of her work, including a book illustration, at the Royal Hibernian Academy (1913).

HARVEY, AGNES BANKIER (1874-1947)

Goldsmith / Silversmith / Enameller / Designer / Artist. Born in Anderton, Glasgow in March 1874. The daughter of William Gourlay Harvey and Sarah Tennant Sloan. One of at least six children (Francis, David, Charles, Agnes, Lawrence and Lennant). Educated at the Cheltenham Ladies' College. Studied at the Glasgow School of Art and at the London School of Silversmithing. A silver medallist in design at the National Competition of Schools of Art at South Kensington, London. A Leander Bequest prizeman in 1928. Spent much of her life and career in Scotland, in Glasgow, at Gourock and, latterly, at Greengate Close, Kirkcudbright. Fellow artist and friend Jessie M. King also spent time at Kirkcudbright, where an artists' colony formed for a while. Harvey acted as instructor of silversmithing at the Glasgow School of Art in the early 1900s. Produced a variety of work during her lengthy career, which lasted from at least 1899 until at least 1934. Designed and executed enamelled jewellery but also worked in brass and beaten repoussé as well as executing black & white drawings. Produced a wide variety of items including altar crosses, metal boxes, door plates and other decorative metalwork.

Commissions were equally wide and varied, and included a Coat of Arms in metal for the Gourock Town Council. Also, a panel for the Gourock Yacht Club. Produced gun tompions and boat badges for H.M.S. Ajax. Two fingerplates in decorative metalwork by Harvey were illustrated in The Studio, Vol.19, 1900, p.241. Exhibited her work, including at the Royal Scottish Academy (1904), the Royal Glasgow Institute (1899-1916), in London, Turin, Budapest, Paris, Cork and Berlin. Also, with the Scottish Guild of Handicraft (certainly in 1905) and with the Glasgow Society of Lady Artists' Club. Elected a Member of the latter. At the 1902 Turin Exhibition, she showed enamels in the Scottish Section. Exhibited at the annual Glasgow School of Art Club exhibition, including in 1903. Some of her exhibits on that occasion, including enamelled jewellery, were illustrated in The Studio, Vol.30, 1903. Awarded a silver medal in London for metalwork shown. Other exhibited works included: Sea Nymphs, The White Swan (black & white), The Persian Rose (enamel) and The Crystal Gazer (enamel pastel). Some of her tapestry designs were illustrated in L'Art Nouveau. Harvey developed an interest in yachting.

HARWOOD, EDITH (active 1890s-1900s)
Painter / Illustrator / Craftswoman / Illuminator. Based in London, using Canwell Studio, Tite Street, Chelsea for a time. Exhibited at the Society of Women Artists (1895-1908). Exhibited works included: Miss Monypenny at Work (watercolour), Sea Lavender (watercolour), Westminster Abbey (watercolour) and Old English Singing Game. Exhibited handicrafts too. Worked as a book illustrator. Contributed ornamental letters and illustrations to Chaucer's Flower and the Leaf printed by the Essex House Press in 1902. An example of her illumination work, Milton's Ode to Time, with contributions by Graily Hewitt, was reproduced in The Studio, Vol.34, February 1905, p.159.

HASTINGS-GRAY, ERICA MARGARET (1890-1967)
Painter / Artist in Illumination and Lettering. Born in London. The daughter of Bruno Butler Bowdon, who had private income, and Constance. Had at least one sibling, Dorothy. Raised in Dorchester, Dorset. Educated at Princethorpe Priory, Rugby and privately. Studied at the London School of Art between 1914 and 1916 under Ernest Borough Johnson and John Hassall. Also, at the Spenlove School of Landscape under Frank Spenlove-Spenlove, and studied under Hesketh Hubbard. Produced landscape paintings in watercolours, illuminations and decorative lettering. Works included, for example, the design and illumination of the Golden Book, presented to Rouen from England on St Joan's quincentenary in 1931. Exhibited her work with the Royal Institute of Painters in Watercolours, the United Society of Artists, the Women's International Art Club and the East Sussex Art Club, Hastings. Elected a Member of the East Sussex Art Club. Based in Hastings, Sussex for part of her career. In 1938 she married William A. Hastings-Gray in Kensington, London. Erica died in Uckfield, Sussex, aged 76.

HATCHER, ROBERTA - SEE EVERETT, R.

HATT, DORIS BRABHAM (1890-1969)
Painter / Wood Engraver / Woodcut Artist / Black & White Artist. Born in Bath, Somerset in September 1890. The daughter of William Edward Hatt and Mary Emily Brabham. The second of at least three children. Had an older sister, Rayonette, and a younger brother, Richard William, who became a journalist. Her father originated from Bath, her mother from London.

Her father was a hairdresser and perfumer who later also became a wigmaker. Her mother was a Professor of Pianoforte and a music teacher. All three children were raised in Bath. Doris was educated at a private school in Bath and in Germany. Studied at the Bath School of Art, followed by the Goldsmiths' College and the Royal College of Art, London. She also spent time in Vienna studying the art of the woodcut under Professor Martin at the Kunst Gewerbe Schule. In 1911, aged 20, and studying at the Bath School of Art, she is listed as a fashion artist. Later, after completing her studies, she concentrated on oil painting, wood engraving, woodcuts and black & white drawing. Concentrated on various subjects, including landscape, portrait and still life. Once qualified, she returned to Somerset and remained in the south-west of England for much of the rest of her life, dying at Weston-super-Mare, aged 79.

Hatt had a successful and extensive career, covering a period of more than 40 years, much of that time spent living at Littlemead in Clevedon, Somerset. For a while, she ran a free painting class once a week for the village children in her studio in Somerset. Exhibited throughout her career, including at the Royal Academy (1923-31), the Society of Women Artists (1923), the Leicester Galleries, the Redfern Gallery, the Zak Gallery in Paris and in New York and Boston. Also, with the International Society of Sculptors, Painters & Gravers, the New English Art Club, the National Portrait Society and at the British Oil Painters' Exhibition in Washington, U.S.A. Also exhibited regionally, in Plymouth (under the Duveen scheme), with the Royal West of England Academy and with the Clifton Arts Club in Bristol. Elected a Member of the Clifton Arts Club. Elected an Associate of the Royal West of England Academy. Exhibited works included: The Yellow Tray, Brown and Gold, Sallow Willows (oil) and Brandon Hill (oil, colour woodcut and wood engraving). Works in The New Art Gallery, Walsall, Staffordshire.

HAUGHTON, JANET MABEL (1870-1951)
Potter / Sculptor. Born in Colne, Lancashire in November 1870. The daughter of Thomas Mason of Alkincoats Hall, Lancashire and Janet Amelia. Her father, who originated from Yorkshire, was a manufacturer of worsted and cotton in Colne, running a large mill where he employed over 175 workers. He was also a J.P. Her mother originated from Liverpool. Janet was the fourth of at least five children (Joseph, Alfred, Ethel May, Janet Mabel and Helen Maud). Her siblings were also born in Colne. All were raised and educated there.

By at least 1891 her father had died, and she had moved to Tunbridge Wells, Kent with her mother and sisters Ethel and Helen. At some point after that, Janet took up pottery, producing mainly figures modelled in china clay. In 1894 she married artist and 'gentleman' Benjamin Alfred Haughton, R.B.A. (1865-1976) in Skipton, Yorkshire. He originated from Cheshire. They lived in various places, including London, Benenden and Cranbrook in Kent, and Ottery St Mary and Barnstaple in Devon. They had two daughters, Bertha and Florence. Janet died in early 1951 in Surrey, aged 80. In 1926 she was elected a Member of the Royal Miniature Society. Also a Member of the Cowdray Club. In 1927 she visited New Zealand. Possibly exhibited at the Royal Academy in 1904, showing Maggie and Essie - plaquettes (lists only Mabel Mason, 20th Century Club, Stanley Gardens, London). Painter Miss Mary Mason, also of Stanley Gardens, who exhibited at the Royal Academy in 1917, may be of the same family.

HAVERS, ALICE MARY (1850-90)

Painter / Illustrator / Photographer. Born in Camberwell. The daughter of Thomas Havers and Ellen Ruding. One of at least four children (Ellen, Dora, Thomas and Alice). In 1851, her father is listed as a general merchant. Later, he is listed as an architect. He originated from Norfolk. Alice grew up in a house with servants. She studied at South Kensington, London. Became a successful watercolour artist and illustrator with an additional interest in photography. Illustrated a number of books, including Hans Andersen, The White Swans (Hildesheimer, 1885), C.W. Faulkner, Cape Town Dicky (Hildesheimer, n.d.) and A Book of Modern Ballads (1890). In 1881 Messrs Hildesheimer & Co. held an Exhibition of Christmas and New Year Cards. Alice won a first prize of £200. She contributed to various journals and magazines including Cassell's Family Magazine. Also a successful exhibiting artist. Exhibited her work widely, including at the Royal Academy (1873-89), the Royal Society of British Artists (1872-82), the Royal Hibernian Academy (1883), the Royal Glasgow Institute (1875-88), the Society of Women Artists (1883-90), the Royal Birmingham Society of Artists, the Paris Salon and in Liverpool and Manchester. Received a Special Mention at the 1888 Salon, and was praised by Queen Victoria, who owned her Ought and Carry One. Exhibited works included: A Knotty Subject, Rush-Cutters, A Christmas Errand and Divided (photogravure). Elected an Honorary Member of the Society of Women Artists (1885-90).

Alice lived mainly in London during her life and career. In April 1872 she married portrait painter Frederick Morgan (b.1848) in Camden. His father, John Morgan, was also an artist. The couple had three children, Valentine (1873-1912), Lillian Emmeline (b.1875) and Reginald Frederick (1881-1919). Valentine later used the surname Havers-Morgan. He married and became an artist, but died young. Reginald appears to have died at the Bethnall House Asylum in Middlesex. The family lived at Cathcart Road, Kensington. Though she continued to work and exhibit after her marriage, indications are that Alice encountered serious difficulties in her private life. Some short time after the birth of her third child, Alice was separated from Morgan and their children, and died alone in Marlborough Road, London, aged only 40. The 1881 national census records her as having no profession, even though she continued to exhibit up to her death. Her will states that by 1890 she was a single woman and 'before now wife of Frederick Morgan'. Her estate of some £2000 was left to her aunt. Somewhat prophetically, her Trouble (with quotation, priced £175) was exhibited at the Society of Women Artists in 1885. Noted in Mahony, Latimer & Folmsbee, Illustrators of Children's Books 1744-1945, Boston, The Horn Book Inc., 1947. Also, in James Thorpe, English Illustration: The Nineties, New York Hacker Art Books Inc, 1975 (first edition 1935). Works in the Southport Art Gallery. Alice's sister, Ellen Havers, was also an artist and exhibited her work at the Royal Society of British Artists (1877 / 78). Frederick Morgan married again, twice, and had other children.

HAWEIS, MARY ELIZA (1848-98)

Decorative Artist / Illustrator / Writer. Born in Chelsea in early 1848. The daughter of artist Thomas Musgrave Joy and Eliza. Her father exhibited his work at the British Institution between 1832 and 1867. Mary had a younger sister, Edith Susannah. Mary was involved in interior decoration and various other aspects of the arts. She wrote and illustrated a number of books for children, including Chaucer for Children. She was the author of a number of other books, including The Art of Dress (c.1879), The Art of Decoration (c.1881) and The Art of Beauty (c.1883). Produced woodcuts for Cassell's Magazine. Also designed book covers. Contributed to women's magazines. Exhibited one work at the Royal Academy in 1866, 'Long I Looked Out for the Lad' (Jean Ingelow). Exhibited one work at the British Institution in 1867, The Cyanus (priced £20), in the same year that her father exhibited there for the last time. Based in London at that time. In late 1867 she married the Rev. Hugh Reginald Haweis, incumbent of St James's, Marylebone, in Middlesex. Mary was then only 19 years of age. Haweis, who originated from Essex, was some 10 years older than his wife. They had three children, Lionel (b.c.1871), Hugolin (b.c.1874) and Stephen (b.c.1879), all born in London. The marriage is believed to have been a difficult one. Mary died in Bath, Somerset, aged 49.

HAWKSLEY, DOROTHY WEBSTER (1884-1970)

Painter / Lithographer / Illustrator. Born in London in November 1884. The daughter of Thomas Paton Hawksley (1839-1908), a surgical instrument maker, and Maria Groves Walters (1846-1930). Her father originated from Yorkshire, her mother from London. One of possibly eight children (also May, Annie, Agnes, Thomas, Bessie, Robert and Charles). The children were raised in London, and Charles subsequently took over his father's business. Dorothy studied at the St John's Wood School of Art, where she was a silver medallist. Also studied at the Royal Academy schools under George Clausen, Solomon and Dicksee. A silver medallist twice at the schools, on one occasion for the category of best painting from the nude. In 1910, she won the Landseer Scholarship of £40 a year. Remained in London after completing her studies, dying in Kensington, aged 85.

Hawksley produced paintings in tempera and watercolours, lithographs, decorative paintings, drawings in wash and pencil studies. Subjects included portraits and figures. Exhibited her work over a period of more than 54 years. Exhibited at the Royal Academy (66 works, 1909-64), the Royal Glasgow Institute (1921-28), the Royal Scottish Academy (1920 & 1957) and the Society of Women Artists (1919-51). Also, with the Royal Institute of Painters in Watercolours, at the Paris Salon and in Liverpool, Brighton, Pittsburg and elsewhere. Exhibited works included: Summer (watercolour), Mary and Elizabeth (tempera), Little Kids (wash) and Fancy Dress Optional. A Paris Salon silver medallist. Elected a Member of the Royal Institute of Painters in Watercolours and of the Society of Women Artists (1935-41).

Illustrated The Gospel of St Luke (The Story of Jesus). Works illustrated in Bystander, including her Adam and Eve. She also contributed Cat Burglar and other works to Sketch. At least two of her works, Christ in the Work Shop and Mary and Martha, were published by the Medici

Society. Her Moonrise was published by Stacey. The Birmingham City Art Gallery acquired her The Nativity. Other works were acquired by the galleries of Liverpool (Jairus's Daughter) and Oldham (Prodigal Son). The National Gallery of Canada acquired her Lung Ching and the Beggar Maid (watercolour) which was illustrated in The Studio, Vols.127 / 128, 1944, p.9. In 1922, Hawksley was the subject of an illustrated article in The Studio, Vol.84, November, pp.257-262. One of the illustrations was of her colour lithograph Peace.

HAYES, EDITH CAROLINE (1860-1948)

Painter / Wood Engraver. Born at Southsea, Hampshire in May 1860. The daughter of Capt. John Montague Hayes of the Royal Navy and Julia. Her mother originated from Portsea, Hampshire. One of at least five children (Montague, Julia, Jessie, Ada and Edith). Edith was registered as deaf. She studied in London at the St John's Wood School of Art and at the Royal Academy schools. Listed as an art student living in Paddington, London from at least 1881. Spent some time in Paris and Dublin in the later 1880s. Also worked as a professional artist in St Ives, Cornwall in the 1890s. From the early 1900s until her death she lived and worked in Great Marlow, Buckinghamshire. Produced oil and watercolour paintings and wood engravings, of landscapes, portraits and other subjects. Exhibited at the New English Art Club (from 1912), the Royal Academy (1889-97) and the Royal Hibernian Academy (1881-91). Possibly exhibited at the Royal Academy between 1907 and 1911. A Miss Hayes also exhibited at Messrs Connell's Gallery in 1909 with Hester Frood and other etchers. Exhibited works included: At Newlyn, The Guitar, Bunol Valencia and Susie and Daffodils. Elected a Member of the Lyceum Club. Listed as still active into the 1930s, in her 70s. Died in Great Marlow, aged 88.

HAYES, GERTRUDE E. - SEE MORGAN, G.E.

HAYES, MARY WINIFRED (1891-1980)

Sculptor / Painter. Known as Winifred. Born in London. The daughter of James Yule and Mary. Became Mrs Hayes on her marriage in 1918. Studied at the Aberdeen School of Art. Also, at the Edinburgh College of Art. Won the highest award as an art student as well as various scholarships. Initially based in India Street, Edinburgh. But spent much of her life and career in London, including at Clanricarde Gardens and Holland Park Avenue. Died in Surrey in June

1980, aged 89. Produced busts and heads in marble, wood and bronze, and paintings of various subjects. Exhibited her work, including at the Society of Women Artists (1936-37), the Royal Academy (1927-49), the Royal Scottish Academy (1913), the Royal Glasgow Institute (1931-33) and the National Portrait Society. Exhibited works included: The Rt Hon. Sir William Bull, Bt, M.P. - Presentation Bust (bronze), Youth (bust, marble), Simon Asquith (head, carved wood) and Printemps (oil). Elected a Member of the Lyceum Club. Her son, Colin Hayes, became a painter. She exhibited at least two portrait sculptures of Colin at the Royal Academy.

HAYNES, GWENDOLYN JOYCE (1917-2001)

Potter. Born in Aldershot. The daughter of Lt. Col. P. Haynes. Educated at the St Helen's School, Abingdon. Studied under Philip Wadsworth and Percy Brown at the Leicester College of Art between 1937 and 1943. Awarded an Art Teachers' Diploma in 1943. Also studied at the Bernard Leach Pottery in 1949. Worked in earthenware and stoneware. Also worked as an art teacher. Was a lecturer in art at the Derby Training College between 1945 and 1947. Then became a pottery teacher at the Scarborough School of Art from 1947. Exhibited her work, including at the Society of Women Artists (1951-53), with the Red Rose Guild, at the galleries of Leicester and Scarborough, in Derby and Nottingham and at the Inn Crafts Exhibitions. Exhibited works included: The Rock (stoneware), King David (soft earthenware) and Fish in the Pool (stoneware). Works purchased by the Leicester Museum, the Argentine State Collection and the N.R.Y. Education Committee. Died in Lincoln, aged 84.

HAYTHORNE, MARGARET CURTIS (1893-1978)

Painter / Wood Engraver / Designer. Born in Liverpool in October 1893. The daughter of Thomas Joseph Scott Haythorne, M.D., B.A., a surgeon, and Elizabeth. Her father originated from Canada, her mother from Swansea. One of at least three children (Winifred, Margaret and Edmund (1898-1974)). Raised in Liverpool. Spent much of her life and career in Liverpool. But died in Cumbria, aged 85. Educated at the Belvedere School, Liverpool. Studied at the Liverpool City School of Art under Will Penn. Also, at the London County Council Central School of Arts and Crafts under Cyril Goldie, Noel Rooke and F.E. Jackson. Awarded a

Queen's Scholarship and the William Atkinson Scholarship. Produced wood engravings, poster designs for the L.C.C. Tramways (in 1922) and other decorative work as well as paintings. Executed decoration on the staircase wall of the L.C.C. Central School of Arts and Crafts and in St Peter's Church, Limehouse.

Margaret exhibited her work, including at the Society of Women Artists (1929), at the Arts and Crafts exhibitions in London, with the New English Art Club, the Society of Present Day Artists, the Society of Wood Engravers, the English Wood Engraving Society and the Royal Academy (1944). Also, at the Royal Cambrian Academy, with the Sandon Studios Society and at the Redfern Gallery. Exhibited works included: Upper Room (wood engraving) and Gethsemane (wood engraving). Elected a Member of the Sandon Studios Society and of the Langbourn Club. Her Deposition was illustrated in the London Mercury. Other works were reproduced in Artwork and Modern Woodcuts. Her Sleep was illustrated in The Studio, Vol.99, March 1930 in an article British Wood Engraving of the Present Day (pp.155-167) by Maximilien Vox. Some of Haythorne's prints were acquired by the Contemporary Art Society, the Whitworth Art Gallery, Manchester and the Aberystwyth University Library.

HEARD, EILEEN MURIEL (1902-87)

Designer / Embroideress / Leatherworker / Bookbinder. Born in London. The daughter of Robert James Heard, a shipping clerk, and Eileen. Had at least one sibling, Leslie. Raised in Kent and London. Educated at the Blackheath High School. Studied at the Blackheath School of Art and in London at the L.C.C. Central School of Arts and Crafts. Also spent some time studying in the Victoria & Albert Museum, London. Awarded three certificates of the Art Advisory Board final examination of City & Guilds of London Institute. Achieved a First Class in design and embroidery. Also awarded a full First Class Teaching Certificate of the London Institute of Plain Needlework. Exhibited her work only occasionally, including at the Royal Academy, the Walker's Gallery, at Wembley and at the Eltham Arts and Crafts Exhibition. Based in London for part of her career, but died in Sussex, aged 84. Sold some of her work through exhibitions held at the Royal Academy. Acted as a visiting teacher.

HEATH, IRENE GWENDOLEN (1905-89)

Painter / Illustrator / Writer. Born in Bedford in May 1905. The daughter of Albert George Heath,

M.B.E., a surveyor, and Marie. One of at least three daughters (Monica, Irene and Olive). Raised and educated in Bedford. Studied in London at the St John's Wood School of Art, at the Heatherley's School of Art and at the Regent Street Polytechnic. Studied under Ronald Ossory Dunlop, Frederick Whiting and Arthur Ralph Middleton Todd. Produced paintings in oils, book illustrations, including for her own children's books for Warne publishers, and contributed to various newspapers and periodicals. Books illustrated included: Good Luck and Good Bye (Hale), Capricorn Colony (Gifford), A Birthday Book For Children, Heard By a Mouse and Sugar and Spice. Exhibited her work, including at the Royal Academy (1947-56), the Royal Institute of Oil Painters, the National Society and the Artists of Chelsea at the Chenil Gallery. Exhibited works included: A New Profession and Chelsea Sunday. A Member of the National Book Club. Based mainly in London, dying there aged 84. Heath married James Brooks, F.R.G.S., and had two daughters.

HECHLE, HILDA MARION (1886-1939)

Painter / Engraver / Illustrator. Born in Brassington, Derbyshire in early 1886. The daughter of Henry John Hechle (b.1858) and Una Marion Breakell (b.1860). Her father originated from Liscard, Cheshire, her mother from Manchester. Her father appeared to have no definite occupation, but had private funds. Hilda was an only child and was raised in Derbyshire and Colwyn Bay, Wales. Studied in London, at the St John's Wood School of Art and at the Royal Academy schools, where she was a medal and prize-winning student. Produced landscape, portrait and figure paintings, engravings and book illustrations. Worked in oils, watercolours and tempera. Evidently travelled to paint, and became known for her Alpine landscapes. Some of those appeared in an exhibition titled Mountain Landscapes held at the Alpine Club Gallery in 1922. The exhibition was made up of the works of Hechle, Katharine Clausen and Clement du Pontet. Also exhibited her work at the Royal Academy (1906-31), the Royal Glasgow Institute (1923), the Royal Society of British Artists, the Royal Institute of Painters in Watercolours, the Walker Art Gallery, Liverpool and the Society of Women Artists (40 works, 1924-39). A Member of the New Autumn Group, which originally consisted of 21 members, all centred around St John's Wood. In 1925 she showed Climbing the Meije Dauphine at their exhibition. The painting was illustrated in The Studio, Vol.90, December 1925, p.346.

Further afield, Hechle exhibited in Budapest and in Washington, U.S.A. at the National Gallery of Art. Held one-woman shows at the St George's Gallery. Also exhibited at the Grosvenor Gallery and under the Duveen scheme. Elected a Member of the Royal Society of British Artists in 1926, and a Member of the Society of Women Artists (1928-38). Exhibited works included: The Matterhorn in Moonlight, Grey Owl, Fire Clay Pit, Derbyshire and Jack Frost (engraving). Works illustrated by her included Stories From the Earthly Paradise (Edward Arnold) and Macbeth and Julius Caesar (Clark Co. Ltd, Toronto). Some of her works were illustrated in Colour (including Study in January 1922), in The Westminster Gazette (The Sphinx) and in Drawing & Design (Vertain Spitze). Also, in Queen and The Sphere (including Christmas drawings). Based in London for much of her career, in Hampstead and in a studio in St John's Wood. Still based in St John's Wood when she died in April 1939, aged 53, but actually died in Surrey. Left her small estate to her father. Hilda was also a Member of the Forum Club.

HECTOR, GERTRUDE MARY (1888-1972)

Designer / Craftswoman. Born in Calcutta, India in December 1888. The daughter of the Rev. John Hector, M.A., D.D. (1845-1934) and Margaret Pittendrigh (1857-1917). Her father was a missionary in India from around 1879, then became Principal of Duff College, Calcutta. He was born in Aberdeen and died there. Gertrude was the youngest of at least six children (Kenneth, John Ernest, Mabel, George, John Masson and Gertrude Mary). John Ernest died at birth or just after. It may have been that which prompted Margaret Hector to return to Aberdeen, when Gertrude was still only around two years of age, with her five surviving children. For at least 10 years (certainly up to 1901) they lived with Margaret Hector's mother, Margaret Pittendrigh, in Aberdeen. Gertrude's sister Mabel later became a doctor in India, at a medical missionary. Gertrude was educated privately. She then studied at the Gray's School of Art, Aberdeen, and at the Battersea School of Art, London. As a student, she was a Byrne Scholar. She then established herself as an expert metalworker, enameller, embroideress and maker of decorative jewellery. Spent most of her life and career in and around Aberdeen, using a studio on Union Street, and later one at Bonaccord Terrace. Her career covered at least three decades. Exhibited her work, including at the Scottish Society of Women Artists, the Aberdeen Artists' Society, the Royal Scottish Academy (1916-18), the Society of

Women Artists (1916-18) and the Walker Art Gallery, Liverpool. Exhibited works included: The Spirit of Youth (cloisonne enamel) and The Spirit of the Night (cloisonne enamel panel). Elected a Member of the Scottish Society of Women Artists (1926). A Member of the Soroptimist Club, Aberdeen. Hector was also the author of Peeps at Arts and Crafts (A.&C. Black, c.1928). She died in January 1972, aged 83, and was buried at Aberdeen.

HEELAS, MABEL MARY ANN (1876-1951)
Painter / Black & White Artist. Born in Wokingham, Berkshire. The daughter of Tyndale William Heelas and Amelia Mary Anne. Her father, a draper and outfitter, originated from Wokingham, her mother from Westminster. One of at least seven children (Arthur, Ernest, Alice, Frank, Mabel, Ethel and Hilda). Raised and educated in Wokingham. Educated privately. Studied art in the local studios. Based at The Warehouse Studio in Wokingham for much of her career. Produced landscape paintings in watercolours and black & white drawings. Exhibited occasionally, including with the British Watercolour Society, in London and in the provinces. Elected an Associate of the British Watercolour Society in 1919. Died in Berkshire, aged 75.

HEINE, ROSIE M. - SEE PITMAN, R.M.

HELLABY, RUTH - SEE HOLLINGSWORTH, R.

HENDERSON, MARY REID (active 1910s-1940s)
Painter / Etcher / Craftswoman / Illuminator / Enameller / Metalworker / Embroideress / Ecclesiastical Artist / Pen & Ink Artist. Born in Glasgow. The daughter of John Henderson, a teacher of French and a Glasgow Education Authority Official. Educated at The High School for Girls, Glasgow. Studied at the Glasgow School of Art, where she was awarded a scholarship, a travelling bursary and various prizes and medals. Awarded a Glasgow School diploma in 1913. Based mainly in Glasgow during her career, but also latterly at Largs, Ayrshire. Acted as teacher of embroidery continuation classes at the Motherwell Technical School. Also acted as head teacher of art at Helensburgh and teacher of drawing and metalwork at Stirling. Produced paintings in oils and watercolours as well as working as a decorative artist / craftswoman. Exhibited her work over a period of at least 26 years, including

at the Royal Glasgow Institute (1915-41) and the Royal Scottish Academy (1918-32). Also, with the Royal West of England Academy, in Toronto, and locally in Stirling, Paisley and elsewhere. Exhibited works included: Piras Japonica (watercolour), Thistle Chapel, St Giles, Edinburgh (drawing), Sunshine and Shadow (etching) and Solitude. Elected a Member of the Glasgow Lady Artists' Club. Works reproduced in The Studio, La Revue Moderne and History of Glasgow, Vol.21, which illustrated her St Enoch's Church and Square at Glasgow, a triptych in enamel and metal and a gold pendant.

HENNES, HILARY M. - SEE MILLER, H.M.

HEPWORTH, BARBARA (1903-75)
Sculptor. Was Jocelyn Barbara, known as Barbara. Arguably one of Britain's best known and most successful women sculptors of the mid-twentieth century. Born in Wakefield, Yorkshire. The eldest child of engineer Herbert Raikes Hepworth and Gertrude Johnson. One of four children. Won a scholarship to the Leeds School of Art where she first encountered Henry Moore (1898-1986). A second scholarship took her to the Royal College of Art, London. A third took her to Italy for two years. Produced various subjects, working in marble, alabaster, stone and wood. Quickly became a prominent force in the world of modern sculpture. Likened to Henry Moore. One of the most comprehensive illustrated articles on Hepworth appeared in The Studio, Vol.171, June 1966, pp.252-257, by Gene Baro. The article included quotations from an autobiographical essay in which Hepworth states:
Sculpture is to me an affirmative statement of our will to live:
whether it be small, to rest in the hand; or larger to be embraced;
or larger still, to force us to move around it and establish our
rhythm of life.
In 1925, Hepworth married fellow sculptor John Skeaping. In 1929 she gave birth to a son, Paul. She continued to work. Exhibited at home and abroad many times. For example, exhibited at the Beaux Art Gallery in 1928 alongside William Morgan and Skeaping. Also showed work at the Tooth's Gallery, the Lefevre Gallery, at the Artists International Association exhibition at the New Burlington Galleries, the Zwemmer Gallery, the Whitechapel Art Gallery, the Festival of Britain, the Bankfield Museum and the Halifax and Wakefield City Art Gallery. Exhibited at the Royal Scottish Academy (1929-51). In 1954 the

Whitechapel Art Gallery held a major retrospective of her work, of carvings and drawings. In 1964 she exhibited at the Galerie Gimpel, Hanover, and in the same year at the Pittsburgh International Exhibition of Contemporary Painting and Sculpture along with Elisabeth Frink and others.

Hepworth's marriage to Skeaping ended, and in 1930 she married painter Ben Nicholson (1894-1982). In 1934 she gave birth to triplets Sarah, Simon and Rachel. Undaunted, she continued to work and to exhibit. In 1939 the family moved from London to Carbis Bay, Cornwall. Hepworth subsequently settled at the Trewyn Studio in St Ives where she worked up until her death. She and Nicholson eventually separated. Her work was discussed frequently in journals of the day, but she was particularly noted for the often huge scale of her sculptures. She was a founder member of the influential if short-lived Unit One, a group of artists, sculptors and architects founded under Paul Nash in 1933 and disbanded in 1934. Also a member of Abstraction-Creation, founded in 1931. With Nicholson, she joined the Seven and Five Society, a group consisting of seven British painters and five sculptors, founded in 1920. A member of the Penwith Society of Arts and Crafts, a breakaway group of the St Ives Society of Artists which included Bernard Leach and Adrian Stokes. Hepworth exhibited with the St Ives Society of Artists too.

During her career, Hepworth won numerous awards for her work, including the Hoffman Wood Trust gold medal for her Biolith (1948-49) which was shown at the 25th Venice Biennale. Awarded honorary degrees by the Universities of Leeds, Exeter, Birmingham and Oxford. In 1968 she was received into the Gorsedd of Cornwall as a Bard in recognition of work done for Cornwall. One of her best-known works was Winged Figure for the exterior of Oxford Street's John Lewis store. In 1953 her son, Paul, was killed on active service with the R.A.F. In his memory, she created Madonna and Child, now in the St Ives Parish Church. She was created C.B.E. in 1957 and made a Dame of the British Empire in 1965.

Hepworth's work can be found reproduced countless times in books, journals and magazines. For example, Apollo, November 1930, pp.347-351 included illustrations of her Infant (carved wood), Mask (Norweigian stone) and Dog (Hornton stone) in an article The New Generation of Sculpture. In 1965, The Studio, Vol.169, March, p.99 included her Pierced Form (Pentelican marble), which measured 50" in height, in an article The Phenomenon of British Sculpture. Noted in books including Private View by John Russell and Bryan Robertson, which

discussed patronage of the arts. Hepworth died in a fire in her studio in 1975. Her studio is now a gallery of her works. In 2003 the Tate Gallery, St Ives held a Centenary Exhibition which combined drawings and sculptures by Hepworth.

HERBERT, GWENDA (1878-1966)

Sculptor / Craftswoman. Was Gwendolen, known as Gwenda. Born at Cahirnane House, Killarney, Co. Kerry. Part of the Herberts of Muckross (landed gentry). In around 1898 she moved to Dublin when the family fortunes dwindled. Studied at the Metropolitan School of Art, Dublin from 1899. Won a studentship in 1900 and studied modelling. From 1904 she studied enamelling and metalwork under P. Oswold Reeves. Associated with the Irish Art Companions, an Irish Revival Industry founded in Dublin in 1904. The Companions produced plaster as well as such things as figures and statues using the plaster. Herbert joined along with Joseph Corre, Mervyn Lawrence and others. Herbert executed some Irish peasant figures and workers. Based in Clyde Road, Dublin for a time. In around 1907, she moved to London where she taught and made garden statues. Exhibited at the Royal Academy in 1907, showing a case of three works in bronze and silver, including a portrait medal for a Physical Training College and Goats of Glendalough. The following year, she exhibited two works at the Royal Hibernian Academy, Andromeda and Reflections. Also exhibited at the Walker Art Gallery, Liverpool and at the Irish International Exhibition, Dublin in 1907. Returned to Ireland in 1929. Works in the National Gallery of Ireland.

HEWETT, IDALIA B. - SEE LITTLEJOHNS, I.B.

HEY, CICELY (1896-1980)

Painter / Draughtsman / Modeller. Was Mary Cicely, known as Cicely. Born in Faringdon. Died in Colwyn Bay, Wales. The daughter of Harold Darwin Hey (1868-1946) and Mary Mallan (1870-1936). Her father was a surgeon. Had at least one sister, Lucy. Raised in Berkshire. Studied in London, at the L.C.C. Central School of Arts and Crafts, and at the Slade School. Became a portrait and figure painter, a draughtsman and a modeller of miniature period figures. Exhibited her work, including with the London Group, the National Society, the Women's International Art Club, the New English Art Club and the Society of Graphic Art. Also contributed to various exhibitions of such things as inn signs and crafts. In 1933 she held a one-woman exhibition of portraits of art celebrities at the Reid & Lefevre galleries. Elected a Member of the National Society and of the London Group. Her portrait of D.S. MacColl was acquired by the British Museum. Hey was evidently at the forefront of developments in British art in the 1930s and 1940s, exhibiting with some of the then ground-breaking artists and art groups. Sickert painted her portrait. She was based in London for part of her career. Some of her works were reproduced in The Studio, the Daily Telegraph, the Radio Times and elsewhere. In 1924 she married Robert Rattray Tatlock (1889-1954) in Middlesex. He was a former student of the Glasgow School of Art, and was art critic to the Daily Telegraph and editor of the Burlington Magazine.

HIBBERD, GLADYS MARY (b.1902)

Pottery Figure Artist. Born and raised in London. The daughter of Frank Joel Hibberd, a builder, and Hannah. One of at least three children (Frank, Eric and Gladys). Studied at the Camberwell School of Arts and Crafts, London. Produced pottery figures, specialising in animals. Exhibited at the Royal Academy 1926 Arts and Crafts exhibition, the Society of Women Artists (1927-38), the Walker Art Gallery, Liverpool, in Stockholm and elsewhere in London. Exhibited works included: Pointer and Setter, The Shepherd, Boy and the Bird and Geese.

HICKMAN, EVELYN AUGUSTA (1859-1943)

Sculptor / Painter / Decorative Metalworker. Born in Newport, Isle of Wight. The daughter of William T. Hickman, an army officer, and Annie De Courcy. One of at least six children (Evelyn, Ada, Louisa, Rose, Dora and Mary). Based in St Leonards, Sussex early in her career. Later based in Chelsea. Died in South Kensington, London. Produced busts in bronze, paintings and decorative metalwork with enamelling. Exhibited at the Royal Academy (1891 & 1922) and at the Society of Women Artists (1902). Also exhibited at the 1900 Leeds Arts and Crafts Exhibition, showing a casket made of copper and enamel, with steel mounts, decorated with a shamrock leaf design on the lock-plate and mounts of the feet. Exhibited at the 1905 Exhibition of Arts and Crafts at the Lyceum Club, showing a copper standing mirror which was illustrated in The Studio, Vol.36, October 1905, p.73. Contributed to the Exhibition of Works of Art by Women Artists held at Waring & Gillow's in May 1916, organised to raise funds for women artists suffering due to war. The exhibition was visited by the Queen and Princess Mary. The Queen purchased one of Hickman's works. Other works by Hickman included Boy Whistling (bust, bronze) and Summer.

HICKMAN-SMITH, EILEEN (1909-70)

Sculptor / Painter / Journalist. Born in Islington, London in March 1909. The daughter of Arthur Ernest Hickman-Smith, F.R.S.A., and Annie. Her father, an artist, was co-founder of, and Honorary Secretary of, the Islington Art Circle. A former student of the Birmingham School of Art, he produced book illustrations and paintings in oils and watercolours, but was also a writer and musician. He died in 1956. Her mother was also a musician. Eileen appears to have been an only child, raised in Islington. Educated at the Highbury Hill High School, London. Subsequently studied at the Regent Street Polytechnic School of Art under Harold Brownsword, F.R.B.S., A.R.C.A. She was a bronze medallist in sculpture as a student. Worked as a painter in oils and a sculptor of figures and reliefs in stone and bronze. Based in London for much of her life and career, at Highbury Quadrant, Islington with her parents. Exhibited her work mainly in London, at the Royal Academy (1941-42), the Royal Society of British Artists, the Women's International Art Club and the Whitechapel Art Gallery. Also exhibited with the Islington Art Circle and the Society of Women Artists. At the latter, she showed two works, Autumn Bunch (oil) in 1965 and Portrait, Carlo Marini in 1969. Other exhibited works included: Otelio (head) and Reflection (statuette). Died in London in early 1970, aged 61.

HIGGINS, KATE ELIZABETH (1881-1960)

Sculptor / Illustrator / Painter. Born in London. The daughter of Henry U. Olver, L.D.S., R.C.S., a dental surgeon, and Alice. Had at least one sibling, Julian. Raised in Surrey. Educated at the Queen's College, Harley Street, London. Studied at the Royal Academy schools, London. Became a book illustrator, a sculptor of statuettes and a painter of landscapes, portraits and figures in oils and watercolours as well as executing works in pencil and chalk. Based largely in London during her career, but also latterly in Northall, Bedfordshire. In 1927, with a well-established career, she married the younger Charles Samson Higgins (1893-1980) in Hampstead. He was a civil engineer, born in Argentina. Charles Higgins was also an author and an oil and watercolour painter who sometimes wrote under the name of Ian Dall.

Kate exhibited her work both before and after her marriage, over a period of more than 39 years. Exhibited at the Royal Academy (38 works, 1910-46), the Royal Scottish Academy (1934), the Royal Glasgow Institute (1922), the Society of Women Artists (1907-39), in Liverpool, at the Paris Salon and with the Royal Society of Portrait Painters. Exhibited works included: The Young Peasant (statuette), Lovely Nonsense, Fisher Girls Resting: Outer Hebrides and Delia (pencil). Elected an Associate of the Society of Women Artists (1934-36) and a Member (1937-39). Produced illustrations for a number of books, including Hilda M. Hankey, Many Moving Pictures (Andrew Melrose, 1917), Robert Louis Stevenson, A Child's Garden of Verse (Collins) and Anna Spyri, Children of the Hills. Some of her works were reproduced in The Studio, the Sphere, The Times and the Observer. Works purchased by the Corporation of Hull. Kate died in London, aged 79. Charles Higgins died in Kensington, aged 87.

HILL, AGNES THOMPSON (1874-1963)

Painter / Decorative Metalworker. Was Agnes Thompson. Born in Liverpool. Educated at the Mount School, York. Studied at the Liverpool University. Produced paintings in watercolours and decorative jewellery. Exhibited her work occasionally, showing jewellery at the second exhibition of the Northern Art Workers' Guild in 1903. Also exhibited jewellery at the Walker Art Gallery, Liverpool, including at their autumn exhibitions of 1906, 1909 and 1914. Also exhibited in Leeds and London. In 1903 she married Edward Faulkner Hill in Liverpool. He was a doctor. They lived at Llanrwst, Wales and later at Victoria Park, Manchester. Agnes died in Manchester, aged 89. Evidently continued to work for some years after her marriage.

HIMSWORTH, JOYCE ROSEMARY (1905-89)

Designer and Craftswoman of Ecclesiastical and Domestic Plate / Jeweller / Enameller. Born at Ecclesall, Yorkshire in August 1905. The daughter of craftsman Joseph Beeston Himsworth (1874-1968) and Dora Elizabeth Gill (b.1870). Educated at the Sheffield High School. Studied at the Sheffield College of Arts and Crafts, and in Italy. Awarded a First Class City & Guilds Full Technological Certificate in goldsmiths' and silversmiths' work, including enamelling. Recipient of the Alfred Chadburn Prize. Also studied at the London County Council Central School of Arts and Crafts. Based for much of her career in Chelsea Road, Sheffield.

Became a leading designer and craftswoman in metalwork, enamelling and jewellery. Highly respected in her day. She was the daughter of an equally gifted craftsman. Joseph Himsworth was the son of a cutlery manufacturer. He became a lecturer, worked in gold, silver, bronze and enamelling, was a stained glass designer and an illuminator. He too studied at the Sheffield College of Arts and Crafts, and was Master and Fellow of the Sheffield Art Crafts Guild. Joyce became a Fellow and Secretary of the Guild in 1925, also exhibiting with the Guild. She was also a Member of the Red Rose Guild.

Joyce evidently had a close relationship with her father, and worked with him from an early age. She signed her work J.B.H.J.R.H. Also exhibited her work at Goldsmiths' Hall, at various arts and crafts exhibitions, at the Walker Art Gallery, Liverpool, and in Oxford, Newlyn, Manchester, Leeds, Newcastle and Doncaster. Further afield, she exhibited in Prague. Contributed to the Art competitions at the 1948 London Summer Games. Taught metalwork and jewellery at the Chesterfield and District School of Arts and Crafts, and at the Rotherham School of Art. Produced a wide range of items during her career, including hair ornaments, cigarette boxes, drinking cups, napkin rings, spoons and all manner of jewellery including bracelets. She incorporated many different styles into her work, including Celtic. Designed a silver cup to celebrate the Coronation of Edward VIII, executed in 1937. The cup was subsequently altered to fit changing events. Purchasers of her work were many and varied. The Worshipful Company of Goldsmiths acquired some of her gold and enamel jewellery. Also executed a pair of lily vases and two chalices for Westminster Cathedral. Her work was illustrated in the National Association of Goldsmiths' Journal and in the Sheffield Telegraph and Independent. She retired in the 1960s. Died in Sheffield in April 1989, aged 83. Works in the Sheffield Museums collection.

HINCHLEY, EDITH MARY (1870-1940)

Miniature and Portrait Painter / Bookplate Artist. Born in January 1870. The daughter of John Mason, a florist and nurseryman, and Frances. Her father, who originated from Essex, employed at least 10 men. He died sometime in the 1880s, whilst Edith was still living at home. One of at least four daughters (Jane, Frances, Edith and Emily), all born and raised in Chelsea. Her mother originated from Dulwich, and after her husband's death worked as a pencil artist. By at least the early 1890s, Edith was already an art student. She studied at the National Art Training School, London, which became the Royal College of Art. Was a silver medallist. Elected an Associate of the Royal College of Art in 1895. By the early 1900s, the four Mason sisters were living together, Frances having apparently died, all unmarried. By that stage, Edith was working as a professional artist. Also living in the house were two boarders, Albert Hall and John William Hinchley (1871-1931). In 1903, Edith and Hinchley were married in Kensington. He was a Professor of Chemical Engineering. After their marriage, Edith continued to work as an artist, and the couple lived mainly in London.

Edith began exhibiting her work more seriously in the late 1890s. Exhibited at the Royal Academy (27 works, 1897-1928), the Royal Hibernian Academy (1898), the Royal Glasgow Institute (1900), the Society of Women Artists (1899-1939), in Liverpool and at the Paris Salon. Also exhibited with the Royal Society of Miniature Painters, including in 1912 when she showed Youth. Other exhibited works included: Professor Hinchley, Mrs Bernard Shaw, H.H. Princess Helena Victoria, Golden Locks and The Tomb of Romeo and Juliet, Verona. Elected a Member of the Royal Society of Miniature Painters (1896) and a Member of the Society of Women Artists (1922-30). Also a Member of the Lyceum Club. The Victoria & Albert Museum, London acquired her Memories. Her career spanned over five decades, and she worked and exhibited up until her death. In her death notice, it is noted that she was killed 'through war operations' in October 1940 and that her body was recovered five days later. She was a widow at that time, living in Redcliffe Road, Kensington.

HINDSON, ALICE MAUDE CHARLOTTE (1896-1984)

Writer / Illuminator / Wood Engraver / Figured Silk Weaver. Born in Andover, Hampshire in October 1896. The daughter of John H. Hindson, a clerk in holy orders, and Lavinia. The fourth of at least five children (Robert, Godfrey, Reginald, Alice and Lavinia), born between 1892 and 1898. By at least 1901 the family had moved to Chester. The children were taught by a governess. Alice was also educated at the Cheltenham Ladies' College. Subsequently studied at the London County Council Central School of Arts and Crafts. Remained in London, working from a studio in Cathcart Road. Later returned to Hampshire, to the New Forest area, where she died, aged 87. Elected a Member of the Society of Scribes and Illuminators in 1923. Served as

Honorary Secretary of the Society between 1928 and 1931.

HODGE, ESME V. - SEE SANDERCOCK, E.V.

HODGE, JESSIE MARY MARGARET (1901-64)

Mural Decorator / Illuminator / Artist. Born in Hammersmith, London in late 1901. The daughter of Albert Hemstock Hodge (1875-1917) and Jessie Dunn. Her parents originated from Scotland. Had at least one younger sibling, Norman. Raised in London. Her father was a sculptor and Member of the Royal Society of British Sculptors. He originally trained to be an architect, but opted to take up sculpture. He studied at the Glasgow School of Art, and executed architectural sculptures for major buildings in England, Wales and Canada. Jessie was educated at the Norland Place School and at Lime Grove. Doubtless influenced by her father, who possibly initially taught the young Jessie. She studied at the Royal Academy schools, London. Won the Royal Academy bronze medal for life painting, and was a Landseer Scholar. Her father did not live to see her succeed as an artist.

Jessie became a highly competent and diverse artist who worked and exhibited until just before her death. Became artist to St Mary's Hospital. Produced works in oils, watercolours and tempera, including watercolours on vellum. Carried out various illumination work, including in commemoration of Sir Ernest Shackleton (an official purchase). Did lettered tablets for the Second Church of Christ Scientist. Did lettering around the Kitchener Memorial for St Paul's Cathedral. Carried out various commissions for interior design, including office decoration for Sir John Burnet, Tait and Larne. Also, fresco panels for the hall at the Eastman Dental Clinic. Produced other interior decoration for Vigo House which was illustrated in the Builder and elsewhere. Executed medical and surgical illustrations for Sir Duke-Elder, Glasgow University and others. Executed book illustrations, including for A Midsummer Night's Dream. Her murals included Friendship, part of a design for the S.S. Uganda in watercolours and tempera which was exhibited at the Society of Women Artists in 1960.

Exhibited her work widely over a period of more than 40 years, including at the Royal Academy (1922-47), the Royal Glasgow Institute (1932-54), the Royal Scottish Academy (1933-49) and the Society of Women Artists (1954-63). Also, at the Walker Art Gallery, Liverpool, the Royal

Society of Miniature Painters and the Paris Salon. Exhibited works included: The Nymph, Canada Geese, Oyster Catchers and The Paper Shop, Carradale. Elected an Associate of the Society of Women Artists (1955-60) and a Member (1961-64). Based in and around London for most of her life and career. Died in Middlesex, aged 63. Works published by The London Press Exchange Ltd.

HODGKIN, ELIZABETH - SEE WATERHOUSE, E.

HOLDEN, EDITH BLACKWELL & EVELYN & VIOLET MARY (1871-1920) & (1877-1969) & (1874-1958)

Artists. Three artist daughters of Arthur Holden and Emma Wearing. Both parents originated from Bristol. The Holdens had at least six children (Winifred, Arthur K., Edith, Violet, Bernard and Evelyn), all born between 1869 and 1877. Arthur Holden was a varnish and paint manufacturer in Solihull, Birmingham, and all the children were born in and around the Midlands. They were raised in Solihull, living at The Elms and, later, The Gowans, with servants. At the age of 75, their father was a widow and still running his own business. At that point, Edith, Winifred and Violet were still living at the family home, aged between 37 and 42, all unmarried.

Edith Holden became a painter and illustrator. She was born in Kings Norton, Birmingham in late 1871. Studied at the Birmingham School of Art between 1885 and 1901. Also studied under Joseph Denoval Adam at Craigmill, Stirling between 1891 and 1892. She taught at private schools between 1906 and 1909. Produced oil and watercolour paintings, usually plants and animals, and book illustrations. Illustrated several books including Helen van Cleve Blankmeyer, Three Goats Gruff (n.d.), Margaret Gatty, Daily Bread (1910), Margaret Rankin, Woodland Whisperings (1911) and Martin Merrythought, Animals Around Us (1912). Contributed illustrations to The Animals' Friend, the magazine of the National Council for Animal Welfare, and to Mrs Strang's Annual for Children. Edith is largely known today for her Country Diary of an Edwardian Lady, which was published by Webb & Bower in 1977. The book contained watercolour sketches of plants found by Edith on her country walks. Although listed as still living at home in 1911, aged 39, in that year she married sculptor Alfred Ernest Smith in Chelsea. The couple lived in Chelsea. On one of her sketching walks, Edith accidentally drowned in the Thames, dying at Richmond, Surrey, aged

48. Exhibited her work in Birmingham and Liverpool, at the Royal Academy (1907 & 1917) and the Society of Women Artists (1903). Exhibited works included: Changing Pasture, The Rowan Tree, Young Bears Playing and The Guardian of the Plaid.

Evelyn Holden was an artist, illustrator and designer. Born in Warwickshire. Like Edith, studied at the Birmingham School of Art. Exhibited in the School's annual exhibitions, including in 1898, showing a design for stained glass which was illustrated in The Studio, Vol.13, April 1898, p.195. Also contributed to the School's 1901 exhibition of student work held at the Society of Arts rooms. There, Evelyn showed a frieze in relief. With Violet Holden and others, contributed to the Birmingham Guild of Handicraft magazine Quest, and to the Yellow Book. Produced book illustrations with Violet, including for Blanche Atkinson, The Real Princess (1894) and Jack and the Bean Stalk (1895). Also for The House That Jack Built (1895) for the Banbury Cross series for Dent & Co. With stained glass artist Florence Camm, whose family glass business was based in Birmingham, Evelyn designed a silver casket with enamel and repoussé, to contain the Freedom of the City of Birmingham. It was presented to J. Thackeray Bunce, J.P. and exhibited at the Spring Exhibition of the Birmingham Society of Artists in 1901. Evelyn also exhibited at the 1903 Arts and Crafts Exhibition held at the New Gallery. Executed a needlework panel with Violet and Mary J. Newill, Gareth and Lyonors, shown at that exhibition. In 1904 Evelyn married Frank Mathews in Warwickshire. She died in Tonbridge, Kent, aged 91.

Violet Holden was an illustrator, artist and craftswoman. Born in Kings Norton, Birmingham. Also studied at the Birmingham School of Art. Showed some of her work in the School's exhibition for 1894. As a student, contributed to the National Competition of Schools of Art, showing a metal buckle in 1895. From around 1904 she taught at the School for Writing and Illumination. Like Evelyn, contributed to the Birmingham Guild of Handicraft magazine, Quest. Contributed to the 1893 Arts and Crafts Exhibition Society exhibition along with others who became known collectively as the Birmingham Group, including Charles Gere, E.H. New and Mary Newill. In the same year, A Book of Christmas Carols was published by George Allen, price 5s. The book was designed by members of the Birmingham School of Art, overseen by Arthur Gaskin. Violet was one of a number of artists to contribute drawings. Others included Mary Newill, Florence Rudland, Mildred Peacock and Bernard Sleigh. Violet also produced book illustrations with Evelyn, and designed bookplates. Designed decorative bookbindings, exhibiting examples in 1899. Contributed to the 1900 exhibition of the Sketch Club of the Birmingham School of Art Union, held in the Municipal School of Art, Birmingham. Other exhibitors included Celia Levetus, Arthur Gaskin, Fred Mason and Kate Bunce. Violet also exhibited at the Fine Art Society. Violet died in Surrey, aged 84. The Holden sisters were noted in R.E.D. Sketchley, English Book Illustration of To-day, London, Kegan Paul, 1903. One of Violet's bookplates was illustrated in Norna Labouchere, Ladies' Book-Plates, London, George Bell, 1895.

HOLDEN, MARGARET T. - SEE JONES, M.T.

HOLDERNESS, HELEN A. - SEE PAGE, H.A.

HOLIDAY, CATHERINE HARRIET (1839-1924)

Embroideress. Born in Preston, Lancashire. The daughter of Thomas Raven and Susannah. Her father, who originated from Norfolk, was a Church of England clergyman. She was raised in Sussex. One of at least five children (John, Jane, James, Eustace and Catherine). In 1864 she married artist / designer Henry George Alexander Holiday (1839-1927) in Denbighshire. Holiday was the son of Geoffrey, a teacher of languages. His mother, who originated from France, taught French and German. Henry Holiday became an influential stained glass designer, initially influenced by the Pre-Raphaelites. The couple initially lived at Marlborough Road, London, but spent much of their marriage at Oak Tree House in Hampstead. They had one daughter, Winifred Raven Holiday.

Possibly under Holiday's influence, Catherine became an expert and accomplished professional embroideress, working in collaboration with William Morris in the 1870s, and is still listed as active professionally in the 1881 and 1891 national census recordings. Embroidery silks were specially dyed to her specification by Thomas Wardle, President of the Silk Association of Great Britain and Ireland (Wardle's wife, Elizabeth, founded the Leek Embroidery Society in 1879). One coverlet alone executed by Mrs Holiday could sell for over £100 through the Morris & Co. firm. Morris provided the designs, and often advised on their execution, though she decided on technique and colour. She was

particularly known for her silk chain stitch hangings of floral design. Her work was praised by Walter Crane in his essay Notes on Needlework in the Present Century, published in association with the Northern Art Workers' Guild Exhibition of 1903, which suggests that Catherine was still active into the early 1900s. She also executed designs for her husband, including a wall hanging executed in around 1887. Catherine died at Chesterford Gardens, Hampstead, aged 85. Henry died some three years later.

HOLLAND, HESTER GASKELL - SEE GORST, H.G.

HOLLAND, ISABEL FISHLEY (b.1914)

Potter. Born in Braunton, Devon in February 1914. The daughter of William Fishley Holland (1889-1969) and Annie Jane. Her father was an earthenware potter. Isabel was educated at the St Andrew's School, Clevedon, Somerset. Her father, who was born in Fremington, Devon, was part of a family of potters who were well known in the area. The Fishley Holland Pottery, where William worked, was founded by George Fishley, who ran it from 1865 to 1906. When it was sold, Isabel's father moved to nearby Braunton, where Isabel was born, and established the Braunton Pottery on behalf of a man named Hooper. He then moved to Clevedon, and established his own pottery, subsequently assisted by Isabel and other members of the family. Isabel executed and exhibited her own work. Showed with the Red Rose Guild in Manchester, and with the Clifton Arts Club. Some of her work was illustrated in The Sphere.

HOLLAND, VERA MARY (1890-1974)

Painter / Embroideress / Tapestry Designer / Pen & Ink Artist. Born in Sileby, Leicestershire. The daughter of William Alfred Holland, a Chief Officer, M.N., and Mary Martin. Her father died whilst she was still a child. Studied under Edgar Lander, and at the Loughborough School of Art under S.B. Potter. Produced paintings in oils and watercolours, and pen & ink drawings. Subjects included flowers, portraits, buildings, figures and birds. Also produced embroideries and tapestry designs. Some of her designs were reproduced by Weldons and by Paton and Baldwins. Others were published in Stitchcraft and in Weldon's periodicals. Exhibited her work, including at the Royal Society of Painters in Watercolours, in the galleries of Leicester and Loughborough, and in Loughborough Town Hall. Also showed over 50 works at the Society of Women Artists between 1952 and 1972. Those included: Arums and

Shells (watercolour), Flatford Mill (pen & ink), Blenheim, Home of Sir Winston Churchill and Wood Sprite (ink & watercolour). Her portrait subjects included Princess Alexandra, Enoch Powell and ballerina Svetlana Berlosova. Elected an Associate of the Society of Women Artists (1954-60) and a Member (1961-75). Also a Member of the Claverden Art Club and of Leicester Sketch. Based in Silesby during her career. Died in Leicestershire, aged 84.

HOLLINGSWORTH, RUTH (1881-1945)

Painter. Born in Clapham, London. The daughter of Alexander Thomas Hollingsworth, who originated from Birmingham, and Charlotte, who originated from London. Her father was the proprietor of Engineering. One of at least eight children (Kate, Allen, Edith, Florence, Beatrice, Louisa, Ruth and Jessie), all born between 1871 and 1882. Raised in Clapham and in Hampstead. Educated at Hamilton House and in Lausanne. Studied in London, at the Slade School and the London School of Art. Became a painter of landscapes, portraits and still life, mainly in oils. Remained in Hampstead initially, but was later based at Holbrook, Suffolk and in Essex. Died in Colchester, Essex in early 1945, aged 63. Exhibited her work at the New English Art Club (from 1910), the Royal Institute of Oil Painters, the Royal Academy (1906-38) and the Society of Women Artists (1914-18). Exhibited at the Women's International Art Club. For example, in 1912 she showed The Bather, and in 1913 showed Anemones. Exhibited at the Grosvenor Gallery at a Colour magazine exhibition held in 1922. Also held several one-woman shows at the Goupil Gallery. Other exhibited works included: Odds and Ends, Long Eliza with Carnation, From a Window at Chelsea and The Way to Florence. Elected a Member of the Women's International Art Club. Elected an Associate of the Society of Women Artists (1916) and a Member (1917-19). Also a Member of the Forum Club. Works illustrated in Colour, Sphere, Homes and Gardens and Pears Annual. Her The Tea-Cup was illustrated in Colour, March 1922.

Hollingsworth was a main contributor to an Exhibition of Works by Women Artists staged at Waring & Gillow's in 1916. She was the Honorary Secretary and organiser. The exhibition aimed to raise funds to assist women artists who were suffering due to war. The Queen and Princess Mary visited and purchased a number of works, including one by Hollingsworth. She was invited to take tea with the Queen. In April 1917 Ruth married artist Richard Sydney Hellaby, the son of Richard Hellaby, a merchant. Hellaby, a

Lieutenant who fought in the First World War, was then 29. She was 35. They married in London. He resumed his career after the war, exhibiting at the Royal Academy (1921-36). Ruth exhibited less after her marriage, but evidently continued to paint until shortly before her death. The couple had two daughters, Lettice (b.1918) and Felicity (b.1921). They travelled to New Zealand, America and South Africa during their marriage. Richard Hellaby survived his wife by some five years, dying in Kensington in early 1950.

HOLMAN, AGNES GLADYS (1885-1966)

Illustrator / Painter / Sculptor. Born in Cheltenham in October 1885. The daughter of Walter Henry Holman, a gentleman farmer, and Agnes Frederica. Both parents originated from Gloucestershire. Had at least one sibling, Walter. Educated at the Oakover Girls' School, Burnham, Somerset. Studied at the St John's Wood School of Art, London. Remained in London for much of her career, but died in Bath, aged 80. Produced animal, portrait, landscape and miniature paintings in oils and watercolours, occasional sculptures and book and general illustrations. Produced illustrations for Messrs G. Bell, for the Oxford Press and for Scout and Guiding publications. She had a keen interest in Girl Guiding. Other works were reproduced in Time and Tide and in the daily press. Sculptures included a memorial tablet to the flood victims for Dalgarrog Church, North Wales.

During the war, Holman worked in the Land Army, and later became a member of the Ex-Service Women's Club. Also had close ties with the Royal Drawing Society, where she was awarded medals and book prizes along with 14 gold stars. Elected a Member of the Society in 1918. Also elected a Member of the Society of Miniaturists in 1912. Acted as examiner and teacher of children's drawing at the Royal Drawing Society. In 1932 she was elected a Knight of the Round Table, Tintagel. Exhibited her work occasionally, including at the Royal Society of Painters in Watercolours and the Society of Women Artists (1909 & 1954). Exhibited works included: St Patrick's Day (miniature portrait), Runaway Water-Cart, Toledo and Gaslight and Washing Day (watercolour).

HOLMES, MADELINE R. - SEE
WELLS, M.R.

HOLT, ROSE GWYNNETH (1909-95)
Sculptor. Known as Gwynneth. Born in Wednesbury, Staffordshire in January 1909. The daughter of Benjamin and Rose Hannah Holt. Her father, a butcher, originated from Darlaston, Walsall, her mother from Wednesbury. Had at least one younger sibling, Beryl. Raised in Wednesbury, at Trouse Lane. Educated at the St Anne's Convent, Birmingham. Studied at the Wolverhampton School of Art under Robert Jackson Emerson, A.R.B.S., between 1925 and 1930. Emerson had a studio in Wolverhampton and carried out various commissions including the R.N.V.R. Memorial at Wolverhampton. Holt became a sculptor, producing figures, groups and other subjects. Worked in wood, stoneware, bronze, copper, terracotta and ivory. She was recipient of the Feodora Gleichen Award for an ivory carving exhibited at the Royal Academy.

Holt had a long and distinguished career which spanned six decades, from the 1930s to the 1980s. Exhibited widely, including at the Royal Scottish Academy (1944-80), the Royal Glasgow Institute (1949-66), the Royal Academy (1938-69), the Scottish Society of Women Artists, the Society of Scottish Artists and the Royal Birmingham Society of Artists. Exhibited one work, Scilla (ivory), at the Society of Women Artists in 1953. Exhibited in the provinces, and with the Aberdeen Artists Society. Also, with the Society of Portrait Sculptors. For example, showed Christobelle (terracotta) with the Society in 1961. Other exhibited works included: Madonna and Child (oak), Magnolia (statuette, ivory), Thinking of Small Things (terracotta) and The Pink Dress (terracotta). Elected an Associate of the Royal Society of British Sculptors in 1943.

In mid-1934, Gwynneth married sculptor Thomas Bayliss Huxley Jones (1908-68). He too studied at the Wolverhampton School of Art, and at the Royal College of Art, London. Initially, Holt was based in Staffordshire, and is listed in Kelly's Directory of Staffordshire for 1932 as a teacher of arts and crafts. However, when Huxley Jones was made Principal of the school of sculpture at the Gray's Art School in Aberdeen, the couple moved to Scotland. Later, in around 1949, they moved to Broomfield, Chelmsford in Essex. Huxley Jones died there, and was buried at the local church of St Mary's. In 1971 Holt married Bishop (George) Eric Gordon in Chelmsford, and moved to Eynsham, Oxfordshire. There, she carried out some carving for the local church of St Leonard's. Gordon died

in 1992, and Gwynneth three years later in February 1995, aged 86. She was buried with Huxley Jones at St Mary's in Essex. During her lifetime her works were illustrated in various publications including The Studio in 1947 (Vol.134, September, p.63), in 1953 (Vols.145 / 146, p.175) and in 1961 (Vol.161, February, p.67). Also, in Sculpture Today and British Sculpture (E. Newton), and in Scottish Sculpture (T.S. Halliday and G. Bruce). Works acquired by the Wolverhampton Art Gallery and the Newport Art Gallery. The Aberdeen Art Gallery acquired her Annunciation. Private collectors of her work included Dr S.A. Schneidman of America who showed an interest in the work of several British women sculptors.

HONE, EVA SYDNEY (1894-1955)
Painter / Stained Glass Artist. One of Ireland's foremost stained glass artists. Known as Evie. Born in Dublin. The daughter of a wealthy businessman. Began her career by studying in London, at the Westminster School of Art and the L.C.C. Central School of Arts and Crafts under Walter Sickert (1860-1942) and Bernard Meninsky (1891-1950). In 1920 she went to Paris where she and lifelong friend Mainie Jellett (1897-1944) studied under Andre L'Hote (1885-1962). In 1921 they became pupils of Albert Gleizes (1881-1962), some of his first. Hone, essentially an abstract painter, became a member of the Abstraction-Creation group to which sculptor Barbara Hepworth belonged. However, Hone was also influenced by medieval Irish stone carvings, and by Georges Rouault (1871-1958). In 1933 she began designing for stained glass, employing her abstract background. Initially, her designs were made by London-based stained glass worker Wilhelmina Geddes (1887-1955). Later, she collaborated with An Tur Gloine (1935-44), an Irish co-operative stained glass workshop run by Sarah Purser. Hone's first window was The Annunciation (1933-34) for St Nahi's Church, Dundrum. She carried out numerous commissions for windows, including for St Michael's Church, Highgate, for the Church of the Immaculate Conception, Farm Street, London (1953) and for as far afield as Washington Cathedral, America. Based largely in Ireland during her career.

Hone eventually opened her own studio at Rathfarnham, Co. Dublin where she executed, among other commissions, The Crucifixion and The Last Supper for Eton College Chapel. Artist Elizabeth Rivers spent some time in Ireland, assisting Hone in her studio. Hone exhibited some of her paintings and stained glass designs at the Royal Hibernian Academy (1931-37), including A Glorious Mystery (stained glass design) and 10 works of no title in oils and gouache. In 1924 she and Jellett held an exhibition of paintings and drawings in Dublin. All 59 works lacked a title, something which caused some controversy and criticism at the time. In 1947 some of Hone's stained glass panels were included in an exhibition titled Living Irish Art held in London. Hone was one of the founders of the Irish Exhibition of Living Art. She had some considerable influence on modern Irish art, campaigning for its wider acceptance. After her death, in 1959, five of her cartoons were exhibited at the Tate Gallery, including one for Eton College Chapel. In the same year, an exhibition of her work was held at the Arts Council Gallery, which included actual stained glass windows designed by Hone.

In 1938 Hone was commissioned to produce a large window for the Irish Pavilion at the New York World Fair. Around the same time, she produced My Four Green Fields (1938-39) for the offices of Coras Iompair Eireann in O'Connell Street, Dublin. In her later career, she executed The Beatitudes (1946) and The Last Supper for the Chapel of St Stanislaus College, Tullabeg, part of a series of five windows. Also designed Ascension (1947-48), a window for the Catholic Church at Kingscourt, Co. Cavan. Before her death, she worked on a window for the Catholic Church at Blackrock, Co. Dublin. Works illustrated in The Studio. Works in the National Gallery of Ireland, the Hugh Lane Municipal Gallery, Dublin, the Crawford Municipal Art Gallery, Cork and the Ulster Museum, Belfast. Noted in E. Liddall Armitage, Stained Glass, 1960.

HOPE, EDITH ANNIE (1871-1942)

Painter / Etcher / Wood Engraver / Lithographer. Born in Sydney, Australia. The daughter of the Hon. Louis Hope of the Coldstream Guards. Educated in England, at the Cheltenham Ladies' College. Studied at the Slade School, London where she won two prizes. Spent much of her career in London (until at least the late 1920s). Spent her final years in Steep, Petersfield. In London, she lived for a while with her elder sister Henrietta. She too was born in Australia. Edith produced paintings in oils and watercolours, etchings, wood engravings and lithographs, various subjects. Exhibited her work, including at the Royal Scottish Academy (1913-25), the Royal Hibernian Academy (1932), the Royal Glasgow Institute (1916-28), the Royal Academy (1910-24), in Paris and America, and with the Women's

International Art Club. At the last of those she showed, for example, Portrait of a Girl in a Fur Hat in 1913. Other exhibited works included: The Porch, Chartres (watercolour), The Black Jug and Boatyard, Venice. In 1908, Hope contributed to an exhibition of work by students of the London School of Art, held at the Stratford Studios. Elected a Member of the Royal Society of British Artists, and of the Forum Club. Her etching The Beer Cellar was illustrated in The Studio, Vol.45, October 1908, p.77. One of her lithographs was purchased by a Canadian gallery.

HOPE, ROSA SOMERVILLE & MURIEL HOLINGER (1902-72) & (1902-63)

Artists. Born in Manchester in June 1902. The twin daughters of Herbert Somerville Hope (b.1872) and Ethel Holinger (b.1871). Both parents originated from Manchester. Herbert was a manufacturer's agent. Ethel was a painter who, in the 1890s, was a teacher of drawing in Warrington. She was the daughter of a commercial clerk. Ethel married Herbert in 1900. She exhibited her work at the Royal Academy in 1922. Perhaps unsurprisingly, both girls also became artists. They were raised in Stockport.

Rosa studied at the Slade School, London where she won a scholarship and various prizes. She was also a final competitor for the Prix de Rome (1926). Also studied at the L.C.C. Central School of Arts and Crafts. Produced etchings, watercolour paintings of various subjects, aquatints and chalk drawings. She was considered an excellent draughtsman. Worked as a teacher. Initially based in London. But by 1935 had moved to South Africa to work at the Michaelis School of Fine Art, Capetown University. In 1938 she then became a Senior Lecturer in Fine Art at the Natal University College, South Africa. She spent the rest of her life there and died there. However, she continued to exhibit her work in Britain.

During her career, Rosa exhibited at the New English Art Club, the Royal Society of Painter-Etchers & Engravers, with the Society of Graphic Art, the Hampstead Society of Artists and at Wembley (1925-26). Also, at the Brighton Art Gallery, the Manchester Art Gallery, the Plymouth and Belfast Art Galleries, the Royal Academy (1927-48), the Royal Scottish Academy (1927), the North British Academy, in Leeds, Glasgow, Hull and Liverpool, in Chicago, Philadelphia, Stockholm, Vienna, Capetown, Johannesburg, Bloemfontein and Durban. Held one-woman shows at the Rembrandt Gallery, London, the Gainsborough Galleries, Johannesburg and in Pietermaritzburg. Exhibited works included: The Victorian Dress (etching & aquatint), Girl with Guitar (chalk), The Adoration of the Shepherds (etching) and The Ballet Dress. Elected an Associate of the Royal Society of Painter-Etchers & Engravers (1923). Elected a Fellow of the South African Society of Artists. Some of her etchings were reproduced by the Fine Art Society. Other works were published by W.B. Paterson, London. Works purchased by the Municipal Gallery of Pietermaritzburg, South Africa, by the Manchester City Art Gallery, the National Gallery, Wales, the British Museum, the Victoria & Albert Museum, London, the South African National Gallery, Capetown, the State Museum, Eastern Slovakia and for the South African War Artists' Collection, Pretoria. Noted in Frank L. Emanuel, Etching and Etchings, London, Pitman & Sons, 1930.

Muriel Hollinger Hope also studied at the Slade School, London, winning a scholarship and a first prize in figure painting. Produced portrait, figure and landscape paintings. Exhibited her work, including at the Royal Academy (1929-50), the Goupil Gallery, the Paris Salon, with the New English Art Club and at the galleries of Bradford, Manchester, Leeds, Plymouth and Belfast. Exhibited works included: In the Fields, John M. Bacon, Esq., M.A., F.R.S.A, Bosham Creek and Sir Lewis Casson. Based in London and, later, Bosham, Sussex. In 1924 she married diplomat Sir John Everard Stephenson, K.C.M.G., C.V.O., O.B.E. (1893-1948). He died at Bosham. Muriel died at Minnadhu Cottage, Cawsand, Cornwall, aged 60.

HOPKINS, MRS ROBERT (active 1890s)
Woodcarver. Based in Birmingham. Largely self-taught. Had some lessons under Mr Claxton of Worcester. Worked as a professional decorative carver rather than as an amateur. Did some teaching in the Midland counties. Held large classes in Walsall and other towns. Her first commission was for a settle for the Senior Tutor of Trinity Hall, Cambridge, with the college arms on the centre panel. One of her carved panels was illustrated in The Studio, Vol.11, 1897, p.124.

HORSMAN, KATHLEEN FINLAY (1911-99)
Potter / Painter. Born in London in April 1911. The daughter of Herbert William Horsman. Educated at the Hornsey High School. Studied at the Hornsey School of Arts and Crafts under John C. Moodie between 1929 and 1933. Also, at the Royal College of Art under William Staite Murray between 1933 and 1937. Elected an Associate of the Royal College of Art in 1936.

Became pottery instructor at the Liverpool City School of Art between 1938 and 1942. In 1942 she took up the post of senior lecturer in ceramics at the Edinburgh College of Art. She was still teaching into the late 1950s. Lived in Edinburgh for much of her career, using a studio at West Bow for part of the time. Died in Scotland. Exhibited her work, including at the Enterprise Scotland (1947), with the Society of Scottish Artists and the Scottish Society of Women Artists. Elected a Member of the Society of Scottish Artists, the Scottish Society of Women Artists and of the Saltire Society. Works purchased by the David Muirhead Bequest. Some of her work was reproduced in Ronald G. Cooper, The Modern Potter. Elected M.B.E. Visited New York several times in the 1950s.

HORTON, SARAH ELIZABETH ROBERTS (1865-1959)
Painter / Gesso Panel Artist / Book Illustrator. Born in Australia in October 1865. The daughter of Thomas Horton, a mining engineer reputed to be the first to discover silver in Australia. Studied at the Bushey School of Art, Hertfordshire under Professor Hubert von Herkomer, and at the Branch Schools of South Kensington. Won various scholarships and medals. Later spent some time living with an aunt in Sydenham, Gt. London. Latterly based in Bath, Somerset where she died, aged 94. She never married and apparently had virtually no family in England. Produced paintings in oils and watercolours, various subjects including portraits, gesso panels and book illustrations. Executed gesso panels for, for example, Lyndhurst Church, St Michael's Church, Golders Green and St Philip's Church at Sydenham. Queen Victoria twice purchased her work. Taught pupils in her own studio. Exhibited her work, including at the Royal Academy (1934-39), the Royal Society of British Artists (1890 / 91), the Royal Institute of Painters in Watercolours, the Society of Women Artists (1889-98) and at various provincial galleries. Exhibited works included: The Library Door (watercolour), Low Tide at Evening (watercolour), Rough Sea, Cornwall and To Let (watercolour). Elected a Member of the British Watercolour Society.

HOUGHTON, ELIZABETH ELLEN (1853-1922)
Illustrator / Painter. Born in Warrington, and died there aged 69. The daughter of James Bolton and Henrietta. Her father died when she was still a child. Raised in Warrington. One of at least four children (James, Henrietta, Elizabeth and

Charles). In 1875 she married Hamlet Newhall Houghton (b.1852) in Liverpool. He was an ironmonger who also originated from Warrington. They lived mainly in Warrington. The couple appears to have had no children. Elizabeth worked as an artist both before and after her marriage, and continued to work after her husband's death in 1908. Later in her career, she was based in Runcorn (where Hamlet died) and at Grappenhall, both Cheshire. Remained active until shortly before her death. Specialised in illustrating children's books. Those included: Abroad For Marcus Ward (with T. Crane, c.1881) and The Adventures of Little Man-Chester (1887). Contributed to The Dome. At the 1899 Exhibition of Pictures & Decorative Art held in Kendal, Westmorland, Houghton showed two pastel sketches, which were designs for panels taken from Tennyson. Exhibited two works, An August Morning and Four O'Clock, at the Society of Women Artists in 1919. Also exhibited in Liverpool and Manchester. Possibly had connections with the Northern Art Workers' Guild. Designed a poster for the Guild's 1898 Manchester exhibition. Possibly the same Ellen Houghton who exhibited embroidery at the same exhibition. Works in the Victoria & Albert Museum, London and in the Delaware Art Museum. Works illustrated in The Studio, Vol.15, November 1898, p.126.

HOUGHTON, EVELYN E. - SEE JARMAIN, E.E.

HOUSEMAN, EDITH GIFFARD (1875-1960)

Artist / Wood Engraver. Born at Bredwardine, Herefordshire in December 1875. Raised in Northamptonshire. The daughter of the Rev. John Houseman and Edith. One of at least four children (John, Leonora, Lucy and Edith). Her father died whilst she was still a child. Educated at home with a governess, and at the Bedford High School. Studied art under Claude Hayes, R.I., Walter Donne and Frank Calderon. Produced paintings in oils and watercolours, wood engravings, pen & ink drawings and portraits in pencil. Subjects also included landscape, still life and buildings. Spent time living with her brother and Leonora in Surrey in her 20s. Later based in Petworth, Sussex, dying in Sussex in 1960, aged 85. Exhibited extensively throughout her career, over a period of more than 54 years. Exhibited at the Royal Scottish Academy (1908-37), the Royal Academy (1906-38), the Royal Hibernian Academy (1913-14), the Royal Society of British Artists, the Scottish Society of Women Artists

and the Royal Institute of Painters in Watercolours. Exhibited 90 works at the Society of Women Artists (1920-60). Exhibited works included: Moel Siabod, Wales, The Seagull's Haunt, Study by Electric Light and The Orange Jar, Late Autumn Roses. Elected an Associate of the Society of Women Artists (1927-47) and a Member (1948-60). Also a Member of the Irish Three Arts Club and of the Faculty of Art. Travelled to paint, including to Ireland. Works in the permanent collection of the Towner Art Gallery, Eastbourne.

HOUSTON, MARY GALWAY (1871-1962)

Designer / Craftswoman. One of Ireland's most prominent and successful early twentieth century craftswomen, whose influence was also felt in England. Born in Coleraine, Co. Londonderry, Ireland in July 1871. The daughter of Thomas Galway Houston and Maud Steen Millar. Raised in Ireland. Studied at the Metropolitan School of Art, Dublin from 1890. In 1894 and 1895 she exhibited lace and crochet at the Royal Dublin Society as well as black & white designs at the Arts and Crafts Society of Ireland. Also won prizes for her leatherwork and repoussé metalwork around that time. In 1896 she moved to London to study at the Royal College of Art, South Kensington, where she was a gold medallist. In the same year, she won a first prize in The Studio magazine competition. In 1898 she contributed to the National Competition of Schools of Art, South Kensington, showing an embossed leather book cover. At the 1899 National Competition, whilst still a student, she showed an embossed leather book cover titled Hand and Soul, and a silver mirror, brush and comb with a design based on the flowing hair of a female figure, suggesting the influence of Art Nouveau in her work. At the same Competition, she showed a silk portiere with a St George and the Dragon design in applique embroidery, demonstrating her diversity and talent in various areas of the decorative arts. Some of the above were illustrated in The Studio, Vol.17, September 1899, pp.251-253.

Houston remained in London for at least the next seven or eight years, establishing herself as a successful craftswoman. She returned to Ireland sometime after 1907. For part of the time, she shared digs in Coulston Street, Chelsea with embroidery designer Mary Bella Canning, who also originated from Ireland. She then spent some time living in Brunswick Square, Camberwell. Although resident in London for a comparatively short time, Houston certainly made a considerable impact with her work, winning a deal of attention and praise. She began to exhibit her work more seriously in 1899 when she presumably finished her studies at South Kensington. In that year she contributed to the sixth Arts and Crafts Exhibition Society exhibition held at the New Gallery, London, showing a binding for the Kelmscott Chaucer which was praised in The Studio as one of the most interesting exhibits of the year. Houston also produced a leather panel which was used in a bookbinding designed and tooled by Johanna Birkenruth titled The Little Mermaid. The binding was illustrated in The Studio, Vol.18, Special Number 1899-1900, p.43 in an article British Tooled Bookbindings and Their Designers. The same panel was illustrated in the Art Journal, 1899, p.317. Houston was clearly not averse to working with others, and subsequently executed an album, in tooled leather with illuminated address and leather medallions, which had an interlaced design by Irish artist Lilian Davidson and silver corners by M.W.C. Wheeler. The album was shown at the 1904 Irish Arts and Crafts Society exhibition held in Dublin and was illustrated in The Studio, Vol.33, January 1905, p.364. Houston executed another leather panel for a binding of Keats's Odes, Sonnets & Lyrics, also bound by Birkenruth in around 1899.

In 1901, Houston exhibited another such panel in stained leather at the First International Studio Exhibition of 1901-02. In the same year, she began to exhibit at the Royal Academy, eventually showing five works there up to 1904 including a panel in leather titled The Return of Kilmeny and two leather medallions titled Sleep and St Cecilia. Although exhibiting predominantly in England, during her time in London she continued to exhibit in Ireland. In 1902 she sent a silver-plated casket to the Cork Exhibition, where a section was set aside for women decorative artists. The casket was illustrated in The Studio, Vol.24-25, 1902, p.296. As always, her work was commended for careful attention to detail, exquisite design and expert execution. In 1903 she contributed to the seventh Arts and Crafts Exhibition Society exhibition, again held at the New Gallery, London. The mere fact that she was included in such a prestigious exhibition again indicates the exceptionally high standard of her work. Also in 1903, Houston became a member of the newly-founded Dress Designers' Exhibition Society and contributed enamels and jewellery to its first exhibition held in 1903 at the Dore Gallery, New Bond Street, London. The Society aimed to improve popular taste in dress and personal adornment and to challenge conventionality. President of the Society was Walter Crane. Other members included Annie Garnett of Windermere.

In the same year, the Art Workers' Quarterly, July, p.121 illustrated a portion of a belt in embossed leather designed by Houston along with working drawings of an embossed leather bag and belt, which accompanied an article Embossing and Chasing Leather written by Houston. The same journal had already illustrated two of her panels for a casket designed and worked by her in leather in October 1902. From at least 1906 (probably earlier) Houston taught box-making at the Camberwell School of Arts and Crafts, yet another aspect of her creativity. In later years she published at least three authoritative books on the subject of costume, including Ancient Egyptian, Assyrian and Persian Costumes (A. & C. Black, 1920, with Florence Hornblower) and Medieval Costume in England and France: 13th, 14th & 15th Centuries (A. & C. Black, 1939). In 1950 John P. Harthan's volume Victoria & Albert Museum Bookbindings was published, containing an illustration of Houston's binding for the Rubaiyat of Omar Khayyam (executed c.1899).

Houston died in Co. Down, Ireland in April 1962, leaving only a small estate. Possibly of the same family was miniature painter Margaret M. Houston of The College, Coleraine, Ireland, who also exhibited at the Royal Academy (1904). Unlike Houston, Mary Bella Canning remained in England, dying in Worthing, Sussex in March 1964, aged 88. Like Houston, Canning was born in Coleraine. She was the daughter of John James Carter Canning, a bank manager, and Annie Bellas. In 1912 she married Freeman Willis Crofts (1879-1957), an engineer. They had no children. He originated from Dublin. The couple moved to Sussex in 1953.

HOW, FRANCES THALIA (1871-1944)

Jeweller / Enameller / Painter / Metalworker. Born in New South Wales, Australia. The daughter of Janet F. Stobbs of Kelso, Scotland. Had at least one sibling, Louisa. Lived in Scotland from at least 1891; probably studied there. Subsequently moved to London with her mother. Had a studio there from at least 1911. Active until at least the early 1930s. Remained in London, dying in Kensington, aged 73. Produced watercolour paintings, enamels, decorative jewellery and metalwork. Exhibited her work, including at the Royal Academy (1913-14), the Society of Women Artists (1930-32), the Royal Scottish Academy (1912-28) and the International Society of Sculptors, Painters & Gravers. Also, at the Salon des Beaux-Arts in

Paris and with the Arts and Crafts Exhibition Society. Exhibited a copper bowl and other items of decorative metalwork at the Edinburgh Arts and Crafts' Club exhibition of 1905. Exhibited works included: The Message (enamels, bassetaille), Charity; Mater Domini (prayer case of bassetaille enamels), A Procession of Life (champleve enamels for triptych) and The Crystal Gazer (enamels, bassetaille). Elected a Member of the Sesame Club.

HOWARD, CONSTANCE MILDRED (1910-2000)

Wood Engraver / Embroideress. Born in Northampton in December 1910. The daughter of Arthur Howard, a schoolmaster, and Mildred. Her father originated from Northampton, her mother from Norfolk. Educated at the Barry Road Girls' Intermediate School. Studied at the Northampton School of Art between 1925 and 1931, under Lewis Duckett between 1929 and 1931, and at the Royal College of Art, London under Professor Ernest William Tristram, Eric Ravilious and Edward Bawden between 1931 and 1935. Elected an Associate of the Royal College of Art in 1935. Produced mainly wood engravings and embroidery. Worked as a part-time lecturer at the Goldsmiths' School of Art. Also acted as art teacher at the Cardiff School of Art between 1935 and 1938. A lecturer on women's crafts at the Eastbourne School of Art between 1938 and 1939 and at the Kingston-upon-Thames School of Art between 1939 and 1946.

Howard exhibited her work, including with the Society of Wood Engravers, the Arts and Crafts Society, the Arts Council travelling exhibitions and the Pictures for Schools exhibitions. Her work was reproduced in The Listener, the Illustrated London News and Sport and Country. In 1955, two of her embroideries, The Sisters and The Visitors, were illustrated in The Studio, Vol.50, September in an article Contemporary Needlework Pictures by Dora Billington. Howard is there described as a 'skilled needlewoman' who used patterned materials in her embroidery and a variety of stitches to create largely decorative works. Howard created a large panel, or wall hanging, which was shown at the South Bank Exhibition and which depicted the activities of the Women's Institutes. She was elected to the Art Workers' Guild in 1974. During her career, she also contributed articles on women's crafts and embroidery to the Odhams Press. Purchasers of her work included the Arts Council, the Festival of Britain and some local Education Committees. In 1945 she married sculptor Harold Wilson Parker (b.1896) in Surrey. They had at least one daughter. For some of the time, they lived in Chelsea. Constance died in Surrey.

HOWARD, FERELYTH A. - SEE WILLS, F.A.

HOWARD, MARGARET MAITLAND (1898-post-1952)

Painter / Illustrator. Born in Friern Barnet, Middlesex in July 1898. The daughter of Henry James Howard and Margaretta Magdalena. Her father was a post office clerk in Barnet. Possibly an only child, raised in Middlesex. Educated privately. Studied in London, at the Byam Shaw and Vicat Cole School of Art and at the Royal Academy schools. Awarded five silver medals, a British Institute Scholarship and extension, and a Certificate Prize for a portrait head at the National Welsh Eisteddfod at Swansea in 1926. Also awarded a Royal Academy Certificate and Society of Arts Certificates in French and Spanish. Produced subject and portrait paintings in oils, illustrations in black & white and colour, works in pastels and watercolours, miniatures and figures. Based in Sutton, Surrey during her career. Illustrated, for example, The Fables of Aesop (Bodley Head) and Rovers and Stay-at-Homes (Dent). Works also reproduced in Academy Illustrated and American Weekly. Worked on three volumes, Through the Green Meadows, Dating the Past and Ancient India. Acted as an artist and research worker for the Institute of Archaeology, University of London. Exhibited her work, including at the Royal Academy (1923-35), the Royal Society of Portrait Painters, the Royal Institute of Oil Painters, the New English Art Club, the Walker Art Gallery, Liverpool, the Hull Municipal Gallery, in Bournemouth and at the Panton Club. Exhibited works included: Thermuthis, Adam and Eve, Apollo and Daphne and The Judgement of Paris. Elected a Fellow of the Zoological Society. Elected a Member of the Ridley Art Club and of the Campden Hill Club.

HOWSON, JOAN (1885-1964)

Artist / Stained Glass Designer. Born at Overton-on-Dee, Flintshire. The daughter of the Rev. George Howson, later Archdeacon of Liverpool. Studied music for a time. But, in around 1909, she began studying at the Liverpool School of Art, concentrating on textile design and stained glass work. Subsequently became an apprentice to stained glass designer Caroline Townshend (1878-1944) in Fulham. During the First World War, Howson went abroad, working with refugees, also establishing employment schemes for women in France. She returned to London in 1920, and formed a stained glass partnership with Townshend. Townshend worked mainly on the designs whilst Howson was largely responsible for their execution. She also specialised in the repair of medieval glass. In 1926 the duo moved to Deodar Road, Putney.

The Second World War caused further disruption, and the two women joined fellow stained glass designer Margaret Rope in caring for evacuated children in Wales. Townshend died in 1944, and after the war Howson continued to produce stained glass at Putney under the Townshend and Howson name until the 1950s. The firm's commissions included a memorial window to a mountain climber for Platt Chapel, Manchester (1921), stained glass for Morpeth Parish Church, Northumberland (1929) and for the Chapel of the Royal Southern Hospital, Liverpool (1931). Also, a memorial window to Bishop James Hannington in Hannington Hall, St Peter's House, Oxford (1928-29), and a three-light window, St Hugh of Lincoln, for Ducklington Church, Oxfordshire (1934). Howson's later solo commissions included stained glass for the Savoy Chapel, London (1952-58) and for Namirembe Cathedral, Uganda (1952-54). Her restoration projects included the repair of windows in the Chapter House, Westminster Abbey (1947). One of the firm's most important repair commissions was carried out for New College, Oxford from 1933 onwards, and involved the repair of its fourteenth-century windows. At the time of her death, Howson was living in a cottage in Wales. Three of her designs were exhibited at the Royal Academy in 1934 and 1935. Those were a Lewis Carroll memorial window, a design for the Church of the Holy Trinity, Leamington and a design for the Empire Hostel, Limehouse.

HUBBALL, ELSIE (1902-93)

Painter / Embroideress / Leatherworker. Born in Wolverhampton. The daughter of Thomas A. Hubball, a toolmaker in the cycle trade, and Annie. Educated at the Higher Grade School, Wolverhampton. Studied at the Wolverhampton School of Art. Awarded the Oxford Junior Certificate. Also, a full Technological Certificate of City & Guilds of London in embroidery. Based in Wolverhampton. Died there, aged 90. Produced watercolour paintings, embroideries and leatherwork. Exhibited her work occasionally, including with the Royal Birmingham Society of Artists, at the Walker Art Gallery, Liverpool and with the Wolverhampton and Dudley Art Circles.

HUDSON, GWYNEDD MAY (1881-1932)

Painter / Illustrator. Born in Kensington, London. The daughter of William Henry Hudson, a bank manager, and Mary. One of at least three children (Gwynedd, Dorothy and George). Raised in Kensington, though the family subsequently moved to Hove, Sussex (between 1891 and 1901). Gwynedd studied at the Brighton Municipal School of Art whilst living at Hove. As a student, she gained a distinction in the National Competition of Schools of Art. At the 1907 National Competition, she showed a design for a mural decoration. Became a book illustrator in black & white and colour, particularly of fairy tales, a painter of various subjects and a poster designer. Books illustrated by her included Lewis Carroll, Alice's Adventures in Wonderland (12 colour plates and text decoration, 1922) and J.M. Barrie, Peter Pan and Wendy (1931). Designed posters for the Underground Group (1926-29), now in the London Transport Museum. Exhibited one work, Winter, at the Royal Academy in 1912. Showed book illustrations at the 1910 Arts and Crafts Exhibition Society exhibition. Also exhibited with the Sussex Women's Art Club in Brighton. Used the Wick Studio, Holland Road, Hove for part of her career. Her sister, Dorothy Cecil Hudson (1882-1935), was also an artist. Neither sister lived to a great age. Gwynedd died in Sussex, aged 51. Gwynedd's The Changeling (watercolour) was illustrated full-page in The Studio, Vol.69, 1916-17, p.151.

HUGGETT, BESSIE (1861-1945)

Ecclesiastical Embroideress / Decorative Artist. A prominent professional embroideress, active in the late nineteenth and early twentieth centuries. Executed work for several prominent design figures of the day. Born in Brighton, Sussex and spent much of her life there. But did spend some time living in London in the 1910s with her sister, Ellen, who was then a secretary superintendent at Guy's Hospital. Bessie died in Hove, Sussex, aged 83. She was the daughter of Bryant Frederick Huggett, a grocer, and Elizabeth. Both parents originated from Brighton. One of at least three children (Harriett, Ellen and Bessie). Became particularly well known in her lifetime for working the church embroidery designs of Aymer Vallance (1862-1943) and William Harrison Cowlishaw (1870-1957). Cowlishaw was a London-based architect and potter who produced illuminated manuscripts. Vallance, a Reverend and former Oxford graduate based in London and Sussex, was an artist, designer and writer on art and architecture.

In 1893, Huggett contributed to the Arts and Crafts Exhibition Society exhibition, showing a stole designed by Vallance and worked by her. She also showed part of a portiere, also designed by Vallance. At the 1896 Arts and Crafts exhibition, she contributed a painted vellum binding worked by her to the design of Vallance and shown under his name. In 1899 she showed a book cover worked by her to a design by Vallance at the Exhibition of Pictures & Decorative Art held in Kendal, Westmorland. Two banners designed by Vallance and executed by Bessie were illustrated in The Studio, Vol.19, February 1900, p.43. A frontal cloth for a Rosary Altar designed by Cowlishaw and worked by Bessie was illustrated in the same edition (p.49). The frontal was made of white satin with a gold fringe, with leaves and roses of green satin and pink velvet, with embroidery. The 15 roses incorporated into the design represented the 15 mysteries of the Rosary.

HUGHES, CATHERINE EDITH (1871-1934)

Enameller / Artist. Born and raised in Bristol. Studied in London and Paris. Spent some time in Sheffield in the early 1890s, where she was a boarder with William Straw, a metal traders' agent. She returned to Bristol in the early 1900s, subsequently living at Letchworth, Hertfordshire in the early 1910s before returning to Bristol by at least the very early 1930s. She died in Bristol, aged 63. Early in her career, she is listed as a printer-artist. But she was better known for her enamelling on metal. She executed the Royal Badge of the Welsh Dragon, in translucent enamels, which was illustrated in The Studio, Vol.38, June 1906, p.72. The badge was mounted in a silver setting of a leek design and received the approbation of H.R.H. the Prince of Wales when he laid the foundation stone of the University buildings at Cardiff, where it formed one of the decorations of his private rooms. He later accepted it as a reminder of his visit. Her enamels were much sought after and highly regarded in her day. She was known for her exquisite use of colour and originality. Exhibited her work occasionally, including at the Royal West of England Academy and at various Arts and Crafts exhibitions. Elected a Member of the Royal West of England Academy. Used St Vincent's Studio, Redland, Bristol during her later career.

HUMPHREYS, AILEEN MAUDE (1891-1975)

Silversmith / Goldsmith / Enameller / Jeweller. Born at Escrick, Yorkshire in September 1891.

The daughter of Charles I. Faulkner, a physician and surgeon, and Alice. Raised in Escrick. Educated at the Queen Margaret's School, Scarborough. Studied in London at the L.C.C. Central School of Arts and Crafts. Based in London for part of her career. Exhibited her work at the Arts and Crafts Exhibitions in London and at Wembley (1924-25). In 1927 she married Christmas Humphreys in Brentford, Middlesex. She died in Middlesex, aged 84.

HUNT, AMY HENRIETTA (1856-91)

Sculptor. Born in Westminster, London. The daughter of James Hunt (1833-69) and Henrietta Maria. One of at least five children (Mary Ann, Eliza, Jane, Amy and James), all raised in London. Her father is listed in the Dictionary of National Biography as an ethnologist and writer who specialised in the subject of stammers and stammering, but also as having a testing personality, to the detriment of his career. Amy studied sculpture in London, and is listed as an art student in 1881, lodging with other students, including other female art students. She was subsequently based at the Kensington Studios and at the Stratford Studios, Kensington, working as a sculptor of heads and busts in terracotta. Exhibited her work, including at the Royal Academy (1888-91), the Royal Society of British Artists (1887-89) and the Society of Women Artists (1888-90). Exhibited works included: La Grandmere (bust), Pensive (bust), An Armenian (bust) and Volumnia (head). Amy's career was curtailed by her premature death in Windsor, Berkshire, aged 34. Also at the Stratford Studios was painter Mary Hunt, who exhibited her work at the Royal Hibernian Academy and the Royal Glasgow Institute. She appears not to have been directly related to Amy. Mary Ann, Amy's sister, became a music teacher.

HUNT, GLADYS MILLAIS MULOCK HOLMAN (1876-1952)

Sculptor. Born in Jerusalem. The daughter of eminent Pre-Raphaelite artist William Holman Hunt (1827-1910) and his second wife, Marion Edith. They also had a son, Hilary. Gladys was raised in London. Studied sculpture, probably in London or Paris. Produced statuettes and busts in bronze. Exhibited her work, including at the Royal Academy (1911-20) and with the International Society of Sculptors, Painters & Gravers, including in 1911. Exhibited works included: The Refugee (bust), Phyllida Flouts Me (bust, bronze), Bereft (bust) and Daphne (statuette). In 1918 she married Henry Michael

Joseph in Kensington. He was a doctor. Gladys died in London, aged 76.

HUNT, WINIFRED FLORENCE (b.1878)

Sculptor. Born in Japan. The daughter of Henry J. Hunt and Clara. Her father was a tea manufacturer in Japan. One of at least three children (Edith, Winifred and Edward). Based in Wimbledon and Putney during her career. Produced busts and statuettes in ivory, marble and bronze. Exhibited only occasionally. Showed two works at the Royal Academy, Miss Edith Hunt (bust, marble & bronze) in 1903 and Lamia (statuette, ivory) in 1904.

HUNTON, CHARLOTTE ELIZABETH (1857-1925)

Sculptor. Born in Tottenham. The daughter of Thomas Hunton, a teacher, and Charlotte. Her father originated from Norfolk, her mother from Ireland. The second of at least three children (Theodore, Charlotte and Alfred), born between 1855 and 1859. Her mother died young, and the family moved to Devon sometime prior to 1861. By at least 1871 they were based at Brows Hill, Torquay, where Charlotte was still living in the 1890s. Charlotte studied sculpture, possibly in Torquay. Produced heads and statuettes in bronze. Exhibited occasionally, including at the Royal Academy (1892-93). Exhibited works included: A Young Bacchante (statuette, bronze), Bacchante: Head and Vanity (statuette). In 1893 Charlotte married Henry William Jacob in Newton Abbot, Devon. Jacob was a medical practitioner who originated from Dublin, Ireland. The couple lived in Worcestershire. It is difficult to ascertain if Charlotte continued to work after her marriage. She died in Worcestershire, aged 68. Jacob died three years later, also in Worcestershire.

HURD, MARGARET McFARLANE (1902-91)

Etcher / Painter / Leatherworker / Craftswoman. Born in Bothwell near East Kilbride, Scotland in September 1902. The daughter of F.W. Hurd, a consulting engineer. Educated at a private school for the deaf at Callander, Perthshire. Studied at the Harrow School of Art, Gt. London, and at private classes. Travelled in Britain and abroad to paint. Based in Middlesex for much of her career, but latterly based at Grindleford, Derbyshire. Died in Derbyshire, aged 88. Awarded a gold medal by the Panton Art Club, and a bronze medal by The Artist magazine. Painted flowers, landscapes and buildings in oils and watercolours, produced etchings, leatherwork

and other craftwork. Exhibited extensively over a period of more than 26 years, including at the Royal Scottish Academy (1929-52), the Royal Glasgow Institute (1930-54), the Royal Academy (1929-48) and the Society of Women Artists (1928-54). Also, at the Royal Cambrian Academy, with the Scottish Society of Women Artists, the Society of Graphic Art, the Aberdeen Art Society, the United Society of Artists and at the Paisley Art Institute. Exhibited works included: Lupins (oil), At Limehouse, London (watercolour), In the Forum, Rome (etching) and In the Market, Florence (etching). Elected a Member of the Glasgow Lady Artists' Club and of the Scottish Society of Women Artists. Her Three Sisters, Glencoe was illustrated in The Artist. Her etching of St Bride's Parish Church, Bothwell was published by S. & G. Ponton Ltd.

HUTCHINSON, CONSTANCE E. - SEE ROWLANDS, C.E.

HYNES, GLADYS MARGARET JERMYN (1888-1958)

Painter / Sculptor / Decorative Artist. Born in Indore, India. The daughter of Harry Hugh Hynes, a banker, and Edith Power. One of at least five children (Harry, Eileen, Gladys, Hugh and Ernest). Educated privately. Studied under Cornish-based artist Stanhope Alexander Forbes, and at the London School of Art. Spent much of her career in London, but also later spent time living and working in Penzance, Cornwall. Died in Harrow, aged 70. Produced paintings and portrait sculptures, illustrations and decorative work. Provided illustrations for Ezra Pound, Cantos (John Rodker). Exhibited her work occasionally, including at the Royal Academy (1912-33), the Salon des Artistes Francais, the Venice International, with the London Group and with the International Society of Sculptors, Painters & Gravers. Works included: Oakley Crescent, Chelsea, The Fowler, Woman with Clasped Hands (carving) and Underground. Her The Chalk Quarry was illustrated in Modern Art. Her Noah's Ark was illustrated in the Daily Express. During her time in Cornwall, Hynes mixed with other locally-based artists, and became involved with some of those on the interior decoration of St Hilary Church at Marazion, just outside Penzance. Under the influence of Bernard Walke, Vicar of St Hilary and husband of artist Annie Walke, Hynes and others including Harold Harvey, Harold Knight, Ernest Procter and Alethea Garstin carried out various decorative projects during the 1920s and 1930s. Hynes produced a carving of the Madonna and Child, and contributed to a series of paintings for the front of the choir stalls, the design for which was based on the lives of the Cornish saints. Hynes was noted in Bernard Walke's autobiography, Twenty Years at St Hilary, London, Methuen, 1935.

I

IBBOTSON, HELENA MARY (1877-1962)

Enameller / Metalworker. Born in Sheffield, Yorkshire. Raised there and remained there all her life, mainly at Rustlings Road, but died in a nursing home in Kent, aged 85. The daughter of Henry Ibbotson, a corn miller who originated from Yorkshire, and Susan Ann, who originated from Cornwall. One of at least four children (Henry, Charles, Helena and Muriel). Helena studied at Sheffield University and abroad. Awarded an art masters' diploma by Sheffield University in 1917. Then studied at the Sheffield College of Arts and Crafts and in the London museums. Won a national bronze medal as a student, and was awarded art teaching certificates. During her career, she taught at the Woodhouse Secondary School. Also, at the Pupil Teachers' Centre, Sheffield and The Training College, Sheffield. Acted as head teacher of the Firshill Branch School of Art.

Ibbotson also worked as an enameller and in gold and silver. Her work included an enamelled bowl presented to the King, enamelled covers presented to Princess Mary, various trophies and an enamelled corporation plate. Elected to the National Society of Art Masters. Elected a Member of the Art Crafts Guild and of the Society of Artists, Sheffield. Exhibited her work occasionally, including in Liverpool, London, Glasgow and Sheffield. A gold and enamel cup by Ibbotson was purchased by the Worshipful Company of Goldsmiths for their private collection. Some of her works were illustrated in the Goldsmiths' Journal, the Watchmakers' Journal and the Sheffield Telegraph. Also listed as active in Sheffield, at The Decor Studio, Thornsett Road, is decorative metalworker Miss Marjorie Ibbotson. She exhibited at the Royal Scottish Academy (1939) and the Society of Women Artists (1936-49). Possibly a member of the same family.

ILLINGWORTH, ADELINE SARAH (1858-1942)

Etcher / Engraver / Artist. Born in Bradford, Yorkshire. The daughter of Thomas Illingworth and Sarah, both of whom originated from Halifax.

Her father was a manufacturing chemist and, later, a grocer. Adeline was one of at least six children (Edith, Ernest, Adeline, Agnes, Ethel and Letitia). The children were raised in Bradford and at Ilkley, Yorkshire. By at least 1891 Adeline was living in Chelsea, London and working as an artist and art teacher. This would suggest that she studied in London in the 1880s and possibly chose to remain there. She spent much of her career in Chelsea, at Glebe Place and then Cheyne Walk, but died in Surrey. Produced etchings and engravings (working on copper), watercolours and pen drawings. Best known for her architectural studies. She was evidently well travelled and executed studies of buildings in Italy, France, Bavaria, London and elsewhere.

Illingworth exhibited her work extensively over a period of more than 30 years, including at the Royal Academy (21 works, 1897-1916), the Society of Women Artists (18 works, 1896-1924), the Royal Scottish Academy ((1910-28), the Royal Hibernian Academy (1903-14) and the Royal Glasgow Institute (1909-21). Also, with the Glasgow Society of Lady Artists' Club (certainly in 1908) and the Royal Society of Painter-Etchers & Engravers (including in 1910 when she showed Rothenburg, Bavaria). Other exhibited works included: Ponte Vecchio, Venice, Vanished Chelsea, The Towers of Chartres and The South Ambulatory, Westminster Abbey. Elected an Associate of the Royal Society of Painter-Etchers & Engravers. Works illustrated in The Studio, Vol.23, 1901, p.273. Evidently still active in the late 1920s.

INCE, EVELYN GRACE (1886-1941)

Painter / Illustrator. The fourth and youngest daughter of the Rev. John Cook Ince, who originated from Ireland. Her mother died when Evelyn was very young. All the Ince girls (Eliza, Mabel, Alice and Evelyn) were born in Bengal, India, but moved to England sometime between 1886 and 1891 when their father became Curate of Gurnard near Cowes on the Isle of Wight. John Ince remained on the island until his death in 1922, having apparently never remarried. None of the Ince sisters ever married. By at least 1911 Evelyn was working from home as a black & white artist, as was Mabel. It is probable that both sisters had some tuition locally. However, Evelyn subsequently moved to London to study at the Byam Shaw and Vicat Cole School of Art, winning a scholarship in 1913. She remained in London for a while before moving to Petworth, Sussex, then Hampstead, then Letchworth, Hertfordshire. She died in Letchworth in May 1941, leaving her small estate to Eliza Ince. Her sister Mabel, who lived with Evelyn, also died in 1941. Eliza and Alice Ince lived together in Farnham, Surrey and died a few years later. Evelyn died only in her mid-50s, her career prematurely curtailed. Between 1917 and 1918 she spent time as a land worker.

Evelyn Ince worked as a painter in oils, watercolours and tempera. Subjects included landscapes and portraits. Latterly, she concentrated on flowers. Early in her career, she worked as an illustrator, mainly for children, and as an art teacher. Exhibited her work, including at the Royal Academy (1917-41), the Society of Women Artists (1930-32), the Royal Society of Portrait Painters, the Royal Society of British Artists, the International Society of Sculptors, Painters & Gravers, the International Exhibition and the Carnegie Institute. Exhibited works included: Bank Holiday, Hampstead, Hitchin Church and Dahlias. Her Flower-Piece in tempera was a Chantrey Bequest. Her Flowers in a Black Vase, also in tempera, was a Stott Bequest. Elected a Member of the Royal Society of British Artists in 1926. Works reproduced in Colour.

INCLEDON, MARJORIE MAY (1891-1973)

Oil Painter / Stained Glass Designer. Born in October 1891 in North Bromsgrove, Worcestershire. The daughter of Walter Bury Incledon and Edith May. He originated from Sheffield, her mother from Moseley, Worcestershire. Her father was a hardware merchant who employed staff and servants. Marjorie had at least one sister, Friede Mary (b.1895). Marjorie was educated at the Berkhamsted Grammar School. Whilst still at home, she studied at the Birmingham College of Art under R. Stubbington between 1911 and 1914. She then studied at the London County Council Central School of Arts and Crafts under Butterfield between 1917 and 1918. She later returned to the Birmingham College between 1941 and 1942, followed by the Brighton College of Art between 1942 and 1945, studying under Charles Knight and Dorothy Coke. Latterly, she was based in Sussex, at Rottingdean and Ditchling. Produced stained glass designs and oil paintings of various subjects including still life and landscape. Exhibited more, later in her career. Exhibited at the Royal Academy (1945-57), the Society of Women Artists (1952-58), the Royal Institute of Oil Painters, the Royal Society of British Artists, with the Sussex Artists, the Brighton United Artists and elsewhere. Exhibited works included: Christmas Still Life (oil), In the Loft (oil), Kitchen Table and Winter Tangle. Elected a Member of the Sussex Women's Art

Club. Marjorie died in Eastbourne, Sussex, aged 82. Friede Incledon died in Westminster in 1940, aged 45.

INGAMELLS, IVY K. - SEE ROLLETT, I.K.

INGLIS, HESTER (1571-1624)

Calligrapher / Book Decorator. Born in Edinburgh to French Huguenot parents, Nicholas Langlois and Marie Presot. In around 1596 she married Bartholomew Kello, a poor clergyman of an Essex parish. They had six children. In the early 1600s, Hester changed her name to Inglis. She decorated around 50 manuscripts, some bound in vellum, some in velvet, silk, or gold-tooled leather, between around 1591 and the time of her death. Fabric bindings were embroidered with silk or metal threads. She probably executed the embroidery herself. According to C.E. Clement, author of Women in the Fine Arts, New York, The Riverside Press, 1904, in the Library of Christ Church College, Oxford there is an example of the Psalms, in French, written and decorated by Inglis, which formerly belonged to Queen Elizabeth. In the Royal Library of the British Museum, there is also, according to Clement, a 'Book of Emblems in her hand'. Inglis is also noted in Marianne Tidcombe, Women Bookbinders 1880-1920, Oak Knoll Press / The British Library, 1996.

INGREY, MABEL CONSTANCE ELLEN (1872-1955)

Artist / Illuminator. Born in Paddington, London. The daughter of Charles Ingrey, a consulting engineer, and Ellen. One of at least four children, Charles, who became a chemist, Ernest, who became a bookkeeper, Mabel and Olive Magdalene Evelyn (1875-1956). Mabel and Olive studied art, probably in London, and both became fashion artists. They were raised in London and remained there until their deaths. Mabel also produced illumination work. Six of her illuminations were exhibited at the Society of Women Artists (1918-20). Those included an illuminated coat of arms, three illuminated prayers by the late Ven. Archdeacon Wilberforce, Mine Eyes Have Seen the Glory and The Heavens Declare the Glory of God.

IRELAND, EDITH MARY (1891-1980)

Decorative Artist / Painter / Writer / Lecturer. Known as Mary. Born in Stockingford, Warwickshire. The daughter of George Henry Morris and Mary Ada. Her father, a colliery secretary, originated from Worcester, her mother from Surrey. Had at least one sister, Frances. Raised in Stockingford. Educated at the Edgbaston Church of England College and at Montrose. Studied at the Birmingham Municipal School of Art under Robert Catterson-Smith between 1912 and 1917. Catterson-Smith was a Member of the Art Workers' Guild, a painter, a black & white artist and a silversmith. Mary also studied at Newlyn under Stanhope Alexander Forbes. She became an artist in silk textiles, a stained glass artist, an illuminator on vellum and a painter in watercolours as well as a writer and lecturer.

Mary exhibited her work, including at the Royal Academy (1915), the Society of Women Artists (1932-53), at the Graham Gallery and at the Arlington, Burlington, Folkestone, Westminster, Eastbourne and Crowborough Galleries. Her work also appeared on television and in films. Exhibited works included Decoration: The Dressing Room and Madonna With the Ball. Executed the Dover Patrol Book of Remembrance for Dover Town Hall. Executed a decorative panel St George which was presented by the Royal Society of St George (Malta), and various reredos and altar pieces for churches. Her work was reproduced in the Sunday Times of Malta, La Revue Moderne, Sketch, Home Chat, Good Housekeeping, the Daily Mail, Star, Queen and the South Wales Echo among other publications. Elected a Member of the Lyceum Club and of the National Book League. Initially based in Nuneaton during her career. In 1921 she married James A. Ireland in Nuneaton. They subsequently lived in Folkestone, Kent where Mary had a studio. She died in Kent, aged 89.

J

JACKSON, MURIEL AMY (1902-89)

Illustrator / Artist. Born in London. The daughter of Albert Edward Jackson (b.1873) and Eva Amy. Her father was a painter and illustrator and a Member of the East Sussex Arts Club. Muriel was one of at least five children (three sons and two daughters). Educated at the Berkhamsted High School. Studied at the Hastings School of Art, and at the London County Council Central School of Arts and Crafts under A.E. Jackson between 1915 and 1918. Also, under E. Leslie Badham, R.B.A., F.R.S.A. and Philip William Cole, R.B.A., A.R.C.A. between 1918 and 1922. Produced flower paintings in oils, black & white drawings, and children's illustrations for the Amalgamated Press from 1919. Illustrated for children's annuals and magazines. Exhibited her

work occasionally, including with the Highgate Artists Society, the Thames Valley Arts Club and the East Sussex Arts Club. Elected a Member of the East Sussex Arts Club, like her father, and like Philip W. Cole, Headmaster of the Hastings School of Art. Based in Hastings for much of her life and career. She was still living at the family home with her father into the 1950s. Died in East Sussex, aged 86.

JACKSON, MURIEL BLOMFIELD (1901-77)

Mural Decorator / Wood Engraver / Painter. Born in London in March 1901. The daughter of Arthur Blomfield Jackson, an architect, and Ida Mary Phipps. One of at least three children (Mary, Muriel and Richard). Raised in London. Educated at the Hampstead Day School. Studied at the London County Council Central School of Arts and Crafts, a pupil of Noel Rooke. During that time she was selected for the final competition of the Rome Scholarship in 1925 in the painting section. Based mainly in London thereafter, where she died. Produced decorative murals, wood engravings and portrait paintings in oils and tempera.

Jackson exhibited her work, including at the New English Art Club, the Royal Academy (1927-66), with the Society of Wood Engravers, at the Redfern Gallery and in Paris (1925). Awarded a First Prize and the Logan Medal at the Third International Exhibition of Lithography and Wood Engraving in Chicago in 1931. Her wood engravings included: Reapers in Italy and Seven Ages of Man. Her engraving Motor-Bike was illustrated in Drawing & Design. Executed mural decoration for St Peter's Church, Limehouse which was illustrated in The Studio. Other mural designs included Ice-Cream Stall. Her portraits included The Child's Dulcimer (tempera), Nanny (oil & tempera) and District Judge, India. In 1931, Jackson exhibited with the Society of Wood Engravers along with Iain MacNab, Ethelbert White and others. She showed an enormous print of a caravan encampment which was considered possibly too large to make an acceptable woodblock print purely on its scale. Jackson, however, appears to have achieved her aim. She was elected an Associate of the Society of Wood Engravers. Her wood engraving Balaam's Ass was illustrated in The Studio, Vol.141, June 1951, p.172. In 1928 she married Francis Courteney Mason in Hampstead. Evidently continued to work long after her marriage.

JACOB, ALICE (1862-1921)
Painter / Designer. Raised in Dublin in a family of Quakers. They moved to New Zealand for a time, but returned to Dublin. Alice studied at the Metropolitan School of Art, Dublin in the 1880s. Won several prizes and scholarships. In 1891 she completed a summer course at South Kensington, London. Taught elementary design at the Dublin and Cork Schools of Art and later at the Rathmines Technical School. One of her pupils was Kathleen Quigly. Jacob produced lace, embroidery and crochet designs, painted silks and watercolour paintings. Executed orchid studies for the Botanic Gardens Collection at Glasnevin (1907-20). Also produced embossed designs for leather. Decorated a set of Belleek porcelain for Dr Perceval Wright, Professor of Botany at Trinity College, Dublin. Favoured Celtic design in some of her work. Also inspired by nature. A Member of the Gaelic League. Worked at the Dublin School of Art almost until her death. Died in Dublin, aged 58.

JACOB, CHARLOTTE E. - SEE HUNTON, C.E.

JACOBS, LOUISA (1857-1936)
Sculptor. Born in Cheltenham, Gloucestershire. The daughter of Frederick Alexander Jacobs, an agent. Based in London for much of her life and career, dying there, aged 78. Probably studied in London. Produced busts and figures in terracotta. Exhibited her work, including at the Royal Academy (1886-87) and the Royal Society of British Artists (1887-89). Exhibited works included: Childhood (bust), Day Dreams (terracotta), Fiat Voluntas Tua (bust, terracotta) and Nancy (terracotta). In 1890 Jacobs married James Blewitt Spurge in London. He was an engineer in the nitrous oxide gas compressor. They had one daughter, Grace, who became an art student in London. James Spurge died in Kent in 1932. Louisa was still listed as a sculptor in 1891, after her marriage. But she appears to have ceased exhibiting her work by that time.

JACOBS, LOUISE RICA (1880-1946)
Painter / Illustrator / Engraver. Born in Hull, Yorkshire. The daughter of Benjamin Septimus Jacobs, an architect, and Isabel Kisch. One of at least three children (Ethel, Louise and Bethel). Raised in Hull. Produced landscape, flower, figure and portrait paintings, poster designs, colour lithographs and illustrations. Her career spanned over at least three decades, from the 1910s to the late 1930s. Based in Hull initially, but by at least 1910 she was living and working in London. Later in her career, she spent time back in Hull and, latterly, in New Malden, Surrey. Died in Camberwell, aged 66. Exhibited her work, including at the Royal Scottish Academy (1935-37), the Royal Hibernian Academy (1930-38), the Royal Academy (1910-38) and the Society of Women Artists (1910-36). Exhibited works included: Red Roofs of Whitby, The Mother (colour lithograph), The Black Hat and In the Shadow (lithograph). The Museum of London has reproduced her poster Appeal of Womanhood (1912) for sale.

JAGGER, MARGARET LEAH - SEE BLUNDELL, M.L.

JAMES, ELIZABETH CAMPBELL (b.1923)
Artist / Etcher / Engraver. Born in Hampstead in November 1923. The daughter of Norman Walker James, a designer and Member of the Art Workers' Guild. Educated at the P.N.E.U. School, Temple Fortune and at the South Hampstead High School. Studied at the Hornsey School of Arts and Crafts under John Charles Moody, Norman Janes, W.E. King and H. Youngman. Awarded an Art Teachers' Diploma in 1946. Worked as an artist in oils and pen & wash. Produced engravings, etchings and linocuts. Based in Enfield, Middlesex for part of her career. Acted as an art teacher at the Enfield County School for Girls from 1946. Exhibited her work, including at the Royal Academy (1947-64), with the Society of Graphic Art and with the Artists and Designers Group. Exhibited works included: Clowns (wood engraving), The Blind Fiddler and Nine Maidens, Boscawen (linocut), The Old Tree (wood engraving) and Badgers in the Snow. Elected a Member of the Society of Graphic Art in 1948. In 1949 she married Godfrey William Hargrave in Middlesex. Evidently continued to work after her marriage.

JAMIESON, DOROTHEA M. - SEE SELOUS, D.M.

JARMAIN, EVELYN ETHEL (1908-83)
Artist / Needlewoman / Engraver. Born in Sagaing, Burma in November 1908. The daughter of Bernard Houghton of the Indian Civil Service. Possibly one of up to six children. As a small child, she spent some time living in Westbury, Wiltshire. Educated at the Hove High School. Studied at the Ruskin School of Drawing under Sydney Carling, John Nash, Richard Carline and Gilbert Spencer. Also studied at the Royal Academy schools under Sir W.W. Russell and Walter Monnington. Awarded a silver medal at

the Royal Academy schools in 1929. Worked as an artist in oils, watercolours and pencil, produced wood engravings and executed fine needlework. Acted as art mistress at Acton Reynold, Shrewsbury (1945) and at the Mount School, York (1946). Exhibited her work at the Royal Academy (1931), in Brighton, at the National Gallery of Canada in the British Artists Exhibition (1931) and with the East Kent Art Society (from 1949). Exhibited works included: Lady With a Fan. Elected a Member of the East Kent Art Society and of the Imperial Arts League. Based in Burford, Oxfordshire for a time. But based mainly in Kent, where she died, aged 74. Signed her work Eve Houghton. In 1934 she married John (William J.F.) Jarmain in Westminster. He was an author and poet. They had at least one son and one daughter. Some of Evelyn's work was used to illustrate a volume of John Jarmain's poems, published in 1945.

JARRETT, MARCIA LANE (1897-1983)

Engraver / Illustrator. Was Nellie Marcia Lane Foster, known as Marcia. Born in Seaton, Devon in August 1897. The daughter of Henry Llewellyn Thomas Foster, an electrical engineer, and Ellen Lane. Raised in Manchester. One of at least four children. Subsequently based in London and Huntingdon, Cambridgeshire. Died in Somerset, aged 86. Studied in London, at the St John's Wood School of Art and at the L.C.C. Central School of Arts and Crafts under Noel Rooke. Won a silver medal for figure painting (1920-21). Best known for her distinctive wood engravings, but also produced drawings and portrait paintings. Worked for a number of book publishers. Illustrated books including William J. Locke, The Golden Journey of Mr Paradyne, Kenneth Grahame, The Headswoman, Anatole France, Little Sea Dogs and Other Tales (1925), Kitty Barne, Dusty's Windmill (1949), Viola Bayley, Paris Adventure (1954) and Scottish Adventure (1965). Produced a set of 16 wood engravings for Anatole France, The Merrie Tales of Jacques Tournebroche, acquired by the British Museum. Also worked in advertising. For around 20 years she worked for William Hollins & Co. Designed children's wear advertising for Viyella and Clydella. Produced promotional material for Cadbury, Nestle, Kodak, Bovril, T.C.P. and Clark's shoes.

   Jarrett exhibited her work, including at the Royal Academy (1952-64), the New English Art Club, the Paris Salon and the Society of Women Artists (1923-35). Exhibited works included: Cutcombe Cattle Market (wood engraving), Tarring the Boat (wood engraving), Mugs (wood

engraving) and Hole in the Road (wood engraving). Elected a Member of the Arts and Crafts Exhibition Society. Elected an Associate of the Royal Society of Painter-Etchers & Engravers (1959). Her wood engraving The Organ Grinder was reproduced in Campbell Dodgson's volume Contemporary Woodcuts, London, Duckworth & Co., 1922. Only 500 copies of the book were produced, and only a comparatively small number of woodcuts chosen for inclusion. Some of her illustrations to The Merrie Tales of Jacques Tournebroche were reproduced in Herbert Furst, The Modern Woodcut, London, John Lane, 1924. Also noted in Bernard Sleigh, Wood Engraving Since 1890, London, Pitman, 1932. Noted by Sleigh as needing to adopt 'a less coarse handling of the graver' (p.82). Despite such a comment, Jarrett became one of the most successful artists of her generation. In 1925, she married Howard Dudley Jarrett (1894-1980) in Bodmin, Cornwall. He was an artist and author. He too died in Somerset.

JEBB, KATHLEEN MARY (1878-1957)

Painter / Engraver / Black & White Artist.
Born in Liverpool in April 1878. The daughter of William Jebb, Surveyor of Customs, and Julia. One of at least three children (Lilly, Kathleen and William). Raised in West Derby, Liverpool and at Westbury-on-Trym, Bristol. Remained in Bristol for much of the rest of her life and career, dying at Westbury-on-Trym, aged 78. Possibly studied in Bristol. A bronze medallist at the National Competition of Schools of Art, South Kensington, and a book prizeman. Chiefly a black & white artist, but also a painter in watercolours and an engraver in aquatint and drypoint. Acted as assistant evening teacher at the Bristol Municipal School of Art in the 1910s. Exhibited her work, including at the Royal Academy (1914-28), the Royal Scottish Academy (1924-28), the Walker Art Gallery, Liverpool and the Royal West of England Academy. Works included: The Wye at Symonds Yat (etching), The Distant Severn (etching), The Severn at Old Passage (drypoint) and The Monnow Bridge, Monmouth (aquatint). Elected an Associate of the Royal West of England Academy.

JEFFERIES, KATHERINE G. - SEE HARTNELL, K.G.

JEKYLL, GERTRUDE (1843-1932)

Garden Designer / Painter. Born in London, but raised in Surrey from around 1847. The daughter of Edward Jekyll of Wargrave Hill, Berkshire where the family also spent time. He was a

Captain in the Grenadier Guards. One of five children, Gertrude was taught by a governess. Showed an early interest in art and horticulture. With the support of her parents, in 1861 she enrolled at the South Kensington School of Art, remaining there for two years, intending to become a painter. Early in her career, she was involved in embroidery, wall painting, metalwork, photography, inlay in gold and silver, wood inlay and ivory inlay. In the early 1860s, she travelled abroad. Subsequently exhibited eight of her works at the Society of Women Artists (1867-70), including Donkey Foal, Life Size, Mr Punch's Dog Toby and Thomas, a Favourite Cat, in the Character of Puss in Boots. Also exhibited one work at the Royal Academy in 1865, Cheeky, 64 Regt, a Native of Cawnpore. After spending time in Berkshire with her parents, in 1876 her father died, and the family moved back to Surrey, where architect J.J. Stevenson built a home at Munstead.

Jekyll intended to become a professional artist, but an eye condition prevented this, and she turned to garden design instead. Despite her success, she always described her work as merely 'gardening'. Often linked to the Arts and Crafts movement, being influenced by John Ruskin (1819-1900) and William Morris (1834-96), although she learnt about colour from watercolour painter Hercules Brabazon. Jekyll believed that no plant should be seen in isolation because its value could be appreciated only when it was seen next to other colours. Much of her gardening knowledge was gained by developing Munstead Wood in the early 1880s, a large plot of land close to the family home in Surrey, where architect and friend Edwin Lutyens (1869-1944) later built Munstead House for Jekyll. The house was finished in 1896.

From a nursery at Munstead, Jekyll was able to supply clients with trees, shrubs and plants, and influenced a new use of herbaceous and woodland plants in gardening which is still evident today. She also brought a new awareness of the relationship of a house to its garden, something which also interested Lutyens, whom Jekyll first met in 1889. Jekyll worked by the maxim 'simplicity is the beginning and the end of all good things in gardening'. During her distinguished career, she produced over 350 garden designs. Her gardens, with their often labour intensive herbaceous borders, could be found across Britain. For example, in Strathclyde, Somerset, Hampshire, Buckinghamshire and North Wales. Three commissions were carried out for clients in America, the first in Ohio in 1914. Another of her commissions, for three acres of garden at Tigbourne Court, Surrey, a house

designed by Lutyens and built in 1899, was discussed in The Studio, Vol.26, June 1902, pp.21-24.

Jekyll wrote extensively on gardens and garden design, producing over 1000 articles for periodicals such as Country Life and Edinburgh Review. Some of her articles have been published collectively as A Gardener's Testament (1937). Also wrote a number of books including Wood and Garden (1899), Lilies for English Gardens (1901), Roses For English Gardens (1902), Children and Gardens (1908), Gardens For Small Country Houses (with architect Lawrence Weaver, 1912) and Garden Ornament (1918). The majority of her designs are now in the Reef Point Collection, University of California. Noted in Ellen C. Clayton's two volumes, English Female Artists, London, Tinsley, 1876. Painter William Nicholson executed a painting of Miss Jekyll's Gardening Boots which was illustrated in Herbert Furst's volume The Art of Still-Life Painting, London, Chapman & Hall, 1927. The black lace-up boots were, expectedly, well worn and well used. Nicholson also executed a portrait of Jekyll which was owned by the Tate Gallery.

JENKINS, EVELINE ANNIE (1893-1976)

Artist in Wax / Artist in Black & White / Botanical Artist / Painter. Born in Monmouthshire in July 1893. The daughter of William Herbert Jenkins, a civil servant, and Eveline. One of at least three children (Eveline, William and Ella). Raised in Monmouthshire. Educated at the Newport Girls' High School. Then attended University College, Aberystwyth. Awarded a B.Sc. (Wales, 1919). Studied art only in her spare time. Attended the Aberystwyth Art School between 1912 and 1913. Studied under Stanhope A. Forbes for six weeks in Newlyn in 1916. Attended the Newport Art School for four months in 1927, and attended evening classes at Cardiff in 1929. Worked in wax. Produced black & white drawings and studies in oils, watercolours and pastels. Excelled as a botanical artist, working in that capacity for the National Museum of Wales, Cardiff from 1927, and was placed on the staff there from 1936.

Her botanical studies were used chiefly in museum publications. For example, Jenkins illustrated The Preparation of Fungus Models in the Museum's Journal (38, 1938, pp.51-55, pp.116-122). Also, Some Welsh Fungi (p.50, Cardiff, 1948) and Museum Guide to Fungus Models (c.1948). Exhibited her work, including at the Foyle's Art Gallery, at Turner House, Penarth, at the Newport Museum and Art Gallery and with the South Wales Group. Elected a

Member of the British Federation of University Women, of the South Wales Art Society and of the Newport Art Society. Some of her work was linked to the British Mycological Society. Some of her models were in the collection of the National Museum of Wales, Cardiff. Based in Cardiff for part of her career. She died in South Glamorgan, aged 83.

JOCE, EVELYN DOROTHY (1900-73)

Bookbinder / Textile Designer / Wood Engraver / Print Artist of Scarves, Dresses and Jumpers. Born in Edinburgh in June 1900. The daughter of Frank Sidney Goggs, A.I.A. (American Institute of Architecture), F.C.I.S., F.C.I.I., and Eleanor. Raised in Edinburgh. Educated at Craigmount, Edinburgh and the Wimbledon High School. Studied in London at the L.C.C. Central School of Arts and Crafts. As a student, she won a 10 guinea prize in a competition of industrial designs in 1925. In the same year, she won the Owen Jones medal for designs for endpapers in books, and a gold medal for textile designs at the Paris International Exhibition. Exhibited her work at Wembley (1925), Paris (1925), the 1926 Arts and Crafts Exhibition, the 1926 Liverpool Exhibition of Modern Art, and in Leipzig in 1927. Her design for a Nicolas Poussin binding and a scarf were purchased by the British Institute of Industrial Art. Her design for a block-printed jumper was illustrated in The Studio. Some of her bindings, and a design for cretonne, were illustrated in Drawing & Design. Executed bindings for, for example, Shelley and His Poetry, Russian Wonder Tales and Northanger Abbey. The subject of a brief illustrated article in The Studio, Vol.92, September 1926, pp.168-170. Based in London for part of her career. In 1928 she married Owen P. Joce in Surrey. She died in Aldershot, Hampshire, aged 73.

JOEL, BETTY (1894-1985)

Furniture and Textile Designer. Born in Hong Kong. The daughter of Sir James Haldane Stewart Lockhart, K.C.M.G., LL.D. (d.1937) and Edith Louise Rider. Records suggest her name was Mary Stewart Lockhart, but was always known as Betty. She moved to England at some point, and shortly after the First World War founded a furniture workshop, Betty Joel Ltd, with her husband, David Joel (1891-1971). Apparently, the couple had no formal training in design. The workshop was based at Hayling Island. David Joel had been in the navy, but retired around 1923 to make quality furniture to good design with Betty. Soon after, a factory was opened in Portsmouth and a shop in Sloane Street,

London. The furniture was made to Betty's designs which, initially, tended towards Arts and Crafts. But her work quickly became more modern, reflecting current design trends, but always from a female perspective.

Betty Joel was a contemporary of Marion Dorn and Marion Pepler, who also made significant contributions to interior design in the late 1920s and 1930s. Joel's career as a designer evidently peaked in the 1930s, with a number of her designs illustrated in The Studio magazine. In May 1932, for example, the magazine illustrated some of her latest pieces in an article Metal and Furniture (pp.260-265). Those included a large writing desk and two smaller cocktail tables. The bases of the tables were staybrite steel whilst the wood was cellulosed black and red. Also in 1932, Joel was one of a series of designers featured in articles in The Studio titled British Interior Architects of To-day (Vol.104, November, p.276). Joel was described as one of the pioneers of the Modern movement in Britain, who sought to create new furniture to fit modern homes rather than adapting the old. Joel was noted as having three basic aims in her work:

1. To achieve beauty by line, form and proportion rather than by ornament.
2. To use quality materials.
3. To adopt a high standard of workmanship as in the past.

The success of Joel's work saw her create a set design for the film Sleeping Car in the 1930s, which included furniture. She was also praised in other arts journals of the day, including Architectural Review, but also Colour magazine, which in December 1929 (pp.23-24) offered an illustrated article by Joel titled At Last a Modern Period. There, she discussed Modernism and the Modern furniture movement in Britain. She also noted that she had recently taken a stand at the Ideal Home Exhibition in London, where she had been visited by the Duchess of York. The Duchess had suggested the use of Queensland Silky Oak, which Joel used in furniture thereafter. Joel saw Modernism as an opportunity for testing new woods.

Joel executed a number of important commissions during her career, including a study at Lord Louis Mountbatten's pre-war penthouse, in which she used Honduras cedar, unpolished. Other commissions included a consulting room for eye specialist F.A. Williamson-Noble (c.1928). Joel eventually built a new works on the Kingston bypass which was designed by H.S. Goodhart Rendel who, in 1937, also designed the new front for Joel's already established Knightsbridge showrooms. The showrooms were used to display Joel's own work, but were also used to display other work, including prints by various artists. Exhibitions were also held there. In May 1930, for example, an exhibition of the work of Frederick Whiting was held. And in late 1935 a selection of paintings and sculptures for loan purposes was held by Picture Hire Ltd.

Betty Joel also ventured into carpets (made to her design in China) and fabrics (woven to her design in France) which were often abstract in design. Always at the forefront of contemporary design, in 1937 she exhibited chairs with Aubusson tapestry covers designed by leading artist Anna Zinkeisen. Her work was exhibited elsewhere too. In 1935, for example, her revolving bed was shown at the British Art in Industry Exhibition held at the Royal Academy. In 1937 she held a large exhibition at her Knightsbridge showrooms, with furniture set out as rooms. It was titled Betty Joel's Coronation Exhibition. Pieces included a serpentine-fronted sideboard and a desk with white shell-shaped handles. Mural decorations were provided by Anna Zinkeisen.

Joel also wrote enthusiastically on her subject. In June 1935 she contributed an illustrated article to The Studio, Vol.109, pp.302-311, titled Antiques and the Modern Setting. Some of her sketches were included along with a photograph of an interior designed by Joel for a Mrs Millard of Fitzjohn's Avenue, Hampstead. The design incorporated period furniture, including a spinet in mahogany decorated by Angelica Kauffman. Other design schemes by Joel were included in the article. In August 1936, The Studio, Vol.112, pp.89-90, published another article by Joel titled Interior Decoration - Space Saving in the Small Flat, complete with diagrams. Joel retired in around 1938. In 1953 some of her furniture was illustrated in David Joel, The Adventure of British Furniture 1851-1951, London, Ernest Benn Ltd., including a single wardrobe in American black walnut (1926) and a wardrobe in Indian silver greywood (1929). David Joel instigated a brief revival of Joel furniture after the Second World War under the name David Joel Ltd. Joel furniture can be found in the collection of the Victoria & Albert Museum, London. Betty died in Hampshire, aged 90.

JOHNSON, EDITH (b.1902)

Painter / Illuminator / Embroideress. Born in Leicester in September 1902. The daughter of Thomas Johnson, a gas engineer, and Maria. One of at least six children (Frederick, Edith, Amy, Ruth, Bertha and Maria). Raised in Leicestershire, but moved to Derbyshire. Studied at the Derby School of Art. Awarded a Board of Education Certificate in industrial design and illumination. Also, a full technological certificate of City & Guilds for embroidery. Produced portrait paintings in miniature, illuminations and decorative embroidery. Worked as an art teacher for a time. Exhibited her work occasionally, including at the Royal Academy (1923-36), the Walker Art Gallery, Liverpool and with the Royal Society of Miniature Painters (from 1923). Exhibited works included: Sicily, Study of an Old Man and Dorothy. Elected a Member of the Derby Women's Arts Club. Based in Alvaston, Derbyshire for part of her career.

JOHNSTON, ARNRID BANNIZA (1895-1972)

Carver / Modeller / Artist. Born in Uddevalla, Sweden in August 1895. The daughter of Arthur Sannox Johnston, a merchant. Educated at St Helen's, Blackheath, London. Studied at the Slade School, London. Won the Slade Scholarship, two prizes and the Countess Feodora Gleichen memorial prize two years running. Worked as a carver in stone, marble and wood, a modeller in lead and bronze, and an artist in pen & wash. Produced groups of animals, garden ornaments and figures. Based in Chelsea for part of her career. Died in Wandsworth, aged 79. Exhibited her work at the Goupil Gallery, with the New English Art Club, at the Whitechapel Art Gallery, at Wembley, at the Chenil Gallery and under the Duveen scheme. Showed one work at the Royal Academy in 1940, Land Girls Milking (pen & wash). Other works included: Pastoral (a relief in black marble) and a bronze baby executed for the Child Welfare organisations in Egypt. Works illustrated in The Studio, Architectural Review, Architect's Journal and Tatler.

JOHNSTONE, DORIS - SEE ZINKEISEN, D.

JOLLIFF, GRACE HELEN M. (1878-1962)

Painter. Born in Llanelly, Glamorgan, Wales in August 1878. The daughter of John H. Rogers and Eliza. Her father was an iron, steel and tinplate merchant in Llanelly, employing around 900 people in the 1880s. The family presumably had an affluent lifestyle, given the scale of the business, and employed several servants at their home. Later, in the 1920s and 1930s, her father is listed as a woodcarver. By at least the early 1900s the family was based in London, living in Hampstead by at least 1911. Grace was one of at least four children. Her sister Dorothy became a musician. Grace was educated at the Queen's

College, Harley Street, London and became a watercolour painter, chiefly of landscapes. As a student, she was twice presented with a First Prize by landscape painter Sir David Murray. She was still living in London in the 1920s and 1930s. In late 1927, at the age of around 49, she married Reginald Jolliff in Hampstead. Latterly spent time in Cornwall. Died in Camelford, Cornwall in June 1962. Her exhibiting career spanned over four decades. Exhibited her work at the Women's International Art Club, the New English Art Club, the International Society of Sculptors, Painters & Gravers, the Royal Institute of Painters in Watercolours, the National Society (certainly in 1936) and the Society of Women Artists (1906). Exhibited works included: Afterglow in St Ives Harbour and Grey Day at St Ives. Elected a Member of the Women's International Art Club.

JONES, CLARA ELLEN - SEE BILLING, C.E.

JONES, GWENDOLINE M. - SEE WHITE, G.M.

JONES, MARGARET TALBOT (1894-1996)
Embroideress / Illuminator. Born in Liverpool in April 1894. The daughter of William Stackhouse Holden and Margaret. Her father, a solicitor, originated from Liverpool. One of at least three children. Her brother Guy studied law. Raised in Liverpool, in a house with servants. Educated at the Belvedere School, Liverpool. Studied at the Liverpool School of Art, followed by the Royal College of Art, London on a scholarship. Elected an Associate of the Royal College of Art in 1919. Subsequently taught at the Blackheath School of Art. Also spent time teaching art in Boston, and at the Chicago Art Institute and Academy. This was probably in around 1923, when she sailed from Southampton to New York at the age of 29. Produced embroideries and illuminations, but also painted flowers as a hobby. Elected to the Society of Scribes and Illuminators in 1922.

Jones exhibited her work, including at the Arts and Crafts Exhibition in London, at the International Exhibition in Paris, in New York, Boston, Chicago and New Zealand. The Museum of Art, Detroit purchased her embroidered panel, Truth. Other work included a war memorial for the Surveyors' Institute. Also, various presentations, including to Dr Eliot of Harvard University. A petit point brooch and a stud box by her were illustrated in two French magazines. Like a number of British artists and designers, Jones was perhaps more appreciated abroad. Based in London for part of her career, at Anerley Hill in the 1930s. In 1927 she married Arthur

Percy Jones in Croydon. She died in East Sussex, aged 101.

JONES, MARJORIE - SEE MEGGITT, M.

JONES, OLIVE L. - SEE WHITE, O.L.

JONES, PEARL - SEE BINDER, P.

JONES, ROSE G. - SEE HOLT, G.

JONES, VIVIEN MASSIE - SEE GRIBBLE, V.M.

JOSEPH, AGNES ELEANOR HOPE (1878-c.1953)
Painter / Poster Artist / Illustrator / Pottery Artist / Woodcut Artist. Born in Ajmere, India. The daughter of Lieut.-Col. F.W. Joseph. Educated at the Clifton High School. By at least 1901 she was based in Newlyn, Cornwall, also working at Zennor and Penzance in the county. Subsequently worked in London and at Ashtead, Surrey. Possibly died in Hitchin, Hertfordshire, aged 75, though this needs absolute clarification. She also spent time in Paris and elsewhere in France. Studied art at Newlyn under Stanhope A. Forbes and in Paris. Produced portraits, flowers and landscapes, miniatures, poster designs, woodcuts, pottery decoration and illustrations. Exhibited her work, including with the Women's International Art Club, at the Paris Salon, the Royal Scottish Academy (1908), the Royal Academy (1907-33), the Royal Hibernian Academy (1908), the Society of Women Artists (1904-36), with the Royal Institute of Oil Painters and the Royal Society of Portrait Painters. Exhibited works included: Newlyn Fishermen (miniature), White Tulips, The Red Lantern and By the Seine in Paris. Works reproduced in Artwork (Garcon au Beret), Colour and Drawing & Design.

JOSEPH, GLADYS - SEE HUNT, G.

JOY, MARY ELIZA - SEE HAWEIS, M.E.

JUDD-MORRIS, LOUISA E.E. - SEE WOOLLATT, L.E.E.

JUKES, EDITH ELIZABETH (1910-post-1966)
Sculptor. Also known as Betty or Beth. Born in Shillong, Assam. The daughter of Captain Andrew Monro Jukes, M.D., I.M.S. and Gertrude Elizabeth King. Her father died young, in Egypt in 1918, having been married for only nine years. She and her mother returned to England when Edith was small, and her mother died in 1958,

leaving her small estate to Edith. Apparently an only child, Edith was educated at the Norland Place School in Kensington, London. Studied sculpture at the Royal College of Art, London between 1928 and 1932 under Richard Garbe, Henry Moore and Herbert Palliser. Elected an Associate of the Royal College of Art in 1932. Remained in London, using a studio at Glebe Place, Chelsea for a time. Produced mainly figures and portrait works in coloured plaster, clay, wood, stone, cement and bronze.

Jukes began to exhibit her work from around 1935. Exhibited at the Royal Academy (18 works, 1935-66), the Royal Glasgow Institute (1950) and the Society of Women Artists (1936). Exhibited works included: Proserpine (garden ornament, bronze), The Cradle (carving in stone wood), The Gull's Way and the Wind's Way (relief, wood) and The Little Immigrant (statue, cement fondu). Her work was temporarily interrupted by the Second World War, and she qualified as a State Registered Nurse in 1945, indicating that she carried out important work during the war. From 1947 she taught at the Sir John Cass College School of Art. In 1948 she was elected an Associate of the Royal Society of British Sculptors. Also a Member of the Ski Club of Great Britain. Evidently a talented and highly active individual.

K

KAPP, HELEN BABETTE (1901-78)

Painter / Illustrator / Wood Engraver. Born in Hampstead, London in December 1901. Raised there. Died in Ipswich, Suffolk, aged 77. The daughter of Emil Benjamin Kapp and Bella. Her father, a merchant and later an agent, originated from Russia, her mother from America. One of at least three children (Edmond, Harold and Helen). Edmond (1890-1978) became a successful painter, lithographer and draughtsman, and was an official war artist with a studio in London and one in Paris. Helen was educated at the Maria Grey Brondesbury and Kilburn High School. Studied in London, at the Slade School and the L.C.C. Central School of Arts and Crafts. Also, in Paris. Produced paintings and illustrations in oils, watercolours and pen & wash, and wood engravings.

Kapp illustrated a number of books during her lengthy career for Dent, Gollancz, Routledge & Kegan Paul, Robert Hale, the Medici Society and others. Those included Gerald Bullett (ed.), Seed of Israel: Tales From the English Bible (1927), Basil Collier & Helen Kapp, Take Forty Eggs

(1938), Harold Morland, Fables and Satires (1945) and James Laver, Toying With a Fancy (1948). Kapp acted as Director of Wakefield City Art Gallery (1951-61). Then as Director of Abbot Hall Art Gallery, Kendal (1961-67). She was also an Arts Council Lecturer (1940-45) and a War Office Lecturer (1940-48). Was the author of Enjoying Pictures (Routledge & Kegan Paul, 1975). Exhibited her work, including at the Royal Academy (1940), the American Institute of Architecture, with the London group, at the Redfern Gallery, the St George's Gallery, with the Society of Wood Engravers and under the Duveen scheme. Held one-woman shows at the Nicholson's Gallery and with the British Council in 1946. Exhibited works included: Plain Near Perpignan (pen & wash).

KAUFMANN, LILY ELIZABETH JEAN (1870-1947)

Painter / Miniaturist / Designer. Born and raised in Liverpool. The daughter of Joseph Nairn Skeaping and Mary. Her father was an art master and a designer and sculptor in wood. Lily was one of at least four children (Margaret, John, Elizabeth and Nellie). Nellie also became an art student. Lily studied at the Liverpool School of Art, also studying in the European galleries. Won prizes in the National Competition Science and Art Department. Also won Director's Prizes and a silver medal. In 1898 she married Bernard Kaufmann, L.A.A., in Liverpool and had one daughter. Lily was widowed young. Produced paintings of figures and landscapes in oils and watercolours, miniatures and designs. Worked as an art teacher in Liverpool after her marriage. Taught at the Liverpool Technical Institute and taught dress design at the St Helen's School of Art. Exhibited her work, including at the Walker Art Gallery, Liverpool, the Royal Institute of Painters in Watercolours and in Leeds and Manchester. Works included: Merry Goes the Time, Sister Blossoms and Her Favourite Singer. Elected to the National Society of Art Masters. The Blackpool Art Gallery acquired her Dear Child of Nature. Latterly, she had a studio in Prescot, Lancashire. Died in Liverpool, aged 77.

KAY, NORA ELIZABETH (1913-2005)

Decorative Artist / Designer / Calligrapher / Potter. The daughter of Alexander Berridge Kay. Educated at the High Wycombe High School. Studied in London, at the St Martin's School of Art under J.H. Rowe between 1932 and 1934. Also, at the Royal College of Art under Professor Ernest W. Tristram, Edward Bawden and Eric Ravilious between 1934 and 1937. Elected an

Associate of the Royal College of Art in 1937. Worked as an artist in cut paper, a calligrapher, a display and advertising artist in black & white and colour, including posters, a studio potter and a linocut artist. Worked for, for example, Yardley & Co. (1938) and Jenners Ltd (1940). Executed at least one London Transport poster, in 1948. Executed other general design work, including for Christmas cards, and for packaging and designs for fabrics and table mats. Also involved in children's books. Worked as a teacher at the St Martin's School of Art from 1940, and taught at the High Wycombe School of Art. Exhibited three works at the Society of Women Artists in 1954: The Magpie (linocut), The Lodge, Langley Broom and Staffordshire Dog (linocut). Elected a Member of the Society of Industrial Artists in 1945. Spent much of her career at Gerrards Cross, Buckinghamshire. Died in Buckinghamshire, aged 92.

KAYLEY, MARGARET CLARA (1907-99)

Poster and Advertisement Artist. Born in Southport, Lancashire in March 1907. The daughter of George Kayley and Blanche Adelaide Lamb. Her father, who originated from Southport, was the Secretary and a schoolmaster of the Southport University School and later an accountant. One of at least four daughters (Helen, Ruth, Margaret and Mary). Educated at the Girls' Secondary School. Studied at the Victoria School of Art. Based largely in Southport during her career. Died in Chelsea. Work included advertisements for Woodhead's Cafes and a poster for Southport Opera House. Executed advertisements for the back of the Railway Guide for the Visitor Printing Works, Southport. Exhibited her work only occasionally, including at the Victoria & Albert Museum, London.

KEATING, RUTH MONICA (1910-2006)

Theatrical Designer. Born in London. The daughter of Joseph Keating, a mercantile clerk at a varnish factory, and Berry. One of at least three children (Frances, John and Ruth). Raised in London. Educated at the St Paul's Girls' School. Studied in London at the L.C.C. Central School of Arts and Crafts. Works included, for example, the design for the Gentle Shepherd at the Edinburgh Festival Society. Also, the design for the Barber of Seville at Sadler's Wells. In 1935 she married Hubert E.S. Pearson, M.D., M.B., M.R.C.P. in London. They had at least one son and two daughters. She is listed as still active into the 1950s, after her marriage. Spent part of her career in Surrey. Died in Ross, Herefordshire, aged 96.

KEATINGE, ALYS F. - SEE TROTTER, A.F.

KELL, LORNA BEATRICE (1914-95)

Textile Designer / Artist / Wood Engraver. Born in London in January 1914. The daughter of George and Beatrice Prince. Educated at the East Finchley Grammar School. Studied at the Hornsey School of Arts and Crafts under John Charles Moody, Edith Lindquist, Norman Janes and Frank Winter. Based in New Barnet, Hertfordshire for part of her career. Produced pen & wash studies, watercolours, textiles and wood engravings. Exhibited at the Royal Academy (1951-65), the Royal Society of British Artists, the Society of Graphic Art, at the Guildhall, City of London and at local exhibitions. Exhibited works included: Rhododendron (wood engraving), Protea (wood engraving) and Reminiscences of Wales (pen & wash). In 1939 she married textile designer H. Lorraine Kell in Middlesex. She died in Middlesex, aged 82.

KEMP, MARJORIE BOYCE (1886-1975)

Stained Glass Artist. Born in Blairgowrie, Perthshire. The daughter of the Rev. Robert Kemp. Educated at the Ministers' Daughters' College, Edinburgh. Studied at the Glasgow School of Art. Awarded a diploma. Established herself as a stained glass artist. Initially worked at the Abbey Studio in Glasgow. There, she met fellow stained glass artist Margaret Chilton (1875-1962) who joined the studio as a designer in 1918. In 1922 they formed a partnership and established their own stained glass studio in George Street, Edinburgh, later moving to Queen Street. After the Second World War, the studio moved to Fettes Row in Edinburgh. The firm was known as Chilton & Kemp. Each produced their own designs, but jointly executed them.

Many of the firm's commissions can be found in Scotland. For example, in Edinburgh's City Chambers, for which the firm executed heraldic windows. Also executed a window for St John's Church, Perth; a panel for St Ninian's Church, Aberdeen; a Henry V design for a door panel at Colinton, Midlothian; stained glass for Greyfriar's Church, Edinburgh and Hill Parish Church, Blairgowrie among others. Kemp's designs included a three-light east window for the East Church of St Nicholas, Aberdeen (1936) based on Crucifixion, Resurrection, Acts of Mercy. Appropriately, she produced a design for a staircase window for the Ministers' Daughters' College she had earlier attended.

Smaller commissions included a nursery window for Monkwood House, Edinburgh and a staircase window for Esdaile School, Edinburgh based on St Joan. In around 1938 the firm executed a stained glass window for the Church of Scotland Building for the Empire Exhibition, Glasgow. Outside Scotland, executed a two-light and a three-light window, based on St Luke and St Michael, for Milburn Church, Westmorland. Further afield, the firm's designs can be found in St Andrew's Church, Buenos Aires and in South Africa.

Kemp exhibited her designs throughout much of her career, including at the Royal Scottish Academy (1925-50), the Royal Glasgow Institute (1934-55), the Royal Academy (1930-36) and the Society of Scottish Artists. Possibly exhibited one work at the Society of Women Artists in 1969 (Mrs Marjorie Kemp, no address, needs clarification). After Chilton's death, Kemp retired and continued to live in Edinburgh. She died in the city some 13 years after her business partner. Works illustrated in The Builder. Works included in an exhibition Women Stained Glass Artists of the Arts and Crafts Movement held at the William Morris Gallery, London, 1985-86.

KENDALL, ALICE (b.c.1896)

Painter / Writer / Musician. Born in Little Hulton, Lancashire. The daughter of Thomas Henry Tyldesley. Educated privately and at the Manchester College of Music. Studied art in New York, and at the Edinburgh College of Art under Gerald Moira, David Allison, David Foggie and Henry Lintott. Produced paintings in watercolours and oils, various subjects. Exhibited with the Society of Scottish Artists, the Women's International Art Club, the Royal Society of British Artists, the United Society of Artists, the Royal Institute of Oil Painters and the Royal Institute of Painters in Watercolours. Exhibited one work, Raining Cats and Dogs (oil), at the Society of Women Artists in 1949. A Member of the United Society of Artists, and of the Society for Education in Art. Works reproduced in La Revue Moderne, the Scotsman and the Scottish Daily Express. Written articles were reproduced in the Scotsman, the Manchester Guardian and the Christian Science Monitor. Based in New York, Edinburgh and Edith Grove, London. She married Professor James Pickering Kendall, F.R.S., P.R.S.E, (1889-1978), an expert in solution chemistry. He worked in New York, where Alice studied. James Pickering attained a full Professorship at Columbia in 1922, and in 1926 became Head of the Department of Chemistry at Washington Square College. They had at least three children, Alice R., James and

Isobelle (also possibly Jean). Alice R. Kendall became an artist. SEE: KENDALL, ALICE R.

KENDALL, ALICE R. (b.c.1922-post-1993)

Painter / Illustrator / Writer / Textile Designer. Born in New York. The daughter of chemist Professor James Pickering Kendall, F.R.S., P.R.S.E. (1889-1978) and writer, artist and musician Alice Kendall. Her parents were British, but her father worked in America for some years, attaining a full Professorship at Columbia in 1922. One of at least three children. Educated at the Horace Mann School in New York, and at the St Trinnean's School, Edinburgh. The family returned to Britain whilst Alice was still a child, in around 1928. She studied at the Edinburgh College of Art between 1939 and 1943 under David Allison, William Gillies, Donald Moodie, R.H. Westwater, Joan Hassall and C.T. Howieson. Based in Edinburgh, but subsequently (sometime in the 1940s) moved to Edith Grove and then Beaufort Gardens, London. Awarded a Diploma of the Edinburgh College of Art. Produced paintings in oils and watercolours, pen & ink drawings, sepia drawings, murals, illustrations and textile designs. Subjects included portraits, still life, figures and animals.

Kendall exhibited widely, including at the Royal Glasgow Institute (1945-50), the Royal Academy (1944-61), the Society of Women Artists (123 works, 1949-93), the Royal Scottish Academy (1943-46), the Society of Scottish Artists, the Women's International Art Club, with the United Society, at the Guildhall, the Chenil Gallery and the Society of Graphic Art. Exhibited works included: Tranquility, The Magic Bough, Pooh's 21st Birthday Party and Tatties. Executed a portrait of her father which was purchased by the Royal Society of Edinburgh in 1956. The portrait was exhibited in London at a private show in 1956.

Kendall executed murals for the British Council and for the Ministry of Labour. Her Adoration of the Toys was reproduced in Scottish Field. Illustrated poems by Jean Kendall for the Epworth Press. Contributed illustrations to Funny Fishes, and to journals including Art and Design, Punch, the Strand, Truth, Somerset Countryman, Wild Life and Scottish Zoo. Elected a Fellow of the Royal Zoological Society (of Scotland). A Member of the United Society of Artists, and of the Royal Glasgow Institute. Elected a Member of the Society for Education in Art, as was her mother. Elected an Associate of the Society of Women Artists (1958-60), and a Member from 1961. Acted as Vice President of the Society (1972-76), and as Honorary Treasurer (1965-72).

Became President of the Society of Women Artists (1977-82), having acted as Acting President between 1973 and 1976 whilst Muriel Wheeler was President. Also a Fellow of the Royal Society of Arts. SEE: KENDALL, ALICE

KENDRICK, FLORENCE ADA (1880-1969)
Sculptor / Modeller / Painter / Designer. Known as Flora. Born in Margate, Kent. The daughter of Joseph Thomas Kendrick, an engraver. Studied at the Royal College of Art, London. Lived with her father in Ealing, London after that. Became a sculptor of busts and statuettes in bronze, but also executed masks in bronze, pottery statuettes and designs for printed fabrics. Also a watercolour painter and an art teacher for a time. Exhibited her work, including at the Royal Academy (1910-57), the Royal Glasgow Institute (1916) and the Royal Scottish Academy (1916). Also, at the Paris Salon, in Leeds and Manchester, with the Royal West of England Academy and at the 1906 exhibition of the Arts and Crafts Exhibition Society. Other works shown at the Walker Art Gallery, Liverpool, with the International Society of Sculptors, Painters & Gravers, under the Duveen scheme, and with the Society of Women Artists (1908-19). Exhibited works included: The Herald of the Coming Age, The Merry Peasant (bronze), Puck (statuette, bronze) and Siamese (statuette, pottery). Also executed at least one portrait work of her father. Elected an Associate of the Royal Society of British Sculptors. In 1919 she married Horace Shipp (1891-1961) in Richmond, Surrey. Thereafter, remained in London, latterly at The Gables, Hampstead Heath. Flora died in Hampstead, aged 89.

KENNEDY, HAZEL RUTHVEN - SEE ARMOUR, H.R.

KETTLEWELL, FRANCES - SEE CRAWSHAW, F.

KIDMAN, LILIAN LEIGH (1879-1956)
Illustrator / Poster Artist / Painter. Born at Gt Nast Hyde, St Albans, Hertfordshire. The daughter of Henry Oscar Kidman, a gentleman farmer, and Louisa Rosetta. Initially raised at Nast Hyde Farm, but later based at Buttermere, Wiltshire and in Surrey. One of at least four children (Walter, Lilian, Ella and Lester). Educated privately. Took up art relatively late. Listed as an art student in 1911, aged 30, whilst living in Surrey with her parents and Ella. Studied under Richard Jack, John Hassall and E. Sullivan, at the London School of Art and at Calderon's School of Animal Painting. Produced illustrations for annuals and children's books for Blackie, Nelson, Ward Lock, Wells Gardner Darton and the Epworth Press. Exhibited her work occasionally, including at the Gieves Gallery and the Society of Women Artists (14 works, 1924-31). Exhibited works included: Saturday, No Luck At All, Gossip in High Places, True Dignity and The Knitting Lesson. Elected an Associate of the Society of Women Artists (1926-31). Based in London for part of her career. Died at Kings Langley, Hertfordshire, aged 76.

KIMBALL, KATHARINE L. (1866-1949)
Painter / Artist in Pen & Ink / Illustrator. Although born in Fitzwilliam, New Hampshire, U.S.A., Kimball spent over half her life and most of her career in England, moving to London in around 1900, dying in Bath, Somerset. She was the daughter of John Richardson Kimball and Catherine. She was also cousin to Mr Fiske Kimball (b.1888), Director of the Philadelphia Museum of Art. Prior to 1900, she spent some time in Boston, Massachusetts and studied at the National Academy of Design in New York. She then studied at the Royal College of Art, London. She was best known for her visually appealing pen & ink drawings of towns and cities, and illustrated a number of topographical books and articles, some for American magazines. Works illustrated by Kimball included Paris (Okey, 1904), Brussels (Gilliat Smith, 1906), Canterbury (Sterling Taylor, 1912) and Rochester (1912). She also contributed to The Century, The Artist, The Queen and the Gazette Des Beaux Arts.

Kimball held what was possibly her first exhibition in England in 1902, showing some of her drawings at the Clifford Gallery in the Haymarket. Two of her exhibits were illustrated in The Studio, Vols.24-25, 1902, pp.282-283. Also exhibited her work at the Royal Academy (1907-19), in Liverpool and with the Royal Society of Painter-Etchers & Engravers. In 1907 she contributed to an exhibition at the Ryder Gallery. Other exhibitors on that occasion included Blanche Baker. Kimball's exhibited works included: A Corner of Old Paris, The Cathedral, Bruges, Noah's Ark, Lannion and Hintersteinebach, Switzerland. She was elected an Associate of the Royal Society of Painter-Etchers & Engravers in 1909. In 1907, The Studio, Vol.40, March, p.152, illustrated her drawings of Notre Dame, Paris and San Giorgio Maggiore, Venice. In 1900, artist Grace R. Lewis exhibited a portrait of Miss Kimball at the Royal Academy.

KIMBER, SARAH VIRGINIA MAY (b.1891)
Illuminator / Decorative Artist. Born in Kilburn, London. A student of the Brighton Municipal School of Art. Produced illuminations on vellum and other decorative work including memorial cards. Based in London for much of her career. Exhibited eight works at the Society of Women Artists between 1920 and 1930. Those included: The Covenant, The Sermon on the Mount, Love's Rhapsody and The Word Was Made Flesh (illumination on vellum). In 1917 she contributed to a joint exhibition of the Royal Society of Portrait Painters and the Royal Society of Miniature Painters held at the Grafton Galleries, London. Kimber showed two of her illuminations, Mater Christi and Prayer. Used the names Sarah, Virginia and May at different times during her career.

KING, MARY ANN - SEE RAEMAEKERS, M.A.

KINGHAM, SYLVIA SARAH (1895-1980)
Sculptor / Painter / Decorative Artist. Sometimes recorded as Sylva. Born in Reading, Berkshire. The daughter of journalist George Hollock Wynn and Sylvia. Had at least one elder sibling, George. Raised in Redbourn, Hertfordshire. Educated at St Albans. Studied under Professor (Louis) Richard Garbe at the London County Council Central School of Arts and Crafts. Garbe was Professor of Sculpture at the Royal College of Art as well as teacher of sculpture at the Central School. Kingham spent much of her life in London and Middlesex, dying in Westminster, aged 86. Produced animals, birds, figures, portraits and decorative works in bronze, lead, concrete, cement fondu, plaster, Hoptonwood stone, wood, coloured plaster, gunmetal, copper and imitation stone. Also executed paintings in oils and watercolours. Produced decorative pieces such as mascots and door knockers.

Exhibited her work consistently over a period of at least 51 years, including at the Royal Academy (1925), the Royal Glasgow Institute (1926), the Walker Art Gallery, Liverpool, with the Women's International Art Club and in Toronto. Held at least one solo show at the Redfern Gallery. At the Society of Women Artists, she showed at least 61 works between 1925 and 1976, indicating that she was active and productive until a very short time before her death. Exhibited works included: Decorative Stag (lead), Watchful Repose (concrete), Cow Jumped Over the Moon (door knocker) and Sea Lion (statuette, bronze). Elected an Associate of the Society of Women Artists (1950-52) and a Member (1953-80). Also

elected Vice Chairman of the Women's International Art Club. Some of her works were illustrated in The Studio and the Illustrated London News. Purchasers of her work included the Contemporary Art Society. In 1921 she married William Randolph Kingham, M.A., F.R.H.S., in Kent. She executed and exhibited at least one sculpture of her husband, and a study of her daughter in fondu.

KINGSFORD, FLORENCE KATE (1872-1949)
Illuminator / Bookbinder / Artist. Born in Lewisham, London in October 1872. Her father, Charles Tomson Kingsford (1843-1902), was a corn and flour factor at the Corn Exchange, London, and later worked as a financial agent and broker. Her mother was Anne Harriet Moseley (1842-1930). Her father originated from London, her mother from Camberwell. Florence was raised in London. One of at least seven children (six girls and one boy). Two of her sisters became governesses. By the age of at least 18, Florence was already an art student in London. Studied at the London County Council Central School of Arts and Crafts. Became a painter and decorative artist working in various fields including illumination and bookbinding. Always regarded as an excellent calligrapher. One of her earlier illuminations was illustrated in The Studio, Vol.21, p.55 in 1900, by which time she was working from a studio at Stratford Place, Kensington where other artists had studios.

Kingsford carried out work for various private presses, including the Ashendene Press which was based in Chelsea, and which flourished under the guidance of St John Hornby from around 1895. In 1902 the Press produced 40 copies of The Song of Songs, all printed on vellum, illuminated by Florence Kingsford and bound by Katharine Adams, Alice Pattinson and Florence Paget. Two pages from that were reproduced in colour in The Studio, Vol.56, June 1912, pp.45-58, in an article Some Modern Illuminations. Kingsford also worked for the Essex House Press of Charles R. Ashbee's Guild of Handicraft. The Press flourished from the late 1890s until around 1909. Florence designed initial letters for the Press, and decorated editions of Tam O'Shanter and The Rime of the Ancient Mariner among others, also hand-colouring The Flower and the Leaf, a medieval poem. Others who worked for the Press included Edith Harwood. Florence was also a regular contributor to the exhibitions of the Arts and Crafts Exhibition Society, including in 1906. At the 1910 Exhibition, she showed a manuscript executed in collaboration with Graily

Hewitt. Also exhibited three works at the Royal Academy early in her career, Greek Girls Playing at Ball in 1899, and Harmony and "1844" in 1900.

In 1907, aged around 35, Florence married Sydney Carlyle Cockerell (1867-1962) in London. Cockerell became Director of the Fitzwilliam Museum, Cambridge (1908-37) as well as acting as secretary to William Morris at the Kelmscott Press. Born in Brighton, Sussex, he was the son of Sydney John Cockerell (1842-77), and elder brother to Douglas B. Cockerell (1870-1945), a bookbinder and teacher of bookbinding at the L.C.C. Central School of Arts and Crafts. The Cockerell family had strong artistic leanings. Douglas and Sydney had a sister, Olive Cockerell (1869-1910), who was a book illustrator, but who died young. Douglas's daughter was jeweller and silversmith Catherine Anne Cockerell (b.1903). Their father, Sydney John Cockerell, was, perhaps surprisingly, a local coal merchant who apparently had no obvious artistic interests. Sydney always referred to Florence as Kate. They had three children, Margaret Kate (1908-86), Christopher Sydney (1910-99) and Katherine O. (1911-96). Christopher was the inventor of the hovercraft. Bookbinder Katharine Adams was godmother to Katherine.

After their marriage, Florence continued to work. In 1914 her illuminated manuscript The Book of Job with calligraphy by Graily Hewitt was exhibited at the Exposition des Arts Decoratifs in Paris. In March 1916, Colour magazine, Vol.4, illustrated a colour facsimile of an illuminated address which had been presented by Queen Alexandra at Marlborough House on 17th December 1915, on behalf of the British Red Cross Society to the Japanese Red Cross Society, in recognition of the services of their mission in the British Red Cross Hospital at Netley between January and December 1915. The design was by Florence and the lettering by Graily Hewitt. Later in her career, Florence exhibited The Wood Beyond the World at the Royal Glasgow Institute in 1924, then living in Cambridge. In 1937, and now Lady Cockerell, she exhibited Phlox at the Society of Women Artists, then living at Holland Park, London. She died in Middlesex, aged 76. Sydney Cockerell subsequently lived at Kew, Surrey, and survived his wife by some 12 years, reaching the age of 94, dying in Surrey.

KINKEAD, ALICE SARAH (1871-1926)
Painter / Artist / Craftswoman. Born in Galway, Ireland in February 1871. The daughter of Richard John Kinkead and Alice Sarah Laughy. Probably studied in Ireland. Initially based in Galway, but some time between 1897 and 1898

she moved to London. There, she used the Pomona Studios in the New King's Road and later the Yeoman's Row Studios, Brompton. For a while, she was neighbour to Adolphus Birkenruth, an artist and brother to Johanna, a bookbinder. Alice remained in London, dying at Bedford Gardens, where she lived latterly, aged 55. Produced portrait and landscape paintings, various handicrafts, and Chromo-xylographs which were used for bookplates and greetings cards. Exhibited her work in Ireland, England and Scotland. Exhibited at the Royal Glasgow Institute (1905), the Royal Academy (1915), the Royal Hibernian Academy (1897-1920) and the Society of Women Artists (1901-24). Also contributed to the 1911 Sir John Cass Arts and Crafts Society exhibition held at Sloane Street, London. The Society was made up of students and staff of the School of Art, indicating that Kinkead may have studied or worked there. Exhibited works included: W.B. Yeats, Esq., Lieut. A. Haslam, M.C., D.F.C., R.F.A., R.A.F., Dick, Son of Robert Allan, Esq., M.B., F.R.C.S.I. and The Village of Piana, Corsica. Her portrait of Joseph Conrad was praised and illustrated in The Studio, Vol.88, September 1924, p.157.

KIRK, ELIZA (1814-71)
Sculptor. Born in Dublin, Ireland in December 1814. The daughter of Thomas Kirk (1781-1845) and Eliza Robinson (1788-1869). Her father was a reputable sculptor who exhibited his work at the Royal Hibernian Academy (1826-52) and was elected a Royal Hibernian Academician. Eliza was one of at least three children. Her brother Joseph (b.1820) became a sculptor too. He was also elected a Royal Hibernian Academician, exhibiting his work between 1840 and 1871. He died in America in 1894. Another brother, William, also became a sculptor and exhibited at the Royal Hibernian Academy (1844-56). Eliza worked over at least three decades, producing mainly small and miniature busts in marble. Although based in Dublin, she had a wide range of sitters not only from Ireland but from England too. Those included Robert Marshall, Esq. of Liverpool, for whom she executed a bust in miniature. Eliza too exhibited predominantly at the Royal Hibernian Academy, showing 18 works there between 1837 and 1859. Exhibited works included: The Rt Hon. Frederick Shaw, M.P. (miniature bust), King William III (miniature bust), The Juvenile Recreations of an Anti-Teetotaller Deity and Child and Butterfly.

KIRKPATRICK, ETHEL ALICE & IDA MARION (1870-1966) & (1867-1950)

Artists / Painters / Craftswomen. The daughters of Capt. T. Sutton Kirkpatrick, of the 3rd Dragoon Guards, and Rosa. Their father, who originated from Ireland, subsequently worked at Her Majesty's Prison, Clerkenwell, and later became Governor of Wormwood Scrubs Prison, London. They were two of at least five children (Ida, Ethel, Muriel, Claude and Cyril).

Ethel Kirkpatrick was born in Clerkenwell, London, and died in Harrow, aged 97. She spent much of her career living at The Gables, Harrow. Studied in London, at the Royal Academy schools and at the L.C.C. Central School of Arts and Crafts. Became a painter of landscapes, flowers, figures and portraits in oils and watercolours. Also worked as a designer, a decorative craftswoman and a colour woodcut artist. Exhibited her work, including at the Royal Academy (1895-1941), the Royal Society of British Artists (1888-94), the Royal Glasgow Institute (1900 & 1924) and the Society of Women Artists (1890-1907). Also, at the Venice International, at Wembley, at the Graphic Arts exhibition, Zurich, at the Rio de Janeiro International Exhibition, with the Society of Graver-Printers and with the Colour Woodcut Society. Held joint shows with Ida. Also contributed to the Arts and Crafts Exhibition Society exhibitions, including in 1916 when she showed a colour woodcut, Mount's Bay, which was illustrated in The Studio, Vol.69, 1917. Her watercolour painting Evening – Venice, priced £7 7s, was shown at the 1899 Exhibition of Pictures & Decorative Art held in Kendal, Westmorland. Exhibited works included: Venetian Beads, Against the Red Curtain, The Niesen Lake Thun (colour woodcut) and Fishing Boats at Tenby (watercolour). Both sisters exhibited decorative jewellery at the 1908 Mr John Baillie's Annual Exhibition of Arts and Crafts. A necklace by Ethel, titled Daisy Chain, was illustrated in The Studio, Vol.33, January 1905. Elected a Member of the Society of Graver-Printers, of the Colour Woodcut Society and of the Arts and Crafts Exhibition Society. Noted in Herbert Furst's volume The Modern Woodcut, London, John Lane, 1924. Works acquired by the Print Rooms of the British Museum and by the South Kensington Museum.

Ida Kirkpatrick was born in Jersey. Educated at the Queen's College, London and in Lausanne, Switzerland. Studied at the Royal Female School of Art, London and at Julian's in Paris. Awarded a National Gilchrist Scholarship of £50 for two years, and a Queen's Scholarship of £60 for one year. Also awarded a Diploma at the Royal Female School and an Art Class Teachers' Certificate. Principally a landscape, portrait and flower painter in oils and watercolours. Spent all her life living with Ethel. Into their 40s, the sisters were still also living with their widowed mother. Ida exhibited her work, including at the Royal Academy (1895-1924), the Royal Society of British Artists (1887-93), the Society of Women Artists (30 works, 1890-1913), the International Society of Sculptors, Painters & Gravers, the Royal Institute of Painters in Watercolours and the Royal Institute of Oil Painters. Also, with the Women's International Art Club, in the provinces, and at private shows with Ethel, including at the Alpine Club Gallery and other London galleries. Exhibited works included: A Still Salt Pool (watercolour), Pear Blossom (watercolour), Silence and Old Yorkshire Fishing Town. Her Nasturtiums was reproduced in Colour, July 1919. Other works were reproduced in The Artist, Queen and Lady's Pictorial. Elected a Member of the Halcyon Club. Ida also died in Harrow, aged 83. She appears to have been involved in the designing and making of decorative jewellery with Ethel.

KIRKWOOD, ELIZABETH H. & CONSTANCE ROBINA B. (b.c.1882) & (1883-1975)

Decorative Artists. Born and raised in Edinburgh. The daughters of Henry B. Kirkwood and Elizabeth. Part of a large family, of at least eight children (Jessie, Elizabeth, Constance, Marjorie, Dorothy, James, Olive and Phillis).

Constance Kirkwood studied in Dublin, at the L.C.C. Central School of Arts and Crafts in London and at the Edinburgh College of Art. She worked as a pottery artist, a designer, a lithographer and an etcher, with a studio in Frederick Street, Edinburgh. During her career, she was also an art teacher at the St Oran's School, Edinburgh. Exhibited her work, including at the Royal Scottish Academy (1916-19) and the Society of Scottish Artists. Exhibited works included: The Night of the Full Moon (lithograph), Pine Trees (etching) and Miss Muriel Graham Watson. Although she spent much of her life in Edinburgh, Constance died at Ringwood, Hampshire, aged 91. She produced numerous designs worked in enamels and exhibited by Elizabeth. She remained active into the 1930s.

Elizabeth Kirkwood also probably studied in Edinburgh, and spent much of her life there. She worked in enamels, often using designs by Constance. Elizabeth had a studio in Thistle

Street, and then George Street, Edinburgh. Produced some highly decorative pieces, such as a Celtic Processional Cross (designed by Constance), enamel pendants (designed by Constance) and a stall plate in enamels for the Thistle Chapel. Exhibited her work, including at the Royal Scottish Academy (1909-20), the Royal Glasgow Institute (1911) and the Royal Academy (1910-20). Exhibited works included: There Was Once a Prince (enamel, designed by Constance), Kippen and 1916. Still active into the 1920s.

KIRMSE, MARGUERITE (1885-1954)

Etcher / Painter / Sculptor. Born in Bournemouth. The daughter of Richard Kirmse and Lea. Her father originated from Germany, her mother from Switzerland. Richard Kirmse was a teacher who ran a school in Bournemouth for a number of years. Marguerite was one of at least three children. Attended the Fontainebleau School for Girls (probably her father's school). Initially, she showed an interest in music and studied at the Royal Academy of Music, London. Originally intended to become a musician and played the harp. But she was also interested in art, which she studied at Frank Calderon's School of Animal Painting and the Polytechnic School of Art. Her love of animals dictated her subjects. She began drawing at the London Zoo and at various dog shows. She continued with her music initially, but eventually gave it up in order to concentrate on art. Won a wide reputation as a painter of dogs and horses. Worked for various publications. Worked in oils, pastels, crayon and pencil. Also produced a number of bronzes of dogs and etchings in drypoint. In 1910 she emigrated to America where she won numerous commissions. She visited England occasionally after 1910. Sometime prior to 1930, she married George W. Cole, who shared her passion for animals. They lived on a farm at Bridgewater, Connecticut and she had a studio in New York. Used her own dogs as models. Illustrated a number of books, including Greyfriars Bobby (Atkinson, Harper, 1912), The Disappointed Squirrel (Hudson, Doubleday, 1925) and Lassie Come Home (Knight, Winston, 1940). Noted in Mahony, Latimer & Folmsbee, Illustrators of Children's Books 1744-1945, The Horn Book Inc., Boston, 1947.

KITCHENER, FRANCES MADGE (1889-1974)

Sculptor. Also known as Madge. Born in India in August 1889. The daughter of General Sir Walter Kitchener, K.C.B., and Caroline. Her mother was also born in India. One of at least three children

(Frances, Mary and Phillippe). Educated at Wycombe Abbey. As a child, she spent time in Farnborough, Hampshire. Studied at the Slade School, London, in Paris, under Charles Hawthorne and in America. Spent much of her career based in Surrey, at The Little Gallery in Ashtead. Died in Surrey, aged 84. Became a numismatic and heraldic sculptor and a painter. Produced portrait medals and medallions in bronze. Executed a plaquette, "London 1924", for the Royal Mint. Produced a portrait medal of Sybil Thorndike as Saint Joan, just over 3" in size, which was illustrated in The Studio, Vol.89, February 1925, p.105. Thorndike owned a bronze cast of the medal. Other subjects included Francis Derwent Wood, R.A., a medallion in bronze which was her only exhibit at the Society of Women Artists, in 1930. Also, the Rev. Canon A.G. Hunter, M.A., St Christopher and Pere Martin. Also exhibited her work at the Royal Academy (1926-29), the Paris Salon, in Liverpool, at Wembley and in New York.

KNIGHT, EVA ANN (1881-1961)

Sculptor / Painter. Born in Countisbury, Devon. The daughter of Frederick J. North (b.1848) and Louisa Lettey (1849-1935). Her father was a gamekeeper. Both parents originated from Porlock, Somerset. Eva was one of at least three children (Robert, Kate and Eva). Raised in Somerset, in Porlock, Minehead and Wiveliscombe. Educated privately. Studied at the Bristol School of Art. Produced paintings in oils and watercolours and sculptures. Exhibited her work, including at the Royal West of England Academy, the Victoria Art Gallery, Bath and with the Bath Society of Artists. Exhibited works included: The Little Paddler, Spring (sculpture), Playmates and Girl With Dove. Elected an Associate of the Bath Society of Artists. Later based at Ilfracombe, Devon and Chipping Sodbury near Bristol. She died in Yeovil, Somerset, aged 80. In 1908 she married Charles Knight in Somerset. He was an elementary teacher who originated from Wiveliscombe.

KNOBLOCK, GERTRUDE (1880-1964)

Sculptor. Although born in New York, Knoblock was based in Britain for several decades, from at least 1902 until her death some 62 years later, at the age of 83. She was the daughter of Charles Knoblock, and was educated privately. She studied at the Art League of New York under George Barnard, at the Academie Julian in Paris under Verlet, and at the Royal College of Art, London under Professor Edouard Lanteri between 1902 and 1907. Based in London thereafter. Produced garden figures, animals, fountains and statuettes in lead, stone, plaster and bronze. Exhibited at the Royal Academy (1906-41), the Royal Scottish Academy (1939-40), the Royal Glasgow Institute (1938), the Society of Women Artists (1927-51) and elsewhere. Exhibited works included: The Watchman (garden figure, lead), Girl Snail Rider (garden ornament, lead), Artemis Brauronia (statuette, bronze) and Faun (statuette, bronze). One of her commissions was for a bronze statuette of Florence Nightingale which was to be placed in a niche at her former home. Knoblock also executed a bronze statuette of Tchernicheva in the role of Francesca. Whilst living in London, she visited New York. Elected a Member of the Three Arts Club. Also elected a Member of the Society of Women Artists (1948-60).

KNOWLES, CAMILLE B. - SEE WOOD, C.B.

KOENIG, GHISHA (1922-93)

Sculptor. Born in Kensington, London. Died in London, aged 71. The daughter of Leo Koenig, a poet, writer and art critic. Her mother's name was Hildebrand. Studied at the Hornsey College of Art for two years, from 1939. Her studies were interrupted by the Second World War. In 1946 she joined Henry Moore's class at the Chelsea School of Art. Subsequently spent two years at the Slade School (1948-49) under Frederick Edward McWilliam. She then worked from home, also doing menial jobs to survive. In 1950 the Ministry of Works commissioned a large carved wood panel depicting the building industry for the Festival of Britain. The following year, she was commissioned to produce a large terracotta figure for the Poplar housing scheme. An admirer of Rodin, she concentrated on figures and portraits rather than the then-popular abstract forms. Her belief was that art and life are interrelated. She developed a particular interest in industrial subjects, and visited factories and other places for inspiration, producing works such as Men on Scaffolding II (terracotta, 1959) and three groups in terracotta titled Miners at Work. Worked in terracotta, bronze, polyester and other materials.

Initially, Koenig worked in London. But in 1951 she married Emanuel Tuckman (b.1921) in Kent. Thereafter, she was based largely at St Mary Cray in Kent, where her husband was a doctor. There, she found further inspiration. She was asked to work in local factories, and spent six years concentrating on that. First, she made preliminary studies in local paint factories, paper mills and industrial bakeries. Then, she would return to her studio and experiment with various materials. Around 1955 / 56 she began to create large figures in concrete, of men at their machines. One of those, The Machine Minders, was exhibited at the Whitechapel Art Gallery in 1956 and was praised in The Times and the Manchester Guardian. She also executed large bas-reliefs of women workers.

In 1959, Koenig gained permission from the Coal Board to make drawings below ground at the Chislet pits near Canterbury. She spent three days there, at one point for seven hours, crawling with her sketchbook. From that, she executed five terracotta works, three of the miners and two of the canteen. Also produced reliefs of scaffolders working at the local railway station. Exhibited her work elsewhere, including at the Royal Academy (1955-63). In 1962 she exhibited with the Society of Portrait Sculptors (founded in 1953), showing Christine. In 1963 exhibited Rag Trade I at the Grosvenor Gallery. Other exhibited works included: Twisters (statuette group, polyester), The Survivor (bas-relief, bronze) and Jane (head, bronze). Other works included Ezekiel, a bronze in memory of the Holocaust survivors. The subject of an illustrated article in The Studio, Vol.160, January 1960, pp.22-23.

KRAUSS, AMY ELIZA (1876-1961)

Potter / Painter. Born in Bristol. The daughter of August Krauss, a building contractor, and Alice Elliott. Her father originated from Germany, her mother from London. Her mother died in the 1880s, whilst Amy was still a child, and the family was cared for by her mother's sister. The second of at least five children (August, Amy, Alice, Daisy and Agnes), all raised in Bristol. Amy subsequently studied art in Paris. Became a pottery artist and a watercolour painter. Returned to Bristol and established herself as an exhibiting artist. Exhibited at the Royal Academy (1912), the New English Art Club (from 1914), the Paris Salon and the Royal West of England Academy. Exhibited works included: A Spring Morning and Flower Study. Elected a Member of the Royal West of England Academy. Subsequently (from at least the early 1930s) established a pottery studio at Red Lane Cottage, East Street in the village of Corfe in Dorset. Remained there until her death in December 1961.

KYLE, GEORGINA MOUTRAY (1865-1950)

Painter. A highly productive artist who travelled abroad to paint, but who also painted a deal of Ireland and Irish subjects. Concentrated on landscapes, street scenes, figures, portraits and still life. Worked in pastels, watercolours and oils. Born in Craigavad, Co. Down, Ireland. The daughter of George Wilson Kyle. Part of a prosperous business family. Spent much of her career in Belfast, including at West Elmwood. Educated at home. Studied art at the Academie Colarossi in Paris. Returned to Belfast. Joined the Belfast Ramblers' Sketching Club in 1889, and its successor the Belfast Art Society. There, acted as Secretary of the Ladies' Life Class. Exhibited widely, including at the Societe des Artistes Francais, the Walker Art Gallery, Liverpool, the Royal Glasgow Institute (1921-30), the Royal Scottish Academy (1931-37), the Royal Hibernian Academy, the Belfast Art Society, the Royal Institute of Oil Painters, the Society of Women Artists (1939) and with the Ulster Academy of Arts. Exhibited works included: The Lifting of the Fog at the Gas Works, Belfast, An Autumn Market in France, The Herring Buoy at Ardglass, The Girls of the Fishery and Her Feather Fan. Elected an Academician of the Ulster Academy of Arts. Several of her works were reproduced, including her Le Marche in Colour. Five of her works, including A Market in Ireland, were reproduced in the Paris Salon Catalogue. Purchasers of her work included the Belfast Art Galleries who acquired her A Busy Day at Smithfield and Le Marche Concarneau. Works also in the Ulster Museum, the Armagh Museum, the Queen's University, Belfast and Bangor Town Hall, Co. Down. Politically active. Travelled extensively and painted for over 50 years. Often gave away her paintings.

L

LACEY, CONSTANCE MARY (1884-1961)

Designer / Illuminator / Embroideress / Painter. The daughter of George Lacey and Fanny. Her father, a farmer, originated from Cotes, Leicestershire, her mother from Nottingham. Constance was the eldest of at least four daughters (Constance, Kathleen, Dora and Ethel), all born and raised in Cotes. Educated at the Loughborough High School, and in Germany. Then studied at Sir Arthur Cope's School of Painting, followed by the Royal College of Art, London. Won a medal at Cope's School. Awarded two prizes at the Royal College of Art and a diploma. Also awarded a technological certificate for embroidery by the City & Guilds of London Institute. Elected an Associate of the Royal College of Art in 1907. Subsequently acted as an examiner in embroidery for the Union of

Lancashire and Cheshire Institutes. Acted as assistant at the Derby School of Art. Also acted as assistant at the Ipswich School of Art, and was a visiting teacher of arts and crafts under London County Council. Exhibited her work occasionally, including at the Arts and Crafts Exhibitions held in London in 1909 and 1926. Also, at the Derby Art Gallery in 1924 and 1927. An embroidered chalice and veil executed by Constance was illustrated in the Art Journal, 1910, p.250 in an article Embroidery and Needlework. By the 1930s, she was living in Derby. Died in Brixworth, Northamptonshire in late 1961, aged 77.

LACK, BARBARA DACIA (1907-2004)

Painter / Engraver / Textile Designer. Born in Chesterton, Cambridgeshire. The daughter of Charles Tibbit Lack, M.I.M.E., A.M.I.E.E., and Florence Daisy. Her father, an engineering consultant, originated from Cambridge, her mother from Essex. Had an older brother, Eric. Raised in Cambridge and spent much of her career there. Died in Penrith, Cumbria, aged 97. Educated at the Perse School, Cambridge. Studied at the Cambridge School of Art and the Royal College of Art, London. Elected an Associate of the Royal College of Art. Became a teacher and artist in painting, engraving and textile design. Taught at the School of Art, Cambridge Technical School and at several private schools. Exhibited her work occasionally. Showed paintings and engravings at the Royal College of Art Association Exhibition held at the Royal Academy in 1948, and in the provinces. Also, elsewhere in London, and in Edinburgh and Copenhagen. Two of her works were purchased by Messrs J.&P. Coats in 1945. Works reproduced in various journals including The Studio and Embroideress.

LAIDMAN, EDITH ANNIE (1880-1943)

Sculptor / Miniature Painter / Potter. Born in India. The daughter of George John Laidman (1845-86), of the Indian Civil Service, and Charlotte Smith (1846-1934). The youngest of five children (George Henry, Charlotte Mary, William Ernest, Ida Frances and Edith Annie). Her brother William became a clergyman in Yorkshire. Ida Laidman (1878-1962) became a painter of portraits and miniatures, and was a singer. Both Edith and Ida were educated on the Continent. Ida studied art at Bushey, Hertfordshire in the early 1900s, at the Herkomer School. Since Edith was also based at Bushey at that time, it can be presumed that she too studied there.

After Bushey, Edith lived and worked at Godalming, Surrey (from at least 1908), and died there in April 1943, aged 62. Ida lived with Edith at Bushey and at Surrey, but was later based at Albert Lodge Studio, Albert Place, Kensington and Victoria Park, Kensington. Ida died in Kensington in June 1962, aged 84. For a time, they were joined in Surrey by their sister Charlotte, who was known as Mary. None of the sisters married. Edith produced sculptures in marble and terracotta. Subjects included animals, portraits and figures. Also produced portrait miniatures and pottery.

Edith exhibited her work over a period of more than 30 years. Exhibited at the Royal Academy (1904-34), the Royal Glasgow Institute (1927), the Walker Art Gallery, Liverpool, the Chester Gallery, the Royal Drawing Society and the Gieves Gallery. Exhibited works included: The Artist's Mother (bust, marble), Toilers of the Land (statuette group, terracotta), The Rev. R. Nattrass, Eveline (miniature) and My Sister Mary. On her death, Edith left her estate to Charlotte. Ida exhibited her work for over 55 years. She exhibited at the Royal Academy (1905-60) and the Royal Society of Miniature Painters. Elected an Associate of the latter in 1920. Charlotte executed portraits of, for example, H.R.H. Princess Christian of Hesse, H.R.H. Prince Vladimir of Russia, Lady May Cambridge and Mrs Cornelius Vanderbilt Jnr. She travelled to Europe, America and Canada. Evidently a society portrait painter.

LAKE, EVELYN FRANCES COOTE (1886-1979)

Painter / Decorative Artist / Writer. Born in St Pancras, London. The daughter of Joseph Fosbrey Lake (d.1932) and Elizabeth. Her father, a jeweller, originated from Essex, her mother from London. Had at least three siblings, Harold, Cuthbert and Hilda. All the Lake children were well educated. Harold became a jeweller. Cuthbert became a surveyor. Evelyn was raised in London and spent much of her life there, dying in Haringey, Gt. London, aged 93. Also spent some time in Hertfordshire. She only took up art seriously in the 1930s. Initially studied at the North London Collegiate School, then the Royal College of Music, and the London School of Economics. She studied art at the Camden and Hornsey Schools of Art as well as in Europe. Became an artist in watercolours, crayon, charcoal, wash, chalk and pastels. Also a miniature painter. Specialised in cats and birds. Also a writer on folklore. Became a regular contributor to Folk Lore magazine from 1949.

Contributed articles to other journals, and occasionally verse. Executed decorative drawings for a cat encyclopedia by Kit Wilson. One of her commissions involved painting champion cats Hendon Defendant and Barney of Bedale. Exhibited her work, including at the Royal Society of Painters in Watercolours, the Royal Society of Miniature Painters, the Paris Salon, the Society of Women Artists (1939-63) and in the provinces. Held one-woman shows at Walker's Gallery in 1949 and 1951. Exhibited works included: Tabby Cat (pastel) and Pheasant (crayon). Elected a Member of the Committee of the Royal Society of Painters in Watercolours Art Club (1939-49). Elected an Associate of the Royal Society of Miniature Painters (1947) and a Member of the Council of the Ridley Art Club (from 1949). Also a Member of the Royal Empire Club. Lake was still painting and exhibiting into the 1960s.

LALL, DIANA METFORD (1886-1980)

Painter / Engraver. Born in Bridgwater, Somerset in April 1886. The daughter of Carveth Read, Professor of Philosophy at the University of London. Educated at the Norland Place School, London. Studied at the Crystal Palace School of Art for a year. Then studied at the Slade School for one year, followed by the St John's Wood School of Art for 18 months, and at the Royal Academy schools for three years. Also spent three months at the British Academy in Rome. Won a silver medal for antique drawing at the Crystal Palace School in 1903. Awarded a First Class Certificate for life drawing at the Slade School. Awarded a Bachelor of Arts in 1926. Became a painter in oils, watercolours and tempera, a wood engraver and woodcut artist. Spent time in Italy and India. Later based in Birmingham and Newcastle. Died in Surrey, aged 93.

Latterly, Lall became a lecturer in art at the Armstrong College, Department of Fine Art, Newcastle. Exhibited her work regionally, wherever she was living. Exhibited in Calcutta, Bombay, Birmingham and Newcastle. Exhibited works included: Isis and Osiris (tempera). Executed decorative works, including a wall painting for the Bensham Grove Nursery School in Gateshead. One of her woodcut prints, Everest, was acquired by the British Museum Print Room. Work published included: Krishna and Radhika in Swarga (Calcutta, 1916). Did illustrations to Dick, Gerry and Miranda (Elliot Stock, London, 1910) and to Ramayana and a Sikh poem (India, 1917). Wrote articles and reviews for The Forum of Education (Longmans Green & Co., London).

Married Kindan Lall in Elham, Kent in 1913. Had at least one daughter.

LAMB, HELEN ADELAIDE (d.c.1981)

Illuminator / Painter / Pencil Artist / Embroideress. Born in Scotland. Educated privately. Studied at the Glasgow School of Art. Awarded a diploma, a travelling bursary and a post-diploma maintenance scholarship. Based mainly in Glasgow and Dunblane during her career. Worked principally as an illuminator, receiving commissions. But also produced paintings in watercolours, drawings and decorative embroideries much in the style established at the Glasgow School of Art by Jessie Newbery. Also worked as an art teacher at the St Columba's School, Kilmacolm. Elected an Associate of the Glasgow School of Art. A Member of the Glasgow Society of Lady Artists' Club. Elected to the Society of Scribes and Illuminators in 1921. Exhibited her work occasionally, including at the Royal Scottish Academy (1924-61), the Royal Glasgow Institute (1919-63), the Edinburgh Academy and in Liverpool and Stirling. Exhibited works included: St Columba (illumination), Peace Be To Thee, Iona, Silver Birch (black & white) and Near Arisaig (watercolour).

Other works executed by Lamb included an Illuminated Prayer shown at the Church of Scotland Empire Exhibition. Also, a Cradle Roll for the United Youth Committees of the Church of Scotland and the United Free Church of Scotland. Executed Rolls of Honour for Dunblane Cathedral, St Cuthbert's Church, Edinburgh and Troon Golf Club. Contributed to the Glasgow School of Art exhibitions. In 1909, for example, Lamb showed an embroidered panel which was illustrated in The Studio, May 1909, p.333. In 1910, The Studio, Vol.50, p.133 illustrated her design for an embroidered panel in an article The Glasgow School of Embroidery by J. Taylor. Lamb was active from at least 1909 until at least 1963. At the same address was artist Mildred Richley Lamb (1900-47). She also exhibited at the Royal Scottish Academy (1935-37) and the Royal Glasgow Institute (1930-41). Mildred produced pen & ink drawings, chalk drawings, paintings and pencil drawings.

LAMB, MARGARET CAROLINE (1873-1940)

Sculptor / Painter. Was Margaret Caroline Thurton Godfrey Thurlow. Born in Teddington, Middlesex. The daughter of William Thurlow Godfrey Thurlow (b.1843) and Margaret Clopton Brewster (b.1844). Her father, a clerk to the Admiralty, was born in the East Indies, her mother in Essex. Margaret was one of at least six children, all of whom were given lengthy names. She spent her childhood in Swanscombe, Kent. By the age of at least 18, she was a student at the Wimbledon College of Art, London. Whilst there, at the age of 19, she exhibited Sleeping Dog at the Royal Academy in 1892, a life-size sculpture of a dog. She also studied at the South Kensington Art School and the Royal Academy schools. Awarded a silver medal at the latter. Produced watercolour paintings and sculptures. However, she gave up sculpture when she married at the age of 22, but took it up again in 1918, almost 24 years later.

Margaret married solicitor John Frederick Lamb in Lambeth, London in 1895. He was 12 years her senior. At the time of their marriage, John Lamb was living in Chorlton-cum-Hardy, Lancashire. The couple subsequently lived in the north of England, including in Prestwich, Bowdon and Hale. They had two children, Arthur (b.1896) and Violet (b.1899). Latterly, Margaret lived in Southport, Lancashire where she died in October 1940, aged 67. Her husband outlived her. She began to work again on a more professional level once her children had grown up, around the time that the First World War came to a close. She began to exhibit again more seriously in the early 1920s, continuing until shortly before her death. Also exhibited at the Royal Hibernian Academy (1934-38), the Society of Women Artists (1924-27), in Liverpool, at the Government Pavilion at Wembley, at the Paris Salon, in Toronto and elsewhere. Exhibited groups, bas-reliefs, busts and figures in plaster, marble, bronze and copper, mainly animals. Exhibited works included: Russian Troika Horses (bas-relief, exhibited Paris Salon, 1923), The Late Walter Winans (bust, exhibited Paris Salon, 1924), London Mounted Police (bas-relief, exhibited Paris Salon, 1925), Tortoise (bronze, exhibited Paris Salon, 1926), Cocker Spaniel (bronze on Irish marble) and Young Rabbit (bronze).

LAMB, MARY (1764-1847)

Embroideress. Born in London. The daughter of John Lamb, a lawyer's clerk, and Elizabeth Field. Sister to writer and poet Charles Lamb (1775-1834). His first sonnet was published in 1794. Mental instability ran in the family, however, and both Mary and Charles were affected to varying degrees. In 1796 Mary killed her mother in a fit of madness, after which she spent time in an asylum. On her release, Charles acted as her guardian. Neither ever married. When he died, Mary's condition deteriorated considerably. She is buried in the same grave as Charles. Mary and Charles worked together on a volume titled Tales From Shakespeare (1807). Mary was also a skilled needlewoman and worked professionally for around 11 years. In 1815 she wrote and had published an essay titled On Needlework, in which she assessed the differences between the work of men and women.

LAMB, MILDRED RICHLEY - SEE LAMB, HELEN ADELAIDE

LAMBERT, HELEN G.C. - SEE MARSH, H.G.C.

LA MONTE, ELISH (1816-70)
Miniature Painter. Also sometimes Lamont. Born in Belfast. Came from a family of printers and stationers. Studied miniature painting in London in 1837. From 1838 exhibited with the Belfast Association of Artists. Also exhibited at the Royal Hibernian Academy (24 works, 1842-70) and the Royal Academy (1856-59). Concentrated on portraits. Subjects included the Earl of Belfast (watercolour), the Marquis of Headfort (watercolour), Lady Dufferin, Miss Agnew of Cairn Castle and the Hon. Mrs William Trevor Stamer. Based largely in Belfast during her career. In 1845 she published a series of prints illustrating Moore's Irish Melodies. Some of her miniatures were presented to Queen Victoria on her visit to Dublin in 1853. Engravings after her miniatures of Lady Dufferin and the Dowager Duchess of Manchester were included in The Court Album which was published annually in London between 1850 and 1857. The Album consisted of portraits of female aristocracy. La Monte may have produced some illustrations for Swain in the 1860s. Also an author and a schoolmistress. Literary works included a book of ballads, Christmas Rhymes, compiled with her sister in 1846, and Impressions, Thoughts and Sketches During Two Years in Switzerland. Won a second prize at the Victoria Fete in Belfast in a poetry competition in 1850 for her poem The Island Queen. She ran a boarding school in Belfast for a short time from 1851. Latterly, lived in Rochester, Kent. She died in Kent, aged 54.

LANCASTER, CLARE BRACEBRIDGE (1875-1954)
Painter. Born in Hong Kong. The daughter of Alfred Thomas Manger, J.P. From a young age, lived with her grandfather, an oil merchant, in London. Educated in Brussels. Studied at the Byam Shaw and Vicat Cole School of Art, London. But also studied in the studio of M.

Argemans, under H. Moore and G.F. Watts, and at St Ives, Cornwall under Algernon Talmage. Based mainly in London during her life and career. Produced portraits, still life, landscapes and other subjects in oils and watercolours. In 1907 she married Robert Lancaster (b.1880) in Kensington. He was listed as a gentleman of no profession at the time of their marriage, but subsequently became a publisher. They had at least one son, Osbert (b.1908), who became a successful oil painter, black & white artist and theatrical designer. Clare exhibited more after her marriage. Exhibited at the Royal Academy (1932), the Society of Women Artists (1924-33), the Royal Institute of Oil Painters, the New English Art Club and elsewhere. Exhibited works included: The Incense-Burner, Old London Houses, Cyclamen and Rue Pie, Roquebrun. Elected a Member of the Halcyon Club, of the Forum Club and of the Royal Society of British Artists Art Club. Died in Kensington, aged 79.

LANCASTER, LILIAN ADELAIDE (1887-1973)
Designer / Decorative Painter. Born in Hammersmith, London in October 1887. Raised in London and remained there for much of her life. The daughter of William James Lancaster, a theatrical agent and later 'gentleman', and Margaret. Had an older sister, Theodora, who trained to be a teacher. Educated at Crawford House, Maidenhead. Studied at the Slade School, London, the Westminster School of Art and the Brighton School of Art. A pupil of the highly influential painter Walter Sickert (1860-1942). In 1913 Lilian was chosen as one of four to compete in the Roman Scholarship Competition for decorative painting. The Scholarship was awarded by the Commissioners of the Exhibition of 1851 (British School at Rome).

Lilian became a designer and decorator, producing cartoons for decoration. Also produced landscape, figure and flower paintings. Worked in pastels, chalk and oils. Taught life drawing and painting at the Brighton School of Art, and at the Eastbourne School of Art during the First World War. Exhibited at the Salon D'Automne, the New English Art Club (from 1911), the National Portrait Society, the Royal Society of Portrait Painters, the Royal Academy (1927-66), the Society of Women Artists (1929-65) and in Stockholm. Exhibited in Germany by invitation of the Grosse Berliner Kunstanstellung. Exhibited works included: The White Jersey, Young Women at Their Toilet (decoration for bathroom), War (cartoon for decoration), Wild Roses and Gentle Cynthia (oil).

In 1921, Lilian married Alfred Clive Gardiner (1891-1960) in Chelsea. Born in Blackburn, Lancashire, he was a pupil of the Slade School and the Royal Academy schools. From 1929 he taught at the Goldsmiths' College of Art, and became its Principal from 1952. The couple appears to have had at least two sons, one being Stephen, whose portrait was exhibited at the Society of Women Artists in 1929. Alfred died in Chelsea, aged 69. Latterly, Lilian lived in Oxfordshire. She died at Abingdon, Oxfordshire, aged 86. Her career eventually covered five decades.

LANCE, EVELYN DELA BELINGE (1866-1937)

Artist / Illustrator. Also sometimes Eveline. Born in Barley, Hertfordshire. The daughter of Thomas Lance, who died young, and Evelyn Ann. One of at least five children (Thomas, Robert, William, Arthur and Evelyn). Raised in Middlesex. Later based in Chelsea. Died in Godalming, Surrey in December 1937. Became a painter of landscapes and buildings. Also an illustrator for The Religious Tract Society, and for Ernest Nister in the 1890s. Books illustrated by her included A Puzzling Pair (1898), Bulbs and Blossoms (1898) and His Birthday (1909) by Amy Le Feuvre. Also, My Seaside Story Book (with others, n.d.), Evelyn Everett-Green, Short Tales From Storyland (1902), and Lance's own Holiday Friends (1901) and Happy Playtimes (1901). Exhibited her work at the Royal Society of British Artists (1892-94) and the Society of Women Artists (1893-96). Exhibited works included: In a Dry and Thirsty Land, The Churchyard, Goudhurst, Kent, Old Gateway, Winchelsea (watercolour) and Nell Gwynn's House at Highgate. Arthur Lance also became an art student. Later in her life, Evelyn lived with her unmarried brother William, who was a Priest of the Apostolic Church. In the early 1880s, Evelyn's mother worked as a schoolteacher to support her family, but also took in lodgers. One of those was artist and author Mary P. Blyth who originated from Beverley, Yorkshire. It is feasible that Blyth had some influence over Evelyn and possibly taught her. On her death, Evelyn left her small estate to Mary Popham Blyth and Emily M.E. Blyth. At the age of 15, Evelyn is listed as a schoolteacher, so possibly assisted her mother.

LANCE, MARJORIE (1900-67)

Artist. Born in Scarborough, Yorkshire. The daughter of George William Lance and Mary Ethel Clark. Her father, a wholesale grocer, originated from Yorkshire, as did her mother.

Had at least two siblings, Doreen and George. Raised in Scarborough. Educated at Queenswood, Hatfield, Hertfordshire. Studied at the Slade School, London under Professor Henry Tonks, Philip Wilson Steer and Professor John Wheatley between 1919 and 1923. Awarded certificates for drawing, painting and design. Worked in oils, watercolours and pastels. Subjects included landscapes, portraits, figures and flowers. Exhibited widely, including at the Royal Scottish Academy (1940), the Royal Academy (1957-62), the Society of Women Artists (1952), at the Goupil Gallery, the Leicester Galleries, at Heals, with the New English Art Club and the Royal Society of British Artists. Also, at the Royal Society of Portrait Painters, the Pastel Society, the British Dominion Exhibition, in Leeds and Hull, at the Artists' Aid to China Exhibition, at the Wallace Collection and the Society of Marine Artists. Exhibited works included: The Victorian Chair, Evening, Villefranche, Winter Landscape and Petunias With Cactus. In 1931 she married Henry Carlyon Webb, A.R.S.M., E.M., in Yorkshire. Based in London, Middlesex and Hampshire during her career. Died in Hampstead, London.

LANCHESTER, MARY (1864-1942)

Painter / Colour Print Artist / Le Begue Water-Wax Artist. Born in November 1864 in Lewisham, London. The daughter of Henry Jones Lanchester (1834-1914) and Octavia Ward (1834-1916). Her father, an architect and Fellow of the Royal Institute of British Architects, originated from Islington, her mother from Middlesex. One of at least seven children (Henry Vaughan, Mary, Frederick, Francis, Edith, Edward and George), all born between 1863 and 1874. Mary studied at the Brighton School of Art, and at South Kensington. Won awards and certificates including an Art Masters' Certificate. In her 20s she was living as a boarder in a house in Brighton, and was a teacher of drawing and painting. But by her 30s, she was living with her retired parents in New Malden, Surrey, working as an artist. By at least 1911, she was living with her brother, Henry (1863-1953), in Weybridge, Surrey. Henry became an architect and was a Member of the prestigious Art Workers' Guild. Mary was still working as an artist at that point. Later, she was based at Haywards Heath, Sussex. She died there in January 1942, leaving her small estate to Henry.

Mary produced paintings in oils, watercolours and tempera. Subjects included landscapes and flowers. Also a colour print artist. Was a recognised expert in the Le Begue water-wax medium, and wrote a paper on the subject which was published in the papers of the Society of Mural Decorators and Painters in Tempera (The Dolphin Press). Lanchester was elected Honorary Secretary of the Society. The National Art Library acquired her The France Book for infants, hand-done and published by herself. Her River Severn was purchased by T. Murphy. Exhibited her work, mainly in the late 1890s and early 1900s. Exhibited at the Society of Women Artists (1896-1903), the Royal Academy (1900), the Royal Society of British Artists, the Royal Institute of Painters in Watercolours and in the provinces. Exhibited works included: Farm on the South Coast, Cowslips and Primroses, The Village Laundry and Orchard in Spring (watercolour).

LANGDON, BEATRICE AMY MILLICENT (1898-1986)

Artist. Born in Chorlton, Manchester. The daughter of Adolph Max Langdon, King's Council, and Amy Henrietta. Had at least two siblings, Ernest and Stephen. Based in London for much of her life and career. Spent some time in Budleigh Salterton, Devon. Died in Surrey, aged 87. Educated at the St Paul's Girls' School. Studied at the Byam Shaw and Vicat Cole School of Art, London. Produced landscapes and other subjects. Exhibited her work, including at the Royal Academy (1932-56), the Royal Scottish Academy (1937), the Royal Glasgow Institute (1936-37) and the Paris Salon (certainly in 1925). Also exhibited at the Royal Institute of Oil Painters (certainly in 1924 and 1925), in Hull, Birmingham and Liverpool and at the Royal Society of British Artists. Held a one-woman show at the Arlington Gallery. Exhibited works included: Lincoln's Inn, London: The Bencher's Walk, The Road to Tavistock, Near Fernhurst, Sussex and Victoria Grove, Kensington.

LANGHORNE, MARY (1909-84)

Painter / Textile Designer. Was Winifred Mary, known as Mary. Born in Exeter, Devon. The daughter of the Rev. Richard William Bailey Langhorne, M.A. (Oxon.) and Victoria Winifred Helen Poole. Her father originated from London, her mother from Somerset. Had at least one older sibling, Edward J.B. Langhorne. Raised in Exeter and spent much of her life and career there. Died in Exeter, aged 75. Educated at the Queen Anne's School, Caversham. Studied at the Royal Academy of Music. Also studied at the Exeter School of Art between 1928 and 1930, and at the L.C.C. Central School of Arts and Crafts, London between 1930 and 1932 under Bernard Adeney

and Graily Hewitt. Became a painter in oils and watercolours and a textile designer. Also became a teacher. Exhibited her work occasionally, including at the Royal West of England Academy, the Royal Institute of Painters in Watercolours and various provincial galleries. Works in the permanent collection of the Bristol City Art Gallery.

LANGLEY, HELEN ISABELLA (1861-1943)

Sculptor / Decorative Artist. Born in Eltham, Gt. London. The daughter of Edward Langley (b.1821) and Elizabeth (1824-1911). Her father, a bullion dealer and American banker, made sufficient money to enable him to retire from working whilst Helen was still young. She was one of at least six children (Leonard, Walter, Emily, John, Grace and Helen), all born between 1853 and 1861. The eldest, Leonard, who became a bank clerk, was born in Shanghai, China. John became a medical student, in his early 30s. The Langley children were raised and educated in London. Helen presumably studied in London. Became a sculptor and decorative artist, producing medallions, busts, reliefs, memorial tablets, decorative plaster friezes, decorative plaster panels, ceiling panels, mural decorations and designs for such things as door knockers in bronze, keyholes in bronze, bell-pushes, letter boxes and playing cards. Worked in various materials including silver, bronze, plaster, charcoal, coloured chalk and pencil.

Helen was based mainly in London during her career, but spent a short time in Bath, Somerset where, in the 1890s, her parents lived at Charlcombe Manor. Her mother originated from Somerset. By at least the early 1900s, Helen, her widowed mother and her sister Emily were back in London, and Helen was now listed as an independent sculptor earning her own living. In 1911 her mother died, at which time Helen was living with her unmarried brother, Leonard, in London. Helen died in London in July 1943, aged 82. She remained active as a sculptor until shortly before her death.

Langley had a long, successful and productive career, exhibiting her work over a period of more than 42 years. The fact that she began to exhibit her work in around 1897, at the age of 36, and is not listed as a sculptor on the 1891 National Census, would indicate that she took up sculpture some time in the early to mid 1890s, possibly when the family returned to London from Somerset, after her father's death. In 1897 she exhibited at the Royal Academy and the Society of Women Artists for the first time. At the Royal Academy, she showed 19 works up to 1927, including The New Book (relief), A Humble Task (relief) and A Young Girl (head, bronze). At the Society of Women Artists, she showed a considerable number of individual works, over 97 in total, the last in 1939. Those included: Querida (bust in bronzed plaster), Fairy Tales (panel in coloured plaster) and Peacock Frieze (coloured plaster). Exhibited with the Arts and Crafts Exhibition Society, including in 1899 when she showed a plaster relief. In 1899, two of her works, a Peacock frieze in coloured plaster and a design for a panel in plaster, were shown at the Exhibition of Pictures & Decorative Art held in Kendal, Westmorland. In 1901 she showed a panel in silvered relief at the Glasgow Exhibition alongside the work of Ann Macbeth, May Morris and other leading arts figures of the day. Exhibited at the First International Studio Exhibition, held in 1901-02, showing a coloured plaster panel.

In 1904 Langley contributed a plaster study of a child to the Clarion Guild of Handicraft Exhibition held in Manchester. She had ties with the Guild's London branch. Founded in 1902, the Clarion Guild concerned itself with Arts and Crafts philosophies, but also advocated the use of machines. Helen contributed to other Guild exhibitions, including that held in 1905. Also in 1904, she exhibited Seasons, a plasterwork to be used as an overmantel, at the City of Bradford Industrial Exhibition. The exhibition included handicrafts practised by women. Also contributed to the exhibitions of the Lyceum Club, including in 1906 when she showed two reliefs. Exhibited at the Walker Art Gallery, Liverpool, including in 1907. Elected an Associate of the Society of Women Artists (1908-47). Two of her coloured plaster panels and a bronze relief titled Jeune Mere were illustrated in The Studio, Vol.38, June 1906, pp.70-71.

Langley also designed a ceiling panel with modelled figures for architect T.E. Collcutt, for a house for one of his clients, along with a frieze. Both were exhibited at the Royal Academy in 1898. The ceiling panel had a central design of two winged children, one playing a horn, the other holding a scroll of music. At the 1899 Arts and Crafts exhibition, she showed a replica of the frieze, coloured, with a gilt background, with five children incorporated into the design. Both were illustrated in The Studio, Vol.18, 1899, p.271. During the First World War, she was commissioned to produce war memorials, including one titled Angels of Pity Comforting Sorrow which was exhibited at the Royal Academy in 1914.

LAPTHORN, MABEL DICKENSON (1889-1975)

Painter / Linocut Artist / Decorative Artist. Born in London. The daughter of George Lapthorn, a chemist, and Gertrude. Her father originated from Gosport, Hampshire, her mother from Staffordshire. The eldest of at least three daughters, also Gertrude, who became a pharmacy student, and Eileen. Raised in London. Studied in London, whilst living at the family home in Abbey Road, St John's Wood. Produced paintings in oils and watercolours, linocuts and decorative designs for masks. Exhibited two works at the Royal Academy, Pelleas and Melisande in 1913 and A Sleep and a Forgetting in 1914. Two of her works were illustrated in Colour magazine, an oil painting in May 1929, p.24 and Oriental Mask in September 1929, p.27. Three of her works were illustrated in The Studio, Vol. 93, 1927. Those were a mask titled Aquarius, a watercolour painting titled Cave Near Land's End (both p.352) and a linocut City of Dreadful Night (p.355). Lapthorn died in Hendon, London, aged 86.

LARCOMBE, LAURA ETHEL (1876-1940)

Artist / Illustrator / Designer. Known as Ethel. Born in Exeter, Devon. Remained there for much of her life, and died there in late 1940, aged 64. One of at least seven children of John Samuel Larcombe and Louisa Jane. Her father was a schoolmaster who ran the St John's Hospital School and Orphanage in Exeter, and her mother acted as mistress of the institution. Her father originated from Uplyme, Devon, her mother from Southwark, Gt. London. All the remaining Larcombe children were also born in Exeter. Ethel probably studied at the Exeter School of Art. She won numerous awards in The Studio magazine competitions for design. For example, won an Honourable Mention in 1900 for a design for a title page; won an Honourable Mention in 1900 for a 'Design Symbolic of Winter'; and another Honourable Mention for a Christmas card design and a Second Prize for a Christmas card design, again in 1900. She showed her work in The Studio competitions under the name Isca. Eventually, over a 10-year period, she won some 23 First Prizes, 17 Second Prizes and around 40 Honourable Mentions.

A diverse and talented artist, Larcombe produced not only Christmas card designs but advertisement designs, type designs, other greetings cards and bookplates. Also executed illustrations for children's books, including for Lollypop Lays for Dean's Rag Book (c.1914), and for Timmy the Elfin Taylor (Pixie Series, Rutley,

Dean, n.d.). She mixed with leading artists of the day. Talwin Morris (1865-1911) approved of her work and persuaded her to work for Blackie & Sons publishers, for whom he acted as art manager. She eventually worked for Blackie for around eight years, between 1904 and 1912. Produced decorative design work for other publishers including J.M. Dent, Delgado, Hills & Co., A.R. Mowbray, E.W. Savory and Carfax. Produced decorative postcards for Liberty, E.W. Savory and the Clifton Series. Produced decorative bookbindings, including for Bessie Marchant, A Heroine at Sea (Blackie), Charlotte M. Yonge, The Lances of Lynwood (Blackie) and Susan Coolidge, What Katy Did (Blackie). Some of her decorative bookbindings were exhibited in 1904. In 1909, Larcombe joined Jessie M. King and Dora Stone in creating a set of three Christmas card designs, available for purchase through The Studio magazine. The cards were advertised in the July 1909 issue, 50 cards for 15 / -. Later in her career, from at least 1911, Larcombe concentrated on teaching in her parents' school in Exeter along with two of her sisters, Marie and Amy. On her death, she left her small estate to Amy Larcombe, who also never married.

LARKING, LOUISA MARGARET (1898-1978)

Artist / Etcher. Born in Malvern, Victoria in Australia in January 1898. The daughter of Richard Jas Larking, a merchant, and Ethel Maude Peterson. Educated in Cambridge, Paris and Munich. Studied in London at the Slade School, the L.C.C. Central School of Arts and Crafts and the Royal College of Art. Produced etchings and pen & sepia drawings. Had addresses in London, Dorset, Melbourne in Australia and St Ives, Cornwall. Died in Cornwall, aged 80, her death registered in Penzance. Elected a Member of the Society of Graphic Art in 1924. Also a Member of the St Ives Society of Artists (1932-34). Exhibited with the Society in 1934 and 1938. Also a Member of the Three Arts Club and of the Print Collectors' Club. Works included: The Cornish Valley. Her The Mysterious House was reproduced in The Studio. A lifelong companion of artist Marjorie Heudebourck Ballance.

LASSAM, SUSIE (1875-1962)

Miniature Painter / Modeller / Metalworker. Born in Dulwich Village in December 1875. The daughter of Frederick Lassam, a baker and confectioner who employed at least seven people in his business, and Susannah. Her father originated from Dulwich, her mother from Middlesex. One of at least three children (Susie, John Errington and Margaret). Raised in Camberwell. Educated at the James Allan Girls' School, Dulwich. Remained at home into her 20s and 30s, by which time her father had retired. By her 30s, they were living at Rose Cottage in Dulwich Village, and Susie was then working as an artist. She studied at the Lambeth School of Art, the Royal College of Art and the L.C.C. Central School of Arts and Crafts. Had a long and productive career. Produced portraits in miniature and decorative metalwork. Also a modeller.

Lassam exhibited her work, including at the Royal Academy (1908-36), the Paris Salon, the Walker Art Gallery, Liverpool and the Royal Glasgow Institute (1911). Exhibited most prolifically at the Society of Women Artists, showing 103 works between 1915 and 1959. Exhibited works included: Lady Teazle, The Gay Deceiver, The Striped Bodice and Geoffrey (miniature on ivory). Elected an Associate of the Society of Women Artists (1931-39) and a Member (1940-61). Elected a Member of the Society of Miniaturists and an Associate of the Royal Society of Miniature Painters. Also a Member of the Overseas Club. By the 1940s, Lassam was living at The Cottage, Galmpton, Devon. She remained there until her death in March 1962, aged 86. She continued to work until shortly before her death and exhibited until at least 1959. She left her small estate to her brother, John Errington Lassam.

LATHAM, ANGELA (1894-1980)

Painter / Decorator / Fresco Artist. Born in Wolverhampton. The daughter of Francis Gibbons. Educated at the Convent of the Holy Child, Cavendish Square, London. A young talent, she studied at the Wolverhampton School of Art between the ages of 12 and 16. Then completed short courses in Oxfordshire and London. Also studied under George Thompson at South Villa. Painted for a time with Maurice Denis at his studio at St Germain-en-Laye, Paris. During the First World War, she carried out Voluntary Aid Detachment duty between 1915 and 1918. After the war, she divided her time between Penn Hall, Wolverhampton and Abbey Road, London. Worked as a painter in tempera and a decorative and fresco artist.

Latham began exhibiting her work in the early 1920s, and was still exhibiting in the mid-1960s, covering at least five decades. Exhibited at the Royal Academy (1923-65), the Royal Institute of Painters in Watercolours, the Royal Institute of Oil Painters, the National Portrait Society, the

Society of Women Artists (1924-35) and elsewhere. Exhibited works included: Chinese Coat, Madonna and Child, At Kynance Cove and The Lord Warrington of Clyffe. Also, Descent From the Cross, one of 14 Stations of the Cross executed for All Souls' Church, Warwickshire. Latham became particularly known for her portraits in tempera and for her fresco painting on walls. Elected a Member of the Society of Mural Decorators and Painters in Tempera. Also a Member of the Halcyon Club. Acted as Honorary Secretary of the Anglo-French Society of Staffordshire for a time. Executed a number of important commissions during her lengthy career. Those included an altar panel for the Birmingham War Memorial Church which measured a substantial 149sq.ft. Also executed an altarpiece for St Benet's Hall, Oxfordshire, and a fresco for the music room of The Beeches, Penn, Staffordshire. Her Girl in Red Coat was reproduced in Colour magazine. Her fresco Harlequin and Columbine was reproduced in The Queen. In 1925 she married Peter Morton Sturges Latham, M.A. (Oxon.) in Wolverhampton.

LATTER, RUTH (1868-1949)

Painter. Born in Todmorden, Lancashire. Was Ruth Beechey. Produced flower, landscape and portrait studies in oils and pastels. In 1893 married Cecil Latter in Yorkshire. He originated from Hertfordshire. They had at least one son, John (b.1897). Cecil died young, so Ruth worked as an artist to support herself. Based mainly in Battersea during her career, having formerly lived in Folkestone, Kent. Exhibited occasionally, including at the Royal Academy (1906-37), the Society of Women Artists (1922), the Salon des Beaux-Arts, the Salon des Artistes Francais and the Walker Art Gallery, Liverpool. Exhibited works included: Count Georges von Dardel, Madonna Lilies in a Cottage Garden, The Open Window and Primroses. Works purchased by the Oldham Municipal Art Gallery. Died in Battersea, aged 80.

LAURIE, KATHLEEN FRANCES (1900-97)

Artist / Academic. Born in Ceylon. The daughter of Frank Maxwell Laurie and Annie Elizabeth. Her father, who originated from Bedfordshire, was a tea planter in Ceylon, and her mother and two elder sisters, Irene and Beatrice, were also born in Ceylon. Kathleen moved to England when her father retired, whilst she was still a young child. The family lived in Wimbledon. Kathleen was educated at the Wimbledon High School. Evidently began her career as an academic rather than as an artist, studying at the

University College, London and the London School of Economics. She was awarded a B.A. Hons degree in 1923, and an M.A. in 1929. Was a Rosa Morrison Literary Research Scholar at the University College between 1927 and 1929. Also awarded a University of London Teachers' Diploma in 1924, a Diploma in Mental Health in 1938 and a University of Oxford Art Diploma in 1949. Became a senior English mistress in several schools, teaching some art between 1924 and 1932. Also involved in social work under the Education Committee (1933-37) and in psychiatric social and employment work with the Mental After Care Association Hospital and County Child Guidance Clinics (1938-46).

Between 1946 and 1947, Laurie studied art under Peter Greenham and Hubert Hennes at the Oxford City Art School. Between 1947 and 1949 she studied under Albert Rutherston, Percy Horton and Naish, Huskisson, Friedman and Gwyn-Jones at the Ruskin School of Art. Became an artist in watercolours, pen & wash. Exhibited at the Royal Academy (1951), the Society of Women Artists (1951), the Royal West of England Academy, the Royal Institute of Painters in Watercolours, the Scottish Society of Women Artists and the Society of Graphic Art. Also, with the Irish Art Society, the Oxford Art Society, the Festival Travelling Exhibitions, Derby Corporation and elsewhere. Exhibited works included: Grayshott, The Aquinas Castle, Roccasecca, Italy (watercolour) and The Heads at Trebarwith, North Cornwall (watercolour). Wrote a number of articles on employment for the Press. Based in Beckenham, Kent during her career.

LAVEROCK, FLORENCE HILDA (1879-1948)

Painter / Decorative Artist. Born in early 1879 in Warrington, Lancashire. The daughter of John Laverock and Eva, both of whom originated from Warrington. Had at least two sisters, Mary and Eva, also born in Warrington. All were raised in the town. There, their father was a tailor and woollen-draper, running the family business which he had taken over from his father, James Laverock. James was married to Mary, Florence's grandmother. Her father John had a sister, Eliza (1850-1917), also born in Warrington, who was a teacher of art needlework and other subjects. Eliza subsequently lived with her stepmother Elizabeth, James Laverock's second wife, and left her small estate to Florence when she died. Elizabeth and James had a son, Arthur, who was Florence's half-uncle. For many years, Elizabeth, Eliza and Arthur lived in the same street as

Florence and her family. It is probable that her Aunt Eliza had some artistic influence over Florence since Florence subsequently studied art needlework at art college.

By at least 1901 Florence had become a student at the Liverpool School of Art, Mount Street which, at that time, had Fred V. Burridge as its Principal. Burridge had a considerable influence on the School, and under his direction, in 1901 a needlework class was formed, with Florence as one of its earliest students. The class aimed to explore needlework and its design in a way not dissimilar to that taking place at the Glasgow School of Art. Florence's contemporaries at the Liverpool School of Art included Jessica Walker, Frances A. Jones and Gwendolen Parry. Like her aunt, Florence studied other subjects, producing not only applique and embroideries but metalwork, jewellery, enamels, lithographs, colour prints and black & white drawings. Whilst still a student, three of her colour prints were illustrated in The Studio, Vol.30, 1903, a journal which clearly recognised her burgeoning talents.

As a student, Florence showed work at the School's own exhibitions, and in 1901 showed a number of items in silver and enamel, including pins, brooches, buckles and pendants. The School held exhibitions on an annual basis, and Florence contributed until at least 1907. In 1907, she exhibited a series of panels illustrating Historic Fashion, lithographed by her. One of the panels was illustrated in The Studio, Vol.41, June 1907, p.167. The panels were the result of a commission from a firm who wanted them for a costumier's showroom, illustrating costumes of various periods in English history. The 1907 Liverpool School of Art exhibition of students' work was held at the Walker Art Gallery, Liverpool. Laverock also contributed to the National Competition of Schools of Art, South Kensington, including in 1903 when she showed, among other things, a colour print Days of the Week. She also certainly exhibited at the National Competition in 1904. One of her print decorations was illustrated in The Studio, Vol.38, June 1906, p.76.

Laverock particularly excelled in embroidery. In 1904, The Studio, Vol.33, offered a full-page colour illustration of her applique and embroidered hand screen. In the same year, the Art Journal, pp.70-71, illustrated one of three panels in applique and embroidery intended for a three-fold draught screen, and two panels which were part of a scheme for a Lewis Carroll schoolroom. The letter design incorporated sea creatures. Even as a student, Laverock was noted as having a solid approach to design and a keen eye for strong pattern. Whilst at the Liverpool

School, she lived at home with her widowed mother and sister Eva in Warrington. After leaving the School sometime around 1907 or 1908, she became an art teacher at a girls' school. Indications are that no more of her work appeared in The Studio after 1907, and it would also appear that she declined to exhibit after 1907. In 1911 she is listed as a teacher, living in Grappenhall, Cheshire with her mother and both her unmarried sisters. She died in Merioneth, Wales in October 1948, leaving her estate to Mary Laverock.

LAW, VERA (1900-85)

Illuminator. A founder member of the Society of Scribes and Illuminators. Sat on its initial committee, founded in 1921. Served as Honorary Secretary of the Society between 1937 and 1942. Studied under Lawrence Christie and Graily Hewitt. Died in Cambridgeshire.

LAW ADAM, EDITH CONSTANCE (1870-1951)

Painter / Silversmith. Known as Constance. Born in London. Was Edith Constance Elmore. In 1897 married John Law Adam in London. Lived in London, Hampshire and Surrey. Died in Surrey. Produced paintings in watercolours, mainly still life, and worked in silver. Exhibited at the Royal Academy (1925-40), the Society of Women Artists (1899-1924) and in Liverpool, Birmingham, Brighton and elsewhere. Exhibited works included: Moonrise, Rhododendrons, Green Bowl and Roses and Out of My Garden. Elected a Member of the Women's International Art Club. Also a Member of the Faculty of Arts and of the Ridley Art Club.

LAWRENCE, EDITH MARY (1890-1973)

Painter / Designer / Ceramic and Print Artist. Born in Surrey in March 1890. The daughter of George Adams Lawrence (1846-1927) and Clara Hayward (b.1854). Her father, a wine merchant and tea dealer, originated from Dorset, her mother from Holloway. Had at least one sister, Constance (1886-1973). Raised in London, and spent much of her life and career there. Educated at Queen's College, London. Studied at the Slade School, London. Won the Wilson Steer special painting prize and Slade First Class Certificates for painting and drawing. Became a landscape and portrait painter in oils and watercolours, a designer of textiles, a colour print artist, an interior designer and a stained glass designer. Taught colour printing privately. Also worked as an art teacher at Runton Hill, Langford Grove and Browning House.

Lawrence exhibited her work, including at the Society of Women Artists (1917-18), the Royal Scottish Academy (1938), the Royal Academy (1922) and the New English Art Club. Also, at the Royal Institute of Painters in Watercolours, with the National Portrait Society, with the Seven and Five Society and the Friday Club. Exhibited works included: On the Mole, On the Loire, Letters (oil) and Mother and Child (oil). Her Young Women was reproduced in Punch. Her Door Curtain was reproduced in the Daily News. Her watercolour French Chateau was illustrated in Colour, October 1930. Her stained glass designs included The Kingdom of the Future which was exhibited at the Royal Academy in 1922. Executed designs for tapestries too, including Cornwall. Lawrence developed a close relationship with (Walter) Claude Flight (1881-1955), though they never married. He began his career as a clerk, but took up art in his late 20s. In 1915 he married Helen Clare James, but evidently subsequently became close to Lawrence. In the 1930s she worked with Flight on some of his interior design schemes. Flight died in Salisbury, leaving his estate to Lawrence. She also died in Salisbury, some 18 years later. Helen Flight died in Sussex in 1983.

LAWRENCE, MADELINE CONSTANCE (1896-1952)

Textile Designer. Born in Islington, London. The daughter of Edward Lawrence and Martha. Her father, a commercial traveller and later a Fellow of the Royal Anthropological Institute and Member of the Geological Society, originated from London. Her mother originated from Shrewsbury. Had at least two younger sisters, Irene and Patricia. Raised partly in Leigh-on-Sea, Southend. Educated in Westcliff-on-Sea, Southend. Studied at the Southend-on-Sea School of Art between 1915 and 1919. Became a textile designer for the Silver Studio until 1944. The Studio was originally founded by Arthur Silver (1853-96) in London in 1880. It was later run by his two sons, Rex and Harry. It closed in 1963, having produced countless wallpaper and textile designs. Lawrence was elected a Member and Licentiate of the Society of Industrial Artists. Later in her career, she was based at Kenton, Middlesex. She died in Middlesex, aged 56.

LAWSON, DOROTHY PRENTICE (active 1930s)

Sculptor. Based in Roehampton Lane and Princes Gate, London. Exhibited four works at the Society of Women Artists: Mushroom, Portrait of a Thoroughbred and Fawn (garden ornament, bronze) in 1934, and Cart Horse (oak) and Car Mascot (plated bronze) in 1936. Otherwise, remains difficult to trace.

LAWSON, JESSIE MUTTER (1885-1965)

Sculptor. Born in Leith, Midlothian in February 1885. The daughter of corn merchant William Lawson and Jessie. One of at least five children. Raised in Midlothian. Initially studied at the Edinburgh College of Art. Then studied sculpture at the Royal College of Art, South Kensington between around 1908 and 1911. In 1908 she contributed with other students to an exhibition at South Kensington which consisted of 400 exhibits, all vying for 33 vacation prizes offered mostly by the teaching staff at the Royal College of Art. Lawson won a first prize and was awarded a special additional prize given by the sculpture judge. Lawson was again a prize-winning student at the Royal College of Art in 1909. By 1911 she was still an art student but also a visiting teacher. She was a contemporary of Anne Crawford Acheson, also a sculptor, with whom she shared digs. Lawson remained in London, working from Pembroke Studios, Kensington. Sometime around the end of the First World War, she married Howard Marriott Peacey and took his name when exhibiting her work. Peacey was a Cambridge scholar who trained as an accountant. He served in the war, and became a successful playwright. His works included The Fifth of November, El Dorado and Majestic House. The couple remained in England until the late 1930s when, effectively, Jessie ceased to exhibit in Britain.

Whilst living in England, Jessie exhibited at the Royal Academy (1910-38), the Royal Scottish Academy (1911-37), the Royal Glasgow Institute (1914-35) and the Society of Women Artists (61 works, 1922-37). Elected an Associate of the Society of Women Artists (1922) and a Member (1923-49). Also elected to the Royal Society of British Sculptors. Whilst in Britain, Jessie remained active and productive after her marriage. Produced portrait busts, groups, statuettes, panels, pottery groups, glazed earthenware figures, garden figures, bas-reliefs and studies of animals. Worked in plaster, stone, lead, terracotta, bronze, polychrome, wood and lacquer. Her portrait works included studies of Lord Fisher of Kilverstone, Miss Sybil Thorndyke as St Joan and Mrs Victor Gollancz. Exhibited works included: The Wrestlers, Seed-Time and Harvest (plaster), The Young Archer (bronze statuette), Javanese Dance (lacquered plaster plaque) and The Dance of the Cymbals (bronze statuette). Her Plunder (a garden group, lead) exhibited at the British Empire Exhibition, was illustrated in The Studio, Vol.88, July 1924, p.38.

In the late 1930s, the Lawsons left England. By 1938 they had travelled from Australia to San Francisco, and by 1940 were based in New York. Jessie had already visited New York in 1917, at the age of 32. It remains unclear if she ceased to work after 1938, but she remained a Member of the Society of Women Artists until 1949, if not an exhibitor. The Lawsons subsequently moved back to California. Howard Peacey died in California in May 1957. Jessie died there in June 1965.

LAWSON, LIZZIE (b.1859)

Painter / Illustrator. Was Elizabeth Ann, known as Lizzie. Born in Dunfermline, Scotland. The daughter of John Lawson, an artist and figure designer, and Martha. Both parents originated from Scotland. Records suggest that Lawson was one of at least five children (Lizzie, Martha, Edwin, William and Minnie). Sometime between 1871 and 1881 the family moved to Chelsea, and by the early 1900s, Lizzie was living with her parents in Fulham, aged 42. In 1886 she had married Robert Ellis Mack (1856-1939) in Fulham. Mack was an artist who originated from Bristol, but lived and worked in London. However, indications are that within a short time of the marriage taking place, Mack and Lizzie were living separate lives. She may have studied under her father, or even under Mack, and worked as an artist into the early 1900s. Produced figure paintings and illustrations, including pen & ink drawings. Contributed illustrations to Old Proverbs published by Cassell. Also contributed illustrations to Little Folks. Exhibited her work, including at the Royal Academy (1896-1902) and the Royal Scottish Academy (1902). Exhibited works included: Child on Stool, Child With Kittens, A Haven of Rest and Children With Toy Donkey. Possibly the same Lizzie Mack who died in Aylesbury, Buckinghamshire in 1958, aged 99.

LAWSON, VIVIEN SHERWOOD (1905-68)

Sketcher in Oils and Watercolours / Lithographer. Born in East Sheen, Surrey in August 1905. The daughter of Dr Frederick James Lawson, M.R.C.S., L.R.C.P., M.D., and Ethel. Her parents originated from London. Possibly an only child. Raised in London and spent much of her career there. Died in Bournemouth, aged 62. Educated at the Frances Holland School and University College, London. Studied at the Chelsea Polytechnic and the Royal College of Art. A prize-winning student. Elected an Associate of the Royal College of Art in 1930. Exhibited her work, including at the Royal Academy (1931), with the New English Art Club, at the Senefelder Club, the XXI Gallery, at the Young Artists' Exhibition, the Burlington Galleries and the Zwemmer Gallery. In 1931, she contributed to the Seventeen Artists Second Exhibition at the Zwemmer Gallery. Other exhibitors on that occasion included Barbara Hepworth, Sine McKinnon and Edna Ginesi. Works included: Chilworth Fields, Hampshire (oil), Unjust Steward (watercolour), Dairy Show (watercolour) and Salva and the Dragon (lithograph).

LAYNG, MABEL FRANCES (1881-1937)

Painter / Decorative Artist. Born in Macclesfield, Cheshire. The daughter of Alfred E. Layng, a schoolmaster. Her mother died whilst Mabel was still young, and her father spent some years living with his mother and sisters in Staffordshire, with Mabel and her sister Ada Clarice (1882-1977). Mabel studied at the London School of Art, at that time run under J.M. Swan and Frank Brangwyn among others. She contributed to exhibitions of students' work held by the London School at the Stratford Studios, Kensington, including in 1906 and 1908. On the latter occasion, she won a second prize. Other exhibitors included Helen Wilson and Janet Procter. Ada Layng also studied art in London, having formerly been a pupil at the Wycombe Abbey School in High Wycombe, Buckinghamshire.

After completing their studies, the Layng sisters lived together at Nevern Square, Kensington, working as artists. Mabel was the more productive, producing paintings in watercolours and decorative works of various subjects. One of her decorative compositions was illustrated in The Studio, Vol.45, October 1908, p.75. She exhibited at the Royal Glasgow Institute (1921-28) and the Royal Academy (1916-28). Also exhibited with the International Society of Sculptors, Painters & Gravers, including in 1921 when she showed her watercolour The Hat Shop. The painting was illustrated in The Studio, Vol.82, July 1921, p.28. Exhibited with the Women's International Art Club, including in 1913 when she showed Reading Aloud. Other exhibited works included: Crossing the Road, The Strolling Players and The Workroom. Later in her career, Mabel lived at Ealing, also using the St Albans Studios, London. She died in Camberwell, aged 55. Ada appeared never to exhibit at any of the major London galleries. She died some 40 years after Mabel, in Ealing, aged 94.

LEA, SHEILA (1901-92)

Sculptor. Born in London. The daughter of Norman Maclagan, who had independent means, and Olive. Her father originated from Dundee, her mother from Cornwall. Had at least one younger sibling, Thomas. Spent part of her childhood in Bruton, Somerset. Studied at the Bournemouth School of Art and at the Regent Street Polytechnic, London. Based largely in Bournemouth during her career, dying there aged 91. Produced statuettes and groups in plaster and bronze. Exhibited occasionally, including at the Royal Academy (1946-51), the Society of Women Artists (1955) and in Paris. Exhibited works included: Madonna (plaster), Sudanese Woman and Child (statuette group) and Slugs and Snails and Puppy Dogs' Tails (statuette group). In 1931 she married Cyril A.E. Lea in Bournemouth.

LEACH, JANET (1918-97)

Potter. Although essentially American, Leach spent much of her career in England and, for a time, became the driving force behind the Leach Pottery in St Ives, Cornwall. She was born in Texas, the daughter of Charles W. Darnell, a clerk, and Ollie. She is listed as a student in Texas, aged 22. Studied sculpture initially, then studied pottery in New York. She met influential British potter Bernard Howell Leach (d.1972, aged 92) and his contemporary and friend Shoji Hamada at a pottery seminar they were conducting. In 1954 she visited Japan where she worked with Hamada, spending a winter in a Japanese pottery in the remote mountains. She met Leach again in Hamada's workshop, and in 1956 moved to England. She married Leach in 1956 in Penzance. The couple based themselves in St Ives and established a successful pottery workshop.

Janet Leach was keen on texture in her pottery and experimented with various glazes. Became particularly known for her large bottles and dishes. One of her stoneware pots in grey glaze with black slip decoration was illustrated in The Studio, Vol.159, June 1960, p.197. She exhibited some of her work with William Marshall, a senior potter at the Leach Pottery. Noted in Muriel Rose, Artist Potters in England, London, Faber & Faber, 1955 / 1970. Rose illustrated four of Leach's stoneware jars in her second edition, all dated between 1963 and 1965. Also noted in Pottery Quarterly, IX, 1967, Janet Darnell Leach by J.P. Hodin. Janet Leach died in Cornwall, aged 79. The Tate, St Ives held a retrospective of her work in 2006 / 07.

LE BAS, MOLLY ROSE (b.1903)

Sculptor. Born in Stoke Newington, London in June 1903. The daughter of Edward Le Bas, an iron and steel merchant, and Anna. Her parents originated from Jersey. One of at least three children (Gwendoline, Molly and Edward). Raised in London and remained there for much of her life and career, but did spend some time in Angmering, Sussex. Educated privately and at Broomfield Hall. Studied in Paris. Became a sculptor of busts and statuettes in stone, marble and bronze. Exhibited her work, including at the Royal Glasgow Institute (1928), the Royal Academy (1925-31), the Paris Salon and the Walker Art Gallery, Liverpool. Exhibited works included: April (bust, bronze), Gwendoline Anna (bust, marble), Aphrodite (statuette, stone) and The Ring (half-figure, marble). Possibly the same Molly Le Bas who married Montagu B. Burrows (1894-1967) in London in 1932. She may have died in London in October 1996, aged 93. Her brother, Edward Le Bas (1904-66), became a painter, also based in London. He exhibited at the Royal Scottish Academy (1946-56).

LE BAS, RACHEL ANN (1923-post-1969)

Painter / Engraver. Born in April 1923. The daughter of Captain R.S. Le Bas of the Somerset Light Infantry. Educated at the West Heath School, Sevenoaks, Kent. Studied for her City & Guilds at the London School of Art from 1946 under Arthur Ralph Middleton Todd. Produced engravings and landscape paintings in oils. Exhibited at the Royal Academy (1945-68), the Royal Society of British Artists, the New English Art Club and with the London Group. Exhibited works included: The Exe Below Winsford, September Evening: An Old Wych Elm, A Market Garden Near Cahors, France (line engraving) and Spacewings. A Member of the United University Club. Based in Minehead, Somerset and London during her career. Line engraver, painter and etcher Ann Le Bas, possibly the same artist, was elected to the Art Workers' Guild in 1969.

LE COCQ, DORIS ROSEMALE (active 1920s-1930s)

Potter / Sculptor. Born in Blackheath, London. The daughter of W.A.R. Le Cocq, a journalist. Educated in Alberta, Canada. Studied in London at the L.C.C. Central School of Arts and Crafts and at the Royal College of Art. Produced ceramics and bronzes, usually animal portraits and groups. Spent time abroad during her life and career, studying animal life in the Canadian Rockies for part of that time. Acted as pottery instructor for the L.C.C. Campden Hill Technical Institute. Exhibited her work occasionally, including at the Royal Academy (1935), the Society of Women Artists (1929), the Royal Society of Miniature Painters and in Toronto and Milan. Exhibited works included: Sea Spray (statuette group, bronze), Canadian Racoons (porcelain) and Rocky Mountain Bears (glazed earthenware).

LEDGER, MILDRED MAI (1879-1939)

Commercial Artist / Painter. Born in Hackney, London. The daughter of Henry Ledger, a South African merchant, and Mary. Her father originated from London, her mother from Hampshire. Raised in London. Studied at the St John's Wood School of Art and the Royal Academy schools. Became a commercial artist producing designs for such things as book covers and posters. Some of her posters and showcards were illustrated in Posters and Publicity. Commission work included book covers for Heinemann, showcards for Park Davis and work for Dalcroze Eurythmics. Also executed portrait paintings. Exhibited her work, including at the Royal Academy (1901-18), the Society of Women Artists (1918-34), the Royal Institute of Painters in Watercolours and the Beaux Art Gallery. Exhibited works included: Mrs Henry Ledger, A Royal Princess - Christina Rossetti, The Grey Dress and The Pink Hat. Signed her paintings Mildred M. Ledger and her commercial work M. Ledger. Later in her career, she moved to Ipswich, remaining there until her death.

LEE, ANNIE LOTTIE (1869-1939)

Painter / Artist. Born in Chelsea. The daughter of Henry Lee, a merchant, and Sarah Ann. Studied at the Bromley School of Art, Spenlove's Yellow Door Studio and the London School of Art. As a student, awarded a bronze medal by the Society of Science, Letters and Arts. Spent much of her career living in Kent, but also spent time in London and Harrow. Was a visiting art teacher in various schools and classes including The Oaks School, Harrow. Produced paintings in oils and watercolours, worked in pastels and executed line drawings, sometimes with watercolour wash. Subjects included buildings, landscapes and portraits. Exhibited her work occasionally, including in Cheltenham, Bradford, Salford and Bromley, and at the Kent County Exhibition. May have exhibited at the Royal Society of British Artists (1891) and at the Royal Academy (1897) (states only A. Lee). Exhibited works included: Roses (watercolour), The Little Balloon Boy (oil), Toilers at Break of Day (pastel) and A

Spring Pastoral (line & watercolour). Elected an Associate of the British Watercolour Society (1914) and of the Royal Drawing Society (1927). Three of her works, A May Day in Kew Gardens, Mermaid Inn, Rye and West Street, Rye, were purchased by provincial galleries. Lee died in Kent, aged 70.

LEE, ERICA (1888-1981)

Sculptor. Born in Prestwich, Lancashire. The daughter of lawyer Walter Lee of Manchester. Also appears to have been the daughter of Annie or Eliza Clapham, who was widowed young, and to have had an older sister, Claire Millicent Lee. However, records are unclear. Erica was educated at the Brighton High School, Rathgowry and at Eastbourne. By at least 1911, aged 22, Erica was based in Hampstead, London with her mother and sister. There, she studied sculpture under Edwin Whitney Smith, R.B.S. and Sir William Reid Dick, R.A., two high profile figures in the British arts at that time. Became a professional sculptor, living and working in London, dying in Westminster, aged 92. Used a studio at St John's Wood for a time. Latterly based at Acacia Road. Produced heads, busts, figures and portrait reliefs. Worked in terracotta, bronze and plaster. Executed portrait works of numerous sitters including Nina Verchinina in Les Presages and The Hon. Mrs Eric Harmsworth.

Lee exhibited her work over six decades, from at least the 1920s until at least the early 1970s. Exhibited at the Royal Scottish Academy (1922-34), the Royal Glasgow Institute (1924-59), the Royal Academy (43 works, 1920-60), the Walker Art Gallery, Liverpool and in Manchester and Scotland as well as various smaller provincial galleries. At the Society of Women Artists, she showed 18 works between 1923 and 1972 which included: Maud (statuette, bronze), Elizabeth Melville (plaster), The Five Foolish Virgins, Woman in a Wind (bronze resin) and The Naughty Child (plaster). Also exhibited at the Paris Salon, where she won an Honourable Mention in 1930. Her bronzes sold for around £100-£150; her works in plaster and terracotta sold for around £40-£50. Elected an Associate of the Royal Society of British Sculptors in 1938. Elected to the Societe Des Artistes Francais. Subsequently made a Fellow of the Royal Society of British Sculptors. Also a Member of the English Speaking Union. The Newport Art Gallery acquired her The Nymph in 1930. Works illustrated in Colour (1921), Builder (1930), Modern Sculpture (R.B.S.), Good Housekeeping (1931) and The Sketch (1941).

LEECH, BEATRICE MARY SECCOMBE (1880-1945)

Painter. Born in Eccles, Lancashire in May 1880. The only child of the marriage of Joseph Farran Leech (b.1846) and Beatrice J. Seccombe (b.1846). Her father subsequently married Alice E. Walker (1864-1934) and had three more children, Hugh, Sylvia and Cecil, Beatrice's half-siblings, all born in Eccles between 1890 and 1893. Her father, a bank manager who worked in Manchester, originated from Tyrone, Ireland. Her mother originated from Cornwall. Beatrice was raised in Eccles. Educated at the Royal School, Bath and in Brussels. Studied art at W.H. Wilkinson's studio in Manchester. Based in the north of England for much of her life and career, though sold her works through the London-based agent J. Bourlet & Sons of Nassau Street. Became a painter of landscapes and genre, usually in watercolours. Predominantly active in the 1930s and 1940s.

Beatrice exhibited her work, including at the Royal Scottish Academy (1937), the Royal Hibernian Academy (1937-39), the Royal Academy (1942-43) and in Manchester. Exhibited works included: Edinburgh: View From Princes Street, Cathedral, Westminster, Milano, 1932 and Horns and Hoofs. Elected an Associate of the Manchester Academy of Fine Art. Elected a Member of the Women's International Art Club, of the Attic Club and of the Manchester Society of Women Artists. During the First World War, she was on Voluntary Aid Detachment, attached to the Derbyshire headquarters of the British Red Cross Society (1917-26). Sometime prior to her death, she was based in Altrincham. Died in June 1945, aged 65, in a Cheshire nursing home.

LEE-HANKEY, EDITH MARY (1881-1956)

Painter / Etcher. The second wife of artist William Lee-Hankey (1869-1952). Born in Wasperton, Warwickshire in August 1881. The daughter of George Garner and Mary. Her father was a tenant farmer who originated from Wasperton. One of at least three children (Edith, John and George). Educated at the North London Collegiate School. Studied at the Slade School, London and in Paris. Produced landscape and figure paintings in oils and watercolours, drawings and etchings. Some of her etchings of Warwick, and some of her drawings of Coventry, were published. Exhibited her work, including at the Royal Academy (1915-38), the Royal Glasgow Institute (1921), the Society of Women Artists (1936-52), at the Walker Art Gallery, Liverpool and the Royal Institute of Oil Painters.

Also, at the Royal Institute of Painters in Watercolours, with the National Society, the Women's International Art Club and at the Walker's Gallery. Exhibited works included: Shepherd's Market (watercolour), Black and Gold (oil), St Riquier and The Gateway, Granada. In 1933 an exhibition of her work, Shell Mex in Construction, was held at the Walker's Gallery, charting the architectural changes taking place in London at that time.

Edith was elected an Associate of the Society of Women Artists (1951-52). Elected a Member of the Royal Institute of Oil Painters, of the Women's International Art Club, of the Three Arts Club and of the Arts Theatre Club. Her Romford Market was reproduced in Colour in November 1918. Her career lasted over 37 years. She spent much of her life in London, but also spent some time in France. She died in Sussex, aged 75. In 1917 she married William Lee-Hankey in London. He produced engravings and paintings in oils and watercolours, and was Vice President of the Royal Society of Painters in Watercolours. He and Nelson Dawson taught at the School of Colour-Printing at St Peter's Square, Hammersmith, where Edith was also a student.

William Lee-Hankey's first wife was artist Mabel E. Hobson (1869-1943), whom he married in London in 1896. Mabel was born in Bath, Somerset and raised in London. She too studied under her husband. Her father was landscape painter Henry Edrington Hobson. Her mother, Ada Hobson, was a portrait painter. Mabel's brother, Henry, became a draughtsman, and another brother, Cecil, became a painter. Mabel produced miniature paintings, including flower studies and portraits, and colour prints, one of which was illustrated in The Studio, Vol.55, April 1912. She too had a lengthy career, lasting more than 47 years. Exhibited her work, including at the Royal Academy (84 works, 1889-1936), the Society of Women Artists (1918-34) and the Royal Society of Miniature Painters. Exhibited works included: Lady Margaret Herbert, Anemones, H.R.H. The Duchess of York and Edwin Fagg, Esq., F.R.S. Mabel too spent much of her career in London, but also died in Sussex, aged 74, having apparently never remarried.

LEIGH, FRANCES E. - SEE RYDER, F.E.

LEISCHNER, MARGARET FREDA (1907-c.70)

Designer. Born in April 1907. Studied at the Bauhaus-Dessau between 1928 and 1931 under Paul Klee and Gunta Sharon-Stolz. Awarded a

Bauhaus Diploma. Worked in London as a designer of woven fabrics. Became Head of the Weaving Department at the Royal College of Art. Exhibited at the Britain Can Make It exhibition. Elected a Fellow of the Society of Industrial Artists. Possibly died in Sussex, aged 63.

LEISENRING, ALICE (1904-86)

Painter / Pencil Artist. Born in Sandy Run, U.S.A. The daughter of Walter and Winifred Wilson Leisenring. Educated at the St Christopher's School, Hampstead, London. Studied at the Slade School, London. Exhibited her work occasionally, including at the Royal Academy (1933), the Royal Scottish Academy (1934-35) and the New English Art Club. Exhibited works included: Clematis, Peonies and Honeysuckle and Wild Daffodils. Spent much of her career in Suffolk, where she died, aged 82.

LEMANN, ELIZA ANNE (1851-1938)

Painter / Illustrator. Born in Victoria, Australia. The daughter of Henry R.W. Lemann and Mary. Her father had money, and originated from London, as did her mother. Eliza had at least one elder sister, Kate, also born in Australia. The sisters were raised mainly in Bathampton, Somerset, and spent most of their lives there. Eliza died in Somerset in September 1938, aged 86. She became a painter in watercolours of landscapes, flowers and other subjects, and a book illustrator, mainly for children. Illustrated, for example, Andrew Lang, The Cold of Farnilee, H.C. Davidson, King Diddle and Maurice Noel, Under the Water (c.1899). Exhibited her work occasionally, including at the Royal Society of British Artists (1878) and the Society of Women Artists (1879-85). Exhibited works included: The Trespassers, February, On the Dorset Coast and An August Evening, Bournemouth. Works in the collection of the Fox Talbot Museum, Wiltshire.

LE QUESNE, ROSE (active 1880s-1890s)

Painter / Sculptor / Illustrator. Based in London and Jersey. Produced heads, reliefs, medallions and bas-reliefs in terracotta. Produced designs for decorative purposes, including Dancing Girls, a design for a mantelpiece. Also produced flower subjects in pastels and paintings. Produced illustrations for The Strand Magazine (1891). Exhibited her work, including at the Royal Academy (1886-95), the Royal Society of British Artists (1891), the New English Art Club (1892) and in Liverpool. Exhibited works included: Cornflowers, Spring (relief), The Dance (medallion) and The Snake-Charmer (relief).

LESSORE, ADA L. - SEE POWELL, A.L.

LESSORE, ELAINE THERESE (1884-1945)

Painter / Designer / Embroideress. Known as Therese. Born in Southwick, West Sussex. Raised in Sussex. The granddaughter of French-born Emile Lessore (1805-76), the renowned decorator of Wedgwood pottery (c.1858-75). The daughter of marine painter Jules A. Lessore (1849-92) and Ada. Her sister (Ada) Louise (1882-1956) became an illuminator, embroideress, furniture decorator and designer who married architect / designer Alfred Hoare Powell. The Powells also worked for Wedgwood. Her brother, Frederick Lessore (1879-1951), became a sculptor, and was founder of the Beaux Art Gallery. Her aunt, Therese Lessore, was an artist who painted and designed for Wedgwood. The young Therese studied art at the Slade School, London. Worked as a designer for Wedgwood in the 1920s. Also a painter of landscapes and other subjects. Exhibited her work occasionally, including at the Royal Scottish Academy (1933) and the Society of Women Artists (1909 & 1940). Exhibited works included: A Railway Journey and The Side Street. Based mainly in London during her career. Died in London.

Like Louise, Therese also produced embroideries, some of which were shown at the Brighton Guild of Applied Arts exhibition of 1911. One of those was illustrated in The Studio, Vol.52, May 1911, p.316. Fellow exhibitors on that occasion included Gwendoline Morris and Georgina Gaskin. In 1909 she married artist (William) Bernard Adeney in Stroud, Gloucestershire where Louise also spent time. Together, Therese and Adeney founded the London Group in 1913. The Group succeeded the New English Art Club as London's leading progressive art exhibition. Members included Jessica Dismorr. First President was Harold Gilman. Therese exhibited with the Group on numerous occasions, including in 1931 at the Burlington Galleries when she showed Hampstead Heath. Fellow exhibitors on that occasion included Vera Cuningham.

Clearly at the forefront of developments in art in Britain, Lessore also joined the London Artists' Association around 1932. At that year's exhibition, she showed some of her circus subjects. Also like Louise, Therese exhibited with the Arts and Crafts Exhibition Society. For example, at the 1906 exhibition, she showed a child's frock and cap with a forget-me-not design, embroidered on linen. At the Society's 1910 exhibition she showed embroidered hangings and covers. Therese also had associations with the

Bloomsbury Group. As a result, some of the Group also worked for Wedgwood. In 1918, Therese held an exhibition of her paintings at the Eldar Gallery, Great Marlborough Street, London. Artist Walter Sickert (1860-1942) wrote a glowing Preface to the exhibition catalogue, describing Therese as 'a designer of genius'. The preface was published in Colour magazine in November 1918, Vol.9, p.xvii. Her marriage to Adeney did not last, and in 1926 Therese married Walter Sickert in Kent. She was his third wife. She continued to work until shortly before her death. SEE: POWELL, ADA LOUISE

LEVETUS, CELIA ANNA (1874-1936)

Artist / Black & White Illustrator. Born in Montreal, Canada to Jewish parents. Her father, Edward Moses Levetus, was born in Birmingham. Her mother, Sarah Isabella Himes, originated from London. They were married in Canada in 1870. Celia was one of at least six children (Edward, Florence, Celia, Arthur, Daisy and Frank). Her father was a merchant. Her brother, Edward Lewis Levetus, became an eastern export merchant and an occasional writer. Her sister Daisy became a pianoforte teacher. Edward, Florence and Arthur were also born in Canada. Daisy and Frank were born in London. The family returned from Canada in 1878, living in Paddington, London. Sometime in the mid-1880s they moved to Edgbaston, Birmingham.

In the 1890s, Celia enrolled at the Birmingham Municipal School of Art, studying book illustration and decoration under Arthur Gaskin, but also studied Limoges enamelling, decorative needlework, stained glass design, modelling and painting. Such was her artistic talent, she won a South Kensington scholarship as a student. Her work was praised early on by G.F. Watts, Walter Crane and Holman Hunt. Holman Hunt owned one of her bookplate designs, which was illustrated in the Art Journal in 1900. Her speciality was decorative black & white work. Particularly known for her bookplates, another of which was illustrated in The Studio, Vol.7, March 1896, p.94 in an article Some Recent Book-Plates by Gleeson White.

Celia's first patron in publishing was Mr Darton of Wells, Gardner, Darton & Co., who in 1899 published her take on William Blake's The Songs of Innocence (25 illustrations). David Nutt published her take on Blake's The Songs of Experience. Working on Blake had been entirely her own idea. Some of her illustrations to Blake were given in the Art Journal, 1900, pp.237-239 in an article An Illustrator of Blake. The article included a portrait photograph of Levetus. She illustrated a number of other books, including Turkish Fairy Tales (10 illustrations, Lawrence & Bullen, 1896) and Verses Fancies (Chapman & Hall, 1898). The latter was written by Edward Lewis Levetus. Celia was also one of 18 contributors to Quest, a magazine produced by the Birmingham Guild of Handicraft in the 1890s. In 1900, Levetus contributed to an exhibition of the Sketch Club of the Birmingham Municipal School of Art Union, held at the Municipal School of Art. Other contributors included Kate Bunce and E.H. New. Levetus was part of a wave of successful artists and designers to come out of the Birmingham School in the 1890s and early 1900s, and was certainly one of the most talented book illustrators. But she also produced greetings cards and contributed to various periodicals including The English Illustrated Magazine (1896) and the Yellow Book (1896).

In 1895, her father died, by which time he was listed as a jewellery manufacturer living in Carpenter Road, Edgbaston, Birmingham. Celia continued to live with her mother, as did her siblings, but by at least 1901 they were based in King's Norton, Worcestershire. Celia is listed as a black & white artist living on her own means by that time. In 1902 she married Eric Pearson Nicholson in Worcestershire. They apparently had no children, and she appeared to give up her illustration work, but did continue to draw and paint. She also wrote novels under her married name, C.A. Nicholson, and under the name Diana Forbes. In 1911 a small book of verses by her, The Comfort-Lady, was published. One of her nieces became an artist. Her father's sister, Amelia Sarah Levetus, who was born in Birmingham in 1854, was also involved in the arts. From 1899 Amelia acted as a correspondent of The Studio magazine, was President of the John Ruskin Club, and was a teacher in Vienna, where she lived. She was also a specialist in modern and decorative art. Amelia wrote on various subjects, including Frank Brangwyn, art in Vienna and peasant art in Austria and Hungary. Celia died in Marylebone, London, aged 61. A portrait photograph of Levetus was given in the Art Journal, 1900, p.237. Her work was noted in R.E.D. Sketchley's volume English Book Illustration of To-day, London, Kegan Paul, 1903, and in Mahony, Latimer & Folmsbee, Illustrators of Children's Books 1744-1945, Boston, The Horn Book Inc., 1947. Works also illustrated in Norna Labouchere, Ladies' Book-Plates, London, George Bell & Sons, 1895.

LEVICK, RUBY WINIFRED (1872-1940)

Sculptor. Born in Llandaff, Glamorganshire. The daughter of George Levick, a civil engineer, and Jeannie. Her father originated from Monmouth, her mother from Durham. The eldest of three children. Her sister Lorna (b.1873), who was also born in Llandaff, became a musician. Her brother George (b.1877) was born in Newcastle. As a consequence of George Levick's job, the family moved around, later living in Acton, Middlesex. By at least 1891, aged 19, Levick was already a student of modelling at the prestigious Royal College of Art, London, studying under Edouard Lanteri. Whilst at college, Levick lived with her grandmother in Kensington.

An exceptional student, Levick won numerous awards and prizes. Within a year of beginning her studies, she had won a free studentship. Other awards included a prize for figure design, a medal for a study of a head from life, and various medals at the National Competition of Schools of Art. Also won a British Institution scholarship for modelling in 1896, and a gold medal and the Princess of Wales Scholarship in 1897. Levick became a sculptor of statuettes, portrait medallions, small figures and heads of children. Worked in marble, bronze, plaster, silver, stone and other materials. Also produced designs for stained glass, designs for shop fronts, memorial sculptures, silver panels, coloured plaster panels and other decorative panels.

Levick exhibited throughout her career, which covered a period of at least 30 years. She began exhibiting at the Royal Academy in 1894, whilst still a student and only 22 years of age. Exhibited 28 works there, the last in 1919. In 1896 she exhibited some of her panels with the Royal College of Art Sketching Club. Also exhibited with the Women's International Art Club (winning at least one gold medal), the International Society of Sculptors, Painters & Gravers, and at various Arts and Crafts Exhibitions. For example, in 1905 / 06 she exhibited decorative modelling at the Second Exhibition of Arts and Crafts held at the Lyceum Club. In 1910 exhibited with the Ridley Art Club. In 1925 exhibited at the International Exhibition of Modern Decorative Art in Paris and won a gold medal. Elected a Member of the Ridley Club.

By 1901, aged 29, Levick had completed her studies at the Royal College of Art, and remained in Kensington, working as a professional sculptor. At that time, she shared a house with her brother and sister. George Levick was then a medical student. Ruby's commissions included two decorative panels, Our Lady and St Edmund, for St Edmund's Chapel at Hunstanton, Norfolk.

Produced a reredos panel and a memorial tablet for St Brelade's Church, Jersey. Also designed two stained glass windows for St Edmund's Chapel. Produced a decoration for a shop front in Sloane Street, London. Produced decorative silver panels such as a fairy kissing hollyhocks. Another was titled Sea Urchin. Her plaster reliefs included Sleep. Other works by Levick included Sledgehammers, The Hammer Thrower, Boys Wrestling and Fishermen Hauling in a Net. There is an appealing element of rawness in Levick's sculptures, as well as an element of sentimental romance and imagination in her more decorative pieces.

In 1905, Levick married architect Gervase Bailey and had two children. She continued to work and to exhibit. Lived mainly in Kensington during her career. Used the St Paul's Studios, Kensington and the Leighton Lodge Studios in Edwardes Square. Levick died in Westminster, London, aged 68. Arguably the most successful and accomplished woman sculptor to come out of Wales. The subject of an article in The Studio, Vol.34, March 1905, pp.100-107, titled A Decorative Sculptor: Miss Ruby Levick, written by T. Martin Wood. Noted in M.H. Spielmann, British Sculpture and Sculptors of To-day, London, Cassell & Co. Ltd, 1901. Spielmann includes an illustration of her Figure of a Boy.

LEVIN, VICTORIA AMELIA (1851-96)

Painter / Decorative Artist. Born in Berlin. The daughter of artist Pheolos Levin and Emily. Her father originated from Berlin, her mother from London. Her father was active in Britain from at least 1858, which indicates that Victoria grew up mainly in London. He exhibited at the Royal Hibernian Academy and the Royal Society of British Artists, and was elected a Member of the latter in 1862. As an adult, Victoria lived with her parents in London. She died in St Pancras, London, aged only 45. Probably studied under her father. Produced enamels and watercolours. Subjects included landscapes and still life. Also produced decorative fans painted on silk, one of which was titled Fun and Frolics. Began exhibiting her work in Britain in at least 1869, aged 18. Exhibited at the Royal Society of British Artists (18 works, 1869-87), the Royal Hibernian Academy (1890) and the Society of Women Artists (1871-84). Exhibited works included: Holiness (enamel), Innocence (enamel) and A Piece of Underglazed Pottery (watercolour).

LEVISON, RACHEL (b.1837)

Sculptor. Born in Doncaster, Yorkshire. The daughter of Jacob Leslie Levison and Catherine.

Had at least one younger sibling, Mary (b.1838). Raised in Doncaster, in Brighton, Sussex and in London. Probably studied in London. Worked as a sculptor in London, at Dorset Place and St John's Wood, from at least 1856 until at least 1859. Produced busts, medallions, bas-reliefs and groups in marble and other materials. Exhibited her work, including at the Royal Academy (1856-59) and the Society of Women Artists (1857-59). One of the Society's earliest exhibitors. Exhibited works included: The Sisters (group), Napoleon F. Zaba (bust), Mercy and Truth are Met Together and Eli Blessing Hannah and Samuel. Possibly the same Rachel Levison who married Michael Heaton in Yorkshire in 1863.

LEVY, MABEL ANNIE (1884-1968)

Painter / Etcher / Drypoint Artist. Born in Nottingham. The daughter of Abraham Levy, a lace manufacturer, and Florence Annie. Her father originated from Nottinghamshire, her mother from Lincolnshire. Had at least two younger siblings. Raised in West Bridgford, Nottinghamshire. Educated in West Bridgford, but also in Belgium. Studied at the Nottingham School of Art. Became a painter in watercolours, an etcher and a drypoint artist. Exhibited her work, including at the Walker Art Gallery, Liverpool, with the Royal West of England Academy, the Faculty of Arts and the Corporation Art Gallery of Derby. Remained in Nottinghamshire throughout her life and career, dying there aged 83.

LEWIS, DOROTHY (1882-post-1940)

Painter / Miniaturist. Born in Finchley, London. The daughter of Henry F. Cox and Emma Mary. Her father appeared to spend time away with his job. In 1901, Dorothy is listed as an art student in London, living in Croydon with her mother. She continued to live with her mother in London whilst working as an artist. Produced miniatures and paintings in watercolours with the use of line. Subjects included portraits and landscapes. Exhibited her work from at least 1899, when still only 17 years of age, until at least 1940. Exhibited at the Royal Academy (1899-1940), the Royal Glasgow Institute (1900), the Royal Hibernian Academy (1916-24) and the Society of Women Artists (1899). Exhibited works included: Sheep on a Hill, The Gardener, The Water Troughs and Marigold. In 1910, Cox married Llewellyn W. Lewis in Kensington, but was still living with her mother in 1911. Later in her career, she moved to Shoreham-by-Sea in West Sussex and then to Bournemouth.

LEWIS, EFFIE MAY (1886-c.1959)

Chinese Lacquer and Italian Renaissance Artist / Fruit and Flower Modeller. Born in New Zealand in May 1886. Based at Gilston Rectory, Harlow, Essex for part of her career. Active into the 1930s at least. Exhibited some of her work in Britain, at the Home Arts and Industries Association exhibitions and at the Essex Handicrafts Exhibition. Otherwise, remains untraced.

LEWIS, JANE MARY - SEE DEALY, J.M.

LIMRICK, MARY FRANCES ROSE (1890-1980)

Painter / Engraver / Craftworker. Born in Liverpool in August 1890. The daughter of Osborne Edward Barber Limrick, a physician and surgeon, and Mary Jane Tait. Her parents originated from Ireland. Mary was raised in Liverpool. One of at least four children (Mary, Kathleen, Aileen and Paul). All were well educated. Mary studied at the Bedford College in Liverpool, and at Liverpool University, where she was awarded a diploma in education. She became an Assistant Inspector for the Ministry of Health Insurance Department. But she also became an artist in oils and watercolours, a lino engraver and a barbola worker. Barbola work is the craft of making small models, usually of flowers or fruit, from plaster paste. Mary exhibited her work occasionally, including at the Walker Art Gallery, Liverpool, at the Civil Service Exhibition at South Kensington and with the Wallasey Art Society and the Liver Sketching Club. Elected a Member of the Wallasey Art Society, of the Liver Sketching Club and of the Ministry of Health Art Club. Based in Wallasey for much of her career. Her death, at the age of 90, was registered in Stockport.

LINDNER, DORIS LEXEY MARGARET (1896-1979)

Sculptor. Born in Llanyre, Radnorshire, Wales in July 1896. The daughter of George M. Lindner and Lexey. Her father originated from Edgbaston, Birmingham, her mother from Wales. One of at least six children (George, Doris, Charlotte, Charles, Courtenay and Helen). Raised in Llanyre initially, but moved to Abbey Lodge, Winchester, Hampshire whilst still a child. Her father had private means and appeared to have no necessity to work as Doris grew up. The family had several servants. Doris studied at Frank Calderon's School of Animal Painting, the St Martin's School of Art, London and the British School in Rome. Concentrated on sculpture, specialising in birds, animals and portrait works. A number of her figures were reproduced in porcelain by Royal Worcester. Worked in bronze, wood, stone, concrete and plaster. Based in London initially, then also Addlestone, Surrey. Doris died in Maidstone, Kent, aged 82.

Lindner exhibited her work, including with the Royal Society of British Sculptors, at the Leicester Galleries, the Royal Glasgow Institute (1949) and the Royal Academy (1927-57). Exhibited works included: H.R.H. The Princess Elizabeth (equestrian statuette, bronze), Angelo (statuette, bronze), Wing Commander T.R. Bird (head) and Horse (statuette, Indian Rosewood). In 1938 Lindner achieved a flying certificate at the Herts and Essex Aero Club. At that time she had a sculpture studio at Chalcot Gardens, London. Evidently had a passion for flying as well as sculpture. In 1960, aged 64, she visited New York. Still listed as a sculptor at that point.

LINDQUIST, EDITH CATHERINA ELIZABETH (1877-1951)

Sculptor / Painter. Born in Newcastle-upon-Tyne. The daughter of Asker Lancelot Lindquist and Alice. Her father was a clerk. Edith was one of at least three children. During her lifetime she spent time in Newcastle, Essex, Surrey and London. Died in London. Studied at the Slade School in the early 1900s. In 1908 she was awarded a £3 prize for anatomy at the School's 1907-08 session. From at least 1901 she was a pupil-teacher whilst living at Langdon Park Road, Surrey. Worked as an art teacher for most of her career. Latterly, she taught at the Hornsey School of Arts and Crafts. One of her pupils was Lorna Beatrice Kell. Produced medallions, paintings in watercolours and miniatures. Exhibited her work, including at the Royal Academy (1901) and the Society of Women Artists (1902-04). Exhibited works included: The Triumph of Good Over Evil (medallion), The Library (watercolour), T'Auld Peggy, Runswick (watercolour) and At Thornton Dale, Yorkshire (miniature).

LINDSAY, GERTRUDE (1877-1961)

Painter / Illustrator. Born in Belfast, Ireland. The daughter of Thomas M. Lindsay and Ruth. Her father was an artist and teacher of art. He originated from Lancashire, her mother from London. Gertrude was one of at least four children (Katharine, Courtney, Gertrude and Pauline). For some years the family was based in Rugby, at the curator's house to the Temple Art Museum. Her father presumably worked at the Museum. In the late 1890s, Gertrude went to London to study at the Royal Academy schools. There, she shared digs at Alexander House with a

considerable number of other female students of art and music, including Mary Buzzard, Frances Darlington and Nina Oliver.

As a student, Lindsay won at least three silver medals. One of those was in 1900 for a painting of the draped figure, in a competition open to female students only, since male students were at liberty to study the naked form (women were not). The draped figure was seen as more acceptable for women students to draw, however redundant that actually was as an exercise in learning. Sometime after completing her studies, Gertrude returned to Rugby and worked as a painter of miniatures and figures, and as an illustrator. She lived for a time at Pennington Street in Rugby, with her unmarried younger sister Pauline, who then worked as a governess. Lindsay also kept a London studio. She died in London in May 1961, aged 83. Exhibited her work occasionally, including at the Royal Academy (1906-35) and the Society of Women Artists (1931). Exhibited works included: The Sorceress, Beauty, The Nightingale and Spring Comes to Town.

LINDSLEY-SIMS, CATHARYNE ELISE (b.1909)

Designer / Illustrator / Painter / Decorative Artist / Decorator. Also Catherine or Katherine on records. Born in Ben Rhydding, Yorkshire in February 1909. The daughter of Archibald William Lindsley-Sims (1865-1936) and Elsie Mary Davey (1868-1950). Her father, who originated from Lincoln, was a mechanical engineer and member of the Institute of Mechanical Engineers. Her mother, who originated from Crewe, Cheshire, was a talented and equally diverse artist. Catharyne was educated at the Hiatt Ladies' College. The family lived in various places including Yorkshire. Catharyne elected to follow in her mother's footsteps, and attended the Shrewsbury School of Art (1922), then studied at the Wolverhampton School of Art (1923-25), followed by the Birmingham Central School of Art (1927).

Catharyne was a prize-winning student at Wolverhampton. Awarded two firsts and a third prize, presented by Sir Frank Dicksee, P.R.A., won in open competition. One of her prizes was an original etching by Sir Frank Short, won for a poster design advertising an exhibition of the works of Albert Goodwin, R.A. Based in London for part of her career. Became a designer of period dolls for Chad Valley Co. Ltd, an illustrator, a decorative and interior designer and a painter of portraits in oils. Decorative works included a standard lampshade with six decorative panels of figures painted on vellum (owned by a Mrs G.A. Norton of Claverley). Also, a decorative poster acquired by the Wolverhampton Municipal Art Gallery. Exhibited works included portraits of Geoffrey Marcus Fletcher and Reuben Astley (oils), and The Sea God. Exhibited her work occasionally in Bradford and at the Wolverhampton Municipal Art Gallery. Possibly the same Catherine E.L. Sims who married James Cockett in Dartford, Kent in early 1940. SEE: LINDSLEY-SIMS, ELSIE MARY

LINDSLEY-SIMS, ELSIE MARY (1868-1950)

Painter / Modeller / Metalworker / Embroideress / Artist in Gesso / Leatherworker. Born in Crewe, Cheshire. The daughter of the Rev. Austin Davey and Annie. Her father, a Wesleyan minister, originated from Dublin, her mother from Worcestershire. Spent time in Gateshead and in Cheltenham, Gloucestershire prior to her marriage. Educated in Gateshead and Highbury, and at the Cheltenham Ladies' College. Studied art at the Royal College of Art, London and at the Leeds, Wolverhampton and Taunton Schools of Art. A prize-winning student at the Royal College of Art. Became a painter of landscapes, still life and portraits, a modeller, a metalworker, embroideress, leatherworker and gesso artist. Based in Ilkley, Yorkshire, Wellington, Bromley, Westminster and elsewhere during her career. Died in Middlesex in May 1950, aged 82.

Exhibited her work, including at the Victoria & Albert Museum, London, the Society of Women Artists (1924-27), the Royal Cambrian Academy, the Walker Art Gallery, Liverpool, with the Royal Birmingham Society of Artists and at the Maddox Galleries. Also, with the Old Dudley Art Society and in Bradford, Doncaster and Wolverhampton. Exhibited works included various handicrafts along with, for example, Honesty: Still Life, On the Llugy, Newlyn and The Nun of St Saviour's. Elected a Licentiate Incorporated Faculty of Arts and an Associate of the National Society of Art Masters. Awarded an Art Masters' Teaching Certificate. Acted as a lecturer under the National Society of Art Masters. Her works were purchased by various private collectors, including in Canada. In 1900, she married Archibald William Lindsley-Sims (1865-1936) in East Grinstead, West Sussex. Lindsley-Sims, who originated from Lincoln, was a mechanical engineer. The couple had one daughter, Catharyne Elise, whilst in Yorkshire in 1909. Like her mother, Catharyne became a talented artist. Elsie Lindsley-Sims was still active into the

1930s. SEE: LINDSLEY-SIMS, CATHARYNE ELISE

LINES, GLADYS (1894-1955)

Pictorial Artist. Born in Adlington, Lancashire in February 1894. The daughter of John Entwistle and Martha. Her father, who originated from Blackburn, was a market gardener and then a jobbing gardener. Her mother, who originated from Bolton, was a schoolmistress. Gladys appears to have been an only child, and was raised in Anderton and then Lytham, Lancashire. She then studied at the St Anne's-on-Sea School of Art from at least 1911. Produced landscape paintings in oils and watercolours. Exhibited her work, including at the Society of Women Artists (1950-53) and the Royal College of Art. Exhibited works included: The End of the Road (oil), Windswept Trees (watercolour) and In a Farmyard (oil). Became an art teacher in Colwyn Bay, Wales. In 1924, she married schoolmaster Leslie Lines (d.1963) in Conway. Gladys died in Wales, having remained active until almost the time of her death.

LINGSTROM, FREDA VIOLET (1893-1989)

Painter / Poster Designer. Born in Chelsea, London in July 1893. The daughter of George Louis Lingstrom, Secretary of the Friendly Society, and Alice Clarey Anniss. Had Swedish grandparents. One of at least three children (Elsie, Freda and Marjorie). Raised in Hornsey and Wood Green, Middlesex, and in Chelsea. Elsie Lingstrom studied at training college. Freda was educated at the Wood Green Higher Grade School. Then studied at the L.C.C. Central School of Arts and Crafts and at the Heatherley's School, both London. Produced poster designs and decorative landscape paintings. Based in London during her career and, latterly, in Kent. Died in Tunbridge Wells, Kent, aged 95.

Lingstrom was elected a Member of the British Society of Poster Designers. Some of her landscapes were used in advertising for the L.N.E.R., the Cunard Line, the London Underground and the Norwegian state railways. She also wrote about Norway. She was sent by the Norwegian Government to execute drawings of Norway for English travel promotions. Carried out a similar commission for the Swedish Government. Some of her works were illustrated in The Studio poster book (railway posters). In America, her work was reproduced in Printer's Ink, and in Germany in Gebrauchsgraphik. Some of her posters were acquired by the Victoria & Albert Museum, London. In 1934 she is listed as working on a book Plant Form for Batsford. Also became a successful B.B.C. producer and executive associated with children's television, including Andy Pandy. In 1958 she travelled to New York as a B.B.C. employee.

LINNELL, EDITH MADELEINE (1877-1961)

Decorative Jeweller / Metalworker / Carver / Designer. Born in Birmingham. The daughter of Thomas Grimley, a bank cashier, and Annie Gertrude. Her father originated from Birmingham, her mother from Northamptonshire. One of at least three daughters (Annie, Maude and Edith). Raised in Birmingham. Educated privately. Studied at the Birmingham School of Art from the late 1890s into the early 1900s. Exhibited at the Birmingham School of Art students' exhibition, including in 1904. Some of her exhibits were chosen for the 1904 St Louis Exhibition. As a student, also showed work at the National Competition of Schools of Art, South Kensington. At the 1902 exhibition, she won a bronze medal for design and jewellery. At the 1903 competition, she won a gold medal for art jewellery. Linnell established herself as a designer and maker of decorative jewellery, a decorative metalworker and a carver in ivory. Initially based in Birmingham. Subsequently based in Knightsbridge, London. Died in Surrey, aged 85.

In 1897, before completing her studies, Linnell married Joseph Sydney Linnell in Wolverhampton. The marriage was short-lived and ended in divorce in 1908. Records indicate that she had left her husband sometime before 1901, since she was living with her sister, Maude, in Moseley, Birmingham by that time. Maude was then working as a secretary. The Linnells had one daughter, Violet Gwendoline, born in Liverpool in 1898. Edith was still active as an artist into the 1930s. Exhibited her work throughout much of her career. Exhibited with the Society of Women Artists (1909-25). Also, at Mr John Baillie's Annual Arts and Crafts Exhibition (including in 1908). There, she exhibited alongside other leading designers and craftworkers, including Jessie Bayes, Florence Stern and Dora Stone. Also exhibited at the Walker Art Gallery, Liverpool (including in 1909), and at the Festival of Empire, Imperial Exhibition in 1911. Exhibited at the Paris Exhibition of 1925, where she won a silver medal. Also, with the Royal Society of Miniature Painters, and at the North-East Coast Exhibition, Newcastle-upon-Tyne, winning a First Class for jewellery and a Highly Commended for metalwork in 1929. Exhibited at the Palace of Arts, Wembley and in Venice and Ghent. At the 1921 Ghent Exhibition, she was awarded a Certificate of Honour for design and jewellery. Elected an Associate of the Royal Society of Miniature Painters. Purchasers of her work included the Victoria & Albert Museum, London, the Duchess of Buckingham and Chandos, the Duchess of Leeds, the Duchess of Grafton, Sir John Walker, Sir John Wallis and Lord Wavertree.

LINTON, MURIEL (1886-1968)

Artist / Potter. Born in Hay, New South Wales, Australia. The daughter of Sydney Linton and Jane. Her father was the first Bishop of Riverina, Australia. Indications are that the family moved to Australia from Norfolk, England. But by at least 1901 they had returned to England, and lived in Oxford thereafter. Muriel was educated at the Oxford High School. Then studied in London at the Grosvenor School of Art and the Slade School. Produced miniatures, portraits and pottery. Spent most of her career in Oxford, dying there, aged 82. Exhibited four works at the Royal Academy between 1911 and 1916, Portrait, Summer, Maudie and Christopher Tripp. Also exhibited at the Walker Art Gallery, Liverpool.

LINWOOD, MARY (1756-1845)

Embroideress. An expert needlewoman, Linwood produced worsted and crewel copies of old master paintings in the late eighteenth century. Between 1776 and 1778 she exhibited her needlework twice at the Society of Artists of Great Britain, showing a study of flowers and a landscape. In 1787 over 100 of her framed embroideries were exhibited at the Hanover Square Rooms in London before touring the country. Her embroideries were highly regarded and commanded considerable fees. Her work was praised in The Hand-Book of Needlework (1842) by Miss Lambert. Linwood had a permanent exhibition of her embroidered pictures at Leicester Square, London. In 1787 miniature painter Sarah Pierce of London exhibited a portrait of Miss Linwood at the Royal Academy. This was probably Mary, given her importance, and that in the same year her touring exhibition was in full flow. Her reputation long outlived her, and she was occasionally mentioned in arts journals even into the twentieth century. In the early 1900s, embroideress Violet Turner produced needlework pictures not unlike Linwood's. In 1901, one of Linwood's works was exhibited at the Society of Women Artists, courtesy of Messrs Toye of Clerkenwell Road, London.

LIPSCOMB, JESSIE - SEE ELBORNE, J.

LISTER, FANNY D.H. - SEE CALDER, F.D.H.

LITHIBY, BEATRICE ETHEL (1889-1966)
Painter / Decorative Artist. Born in Richmond, Surrey in December 1889. The daughter of Sir John Lithiby, C.B., a barrister and civil servant, and Lady Ethel Stewart Lithiby (nee Smith), the daughter of a gentleman and merchant. Her father originated from Devon, her mother from Paddington, London. Her parents married in Middlesex in 1888. Beatrice had at least one brother, John S. Lithiby who was born in Richmond in 1893. He fought in, and survived, the First World War, distinguishing himself with medals in the Manchester Regiment. Both siblings were raised in Paddington. Beatrice was educated at the St Mary's College, Paddington. She then studied at the Royal Academy schools, London. Became a painter of landscapes in oils and watercolours, and a painter of church decoration. Her decorative schemes included a design for a wall painting for Holy Trinity Church, Paddington. Such works, along with her later associations with The Guildry of St Mary, Belmont, Wantage in Berkshire, suggest some religious conviction. She was based in London and Berkshire during her career. Died in Oxford, aged 76.

Lithiby exhibited her work, including at the Royal Academy (1924-30) and the Royal Society of British Artists. Exhibited at the Walker Art Gallery, Liverpool and at the Walker's Gallery, London, on one occasion showing paintings of Assisi and Ypres at the latter. Also exhibited at the Society of Women Artists (26 works, 1920-55). Exhibited works included: Delville Wood - Autumn 1919, The Cathedral, Ypres, Julian in the Alps and Sussex Downs. Elected a Member of the Society of Women Artists (1934-40). Elected a Member of the Royal Society of British Artists (1930). Made M.B.E. in 1919, and O.B.E. in 1944. A Member of the Service Women's Club. She has at least one work in the collection of the Imperial War Museum - An Auxiliary Territorial Service Camp at Tuxford, Nottingham (1958).

LITTLEJOHNS, IDALIA BLANCHE (1893-1968)
Painter / Craftswoman. Born in Kidderminster. The daughter of Reginald W. Hewett and Minnie. Her father, a poultry and fruit dealer, originated from Birmingham. Her mother originated from Herefordshire. Had at least one sister, Pearl. Raised in Herefordshire. Later based in London,

at the Orchard Studios. Died in Sussex, aged 75. Worked as a painter, craftswoman and lecturer. Wrote on various crafts. For example, Ornamental Homecrafts for Pitman & Sons. Also the author of Painted Fabrics (Pitman's Craft-For-All Series, 1930), Gesso, Beadcraft and Prints and Patterns. Exhibited her work occasionally, including at the Society of Women Artists (1923), the Royal Institute of Oil Painters, the Walker's Gallery, the Suffolk Street Galleries and the Alpine Club Gallery. Exhibited works included: Tinsel. Elected a Member of the Women's International Art Club. In 1916 she married painter / illustrator / lecturer John Littlejohns (b.1874) in Hammersmith. He originated from Devon. He too worked at the Orchard Studios. For a time, he was art master at the Westminster City School. He was elected a Member of the Art Workers' Guild.

LITTLER, HILDA MARGARET (1909-84)
Sculptor. Records indicate (but do not absolutely confirm) that Hilda Littler was born in Liverpool, the daughter of Robert E. Ellis and Margaret. Both parents originated from Liverpool. Robert Ellis was an insurance assistant superintendent. Hilda had at least one sibling, Robert. In 1945 she married Eric H. Littler in Southport. They lived in Ainsdale, Southport for much of their marriage. Her death, in May 1984, was registered in Sefton North, Merseyside. Possibly studied in Liverpool. Worked as a sculptor of statuettes, groups, heads and reliefs in materials including oak, mahogany, beech, obeche and elm. Began to exhibit her work shortly after her marriage. Exhibited at the Royal Academy (1946-56), the Royal Glasgow Institute (1946-63) and the Society of Women Artists (1953-54). Exhibited works included: Resting (statuette group, mahogany), The Infant St Francis (statuette group, mahogany), Grief (figure, beech) and Sun Bather (woodcarving, obeche). A sculpted head by Littler is currently owned by the Southport Art Gallery.

LLOYD, EDITH (1868-post-1934)
Painter / Black & White Artist. Born in Isleham, Cambridgeshire. The daughter of John Boyce and Esther. Had at least one sibling, Herbert. Raised in Cambridgeshire and in Gazeley, Suffolk. Returned to Cambridgeshire and in the early 1890s worked as a saleswoman. By the early 1900s, however, she had undertaken private tuition in art and had become an artist in watercolours and in black & white. Based in London during her career. Exhibited her work occasionally, including at the Royal Society of

British Artists, with the Women's International Art Club and with the National Association of Women Painters and Sculptors, New York. In 1904 she married John Price Lloyd (b.1874) in Cambridgeshire. He was a civil servant who originated from Somerset. Edith is listed as still active into the 1930s.

LLOYD, KATHARINE CONSTANCE (1884-1974)

Painter / Illustrator. Born and raised at Hartley Wintney, Hampshire. Spent much of her life at Hartford House there, but later also used a studio, the Lillingstone Studios, at Redcliffe Road, London. She died at Battle, Sussex, aged 90. The daughter of headmaster Edward Wynell Mayra Lloyd (d.1928) and Eleanor Elizabeth. Her father, who was born in India, was a Cambridge scholar. Her mother originated from Worcestershire. Katharine was one of at least seven children (Katharine, Charles, Edward, Eleanor, Gladys, Wynell and Robert). Katharine studied at the Slade School, London under Professor Henry Tonks and Philip Wilson Steer. A prize-winning student. Became a painter of portraits, landscapes and flowers in oils and an illustrator of children's books. Exhibited her work, including at the Royal Academy (1933-46), the Society of Women Artists (1929), the New English Art Club, the Royal Society of Portrait Painters, the Portrait Society, Brighton and the Duveen Exhibition at Hull. Exhibited works included: His Honour Judge Gamon, Picked in September, Gwendoline and Niton, Isle of Wight. Her portrait of Dr Winnington Ingram, Bishop of London was reproduced in The Times and in R.A. Illustrated.

LLOYD-JONES, AUDREY (1902-89)

Painter / Black & White Artist. Was Constance Audrey, known as Audrey. Born in Cambridge. The daughter of Ernest Lloyd-Jones, a consultant physician, and Constance Mary. Educated at Abbotshill, Malvern and North Foreland Lodge, Broadstairs. Studied art privately, with A.G.G.S. Amarasekara between 1940 and 1941. Became an artist in pastels and watercolours and in black & white. Based in Cambridge during her career. Died in Cambridge, aged 86. Exhibited her work occasionally, including with the Pastel Society and the Royal Cambrian Academy. Works reproduced in the Journal of British Grassland Society and in other scientific and agricultural publications.

LOCKE, MABEL RENEE (1883-post-1940)

Sculptor / Pencil Artist / Painter. Born in Selkirk, Scotland. The daughter of James Locke, a manufacturer, and Wilhelmina. Studied in Edinburgh. Produced figures and heads in bronze and plaster, bas-reliefs, garden sculptures and decorative pieces. Also produced pencil drawings and oil paintings. Based mainly in Edinburgh and Hawick during her career. Exhibited at the Royal Scottish Academy (1905-37), the Royal Glasgow Institute (1911-40), with the Society of Scottish Artists, the Scottish Society of Women Artists, the United British Artists, at Crystal Palace, with the Aberdeen Artists' Society and in Leeds. Exhibited works included: Sea Tangle, Remorse, Josephine and La Tristesse. Elected a Member of the Society of Scottish Artists and of the Scottish Society of Women Artists. The George Watson Ladies' College, Edinburgh acquired one of her statuettes. Produced figures for the Royal Crown Derby Company. Executed a font for Colinton Church. One of her sundials was placed at Greenock. Executed a number of portrait works of distinguished individuals including Sir James Caird, The Rt Hon. the Earl of Home and Hebridean musician Duncan Morrison. Locke was active into the 1940s.

LOCKHART, BETTY - SEE JOEL, B.

LOGAN, GLADYS CAROLINE - SEE BARRON, G.C.

LOMAS, CHRISTINE - SEE CONNELL, C.

LOOSELY, ANNE (1906-92)

Textile Designer. Born at Bidford-on-Avon, Warwickshire. The daughter of portrait painter George Frederick Loosely (1864-1934) and bookbinder Annie Isabel Power (1873-1960). Her father originated from London, her mother from Whitby, Yorkshire. Had one brother, George Henry Hugh Loosely (1916-2000), who became a company director. He was born in Hemel Hempstead, Hertfordshire. Anne was educated at Kings Langley Priory, Hertfordshire. Raised mainly at The Firs, Kings Langley in Hertfordshire, where the family lived for a considerable number of years, and where both her parents died. She studied art at the L'Union Central des Arts Decorative under M. Rapin between 1925 and 1926. Also, at the Regent Street Polytechnic School, London under George Percival Gaskell, Harry George Theaker, Winifred Stamp, Miss Smith and Mr Tresillian. Concentrated on hand-printed textile designs. Exhibited her work at the Arts and Crafts Exhibition, Central Hall, Westminster, the Ideal Home Exhibition, with the British Council, Sweden, at the Britain Can Make It Exhibition, the Festival of Britain, at the Society of Industrial

Artists Exhibitions and with the Cotton Board, Manchester. Travelled abroad with her work. Purchasers of her designs included the Office of Works, the British Railways and the Cunard White Star Line. Some of her designs were reproduced in Ideal Home and Designers in Britain. Elected Licentiate of the Society of Industrial Artists (1947) and a Member of the Society of Industrial Artists (1950). Based mainly in London. Died in Richmond-upon-Thames in December 1992, aged 87. SEE: POWER, ANNIE I.

LOOSELY, ANNIE ISABEL - SEE POWER, A.I.

LORD, ELYSE ASHE (1885-1971)

Painter / Engraver / Decorative Artist. Born in March 1885. Died in Berkshire, aged 86. Has proved elusive in research, and may have originated from overseas. Active in Britain from at least 1920, and lived in Kent and Berkshire. She was still active as an artist into the 1950s. Produced colour prints and watercolours. Specialised in Far Eastern subjects. Exhibited her work, including at the Royal Scottish Academy (1923-39 & 1953), the Royal Glasgow Institute (1925), the Royal Academy (1920-22) and the Paris Salon, where she was a silver medallist for her colour prints. Also exhibited with the Royal Institute of Painters in Watercolours, and with the Society of Graver-Printers in Colour. She was elected a Member of both. In 1931 she exhibited watercolours at Messrs Bull & Saunders Gallery in Cork Street. Exhibited works included: The Drummer, Springtime in Loyang, The Blue Beads and Ode to the Blackthorn. Noted in Frank Emanuel's volume Etching and Etchings, London, Pitman & Sons, 1930. Noted by Emanuel as a 'British, Aquatinter'. In 1927, The Studio magazine published a folio of her work under the Masters of the Colour Print series. Hers was the first folio to be published in 1927 and was noted as a great success, and was to be followed shortly after by a monograph on John Raphael Smith. In 1944, The Studio, Vol.127 / 128, October, pp.114-116, reproduced some of her work, including Biwa Player and At the Shrine.

LOSH, SARAH (1785-1853)

Designer. The daughter of John Losh of Woodside near Wreay, Cumberland. John Losh originated from Cumberland, and was educated at Sedbergh, followed by Cambridge University. He made his fortune in founding an alkali works at Walker near Newcastle. In 1809 he established the Walker Iron Works which was run by his brother, William. John Losh had another daughter, Katherine. Sarah Losh was educated in London and Bath, was fluent in several languages, good at mathematics, and had a keen interest in architecture. She travelled to Italy and France, which influenced her work in architecture, sculpture and design. Although strictly an untrained amateur, she produced some interesting work, principally St Mary's Church at Wreay, which cost £1200 to build and which was consecrated in 1842. Romanesque in influence, but essentially a mix of styles, the Church was built as a memorial to Katherine, who died young in 1835. Animals, birds, flowers and all manner of other natural life were incorporated into the design by Losh. In executing the sculptures she designed for the Church, Losh employed a local man, William Hindson, but produced her own mouldings in clay, from which he worked. Losh also designed a mausoleum in Katherine's memory, in front of which is a cross designed by Losh around 1835 and dedicated to her parents. Losh's work was praised in Nikolaus Pevsner's Buildings of England series, published in 1967. Photographs and a description of Losh's church also appeared in Country Life, 4th November 1971, in A Memorial to Two Sisters by M.A.Wood. More recently, Losh was the subject of a book, The Pinecone (Faber & Faber) by Jenny Uglow.

LOVEDAY, DOROTHY (1883-1974)

Bookbinder / Sculptor. Born and raised in Wardington, Oxfordshire. The daughter of George Loveday, a magistrate, and Magdalene. One of at least seven children (Laura, Ethel, Dorothy, Cecilia, Paulina, Katharine and Clement). All were well educated. Cecilia became an assistant teacher, and Paulina became a music student. Dorothy studied art in Birmingham, then moved to London with her mother, Cecilia and Paulina, working as a bookbinder. In London, Magdalene took in lodgers, including violinist Emma Schuly. Dorothy was friends with Alice F. Richardson, also a bookbinder. Dorothy later lived at Nut Tree Cottage, Bloxham, Banbury and died in Honiton, Devon, aged 90. In the 1920s and 1930s, she also worked as a sculptor in wood. Exhibited four works at the Royal Academy, The Madonna of the Pines (relief, carved wood) in 1929, A Negro's Head (carved wood) in 1931, Dr Frances Rendel (relief, wood) in 1935 and M.F. Nicholls Esq., F.R.C.S. (relief, carved wood) in 1938. Also exhibited Negro at the Royal Scottish Academy in 1935.

**LOVELY, MAUREEN P. - SEE
PROUDMAN, M.P.**

LOW, DIANA MABEL (1911-75)
Painter / Textile Designer. Born in London in
February 1911. The daughter of Vincent Warren
Low, a surgeon, and Mabel. Her father originated
from Surrey, her mother from Middlesex. One of
at least four children (Marcus, Roger, Margaret
and Diana). Raised in London. For a time, the
family lived at Harley Street. Diana was educated
at the Cheltenham Ladies' College. Then studied
at the Academie Ranson under M. de la Pateliere.
Also, at the Slade School, London under
Professor Randolph Schwabe, and worked under
Sir William Nicholson. Produced textile designs,
paintings in oils and pastel studies. Subjects
included flowers and landscapes. Exhibited her
work, including at the Royal Scottish Academy
(1966-69), the Royal Academy (1949-65), at the
New English Art Club and the Paris International
Exhibition. Exhibited works included: Orchard in
Winter, Chrysanthemums, Father and Children
and Underhill Farm - Early Spring. Based for part
of her career in Kent. Died in Marylebone,
London. In 1934 she married Richard Clissold
Tuely (1908-2001) in Marylebone. They had
three children. Evidently continued to work and
to exhibit long after her marriage. Works in the
permanent collection of the Hanley Art Gallery,
Stoke-on-Trent.

LOW, MABEL BRUCE (1883-1972)
Painter / Woodcut Artist. Born in Edinburgh. The
daughter of Robert Bruce Low, C.B., M.D., and
Henrietta. Her father, the assistant medical officer
to the Local Government Board, originated from
Edinburgh, her mother from Lincolnshire. The
family moved around, also living in Yorkshire
and London. Mabel was one of at least six
children (John, Mary, Constance, Blanche,
Robert and Mabel). All were well educated.
Constance later became a lecturer. At least four
of the children, including Mabel, were still living
at the family home in Battersea into their 30s.
Mabel was educated at the Dulwich High School
and in Dresden. She then studied at the
Westminster School of Art under Mouat Loudon
and Walter Sickert. Also studied at the Edinburgh
College of Art under Robert Burns, R.S.A., and
at the London School of Art under Richard Jack,
R.A. Produced paintings in watercolours, oils and
gouache and colour woodcuts. Subjects included
flowers, portraits, buildings and landscapes.
Based in Battersea early in her career, then in
Chelsea and latterly in Bournemouth. Died in
Bournemouth, aged 89.

Low exhibited her work over a period of eight
decades, including at the Royal Academy (1909-
54), the Royal Scottish Academy (1906-16) and
the Society of Women Artists (over 121 works,
1905-71). Also exhibited at the International
Society of Sculptors, Painters & Gravers, the
New English Art Club, the Royal Society of
British Artists, the Royal Society of Portrait
Painters, the Royal Institute of Painters in
Watercolours and in Liverpool. Exhibited works
included: Dordrecht Cathedral, Hydrangeas and
Pink Lily (watercolour), Low Tide, Honfleur
(gouache) and Rowena. Low exhibited at the
Society of Women Artists virtually throughout
her entire career. She was elected a Member of
the Society (1931-71), acted as Honorary
Treasurer (1934-35) and as Vice President (1964-
70). Elected a Member of the Royal Society of
British Artists (1919). Also a Member of the
Forum Club and of the Three Arts Club. The
Contemporary Art Society purchased one of her
colour prints for the British Museum. The Art
Galleries of Sunderland (colour print) and
Bournemouth (watercolour) also purchased
works. Some of her works were reproduced by
Warren Johns Ltd and by the Autotype Co. In
1933 Low married Alexander Chisholm in
Chelsea. A few years after the marriage, they
moved to Bournemouth.

LOWNDES, MARY (1857-1929)
Stained Glass Artist. Born in Ampney Crucis,
Gloucestershire in early 1857. The daughter of
Richard and Annie Harriet Lowndes. Both her
parents originated from Middlesex, but by the
time Mary was born they had already moved to
Gloucestershire. Whilst she was a small child, her
father was Rector of Poole Keynes,
Gloucestershire. She was one of at least eight
children (four boys, four girls). Around 1863 the
family moved to Dorset, where Richard Lowndes
became Vicar of Sturminster Newton and a
Canon of Salisbury Cathedral. In the early 1880s,
Mary began studying at the Slade School in
London. She then became a pupil of Henry
Holiday (1839-1927), a leading designer in
British stained glass. Holiday, who was heavily
influenced by Rossetti and Burne-Jones, taught
her cartooning. In 1885 she designed her first
stained glass window, a memorial to her mother
situated in Sturminster Newton Church.
In the 1890s, Lowndes began to teach herself
glass painting and was given a studio in which she
could work at the firm of Britten & Gilson in
London. At that time, she encountered
Christopher Whall (1849-1924), a Member of the
Art Workers' Guild and one of the most

influential designers in Arts and Crafts stained glass. Lowndes was also influenced by Edward V. Prior (1852-1932), whose suggestions on types of glass she adopted. She used small pieces of moulded dull glass of varying thicknesses rather than pieces of rolled or blown glass in her windows. That made the finished window brilliant yet not transparent, giving it a solidity. However, the method was costly. In 1896 art critic Fred Miller visited Lowndes in her London studio. He then included her in his article Women Workers in the Arts and Crafts which was published in the Art Journal, 1896, pp.116-118. Miller included two examples of her work.

In 1897 Lowndes set up the firm of Lowndes & Drury, Stained Glass Workers in Chelsea with Alfred Drury (1856-1944). Drury had been head glazier at Britten & Gilson. In 1906 the firm moved to larger workshops in Lettice Street, Fulham which were known as The Glass House. For much of her career, Lowndes lived in Chelsea. By 1911 her private address was Brittany Studio, King's Road, Chelsea, which she shared with several others, including her lifelong companion Barbara Geraldine Forbes. Forbes, a stained glass painter who originated from Richmond, Surrey, was then acting as Secretary to the Artists' Suffrage League. Lowndes was Chairman of the League in the early 1900s and was a Member of the London Society for Women's Suffrage. In 1909 Lowndes took part in designing embroidered placards and banners for the Pageant of Women's Trades and Professions, held at the Albert Hall as part of the International Women Suffrage Alliance Congress. In 1916 she was one of the organisers of the Women Welder's Union for women involved in war work. She and Forbes lived together from at least 1901, and Lowndes left her sizeable estate (over £15,000) to Barbara Forbes on her death.

Moving into larger workshops from 1906 provided Lowndes with a kiln room, a glazing workshop and a drawing office. She designed over 100 windows for churches, houses and other premises during her career, occasionally working in collaboration with others. She also produced a number of war memorial windows. Between 1901 and 1902 she made several windows to the designs of Isobel Gloag (1865-1917), including a memorial window to her father for Sturminster Newton church (1901) and St Mary Magdalene for St Peter's Church, Henfield, Sussex (1901). Some years later (c.1919) she collaborated with artist and fellow suffragist Emily Ford (1851-1930). Lowndes also made up designs by Henry Holiday, including a memorial window which was commissioned by artist Ida Perrin and her husband for their local church, St Peter's at Bushey, Hertfordshire.

Other designs by Lowndes included The Supper of Emmaus, a three-light window for Holy Trinity Church, Sutton Coldfield (c.1910), and the chancel windows for St George's Church, Altrincham (1895). Also, designs for decorative glazing for Messrs Wallis & Co.'s showrooms (c.1910). Produced designs for fan lights and lunette windows too. Lowndes & Drury were also responsible for the restoration of the glass in Salisbury Cathedral. Lowndes did everything herself in the production of a window, except the cutting and leading. She selected every piece of glass used in the making of a window.

Lowndes occasionally exhibited her work. Some of her stained glass designs were shown at the first exhibition held at the Permanent Gallery of Decorative Art at Harrington Road, South Kensington in 1899. The exhibition aimed to draw attention to the decorative arts and win artists commissions. Other exhibitors on that occasion included Hilda Pemberton and Ellen M. Rope. In 1925 Lowndes contributed stained glass designs to the New Forest Exhibition held at the Mansard Galleries which had the theme of art in libraries. Lowndes was included in an exhibition Women Stained Glass Artists of the Arts and Crafts Movement held at the William Morris Gallery, London between December 1985 and March 1986. She also exhibited at the Royal Society of British Artists (1886-87) and the Society of Women Artists (1887-88), though these appear to have been paintings rather than stained glass designs, executed before she had established her design career. Also a Member of the eminent Church Crafts League, a body of reputable artists and designers who sought to maintain standards in church art. Some of her designs were kept at the Fawcett Library, City of London Polytechnic. Lowndes died in Chelsea in early 1929, aged 72.

LUDGATE, PATRICIA KATHLEEN (1895-1963)

Sculptor. Born in the Basque Polynesian Chincha Islands, South Africa. Her father died whilst she was still a small child. Lived with her widowed mother, Alice, in Portsmouth, then in Lee, London. Had one sister, Lucy, who was born in Portsmouth, as was her mother. Studied sculpture, probably in London. Produced statuettes and garden sculptures in bronze and lead. Exhibited her work occasionally, including at the Royal Academy (1916-19) and the Society of Women Artists (1940). Exhibited works included: Tortoise Group (lead), Echo (bronze),

A Sprite (statuette, bronze) and Ariel (statuette, bronze). Based, for much of her life and career, in London. Died in Bromley, Kent. Her career covered at least four decades, from the 1910s into the 1940s.

LUNGLEY, EDITH AMELIA & DOROTHY (1876-1939) & (1886-1962)

Artists / Craftswomen. The daughters of Arthur Robert Lungley and Margaret Elizabeth Ayers. Both girls were born, raised and educated in Australia. However, both came to England to study at the Royal College of Art, London. Edith, by that time in her 30s, studied stained glass under Herbert Hendrie, A.R.C.A., and was awarded a diploma in design at the College in 1913. She was elected an Associate of the Royal College of Art. Then established herself as a stained glass designer based at various addresses in London, including Thurloe Court and Peckham Crescent. But she also spent time at a cottage at Sheethanger Common, Boxmoor in Hertfordshire.

Edith worked and exhibited consistently until her death, executing a number of important commissions. For example, she produced stained glass designs for a memorial window to the late Professor Thorburn Brailsford Robertson; a window for the College Library based on St Catherine of Alexandria; a window for Creighton House chapel; a memorial window for the University of Adelaide, and a window for St Margaret's Church, Rottingdean. She also produced decorative panels such as Architecture and Cockatoo, but also paintings and drawings including Artichoke. Exhibited her work, including at the Royal Academy (1928-38), various Arts and Crafts exhibitions in London, with the Women's International Art Club, at the Walker Art Gallery, Liverpool and the Society of Women Artists (1924-39). Elected a Fellow of the British Society of Master Glass Painters. Elected a Member of the Society of Women Artists (1931-39) and of the Women's International Art Club. Edith died at Sheethanger Common, Hertfordshire.

Dorothy Lungley became a colour woodcut artist, a pottery artist, an embroideress and a designer. She too was based in London and Hertfordshire, sharing addresses with Edith until Edith's death. Dorothy also exhibited her work, including at the Society of Women Artists (1924-35), with the Society of Graver-Printers in Colour, the Colour Woodcut Society, at Wembley and in Canada, Australia and America. Exhibited works included: In a Forest (colour woodcut), Kingfisher Blue (colour woodcut), A Fantasy and The Sentinel. Elected a Member of the Society of Graver-Printers in Colour. Dorothy and Edith lived with another sister, Beatrice Margaret Lungley (1881-1962), whilst in London. After Edith's death, Dorothy and Beatrice lived at Hove, Sussex, but not together. Both died at Hove in the same year.

LUXMOORE, MYRA ELIZABETH (1865-1918)

Painter / Illustrator. Produced miniature paintings, portraits, landscapes and illustrations. Illustrated, for example, A Village Tragedy and Hans Andersen's The Princess and the Nettles. Active for over 25 years, yet remains difficult to trace. Exhibited her work, including at the Royal Academy (1893-1918), the Royal Society of British Artists (1887 / 88), the Paris Salon and the Society of Women Artists (20 works, 1888-1911). Exhibited works included: From Gutter to Gorse, Miss Edith Vicary (miniature), So Delicate With Her Needle and The Black Hat. Elected an Associate of the Society of Women Artists (1908-11). Spent most of her career in London, but also in Newton Abbot, Devon. In 1904 she advertised classes in painting and drawing at her Campden Hill Studio in The Studio magazine. Died at Redcliffe Road, London, aged only 53.

M

McADOO, ANNIE FLORENCE VIOLET (active 1925-65)

Painter. Known as Violet. Born in Cookstown, Co. Tyrone, Ireland. The daughter of Hugh W. McAdoo. Educated at the Girls' School, Cookstown. Studied at the Belfast School of Art. Then studied at the Royal College of Art, London. Elected an Associate of the Royal College of Art in 1927. Worked as a painter in oils and watercolours; various subjects but mainly landscapes. Became an art teacher. Based mainly in Belfast, at Rugby Road for part of the time. Exhibited at the Society of Women Artists (1949-53), the Royal Hibernian Academy (1941-46), the Ulster Academy, the Royal Ulster Academy, the United Society of Artists and the Watercolour Society of Ireland. Exhibited works included: Leeks (watercolour), The Road to the Hills (watercolour), Farmyard, Normandy (watercolour) and The Open Gate. Elected a Member of the Royal Ulster Academy and of the Watercolour Society of Ireland. Works acquired by the Belfast Museum and Art Gallery (Tiled Roofs and Hay Stacks).

McBEAN, ISABEL (1874-1952)

Metalworker / Designer / Enameller / Jeweller. Born in Peckham, London. The daughter of Lachlan McBean (1833-79) and Emma Norton (1844-1929). Her father, a commercial clerk, originated from Inverness, her mother from Norfolk. Her father died whilst Isabel was still a small child. She was raised in London by her widowed mother. One of at least seven children (Jessie, John, William, Geoffrey, Isabel, Susan and Donald). Isabel studied at the Goldsmiths' College of Art, London in the late 1890s until around 1900. As a student, she contributed to the National Competition of Schools of Art. In 1898, for example, she showed a design for a silver cup and a design for a silver bowl, both of which were illustrated and praised in The Studio, Vol.14, September 1898, pp. 263-264. At the 1900 National Competition, she showed designs for enamels and a series of studies for church metalwork and electric lamps. Fellow students at Goldsmiths' included Katharine Coggin, Edith Pickett and Hilda Pemberton.

After leaving the School, Mc Bean taught decorative metalwork at the Keswick School of Industrial Arts in the Lake District. She was there only a short time, between 1901 and 1902. However, she clearly had some impact whilst at the Keswick School, exhibiting work at the annual Home Arts and Industries Association exhibition in London. In 1902, for example, she exhibited a jug designed and executed by her at the School. The jug was illustrated in The Studio, Vol.26, July 1902, p.132. After leaving the School, she appears to have produced and exhibited little on a professional level. She returned to live with her mother, in Boscombe, Hampshire, and several of her adult siblings. She died in Bournemouth, aged 77.

MacCABE, GLADYS (1918-post-1980)

Painter / Artist. Born in Randalstown, Northern Ireland. The daughter of George Chalmers, an artist and commissioned officer (Gordon Highlanders). Educated at the Brookvale Collegiate School, Belfast. Studied fashion design, commercial art and sculpture at the Belfast School of Art between 1934 and 1938. Self-taught as a painter. Produced paintings in oils and watercolours, various subjects including still life, landscape and figures. Married painter and Official of the Fine Art and General Insurance Co. Ltd Max MacCabe. He was born in Belfast in 1917 and was the son of journalist and poet Matthew MacCabe. Max MacCabe exhibited his work widely. The couple had at least one son. Gladys was based in Belfast for much of her life and career.

Gladys also exhibited her work, including at the Society of Women Artists (1948), the Royal Scottish Academy (1948), at the Irish Exhibition of Living Art, at the Royal Ulster Academy and with the Watercolour Society of Ireland. Also, at the Victor Waddington Gallery, Dublin, the Grafton Galleries, the Dawson Gallery, Dublin, the Leicester Galleries, London, the Kensington Art Gallery, London, with the American Institute of Architecture and the Oireachtas, Dublin, in Canada and America, and with C.E.M.A. (Northern Ireland). She held several two-man shows with her husband, including in Dublin, Belfast, Edinburgh and London. Works exhibited by Gladys included: Winter Landscape, Still Life and Rides on the Beach (oil). She was elected an Associate of the Royal Ulster Academy (1950). Also acted as a committee member for the Belfast Feis (arts and crafts section, 1943-45). Elected to the American Institute of Architecture (to the Northern Ireland affiliated group). Acted as a Member of the hanging committee for the Ulster Academy of Arts (certainly in 1946, 1947 and 1949). Also elected a Member of the Council for the Royal Ulster Academy (1950).

Some of her works were reproduced in Irish Tatler, Sketch and the Standard Catalogue of Contemporary Irish Painting (U.S.A. and Canada). Purchasers of her work included Belfast Corporation, the Haverty Trust and C.E.M.A. (Northern Ireland). Works in the permanent collections of the Belfast Municipal Museum and Art Gallery, the Queen's University, Belfast, C.E.M.A. (Northern Ireland) and in the private collections of Sir Thomas McMullan, Maj.-Gen. W. Brooke-Rurdon, Professor O.H. Meredith and Maj.-Gen. Symen-Maxwell among others. Five works in the Imperial War Museum Collection dated 1979-80, including Street Incident, Londonderry (oil, 1979).

McCANN, WILHELMINA L. - SEE NEUWIRTH, W.L.

McCANNELL, URSULA VIVIAN (1923-post-1970)

Artist / Illustrator. Born in Hampstead in June 1923. The daughter of painter and Principal of the Farnham School of Art, William Otway McCannell (1883-1969). Educated at Frensham Heights. Studied at the Farnham School of Art between 1940 and 1942. Then studied at the Royal College of Art between 1942 and 1944. Elected an Associate of the Royal College of Art in 1944. Became a painter of landscapes, portraits and other subjects in oils, watercolours and tempera, and an illustrator. Exhibited her work at the Royal Academy (1940-70), the Leicester Galleries, the Royal Society of Portrait Painters, with the London Group, at the Arcade Galleries and the Society of Women Artists (1937). Held one-woman shows at the Redfern, Leger and Modern Arts Galleries. Contributed to other exhibitions. For example, in 1945 contributed to an exhibition at the Peter Jones Gallery, London titled Loaves and Fishes. Other exhibitors on that occasion included Leonard Greaves, Mervyn Peake and Edward Wolfe. Exhibited works included: Man in Dark Landscape, Dreamers, Souls in Torment and Waterhead, Ambleside (tempera). In 1946, her The Land of Illusion was illustrated in The Studio, Vol.131 / 132, pp.65-78 in an article The Younger British Artists. Other works reproduced in The Moderns. Based mainly in Farnham, Surrey. Works in the permanent collection of the Manchester Art Gallery. In 1945 she married Peter W.G. Roberts in Surrey. They had two sons.

MacCARTHY, AMELIA & GERTRUDE (active 1830s-1850s)

Sculptors. Members of a distinguished family of sculptors. The daughters of stonemason John James MacCarthy, sisters to sculptors Carlton, Hamilton and Saxon MacCarthy. Carlton and Hamilton collaborated, as did Amelia and Gertrude. Hamilton's son, Hamilton Patrick MacCarthy, also became a sculptor, as did Mrs Saxon MacCarthy. All five MacCarthy siblings exhibited at the Royal Academy, and carried out prestigious commissions. Amelia exhibited two works at the Royal Academy in 1843, a miniature bust of Mrs Col. Finch and a miniature full-length figure of Miss Blanch Kelly, both executed with Gertrude. Gertrude exhibited two works at the Royal Academy in 1838 and 1839, and exhibited at the British Institution in 1853. A Miss F. MacCarthy exhibited sculptures at the Royal Academy in 1856 and 1857, possibly of the same family. Mrs H. MacCarthy exhibited sculptures at the Royal Academy in 1857. Mrs Saxon MacCarthy exhibited sculptures at the British Institution between 1853 and 1858. To complicate matters further, a Mrs MacCarthy exhibited sculptures at the Society of Women Artists in 1857, including a bust of Lord Lyons and The Favourite - Master A. Thomas. The family was based largely in London.

McCLINTOCK, MARY HOWARD (1888-1965)

Painter / Modeller / Woodcut Artist. Known as Maidhi. Born in Bagshot, Surrey in May 1888. The daughter of Major-General Sir F. Howard Elphinstone, K.C.B., V.C. and Annie (d.1938). Her father, who was born in Russia to British parents, died in 1890 whilst Mary was still a small child. She was the youngest of at least four daughters (Victoria, Irene, Olive and Mary). Had a private education. Studied at the Slade School, London. Produced woodcuts, paintings in oils and watercolours, including landscapes, and worked as a modeller. Based in Edinburgh, Kent and Surrey during her career. Died in Surrey. In 1909 she married Col. Robert Singleton McClintock, D.S.O., and had two sons and two daughters. She continued with her career after her marriage. Exhibited her work at the Royal Scottish Academy (1928-34), the Royal Academy (1929-30), the Society of Women Artists (1928), the Royal Institute of Painters in Watercolours and the Goupil Gallery. Exhibited works included: Chinese Boats, Bangkok, The Log of the Cutty Sark, The Bathers and Seville Cathedral. Works illustrated in The Studio.

MacCOLL, ELIZABETH MATHIESON (1863-1951)

Bookbinder / Book Decorator. Born in Glasgow, Scotland in January 1863. The daughter of the Rev. Dugald MacColl (1827-82) and Janet Scott Mathieson (b.1831). Her parents originated from Scotland. Her father was a Minister of the Briggate and previously of Wynd Church. Her mother was the daughter of William Mathieson, a junior partner in the West Indies firm of James Ewing. Elizabeth was the fourth of at least six children (Margaret, Dugald, Janet, Elizabeth, Letitia and Rebecca). All were initially raised in Scotland. However, in 1873 their father moved to a church at Wandsworth, London and the family moved with him. In 1877 he then moved to Allen Street Church in Kensington. In the early 1880s, Elizabeth became an art student in London, studying at the South Kensington and Westminster Schools of Art. She also subsequently studied bookbinding under Sarah T. Prideaux from 1891. Another of Prideaux's pupils was Katharine Adams. Elizabeth may have been Prideaux's first pupil. A notebook belonging to her, containing notes taken during Prideaux's lessons, is in the Victoria & Albert Museum, London. Elizabeth's brother, Dugald Southerland MacColl (1859-1948), was a B.A. student at the London University, and subsequently became an art critic, painter and designer and Keeper of the

Tate Gallery in 1906, and later of the Wallace Collection. He was also elected a Member of the prestigious Art Workers' Guild, and exhibited his work at the Royal Scottish Academy (1912-39).

Elizabeth MacColl became a proficient and accomplished bookbinder, working on at least 25 printed books as well as various prayer books, albums, blotters, card cases and visitor's books. She also executed panels inlaid with various coloured leathers, with gilt applied to create pictures. It would appear that all the designs she worked were produced by her brother, Dugald, and that the siblings worked successfully together spasmodically for over 30 years. Dugald also designed a small number of bindings at the request of Sarah T. Prideaux, principally for Andrew Lang's Grass of Parnassus, Walter Pater's The Renaissance and D.G. Rossetti's Poems. However, these appear to have been executed by a firm rather than by Prideaux herself. Dugald MacColl's designs were highly original and, in some respects, modern, with a reliance on line which almost pre-empted the Art Deco style of the 1920s. He incorporated minimal use of decoration in his designs, which were often symmetrical, sometimes abstract, sometimes pictorial. Elizabeth first impressed the design on the leather, then applied gold leaf which was pressed into the lines. She never imitated her contemporaries in either design or technique, and was constantly experimenting with bookbinding techniques. She even developed a leather tool to her own design.

Elizabeth was active as a bookbinder from at least 1889. In that year she executed a binding for the Catalogue of the Second Exhibition of the Arts and Crafts Exhibition Society. The design incorporated a peacock and a fountain. A list of other bindings by her can be found in Marianne Tidcombe, Women Bookbinders 1880 to 1920, Oak Knoll Press / The British Library, 1996. Those also included William Morris (transl.), The Tale of King Florus and the Fair Jehane (Kelmscott Press, 1893) which was executed in green goatskin with gold-tooling in 1894 (now in the John Rylands Library, Manchester). Also, Charles Newton Robinson, The Golden Hind (published in London in 1880) which she worked in olive green goatskin with gold-tooling. And, Edward F. Strange, Alphabets, D.S. MacColl, A Merry New Ballad of Dr Woodrow Wilson (Glasgow, 1915) and Charles Newton Robinson, Tintinnabula (1890).

The MacColls exhibited their work regularly, including at a small exhibition of arts and crafts held at the Woodbury Gallery in 1903. One of Elizabeth's bindings from that particular exhibition was illustrated in The Studio, Vol.30,

1903, p.339. Other contributors included Ellen Mary Rope. Elizabeth also contributed to the 1901 Glasgow Exhibition. The Art Journal, 1901, p.329, singled out her work for special mention and described her use of 'the wheel' which she had devised for decorating purposes. Showed other works at the 1893, 1896 and 1903 Arts and Crafts Exhibition Society exhibitions. Three bindings designed by Dugald and executed by Elizabeth, and shown at the 1893 Exhibition, were illustrated in The Studio, Vol.2, October 1893, p.26 (reproduced as sketches). Also exhibited at the Goupil Gallery. For example, in 1898 she showed a binding for Walter Crane, Decorative Illustration of Books. Dugald MacColl sent specimens of work to the 1902 Turin Exhibition, which presumably included Elizabeth's bindings. Four of her bindings were shown at Karslake's in London in 1897. Karslake instigated the founding of the short-lived Guild of Women Binders in the following year, though Elizabeth was not a member of the Guild.

Art journals of the day proved particularly supportive of the MacColls. In 1896 Dugald contributed an article Miss E.M. MacColl's Bookbindings A New Technique in Tooling to the Art Journal (pp.147-152). Though Elizabeth is scarcely mentioned, 11 examples of her bindings are illustrated, including Lives of the Fathers, Tennyson's The Princess, and The Divine Comedy. In The Studio, Vol.10, February 1897, pp.40-47, Gleeson White offered an article on Some Recent Bookbindings, with further examples of Elizabeth's work. White praises Elizabeth, discussing her work in relation to that of T.J. Cobden-Sanderson. Four more of her bindings were then illustrated in The Studio, Vol.18, pp.3-37, in an article Modern Bookbindings and Their Designers by Esther Wood in a Special Winter Number, 1899-1900. One of her bindings was owned by designer Charles R. Ashbee, another by Mrs Charles Strachey.

In 1906 Sarah T. Prideaux included Elizabeth's binding for Monica Turnbull's A Short Day's Work (exhibited at the 1903 Arts and Crafts Exhibition) in her volume Modern Bookbindings: Their Design and Decoration, London, Archibald Constable & Co. On page 54 Prideaux notes:

Miss MacColl's books have for some time excited interest both on account of the character of her brother's designs and her manner of executing them by means of a small wheel which is an attempt to overcome the restrictions of the finisher's ordinary methods.

Elizabeth remained in London for the rest of her life, her choice of career eventually affected by failing eyesight. However, she was able to continue bookbinding in a lesser way up to 1924. During the First World War, she worked on the design and construction of surgical footgear for disabled soldiers. She died in a nursing home in Haslemere, Surrey in January 1951, though her home address at that time was Hampstead Garden Suburb. She left an estate of some £7955.

McCURDY, SYLVIA W.A. - SEE STEBBING, S.W.A.

MACDONALD, ANNIE SMITH (1851-1924)

Bookbinder. Born in Glasgow. Was Ann Smith Johnston, known as Annie. Possibly the daughter of Frederick and Lucy Johnston. In 1880 she married William Rae Macdonald (b.1843) in Scotland. They lived in Edinburgh, where William was an actuary. There are no children listed on census recordings. Annie took up decorative bookbinding without any formal tuition. She already had an interest in bookbinding and was inspired by old bindings she had seen. She did, however, visit Walter B. Blaikie of A. & J. Constable along with several other interested pupils, including Blaikie's two cousins, the Misses Balfour, in the 1890s. Mrs Macdonald largely developed her own technique, however. She produced bindings in undressed morocco and declined to use gold-tooling. Like Mary G. Houston, her designs were modelled rather than added. This produced a slightly less colourful result, but the design was often finer and more detailed.

Mrs Macdonald incorporated angels and figures into her designs, but also revealed the influence of Celtic design in her work. She was always known for her high standard of craftsmanship. Executed around 50 bindings during her career, including at least seven copies of the Kelmscott Chaucer. One of those, completed in 1899, was made of natural goatskin modelled and bound by her. Also executed a modelled leather binding for The Song of Solomon in 1901. Executed a visitor's book cover for the Scottish Children's League of Pity, and a cover for the Antiquaries' Club, founded in 1901. She executed other designs for visitor's books, club rolls and for regimental purposes. Another of her bindings was for Amor Lachrymosus along with one for the poems of two women known by the pseudonym Michael Field.

Mrs Macdonald ran a class in Edinburgh for modelled leatherwork which had ties with the Edinburgh Arts and Crafts' Club. Also active in bookbinding at that time were Phoebe Traquair, Jessie MacGibbon, Mrs Douglas MacLagan and Jean Pagin. Mrs Macdonald was particularly supportive of the Guild of Women Binders, founded in around 1897, though it proved to be short-lived. The Guild's first exhibition was held in 1897, its second in 1898. Mrs Macdonald showed some of her own bindings. The Guild also worked some of her designs. In 1897 she had already contributed to the Victorian Era Exhibition at Earl's Court, London. In 1901 she won a bronze medal at The Studio Exhibition, staged by the magazine. In 1905 she showed some of her bindings at the Edinburgh Arts and Crafts' Club exhibition. Some of her works were illustrated in The Studio. For example, two of her designs were illustrated in an article Modern Bookbindings and Their Designers (Vol.18, Special Winter No. 1899-1900, pp.3-37) by Esther Wood. In 1905 The Studio, Vol.34, February, pp.60-64, offered a short piece about her work. See also, Annie S. Macdonald, Modelled Bookbindings, The Book Lover's Magazine, Vol.VII, Pt III, 1907, pp.111-113.

MACDONALD, FRANCES & MARGARET (1873-1921) & (1865-1933)

Craftswomen / Decorative Artists / Painters. The daughters of John Macdonald (1825-95) and Frances. Their father, a colliery manager and later an engineer, originated from Scotland. Their mother originated from Worcestershire. They had at least three brothers, John, Archibald and Charles. Charles studied law. In the 1880s they are listed as living in Stoke-on-Trent. But by at least 1890 the family had returned to Glasgow, and Margaret had become a student at the Glasgow School of Art, closely followed by Frances.

Frances Macdonald was born at Wolstanton, Staffordshire. She studied at the Glasgow School of Art until at least 1894, and subsequently became a teacher there. At the School, the Macdonald sisters became closely associated with fellow students James Herbert MacNair (1868-1955) and Charles Rennie Mackintosh (1868-1928), and became known informally as The Four or The Spook School, because of their ghostly figure drawings. The sisters often collaborated during their early careers, but also worked with MacNair and Mackintosh on design projects. Like Margaret, Frances was multi-talented and worked in stained glass, oil and watercolour painting, embroidery, design, illustration, illumination, furniture, metalwork, enamelling and poster design.

By 1895 the Macdonald sisters had set up their own design studio in Hope Street, Glasgow. Because they worked together and independently, it is sometimes difficult to identify exactly who produced what. Some of their poster designs were exhibited at the Salon de l'Art Nouveau, Paris in 1895. In the same year, examples of their decorative art and furniture were exhibited at the Queen's Rooms, Glasgow. In 1896, some of their posters were exhibited at the Royal Aquarium, London, and in the same year they exhibited at the Walker Art Gallery, Liverpool Autumn Exhibition. Frances showed posters at the Societe des Beaux-Arts, Glasgow in 1896, and contributed to that year's Arts and Crafts Exhibition Society exhibition. The sisters also exhibited in Venice in 1899, in Vienna in 1900 and in Turin in 1902. Frances also exhibited at the Royal Scottish Society of Painters in Watercolours in 1898, with the International Society of Sculptors, Painters & Gravers in 1899, in Dresden in 1901 and in Moscow in 1902. At the Royal Glasgow Institute, she showed three works between 1893 and 1897 including The Annunciation (relief, with Margaret) and Corn Flowers (watercolour). Two of her paintings appeared in The Yellow Book in 1896.

In 1898 MacNair moved to Liverpool to work as design instructor at the new School of Architecture and Applied Art at the University College. In 1899 MacNair and Frances married in Scotland, and lived in Oxford Street, Liverpool. After that, she no longer collaborated with Margaret, who remained in Glasgow at that time. In 1900 Frances gave birth to her only child, a son, Sylvan, who later became a motor dealer. She continued to execute work, including a cover design for Das Eigenkleid der Frau (Krefeld, Kramer & Baum, 1903) by Anna Muthesius. The book, devoted to women's fashions, included photographs of Frances and Margaret. Whilst in Liverpool, Frances studied enamelling under Lily Day, and taught embroidery for a time. She and MacNair designed costumes for amateur theatre too. Both exhibited locally with the Sandon Society, but also at the London Salon of the Allied Artists' Association. In 1904 the MacNairs exhibited at the Port Sunlight exhibition.

Sometime in the early 1900s, the MacNairs returned to Glasgow. For a time, Frances taught enamelling and metalwork at the Glasgow School of Art, but MacNair struggled to find work. He took to drink, and after 1910 neither had any real artistic success. Frances died in 1921, presumed to have taken her own life. MacNair destroyed much of their work. At its peak, work by Frances and Margaret had featured in The Studio and Dekorative Kunst among other leading journals. The work of the MacNairs featured in a recent exhibition, Doves and Dreams held at the Hunterian Art Gallery, Glasgow and the Walker Art Gallery, Liverpool in 2006-07.

Margaret Macdonald was also born and raised in Staffordshire. She attended the Orme's School for Girls at Newcastle-under-Lyme, Staffordshire. Whilst Frances suffered poor health and a difficult marriage, Margaret appeared to thrive in her private as well as work life. In 1900 she married architect and designer Charles Rennie Mackintosh, with whom she sometimes collaborated. With Frances, she created a recognisable style which reflected their interests in myth and legend, with pale, willowy figures, ghostly maidens, stylised flowers, butterflies and birds. However, it was a style that would fall out of favour in later years. Like Frances and MacNair, Margaret and Mackintosh worked together after their marriage and sometimes exhibited jointly. Margaret exhibited her work at the Royal Scottish Society of Painters in Watercolours, and at the Fine Art Society in 1911. In The Studio, Vol.52, May 1911, p.316, she is noted as 'gifted'. At the 1902 Turin Exhibition, she showed panels in coloured plaster, panels in coloured gesso, needlework panels and silver and gesso panels. She also contributed to the 1900 Vienna Exhibition, the 1901 Glasgow Exhibition and with the Glasgow Society of Lady Artists' Club. Exhibited at the Royal Scottish Academy (1906) and at the Royal Glasgow Institute (1880-1913). Elected a Member of the Royal Scottish Society of Painters in Watercolours in 1898.

Both Frances and Margaret were jointly, and independently, involved in almost every aspect of the decorative arts. In metalwork alone, they designed and executed all manner of items including mirror frames, clocks, candlesticks, panels and sconces. They designed and worked their own embroideries, additionally producing such things as bookplates, illuminations, graphic designs and pastels. With Mackintosh, Margaret worked on a number of important projects, including the Willow Tea Rooms in Glasgow. She also produced four decorative panels, The Four Queens (1909), for the card room of a house designed by Mackintosh for Miss Cranston. Also for Miss Cranston, she designed menu cards. Margaret occasionally designed panels to decorate furniture designed by her husband.

During their early marriage, Margaret and Mackintosh remained in Glasgow. But disillusioned, they moved to London, and are recorded as living there in 1911. They subsequently spent time in France, then returned to London shortly before Mackintosh died. Margaret's work, including with Frances, was noted and illustrated in numerous journals. For example, The Studio, Vol.11, July 1897, included an article Some Glasgow Designers and Their

Work (pp.86-100). Included in the article were illustrations of candlesticks in beaten brass by Frances and owned by Talwin Morris. Also, a panel The Sleeping Princess by Frances, with a frame of silvered copper; a pair of sconces in beaten brass by both sisters; a clock in brass and ivory by the sisters, and a poster for the Nomad Art Club by the sisters. Like Frances, Margaret struggled in her later career, and gradually lost her popularity. Their impact on the design world, however, remains evident today.

McDOWELL, HILDA M. - SEE SELIGMAN, H.M.

McGEEHAN, ANIZA (1874-1962)

Sculptor / Painter. Annie Louise, known as Aniza. Born in Airdrie, Lanarkshire, Scotland, part of an artistic family. Her father, Patrick McGeehan, was a painter who exhibited at the Royal Scottish Academy in 1879. Her sisters Jessie, Mary Catherine and Lizzie also became artists. All four sisters studied at the Glasgow School of Art at various times. The McGeehan sisters won various prizes and free scholarships as students. Jessie (1872-1950) also studied in Paris, and had a studio in Glasgow. She executed glass mosaic panels and carried out other church decoration including stained glass windows. One of her glass mosaics, Stations of the Cross, was executed for St Aloysius Church, Garnethill, Glasgow; another was made for St Mary's Church, St Helens, Lancashire. Mary Catherine (1877-1960) became an art teacher at the Training College, Dowanhill, Glasgow. She executed illuminations, illustrations and watercolour paintings and worked on stained glass. Lizzie died young, in 1918. Two brothers were also lost in the First World War. They had at least one other sister, Agnes.

Aniza McGeehan chose to concentrate on sculpture. Initially, she worked in Airdrie, but moved to Glasgow in the late 1890s, studying in Paris at Colarossi's for a short time. Sometime around 1900, she married Liverpool-born timber importer Vincent Murphy and moved to Waterloo Park, Liverpool. They had two surviving children, Mariel and John Vincent. They also lived at Hampstead, London and Blundellsands, Liverpool. Mariel died young. John Vincent went on to become a company director. Aniza died a widow in a nursing home in Conway, Wales, aged 87. She enjoyed a long and fruitful career, working and exhibiting from the early 1890s until at least the 1930s. Produced statuettes and busts, working mainly in bronze. Had a number of eminent sitters including the Rev. Ignatius Ireland

and the Rt Rev. Monsignor Nugent. Also executed a portrait work of her sister Jessie, a bust of her husband, Vincent, and a head of her son, John Vincent. Carried out various other commissions, including 10 sculptures for the Pettigrew & Stephen's Store in Sauchiehall Street, Glasgow. Exhibited her work through at least five decades, including at the Royal Academy (1902-31), the Royal Scottish Academy (1894-99), the Royal Glasgow Institute (1894-1930) and the Walker Art Gallery, Liverpool. Exhibited works included: Innocence (statuette), James Smith, LL.D., H.M.I.S., Maiden Meditation, The Castanet Player and Amy Gilmour (bust, bronze).

MacGREGOR, PHYLLIS M.H. - SEE BUSH, P.M.H.

McGUINNESS, NORAH M. (1901-80)

Artist / Illustrator / Costume Designer. Born in Derry, Ireland. The daughter of a shipowner. Began studying at the Dublin Metropolitan School of Art from 1921 under Harry Clarke and Patrick Tuohy. Won a scholarship tenable for three years. In 1923 she won a medal for some of her drawings at the Tailteann competition. Also awarded a medal by the Royal Dublin Society early in her career. After leaving the Dublin School, she went to study at the Chelsea School of Art, London in 1924. Immediately on leaving, some of her black & white drawings appeared in a number of leading periodicals. In 1925 she completed a series of designs for a deluxe edition of Laurence Sterne's Sentimental Journey (published in 1926). McGuinness illustrated other works during her lengthy career, including W.B. Yeats, Stories of Red Hanrahan (1927), Maria Edgeworth, The Most Unfortunate Day of My Life (1931), Eileen O'Faolain, Miss Pennyfeather and the Pooka (1944) and Elizabeth Bowen, The Shelbourne (1951). Also illustrated Coleridge's Christabel.

McGuinness also produced costume designs and stage masks for Irish theatre. For W.B. Yeats's masque The Jealousy of Emir she designed the mask and death mask of Cuchulainn and the mask of the Wonma of the Shi. Produced paintings in watercolours, oils and gouache, various subjects including portraits. Stylistically, a broad influence in her design work, including Celtic and Art Deco. Between 1929 and 1931 she studied in Paris, at Andre L'Hote's studio. Otherwise, lived mainly in Ireland, at Wicklow and Dublin. She married poet Geoffrey Phibbs.

McGuinness exhibited widely, including at the Royal Hibernian Academy (46 works, 1924-79).

Also, at the Zwemmer Gallery, the Wertheim Gallery, the Leicester Galleries and the Mercury Gallery, all London; at the Taylor Galleries, the Dawson Gallery, the Contemporary Pictures Gallery, The Gallery and the Victor Waddington Gallery, all Dublin. Also, at the Sullivan Gallery and the Paul Reinhart Gallery, both New York. Contributed to an Exhibition of Contemporary Irish Painting held in America and to an exhibition Twelve Irish Painters held at the Art Center, New York. In 1938 she contributed to an exhibition Lithographs in Colour held at the Leicester Galleries. Contributed to an exhibition Living Irish Art held in London in 1947, showing The Yellow House. Other exhibited works included: The Idol, The Canal (gouache), Portrait of Michael O'Higgins and The May Tree (watercolour). Elected an Honorary Royal Hibernian Academician. Awarded an Honorary Degree, D.Litt., by Trinity College, Dublin in 1973. Continued to work almost until her death, showing possibly her last exhibited work, Green Seaweed Patches, at the Royal Hibernian Academy in 1979. The subject of an article in The Studio, Vol.90, September 1925, pp.168-171. The article included three illustrations of her work: a pen drawing titled Geraldine (executed for Coleridge's Christabel), and two watercolours, The Widow and The Grave Digger and The Mocking Elf. A reproduction of her Landscape was included in The Studio, Vol.139, 1950, pp.72-77, in an article Irish Painters of To-day by James White. Works in various Irish galleries.

MacKAY, HELEN VICTORIA (1897-1973)

Sculptor. Born in Cardiff in April 1897. The daughter of George Donald MacKay, a railway contractor and quarry owner, and Helen Wate. Her father died whilst Helen was still a child. Subsequently raised in Wales by her widowed mother. One of at least five children (Donald, May, Lilian, George and Helen). Educated at the Cheltenham Ladies' College. Studied at the Regent Street Polytechnic School of Art, London under G.P. Gaskell and Harold Bruninskow. As a student, she was a bronze, silver and gold medallist. Became a sculptor of heads, statuettes and garden ornaments in bronze, stone, lead and wood. Based mainly in London. Died in Fulham.
Helen exhibited her work, including at the Royal Scottish Academy (1923-51), the Royal Glasgow Institute (1931), the Royal Academy (1922-55), the Society of Women Artists (1927 & 1936) and the Walker Art Gallery, Liverpool. Also, at the Grosvenor Gallery and with the Royal Institute of Painters in Watercolours. Exhibited works

included: The Holy Child (bronze), The Trembling Heart (statuette), The Coat Without a Seam (statuette) and The Happy Fish (garden ornament, bronze). Elected an Associate of the Royal Society of British Sculptors in 1938. Works reproduced in Royal Society of British Sculptors, Modern Sculpture (1938) and British Sculpture (1944-46). Works also reproduced in the Illustrated London News and The Parthenon. One of her most prestigious works was a portrait of the Viscount St Davids.

MacKAY, JEAN (active 1930s)

Painter / Designer. Born in Glasgow. The daughter of Charles MacKay, a shipping agent. Educated at the Ardrossan Academy and the Methodist College, Belfast. Studied art in Belfast, winning a bronze medal for life drawing and a number of first prizes. Maintained ties with Ireland, but also spent time in London. Became a portrait painter, a freelance designer and an embroidery and textile designer. Produced furnishing fabric designs for T.F. Firth & Sons Ltd. Executed nursery friezes. Exhibited her work occasionally, including with the Belfast Art Society, in Leeds and at Cartwright Hall, Bradford. Works included: Pleasure and Time and Industrial Peace. Elected a Member of the Belfast Art Society and of the Bradford Art Club. One of her portraits, Eileen, was illustrated in the Bradford Telegraph.

McKIE, HELEN MADELEINE (1889-1957)

Illustrator / Decorative Artist. Born in London. The daughter of Douglas Allan McKie, a bank official, and Lucy Annie. Her father was born in Brisbane, Australia, her mother in Berkshire. One of at least three children (Helen, Douglas and Katharine). Raised in London. Worked and died in London. Studied at the Lambeth School of Art. Worked as an illustrator for The Bystander. Contributed to other periodicals including The Graphic and Sphere. Her illustrations also appeared in, for example, Beau Geste and in translations of Pierre Mille's books. Contributed architectural drawings and interiors to English Life. Executed poster designs, including for the railways. Exhibited her work occasionally, including at the Society of Women Artists (1921-34), the Walker's Gallery and the Brook Street Art Galleries. Exhibited works included: Chelsea Pensioners, Profiteer, Pack Drill and Ruins of Arras Cathedral. The Queen purchased one of her works at an exhibition in June 1928. At least one of her posters, Waterloo Station (1948), executed for the Southern Railways to mark a centenary of uninterrupted service (1848-1948), is owned by the National Railway Museum.

MacKIE, KATHLEEN ISABELLA (b.1899)

Painter. Born in Belfast, Ireland in July 1899. The daughter of Arthur Metcalfe, a flax spinner. Educated at the Highcliff School, Scarborough. Then went to the Alexandra College, Dublin. Won a scholarship to the Royal Academy schools, London. Also studied at the Belfast School of Art. Studied under Gerald Kelly, William Orpen and George Clausen. Won the Ardilaun Scholarship and the Taylor Bequest of £50 in 1922. Also awarded a British Institute Scholarship of £75 for two years and an extension. Won various watercolour prizes. Produced portrait and landscape paintings. In 1926 she married John Pringle MacKie and had at least one son. Lived mainly in Ireland, in Belfast and Co. Down. Continued to paint after her marriage, but exhibited less after 1927. Exhibited at the Royal Hibernian Academy (1926-27), the Paris Salon and with the Belfast Art Society. Exhibited works included: Delphiniums Blue, Slemish Mountain, At the "Point to Point" and Chalet Wengen. At the age of 86, had a retrospective exhibition. Works in the Royal Ulster Academy.

MacKINLAY, GEORGIA ANNIE ELIZABETH (1871-1946)

Painter / Leatherworker / Embroideress. Also sometimes Annie Elizabeth Georgina. Born in Woolwich. Her mother was Jemima, who originated from Glasgow. Georgia had at least one sibling, Margaret. Based mainly in London. Died in Lewes, Sussex, aged 75. Studied in London, at the Royal College of Art and at the Clapham School of Art. As a student, exhibited at the National Competition of Schools of Art, winning bronze and silver medals. Also an exhibitioner and holder of the National Scholarship. Produced embossed leatherwork, embroideries, miniature paintings and paintings in oils, watercolours and pastels. Exhibited at the Royal Academy (1898-1926), the Royal Scottish Academy (1913), the Royal Hibernian Academy (1904) and the Society of Women Artists (1923-27). Also, at the Royal Institute of Painters in Watercolours and the Walker Art Gallery, Liverpool. Exhibited works included: Apple Blossom, Miss Marjorie Garratt, Daddy and Lieut.-Col. Hall. Queen Mary purchased her miniature of a group of flowers, shown at the Royal Institute of Painters in Watercolours in 1926. Acted as an art teacher for the London County Council, teaching drawing.

MacLAGAN, SHEILA - SEE LEA, S.

MacLAREN, OTTILIE H. (1875-1947)

Sculptor. Born in Edinburgh. Her father was John, the Hon. Lord MacLaren (1831-1910), Senator of the College of Justice. Her mother was Ottilie Augusta Schwabe. One of a large family. Educated at the St Leonard's School, St Andrews. Spent her early years in Scotland, but later lived and worked in London. Studied sculpture in Paris, becoming a pupil of Auguste Rodin (1840-1917). Her address in 1900, when she first began exhibiting her work seriously, was Rue de l'Universite, Paris, after which she spent a short time in Edinburgh. In 1905 she married William Wallace, M.D., F.R.A.M., who originated from Greenock, Scotland. Wallace was 15 years older and was a composer as well as medically qualified. The couple lived in London. Ottilie took a studio at Selwood Place, London, and later at Clarendon Road, London. She carried out war service with the British Red Cross Society and the Women's Royal Naval Service, during which her exhibiting career appeared to dwindle. However, by 1920 she had fully resumed her career.

Ottilie exhibited her work at the Royal Scottish Academy (1900-11), the Royal Academy (1905, 1920-26) and the Society of Women Artists (1936). Also exhibited with the International Society of Sculptors, Painters & Gravers. Elected an Associate of the Society in 1922. Awarded the O.B.E. in 1918. Produced works in various media, including marble and bronze. Also produced enamels. Exhibited works included: The Rt Hon. Lord Young (bust), The Countess of Seafield (bust) and John B. McEwen, Esq., Principal, Royal Academy of Music (bust). Acted as Chairman and Governor of The Three Arts Club. Produced a number of memorials which were sited in London, Paris, New York, Buenos Aires and Valparaiso. Executed a portrait bust in marble of Lord MacLaren for Parliament House, Edinburgh. Other works included a memorial to Princess Pocohantas. William Wallace died in Wiltshire in 1940. Ottilie died in London a few years later.

McLEISH, ANNIE MATILDA & MINNIE (1878-1919) & (1876-1957)

Decorative Artists / Designers. The daughters of James McLeish, at one time a boiler inspector for an insurance company. He was born in Liverpool in 1849 and married Mary Fox (b.1848), also of Liverpool. She was later a draper. They had at least five children, Minnie, Annie, Phoebe, James and Harry (b.1884). The family spent some time in Handsworth, Birmingham whilst the children were young, but returned to Liverpool. By the early 1890s, James McLeish senior had died and the remaining family were living with Mary's brother, George Fox of Kirkdale, Liverpool, along with another sister, Hannah Day and her daughter Sarah Day. The three McLeish girls were all artistic, while the two sons initially took work as a clerk and in telephones. By the late 1890s, the girls were studying at the Liverpool School of Art, Mount Street, at that time under Fred Burridge. Like the Glasgow School of Art, the Liverpool School was keen to promote the decorative arts in order that its students had greater skills when seeking employment.

Annie McLeish was born in West Derby, Lancashire. At the Liverpool School of Art, she experimented in various areas of design and the decorative arts. Fellow students included Florence Laverock and May Cooksey. Within a short time of her becoming a student, her work began to appear in The Studio magazine. In 1898 some of her designs for menu cards were illustrated in Vol.13, April 1898, pp.192-193. In 1900 she was awarded prizes for her work. In 1901 she won a gold medal at the National Competition of Schools of Art. In 1902 her student entry for the National Competition, a cartoon for a dining room panel titled The Blind Beggar's Daughter, was illustrated in The Studio, Vols.24-25, p.269. In the same year, the same journal illustrated her chamber organ design which had an exterior of walnut wood inlaid with ebony and satinwood, the inside of the folding doors decorated with Pan and Orpheus. Possibly the same design illustrated in The Artist, 1901, p.67 and shown at the National Competition for 1901.

Some of Annie's lithographs in three colours were illustrated in The Studio, Vol.21, January, p.267 in 1901.The lithographs were included in an exhibition of students' work. At the same exhibition, she showed a decorated page titled March Weather along with several poster designs, a silver and enamel belt, a buckle and several brooches. In around 1900 the Liverpool School had acquired equipment for lithographic colour-printing and for copper-plate etching which enabled students like Annie McLeish to design and print, including posters. Some of her menu cards and book illustrations were exhibited at the Walker Art Gallery, Liverpool in 1898. The three McLeish girls continued to live together once they had left the School, and were based for a time in Wavertree, working as independent artists. James and Harry also continued to live with their sisters, along with their cousin, Sarah Day, who was a dressmaker. Having never married, and having spent only a few short years supporting herself as an artist, Annie died in Prescot, Lancashire, aged only 41. She exhibited little.

Minnie McLeish was also born in West Derby, Lancashire. Equally talented, she also drew attention as a student. By 1900, she was already winning prizes for her work and was being noted in The Studio. In 1900, the journal (Vol.19, p.133) illustrated her design for a repoussé clock case with enamelled door panel and (p.135) a portion of a title page for As You Like It, indicating that she too experimented in various areas of the decorative arts. She had a longer career than Annie, working for over 30 years, dying in Hammersmith, aged 81. She was involved in textile design, metalwork, ceramic design, printing and embroidery. Like Annie, showed her work at the annual exhibition of students' work. One of her exhibits, an embroidered banner titled St Nicholas, was illustrated in The Studio, Vol.21, p.268) in January 1901. Also exhibited posters on that occasion along with silver and enamel brooches, pins, buckles and pendants. Her later textile designs included an Art Deco style print for William Foxton, a roller-printed cotton dated 1921, a sample of which is in the Victoria & Albert Museum, London.

Minnie exhibited some of her textile designs at the 1927 Leipzig European Arts and Crafts show. Other exhibitors on that occasion, in the British section, included Dorothy Larcher and Eric Gill. Her ceramic designs included a tea service produced by W.T. Copeland & Son for Heal & Son Ltd which was illustrated in The Studio, Vol.96, September 1928, p.182. The design was a dainty flower pattern. Minnie is also presumed to have produced designs for Poole Pottery, Dorset where her sister Phoebe worked for a while. In 1910, Minnie travelled to the United States. Also a writer, she was the author of Decentralisation & Art Education, a series of articles published in The Studio, Vol.121, 1941. Also the author of Beginnings - Teaching Art to Children, London, Studio Publications, 1941. She notes that, as she wrote the preface to the book, an air raid was taking place. Clearly profoundly disturbed by the concept of war, and shows a quick, intelligent, sharp mind. Evidently keen on teaching children to enjoy art, noting, 'Art does not lead, it reveals. It requires us to look and learn'. SEE: STABLER, PHOEBE

McLEISH, PHOEBE G. - SEE STABLER, P.G.

MacMILLAN, MARY E. (active 1900s-1930s)
Painter / Etcher. Born in South Africa. The daughter of the Rev. Dugald MacMillan and Margaret. One of at least six children (Margaretta, Mary, Neil, Ada, John and Dugald). Studied painting and drawing under Robert MacGregor. Studied etching under M. Leon in Paris and miniature painting under Mme Lefarge in Paris. Produced paintings, portraits in miniature and woodcuts. Subjects included buildings and street scenes as well as portraits on ivory. Based in Edinburgh for much of her career. Exhibited at the Royal Scottish Academy (1913-32), the Royal Glasgow Institute (1901-32) and in Birmingham and Liverpool. Exhibited works included: Lady Margaret Sackville (miniature), Moonlight - Greengate Close, Kirkcudbright (woodcut), Old Book Stalls on the Quai Near Notre Dame and Dolly's Decorations. Elected a Member of the Faculty of Arts.

McMURDIE, GERTRUDE - SEE HAMMOND, G.

MacNAIR, FRANCES - SEE MACDONALD, F.

MACBETH, ANN (1875-1948)
Embroideress / Designer. Also known as Annie. Born in Bolton, Lancashire in September 1875. The daughter of Norman Macbeth, a civil engineer, and Annie McNichol. Both parents originated from Scotland. One of a large family, of at least seven children. Her grandfather was the artist Norman Macbeth, a Member of the Royal Scottish Academy. Due to her father's job, the family moved to Lancashire, where Ann was born. They were still in the area in the 1890s. In 1897 Ann began her studies at the Glasgow School of Art, at that time under Francis H. Newbery. Under Newbery's influence, the School was then producing a high number of successful women who were not only artists but designers and craftswomen, who were better able to find work once their studies were completed. As a student, two of Macbeth's decorative workbags were illustrated in The Studio, Vol.19, 1900, p.234 & p.236, in an article about the School's students.

So successful was Macbeth that, shortly after her arrival, she began to assist Jessie Newbery (Newbery's wife) in needlework classes. With Annie French, she also subsequently took over Jessie King's classes in ceramic decoration and book design and decoration in 1907. In around 1910, she took over completely from Mrs Newbery, and became widely known as something of a pioneer in her approach to needlework. In 1910, she was described by J. Taylor in The Studio as 'Professor of Embroidery' in an article The Glasgow School of Art (Vol.50, pp.124-135). Taylor also noted that Macbeth was then developing a revolutionary new scheme of teaching needlework with Miss Margaret Swanson. Macbeth is generally associated with Frances and Margaret Macdonald, Charles Rennie Mackintosh, Jessie King and other former Glasgow School pupils who, chronologically, came just after William Morris and the Arts and Crafts movement.

During her lengthy, productive and successful career, Macbeth completed numerous commissions as well as carrying out her teaching. Those included an ornamental panel for one of Miss Cranston's tearooms, and a frontal for Glasgow Cathedral. Like Jessie King, she executed designs for Liberty & Co. of London. Alexander Morton of Carlisle also commissioned carpet designs from her. During her career, she also executed a small number of leather bookbindings of discreet, minimalist design, one of which, for The Pilgrim's Progress, was completed with George Turnbull and illustrated in The Studio, Vol.56, September, 1912, p.318. Some of her bookbinding designs were executed by James MacLehose & Sons. Such was her success that, in 1902, she was already the subject of an article, An Appreciation of the Work of Ann Macbeth, in The Studio, Vol.27, pp.40-49, written by Francis Newbery, with colour illustrations. Examples of her work reproduced in the article included embroidered table mats and tablecloths and some of her portrait studies and designs. Newbery notes that her chief aim was to beautify everything in daily life. She was also described during her career as a good draughtsman who then applied that to her design work, which was her underlying success. Other works included embroidered book covers, and the design for the British Association banner for the Glasgow Meeting of 1901 which was illustrated in The Studio in January 1902.

During her career, Macbeth exhibited her work extensively, in Britain and abroad. For example, she contributed regularly to the exhibitions of the Glasgow Society of Lady Artists' Club (founded 1882), and to the First International "Studio" Exhibition in 1901. Other works were included in the 1901 Glasgow Exhibition, the 1902 Turin Exhibition, the 1902 Bristol and Clifton Arts and Crafts Society "Art Work" Exhibition and with the Arts and Crafts Exhibition Society in London.

In 1903 she contributed to the Second Exhibition held by the Worshipful Company of Broderers, to the 1903 Clarion Guild of Handicrafts exhibition, and to the 1904 Leicester Arts and Crafts Exhibition. Also exhibited with the Scottish Guild of Handicraft and at the John Baillie Gallery on several occasions, including in 1905. Locally, she contributed to the Glasgow School of Art exhibitions, including in 1905 when she showed The Angel of the North and other works. Later, in 1916, she contributed to a 'Needlework Exhibition' held at the Glasgow School. At the Royal Glasgow Institute, Macbeth showed seven works between 1902 and 1916. With the Macdonald sisters and Jessie King, she became the epitome of the Glasgow style into the 1900s, still affected by the Arts and Crafts movement, but also moving into new ground. Her embroidery work, in particular, concentrated on simplicity of design combined with a high standard of execution which proved less taxing and time-consuming than that of her predecessors, though no less visually appealing. She was also, however, capable of great complexity and skill in her work, as shown later in her career in her tapestry work.

Despite her commitments, Macbeth still found time to write a number of books, including Educational Needlecraft (with Margaret Swanson, 1911), School and Fireside Crafts (with May Spence, 1920), Embroidered and Laced Leatherwork (1924) and The Country Woman's Rug Book (1929). Her talents were acknowledged by Walter Shaw Sparrow in his volume Women Painters of the World (Hodder & Stoughton, 1905, p.97). Sometime in the late 1920s, Macbeth retired from the Glasgow School and moved to Patterdale in the Lake District, where she remained until her death. For a short time, she lived with designer May Spence (1857-1957). Macbeth continued to work until her death, contributing to the Lakeland arts exhibitions, coming into contact with other local artists and craftsmen and women. Some of her painted pottery appeared in the exhibitions of the Cumberland and Westmorland Arts and Crafts Society in Carlisle, including in 1914 when she showed 15 examples. She became best known locally for her vivid clothes and painted pots. She also completed a number of large tapestries, of which The Good Shepherd and Peace remain in the possession of the local church at Patterdale. Her The Nativity, though kept in the Glasgow Museum, is very much a Lakeland tapestry. As with The Good Shepherd, its background landscape was inspired by the valley where its creator chose to have her ashes scattered in 1948. In 1930 she received the Lauder Award.

MACBETH-RAEBURN, MARJORIE M. - SEE BACON, M.M.

MACK, HILDA MURIEL (1895-1983)
Painter / Etcher. Born in Glasgow in May 1895. The daughter of William Henry Watkinson, a Professor of Engineering at Liverpool University, and Emma Crabtree. Her father originated from Keighley, Yorkshire, her mother from Worcestershire. Raised in Glasgow and Liverpool. One of at least four children (Gwendolen, Arthur, Hilda and Geoffrey). Hilda studied at the Slade School, London and at Colarossi's in Paris. She returned to Liverpool. There, in 1924 she married Lovel Durant Mack. They had at least three children. She worked as a painter and etcher, exhibiting her work at the New English Art Club, at Burlington House, in Liverpool and in Cardiff. Elected a Member of the Sandon Studios Society, Liverpool.

MACK, LIZZIE - SEE LAWSON, L.

MACK, MARY HAMILTON (1901-84)
Painter / Woodcut Artist. Born in Bow, London in January 1901. The daughter of Hans Hamilton Mack, L.R.C.P., M.A. (Lond.), a physician and surgeon, and Susie. Raised in London. Educated at the West Ham High School, St. Catherine's Convent and the University College, London. Studied at the Slade School, London under Professor Henry Tonks, Philip Wilson Steer and Russell. Won a Slade Scholarship and the Melville Nettleship Scholarship. Awarded an Honorary Distinction for painting and composition. Produced portraits and landscapes in watercolours, oils and pen & wash, and woodcuts. Spent some time (pre-1930) working in Sydney, New South Wales and in Western Australia early in her career. She returned to England and was based in London, Rotherham and Surrey thereafter. Taught art at the Rotherham Technical School and at the Spurley Hey School. Later taught at the Fulham County Secondary School. She died in Abingdon, Oxfordshire, aged 83.

Mack exhibited her work, including at the Royal Academy (1930-66), the Society of Women Artists (1932), with the New English Art Club and at the Goupil Gallery. Also, with the Sydney Society of Artists, New South Wales, with the Sheffield Society of Artists, the Royal Society of British Artists and at the Doncaster Art Gallery. Works included: Arnold Mason, Painter (pencil & wash), Teenagers in the Snow, Thames Bridge and Eve (drawing). Other portrait subjects included: Serge Jaroff, the Rt Hon. J.H. Scullin and Dr Mengelberg. One of her portraits, of Professor Sadler, was illustrated in Art in Australia. Some of her work, including two portraits of Jess and My Grandmother, was sold in Sydney. Elected a Member of the English Speaking Union.

MACKINTOSH, MARGARET - SEE MACDONALD, M.

MAHLER, MARIANNE (1909-83)
Illustrator / Textile Designer / Commercial Artist. Born in Austria. Educated to elementary and secondary level in Vienna. Studied at the Kunst Gewerbe Schule, Vienna under Professor Josef Hoffmann (architect) between 1929 and 1932. Also studied at the Royal Academy schools, London under Professor Larvin. Based mainly in London thereafter. Worked as a freelance designer. Qualified as an art teacher. Produced designs for textiles, furnishing fabrics, wallpapers, posters and showcards. Wrote and illustrated children's books, signed 'Marian'. Worked for Penguin publishers. Some of her designs featured in Vogue, The Studio, Design in Britain, British Textiles and British Achievement in Design. Exhibited her work at the 1936 Paris Exhibition. Also, in Vienna, London, New York and Manchester. Elected a Member of the Society of Industrial Artists. Died in London. Works in the Edinburgh University Library.

MAHONEY, DOROTHY LOUISE (1902-84)
Illuminator / Wood Engraver / Craftswoman. Born in September 1902 at Wednesbury, Staffordshire. The daughter of William Booth Bishop (b.1877) and Louise (b.1877). Her father worked in industry, at a tube works. Dorothy was one of at least three children (Dorothy Louise, Marjorie Booth and William Albert), all raised in Wednesbury. Educated at the St Bartholomew's Girls' School, Wednesbury. She initially studied at the Ryland Memorial School of Art in West Bromwich between 1919 and 1924. Then moved to the Royal College of Art, London, studying under Sir William Rothenstein and Professor of Design Ernest William Tristram between 1924 and 1928. Elected an Associate of the Royal College of Art.

Dorothy concentrated on calligraphy, but also studied wood engraving, pottery, embroidery and bookbinding. She became a teacher of calligraphy at the Royal College of Art. Wrote a series of articles on Lettering in Art and Craft Education, and contributed articles to various art magazines. Elected a Member of the Arts and Crafts Exhibition Society, and of the Society of Scribes

and Illuminators (elected 1927). An example of her work was illustrated in The Studio, Vol.138, July 1949, pp.1-5 in an article about the Society of Scribes and Illuminators, written by fellow member Claire Evans. The article showed pages from a Roll of Honour executed by Mahoney. The Society was founded in 1921, making Mahoney one of its earliest members. She exhibited her work occasionally, including at the Arts and Crafts Exhibition Society exhibitions, and at the Craft Centre. Exhibited two works at the Society of Women Artists in 1950: The Valley and A Courtyard, West Wycombe (wood engravings), priced at £3 each. In 1941 she married artist / mural decorator Charles Mahoney (1903-68) in Westmorland. Born in London, he also studied at, and taught at, the Royal College of Art, in the Painting School. He was a member of the distinguished Art Workers' Guild. They had at least one daughter. The couple spent time in London, but also at Wrotham near Sevenoaks, Kent. Dorothy died in Kent in May 1984, aged 81.

MAIRET, ETHEL MARY (1872-1952)
Weaver / Dyer. Born in Barnstaple, Devon in February 1872. The daughter of James Partridge, a druggist and chemist, and Mary. Both originated from Devon. One of at least three children (also Alice and Frederick). Spent her childhood and early adulthood in Devon. Studied at the Municipal Science and Art School in Barnstaple before moving to the Royal Academy of Music in the 1890s, gaining a teaching diploma in pianoforte. She subsequently worked as a governess in London and Germany. Returned to England, and in 1902 married geologist Ananda Coomaraswamy (1877-1947). Ethel then met Charles R. Ashbee and moved for a short time to Chipping Campden, Gloucestershire where Ashbee had recently established an artistic community. In 1903 the couple moved to Ceylon, and this fired Ethel's interest in textiles. With her husband, she produced a book on Sri Lankan craft and culture. They returned to England in 1907 and were based at Broad Campden in the Cotswolds. There, Ethel concentrated on hand weaving and dyeing. Her marriage foundered, however, and the couple divorced.

In 1913 Ethel married Philippe Auguste Mairet (1886-1975) in Holborn, London. They moved to Shottery near Stratford-upon-Avon, where she established a weaving workshop. By 1915, the couple had moved to Ditchling in East Sussex where Eric Gill and others were beginning to form an artistic community. There, Ethel built her own home and workshop, Gospels, and remained there until her death in 1952. She maintained some ties with the Cotswolds, contributing to an 'Exhibition of the Work of Cotswolds Artists and Craftsmen' in 1932. At Ditchling, she took on workers and apprentices, but also pupils such as Elizabeth Peacock. The workshop produced furniture and dress fabrics in wool, cotton and silk, and produced items such as scarves. Mairet became an expert in her field, and wrote a number of books including Vegetable Dyes (1916), Hand-Weaving Today: Traditions and Changes (1939), Hand-Weaving and Education (1940) and Hand-Weaving Notes For Teachers (1948). Her study on vegetable dyes was still in print as late as 2009. She always promoted natural dyes and hand production, and admired William Morris's efforts to return to traditional handcrafts.

Mairet was, effectively, a self-taught craftswoman who did not attend any of the large city art schools. Rather, she learnt her skills in various workshops in England and India, and on the Continent. She won widespread praise for her work. She was elected a Member of the Red Rose Guild of Designer Craftsmen (founded 1921) where she was one of its earliest exhibitors. She was also elected a Royal Designer for Industry. Her textiles were exhibited at the Arts and Crafts Exhibitions, at the Bond Street Galleries, London, at the Beaux Art Gallery (including in 1924) and in Paris, Tokyo and elsewhere. Her work was reproduced in numerous publications, including International Textiles and Architectural Review. Although Mairet worked alongside Gill and his fellow Ditchling craftsmen, Ethel remained essentially a free spirit who followed her own individual artistic path. She remained in Ditchling for the rest of her life, whilst Gill left in 1924. Some of his colleagues elected to remain. Philippe Mairet, who was some 14 years younger than his wife, remained in East Sussex until his death, some 23 years after his wife's. She was the subject of a book, A Weaver's Life, Ethel Mairet 1872-1952 by Margot Coatts, published by the Crafts Council in 1983.

MALTWOOD, KATHERINE EMMA (1878-1961)

Sculptor. Born in Woodford, Essex. The daughter of George Saunders Sapsworth and Elizabeth. Her father worked in the leather and tanning trade. Katherine had at least one brother, Arnold. Raised in Essex. Studied at the Slade School, London. Produced figures, reliefs and other works. Exhibited at the Royal Academy (1911), with the International Society of Sculptors, Painters & Gravers, the Ridley Art Club and at Wembley and Olympia. Exhibited works

included: Magna Mater (relief), The Path of Enlightenment, The Vision and Priest of Buddha. Elected a Member of the Ridley Club. In 1901 Katherine married John Maltwood in London. He was an advertising manager. Initially, she was based in London, but after her marriage was also based at Tadworth, Surrey. She died in Canada.

MANGER, CLARE B. - SEE LANCASTER, C.B.

MANLEY, EDNA (1900-87)

Sculptor. Born in Bournemouth. The daughter of Ellis and Elizabeth Swithenbank. Both parents were born in Jamaica. Her father had a private income. Edna was one of at least eight children (Lena, Gladys, Nora, Edna, Winifred, Harvey, Ralph and Kathleen). Lena and Gladys were also born in Jamaica. The family also spent time in Northumberland and Penzance, Cornwall, where Edna went to school. She subsequently studied at the Regent Street Polytechnic and the St Martin's School of Art, both London. During her career, she spent time living in London, but also in Jamaica. In 1921 she married Norman W. Manley in Middlesex. He too was born in Jamaica. Edna produced various subjects, often working in wood, using native woods in Jamaica.

Edna was elected a Member of the London Group. Exhibited with the Group, showing works including Dance, a large frieze in mahogany which was illustrated in Apollo in December 1932, p.308. The frieze consisted of five planks of mahogany joined, and measured around 6ft by 4ft with eight figures in relief. The wood was seasoned in Jamaica. Also exhibited at the French Gallery (including in 1937), the Society of Women Artists (1924-28), the Royal Scottish Academy (1938) and the Goupil Gallery. At the Goupil's Summer Exhibition for 1929, Manley showed a life-size statue carved in wood, also illustrated in Apollo, Vol.10, September 1929, p.185. In 1932 she showed Sixteen at the Goupil Gallery. Her works were often large. Her Crucifix for All Saints Church, Kingston, Jamaica, for example, measured 10ft in height. The mahogany sculpture was illustrated in The Studio, Vol.145, May 1953, p.175. Other exhibited works included: The Beadseller, Wolves and Frog and Torso (golden mahogany). Works also illustrated in Sculpture of To-Day. The Dublin Modern Art Gallery acquired her Woman With Basket. The Graves Art Gallery, Sheffield acquired her Eve (carved mahogany).

MANNERS, ERNA (b.c.1899)

Designer / Pottery Worker / Wood Engraver. Born in South Australia. Records suggest she was Erna Hedwig, the daughter of Ernest A. Manners, M.I.M.E., and Selina. She was educated in Adelaide. By at least 1911 the family had moved to Chiswick, London. Erna subsequently studied at the Royal College of Art, London and in the galleries of Italy, Paris, Vienna and Berlin. Elected an Associate of the Royal College of Art in 1923. Produced wood engravings, pottery and carved figures. Worked as a designer for Poole Pottery in Dorset and as a commission worker. She had her own private pottery studio. Exhibited her work at Wembley, in Paris and Manchester, and at the Society of Women Artists (1924-39). Exhibited works included: Goose (plaque), St Cast, Brittany (coloured wood engraving), Lady in a Shawl (carved alabaster) and Duiker (carved pear). Some of her pottery was illustrated in The Studio and in the Year Books of Decorative Art. Elected an Associate of the Society of Women Artists (1924-49). Possibly the same Erna Manners who died in Australia in 1956, aged 56.

MARCH, ELSIE (1884-1974)

Sculptor. One of nine children, eight of whom became artists, sculptors or craftsmen. The March siblings spent much of their lives together, and occasionally worked together. All the siblings were born in Hull, Yorkshire where their father, George H. March, worked as a seed crusher's foreman. Perhaps surprisingly, neither George March nor his wife, Elizabeth, appeared to have any obvious artistic leanings. The siblings were raised in Hull, but in around 1900 the family moved to London for a time. Subsequently, the siblings were based in Farnborough, Kent, at Goddendene. All the siblings, except for Eva (1881-1964), underwent some formal art training. Edward (1873-c.1966) became a painter. Sydney (1876-1968), Vernon (1891-1930) and Elsie became sculptors. Frederick (c.1880-1962), Dudley (1882-1962), Percival (1878-1953) and Walter (1888-1954) became artist / craftsmen. Elsie remained in Kent until her death, aged 89.

Elsie's career as a sculptor covered at least five decades, from the 1910s to the 1950s. She produced groups, statuettes and heads in plaster, clay, bronze and terracotta. Exhibited her work at the Royal Academy (1919-57), the Society of Women Artists (1935-51), the Royal Society of British Artists, the Royal Glasgow Institute and the Walker Art Gallery, Liverpool. Exhibited works included: Beethoven (head, terracotta), The Dying Yesterday (statuette group, bronze), The Incoming Wave (terracotta) and The World

and the Soul (group, bronze). Elected a Member of the Royal Society of British Artists. Her bronze group, Evening, was purchased by the Canadian National Gallery. Produced a bronze reredos for Ravenscar Church. She collaborated with her brothers on the National War Memorial of Canada, Ottawa. Edward, Sydney and Vernon also exhibited at the Royal Academy. Like Elsie, Sydney, Percival, Frederick, Dudley and Vernon all died at Goddendene. Vernon fought in the First World War. Eva married Charles Newman in Kent in 1916.

MARSH, HELEN GRACE CULVERWELL (1888-1981)

Illustrator / Artist. Born and raised in Bristol. The daughter of Thomas Culverwell Marsh (d.1924), a hosier, and Emily. Her father originated from Somerset, her mother from America. One of at least six children (Florence, Edward, Emily, Helen, Ethel and Ernest). Helen later moved to Barnet, Middlesex with her parents. A young talent. Probably studied in London. She worked for over 27 years as an illustrator of children's books in colour and black & white. Also worked on games, puzzles and pastimes as well as producing greetings card and postcard designs, nursery products, booklets and advertising. Produced advertising for, for example, Colgate toothpaste, Puritan soap and Ovaltine. Worked for companies and publishers including C.W. Faulkner, A.M. Davis, Allday Ltd, The Art & Humour Publishing Co., Dean & Son, Gale & Polden, Collins and Ward Lock. Also, Alpha Publishing, E. Mack, A. Vivian Mansell, Photocrom, E.W. Savory, Blackie and J. Salmon. Books illustrated by Marsh included Betty in the Country (embroidery book, The Art & Humour Publishing Co., n.d.), Me and Mike (Gale & Polden, c.1920), My Lady Betty (with John Hassall, Collins, n.d.), Songs For the Wee Folk (with Charles Lambert, Gale & Polden, 1919), The Cobweb Dress (Lambert's New Playbooks, 1921), Nursery Verse (Ward Lock, 1923) and Jack and the Bean Stalk (1929). Marsh wrote and illustrated her own books, and occasionally worked with her husband. Based in Sidcup and in Paignton, Devon. In 1913 she married Charles Theodore Lambert (1890-1959) in Barnet. He served in the First World War and died in Paignton. They had two children. Helen died in Leicestershire, aged 93.

MARSH, JANET MARY GOOLD (1877-1944)

Illuminator / Pictorial and Decorative Figure Worker. Born in Blandford, Dorset. The daughter of William Ernest Brennand, a solicitor, and Florence Goold. One of at least five children (Clara, William, Janet, John and Florence). Raised in Dorset. Studied at the Royal Academy schools and at the Royal College of Art, London. For a time, as a student, she shared digs with sculptor / modeller Margaret Winser (1868-1944). The two remained friends. By 1911, Marsh is listed as a peripatetic art teacher in London. In 1915 she married the Rev. Edmund Marsh in London. They subsequently moved to King's Lynn, Norfolk, to East Winch vicarage. At King's Lynn, she had her own private studio. Exhibited her work, including at the Royal Academy (1905-24) and the Royal Institute of Oil Painters. Exhibited works included: Art Class in an L.C.C. Cripple School, The Breakfast-Room, Bradbourne House, Kent, Memorial For St Mary's Church, Edmonton and Parkstone, Dorset. Janet died in Norfolk, aged 67.

MARTIN, DOROTHY BURT (1882-1949)

Watercolour Painter / Etcher / Pottery Worker / Embroideress / Artist in Lettering and Illumination. Born in January 1882 in Tettenhall, Staffordshire, near to Wolverhampton. One of at least five children (three girls, two boys). The daughter of George Maynard Martin (b.1848) and Emma Ellis Sharp (1846-1929). Her father, a solicitor and Borough Coroner, originated from Devon. Her mother originated from Staffordshire. Dorothy was the youngest child, along with her twin sister, Margaret Ellis Martin. Raised in Tettenhall. Educated privately. Studied at the Wolverhampton Municipal School of Art. Subsequently went to London to study at the Royal College of Art. Elected an Associate of the Royal College of Art in 1911, whilst living in West Kensington. Gained a Diploma, and an Engraving Diploma in 1924. A promising student, she won silver and bronze medals at the National Competition of Schools of Art. Also gained her Art Masters' Teaching Certificate. Worked in various artistic fields, but also taught widely. She was assistant teacher at the Wolverhampton School of Art. Was art teacher at the Leeds and Wood Green Training Colleges, and visiting teacher at the Peckham L.C.C. Secondary School. She became Head of the Art Department at Roedean School, Brighton. Was still at Roedean into the 1930s. Also taught etching at the Brighton Municipal School of Art. Later, in 1933, she gained a Diploma in the History of Art at the Courtauld Institute.

A diverse and talented artist, Martin exhibited her work over a period of more than 21 years. Exhibited at the Royal Academy (1914-32), the Royal Glasgow Institute (1924), the Society of Women Artists (1918-35), the Wolverhampton Art Gallery, at an Arts and Crafts Exhibition at Worthing and with the Sussex Women's Art Club. Exhibited works included: Wharfedale, Yorkshire (after Cecil Lawson), Cowley's Barn, Ovingdean, Notre Dame, Paris (aquatint), Chand (pottery elephant) and The Jungfrau (aquatint). The Worthing Art Gallery purchased her etching Fiesole. Some of her works were illustrated in leading journals of the day. For example, her studies of fish appeared in the Building News (1908), while a drawing of an Erechtheion frieze appeared in the Builder (1909). An embroidered portiere was illustrated in Art and Decoration (1914). On her death in August 1949, aged 67, Dorothy was living in Askerswell, Dorset at Sherwood Cottage, but died in hospital in Clapham Common, London. She left her £2055 estate to her twin sister Margaret, who also never married. Margaret died in 1957, aged 75, then living in Bridport, Dorset. She outlived Dorothy by some eight years.

MARTIN, EDITH EMMA (1875-1960)

Painter / Craftswoman. Born in Battersea, London. The daughter of Walter S. Dunkley and Elizabeth. Had at least one sibling, Ferdinand. Raised in Battersea. Studied at the Croydon School of Art, the Cathcart Studios, the Yellow Door Studios and in Germany. Produced oil and watercolour paintings, including landscapes, and was involved in various crafts. Based in London, but also Surrey. Died in Surrey, aged 85. In 1896 she married Alfred Stanley Martin, a commercial traveller. They had at least one son, Laurence. It appears that Edith took up art only in her 30s, after she married, since she is listed as an art student in 1911 at the age of 35. As a consequence, she exhibited her work mainly in the 1920s and 1930s. Exhibited at the Royal Academy (1925), the Society of Women Artists (1921-28), with the Royal Institute of Painters in Watercolours and in America. Works included: The Thames at Dusk, A Garden Trophy, Windflowers and Sunday Afternoon in the Green Park. Elected a Member of the Faculty of Arts.

MARTIN, ETHEL SELENA (1876-1963)

Painter / Craftswoman. Born in Walthamstow, Essex. The daughter of Edward John Martin, a commercial clerk and later works manager, and Ellen. Her parents originated from London. Raised in Walthamstow and in Leyton, Essex. One of at least three children (also Ruth and Hilary). Ethel studied at the Liverpool School of Architecture and Applied Art from around 1898 until at least 1903. As a student, in 1903 she was awarded the blue ribbon prize for art students of Liverpool, which was a £60 special art scholarship, tenable for one year's study in London or abroad. The award was presented by the City Council through the Technical Instruction Committee. During her previous four years of study, she had already won other prizes, and for two years in succession won a £30 art scholarship.

Ethel's talents as a student were noted in The Studio, Vol.28, May 1903, p.291. She was particularly praised for an original design for a fountain, and was commended for her drawing and design skills and for her modelling work from life. She became a painter in watercolours of flowers and other subjects, and a craftswoman. She was also art mistress at the Liverpool School of Art. In 1911, she is listed as an art mistress in Yorkshire, boarding with artist and art master George Marples. Marples was Principal of the Hull and Huddersfield Schools of Art, but also, subsequently, the Liverpool School of Art where Ethel worked. In the 1920s, 1930s and 1940s she was based at Hoylake, Cheshire. She died in Ashford, Kent, aged 87. Exhibited her work occasionally, including at the Royal Academy (1926-47) and the Walker Art Gallery, Liverpool. Exhibited works included: Magnolia, Hawthorn and Yellow and Gold. Elected a Member of the Arts and Crafts Society.

MARTIN, HELEN ALICE (b.1889)

Etcher / Poster Designer / Painter. Born in Sheffield in September 1889. The daughter of John Wise Martin (d.1911), a doctor, and Louise. Her parents originated from Ireland. Had at least five older brothers (James, Ernest, John, Robert and Gerald). Raised in Sheffield. Helen was educated privately. Studied at the Sheffield, Eastbourne and Cheltenham Schools of Art and at the Sheffield University. Passed her Board of Education exams in drawing and industrial design. Became an etcher, poster designer and painter of landscapes and portraits. Produced etchings and aquatints. Spent much of her career in Cheltenham. During the First World War, she carried out service as a munition and creche worker. She took up art again in 1918. Exhibited her work occasionally, including at the Society of Women Artists (1927) and in Liverpool and Sheffield. Works included: The Old Forge (etching), Midhurst, Sussex (aquatint) and Mont St Michel (aquatint). Elected an Associate of the Sheffield Society of Artists and of the Eastbourne Society of Artists. Also a Member of the Panton Club, London.

MARTIN, MABEL LILIAN I. (1886-1978)

Artist / Lithographer / Designer. Born in Dover. The daughter of Henry Frederick Martin. Educated at the Girls' Public Day School, Dover. Studied at the Westminster School of Art, the Regent Street Polytechnic (1918-24) under Harry Watson, at the Hornsey College of Art (1933) and in Paris. At the Regent Street Polytechnic, she was awarded two bronze medals for drawing. Awarded a Drawing and Design Board of Education Diploma. Produced miniature paintings, sketches and portraits in oils and watercolours, lithographs and poster designs. Also acted as art mistress at various places including the Grove School, Hindhead, the London County Council Institutes and at Winton House, Ealing. Elected a Member of the Three Arts Club. For 18 months she acted as Secretary to the Art Section of the Three Arts Club. One of her aims was to introduce more colour into everyday life. Based in London and Dover during her career. Died in Dover, aged 91.

Martin executed numerous poster designs during her career, including for Dover and for the Girls' Club, London. Also produced postcards of Dover. Exhibited widely, including at the Royal Academy (1920-50), the Society of Women Artists (1949-59), the Royal Society of British Artists, the Women's International Art Club and with the East Kent Art Society. Also, at the Walker Art Gallery, Liverpool, the Three Arts Club and the Paris Salon. Exhibited works included: An Old Pensioner, Snow at Dover (watercolour), Adele and A Balcony Window, Luchon (oil). Works illustrated in Revue Moderne (A Study, (miniature) and Mrs C.E. Nixon (sketch portrait)) and in Les Artistes d'Aujourdhui (Mrs C.E. Nixon and the Hon. Mrs Hopwood, miniatures).

MARTIN, SOPHIE FREDERIKA - SEE EVA, S.F.

MARX, ENID CRYSTAL DOROTHY (1902-98)

Painter / Engraver / Textile Printer / Designer / Illustrator. Born in Hampstead, London in October 1902. The daughter of Robert Joseph Marx, a consulting engineer, and Annie. Had at least one sister, Marguerite. Raised in London and spent much of her life there, dying in Camden, aged 95. Educated at the Roedean School, Brighton. Studied at the L.C.C. Central School of Arts and Crafts. Also, at the Royal College of Art, London under Bernard Adeney, Paul Nash and Leon Underwood. Became a diverse artist involved in various areas of the decorative arts. Produced woodcuts, paintings, lithographs, linocuts, book illustrations, textile designs, pen & ink drawings and designs for posters, book jackets, greetings cards, endpapers, trademarks and postage stamps. Between 1925 and 1927 she worked with textile designers Phyllis Barron and Dorothy Larcher. She then set up her own studio designing and producing hand block printed textiles during the late 1920s and 1930s, until the start of the Second World War. In 1926, some of her textiles were added to the British Institute of Industrial Art permanent exhibition at the South Kensington Museum. One of those was a hand block print on cotton which was illustrated in The Studio, Vol.92, August 1926, p.121. Textiles by Barron and Larcher were also in the exhibition. The Brooklyn Museum acquired lengths of materials designed and printed by Marx for its collection.

In 1937 Marx designed seating fabric for the Underground trains. In 1942 she was elected a Royal Designer for Industry. In 1946 she was elected a Fellow of the Society of Industrial Artists. From 1944 to 1947 she was also a designer of textiles to the Board of Trade Utility Furniture Design Committee, evidently working as part of the war effort. During her lengthy career, Marx also worked as an illustrator. Worked for publishers including the Curwen Press, Chatto & Windus and Faber & Faber. Books illustrated by her included Francesca Allinson, A Childhood (1937), Margaret Lambert, When Victoria Began to Reign (1937) and Norman Douglas, An Almanac (1945). Illustrated her own books, including A Book of Nursery Rhymes (1938), The Little White Bear (1945), The Pigeon Ace (1946) and Sam and Amy (1972). Also the author of Popular and Traditional Art in England (with Margaret Lambert).

Marx exhibited her work, including at the Royal Scottish Academy (1957-60), the Victoria & Albert Museum, London, at the Redfern Gallery, in Paris and Leipzig, and at the Boston Museum and elsewhere in America. In 1979 some of her works were included in an exhibition of women engravers titled Shall We Join the Ladies? held at the Museum of Oxford. Marx was one of 27 women artists represented. Some of her work was reproduced in journals including International Textiles, Listener, Vogue, Design 46, Architectural Review, House and Garden, The Studio and some Swedish periodicals. From 1965 she was Head of the Dress, Textiles and Ceramics Department of the Croydon College of Art. In 2012 the Pallant House Art Gallery, Chichester held an exhibition of her work. Noted in Janet Adam Smith, Children's Illustrated Books, London, Collins, 1948. Smith includes a woodcut illustration taken from Marx's own Nursery Rhymes.

MARYON, LOUISA EDITH CHURCH (1872-1924)

Sculptor / Decorative Artist. Also known as Edith. Born in St Pancras, London. The daughter of John S. Maryon, a tailor, and Louisa. One of at least six children (John, Louisa, Herbert, George, Mildred and Violet). Raised in London. Lived with her family until 1914, when she moved to Switzerland. John became a railway clerk initially, and George became a mechanical engineer. Herbert (b.1874) became an artist / designer and art lecturer. He spent some time lecturing in Carlisle, and took on the role of designer / teacher in metalwork at the Keswick School of Industrial Arts in the Lake District.* Mildred (b.1881) also became an art student, but appears to have given up art when she married Frank D. Stones in Chelsea in 1906. Louisa studied at the L.C.C. Central School of Arts and Crafts, and at the Royal College of Art, London. Produced busts, reliefs, groups and statuettes in marble and bronze, decorative panels and friezes and works in silver and enamel.

Louisa exhibited her work, including at the Royal Academy (1900-12), the Royal Glasgow Institute (1905), the Society of Women Artists (1900), in Leeds, at the 1901 Glasgow Exhibition and at the Walker Art Gallery, Liverpool. Exhibited works included: A Future Darwin (bust), Psyche (statuette, bronze), Rev. Canon Rawnsley (relief, bronze) and Cupid and Psyche (clasp, silver & enamel). Edith is listed in M.H. Spielmann's British Sculpture and Sculptors of To-day, London, Cassell & Co. Ltd, 1901. Spielmann illustrates her May Morning. Edith was also one of the founders of anthroposophy along with Ita Wegman. In around 1912 she met Rudolf Steiner, its originator, which lead her to move to Switzerland in 1914. She worked with Steiner on the construction of the first Goetheanum in Dornach, Switzerland. Louisa contributed sculpture for the building. She worked as head of the fine arts section at the Goetheanum. She died in Switzerland of tuberculosis, leaving her small estate to her brother Herbert. SEE: Sara Haslam, John Ruskin and the Lakeland Arts Revival 1880-1920, Cardiff, Merton Priory Press, 2004.

MASON, EDITH M. - SEE HINCHLEY, E.M.

MASON, EMILY FLORENCE (1870-c.1940)
Painter / Decorative Artist. Born in Birmingham. The daughter of Robert Crump Mason, a chemist and druggist, and Mary. Her father originated from Birmingham, her mother from Shropshire. The third of at least four children. The eldest child, Jessie, became a governess. The second eldest, Walter, became a commercial traveller. The fourth child was Archibald. Emily was raised in Bromsgrove, Worcestershire. She was still there until at least the age of 20. Subsequently went to London to study at the Royal College of Art. Awarded an Art Class Teachers' Certificate. Became a painter of various subjects, including portraits, but also produced decorative works including gesso panels. She returned to live with her father in Bromsgrove, and was still there in 1901 at the age of 30. Her father was then 68 and widowed. By this stage, Emily is listed as an artist with her own income. Her father died in 1914, leaving his £677 estate to Emily, who was then 44 and unmarried.

At some point, Emily acted as art mistress at Howell's School, Llandaff, Cardiff. She also evidently travelled abroad, and for a time acted as Honorary Secretary of the Ceylon Society of Arts and as an inspector in Ceylon. Latterly, she was based in London. Died sometime in the late 1930s or early 1940s. Exhibited her work, including at the Walker Art Gallery, Liverpool, with the Royal West of England Academy, in Manchester, with the Royal Institute, the Cardiff Art Society and at the Birmingham Art Gallery. Also exhibited four of her gesso panels at the Society of Women Artists in 1921: St Agnes, St Cecilia, St Hild and St Katharine. Other works included: Stories From the Life of Buddha, The Palmist and The Seen and the Unseen. Painted abroad. Several of her Eastern pictures were reproduced.

MASON, JANET M. - SEE HAUGHTON, J.M.

MASON, MURIEL B. - SEE JACKSON, M.B.

MASSEY, GERTRUDE (1868-1957)
Painter / Decorative Artist. Born in Brixton, London in February 1868. The daughter of Gustav Wilhelm Louis Seth and Fanny Elizabeth. Her father, a West African merchant, originated from Germany. Gertrude was the eldest of at least six children (Gertrude, Florence, Eva, Percival, Algernon and Nora). Spent part of her childhood in Croydon, Surrey, at Stethis Lodge, where various other family members and servants lived. She was educated privately. It is unclear if she studied at a recognised school of art. However, she married etcher / painter Henry Gibbs Massey (b.1860) in London in late 1890. He was Principal of the Heatherley's School of Fine Art in London, a post which he held until the 1920s, by which time he had been joined in the post of Principal by Ian MacNab. Gertrude's sister, Florence, studied at Heatherley's and Gertrude taught miniature painting at the school in the early 1900s. The above would suggest that she too studied there. Massey was the son of a merchant. The couple had one daughter, Eva (b.1894), and lived in London for most of their lives and careers. Gertrude produced portraits, miniatures and decorative landscapes in oils and watercolours. She also advertised lessons in miniature painting in The Studio (certainly in 1910).

Interestingly, she appears to have exhibited her work more seriously after her marriage and the birth of her daughter. Exhibited at the Royal Academy (23 works, 1898-1918) and at the Paris Salon. Held several one-woman shows. For example, in late 1925 / early 1926, she held an exhibition of watercolours at the Graham Gallery in New Bond Street, London. Exhibited works included: Eva, Daughter of Mrs Massey, Elsie and Marie, Daughters of Lady Mary Fitzwilliam, Mrs Gertrude Massey and Her Sister and H.H. Princess Toussoun. Evidently favoured by royalty, Gertrude was commissioned at least 24 times by the Royal Family. Subjects included Queen Victoria's Pomeranian Dogs, Turi and Marco, Princess Mary of Wales, the Prince of Wales, Queen Alexandra and the Duke of York. Other subjects included the Queen of Norway and the Dowager Empress of Russia. Works reproduced in various publications including The Studio, Colour and Drawing & Design. For example, in 1908 The Studio offered a colour reproduction of her miniature painting of The Marchioness of Lansdowne (Vol.44, p.177) in an article Modern Miniature Painting. Henry Massey died in July 1934. Gertrude died in Chichester, Sussex, aged 89. Her sister, Florence Seth, also became a successful artist. SEE: SETH, FLORENCE

MATHEWS, EDITH LAURA - SEE CALVERT, E.L.

MATHEWS, EVELYN - SEE HOLDEN, E.

MAUDE, THE HON. ALICE CHARLOTTE (1879-1967)

Painter / Sculptor / Etcher. The daughter of Ludlow E. Maude, an estate agent who originated from Dublin, Ireland. Her mother, Clara, originated from Fareham, Hampshire. One of at least five children (Kathleen, Elinor, Dorothy, Eustace and Alice), all born and raised in Horsmonden, Kent. The family lived at Broadford House, with at least four servants. Eustace later joined the army. Alice was educated privately. She then studied art in London, at the Chelsea, Lambeth and Hammersmith Schools of Art. Also studied at the London County Council Central School of Arts and Crafts. As a student, she was awarded a silver medal for her etchings. Produced sculptures, etchings, watercolour paintings and black & white drawings. Subsequently lived in London, Dorset and Kent. She exhibited two works at the Royal Academy: Problems of the World (statuette, bronze) in 1914 and Peace (relief) in 1917. Both were strongly indicative of what was happening across Europe at that time. Also exhibited with the International Society of Sculptors, Painters & Gravers, at the Society of Women Artists (1917-24) and at various provincial galleries. Exhibited works included: Major The Viscount Hawarden (bronze), The Archer (bronze), Bubbles (bronze), Major Gilbert Green, M.C., R.F.A. (bronze) and Baby's Portrait (bronze). Her design for a memorial wall fountain was illustrated in the Daily Mail. Two of her garden ornaments were illustrated in The Studio Year Book. Other works by her included war memorials for India and Hong Kong. In her 40s, Alice married Alan L. Stewart in Chelsea. She died in Canterbury, Kent, aged 87.

MEARS, NORAH GEDDES (b.1887)

Artist in Paper Silhouettes. Born in Edinburgh in October 1887. The daughter of Sir Patrick Geddes, Kt. (1854-1932) and Anna Morton (1858-1917). Her father was a Professor of Botany, based at St Andrews University for a time. One of at least three children (Norah, Alistair and Arthur). Raised in Edinburgh. Educated at home and abroad. Studied at the Edinburgh College of Art. Became a successful artist in paper silhouettes, but also the author of Intimations and Avowals (Moray Press, Edinburgh), a book of verse. Based in Scotland

for much of her life and career, including at Musselburgh. Elected a Member of the English Speaking Union. In 1915 she married architect and planning consultant Sir Frank C. Mears (1880-1953), P.R.S.A., LL.D., F.R.I.B.A., M.T.P.I., F.R.S.E. He was responsible for, among other projects, the King George Bridge, Aberdeen and the Livingstone Memorial, Blantyre. The couple had three sons, two of whom died young.

MEATS, SARA MURIEL (1904-91)

Etcher / Enameller / Engraver / Silversmith. Known as Muriel. Born in Birmingham in June 1904. The daughter of Robert Livingstone Meats, Manager of the Lloyds Bank, Coventry. Had at least one sibling, Philip. Studied at the Birmingham Central School of Art. Based mainly in Birmingham and Coventry during her career, but latterly based in Cumbria. Died at Grasmere in December 1991, aged 87. Exhibited her work occasionally. Contributed to two Arts and Crafts Exhibitions held at the Royal Academy in 1926 and 1928. Also exhibited with the Royal Birmingham Society of Artists and the Society of Staffordshire Artists. In 1937 one of her cigarette cases, with a design of elephants in enamel, was purchased by the Worshipful Company of Goldsmiths, London.

MEESON, DORA - SEE COATES, D.

MEGGITT, MARJORIE (1906-70)

Sculptor. Born in Sheffield in February 1906. The daughter of John Eyre Meggitt and Helen. Her father originated from Sheffield, her mother from London. One of at least three children (also Jack and Samuel). Raised in Sheffield. Educated at Firs Hill. Studied at the Sheffield College of Art under Francis Jahn. Also, at the Royal Academy schools, London under Sir William Reid Dick and William MacMillan. Also studied at the British School in Rome. Won a Royal Academy schools Gold Medal and a Travelling Scholarship (1930). Awarded the Prix de Rome for sculpture (1932-35). Worked in bronze, plaster, wood and terracotta. Produced reliefs, busts and groups.

Meggitt exhibited her work, including at the Royal Glasgow Institute (1936), the Royal Academy (1930-65) and in the provinces. Exhibited works included: Berenice (statue, terracotta), The Four Races (group, reinforced plaster), Carmen (bust, terracotta) and Springtime (bust, bronze). She spent time working in Sheffield, London and Mousehole, Cornwall. Commissions and purchasers included London County Council; a memorial for the Green-Jackets, Calas (regimental badges); the 49th West

Riding Division (Normandy Arch); Plumstead Hospital Relief Panel; a sculpture for the Children's Shelter in Gilford Street, London and various private commissions. Works reproduced in Architectural Review, The Builder and various other journals. In late 1936 she married Glyn Owen Jones in Fulham, London. They had three daughters, one of whom became an artist. Meggitt worked and exhibited until at least 1965. She died in Hammersmith, London, aged 64.

MELLIAR, GLADYS DEWSBURY FOSTER (1880-1964)

Sculptor. Born in Tostock, Suffolk. The daughter of Andrew Foster Melliar, a Church of England clergyman, and Catherine. One of at least six children (Mabel, Robert, John, Elsie, Gladys and Winifred). Based in Chelsea for a time, and in Sproughton, Suffolk. Probably studied in London. Became a sculptor of busts and statuettes in silver and bronze. Exhibited three works at the Royal Academy: Melisande (statuette, silver) and The Mirror (statuette, bronze) in 1910, and Portrait of a Lady (bust, bronze) in 1913. In 1942 she married Oriel Riviere Burney in Ipswich. He was a music teacher. Gladys died in Ipswich, aged 85. She was a friend of artist Agnes Dora Mason who was also based at Sproughton.

MELVIN, GRACE WILSON (1892-1977)

Illuminator / Bas-relief Artist / Painter. Born in Scotland. The daughter of John Melvin, a produce merchant of Glasgow, and Jessie Jane. Educated at the Glasgow High School for Girls. Studied at the Glasgow School of Art, winning maintenance and travelling scholarships. Won the Lauder Prize of the Glasgow Society of Lady Artists. Became an illuminator, an artist in watercolours, a bas-relief artist and an embroideress. Took charge of the lettering and illumination section of the Glasgow School of Art in the 1920s and 1930s. Designed and executed the Burgess tickets presented by the Corporation of Glasgow for at least five consecutive years. Also designed and executed the Burgess tickets for the Duke of York, Princess Mary and Prince Henry. Also, the Rolls of Honour for Stewart and McDonald Ltd. Exhibited her work with the Society of Scottish Artists and the Glasgow Society of Lady Artists. Elected a Member of the Glasgow Society of Lady Artists' Club. During her career, she travelled to Vancouver and did some teaching at the Vancouver School of Decorative and Applied Arts. One of her bas-reliefs was illustrated in The Studio.

MERCER, ELEANOR LOUISE (1871-c.1900)

Sculptor / Metalworker. Born in Gainsborough, Lincolnshire. The daughter of Henry Mercer who was a seed crusher in Lincolnshire at the time of her birth. He originated from Hull. Her mother, Louise, originated from France. One of at least six children (Walter, Caroline, Eleanor, Arthur, Millicent and Harry). By the early 1890s, the family was living in Sheffield, Yorkshire, where Henry Mercer was employed as an insurance agent. By this stage, Arthur had become a merchant, and Caroline was working as an author and writer for a magazine. Both Millicent and Eleanor (now aged 20) were working as gold and silver chasers, with Eleanor also working as a designer. Shortly after, Eleanor went to London to study sculpture under Professor Edouard Lanteri at the South Kensington School of Art. She had her own studio at Rathbone Place, London. However, her career was cut short by her premature death in around 1899 or 1900. No death is recorded in British records, which suggests she may have died abroad.

Despite being in only the initial stages of her career, Eleanor had already made a considerable impact. Between 1897 and 1899 she exhibited five works at the Royal Academy including: Miss Bertha Sharp (medallion, bronze), Fletcher Mercer, Esq. (medallion, bronze) and a decorative bowl in silver. Also exhibited three works at the Society of Women Artists in 1897: Relief Head (priced £4), Reapers (modelled panels, £3) and An Old Man (bust, £5). At the 1899 Arts and Crafts Exhibition Society exhibition, she showed a decorative panel. Mercer produced portrait works, statuettes, busts, panels, reliefs and works in silver. She won a brief mention in M.H. Spielmann's volume British Sculpture and Sculptors of To-day (London, Cassell & Co. Ltd), published in 1901. Spielmann notes that Mercer had died 'recently', with a promising career ahead of her now curtailed. In 1905 the South Kensington School of Art (the Royal College of Art, London) held a reception for Mercer's former teacher, Lanteri, to mark his 25th year as Master of Sculpture. Past and present students attended, and Lanteri was presented with a silver bowl designed and made by Eleanor Mercer.

MESSENGER, EILEEN C. - SEE GREENWOOD, E.C.

METCALFE, KATHLEEN I. - SEE MacKIE, K.I.

METEYARD, KATE MURIEL M. - SEE EADIE, K.M.M.

MIDDLETON, DORA THACKER - SEE CLARKE, D.T.

MILES, HELEN JANE ARUNDEL (1841-1919)

Artist / Designer. Born in Battersea, London. The daughter of Alfred Miles (c.1797-1851) and Sibella Elizabeth Hatfield (1800-82). Her father was a Commander in the Royal Navy, and later an assistant in the Hydrographic Office of the Admiralty. He was also an artist, and three of his drawings were published by Day & Son with an accompanying poem by his wife. He also edited two editions of Horsburgh's Indian Directory. Her mother, Sibella, was a respected and published poet. She wrote, among other things, the introduction to Te Deum (1877) with illustrations by Helen. Helen had one elder brother, Frederick (b.c.1837). As a child, she spent some time in Jersey. After her father's death, the family returned to London, where Helen remained for much of the rest of her life. She died at Streatham Park.

In London, Helen studied at the South Kensington school for some three years, winning a local and national medal for a set of anatomical drawings. The drawings were later purchased by the Department of Science and Art. She also studied at the Lambeth School of Art, winning a bronze medal for a design for a library door. Her studies were interrupted by Frederick's illness and death. She subsequently began to work as a designer on wood and a book illustrator, living with her mother until Sibella died. She then lived alone or in boarding houses. She also executed pottery designs for Doulton's of Lambeth, including figures of Britomart and Una from Spenser's The Faerie Queene which were shown at the 1874 International Exhibition. She also designed for a number of years for Wedgwood, producing, for example, a set of 12 tiles based on Old English Months. Other tile designs by Helen included characters from A Midsummer Night's Dream (1878).

Helen exhibited her work regularly at the Dudley Gallery, showing watercolour drawings and decorative designs. She also exhibited at the Royal Society of British Artists (1860-78) and at the Society of Women Artists (1874-79).

Exhibited works included: The Warrior's Return (decorative design on oak panel), The Fisherman (watercolour), A Surrey Oatfield and Bertha in the Lane (watercolour). Her work was noted in Ellen C. Clayton's English Female Artists, Vol.II, London, Tinsley, 1876. Some confusion exists over the exact number of works exhibited by Helen at the Society of Women Artists since some may have been submitted by artist Ellen Miles, also of London. Similarly, some of Ellen's works may have been wrongly attributed, and may actually have been executed by Helen.

MILLER, HILARY MARGARET (1919-93)

Illustrator / Painter. Born in London in October 1919. The daughter of Guy Miller, a teacher and curator of the South London Art Gallery. Hilary was educated at the Blackheath High School. Studied in London, at the Blackheath School of Art between 1936 and 1940, and at the Royal College of Art between 1940 and 1943. Elected an Associate of the Royal College of Art in 1943. Produced illustrations and paintings, including in tempera. Based mainly in Oxford and Oxfordshire during her career. Died in Oxfordshire, aged 73. In 1946 she married artist Hubert Hennes, A.R.C.A., in Greenwich. Had at least one son. Exhibited her work at the South London Art Gallery and at the Royal Academy (1948-67). Exhibited works included: Flower Piece (tempera), A Welsh Wall, Wasteland and Dorset Lease. Produced illustrations for, for example, The Living World (Odhams) and Boff's Book of Gardening (Odhams). Acted as a teacher at the South-East Sussex Technical College (1943) and at the Oxford School of Art (1945).

MILLIGAN, FRANCES JANE GRIERSON (b.1919)

Painter / Artist / Artist in Silver and Copper / Illuminator. Born in Northamptonshire in July 1919. The daughter of artist Thomas Vaughan Milligan, A.R.C.A., and Grace Wilson. Her father was an art master at the Llanelly School of Art and at the Herefordshire School of Art. He died in Herefordshire in 1966. Frances was educated at the Hereford High School for Girls, and at the Elms Private School for Young Ladies. She studied at the Herefordshire School of Art under her father. Became an artist in oils, watercolours, black & white and pencil, and worked in silver and copper. Became a student teacher at the School between 1938 and 1942. Acted as the visiting art teacher at the Bromyard Grammar School in 1940, then acted as a full-time teacher at the Herefordshire School of Art and at Bromyard between 1942 and 1945. Acted as a full-time art teacher at the Herefordshire School of Art between 1945 and 1948. Also acted as an art teacher at the Hereford Cathedral Grammar School between 1947 and 1948. Was a swimming instructor at the Hereford Cathedral Preparatory School between 1937 and 1940. Acted as visiting art teacher at the Belmont Convent of the Assumption from 1946. Based mainly in Hereford during her career.

In 1948 Frances married Councillor Alfred Felix Macirone Watkins in Hereford. They had at least one son. Exhibited her work, including at the Royal Academy (1946-48), the Royal Scottish Academy (1947), the Royal Society of British Artists, the Brighton and Hove Autumn Exhibition, with the Midland Contemporary Artists in Birmingham, at the National Eisteddfod of Wales, and at the Herefordshire Arts and Crafts Exhibitions. Held a one-woman exhibition at the Hereford City Art Gallery (of approximately 100 works). Held a display of her works in silver in 1947. Exhibited works included: Introspection (pencil) and Commercial Road, 6am. One of her portraits, of Lady Hawkins, was purchased for presentation to the Lady Hawkins Grammar School, Kington. One of her portraits was illustrated in the Hereford Citizen and Bulletin. One of her illuminated addresses was purchased by the Agricultural Executive Committee. Elected a Member of the Soroptimist Club (Hereford).

MILLS, DOROTHY ANNA HAYWARD (1894-1948)

Illustrator / Painter / Author / Woodcut Artist / Wood Engraver. Born in Frocester, Gloucestershire in April 1894. The only daughter of the Rev. William Lancelot Mills (1840-1909) and Hannah Reading (1852-1942). Her father, a Cambridge scholar and clergyman, originated from Stonehouse, Gloucestershire where Dorothy was raised. Her mother originated from Northampton. Dorothy was educated at the Cheltenham Ladies' College. Studied at the Cheltenham School of Art. Also, in London at the Regent Street Polytechnic and at the St John's Wood School of Art. Based at Battledown near Cheltenham in Gloucestershire during her career. Died in Oxfordshire, aged 53, only a few years after her mother. Dorothy became a book illustrator, a painter of various subjects in oils and watercolours, a writer and, for a short time, an art lecturer. Illustrated, for example, The Polish Folk Tales and Happy Endings. Her paintings included The Lord of Joy (oil), Fowey (oil) and Barbara. Her published works included Bruges, Ghent, Ypres and The Log-Book of a Dream Ship (Burns

& Oates). Works illustrated in The Studio and in Bookman. One of her wood engravings was purchased by Princess Marie Louise. Exhibited her work occasionally, including at the Royal Academy (1919), with the Three Arts Club and with the Cotswolds artists. Was a prize winner at the National Eisteddfod of Wales, Llanelly, for a black & white drawing.

MILLS, ELIZABETH (1842-1929)

Lace Maker. A Buckinghamshire lace maker active in the later nineteenth and early twentieth centuries, part of the general revival of traditional handcrafts. She lived and worked at Gawcott village, close to Buckingham. She took a diploma in lace making and worked traditional 'Old Bucks Point' lace. She created a piece of lace for Queen Victoria's Jubilee in 1887 which included the year and a diamond shape incorporating the word 'Jubilee'. Mrs Mills was able to execute immensely complex pieces of lace by hand. She was born in Gawcott as Elizabeth Blencowe. Her mother, Mary, was also a lace maker, as was her sister, Eliza. Elizabeth is listed on census recordings as a lace maker from at least 1861. In around 1864 Elizabeth married local man Reuben Mills (c.1843-1928), a farm labourer. They lived mainly in Gawcott, and had at least four children (Mary, Sarah, George and Eva). The family spent a short time in Reigate, Surrey, but moved back to Gawcott, where they remained thereafter. In the 1881 census recordings, Elizabeth is still listed as a lace maker, which suggests that her work was paid employment, and that she considered her work to be professional rather than amateur. By 1881, her daughter, Sarah, aged only 12 years, is also listed as a lace maker.

MILLS, ELSIE JANE LOCKGER (1887-1957)

Craftswoman. Born in Wellington, Salop, Shropshire in February 1887. Her father, William Josiah Mills (b.1840), was a schoolmaster and later a headmaster. Her mother was Lucy Jane (b.1845). Had one sister, Bertha (b.1876), who was some 11 years older. Elsie was educated privately. She became a worker in embossed and stained leather and a woodcarver. Also became Principal of the Commercial School. Lived in Southport. Exhibited at the Southport Art Gallery at the Spring Exhibition (at least twice), and at the Walker Art Gallery, Liverpool (certainly in 1925 and 1926). Elsie died in Ormskirk, Lancashire, aged 70.

MILLS, ERNESTINE EVANS (1871-1959)

Metalworker / Enameller. Born in Hastings, Sussex. The daughter of Thomas Evans Bell, a Major (Madras staff) and later author and journalist, and Emily. Her father originated from London, her mother from Manchester. Had one sister, Myme (b.1869). Raised in Kensington, London in a house with servants. As a child, she was taught by painter Frederick Shields who originated from Manchester. Shields had links with the Pre-Raphaelite Brotherhood, and Ernestine later published The Life of Frederick Shields (Longmans). By at least 1891 she was a student of painting, still living in Kensington. By this time, her father had died, and Ernestine was living with her mother, who was teaching. She studied at the Slade School, London, the Royal College of Art and the Finsbury Central Technical College. As a student, she won a prize for enamels, and studied enamelling under the highly respected Alexander Fisher. Became a skilled and talented metalworker and enameller with a career that lasted over 55 years. Worked and exhibited prolifically, establishing herself as an independent craftswoman at St Mary Abbot's Terrace, Kensington and later at Addison Road, Kensington.

Mills exhibited at the Royal Academy (1900-52), the Royal Scottish Academy (1923), the Royal Glasgow Institute (1949) and the Society of Women Artists (1901-61). Exhibits included: Queen of Hearts (enamel on copper), The Late Lady Frances Balfour (enamel on silver), a case of sketches for Heraldic Enamels on silver and copper and Flower of Light (plaque, enamel). Also exhibited with the Royal Society of Miniature Painters, with the Dress Designers' Exhibition Society (in 1903 showing enamels and jewellery), at the Grafton Gallery and further afield in, for example, Toronto, New Zealand, Australia, Boston, Paris, Milan and Detroit. Won a Gold Medal at the Milan International Exhibition. Won a Paris Salon medal for enamels in 1950, and a silver medal in 1955. Contributed to the Arts and Crafts Exhibition Society exhibitions, including its eighth, held in 1906. A regular contributor to the Walker Art Gallery, Liverpool annual exhibitions. For example, at the Gallery's 1906 Autumn Exhibition she showed several items including a silver bowl with enamel decoration, a copper potpourri bowl with enamel decoration and a decorative lid for a silver bowl which were illustrated in The Studio, Vol.39, November 1906, pp.168-169. Mills contributed to numerous other exhibitions including the 1905 exhibition of Arts and Crafts held by the members of the Lyceum Club. Contributed to the May 1916 Exhibition of Works of Art by Women Artists held at Waring & Gillows. The exhibition intended to raise funds to assist women artists who were suffering due to war. It was visited by the Queen and Princess Mary. The Queen purchased one of her works.

Mills was elected an Associate of the Society of Women Artists (1919), a Member (1920-59), Honorary Treasurer (1947-58) and Vice President (1929-34). Also a Member of the Soroptimist Club, of the Arts and Crafts Exhibition Society, of the Ridley Club and of the Council for the Society of Women Artists. She represented the Society of Women Artists on the Council of Central Institute for Art and Design. Also a supporter of the suffrage movement, Mills designed badges in the suffragette colours - purple, white and green. In 1907 she joined the Women's Social and Political Union, and by 1909 was a Member of the Fabian Women's Group. In 1950, Mills was commissioned to make a plaque for the Suffragette Fellowship to commemorate the Brackenbury sisters (Museum of London). Also the author of The Domestic Problem (Castle) and contributed articles to Nation, Englishwoman, Apollo, Westminster, Contemporary Review, Queen and other journals. She also read papers before various societies.

Official purchases of her work included a memorial tablet for the Ethical Church, Bayswater; a triptych for the Manchester Municipal School of Art; a memorial tablet for Brook Hospital, Woolwich; a number of enamels purchased by Queen Mary, and work for the St Clair Club, Trinidad. Produced an enamel portrait of Emperor Haile Selassie in around 1936. Other works reproduced in The Studio. For example, The Studio, Vol.47, September 1909, p.299 included an illustration of three enamels on copper set in a silver frame, shown at the Royal Academy. She also produced paintings in oils and watercolours, some of which were exhibited with the Society of Women Artists. For example, South African Flowers (oil), Us-Once (watercolour), From a Dorset Hedge (oil) and Bombed Studio, Next Morning (watercolour). In 1898 Ernestine married Herbert H. Mills, a doctor. They had at least one daughter. Ernestine remained in Kensington for much of her life. She died in Ealing, Middlesex in February 1959, aged 88. Remained active until shortly before her death. Some of her work was exhibited at the Society of Women Artists two years after her death.

MILMAN, SYLVIA F. - SEE WHITHAM, S.F.

MILNES, SIBYL MARJORY (b.1902)
Painter / Artist in Black & White / Modeller. Born at Gislingham, Suffolk in April 1902. The daughter of John G. Milnes, M.R.C.S., L.R.C.P., a surgeon and physician who originated from Lambeth, London, and Jessie. Educated at the Derby High School. Studied at the Derby School of Art. Also, in London at the Regent Street Polytechnic and the Clapham Schools of Art. Based in Clapham during her career. Did some modelling in clay and stone carvings. Also produced oil and watercolour paintings, mainly of decorative figure compositions, and was a black & white artist who occasionally contributed to Punch. Exhibited her work, including at the Royal Academy (1930-40), the Society of Women Artists (1932), the Societe des Artistes Francais, at the Daily Express Young Artists Exhibition (1927), at the New Irish Salon (1928) and at the Paris Salon (1928). Exhibited works included: The Legend Romance, April and The Three Nuns. Works reproduced in R.A. Illustrated.

MILWARD, FREDA M. - SEE COLEBORN, F.M.

MITCHELL, MAGGIE (1883-1953)
Sculptor. Born in Camberwell, London. The daughter of James Richardson, a customs and excise official, and Lucy Jane. Her father originated from Ireland, her mother from Scotland. Maggie had at least one brother, Kenneth, who became a student of engineering. Maggie studied sculpture in London at the Goldsmiths' College and at the Royal College of Art. Produced portrait works and statuettes in bronze and plaster. Exhibited her work, including at the Royal Academy (1907-47), the Royal Glasgow Institute (1911 & 1947), the Society of Women Artists (1931-40), the Royal Scottish Academy (1921-25) and the Paris Salon. Elected a Member of the Society of Women Artists (1931-49) and a Member of the Royal Society of British Artists (1929). Works included Demobilised, a peace trophy kept by the Southport and Ainsdale Golf Club. Also, bronze busts of Thomas Hardy, O.M., J.G. Lawn, C.B.E., Mining Engineer, Sir William Rothenstein and Lord Snell. Statuettes included Icarus, The Lizard and Love Bound. Based in London, Southport and in Yeovil and Norton sub Hamdon in Somerset. Died in Yeovil, aged 70. In 1912 she married painter George Joseph Mitchell in

Redruth, Cornwall. She worked until shortly before her death.

MOLLER, MURIEL (active 1890s-1900s)
Woodcarver / Bookbinder. Of Swedish origin. Spent some time in England, certainly from the late 1890s until at least 1908, living in London. An expert woodcarver, she knew Kendal-based woodcarver Arthur W. Simpson. May have been taught by Simpson, or influenced by him, since she produced decorative carved panels similar to his, with designs based on nature. Like Simpson, Moller showed precise and careful cutting, avoiding too realistic interpretations of nature in her designs, so that her work was never heavy or florid. Did visually beautiful work which was praised in leading journals of the day, including The Studio, who deemed her work to be the best of its type done at that time. Four of her carved wood panels were illustrated in The Studio, Vol.34, April 1905, p.265. The panels were intended for four sides of a revolving bookcase.

Moller also carved pieces of furniture, some of which were shown at the Society of Art Workers' exhibition held at the Bruton Galleries in late 1905, a small exhibition of arts and crafts. One of her exhibits on that occasion was an oak cabinet made by Arthur Simpson but decorated by her. The cabinet was illustrated in the Art Workers' Quarterly in January 1906, p.47. Also contributed to the Clarion Guild of Handicraft exhibitions, including in 1904, when she showed examples of carved oak panelling, but also some of her bookbindings in embossed leather, including an edition of Omar Khayyam in white morocco. An expert in modelled leather bindings on books. Moller advertised classes in woodcarving and bookbinding in the early 1900s at her London studio. One of her pupils was Katharine Archer. Moller also contributed to the Society of Women Artists exhibitions. Exhibited there from 1897 to 1908, showing various 'handicrafts'. Contributed to the Second Exhibition of Arts and Crafts held at the Lyceum Club in early 1905. Contributed to the exhibitions of the Arts and Crafts Exhibition Society. Awarded gold medals for her work. Other examples of her carved panels were illustrated in The Studio, Vol.38, June 1906, pp.70-71.

MONSELL, ELINOR MARY - SEE DARWIN, E.M.

MONTALBA, HENRIETTA SKERRETT (1856-93)
Sculptor. Born in London. The daughter of Anthony Rubens Montalba and Emmeline. Her

father was Swedish, her mother English. One of four artistic daughters. Clara, Ellen and Hilda took up painting. Henrietta was the only one to choose sculpture. Her father was an exhibiting artist too. The Montalba sisters were all well educated and well travelled. Henrietta lived in Venice as well as London, dying in Venice at a comparatively young age. She studied at South Kensington, then at the Belle Arti in Venice, and later became a pupil of French sculptor M. Jules Dalou. Henrietta produced sculptures in terracotta and bronze. For a time, she used a studio at Campden House Road Mews in London. Exhibited her work up until her death, including at the Royal Academy (1875-93), the Royal Glasgow Institute (1881-82) and the Society of Women Artists (1876-81). Also, at the New Gallery and the Grosvenor Gallery. Works included a bust of Richard Burchett, Head of the National Art Training Schools executed for the South Kensington Art Schools. Also, busts of Lady Sophia Macnamara and Robert Browning. Exhibited works included: At Play and A Venetian Boy (terracotta). Noted briefly in M.H. Spielmann, British Sculpture and Sculptors of To-day, London, Cassell & Co. Ltd, 1901. Spielmann compares her to Mrs Thornycroft stylistically, and notes her as having shown promise. Henrietta also had a brother, Augustus, who was an artist.

MONTGOMERY, MRS (active 1890s-1900s)

Craftswoman. Mrs Montgomery of Blessingbourne founded a metal repoussé class at Fivemiletown, County Tyrone, Ireland in the early 1890s. Essentially a cottage handcraft industry, the class was formed to give the village boys a spare time occupation and to relieve local poverty. Like other handcraft classes across England and Ireland, such as the Keswick School of Industrial Arts and Newlyn, Fivemiletown became a highly successful artistic venture which helped to revive lost handcraft skills, and which brought a new degree of artistic excellence to the decorative arts. Mrs Montgomery taught the class herself, assisted by the local bank manager, with an occasional visit from John Williams, art teacher to Surrey County Council, whose designs were mostly used. His designs were also used at the Newton, Cambridgeshire metalwork class and he executed work at Essex House in connection with the Arts and Crafts movement. Exceeding all expectations, the students made swift progress, and from at least 1894 their work appeared at the annual Home Arts and Industries Association exhibition, held at the Albert Hall, London. The class won numerous gold awards over the

following 12 or so years. Goods were worked chiefly in copper, brass and pewter, and included all manner of mostly domestic items such as mirror frames, trays, fenders, plaques, doorplates, mugs, candlesticks and newspaper racks. By at least 1907, silver was also being worked.

By 1896, Fivemiletown was widely considered to be the leader in metalwork in relation to the Home Arts and Industries Association exhibitions. That was, in part, due to the input of John Williams, but was also due to the dedication of the workers. At the 1896 Home Arts exhibition, the class showed an assortment of items including a mirror frame which was illustrated in The Studio, Vol.8, 1896, p.95, and an owl fender which was illustrated in the same journal (p.100). Both were designed by Williams. At the 1897 Home Arts exhibition, the class showed a fender designed by Williams and worked by Patrick Roche. That too was illustrated in The Studio, Vol.11, July 1897, p.11. The class contributed a number of fenders on that occasion, mostly in brass, one with a squirrel design. Many of the designs were based on nature. The names of the individual workers associated with the class occasionally appeared in journal reviews, and included not only Patrick Roche but Frank Roche, Thomas Adams, Arthur Adams, Robert Mitchell, M. Carruth, J.B. Wilson, W.J. Walker and T. Cumberland. By the time of the 1899 Home Arts exhibition, the class had progressed to making light decorative furniture, more decorative repoussé plaques, and even a copy of an old lantern. One of its later doorplates, in hammered copper, worked by Thomas Adams, had a design of mushrooms. A newspaper rack executed by Thomas Adams to a Williams design and sent to the 1899 exhibition was illustrated in The Studio, Vol.17, July 1899, p.104, along with a tankard designed by Mrs Mary Williams and executed by W.J. Walker (p.105). Again, the designs were inspired by nature.

The Fivemiletown class went on to exhibit at the Home Arts in 1900, and continued to contribute until at least 1906. Although they exhibited locally too, the London exhibitions broadened their market, and they became known for their excellent craftsmanship. In 1900, The Studio, Vol.20, July, p.84, again illustrated several pieces by the class, including a mirror frame in hammered brass and oak, all shown at that year's Home Arts exhibition. Other examples of work by the class were illustrated in The Studio, Vol.40, February 1907, p.67, including an electric light sconce and a tea tray. The class never intended to provide professional, full-time employment. But it did allow creative expression in its workers, to some degree. In 1906 / 07, the work of Patrick Roche, one of the class's foremost craftsmen, won attention at the annual Dublin Exhibition. Roche won a prize for his silver potpourri casket with its stem of enamels. The casket was illustrated and commended in The Studio, Vol.40, February 1907, p.67.

MOORE, ESTHER MARY (1857-1934)
Sculptor / Designer. Born in Burnley, Lancashire in late 1857. The daughter of Henry Moore and Mary E. Margerison. The third of at least eight children (seven girls and one boy). Both parents originated from Burnley, and the other seven children were also born there. Initially, in the 1860s, her father was a master cotton spinner in Burnley, employing over 900 workers, and the family had servants. Subsequently, he ran a cotton spinning business in Rossendale, Lancashire, employing some 500 men, women and children. After her mother's death in the 1870s, the family relocated to Hampshire, where her father acted as a colliery agent. By the early 1890s, the family had moved again, to Chiswick, London, and Henry Moore had retired to become an artist. The family clearly had artistic interests. Florence Moore (b.c.1854), one of Esther's sisters, became an artist who produced drawings for printing. Another sister, Charlotte (b.c.1865), worked for a while as a woodcarver.

Esther's interests lay in sculpture, which she studied at the Royal College of Art, London under Professor Edouard Lanteri, who was modelling master there. She also studied in Paris. She subsequently took a studio in Bedford Park, London, and from 1890 began to exhibit her work at the Royal Academy, eventually showing 19 works there up to 1919. Early works included busts, statuettes and reliefs. In the late 1890s, she turned her attention to applied design, and began to produce designs for such things as electric lamps, panels in silver and bronze, and decorative jewellery such as hair clasps. Moore spent several months in a jeweller's workshop in order to gain experience and knowledge. She was praised in her lifetime for her originality of design and for her graceful use of line. One of her designs was for a silver panel titled Evensong which, along with two smaller silver panels, was intended for the decoration of a piano. Another design, Tragedy, consisted of three small bronze panels intended for the front of a bookcase containing the complete works of Shakespeare. Two of her panels, one a piano front in silver, were illustrated in the Art Journal, 1898, p.28, both with figure designs. One of her electric lights was illustrated in the Art Journal in 1896 in an article Women

Workers in the Art Crafts by Fred Miller (pp.116-118), along with a bas-relief panel.

For her panel reliefs, Moore initially worked in wax, then cast in plaster. A mould was made from the plaster, and a casting taken in silver or bronze. Two of her works, one of which was a bust of her father, were exhibited at the Society of Women Artists in 1896. Also exhibited at the Royal Scottish Academy (1911), at the Walker Art Gallery, Liverpool, and at the Arts and Crafts Exhibition Society exhibitions. At the 1893 Arts and Crafts exhibition, she showed an electric light which was illustrated in The Studio, Vol.2, October 1893, p.18. Exhibited works included: The Awakening Kiss of Parting Day, The Lute of Hope, A Ruffian (head), The Merman and Fantasiuccia (relief). Also produced memorials, sometimes in marble. One of her pupils was Ellen Kathleen Wheeler who also became a successful sculptor. In Chiswick, the Moore family were neighbours to artist / etcher Reginald P. Phillimore, evidently part of the London art scene. Moore spent her final years in Devon, dying there in late 1934, aged 77. Truro Museum and Art Gallery has her At the Gates of the Past (c.1897).

MOORE, GWENDOLINE B. - SEE WHITE, G.B.

MORCOM, FRANCES I. - SEE SWAN, F.I.

MORETON, ALICE BERTHA (1901-77)
Sculptor / Black & White Artist. Born in West Derby, Liverpool in March 1901. The daughter of David Tippin, a builder and contractor, and Marion Close. Had at least one elder sibling, Dora Marion. Educated at the Bootle Secondary School. Studied at the Bootle School of Art. Then went to the Liverpool School of Art where she studied under sculptor Charles John Allen and George Marples (Principal of the School). There, she won at least two scholarships and two studentships. The recipient of the British Institution Scholarship and the Liverpool Travelling Scholarship in 1922. Between 1922 and 1924 she studied in Paris and Rome on her Travelling Scholarship. Also studied at the Royal Academy schools (1924-28) under sculptors Sir George Frampton and Sir William Reid Dick. Won three silver and three bronze medals and the Landseer Scholarship. After completing her studies, Alice returned to the north of England. Based herself in Liverpool and on the Wirral. Later based at Hooton, Cheshire. She died in the region, aged 76.

Alice acted as art mistress at the Belvidere School of Art, Liverpool in the 1920s. Produced mainly sculptures, usually heads and statuettes in various materials, and black & white drawings. Exhibited her work at the Royal Academy (1925-49), the Paris Salon, the Manchester Art Gallery, the Southport Art Gallery, the Walker Art Gallery, Liverpool and with the Merseyside Art Circle. Exhibited works included: Ian (head), David (head) and The Boxer (statuette). Later became a Member of the Sandon Studios Society and of the Wirral Society of Arts. Also a Member of the Faculty of Arts Club. In 1944 she was elected a Fellow of the Central Institute for Art and Design. In 1928, after completing her studies, Alice married John Moreton in West Derby. They had two daughters. Alice was still active into the 1950s.

MORGAN, ALICE MARY - SEE HAVERS, A.M.

MORGAN, GERTRUDE ELLEN (1872-1956)

Painter / Etcher / Repoussé Metalworker. Born in Bloomsbury, London in November 1872. The daughter of James Harmer Hayes and Mary Ann. One of at least three children (Edith, Gertrude and Herbert). Raised in London. Educated privately. Studied at the Royal College of Art, London, and was a Royal Exhibitioner and a recipient of the British Institute Scholarship. Awarded an Art Masters' Certificate and a Training Studentship. Also awarded bronze and silver medals as a student. Produced landscape, flower and figure paintings in oils and watercolours, etchings of buildings and other subjects, drypoint and repoussé metalwork. Exhibited her work, including at the Royal Academy (1896-1927), the Society of Women Artists (83 works, 1895-1939), the Royal Scottish Academy (1928), the Royal Society of Painter-Etchers & Engravers, the Walker Art Gallery, Liverpool and at St Louis. Exhibited works included: Fishing Huts, Whitby (etching), Albogasio (drypoint), French Peasant (oil) and Stonegate, York (etching). Elected a Member of the Society of Women Artists (1921-36) and of the Society of Graphic Art. Elected an Associate of the Royal Society of Painter-Etchers & Engravers.

Morgan evidently had an interest in music since she acted as Honorary Local Secretary to the Royal Academy of Music and the Royal College of Music. She also acted as Head of the Art Centre, Forest Hill. Became assistant art mistress at Rugby School, Warwickshire and repoussé instructor. A number of her works were reproduced, including her Mercery Lane, Canterbury by Raphael Tuck; her St Maclou,

Rouen by Connell's; her Richmond Castle by Graves & Co. and various other works by Benyon of Cheltenham. In 1904 she married painter / etcher Alfred Kedington Morgan (1868-1928). He was also a student of the Royal College of Art and was art master at Rugby School. Prior to her marriage Gertrude lived in London. After her marriage, she lived in and around Warwickshire. In 1936 she married for a second time, to painter / etcher Edwin Maurice Betts (d.1957) who was also art master at Rugby School and at the Nottingham High School. Latterly, she was based in Nottingham, but died in Rugby. Purchasers of her work included the South Kensington Museum, London and the Federal Library, Washington.

MORGAN, JANE (1831-99)

Painter / Sculptor. The daughter of Anthony Morgan of Prospect Hill, Carrigrohane, Co. Cork, Ireland. One of five children. Studied at the Cork School of Design. Subsequently studied modelling in Dublin under sculptor J.R. Kirk. Won a prize for sculpture in the Taylor competition of 1860. Produced monuments, memorials, portrait busts and figures. In 1865 she visited Rome with her sister, Maria, and joined a colony of women artists which included American sculptors Emma Stebbins and Harriet Hosmer. She remained in Rome for a few years. Then studied in Copenhagen, Dusseldorf and Munich, remaining there for 15 years. Whilst in Munich she exhibited two works at the Society of Women Artists: The Mother's Darling and Mamma's Darling. In that year she visited New York to decorate her sister Maria's home. Maria was possibly the first woman journalist to be employed by the New York Times. Jane remained with Maria until her death. She worked almost until her death in April 1899. She also exhibited two works at the Royal Hibernian Academy: a marble bust of Miss Morgan in 1864 and a bust of Joseph R. Kirk, Esq., R.H.A., in 1865. One of her works is in the collection of the Ulster Museum.

MORLEY, RUTH KILLICK (b.1888)

Sculptor. Born in Lambeth, London. The daughter of Samuel Morley, a piano dealer, and Ann. Her father originated from London, her mother from Lambeth. Raised in Lambeth. Had at least one younger sibling, Elizabeth. Educated at the Neuchatel College, where she was awarded a certificate and a diploma. May have studied sculpture in Paris. Produced statuettes, heads and animal and equestrian subjects in bronze and marble. Exhibited at the Royal Scottish Academy

(1924), the Royal Glasgow Institute (1918-27), the Royal Academy (1918-22) and the Society of Women Artists (1924). Also, at the Paris Salon, the Walker Art Gallery, Liverpool, in Turin and elsewhere. Exhibited works included: Pearls (statuette, bronze), Little Girl With Pigeon (bronze), Colt (oval design, bronze) and Faun (statuette, bronze). Based in Paris and in Chelsea during her career. Her Grief was purchased by Queen Alexandra. Other works included an equestrian statuette of Lord Wavertree, a memorial to Sir Graham Hamond-Graeme, Bt., and The Master of the Drag. Elected a Member of the Lyceum Club and of the Panton Arts Club. She may have died abroad. In 1928 Morley is recorded as sailing to New York, at which point she effectively ceased to exhibit at any of the major British galleries.

MORRIS, EDITH M. - SEE IRELAND, E.M.

MORRIS, GERALDINE GERTRUDE (b.c.1881)

Decorative Artist. Records suggest that this is Gertrude Morris who was born in Old Charlton, Kent in 1881. Gertrude, also listed on occasions in census recordings as Geraldine, was the daughter of Ambrose Morris (d.1908), a clergyman of the Church of England, and Ellen Georgina. Her father originated from Ireland, her mother from Surrey. She was one of at least six children (Arthur, Gertrude, Margaret, Maynard, Richard and Cecil), all raised in Kent. By at least 1901 the family was living in Wythall, Worcestershire and Gertrude is listed as an art student. Geraldine Morris is listed as a student of the Birmingham School of Art from at least 1901 until at least 1908. Her work appeared in the annual National Competition of Schools of Art. In 1901, for example, she contributed designs for stained glass based on Hylas and the Water Nymphs. Some of those were illustrated in The Artist, 1901, p.67 and won her a gold medal. In the 1902 Competition, she showed a design for a decorative frieze. In the 1907 Competition, she won another gold medal for a design in enamels illustrating Morte d'Arthur. And in 1908 she won another gold medal for a copper gilt box adorned with Champleve figures.

Morris also contributed to the annual exhibition of works by the students of the Birmingham School of Art. In 1901, for example, she showed four designs for stained glass representing the Four Winds. One of those, North Wind, was illustrated in The Studio, Vol.22, April 1901, p.201. At the 1904 annual exhibition, she showed a tempera design for a piano front and an

overmantel. In 1911 Geraldine exhibited a panel in enamels, Young Sir Tristram (Malory), at the Royal Academy. However, that may also be the Gwendoline Morris who exhibited enamels at the 1911 Brighton Guild of Applied Art Exhibition. She also produced book illustrations. After completing her studies, Morris was based in Newhall Street, Birmingham, but appeared not to exhibit at any of the major galleries again. She remains untraced after 1911.

MORRIS, HILDA GERTRUDE (1883-1963)

Painter / Wood Engraver / Linocut Artist. The daughter of John E. Morris, a physician and surgeon, and Elizabeth Florence. One of at least five children (Florence, Claude, Hilda, Victor and Joan). All were born and raised in Bishop's Stortford, Hertfordshire. Hilda spent much of her life and career in Bishop's Stortford, living for much of the time at the family home at Windhill, and died in Hertfordshire aged 79. She studied at the Slade School, London for a short time, but also studied at Tudor Hart's studio in Paris and under Hannicote. She became a painter in watercolours of buildings, landscapes and other subjects, a wood engraver and a linocut artist. Exhibited at the Society of Women Artists (1928-32), the Paris Salon, the Women's International Art Club and the Panton Club. Exhibited works included: The Hall, Benenden School, Roses, Roscoff Church Porch and Old Houses, Amersfoort.

MORRIS, MARION (active 1950s-1960s)

Sculptor / Potter. Born in Hungary. First studied pottery in Vienna as a child. Then studied art and modelling at the Budapest Royal College of Art. She subsequently studied at the Central School of Arts and Crafts in London and developed her modelling from the thrown shape. She did straight pottery before developing her figure work. Became known for her earthenware, stoneware and porcelain figures. Those were highly individual pieces with faces of character, usually measuring between 10" and 18" in height. Known for her delicate, detailed and graceful work, full of humour and expression, but with limited use of colour. Figures included, for example, Queen Elizabeth I, an earthenware figure, 10" high, in black, white and red with a transparent glaze. Her Meta was a stoneware figure, 18" long, in buff and white with black decoration and partly glazed, in the thrown bell-shape style. Her bottle figures included Oil and Vinegar and Horsewoman. Morris also did figures in motion. All of the above were illustrated in an article The Pottery Figures of

Marion Morris by Noel Heath in The Studio, Vol.150, October 1955, pp.120-121.

Morris exhibited some of her work at the Craft Centre, London. Held a one-woman show there in 1956. Also exhibited elsewhere. For example, at the Royal Academy, she showed 17 works between 1952 and 1961 including: Salome (porcelain), Winter (statuette, earthenware), St George and the Dragon (unglazed stoneware) and Danae (earthenware). In 1952 she also exhibited two works at the Society of Women Artists: 1825 (earthenware, priced £10) and Garden Party (earthenware, priced £13). She was based in Central Parade, Kingsbury, St John's Wood. Also, at Stoke Hammond near Bletchley, Buckinghamshire and Bishop's Stortford, Hertfordshire. She worked predominantly in the 1950s and 1960s.

MORRIS, MAY (1862-1938)

Embroideress / Designer / Craftswoman. Born in Kent. Died in Oxfordshire, aged 76. May was actually Mary, but was always known as May. She was the daughter of eminent designer William Morris (1834-96) and Jane Burden (1839-1914). Had one sister, Jane Alice, known as Jenny, who had a restricted life due to epilepsy. Both girls were sketched by Rossetti in 1871. In 1890, May married Henry Halliday Sparling (1860-1924), but they divorced in 1898. Sparling, who was Secretary of the Socialist League, remarried in 1905. Otherwise, May lived her life unattached, and remained prolifically busy as an embroideress and designer, working in conjunction with her father until his death. She was initially trained by her father, and from 1885, aged 23, she took charge of the embroidery section of the Morris & Co. firm (founded in 1861) in London, dealing with administration as well as design.

At Morris & Co. her talents quickly flourished. She now used designs not only by Morris but by herself and others such as J.H. Dearle. With her assistants, she worked on some of her father's tapestries, including Woodpecker (1885), and on numerous embroidered hangings such as Vine (1890). Some of the firm's wallpaper (including Honeysuckle, 1883) and jewellery designs have also been attributed to May. Her embroidery assistants, who included Lily Yeats (sister of Irish poet W.B. Yeats), Mary De Morgan and Mrs George Jack (wife of the firm's furniture designer), later worked in May's Hammersmith Terrace drawing room. Lily Yeats left her employ to return to Ireland and work with her sister, Elizabeth. Lily is believed to have found May an

exacting mistress who demanded high standards of workmanship.

May Morris was responsible for designing the famous Kelmscott Manor embroidered bed cover and hangings which have been much photographed and written about over the years. The hangings indicate the extent to which Morris influenced his daughter's style. She was also responsible for some of the Morris & Co. church embroideries. Like her father, May was a committed socialist and sewed banners for his political groups. She also edited her father's writings, which were published as The Collected Works of William Morris (24 volumes, London, Longmans, 1910-15). In 1936, not long before her death, her volume William Morris: Artist, Writer, Socialist (Oxford, Basil Blackwell) was published. Occasionally, she worked with other well-known designers. For example, in 1903 she and Walter Cave showed an embroidered mirror frame at the 7th Arts and Crafts Exhibition Society exhibition. The embroidery had been worked by Lady Cave.

May was additionally keen to address the issue of the status of women in the arts and, as a result, in 1907 founded the Women's Guild of Art. Over the years, she wrote a number of articles on needlework, including Line Embroidery which appeared complete with illustrations in the Art Workers' Quarterly, October 1902. She also contributed a series of articles on ecclesiastical embroidery to the Building News, beginning in 1893. Her own book, Decorative Needlework (London, Hughes & Co.), was published in 1893. She found time to lecture, too. From the 1890s into the 1900s, she lectured on embroidery, jewellery and costume and pattern design at various places, including the Birmingham School of Art and the Central School of Arts and Crafts, London (from 1896). In 1910 she lectured in America on the above subjects. Some of her own designs were illustrated in W.G. Paulson Townsend, Modern Decorative Art in England (Batsford, 1922).

May exhibited her work nationally and internationally over a period of more than 30 years. From the outset, she contributed to the Arts and Crafts Exhibition Society exhibitions, beginning in 1888, the first. She was still making an impact in 1916, at the 11th exhibition held by the Society. On that occasion, she designed and arranged a small room with Ernest Gimson which incorporated an ebony china cabinet designed by Gimson. A bedroom displayed at the same exhibition was specially arranged by the Women's Guild of Art. Elsewhere, she contributed to, for example, the 1901 Glasgow Exhibition along with Helen Langley, Ann

Macbeth and others. In 1906 she contributed needlework to the 10th annual exhibition of the Cumberland and Westmorland Society of Arts and Crafts held in Carlisle. Some of the designs on that occasion were her father's. In 1908 she showed jewellery in the Craft Section of the New Gallery exhibition along with an embroidered landscape which was illustrated in the Art Journal, 1908, p.184. In 1916 May contributed to a Needlecraft Exhibition held at the Glasgow School of Art, showing a cushion of pink silk with pearls, embroidered by her to the design of Charles Ricketts. Later, in 1921, embroidered bed hangings by May were included in an exhibition of British Arts and Crafts in Detroit. The hangings were illustrated in The Studio, Vol.82, July 1921, p.41. May also exhibited with the Society of Women Artists, in 1896, 1929 and 1932.

May Morris was a lifelong friend of decorative bookbinder Katharine Adams. In March 1905 they held a joint exhibition of jewellery, embroideries and bookbindings in Mayfair. To a lesser extent, May ventured into book decoration. For example, she decorated a copy of Morris's Love is Enough (1873) with a blue silk, embroidered and decorated with pearls and garnets. She also designed an embroidered binding for A Study of Dante, worked by Mrs Cave and exhibited at the 1890 Arts and Crafts exhibition. It appears unlikely that she did any actual binding herself. Elsewhere, she designed some of the letters used by T.J. Cobden-Sanderson for his books, for the spine of Fabian Essays in Socialism (1889), and for her own Decorative Needlework. In 1909, May acted as an adjudicator at the Royal College of Art exhibition of students' work along with Herbert Dicksee, Philip Wilson Steer and George Clausen.

During her career, her work was praised numerous times in arts journals and other publications. For example, in 1898 her embroidery work was noted in the Catalogue of Works Exhibited by Members of the Northern Art Workers' Guild at the Manchester Art Gallery. In 1905 her work was noted in an article in the Art Journal, pp.256-258. The article included an illustration of a large portiere in silk damask titled The Fruit Garden, designed and worked by May. In 1907 the Art Journal illustrated some of her work in an article Some Modern Embroideries, pp.321-326, by R.E.D. Sketchley. Those included embroidered ecclesiastical gloves designed by Charles Ricketts, a line napkin embroidered in flax thread and a Tussore silk cushion embroidered in brown silk. May's work was still making an impression in 1953. In that year, The Studio, Vol.145, April, p.132, illustrated an embroidered wall hanging, The Orchard, worked to May's design by Theodosia Middlemore in 1894.

It is relevant to note that Jane Morris, May's mother, was also an expert embroideress, also taught by William Morris. Jane was the daughter of Robert Burden, a groom, and Ann. Jane had a brother, William, and a sister, Elizabeth (1842-post-1911). Elizabeth also studied embroidery under William Morris, and worked at the Royal School of Art Needlework. Latterly, after Morris's death, Elizabeth and Jane lived together in Canterbury. Jane died in Bath in 1914, though her address at that time was The Manor House, Kelmscott, Oxfordshire.

MOSS, PHOEBE A. - SEE TRAQUAIR, P.A.

MUDIE-COOKE, OLIVE (1890-1925)
Engraver / Artist. Born in Highgate, Middlesex in February 1890. The daughter of Henry Maggs Cooke (1861-1931) and Beatrice Paulina Mudie (1859-1942). Her father died in London, leaving a substantial estate of almost £58,000. Her mother died whilst living in Hyde Park, London and left the smaller sum of £11,220. Henry Cooke was a wealthy carpet manufacturer and dealer, and in the 1890s the family was based in Torquay, Devon. By the early 1900s, they had moved to London, where they remained thereafter. Olive had at least one sister, Phyllis, who was a student of archaeology. By 1911, Olive is listed as an artist, presumably having studied in London, and is still living with her parents. She produced paintings and lithographs. Her premature death at the age of around 36, however, curtailed her career. Exhibited occasionally before her death, including at the Royal Academy (1921) and the Society of Women Artists (1915). Exhibited works included: Certosa, Florence, Beaulencourt and Church (lithograph) and Paschendael - Hun "Pill Boxes" (lithograph). During the First World War, Olive worked as an ambulance driver and interpreter in France and Italy. She made sketches whilst out there. Spent some time in Newlyn, Cornwall in the early 1920s, working at Orchard Studio. Affected by what she saw during the war, she took her own life on 11 September 1925 in St Remy-de-Provence, France, though her address was The Mall, Parkhill Road, Hampstead at that time. Left a sizeable estate of £11,675 on her death, which was left to her friend, lecturer Eustace Mandeville Tillyard. She died before both her parents. Works in the collection of the Imperial War Museum.

MUNNS, UNA ELAINE (1900-75)

Painter / Jewellery Designer. Born in Olton, Warwickshire in June 1900. Belonged to a family of artists. The only child of portrait painter, illustrator and trade photographer John Bernard Munns (1868-1942) and Theresa Maud Lilley (d.1942). John Munns, who originated from Birmingham, was a Member of the Birmingham Art Circle. He was also the son of portrait painter Henry T. Munns. Una's mother also originated from Birmingham. Una was raised in Olton but also in Edgbaston, Birmingham. She was educated at the Edgbaston Church of England College, Birmingham. Studied at the Birmingham Central School of Art. Became a painter of portraits and landscapes and produced jewellery designs in watercolour. She enjoyed a long and productive career, covering six decades from the 1920s into the 1970s. Based in Birmingham initially, but latterly moved to New Milton, Hampshire. Died at the New Forest, Hampshire, aged 75. Exhibited her work at the New Zealand Exhibition, at the Paris Salon, the Walker Art Gallery, Liverpool and the Society of Women Artists (1923-71). Exhibited works included: Susan (watercolour), Day Dreaming, Design for a Brooch (watercolour) and Design for a Spray of Jewels (watercolour). Elected an Associate of the Society of Women Artists (1925-60) and a Member (1961-74). Also a Member of the New Society of Artists and of the Birmingham Art Circle.

MUNTZ, ELIZABETH (1894-1977)

Sculptor. Born in Toronto, Canada in October 1894. The daughter of Rupert Muntz. Had at least one sibling, Isabelle Hope Muntz, who became a noted historical novelist. Elizabeth was educated at the Bishop Strachan's School, Toronto. Studied at the Ontario College of Art, the Academie Grande Chaumier, Paris (under Emile Antoine Bourdelle), and privately under British sculptor Frank Dobson, who had a studio in Chelsea. Elizabeth produced sculptures in wood, stone, bronze and terracotta, mainly figures, groups, busts and heads. Also executed paintings in oils and tempera. After completing her studies, she was based mainly at Apple Tree Cottage, Dorchester, Dorset. She died in Dorset in March 1977, aged 82.

Muntz exhibited her work, including at the Royal Academy (1952-55), the Society of Women Artists (1952) and the Royal Glasgow Institute (1954-55). Further afield, she exhibited in Paris, New York, Montreal, Berlin and Leipzig. In January 1931 Apollo magazine reported on an exhibition titled Eleven Painters and Sculptors held at the Goupil Gallery. Muntz contributed to the exhibition along with Hooper Rowe, Florence Asher, Ethel Walker, Robert Medley and others. The article in Apollo noted that Muntz was 'an accomplished sculptor' (p.64). In 1932 an exhibition of her sculptures took place at the Allied Artists' Association at the Cooling Galleries in New Bond Street, London. Exhibits included works in wood, stone and bronze along with garden sculptures and drawings. Two of her exhibits, The Sisters (stone carving) and Erda (plaster for bronze), were illustrated in Apollo, May 1932, pp.244-245. Other works exhibited by Muntz included My Gardener's Son (bust, terracotta), The Late R.C. Trevelyan (head, bronze) and Torso (yellow Mansfield stone). Muntz exhibited a portrait work of her sister, (Isabelle) Hope Muntz, in terracotta. Elected a Member of the Sesame Club and of the Isle of Purbeck Arts Club. Also a Member of the London Group. Executed illustrations for The Dolphin Bottle (London, Victor Gollancz) by Elizabeth Sprigge in 1965. Works acquired by the Manchester Art Gallery (Erda, group, bronze) and by the Bristol Art Gallery (stone head of T.F. Powys).

MURE, GEORGINA FREDERICA (1855-1944)

Craftswoman. Born in London. The daughter of George and Elizabeth Dawson. Her stepfather was artist John R. Stanhope. In 1875 she married Arthur Henry Mure (d.1931), a partner in a brewery, in Westminster. They had at least one son. Based in London. From at least 1901 until at least 1912, Mrs Mure was involved in the design and execution of artistic jewellery. She exhibited her work at the Society of Women Artists (1901-12). She also exhibited a pendant at the 1902 Cork Exhibition in Ireland. Other exhibitors on that occasion included Georgina Gaskin and Evelyn Bethune. They were put into a special section set aside for women decorative artists. The pendant was illustrated in The Studio, Vol.26, September 1902, p.299. In 1911, Mrs Mure exhibited at the Society of Women Artists jointly with an artist named only as Mackenzie.

MURPHY, ANIZA - SEE McGEEHAN, A.

MURPHY, DIANA JESSIE (1906-77)

Decorative Artist / Embroidery Designer. Born in London. The daughter of James Murphy. Educated at the London County Council Trade School. Studied in London, at the Clapham School of Art and the Royal College of Art. Won a Royal College of Art Travelling Scholarship.

Elected an Associate of the Royal College of Art. As an artist, Murphy developed an allergy to turpentine and oil, so turned to watercolours and line and wash drawings, mainly of figure subjects, sometimes with a background of the sea or the beach. She was known to be a great draughtsman and designer, also producing highly regarded needlework designs. Particularly influenced by her London origins, by her busy and diverse city upbringing. Attracted to people, costumes, the theatre, animals and comedians in her work. She was an associate of W.B. Yeats and executed drawings interpreting his poems. The drawings were then used by one of Yeats's sisters as embroidery designs. Some of Murphy's embroidery designs were reproduced in Modern Embroidery. Some of her other works were reproduced in The Studio, Drawing & Design and La Revue Moderne.

Murphy exhibited her work, including at the Royal Academy (1940-50), the Society of Women Artists (1931-36 and possibly 1971), the Royal Society of British Artists, the Royal Institute of Painters in Watercolours, the Leicester Galleries, the Leger Galleries, at the Arts Council Exhibitions, with the New English Art Club and the London Group. Also, with the Women's International Art Club, the National Society and at the galleries of Bradford, Birmingham, Sheffield and elsewhere. Exhibited works included: Dancer in Costume (Vera Zorina), Old Lady (pen), In the Country (decorative watercolour) and St Dorothy With the Heavenly Bridegroom. Elected a Member of the Women's International Art Club. Based in London and Surrey. Died in Richmond, Surrey, aged 71. In 1930 she married artist Albert E. Poulter, A.R.C.A., N.R.D., in Wandsworth. Purchasers of her work included the Earl of Iddesleigh and the galleries of Manchester and Carlisle. The Whitworth Art Gallery, Manchester acquired her Faust and Marguerite (watercolour). The subject of an article, The Drawings of Diana Murphy, in The Studio, Vols.145-146, 1953, pp.56-57.

N

NAFTEL, MAUD (1856-90)

Painter / Illustrator. From a family of artists of Guernsey origin. The daughter of artists Paul Jacob Naftel (1816-91) and Isabel Oakley. One of at least three children (also Percy and Cecil). Maud was probably born on Guernsey since the family lived there until the 1860s. By at least the very early 1870s the Naftels were based in

Paddington, London. Maud subsequently studied at the Slade School, London, then in Paris. Thereafter, she was based in London. Produced illustrations and watercolour paintings of flowers, landscapes and other subjects. Although she died young, aged only 34, Maud Naftel accomplished a considerable amount during her shortened career. Exhibited widely, including at the Royal Academy (9 works, 1875-89), the Royal Scottish Academy (1887), the Royal Glasgow Institute (10 works, 1877-90), at the Grosvenor Gallery (certainly in 1881) and at the Eighteenth Exhibition of Water-Colour Drawings at the Dudley Gallery in 1882. She also exhibited in Birmingham, at the Fine Art Society, at the Royal Institute of Painters in Watercolours and the Royal Society of Painters in Watercolours.

Maud exhibited most prolifically, however, at the Society of Women Artists. There, she showed 67 works between 1874 and 1891, the first of those when she was still only 18 years of age, the last around the time of her death. Exhibited works included: A Kentish Farm, Roses in Opal Vase, Daisy Field, Cookham-on-Thames, Unwillingly to School and Primroses. Elected an Associate of the Society of Women Artists (1885) and a Member (1886-89). Elected an Associate of the Royal Society of Painters in Watercolours. Author of Flowers and How to Paint Them (1886). Her mother, Isabel, was also a watercolour painter of various subjects, and an engraver. Isabel exhibited extensively, including at the Royal Academy (1862-89), the Royal Society of British Artists (1857-80), the Royal Glasgow Institute (1875-85) and the Society of Women Artists (1862-92). She too was elected a Member of the Society of Women Artists (1875-92). She outlived her husband and daughter, latterly living at Surrey. Paul Naftel exhibited at the Royal Glasgow Institute (1861-91) and elsewhere. He died in Middlesex within weeks of Maud, who died in Chelsea.

NANCE, ARMOREL MARY YEO MORTON (b.1904)

Sculptor / Painter / Designer / Engraver. Born in Cardiff, Wales. The daughter of Ernest Morton Nance, M.A. (1868-1952) and Sarah Louise Yeo (b.1863). Her father, a Classics student at Oxford, was an art collector. Her uncle, Robert Morton Nance (b.1873), was a painter and illustrator. Armorel was raised in Cardiff and Margate, Kent. She was educated at the King Alfred School, Hampstead. Studied at the Slade School and at the Royal College of Art, London. Also spent time studying abroad, in Rome and at the British School at Athens. During her career, she lived at

Beaconsfield, Buckinghamshire, at Carbis Bay in Cornwall and at Bournemouth. Her father left Armorel a considerable estate, which meant that she had no necessity to work. He died in Cornwall. Her uncle, Robert, also spent some time living in Wales and Cornwall. Armorel exhibited her work only occasionally, including at the Royal Academy (1924) and at the Walker Art Gallery, Liverpool. Exhibited works included Prince (head, bronze).

NAPER, ELLA LOUISE COUSHMAN STEEL (1886-1972)

Jewellery Designer & Maker / Ceramicist. Part of the wave of late nineteenth and early twentieth-century artistic jewellery makers which also included Georgina Gaskin, Cecilia Adams and Mrs Hadaway. Ella was born in London. The daughter of Alfred Coushman Steel Champion and Mary Ann Weeks. Her father was initially an electrician, then an electrical engineer and later Inspector of Electrical Acts Orders. Ella was one of at least seven children (Alice, Ella, Sarah, Marion, Ellen, Henry and Alexander). Raised in London. In 1904, aged 18, and still living at home, Ella began a two-year course at the Camberwell School of Arts and Crafts. Studied design, and made drawings which she used in various crafts. Became involved in copper, enamelling, woodwork and metalwork, and designed bookplates.

Ella was a natural talent whose family background contained no other obvious hints of artistic leanings. Two of her sisters became shorthand typists, and one of her brothers became an office clerk. Ella flourished and won at least one prize in the annual National Competition of Schools of Art at South Kensington. She particularly excelled in jewellery. At Camberwell, she was particularly influenced by Fred Partridge. He had been one of Charles Ashbee's handicraft guild members at Chipping Campden, Gloucestershire. When Ella finished her studies in 1906, she moved to Branscombe in Devon where Partridge established a jewellery workshop which ran as a co-operative. His wife, May Hart, was also there. Ella designed and made her own jewellery at Branscombe, employing natural forms in her designs, including flowers, following the fashion of the period. She remained at Branscombe for three years.

Ella subsequently moved to Cornwall. During her time in Devon, she had met painter Charles William Skipwith Naper (b.1882), a former student of the Royal Academy schools. Ella married Naper in 1910 in London. She continued to make, sell and exhibit her jewellery. Sold mainly through exhibitions, including those held by the Arts and Crafts Exhibition Society. In 1912 the Napers moved permanently to Cornwall, living for the rest of their lives at Trewoofe House. Never affluent, the couple relied on sales of their work. They became part of the artistic community in Cornwall which included Harold and Laura Knight, who became close friends. Laura painted Ella a number of times. She was the model featured in one of Laura Knight's best-known self-portraits. To make more money, Ella diversified and made items such as jewelled photograph frames, some of which were shown at the Fine Art Society, London in June 1915 along with paintings by Lamorna Birch and Laura Knight. Ella also exhibited occasionally at the Society of Women Artists (1913-31) and at the Walker Art Gallery, Liverpool.

During the First World War, Charles Naper went away on active service while Ella worked in a munitions factory in Woolwich, and spent time in London. She produced a number of war memorials. For the family of Benjie Leader, son of artist Benjamin Leader, she created a memorial plaque for St Buryan Church, Cornwall. Also worked on a memorial tablet to the men of the Royal Field Artillery for Exeter Cathedral, and a memorial tablet for a Plymouth family for Charles Church, Plymouth which was destroyed during the Second World War. After the war, the Napers returned to Trewoofe. Ella continued to produce jewellery, also designing and making other items such as butterfly combs carved in horn and applied shell as well as silver brooches set with semi-precious stones or enamels, silver pendants set with hardstones, buttons, hairpins, buckles, spoons, earrings, rings, bracelets and cuff-links. She sold elsewhere through the Grosvenor Gallery, through the Brighton Guild of Applied Art, the Collectors' Gallery in Manchester, the Ruskin Museum, Heal's and the Newlyn Art Gallery among other places. She acquired a number of prestigious clients, including Lady Oppenheimer.

Ella made many hundreds, if not thousands, of pieces of jewellery during her lengthy career, all individually designed and made by hand. She also executed delicate watercolour studies of flowers, and the occasional oil painting. With artist Kate Westrup, Ella later founded the Lamorna Pottery which ran as a co-operative. Ella made ceramic figures, including portraits of herself and Laura Knight. She also produced pots, jugs, vases and other domestic items to sell. Like her jewellery, her pots were bright and vivid. She sold her Lamorna wares through various outlets, including in Liverpool. The pottery closed after Kate's sudden death in 1928.

With no children, the Napers were able to tour the French Alps and Scotland during their careers. Ella also acted on the committee of the Newlyn Art Gallery, exhibiting at the Gallery's summer and winter shows. In 1933 she executed a Mayoral chain for the Mayoress of Penzance, and during her career made enamelled badges for the Penzance Girls' Grammar School. Ella ceased to exhibit or sell her work after the start of war in 1939. But she still made pieces as gifts. Charles Naper died in 1968, some four years before Ella.

NASH, FLORENCE KATE (1862-1939)

Embroideress. The wife of eminent designer / architect Mackay Hugh Baillie Scott (1865-1945). The son of a wealthy Scottish landowner, Baillie Scott not only worked as an architect, but produced designs for stained glass, ironwork, mosaics, applique embroidery, furniture and wallpaper. Florence was the daughter of John Pearson Nash, a surgeon born in India, and Catherine Harper. Born at sea, Florence was raised in London, possibly an only child. She married Baillie Scott in Bath, Somerset in 1889. The couple had at least two children, Mackay H.B. Scott and Enid Maud Scott. Florence executed some of her husband's embroidery designs. Those included two panels in cotton with applique linen, embroidered in coloured silks and gold and silver braid, and glass beads (c.1896). In 1903, The Studio, Vol.28, p.279, published an article by Baillie Scott, Some Experiments in Embroidery. Florence died in Kent, aged 76.

NELSON, IDA (1889-1975)

Sculptor. Born in Manchester in October 1889, and raised there. The daughter of John Culbert Baines Percy and Sarah Ann. Her father, who originated from Lancaster, was a printer and publisher in Manchester. Her mother originated from Manchester. Ida had at least one brother, Arnold. She studied at the Manchester School of Art, then at the Slade School, London. Remained in London, using the Oakley Studios at Upper Cheyne Row, Chelsea, but also kept an address at Victoria Park, Manchester for a number of years. She subsequently moved to Harrow-on-the-Hill, Middlesex. Died in Cheltenham, aged 85. Produced heads and statuettes in bronze. Active for over 30 years. Exhibited her work, including at the Royal Academy (1927-57), the Royal Scottish Academy (1939), the Walker Art Gallery, Liverpool, at the Manchester Art Gallery and with the Manchester Academy of Fine Arts. Exhibited works included: An Irish-Canadian Poet (head, bronze), A New Zealander (head, bronze), Sea Breezes (statuette, bronze) and

Major A.J. Ellis (head). Elected a Member of the Manchester Academy of Fine Arts. Also a Member of the Attic Club, and of the Manchester Society of Women Artists. In 1917 she married William Mornington Nelson (1891-1955), who originated from Salford. The marriage was short-lived, and in 1927 she married again, to Terence Bond in Chelsea.

NEUWIRTH, WILHELMINA LOUISA (1877-1964)

Sculptor. Born and raised in London. The daughter of Frederick Godfred Neuwirth, a musician, and Clementia. In 1901, Wilhelmina is listed as an art student whilst living in Chelsea with her elder sister, Florence Ada Neuwirth (b.1863), who was also a musician. Wilhelmina produced medallions and statuettes. Exhibited two works at the Royal Academy, Undine (statuette) in 1907 and When Day Goes Down (medallion) in 1911. Other works included a medallion to Lord Leighton. Florence married in late 1901, and Wilhelmina continued to live in Chelsea. There, in 1913, she married Ernest Armitage McCann. He was the son of a clergyman and a Secretary. Possibly the Minna McCann who exhibited at the Royal Academy in 1915 and the Society of Women Artists in 1916. Wilhelmina died near Stroud in Gloucestershire, aged 87.

NEWBERY, JESSIE WYLIE (1864-1948)

Painter / Designer / Embroideress / Metalworker. Born in Paisley, Scotland in May 1864. The daughter of William Rowat (b.1831), a shawl manufacturer, and Margaret Downie Hill (1840-73). Educated in Paisley. Studied at the Glasgow School of Art. As Miss Rowat, was a medallist at the National Competition of Schools of Art at South Kensington. In 1889 she married Head of the Glasgow School of Art, Francis Henry Newbery (1855-1946). Newbery originated from Devon, the third of six children of a shoemaker and a dressmaker. He spent his early life in Dorset. A naturally gifted artist, he attended the Bridport School of Art in Dorset. In 1875 he qualified as an art master and moved to London to teach, also continuing with his own studies. In May 1885 he was appointed Head of the Glasgow School. There, he made a considerable impact, not only on the School, but on British art and design. During his time there, the School produced a considerable number of highly successful artists and designers, male and female. He was not, however, the initial motivator of the Glasgow movement, since changes were already underway before his arrival at the School. But the movement certainly flourished under his influence.

After completing her studies, Jessie became a teacher of embroidery, enamelling and mosaic work at the Glasgow School, working there from 1894 until 1908. In 1894 she formed an embroidery class, with lessons held at 3 Rose Street and, later, at Renfrew Street. She was the original driving force in establishing artistic embroidery in Glasgow. She became an equally integral part of developments at the School, and was closely linked to Margaret and Frances Macdonald, Charles Rennie Mackintosh and Herbert MacNair. Embroideress Ann Macbeth also taught at the Glasgow School, and with Jessie quickly established the School as a leader in that particular field. When embroidery became a recognised part of the primary and secondary school curriculum in around 1900, Jessie instructed other teachers in giving classes.

Both Jessie and Francis Newbery had demanding careers at the Glasgow School. Jessie not only taught but had two daughters, Margaret in 1890 and Mary in 1892. She also continued with her own art and design work, appearing regularly in The Studio magazine along with her husband. Like Francis, Jessie held very definite views on life and art. In 1897, The Studio, Vol.12, October, p.48, reported her as saying:

I believe that the greatest thing in the world is for a man to know
  that he is his own, and that the great end of art is the discovery
    of the self of the artist.
Also that:
I believe that nothing is common or unclean; that the design and
  decoration of a pepper pot is as important, in its degree, as the
    conception of a cathedral. I believe in everything being beautiful,
      pleasant, and, if need be, useful.

Such views clearly indicate the influence of the then-thriving Arts and Crafts movement.

Not unexpectedly, Jessie contributed to several of the Arts and Crafts Exhibition Society exhibitions. In 1893, for example, she exhibited a chalice and paten, an altar frontal and a repoussé alms plate worked to her own designs. At the Society's 1896 exhibition she showed several embroidered cushion covers, a mantel border, a book of emblems bound in green morocco gilt and a quilt, also to her own designs. She exhibited her work elsewhere too. In 1899, for example, she contributed to an exhibition of work held annually at the Glasgow Fine Art Institute. Organised by the Glasgow School of Art Club, exhibitors were past and present pupils of the School. On that occasion, Jessie showed examples of needlework along with work by her pupils. Some of her exhibits, including a tea cosy and a square of embroidery designed by her but worked by Bella and Edith Rowat, were illustrated in The Studio, Vol.15, January 1899, p.280. Also in 1899, Jessie contributed to the first exhibition of the Scottish Society of Art Workers. Held in Glasgow, Jessie showed examples of book covers and embroidery at that particular exhibition. Other exhibitors included John Guthrie, Jessie Keppie and Jessie King.

In 1901 Jessie contributed to the Glasgow International Exhibition. One of her exhibits, an embroidered curtain, was illustrated in The Studio, Vol.23, 1901, p.239. She also contributed to the 1902 Turin Exhibition, in the Scottish Section, showing an embroidered curtain, various brooches and belt clasps in pewter and a child's blue linen dress embroidered with a grape pattern in coloured silks. She also showed an Axminster carpet which had been executed by the firm of Alexander Morton & Co. of Darvel, designed by her. A number of Jessie's pupils and contemporaries worked her designs over the years, including Mrs Dekkart who also exhibited at Turin, showing embroideries to Jessie's designs. The following year, two dresses made by Frau. Ann Muthesius, with embroidery designed by Mrs Newbery, were shown at the first exhibition of the Dress Designers' Exhibition Society. Walter Crane (1845-1915) was President of the Society.

Elsewhere, Jessie exhibited with the Glasgow Society of Lady Artists' Club. Other works, including some of her watercolour paintings, were exhibited at the Royal Glasgow Institute (1892-1900). Those included Jeannie (watercolour), The White Cottage (watercolour), A Suffolk Stream (watercolour) and a design for a pulpit fall. Francis Newbery exhibited paintings at the Institute from 1890. In 1894, a Miss Dunlop exhibited one work at the Institute, a design for an altar cloth for the Church of St Bride, Kelvinside. The design was by Jessie Newbery, the embroidery by Miss Dunlop. Jessie exhibited at the Royal Scottish Academy, showing The White Butterfly in 1898. Paintings by Francis were also exhibited there, from 1890 until 1949 (after his death). Although she gave up her teaching work in 1908, in 1916 Jessie contributed to the fourth exhibition of the Artist Teachers' Exhibition Society held at the Glasgow School of Art. One of her exhibits was a watercolour drawing, The Manor House.

The Newberys won almost ceaseless attention for their many successes at the Glasgow School, their work and achievements regularly reported in a number of leading arts journals of the period. Over some 20 years, The Studio, in particular, offered glimpses into their lives and work. In 1897, for example, illustrations of some of Jessie's embroidered panels and cushions featured in an article Some Glasgow Designers and Their Work (Vol.12, October, pp.47-51) by Gleeson White. Such illustrations reveal the most beautifully executed work, a pleasing symmetry in design and attractive colour schemes, all with a simplicity that reflected the abandonment of more traditional, time-consuming embroidery. Further illustrations of her work were given in The Studio, Vol.19, 1900, pp.235-237 in an article about the Glasgow School students. Other examples of Jessie's work were given in the Art Journal. For example, in 1907 in an article Scottish Arts and Crafts (pp.233-241, 318). Those included a dress collar.

Jessie Newbery's work was singled out for mention in the Catalogue of Works Exhibited by Members of the Northern Art Workers' Guild, which accompanied an exhibition held at the Manchester Art Gallery in 1898. This only served to reaffirm her significant links to wider developments in the decorative arts outside Scotland as well as in it. The strain of running the Glasgow School, combined with his own successful painting career, eventually proved too much for Francis Newbery. In 1918, after two mental breakdowns, brought on by overwork and the effects of the First World War, he retired from the School. After spending a short time in Clovelly, Devon, the Newberys settled at Corfe Castle, Dorset in 1919. There, they became part of another artistic circle. In 1933 Jessie delivered an introduction to the Mackintosh Memorial Exhibition held in Glasgow, one of the first retrospective views of the Glasgow School. Both Jessie and Francis died in Dorset. Mary Newbery became a successful exhibiting artist too. SEE: NEWBERY, MARY ARBUCKLE

NEWBERY, MARY ARBUCKLE (1892-1985)

Painter / Artist / Embroideress. Born in Glasgow. Spent much of her life there, and in Edinburgh. The daughter of Francis H. Newbery (1855-1946) and Jessie W. Rowat (1864-1948). Had one sister, Margaret E. Newbery (b.1890). Her father, a gifted painter, was appointed Head of the Glasgow School of Art in 1885, before his daughters were born, and remained at the School until 1918, when ill-health forced him to retire. Her mother was a gifted painter, designer and embroideress who also taught at the Glasgow School. After their retirement, the Newberys

moved to the south of England, where Francis Newbery originated from, living in Devon and then Dorset.

Not surprisingly, Mary became an artist and embroideress, probably studying at the Glasgow School. She produced watercolour paintings, black & white and pen drawings, linocuts and, occasionally, embroideries. In 1918, the year her father retired from the Glasgow School, Mary married Scottish landscape painter Alick Riddell Sturrock. Sturrock was born in Edinburgh in 1885, and was a student of the Edinburgh College of Art. Mary continued to work after her marriage. She exhibited mainly in Scotland, at the Royal Scottish Academy (52 works, 1915-52) and the Royal Glasgow Institute (40 works, 1911-49). Exhibited cushion covers at the 1916 Glasgow School of Art Needlecraft Exhibition. Also exhibited with the Edinburgh Group, including in 1920. Exhibited works, which included portraits, figures, flowers and landscapes, included: Madonna Lilies, The Ravished Orchard, The Weeds That Were Green and Theodora Garland. A portrait of Mary Newbery, by Jean Delville, was exhibited at the Royal Scottish Academy in 1935. SEE: NEWBERY, JESSIE WYLIE

NEWCOMBE, BERTHA (1857-1947)

Artist / Illustrator. Born in Hackney, London. The daughter of Samuel Pront Newcombe, a solicitor, and Hannah. One of at least seven children (Frederick, Mary, Ada, Bertha, Claude, Mabel and Jessy). Raised in London, and presumably studied there sometime before 1880. Spent much of her life in London, but died in Petersfield, Hampshire, aged 90. She was still living with her elderly parents into her 40s, and in her 50s was living with her widowed father and sister Mabel in Chelsea. Bertha was active predominantly from the 1880s to the 1900s, over at least a 26-year period. Produced and exhibited flower, figure and landscape paintings in oils and watercolours. She also produced illustrations for magazines including The English Illustrated Magazine, The Temple Magazine and the Windsor Magazine. For example, she illustrated a serialisation of Love in Our Village for the Windsor Magazine, Vol.XI, December 1899-May 1900, pp.385-393, Ward Locke & Co. Ltd, London. Bertha exhibited her work throughout her career, including at the Royal Academy (1882-1906), the Royal Society of British Artists (1882-91) and the New English Art Club (1888-94). At the Society of Women Artists, she showed 23 works between 1880 and 1893, including The Little Knitter (watercolour), Three Studies of

French Peasants (watercolour), A Lancashire Garden and Waterlilies. Elected a Member of the New English Art Club. Elected an Associate of the Society of Women Artists (1888-89). Works in the Southwark Art Collection.

NEWILL, MARY JANE (1860-1947)

Embroideress / Illustrator / Stained Glass Artist. Born in Admaston, Shropshire. The daughter of Robert D. Newill (1826-86), a solicitor, and Marion (b.1836). The eldest of ten surviving children (Mary, Helene, Edith, Fanny, Lucy, Margaret, Percy, Edward, Ethel and George). All the children were raised in Shropshire. By at least 1881, Mary was a student at the Birmingham Municipal School of Art, but was still living with her family in Shropshire. She is still listed as a student 10 years later, after her father's death. After completing her studies, she became a successful and diverse designer, stained glass artist, painter, illustrator and embroideress. She also became a needlework teacher at the Birmingham School from at least 1892. She was still active at the School some 30 years later.

Newill became part of the Birmingham Group, formed in the 1890s. The Group consisted of Edith and Henry Payne, Margaret and Charles Gere, Arthur and Georgina Gaskin, Sidney Meteyard, Bernard Sleigh and Joseph Southall, all of whom, except Southall, had come under the influence of E.R. Taylor at the Birmingham School. All were highly successful and influential in their own right, and all made valuable contributions to British art and design. Newill was also linked to the Birmingham Guild of Handicraft, supervising its embroidery, contributing to the Guild's magazine, Quest (1894-96). The magazine was distinctly Arts and Crafts in flavour, publishing texts by William Morris, W.R. Lethaby and other notable Arts and Crafts figures. The magazine also included illustrations by some of the Birmingham Group.

By the early 1900s Newill was living with her widowed mother in Edgbaston, subsequently spending time at Knightwick, Worcestershire. She died in Gloucestershire in January 1947, latterly living at The Cross, Painswick. She left her £19,000 estate to her brother, Edward, who was a Church of England cleric. Religion was evidently of some significance to the Newill family. Mary's sister, Helene, became a Bethany Church worker in the early 1900s, and Mary herself executed numerous commissions for churches during her career.

Newill enjoyed not only a long and successful career, but a diverse one. Her roots remained firmly embedded in the Arts and Crafts

movement, always working to Morris's beliefs in the necessity for quality craftsmanship and for beauty as well as function. She was particularly admired for her exquisite embroidery, some of which appeared in prestigious exhibitions around the country. Some of her earlier textiles appeared at the 1893 Fourth Arts and Crafts Exhibition Society exhibition, including a silk embroidered panel titled Innocence Taught of Love. Other examples were shown at the National Competition of Schools of Art, held annually at South Kensington, including in 1895. In 1896 she showed three embroidered panels for a reredos at the Fifth Arts and Crafts exhibition along with an embroidered cover for the Kelmscott Chaucer, designed and executed by her and illustrated in The Studio, Vol.9, 1897, p.278. At the Society's Sixth exhibition, held in 1899, Newill showed two more embroideries, The Red Cross Knight and The Wandering Wood. In 1900, some of her embroideries were made up into a bedroom display at the Paris International Exhibition.

In 1903 the Art Workers' Quarterly, April, p.74, illustrated one of Newill's decorative needlework creations, an overmantel titled Gareth and Lyonors which was worked in crewels and shown at the 1903 Arts and Crafts exhibition held at the New Gallery. The panel was executed by Mary, assisted by Violet and Evelyn Holden, also of the Birmingham School. Newill exhibited other needlework at the 1908 New Gallery exhibition alongside the work of May Morris, Florence Steele, Harold Stabler and others. In 1909 she contributed needlework to the Royal Birmingham Society of Artists exhibition, which included a section of some 300 craft exhibits.

Later, in 1916, Newill contributed an altar frontal, designed and executed by her, to a Needlecraft exhibition held at the Glasgow School of Art. On a slightly less ambitious note, in 1896 a presentation was made to J. Thackeray Bunce by the masters and students of the Birmingham School of Art. Bunce was then 20 years a member of the committee of the School and 20 years Chairman of the Management Committee of the School and of the Corporation Art Gallery. One of the items presented to Bunce was an illuminated address in an embroidered cover designed and executed by Newill and illustrated in The Studio, Vol.7, 1896, p.178. Her embroidered panel, Una and the Red Knight was acquired by the Worcester County Museum, Worcestershire. The panel was originally designed for the dining room of E. Butler's house, Top O' the Hill.

Newill's embroidery included not only decorative pieces such as panels and curtains, but ecclesiastical pieces executed specifically for churches. In her stained glass work too, there was a strong indication of the significance of religion in her life and work, though some designs were entirely secular. By 1906 Newill had her own studio in Birmingham where she designed stained glass windows and decorative glass panels over several decades. Earlier commissions included windows for a house in Handsworth which was built in 1898. The designs depicted Queen Matilda and her ladies working on the Bayeux Tapestry. Newill also designed two windows for a house in Sutton Coldfield depicting John Ball and Watt Tyler. Other commissions included a window for St Mary and Ambrose at Edgbaston (1906). Some of her earliest stained glass was shown at the Birmingham School of Art annual exhibition, including an entire window by Newill which was exhibited in 1898. Some of her glass designs were shown at the 1903 Seventh Arts and Crafts Exhibition. Two of those were based on the Parable of the Good Samaritan and illustrated in The Studio, Vol.29, June 1903, p.24. Her stained glass designs were illustrated elsewhere, including in the Art Journal, 1896, pp.116-118 in an article Women Workers in the Art Crafts by Fred Miller.

During her career, Newill also spent time studying tempera painting in Florence. May Morris temporarily took over her needlework classes at the Birmingham School at that point. However, Newill became better known for her illustration work than for her painting. As part of the Birmingham Group, in the early 1890s, she established a style of illustrative drawing reminiscent of woodcuts. Simple and effective, her drawings were used in a number of children's books. For example, in 1893 some of the Birmingham School, overseen by Arthur Gaskin, produced A Book of Christmas Carols (George Allen, priced 5s). Newill contributed full-page drawings to the book. Other contributors included Florence Rudland, Bernard Sleigh and Henry Payne. Newill also illustrated, for example, Hans Andersen's The Nightingale (c.1894) and a Book of Nursery Songs and Rhymes (Methuen, 1895). Some of her black and white drawings were illustrated in The Studio, Vol.5, May 1895 in an article Some Aspects of the Work of Mary Newill. Later in her career, she exhibited embroideries with the distinguished Embroiderers' Guild. In 1923, for example, at the Guild's first major exhibition, she contributed an embroidered panel of a Welsh landscape which was praised in The Studio Vol.87, January 1924, p.18. She exhibited again at the Guild's 1927 exhibition, by which time she would have been around 67 years of age. The Victoria & Albert

Museum, London has four embroidered curtains executed by Newill, dated around 1906.

NEWMAN, CHARLOTTE ISABELLA (1836-1920)

Artist / Designer / Goldsmith. Born in London. The daughter of George Gibbs, a schools inspector, and Charlotte. In 1860 she married painter Philip Harry Newman (1840-1927) in London. They lived in London, and both died there. The couple had at least two children, Mary Banks Margaret and George Philip. Mary became a musician, but later also assisted her mother in her art and design work. Philip also became a musician and a photographer. Throughout her entire marriage, and almost until her death, Charlotte worked as an interior decorator, a designer and maker of jewellery and a goldsmith. She was also assisted in her work by Philip Newman, as well as her daughter. Charlotte exhibited two designs for wall decoration at the Royal Academy in 1873 and 1882. One of those was titled Consider the Lilies of the Field. The other was a design of painted tiles. Charlotte was still active into her 70s, and lived to the age of 83.

NEWMAN, FLORENCE (1866-1938)

Sculptor. Born in Westminster, London in late 1866. The daughter of Charles Newman, a Jobmaster, and Maria Emmeline. One of at least five children. Had three brothers (Robert, Henry and Charles) and one sister (Catherine), all older. Raised in London and based there for much of her life and career. Lived at the family home whilst studying sculpture at the Slade School of Art, London. Became a successful sculptor producing portrait medallions and coloured wax miniatures. Had a gift for portraits. Worked in wax, bronze and plaster. Her subjects were many and varied, old and young, adults and children. She used the Cleeve Studios at Brondesbury for a time. Exhibited her work, including at the Royal Academy (21 works, 1890-1925), the Royal Scottish Academy (1897-1905), the Royal Glasgow Institute (1903-06) and the Society of Women Artists (1903-07). Also, at the Walker Art Gallery, Liverpool and with the Royal Birmingham Society of Artists. Exhibited works included: Miss Florrie Verrall (bust), Rev. R.C. Kirkpatrick (medallion), Dr James Love, Sir Samuel Wilks, Study of a Child (coloured plaster) and Lionel Brough (plaster medallion). Elected an Associate of the Royal Society of Miniature Painters.

Florence lived with her widowed mother until she married sculptor Frederick Thomas Callcott (b.1853) in St Marylebone, London in mid-1912.

At the time of their marriage, Florence was 45 years of age, and Callcott was then 59. He had previously lived with his married brother, architect and surveyor Charles William Callcott. Frederick was also a sculptor of note, and a Member of the Royal Society of British Sculptors. Already a successful sculptor prior to her marriage, there is no suggestion that Florence married in order to enhance public perception of her work. She continued with her career after her marriage, and into the 1920s. Other works included a bronze medallion of the late Rev. Charles Taylor, D.D., LL.D., for University Library, Cambridge which was exhibited at the Royal Academy in 1909. Florence was a Member of the Halcyon Club, and had an interest in gardening. Latterly, she was based at Golders Green. She died at Woodstock Road, Golders Green in January 1938, leaving a substantial £23,582 in her will. Frederick Callcott died in May 1923 at St Leonards-on-Sea, Sussex, leaving Florence £367 in his will.

NEWTON, IRENE MARGARET (1915-92)

Woven Textile Designer. Born in December 1915. The daughter of J.H. Newton. Educated at the High School for Girls, Truro, Cornwall. Studied at the Truro School of Art under W.P. Hodgkinson between 1934 and 1938. Initially based in Truro. Worked as an assistant at the Stourbridge School of Art. Also, as an assistant at the Hereford School of Art (1946-49). Produced woven textile designs, for weaving by hand and machine. Elected a Fellow of the Royal Society of Arts (1940). Elected Licentiate of the Society of Industrial Artists. Died in Merseyside, aged 76.

NICHOLS, IRENE (1862-1907)

Bookbinder. Born in Paddington, London in January 1862. The daughter of Francis Morgan Nichols (1826-1915) and Mary Buchanan (b.1826). Her parents originated from Middlesex. Had at least four siblings, also born in Paddington. Raised at Lawford Hall, Rochester, a sizeable farming estate which employed a considerable number of staff, including a private tutor. Her father was a qualified barrister but was not in practice. Two of Irene's brothers, Walter and John, studied at Oxford. Irene read English Literature at Lady Margaret Hall, Oxford in the early 1880s. She spent some time travelling abroad, learning basic bookbinding in Rome in 1888. Then went to London and, through artist Barbara Bodichon, encountered bookbinder T.J. Cobden-Sanderson. He gave her further lessons in bookbinding at his London home, where he had a workshop.

Irene then took a studio in Sloane Square, living in a feminist house in the early 1890s, which was run by the Lady's Dwelling Co., along with a number of other women including stained glass artist Mary Lowndes. Irene evidently held an interest in women's issues. Queen Victoria requested to see some of her work. Nichols was not active for long, however, and by 1897 had given up bookbinding. She moved into her father's house in Green Street, Park Lane to look after him. Her mother had died some years before. Irene died of influenza in London in 1907, aged only 45, some eight years before her father died. She left a considerable estate of more than £10,000 to her friend Harriet Urquhart. Irene bound The Germ (c.1892). In 1893 she exhibited at the World's Columbian Exposition in Chicago. Also bound Shakespeare's Songs and Sonnets and Elizabethan Lyrics, both of which were exhibited at the 1893 Arts and Crafts Exhibition Society exhibition. She bound D.G. Rossetti's Poetical Works (1891), worked to a design by Cobden-Sanderson, as was Elizabethan Lyrics.

NICHOLSON, BARBARA - SEE HEPWORTH, B.

NICHOLSON, CELIA ANNA - SEE LEVETUS, C.A.

NORRIE, DAISY M. (b.1899)

Etcher / Aquatinter / Drypoint Artist / Engraver. Born in Fraserburgh, Aberdeenshire in June 1899. The daughter of William Norrie, a professional photographer, and Jane Peterkin. One of at least two children. Raised in Fraserburgh. Studied at the Aberdeen School of Art. Awarded a diploma, an endorsement of diploma and a travelling scholarship. Awarded a Diploma of the Edinburgh College of Art in 1921. Produced etchings, engravings, aquatints and drypoint. Subjects included landscapes. Exhibited her work, including at the Walker Art Gallery, Liverpool, the Royal Scottish Academy (1924-25) and the Royal Glasgow Institute (1924). Exhibited works included: Fraserburgh Bay, At Cairness, Moonlight, Pembroke Castle and Moonlight on a Fountain in Rome. Elected a Member of the Scottish Society of Women Artists. Based in Buckley near Chester in the 1920s and 1930s.

NORRIS, EDITH (active 1920s-1940s)

Stained Glass Artist. Born in Bolton, Lancashire. The daughter of James Walsh, an engineer and draughtsman. Studied art in Bolton under Ernest Hartley, A.R.C.A. In 1928 she married Harry

Norris in Bolton. Exhibited at Burlington House. Elected a Lay Member of the Red Rose Guild of Craftsmen in 1928. Elected an Associate of the British Society of Master Glass-Painters in 1949.

NORRISS, BESS - SEE TAIT, B.

NORTH, EVA A. - SEE KNIGHT, E.A.

NOTTIDGE, CAROLINE - SEE FRY, C.

O

O'BRIEN, CATHERINE A. (d.1963)
Stained Glass Designer. A student of Dublin's Metropolitan School of Art where A.E. Child supervised stained glass. Joined Sarah Purser's (1848-1943) stained glass studio An Tur Gloine (The Tower of Glass) in Dublin, shortly after it opened in 1903. Remained there until its closure in 1963. She produced a substantial number of windows, including Mass in Penal Days (1936) for The Friary, Athlone, Co. Westmeath. Also, The Sower (1953) for Killoughter Church of Ireland, Redhills, Co. Cavan and The Good Samaritan (1960) for the Church of Ireland, Harold's Cross, Dublin. Other works included stained glass for the Church of Ireland, Gorey, Co. Wexford. Also, for St Naithi's, Dundrum, Dublin. O'Brien was particularly talented in opaque stained glass or 'opus-sectile'. Showed examples of her work at the Dublin School of Art exhibition of past and present students in 1910. When An Tur Gloine was formally dissolved as a co-operative in 1944, O'Brien took it over completely and continued to run it alone for another 19 years. One of her colleagues at An Tur Gloine, Evie Hone, opened her own studio in Co. Dublin and continued her own stained glass work.

OLVER, KATE E. - SEE HIGGINS, K.E.

ONIONS, MARTHA AMY (1874-1956)
Sculptor. Born in Yardley, Worcestershire. The daughter of John Collingwood Onions (1841-1904) and Helen Waterhouse (1847-1914). Raised in Worcestershire. One of at least four children (Helen, Simon, Martha and James). Studied at the Birmingham Municipal School of Art in the late 1890s. Submitted work to the National Competition of Schools of Art held at South Kensington. A bas-relief memorial tablet by her, and sent to South Kensington, was illustrated in The Studio, Vol.6, 1895, p.47. Also contributed to the annual exhibition of work by students of the Birmingham School. In 1897, for

example, she showed a model of a nun in prayer in plaster, not dissimilar to the work of Evelyn De Morgan (1855-1919). The modelled head was illustrated in The Studio, Vol.10, March 1897, p.133. In 1898, around the time she completed her studies, Martha married Launcelot Dimmock in Solihull. Records indicate that they had at least three children (Florence, Joyce and James), though this needs absolute clarification. Dimmock was a stocks and shares broker. The couple lived in Worsley, Lancashire for a time, and in Cheshire. Martha died in Gloucestershire, aged 81. She appears to have given up sculpture on her marriage. However, her work was clearly regarded as having artistic merit since it was reproduced in The Studio. Martha appears to have exhibited some of her work with the Royal Birmingham Society of Artists in the 1890s.

OSBORNE, CHARLOTTE ELLEN (1902-94)
Sculptor. Born in April 1902. The daughter of Charles Gordon Gibson, a medical practitioner, and Annie. Her father originated from Edinburgh, her mother from Launceston, Cornwall. One of at least five children (Agnes, Maitland, Charlotte, Annie and Winifred), all born and raised in Launceston, in a house with servants. Charlotte was educated at the Launceston and Devonport High Schools. She then studied at the Regent Street Polytechnic School, London under Harold Brownsword between 1925 and 1931. Won a Special Mention Rome Scholarship in 1931 which took her to Italy for a year (1931-32). She became a sculptor of heads, busts and statuettes in stone, clay, wood, bronze and marble. Based mainly in London during her career, also working as a teacher in the Sculpture School of the Regent Street Polytechnic School of Art from 1933 until at least the 1950s.

Osborne exhibited her work, including at the Royal Scottish Academy (1935), the Royal Glasgow Institute (1937-49), the Royal Academy (1926-49) and at various provincial galleries including Bournemouth. She may also have exhibited one watercolour painting at the Society of Women Artists in 1948. Exhibited works included: Vittoria, Lot's Wife (statuette), Joy (statuette) and The Man Who Found Himself (statue). Elected an Associate of the Royal Society of British Sculptors, then a Fellow in 1951. Works reproduced in Sculpture Today in Great Britain (1940-43). In late 1937 she married etcher / engraver / lithographer / painter / illustrator James Thomas Armour Osborne (b.1907). The son of a farmer, an Associate of the Royal College of Art, a Rome scholar and an

Associate of the Royal Society of Painter-Etchers & Engravers, he was Master at the Regent Street Polytechnic School (1936-39). Charlotte Osborne died in East Sussex in July 1994, aged 92. She was active for more than 25 years.

OSBORNE, NORAH - SEE SIMCOCK, N.

OSBORNE, PHYLLIS ISABELLA (1904-46)
Modeller / Carver. Born in North Ormesby, Yorkshire. The daughter of Joseph Chilton and Ethel. Her father, an engineering draughtsman, originated from Northumberland. Her mother originated from Durham. Had at least one sibling, Elsa, also born in Durham. The family spent time living in Gateshead. Phyllis was educated at the Dame Allan's School, Newcastle-upon-Tyne. Then studied at the Westminster School of Art, London. Awarded a teaching diploma with distinction. Acted as art mistress at the Sawston Village College, Cambridge early in her career. Produced figures in stone, alabaster and brass. Exhibited her work, including at the North East Coast Exhibition, the Valenza Gallery, the Laing Art Gallery, Newcastle, at the Exhibition of Modern Artists, Cambridge and at Heal's Metal and Glass Exhibition. Works included: Venus, Contemplation (Portland stone), Hen (polished brass) and Wind (alabaster). Elected a Member of the National Society of Painters, Sculptors and Gravers. In 1932 she married Harold Osborne in London. They lived in London and Cambridge. Phyllis died in London, aged only 42.

OSBORNE, VERA ERMYNTRUDE CYPRIAN (1904-c.84)
Painter / Decorative Artist / Barbola Worker. Born in Mauritius in June 1904. The daughter of Major William Cyprian Bridge and Ada. One of at least four children (Olga, Ksonia, Vanda and Vera). Olga, a music student, was born in Jersey, Ksonia was born in Surrey and Vanda in Scotland, indicating that the family moved around with William's occupation. Vera was raised in Surrey and educated in Torquay. Studied art under G.K. Kenaway in Torquay, at Reading University and at the Slade School, London. She received a completion certificate for the Royal Drawing Society exams, aged only 15. Produced landscape and still life paintings in oils and watercolours and portraits of children. Worked as a decorative artist. Also, as a barbola worker, which was the art of making small models of fruit or flowers from a plastic paste. Exhibited her work, including at the Society of Women Artists (1952-56) and the Royal Institute of Painters in Watercolours. Exhibited works included:

Industrial Scene, November in London (oil), Snow in London (oil) and Street in Henley (oil). Elected a Member of the Overseas Club. Worked as an art teacher in Camberley, Surrey for a time. In 1932 she married Rene Denis Howard Osborne (1901-78), a barrister. The couple lived in Henley-on-Thames, London and Camberley, Surrey.

OULESS, CATHERINE (1879-1961)
Painter. Born in London in September 1879. The daughter of Walter William Ouless, R.A. (1848-1933). He was a respected portrait painter and Member of the Order of Senior Academicians. Walter was born in Jersey, the son of P.J. Ouless, a painter of marine subjects. Walter married Catherine's mother, Lucy Maitland Chambers, in 1878. Catherine was one of at least three daughters. Walter studied at the Royal Academy schools and won medals for his work. Remained in London thereafter. His portrait subjects included Charles Darwin, Lord Lister and Cardinal Newman. Catherine evidently followed in her father's and grandfather's footsteps, and became a painter, of portraits and landscapes. She too studied at the Royal Academy schools, winning silver medals in the antique and life as well as the Creswick Prize. She worked as a professional artist for over 40 years, and was still living with her family in Bryanston Square, London in 1927 at the age of 48. Remained in London, and died in Kensington on the 4th January 1961.

Catherine exhibited her work, including at the Royal Academy (55 works, 1902-34), the Society of Women Artists (1905-06) and in Liverpool and Manchester. Exhibited works included: Eastern Souvenirs, Ringstead Bay, Gwendoline and In a London Garden, June 1911. More notable portrait subjects included General Gordon, Sir Reginald Wingate, Arthur Somerville, Lady Palmer and Miss C.M.E. Burrows, M.A., Principal of St Hilda's Hall, Oxford, 1910-1919, afterwards Principal of the Society of Oxford Home Students. One of her oil paintings, A Warden's Post in Kensington (c.1941-42), is in the Imperial War Museum collection. Elected an Associate of the Society of Women Artists (1906). A Member of the Sesame Club.

P

PAGE, HELEN ALICE (1886-1973)
Painter / Decorative Worker. Born in Eastbourne in February 1886. The daughter of Sir Thomas William Holderness and Lucy Shepherd. Both

parents were born in India. Her father was an Indian Civil Servant. She had a younger brother, Ernest William. She studied at the Slade School, London. Was a Frederick Ward prizeman and a Nettleship prizeman. Based in London. In 1913 Helen married Charles Max Page in London. Died in Canterbury, Kent, aged 87. Produced oil paintings, various subjects, and some decorative work. Exhibited occasionally, including at the Royal Academy (1933) and the Royal Society of British Artists. Exhibited works included: Dahlias, Magic Casements, Peruvian Lilies and Victoriana.

PAGET, FLORENCE MARY EMILY (1862-1947)

Bookbinder / Book Decorator. Born in Farnham, Surrey. The daughter of Patrick Paget, a Colonel, and Frances. One of at least five children (Gertrude, Violet, Florence, Mildred and Henry). Raised in Farnham. Died in Surrey. Active as a bookbinder and decorator in the late 1890s and early 1900s. A pupil of Douglas Cockerell. Worked on some private press books. Paget worked on Song of Songs, 40 copies of which were produced by the Ashendene Press in 1902, all printed on vellum, illuminated by Florence Kingsford, all bound by Katharine Adams, Alice Pattinson and Florence Paget in 1903. She sold her bindings elsewhere too. Showed some of her work at the 1899 Arts and Crafts Exhibition Society exhibition. Noted in Sarah T. Prideaux's Modern Bookbindings Their Design and Decoration, London, Archibald Constable & Co., 1906. Prideaux noted Paget as being at Farnham, doing 'good honest work of a comparatively simple nature' (pp.53-54). In 1911, Paget is listed as being an antiques dealer in Farnham.

PAGET, WINIFRED - SEE TURNER, W.

PALMER, ADA M. (b.1851)

Sculptor. Born in Chigwell, Essex. Spent much of her life in Chigwell, at Turnour's Hall, but also spent a short time in Kensington, London and Kent in the early 1880s. The daughter of a wealthy landowner, William Palmer, and Matilda. One of at least three children (Mary, Gertrude and Ada). Produced statuettes, heads and figures in bronze. Exhibited her work at the Royal Academy (1884-87), the Royal Society of British Artists (1886 / 87) and the Society of Women Artists (1888). Exhibited works included: Going to Market (group), The Pied Piper of Hamelin (statuette), A Dutch Holiday (bronze) and A Trial Trip (statuette group). Effectively disappeared after 1891.

PALMER, HANNAH EMMA (1881-1965)

Painter / Etcher / Modeller. Born in Bristol, Gloucestershire. The daughter of William Lowell Palmer (1839-1920) and Mary Jefferies (1842-1910). Her father was a solicitor's clerk. One of at least four children (Marion, Hannah, Emily and William), she was raised in Bristol and spent virtually all her life there, at the family home in Auburn Road. She died there, aged 84. Educated at the Burlington House School. Studied at the Bristol School of Art, the Royal College of Art, London and the Royal West of England Academy. A keen observer of nature in her work. Produced oil and watercolour landscape paintings. Early in her career, she worked as an etcher and modeller. Exhibited her work with the British Watercolour Society, the Royal West of England Academy and in London. Works included: A Sunbeam's Farewell, Ruins Still Beautiful, Waning Nature and Ascension Day. Elected an Associate of the British Watercolour Society (1924). Palmer is also listed in census recordings as being a music teacher.

PARBURY, KATHLEEN OPHIR THEODORA (1901-86)

Sculptor. Known as Kate. Born in Elstree, Hertfordshire in August 1901. The daughter of Walter Key Parbury, a physician and surgeon, and Annie Lillian Crouch. Her father originated from New South Wales, Australia, her mother from Heathfield, Sussex. Her parents married in Middlesex in 1889 but lived in Australia after their marriage. They had two daughters whilst there, but returned to England sometime between 1899 and 1900 before having three more daughters. Kate was the third child. She was raised in Shambrook, Bedfordshire. Between 1920 and 1924, Kate studied at the Slade School, London under Professor Henry Tonks and sculptor George Havard Thomas. She subsequently worked as a sculptor, producing portrait works and figures in bronze and other materials.

Exhibited her work, including at the Royal Society of British Sculptors, the Royal Scottish Academy (1941) and the Society of Women Artists (1951). Exhibited works included: J.W.F. Lumsden, Esq., Study of a Boy and J. Lyle Cameron, Esq., M.D., F.R.C.S., F.R.C.O.G. (bronze). Elected a Fellow of the Royal Society of British Sculptors in 1966. Based in Edinburgh for a while in the 1940s, and in London. Also lived on Lindisfarne, Northumberland. She died in Northumberland in September 1986, aged 85.

One of Parbury's best known and possibly largest works was an exterior sculpture The Risen

Christ for the outside west end wall of St Michael and All Angels at Bemerton, Wiltshire. The church was designed by London architect N.F. Cachemaille-Day, F.R.I.B.A. The sculpture was designed to look over the main road and Salisbury Plain. Parbury executed the huge group in her Kensington studio, and it was transported in sections to the site. The risen Christ takes a central position in the design, with two angels, one pointing to the empty tomb and another rolling away the stone. There is also a small group symbolic of the choirs of angels. Christ is seen to be looking across the Plain towards Salisbury Cathedral. The sculpture was illustrated in The Studio, Vol.154, November 1957, p.158. With sculptor Josephina De Vasconcellos, and the Rev. Noel Parry Gore, Parbury organised an exhibition of Christian sculpture at the St John's Wood church.

PARGETER, CONSTANCE M. - SEE SKINNER, C.M.

PARKER, CONSTANCE M. - SEE HOWARD, C.M.

PARKER, LILIAN GERTRUDE (1874-1947)
Sculptor / Painter. Born in Bolton, Lancashire. The daughter of the Rev. Alfred Wells, a Wesleyan minister, and Eliza. Her father originated from Bromsgrove, her mother from Birmingham. One of at least three children (Ethel Mary (b.1873), Lilian and Walter (b.1877)). The family moved around the country with Alfred's job, and the young Lilian spent time in Bromsgrove and Lowestoft in Suffolk. She was educated at Queenswood, Clapham Park. Then studied at the Royal College of Art, London where she was awarded a diploma. She was a gold, silver and bronze medallist and the recipient of two Queen's Prizes in the National Competition of Schools of Art. In the 1898 National Competition, she exhibited a design scheme based on ships and shells. Remained in London for much of her career, at Clapham Road, Hounslow, Wandsworth and Putney Heath. Lilian became a painter in watercolours and a sculptor of busts and figures in terracotta. For a short time, she acted as an art teacher and adviser. Occasionally exhibited her work, including at the Royal Academy (1902-27), with the Royal Drawing Society, the British Watercolour Society, the Salon des Artistes Francais, the Paris Salon (1928), the Walker Art Gallery, Liverpool and in Hull and Manchester as well as at various smaller provincial galleries. Exhibited works included: Charlotte Corday (bust, terracotta), Alfred Wells (bust) and The Artist's Husband

(head). Elected an Associate of the Royal Drawing Society (1902) and an Associate of the British Watercolour Society (1919). A Member of the Royal College of Art Club. In 1908 she married Frank William Parker in Brentford. He was a schoolmaster who originated from London, and was some 11 years older than Lilian. Lilian continued to work as a painter and sculptor into the 1930s. She died in Weston-super-Mare, Somerset in late 1947, aged 73.

PARKINSON, FLORENCE (active 1890s-1910s)
Sculptor / Painter. A little-known artist who remains difficult to trace. She was married to William Parkinson, a painter and Royal Academy exhibitor (1886-95). Based in London. Produced statuettes in bronze and paintings. She exhibited at the Royal Academy (16 works, 1893-1918). Exhibited works included: A Soldier of the Empire (statuette), Cat's Cradle (statuette), St Agnes Eve (statuette) and Sir Joseph Pulley, Bart. In May 1916 she contributed to an Exhibition of Works by Women Artists held at Messrs Waring & Gillow. The exhibition was visited by the Queen, who purchased one of Florence's works.

PARNELL, EDITH CAROLINE - SEE FARMILOE, E.C.

PARNELL, GWENDOLEN / GWENDOLINE MURIEL (1877-1957)
Artist / Pottery Artist. Records suggest that Gwendolen Parnell was born in Gibraltar, the daughter of Arthur Parnell (1841-1914) and Mary Anne Dunn (d.1920). Her father was a Major in the Royal Engineers. She was one of at least 10 children (Edith, Winifred, Barbara, Geoffrey, Gwendolen, Yseulte, Arthur, Bertram, Muriel and Harold). The children spent time in Devon, Sussex and Chelsea. Gwendolen died in Cirencester, Gloucestershire, aged 80. She began as an art student at South Kensington. Then studied painting under Professor Knirr in Munich. She returned to England, set on becoming a portrait painter, but also took up black & white work for illustration as a means of earning money. The start of the First World War in 1914, however, interrupted her work. During that time, when artists were being encouraged to contribute to the war effort, she encountered a small china ornament. That encouraged her to find out more, but no studio potters were making such figures at that time. So she experimented herself with clay, a hairpin and a paperknife to create her first figure. It then took her three years to perfect her technique. So impressive were her early efforts

that she was discussed in The Times. Her figures were small, delicate, intricate and colourful; colour being always important in all her work. Since she was based in Chelsea, her figures became known as Cheyne, after Cheyne Walk in Chelsea.

Parnell's work was difficult to categorise since she never copied old figures such as Dresden, and every piece she created was entirely unique, so quickly became collectable. Her studio in Chelsea was on the site of the old Sprimont pottery, which had thrived some 160 years before. She then needed larger premises and moved to Paradise Walk in Chelsea, establishing the Chelsea Pottery Works in an old chapel and former parish hall (from at least 1921). One of her earliest sets of figures was based on John Gay's The Beggar's Opera, as performed at the Lyric Theatre in Hammersmith. They were acquired by the Royal Scottish Museum, Edinburgh. One of her forebears was poet Thomas Parnell, a friend to Gay and Pope. Parnell was his three times great-grand-niece. She also produced a set based on the Russian Ballet. Other figures created by her included The Apache Kid, the Pierrot Thief and Phillida Flouts Me. Parnell was able to convey the whole gamut of human emotion through her figures. They were figures of joy, of sadness, of the comic and the tragic, of the ridiculous and the beautiful. She evidently had a vivid imagination. Lady Astor owned her Somer is i-comen In which was a figure in a brightly coloured dress, running over the flowers. Her Ballet Girl Resting was a dancer in a pink dress.

Parnell did not use moulds, as the large factories did. Her figures were also occasionally based on real people as well as the imaginary. One of her studies was of Mrs Theodore Roosevelt junior (in biscuit). Most were purely imaginary, however, and also included Abundance, which reflected a medieval influence, and The Clown, which was a study of Death in a Pierrot costume. At Colnaghi's she exhibited a set of figures based on The Cries of London, inspired by a book of 1711, lent by Dr Bellamy Gardner in the 1920s. The amount of time spent on each piece, however, meant that production was limited, with many hours of concentrated work devoted to each figure. Parnell excelled, however, because of her minuteness of observation, which truly set her apart. She exhibited into the 1920s and 1930s. At the Society of Women Artists, she showed her figures between 1921 and 1925. In 1927 she exhibited at the Leicester Galleries.

In 1930 Parnell showed figures at the Fine Art Society, including The Shepherdess, Cupid's Bath and Sophia Unmasked which were illustrated in a review of the exhibition in Apollo,

August 1930, pp.166-167. In 1933 her work was included in an exhibition at Colnaghi's, which also included the work of Phyllis Simpson. One of her figures was illustrated in The Studio, Vol.93, 1927, p.424. Another was illustrated in The Studio, Vol.110, November 1935, p.264 in an article Figurines in Pottery. In 1929 she was the subject of an article, Gwendolen Parnell and Her Chelsea Cheyne Figures, by Mrs Steuart Erskine in the Apollo, Vol.9, February, pp.100-105. Her sister, Edith, also became an artist. SEE: FARMILOE, EDITH C.

PARRY, RUBY (1881-c.1961)

Sculptor. Born in Beddgelert, Wales. The daughter of Sidney Llewelyn Parry (d.1929) and Mary Sophia. Her mother came from a wealthy and titled family. Raised in Wales, but also spent time in Stinsford, Dorset and Kensington, London. The eldest of at least five daughters (Ruby, Pearl, Mary, Olive and Ivy). Olive and Ivy appear to have been twins. Ruby studied sculpture. Produced animals in plaster and bronze. Exhibited her work over a comparatively short time, including at the Royal Scottish Academy (1914-15), the Royal Glasgow Institute (1913) and the Royal Academy (1913). Exhibited works included: Tigers Fighting (bronze), Wolves (plaster, bronze) and Polar Bears Playing. Parry may have died in Hereford in 1961, aged 80, though this needs absolute clarification.

PARSONS, SYBIL (1906-77)

Potter. Born in London in April 1906. The daughter of Horace Finnemore (1878-1967) and Nellie Muriel M.K. Blundell (1876-1964). Her father, a pharmacist and later a university lecturer, originated from Staffordshire, her mother from London. Had at least two sisters, Cicely and Joan. Studied at the L.C.C. Central School of Arts and Crafts, London. Whilst still a student, her work was praised and illustrated in The Studio, Vol.95, January 1928, p.33. The two pots illustrated had been shown at a students' exhibition in Southampton Row. Particularly noted even at that stage for her excellent craftsmanship. Developed a career in making and decorating hand-thrown pottery. Initially based in Croydon. Did some animal subjects. Liked to give the impression of movement.

Whilst Parsons was a student, the Central School of Arts and Crafts produced a number of distinguished potters and developed an admirable success rate, helped by its new kilns which enabled the production of stoneware. In 1929 she married Tom Raymond Parsons in Croydon. They had at least one daughter. With Tom, she subsequently ran The Yellowsands Pottery on the Isle of Wight. It closed in the 1930s, then reopened in 1949 as the Bembridge Pottery, closing in 1961. Sybil died on the Isle of Wight. Exhibited her work, including at the Society of Women Artists in 1928, at the Arts and Crafts Exhibitions and with the Red Rose Guild. Works purchased by the British Institute of Industrial Art. The Victoria & Albert Museum, London acquired a stoneware vase decorated in black on grey slip (1926). Works also in the collection of the Aberystwyth University. Works illustrated in The Studio Yearbook.

PARTRIDGE, ETHEL M. - SEE MAIRET, E.M.

PARTRIDGE, MAY HART (b.1877)

Craftswoman / Jeweller / Enameller / Metalworker. Was Gertrude Mary / May Hart, known as May. Born in Harborne, Staffordshire. Studied metalwork and enamelling at the Birmingham School of Art. In 1900, in response to the new interest in artistic jewellery, the Birmingham School had set up a School of Jewellery and Silversmithing, from which May and others benefitted. From 1902, Head of the new department was Arthur Gaskin. In 1904, May contributed to the exhibition of students' work. Shortly after, some of her works and designs were sent to the St Louis Exhibition. In 1906 May exhibited enamels at the National Competition of Schools of Art, including one titled War. Also in 1906, by which time she appears to have completed her studies, May, along with fellow artist Ethel Agnew, opened a short-lived class in enamelling and jewellery at the Cathcart Studios, Redcliffe Road, London.

In the same year, May married Frederick (Fred) James Partridge (1877-1945), who originated from Barnstaple, Devon. He was also a student of the Birmingham School of Art, and initially became a silversmith for Charles R. Ashbee's Guild of Handicraft at Chipping Campden, Gloucestershire. May also spent a short time producing enamels for Ashbee's Guild. However, she and Fred elected to move to London and work as art jewellers and decorative metalworkers, also teaching at the Camberwell School of Arts and Crafts. One of Fred's students was Ella Naper. When she completed her studies in 1906, Naper went to Branscombe on the Devonshire coast, where Fred established a jewellery workshop which ran as a co-operative. May also worked there. Ella Naper designed and made her own jewellery at Branscombe. In London, May also taught at the Sir John Cass Technical Institute.

Fred was subsequently elected a Member of the Art Workers' Guild. He died in Ditchling, Sussex.

May exhibited her work elsewhere during her career, including at the Royal Academy (1906) and at the exhibitions of the Sir John Cass Institute, including in 1908 at the Walker's Gallery, New Bond Street, London. Occasionally, May worked with other artists, including Harold Stabler. At the above 1908 exhibition, she and Stabler jointly showed a cup in silver, enamel and ivory. Works by May and Fred can be found in the Victoria & Albert Museum, London, given by Joan Partridge.

Fred Partridge was the son of James Partridge, a chemist and druggist, and Mary. He had two sisters, Ethel M. and Alice Maud (b.1873), known as Maud. Maud spent much of her life in Barnstaple, where Fred grew up. Of some significance is that, sometime in the very early 1900s, Maud became involved with the local Guild of Metal Workers. Very little is known of the Guild, but its address was Trinity Street, Barnstaple, then The Red House, Pilton Street, where Maud resided for some years, involved in decorative metalwork. Maud exhibited under the Guild title at the Society of Women Artists between 1903 and 1913. A set of fingerplates by her, designed by G.L.C. Morris and again exhibited under the Guild title, also received an Honorary Mention at the 1903 Bristol and Clifton Arts and Crafts Society 'Art Work' exhibition. Like Fred, Maud died in Ditchling, Sussex, aged 74. It is feasible that Fred, and possibly May, had connections with the Guild.

PASLEY, LOUISA MARIA SABINE (1847-1929)

Sculptor. Born in Kendal, Westmorland. The daughter of Thomas Sabine Pasley, a Baronet and Admiral. One of at least three daughters (also Georgina and Madelene). Raised in Devon and Hampshire. Died in Botley, Hampshire, aged 82. Produced busts and groups in terracotta. Exhibited two works at the Royal Academy, a bust of General Sir Edward Sabine, K.C.B., Late President of the Royal Society, in 1880, and Dog and Cat Playing (group, terracotta) in 1884.

PATERSON, EGLINGTON M. - SEE PEARSON, E.M.

PATRICK, JESSIE G. (b.c.1876)

Decorative Artist / Designer. Born in Glasgow. The daughter of William Patrick and Mary. One of at least nine children (Eliza, John, Harty, Mary, Isabella, Jessie, Kate, George and William). Raised in Glasgow. Studied enamelling.

Exhibited two works at the Royal Glasgow Institute, Head (enamelled) in 1902 and a decorative enamelled panel in 1905. Became Mrs D.N. Rollo.

PATTINSON, ALICE (1869-post-1943)

Bookbinder / Book Decorator. Born in Gateshead near Newcastle. The daughter of John Pattinson (b.1828), an analytical chemist, and Mary Jane (b.1834). Her father originated from Alston, Cumbria, her mother from Gateshead. One of at least eight children (Hugh, Mary, Ethel, Ellen, Katherine, Alice, Bertha and Winifred), all born between 1858 and 1876. Raised in Gateshead. The Pattinson children were well educated. In 1891 Hugh is listed as an analytical chemist whilst Alice is a teacher of music and Bertha is a Classics student. Other family were connected to the printing and selling of books.

Sometime after 1891, Alice gave up music and took up bookbinding. She became a pupil of Douglas Cockerell (1870-1945) in London. He taught bookbinding at the L.C.C. Central School of Arts and Crafts and in his own studio. He was also a Member of the Art Workers' Guild and founder of the Golden Cockerel Press in 1921. Pattinson then set up a bindery in Cockerell's rooms at Gilbert Street, London when he moved to Ewell in 1902. There, she was assisted by Miss Else Hoffman (forwarding) and George Fisher (gold tooling). The designs of her bindings were strictly her own work, and she ran a small workshop where careful attention was paid to detail.

Pattinson was already exhibiting her work in 1899. In that year she contributed to the Arts and Crafts Exhibition Society's exhibition, which indicates the high standard of her work, and she continued to exhibit elsewhere into the early 1900s. In December 1904 she held an exhibition of her own bindings. In the same year, she contributed to the 1904 City of Bradford Exhibition which devoted a small section to artistic handicrafts practised by women. One of her exhibits on that occasion was a Guest Book bound by her. Also contributed to the Second Exhibition of Arts and Crafts held at the Lyceum Club in 1905 / 06. She showed her binding for Omar Khayyam's The Rubaiyat which was illustrated in The Studio, Vol.36, January 1906, p.355. That particular binding, executed in collaboration with Hoffman and Fisher, was light brown with green and red, tooled in gold.

At the Arts and Crafts Exhibition Society's 1906 exhibition she showed a binding for the Book of Common Prayer, which was also illustrated in The Studio, Vol.37, April 1906, p.228. In the same year, that particular binding was illustrated in Sarah T. Prideaux's book Modern Bookbindings Their Design and Decoration, London, Archibald Constable & Co., 1906. Prideaux notes Pattinson's neat and delicate work, and lists her as one of a number of women then doing 'well considered and tasteful work on sound principles' (p.54).

Other binding projects undertaken by Pattinson included an edition of Walter Pater's Greek Studies (1901) in brick-red goatskin with gold tooling (with Hoffman and Fisher). In 1902 the Ashendene Press produced 40 copies of Song of Songs, all printed on vellum, illuminated by Florence Kingsford and bound by Katharine Adams, Florence Paget and Alice Pattinson. Else Hoffman, also a talented craftswoman, exhibited some of her own bindings at the Arts and Crafts exhibitions as well as in Frankfurt in 1906 and Leipzig in 1914. Hoffman lived at Oak House, The Mount, Sydenham, Kent for a time. Pattinson's work was praised in a number of journals other than The Studio, including the Art Journal and The Art of the Book (1914). The Art Workers' Quarterly, January 1905, p.47 offered a small piece describing her bindery and praising her work.

In mid-1906, Pattinson married Raymund Cecil Edward Allen (1864-1943). He was a barrister who originated from Millom, Cumbria. They married in Gateshead. By at least 1908 they were based in Cardiff and had one son, Pattinson Allen, born there in that year. Alice was still listed as a bookbinder in 1911, aged 42, working from home. Raymund died in Bath, Somerset. Alice was still alive when he died.

PAUL, DOROTHEA - SEE BRABY, D.

PAUL, EVELYN MAUDE BLANCHE (1883-1963)

Illustrator. Born in London. The daughter of artist Robert Paul and his second wife, Annie. Her father was some 30 years older than her mother, and she was their only child. Raised in London. Became an art student in London from at least the age of 17. Records suggest that, in the early 1900s, she was a student at the Camden School, Islington. She contributed to the annual National Competition of Schools of Art. For example, in 1906 she showed book illustrations. In 1907 she won a gold medal for designs for colour prints. In 1909 she won another gold medal, for colour prints. One of her 1908 National Competition entries, a coloured lithograph, was illustrated in The Studio, Vol.44, 1908, p.276. Paul was still listed as an art student in 1911, after her father's death. Worked mainly as a book illustrator in London. Produced illustrations for, for example, Mrs Gaskell, Cranford (1910), Susan Cannington, Stories From Dante (1910), Frederick H. Davis, Myths and Legends of Japan (1912), Charles Reade, The Cloister and the Hearth (1922) and W.J. Gordon (ed.), Warne's Pleasure Book For Girls (1928). In 1911, Evelyn married artist Alexander G. Small (1843-1929) in London. She died in London, aged 79.

PAYNE, DOROTHY MARGARET ETHEL (1887-1949)

Illustrator. Born in Walworth, London. The daughter, and possibly only child, of Frederick William Payne and Lucy Maud Harrison. Her father was master at a secondary school. Raised and lived in London, but died in Lostwithiel, Cornwall, aged 61. Studied at the Lambeth School of Art, London (certainly in 1910 and 1911). Exhibited some of her work at the National Competition of Schools of Art in 1910, including designs for bookplates, book decoration and book illustrations. Some of those were illustrated in The Studio, Vol.50, 1910, pp.302-303. Exhibited book illustrations at the 1911 National Competition. Noted in the opening essay of Malcolm C. Salaman's volume Modern Book Illustrators and Their Work, London, The Studio Ltd, 1914, edited by C. Geoffrey Holme & Ernest G. Halton. Salaman offers two of her illustrations, one from La Belle Dame Sans Merci, the other from Joan of Arc.

PEACEY, JESSIE MUTTER - SEE LAWSON, J.M.

PEACOCK, MABEL R. - SEE WHITE, M.R.

PEAKE, ETHELWYN MAY (1899-1987)

Ceramics Artist. Records suggest that Peake was born in Madagascar, but spent virtually all her life in England. Her father, George Peake, was also born in Madagascar, as were three of her siblings. George Peake was a physician and surgeon. Ethelwyn's mother, Agnes, was born in South Africa. Ethelwyn was one of at least five children (Bruce, Ethelwyn, Muriel, Howard and Frank). The family moved to England sometime between 1902 and 1904, initially to Birmingham, where Frank was born, then to Poole in Dorset. Ethelwyn was a student of the Bournemouth Municipal School of Art in the early 1920s. Produced earthenware figures, including animals, one of which was illustrated in The Studio, Vol.94, 1927, p.428. Exhibited two of her works at the Society of Women Artists in 1959, Nymph

and Angel. At that point, she was based in Hatch End, Middlesex. She appears to have married Terence E. Crowley in Southwell, Nottinghamshire in 1939, though this needs absolute clarification. She died in Oxfordshire, aged 88.

PEARSE, DAMARIS (1659-79)

Embroideress. A talented decorative embroideress. The daughter of William Pearse, a Nonconformist minister of Ermington, Devon. One of her works (attributed to her), The Drowning of Pharoah in the Red Sea (c.1673), has survived in the care of the Lady Lever Art Gallery, Port Sunlight, Liverpool. Wooden moulds and wool padding create a three-dimensional effect, with the satin background embroidered with silk, metal thread, mica and seed pearls in a variety of stitches and knots. Since Damaris was ill for the last four years of her short life, the embroidery was probably executed when she was less than 16 years of age. There are indications that she made money from the sale of her embroideries and needlework. In her memory, in 1683 William Pearse published a book titled A Present for Youth and an Example for the Aged: or the Remains of Damaris Pearse in which he referred to her needlework and its importance to her personally. An illustration of her The Drowning of Pharoah in the Red Sea is given in Xanthe Brooke, Catalogue of Embroideries, Lady Lever Art Gallery, Stroud, Alan Sutton, 1992, p.60.

PEARSE, NORAH (1889-1981)

Painter / Woodcut Artist / Aquatint Artist / Linocut Artist. Born in Exeter, Devon. The daughter of Charles Samuel Pearse and Mary Amelia. Her father, who originated from Exeter, ran a drapery business in the city. Norah had at least one sister, Hilda. The girls were raised in Exeter, where Norah attended the Maynard School. She spent much of her life there, though also spent time in Exmouth later in her career. She died in Exeter, aged 92.

Norah studied at the Exeter School of Art under Nathaniel Hughes John Baird and Robert Kirkland Jamieson. Became a painter of various subjects, including landscapes, figures, animals and flowers, in oils and watercolours. Also produced watercolour and chalk drawings, woodcuts, aquatints and linocuts. Some of her paintings were of her local surroundings. However, she evidently travelled, producing studies of, for example, Pollensa, Dieppe, Bavaria, Scotland, Dorset, Wales and the New Forest.

Exhibited her work extensively over more than 45 years, including at the Society of Women Artists where she showed 111 works between 1931 and 1976. Those included: Poor Artist (linocut), Fisherwomen, Dieppe (aquatint), Electricity Cooling Towers, Coleshill and The Old Armchair (oil). Also exhibited at the Royal Hibernian Academy (1940), the Royal Academy (1950), the Royal Scottish Academy (1936-38), the Royal Society of British Artists and the Royal Institute of Painters in Watercolours. Also, at the Paris Salon, the Royal Society of Painters in Watercolours, the Royal West of England Academy, the Walker Art Gallery, Liverpool, the Society of Graphic Art, the Colour Woodcut Society and the Royal Institute of Oil Painters. Elected a Member of the Society of Women Artists (1950-78) and an Honorary Retired Member (1979-81). Also elected a Member of the Society of Graphic Art and of the Royal Society of Painters in Watercolours Art Club. For a time, she acted as art mistress at St Margaret's School, Exeter.

PEARSON, EGLINGTON MARGARET (d.1823)

Painter on Glass. The daughter of Samuel Paterson, a well-known auctioneer and originator of the 'Darien Scheme'. Married artist James Pearson. In 1770 he stained the chapel windows of Brasenose College, Oxford, from cartoons by Mortimer of Christ and the Four Evangelists. In James Dallaway's Anecdotes of the Arts in England, Mrs Pearson is noted as being as talented as her husband in her field, and that the couple often worked together on glass painting projects. One of her works was the Aurora of Guido window for Arundel Castle. In her day, her reputation was also secured by her copies after the cartoons of Raffaelle. Made two sets of those. She exhibited 11 works at the Society of Artists between 1775 and 1777, including A Golden Pheasant and A Paroquet, with Insects. She was then based in Westminster. James Pearson also exhibited with the Society (1775-77). Mrs Pearson was active around the same time as Mrs Lawrie, who is said to have shown distinct promise in stained glass around 1770. Even less is known about her today. Mrs Pearson died in February 1823. Noted in Ellen C. Clayton, English Female Artists, London, Tinsley, 1876.

PEARSON, KATHLEEN MARGARET (1898-1961)

Painter / Equestrian Artist. Born in Knutsford, Cheshire in January 1898. The daughter of Stanley Pearson, a Chartered Accountant, and Edith. Her father originated from Stalybridge, Lancashire, her mother from Birmingham. The youngest of four children (two sons and two daughters). Raised in Cheshire. Educated at the Malvern College. Studied at the Slade School, London (1920), followed by the Royal Academy schools (1921-26). Produced portrait, landscape, animal and still life paintings, mainly in oils but also occasionally pastels. Perhaps best known for her equestrian paintings.

After completing her studies, Kathleen remained in London, at Taviton Street, for a while. By the 1930s she had moved to the Old Manor House, Lymington in the south of England. Subsequently moved to Great Collin Farm, Broadway, Worcestershire, where she remained until her death in April 1961 at the age of 63. Died in Stoke Newington, London. Left part of her estate to her brother John, a farmer. In the countryside, she had an inexhaustible supply of subject matter; in particular, horses.

Pearson exhibited her work widely over a period of five decades, from the early 1920s to the early 1960s. Exhibited at the Royal Scottish Academy (1934-39), the Royal Hibernian Academy (1934-36), the Royal Academy (1924-38), the Society of Women Artists (1936-61) and the Royal West of England Academy. Also, at the Royal College of Art, the Paris Salon, the International Society, the Royal Society of Portrait Painters, the Royal Institute of Oil Painters and in Manchester and Liverpool. In 1933 she exhibited with the United Society of Artists at the Suffolk Street Galleries. Other exhibitors on that occasion included Anne Acheson. Exhibited works included: The Girl With the Flaxen Hair, Plough Monday, Sand-Ponies at Filey, The Flueologist and The Drum-Horse of the IV-VIIth Dragoon Guards. Her highly regarded equestrian studies also included a study of The Stallion Class at the Hunters' Show, the Royal Agricultural Hall (c.1949). Elected an Associate of the Society of Women Artists (1940-48) and a Member (1949-60). Also elected an Associate of the Royal West of England Academy (1939). Works illustrated in Colour. Purchasers of her work included the Russell-Cotes Art Gallery, Bournemouth (The Gipsy Cart). Also, the Sunderland Art Gallery (Head of a Girl).

PEARSON, RUTH M. - SEE KEATING, R.M.

PEART, EVELINE - SEE SIMMONDS, E.

PEASE, MARY AVERN (1885-1960)

Sculptor. Born in Woolwich, London. The daughter of Joseph A. Pease and Mary. Her father, a military tutor, originated from Woolwich, her mother from Chelsea. Mary became an art student in London, lodging with relatives. Subsequently became a sculptor of busts, statuettes and plaquettes. Exhibited occasionally, including at the Royal Academy. There, she showed three works, The Bracelet (statuette) in 1908, Miss Janie Stockwell (bust) in 1909 and Frederick Halnon, Esq. (plaquette) in 1910. Possibly a student of the Royal Academy schools. Died in London, aged 74.

PEATE, ENID MAY MEREDITH (1883-1954)

Painter / Embroideress / Leather and Brass Craftswoman. Born in Willesden, Middlesex in May 1883. The daughter of Samuel Cartwright, a Chartered Accountant, and Alice. One of at least four children (Samuel, Alice, Enid and Hilda), all raised in Willesden. Alice became an insurance clerk. Enid studied at the Willesden Art School and in Oswestry. Awarded an Art Masters' Certificate. Produced paintings in watercolours, worked in leather and brass and executed embroideries. Also worked as an art teacher. Exhibited her work occasionally, including at the Walker Art Gallery, Liverpool and with the Liver Sketching Club. Works included: The Mill Pool and The Mill Silo. Her watercolour Winter Sunshine was bought for the Liverpool Permanent Collection. In 1915 she married Albert Edward Peate (1868-1941) in Hendon, Middlesex. He was a flour miller from Oswestry. They had one son and two daughters. Later lived in Portmadoc. Both died in Wales, Enid aged 71. Enid continued to work until shortly before her death.

PEGRAM, MARY CONSTANCE - SEE BUZZARD, M.C.

PELTON, DOROTHY GENDLE (1885-1969)

Illuminator. Born and raised in Croydon. Died in Cambridge, aged 83. The daughter of John Ollis Pelton, a grocer and wine merchant, and Alice Rose. One of at least three children (May, Dorothy and Norah). Worked as an illuminator. Produced beautifully executed, finely detailed work. Exhibited some of her work at the Society of Women Artists in 1911. Two examples of her work were illustrated in an article Some Modern Illuminators in The Studio, Vol.56, June 1912, pp.45-58 (p.53). One was taken from Matthew Arnold's The Forsaken Merman, the other from Henry W. Longfellow's The Song of Hiawatha. In 1919 she married bank clerk Sidney Packer Dickins in Croydon.

PEMBERTON, HILDA MARY LEIGH (1872-1956)

Painter / Etcher / Decorative Designer. Born in Hammersmith, London. The daughter of Frederick Blake Pemberton and Lucy. Her father was initially a brick maker and later a civil engineer. Hilda was one of at least six children (Amy, Francis, George, Charles, Hilda and Helen). Raised in South Shoreham, Hampshire and in London. Studied at the Goldsmiths' College of Art, London, a contemporary of Katharine Coggin and Isabel McBean. Goldsmiths' College was then particularly strong on the decorative arts and produced a number of highly competent female designer / craftswomen. Hilda also studied at the Royal College of Art, London. Elected an Associate of the Royal College of Art. Exhibited at the National Competition of Schools of Art, including in 1898. As a student, awarded bronze and silver medals.

Hilda was initially based in London. Produced decorative work including designs for embroidery, lace, book covers, posters, wallpaper, jewellery, tapestries, stained glass and bookplates. Also produced designs for items in bronze and silver, such as sugar basins and cups. Exhibited jewellery designs for brooches in enamel and repoussé, some of which were illustrated in The Studio, Vol.14, September 1898, p.264 along with an illustration of her design for an embroidered panel (p.267). Some of her jewellery was included in the 1904 Dress Designers' Exhibition Society exhibition. One of her designs for a silver sugar basin, exhibited at the Society of Women Artists in 1898, was also illustrated in The Studio, Vol.13, April 1898, p.187. She also produced etchings, engravings, mezzotint, lithographs, drypoint, aquatints and woodcuts. Produced paintings in watercolours and oils, and pencil studies, mainly flowers and landscapes.

Exhibited her work elsewhere, including at the Royal Academy (1910-40), the Royal Scottish Academy (1925-32) and the Royal Cambrian Academy. At the Society of Women Artists, she showed 98 works between 1897 and 1955. Exhibited works included: Low-Tide (drypoint), Sight (design for stained glass), Japanese Anemones (watercolour) and Cottage at Blewbury (woodcut). She exhibited work at the first exhibition at the Permanent Gallery of Decorative Art, Harrington Road, South Kensington in 1899. Other exhibitors on that occasion included Mary Lowndes, Ellen M. Rope and W. Glasby. The exhibition aimed to promote decorative artists and win them commissions. A Miss Leigh Pemberton, possibly Hilda, exhibited pottery at Messrs Colnaghi in 1931. Pemberton was elected an Associate of the Society of Women Artists (1923-38) and a Member (1939-55).

Later in her career, Hilda worked as an art teacher for the London County Council. In 1905 she married painter / etcher Eli Marsden Wilson (1877-1965). A former student of the Royal College of Art, he originated from Yorkshire. The couple spent time living and working in London, but later also spent time at Blewbury, Oxfordshire. Hilda died first, in Ealing, aged 84. Eli died some nine years later, in Ealing, aged 88.

PERCY, IDA - SEE NELSON, I.

PERKINS, ATHELINA LOIS GWENDOLINE (1896-1964)

Painter / Modeller / Illuminator / Pewter Worker. Born in Coventry. The daughter of Arthur Edward Perkins and Alethea Jenie. Her father was a nurseryman, seedsman and florist. Had at least one sibling, Gladys Vera. Neither sister ever married. Both were raised in Coventry, lived there and died there, Athelina at the age of 67. She was educated at high school in Coventry. Studied at the Birmingham School of Art. Also, at the Slade School, London, where she was awarded certificates for drawing and painting. Became a painter of portraits and other subjects in oils and watercolours and of miniatures, a modeller, an illuminator and a pewter worker. Exhibited her work, including at the Royal Academy (1920-21), the Walker Gallery, with the Royal Birmingham Society of Artists and the Manchester Society of Miniature Painters. Exhibited works included: Jessie, A Blue-Coat Girl and Niccolo Giomi. Works reproduced in La Revue Moderne. Other works included an altar set and altar rails for St James's House, South Leigh.

PERRIN, IDA SOUTHWELL (1860-1953)

Painter / Illustrator / Pottery Manager. Born in Bayswater, London in November 1860. The daughter of architect Edward John Cookworthy Robins, F.S.A., F.R.I.B.A. (1830-1918) and Elizabeth Southwell (1825-1908). Possibly an only child. Raised in London. Educated at the Hampstead High School. Studied at the Bedford College and at South Kensington. Obtained a drawing certificate. Remained in London and worked as a painter in oils and watercolours of various subjects including landscapes, flowers and portraits. Exhibited her work, including at the Royal Academy (1884-1925), the Royal Society of British Artists (1890-92), the Society of Women Artists (1914-23), the Royal Institute of

Painters in Watercolours and the Paris Salon. Exhibited works included: Azaleas, A Cloister in France, La Signora and Through the Cornfield.

In July 1886, Ida married Henry S. Perrin (1858-1938) in Camden, London. He originated from Paddington, London, and is initially listed as being a warehouseman. The couple lived in Hampstead early in their marriage, and later in Kensington. They had two children, both born in London, Maurice in 1887 and Muriel in 1889. Maurice became a medical student, and Muriel became a student of sculpture at the Royal College of Art. Ida continued to work as an artist, and some of her works were reproduced by Anacker, while her Fancy Head was reproduced by the Autotype Fine Art Company. Henry Perrin subsequently became a considerably wealthy manufacturer and merchant of clothing for women and children. During the early 1900s, he acquired a large property, The Cottage at Bushey Heath, Hertfordshire, and the family lived there as well as in Kensington from around 1905. The Cottage later became the home of scientist and inventor J. Langham Thompson and was eventually demolished.

In 1921, Ida established the De Morgan Pottery Works at The Cottage, named in honour of art potter William De Morgan. A former partner of De Morgan's, Fred Passenger, worked there from 1923 until its closure in 1933. Ida is believed to have instigated Passenger's production of lustre pieces reminiscent of those by De Morgan. Ida acted as manager of the pottery, and The Cottage also became known as the Bushey Heath Pottery. Some of Passenger's works have been on display at the Bushey Museum.

For her work at the pottery, Ida was elected a Member of the Guild of Potters. Also elected a Member of the Artists' Guild and of the Model Theatre Guild. In 1914 Ida contributed 300 drawings to British Flowering Plants, four volumes published by Bernard Quaritch of London, with an introduction by George S. Boulger. The Perrins moved in prominent artistic circles of the day, but also became involved with their local church at Bushey, St Peter's. The Perrins commissioned Henry Holiday to design a memorial window for the church, which was made by Lowndes and Drury of The Glass House, Fulham. The window was dedicated in 1918. Ida Perrin died in a Buckinghamshire nursing home at the age of 93. Henry died in January 1938, leaving a substantial estate.

PETHERICK, ROSA CLEMENTINA (1871-1931)

Illustrator. Born in Croydon. The daughter of Horace William Petherick (1838-1919) and Clementina Augusta Bonney (1837-1909). Her father was an artist and draughtsman, but also later a musical instructor. Rosa was one of at least five daughters (Rosa, Ada, Leila, Evelina and Dora), all raised in Croydon. All were well educated and artistic. Rosa became a book illustrator, Ada a pianist, Leila a vocalist, Evelina a violinist, and Dora a cellist. Early in her career, Rosa competed in The Studio book illustration competitions, including in 1896. Worked as an illustrator from at least the very early 1900s until shortly before her death. Books illustrated by her included Lillian D. Gask, Little Folks of Many Lands (with Kate Fricero, n.d.), Mother Hubbard's Cupboard of Nursery Rhymes (1903), Elsie Oxenham, The Abbey Girls in Town (1925) and Simple Composition Steps (1930). Also contributed to Little Folks periodical. Rosa died in Brighton, Sussex.

PETO, GLADYS EMMA (1890-1977)

Poster Artist / Black & White Artist / Designer / Illustrator. Born in Cookham, Berkshire in June 1890. The daughter of William Peto, a farmer, and Mary Jane. Raised in Cookham. One of at least three children (William, Ernest and Gladys). Educated at the Harvington College, Ealing. Initially studied at the Maidenhead School of Art whilst living at home. Then studied at the London School of Art. Became a diverse and talented artist, working until shortly before her death. Initially based in London. Produced poster designs, advertisement designs, fabric designs and designs for stage settings. Produced black & white drawings, book illustrations and postcards. She was on the staff of Sketch between 1915 and 1926. Works appeared in a number of other weekly and monthly magazines including The Bystander and Pearson's Magazine.

In 1922 she married Major Cuthbert Lindsay Emmerson, R.A.M.C., in Kensington. Between 1924 and 1928 they lived abroad, in Malta, Cyprus and Egypt. Wrote and illustrated her own books, including Gladys Peto's Children's Annual (Sampson Low, 1924), Gladys Peto's Bedtime Stories (Shaw, 1931), Malta and Cyprus (Dent, 1928) and Egypt of the Sojourner (J.M. Dent & Sons). Also illustrated, for example, The Works of Louisa M. Alcott (1914), Daphne and the Fairy and Other Tales (Sampson Low, 1924), Enid L. Hunt, A Fine Lady Upon a White Horse (Sampson Low, 1929) and Twilight Stories (Shaw, 1932). Also worked for J. Salmon and

Allenbury's. Between 1933 and 1938 the Emmersons lived in India. In 1939 they moved to Northern Ireland, where Gladys held several exhibitions of her watercolours. A Member of the Lyceum Club. Gladys died in Ireland.

PETRIE, EMELINE - SEE STEINTHAL, E.

PETRIE, MARIA (1887-1972)

Sculptor / Painter. Born in Frankfurt, Germany in August 1887. The daughter of S. Zimmern, a doctor of medicine. She studied at the Frankfurt College of Art. Also, in Paris with Aristide Maillol, Maurice Denis, Theo von Rysselberghe and Paul Serusier. Spent several decades working in Britain, living in Ilkley, Yorkshire, London and Rocester, Staffordshire. Married Francis Eric Petrie (1886-1974) and had at least one son. Produced portrait busts in bronze and stone, and garden statues. Exhibited her works, including at the Royal Scottish Academy (1928-37), the Royal Academy (1926), the Society of Women Artists (1938), with the Allied Artists in London and in Bradford, Leeds, Liverpool and Manchester. Also, with the London Group (by invitation), at the Gallerie Druet, Paris in 1911 and at the Paris Salon. Exhibited works included: G.K. Chesterton, Esq. (bust, bronze) which was reproduced in Sphere. Also, Portrait of Sir Gerald du Maurier. Her portrait bust in stone of Theo von Rysselberghe was illustrated in Revue Moderne. One of her garden statues was illustrated in the Architect's Journal. Maria died in Santa Barbara, California. Francis Petrie died in West Sussex two years later.

PETTIGREW, HARRIET SELINA (1869-1953)

Sculptor. Also known as Hetty or Hettie. Born in Portsmouth, Hampshire. The daughter of William Pettigrew and Harriet. Her father was a cork cutter. Her mother, who originated from Birmingham, was a needleworker. Harriet was one of at least 11 children (Charles, Richard, Alfred, William, Thomas, Henry, Christine, Harriet, Lilian, Florence and Rosie). They were raised in Portsmouth. Four of the sisters, Christine, Harriet, Lilian and Rosie, moved to Fulham, London sometime in the late 1880s or very early 1890s, when Rosie and Lilian were still in their teens. Christine, the eldest of the four, acted as housekeeper. The other girls became successful, professional artists' models. The sisters posed for such eminent figures as John Everett Millais and James McNeill Whistler. However, Harriet also took up sculpture in London. She produced mainly decorative friezes or panels. Exhibited her work, including at the Royal Glasgow Institute (1893-98). Exhibited works included: An Offering to the Spring, Roses, Jealousy and Adoration of St John. Still active in the 1910s, she later lived in Putney with her widowed mother, Christine and Florence. Only Harriet was working at that stage. She died in Croydon, aged 83.

PHIBBS, NORAH M. - SEE McGUINNESS, N.M.

PHILPOTT, ROSAMOND (1861-1950)
Bookbinder / Book Decorator. Born in Chewton Mendip, Somerset. The daughter of Richard Stammer Philpott and Mary Charlotte. Her father, a Canon of Wells Cathedral, originated from Brighton, Sussex, her mother from London. Rosamond was raised in Chewton Mendip, where her father was vicar of the local church. By at least the early 1890s and into the early 1900s, the family was based in Hammersmith, London. Rosamond was one of at least seven children (Richard, John, Mary Grace, Julia, Charles, Rosamond and Henry). Henry became a Lieutenant in the Royal Navy.

Whilst in London with her family, Rosamond became a teacher of music. Sometime after 1901, however, she moved to Cambridge, and established herself as a bookbinder and decorator, living alone. Indications are that she was a pupil of Francis Longinus Sangorski and George Herbert Sutcliffe. They had a bindery workshop in Bloomsbury, London and taught pupils. They had previously worked with bookbinder and teacher Douglas Cockerell. It is probable that Rosamond taught her own pupils too. She became proficient enough to be noted in Sarah Treverbian Prideaux's volume Modern Bookbindings Their Design and Decoration, London, Archibald Constable & Co., 1906. Prideaux notes that she has 'established herself in Cambridge', and illustrates Philpott's binding for The Church Towers of Somerset. That particular binding was shown at the 1903 Arts and Crafts Exhibition Society exhibition. She showed other works at the Exhibition Society's 1906 exhibition. She also contributed to the Artists at Work Exhibition held at the Grafton Galleries in October 1906. The exhibition was made up of the work of 120 craftsmen and craftswomen. One of her contributions to that particular exhibition was a decorative cover for Lawrence Hope's Indian Love which was illustrated in The Studio, Vol.39, December 1906, p.247. Latterly, Rosamond returned to Somerset, living at Haversham House in Wells. She died there, aged 89.

PHIPPEN, AUBREY PAULINA - SEE EMONET, A.P.

PIATTI, MARIA L. - SEE STEELE, M.L.

PICOT, AVERIL EMILY MARY (1883-1954)
Sculptor. The daughter of George Picot and Nina. Her parents originated from St Helier, Jersey. Averil was one of at least seven children (George, Norman, Averil, Ralph, Dorothy, Grace and Roger). All were born and raised in Leytonstone, Essex, in a house aptly named St Helier's. Averil became a painter and a sculptor of statuettes and medallions in silver. Active for at least 25 years. Exhibited her work, including at the Royal Academy (1916-41) and the Society of Women Artists (1917-24). Exhibited works included: On the Broads, Norfolk, La Jeunesse (statuette), La Meditation (statuette) and Rozel (medallion, silver). Averil died in Essex. In 1955, just after her death, the Averil Picot Scholarship was established. It was founded under her instruction for the purposes of supporting art students.

PIERCE, LUCY ELIZABETH (1887-1950)
Painter / Limoges Enameller. Born and raised in Enfield, Middlesex. The daughter of William George Pierce, a chemist and druggist, and Lucy Schofield. One of at least three children (William, Frederick and Lucy). Frederick became a medical student. William became a chemist's assistant. Lucy studied art. As a student, she won gold and silver medals at the National Competition of Schools of Art held at South Kensington. Based in Enfield throughout her career, and died there. She became a watercolour painter and Limoges enameller. Produced drawings and book illustrations, including for Grimm's Fairy Tales and Omar Khayyam. Paintings included miniatures, portraits, flowers, landscapes, figures and still life.

Pierce exhibited her work, including at the Royal Scottish Academy (1919), the Royal Glasgow Institute (1920-25), the Royal Academy (19 works, 1910-50) and the Society of Women Artists (68 works, 1913-49). Also, with the Royal Institute of Painters in Watercolours, at various provincial galleries and abroad. Exhibited works included: Lace Makers, Bruges, Bergen Fish Market (watercolour), The Night-Piece to Julia and Violets (miniature). Elected an Associate of the Royal Society of Miniature Painters in 1921. Elected an Associate of the Society of Women Artists (1924-40). Works reproduced in The Studio. Two of her watercolours, Interior of an Old Shop and The Bottle Shelf, were purchased by The Wellcome Historical Medical Museum. She remained active until her death.

PILKINGTON, MARGARET (1891-1974)

Painter / Wood Engraver / Woodcut Artist. Born in Salford, Lancashire in November 1891. Died in Macclesfield, Cheshire in 1974, aged 82. The daughter of Lawrence Pilkington (1855-1941) and Mollie (Mary) Stevenson (d.1942). Her father was the co-founder of the Pilkington Lancastrian Pottery and Tile Company at Clifton Junction, Manchester along with his brother, Charles. The business, known for its lustrewares, was successful, enabling the family to live for much of the time at Alderley Edge, Cheshire amongst the affluent. Margaret later became a director of the firm. She had one younger sister, Dorothy (1893-1971). The Pilkington sisters were educated at the Croham Hurst School, Croydon, where Margaret showed an early talent for art. From 1911 until 1913 she studied at the Manchester College of Art. In 1913 she went to London to study at the Slade School of Fine Art, under Henry Tonks, Ambrose McEvoy and Derwent Lees. The following year she moved to the L.C.C. Central School of Arts and Crafts. There, she studied wood engraving under Noel Rooke. Rooke taught a number of women at that time who went on to become exceptional and successful engravers, including Millicent Jackson, Vivien Gribble and Mabel Annesley. Margaret also fell under the influence of Lucien Pissarro.

Her studies were disrupted by the First World War, and Margaret returned to Alderley Edge to live and work as a painter, but primarily as an engraver. She favoured animal subjects, and is also listed as a heraldic designer. Exhibited her work occasionally, though not prolifically given that her career eventually spanned some six decades. Exhibited with the Society of Wood Engravers, at the Manchester Academy of Fine Arts, with the Manchester Society of Modern Painters, at the New English Art Club (certainly in 1916) and the Society of Women Artists (1917). Exhibited works included: Cock and Hen, Ducks and The Spirit of Wilderness. She illustrated a number of books during her career, including Margaret Swanson, Needlecraft for Older Girls (1920) and Katherine Chorley, Hills and Highways (1928). Also illustrated several books by her father, Lawrence Pilkington, including An Alpine Valley and Other Poems (1924), Tattlefold (1926) and The Chimneys of Tattleton (1928). She designed the cover for his last book, Early Climbing Memories (1941).

Margaret also put a deal of time and effort into other aspects of art and design. In 1920 she arranged an exhibition at Houldsworth Hall which proved to be the beginnings of the Red Rose Guild of Artworkers, a northern organization which aimed to promote and exhibit the work of northern craftsmen and craftswomen. Margaret was a founder member of the Guild, which came into existence in January 1921, and acted as Honorary Secretary. She was appointed Chairman in 1927 following the death of Henry Cadness. She was elected a Member of the Society of Wood Engravers, acting as its Honorary Secretary (1924-52) and its Chairman (1952-67). She served on the Council of the Crafts Centre of Great Britain (founded in London in 1947). She was awarded an M.A. by Manchester University in 1942, and was made O.B.E. in 1956. Also acted as Honorary Director of the Whitworth Art Gallery, Manchester (1936-59). In that capacity, she purchased a number of important works for the Gallery, including by Bonington, Munch, Piper, Wheatley, Sutherland and Ravilious. Acted as President of the North West Federation of Museums and Art Galleries from 1945. Elected a Member of the prestigious Art Workers' Guild in 1965.

After her father's death, Margaret continued to live at Alderley Edge with Dorothy. Some of her works were included in an exhibition of women engravers titled Shall We Join the Ladies? held at the Museum of Oxford in October 1979. She was one of only 27 women represented. Noted in Douglas Percy Bliss, A History of Wood-Engraving, London, Spring Books, 1928. One of her woodcuts appeared in Campbell Dodgson's volume Contemporary Woodcuts, London, Duckworth & Co., 1922. The book was a limited edition (500 copies) of modern woodcuts put together by Dodgson to represent the best at that time. Dodgson notes of Margaret Pilkington and Vivien Gribble that they were women artists who 'practised wood engraving with zeal and success'. Papers belonging to Margaret Pilkington can be found in The John Rylands University Library, Manchester. See also: David Blamires, Sarah Hyde & Patricia Jaffe, Margaret Pilkington 1891-1974, Buxton, Hermit Press, c.1995.

PINCOMBE, HELEN (1908-2004)

Potter. Was Edith Helen, known as Helen. Born in India in April 1908. Spent much of her life in England. Died in Cambridge, aged 96. The daughter of William Edwin Pincombe and Helen Martha. Her father was a chief engineer for the Eastern Railways. Educated in Australia. Came to England in 1925 and discovered pottery at the

Camberwell School of Art, also studying at the London County Council Central School of Arts and Crafts. Later became an exhibitioner at the Royal College of Art. But her work was disrupted by the Second World War. The College moved to Ambleside, Cumbria and after taking her Diploma, she was asked to join the staff temporarily to teach pottery. She was inspired by what had previously happened at nearby Burton-in-Lonsdale where slipware had been made over previous centuries. She subsequently set up her own pottery in Oxshott, Surrey, exhibiting her work in England and abroad. In 1956 she held an exhibition with Kathleen Pleydell-Bouverie in London. Elected a Member of the Art Workers' Guild in 1968, and a Committee Member in 1972. Noted in Muriel Rose, Artist Potters in England, London, Faber & Faber, 1970 (first edition 1955). Rose illustrates her squared stoneware jar (1967). Works in the Victoria & Albert Museum, London and in the Eagle Collection, Gateshead Museum.

PINKS, GLADYS ANNIE (1890-1973)

Painter. Born in Brixton in September 1890. The daughter of Edwin Charles Pinks, F.S.I., a surveyor, and Annie Selina. Her parents originated from Surrey. Had an older brother, Edwin, and a younger sister, Elsie. Educated at The Study, London. Studied art at the Grosvenor Studio under Walter Donne (1909-12), and in Paris under Lucien Simon (1912-13). Produced landscapes, still life, figures and portraits in watercolours, oils, chalk and pastels. Particularly known for her portraits of children. Based mainly in London during her career. For part of the time, she worked from The Garden Studio, Bedford Gardens. Exhibited her work over a period of at least 30 years. Exhibited at the Society of Women Artists (1930-58), the Royal Glasgow Institute (1949), the Royal Academy (1939-60), the Royal Institute of Painters in Watercolours, the Women's International Art Club, the Royal Society of Portrait Painters and various provincial galleries. Also exhibited at the Salon des Artistes Francais where, in 1926, she won an Honourable Mention. Exhibited with the Canadian Society of Artists and the Ontario Society of Artists, having spent time visiting her sister in Canada in 1928 and 1948. One of her paintings of Canada, Fishermen's Huts, Ontario, was exhibited at the Society of Women Artists in 1930. Exhibited works included: Deserted and Forlorn, Pink Hydrangea, Child Drawing and Dancer Warming Up (chalk). Several of her works were reproduced. Died in Chelsea, aged 83.

PIPER, ELIZABETH (b.1859)

Etcher / Painter. Born in Bisley, Gloucestershire. The daughter of Solomon and Emma S. Piper. Had a brother, Frederick, two years younger. He later became a clerk. Raised in Gloucestershire at various addresses. Her father, a schoolmaster, originated from Kent, her mother from Bisley. Elizabeth is listed as an art student from at least 1881 whilst still living at home at Winterbourne, Gloucestershire. She studied at the Clifton School of Art in Bristol. Subsequently went to the Royal College of Art, London. Also studied in Belgium and Paris. Won several scholarships. Worked principally as an etcher, but also produced paintings in oils and watercolours.

By at least 1891 Piper was living alone at Oakley Flats, Chelsea, and is listed as a professional artist. In the same flats were artists Beth Amoore, Mary B. Downing and her sister Edith E. Downing. Piper later had a studio in Stanmore, Middlesex. She was particularly known for her exquisitely detailed and accurate etchings of buildings, such as Tower of Two Wardens which was published by W.H. Benyon & Co. of Cheltenham in around 1910. Also produced landscape and interior subjects. Her works were reproduced in a Shakespeare Series for Messrs Henry Graves Ltd, Pall Mall. Also, in the Edinburgh Series for Goupil Ltd, and in the Colleges and Public Schools Series for W.H. Benyon.

Piper's Shakespeare's Hearth was submitted for the Queen's Dolls' House at the invitation of Princess Marie Louise. Exhibited her work, including at the Royal Academy (1897-1903), the Society of Women Artists (1898), the Royal Society of Painter-Etchers & Engravers, the Royal West of England Academy, the Walker Art Gallery, Liverpool and in York, Leeds, America, France and Germany. Exhibited works included: A Lowering Evening on the Thames, Queen Mary's Bedroom, Holyrood Palace, The Sanctuary Knocker, Durham and Bedroom in Which Shakespeare was Born. Elected an Associate of the Royal Society of Painter-Etchers & Engravers, and of the Royal West of England Academy. Also a Member of the Faculty of Arts and of the Lyceum Club. Purchasers of her work included the Leeds Corporation, and the Queen (A Lowering Evening on the Thames).

PISTRUCCI, ELENA & ELISA MARIA (1822-86) & (1824-81)

Gem Engravers / Sculptors. The daughters of Benedetto Pistrucci (1783-1855). He was an Italian gem engraver, sculptor and medallist who originated from Rome and worked in Britain from around 1815. He died in Englefield, Surrey. Pistrucci married Barbara Folchi and had at least six children (one died young), including Elena and Elisa. From around 1816 Pistrucci worked at the Royal Mint, and in 1828 was appointed Chief Medallist. Records indicate that Elena was born in England, but Elisa was born in Rome. Both list their address as the Royal Mint for a number of years.

Both Elena and Elisa became cameo-engravers, probably trained by their father. Elena exhibited some of her work at the British Institution between 1847 and 1848, including Head of a Nymph (in German agate) and Head of a Bacchante. Jointly, the Pistrucci sisters exhibited 40 examples of their work at the Society of Women Artists in 1858. Those consisted of works in wax and of cameos in sardonyx, jasper, chalcedony and agate. Cameos exhibited there included Head of Flora, Head of Psyche and Head of Bacchus. Other exhibits included coin designs such as St George and the Dragon. Some of their works were copies of designs by their father, including a medal for the Royal Humane Society. Elisa made a cameo portrait of her father, and exhibited a sardonyx cameo of the Death of Adonis at the 1862 International Exhibition.

PITMAN, ROSIE MARGARET McLEAN (1868-1947)

Painter / Illustrator. Also known as Rose. Born in Prestwich, Manchester. The daughter of Henry Pitman, a reporter and occasional teacher in phonography, and Helen. One of at least seven children (May, Flora, Frederick, Rose, Lily, Percy and Violet). Raised in Prestwich, in Altrincham and in Burnage, Lancashire. Percy Pitman became a hydraulics engineer. Violet (1876-1964) became a fashion artist. However, she appeared to give up her work on her marriage in 1904 to William Frederick Wilkinson Rhodes. He was a solicitor. Violet died in Yorkshire. Rose became a book illustrator and a painter of various subjects. During her career, she was based in Halifax, Manchester, Derbyshire and London. Worked for publishers including Macmillan. Books illustrated by Rose included: The Countess of Jersey, Maurice, or the Red Jar (Macmillan, 1894), F. De la Motte Fouque, Undine (63 illustrations and decor, Macmillan, 1897), Mrs Molesworth, Magic Nuts (Macmillan, 1898) and Ruby Ring (Macmillan, 1904). Also contributed to Quarto (1896).

Pitman exhibited her work occasionally, including at the Royal Academy (1894-97), the Royal Scottish Academy (1884-86), the Royal Glasgow Institute (1902) and in Liverpool and Manchester. Exhibited works included: Dunham Park, Cheshire and Vegetarian Diet. Noted in R.E.D. Sketchley, English Book Illustration of To-day, London, Kegan Paul, 1903. Also noted in Mahony, Latimer & Folmsbee, Illustrators of Children's Books 1744-1945, Boston, The Horn Book Inc., 1947. In 1905 Rose married Frederick William Albert Heine (b.1867) in Herefordshire. In 1911 she is no longer listed in census recordings or local directories as an artist, and is listed as her mother's companion. Rose died in Yorkshire, aged 78.

PLEYDELL-BOUVERIE, KATHLEEN HARRIOT DUNCOMBE (1895-1985)

Pottery Worker. Born in Coleshill, Highworth, Wiltshire in June 1895. The daughter of the Hon. D. Pleydell-Bouverie. Requested to become a student at St Ives, Cornwall under Bernard Leach (1887-1979) after seeing his work in an exhibition in 1923. But she was, at first, refused. So she went to study at the Central School of Arts and Crafts, London where Dora Billington was teaching pottery. In 1924 she joined Leach's pottery, at a time when Shoji Hamada and Tsurunoske Matsubayashi were there. Norah Braden arrived shortly after, and Michael Cardew was there too. Kathleen left St Ives in 1925, moving back to Coleshill, Wiltshire where she was born. There, at The Mill, she established her own pottery workshop, and in 1928 Norah Braden joined her. They worked together for eight years, producing mainly unglazed pots and bowls for plants. Braden left Coleshill in 1936. Kathleen carried on alone until 1940, when war had started.

In 1946 Kathleen moved to Kilmington Manor in Wiltshire, where she built an oil-fired kiln. Unlike Braden, Kathleen used brush decoration. Still working into the 1950s. Died in Warminster, Wiltshire in January 1985. Exhibited her work occasionally, including with the Society of Women Artists (1928). Also, with the Red Rose Guild of Designer Craftsmen (founded 1921), of which she was a Member. Held an exhibition of stoneware with Norah Braden at Mr Paterson's Gallery in 1930. Their work was described in Apollo, 1930, p.81 as 'chaste in form, beautiful in glaze, restrained in colour'. Exhibits on that occasion included bowls, jars and bottles in subdued colours, in browns, greens and greys. Some of Kathleen's work was illustrated in Muriel Rose, Artist Potters in England, London, Faber & Faber, 1955 (revised 1970), chiefly a stoneware jar (1930) and two stoneware bowls (c.1932), the latter owned by the University College of Wales, Aberystwyth. Other purchasers of her work included the Victoria & Albert Museum, London and the Contemporary Art Society. See also, Artwork 6, No.24, 1930, N. Braden and K. Pleydell-Bouverie, English Stoneware Pottery by W.A. Thorpe. Also, Apollo 38, December 1943, K. Pleydell-Bouverie and D.K.N. Braden, Studio Potters of Coleshill, Wiltshire by Ernest Marsh. Works in the Royal Cornwall Museum, Truro, Cornwall. An example of her thrown and turned stoneware is in the Cheltenham Collections. SEE: BRADEN, DOROTHY KATHLEEN NORAH

POCOCK, HILDA JOYCE - SEE STEWART, H.J.

POCOCK, JULIA - SEE STEWART, H.J.

POCOCK, LILIAN JOSEPHINE (1883-1974)
Painter / Illustrator / Stained Glass Artist. Born in London in May 1883. Part of a family of distinguished artists which included Lexden Lewis Pocock (her father), Alicia J. Shellshear (her mother), Hilda Stewart (her sister), Alfred Lyndhurst Pocock (her brother) and Julia Pocock (her aunt). One of at least eight children, all raised in London. Initially attended the Royal Academy schools. Then went to the Regent Street Polytechnic, London in the late 1890s and early 1900s. She won prizes in the National Competition of Schools of Art in 1899, 1904, 1905 and 1906 for stained glass designs. In 1906 she began studying at the London County Council Central School of Arts and Crafts, specialising in stained glass. There, she studied under Christopher Whall (1849-1924), Karl Parsons (1884-1934) and Alfred Drury (of Lowndes & Drury). In 1907 one of her cartoons and one of her stained glass panels were illustrated in the Art Journal (p.272).

Lilian left the Central School in around 1910. For a short time, she became assistant to Karl Parsons who was then working on a series of windows for Capetown Cathedral. She subsequently worked from a studio at home in Blomfield Road, Maida Vale, and later (from 1924) at Warwick Avenue, also London. She continued to use Lowndes & Drury in the actual execution of her stained glass. Pocock completed her first church window in 1915 for St Christopher & St Nicholas, Little Marlow, Buckinghamshire. Shortly after, she produced three large windows for Tonbridge School Chapel, Kent (including St Denis), a complete scheme for Wilton Church near Hawick, Scotland, and five windows for the Catholic Apostolic Church in Gordon Square, London.

Pocock worked consistently until her eyesight began to fail in her latter years. Other stained glass commissions included for, for example, Dryfesdale Church, Lockerbie and Christ as the Good Samaritan for Llanfachraeth Parish Church (single-light, 1918). Later works included a single-light window for Queen Alexandra's Hospital Home Chapel, Gifford House, Worthing, Sussex (1946). Also a gifted watercolour artist and book illustrator. Her watercolour paintings included The Return of the Spies and A Romance. Produced book illustrations for, for example, E.E. Holmes, In Praise of Legend (1913) and And Mary Sings Magnificat (1915). Illustrated her own volume of poems, December on the Downs, De La More Press, 1939.

Lilian exhibited her work, including at the Royal Scottish Academy (1924-25), the Society of Women Artists (1908-24), the Royal Academy (1908-41), at the International Exhibition in 1913 and at the Paris International Exhibition of 1914. Also, with the Arts and Crafts Exhibition Society. At their 1916 exhibition, she showed, among other things, a drawing titled The Adoration of the Magi which was illustrated in The Studio, Vol.70, February 1917 in a review of the exhibition. Elected a Member of the Arts and Crafts Exhibition Society. Elected an Associate of the Society of Women Artists (1909-11). Works included in an exhibition Women Stained Glass Artists of the Arts and Crafts Movement held at the William Morris Gallery, London, 1985-86. SEE: STEWART, HILDA J.

POLUNIN, ELIZABETH VIOLET (1887-1950)
Painter / Scenery and Costume Designer. Born in Ashford, Kent in May 1887. The daughter of Stephen Hart, a farmer. Educated at St Swithin's, Winchester. Studied at Colarossi's in Paris, at Lucien Simon's School, the Ecole des Beaux-Arts, Paris, at Leon Bakst's School, St Petersburg and under Walter Sickert at the Westminster School of Art, London. Was a bronze medallist as a student. Became a portrait painter and a scenery and costume designer. She worked as a scene painter to Serge Diaghilev's Russian ballet. Sometime just before 1911, she married Vladimir Polunin (1880-1957). He originated from Moscow, but worked in London as a decorative and stage designer. He was also a teacher at the Slade School, London and a designer for Sir T. Beecham's opera and Diaghilev's Russian ballet. They had three sons and one daughter. The couple lived in Reading, Chiswick in London and Petersfield, Hampshire. Elizabeth died in

Kensington, aged 72. Polunin died a few years later, in Surrey, aged 76.

Elizabeth exhibited her work, including at the Royal Academy (1924-41), the Society of Women Artists (1940), the Royal Society of Portrait Painters, the New English Art Club (from 1917), with the London Group and the Royal Society of British Artists. She held two one-woman shows at the Claridge Gallery. Exhibited works included: Daphne Austen, Professor Constable and Anthony Crossley, Esq., M.P. Other works included portraits of Diaghilev and Chaliapin. The Victoria & Albert Museum, London purchased some of her costume designs. She produced the decor and costumes for The Snow Maiden at Sadler's Wells.

POPE, HILDA CHANCELLOR (1912-84)

Painter / Decorative Artist / Puppet Maker. Born in Catford, London in December 1912. The daughter of John Chancellor Pope. Educated in Catford. Studied at Bromley under painter and mural decorator Herbert Ashwin Budd between 1928 and 1932. Also, at Beckenham under Henry Carr, and under Sir William Rothenstein at the Royal College of Art, London between 1932 and 1935. Elected an Associate of the Royal College of Art. Awarded a Travelling Scholarship. Produced paintings of landscapes and other subjects in watercolours and tempera. Worked as a mural decorator and a puppet maker. Also worked as a freelance art teacher.

In 1939 Hilda married Edward H.D. Scott in Bromley, Kent. Scott was a cabinet designer and craftsman. They had at least one son. The couple lived near Andover in Hampshire, and near Woking in Surrey for a time. Hilda died in Bromley, Kent, aged 72. She exhibited her work, including at the Royal Scottish Academy (1956) and the Royal Academy (28 works, 1949-68). Also, with the New English Art Club, at the Royal Institute Galleries, at the Whitechapel Art Gallery, with the Bromley Art Club, at the Goupil Gallery, the Graves Art Gallery in Sheffield, with the Kent Art Society, in Southampton, with the Andover Art Society and at the American Institute of Architecture. Pope executed a mural painting for the Dome of Discovery at the 1951 Festival of Britain. Exhibited works included: Threshing in Hampshire, Blossom in the Churchyard, The Flower Stall and Over the Roof-Tops, Guildford. Elected a Member of the American Institute of Architecture Club. Works in the collections of the Graves Art Gallery, Sheffield and the University of London.

POPHAM, ROSALIND - SEE THORNYCROFT, R.

PORTER, MURIEL G. - SEE VALLIS, M.G.

PORTWAY, HEBE - SEE COX, H.

POTT, CONSTANCE MARY (1862-1957)

Painter / Etcher. Born in West Wickham, Kent. The daughter of Henry Pott (1828-1910) and Constance (1836-1915). Based in London throughout much of her life and career, mainly at Cornwall Gardens, South Kensington. Still living with her widowed mother in her 40s. One of a large family of up to nine children. One of her brothers, Francis, became a medical student. Indications are that Constance studied at South Kensington, and was also possibly a pupil of C.W. Sherborn. Produced etchings, paintings in oils and watercolours and bookplates. Subjects included landscapes, buildings and figures. She was particularly known for her soft ground etchings.

Pott exhibited her work, including at the Royal Academy (1897-1922), the Society of Women Artists (1893-94) and with the Royal Society of Painter-Etchers and Engravers. Exhibited works included: Worcester Cathedral (etching), Southampton Water (etching), East Cliff, Hastings (etching) and St Benet's Abbey, Norfolk. Her work was noted in several major publications during her career. In 1901 The Studio, Vol.23, June, p.18 reproduced one of her etchings, Study of Willows, in an article Recent Etching and Engraving. In 1909 some of her work was reproduced in Sarah T. Prideaux's volume Aquatint Engraving: A Chapter in the History of Book Illustration, London, Duckworth & Co. In 1911 one of her works was illustrated in an article The Royal College of Art Engraving School by Malcolm C. Salaman which appeared in The Studio, May, pp.280-290. Later, in 1930, Pott was noted in Frank L. Emanuel's volume Etching and Etchings, London, Pitman & Sons. Emanuel noted her to be a Member of the Royal Society of Painter-Etchers and Engravers. Pott died at the age of 94, and was still living at Cornwall Gardens at the time of her death.

POULTER, DIANA J. - SEE MURPHY, D.J.

POWELL, ADA LOUISE (1882-1956)

Embroideress / Dress Designer / Ceramic Designer / Furniture Decorator / Artist. Known as Louise. The granddaughter of French-born Emile Lessore, the renowned decorator of Wedgwood pottery in the mid-nineteenth century. He also worked briefly for Minton. The daughter of marine painter and Royal Academy exhibitor Jules A. Lessore and Ada. Louise was born and raised in Southwick, West Sussex. She had a sister, Elaine Therese Lessore (1884-1945), who became an embroideress and painter, who also co-founded the London Group, and who worked as a designer for Wedgwood in the 1920s. Their brother, Frederick Lessore (1879-1951), became a sculptor, a Member of the Art Workers' Guild and winner of the medal of the Royal Academy schools in 1906. Their aunt, artist Therese Lessore, was also a painter and designer for Wedgwood in the 1870s. Louise studied at the L.C.C. Central School of Arts and Crafts in London (c.1900-06), at that time under W.R. Lethaby. She exhibited at the National Competition of Schools of Art. In 1900 she showed designs for four dessert plates which were illustrated in The Studio, Vol.20, 1900, p.65. In 1906 she showed a book illumination and an embroidered book cover. She became a talented and diverse artist involved in various areas of the decorative arts.

In 1906 Louise married architect / designer Alfred Hoare Powell (1865-1960) in London. He originated from Berkshire. Sometime in the early 1900s, around 1903, Alfred Powell had begun to design for Wedgwood, and from around 1905 he and Louise worked together for the pottery manufacturer, employed specifically to develop its art wares. They remained associated with the firm until 1940, with Louise designing both shapes and decoration. By the 1920s, at least 50 of their designs were in production at Wedgwood. Louise was also a gifted calligrapher and book decorator, decorating books by lettering expert and bookbinder Alfred Fairbank. Also worked on several commissions with Graily Hewitt, including two incomplete Morris manuscripts. Louise was elected a Member of the respected Society of Scribes and Illuminators (founded 1921) in 1921. She also sat on its committee. Exhibited some of her illuminations at the 1906 Arts and Crafts Exhibition Society exhibition, held at the Grafton Galleries. One of her illuminations, taken from The Gospel of Peace and executed on purple vellum, was illustrated in The Studio, Vol.56, June 1912, p.52 in an article Some Modern Illuminations (pp.45-58).

During their marriage, the Powells divided their time between London, Stoke-upon-Trent and Stroud, Gloucestershire. Their associations with Gloucestershire brought them into contact with Ernest Gimson and the Barnsley brothers, who were part of what became known as the Cotswold School. Louise painted furniture made by various members of the School, but particularly Ernest Gimson and Sidney Barnsley. In 1916 she laid out a room at that year's Arts and Crafts exhibition, which included 12 panels painted in egg tempera, mounted on a plaster frieze designed and modelled by Ernest Gimson. Louise completed other furniture projects, and on occasions worked in collaboration with Diana Hornby, daughter of C.H. St John Hornby. One of their joint projects was the design and decoration of a suite of bedroom furniture. C.H. St John Hornby was a craftsman and patron of the Arts and Crafts movement, supporting, among others, Gimson. Grace Barnsley, daughter of Sidney Barnsley, trained as a decorator of pottery with the Powells. The Powells had set up a studio for ceramic painting in around 1904, in Millwall, before moving to Red Lion Square, London. They concentrated on lustre and underglaze painting, and were instrumental in reviving the employment of freelance decoration by Wedgwood of Staffordshire. They ran the studio until 1939. The Powells were also responsible for training decorators at Wedgwood, including Millicent Taplin and Star Wedgwood. Taplin worked for the firm into the 1950s.

Louise also executed exquisite embroidery and needlework, some of which was exhibited at the 1906 Arts and Crafts Exhibition Society exhibition. An embroidered bag by Louise, owned by Mrs C.H. St John Hornby, was illustrated in the Art Journal in 1907 (p.322) as part of an article Some Modern Embroideries by R.E.D. Sketchley (pp.321-326). The same journal, same edition (p.378), also illustrated an altar frontal for St Andrew's Church, Monkwearmouth, Sunderland designed by Louise and worked by her and Frances Channer. The church is described in 1907 as 'recently consecrated'. The frontal was worked in silks on a Morris silk damask in reds, blues and greens. The Powells exhibited their work regularly with the Arts and Crafts Exhibition Society, not only in 1906 but in 1910, when they showed, among other items, a two-handled jar designed by Louise. At the 1912 exhibition, they showed more pottery, including mugs, vases, bowls, dishes, jardinieres and china napkin rings, painted by Alfred and Louise and executed by J. Wedgwood & Sons. At the 1916 Arts and Crafts exhibition, they showed a painted ebony and walnut cabinet designed by Louise and executed by Louise and Sidney Barnsley. The large decorative piece had seven drawers and was illustrated in The Studio, Vol.69, January 1917. The Powells also exhibited more pottery on that occasion, some of which was illustrated in the same edition of The Studio (p.191). Items shown on that occasion included a blue and white jar, a lustre jug with an oak tree design and a round dish decorated with a stag design, all of which were displayed in a case.

In the same year, Alfred Powell was elected to the Art Workers' Guild, and acted as a Committee Member between 1918 and 1920. In late 1919 the Powells exhibited pottery at the Twenty-One Gallery, London. In 1922 they held another exhibition of their pottery at the Brook Street Art Gallery, London. Louise exhibited various handicrafts at the Society of Women Artists in 1909 and 1924. Louise died in London in September 1956. Alfred Powell died in London in May 1960. SEE: LESSORE, ELAINE THERESE; SEE: BARNSLEY, GRACE

POWER, ANNIE ISABEL (1873-1960)

Bookbinder. Born in Whitby, Yorkshire. The daughter of Henry Power, a surgeon, and Ann. Her father originated from Nance, France, her mother from Whitby. One of at least six children (Darcy, Alice, Francis, Lucy, Hilda and Annie), with records suggesting possibly three more. Annie may have been Anastasia. Raised partly in London. Became a pupil of Douglas Cockerell (1870-1945), who taught a number of women the art of bookbinding in London. Cockerell was the author of Bookbinding and the Care of Books and Some Notes on Bookbinding, and taught bookbinding at the London County Council Central School of Arts and Crafts. Power then set up a workshop in Museum Street, London with Sylvia Stebbing, also a pupil of Cockerell. They purchased their own presses, tools and supplies. Virginia Woolf (then Stephen) became a friend of Stebbing and undertook a few lessons in binding at their workshop. Power took on pupils to earn additional income.

Power subsequently went on to work for Charles R. Ashbee (1863-1942). For a number of years, she had ties with Ashbee's Guild of Handicraft, and took charge of the Essex House Bindery which ran in conjunction with Ashbee's Essex House Press (1898-1909). Opened in around 1902, the Bindery was based at Chipping Campden, Gloucestershire, Ashbee having left London for the countryside. Books of all types were bound there in various leathers, with ebony, rose and holly woods as well as silver and enamels used in the designs. Most of the designs were by Ashbee. Annie Power also trained workers at the Bindery. She was assisted in her work by Edgar Green, and by Nellie Binning and Lottie Eatley. Nellie Binning may have been related to Tom Binning who had worked at the Kelmscott Press until 1898, when workers and presses had been transferred to the Essex House

Press, and Lottie Eatley may have been related to Dick Eatley, pressman.

At Chipping Campden, Power lived in a small cottage. Sylvia Stebbing visited her there. However, Power had a dispute with Janet Ashbee, and when she married artist George Frederick Loosely (1864-1934) in Whitby in 1905, she left the Guild, but continued to work in bookbinding. She remained in Chipping Campden for a few years, using her own studio, then moved back to Whitby, then to London before settling at The Firs in Kings Langley, Hertfordshire. She died in Hertfordshire in December 1960, aged 86.

Power exhibited her work occasionally, showing bindings at the Arts and Crafts Exhibition Society's 1903 (seventh) exhibition. She was possibly the A. Power who exhibited two 'handicrafts' at the Society of Women Artists in 1901 (address given as Russell Street, London). As Mrs Loosely she exhibited at the Society of Women Artists between 1907 and 1931, showing well over 75 items. She was elected an Associate of the Society (1913-18) and a Member (1919-32). A cabinet designed by Ashbee and kept in the Victoria & Albert Museum, London, has leatherwork decoration executed by Power. The cabinet was shown at the Arts and Crafts Exhibition Society's 1906 (eighth) exhibition. The cabinet has been dated approximately 1905.

Power's work included bindings for Blake's Jerusalem, now in the British Library, and for Coleridge's Rime of the Ancient Mariner. Another of her bindings, for Maud I. Croft's Women Under English Law (1925), was bound for Queen Mary and was in the Royal Library at Windsor. One of her more prestigious bindings was for The History of St Bartholomew's Hospital by Sir D'Arcy Power, K.B.E., F.R.C.S. The Governors of the Hospital presented it to the King in 1924, on the 800th anniversary of the founding of St Bartholomew's. The binding was illustrated in The Studio, Vol.89, June 1925, p.330.

In 1925, Power held a one-woman show of her work. She was also a Member of the Panton Club. In 1906, she was mentioned in Sarah T. Prideaux's volume Modern Bindings Their Design and Decoration, London, Archibald Constable & Co. Prideaux notes that Miss Power had been recently responsible 'in the main' for the Essex House execution of designs by Ashbee for bindings. Despite a full career, Power had two children, Anne (1906-92) and George H.H. (1916-2000). Anne became a successful textile designer. SEE: LOOSELY, ANNE

POWER, MAY (1904-post-1961)

Sculptor / Painter. Was Mary Elisabeth Power, known as May. Born in Dublin in September 1904. The daughter of sculptor Albert George Power (1883-1945), a Royal Hibernian Academician. Educated privately. Studied at the Royal Irish Academy of Music. Studied sculpture under her father, and at Dublin's National College of Art under Oliver Sheppard, R.H.A., and John Keating, R.H.A. Produced mainly portrait works, figures and busts in plaster and bronze. Also produced watercolour paintings. Signed her work 'May Power'. Based in Dublin throughout her career, mostly at Geraldine Street. Taught at the Academy of Christian Art, Dublin (1939-45). Exhibited at the Royal Hibernian Academy (19 works, 1933-61). Also contributed to the Oireachtas Exhibition, Dublin, and to the Sport in Art Exhibition held at the Victoria & Albert Museum, London in 1948. Held a one-woman show in Dublin in 1938. Exhibited works included: Fatigued (plaster), The Late Miss Annie Lord, F.R.I.A.M., The Late Count Plunkett and Father William (portrait bust). Of the same family was sculptor James Power, who also exhibited at the Royal Hibernian Academy (1940-74).

POWNALL, MARY - SEE BROMET, M.

PRESTEL, MARIA CATHARINE (c.1744-94)

Engraver. The wife of German painter and engraver John Gotlieb Prestel. She assisted him in his work, particularly on his landscapes. However, the marriage did not last. In 1786 she moved to England alone. There, she engraved prints which were widely praised. She executed etchings and finished in aquatint in a picturesque manner. She died in London. Noted in Mrs E.F. Ellet's Women Artists in All Ages and Countries, London, Bentley, 1859.

PRICE, ELEANOR CHILTON (1901-85)

Etcher / Designer / Leatherworker. Born in Bath, Somerset in March 1901. The daughter of John Chilton Price, a commercial traveller in leather, and Lucy. Her parents originated from Salop. Had at least one sibling, Mary Chilton Price. Raised in Bath. Educated at a private secondary school there. Studied at the Bath School of Art and at the Bristol School of Art. Studied etching at the latter. As a student, won a scholarship of £5 and a Maintenance Grant of £20. Won a First Prize for a cretonne design in the Textile Recorder competition. Worked in various areas of the decorative arts. Early in her career, she worked as a wallpaper stenciller and furniture painter.

Designed Christmas cards, calendars and leatherwork for E.W. Savory Ltd of Bristol. Designed posters, one of which was sold to the Health and Cleanliness Council. Executed showcards for local firms during the Bath shopping week. Drew fish for the Bristol Zoo Aquarium. Exhibited some of her etchings with the Bath Society of Artists. Also exhibited with the Royal Society of Arts. She had an interest in legend and folklore, which may have inspired her work. Worked in Bath, but died in South Glamorgan, Wales, aged 84.

PRIDEAUX, SARAH TREVERBIAN (1853-1933)

Bookbinder / Book Decorator. One of Britain's first true professional women bookbinders and decorators. Born in London. The daughter of Walter Prideaux and Elizabeth. Her father, a solicitor, businessman and Clerk to the Goldsmiths' Company, originated from Devon. Her mother was the daughter of General Sherburne Williams of Cattsfield near Battle, Sussex. The Prideaux family had a house, Faircrouch, at Wadhurst, Sussex and lived at Goldsmiths' Hall in London. Sarah spent time in Sussex and in London. She had at least two siblings, Ada and Arthur. Initially, she was educated at home. In 1877, aged 23, she entered Newnham College, Cambridge, but stayed only a short time, returning home to look after her ailing father. He died in 1889. Before his death, Sarah taught English alongside Octavia Hill at a school run by Hill's sister Miranda in Marylebone, London.

In the late 1880s, around the age of 35, Sarah took up bookbinding whilst living with her mother and five servants at Norfolk Square, London. For a short time, she worked with friend and fellow bookbinder Olive Macmillan near the Strand. In 1888 she began lessons with Joseph Zaehnsdorf in London. Also went to Paris for lessons at Leon Gruel's. By the early 1890s, she had established herself independently in London, at Norfolk Square. By the time of her death, in March 1933, she was living at Hornton Street, Kensington and left a considerable sum of more than £14,000 in her will. At the time Prideaux was first active, women were still excluded from bookbinding classes held at the London County Council Central School of Arts and Crafts. So Prideaux took on her own pupils, Elizabeth MacColl, Katharine Adams and Maude Nathan. Adams was particularly successful and went on to establish the Eadburgha Bindery at Broadway, Worcestershire in 1909. MacColl and Nathan experienced similar success as independent bookbinders, their work noted and praised in leading arts journals of the day.

Prideaux also played a role in the founding of the Guild of Women Binders in around 1897. The Guild was formed following the success of the Exhibition of Women's Bindings held in London in 1897. The Guild initially comprised some 67 women from around the country. They not only exhibited their work, but aimed to reject mechanical design and to promote originality. In 1900 Prideaux and Adams printed A Catalogue of Books Bound by S.T. Prideaux Between 1890 and 1900, with 26 illustrations. Prideaux became a leading authority on her subject and produced a number of books of technical, historical and academic value. Those included An Historical Sketch of Bookbinding (London, Lawrence & Bullen, 1893) and Bookbinders and Their Craft (London, Zaehnsdorf, 1903). In her 1906 volume Modern Bookbindings Their Design and Decoration (London, Archibald Constable & Co.) Prideaux revealed the extent of her knowledge of the history of British and French bookbinding.

In 1909 Prideaux wrote with equal expertise on Aquatint Engraving: A Chapter in the History of Book Illustration (London, Duckworth & Co.). The volume was advertised in The Studio in 1910, priced 15s, and contained illustrations of the works of Constance M. Pott, R.E. All Prideaux's literary endeavours contained her trademark double acorn above her initials. As early as 1891, Prideaux had contributed an introduction to the catalogue for an exhibition of bookbindings held by the Burlington Fine Arts Club in 1891, revealing her already burgeoning talents as a binder and a writer. She was more than familiar with the Arts and Crafts movement, and might best be described as an Arts and Crafts craftswoman, following in the mode of Morris, Ashbee and others who adopted the basic principles of quality hand work, quality materials and artistic excellence.

By 1900 Prideaux had executed designs for at least 175 bindings, the number rising to around 300 in total, with some repeat designs. One of those was a binding for Autres Poesies (P. Villon, London, 1901). In 1902 she executed a red goatskin binding, gold-tooled, for Omar Khayyam's The Rubaiyat (Vale Press, 1901). Other books bound by Prideaux included Matthew Arnold's Selected Poems (1893), Ralph Caldecott's The Owls of Olynn Belfry (London, 1886), Cyril Davenport's The Cantor Lectures on Jewellery (bound 1903) and Michael Field's Fair Rosamund (Vale Press, 1899). Produced a binding for a copy of her own Bookbinders and Their Craft (1903) for Samuel Putnam Avery, now in the Spencer Collection, New York Public

Library. Although she mostly worked her own designs, Prideaux did a small number of bindings to the designs of others. Those included D.S. MacColl, brother to Elizabeth, her former pupil. For MacColl, she executed bindings for, for example, Andrew Lang's Grass of Parnassus, Walter Pater's The Renaissance and D.G. Rossetti's Poems which was illustrated in the Art Journal, 1896, p.148.

Prideaux exhibited her work occasionally. For example, in 1893 when she sent leather and embroidered velvet bindings to the World's Columbian Exposition in Chicago. In 1896 she gave a series of lectures on The History and Ornament of Bookbinding to the Ladies' Department of King's College, London. In 1899 she took charge of designing and producing the King's College Magazine for the Ladies' Department. Along with her friend Mabel Winkworth (Mrs Lamb) she acted as director of the Women's Printing Society, a co-operative women's press based at 66 Whitcomb Street, London, where the magazine was printed. Prideaux always supported education for women, and had an interest in photography. She wrote numerous articles on bookbinding in the 1890s, for journals such as the Magazine of Art. Compiled a Bibliography of Works Relating to Bookbinding published in The Bookbinder in 1888, and in The Library in 1892. Some of her writings were published in America too.

Prideaux was noted in an article British Tooled Bookbindings and Their Designs in The Studio, Vol.18, Special No., 1899-1900. There it is stated she was 'the first woman book-binder in this country' (p.44). The journal also describes her work as intelligent, refined and thoughtful in design and craftsmanship, with a fine feeling for material and a deft and efficient use of tools. It was noted that her volume on bookbinding was a standard history of the craft and widely used. The article included illustrations of her bindings for The Tale of the Emperor and a volume of Percy Bysshe Shelley. Prideaux remained in contact with Katharine Adams, and Adams wrote a tribute to her former teacher after her death, which was printed in a limited edition of 25 copies with the title Sarah Prideaux: A Pupil's Tribute published by the Bancroft Library Press. Adams also wrote an obituary titled In Memoriam for The Times in tribute to Prideaux.

PRINCE, LORNA B. - SEE KELL, L.B.

PRINCEP, AMY ELISE (1878-1950)
Designer / Etcher / Painter / Embroideress / Jewellery Worker. Born and raised in Bristol. The

daughter of John Walter Princep, a timber merchant, and Elise. One of at least three children (Amy, Janet and Martha). Educated at the Clarendon College, Clifton, Bristol. Studied in Clifton, and at the Royal College of Art, London. Awarded an Art Masters' Teaching Certificate in 1908. Elected an Associate of the Royal College of Art in 1912. As a student, she won a prize for light and shade in 1904, and the King's Prize for life painting in 1908. In 1909 she was awarded a student in training scholarship at the Royal College of Art. Produced paintings in watercolours, designs, etchings, embroideries and decorative jewellery. Acted as an art mistress for intermediate schools in Glamorgan, Wales. Also acted as a part-time assistant in Clifton and elsewhere. Based mainly in Bristol and Glamorgan during her career, but died in Weston-super-Mare, Somerset, aged 72. Exhibited her work, including at the Society of Women Artists (1930-31), with the Royal West of England Academy, the South Wales Art Society and at the National Eisteddfod, Swansea in 1926. Exhibited works included: Chipping Campden, Gloucestershire and Fowey, Cornwall. Dame Margaret Lloyd George purchased her etching of Chipping Campden.

PRINGLE, SYBIL NORAH (b.1913)
Metalworker / Designer. Born in Barrow-in-Furness, Lancashire in November 1913. The daughter of John Pringle. Educated privately. Studied at the Edinburgh College of Art between 1939 and 1942 under Hubert Lindsay Wellington, then at the same college under Robert Lyon between 1942 and 1943, and 1946 to 1947. Also studied under painter and stained glass artist Herbert Hendrie, Head of Design at the Edinburgh College of Art, and under Charles Creswick. Awarded a B.A. (Edin.) in 1943. Awarded a postgraduate scholarship. Became an artist in silver, copper and brass. Based in Newcastle for part of her career. Exhibited her work at the Enterprise Scotland exhibition of 1947, with the Society of Scottish Artists, the Scottish Society of Women Artists and at Outlook Tower. Work reproduced in Decorative Art 1943-48. Married Eric Fenwick sometime prior to 1952.

PROUDFOOT, IVY H. - SEE GARDNER, I.H.

PROUDMAN, MAUREEN PATEY (1906-88)
Painter / Engraver / Designer. Born in Birkenhead, Cheshire in May 1906. The daughter of Percy George Patey Eyre (1866-1914) and Mabel Beatrice (d.1958). Her father was a pensioned insurance secretary. Maureen was raised in Birkenhead. Educated at Godolphin, Salisbury. Studied at the British Academy in Rome under Professor Lipinski. Also studied at the Royal College of Art, London under Sir William Rothenstein and Professor Ernest W. Tristram. Elected an Associate of the Royal College of Art. Became a painter in oils and tempera, an engraver and a designer of posters, textiles, china, book jackets and carpets. Exhibited her work, including in Rome and Simla, at the Leicester Galleries, the Walker Art Gallery, Liverpool, various smaller provincial galleries and at Burlington House. Works included a 70ft poster for Messrs Yardley Industrial Works (1931). Also, a poster for Jodhpur Fort for the Indian State Railways used as a cover of a magazine (1937). Maureen married Philip Arthur Proudman (d.1951) and had two sons. In 1974 she married again, to Ernest W. Lovely, in Romsey, Hampshire. She also spent time during her career in Roehampton, London. She died in Winchester, Hampshire, aged 82.

PROUT, EDITH MARY (1862-1927)
Painter. Born in December 1862 in Plymouth, Devon. The daughter of Henry Ebenezer Prout, a pianoforte and music seller, and Emily. One of at least six children (Ernest, Harry, Edith, Beatrice, Ethel and Victor), all born between 1859 and 1872. Educated at home. Raised in Plymouth and remained there with her parents until at least 1901, aged 39. The family had relatives in Cornwall, and Edith later moved there, living at Newquay. Died in St Columb, Cornwall in September 1927, aged 65. Became a seascape and landscape painter in oils and watercolours. May have studied locally or privately. Exhibited at the Royal Birmingham Society of Artists and with the Old Dudley Art Society. At the Society of Women Artists, she exhibited two works in 1906 and 1907, Toilers of the Sea and Once More 'tis Eventide. Other works included: Rocky Valley, Tintagel and Slate Quarry, Tintagel. Works reproduced in Paris in Revue Moderne, including a study of Mother Ivy's Bay. Falmouth Polytechnic acquired her Rough Sea.

PUGHE, BUDDIG ANWYLINI (1857-1939)
Painter. Born in December 1857 in Aberdovey, Wales. The daughter of John Pughe, a surgeon, and Catherine. Her mother died young, and her father married again, to Maria. Buddig was one of a large family, possibly one of up to 10 children. She grew up in Wales and spent much

of her life there. Studied at the Liverpool School of Art under Finnie, and in Paris and Rome. A silver medallist at South Kensington. Returned to Wales, but spent some time in London in the early 1920s. Also maintained ties with Liverpool, dying there in early 1939, aged 81. In Wales, she spent time living at Rossetti House, Aberdovey as well as at Towyn and elsewhere. Produced mainly landscapes and portraits. One of her works was a study of Liverpool Cathedral which was acquired by the Liverpool Art Gallery. Buddig travelled to paint, visiting Bruges, France, Spain, Venice, Switzerland and elsewhere. Also painted in Britain, producing studies of Wales, Warwickshire and elsewhere.

Pughe exhibited frequently at the Walker Art Gallery, Liverpool. Also exhibited at the Royal Academy (1886-1917), the Royal Hibernian Academy (1912-20), the Society of Women Artists (1901-24), the Royal Institute of Painters in Watercolours and elsewhere. Exhibited works included: Miss Bolton, Coronation Day, Caernarvon, The Drink-Shop, Moonlight and Blue Flowers in the Tyrol. A number of her works were reproduced, including by Anacker of Soho Square, London. One of her watercolours, of The Shakespeare Memorial Theatre, Stratford-upon-Avon, was illustrated in The Studio, Vol.67, May 1916, p.267. Elected a Member of the Liverpool Academy of Arts. A Member of the Sandon Studio Club. One of her portraits was acquired by the Aberdovey Literary Institute. She was still active into the 1920s.

PULLER, LOUISA (1885-1964)

Illuminator. Born in Haslemere, Surrey. The daughter of Charles Giles Puller, a magistrate, and Emmeline. One of at least five children (Christopher, Francis, Katherine, Louisa and Margaret). Raised in Haslemere, and in Wadesmill and High Cross, both Hertfordshire. In the early 1900s, her family was sufficiently wealthy to employ eight servants. Francis Puller became agent to the Youngsbury estate in Ware, Hertfordshire, where Louisa spent some time along with Katherine. She studied at the Slade School, London, and taught calligraphy and illumination there between 1928 and 1957. She was elected a Member of the Society of Scribes and Illuminators (founded 1921), and was a founder member. She acted as Honorary Secretary of the Society between 1921 and 1925. Also produced paintings and drawings. She exhibited Winter Landscape at the Royal Academy in 1940. Some of her paintings are in the collection of the Victoria & Albert Museum, London. Two of her drawings are in the collection

of the Imperial War Museum, purchased in 1941. Louisa died in Chelsea, aged 78.

PULLING, PHYLLIS MARY (1892-1949)

Painter / Decorative Artist / Poster Artist. Born in Kensington, London in May 1892. The daughter of Alexander Pulling, C.B. (b.1858), a barrister, and Margaret Ellen (b.1864). One of at least six children (Phyllis, Joan, Norah, Stella, George and Christopher). Raised in London and in Hitchin, Hertfordshire. Educated at the Kensington High School, and at the King's College for Women. Studied at the London School of Art, at the St John's Wood School of Art, and at the Royal College of Art, London. Awarded a scholarship for life drawing at the London School of Art. Produced paintings in watercolours, oils and tempera, studies in pen & wash, etchings, decorative painted panels, bookplates and poster designs. Spent part of her career in London and then Exeter. In the 1930s she moved to Cornwall, working mainly at the Piazza Studios at St Ives. By the 1940s she had returned to London, and died in Kensington, aged 57.

Pulling exhibited her work, including at the Royal Academy (1927-47), the Society of Women Artists (1921-48), the Royal Institute of Oil Painters, with the International Society of Sculptors, Painters & Gravers, at the Goupil Gallery and with the Royal Institute of Painters in Watercolours. Also exhibited with the New Society of Artists, at the Walker Art Gallery, Liverpool and in Cornwall with the St Ives Society of Artists. Elected a Member of the St Ives Society of Artists (1932-40). Exhibited works included: The Green Tarpaulin, Three Sisters (pen & wash), Anemones and Patchwork and Pea-pickers (tempera). Travelled during her career, and produced watercolours of Sicily, Venice and Majorca. She returned to London during the war, and carried out decorations for bomb-damaged shopfronts. One of her posters was illustrated in Colour. Her posters for the Burma section at Wembley were bought by the Office of the High Commissioner for India.

PURSER, SARAH HENRIETTA (1848-1943)

Painter / Stained Glass Artist. An Irish portrait painter who founded a stained glass co-operative, An Túr Gloine. Better known today for her stained glass. The daughter of Benjamin Purser and Anne Mallett. Their families were linked to engineering and brewing in Dublin. The family had an academic background. Purser was related to painters Frederick Burton and William and Walter Osborne. She was educated in Switzerland and was an intellectual as well as an artist and designer. In 1873 her father suffered financial collapse, after which Purser endured several years of poverty. She studied at the Metropolitan School of Art, Dublin. Then went to the Academie Julian (1878-79). There, she met Swiss artist Louise Breslau and Italian singer Maria Feller. Feller posed for Purser's painting Petit Dejeuner in the early 1880s (now in the National Gallery of Ireland).

From around 1872 Purser established herself as a painter of note, particularly of figures and portraits, but also of landscapes on occasion. Began exhibiting her work from 1872 at the Royal Hibernian Academy, and continued to do so regularly until the end of her life and career. Some of her works were exhibited there just after her death, in 1944. President of the Academy Dermod O'Brien owned her Kerry Fish Wife (No.3). Purser showed 178 works at the Royal Hibernian Academy including Coming From Mass, Fish Wives Gossiping, Penny Dinners in Kevin Street and Viscount Powerscourt. She executed a considerable number of portraits of Ireland's notables, including the Rev. Dr Jellett, late Provost of Trinity College, the Rev. Dr Haughton, President of the Royal Irish Academy and the Right Rev. Charles Graves, Lord Bishop of Limerick. She also exhibited two portraits at the Royal Academy in 1885 and 1886, one of Viscountess Dalrymple. Purser was elected an Associate Royal Hibernian Academician in 1923 and an Academician in 1925.

Despite the considerable amount of time Purser spent on her painting, she also found time to establish An Tur Gloine (The Tower of Glass) in Dublin. An Tur Gloine was a stained glass workshop and studio founded by Purser in 1903 under the influence of Edward Martyn. He was patron of the Abbey Theatre, founder of the Palestrina Choir at Dublin's Cathedral and a Catholic landlord from Co. Galway. He persuaded Purser to found the workshop so that stained glass could be both designed and made in Ireland rather than abroad for Irish churches. Around the same time, the Metropolitan School of Art in Dublin developed a stained glass department which was run by Alfred E. Child. Child accepted the role of manager at An Tur Gloine. Purser was around 50 years of age when she began the workshop. She made very few actual glass panels herself, but created designs including Cormac of Cashel for St Patrick's Cathedral, Dublin (1906). The workshop carried out numerous commissions, including six windows for Loughrea church. Michael Healy (1873-1941) was a foundation member of An Tur Gloine too.

Purser's workshop ran until 1944, when it was dissolved as a co-operative and Catherine O'Brien took it over, running it until 1963. Although it was not intended to be an all-female enterprise, An Tur Gloine was assisted by several leading women artists during its lifetime, including Beatrice Elvery, Ethel Rhind, Wilhelmina Geddes and Evie Hone. Occasionally, the workshop exhibited its work. For example, in 1904 three small panels of stained glass were shown at the Irish Arts and Crafts Society exhibition in Dublin. Stained glass and mosaic work also appeared at the 1906 Royal Dublin Society's Art Industries annual exhibition. Members of An Tur Gloine were encouraged to join the Guild of Irish Art Workers (founded 1909) in the early years.

Purser was based in Dublin for most of her life, and from 1910 was living at Mespil House. There, she held meetings of Ireland's academic elite. She was also an ardent supporter of modern art, and was an art collector herself. Evidence would suggest that Purser was a tough and determined character, but she clearly used that strength to support other artists. With Edward Martyn, she organised an exhibition of the work of John Butler Yeats in 1901. It was a success. Yeats executed a drawing of Sarah Purser Painting. Fellow Irish artist Lilian Davidson exhibited a portrait of Purser at the Royal Hibernian Academy in 1944. Purser also supported the opening of the Gallery of Modern Art in Dublin, taking an active role in other such projects.

PUTTICK, LAURA GRACE (b.1877)
Illuminator. Born in Brighton, Sussex. The daughter of Walter Puttick, a chief cashier with Barclays Bank, and Emma Mildred. Her father originated from Brighton, her mother from London. Raised in Brighton and elsewhere in Sussex. One of at least three children (Alick, Laura and Ethel). Laura was a student at the Brighton School of Art in her early 30s, whilst still living with her parents. She became an illuminator. Two examples of her illuminated texts were given in The Studio, Vol.56, June 1912, p.58 in an article Some Modern Illuminations (pp.45-48). Those particular designs show some Celtic influence. Records indicate that in 1917 Puttick married Samuel White in Brighton. If records are correct, it would appear that she died in Essex in 1957, aged 79.

PYE, SYBIL (1879-1958)
Bookbinder / Book Decorator. Was Anna Sybella, known as Sybil. Born in Marylebone,

London in November 1879. The daughter of William Arthur Pye, a wine merchant, and Margaret Thomson. Her father originated from Exeter, Devon, her mother from Glasgow. One of seven children (Edith, Edmund, Anna, Margaret, Kellow, David and Edwin). Initially raised in Marylebone. By the early 1890s, her father had become a general merchant and the family had relocated to Hampstead. By at least the early 1900s they were in Surrey, living in a large house, Priest Hill, at Limpsfield. Sybil had a private education, at home. She subsequently became a nursery teacher, but was forced to give it up due to ill-health. Her younger sister, Margaret Ethel, studied at the Slade School and became a painter and sculptor who exhibited at the Royal Scottish Academy (1910) and the Society of Women Artists (from 1949). Margaret Ethel was elected an Associate of the Society of Women Artists (1950-51). She and Sybil lived together all their lives.

After their father's death, the sisters moved to Tulip Tree Cottage in Newick, East Sussex, then to Hill Cottage in Newick. Sybil had no formal art training, but with the aid of Douglas Cockerell's manual Bookbinding and the Care of Books she became a professional bookbinder. She began exhibiting her work from at least 1910, when she contributed to that year's Arts and Crafts Exhibition Society exhibition. That would suggest that she took up bookbinding in around 1906. Over the following decades, she worked prolifically on some 174 books and became a leader in the field of book decoration. She worked for some of the most prominent presses of the day, including the Vale Press, the Eragny Press, the Ashendene Press, the Kelmscott Press, the Dove's Press and the Gregynog Press.

For the Dove's Press Pye bound editions of Emerson's Essays and Milton's Paradise Lost and Paradise Regained. For the Vale Press, she bound, for example, Lucius Apuleius, De Cupidnis et Psyches Amoribus in 1910. For the Eragny Press, she bound, for example, Thomas Sturge Moore, The Little School (1905), printed on vellum. For that particular book, she chose green and white with gold tooling, typical of her bold, almost architectural designs combined with striking colour, heavily suggestive of the influence of Art Deco later in her career. She executed another edition of Moore's book in turquoise, jade green and red with gold tooling in 1940. Moore, an artist and poet, wanted to marry Sybil Pye, but she declined. They remained friends, however, and she proof-read his work. He dedicated a collection of his work to her.

It was through Moore that Sybil came under the influence of Charles Ricketts, founder of the Vale Press. Ricketts was an artist and book designer. But she also admired poet Rupert Brooke and met him several times during the war years. She subsequently published Rupert Brooke: Life and Letters in 1929. In 1925 she spent three months rebinding the 10th-century Benedictional of Saint Aethelwold for the Duke of Devonshire. Other books to receive her attention over the years included Dante Gabriel Rossetti, Hand and Soul (Vale Press, 1899, bound 1907), Michael Field, The Race of Leaves (Vale Press, 1902, bound c.1912), Laurence Binyon, The Sirens (Stanton Press, 1924, bound 1928) and Henry Vaughan, The Sacred Poems (Vale Press, 1897, bound 1946). Sometimes, Pye bound more than one copy of a book, sometimes years apart, and bound a number of different books by the same author. Such was her skill, Pye designed some of her own tools to create the effects she desired.

Pye exhibited her work throughout her career, in England and abroad. For example, she contributed to exhibitions in Buenos Aires, Sao Paulo, Paris, Leipzig, Ghent, Stockholm, New York, Brussels, Berlin, Hamburg, Oslo, Cologne, Amsterdam and Utrecht. Also, at the First Edition Club, of which she was elected a Member. Also a Member of the Halcyon Club. Exhibited at the 1913 Arts and Crafts Exhibition, as well as the 1910, showing her bindings for The Race of Leaves and Cupid and Psyche. Also exhibited at Wembley and in Birmingham, Cambridge, Hove, Newcastle and Manchester. Exhibited with the Women's International Art Club, including in 1932 when Apollo magazine described her work as 'of original design and beautiful workmanship' (Vol.15, 1932, p.141). She exhibited latterly at the Golden Gate Exhibition, San Francisco in 1939, and in the same year exhibited at the Society of Women Artists. She worked almost until her death. Works illustrated in Apollo and some German magazines. Two of her bindings were illustrated in The Art of the Book, London, Studio, 1914. Works also illustrated in John Harkhan's Victoria & Albert Museum: Bookbindings (1950). Works acquired by the Victoria & Albert Museum, London and by the McGill University Library, Montreal.

PYKE-NOTT, CAROLINE EVELYN EUNICE (1870-1960)

Painter / Decorative Artist. Known as Evelyn. Born in Exeter, Devon. The daughter of John Nott Pyke-Nott and Caroline. Her father, a landowner, originated from Barnstaple, Devon, her mother from Rochester, Kent. The third of at least five children (John, James, Caroline, Edmund and Isabel). The family was sufficiently wealthy to employ six servants. Whilst the children were still young, the family moved to Bath, Somerset. By at least 1891 they had moved to London. Four of the Pyke-Nott children took up art. James and Edmund became painters. Evelyn and Isabel studied at the Royal Academy schools. Both girls excelled, with Evelyn winning a silver medal as a student (1893 / 94). Evelyn spent much of her career in London but died in Henley, Oxfordshire, aged 89.

During her career, Evelyn produced miniature and decorative paintings, mainly portraits and figures. In June 1899 she married artist John Byam Liston Shaw (1872-1919). He ran a successful school of art in London with painter Vicat Cole. The couple had five children in quick succession, George, Barbara, James, Glencairn and David, between 1900 and 1906. However, John Byam Shaw died in Middlesex at the comparatively young age of 46, leaving Evelyn as sole provider for her family. She worked as an artist before, during and after her marriage, exhibiting her work into the 1930s (at least). Exhibited at the Royal Academy (59 works, 1891-1937), the Royal Hibernian Academy (1898-99), the Royal Glasgow Institute (1903) and the Society of Women Artists (1923-28). Elected a Member of the Society of Women Artists (1923-28). Exhibited works included: Her Hair Fine Threads of Finest Gold, At the Door, Violet, Daughter of the Late Major Gardiner, The Green Feather and The Honourable Mrs Frank Hopwood. Her Justified Rather Than the Other was illustrated in The Studio, Vol.13, 1898, p.108 in a special section on British art of 1898. A portrait of Evelyn was exhibited at the Royal Academy in 1894 by Miss Mildred H. Collyer. Evelyn exhibited a portrait of her sister Isabel at the Royal Academy in 1897.

PYMAN, LILIAN JOAN (1901-c.77)

Sculptor. Born and raised in Hampstead, London. The daughter of Frederick H. Pyman and Edith. Her father, a shipowner, originated from Durham. Her mother was born in India. One of a large family, of at least 11 children (Mary, Margaret, Dorothy, Joyce, Elizabeth, Ruth, Alan, Blanche, Esther, Lilian and Keith). Educated at a school in Hampstead. Probably studied sculpture in London. Produced busts, figures and heads in bronze, marble, plaster and wood. Active for at least 28 years. Exhibited at the Royal Academy (1921-31), the Society of Women Artists (1922-38) and the Royal Glasgow Institute (1923-24). Exhibited works included: Evensong (statue), A Whitby Fisherman (half-figure), Idol (bronze & wood) and The Rev. W.E. Orchard, D.D. (half-

figure). Elected an Associate of the Society of Women Artists (1922-49). Based in London during her career, but also in Chalfont St Giles, Buckinghamshire. In 1926 she married George D. Stewart in London. She died in Hove, Sussex.

Q

QUICK, HILDA MARGARET (1895-1978)

Engraver / Illustrator. Born in Penzance, Cornwall. The daughter of Richard H. Quick and Gertrude Webb Ball. Initially, her father was a bank cashier. Later, he became a bank manager. He was also born in Penzance. Hilda was an only child, raised in Cornwall in a house with servants. She subsequently studied at the L.C.C. Central School of Arts and Crafts, London, specialising in wood engraving under Noel Rooke. Later also studied in Paris. She returned to Cornwall and lived mostly at Penzance. In 1947 her father died, and in 1951 her mother died. From 1951 Hilda lived on the Scilly Isles, at Priglis Cottage, St Agnes. She was friends with Daphne Gould (d.2003) who had a summer house on St Agnes. Hilda worked until her death, aged 83.

Quick produced wood engravings and book illustrations. Some were studies of Cornwall, such as Newlyn Fish Market. Also produced Christmas cards. But she was particularly known for her studies of birds. In the 1930s she illustrated the Complete Works of Edmund Spenser for the Shakespeare Head Press. Also wrote and illustrated Marsh and Shore, a best-seller in 1948. In 1964 she illustrated Birds of the Scilly Isles. She had a particular interest in birds and became editor of the Journal of the Cornwall Birdwatching and Preservation Society. Quick was a close friend of Rowena Cade, founder and builder of the Minack Theatre at Porthcurno, Cornwall. Quick was linked to the Minack and its productions for many years. In the 1930s she produced poster and programme designs for the Minack. She also collaborated with Cade on costume and set designs. Some of her designs have been on show at the Minack Theatre in more recent times, some with bold, bright colour schemes, evidently influenced by Art Deco.

In 1936 Hilda was elected to the Newlyn Art Gallery Arranging Committee for the Cornish Loan Exhibition for that year along with Cade. She spent some time working in Brittany and Normandy. Exhibited her work occasionally, in London, Newlyn and elsewhere. Exhibited one work at the Royal Hibernian Academy in 1931, Staircase Light (unframed). Exhibited two works at the Society of Women Artists in 1927: Drying

Time (colour woodcut) and Gurnards (colour print). She was then based at Lansdowne Place, London. Exhibited with the Society of Wood Engravers, including in 1931 at the Redfern Gallery showing, among other works, Masons. Also exhibited with the English Wood-Engraving Society, including in 1931 at the St George's Gallery with The Staircase Light. Her The Weavers was included in an article British Wood Engraving of the Present Day by Maximilien Vox in The Studio, Vol.99, March 1930, pp.155-167.

QUIGLY, KATHLEEN M. (1888-1981)

Stained Glass Artist / Wood Engraver / Illuminator / Painter / Illustrator. Born in Dublin, Ireland. The daughter of Richard Quigly, M.I.C.E. (Member of the Institute of Civil Engineers). The family moved around with her father's job. Educated in Dublin and London. Returned to Dublin and remained there until 1934, when she emigrated to South Africa. In 1911 exhibited at the National Competition of Schools of Art. She was then based in Dublin, so presumably studied at the Metropolitan School of Art, Dublin. She was known to be a pupil of Alice Jacob who taught at the Dublin School. Quigly became a stained glass artist, a wood engraver, an illuminator and illustrator. Also produced linocuts, enamels, leatherwork and miniature paintings. In Dublin, she worked with Harry Clarke and for An Tur Gloine (The Tower of Glass), Sarah Purser's stained glass workshop.

Quigly set up her own studio at Westmoreland Street, at the Columban Studios. There, she advertised illuminating on vellum and miniature painting. Elected Master of the Guild of Irish Art Workers (1926-28). Produced stained glass for the Treasure House of Eu Tong Sen in Singapore, for St Joseph's, Belton, Harrogate, and for the S.H. Convent, Boston, U.S.A. Produced the windows for Titania's Palace, of plique-à-jour enamel. Executed a charter and certificate for the Irish Theosophical Society in 1921. Exhibited at the Royal Hibernian Academy (13 works, 1917-34). Showed enamels and leatherwork at the 1910 Arts and Crafts Society of Ireland exhibition. In 1925 exhibited a poster for poultry food. Exhibited at the Aonach Tailteann exhibition of 1932. Exhibited works included: The Apprentice, Mrs T. Kettle and Study in Character. Of the same family was Miss Ethel M. Quigly who also exhibited at the Royal Hibernian Academy (1918).

R

RADFORD, HESTER MAITLAND (1887-1965)

Lacquer Screen Worker / Painter. Born in Hammersmith, London in February 1887. Raised in London. The daughter of Ernest Radford (1857-1919) and Caroline Dollie Maitland (1858-1920). Her father was a barrister and journalist who acted as an art critic of poetry. Her mother was a poet and writer, known as Dollie Radford. Hester was one of at least three children. Her brother Maitland became a medical student and a poet. Her sister Margaret also became a part-time student and a poet. Hester was educated at the King Alfred School, and at Miss Horton's School at Hampstead. She took up art and studied at the Slade School, London. Produced paintings in watercolours, including Her Husband's Letter. But she became equally well known for her highly decorative lacquered screens and screens on silk. Exhibited her work at the New English Art Club (from 1913), with the Arts and Crafts Society, the International Society of Sculptors, Painters & Gravers, at the Walker Art Gallery, Liverpool, with the Royal Society of British Artists and at the Beaux Art Gallery. Some of her works were illustrated in the Sphere, the Graphic and The Studio. Spent much of her career in London, but also in Stroud, Gloucestershire. Died in London, aged 79.

RAEMAEKERS, MARY ANN (c.1839-95)

Sculptor. Was Mary Ann King. Born and raised in London. In 1863, she married sculptor John Adrien Raemaekers (1832-94). He was born in Belgium but worked and exhibited in London. There are no children listed on census recordings. It is feasible that Mary studied under her husband. She exhibited one work, The Whistling Birds (terracotta), at the Royal Society of British Artists in 1883 / 84. She died in London, aged 56.

RAMSAY, FRANCES LOUISA MARGARET & VIOLET GRACE MARY (1858-1928) & (1866-1948)

Artists / Decorative Artists. The daughters of Andrew C. Ramsay, LL.D., F.R.S., and Mary Louisa. Their father was Director of the Geographical Survey of England. The Ramsays had at least two other daughters, Dorothea and Elizabeth Eleanor (1853-1930), also known as Eleanor. The girls were raised in a London house with servants. Frances, Violet, and Elizabeth spent much of their lives living together, spending time in London, Beaumaris (where their mother was born) on Anglesey and Chipping

Campden, Gloucestershire. All three died in Wales. Elizabeth, who was born in Beaumaris, became a landscape painter. As Eleanor Ramsay, she exhibited at the Royal Academy, the Royal Scottish Academy and the Royal Hibernian Academy between 1886 and 1908. She died at the age of 77.

Frances Ramsay, who was born in Kensington, became a painter of portraits and other subjects. She exhibited her work at the Royal Glasgow Institute (1892), the Royal Academy (1912) and the Society of Women Artists (73 works, 1882-1920). Exhibited works included: Orchids, Souvenirs of the First Empire, The Shady Hat and Red Cross Worker at Chipping Campden. Frances was elected an Associate of the Society of Women Artists (1908-22). She also designed and made decorative jewellery. She died at the age of 69.

Violet Ramsay, who was also born in London, also became a designer and maker of decorative jewellery. Violet and Frances occasionally exhibited their work jointly. Violet was a student of the Sir John Cass Technical Institute in London. She exhibited her work for at least 19 years, including at the '91 Art Club Exhibition held at the Alpine Club in 1905. Also, at the Society of Women Artists (1916). She showed work regularly at the exhibitions of the Sir John Cass Arts and Crafts Society in London, including in 1908, 1909, 1911 and 1913. The Society was made up of students and staff of the Sir John Cass Technical Institute. At the 1908 exhibition, other exhibitors included Ethel Agnew, Phoebe Stabler, and May Hart Partridge. That particular exhibition was held at the Walker's Gallery, New Bond Street, London. Both Violet and Frances contributed jewellery to the 1912 Arts and Crafts Exhibition Society exhibition. Violet's exhibits on that occasion included a gold and silver vine necklace and a silver necklace with moonstones. Frances contributed a gold and silver pendant set with opals. Some of those were illustrated in The Studio, Vol.57, January 1913, p.293. The sisters also contributed jewellery to a small exhibition of local arts and crafts held at Chipping Campden in August 1924. All exhibits on that occasion were by locally based artists and craftworkers, including Arthur and Georgina Gaskin. Violet died at the age of 81.

RATE, LETTICE M. - SEE SANDFORD, L.M.

RAVEN, CATHERINE H. - SEE HOLIDAY, C.H.

RAWLINS, OLIVIA BEATRICE EMILY (1880-1934)
Sculptor / Decorative Artist. Born and raised in Liverpool. The daughter of Washington C. Rawlins, a civil engineer, and Hester. Had at least one sibling, George. Studied at the Liverpool School of Art in the early 1900s. Showed a pierced and chased silver panel for a piano at the exhibition of students' work held at the School in 1900. Also in the early 1900s (c.1906), she spent some time in Kensington, London, then returned to live with her parents in Liverpool. Exhibited one work at the Royal Academy in 1906, Dawn (relief panel). The same piece was also shown at Liverpool, at the Walker Art Gallery's 1906 Autumn Exhibition. The plaster relief was illustrated in The Studio, Vol.39, November 1906, p.170. Olivia died at Little Waltham Rectory, Chelmsford, aged 54.

RAWNSLEY, EDITH (1846-1916)
Painter / Craftswoman. Born in Bolton-le-Moors, Lancashire, the daughter of John Fletcher and Elizabeth. Her father was a coal mine proprietor, and J.P. Edith was one of several children raised in Bolton-le-Moors. The family later moved to Ambleside in the Lake District. Edith had some early training in the arts and was a competent watercolour artist who exhibited her first work in London in 1876. She was also an avid reader of John Ruskin's writings. In 1878 she married Hardwicke Drummond Rawnsley (1851-1920), a fellow devotee of Ruskin, who had moved to Wray in the Lake District in 1877 after deciding to join the ministry. Their marriage took place at Brathay Church, where John Fletcher was buried, and as they left the church, Edith laid her wedding bouquet on his grave. Moved by the incident, the poet Charles Tennyson Turner wrote a sonnet, The Wedding Posy. In 1879 the couple travelled abroad. But by 1880 they had returned to Wray to settle into the village life which would see the birth of their only son, Noel (1880-1952). In the same year, the Rawnsleys decided to act upon Ruskin's teachings and, under his direct guidance from his home, Brantwood at nearby Coniston, established a woodcarving class for the Wray parishioners. There, Edith could apply her artistic talents.

By 1883 the Rawnsleys had moved to St Kentigern's Church at Crosthwaite, Keswick, and the Wray class was disbanded. Encouraged by their success at Wray, the Rawnsleys decided to establish a similar endeavour at Keswick. But, since Keswick was much larger than Wray, this time it would be a much larger and more ambitious project, and was given the name the Keswick School of Industrial Arts. Still run along Ruskin's teachings, and guided by him, the School aimed to revive lost handcrafts and to offer individuals the opportunity to design and create. Woodcarving, metalwork and embroidery were taught, joined in 1889 by classes in the art of hand spinning, a Lakeland craft re-established elsewhere in Lakeland in 1883 by Ruskin devotee Marian Twelves and her Langdale Linen Industry. Also a skilled needlewoman, Edith Rawnsley took the embroidery class as well as supervising the metalwork. The School ran until 1984, closing just prior to its centenary. Its success was almost entirely due to Edith's early efforts, and she worked tirelessly, also continuing with her artwork, and assisting her husband in his role as writer, cleric and creator of many Lakeland protection and conservation groups.

Whilst at Wray, in 1882 Edith had exhibited A Bit of Helvellyn, Wythburn at the Royal Academy, and she continued to exhibit her paintings after the move to Keswick, showing two works at the New Watercolour Society. In 1904 she contributed a number of sketches to her husband's book Flower-Time in the Oberland (1904). In the same year, she became a Member of the Lake Artists' Society which was co-founded by Ruskin's secretary, William Gershom Collingwood (1854-1932), husband of artist Dorrie Collingwood, also a Member of the Society. The Lake Artists' Society was a deliberate attempt to promote Lakeland artists.

Edith Rawnsley was always a talented designer, and the Keswick School of Industrial Arts produced many pieces designed by her. Those included three gilded panels (c.1893) representing the birth, death and resurrection of Christ which can still be found inside St Kentigern's Church. She was also responsible for the Keswick School's early textile designs, including the Church Congress Banner which was worked by the ladies of the diocese and shown at the 1906 Barrow-in-Furness Ecclesiastical Art Exhibition. Under Marian Twelves's direction, Edith was also a maker of Ruskin lace, a form of textile decoration similar to Greek lace which was created by Miss Twelves and which was unique to the Lake District. After a period of ill-health, Edith died and was buried in Crosthwaite churchyard. The Keswick School continued to thrive, no doubt due to her early

efforts. Information taken from papers currently held in Cumbria Record Office, Carlisle, DB111.

RAYMOND, RUTH (1897-1986)

Calligrapher / Illuminator / Painter / Weaver. Was Florence Laura Ruth, known as Ruth. Born in Greenwich. The daughter of Henry James Raymond and Florence Agnes. Her father, like her mother, originated from Kent. He worked for the Inland Revenue. One of at least four children (Ruth, Henry, Clifford and Norman). Raised in Greenwich. Educated at the Roan School, Greenwich. Studied at the Camberwell School of Art between 1914 and 1917, at the Woolwich Polytechnic between 1917 and 1919, and at the Royal College of Art, London under Professor Ernest William Tristram, Edward Jonston and Robert Anning Bell between 1919 and 1921. Elected an Associate of the Royal College of Art in 1921. Remained in London for a number of years after completing her studies.

Raymond produced paintings in watercolours, illuminations and calligraphy, and worked as a hand weaver. By at least 1937 she had taken the post of teaching of weaving at the Gloucester School of Arts and Crafts. She was still in Gloucestershire, teaching, in the 1950s. She died in Hampshire, aged 88. Exhibited her work, including at the Arts and Crafts Exhibitions at Burlington House (1920-45). Also, with the Guild of Gloucester Craftsmen, at the Festival of Britain Exhibitions, in Gloucester, Cheltenham, Cirencester and elsewhere. Elected a Member of the Gloucester Artists Club and of the Guild of Gloucester Craftsmen. Her illumination and calligraphy work saw her working as assistant illuminator to Graily Hewitt on Books of Remembrance in Westminster Abbey and the Cathedrals of Canterbury, Winchester and Gloucester. She also worked on the Record Book in Gloucester Cathedral. Some of her hand weaving was in the permanent collections of Messrs Heals, Messrs Dryad and the Rural Industries Bureau. Records indicate that in 1924 Ruth married Staffordshire-born artist / sculptor / designer and former student of the Royal College of Art Reco Capey (1895-1961) in Kensington, London. In 1935 Capey married Katharine B. Stone.

READ, DIANA M. - SEE LALL, D.M.

RECKITT, RACHEL BEATRICE (1908-95)

Wood Engraver / Sculptor / Designer of Wrought Iron Work. Born in November 1908 in St Albans, Hertfordshire. The daughter of Frank Norman Reckitt (1872-1940) and Beatrice Margaret

Hewett (b.1878). Her father was an architect who originated from Yorkshire. Her mother originated from Gloucestershire. The youngest of at least three children (also Vera Maud (b.1904) and Basil Norman (b.1906)). Rachel was aunt to writer Penelope Lively, author of A House Unlocked (2001). Basil Reckitt was author of several books including The Lindley Affair - a Diary of the Boer War (1972). Evidently, Rachel was part of a creative family.

Rachel studied wood engraving at the Grosvenor School of Modern Art, London between 1933 and 1937 under Iain MacNab, and studied lithography at the Central School of Arts and Crafts, London. She produced wood engravings, sculptures in wood, stone and metal, carved inn signs in relief and church screens. Some of her work can be found in St Bartholomew's Church, Rodhuish, Somerset. Her engravings were used in a number of books including A.R.J. Wise & R.A. Smith (ed.), Voices on the Green Anthology of Poetry (1945), Sam Price Myers, London South of the River (1949), Walter de la Mare & Others, English Country Short Stories (1949) and Mary Bosanquet, People With Six Legs (1953). One of the last books she illustrated was Seven Psalms (1981).

Reckitt exhibited her work. Showed two works at the Society of Women Artists, Combe Sydenham in 1935 and Agricultural Show in 1936. Also exhibited with the Society of Wood Engravers, of which she was elected a Member in 1950, the New English Art Club and various other London galleries. Sometime prior to 1935, her parents moved to Golsoncott, an Edwardian house in Washford, West Somerset. Reckitt lived at the house through several decades, dying in West Somerset, aged 86. She was elected to the Somerset Guild of Craftsmen in 1970. During the Second World War, she ran a branch of the Citizen's Advice Bureau at the Toynbee Hall, Whitechapel, East London, and a C.A.B. Mobile Unit touring bombed cities. Some of her works were included in an exhibition of women wood engravers held at the Museum of Oxford in October 1979, one of only 27 women chosen. In the late 1950s, Reckitt visited Spain. Her mother, Beatrice, was an expert needlewoman who also produced work for St Bartholomew's Church, including kneelers, banners and altar curtains. Beatrice exhibited her work at the Society of Women Artists in 1937, following her daughter's example.

REED, ETHEL (1874-1912)
Painter / Illustrator / Designer. Although essentially American, Ethel Reed had some impact on British art and design in the late nineteenth and early twentieth centuries. She was born in Newburyport in America, the daughter of Edgar Eugene Reed, and died young in Fulham, London. She studied at the Cowles Art School, Boston, and was engaged for a short time. She is recorded as living in London, England from at least 1901 until her death in 1912. She probably moved to England in around 1897, when her work featured in The Studio magazine. In 1901 she was living in Grosvenor Road with one servant, but also with a son, Anthony, then four months old. She went on to have another child, and eventually married the father, Arthur Warwick, an English army officer. However, she died not long after.

During her career, Reed produced black & white drawings, pen drawings, pastels, book illustrations and poster designs. She specialised in baby and children's books which were published in America and England. Perhaps best known for the Arabella and Araminta Stories by Gertrude Smith (priced two dollars), for which Reed produced 15 pictures and an advertising poster. Noted for her delicate drawings, her solid black silhouettes and sweeping lines, which were, according to the critics of the day, essentially feminine. Her black & white work was done with a brush. Most of her work was fantasy, including a series of Pierrots whose titles included Pierrot Amoreux, Sleepy Pierrot and Temptation.

Regarded as a good draughtsman, Reed also illustrated a volume of Verses by Mrs Louise Chandler Moulton. Produced a number of successful poster designs, including for Field Flowers and for Behind the Arras by Bliss Carman, published by Lawson, Wolfe & Co., Boston & New York. Her poster for Miss Trauweiri was reproduced and sold in England. Her poster for The Quest for the Golden Girl in yellow and black on brown paper was put up around London. She also contributed to the Yellow Book (1897, cover & illustration). Reed was the subject of an article in The Studio, Vol.10, 1897, pp.230-236, The Work of Miss Ethel Reed, with illustrations. SEE: William S. Peterson, The Beautiful Poster Lady, Oak Knoll Press, 2013.

REED, LILLIE (1875-1948)
Sculptor. Born in London. The daughter of Edward J. Reed, a licensed victualler, and Maria. One of at least four children (Lillie, Marion, Ruby and Edward). Raised in London, but later based in Hastings, Sussex (from at least 1901). Still spent time in London, but died in Hastings, aged 73. Possibly a student of the Slade School, London. Produced groups and statuettes in

bronze, and decorative pieces such as electric light switches. Exhibited her work, including at the Royal Academy (1904-10) and at the Leeds City Art Gallery (certainly in 1909). Exhibited works included: The Magic Shell (statuette), Research (statue), Love, Pain and Solitude (group) and Night and Day (electric light switch, group, bronze). Lillie executed some of the carving on the exterior porch to the Lady Chapel of the Anglican Cathedral, Liverpool. Most was done by another carver from her models, but she finished the project. The design was based on children.

REEKS, MARIA ELLEN (1859-1929)

Decorative Woodcarver. Born in London. The daughter of Trenham Reeks (1823-79) and Christiana Caroline Howard (1818-93). Her father, who was born in Lambeth, London, was a Registrar in the Department of Science and Art at one of London's large educational establishments. Her mother was also born in London. Maria was one of at least four children (Trenham, Matilda, Margaret and Maria), all raised in London. Trenham became an analytical chemist. Margaret (1855-1937) became an artist and art teacher. Maria became a decorative woodcarver, producing highly detailed and meticulous work. She also became an assistant teacher at the School of Woodcarving, South Kensington, one of two assistants who worked under a female manager at the School. Later, she became manager, possibly taking over from Eleanor Rowe. Many of the School's pupils were female. Later (in 1911), Maria is listed as sharing lodgings with the School's clerk, Ethel Eugenie Hendrey.

Maria exhibited her work occasionally, including at the Society of Women Artists (1896-1910) under the school's address of South Kensington. Also contributed to the Arts and Crafts Exhibition Society's 1893 exhibition, including a panel for a three-fold screen carved by her but not to her design. The panel was illustrated in The Studio, Vol.2, October 1893, p.25. In 1899 she showed a panel for a screen at the Exhibition of Pictures & Decorative Art held in Kendal, Westmorland. At the same exhibition, Henry Sanders, also of the School of Woodcarving, showed examples of Gothic lettering. Also contributed to the 1910 Arts and Crafts Exhibition Society exhibition, including a carved chest in walnut, but also a walnut cradle executed jointly with Miss F. Steele and Miss A.C. Burton, also of the School of Woodcarving. A presentation book cover designed and carved by Maria was illustrated in the Art Journal, 1896, pp.116-118, in an article Women Workers in the

Art Crafts by Fred Miller. Maria was the author of Woodcarving (1903). She died in London, aged 70. SEE: ROWE, ELEANOR

REES, GLADYS MARY (1898-1985)

Painter / Etcher / Book Illustrator / Poster Artist. Born in London in June 1898. The daughter of Joseph Edward Rees and Edith. Her father, who originated from Wales, was an assistant manager in typewriters. Her mother also originated from Wales. Gladys was raised in London and Ilfracombe, Devon. One of at least four children (Edith, Gladys, Cecil and Walter). Educated at the Putney Secondary School. Studied at the Chelsea School of Art. Awarded a Board of Education drawing certificate and a painting diploma. Taught at the Chelsea School in the early 1920s, whilst John D. Revel was in charge.

Rees became an oil and watercolour painter of portraits, landscapes, figures and flowers. Also produced etchings and woodcuts, poster designs and decorative work, also working in pen & ink and scraperboard. Executed posters for the Underground. Produced illustrations for children's and educational books for the University of London Press, Jonathan Cape, Evan Bros and George Bell & Sons. Books illustrated included H.E. Chapman, Barbara in Pixieland (1922), J.A. Bentham, The City of Wishes (1922), F. Claremont, The Book of the Cat Jeremiah (1929) and B. Lovett, The Princess Who Got Out of Bed on the Wrong Side (1945). Illustrated her own writings, including A Book of Verse (1936), Loosey and Lankey (1945) and XYZ and After (1952). Works also reproduced in the Sphere. Initially based in London, then in West Peeping near Peterborough and in Uffington, Stamford, Lincolnshire. Exhibited her work, including at the Society of Women Artists (147 works, 1923-84), the New English Art Club and the Women's International Art Club. Exhibited works included: The Seagulls (woodcut), Sea Marsh (watercolour), Straw Bales and Vapour Trails (oil) and Kingston Vale (etching). Elected an Associate of the Society of Women Artists (1925-38) and a Member (1939-85). A Member of the Faculty of Arts. In 1927 she married John Pickworth Teesdale in Wandsworth. They had at least two sons and a daughter.

RENNELL, PHOEBE (1883-1972)

Script and Illuminating Artist. Born in London in September 1883. The daughter of Ernest Rennell, a commercial clerk and accountant, and Elizabeth. One of at least four children (Phoebe, Richard, Clarence and Annie). Her father originated from London, her mother from Sydney, Australia. The family remained in London as Phoebe grew up, living in the parish of Lambeth. She studied at the Clapton School of Art and won a bronze medal in the National Competition of Schools of Art. Turned her attention to illumination and calligraphy. Two examples of her lettering and illumination were given in The Studio, Vol.56, June 1912, pp.49 & 54 in an article Some Modern Illuminators (pp.45-58). One was an illuminated page Farewell to Arms. The other was an illuminated title page A Thanks Giving to God for His House by Robert Herrick. Elected a Member of the Society of Scribes and Illuminators (founded 1921). Exhibited her work with the Arts and Crafts Society, at Wembley, in Lincoln, Glastonbury and Edinburgh and, further afield, in Paris, Ghent and Detroit. Later, certainly from the early 1930s, she lived at Spilsby, Lincolnshire where she died, aged 89.

REYNOLDS, LILIAN MARY (1864-1952)

Painter. Born in Hammersmith, London in April 1864. The daughter of Charles Etherington, a solicitor, and Lucy. One of at least six children (Charles, Ambrose, Lucy, Edward, Eleanor and Lilian), all raised in Hammersmith. Ambrose Etherington also became a solicitor. By the age of 16, Lilian was already an art student in London. Studied at Ridley's Art School and in Brussels. By the early 1890s, she was living in Kensington with relatives and was working as a portrait and figure painter. Head of the house was John Williams, an author and editor. By the early 1900s, she was based at St Paul's Studios, Hammersmith in an area full of artists. Her neighbours included painter / illustrator Gertrude Hammond, art student Dorothea Williams and painter Herbert Sidney.

In early 1903 Lilian married civil engineer John Francis Jodrell Reynolds who was eight years younger. The couple lived in Chelsea, but subsequently spent time living with his parents in Haslemere, Surrey before moving back to London. John Reynolds died in Wandsworth in 1948. Lilian died in Wandsworth, aged 87. They had one child who is listed as deceased shortly after birth. Lilian exhibited her work early in her career, but showed less after her marriage. Exhibited at the Royal Academy (1885-1906), the Royal Society of British Artists (1884-89), the Society of Women Artists (1885-89) and in Liverpool, Manchester and Bombay. Exhibited works included: An Idle Boy, The Turn of the Leaf, Greed for Gold, Little Lord Fauntleroy and

Fledgelings. Elected a Member of the Ridley Art Club.

RHIND, ETHEL MARY (c.1878-1952)

Stained Glass Artist / Painter. Born in Bengal. The daughter of an engineer. Educated at the Derry High School. Lived in Belfast. In 1902 she won a scholarship to study mosaic at the Metropolitan School of Art, Dublin for three years. In 1904 she exhibited a mosaic, Head of Juno, and in 1907 exhibited three stained glass panels. In around 1907 she joined Sarah Purser's stained glass workshop An Tur Gloine (The Tower of Glass) in Dublin, and remained there until around 1939. She became Ireland's leading artist in opus sectile and glass.

Works executed by Rhind included Stations of the Cross for Spiddal Catholic Church (1918-28) and other works for Loughrea Cathedral (1929-33) and for the Friary, Athlone (1934-36). Exhibited watercolours and stained glass at an exhibition of work by past and present students of the Dublin School of Art held in 1910, the first of its kind. Other exhibitors on that occasion included Beatrice Elvery, Florence Gillespie and William Orpen. In 1912 she designed a tapestry for the Dun Emer Guild, later in the care of the National Museum of Ireland. In 1913 she was depicted as Salome by Irish painter Harry Clarke. In the same year, she exhibited a panel for stained glass at the Royal Hibernian Academy, the only time she would exhibit there. She occasionally worked in collaboration with Wilhelmina Geddes. Exhibited regularly with the Arts and Crafts Society of Ireland. In 1917, for example, she showed stained glass designs at the Society's fifth exhibition, held in Dublin, then in Belfast, then Cork. Elected a Member of the Guild of Irish Art Workers (founded 1909).

RHOADES, MARJORIE VIOLET M. (1904-70)

Designer / Artist. Born in Gosport, Hampshire in March 1904. The daughter of Col. Cyril Field, R.M., an author and artist. Educated at the Belvedere School, Liverpool. Studied art in Liverpool, at the Regent Street Polytechnic, London and in Paris. Became a designer, including of costume, textiles, silver and wallpaper. Also an artist in line, wash and watercolour. From 1948 she was a lecturer at the Royal College of Art Fashion School. Linked to the Fashion Design Group and the Society of Industrial Artists. Elected a Fellow of the Society of Industrial Artists. Exhibited her work, including at the Cooling Galleries, with the Cotton Board, Manchester, at the Isle of Sark Art

Gallery and at the British Pavilion of the Paris International Exhibition of 1937. Some of her work was reproduced in Harper's Bazaar, Vogue, Queen, Sketch and International Textiles. Also a Member of the Curzon House Club. Based in London for much of her career. In 1942 she married Ivo Nicholson Rhoades (1912-71) in Chelsea. She died in Sussex, aged 66. He died in Sussex shortly after.

RICHARDSON, MAGGIE - SEE MITCHELL, M.

RICHARDSON, NELLIE - SEE BLACKLOCK, N.

RICHES, KATE WINIFRED (1891-1938)

Painter / Interior Decorator / Illustrator. Born in London in March 1891. The daughter of James Riches, the Consul General for Siam, and Alice Mary Mallett. One of at least six children (Bertha, Margaret, Sidney, Dorothy, Kate and Walter). Raised in London. Educated at the Clapham Modern and High Schools. Studied at the Clapham School of Art, and at the City and Guilds Technical Institute, Kensington. Became a miniature and portrait painter in oils. Worked as an interior decorator for a West End firm of decorators. Produced illustrations for A Tale of Old Japan (Blackwood). Had a studio on Bushnell Road, London. Exhibited her work, including at the Royal Society of Miniature Painters. Died in Southampton Hospital, aged only 47. Her address at that time was Farnham, Surrey.

RICHTER, FLORENCE GERTRUDE (1879-1960)

Craftswoman. Known as Gertrude. Born in Birmingham in November 1879. The daughter of William L. Barber and Sarah. Her father, who originated from Cheshire, was an umbrella and furniture manufacturer listed as employing 115 women, 15 men and one boy in 1881. He was also an alderman. Her mother originated from London. One of a large family, of at least 11 children (William, Joshua, Frances, Elizabeth, Annie, Frederick, Ernest, Alice, Howard, Florence and Winifred). Raised in Edgbaston and Aston, both Birmingham. Florence was educated at the Edgbaston College. Studied art under Herbert Davis Richter (1874-1955), whom she married in Birmingham in 1907. He was a decorative artist, furniture designer and lecturer who originated from Brighton. His father was a stud groom on a large estate, and originated from Russia.

Herbert Richter was a Member of the Royal Society of British Artists, the Royal Institute of Oil Painters, the Royal Institute of Painters in Watercolours and the Pastel Society as well as a Member of the Arts and Crafts Society, Vice President of the Royal Institute of Oil Painters and President of the Pastel Society and of the Bath Society of Artists. By at least 1911 the couple had moved to Redcliffe Square, London, where they remained until their deaths. Herbert Richter's brother, Charles (1867-1946), was a furniture draughtsman, and worked with Herbert for the Bath Cabinet Makers Ltd until Herbert left to concentrate on painting. Herbert's sister, Florence Schottler, joined forces with Florence Richter to launch the Guild of Handicraft and Design, intending to make soft furnishings, with contracts coming from India, America and Germany. Florence Schottler was married to musician and musical director William Frederick Charles Schottler, who originated from Germany. Florence Richter exhibited her work, including at the Arts and Crafts Exhibitions in London, and in Liverpool, Birmingham, Doncaster, Paris, Toronto, Dunedin and Stockholm. Also, at the Royal Academy (1908) and at the Society of Women Artists (1917-28). Elected an Associate of the Society of Women Artists (1918-19) and a Member (1920-28). Elected Vice President of the Society (1927-28). Works illustrated in The Studio.

RIDGWAY, GWENDOLINE (b.1901)

Bookbinder. Born in November 1901. The daughter of Brig.-General Ridgway, C.B., Indian Army. Educated at the Royal School, Bath. Studied at the London County Council Central School of Arts and Crafts. Exhibited at the Royal Academy Arts and Crafts Exhibition of 1926. Also exhibited at the Society of Women Artists (1928). Works illustrated in the Journal of the Library Association in 1926 (binding). Based in Campden Hill, London.

RIDING, JESSIE MARY (1884-1957)

Sculptor. Records suggest that Jessie was born in Liverpool, the daughter of William Riding, a bricklayer, and Mary. Raised in Liverpool. It also appears that she was the second wife of sculptor Frederick Edward Charles Gardner (1891-1963), whom Jessie married in Leicester in 1920. His first wife, Dolly (Dorothy) Jackson, died in 1918. Frederick Gardner, who originated from Worcester, was a former student of the Royal College of Art, then taught modelling at the Leicester School of Art. Jessie died first, in Ormskirk, Lancashire, aged 73. Gardner died in

Worcester, some six years later. Jessie lived in Barnes and Leicester during her career. She produced portrait medallions, busts and statuettes in bronze. Also worked as a modeller for Wedgwood. Executed a portrait medallion of Georges Clemenceau in 1919. Active until at least the early 1920s. Exhibited her work, including at the Royal Academy (1915-21). Exhibited works included: F.E.C. Gardner, Esq. (bust), A Young Faun (statuette, bronze), Plumpy Bacchus (statuette, bronze) and Temptation (statuette).

RIDLEY, MURIEL E. (b.1883)

Artist / Illuminator. Born in Wandsworth, London. The daughter of William Ridley, a civil engineer, and Mary. One of at least three children (Mabel, Maud and Muriel). Raised partly in East Grinstead, Sussex. Later based at Oxted, Surrey. Possibly the same Muriel Ridley who married in East Grinstead in 1910. Examples of her work were shown at the Society of Women Artists (1907-12). Those included illustrations from Tennyson's Idylls of the King and for The Earthly Paradise. Also, illustrations, a cover and a title page for Sleeping Beauty.

RIE, LUCIE (1902-95)

Potter. Born in Austria. Trained at the Kunst Gewerbe Schule, Vienna where Michael Powolny was Professor of Ceramics and where she studied ceramic chemistry. Rie established herself as a potter of note in Vienna, winning gold medals in international exhibitions held in Brussels and Paris, and at the Milan Triennale and elsewhere. She moved to England in around 1936, just prior to the Second World War. English potter Bernard Leach was so impressed with Rie that he invited her to visit his pottery at Shinner's Bridge in South Devon.

Rie established her own workshop in London, but war intervened, and she did not begin production fully until 1945 / 46. Began by producing ceramic buttons and beads, assisted by, among others, sculptor-turned-potter Hans Coper (b.1920). Coper had also moved to England just prior to the onset of war, in 1939, from Germany. He established his own pottery at Welwyn. In 1949 Rie exhibited some of her pots at the Berkeley Galleries. With Coper, she developed a range of domestic wares, and shared exhibitions with him at the Berkeley Galleries. Rie also sold in New York through Bonniers, where she held a one-woman show in 1954. Rie exhibited as part of a larger exhibition, staged in 1959, which was launched by the Smithsonian Institute of British Artist-Craftsmen, which toured the United States

for a year. The exhibition consisted of 175 pieces, with a large section devoted to ceramics. Sponsors of the exhibition included Sir Kenneth Clark, Henry Moore and Basil Spence. The select committee included John Piper.

Coper and Rie were chosen to represent England at the Milan Triennale in 1954. Rie also exhibited in Minneapolis, Tokyo and in Rotterdam in 1960 and 1967. In 1967 the Arts Council held a large retrospective of her work, then only the second living potter to receive this honour. She contributed to numerous other exhibitions. Since her death, her work has continued to be exhibited, including as part of a larger exhibition held at the Tate Gallery, St Ives in 2009. In the last years of her life five of her works were included in an exhibition The New Look held at the Manchester Art Gallery, 1991-92.

After arriving in England, Rie developed her work further. Always produced elegant, stylish ceramics. In 1953 The Studio (Vols.145-146, p.78) illustrated some of her porcelain bowls, thrown and turned, and decorated with bands of colour, incised with fine lines. She usually used restrained colours, including greys, black and yellow, highly reflective of what was happening generally in ceramics in the 1950s and 1960s. By 1960, Rie was working exclusively in porcelain and oxidized stoneware produced in an electric kiln. She now used sgraffito as a more frequent means of decoration, still using fine lines and cross-hatching as decoration, and a limited palette of browns, blues and white in porcelain. In her stoneware, she used black, white, lime or blue. Made larger dishes in coarser clay. Latterly, also made large pieces for Japanese tree planting. Rie mainly concentrated on pieces for everyday use such as bowls, cups, saucers and teapots.

Her wares were popular in America, Australia and New Zealand as well as Britain. A porcelain bowl with inlaid decoration by Rie was illustrated in The Studio, Vol.159, June 1960, p.199. Also noted in Muriel Rose, Artist Potters in England, London, Faber & Faber, published in 1955 and reissued in 1970. Rose included 18 illustrations of Rie's work in her volume, including a porcelain bowl owned by the Birmingham City Museum and Art Gallery, and an asymmetrical porcelain bottle and a stoneware bottle owned by the Rotterdam Museum. Rose also included two pieces made early on in Rie's career in Vienna, in terracotta and earthenware in 1936, and a later piece of stoneware dated 1967.

Rie has been the subject of numerous articles, including in Apollo (59, February 1954, Lucie Rie Potter by A.C. Sewter). Also, in Design (226, October 1967, Pottery of Lucie Rie by T. Davenport), in Design Quarterly (39, 1957, Lucie

Rie, Minneapolis, U.S.A.), in Pottery Quarterly (III, 1956, Lucie Rie and Hans Coper, exhibiting at the Berkeley Galleries) and in Architectural Review (116, September 1954, Hans Coper and Lucie Rie by R. Melville). Rie is also noted in Dora Billington's article The Young English Potters in The Studio, Vol.145, 1953. Rie died in London, aged 93.

RIGBY, HONORA MARY (1864-1916)

Sculptor / Miniature Painter. Born and raised in Chester. Worked there, and died there, aged 51. The daughter of Joseph Rigby, a union clerk, and Frances. One of at least four children (Frank, Agnes, Honora and Ernest). Produced miniature paintings of various subjects, decorative panels, decorative designs, such as wall fountains, busts and statuettes in marble, bronze and plaster. Exhibited her work for at least 25 years, including at the Royal Academy (1893-1915), the Royal Scottish Academy (1889-1913), the Royal Hibernian Academy (1901-14), the Royal Glasgow Institute (1901-12), with the Royal Birmingham Society of Artists, in Leeds and Manchester, and at the Walker Art Gallery, Liverpool. Exhibited works included: Les Pensees (bronze), Childhood (marble), Melody (plaster bust) and Sweet Rusticity (statuette). Worked until her death.

RIVERS, ELIZABETH JOYCE (1903-64)

Painter / Wood Engraver. Born in Bishop's Stortford, Hertfordshire in August 1903. The daughter of Thomas Alfred Hewitt Rivers (1863-1915) and Mabel Lucy Hall (1866-1938). One of at least five children (Frances, Thomas, Elizabeth, Edward and Maynard), all born between 1900 and 1907. Her father was a Fellow of the Royal Horticultural Society and ran a large nursery in Sawbridgeworth, Hertfordshire where Elizabeth grew up. The business had been started by Elizabeth's grandfather, Thomas F. Rivers. Her father had at least two sisters who became artists, Mary Laura Rivers (1862-1939) and Alice Werry Rivers (1868-1921). For a time, her Aunt Mary lived with Elizabeth and her family, at Little Pennys in Sawbridgeworth.

Elizabeth Rivers was educated at the St Catherine's School, Bramley, Surrey. She subsequently studied at the Goldsmiths' College, London under E.J. Sullivan between 1921 and 1924. Then studied at the Royal Academy schools under Sims, Walter Sickert, F.E. Jackson and Walter Russell between 1925 and 1930. Between 1931 and 1934 she studied in Paris under Andre L'Hote and Severini and at the Ecole de Fresque. She returned to London in 1934 and

became an artist in watercolours, oils and chalk of various subjects, produced woodcuts and wood engravings and pen & ink drawings for book illustration. Although based in London during her career, Rivers also spent time in Ireland, and died in Dublin in July 1964, aged 60. Spent time living at Aran, at Inis Mor and at Dundrum, Co. Dublin where she used the Knockrabo Studio.

During the Second World War she worked as a fire warden in London, but returned to Aran, publishing A Stranger in Aran with Ireland's Cuala Press in 1946. Between 1946 and 1955 she painted in Dublin and assisted Evie Hone in her stained glass studio. Rivers contributed regularly to the Irish Exhibition of Living Art. Also exhibited with the Royal Hibernian Academy (1936-48). Held a one-woman show at the Nicholson Gallery in Dublin in 1939, and another at the Dawson Gallery, Dublin in 1960. In 1966 a memorial exhibition was held in Dublin.

Rivers exhibited elsewhere during her career, including at the St George's Gallery, the Redfern Gallery, with the Society of Wood Engravers, with the New English Art Club, with the London Group and with the Royal Society of British Artists. Held a one-woman show at the Wertheim Gallery in 1933. Also exhibited with the Society of Women Artists (1927-49) and at the Royal Academy (1928-44). Exhibited works included: Mackerel Harvest, Old Woman (oil), Scything (chalk), Crucifixion (wood engraving) and When I Consider Thy Heavens (woodcut). Elected a Member of the Society of Women Artists (1939-49). A Member of the Arts Theatre Club. Five of her engravings were purchased by the British Museum Print Room. Some of her works were reproduced in the London Mercury, the Times Literary Supplement and elsewhere. In 1930 she travelled to Japan with her brother Maynard, who also became a nurseryman. Rivers illustrated a number of books during her career including Walter de la Mare, On the Edge (1930), Sean Dorman, Valley of Graneon (1944), E.E. Mannin, Connemara Journal (1947) and Patricia Lynch, The Mad O'Haras (1948). Illustrated her own books too, including This Man (Guyon Press, 1939) and Out of Bondage (1957) which was her last book. The National Library of Ireland owns some of her paintings and drawings.

ROBERTS, HILDA (1901-82)

Painter / Sculptor / Illustrator. Born in Dublin to a family of Quakers. Revealed an early talent. Educated at Nightingale Hall. Studied at the Metropolitan School of Art, Dublin from 1919. Spent two years there, studying under Patrick Tuohy. Whilst still a student, she executed 24 illustrations for Persian Tales, published by Macmillan. In the early 1920s, she spent two years at the London Polytechnic studying painting, drawing and anatomy. She returned to Dublin in around 1923 and studied sculpture under Oliver Sheppard, son of sculptor Simpson Sheppard. Roberts won three awards for modelling in 1924 and 1925 which gave her the opportunity to visit France. By 1929, she had returned to Ireland, but gave up sculpture to concentrate on portrait painting. Also produced flowers and landscapes in oils and watercolours, drawings and illustrations. She spent some time in the West of Ireland painting children.

Roberts held exhibitions of her work at the St Stephen's Green Gallery in 1930 and 1931. Also exhibited 60 works at the Royal Hibernian Academy between 1922 and 1979 including A Ghost Story, District Justice Reddin, The Egoist at the Dinner Party, Old Waterford Man and Head of a Cripple Boy. Elected an Honorary Royal Hibernian Academician, and a Member of the Dublin Painters Society. Also a prize winner at the Aonach Tailteann Exhibition of 1932. Won critical acclaim as an excellent draughtsman during her career. She married headmaster Arnold Marsh of Newtown School, Waterford, where the couple lived before returning to Dublin. Then spent time at Drogheda Grammar School, Co. Louth and, latterly, at Woodtown. Hilda also spent time at Bray prior to her marriage. After her marriage, she continued to work, and exhibited until at least three years before her death. She was also involved in needlework and stained glass during her career. Works in the Hugh Lane Municipal Gallery, Dublin, the Ulster Museum and the Waterford Municipal Collection.

ROBERTS, URSULA V. - SEE McCANNELL, U.V.

ROBERTSON, KATHLEEN M. - SEE WALKER, K.M.

ROBERTSON, NAN - SEE WEST, N.

ROBINS, IDA S. - SEE PERRIN, I.S.

ROBINSON, EDITH BREAREY - SEE DAWSON, E.B.

ROCK, HELEN FRAZER (1878-1932)
Sculptor / Potter. Born in Kingston, Surrey. The daughter of Joseph Rock, an East India agent, and Mary. One of a large family of at least 10 children (Catherine, Edwin, Amy, Evelyn, Helen, Leonard, Muriel, Eric, Florence and Annie). Her father may have married twice. Raised in Wimbledon. Studied at the Royal Academy schools, London. As a student, awarded a silver medal in 1904, a silver medal in 1906 and a second prize of £15 for a set of four models in 1907. Produced figure and portrait sculptures in marble, and porcelain figures. Spent her career in Wimbledon and Kensington, dying in Wimbledon. Exhibited her work, including at the Royal Academy (11 works, 1909-23), the Society of Women Artists (1907-25) and the International Society of Sculptors, Painters & Gravers. In 1927 exhibited some of her porcelain figures at the Cooling Galleries, New Bond Street, London along with watercolours by Madeleine Green. Exhibited works included: The Little Mermaid (statuette), Domini Mater (group), Fruition (statuette) and Peace (head, marble). A carved Madonna and Child by Rock can be found in the church of St Andrew, Chedworth, Gloucestershire.

RODGERS, GWLADYS MARY (1887-1946)
Pottery Designer / Decorator. Born in Bedale, Yorkshire. Possibly the only child of John William Rodgers (b.1844), a railway labourer and later a dairyman. Her father was born in Sheffield, though the family had Welsh connections. Her mother appears to have died young. Gwladys lived with her father for many years, spending time in Salford, Lancashire in her youth. She remained in Lancashire, dying in Swinton. She studied locally at the Levenshulme School of Art. As a student, she contributed to the National Competition of Schools of Art, including in 1908. One of her exhibits, an earthenware bowl in silver and ruby lustre, was illustrated in The Studio, Vol.44, 1908, p.273.

Gwladys subsequently worked for the pottery studios of the Pilkington Tile & Pottery Company who, like other businesses at that time, sought to explore the more artistic side of pottery manufacturing. The Pilkington firm was established in 1892 at Clifton Junction. Rodgers was one of four women artists to work for the firm, and specialised in lustre glazes. Her career there lasted from around 1908 to 1938. Her work included developing styles such as Lapis Ware (from 1928). Three examples of her work for Pilkington's were illustrated in The Studio, Vol.96, 1928, p.179 & pp.362-363.

Pilkington's developed the Lancastrian Lapis Ware to reveal the qualities inherent in glazed pottery, with simple brush-work decoration. The pottery was thrown and finished by hand on the potter's wheel, and each piece designed and decorated by one of the artists. The glazes were translucent with a shell-like finish. Examples of Pilkington's wares were on view at Heal's in the late 1920s. Their work showed that Pilkington's were making serious art pottery and employing highly reputable designers including Gwladys. A photograph of Gwladys was included in Abraham Lomax's book Royal Lancastrian Pottery 1900-1938 published in 1957. Works in the Victoria & Albert Museum, London.

ROFF, LETA ROSINA (1878-1969)

Sculptor. Born in Colchester, Essex. The daughter of John Ebenezer Roff, a schoolmaster, and Eliza. One of at least 10 children (John, Harry, Ada, Edith, Charlotte, Arthur, Emily, Marianne, Leta and Lilian). Raised in Colchester. By at least 1901 she was an art student. By at least 1906 she was based in London and remained there for a number of years, until at least 1937. However, she eventually returned to Colchester, where she died, aged 91. In London, she worked as an art teacher and secondary school French teacher, based at Cheyne Walk, Chelsea. She exhibited medallions, busts and statuettes in plaster and bronze at the Royal Glasgow Institute (1909) and at the Royal Academy (1906-13) whilst in London, but appears to have exhibited little else. Exhibited works included: A Baby (statuette, bronze), Muriel (bust), John Ebenezer Roff, Esq. (medallion) and The Snowball (statuette, plaster).

ROGERS, FRANCES CLARA (1890-1967)

Illustrator. Born in Southport, Lancashire. The daughter of the Rev. Joseph Thomas Woodhouse (b.1837), a Congregational Minister, and Clara (b.1856). Her father originated from Lincolnshire, her mother from Sussex. One of at least six children (John, Frances, Leslie, Sydney, Clara and Joyce). The children spent time in, and were born in, various places including not only Southport but Kent, Surrey, Devon and King's Norton in Worcestershire. Frances was educated in Switzerland, at the Bournemouth Collegiate School and at the King Edward's High School, Birmingham. She studied at the Birmingham School of Art, at the Belli Arti, Florence and at the Goldsmiths' College, London.

Frances became principally an illustrator of children's books. Those included several books of collected children's stories and poems. Also illustrated, for example, Stephen Southwold, Ten Minute Stories (Longman's) and Marion St John Webb, Mr Papingay's Caravan (Collins), Mr Papingay's Flying Shop (Collins) and Twice Ten Stories (University of London Press). Exhibited her work occasionally, including at the Royal Academy (1922). Elected a Member of the Faculty of Arts. In 1913 she married Stanley Reginald Harry Rogers (1887-1953). He originated from Nottinghamshire and was also an art student at Goldsmiths'. He was a painter and illustrator who served as a Naval Camouflage Officer for the Admiralty (1941-45). The couple had one son and lived in London, but later lived in Cornwall. Stanley died in Cornwall, aged 66, as did Frances, aged 76.

ROGERS, GRACE EVELYN (1882-1962)

Painter / Wood Engraver / Lithographer / Artist in Black & White / Designer. Born in London. The daughter of Samuel James Rogers (d.1911), a stockbroker, and Fanny (1854-1939). One of at least five children (Grace, John, Winifred, Samuel and Victor). Raised in London and Middlesex. Educated at the Abbotsford College. Studied at the Slade School, London. Produced paintings, wood engravings, lithographs and black & white drawings. Also worked as a designer for the theatre, and as a writer. Worked as a cartoonist for Architecture early in her career. Her woodcuts included The Shipwreck, The Three Follies and St Cecilia, all of which were published by the St George's Gallery. Exhibited her work, including at the St George's Gallery, the Whitechapel Art Gallery and with the Society of Independent Artists. Showed one work, Anemones, at the Royal Academy in 1954. In 1909 she married salesman George Owen Sharman (1883-1971) in Harringay, London. They had at least one son and two daughters. For a time they were based in West Derby, Liverpool. They divorced in 1928 in Liverpool. Grace married again, to Lawrence H. Bradshaw.

ROGERS, GRACE H.M. - SEE JOLLIFF, G.H.M.

ROLLETT, IVY KATHLEEN (1898-1980)

Painter. Born in Grimsby, Lincolnshire in August 1898. The daughter of Herbert Rollett (1872-1932) and Susannah. Had one sister, Gladys. Herbert Rollett was the son of a farmer, and initially, in the early 1900s, worked as a grocer and shopkeeper in Grimsby. However, he was also a landscape painter, exhibiting his work at the Royal Scottish Academy between 1925 and 1930. Ivy became a landscape painter in watercolours, so feasibly studied under her father. Ivy's career, like her father's, appeared to peak in the 1920s, when she began exhibiting more widely. She exhibited at the Royal Scottish Academy (1927-30), the Royal Glasgow Institute (1929), the Royal Academy (1928), at the Paris

Salon, the Walker Art Gallery, Liverpool and with the Royal Birmingham Society of Artists. Exhibited works included: Circles, Willows, Unsettled Weather and Wold Lands. Based in Grimsby for much of her career. In 1932 she married Bernard P. Ingamells in Grimsby. Ivy died in Exeter, aged 81.

ROLLO, JESSIE G. - SEE PATRICK, J.G.

ROLLS, FRANCES ADELAIDE (1869-1951)
Sculptor. Born in Surbiton, Surrey. The daughter of Dudley Rolls and Diana. Her father, a wholesale stationer, originated from Lambeth, her mother from Spitalfields. One of at least six children (Florence, Dudley, Edward, Lucy, Esther and Frances). Raised in Kingston, Surrey. But subsequently moved to 'Dilston' at Eastbourne. She lived there with her elderly parents and with Lucy and Esther until the girls were all at least in their 40s and all unmarried. Only Frances worked, as a sculptor. Produced portrait medallions and reliefs. Exhibited her work at the Royal Academy (eight works, 1893-1905), including Miss Barrell (medallion), Head of a Girl, An April Shower and Lucy (medallion). Still active in 1911. Frances died in Sussex, aged 82.

ROOS, EVA (1872-post-1934)
Painter / Illustrator. Produced portrait and figure paintings. Specialised in portraits of children in oils and pastels. Also produced charcoal drawings for the press in her early career, and executed black & white illustrations for children's books. Born in London in April 1872. The daughter of G.C.W. Roos, a stockbroker. Studied at the schools of Colarossi and Delecluse in Paris. Married animal painter and sculptor Simon Harman Vedder (1866-1937). He originated from Amsterdam and exhibited at the Royal Academy (1896-1931). They had one son. Eva was based in London for most of her life and career. She worked for over 35 years as an artist.

Eva exhibited her work, including at the Royal Academy (1898-1919), the Paris Salon, in Birmingham, Liverpool, Bristol and Manchester. Also, with the Royal Institute of Oil Painters and the Pastel Society. Held one-woman shows at the Maddox Gallery. Contributed to an exhibition of paintings of children held at the Baillie Gallery in 1909. Other exhibitors on that occasion included Helen Bedford, Clare Atwood and Amy Atkinson. Exhibited works included: A Little Convalescent, The Hoop Race, Home Lessons and Our Future Defenders. Won an Honourable Mention at the Artistes Francais. Elected a Member of the Pastel Society (1917). Won an Honourable Mention for her The Passer By. After exhibiting her Home Lessons at the Royal Academy in 1903, she was invited to show at the St Louis Exhibition. Contributed to The Graphic (1910). Illustrated Lullabies and Baby Songs for J.M. Dent (1900). Some of her works, including The Magic Pipe, were illustrated in Colour and Woman's Home Companion. She was still active in the 1930s. Possibly died in Christchurch, Hampshire in late 1958.

ROPE, DOROTHY ANNE ALDRICH (1883-1971)
Sculptor / Modeller. Born in Blaxhall, Suffolk. The daughter of Arthur Mingay Rope (1850-1945) and Agnes Maud Aldrich (1855-1943). The eldest of at least five children (Dorothy, Frederica, Phyllis, Arthur and Margaret), all raised in Leiston, Suffolk. Her father was a farmer. He came from a large family, several of whom became involved in the arts. His sister Ellen Mary Rope (1855-1934) became a successful decorative sculptor, working in London for several decades. His brother George became a painter, and another brother Edwin studied architecture in London. Another relative, Margaret Agnes Rope (1882-1953), became involved in stained glass, as did Dorothy's sister, Margaret Edith Aldrich Rope (1891-1988).

By at least 1901, still aged only 17, Dorothy had moved to London and was living with her aunt Ellen in Marylebone. Their next door neighbour was sculptor / painter May Heatherington Barker (1857-1912) who subsequently lived with Ellen and Dorothy at Marylebone Road. Dorothy studied under Ellen, and possibly under May Barker, and eventually worked with her aunt as well as independently. They shared accommodation until at least 1927, when Ellen appears to have left London and returned to Blaxhall, Suffolk, to the family farm. Dorothy remained in London until at least 1934, the year Ellen died. Dorothy eventually returned to Suffolk too, dying there, aged 87.

Although not as productive as her aunt, Dorothy experienced some success as a decorative sculptor, producing work not dissimilar to Ellen's. Like Ellen, she concentrated on decorative plaster panels, reliefs in silver and bronze, and statuettes in plaster and bronze. She began to exhibit her work from around 1903, when she was still only 20 years of age, and continued to do so until around 1927 when Ellen left London. She exhibited at the Royal Academy (1903-17) and the Society of Women Artists (1916-27). Exhibited works included: Child With Rabbits (plaster panel), Madonna and Child (plaster statuette), Capriccio (relief, bronze) and Summer is ycummin in (low relief, silver). Exhibited several works executed jointly with Ellen, including The Blessed Virgin (statuette, bronze) which was shown at the Royal Academy in 1911. Along with Ellen, Dorothy was a Member of the Church Crafts League (founded 1899), and showed work at the League's exhibitions.

ROPE, ELLEN MARY (1855-1934)

Sculptor / Modeller. Born in Blaxhall, Suffolk. The seventh child of George Rope (1814-1912), a farmer, and Anne Pope (1821-82). There were at least nine Rope children in total (Anne, George, Henry, Hannah, Arthur, Richard, Ellen, Edith and Edwin), born between 1845 and 1860. All were raised in Blaxhall. As a child, Ellen was known as Nell. From around 1870 she studied at Octavia Hill's Nottingham Place School in Marylebone, London. One of her subjects was drawing. She showed sufficient talent to enroll at the Ipswich School of Art, and in 1877 moved to the Slade School, London.

Initially, Ellen concentrated on painting and drawing. But from around 1880 she began to study modelling and sculpture, which would become her chosen career. Fellow students at the Slade included Elinor Halle, with whom she may have shared a studio. Ellen remained in London after completing her studies. Based at Marylebone Road until 1916, then at Fulham Road from 1917. Eventually returned to Blaxhall, to the family farm, sometime around 1927 or 1928. She died at Blaxhall in September 1934, aged 79, having experienced a long, successful and productive career.

Ellen Rope quickly established herself as a sculptor of note. However, she was not the only member of the Rope family to succeed in the arts. Her eldest brother George became a painter. Another brother Edwin became a student of architecture in London, living with Ellen in the early 1880s. Two other relatives, Margaret Agnes Rope and Margaret Edith Aldrich Rope, became involved in stained glass. Arguably her closest relationship was with her niece, sculptor Dorothy A.A. Rope. Dorothy was the daughter of Ellen's brother Arthur who was also a farmer. Dorothy joined Ellen in London, and studied under her aunt, subsequently working with her as well as independently. The two women shared accommodation for a number of years, from at least 1901, when Dorothy was still only 17 years of age. At that time, their neighbour was sculptor / painter and art teacher May Heatherington Barker (1857-1912), who later lived with Ellen

and Dorothy until her death. Dorothy remained in London after Ellen returned to Blaxhall, but she too subsequently returned to Suffolk, dying there in 1971, aged 87. On her death, Ellen left her estate to Dorothy and Margaret Edith Rope.

Ellen Rope's career lasted over 40 years. During that time she produced a considerable body of work, including numerous commissions. Also exhibited widely, from at least 1885 until at least 1927, when she would have been around 72 years of age. Produced mainly reliefs, statuettes and decorative panels, working in marble, bronze, pottery and plaster. Had a preference for figures, but particularly children. She executed highly decorative panels such as Christ Blessing Little Children and The Morning of Life which depicted children playing on the seashore. Evidently had an empathy with children, and executed a number of commissions related to childhood. For example, at the 1912 Arts and Crafts Exhibition Society exhibition, she showed a panel for an altarpiece in a children's chapel which was also illustrated in The Studio, Vol.58, February 1913, p.27. Such works undoubtedly held great charm and appeal, but also reflected her keen eye for immense detail, and her passion for her subject.

During her career, her work proved popular, and was highly regarded artistically. Indeed, in 1901 she was praised by M.H. Spielmann in his volume British Sculpture and Sculptors of To-day, London, Cassell & Co. Ltd. Spielmann notes some of her more prestigious commissions, including four panels, Faith, Hope, Charity and Heavenly Wisdom executed by Rope for the Women's Building at the Chicago Exposition of 1893. They were later set up in the Ladies' Dwelling in Chenies Street, London. Each panel measured 4'6" in length. Spielmann also commends her memorial panel for Salisbury Cathedral, her Pied Piper for Shelley House and her large frieze for the Rotherhithe Town Hall which measured 20ft in length.

Rope evidently had a ready market for her particular style of decorative work, and was frequently praised in journals such as The Studio and the Art Journal. Although not entirely unique, with other decorative sculptors such as Helen Langley producing similar work, Rope was certainly a leader in her field. She exhibited widely, including at the Royal Academy (45 works, 1885-1918), the Royal Society of British Artists (1890), the Royal Glasgow Institute (1905-09) and the Society of Women Artists (26 works, 1905-27). On several occasions, she exhibited jointly with Dorothy. Exhibited works revealed her ability to diversify and included portrait reliefs in bronze, plaques, bas-reliefs and statuettes, but also such things as decorative door furniture and electric bell pushes.

Other works by Rope were shown at the Walker Art Gallery, Liverpool. In 1899 a new exhibition was opened at Harrington Road, South Kensington at the Permanent Gallery of Decorative Art. The exhibition aimed to show work by decorative artists and to help win them commissions. Exhibitors included Ellen Rope, W. Glasby, Mary Lowndes and Hilda Pemberton. Two of Ellen's exhibits on that occasion were a panel relief for an overmantel and Sea Chariot, a panel in relief. Both were illustrated in the Art Journal, 1899, pp.25-26. In 1903, Rope contributed to a small exhibition of arts and crafts which included the work of bookbinder Elizabeth M. MacColl, held at the Woodbury Gallery. She also exhibited at the 1904 City of Bradford Exhibition with Dorothy, which had a section devoted to artistic handcrafts practised by women. In 1905 / 06, Ellen contributed to the Second Exhibition of Arts and Crafts held at the Lyceum Club, showing decorative works such as Guardian Angel, a silver bronze panel. Also contributed to several of the Arts and Crafts Exhibition Society exhibitions. Ellen and Dorothy also exhibited with the Church Crafts League (founded 1899), jointly and independently. For example, at the League's 1902 exhibition Ellen showed a reredos in coloured plaster titled Adoration by Children, designed for a children's hospital. Both were active members of the Church Crafts League, and Ellen also sat on its committee.

The Rope family evidently came from a religious background, executing works for numerous churches and chapels, including at Blaxhall, Suffolk, from where they originated. Ellen may also have been involved with the Clergy and Artists' Association. Three panels in relief by Ellen, intended for a hospital chapel or church, were illustrated in the Art Journal in 1898 (p.110) in an article What the Clergy and Artists' Association is Doing For English Church Art of To-day. Like the Church Crafts League, the Association expressed considerable concern over falling standards in church art. At various times, Ellen Rope worked with other artists and sculptors. At the 1906 Walker Art Gallery Autumn Exhibition Ellen showed a silver and bronze cabinet made jointly with Ellen Woodward and illustrated in The Studio, Vol.39, November 1906, p.169.

During her already demanding career, Ellen also designed for the Della Robbia Pottery at Birkenhead, from the early 1890s until its closure in 1906. Themes in her work for the pottery were typically reliefs, or designs based on children and fairies. The pottery, founded by Harold Rathbone, produced enamelled and coloured earthenware in the style of Della Robbia. Several of Rope's pieces for Della Robbia, including a panel for overmantel insertion and two panels of praying angels, were illustrated in the Art Journal, 1898, pp.27-28. At the Walker Art Gallery's 1898 Spring Exhibition Ellen showed two Della Robbia panels, Boy and Dolphin and Melody, which were designed by her and painted by Miss E.M. Wood. The Melody panel was illustrated in The Studio, Vol.13, April 1898, p.190. Ellen produced at least one design for stained glass, which was executed by one of the Margaret Ropes for Blaxhall church.

ROPE, MARGARET AGNES (1882-1953)

Stained Glass Designer. Born in Shrewsbury, Shropshire. The second child of Henry John Rope (1847-99), a doctor, and Agnes Maud Burd (1857-1948). One of at least six children, raised in Shrewsbury. The early death of her father meant that they were brought up with little money. Most of the family converted to Catholicism. Margaret and her sister Monica eventually became nuns, and their brother Harry became a priest. Another sister, Irene, became a botanist. Two other brothers, Michael and Denys, became an aeronautical engineer and a doctor. Michael died young.

Margaret took up art and in 1900 began studying at the Birmingham Municipal School of Art. She studied enamelling, lettering and stained glass under Sidney Meteyard, E.G. Treglown and Henry Payne. As a student, she won an Honourable Mention for a Christmas card design in The Studio competition for 1900 under the name 'Jemima'. Also contributed to the National Competition of Schools of Art between 1903 and 1909. In 1909 she submitted a set of designs, one for stained glass. She was awarded a National Silver Medal by the judges, who were Messrs Byam Shaw, Lewis F. Day and Alexander Fisher. Rope was also given a Special Mention in the official report. In the same year, her stained glass design Judith was illustrated in the Building News, Vol.96, 29 January, p.178. She spent some nine years at the Birmingham School, winning an assortment of scholarships, medals, prizes and commendations. Left in 1909, working for a short period of time at the family home, The Priory, in Shrewsbury. In 1910 she began the first of a series of seven windows for Shrewsbury Cathedral completed only in the 1920s.

In 1911 Margaret moved to London, renting a studio at The Glass House in Fulham where she could concentrate on stained glass. Worked with her cousin, Margaret Edith Aldrich Rope (1891-1988), as well as independently. Together, they worked on the Rope memorial window for Blaxhall church, Suffolk (1911-12). Other commissions included windows for Newport Catholic Church, Shropshire and the Catholic Cathedral at Geraldton, West Australia. A number of war memorial windows followed. In 1923 she left London and entered the Carmelite monastery at Woodbridge, Suffolk. There, as Sister Margaret, she continued with her stained glass work, in a small studio. The Glass House supplied her with glass cut to her cartoons which, once painted, was returned there for firing and glazing.

Margaret subsequently moved to Rushmere near Ipswich. After the Second World War, the monastery moved to Quidenham, Norfolk. Rope made preliminary sketches for the new windows at Quidenham, but due to ill-health, they were executed by her cousin. She occasionally used her brother Michael as a model for her earlier windows. Other windows executed by her included a glass panel based on Christina Rossetti's Goblin Market (1905). Also, The Last Supper for St Mary's Catholic Church, Lanark (1915), David and Isaiah for the former Franciscan Convent Chapel, East Bergholt, Suffolk (c.1910) and St Michael the Archangel for Michaelhouse School Chapel, Balgowan, nr Pietermaritzburg, South Africa (1920s).

Rope died in December 1953. A memorial window to her can be found at the Church of the Holy Family and St Michael at Kesgrave near Ipswich. Some of her archive can be found at the Birmingham Art Gallery and Museum. Exhibited her work occasionally, including at the Arts and Crafts Exhibition Society exhibitions. In 1916, for example, she showed two drawings for glass roundels at Tyburn Convent which were illustrated in The Studio, Vol.69, January 1917, p.196. Some of her work was included in an exhibition Women Stained Glass Artists of the Arts and Crafts Movement held at the William Morris Gallery, London, 1985-86. Margaret Agnes Rope was part of the artistic Rope family which also included Dorothy A.A. Rope, Ellen Mary Rope and Margaret Edith Aldrich Rope.

ROPE, MARGARET EDITH ALDRICH (1891-1988)

Stained Glass Designer. Born at Leiston, Suffolk. The granddaughter of George Rope (1814-1912), a farmer. The fifth child of Arthur Mingay Rope, also a farmer, and Agnes Maud. Part of an artistic family. George's daughter, Ellen Mary Rope (1855-1934), Margaret's aunt, was a successful decorative sculptor. Her uncle, George Rope, was a painter. Her sister, Dorothy A.A. Rope, also became a decorative sculptor. Stained glass designer Margaret Agnes Rope was her cousin. Margaret Edith began her studies at the Chelsea School of Art. Then moved to the London County Council Central School of Arts and Crafts. At the latter, she studied stained glass under Karl Parsons and Alfred J. Drury who, with Mary Lowndes, founded Lowndes and Drury, later based at The Glass House in Fulham.

From 1911 Margaret worked at The Glass House, assisting her cousin Margaret Agnes Rope, working with her on the Rope family memorial window for Blaxhall church, Suffolk (1911-12). During the First World War, she served with the Women's Land Army. After the war, she returned to The Glass House and continued to work with her cousin. Also carried out her own commissions, including Christ With Children, a stained glass window for Clippesby Church, Norfolk (c.1919). In 1923 her cousin Margaret left Fulham to become a nun, but Margaret Edith remained at The Glass House, living in Deodar Road in a house shared with stained glass designers Caroline Townshend and Joan Howson.

During the Second World War, Rope, Townshend and Howson joined forces and cared for evacuated children in Wales. Also spent time in Sussex. After the war, she returned to London and worked from a different house in Deodar Road. There, she had a studio and workshop with a kiln also used by stained glass designer Rachel Tancock. In the following years, Rope was responsible, with the assistance of friend and pupil Clare Dawson, for yet more stained glass windows. Her career eventually covered over 50 years, with some work completed when she was in her 70s.

Her commissions over the years also included windows for the Carmelite church at Quidenham, Norfolk, originally begun by her cousin. Also, for St Chad's, Far Headingley, Leeds, All Saints, Hereford and St John's, Coventry. Executed a single-light window for Bishop Otter College Chapel, Chichester (1928) and an east window for Ickleton Parish Church, Essex (1929). She eventually returned to Suffolk, dying there in early 1988, aged 96. Converted to Catholicism, as did Margaret Agnes Rope. Works included in an exhibition Women Stained Glass Artists of the Arts and Crafts Movement held at the William Morris Gallery, London, 1985-86.

ROSE, GWENDOLEN BEATRICE (1890-1966)

Sculptor. Born in Shadwell, London. The daughter of Harry Alfred Rose, a barge builder, and Rebecca. Her father originated from Shadwell, and lived in a community of boat and barge builders. Gwendolen was one of at least five children (Harry, Isabel, William, Bessie and Gwendolen). Her brother Harry also became a barge builder. Bessie and Gwendolen became art students in London. Gwendolen became a sculptor of reliefs and statuettes in bronze. Exhibited her work occasionally, including at the Royal Academy (1914-24) and at the 1916 Arts and Crafts Exhibition Society exhibition. Exhibited works included: A Reverie (statuette, bronze), Portrait (relief) and Daydreams. In 1916 she married stockbroker Percy Grout Smith (1888-1959) in Shadwell, London. She died in Chichester, aged 76.

ROSS-CRAIG, STELLA (1906-2006)

Botanical Artist. Born and raised in Aldershot, Hampshire in March 1906. The daughter of John Ross-Craig, M.P.S., a pharmacist, and Christina. One of at least three children (Bertram, Stella and Eunice). Educated privately. Studied at the Thanet Schools of Art. Studied botany at the Chelsea Polytechnic School of Art. Became a botanical artist in pen & ink, pencil and watercolours. Worked as an artist at the Herbarium at the Royal Botanic Gardens, Kew. Also worked as an artist for the Royal Horticultural Society from 1929. Approximately 500 of her watercolours and several hundred of her pen & ink and pencil drawings were kept in the Reference Collection of the Herbarium at Kew. The Royal Horticultural Society also had examples of her watercolours in its collection. Her work was reproduced in Hooker's Icones Plantarum, in Hutchinson & Dalziel's Flora of Western Tropical Africa, in White & Sloane's The Stapelieae, in Snowden's The Sorghums and in numerous scientific publications including Botanical Magazine and Kew Bulletin. Some of her drawings of British plants were also published. Elected a Fellow of the Linnean Society. In 1936 she married Joseph Robert Sealy, B.Sc. and Fellow of the Linnean Society, in Middlesex. Stella died in London, aged 100.

ROWAT, JESSIE W. - SEE NEWBERY, J.W.

ROWE, ELEANOR (1853-1920)

Woodcarver. Born in Kilburn, Middlesex. The daughter of Richard Rowe, an East India merchant, and Eliza. One of at least 11 children (Elsie, Henrietta, Eleanor, Margaret, Alfred, Richard, Adelaide, Fanny, Elizabeth, George and Cecil). Raised in Middlesex and Hampstead. Based in London during her career. Died in Kensington, aged 67. Eleanor trained in woodcarving, probably in London, and was certainly active in the 1880s and 1890s. For a number of years, she was manager of the School of Art Wood Carving at South Kensington. She was the author of French Wood Carvings From the National Museum, London, B.T. Batsford, second edition published 1896, third edition published in 1897. Exhibited her work at the Society of Women Artists (1896-1907). Elected an Honorary Member of the Society (1901-21). According to The Year's Art, 1896, p131, the School of Art Wood Carving was established with a view to encouraging art woodcarving in Britain. It was a City & Guilds Institute and provided 12 free places. The School was open to amateurs. Students of its day classes were charged £2 per month or £5 per quarter. Evening classes were also run. Some tuition was available via correspondence. Secretary of the School in 1896 was Thomas Healey. Instructors included W.T. Ross and W.H. Grimwood. Rowe may have been superseded by Maria Reeks. SEE: REEKS, MARIA

ROWE, ELSIE - SEE THOMAS, E.

ROWLANDS, CONSTANCE ETHEL (1891-1930)

Illustrator. Born in Fukuoka, Japan in March 1891. The daughter of the Venerable Archdeacon Hutchinson. He was Archdeacon of Kiushiu, Japan. Constance was educated at St Michael's, Limpsfield, Surrey. Studied at the Regent Street Polytechnic, London, at the Kensington School of Art, London and in Bristol. A bronze medallist in the National Competition of Schools of Art. A gold and bronze medallist at the Royal Drawing Society. Became a successful illustrator. Illustrated a number of books including Tales of Our Ancestors (Dent, three volumes), Wonder Tales (P. Allen, five volumes), Uncle Parker and The Happy Dragon (P. Allen), Rif (Hutchinson) and The Blessed Damozel (Bodley Head). In 1915 she married schoolmaster Charles Rowlands in Bristol. He originated from Bristol. They lived at Winscombe, Somerset. She exhibited two works at the Royal Academy, The Devout Knight in 1928 and Romance in 1930. Also exhibited with the Royal West of England Academy. Her career was cut short by her untimely death in a Bristol hospital in July 1930, aged 39.

ROWLES, LILIAN MAY BEVIS (1892-1953)

Painter / Commercial Artist. Born in Newport, Monmouthshire. The daughter of the Rev. George Hall, a Congregational minister, and Tudda Bevis. Her father originated from Northumberland. Lilian had at least one sibling, Leslie G.B. Hall (b.1893). Raised partly in West Ham, London. Educated at the Milton Mount College. Studied at the West Bromwich Municipal School of Art near Birmingham. As a student, she was a National silver and bronze medallist and a Senior King's prize winner. Became a painter of portraits and a commercial artist in advertising and illustration. Based mainly in London but also in Congleton, Cheshire for a short time. Exhibited her work widely. Showed all types of commercial art in France, Germany, Britain and elsewhere in Europe, and in America. Also exhibited at the Royal Academy (16 works, 1908-23) and with the Society of Graphic Art. Exhibited works included: Ernest Wild, Esq., K.C., Sir Robert Garran, K.C.M.G., Mrs Maskery and H.R.H. Princess Patricia of Connaught.

In late 1915 Lilian married Stanley Charles Rowles (1887-1966) in Wandsworth, London. Rowles, an Associate of the Royal College of Art, was also a commercial artist and former deputy headmaster of the West Bromwich Municipal School of Art. The son of a headmaster, he designed shipping and railway posters, among other things. The couple lived mainly in London. Lilian used various studios, including the Trafalgar Studios and the St Albans Studios. They had one son and one daughter. Lilian continued with her work after her marriage but appeared to exhibit less into the 1930s. Lilian died in Surrey, where they lived latterly, aged 61.

RUDLAND, FLORENCE MAY (1872-1903)

Painter / Illustrator. Born in Balsall Heath, Worcestershire. Raised in Worcestershire and in Edgbaston, Birmingham. The daughter of William Rudland and Ellen. Her father, a furnishing warehouseman, originated from Suffolk, her mother from Birmingham. Florence was the eldest of at least nine children (Florence, William, Ernest, Beatrice, Frank, Anna, Elsie, Isabel and Percy). Despite a less than affluent background, the children were, apparently, well educated. William became a furniture dealer, Ernest an accounts clerk and Frank a bank clerk. Florence chose art, and in the early 1890s (from at least 1891), whilst still living at the family home, she began at the Birmingham Municipal

School of Art. She contributed to the annual National Competition of Schools of Art, including in 1893 when she won a silver medal for her designs for La Motte Fouque's Undine. The book was reissued in 1897 with Florence's illustrations and a translation by Sir Edmund Gosse. Florence also contributed drawings to the 1895 National Competition. One of those was reproduced in The Studio, Vol.6, October 1895, p.50. She also contributed to the Birmingham School's own annual exhibition of students' work.

Rudland quickly became associated with the Birmingham School of illustration, which also included E.H. New, Violet Holden, Arthur and Georgina Gaskin and Mary Newill. In 1893 she contributed drawings to A Book of Christmas Carols (George Allen, priced 5s), a collective effort which was overseen by Arthur Gaskin. Other contributors included Bernard Sleigh, Mildred Peacock, Mary Newill and Arthur Gaskin. In the same year, some of her work was included in the Arts and Crafts Exhibition Society exhibition. By at least 1896 (April), Rudland was also contributing to The Yellow Book. After completing her studies, she worked as an illustrator, but was responsible for only a small body of work. Books illustrated by her included Mary Martha Sherwood, The Fairchild Family. Rudland's highly promising career was curtailed by her untimely death in Birmingham, aged 30. Up until that point, she was still living at the family home with several of her adult siblings. Noted in Mahony, Latimer & Folmsbee, Illustrators of Children's Books 1744-1945, Boston, The Horn Book Inc., 1947.

RUMBALL, MARJORIE E. - SEE TAYLOR, M.E.

RUSBRIDGE, LILIAN - SEE ANDREWS, L.

RUSHTON, DOROTHY MARION (1884-post-1952)

Painter / Mural Decorator / Etcher. Born in Greenhithe, Kent in September 1884. The daughter of George A. Rushton, a London stockbroker and agent, and Florence. Both her parents originated from London. Had a brother, Cecil, a year older, also born in Greenhithe. Educated at the Queen Elizabeth School and in Hanover. Studied in London at Cope's Art School and the Royal Academy schools. Produced oil and watercolour paintings, mural decorations and etchings, mainly buildings and landscapes. Exhibited at the Society of Women Artists (1916-22), the Walker Art Gallery, Liverpool, with the Women's International Art Club, the Royal Hibernian Academy (1916) and in some provincial galleries in Britain and France. Also, with the British Watercolour Society and the Aberdeen Art Society. Elected a Member of both. Also a Member of the Royal Scottish Society of Painters in Watercolours Art Club and of the Forum Club. Exhibited works included: Ashford's Yard, Saxmundham, Ravello, South Italy (etching), The Portfolio and Leicester Hospital, Warwick (etching). Mural decorations included for the Hall of St George's-in-the-East. Acted as an art teacher for a while. Works illustrated in the Art Chronicle. Active for over 35 years. Based mainly in London.

RUSHTON, ELLEN (active early 1900s)

Engraver. Based in a studio in Gloucester Street, London. Produced chromo-lithographs. Exhibited 16 of those at the Society of Women Artists between 1903 and 1904, including The Mirror, Garden Poppies, A Merry Jest and Birds' Eggs for Naturalists. Otherwise, remains difficult to trace.

RUSHTON, WINIFRED (b.1901)

Designer / Craftswoman. Born in Ryton-on-Tyne, Northumberland in November 1901. The daughter of George Robert Rushton (b.1869) and Edith. Her father was an artist and decorative worker, master of a School of Art in Ipswich and advisor on the committee of the Ipswich Museum and Art Gallery. Winifred had at least one sister, Enid. Raised mainly in Ipswich. Educated at the local High School. Studied at the Ipswich School of Art and at the Brighton School of Art. Awarded a complete certificate of the Board of Education. Awarded a First Class City & Guilds of London Institute in embroidery. Also awarded a teaching certificate in 1925. Became a designer, an embroideress, a weaver, an illuminator and a leatherworker. Became craft mistress at the Eastbourne School of Art. In the 1930s she was based in Blewbury, Oxfordshire. Exhibited her work occasionally, including with the Eastbourne Society of Artists and the Ipswich Fine Art Club.

RUSSELL, HILDA GERTRUDE (1890-1965)

Painter / Woodcut Artist / Embroideress. Born in Camberwell, London in February 1890. The daughter of Thomas Russell, a watchmaker, and Alice. One of at least four children (Sidney, Adelaide, Alice and Hilda). Raised in London. Died in Worthing, Sussex, aged 75. Educated at the Roan School for Girls, Blackheath, London. Studied at the Camberwell School of Art. A City & Guilds bronze medallist. Produced landscape paintings, woodcuts and embroideries. Exhibited at the Royal Society of British Artists, with the South London Group and at the Royal Academy (1936). Exhibited works included: Willow by River, The Teme Valley, An Old Street and Ludlow Landscape. Became a teacher of art. During the war, she worked in the Admiralty Drawing Office.

RUTHERFORD, ROSEMARY ELLEN (1912-72)

Stained Glass Artist / Etcher / Painter. Born in September 1912 in King's Norton, Worcestershire. The daughter of John Finley Rutherford, a clerk in holy orders, and Florence Ellen Edge. Her father originated from Co. Down, Ireland, her mother from Birmingham. Had at least one brother, John Allarton Edge Rutherford (b.1910). Immediately prior to her birth, her parents were based at The Parsonage House at Northfield near Birmingham, in the district of King's Norton. Rosemary studied at the Slade School, London. Her brother followed in his father's footsteps and joined the Church. Rosemary became an artist in watercolours, pen & ink, an etcher and a stained glass designer. Produced various subjects including figures and still life.

Exhibited her work, including at the Royal Academy in 1937 and 1947 whilst living in London. Also exhibited with the New English Art Club. Exhibited works included: In the Larder and Late Roses. Elected a Member of the distinguished Art Workers' Guild in 1970. When war broke out, Rutherford joined the Red Cross as a volunteer. She was given permission by the War Artists' Advisory Committee to record her work as a V.A.D. One of her works was Off Duty Nurse Darning Stockings (watercolour, c.1941). Her voluntary work eventually took her to Ceylon. Her etchings included The Empty Tomb. Stained glass designs included Madonna and Child. Her brother was rector at St Mary's at Walsham le Willows, Suffolk, and later in her career Rosemary had a studio there, and worshipped in the church. She also worked at Boxford and Hinderclay in Suffolk, and at Gaywood in Norfolk. Associated with Cedric Morris and the East Anglian School of Painting and Drawing at Hadleigh, Suffolk. A memorial window to Rosemary can be found at Walsham le Willows church. She died at the comparatively young age of 59 in Lambeth, London.

RYDER, FRANCES ELIZABETH (1886-1976)

Potter / Etcher / Painter. Born at Stoke-on-Trent, Staffordshire in December 1886. The daughter of Thomas Leigh (1865-1936), an accountant, and

Fanny Woolliscroft Rhead (1866-1931). Her father, who originated from Stoke-on-Trent, was, for a time, an accountant for the railways. Her mother was part of the local Rhead dynasty of potters, the daughter of George Woolliscroft Rhead. Frances was one of at least nine children (Frances, Minnie, Phyllis, Dorothy, Gladys, Ethel, Catherine, William and Cyril). Following in the Rhead family tradition, Frances, Minnie and Phyllis all became pottery workers, with Frances and Minnie working as majolica tile decorators for a while. Dorothy became a music student and Gladys a dressmaker's apprentice. Frances studied art at Burslem, and became not only a pottery worker but an etcher and a landscape artist in line & wash, oils and watercolours.

In 1917 Frances married George Ryder (b.1887) in Wolstanton, Staffordshire. He was born in Hanley, Stoke-on-Trent and studied at the Hanley School of Art and at the Royal College of Art, London. He became a Member of the distinguished Art Workers' Guild and, for a time, was art director for a pottery manufacturer. The couple spent much of their marriage (over 40 years) in London. There, Frances exhibited her work, including at the Society of Women Artists (87 works, 1925-65), with the South London Group, with the Blackheath Art Society and at the Macrae Gallery. Exhibited works included: Fishermen's Cottages, Ludlow Church (line & wash), Abel Fletcher's Mill and Roofs and Chimneys, Ironbridge (watercolour). Elected an Associate of the Society of Women Artists (1926-60) and a Member (1961-66). Frances died in Derbyshire, aged 89.

RYLAND, ADOLFINE MARY KONCELIK (1903-83)

Sculptor / Artist. Born in Windsor, Berkshire. The daughter of Frank Theodore Ryland and Adolfine Augusta. Her father, a solicitor, originated from Surrey. Her mother originated from Australia but was a British subject by marriage. Adolfine was one of at least three children, all born in Windsor, all given the middle name Koncelik, their mother's maiden name. Adolfine spent her childhood in Windsor, at Osborne Villas in the parish of Clewer Within. Studied at the Heatherley's School of Art in the 1920s. Also studied at the Grosvenor School of Modern Art under Claude Flight. Produced sculptures, paintings, prints and decorative works. Exhibited two works at the Society of Women Artists in 1924: Afternoon and Trevalga, North Cornwall. Also exhibited with the Women's International Art Club between 1927

and 1954. Elected a Member of the Club between 1936 and 1954. One of her commissions was for London County Council, to design low reliefs for several buildings including the St Martin's School of Art and the School of Butchers. Some of her works were included in an exhibition of printmakers of the 1920s and 1930s held in 1987 at the Michael Parkin Gallery, London. Adolfine died in Bullingdon, Oxfordshire, aged 80. Works in the Tate Gallery, London.

S

SAMS, ISABELLA M. - SEE HARRISON, I.M.

SANCTUARY, MAISIE TOPPIN (1905-93)

Sculptor. Based in Bridport, Dorset and in Laleham-on-Thames, Middlesex during her career. Died in Surrey, aged 88. Active from the 1930s to the 1960s at least. Produced figures in earthenware, stoneware and terracotta. Exhibited her work, including at the Royal Hibernian Academy (18 works, 1935-63), the Royal Academy (1952) and the Society of Women Artists (1951). Exhibited works included: Mother and Child (terracotta), Bantam Cock (pottery), Choirboy (stoneware) and Abyssinian Goose (earthenware).

SANDERCOCK, ESME VIOLET (1909-2003)

Wood Engraver / Drypoint Artist. Born in Croydon. Died in Oxfordshire, aged 94. The daughter of Leslie Sandercock, a civil servant, and Violet Florence. Possibly a student of the Royal College of Art, London. In 1934 she married art master Rodney Hellyer Hodge in Horley, Surrey. He was the son of art master David Henry Hodge. Exhibited her work at the Royal Academy (1930). Also, with the Society of Wood Engravers, including in 1931 at the Redfern Gallery. One of her exhibits on that occasion, The New Baby, was illustrated in The Studio, Vol.101, March 1931, p.196. Other works included Mother and Child and Bedtime (drypoint).

SANDERS, VIOLET E.C. (b.1904)

Draughtsman / Wood Engraver / Heraldic Illuminator / Clay Modeller / Painter. A gifted and versatile artist. Born in Mexico City in March 1904. The daughter of James McConnell Sanders, F.C.S., F.I.C. Educated at the Blackheath High School and at a private school in Eastbourne. Studied at the Blackheath School of Art between

1922 and 1923, the Harrow Technical School between 1923 and 1925, the Willesden Polytechnic between 1925 and 1928 and the Willesden Technical College in 1931, under headmaster J.R. Locke. Also studied engraving under Ernest Heber Thompson, R.E.

Sanders was involved in various areas of art and the decorative arts over some 40 years. Her work included designing bookplates, engraving frontispieces, heraldic designs, wood engravings and modelling in clay. Acted as heraldic artist to the College of Arms between 1936 and 1939. Produced paintings in oils and watercolours. Designed an illuminated Central Statistical Office Christmas card to the U.N.O. in Washington in 1949. Produced designs for Masonic lodge badges. Executed industrial designs for I.C.I. Produced a set of original designs for a commemorative medal and stamps illustrating 900 years since the Norman Conquest. Acted as Admiralty map draughtsman between 1940 and 1947. Also draughtsman to the Cabinet Office, Westminster.

Sanders exhibited her work, including at the Royal Academy (1937-49), which resulted in private purchases. Also, at the Derby Art Gallery (by invitation), the Whitechapel Art Gallery, with the Bath Artists' Society, the National Society, the Society of Graphic Art and the Society of Women Artists (1940-67). Exhibited works included: The Three Marys, Christabel, We Meet Brother Squirrel and In Exile (all wood engravings). Elected a Member of the Society of Graphic Art and of the Bath Artists' Society. Works published in various periodicals. Based at Pinner, Middlesex for much of her career, latterly at Lavender Cottage.

SANDFORD, LETTICE MACKINTOSH (1902-93)

Engraver / Illustrator / Decorative Artist. Born in St Albans, Hertfordshire. The daughter of Lachlan Rate and Ada. Her father had personal wealth. One of at least four daughters (Muriel, Alice, Lettice and Elizabeth). Raised in Haywards Heath, Sussex in a house with servants. Studied at the Byam Shaw and Vicat Cole School of Art in London and at the Chelsea Polytechnic under Percy Jowett. Also taught by Robert Day and Graham Sutherland. Produced wood, copper and zinc engravings along with decorative work and book illustrations. In 1929 she married book designer and publisher Christopher Sandford (1902-83) in Dorking, Surrey. He originated from Ireland. They had one son and two daughters.

Lettice produced engravings for the Boar's Head Press. Christopher Sandford learned the techniques of printing at the Chiswick Press, and from 1933 was director of the Golden Cockerel Press, for whom Lettice also worked. Sandford bought the Press from Robert Gibbins. In 1975 Sandford published a Bibliography of the Golden Cockerel Press. Lettice illustrated a number of books during her career, but was particularly active in the 1930s. Those included Christopher Marlowe, Hero and Leander (Golden Cockerel Press, 1933), for which she produced engravings. Also, The Golden Bed of Kydno, translated by P. Mathers. Lettice produced a design for the upper board and 12 line engravings as well as illustration work. This was a limited edition printed by the Golden Cockerel Press in 1935. And, F.L. Lucas (ed.), The Golden Cockerel Greek Anthology, a selection of poems with 20 line engravings (18 full-page) printed on watermarked Barcham Green handmade rough grey paper, published by the Golden Cockerel Press in 1937. Some 74 specially bound copies were printed.

Other books illustrated by Lettice included Christopher Sandford, The Magic Forest (1931), E.M. Cox (transl.), Sappho (1932), Edmund Spencer, Thalamos (1932), Lucius Apuleius, Cupid and Psyche (1934) and Christopher Whitfield, Lady From Yesterday (1939). Lettice also wrote and illustrated two children's books, Roo Coo and Panessa (1938) and Coo My Doo (1943), and wrote Decorative Straw Work and Corn Dollies published in 1964. Later in their careers, Lettice and Sandford lived at Eye Manor, Leominster, Herefordshire, where they both died. Some of her works were included in an exhibition of women wood engravers held at the Museum of Oxford in 1979. Lettice was one of 27 women represented. She was awarded a Diploma at the 1937 International Exhibition of Art & Industry in Paris.

SANDHEIM, AMY ALICE (1875-1958)

Sculptor / Metalworker. Born in Kensington, London. The daughter of Edmund Wilkins, a cordwainer (shoemaker), and Frances. One of at least 10 children (William, Edmund, Amy, Frances, John, Cecil, Sydney, George, Arthur and Rosamund). Raised in London. Listed in census recordings for 1901 as a sculptor. In 1907, she married Julius Woolfe Sandheim in London. The couple lived in London, and had at least one child, Dorothea. Julius was an art jeweller, and Amy is listed in census recordings for 1911 as an 'art jeweller assistant', indicating that she worked with her husband. She exhibited examples of her work at the Society of Women Artists (1919-28). Amy died in Hammersmith, aged 82.

**SANDISON, MARY S.L. - SEE
WHITE, M.S.L.**

SANFORD, SUSAN ELLEN (1865-post-1922)
Painter / Illuminator. Born in Sutton Coldfield, Staffordshire. The daughter of Henry Sanford, an ironmonger, and Susan. Had at least one brother, Henry. Raised in Croydon. Based in Bassett Road, Kensington during her early career, but subsequently moved around, living in Surrey, Oxfordshire, Berkshire and Sussex at various times. Lived with her widowed mother for some of the time. Produced paintings in watercolours and tempera, including landscapes, still life, portraits and figures. Also, illuminations on vellum. Appears to have exhibited her work predominantly at the Society of Women Artists. Showed 59 works there between 1886 and 1921. Those included: Wild Plums, Trifle Not, Your Time is But Short (watercolour), Psalm 91 (illumination on vellum) and The Flock (tempera). Also exhibited at the Royal Academy (1894-1914). Elected an Associate of the Society of Women Artists (1902-22). During her career, Sanford spent some time in Wantage, Berkshire, close to the Sisters of Wantage. She also spent time in Ascot, Berkshire, close to the Society of the Most Holy Trinity. Both produced embroidery during their existence.

**SAPSWORTH, KATHERINE E. - SEE
MALTWOOD, K.E.**

SARE, HILDA MARY (1879-1938)
Illustrator / Painter. Born in Hitchin, Hertfordshire in January 1879. The daughter of Maurice Farhall, a bank manager, and Clara, a bank clerk. Her father originated from Sussex, her mother from London. Raised in Dover and Chichester, Sussex. Had at least one younger sibling, Maurice. Educated at Merton College and Oakfield, Thurlow Park Road, Dulwich. Studied in London at the Westminster and Lambeth Schools of Art and at the Regent Street Polytechnic. Awarded an Ablett's Art Teaching Certificate. Became a black & white illustrator, a miniature painter and a painter of flowers and portraits in oils and watercolours. Worked as an art teacher for 25 years.

Sare exhibited widely, including at the Royal Academy (1905-28), the Walker Art Gallery, Liverpool, the Society of Miniaturists, with the Streatham Art Society, the Croydon Art Society, in Worthing, at Alexandra House, with the Royal Institute of Painters in Watercolours (as a 10-year old) and in Raphael Tuck's Competition. Exhibited works included: The Late Mr and Mrs

H. Webber, Cassie, Daughter of the Late J.C. Hodson, Esq., Violet and Dreams - a Portrait Study. Her watercolours included: Purity and Old Silver. Some of her flower paintings were published by Eyre & Spottiswoode, V. Mansell, J. Harrap, W.H. MacKenzie & Sons and Dennis & Sons, Holborn. Based in London for much of her life and career. In 1909 she married Thomas Henry Sare (1876-1940) in Southwark, London. He was an insurance clerk. They had a son, Geoffrey, and a daughter. Hilda died in Croydon in August 1938, aged 59.

SASSOON, DULCIE F. (1892-1968)
Sculptor / Painter / Wax Modeller. Born in London. The daughter of Frederick S. Franklin, a banker, and Lucy. One of at least four children (Dulcie, Alan, Margaret and Dorothy). Produced portrait medallions in wax and bronze, and portraits in watercolours. Exhibited at the Royal Academy (1919-27). Exhibited works included: Beatrice (medallion, wax), The Artist's Father (medallion, bronze) and Penelope (watercolour). In 1919 she married Captain Sassoon J. Sassoon in London. They had one daughter. Spent much of her life and career in London. Died in London, aged 75. A Member of the Writers' Ranelagh Club.

SAVORY, EVA (1882-1938)
Flower Painter. Was Alicia Eva Theresa, known as Eva. Born in early 1882 in Weybridge, Surrey. The daughter of Ronald Herbert Savory (d.1931), a stockbroker, and J. Alicia M. Torry (d.1951). Her father originated from London, her mother from Surrey. Had a younger brother, Rudolph. Initially, the family lived in Hampstead, London, but by at least 1901 had moved to Chertsey, Surrey. It remains unclear if she had any formal tuition. However, she became an expert and productive flower painter. Her career, which covered at least two decades, was cut short by her untimely death in October 1938 at the age of 55. She spent her career living at the family home, Sandgates, in Chertsey. Her mother outlived her by some 13 years.

Eva's paintings were highly regarded, and were botanically accurate as well as visually appealing. She was awarded at least 16 medals by the Royal Horticultural Society for collections of flower paintings. Awarded the silver Banksian Medal by the Society (1920-21), and the silver Grenfell Medal at the Chelsea Spring Exhibition (1926) for a collection of flower paintings. Occasionally painted other subjects too. Exhibited her work extensively during the 1920s and 1930s, also showing at the Royal Academy (1924-27), the

Royal Institute of Painters in Watercolours, the Royal West of England Academy, the Royal Hibernian Academy (1932-36) and the Society of Women Artists (16 works, 1921-37). Also, at the Paris Salon (1926, 1930, 1931, 1932), the Walker Art Gallery, Liverpool, the New Society of Artists (certainly in 1927 & 1928) which was founded only in 1921, at the Gieves Gallery, the International Exhibitions of Watercolours, Milan and the International Exhibitions, Paris (1926 & 1927). Exhibited works included: Orange Bedder, In Spite of March, Medlars, Treasures of the Garden and After John's Bunch. Elected a Member of the Faculty of Arts. Works illustrated in Colour, including in November 1930, p.9. Her watercolour Glorious Cinerarias was illustrated in Colour, January 1931, p.10.

SAWYER, AMY (1863-1945)

Painter / Decorative Artist / Designer / Illustrator. Born in East Grinstead, Sussex. The daughter of Charles Sawyer and Eliza. Her father, who originated from East Grinstead, was initially a draper and grocer, but subsequently became a brush, mat and matting manufacturer. Her mother originated from Brighton. Amy was one of at least seven children (Amy, Charles, George, William, Frederick, Harry and Mabel). Her siblings were also born in East Grinstead. The children were initially raised there, but by at least the early 1880s the family had moved to Croydon. Amy then studied at Hubert Herkomer's School of Art at Bushey, Hertfordshire, from the late 1880s into the early 1890s. In 1895 The Studio, Vol.6, pp.3-17, offered an article on the Herkomer School, with illustrations by Amy and fellow student and future Principal of the School Lucy Kemp-Welch.

Whilst at the Herkomer School, Amy lived at Caldicote Hill in Bushey, also using Meadow Studios. In around 1900 she moved to Ditchling, Sussex, living at Russell House and later the Blue House. She was still living at the latter when she died in October 1945. In 1901, Amy is recorded as visiting artist Annie Spong (b.1871) who originated from Fulham. Spong also took a studio at Ditchling in the early 1900s. Amy became a diverse artist. Produced watercolour paintings of various subjects including figures as well as decorative paintings and drawings for book illustration. She also ventured into other areas of the decorative arts, producing, for example, decorative panelled screens, calendar designs, postcard designs, painted furniture, including cupboard doors, and fan designs. One of her highly decorative painted screens was shown at the 1893 Arts and Crafts Exhibition Society

exhibition and illustrated in The Studio, Vol.2, October 1893, p.25. Another of her decorative screens (four-fold) was shown at the Arts and Crafts Exhibition Society exhibition for 1896, sketches of which were given in The Studio, Vol.9, 1896, pp.276-277. Another of her screens was illustrated in Walter Shaw Sparrow's volume Women Painters of the World, London, Hodder & Stoughton, 1905, p.159.

One of Amy's fan designs, bearing several decorative figures, was illustrated in The Studio, Vol.6, October 1895, p.3 in the aforementioned article on the Herkomer School. Amy also contributed illustrations to The Windmill, a follower of The Yellow Book and The Savoy. Exhibited her work elsewhere, including at the Royal Academy (16 works, 1887-1909), with the Pastel Society and at the Society of Women Artists (1900-10). Exhibited works included: A Yorkshire Litany (watercolour), The Beggars Are Coming to Town (watercolour), Titania and the Changeling (watercolour), The Dew Rises, the Dew Falls (painted screen) and The Girl Who Got Lost in the Toadstool Country. Elected an Associate of the Society of Women Artists (1901-08). Noted in James Thorpe, English Illustration: The Nineties published in 1935. In 1936 artist Rose C. Cobban exhibited a portrait of Miss Amy Sawyer at the Royal Academy. Amy also produced embroideries, and took an interest in writing in Sussex dialect.

SAYERS, FREDA IRENE (1902-76)

Sculptor / Painter. Born in Dereham, Norfolk in September 1902. Possibly the only child of Ernest Robert Sayers (1873-1946) and Jane Bacchus Press (1873-1942), both of whom originated from Great Yarmouth, Norfolk. Her father was a premises manager for Barclay's Bank. Whilst Freda was still a small child, the family moved to Ipswich, Suffolk. She was educated at the Ipswich High School. Studied at the Ipswich School of Art, followed by the Regent Street Polytechnic, London. As a student, she won a bronze medal for life drawing, and a silver medal for modelling at the Polytechnic. Based mainly in London during her career, spending time working at St Oswald's Studios and Scarsdale Studios as well as elsewhere. However, she maintained ties with Ipswich and exhibited with the Ipswich Fine Art Club. Produced watercolour paintings and sculptures in wood, bronze, plaster and alabaster, mainly statuettes and figures. Also exhibited at the Royal Academy (1931-39) and the Society of Women Artists (1930-38). Exhibited works included: Echo (statuette, wood), Sorrowing Woman (statuette, wood), Reverie (statuette, bronze), Madonna and Child (alabaster) and Thirty Pieces of Silver (statuette, carved wood). Freda died in Fulham, London in August 1976, aged 73.

SCANNELL, EDITH MAUD SUSANNA (1852-1940)

Painter / Illustrator. Born in London. The daughter of Matilda Scannell (1819-1909). Her father, who was possibly Daniel Scannell, died young, leaving Matilda to raise Edith and her elder sister Florence (1848-1922). Neither sister ever married, and both lived mostly with their mother, who lived to the age of around 90. Edith probably studied in London, since she lived there all her life, dying in Chelsea at the age of 88. She became a painter of miniatures and watercolours, mainly figures and portraits, but occasionally flowers too. Also became a children's illustrator. Scannell specialised in fairy-like children and in a type of romanticised, idealised portraiture not dissimilar to that of Kate Greenaway.

Edith began exhibiting her work from around 1870 and continued to do so until at least 1920, covering a period of at least 50 years. Exhibited widely, including at the Royal Academy (1870-1902), the Royal Society of British Artists (1885-86), the Royal Scottish Academy (1885), the Royal Hibernian Academy (1885-97) and with the Bath Society of Artists (for example, showing The Gentle Angler in 1905). Evidently had close ties with the Society of Women Artists. Exhibited 92 works there between 1872 and 1920, showing a variety of watercolours, profile silhouettes, miniatures and miniatures on vellum. Exhibited works included: Capri Fisherboy, The Poor Relation, In the Spell of Fairies, The Enchanted Wood and The Torn Frock. Also exhibited a portrait of Madeline Marrable, President of the Society of Women Artists, at the Society's 1905 exhibition. Elected an Associate of the Society of Women Artists (1898-1922).

Scannell illustrated a number of books for children during her career, including some written by herself and some by her sister Florence. For example, Play, a Picture Book (S.K. Cowan, 1884), Sylvia's Daughters (F. Scannell, 1886), Pets and Playmates (E. Keary, 1887), The Highwaymen (E. & F. Scannell, 1888), The Child of the Caravan (E.M.Green, 1889), Indian Fairy Tales (M. Thornhill, 1889), Cinderella's Sisters (F. Scannell, 1914) and The Cousin From India (E. Scannell, 1919).

SCANTLEBURY, EDITH ALICE (1873-1940)

Painter / Illustrator. Born in Haddenham, Buckinghamshire. The daughter of George T. Scantlebury (1837-1910) and Martha Hughes Cooling (1839-1927). Her father originated from Kent, her mother from Buckinghamshire. Her father had no profession, having a private income. Edith was one of at least four children (Herbert, Gilbert, Edith and Ethel). Only Gilbert appeared to work, as a timber broker. The children were raised in Willesden, London. Edith remained in Willesden after her mother's death, but died in Stanmore, Middlesex in December 1940. Edith was active as a painter and illustrator primarily between 1901 and 1909. She produced watercolour paintings and designs for book illustration. Subjects included landscapes and figures. Exhibited 12 works at the Society of Women Artists (1901-09) and one work at the Royal Academy (1908). Exhibited works included: The Model, Spinning Flax in Holland, At Work and Sunset on the Yealm.

SCHIMMER, ANNA CATHERINA (b.1898)

Designer / Silversmith / Jeweller / Leatherworker. Born in Edmonton, London in February 1898. The daughter of Carl Schimmer and Anna. Her father, a merchant and manufacturers' agent, originated from Germany. Her mother was born in England. Had at least one brother, Robert. Anna Catherina is also listed in records as Catherina or Katherine Anna. Educated privately. Based in London. Exhibited at Wembley, with the Society of Scottish Artists and at the British Institute of Industrial Art.

SCHMIDT, MARGARET FRANCES (b.1899)

Sculptor. Born in London in June 1899. The daughter of Robert Louis Emil Schmidt, a merchant, and Frances Louise. One of at least three children. Raised in London. Studied at the Goldsmiths' College Art School, London. Produced statuettes in bronze. Remained in London, at Southacre, Crystal Palace Road for much of her career. Most active in the 1920s and 1930s. Exhibited at the Royal Academy (1926), the Royal Scottish Academy (1928), the Paris Salon and the Walker Art Gallery, Liverpool. Exhibited works included: Contemplation (statuette) and Reverie (bronze statuette). One of her bird baths was illustrated in Town and Country News.

SCOTT, FLORENCE K. - SEE NASH, F.K.

SCOTT, HELENA ALICE - SEE CUNDELL, H.A.

SCOTT, HILDA C. - SEE POPE, H.C.

SCOTT, HILDA MARY - SEE CHIRM, H.M.

SCOTT, JANET - SEE HAIG, J.

SCOTT-MOORE, ELIZABETH (1902-93)
Painter / Illustrator. Was Edith Elizabeth, known as Elizabeth. Born in Dartford, Kent in October 1902. The daughter of Henry Brier (1858-1938), a Member of the Institute of Mechanical Engineers and President of the Society of Ice and Cold Storage, and Victoria Mary Carruthers (1872-1967). Her father originated from Bollington, Cheshire, her mother from Glasgow. Victoria Carruthers was a student of the Glasgow School of Art. She exhibited her work at the Royal Glasgow Institute (1892-94), and became an illustrator of children's books to provide income after her marriage. Elizabeth was the third of at least four children (John, Victoria, Edith and Ronald). The children were raised and educated mainly in Dartford, though John was born in Glasgow.

Elizabeth studied at the Goldsmiths' College, London, the L.C.C. Central School of Arts and Crafts, and in Italy. She was also influenced by artist and friend Alfred Heyward. She became an illustrator of children's books, like her mother, working for, among others, the Oxford University Press, Nelson, Blackie and Cassell. Some of her work also appeared in the Daily Mail, the Daily Sketch and in various children's magazines. Also a painter of portraits and landscapes in oils and watercolours.

Elizabeth exhibited her work, including at the Royal Academy (1948-67), the Royal Society of Painters in Watercolours, the New English Art Club, the Women's International Art Club and the Society of Women Artists (1951). Also, at the Royal Glasgow Institute (1959), the Society of Graphic Art, with the United Artists, at the Kensington Art Gallery and with the Times Book Club. At the Paris Salon, she won a Gold Medal in 1962 for a portrait of Alfred Heyward. Exhibited works included: In My Studio - August (watercolour), Rough Grass, Wentworth, The Collector, The Foreshore, Lyme Regis (watercolour) and The Tajo, Toledo, Spain. She was elected to the Royal Institute of Painters in Watercolours in 1959. Elected an Associate of the Royal Society of Painters in Watercolours,

becoming a full Member in 1975, and in 1986 became its first woman trustee. In late 1937 she married Joseph Scott-Moore, F.S.S., F.S.A.A. (1880-1947) in Westminster, London. They lived at Brier Cottage, Wentworth, Surrey. He died only 10 years into the marriage, after which Elizabeth largely gave up illustration but continued to paint and exhibit. She died in Surrey in August 1993, aged 90.

SEALY, STELLA - SEE ROSS-CRAIG, S.

SEELEY, EMMA LOUISE (1848-1927)
Painter / Illustrator. Born in London. The daughter of Robert Benton Seeley, a bookseller and publisher, and Mary Ann. One of a large family, of at least 11 children (Mary, Richmond, John, Harriet, Anne, Walter, Edith, Elizabeth, Emma, Leonard and Ada). All were raised in London and were well educated. Leonard later became a barrister. Richmond became a publisher. Emma, Edith and Ada all became involved in teaching. Later in their lives, all three sisters, unmarried, lived with Richmond, who was by then widowed. Emma eventually became Principal of a girl's school, Edith became Principal of a boy's school, and Ada became a history teacher. Emma concentrated on art early in her career, but appears to have produced and exhibited less after 1881. Spent much of her career in London, but also spent time teaching in Beccles, Suffolk in the early 1900s, whilst living with Ada. Emma died in Reigate, Surrey, leaving her small estate to Ada. Emma produced figure paintings and book illustrations. Exhibited her work, including at the Royal Academy (1873-75), the Royal Scottish Academy (1877) and the Society of Women Artists (1875-80). Exhibited works included: Nobody's Dog, The Old Barn Door, The Gamekeeper and Misgivings. Illustrated books including Eva's Mulberry Tree (c.1880).

SELIGMAN, AUDREY - SEE BLACKMAN, A.

SELIGMAN, HILDA MARY (1882-1964)
Sculptor / Painter. Was Hilda Mary McDowell. Born in Blackburn, Lancashire in early 1882. In 1906 she married chemist and chemical engineer Dr Richard Seligman in London. They had at least two children, Audrey (b.1907) and Adrian (b.1909). The couple spent some time living in Leatherhead, Surrey early in their marriage. Later based in London, including at Wimbledon. She became a sculptor of portrait works in plaster and bronze and a watercolour artist of various

subjects. Her daughter, Audrey, became a sculptor, studying in the 1920s and early 1930s. Hilda worked at around the same time as her daughter, similarly exhibiting her work from the late 1930s to the early 1960s. This would suggest that Hilda may have temporarily halted her career to raise her children, or that she studied at around the same time as Audrey. It may also be possible, of course, that Audrey taught her mother.

Hilda exhibited her work, including at the Royal Glasgow Institute (1943), the Royal Academy (1943) and the Society of Women Artists (35 works, 1939-64). Exhibited works included: Mount Kenya at Mid-day (watercolour), Dr Richard Seligman (bronze), Innocence (bronze) and Badger's Set (watercolour). Elected an Associate of the Society of Women Artists (1950-52) and a Member (1953-66). Executed a number of important portrait works, including of Haile Selassie (who sat for her and was known to the family), The Princess of Berar, Chandra, Emperor of India and J.P. Blake, Chairman of the London County Council. She exhibited until 1964, when she would have been around 82 years of age. She died in late December of that year in Chelsea, London, aged 82. SEE: BLACKMAN, AUDREY

SELLER, CHRISTINE MARY (1906-76)
Painter / Commercial Artist. Born in Harrow. The daughter of Frank Russell Seller, a surveyor to an insurance company, and Winifred Maud. Had at least one sister, Margaret. Raised in Beaconsfield, Buckinghamshire. Studied at the Regent Street Polytechnic, London. Had an interest in Oriental art. Produced watercolour paintings, including figure studies. Also worked as a commercial artist. In 1929 she married Kenneth W. Clark in Amersham, Buckinghamshire. Lived in London. Died in Surrey, aged 70. Exhibited her work, mainly with the Society of Women Artists (1924-52), but also with the Royal Society of Painters in Watercolours. Exhibited works included: The Drowned Baby, Lanterns Full of Moonfire, The Number One Wife and The Passionate Shepherd.

SELOUS, DOROTHEA MEDLEY (1881-1968)
Painter / Potter. Born in April 1881. The daughter of Lt.-Col. Edric Selous, M.D., I.M.S., a surgeon in the Indian Army, and Caroline Josephine. One of at least seven children (E.N., Harry, Reginald, Cuthbert, Julia, Dorothea and Bertha), all born between 1873 and 1886. Five of the children were born in India, which indicates that Edric Selous returned to England sometime between 1879 and 1881. Dorothea was the only child born in London. The youngest, Bertha, was born in

Switzerland. The children were raised largely in London. Later, in her late 20s, Dorothea spent time on the Isle of Wight, living with her widowed mother along with Cuthbert and his family and Julia. Dorothea had a private education. At some point, possibly in the early 1900s, Dorothea studied in London at the Royal Academy schools and in Paris. Thereafter, she was based mainly in London, but latterly spent time in Brighton and then Oxford.

Selous produced landscape, flower, still life and portrait paintings, mostly in oils, and pencil drawings, but was also an artist potter. Exhibited her work over seven decades, from the very early 1900s until virtually her death. Exhibited at the Royal Academy (1908-52), the Paris Salon, with the Royal Photographic Society, with the London Group, and at the Royal Society of British Artists where she was awarded the de Loglo bronze medal in 1933. Also exhibited at the Ghent International Exhibition, under the Duveen Scheme at Liverpool and Glasgow, with the New English Art Club and the Society of Women Artists (18 works, 1923-61). Exhibited works included: The Green Jar, Mrs Cecil Home, Marine Phantasy, Wastage (oil) and Daphne (pencil). Elected a Member of the Royal Society of British Artists. Elected a Member of the Society of Women Artists (1914-50). Was also Acting President of the Society of Women Artists between 1947 and 1948, during which time Laura Knight was President (1932-67). Works reproduced in The Studio, including her portrait Norah which was shown at the Royal Society of British Artists in 1935 and illustrated in Vol.110, September 1935, p.137. Purchasers of her work included the Belfast Art Gallery. In 1920 Selous married painter Robert Kirkland Jamieson (1881-1950) in Hailsham, Sussex. Jamieson originated from Lanark, Scotland. A landscape painter and art lecturer, he was a Member of the Chelsea Art Club, the Royal Society of British Artists and the Art Workers' Guild. He died in Sussex, aged 69. Dorothea died in late 1968 in Oxford, aged 87.

SETH, FLORENCE (1870-1952)
Painter / Designer / Illustrator. Born in Brixton, London. The daughter of Gustav Wilhelm Louis Seth and Fanny Elizabeth. Her father, a West African merchant, originated from Germany. Her mother originated from London. Florence was one of at least six children (Gertrude, Florence, Eva, Percival, Algernon and Nora). Spent part of her childhood in Croydon, at Stethis Lodge, where various other family members and servants lived. Her sister Gertrude became a miniature painter and decorative artist based in London.

Florence studied art at South Kensington, where she was certified in model and freehand at the age of only 14. Also studied at the Heatherley's School of Fine Art and in Paris. Remained in London thereafter, dying in Chelsea in December 1952. For a time, she was a boarder with the family of music teacher David Zeidenrust in St John's Wood.

Florence worked as a miniature, portrait and landscape painter in oils and watercolours, an illustrator in colour, line and wash and a designer on pottery and china. Exhibited her work, including at the Royal Academy (1908-49), the Society of Women Artists (1934-35), the Dore Gallery, the Ryder Gallery and the Seth Gallery. Exhibited works included: Major General G.C. Stockwell, D.S.O., The Rt Rev. Bishop James, W.B. Jacob, Esq. and Mrs Windeler. Seth produced illustration work for Hutchinson, Pitman and Macmillan. Books illustrated by her included The Living Races of Mankind, Customs of the World, Natural History of Australia, Hints and Wrinkles on Sea Fishing and My Friends in the Fifties. SEE: MASSEY, GERTRUDE

SETH, GERTRUDE - SEE MASSEY, G.

SHARMAN, GRACE E. - SEE ROGERS, G.E.

SHARPLESS, MRS (active 1780s)
Needle Weaver. Active in the late eighteenth century. Based in Gerrard Street, Soho, London. Listed in records as 'Embroideress to Her Majesty'. Exhibited one work at the Society of Artists, A Fruit Piece in 1783.

SHAW, CAROLINE E.E. - SEE PYKE-NOTT, C.E.E.

SHAW, ELIZABETH CONSTANCE (1870-post-1934)
Painter / Embroideress / Craftswoman. Born in Merton, Surrey. The daughter of Henry Vincent Shaw and Mary Ann. Her father, who owned property, originated from London, as did her mother. One of at least six children (John, Mary, Elizabeth, Edward, Amelia and Isabel), all of whom lived at the family home well into their 20s and 30s, all unmarried (in 1901). Initially, the family was based in Merton, Surrey, but subsequently moved to Sussex, then to Forest Hill, London where they employed several servants. Elizabeth studied at the Richmond School of Art, the Grosvenor School of Art and the Brighton School of Art. Produced paintings in watercolours, raffia work and art needlework.

Exhibited with the British Watercolour Society. Elected an Associate of the Society in 1923. During her career, she was based at Richmond, Surrey. Possibly died in Monmouthshire in 1951, aged 81.

SHAW, HELENA (active early 1900s)
Embroideress. A pupil of the Liverpool School of Art, Mount Street. A needlework class was formed at the School in around 1901 under the instigation of its Principal, Fred V. Burridge. Shaw was one of its earliest pupils. She was part of the class (certainly) between 1902 and 1904. She was a contemporary of Gwendolen Parry, Frances A. Jones and Florence Laverock. In 1902 the Art Workers' Quarterly illustrated a sideboard cloth in applique designed by Shaw. Another of her embroideries, a piano front decorated with the words 'Rouse the Night-owl in a Catch', was illustrated in The Studio, Vol.33, November 1904, p.150. Exhibited embroideries at the Liverpool School of Art annual exhibition of students' work in 1903. Otherwise, remains untraced.

SHAW, KATHLEEN TROUSDELL (c.1867-1958)
Sculptor. Born in Edmonton, Middlesex. Dates of her birth vary in official records, some stating that she was born in 1865, 1867, 1869 or 1870. Other details of her early life remain unclear. At some point, she became the adopted daughter of Rosamond Venning of Belsize Park Gardens, London and Pit Cottage at Cadmore End, High Wycombe, Buckinghamshire. Kathleen lived with Venning at both addresses, and Venning left her small estate to Kathleen on her death in 1928. Kathleen was still at Pit Cottage at the time of her own death some 30 years later, in June 1958, aged 91.

Shaw studied in Dublin, Paris, Rome and London. She lived mostly in London, working as a professional sculptor, but also spent some time working in a studio in Knutsford, Cheshire. Produced figures, medallions, busts and reliefs as well as decorative works. Worked in marble, silver and bronze. Exhibited her work, including at the Royal Academy (1889-1914), the Society of Women Artists (1888-91), the Royal Glasgow Institute (1894-1901), the Royal Scottish Academy (1894-1910) and the Royal Hibernian Academy (52 works, 1887-1906). Also contributed to exhibitions held by the Leeds City Art Gallery, the Manchester Art Gallery and the Walker Art Gallery, Liverpool as well as the International Exhibition in Dublin (1907). Possibly exhibited at the Royal Society of British

Artists (1886-90). Works included: Mowgli (Rudyard Kipling, statue) and studies of Lord Avebury, Mrs Bram Stoker, Earl Egerton of Tatton, Prince Edward of Saxe-Weimer, His Grace the Primate of Ireland and the Archbishop of Armagh. Other works included: An Athenian Beggar (bust), Aurora (decorative panel), Psyche (bronze) and three decorative panels titled Music, Pottery and Painting for an overmantel (bronze). Elected an Honorary Royal Hibernian Academician.

SHELDON, EDYTH MAY (1897-1988)

Painter / Colour Print & Woodcut Artist. Born in Reading, Berkshire in October 1897. The daughter of Theophilus Sheldon and Louisa Thomson. Her father, who originated from Tipton, Staffordshire, was a commercial clerk with a biscuit manufacturer. Her mother originated from Reading. Edyth had at least two younger sisters, Margaret (b.c.1899) and Dorothy (b.c.1901). The girls were raised in Reading and Edyth spent much of her life there, dying in Reading, aged 91. She also spent some time in Tenby, South Wales. Educated at the St Joseph's High School, Reading and at Wilton House, Reading. Studied at the University of Reading, obtaining a Diploma in Fine Art. Elected an Associate in Fine Art of Reading University. Produced colour prints from woodblocks, woodcuts and watercolour paintings. Also became an art teacher. Exhibited her work occasionally, including at the Macrae Gallery, London and at the Edinburgh, Cheltenham and Reading Art Galleries. Elected a Member of the Colour Woodcut Society in 1924. Works included: The Green Gnome (watercolour), The Crystal Gazer (colour print) and The Witch (woodcut). Her Theatrical Scene: Stars of the East was purchased by the Museum of Petrograd.

SHENTON, ELLEN MARIAN (1828-62)

Sculptor. The daughter of Henry Chawner Shenton (1803-66), an artist and engraver of historical subjects, and Mary Ann Warren. Henry exhibited his work at the Royal Academy (1846-60). Mary Ann was the daughter of Henry's tutor. She originated from St Pancras, Middlesex. Henry originated from Harpenden, Hertfordshire where Ellen was born. Ellen was one of at least seven children (Henry Chawner, Ellen, Ada, Adelaide, Francis, William and Edward). All were raised largely in St Pancras. Henry Chawner junior (1825-46) became a sculptor, but died young. William (1836-77) also became an art student and a sculptor who exhibited at the Royal Academy (1857-71). Ellen too became a sculptor, possibly studying in London. She produced figures and groups in plaster and other materials. She exhibited her work at the Royal Academy (1850-59) and at the Society of Women Artists (1858). Exhibited works included: Sketch in Plaster: Hagar and Ishmael, Genesis xxi, 18, Sybil, Cordelia - King Lear, Act iv, sc.14 and How Sleep the Brave Who Sink to Rest (Collins). Based in London throughout her career, including at St James's Terrace, Kentish Town and Rutland Street, Regent's Park. In May 1859, Ellen married widower and solicitor John Evans (1826-1901) of Holborn in Hendon, Middlesex. Ellen appears to have ceased exhibiting after her marriage. She died only three years later, in Barnet, Middlesex, in June 1862, aged only 34.

SHEPHERD, ALICE (b.1874)

Bookbinder / Book Decorator / Painter / Craftswoman. Born in Leighton Buzzard, Bedfordshire. Became a successful bookbinder and book decorator as well as a painter / artist. It remains unclear if she had any formal art training. However, she did train in bookbinding and leatherwork with Mary Ann Bassett of Leighton Buzzard. Bassett founded and ran a handcraft class there from at least the early 1890s. Initially, the class was a philanthropic enterprise begun to provide employment for some of the region's poorer crippled girls. However, like other handcraft ventures of the period, Leighton Buzzard far exceeded its initial aim, producing decorative work of an exacting standard which was widely praised. The class was associated with the Home Arts and Industries Association and exhibited regularly at its annual exhibition in London. Leighton Buzzard produced a number of excellent craftswomen and craftsmen such as Minnie King. But Alice Shepherd rates as one of its finest.

After her initial training under Miss Bassett, Shepherd worked in association with the Leighton Buzzard class for a few short years. During that time, she contributed to the Home Arts exhibitions. Some of her decorative leatherwork, shown at the Association's 1896 exhibition, was illustrated in The Studio, Vol.8, 1896, p.98. In that year, she also contributed to the Arts and Crafts Exhibition Society's fifth exhibition, indicating the high standard of her work. In 1897, and still under the auspices of the Leighton Buzzard class, she exhibited items including a folding photograph screen in leather at that year's Home Arts exhibition. Also in 1897, three of her bindings were illustrated in the Art Journal, p.317.

Sometime between 1897 and 1898, Alice left Bedfordshire and moved to Somerset to work for the Cedric Chivers Bindery in Bath, living at Weston for part of the time. Although technically freelance, she worked in collaboration with Mr H. Granville-Fenn (artist advisor) and Mr Samuel Poole in the execution of work. At Chivers, Alice was in charge of a department of around five women, all carrying out cut and modelled calf work. Chivers employed around 40 women at various times over the years, including Dorothy C. Smyth, Agatha Gales and Muriel Taylor, who worked in book production and decoration at some point. Some worked from home, some in studios. Shepherd appears to have maintained some ties with Mary Ann Bassett since they jointly designed a small handbag with steel fittings and ornamented by Arthur Smallbones of Leighton Buzzard which was exhibited at the 1900 Home Arts exhibition.

At Chivers, Alice became best known for her cut and embossed leatherwork. She also carried out some designs for gold-tooled bindings for Chivers, and for gold tooling around vellucent panels. Her designs, which often incorporated flowers, were never repeated. Work carried out by her included a set of twelve volumes of the works of Tennyson, each binding with an individual design, now in the Hornby Library, Liverpool. Alice was also responsible for some of the Chivers designs for paintings as vellucent panels. One such panel, used on the cover of The Book of Common Prayer (Cambridge University Press, c.1900), was painted by Alice, presumably to her own design. Some of her work appeared in the Chivers Books in Beautiful Bindings, an illustrated catalogue of 99 different types of bindings. Her department at Chivers also produced more mundane items in decorative leather, including address books, blotters, purses, cardcases and photograph frames.

Artistically, Alice Shepherd clearly excelled at Chivers. Other work undertaken by her included a binding for Algernon Charles Swinburne's Atalanta in Calydon (1865) in brown calf with vellucent panels, bound by Chivers and now kept in the John M. Olin Library, Washington University. Alice also continued to exhibit her work under her own name. In 1897 Chivers showed some of her work at his Library Bureau, Bloomsbury Street, London. In 1901-02, she contributed to the First International Studio Exhibition. In 1902 she showed two examples at the Society of Women Artists (c / o Chivers of Bath), and in 1904 she contributed to the Leicester Arts and Crafts Exhibition along with Samuel Poole, showing a number of items including an embossed leather cardcase.

In 1909 The Studio, Vol.47, September, p.299, illustrated one of her most ambitious works, the gold tooling on the cover of an Illuminated Trophy and Role of Honour designed and executed by Samuel Poole, bound at the Chivers bindery and presented to the Council of the Shakespeare Festival, Stratford-upon-Avon. The Roll was to contain the names of winners in the old English games and sports held at the annual Festival. Alice was noted in Sarah T. Prideaux's Modern Bindings Their Design and Decoration, London, Archibald Constable & Co., 1906. A binding designed by Alice and Miss Bassett was illustrated in John P. Harthan's Victoria & Albert Museum Bookbindings, London, 1950. That particular binding was bound by Arthur Smallbones and W. Fazakerley of Leighton Buzzard. SEE: BASSETT, MARY ANN

SHERIDAN, CLARE CONSUELO (1885-1970)

Sculptor. Born in London in September 1885. The daughter of Englishman Moreton Frewen (1853-1924) and American socialite Clarita Clara Jerome (1851-1935). Clare was cousin to Jack and Winston Churchill. She was educated at the Convent of the Assumption, Paris. In 1896 her father, an M.P., inherited a substantial estate in Co. Cork, Ireland. Clare studied sculpture in London, at the Royal College of Art, under Professor Edouard Lanteri, and studied under sculptor John Tweed, R.A. Tweed, an Associate of the Societe Nationale des Beaux-Arts, was responsible for such works as a memorial to Lord Beresford for St Paul's Cathedral and a marble bust of the Right Hon. J. Chamberlain for Westminster Abbey. In 1910, with her career barely established, she married William Frederick Temple Sheridan (1879-1915) in London. He was a stockbroker. The couple had three children, Margaret (1913-80), Elizabeth (b.1914) and Richard (1915-37). Elizabeth died in infancy in 1914, of tuberculosis, and this prompted Clare to design a model in clay as a memorial. She then completed a second memorial for the family church in Dorset. From that point, she took up sculpture more seriously. During her career, Clare spent time in Dorset, London and Sussex, but also Ireland, Algeria and America. She died in Dorset in May 1970, aged 84.

When her husband died in 1915, just after the birth of Richard, Clare took up sculpture professionally to survive, becoming a society sculptor. Worked in bronze, wood and stone. Produced mainly busts and masks. Early subjects included H.G. Wells and Gladys Cooper. Produced several busts of Winston Churchill along with portrait works of Asquith, Marconi, Lenin, Trotsky and other major international figures. Studied for a short time in the Kremlin on a visit to the U.S.S.R. She was influenced by Epstein at one point. Exhibited her work, including at the Royal Academy (1924-42), the Royal Glasgow Institute (1924), the Royal Scottish Academy (1944), the Royal Hibernian Academy (1949-51), the Paris Salon and the National Academy of Design, New York. Exhibited works included: Winston Churchill, Prime Minister (owned by Edinburgh Corporation), Archangel Gabriel (bronze), Mrs Oswald Birley (mask, bronze) and Madonna.

Later in her career, Sheridan also turned to writing books and journalism. Published an autobiography Nuda Veritas. She was also the author of, among other books, Russian Portraits (1921), My American Diary (1922), A Turkish Kaleidoscope (1926), Arabs Interlude (1943), My Crowded Solitude and Redskin Interlude. After her son's death in 1937, Sheridan turned to carving in wood, with some religious themes. In 1947 she was received into the Catholic Church, at Assisi. In 1957 she published To The Four Winds (autobiography). Works acquired by the Imperial War Museum, the Oxford Union, the Bombay Museum and Moscow.

SHIPP, FLORENCE A. - SEE KENDRICK, F.A.

SHUTER, AGNES (1851-1941)
Sculptor. Active in the late nineteenth century. Born in London. The daughter of James Legasick Shuter, a merchant, and Ann Rebecca. One of at least three children (James, Mary Ann and Agnes). Her brother James became a surgeon. The family lived in and around London, including in Islington. Agnes studied sculpture, probably in London. Exhibited her work rarely. Showed three works at the Royal Academy between 1881 and 1884: Mrs Shuter (bust), a bas-relief and Little Aggie, Daughter of G. Acton Davis, Esq. In 1886 Shuter married Henry Work Dodd (d.1921) in Hampstead. Agnes was nine years older. Dodd originated from Canada and was an ophthalmic surgeon and Fellow of the Royal College of Surgeons. They had three children, Ruth, Charles and Roderic, all born between 1887 and 1895. The family lived in Harrow for a time, then in Harley Street, London. Shuter appears to have given up sculpture on her marriage.

SICKERT, CHRISTINE DRUMMOND - SEE ANGUS, C.D.

SICKERT, ELAINE THERESE - SEE LESSORE, E.T.

SILVER, LEONORA K. - SEE GREEN, L.K.

SIMCOCK, NORAH (1906-59)
Painter / Advertisement Designer. Born in Stockport, Cheshire in May 1906. The daughter of James Simcock, a doctor, and Jane Hannah. Her father originated from Ollerton, Cheshire, her mother from Ardwick, Lancashire. The third of at least three children (also Margaret and Eileen). Raised in Stockport. Educated at the St Leonard's School, St Andrews, Fife. Studied at the Manchester School of Art. Produced landscape paintings in oils and watercolours along with posters and commercial designs. Exhibited her work at the Societe Nationale des Beaux-Arts, Paris, the Salon d'Automne, Paris, the Royal Academy (1932 & 1954) and the Society of Women Artists (1927-35, 1955). Also, at the International Exhibition of Modern Decorative Art, Italy. Held a one-woman show in Liverpool. Exhibited works included: On the Buxton Road, Near Sevenoaks, Kent and South Coast: Spring 1954. Initially, she was based at Heaton Moor, Manchester, but spent some time in London in the 1930s. In 1934 she married company director William Edgar Osborne in Stockport, Cheshire. They subsequently moved to Weybridge, Surrey. Norah died there in April 1959, aged only 52. Worked and exhibited until shortly before her death.

SIMEON, EUNICE & MARGARET (1906-2001) & (1910-99)
Artists. The daughters of Harry Simeon (1871-1953) and Amy Sykes. Harry Simeon studied sculpture at the Huddersfield School of Art, subsequently studying at the Royal College of Art, London. He became a leading artist and ceramic designer at Doulton's of Lambeth. His father, David Simeon, was a monumental mason. Harry and Amy married in a Wesleyan chapel in August 1901. Amy was a dressmaker from Huddersfield. They had two artist daughters, Eunice and Margaret.

Eunice Simeon was born in Wandsworth, London in July 1906. She studied at the Chelsea School of Art and became a painter of landscapes and still life in oils. For much of her career, she was based at Clapham Common, London, living with Margaret. She exhibited her work at the Royal Academy (1929-45), the Royal Scottish

Academy (1933-40), the New English Art Club and the Society of Women Artists (1930). Exhibited works included: Smith Street, Chelsea, The Mulberry Tree, The Coachbuilders and White Hyacinths. She died in Surrey, aged 94.

Margaret Simeon was also born in Wandsworth and died in Surrey. She too studied at the Chelsea School of Art, between 1926 and 1930. But, like her father, she went on to study at the Royal College of Art, between 1931 and 1935. In 1933 she was elected an Associate of the Royal College of Art. In 1934 she was awarded the Royal College of Art Travelling Scholarship, the first textile design student to be awarded the honour. She became a textile designer, teaching textile design and printing at the Royal College of Art from 1936 to 1940. However, she left to concentrate on fabric design and production, though she did teach a little elsewhere. Taught at the Wimbledon School of Art where one of her pupils was Noreen Bennett. Elected a Member of the Society of Industrial Artists in 1945. Also a Council Member of the Arts and Crafts Exhibition Society.

Some of Margaret's designs were illustrated in The Studio, Vol.137, May, pp.150-151 in 1949. Produced attractive, busy textiles with bold repeat patterns. Her work reflected an economy of colour, possibly influenced by her earlier work as a hand-block craftswoman. Rarely used more than five colours. Some of her most successful textiles consisted of only one colour, usually white on a coloured ground. One of her textile designs, produced by the Edinburgh Weavers, based on a repeat pattern of bows and bouquets, was illustrated in David Joel, The Adventure of British Furniture 1851-1951, London, Ernest Benn, 1953, p.246. She did full-size brush designs to begin with, so enlargement for machine production wasn't necessary. Then she did accurate designs for the manufacturer. Also printed hand-blocked materials for exhibition, some of which were used as prototypes for industry.

Margaret also designed for woven fabrics, wallpaper, pottery, glass and carpets. One of her designs was a furnishing satin produced by Messrs John Lewis & Co., who also printed one of her single-colour, machine printed furnishing cottons. One of her screen-print satins was printed by Messrs Allan Walton Textiles. Another of her screen-printed furnishing satins was printed by the Edinburgh Weavers. Exhibited her work widely, including at the International Exhibitions in Paris, Stockholm and New York. Also, with the Arts and Crafts Exhibition Society (between at least 1935 and 1951). Also, at the Britain Can Make It Exhibition of 1946 and the Festival of Britain, South Bank in 1951. Her work was reproduced in a number of journals including The Studio, International Textiles, Architectural Review, Designers in Britain and Decorative Art. Her essay on textile printing was reproduced in Fifteen Craftsmen and Their Crafts.

SIMMONDS, EVELINE (1884-1978)
Decorative Embroideress. Born in Walthamstow, Greater London in October 1884. The daughter of Benjamin Peart, a timber merchant, and Mary Ann. Her father originated from Bethnal Green, London. Her mother originated from Marldon, Devon. Benjamin Peart was some 24 years older than Mary Ann, and was around 61 years of age when Eveline was born. Eveline appears to have been the youngest of at least seven children (Alice, Arthur, Frederick, Rosina, Lilian, Herbert and Eveline), all born between 1875 and 1884. Whilst Eveline was still a child, her father died and her mother raised the family in Ealing. At least three of the Peart children showed artistic ability. Frederick and Herbert studied to become artists whilst Eveline moved to Paddington, London to study at the Westminster School of Art. She was still listed as a student at the age of 26, in 1911.

In early 1912 Eveline married woodcarver, sculptor, painter and puppeteer William George Simmonds (1876-1968). The son of an architect, he studied at the Royal College of Art and the Royal Academy schools, London, and served in the First World War. He was elected to the Art Workers' Guild in 1923. Eveline appears to have concentrated on embroidery during their marriage. Although the couple married in Wandsworth, London, they spent the greater part of their marriage living in Stroud, Gloucestershire. Eveline died there in October 1978, 10 years after her husband, aged 93. W.G. Simmonds belonged to the Cheltenham Group of artists, but also had ties with the Arts and Crafts Exhibition Society, as did Eveline. She did exhibit her work, though not prolifically, including with the Arts and Crafts Exhibition Society, at the International Arts and Crafts exhibitions held in Paris, Ghent and Leipzig, and at an Exhibition of Modern Embroidery held at the Victoria & Albert Museum, London. A sampler of embroidered wildflowers, dated 1916, is currently in the Cheltenham Collections. Eveline cultivated a garden at Gloucestershire, which gave her inspiration in her embroideries.

SIMON, NAOMI BIRDIE (1888-1979)
Painter / Decorative Artist. Born in Sydney, Australia. The daughter of William Graham

Simon. From a young age (at least 10 and 12), Naomi and her sister, Eva Mollie Simon (1890-1972), lived in England with their British-born maiden aunts, also called Naomi and Eva. The girls lived with their aunts until the aunts died. They then remained in London until their own deaths, based at Arundel Gardens and, subsequently, Colville Gardens. Eva died in London, aged 82. Naomi died in Middlesex in March 1979, aged 90. Eva became an insurance clerk. Naomi was educated at the Notting Hill High School. She then studied at the King's College for Women, at the Hammersmith School of Arts and Crafts, and at the Byam Shaw and Vicat Cole School of Art, London. Whilst studying art, Naomi also acted as an art pupil-teacher. She became a portrait, figure, flower and landscape painter in oils and watercolours, a miniaturist and a black & white and lettering artist.

Naomi exhibited her work, including at the Royal Academy (1923-24), the Society of Women Artists (1919-36), the Royal Institute of Oil Painters, the Royal Institute of Painters in Watercolours, the International Society of Sculptors, Painters & Gravers, with the New English Art Club, at the Grosvenor Gallery and the Paris Salon. Also, at the Carnegie Institute and in Manchester, Bradford, Plymouth, Liverpool, Glasgow and Hull as well as under the Duveen Scheme. Exhibited works included: Winter in Kensington, The Artist's Studio, The Crinoline and There Is No War. Exhibited some of her bookplates. Executed at least one portrait of her sister Eva. Some of her pen & ink drawings were reproduced in The Studio. Elected a Member of the Ridley Art Club and of the Campden Hill Club. Acted as Honorary Secretary of the Campden Hill Club.

SIMPSON, IDA MACKINTOSH (1898-1977)

Painter / Maker of Masks. Born in Ackworth, Yorkshire. The daughter of Cecil Harold Simpson, a soap manufacturer, and Annie Elizabeth. Her father originated from Yorkshire, her mother from Edinburgh. Had at least one younger sibling, Helen Elspeth Mackintosh Simpson. Raised in Southwell, Nottinghamshire. Studied in London at the Byam Shaw School of Art, the Westminster School of Art and the Royal Academy schools. Produced paintings, mainly portraits and still life, and decorative masks. Exhibited at the Royal Academy (1931-32), the International Society of Sculptors, Painters & Gravers, the Royal Society of Portrait Painters, the New English Art Club, the Goupil Gallery, with the Women's International Art Club and the Yorkshire Artists. Held a one-woman show of masks at Hartyan's, Knightsbridge. Exhibited works included: Inez and Flower Piece. Works illustrated in The Studio, Sketch and Harpers Bazaar. Based in Chelsea during her career. Died in Kensington, aged 78.

SIMPSON, JANET SCOTT CHISHOLM (1873-1968)

Etcher / Painter. Born in Camberwell, London in late 1873. The daughter of David Goudie Simpson, manager of the Scottish Provincial Assurance Company, and Janet. Her father originated from London, her mother from Scotland. Janet was the fourth of at least six children (four girls, two boys). Mary Goudie Simpson, the eldest child, also became an artist. Another sister, Agnes Wardrop Simpson (b.1879), was an art student in the early 1900s and exhibited handicrafts at the Society of Women Artists in 1911. Janet was raised in Camberwell in a large house with servants. She was educated at the Mary Datchelor School. Studied at the Lambeth School of Art and at the Royal College of Art, London. Won one silver and two bronze medals and various book prizes at the Royal College of Art. Janet and Mary studied at Lambeth at around the same time, and both exhibited book illustrations in the 1900 National Competition of Schools of Art whilst there.

Janet, however, subsequently went to the Royal College of Art, South Kensington to study engraving. Elected an Associate of the Royal College of Art in 1924 (for engraving). She had already been elected an Associate of the Royal Society of Painter-Etchers & Engravers in 1912, some eight years after beginning to exhibit her work nationally and more seriously. Produced etchings and watercolour paintings, mainly landscapes and buildings. All the Simpson siblings remained at home well into adulthood, and at least five of them were still living in Camberwell with their parents in the early 1900s, when Mary was 32 and Janet was 27. The family subsequently moved to Bromley, Kent, some years after David Simpson had retired from insurance, by which time Janet was in her late 30s. Janet remained in Kent thereafter, living in Brenchley, dying in Tonbridge, aged 94.

Latterly, Janet and Mary lived at separate addresses in Kent, both unmarried. Like Mary, Janet clearly enjoyed travel, and painted on her travels at home and abroad. She began exhibiting around 1904, at the Royal Academy, and eventually showed some 29 works there, the last in 1933. Also exhibited at the Society of Women Artists (1904-35), the Royal Scottish Academy

(1921-25), the Paris Salon, the Walker Art Gallery, Liverpool and the International Society of Sculptors, Painters & Gravers. Exhibited works included: Sea Fairies, A Venetian Byway, Advocate's Close, The Fruit Market, Bruges and September Evening (etching). Elected a Member of the Society of Women Artists (1935). Works illustrated in The Studio and The Builder. Some were published by Virtue & Co., and Deighton. Official purchases of her work included an etching Lyme Regis for the Walker Art Gallery, Liverpool. SEE: SIMPSON, MARY GOUDIE

SIMPSON, MARY GOUDIE (1868-1934)
Craftswoman / Designer / Painter. Sister to artist Janet S.C. Simpson. Born in Camberwell, London. Like Janet, she attended the Lambeth School of Art, London. Won a silver medal for painting as well as prizes for design and craftwork shown at the National Competition of Schools of Art. Produced paintings in watercolours, mainly landscapes and buildings, and other work including book illustrations, book covers and designs for Carrickmacross lace. Also became an art teacher. She was the visiting art teacher at the Kinnaird Park School for Girls at Bromley, the St Hugh's Preparatory School for Boys at Bickley, at the Carn-Brea Preparatory School for Boys at Bromley, the Belmont School for Girls at Bickley and The Old Palace School for Girls at Bromley. Like Janet, Mary travelled and painted on her travels. Painted the markets of Bruges and the medieval towns of France, Italy and Belgium.

Mary began exhibiting her work just before Janet. Exhibited at the Royal Hibernian Academy (1891-95), the Royal Scottish Academy (1908), the Walker Art Gallery, Liverpool, at Glasgow, Stockholm, Melbourne, Toronto and Paris, and with the Old Dudley Art Society. Exhibited 103 works at the Society of Women Artists between 1903 and 1935. Exhibited works included: A Fruit Shop, Venice, Homes of the Shrimpers, France, A Sussex Mill, Near the Coast, The Spinster and Edinburgh Castle From Greyfriars. Elected a Member of the Society of Women Artists (1908-34). Elected a Member of the Royal Society of British Artists (1915) and of the National Society of Art Masters (1922). A Member of the Forum Club. Works illustrated in Colour (Market Day) and The Studio. Mary spent her early years in Camberwell, London, later moving to Bromley, Kent with the Simpson family, including Janet. Latterly she lived at Keston and Benenden in Kent. Died in Bromley, Kent, aged 66. Left her £6398 estate to David

Chisholm Simpson and William Murray Simpson. SEE: SIMPSON, JANET S.C.

SINGER, AMY MARY (1862-1941)
Sculptor. Born and raised in Frome, Somerset. The daughter of John Webb Singer (1819-1904) and Sarah (b.1830). Her mother originated from Devon. Her father, who originated from Frome, was a highly regarded silversmith and art metalworker who was based in Frome throughout his life and career. He established a successful metalwork business, employing around 20 men at its peak. Amy had at least three older siblings - Mabel, Walter Herbert (1854-1922) and Edgar Radcliffe (1857-1947). Edgar and Walter (who was known as Herbert) both became art metalworkers too. Edgar, a Royal Academy exhibitor, eventually took over the family business. Edgar, who was also a bell-founder, was elected to the prestigious Art Workers' Guild in 1889.

Amy studied sculpture, probably in London or Paris. She worked mainly in terracotta, producing busts and statuettes. Exhibited her work occasionally. Showed nine works at the Royal Academy (1882-89) including General Sir Charles Staveley, K.C.B. (bust), Samuel Carter Hall, Esq. (bust, terracotta), Seventy (statuette, terracotta), Beryl (bust, terracotta) and Supplication (statuette). In 1889 Amy married Fountain Peter Elwin, a wealthy gentleman of no profession, in Frome. Early in the marriage, they lived at Melcombe Regis in Weymouth, Dorset. Later, they moved to The Manor House at Booton, Norfolk. Amy apparently gave up exhibiting on her marriage, and possibly gave up sculpture. She died in Norfolk in late 1941, aged 79. Elwin died in 1943, leaving part of his considerable estate to Lady Emily Lutyens, wife of architect Edwin Lutyens. Edgar Singer died in Frome just a few years later, having never married. Walter, who married Kate Isabel Long and had children, also died in Frome.

SINGLEMAN, BARBARA - SEE TRIBE, B.

SKEAPING, BARBARA - SEE HEPWORTH, B.

SKEAPING, LILY E.J. - SEE KAUFMANN, L.E.J.

SKEMPTON, MARY NANCY (1913-93)
Wood Engraver / Painter / Bookbinder. Possibly Mary N. Wood who, in 1940, married Alec W. Skempton in Watford, Hertfordshire. Had two daughters. Based in London and Watford during

her career, dying in Wandsworth, London, aged 80. Educated at the Scarborough Girls' High School. Studied at the Scarborough School of Art, then the Royal College of Art, London. Elected an Associate of the Royal College of Art. Exhibited her work at the American Institute of Architecture, the Royal Society of British Artists and in Newcastle and Bradford. Exhibited one work at the Royal Academy in 1946, Red Mount Chapel, King's Lynn.

SKINNER, CONSTANCE MARY (1884-1945)

Sculptor. Born in Camberwell, London. The daughter of Robert Skinner and Louisa Emily Dix. One of several children including Gertrude Ivy who became a violinist. Raised in London. Studied at the Hammersmith School of Art. Won several medals as a student. Worked for over 21 years as a sculptor, producing portrait medallions and statuettes in bronze. Lived with Gertrude in London during her early career. In 1914 she married Alexander Edward Pargeter in London. Spent much of her life in London, but died in Weston-super-Mare, Somerset, aged 61. Exhibited her work before and after her marriage, including at the Royal Academy (1911-32) and the Royal Glasgow Institute (1929). Exhibited works included: Stylite (statuette, bronze), Seaweed (statuette), Little Miss Prim (medallion) and Knucklebones (statuette).

SLOANE, MARY ANNIE (1867-1961)

Painter / Etcher / Engraver / Illustrator. Born in December 1867. The daughter of John Sloane and Sarah. Her father, who originated from Ireland, was a General Practitioner and later a surgeon. Her mother originated from Leicester. Mary was one of at least five children (Eleanor, Mary, John, Sarah and Hans). All were born and raised in Leicester in a house with several servants. By the late 1880s, Mary was in London, possibly the time that she studied at the Royal College of Art. From around 1891 she began studying at the Herkomer School of Art at Bushey, Hertfordshire. Hubert von Herkomer's (1849-1914) school was highly successful and trained a considerable number of women artists, including Lucy Kemp-Welch, who went on to enjoy long and productive careers.

By 1896 Sloane was back in London and remained there until her death in November 1961, aged 93. At the time of her death, she had a home in Hammersmith Terrace, London, but also kept a home in Leicester which, latterly, was The Nook at Enderby. She died in a nursing home in Leicester. Mary lived at various addresses in London over the years. In the early 1900s, she shared a house with several others including artist George Spencer Watson (1869-1934). Next door was Ada M. Shrimpton (b.1866, later Mrs Giles), an equally successful artist. Shrimpton exhibited her work at the Royal Academy (1891-1924), the Royal Society of British Artists (1889-93), the Royal Glasgow Institute (1924) and elsewhere.

Mary Sloane produced oil and watercolour paintings, engravings, etchings, illustrations and mezzotints. Subjects were predominantly figures and landscapes. She evidently travelled to paint, visiting Florence, Gloucestershire, Devon, Oxford, Bedfordshire and elsewhere. In 1911 she visited the Scilly Isles with her widowed mother. She also visited William Morris's former home, Kelmscott Manor, executing a study of the Tapestry Room which was exhibited at the Society of Women Artists in 1915. Sloane exhibited her work over a period of more than 59 years, including at the Royal Society of Painter-Etchers & Engravers, the Royal Academy (1896-1924), the Royal Society of British Artists (from 1889) and the Paris Salon.

Mary also exhibited an impressive 153 works at the Society of Women Artists (1888-1947), including a drypoint of Laura Pendennis and a print of The Old Town Hall, Leicester. Some of her works were social documents of the times such as A Bedfordshire Lacemaker, Silk Weaving in Bethnal Green, Wheelwright's Shop, Enderby, The Village Clockmaker's Home and A Huguenot Silk-Weaver. Elected an Associate of the Royal Society of Painter-Etchers and Engravers. Elected an Honorary Member of the Paris Salon in 1903. A Member of the Lyceum Club. Elected an Associate of the Society of Women Artists (1902-04) and a Member (1905-56). Her Leicestershire Stockinger's Shop was purchased by the Victoria & Albert Museum, London. Her Old Bridge, Enderby was purchased by the National Gallery of Canada.

SMALL, EVELYN M.B. - SEE PAUL, E.M.B.

SMEDLEY, CONSTANCE - SEE ARMFIELD, C.

SMITH, ANNE MAY (b.1906)

Painter / Etcher / Engraver / Designer. Born in Simla, India in June 1906. The daughter of Sir Joseph Smith, a civil engineer. Educated at the Diocesan High School, Auckland, New Zealand. Moved to London to study at the Royal College of Art. Elected an Associate of the Royal College of Art in 1931. Worked in London until at least 1934, but subsequently disappears. Appears to have visited India several times as an adult. Produced paintings, etchings, engravings on wood and copper, textile designs and printed fabrics. Exhibited her work at the Imperial Institute, the Wertheim Gallery, the Albany Gallery and in New Zealand. Purchasers of her work included the British Museum and the Auckland Art Gallery. Also signed her work Anne Sloane, so possibly married.

SMITH, CATHERINE (1874-1955)

Painter / Etcher / Designer. Born in Paddington, London in June 1874. The daughter of William Smith, a chemist and druggist, and Sarah. One of at least eight children (Elizabeth, Alice, Gertrude, Gilbert, Ellen, Catherine, William and Charlotte). All raised in Paddington. Educated at the Notting Hill High School. Studied at the Royal College of Art, London. Also travelled to Italy in 1901, visiting galleries. Became a painter of landscapes and other subjects, an etcher and a designer of linens and lace. Awarded an Art Masters' Teaching Certificate and taught in several public and private schools in London.

Smith exhibited her work occasionally, including at the Royal Academy (1898-1911) and the Paris Salon. Exhibited works included: St William's College, York, The Bells of the Leaning Tower of Pisa, The Final Surrender and The Forerunners of Night. Based in London throughout her life and career, latterly at Porchester Road and Gloucester Terrace. Died in Islington, aged 81. Left her small estate to her unmarried sister, Ellen. Her sister Gertrude became a sculptor who married sculptor Gilbert Bayes. Catherine lived with her widowed father along with Elizabeth, who became a church worker, and Ellen (or Helen) who acted as housekeeper. Catherine also developed an interest in photography. Still active in the 1930s.

SMITH, EDITH - SEE HOLDEN, E.

SMITH, EFFIE SPRING (1907-74)

Painter / Illustrator. Records indicate that Effie Spring Smith was the illegitimate daughter of Witford G. Smith and Annie Derby. Derby, who originated from Liverpool, was Witford G. Smith's cook at his home, Doric House in Woodbridge, Suffolk, where Effie was born. Records also indicate that the couple had already had a son, Digby, two years earlier. Effie was raised in Suffolk and was educated at the Ipswich High School. She then studied at the Ipswich School of Art under George Robert Rushton who also acted as a member of the advisory committee to the Ipswich Museum and Art Gallery. He was

known for his large decorative panels and his watercolours of East Anglia. Effie also studied at the Slade School, London under Professor Henry Tonks between 1925 and 1929. She proved to be an exceptional student at both Schools, winning at least 11 prizes, including a summer exhibition competition as well as the Clayden Travelling Scholarship and the Slade Diploma and Scholarship. She was a prizeman for figure painting, anatomy, head painting, landscape and figure composition.

Effie became a painter of figures, portraits and landscapes in oils and watercolours, and an illustrator for magazines. Some of her work appeared in Sketch, Sphere and Graphic. Her works were reproduced by Messrs Valentine and by Philately. She was still active in the 1950s. Exhibited her work, including at the Royal Academy (1931-49), the Royal Scottish Academy (1937), the Royal Glasgow Institute (1935), the Society of Women Artists (1937), the Royal Society of British Artists, the Royal Institute of Oil Painters and the Royal Society of Portrait Painters. Also, at the Paris Salon, with the London Portrait Society, the New English Art Club, the Royal West of England Academy, at the Walker Art Gallery, Liverpool and in Ipswich, Doncaster, Derby and Manchester. Exhibited works included: Harbour Scene, St Ives, The Nodding Mandarin, Artist's Agent, Off Duty and My Daughter Stephanie. Elected an Honorary Member of the Paris Salon (1936). Elected to the Royal Society of British Artists (1939). Also a Member of the London Club and of the Lyceum Club. Based in London throughout her career. Died in Bromley, Kent. The Felix Cobbold Bequest, Ipswich purchased her The Forum, Rome and a self-portrait. Her Cricket in 1760 was intended for the members' refreshment room at Lords. In late 1939 Effie married Herbert Cutner in Hampstead. Cutner was an artist, journalist and Member of the Society of Graphic Art. They had at least one son and one daughter.

SMITH, GERTRUDE - SEE BAYES, G.

SMITH, GWENDOLEN B. - SEE ROSE, G.B.

SMITH, MARY SOPHIA LYNDON (1863-1957)

Bookbinder / Book Decorator / Woodcarver / Enameller. Born in Leeds, Yorkshire. The daughter of William Lyndon Smith (1836-65) and Eleanor Beard Morgan (1841-93). William died young. Mary had at least two siblings, Charles and Eleanor. Eleanor became a governess. The children were raised in Leeds. In the early 1890s, Mary spent some time in Kirkby Lonsdale, boarding with Alfred and Anne Harris at their Lunefield estate. Alfred was a magistrate and a banker prior to his retirement. Mary spent around four years there, studying decorative leatherwork at the local Kirkby Lonsdale handicraft classes, with which the Harris family was closely involved. In 1899 several examples of her work were shown at the Exhibition of Pictures & Decorative Art held in Kendal, including a blotter. She also spent some time training at the School of Woodcarving, South Kensington, becoming a talented and prize-winning woodcarver and designer. After leaving Kirkby Lonsdale, Mary became a teacher at the Cheltenham Ladies' College in Gloucestershire, teaching inlaid woodwork, cut and modelled leatherwork and enamelling. She taught woodcarving elsewhere in England and Ireland during her career.

As a bookbinder, Mary worked independently rather than with any class or group. But she did exhibit with the Guild of Women Binders in London in 1898-99. One of her bindings, for Alice in Wonderland, designed and executed by her, was illustrated in The Studio, Vol.16, p.49 around the same time. Mary had already exhibited bookbindings at Frank Karslake's in London in 1897, just before Karslake instigated the founding of the Guild of Women Binders. Other bindings by Mary included for Walter Crane's Flora's Feast and for William Cowper's The Diverting History of John Gilpin (1899). In 1900 she exhibited a carved fire screen in unpolished oak at the Leeds Arts and Crafts Exhibition. Mary died in Harrogate, Yorkshire.

SMITH, PAMELA COLMAN (1878-1951)

Illustrator / Artist. Was Corinne Pamela Mary Colman Smith, known as Pamela. Born in London. The daughter of Charles Edward Smith (1846-99) and Corinne Colman (1834-96). Her father was an American merchant, from Brooklyn. Her mother was Jamaican. Pamela was based in Manchester as a child. But she moved to Jamaica in 1889, living at Kingston for a few years. She then enrolled at the Pratt Institute in Brooklyn in 1893, studying under Arthur Wesley Dow. In 1899 she returned to England and worked as an illustrator and theatrical designer for a miniature theatre. She also worked on theatre costume and stage design.

Works illustrated by her included The Illustrated Verses of William Butler Yeats and Others, The Golden Vanity and the Green Bed (London, Elkin Mathews, 1902) and Bram Stoker's first book, The Lair of the White Worm, in 1911. Illustrated

two of her own books, Widdicombe Fair and Fair Vanity. Exhibited some of her work in New York. Held an exhibition of her work at the Baillie Gallery, London in 1911. Showed three works at the Society of Women Artists in 1917: Lay Not Up Treasure, A Gate of Dream and a poster design. Also involved in women's suffrage. In 1911 she converted to Catholicism. She bought a house in Bude, Cornwall with an inheritance, having previously spent time in London. Died in Bude, aged 73.

SMITH, WINIFRED - SEE GREEN, W.

SMYTH, DOROTHY CARLETON & OLIVE CARLETON (1880-1933) & (1882-1949)

Decorative Artists. The multi-talented daughters of engineer and merchant William Hugh Smyth and Elizabeth Ramage. Their father originated from Ireland, their mother from France. Both girls were born in Glasgow. Two of at least six children (Jane, Rose, William, Eleanor, Dorothy and Olive). In the 1880s the family moved to Manchester when William was made managing director of the Openshaw Oilcloth Company. However, both Dorothy and Olive later returned to Glasgow to study. Rose became a music composer.

Dorothy Smyth initially studied at the Manchester School of Art between 1895 and 1898. There, she fell under the influence of Walter Crane who then had a visiting directorship at the School. From 1898 until 1905 she attended the Glasgow School of Art, remaining in the city for much of the rest of her life. At the School, she studied theatre and costume, stained glass, drawing and painting. As a student, she won a number of awards in the National Competition of Schools of Art, including a bronze medal in 1899 for a poster design, a silver medal in 1900 for book illustration and a bronze medal for stained glass design. At the age of 21, and still a student, she showed her stained glass window Tristan and Iseult at the 1901 Glasgow Exhibition. The previous year, two of her low-relief heads in gesso on wood panels had been noted as 'excellent' in The Studio, Vol.19, 1900.

Dorothy began her diverse career as a portrait painter, but through producer F.R. Benson became involved in theatre work in London and France. She designed for a number of notable productions including Matheson Lang's Othello and John Martin Harvey's Richard III. In 1914 she designed the costumes for Granville Barker's A Midsummer Night's Dream. She was appointed head of the Design Department at the Glasgow

School. She taught costume, lithography and illustration. Also continued to execute portraits, including a self-portrait in 1921. Locally, she produced plays in Glasgow, and worked with Charles Rennie Mackintosh and others on decoration. As a book illustrator she worked for Blackie and Collins. Also executed postcard designs, worked in silver, designed panels for cruise liners and produced stone carvings, bronzes and murals. She delivered lectures, wrote, and gave talks on the radio for children. For a time, she worked with Chivers of Bath, producing decorative bookbindings which she designed and painted, and Chivers bound. Her painted parchment book cover Siegfried was shown at the 1903 annual Glasgow School of Art Club exhibition and illustrated in The Studio, Vol.30, 1903, p.108.

Dorothy exhibited her work widely, including at the Royal Scottish Academy (1921), the Royal Glasgow Institute (1904-33) and the Royal Academy (1922). In the Scottish Section of the 1902 Turin Exhibition, she showed some of her line drawings for Ogier the Dane along with a gesso panel, Little Bo-Peep, and stained glass work. At the 1905 Exhibition of Arts and Crafts at the Lyceum Club, she showed pen drawings, including Papillons which was reproduced in The Studio, Vol.36, January 1906, p.356. She had a light, airy, fine drawing style not dissimilar to that of Annie French and Jessie King, but with her own twist. Other exhibited works included: Sparrows, Miss Beatrice Hamilton (watercolour), Cupid's Garden (watercolour) and Contemplation.

In 1905 a quaich, or Scottish drinking bowl, designed by Dorothy and executed by the Glasgow School of Art, was presented to Sir Henry Craik on his retirement from the Secretaryship of the Scottish Education Department. The bowl was executed in hammered silver with a border of laurel repoussé. Inside was a Gaelic motto 'Everyday - present or absent'. The quaich was illustrated in the Art Journal, 1905, p.186 and in The Studio, Vol.35, July 1905, p.156. Dorothy also had ties with the Glasgow Society of Lady Artists' Club.

Olive Smyth also studied at the Glasgow School of Art, between 1900 and 1909. Under the influence of head Francis Newbery, she worked as a tutor whilst still a student. She taught sgraffito, illumination and gesso from 1902 until 1914. She also worked as a portrait and fresco artist. With her artist friends, she frequented the Willow Tea Rooms in Glasgow, designed by Mackintosh. Exhibited her work, including in the Scottish Section of the 1902 Turin Exhibition, showing drawings including Bad Company.

Exhibited in Cork, Toronto, Paris and Munich. Also, at the Royal Academy (1915-31), the Royal Glasgow Institute (1904-48), the Royal Hibernian Academy (1914-27) and the Royal Scottish Academy (1915-38). Exhibited works included: Bacchus in India, Head of Christ, Nigel (pastel) and Searchlights (tempera).

In 1905 Olive became a Member of the Glasgow Society of Lady Artists' Club, where she and Dorothy exhibited. Olive also exhibited at the Paris Salon in 1913, and in the Fine Arts Section of the Foire de Lyon in France in 1917. Her first one-woman exhibition was held in Glasgow in 1937. In 1933 she succeeded Dorothy as head of the Design Department at the Glasgow School of Art, retiring in 1937. Olive also shared Dorothy's interest in the theatre. One of her illuminated panels was illustrated in an article Some Modern Illuminations in The Studio, Vol.56, June 1912, pp.45-58. Like Dorothy, Olive spent much of her life and career in Glasgow and at nearby Cambuslang, Lanarkshire. They appear to have lived together. Works acquired by the National Gallery, Toronto and Tokyo.

SMYTH, MOTHER MARGARET

A nun in the Presentation Convent, Co. Cork, Ireland, and the creator of Youghal lace. The lace was exceptionally difficult to make, worked stitch by stitch without any base or foundation. The Youghal lace industry was founded in Ireland in 1847, the year of the Irish famine, as a means of providing the starving and destitute with paid employment in order to buy food. The lace was created by Mother Margaret after studying ancient Italian laces. After much effort and experimentation, she was able to start a lace school which, by the early 1900s, was widely known. The workers gradually invented many new stitches, making changes to the original pattern used in the needlepoint lace, creating their own unique laces. Most of the lace was made by young girls in the convent, under the supervision of the nuns. But some was made in the surrounding homes by both single and married women. For some, it was a sole source of income. For others, it was an additional income, as in the case of the Ruskin lace makers in the Lake District in the early 1900s. The Youghal industry was noted and commended in The Studio, Vol.29, August 1903, pp.212-215.

SNELLING, LILIAN (c.1879-1972)

Botanical Artist. Born in St Mary Cray near Orpington, Kent. She spent most of her life there. The daughter of John C. Snelling and Margaret. Her father, a brewer and miller, originated from

Kent. Her mother originated from Surrey. Lilian had at least two siblings, Margaret and Edith. Educated in Tunbridge Wells. Became a botanical artist. An album of her early drawings was acquired by The Lindley Library. The album contained studies of wildflowers native to the region. Considered to be an amateur rather than professional. Works reproduced by the Medici Society.

SOMERSET, NINA EVELYN MARY (1898-1980)

Decorative Artist / Ecclesiastical Artist / Illuminator. Born in Saltash, Cornwall. The daughter of William H. Somerset, a Captain in the Royal Navy, and Kate. Her father was born in South Africa. Her mother died young. Nina was possibly an only child. Spent her career in London and Bournemouth. Died in Bournemouth, aged 81. Exhibited her work, including at the Paris Salon, the Society of Women Artists (1920-27) and the Royal Society of Miniature Painters. Exhibited works included: Plumes of Paradise, The Descent From the Cross, The Anchoress and Alpha and Omega.

SORRELL, MABEL ELIZABETH (1916-91)

Painter / Designer. Known as Elizabeth. Born at New Skelton-in-Cleveland, Yorkshire in October 1916. The daughter of George Tanner. Educated at the Eastbourne High School. Studied at the Eastbourne School of Art between 1934 and 1938, and at the Royal College of Art, London between 1938 and 1942 under Professor Ernest W. Tristram. Elected an Associate of the Royal College of Art. Worked as a painter and designer in watercolours and gouache. Exhibited her work, including at the Royal Academy (47 works, 1948-70), the New English Art Club, various provincial galleries, the British Industries Fair, the Britain Can Make It Exhibition, the Ideal Home Exhibitions and the Royal Glasgow Institute (1969). Exhibited works included: Ferns in the Conservatory (Chantrey Bequest purchase), Early Violets, Fisherman's Fancy and The Boy in the Garden (watercolour). Works in the Tate Gallery (a Chantrey Bequest purchase, 1950) and in the Towner Art Gallery, Eastbourne. Works reproduced in Architectural Review and other journals. In 1947 she married artist / illustrator / lithographer Alan Sorrell (b.1904) in Eastbourne. The son of a watchmaker and craftsman, he studied at the Southend School of Art, the Royal College of Art and in Rome. He became a senior assistant instructor at the Royal College of Art. They had at least one son. They subsequently lived at Thors Mead in Thundersley, Essex.

Elizabeth Sorrell died at Southend-on-Sea, Essex, aged 74.

SOUTH, EDITH MABEL (1877-1970)

Sculptor. Known as Mabel. Born in Richmond, Surrey in February 1877. The daughter of Henry James South, an organist and Professor of Music, and Ann Maria. Both parents originated from London. Edith was raised in Richmond. Studied at the Heatherley's School of Art and at the Ecole des Beaux-Arts in Paris. Worked mainly in London, using the Mall Studios, Parkhill Road for a time. Produced animals, statuettes, busts and groups. Worked in marble, plaster, rock, bronze, wood, stone, ebony and terracotta. Exhibited her work, including at the Paris Salon, the Royal Scottish Academy (1925-37), the Royal Glasgow Institute (1925-40), the Royal Academy (1916-57), the Society of Women Artists (1954), and in Glasgow, Bradford and Liverpool as well as some smaller provincial galleries. Exhibited works included: Mandarin Duck (stone), The Song of Birds (bust), Lion Cub (terracotta) and A Nymph of Pan. Elected an Associate of the Royal Society of British Sculptors. The Hull Art Gallery acquired her The Spring Song. Works illustrated in Sphere, Sketch and Tatler. Her figure To the Moon was illustrated in The Studio, Vol.87, June 1924, p.306. In 1904 she married Allan Gabriel in London. He was killed in 1916 in France, during the First World War, as part of the Nottinghamshire and Derbyshire Regiment. Edith died in London, aged 93.

SOUTHALL, ELIZA MARIA (1834-1923)

Craftswoman. Was Eliza M. Baker. The mother of artist Joseph Edward Southall (1861-1944). She originated from Birmingham. Joseph was born in Nottingham. His father was Joseph Sturge Southall (1836-62), a member of a firm of grocers. He originated from Leominster and was a quaker. Joseph Sturge Southall died young, leaving Eliza and Joseph to live off the business. They lived comfortably enough to employ two servants. Joseph Edward studied art, and began as an architect's pupil whilst he and his mother lived at Edgbaston, Warwickshire. He eventually became an artist, producing frescoes and works in tempera, oils and watercolours. He was associated with the Society of Painters in Tempera, and with the Birmingham Group. Most of the Group came under the influence of E.R. Taylor at the Birmingham Municipal School of Art, though Southall did not. He exhibited his work at the Royal Academy (1895-97), at the New English Art Club and elsewhere.

However, Joseph also produced textile designs, including for what was described as 'Greek lace'. Eliza executed his designs, and the end results were exhibited at various venues. Her work included cut and embroidered Langdale linen. The linen came from the Lake District, made by a handcraft industry set up in the village of Elterwater in the late nineteenth century. The Southalls exhibited their work at the Arts and Crafts Exhibition Society's exhibitions. At the Society's 1899 exhibition they showed two examples of Greek lace which were illustrated in The Studio, Vol.18, January 1900, pp.262-263 along with a brief explanation of what Greek lace was. The cutwork was done first, then worked on stitch by stitch. In the Lake District, a similar type of lace, known locally as Ruskin lace, was created, and it is possible that Mrs Southall had learnt the art of lace making there, but chose to call it Greek lace outside the area.

At the Arts and Crafts Exhibition Society's 1903 exhibition the Southalls showed cutwork on Langdale linen, designed by Joseph and executed by Mrs Southall. Again, one of her exhibits was illustrated in The Studio, Vol.28, February 1903, p.36. Joseph also exhibited a number of miniature paintings as pendants on that occasion. At the Society's 1906 exhibition they showed a fire screen which was also illustrated in The Studio, Vol.37, March 1906, p.134. Joseph also exhibited enamel miniatures. At the 1904 Leicester Arts and Crafts Exhibition the Southalls showed other examples of Greek lace worked on Langdale linen. In 1911 Eliza showed a handmade linen screen, the screen made by Joseph, the linen worked by her, at the Second Exhibition of the Arts and Crafts in connection with the Society of Artists. The exhibition was designed to show that good craftwork could be done in the city as well as in the countryside. Eliza died in Birmingham, having worked her son's designs for well over a decade.

SOWERBY, MABEL MARGUERITE - SEE ANNESLEY, M.M.

SPARKS, ELLEN (1863-post-1911)

Decorative Leatherworker / Designer / Painter. An expert professional artist in decorative leatherwork and watercolour painter who was active in London in the 1890s and early 1900s. By 1911, aged 48, she is listed in census recordings as a 'retired artist' and living in Salisbury, Wiltshire. Records suggest that Ellen Sparks was born in Islington, the daughter of John Sparks, a publisher and bookseller, and Jane. One of at least six children (Mary, Amy, Florence, Ellen, Jane and William), all raised in Islington. Other details of her private life remain difficult to trace. She was certainly active from at least 1891 until some time after 1906. She was also a member of staff at the South Kensington School of Art, and during her career lived in Chelsea. In the very early 1900s, she advertised design and leatherwork from her studio in Tite Street, offering private tuition along with the sale of every type of decorative leatherwork. By 1904 she was advertising herself as a gold medallist. Sparks exhibited some of her watercolour paintings and leatherwork along with examples of her bookplates at the Society of Women Artists between 1891 and 1904. Exhibited works included: The Old Parsonage, Eastbourne, Changing Pastures and Suspense.

Exhibited elsewhere during her career, including at the Leeds Arts and Crafts Exhibition of 1900. There, she showed a screen panel in leather and a three-fold screen with full-length panels representing Earth, Air and Water. The designs were her own and she executed all the work herself. One of her exhibits on that occasion was illustrated in The Studio, Vol.21, 1901, p.254, revealing highly intricate and detailed work. Exhibited leatherwork at the 1904 City of Bradford Exhibition, which had a section devoted to artistic handicrafts practised by women. Ellen acted as Honorary Secretary of the leatherwork section. She also contributed to the 1906 Society of Artists at Work Exhibition held at the Grafton Galleries. The Society was organised by Mrs Charles Muller to encourage the sale of artistic handicrafts.

Sparks became particularly well known for her embossed leather panels, leather boxes and book covers. Some of her book covers were exhibited in Kidderminster. One of her leather panels was illustrated in The Studio, Vol.10, 1897, p.189. A chair-back in cut and embossed leather was illustrated in the Art Workers' Quarterly in July 1904. During her career, Sparks was commissioned by the Director of the Baroda State Museum, India to execute a series of cut and embossed leather panels intended to form a box. Those included a panel decorated with St George and the Dragon, with inscriptions and a quotation from Emerson. In 1897 sculptor Edith Downing exhibited a portrait panel of Ellen Sparks at the Society of Women Artists. Women like Sparks were particularly important in the British decorative arts at that time, demonstrating that they could earn a living as craftswomen, and teach other women skills which might lead to some form of independence.

SPARLING, MAY - SEE MORRIS, M.

SPIERS, CHARLOTTE HORN (1845-1914)

China Painter / Decorative Artist / Painter. Born in Oxford. The daughter of Richard Spiers and Elizabeth. Her father was a china merchant and a manufacturer, an alderman and a magistrate. One of at least 10 children (Richard, Elizabeth, Agnes, Charlotte, Alice, Arthur, Samuel, Ernest, Florence and Walter). Raised in the parish of St Giles, Oxfordshire. After her mother's death (some time prior to 1861), the family moved to St Pancras, London. For the rest of her life, Charlotte lived in London, with various members of her family, but mostly with her brother Richard Phene Spiers, who became an architect. Elizabeth Joy Spiers (1844-1901), also known as Bessie, also became an artist. Walter became an architect and surveyor, and Agnes became a governess. Elizabeth, Walter and Agnes lived with Richard and Charlotte over the years. Charlotte and Elizabeth died in London, and Charlotte left her small estate to Richard, who also never married. Ernest Spiers became a solicitor, which would indicate that the children were all well educated. Charlotte spent over 40 years working as an artist, but particularly as a painter of china. Subjects included flowers and landscapes. She evidently travelled around Britain with Elizabeth, producing paintings of, for example, Norfolk, Suffolk, Sussex, Yorkshire, Dorset and Shropshire.

Charlotte exhibited her work extensively, including at the Royal Academy (1881-1911), the Royal Society of British Artists (1882-88), the Royal Hibernian Academy (1886) and the Society of Women Artists (133 works, 1876-1915). Also exhibited at the Dudley Gallery, including in 1880. Exhibited china at the annual exhibition of women's work at the Howell & James, Regent Street, London showrooms. The exhibition was open to amateurs and professionals, with prizes offered. Judges included professional artists E.W. Cooke and F. Goodall. In 1878 Charlotte won a second prize for a plaque ornamented with a large hollyhock. Her work was also highly commended by the judges. She contributed several works to an exhibition held at the Paragon Art Studio in Bath in 1879, when 'art' pottery was still very much in its infancy. The exhibition was staged to display paintings on china, to educate those unfamiliar with it. Around 200 works were on view for a month. Most of the exhibitors were women. Works exhibited during her lengthy career included: Lane's Asylum, Ludlow, The Old Wheel Shed, Bosham, St John's College, Oxford

and Poppies (panel). Elected an Associate of the Society of Women Artists (1893-1914). Elizabeth Spiers worked as a landscape painter, also exhibiting extensively at the Society of Women Artists (1878-1902). She too was elected an Associate of the Society (1893-1901). Like Charlotte, Elizabeth worked until her death.

SPOONER, GERALDINE - SEE CARR, G.

SPOONER, MINNIE DIBDIN (1867-1949)

Painter / Illustrator / Etcher. Born in London. The daughter of Joseph Davison, an oil man, and Eliza. One of at least seven daughters (Emily, Ada, Florence, Minnie, Eliza, Louise and Rose). Raised in London. Probably studied in London. Produced portrait paintings and etchings. Illustrated children's books, including The Gold Staircase Poems and Verses For Children (by Louey Chisholm, T.C. & E.C. Jack, 1906). Exhibited three works at the Royal Academy (1919-27) including: Miss Maud Worsfold and Bridget, Daughter of Nevill Bosworth-Smith, Esq. In 1900 she married Charles Sydney Spooner (1862-1938) in London. Spooner was an architect, a teacher with the London County Council and a Member of the Art Workers' Guild. The couple lived at Eyot Cottage, Chiswick Mall for much of their marriage. Apparently had no children. Minnie died in London, as did Charles.

SPURGE, LOUISA - SEE JACOBS, L.

STABLER, PHOEBE GERTRUDE (1879-1955)

Sculptor / Potter / Black & White Artist / Metalworker / Enameller / Woodcarver. Born in Handsworth, Birmingham. The daughter of James McLeish and Mary Fox, both of Liverpool. One of at least five children (Minnie, Annie, Phoebe, James and Harry). Raised mainly in Liverpool. By the early 1890s, James McLeish had died and the remaining family were living with Mary's brother, George Fox of Kirkdale, Liverpool, along with another sister, Hannah Day, and her daughter Sarah Day. The three McLeish girls were all artistic. By the late 1890s the girls were studying at the Liverpool School of Art, Mount Street, then under Fred V. Burridge. There, Phoebe held the City Scholarship of £30 per annum for two years, and won the municipality's Travelling Scholarship of £60.

After completing her studies at Liverpool (c.1904), Phoebe left the Liverpool home she shared with her sisters and moved to London to study at the Royal College of Art. As a student in Liverpool, she studied modelling under Charles J.

Allen, drawing and painting under David Muirhead and design under Herbert MacNair. Later, she studied under Professor Edouard Lanteri, Augustus John and Richard Garbe. Whilst Annie McLeish died comparatively young, Minnie and Phoebe went on to have long and successful careers in art and design. However, Phoebe was the only one to marry, though apparently did not have children.

In 1906 Phoebe married sculptor and decorative artist Harold Stabler (1872-1945). He originated from Levens, Westmorland. The marriage took place in London and the couple remained there until their deaths, spending much of their time at Upper Mall, Hammersmith where they shared a studio and often worked together. Phoebe was always successful in her own right, however, and over a period of more than 45 years produced a substantial body of work, covering most areas of art and design. She produced panels, statuettes, plaques, figures, garden ornaments and car mascots, working in lead, stone, bronze, terracotta, marble, ivory plaster and other materials. Also worked in porcelain, pottery, stoneware and glazed earthenware. Executed black & white drawings for journals including the Burlington Magazine, and produced poster designs. Executed jewellery and enamels, pencil drawings, charcoal drawings, embroidery, stained glass designs, other decorative metalwork and furniture.

Phoebe exhibited her work extensively, independently and with Stabler, including at the Royal Glasgow Institute (77 works, 1911-56), at the Society of Women Artists (48 works, 1921-55) and the Royal Academy (27 works, 1911-46). Also, at Wembley, the Walker Art Gallery, Liverpool, in Paris and with the Women's International Art Club. Exhibited regularly at the Sir John Cass Arts and Crafts Society exhibitions, including at its third, held in 1908. On that occasion the exhibition was held at the Walker's Gallery, New Bond Street, London, and Phoebe contributed several small bronzes. At the 1913 exhibition, she showed two small bronzes and a small figure, Sauce. Harold Stabler was Head of the Art Department at the Sir John Cass Institute for a number of years, and acted as instructor of metalwork, jewellery and enamelling at the Royal College of Art after Henry Wilson.

The Stablers both exhibited with the Arts and Crafts Exhibition Society. At the 1912 exhibition, for example, Phoebe showed a glazed earthenware figure, Lavender Woman, designed and executed by her and Harold. The figure was illustrated in The Studio, Vol.58, February 1913, p.28. She also exhibited a nearly life-size group, Madonna and Child, along with some smaller pieces executed with Harold, including Baby's Head in terracotta. At the 1916 Arts and Crafts exhibition, Phoebe showed a number of works including Piping Faun (lead roundel) and a bird bath and garden figure, both in lead. Also, a glazed stoneware group and several medallions by her and Harold jointly. Some of those were illustrated in The Studio, Vol.69, October 1916, p.72.

Together, the Stablers exhibited enamels under the auspices of the British Institute of Industrial Art in 1922. In 1914, Phoebe contributed to an exhibition of arts and crafts held at the Old Monastery, Rye, Sussex. Other contributors on that occasion included Heywood Sumner, James Guthrie and Walter Crane. Phoebe Stabler was elected an Associate of the Royal Society of British Sculptors in 1923. Elected a Member of the Society of Women Artists (1921-33, 1950-55). A Member of the Garden Club, and of the Women's Provincial Club. She was also a founder member of the New Forest Group. Devised in 1923, the Group's inaugural exhibition was held at the Mansard Gallery, Tottenham Court Road, London in September 1924. Phoebe exhibited several sculptures. The Group initially had seven members including Phoebe, Marjorie Whittington, Hesketh Hubbard and Maxwell Armfield. Most of the Group lived within a short distance of the New Forest, hence the name. But they did not paint or sculpt exclusively New Forest subjects. At the Group's 1927 exhibition, held at the Arlington Gallery, Phoebe showed a keystone which was illustrated in The Studio, Vol.93, 1927, p.432. Her works were frequently illustrated in journals and newspapers including The Studio, The Times, Colour, Arts and Crafts and the Architectural Journal. In particular, The Studio reproduced some of her works full-page such as her The Young Mother, a concrete garden figure illustrated in Vol.80, September 1920, p.69.

Official purchasers of her work included the Leicester Art Gallery, the Liverpool Art Gallery (a bronze) and the Helsingfors Museum. Also, the Ceramic Museum, New York. She executed numerous war memorials, including for Durban, South Africa, for Rugby, for a church in Hull and the Underground Railway. Executed the Wakefield Speed Trophy. Two of her figures were purchased for the International Museum of Ceramics, Faenza, Italy. Harold Stabler was an equally gifted and successful artist and craftsman, and was the subject of an article in The Studio, Vol.64, February 1915, pp.34-41. He produced metalwork including caskets, enamel panels, jewellery, cream jugs, sugar bowls, altar candlesticks, altar rails in gilded metal, altar crosses, chalices and trays. Also a modeller. During the war, he was a Member of the Civic Arts Association Committee, organised to give advice on war memorials and other issues relating to war and the arts. He particularly campaigned for artists who were not fit for active service to be given work during the First World War.

The Stablers also jointly became associated with the Poole Pottery in Dorset under the Carter, Stabler, Adams partnership. With Truda Carter (Adams) and John Adams, the Stablers worked successfully for Poole from around 1920 until at least the 1930s. Each piece produced by the partnership was hand thrown and decorated, mainly to the designs of Harold and Phoebe. Both had designed and executed their own pottery for a number of years prior to Poole, using a kiln installed in their Hammersmith studio. Some of their earlier designs were later produced in editions by Carter, Stabler, Adams. The partnership exhibited their wares, including at the 1927 Leipzig European Arts and Crafts show in the British Section, and at the Monza Exhibition of Industrial and Decorative Art in 1930. Phoebe also produced designs for Royal Doulton, Royal Worcester and the Ashtead Pottery (founded 1923).

Harold and Phoebe also designed and modelled facades for buildings and monuments which were marketed as 'Constructional Della Robbia'. Harold Stabler died in Hammersmith in mid-1945, aged 72. Phoebe also died in Hammersmith, in late 1955, aged 76. At the time of her death, she was still living at Upper Mall. SEE: McLEISH, ANNIE & MINNIE

STAMP, WINIFRED LOUISE (1881-1948)

Painter / Decorative Artist / Illustrator. Born and raised in Hampstead. The daughter of Edward Blanshaw Stamp and Alice Hopkins Peters. Her father was a chemist and druggist. One of at least eight children (Albert, Francis, Alice, Winifred, John, Charles, George and Dorothy). Studied at the Regent Street Polytechnic, London in the very early 1900s. As a student, she exhibited her work at the National Competition of Schools of Art held at South Kensington. In the 1903 Competition, her exhibits included a design for a colour print, which won her a book prize. The design was illustrated in the Art Journal, 1903, p.315. At the 1905 Competition, she showed a number of decorative illustrations.

Stamp worked as a figure and portrait painter, including miniatures, a decorative artist and an illustrator. Some of her work was included in an exhibition held at Crosby Hall in 1912. Other exhibitors included George H. Day and Jessie Bayes. In the same year, The Studio, Vol.56, August 1912, p.227, illustrated her design for a frieze for the entrance hall of the Regent Street Polytechnic. Also exhibited her work at the Royal Academy (1900-01) and the Royal Society of Miniature Painters. Exhibited works included: Welthin and Winnie, La Princesse Lointaine, The Babes in the Wood and Winifred. Remained in London during her career, but died in Hampshire, aged 66. Records indicate that Winifred taught at the Regent Street Polytechnic, and was still there in 1938, when Harold Brownsword was Head. One of her pupils was textile designer Anne Loosely (1906-92).

STANFIELD, MARION WILLIS (1891-1965)

Sculptor / Decorative Artist. Born in Plymouth, Devon. The daughter of the Rev. John Charles Stanfield, a Wesleyan Methodist minister, and Sarah Jane. Her father originated from Longsight, Manchester, her mother from Bristol, Somerset. One of at least three children (Marion, Joseph and George). Raised initially in Plymouth, but subsequently based in Redditch, Worcestershire with her parents. Studied at the Goldsmiths' College of Art, London, in Paris under Emile Antoine Bourdelle (1861-1929), and in Florence. Became a sculptor in bronze, stone, lead and marble. Also a decorative worker in chromium plating. Produced mainly figures and portrait works.

Marion exhibited her work regularly for more than 33 years, working until shortly before her death. Exhibited at the Royal Academy (1932-59), the Royal Glasgow Institute (1926-55), the Royal Scottish Academy (1950) and the Society of Women Artists (1927-53). Also, at the Paris Salon, the Leicester Galleries and elsewhere. Exhibited works included: April (head, marble), Joy and Gladness (statuette group, bronze), Isaac and His Faggots (statuette), Christopher Robin & Mary Jane (bookends, lead) and A Troubled Cupid (sketch in bronze). Produced garden ornaments too. Elected an Associate of the Royal Society of British Sculptors. Elected a Fellow of the Royal Society of Arts. Also acted as assistant art lecturer at Whitelands Training College, Putney, London. Acted as lecturer in sculpture at Reading University (1947). Based largely in London during her career, including at the Joubert Studios, Jubilee Place, Chelsea and the Bolton Studios, Redcliffe Road. Purchasers of her work included H.R.H. The Princess Royal (angel in marble). Produced Stations of the Cross in Caenstone for St Mary's Church, Chislehurst. Also, two angels in brown Hornton stone for the

Whitelands College Chapel, as well as a number of bronze portrait busts. Comparatively late in life, she married woollen merchant Walter Braun in London in 1950. She died in March 1965 in London, before Walter.

STATHAM, MILDRED ELLINOR (c.1884-1964)

Embroideress / Craftswoman. Born in Brazil. The daughter of John Statham, a shipping merchant, and Alice. Raised mainly in Hale, Cheshire. One of at least seven children (William, Florence, Mildred, Mary, Richard, Alfred and Herbert). Studied at the South Kensington art school, London. Worked as a decorative embroideress and in various handicrafts. Based in London and at Homecrafts, High Street, Dorking, Surrey during her career. Died in Alderley Edge, Cheshire, aged 80. Exhibited her work, including at the Walker Art Gallery, Liverpool, the British Institute of Industrial Art and at the Society of Women Artists (1910-39). Elected a Member of the Arts and Crafts Exhibition Society, of the Faculty of Arts and of the Embroiderers' Guild. Also a Member of the Forum Club. A stool worked in petit point by Mildred was illustrated in The Studio.

STEADMAN, ELLEN MAUDE (1863-1953)

Painter / Decorative Artist / Illuminator. Born and raised in Bristol. The daughter of John Joseph Steadman, a manufacturer, and Elizabeth. One of at least four children (Frances, Charles, Ellen and William). Studied at the Bristol School of Art. By at least 1891 she had moved to London and spent several years there working as an interior decorator. At the same time, she studied life drawing at Heatherley's School. In the late 1890s, she set up an interior design studio in London with Katherine Rayment. They had showrooms in Bond Street. Among other things, they executed stencilled fabrics and painted friezes. A frieze and a wall decoration by the studio were illustrated in The Studio, Vol.14, 1898, p.195. Two stencilled designs by Rayment were illustrated in The Studio, Vol.19, 1900, p.267. Steadman also worked in illumination, studying at the Manuscript Room of the British Museum. As a result, she was commissioned to produce a small number of copies of the Hymns of Thomas Aquinas, and the Great Choir Books of two monasteries. She spent her spare time producing landscape paintings. One of her main influences was William T. Wood, R.W.S., R.O.I. One of her works was illustrated in Apollo, Vol.14, November 1931, p.303. By 1911, Steadman was based at the Sisters of Mercy, Ranelagh Road, Worcestershire, possibly working as an illuminator. She died in Sudbury, Middlesex, aged 90. Her address at that time was The Little Company.

STEBBING, HELEN LILIAN (1883-1937)

Embroideress. Born in London. The daughter of Alfred Stebbing, a general merchant, and Elizabeth. One of at least six children (Edith, Harry, Bertram, Helen, George and Lizzie). Raised in London. Died in Hendon, Middlesex. Worked as an art teacher in London whilst based in West Kensington. Probably the same Helen Stebbing who was a Member of the Church Crafts League, one of its embroiderers. The League (founded in 1899) aimed to maintain standards in church art during the early twentieth century. By 1920 some 73 artists, craftsmen and craftswomen were working in association with the League, including Henry Holiday, Nelson Dawson, Emily Ford and Jessie Bayes. Helen Stebbing of London exhibited handicrafts at the Society of Women Artists in 1929, possibly the same.

STEBBING, SYLVIA WINIFRED ANNETTE (1876-1976)

Bookbinder / Book Decorator. Born in Bloomsbury, London. The daughter of William Stebbing, a barrister and writer, and Anne. Raised in London and Surrey. One of at least five children (William, Henry, Sylvia, Rachel and Nigel). Received some tuition at the Albert Hall under a lady tutor, and from Agnes Ashbee, sister of designer Charles R. Ashbee who taught bookbinding at Cheyne Walk, Chelsea. She then studied under Douglas Cockerell. He had two other pupils at that time, Annie Power and Audrey Ricketts. Sylvia and Annie Power subsequently set up a workshop together in Museum Street, London, buying their own tools, presses and materials. Virginia Woolf (then Stephen) came for a few lessons.

After a while, Annie Power went to work for Charles R. Ashbee, and Sylvia moved to Queen's Road, Bayswater. Sylvia spent some time with Dr and Mrs Henry Daniel at Worcester College, Oxford. Dr Daniel printed his own private press books at the College, and Sylvia bound some of those, including her father's Outlines. Mrs Daniel (Emily) also did bookbinding. Sylvia bound some of her father's other published works. Also bound Charles Kingsley, The Water Babies (1886) in 1904. And, Edward Alexander C. McCurdy, The Roses of Paestum (1900) in 1906. She exhibited two examples of her work at the Society of Women Artists in 1902 (whilst at Museum Street). Sold some of her work in New York.

Executed some 43 bindings during her career. Noted in Sarah Treverbian Prideaux's Modern Bookbindings Their Design and Decoration (London, Archibald Constable & Co., 1906). Stebbing was also the author of A Victorian Childhood (Eastland Press, 1972). She gave up her career when she married author Edward Alexander C. McCurdy in 1906 in Surrey. They lived in Surrey and had six children. Sylvia died just before her 100th birthday.

STEELE, FLORENCE HARRIET (1857-1948)

Designer / Modeller / Metalworker. Born in Reigate, Surrey in January 1857. The daughter of John Sisson Steele, a doctor, and Harriet. Her father originated from Reigate, her mother from Sussex. The youngest of at least eight children (five boys and three girls), the rest of whom were also born in Reigate. Raised in Reigate. Interestingly, Florence and her two sisters, Mary Elizabeth (b.1849) and Eleanor Lucy (b.1854), were all baptised in 1879, when they were in their 20s. One of her brothers, Louis (b.1842), became an artist. He married miniature painter Maria Louise Piatti (b.1849), the daughter of Italian painter Joseph Piatti. John Sisson Steele died in Reigate in 1889, when Florence was around 32 years of age. In 1891, or just after, Florence moved to London and became an art student. At the comparatively late age of 38, she contributed to the National Competition of Schools of Art in 1895, suggesting that she had been unable to study until after her father's death. She showed a design modelled for a bronze door-knocker and designs for glazed tiles at the 1895 Competition, where most of her fellow exhibitors would have been in their early 20s or younger. Nonetheless, by 1896 she was living in London and working as an independent designer and craftswoman at a studio in Hammersmith.

Despite her delayed start, Florence quickly established herself as one of Britain's most accomplished, prominent and productive designers, executing a number of important commissions. She worked and exhibited until at least 1919, when she would have been around 62 years of age. She spent her later career working at Brook Green, London, but spent her final years back in Reigate, at Geranium Cottage. She died in Surrey in January 1948, aged 90, leaving the respectable sum of £7142.

During her career, Steele produced a considerable body of work, in silver, bronze and enamel, and produced the occasional decorative figure. Much of what she designed and made was not unusual, such as decorative silver bottles, silver hand mirrors, buckles, walking stick heads, silver christening cups and alms dishes, bronze sundials and bronze portrait medallions. Yet everything was praised for its high quality of design and craftsmanship as well as its beauty. Her talent for figure work was particularly noted during her lifetime, including on, for example, her silver hand mirror with two mermaids intertwined on the back.

Other work, however, was significantly more important. For example, a silver and enamel triptych designed for the town of Preston, Lancashire for presentation to the Earl of Derby, with the freedom of the town. The Earl had been Mayor during the Guild Merchant Celebration of 1902. On either side of the doors of the triptych were figures of Justice and Energy. Also on the doors were the coats of arms of Lord Derby and the town of Preston. The doors opened to reveal a wording in enamel. The triptych was illustrated in the Art Journal, 1903, p.319 and in the Art Workers' Quarterly, 1904, p.214 along with a silver stick head by Steele. She also designed the chain for the Mayoress of Preston, a portion of which was exhibited at the 1906 Arts and Crafts Exhibition Society's exhibition and illustrated in the Art Journal, 1906, p.125. The design for the chain was also exhibited at the Royal Academy in 1903, and subsequently at the New Gallery exhibition of 1908 as well as being illustrated in The Studio magazine, Vol.44, p.55 along with a silver bowl (p.56) and two silver mirrors also designed and executed by her and shown at the New Gallery (p.60).

Steele's work appeared in numerous exhibitions during her career, including at the Royal Academy. There, she showed 34 examples between 1896 and 1918, including a bronze medallion of George Clark, Esq., a decorative panel, a design for a silver writing case, Hero Finding the Body of Leander (group) and Dawn Dispelling Night and Sleep. In 1914 she also exhibited a design for a medal in Clinical Medicine for the Women's School of Medicine at the Royal Academy, indicating that she was not unsympathetic to women's liberation through study. Other works, as already noted, appeared at the Arts and Crafts Exhibition Society's exhibitions, certainly in 1896, 1903, 1906 and 1910. At the 1896 exhibition, the Society's fifth held, she showed a number of items including a highly decorative lock-plate with a figure design. Also sent metalwork to the 1901 Glasgow Exhibition, and to the 1904 City of Bradford Exhibition which had a section devoted to artistic handcrafts practised by women. Contributed to the 1905 / 06 Permanent Exhibition of Artistic Handcrafts at the Lyceum Club, including one of her metal caskets which was illustrated in the Art Workers' Quarterly, 1906, p.61.

During her career, Steele was elected a Member of the Church Crafts League, there listed as a modeller. The League was founded in late 1899 and was initially based at The Church House, Dean's Yard, Westminster. Its aim was to infuse new life into the building, decorating and furnishing of churches, ably assisted by its members. Foundation patrons of the League were John Ruskin and G.F. Watts. Steele occasionally diversified, and in 1917 was commissioned to produce a design for a monument for the grave of the Waddell family of Glasgow. The design was executed in Hoptonwood stone and illustrated in The Studio, Vol.72, 1917, p.121. A memorial tablet designed by her was also illustrated in The Studio, Vol.74, 1919, p.31, apparently her last appearance in the magazine. Her name has appeared in other sources too, but mostly in her lifetime. For example, in his volume British Sculpture and Sculptors of To-day, London, Cassell & Co. Ltd, 1901, M.H. Spielmann notes that her work was mainly centred on the applied arts, and that she attracted much attention for the delicacy of her portrait medallions. Her designs, he noted, were used by others, including Elkington's and Pilkington's. A silver casket designed by Florence and executed by Elkington & Co. was illustrated in the Art Journal, 1903, p.89 and shown at the 1903 Arts and Crafts exhibition. In The Studio, Vol.44, 1908, p.60, she is noted as 'a designer of skill'. She was also noted in an article in the Art Journal, 1907, p.172, titled Metalwork and Jewellery by R.E.D. Sketchley, which included an illustration of a bell-push by Steele. Her work was also praised in The Studio Year-Book of Decorative Art.

STEELE, MARIA LOUISE (b.1849)

Enamel Artist / Miniature Painter. Also known as Louise. Born in Paris. The daughter of Italian painter Joseph Piatti. She married painter / etcher Louis John Steele (1842-1918). Born in Reigate, he was the son of John Sisson Steele, a doctor, and Harriet. He was one of at least eight children. His sister was modeller / designer / metalworker Florence H. Steele. Louis and Maria had two children, Louis John Sisson Piatti Steele (1871-1946) and Ernest Henry Steele (b.1872). Louis Snr exhibited his work at the Royal Academy between 1872 and 1886. Maria also exhibited there, showing four portraits of family enamelled on gold between 1875 and 1877. The couple lived in London. In 1886 Louis Steele emigrated to Auckland, New Zealand and died there in 1918.

Maria remained in London with her children. She continued to work until at least 1911.

STEINFORTH, LAURA GERALDINE SUSANNA (1874-1958)

Decorative Illustrator / Painter. Born in Liverpool. The daughter of Raymond Steinforth (d.1916) and Ermenilda Clements (d.1922). Her father, a solicitor and foreign law agent, was born in Calcutta. Laura had at least one sister, Edith. Educated at the Convent of Notre Dame. Studied at the Liverpool School of Art. Remained in Liverpool for the rest of her life, dying there aged 84. Produced decorative illustrations in watercolours and portrait paintings in oils. Painted fairy tales and fantastic and imaginary pictures. Exhibited her work at the Walker Art Gallery, Liverpool. Held a one-woman show of 15 of her works at the Liverpool Playhouse in November 1925. Works included: Palace of Art, The Lady of the Emeralds, Enchantment and Beatrice and Primavera. She was known to enjoy poetry, which may have inspired her painting. Elected a Member of the Liver Sketching Club.

STEINTHAL, EMELINE (1855-1921)

Sculptor / Painter. Born in Rochdale, Lancashire. The daughter of George Petrie, an engineer and iron founder, and Sarah Anne. Raised in Rochdale. One of at least three children. Studied sculpture and painting. Produced busts and portrait works. In 1882 she married Francis Frederick Steinthal in Rochdale. He originated from Bradford and was a yarn merchant. The couple lived in Ilkley, Yorkshire, where Emeline died, aged 66. They had at least two sons and two daughters. One of their sons, Paul, also became a yarn merchant. Emeline exhibited her work predominantly after her marriage, which suggests her husband encouraged her in her work, or that she studied after her marriage with his approval. She exhibited five works at the Royal Academy between 1890 and 1905, including: After a Hard Life (bust), A Worker (bust) and Mrs W.E. Forster (bust).

STEPHENS, OLIVE BERTHA (1885-1935)

Etcher / Painter. Also sometimes Bertha Olive, known as Olive. Born in Clifton, Bristol. The daughter of Sidman Thomas Stephens, a corn merchant, and Eliza Clarke. Her parents originated from Bristol. The youngest of three daughters (also Florence (b.1871) and Eliza Kate (b.1873)). Raised in Bristol. Educated at the Redland High School. Her father died in 1906, after which she lived with her mother and sister Kate. Studied at the School of Art, Queen's Road,

Bristol. Then went to London to study at the L.C.C. Central School of Arts and Crafts. Won bronze and silver medals as a student. Won the King's Prize in a national competition. Awarded an Art Class Teachers' Certificate. Returned to Bristol and remained there for much of her life, using various addresses.

Olive became a copperplate etcher and a painter of landscapes in watercolours. Also a printer of artists' proofs. Taught etching for a while. Acted as a teacher at the Branch School of Art and at various private schools. One of her etchings was requested for the Queen's doll's house. Exhibited at the Royal Hibernian Academy (1913), the Royal Academy (1913-18), in Liverpool, Bristol and Conway, and at the Welsh Eisteddfod. Also, with the Print Makers' Society of Los Angeles and the Chicago Society of Etchers. Exhibited works included: Hay Tor From Across the Seigne, The Willow Pool, Stoke, near Bristol, Near Nailsea and Near Henbury Gold Links, Bristol. Elected an Associate of the Royal West of England Academy. Died in Bristol in July 1935, aged 50. Still working and exhibiting in 1934, just prior to her death.

STERN, FLORENCE SARAH (1868-1952)

Decorative Metalworker. Born in Birmingham. The daughter of Moritz Stern and Fanny. Her parents originated from Munich. Her father was an export merchant in Birmingham. Florence was one of at least seven children (Arthur, Florence, Rosa, Marcus, James, Helen and Margaret). All were raised in Birmingham, in a house with several servants. Florence, Helen and Margaret remained at the family home, unmarried, into their 30s and 40s. Florence died in Watford, Hertfordshire, aged 84. James and Helen became commercial clerks. Marcus became an engineer draughtsman. Florence studied at the Birmingham Municipal School of Art. She exhibited at the School's annual exhibition of student work from at least 1894 until at least 1899. One of her exhibits, a repoussé copper panel intended to be a nameplate for the Technical School, was illustrated in The Studio, Vol.13, April 1898, p.194. The panel won her a first prize. At the 1899 exhibition of student work, she showed a clasp in silver repoussé which was also illustrated in The Studio, Vol.16, 1899, p.199. On that occasion, she also showed an altar cross in copper and ivory made for a Birmingham church.

Florence became a decorative metalworker. Exhibited her work elsewhere. For example, in 1908 she contributed to the Liverpool Crafts Exhibition held at the Old Bluecoat School. In the same year, she contributed to Mr John Baillie's Annual Arts and Crafts Exhibition, showing jewellery. Other exhibitors on that occasion included Georgina Gaskin, Jessie Bayes and Dora Stone. Exhibited at the Walker Art Gallery, Liverpool, including at the Autumn Exhibitions of 1909 and 1914. Exhibited at the Society of Women Artists (1906-12), alone and jointly with Gertrude Connolly. Also exhibited locally, with the Royal Birmingham Society of Artists. In 1916 Florence contributed to an exhibition of works by women artists held at Messrs Waring & Gillow in May of that year. The Queen visited and purchased some of Stern's work. The exhibition aimed to raise funds for women artists suffering due to war.

STEWART, ALICE C. - SEE MAUDE, A.C.

STEWART, ETHEL (1869-post-1913)

Decorative Artist / Etcher / Painter. Records suggest that this was Jane Ethel Balfour Stewart, known as Ethel. Born in Richmond, Surrey. The daughter of Balfour Stewart (1828-87) and Katharine Stevens (b.1844). Her father, a Professor of Natural Philosophy, originated from Edinburgh. Her mother originated from London. One of at least three children (also Charles and William). Charles Stewart entered the medical profession. Ethel was raised in Withington, Lancashire. More certain is that Ethel became a student at the Mount Street School of Art, Liverpool in the early 1900s. A contemporary of Florence Laverock, Gwendoline Parry and Edith Walters.

Ethel produced colour prints, etchings, stencils and landscape paintings. Exhibited at the annual National Competition of Schools of Art, South Kensington from at least 1903. In 1904 she showed a stencilled decoration, but also a decorative panel which was illustrated in The Studio, Vol.32, September 1904, p.327. Also exhibited at the Liverpool School of Art annual student exhibition. In 1905 she exhibited coloured stencilled marine and street scenes and etchings. In 1906 she showed a stencil in colours of The Old Wool Market in Dunster which was illustrated in The Studio, Vol.38, June 1906, p.75. Other works were illustrated in the Art Journal. For example, in 1904 one of her colour prints was reproduced (p.72). In 1907 the same journal illustrated her etching The Borderland of Wales. Exhibited her work with the Royal Society of Painter-Etchers & Engravers, including in 1912. Elected a Member of the Society. Also exhibited at the Royal Scottish Academy (1911), the Royal Glasgow Institute (1911) and the Royal Academy

(1909-13). Exhibited works included: Deer Sound in the Orkneys, The River Wall on the Mersey (black & white), The Tithe Barn on the High Croft and On the Eden. Based at Bebington, Cheshire during her career, and at Highbridge, Somerset.

STEWART, HARRIET SANDERSON (1874-1971)

Sculptor. Born in London. The daughter of Francis Stewart, a Church of England priest who was born in the West Indies, and Sarah. Possibly an only child. Raised in Essex, where her father was Rector of Doddinghurst Church in the 1880s and 1890s. Subsequently based in London, where she worked as a sculptor. Lived with her widowed father for part of the time. Died in Malvern, Worcestershire, aged 95. Produced busts, portrait medallions and plaquettes in bronze and plaster. Exhibited her work, including at the Royal Academy (1910-16) and at the Royal Glasgow Institute (1911). Exhibited works included: The Tanner (bust), The Rev. Francis Stewart (plaquette, bronze), The Bands of Sloth (statuette, bronze) and Miss Ysabel Seaton (bust, plaster).

STEWART, HILDA JOYCE (b.1892)

Painter. Born in July 1892 into a family of artists. The daughter of eminent painter / sculptor Lexden Lewis Pocock (1850-1919) who originated from London. Her mother was Alicia Josephine Shellshear (1852-1914) who was born in Russia to British parents. Alicia was also an artist and exhibited her work at the Royal Academy (1877-87) and the Royal Society of British Artists (1873-75). Alicia and Lexden married in Kensington in 1879. Lexden exhibited at the Royal Academy (1875-1914), the Royal Hibernian Academy (1876-89) and elsewhere. Hilda was the seventh of at least eight children (Edith, Alfred, Lilian, Mabel, Roy, Eva, Hilda and Hugh), all born and raised in London. At least three of the Pocock children became artists. Lilian Josephine Pocock (1883-1974) excelled as a painter, book illustrator and stained glass artist. Alfred Lyndhurst Pocock (b.1881), a Member of the Royal Society of Miniature Painters, became a gem sculptor to the Russian Court jewellers for a time. He studied at the Royal Academy schools, as did Lilian, and exhibited at the Royal Academy (1909-30).

Hilda's aunt (Lexden's sister), Julia Pocock (1842-1922), was also a watercolour painter, sculptor and illustrator. Julia and Lexden were the children of Lewis and Eliza Pocock. Lewis was a landed proprietor. Julia exhibited at the Royal Academy (1871-1903), the Royal Society of British Artists (1872), the Royal Scottish Academy (1876-77), the Royal Hibernian Academy (1876-77) and the Society of Women Artists (1861-75). She produced mainly figure and portrait works. Julia had ties with the Female School of Art in Queen Square, London, possibly teaching there.

Hilda Pocock was initially educated at home, and was doubtless influenced by her parents in art. She then went to the Regent Street Polytechnic in London, where Lilian also studied. Hilda completed her studies in around 1917. She chose to concentrate on portrait miniatures. Immediately on completing her studies she exhibited a triptych in stained wood and gesso at the Grafton Galleries in London in a joint exhibition of the Royal Society of Portrait Painters and the Royal Society of Miniature Painters held in 1917. The triptych was illustrated in The Studio, Vol.72, 1917, p.121. In the same year she exhibited at the Society of Women Artists, the only time she would do so. Awarded a Diploma in Miniature Painting by the Royal Society of Miniature Painters in 1927. Elected a Member of the Society.

Hilda executed portrait commissions and copied old masters until her marriage, but did continue to paint after her marriage. She married John Hutchinson Stewart and moved to Canada. They had at least two daughters. During her career, Hilda also exhibited at the Royal Academy (1911-21, and possibly 1928), and in Liverpool, Manchester and Birmingham as well as elsewhere in London. Also, in Toronto, at the Women's Art Association of Canada (Toronto) and with the Canadian Handicraft Guild in Montreal. Other works included a miniature of her father, Lexden Lewis Pocock. Also, His Honour Lieut. Gov. H.E. Munroe, The Rt Rev. William T. Hallam, M.A., D.D., Bishop of Saskatoon and Molly Josephine. Her Emily (a diploma work) was kept for the permanent exhibition by the Royal Society of Miniature Painters. The Canadian Handicraft Guild acquired a triptych in stained wood by her. Presumed to have died in Canada. SEE: POCOCK, LILIAN J.

STIRLING, EVANGELINE (1853-1930)

Sculptor. Born in West Derby, Lancashire. The daughter of Edwin Stirling (1819-67) and Mary. Mary originated from Ulverston, Lancashire. Edwin, a sculptor, originated from Scotland. He studied at the Edinburgh School of Art, but subsequently moved to Liverpool. He died there whilst Evangeline was still young. She was the second of three children (also Lucy Annie Jane and Norman). Raised in Liverpool. Evidently inherited her father's passion for sculpture, studying sculpture and modelling in London, living in Kensington. She returned to Liverpool for a short time before becoming an art teacher at the Cheltenham Ladies' College in Gloucestershire. Produced busts, working in various materials including terracotta. Exhibited four works at the Royal Academy between 1880 and 1894: One of Our Organ-grinders, Irene, a Study, Meditation and Miss Beale, Principal of the Cheltenham Ladies' College. Also exhibited at the Walker Art Gallery, Liverpool. By her 50s, she had retired from teaching and was living with her sister Lucy in Ulverston. In 1923 she emigrated to California at the age of 69, and died there seven years later. She appears to have lived latterly with her brother Norman. She left her £4829 estate to publisher Harold Edgar Young.

STOCKDALE, CHRISTINE
(active 1920s-1930s)

Sculptor. Some confusion currently exists over the correct identity of sculptor Christine Stockdale. Recent sources state that she was the daughter of Henry Stockdale, Rector of East Retford, Nottinghamshire, and that she was born in 1851, dying in 1931 at Bromsgrove, Worcestershire. She spent her later years living with her brother, Charles Stockdale, who was Rector at Stoke Prior, Bromsgrove. However, records indicate that another, younger Christine Stockdale also spent time living at the Rectory at Stoke Prior, and that she may have been the niece of Charles and Christine. The younger Christine was born in around 1881, and may have been the daughter of Henry Stockdale junior, who spent most of his life in South Africa. It was probably the younger Christine who exhibited two works at the Royal Academy: Before Eve (group, stone) in 1921 and "Ons Land", Afrikander Bull (stone) in 1930. And it was probably the younger Christine who spent time in London in the 1920s, teaching figure and animal modelling at the Grosvenor School of Modern Art (certainly in 1927). Documents relating to travel overseas reveal that the younger Christine visited South Africa and elsewhere abroad, and was a sculptor who in 1929 was aged 48. There are no indications that the elder Christine Stockdale worked as a sculptor. No birth or death records exist for the younger Christine, and since she appeared not to exhibit after around 1930, she probably moved abroad later in her career.

STONE, MELICENT (1868-1922)

Artist / Sculptor. Born in Havant, Hampshire. The daughter of William Henry Stone and Melicent. Her father, who originated from Surrey, was a J.P, D.L. and M.A., and an East India merchant. Her mother originated from London. Melicent had at least one sibling, Arthur. The children were raised in Hampshire and London. Melicent spent some time in Surrey with her parents as an adult. Otherwise, she spent much of her career in London, where she died, aged 54. Studied sculpture and painting, probably in London. Produced statuettes and heads in bronze. Produced illustrations for several children's books, including for Grimm, and portrait works. Exhibited her work, including at the Royal Academy (1908-21), the Royal Scottish Academy (1921) and the Society of Women Artists (1895-98). Exhibited works included: The Piper (statuette, bronze), The Butterfly (statuette, bronze), The Two King's Children - Grimm (watercolour) and A Cheerful Countenance (head). For part of the time (1911 certainly) Stone shared digs with artist Beatrice Stella Campbell, but also lived alone in London.

STRATTON, HELEN (c.1866-1961)

Illustrator / Painter. Possibly Helen Isobel Mansfield Ramsay Stratton. Born in India, though the exact year is unclear. The daughter of an Officer who spent much time abroad, and Georgina. One of at least five children (Wallace, Agnes, Margaret, Helen and Janet). By at least the very early 1870s, Georgina and the children were living in Bath, Somerset. Helen died there, aged 95, in a nursing home. By at least 1891, Helen was an art student in London, sharing digs with a number of other women. She remained in London for much of her life and career. She was active as a book illustrator and a painter of landscapes, flowers, buildings and figures in watercolours and oils for over 30 years.

Books illustrated by Stratton included Norman Gale, Songs for Little People (Constable, 1896, 119 illustrations with decor), Walter D. Campbell, Beyond the Border (Constable, 1898, 167 illustrations), Hans Andersen, Fairy Tales (George Newnes Ltd, 1899, 6d each for 14 parts), Marie, Crown Princess of Roumania, The Lily of Life (Hodder & Stoughton, 1913) and Lady E.C. Barnes, As the Water Flows (1920). Also contributed to Little Folk (periodical). Exhibited her work, including at the Society of Women Artists (19 works, 1893-1924), the Royal Academy (1894-1917), the Royal Hibernian Academy (1913), the Royal Society of British Artists (1892-93), in Liverpool and at the Royal

Institute of Painters in Watercolours. Noted in R.E.D. Sketchley, English Book Illustration of To-day, London, Kegan Paul, 1903. Also noted in Mahony, Latimer & Folmsbee, Illustrators of Children's Books 1744-1945, Boston, The Horn Book Inc., 1947.

STURROCK, MARY A. - SEE NEWBERY, M.A.

SUNDERLAND, FRANCES (1866-post-1934)
Painter / Craftswoman. Born in Keighley, Yorkshire in September 1866. The daughter of Wilkinson Watson and Elizabeth Agnes. Her father was a butcher in Keighley. Her mother originated from York. Frances had a younger brother, Charles. She studied locally, at the Keighley School of Art, winning an award in the National Competition of Schools of Art. Awarded an Art Masters' Teaching Certificate in 1893. Became a watercolour painter of landscapes and seascapes, particularly of Yorkshire. Also took up various crafts. Became a teacher of arts and crafts. Taught at the Keighley School of Art and the Yorkshire Art Classes. Elected a Member of the Keighley Art Club. Still listed as an art teacher into the 1910s, and as an artist into the 1930s. She remained at the family home until her marriage in 1908, at the age of around 42, by which time her father had died.
Frances exhibited her work occasionally, including at the Royal Glasgow Institute (1896 & 1921), the Royal Cambrian Academy, the Royal West of England Academy and the Walker Art Gallery, Liverpool. Exhibited works included: Noontide in the Harbour, Whitby, Clifford's Tomb, Bolton Abbey and The Shipbreakers, Whitby. Several of her works of old Keighley were purchased by the Mayor and Corporation of Keighley. Some of her works were reproduced in Lady's Pictorial and Artist. She married Asa Sunderland (1875-1926), a plumber and journeyman, in Keighley. He also originated from Yorkshire, where they remained after their marriage.

SUTCLIFFE, IRENE (1883-1959)
Painter / Woodcut Artist. Born near Whitby, Yorkshire in March 1883. The daughter of Francis Meadow Sutcliffe (1853-1941) and Eliza Weatherill Duck (1843-1914). Her father was a photographer and curator of Whitby Museum. One of at least six children (Kathleen, Eveleen, Horace, Louise, Irene and Zoe). Raised in Yorkshire. Based there for most of her career. Died in Whitby, aged 76. Educated privately. Produced portraits in miniature and woodcuts.

Exhibited her work occasionally, including at the Royal Scottish Academy (1923-24) and the Royal Academy (1913-24). Exhibited works included: Daphne, Muriel and Miss Jean Brodrick-English.

SWAINE, AGNES KEMPSON (1892-1971)
Painter / Designer / Etcher / Illustrator. Born in Wales in March 1892. The daughter of John Swaine and Amelia. Her father, who originated from Staffordshire, was a mechanical engineer, but also an artist. Her mother originated from Lichfield. Agnes was one of at least three children (Agnes, Ida and Ronald). Raised in Wales and Somerset. Educated at Weston-super-Mare, Somerset. Studied at Cheltenham, Gloucestershire under Arthur Richardson, R.B.A., and at Newlyn, Cornwall under Stanhope Forbes. Produced landscape paintings, bookplate designs, etchings and book illustrations. During her career, she was based in West Malvern, Worcestershire, Clifton in Bristol and Nailsea, Somerset. Died in Weston-super-Mare, aged 79. Worked as an artist for much of her life. Visited abroad, including Buenos Aires, the Yemen, Mozambique and Kenya. Exhibited her work, including at the Royal Institute of Painters in Watercolours, the Walker Art Gallery, Liverpool, the Royal Birmingham Society of Artists and the Bath Society of Artists. Won an award of merit for England at the Bookplate Association International Exhibition, Los Angeles in May 1926. Works included: A Shady Lane, An Exmoor Farm and Castle Hill, Edinburgh. Elected a Member of the English Bookplate Society. Elected an Associate of the Bath Society of Artists. Her A Flower Garland was reproduced by Selwyn & Blount Ltd.

SWAINSON, LILIAN - SEE HAMILTON, L.

SWAN, FRANCES ISABEL (1876-1941)
Sculptor. Born at Lowfell, Durham. The daughter of Joseph Wilson Swan, an electrical engineer and chemist, and Hannah. One of at least six children (Mary Edmonds, Hilda, Frances, Kenneth, Percivale and Dorothy). All were well educated and raised in a comfortable home with several servants. Kenneth became a barrister, Percivale was a Cambridge graduate and engineer, Mary became an artist and Frances studied sculpture. They were raised in Durham, in Bromley, Kent and in London. Frances and Mary presumably studied in London or abroad. Frances produced statuettes and busts in bronze. Exhibited her work, including at the Royal Academy (1895-1903). Exhibited works included: Marbles (statuette, bronze), Adeline

(bust, bronze) and Pietro Corsi (bust). In 1904 Frances married Cambridge graduate Reginald Keble Morcom. They had at least one son, Alfred, who became a research chemist. Frances died in Bromsgrove, Worcestershire. Mary Edmonds Swan (1864-1951) worked as a painter for some 20 years, living in Surrey, dying in Kent. She never married. She exhibited her work, including at the Royal Academy (1890-94), showing Miss White and Oranges and Lemons. Possibly of the same family was sculptor Miss Isabel Morcom, also of Bromsgrove. She exhibited one work at the Royal Academy in 1924, a statuette of Sir Joseph Swan, F.R.S.

SWETENHAM, VIOLET HILDA - SEE DRUMMOND, V.H.

SWINSTEAD, EULALIA HILLYARD (1893-1978)

Painter / Vocalist. Born in Crouch End, London in November 1893. The daughter of George Hillyard Swinstead (1860-1926) and Rosalie Edmonds (1867-1956). Her father, who originated from Chelsea, was a successful artist. He was a Member of the Royal Institute of Painters in Watercolours, a Member of the Royal Society of British Artists and an Associate of the Royal British Colonial Society of Artists. Eulalia had at least one older sister, Valerie. Raised in London. Initially studied music under Francis Korbay and L. Lehmann. Subsequently studied art in London, possibly influenced by her father. Elected an Associate of the Royal College of Art in 1926. Became a painter of portraits in miniature. Remained in London. Exhibited her work occasionally, including at the Royal Academy (1918-26) and the Royal Cambrian Academy. Exhibited works included: Mrs G. Hillyard Swinstead, Lady Kathleen Rollo and Portrait of the Artist. Her father also exhibited at the Royal Academy (1905-19). In 1934 she married Charles G. Weld (1878-1964) in Hampstead, London. Weld was a solicitor who was born in India but lived in London. He was awarded a medal for services during the First World War. The couple had no children. They eventually moved to Sussex. Weld died in Sussex in March 1964. Eulalia died in Lewes, Sussex, aged 84. She exhibited little after her marriage.

Eulalia's father came from an artistic background, which may have influenced her. George's father, Charles, was headmaster of the London School of Art. Charles and his wife Jane had six children, five of whom, including George, became involved in art. Charles junior (1851-1921) became an artist and teacher of drawing at a school. Alfred (b.1852) became an artist and headmaster of a school of art in London. Paul (1856-1924) became a schoolteacher. Eliza Jane (1858-1944) became an artist and teacher of drawing, and Frank (1863-1937) became an artist, a teacher of drawing and headmaster of the Hornsey School of Art. Eliza exhibited two flower studies at the Royal Society of British Artists in 1881 / 82, but after her marriage to Sydney Hayworth, in 1884, she appeared largely to give up art. Alfred had two artistic sons, Felix who became a Professor of Music and Charles Ray who became an artist. It is entirely feasible that any or all of her aunts and uncles taught or influenced Eulalia.

SWITHENBANK, EDNA - SEE MANLEY, E.

SYKES, ANGELA CHRISTINA - SEE ANTRIM, COUNTESS OF

SYMONDS, MARY (1867-1948)

Embroideress. An expert embroideress based at No.399 Oxford Street, London in the early 1900s. The firm of Morris & Co. was, at that time, based at No.449 Oxford Street. Symonds worked under the title 'Needlecraft'. She executed ecclesiastical embroideries of all kinds, and provided traces of embroideries for others to execute. Also executed designs by well-known artists, and provided services for cleaning and restoring old lace and tapestries. She gave lessons in embroidery, smocking and lace making, with special terms for classes and schools. These were advertised, including in the Catalogue to the 1906 Ecclesiastical Art Exhibition held in Barrow-in-Furness. Symonds exhibited her work, including at the 1903 Worshipful Company of Broderers Exhibition in London. The Company expressed a clear desire to encourage sound workmanship and artistic taste, and awarded prizes accordingly. Mary won a prize of £5 5s. One of her exhibits on that occasion was a karro curtain designed by Miss Rosalie Vigers and executed by Mary.

Some of Mary's work was chosen by the Royal Commissioners to represent London at the 1904 St Louis Exhibition where it won bronze and gold medals. One of her exhibits on that occasion was a stole designed by Mr Vigers and embroidered by Mary. The stole had a border of thorns worked in Japanese gold thread, couched with silks in brown to dark green and to reddish brown. The centre line of the border was black, with Alpha and Omega and crosses in bullion, decorated with beads and gold angels. An end of the stole was described and illustrated in the Art Workers' Quarterly, 1904, p.74.

In 1905, Mary exhibited at an Exhibition of Arts and Crafts held at the Lyceum Club. One of her exhibits was a cushion with a design of flowers executed by her and illustrated in The Studio, Vol.36, October 1905, p.74. In 1906 she exhibited at the Paris Exhibition, and at the Arts and Crafts Exhibition Society exhibition in London. She evidently had ties with those at the centre of the then-popular Arts and Crafts movement. She was also a member of the highly regarded Church Crafts League (founded 1899), one of six embroiderers listed in the League's papers. Their principal purpose was to restore standards in church art throughout England. Over a period of years, the League attracted the support of numerous artists, architects, craftsmen and craftswomen, including Dorothy Rope, Emily Ford, Helen Stebbing, Mabel Esplin, Charles Baker and Robert Marchant. Symonds is also listed in various sources as 'Embroideress to the King'. She additionally had ties with the Ladies' Work Society. The Society was formed in around 1875 under the patronage of Princess Louise, Marchioness of Lorne, who executed designs for its embroiderers to work. The Society was founded to help gentlewomen find suitable employment if they found themselves in difficult circumstances. Symonds guided the Society (certainly in 1900), and under her supervision they produced, among other things, a large banner designed by Selwyn Image (1849-1930). Image also designed embroideries for the Royal School of Art Needlework. The Image banner was illustrated in The Studio, Vol.19, 1900, p.51.

On a more personal note, Symonds remains difficult to trace. She appears, from national census recordings, to have been born in Lambourne, Essex in 1867, the daughter of William Symonds and Anna. Her father, a farmer, originated from Woodford, Essex, her mother from Suffolk. Mary was one of at least six children, raised in Essex. By at least 1891, whilst still living in Essex with her family, Mary is listed as working as an embroideress. By this time, her mother had died. By at least 1901, however, she had moved to West Ham, London, and is listed in census recordings as 'manager of an Arts Needlework School'. She was then living with her brother William, a clerk, and one of her sisters, Annie, a horticulturalist. By 1911, she and Annie were living alone in Middlesex. Mary was then still working as an embroideress, and Annie was acting as housekeeper for Mary.

It would also appear, however, that by 1913 Mary had married Guy Howard Antrobus in Hambledon, Surrey. Mary was then 46 years of age. Antrobus was 33. He originated from Handsworth, Staffordshire, but worked in Woking, Surrey as a jewellery manufacturer. However, he died soon after in 1914, just as the First World War loomed. Antrobus left Mary the sum of £5700. Mary, now a widow, continued with her work, and subsequently wrote at least three books on the subject of needlework, suggesting an intelligent mind and a continued passion for her subject, but also a willingness to earn her own money. Her literary endeavours included Elementary Embroidery (Pitman, 1915), Needlework in Religion (with Louisa Preece, Pitman, 1924) and Needlework Through the Ages (with Preece, Hodder & Stoughton, 1928). How long Mary continued to work in needlework after 1928 is not clear. She died in Ealing in 1948, aged 81, having apparently experienced a long, productive and artistically accomplished life and career.

T

TAIT, BESS (1878-1939)
Painter. Was Elizabeth May, known as Bess. Born in Melbourne, Australia. The daughter of Thomas W. Norriss, a scientific chemist. First studied under Jane Sutherland, and at the Melbourne Art Gallery School. Then moved to London to study at the Slade School. Produced portraits, including miniatures on ivory, watercolours on vellum and pastel studies. In 1908 she married James Nevin (or Nevis) Tait in Kensington, London. He was the British representative of the Australian Theatre Company of J.C. Williamson Ltd. They had at least one son and one daughter, and lived for much of their marriage in Church Street, Chelsea, where Bess died, aged 61.

Bess was active for more than 30 years, working and exhibiting up until her death. She exhibited her work regularly throughout her career, including at the Royal Academy (1908-36), the Society of Women Artists (1934-39), the New English Art Club, with the International Society of Sculptors, Painters & Gravers, at the Goupil Gallery, the Grosvenor Gallery and the Paris Salon. Also, with the Royal Society of Miniature Painters, the National Portrait Society, the Royal Society of Portrait Painters and in Brussels. Exhibited works included: The Pink Hat, The Cave of Wings (watercolour on vellum), Sleeping Girl (pastel) and Woman and Baby (on ivory). Elected an Associate of the Society of Women Artists (1937-39). Elected a Member of the Royal Society of Miniature Painters, of the Royal Society of Portrait Painters and of the Society of Present Day Artists.

Her works were reproduced in numerous journals including The Studio, Colour, the Connoisseur and several of the leading Paris papers. For example, her Portrait was reproduced in Colour, December 1921, p.111, as was her portrait of Mrs W. Russell Sheppard in January 1922, p.127. Her watercolour The Artist's Son was reproduced in The Studio, Vol.88, November 1924, p.279. In 1924 Colour magazine published a volume containing colour and black & white reproductions of her work. Three of her miniatures were acquired for the Queen's Doll's House. Works purchased by the Walker Art Gallery, Liverpool, Toronto Art Gallery and the Sydney and Melbourne Art Galleries. A bronze bust of Bess, by F. Derwent Wood, R.A., was purchased by the Chantrey Bequest for the National Gallery, Millbank.

TALBOT, DOROTHY (active early 1900s)

Bookbinder / Book Decorator. Produced 'Sutherland Bindings'. These had a specific type of vellum decoration and were produced by George Thomas Bagguley who owned a bindery and bookshop in Newcastle-under-Lyme, Staffordshire. Bagguley employed a number of artists to produce these bindings, including Leon V. Solon. But also the Duchess of Sutherland, the patron after whom they were named. Also, Dorothy Talbot, a gifted artist who produced some of the best designs. Noted in Kineton Parkes, The Sutherland Bookbinding in The Artist magazine, April 1901, p.188. Also noted in Sarah Treverbian Prideaux, Modern Bookbindings Their Design and Decoration, London, Archibald Constable & Co., 1906. Acknowledged for her delicate and attractive work.

TANCOCK, RACHEL MARION (1891-1961)

Stained Glass Designer. Born in Fleetwood, Lancashire. The daughter of the Rev. Charles Tancock, DD, Headmaster of Rossall School, and Marion Alma. Had an older sister, Margaret. In 1897 the family moved to Kent where her father was appointed Headmaster of Tonbridge School. Rachel showed early artistic promise. At that time, they met Christopher Whall who had been commissioned to design a set of windows for the school's new chapel. Initially, she was educated at the Heathfield School, Ascot. Later she became one of Whall's pupils. She began her career by studying painting under Whall, but moved to stained glass work. She assisted in Whall's studio and there met a number of leading designers in stained glass, including Edward Woore, Arnold Robinson and Karl Parsons. Through her painting, she was accepted into the Royal Academy schools in 1914, but as war loomed, she enrolled as a volunteer nurse. Her name was published in the London Gazette in recognition of her outstanding services to nursing.

After the war, Rachel took up her studies once again and became an assistant to Edward Woore. Woore had just established his own stained glass studio in St Peter's Square, Hammersmith, London, but also worked as manager at Whall & Whall Ltd (Christopher and Veronica Whall's stained glass studio) in the early 1920s. In 1925 Woore moved to a studio in Deodar Road, Putney, where a number of successful stained glass studios were in operation. Tancock continued to work as his assistant, but by that time she was also carrying out commissions of her own. Those included a two-light memorial window for St Botolph's, Cambridge, and a memorial window for Rottingdean School. In 1931 she married artist Miles Fletcher de Montmorency (b.1893) who occasionally assisted in her work. He inherited the family baronetcy during the Second World War, and Rachel became Lady de Montmorency.

Most of Tancock's later stained glass was made in the same Deodar Road studios and workshops used by Margaret Aldrich Rope. At that time her home was in Rusholme Road, Putney, close to Deodar Road. In 1959 Tancock was responsible for a memorial window for Tonbridge School chapel dedicated to her father. The window joined those designed earlier by Christopher Whall, along with Karl Parsons and Lilian Pocock. Other commissions carried out by Tancock included an east window for Street Parish Church, Somerset (1949), two west windows, an east window, a rose window and a two-light chancel window for Christ Church, Mitcham, Surrey (c.1954), and an east window for St Saviour's Church, Guernsey (1955).

Other stained glass produced by Tancock included for Ickleton Parish Church, Essex (1929) and St Michael's Church, Eastbourne (1950). She took part in the execution of windows for Winchester College, for which Professor R.M.Y. Glendower was responsible. During the Second World War, she executed two small windows for Cheltenham College also designed by Glendower, and designed two windows for St John's, Fulham. Her last project was a large window for Tonbridge chapel, in continuation of the series begun by Christopher Whall. In her later years, Tancock suffered from arthritis, but continued to work to within one week of her death in November 1961.

Tancock executed numerous studies of plants, small watercolours, life studies and drawings of drapery during her career. She exhibited her stained glass designs at the Royal Scottish Academy (1922) and the Royal Academy (1920-38). She was elected a Member of the British Society of Master Glass-Painters, and was the first woman to be elected to its Council, of which she remained a member until her death. Her obituary was given in the Journal of the British Society of Master Glass-Painters, Vol.XIII, No.4, 1962-63, p.589-590. Her designs were included in an exhibition Women Stained Glass Artists of the Arts and Crafts Movement, held at the William Morris Gallery, London, 1985-86.

TANN, ELIZABETH HANNAH & EDITH MARY (1872-post-1911) & (1875-1947)

The daughters of Edward Tann (1841-95), a stationer, and Jane Elizabeth Powling (1842-1912). Their father originated from Middlesex, their mother from Illinois, U.S.A. The girls had two sisters, Jane (1865-85) and Grace (1879-1956), and a brother, Edward James (1869-1918). Jane and Edward died young. Elizabeth was born in Holborn, London, Edith in St Pancras. The family lived in Essex for a time, but later, after Edward senior's death, lived at Heathfield House, Twickenham. Elizabeth became a student of the Royal School of Art Needlework, South Kensington in the late 1890s and early 1900s. Edith is listed as an art student at the same time, though it is unclear if she too studied at the Royal School. Edith also became an embroideress, but was also proficient in woodcarving, lettering, illumination and metalwork. Since both girls are frequently listed in journals and records as Miss Tann or Miss E. Tann, it is difficult now to separate their careers. But it appears that Elizabeth completed her needlework studies in 1902, when she was sent by the Royal School to teach embroidery at the Newark School of Science and Art, in classes only recently established. She is noted in The Studio as achieving excellent results there within a short time.

Elizabeth also contributed articles on her subject to the short-lived Art Workers' Quarterly in the early 1900s. For example, in October 1902 she contributed Notes on Tambour Work (from p.148), and in October 1903 contributed Drawn Thread Work (from p.181). In October 1904 she contributed Notes on Eastern Embroideries (from p.147). Also in 1904, Elizabeth advertised classes in art or plain needlework in The Studio magazine. Her address at that time was Heathfield House, and she describes herself in the advert as a 'diplomee of the Royal School of Art Needlework'. Elizabeth was still at Heathfield House in 1911 and was working as a teacher and repairer of tapestry. She effectively disappeared after that date, her death proving difficult to trace.

Edith was evidently a more diverse artist, designing for embroidery as well as working as a woodcarver and metalworker, and in lettering and illumination. In 1911 she is listed as a hospital patient in London, so evidently suffered some ill-health at that point. She became an illuminator with the Church Crafts League (founded 1899), and is listed in their papers for 1920. The League was made up of a body of prestigious artists, craftsmen and craftswomen whose principal aim was to restore falling standards in church arts. Other members included Evelyn Barrow, Henry Holiday, Nelson Dawson, Mary Symonds, Jessie Bayes and Helen Stebbing. Like Elizabeth, Edith advertised tuition to private pupils in The Studio, including in 1910. Also like Elizabeth, Edith contributed to the Art Workers' Quarterly. In January 1902, for example, she contributed a design for an embroidered border and drawn thread patterns. She may also have contributed a design for an embroidered figure panel (listed only as Miss Tann). Edith never married and died in Surrey, aged 71. Grace Tann also never married.

TANNER, MABEL E. - SEE SORRELL, M.E.

TATHAM, AGNES CLARA (1893-1972)

Painter / Illustrator. Born in Abingdon, Oxfordshire in January 1893. The daughter of Meaburn Talbot Tatham, M.A., a private tutor, and Clara Susan. Her father originated from London, her mother from Birmingham. One of at least four daughters (Silvia, Mary, Agnes and Evelyn). Raised in Abingdon, at Northcourt House, with several servants. Educated at the St Helen's School, Abingdon and at the Oxford High School. Studied at the Byam Shaw and Vicat Cole School of Art, and at the Royal Academy schools, London between 1915 and 1920. As a student, she won one gold, three silver and two bronze medals for painting. At the Royal Academy schools, she won the Turner Gold Medal. Produced landscapes, portraits and other subjects in oils, watercolours and tempera. Also produced illustrations for children's books. Based in London for much of her career, but still spent time at Northcourt House, Abingdon. Died in Banbury, Oxfordshire, aged 79.

Tatham exhibited her work, including at the Royal Academy (50 works, 1916-61), the Royal

Glasgow Institute (1928), the Royal Society of Portrait Painters, the Royal Society of British Artists, the Paris Salon and with the International Society of Sculptors, Painters & Gravers. Also, at the Carnegie Institute, Pittsburgh, the Walker Art Gallery, Liverpool and in the provinces, including Eastbourne, Bournemouth and Brighton. Exhibited works included: Music, In the Beginning (tempera), Silhouette (tempera) and St David's Cathedral. Elected an Associate of the Royal British Colonial Society of Artists in 1927 and a Member of the Royal Society of British Artists. Also a Member of the Ridley Art Club and of the Campden Hill Club. Some of her works were reproduced in R.A. Illustrated. Her Mercy and Truth Are Met Together (tempera) was purchased by the Birmingham City Art Gallery. Her The Bandaged Thumb was purchased by the Prince of Wales Museum, Bombay.

TATHAM, HELEN SOPHIA (1848-92)

Painter / Illustrator. Born in Huddersfield, Yorkshire. The daughter of Thomas R. Tatham, a surgeon, and Sophia. One of at least four children (Mary, Helen, Catherine and Lewis). Raised in Huddersfield. Later based in Edgbaston, Birmingham. However, by at least 1881 Helen was living in Shanklin on the Isle of Wight with her widowed mother. Helen died there, aged only 44. She worked as a landscape and figure painter in watercolours and an illustrator. Illustrated, for example, Little Margaret's Ride (1878). Exhibited her work, including at the Royal Academy (1891), the Royal Society of British Artists (1878-85) and the Society of Women Artists (29 works, 1877-90). Exhibited works included: Knitting Father's Stockings, Feeding the Rabbits, Dolly's Favourite Corner and Pandy Oak, Betws-y-Coed.

TATLOCK, CICELY - SEE HEY, C.

TAWSE, SYBIL (1887-1971)

Painter / Illustrator / Decorative Artist / Poster Artist. The daughter of George Tawse, a house painter and decorator, and Elizabeth Ann Harrison. Her father originated from Aberdeen, Scotland, her mother from Sunderland. The youngest of at least five daughters (Catherine, Florence, Gertrude, Gladys and Sybil), all born in Co. Durham between 1874 and 1886. Raised in Sunderland. Sybil moved to London to study at the Lambeth School of Art, then the Royal College of Art. As a student, she won the King's Prize scholarship and various bronze and silver medals. Became a portrait, landscape and still life painter, a poster designer, a decorative artist and a book illustrator. Initially remained in London. In 1911 she is listed as living with her sister Gladys (1885-1967) in Gloucester Road, Kensington, London. At that time, Gladys was working from home as a jeweller. Gladys subsequently became a nurse and travelled abroad. Sybil remained in London until at least the late 1920s, based in Cheyne Walk, Chelsea for part of the time. She then moved to Hythe, Kent. She also spent some time in Bath and in London again, but appears to have died in Portsmouth in March 1971, aged 83 (dates vary and records are inconclusive).

Tawse worked as an illustrator from at least 1910 until at least 1933. Illustrated books including Charles Lamb, The Essays of Elia (1910), M.M. Butt, The Fairchild Family (1913), Charles Kingsley, The Heroes (1915), Alexander Dumas, Count of Monte Cristo (1920) and Lucy Maud Montgomery, Anne of Green Gables (1933). Noted in Mahony, Latimer & Folmsbee, Illustrators of Children's Books 1744-1945, Boston, The Horn Book Inc., 1947. Exhibited her work occasionally. Showed two book illustrations at the Society of Women Artists in 1925. Also exhibited at the Royal Academy (1925-26) and at the Brighton Art Gallery. Other exhibited works included: The Artist's Mother, Spring Flowers, Pulteney Bridge, Bath and Boulevard Abbas, Heliopolis.

TAYLOR, ALICE B. - SEE WINNICOTT, A.B.

TAYLOR, BARBARA PENSON AUSTIN (1891-1951)

Sculptor. Born in West Derby. The daughter of Austin Taylor, M.A. and possibly Lucia. By at least the age of 19, she was living in London with two of her sisters, Dorothea Austin and Joyce Austin. Barbara studied in London, at the Westminster School of Art and at the Grosvenor School of Art. Also studied in Rome. She studied stone carving in a monumental mason's workshop. Produced heads, busts and figures in stone, plaster and bronze. Based in London, primarily at the Oakley Studios in Upper Cheyne Row, Chelsea. She worked and exhibited until a short time before her death in London, aged 59. Exhibited her work, including at the Society of Women Artists (1919-30), the Royal Academy (1932-47), the Royal Glasgow Institute (1945) and with the London Group. Also, with the National Society (including in 1936) and the Royal Society of British Artists as well as in Liverpool and Bradford. Exhibited works included: Robert Sauvage, Esq. (head, bronze), Lt. Col. G.B. Byrne (head, bronze), Driver E. Wheatley, Heavy Rescue, Civil Defence, Chelsea (bust) and Ramos (plaster portrait). Purchasers of her work included the Manchester City Art Gallery. A Member of the Camera Club and of The Arts Theatre Club. In 1939 Stafford Art Gallery held an exhibition of her work.

TAYLOR, MARJORIE EMMA (1904-87)

Wood Engraver / Book Illustrator. Born in Birmingham in February 1904. The daughter of Edward Albert Taylor (b.1874), a gold cutter, and Alice Honour Mountford (1877-1926). She had at least one sister, Dorothy Alice. Marjorie was educated at the Birmingham University and the Birmingham Central School of Art. Based in the city thereafter, and died there. Worked as a teacher, but also as a wood engraver and book illustrator. Exhibited principally with the Royal Birmingham Society of Artists. Works illustrated by her included The Faerie Sentinel, A Fairy's Song and Lyrics From Shakespeare. Elected a Member of the National Froebel Union (1926) and of the Birmingham University Art Craft Club. Taylor was noted in Bernard Sleigh's volume Wood Engraving Since 1890, London, Pitman, 1932. Sleigh notes, 'Miss Marjorie Taylor's Chapel on the Walls, Wareham, possesses fine qualities of tone; its simplicity and directness are so pleasing to the eye, and as admirable in their restraint, as her rhyme sheet of Lilac Time' (p.82). In 1933 Taylor married Geoffrey Rumball in Birmingham.

TAYLOR, NORAH HELEN (1885-1974)

Painter. Born in London. The daughter of physician Sir Frederick Taylor, Bt, M.D., who originated from Kensington, London. Her mother was Helen Mary. Norah was the eldest child. Had at least two siblings, Eric Stuart born in 1890, and Harold C. born in 1893. Raised in Marylebone, London in a house with servants. She was educated privately. Then studied at the Slade School, London under Professors Brown, Tonks, Russell and Steer. She also studied under miniature painter Edwin S. Morgan, R.M.S. Norah produced paintings and miniatures, mainly portraits. Exhibited her work, including at the Royal Academy (22 works, 1916-34), the Royal Scottish Academy (1930), the Society of Women Artists (37 works, 1917-35), the Royal Glasgow Institute (1916), in Liverpool, Toronto, Stockholm, Philadelphia, South Africa and at the Paris Salon. Exhibited works included: Grandpapa, The Veteran, A Modern Mona Lisa, The Soldier and The Fortune-Teller. Also listed as exhibiting handicrafts at the Society of Women Artists (not specified). Elected an Associate of the Society of Women Artists (1928-37). Elected an Associate of the Royal Society of Miniature Painters in 1920 and a Member in 1929. Won an Honorary Mention at the Paris Salon in 1931 and a silver medal in 1932. Works reproduced in several French art papers and in R.A. Illustrated. Norah died in Stratford-upon-Avon, Warwickshire, aged 88.

TAYLOR, UNA MARY ASHWORTH (1859-1922)

Embroideress. An expert embroideress who mainly executed the designs of others. Her work easily equalled that of May Morris and others of the late nineteenth and early twentieth centuries. Records indicate that Una Taylor was born in Mayfair, London into a privileged family. Her father was Henry Taylor (1800-86), a Knight Commander of the Order of St Michael and St George, a poet and essayist, and a senior clerk. Her mother was the Hon. Theodosia Frances Alicia Spring Rice (1817-91). Una was one of at least five children (Aubrey Charles Ashworth, Eleanor, Ida Alice Ashworth, Henry (known as Harry) and Una). The children were raised in London, in Mortlake, Surrey and at Holdenhurst, Hampshire. Una died in New Milton, Hampshire, aged 64. She spent virtually her entire life living with Ida (1850-1929). Neither ever married. On national census recordings for 1911, Una and Ida list their income as from 'literature and private means', which suggests that they followed their father's example and later took up writing. Una did not state her profession as 'embroideress' on any census recordings, so presumably did not consider her work to be regular paid employment. However, she was certainly at the forefront of artistic embroidery for a period of more than 20 years, from at least 1889 until at least 1911.

When and where Una Taylor learnt the art of embroidery remains unclear. But she was evidently highly proficient, producing a range of intricately worked items including embroidered bookbindings, panelled screens and chair covers. In 1889 she made her mark by showing an embroidered bookbinding at that year's Arts and Crafts Exhibition Society exhibition in London. The binding was designed by Walter Crane and executed by Una. Crane was an enthusiastic supporter of Una Taylor, and praised her work in his essay Notes on Needlework, published in 1903. In 1898 she had already been noted and praised in the Catalogue of Works Exhibited by Members of the Northern Art Workers' Guild at the Manchester Art Gallery. Crane had strong ties with the Guild. At the 1893 Arts and Crafts exhibition, Una showed five decorative and time-consuming needlework panels titled A Midsummer Night's Dream, worked to the designs of Heywood Sumner. At the same exhibition, an armchair designed by Reginald Blomfield and executed by A.G. Mason was shown, with needlework decoration executed by Una and, again, worked to the design of Sumner. Some of the above were illustrated in The Studio, Vol.2, October 1893, pp.13-15.

In 1901 Taylor contributed embroideries to the Glasgow Exhibition. By this time, her work was considered so precise, neat and uniform that it gave the appearance of machine stitching. In 1904 she contributed to the St Louis Exhibition, again showing silk embroideries. Other examples of her work were shown at the 1906 Arts and Crafts Exhibition Society exhibition; worked to the designs of W. Graham Robertson. Several examples of her work were illustrated in the Art Journal in 1910 (pp.214-218 & p.251) in an article Embroidery and Needlework, including those designed by Robertson, and a panel intended for the top of a glass table.

Una Taylor also proffered support elsewhere in the arts. In 1911, when Mrs G.F. Watts was President of Miss Farmer's Club for girls employed as artists' models, Taylor lent her support to Mrs Watts along with Mrs Lewis F. Day and others when the Club was reorganised. Based at 46 Markham Square, Chelsea, the Club endeavoured to keep a register of the models, for their own benefit and safety. After 1911, Una's career appears to have curtailed. Her niece, Una E. Taylor (b.1887), the daughter of Harry and Minna Taylor, became a sculptor. Una junior married the considerably older and widowed Ernest Troubridge, Rear Admiral of the Royal Navy. She exhibited her sculptures at the Royal Academy (1906-16), both before and after her marriage. She produced statuettes and busts in bronze, including Hypnos, God of Sleep (statuette, bronze) and Commodore Troubridge (statuette).

TEESDALE, GLADYS M. - SEE REES, G.M.

TERRY, SARAH ANN (1839-1913)
Sculptor. Born and raised in Aylesbury, Buckinghamshire. The daughter of Edward Terry, a master brewer, and Susan. One of at least five children (Edward, Jane, Fanny, Sarah and John). Studied sculpture. Subsequently based in Aylesbury and in Richmond, Surrey. For the last decade or so of her life, when she was apparently

no longer active as a sculptor, she lived in St Leonards-on-Sea, Sussex with her widowed sister, Fanny. Sarah died in St Leonards-on-Sea. Listed as producing portrait medallions in marble. Exhibited her work, including at the Royal Academy (1862-79) and the Society of Women Artists (1874-80). Exhibited works included: Maidenhood (medallion), En Fete: Jeanette, Chitty: Queen's Waterman and Portrait of a Child (medallion).

THEOBALD, HILDA (1901-85)
Modeller. Born in Soham, Cambridgeshire in April 1901. The daughter of James Theobald, a farmer, and Elizabeth. Her father originated from Norfolk, her mother from Cambridgeshire. Possibly an only child. Raised in Mundford, Norfolk at West Hall Farm. Educated at the St Edmund's School, Hunstanton, Norfolk. Studied at the Norwich School of Art. Became a modeller in clay and an art teacher. Exhibited with the Norfolk and Norwich Art Circle (1947-48). Latterly based in East Dereham, Norfolk. Died there in October 1985, aged 84.

THEYRE, MARGARET ISABEL (1897-1977)
Painter / Craftswoman / Modeller. Born in Northamptonshire. The daughter of a clergyman. In the 1920s and 1930s, she spent time in London. She then moved to Southwater, Sussex. Died in Surrey, aged 80. Produced landscape and portrait paintings in oils and watercolours, various handcrafts and works in terracotta. Exhibited her work over at least five decades, from the 1920s into the 1960s, including at the Royal Institute of Painters in Watercolours, the Paris Salon, the Walker Art Gallery, Liverpool and the Grosvenor Gallery. Also, at the Royal Scottish Academy (1934-45), the Royal Hibernian Academy (1938-40), the Royal Glasgow Institute (1928), the Royal Academy (1938-39) and the Society of Women Artists (22 works, 1925-61). Exhibited works included: Portrait of a Musician, An Anglesey Farm (watercolour), Conspirators (watercolour) and Goats.

THOMAS, ELSIE HUGO (1890-1983)
Painter / Etcher. Born in Halifax, Yorkshire. Possibly the only child of Stephen Rowe, a solicitor, and Catherine Hugo. Her parents originated from Cornwall. Raised in Hampstead, London and Finchley. Educated privately at Finchley, and in France. Studied at the Slade School, London. Then, at the Studio Simon and Menard, Rue de la Grande Chaumiere, Paris. Also studied landscape painting with Bertram

Priestman, R.A., and received some instruction on figure landscape from Walter Sickert. Became a painter of landscapes, still life, interiors and small decorative pictures, an etcher and a pencil artist. Initially, she was based in Barnes, London, but moved to Birmingham and, latterly, Devon. Died in Honiton, Devon, aged 93. In 1918 she married Howard Gordon Rhys Thomas in Richmond, Surrey. At that time he was a captain in the army. He died in Birmingham in mid-1953, aged 65.

Elsie began exhibiting her work from at least 1916, which indicates that she was probably an art student at the time of the First World War. Exhibited at the Royal Academy (6 works, 1918-48), at least twice on the line. Also exhibited at the Paris Salon, with the International Society of Sculptors, Painters & Gravers (certainly in 1916, 1918 and 1919), at the Goupil Gallery, the Grosvenor Gallery and the Walker Art Gallery, Liverpool (1918-21 at least). She showed other works with the Women's International Art Club, with the Yorkshire Artists, the London Group, the Birmingham Group and the Society of Women Artists (1919-21). Exhibited works included: The Panelled Room, Evening Shadows, Polperro, My Peacock Tea Service and 'Everlasting' Flowers (oil) and Baptist Chapel, Harborne. Elected a Member of the International Society of Sculptors, Painters & Gravers. Also a Member of the Birmingham Group and of the Women's International Art Club, and the I.3.A. Club. Works illustrated in Colour. Her study of Windmill, Rye was published by Anacker.

THOMAS, MILDRED ELSIE - SEE ELDRIDGE, M.E.

THOMPSON, AGNES - SEE HILL, A.

THOMPSON, CONSTANCE (1882-1964)

Painter / Stained Glass Artist / Black & White Artist / Lithographer. Born in St Helens, Lancashire in October 1882. The daughter of John Joseph Dutton and Betsy. Her father, who originated from Stockport, was Headmaster of the Cowley Boys' School in St Helens. Her mother originated from Bolton, Lancashire. One of at least seven children (Horace, Ethel, Arthur, Percy, Charles, Constance and William). Raised in St Helens. Educated at the Cowley Girls' Grammar School, St Helens. Then studied at the St Helens School of Art under John Skeaping, and at the Liverpool School of Art. As a student, awarded book prizes and honours in design. She spent much of her career in Liverpool, dying there aged 82. Executed oil and watercolour paintings, stained glass work, black & white drawings,

lithographs and works in pastels. Exhibited her work, including at the Walker Art Gallery, Liverpool, with the Liver Sketching Club, at the Royal Cambrian Academy, the Royal Society of British Artists, with the United Artists and in London and Conway. Elected a Member of the Royal College of Art, of the Liver Sketching Club, of the Royal Cambrian Academy and of the Liverpool Academy. She was art mistress at the St Helens Higher Grade School, and assistant art mistress at the St Helens School of Art. Works acquired by the Preston Art Gallery and the Shipley Art Gallery. In 1913 she married Edwin Thompson in Prescot, Lancashire.

THOMSON, EMILY GERTRUDE (1851-1929)

Painter / Black & White Artist / Book Illustrator / Stained Glass Designer. Born in Glasgow. The daughter of the Rev. Alexander Thomson, M.A., DD, LL.D., a minister and Professor of Greek and Hebrew at the Lancashire Independent College, and Emma. Her father originated from Aberdeen, her mother from Birmingham. One of at least four daughters (Emma, Emily, Helen and Ann). Her sisters were also born in Glasgow. From at least the very early 1860s the family lived at Chorlton, Manchester. But by at least the early 1900s, Emily was living alone in London. She died in Hammersmith, aged 78. Initially, she was educated at home. Then studied at the Manchester School of Art. As a student, she won several Queen's Prizes from the South Kensington Museum, and a bronze medal for black & white designs.

During her career, Emily produced portraits in colour on Japanese vellum, subject pictures in oils, fairy designs, portraits in pastels, black & white book illustrations, stained glass designs and miniature paintings. Several sets of her fairy designs were reproduced by Arthur Ackermann and Messrs de la Rue. She executed fairy designs for Lewis Carroll's Three Sunsets and Other Poems. Produced four Spenser stained glass windows for Cheltenham College. Produced the design for the Margaret Reynolds memorial window in the Church of St John the Divine, Brooklands, Cheshire. Illustrated other books including A Soldier's Children (with E. Stuart Hardy, 1897). Exhibited her work, including in Manchester, Liverpool, London, Brussels and Canada, and with the Royal Society of Miniature Painters. Elected a Member of the Royal Society of Miniature Painters. One of her miniatures was in the Victoria & Albert Museum, London. Works also in the Manchester Art Gallery. Thomson was still working as an artist into her

60s. One of her friends was artist Kathleen Maxwell who originated from Ireland.

THOMSON, MARGARET STANLEY (1891-1975)

Painter / Etcher / Wood Engraver / Craftswoman / Embroideress. Born in Ormskirk, Lancashire in March 1891. The daughter of James Stanley Thomson (b.1858), a bank manager, and Frances Margaret. Possibly an only child. Raised in Ormskirk and in Southport. Educated in Southport. Studied in Eastbourne. Produced watercolour paintings, etchings, engravings, embroideries, leatherwork and other handcrafts. Exhibited her work, including at the Royal Scottish Academy (1923), the Walker Art Gallery, Liverpool, in Glasgow, with the Red Rose Guild, at the Atkinson Art Gallery in Southport, in Bond Street, London and in Toronto. Also exhibited with the Society of Wood Engravers. In 1924, for example, showed A Normandy Gleaner with the Society at the Redfern Gallery. Other works included: The Road to Mount St Michael, Brittany which was exhibited at the Royal Scottish Academy in 1923. Spent much of her career in Southport. Taught embroidery and leatherwork at the Southport School of Art. Died in the area, aged 84.

THORNYCROFT, HELEN (1848-1937)

Painter / Sculptor. Born in London. The daughter of sculptors Thomas Thornycroft and Mary Francis. The youngest of at least five children. Several of her siblings became involved in the arts. Her sister Alice took up painting and sculpture. Another sister, Theresa, took up painting. Her brother William Hamo Thornycroft also became a sculptor. Like Alice, Helen probably studied under her parents. She lived and worked mainly in London, working for much of the time from the family home. Helen died in Kensington, but did spend some time in the 1910s living at Yew Tree Cottage, Monmouthshire, still working as a painter in her 60s. She enjoyed a long, successful and productive career, exhibiting from at least 1864 (aged 16) until at least 1917. Evidently a young talent, like her mother. Helen produced watercolour paintings of landscapes, flowers and other subjects, and portrait and animal sculptures.

She exhibited her work, including at the Royal Academy (30 works, 1864-1912), the Royal Society of British Artists (1875-81), the Royal Glasgow Institute (1881-89) and the Society of Women Artists (170 works, 1866-1917). Also exhibited at the Dudley Gallery on several occasions. In 1878, at the Gallery's 14th General Exhibition of Watercolours, she showed Rosalind in the Forest of Arden. The Art Journal, 1878, p.21 described it as 'the best picture she ever painted'. Also exhibited at the Gallery in 1880 and 1881 at least. In 1899 she held a private exhibition of flower paintings at the family home in Melbury Road which was reported in the Art Journal in that year. Exhibited works included: The Strayed Fawn (sculpture), F.S. Thornycroft (sculpture) and Chrysanthemums (watercolour). Elected an Associate of the Society of Women Artists (1880-86), a Member (1887-1908) and an Honorary Member (from 1909 to 1913, or possibly 1930, records are unclear). A portrait photograph of Helen appeared in The Year's Art in 1896, one of a series of portraits of lady artists in that particular volume. There, she is listed as Vice-President of the Society of Women Artists. SEE: THORNYCROFT, MARY ALICE, THORNYCROFT, ROSALIND & FRANCIS, MARY

THORNYCROFT, MARY - SEE FRANCIS, M.

THORNYCROFT, MARY ALICE / ALYCE (1845-1906)

Sculptor / Painter. Was Mary Alice. Also known as Alice and, later, Alyce. Born in London. The daughter of sculptors Thomas Thornycroft and Mary Francis. Alice's grandfather was sculptor John Francis (1780-1861). Records indicate that Alice was the eldest of five children (Alice, Frances, Helen, William and Theresa). William Hamo Thornycroft (1850-1925) also became a sculptor, and his daughter Rosalind became an artist. Helen and Theresa became sculptor / painters. Alice spent most of her life and career at the family home in London, first at Wilton Place, then at Melbury Road. Several of her siblings remained there well into adulthood too. She probably trained under her parents, and had a long and productive career, working and exhibiting for over 25 years.

Alice produced watercolour paintings, portrait medallions and busts. Exhibited her work, including at the Royal Academy (1864-92), the Royal Society of British Artists (1875 / 76), the British Institution (1865-66) and the Society of Women Artists (1866-91). Exhibited works included: Ophelia at the Brook (sculpture), Edith in Search of the Body of Harold (sculpture), My Mother (bust, bronze), Lady Mary Stanhope (basso relievo) and The Countess Beauchamp (medallion). Alice died unmarried in Wandsworth, London, aged 62. Her address at that time was The Priory, Roehampton, Surrey.

She left her small estate to her brother William. In Algernon Graves, The British Institution 1806-1867, London, G. Bell, 1908 it is stated that Mr Hamo Thornycroft, R.A., wrote to Graves that Miss Alice Thornycroft changed the spelling of her name in around 1865.

Theresa Georgina (1853-1947), also known as Georgina and Georgia, exhibited her work less frequently than her siblings. Showed at the Royal Academy (1875-83). Exhibited works included: Design From the Parable of the Ten Virgins, Dives and Lazarus and Dawn at Bethlehem. In 1884 she married Oxford graduate Alfred Sassoon, who died young in 1895. The couple lived in Kent, where Theresa died. She left her small estate to author Siegfried Loraine Sassoon. SEE: FRANCIS, MARY, THORNYCROFT, HELEN & THORNYCROFT, ROSALIND

THORNYCROFT, ROSALIND (1891-1973)

Artist / Illustrator. Born in Frimley Green, Surrey in September 1891. The daughter of sculptor William Hamo Thornycroft (1850-1925) and Agatha Cox. Part of a distinguished artistic family. Her father was the son of sculptors Thomas Thornycroft and Mary Francis. Mary Francis was the daughter of sculptor John Francis. Her three aunts, Mary Alice, Theresa Georgina and Helen Thornycroft, all became sculptor / painters. Rosalind spent her childhood in London. One of at least four children (Oliver, Joan, Rosalind and Elfrida). Educated at the King Alfred School. Studied at the London School of Economics, the Slade School, London and the Academie Julian in Paris. Encouraged by her family, she also admired Walter Crane and the Pre-Raphaelite artists, and later Diaghilev's ballet, which inspired Laura Knight and other artists of the period.

In 1926 Rosalind married Arthur Ewart Popham (b.1889) in Richmond, Surrey. He was Keeper of Prints and Drawings at the British Museum. They had two sons and a daughter. Whilst the children were young, the family lived in Italy. On her return to England, she began illustrating books written by Herbert and Eleanor Farjeon. Those included: Nuts in May (1926), Italian Peepshow and Other Tales (Stokes, 1926), Kings and Queens (Gollancz, 1932) and Heroes and Heroines (Gollancz, 1933). Rosalind collaborated with her daughter on making hand-printed materials. She also took part in miniature photography of old master drawings in relation to her husband's work. She died in Somerset, aged 81. Noted in Mahony, Latimer & Folmsbee, Illustrators of Children's Books 1744-1945, Boston, The Horn Book Inc., 1947. SEE:

FRANCIS, MARY, THORNYCROFT, HELEN & THORNYCROFT, MARY ALICE

THORRINGTON, HILDA MARGARET LANG & MARGARET DOROTHY WILTON (1888-1971) & (1885-1961)

Decorative Artists / Craftswomen. The daughters of Thomas Thorrington, who worked for the Inland Revenue, and Eliza Margaret. Their father originated from Devon, their mother from Cornwall. Initially, the family lived in Hunslet, Yorkshire, but later lived in London. Both girls died in Winchester.

Hilda Thorrington was born in Hunslet in February 1888. She produced embroideries, lettering, leatherwork, pewter, suede work, stencilling, painted woodwork, cane and basketwork, raffia work, lace, brass and batik. Also an amateur photographer. Exhibited her work at the London Arts and Crafts Exhibitions. Also, in Melbourne, where one of her embroidery exhibits was chosen to give to the museum there. She became a teacher of embroidery and crafts at various London County Council Institutes from 1909. Also acted as embroidery mistress at the Leyton School of Art.

Margaret Thorrington was born in Rame, Cornwall. Educated at private school and the Mary Datchelor Collegiate. Elected an Associate of the Royal College of Art in 1915. Worked as a pattern and costume designer, an applied art and craft worker, a lettering artist, an embroideress and a painter of woodwork. She became Director of Education Staff, Hampshire. Also acted as art mistress at the Trade School, Paddington Institute between 1906 and 1910, and assistant mistress at the London County Council Camden School of Art between 1910 and 1913. Served as V.A.D. in the Second World War. Elected a Member of the National Society of Art Masters.

THRUSH, MILLICENT KATE AMY (1909-90)

Painter / Artist / Designer. Born in Barry, Glamorgan in Wales in June 1909. Died in Chippenham, Wiltshire. The daughter of Frederick James Thrush, a turf commission agent, and Rose Amy Garlick. Had at least one brother, Bertrand. Raised in Barry. Educated at the St Osyth School and at the Girls' County School, Barry. Studied at the School of Art, Technical School, Cardiff under Wilson Jagger, A.R.C.A., between 1925 and 1930. Awarded an internal scholarship at Cardiff. Also attended evening classes at the School of Lithography and Photo Engraving at Bolt Court, and at the Regent Street Polytechnic, both London.

Thrush enjoyed a varied and diverse career. Produced portrait paintings in oils, for which she was awarded the Mrs Godfrey Clark Silver Medal. Worked as a press fashion artist, a designer of fixed boxes for the luxury trades and tiled floors, and was sole fashion artist employed by Messrs David Morgan Ltd, Cardiff between 1930 and 1932. Also during her career, she worked as a general commercial artist and retoucher for Messrs W.G. Briggs in London between 1932 and 1935. Also, for Messrs E.S. and A. Robinson Ltd of Bristol between 1936 and 1939. In 1939 she worked as a designer of asphalt tile floors for associated firms. Between 1940 and 1945 she carried out war work. On her return, in 1945 she joined the staff of the publicity department at the Western Mail and Echo Ltd. In 1947 she took on the role of part-time teacher of art at the Cardiff School of Art, returning to live in Barry. Between 1948 and 1949 she rejoined one of her pre-war employers as a designer of coloured tiled floors. Then joined the Limmer and Trinidad Lake Asphalt Co. Ltd, London as a designer of asphalt tile and linoleum flooring, also designing for other associated and subsidiary companies from 1949. Exhibited her work occasionally, including with the South Wales Art Society, at Turner House, Penarth (in 1946), in Newport (in 1946) and with the Newport and Monmouthshire Art and Craft Society.

THURLOW, MARGARET C. - SEE LAMB, M.C.

TIPPIN, ALICE B. - SEE MORETON, A.B.

TIZARD, CATHERINE MARY (1853-1943)
Sculptor. Known as Kate. Something of an elusive figure who has proved difficult to trace. Born at Tisbury, Wiltshire in June 1853. The daughter of Henry Tizard (1824-91), a graduate of St Andrews University. He originated from Weymouth, Dorset. Whilst Kate was a child, he was a General Practitioner in Weymouth. Kate had at least one sibling, Ethel, who was two years younger. Their mother died whilst the girls were still young, and they were raised, initially, by an aunt, Sarah Tizard, who lived at the family home. Henry Tizard subsequently married again, and Kate had at least five half-siblings, including twins, all born in Weymouth. At the age of 27, in 1881, Kate is listed on national census recordings as a boarder, living at Holdenhurst, Hampshire with Ethel, acting as assistants to William Dowling, a corn miller. However, by 1891 she is listed as a sculptor and living at Millbrook, Hampshire with Ethel and her husband, George Turner, a solicitor.

In 1891 Kate began to exhibit her work and was using the Queensborough Studios in Bayswater, London. She spent time working in London until at least 1900. It remains unclear where or when she studied sculpture, or if she was self-taught. Nonetheless, she enjoyed a lengthy career, still working and exhibiting into the early 1930s, when she would have been in her late 70s. Between 1900 and 1929, Tizard effectively vanished, and it has been presumed that she was based in France since her work was exhibited there during that period. However, she was back in London certainly by 1929, and remained there for some years. She died in hospital in Chichester, Sussex in October 1943, aged 90, her home address then being Worthing, Sussex. She left a small estate of just over £200. Tizard exhibited her work somewhat spasmodically, including at the Royal Academy (1891-1900), the Royal Glasgow Institute (1929-31), the Walker Art Gallery, Liverpool and with the International Society of Sculptors, Painters & Gravers. Exhibited works included: Hypnos (bust, bronze), Pansy (bust), Adolescence (statuette, bronze) and Youth (statuette, bronze). Evidently produced busts and statuettes in bronze, but also exhibited one watercolour painting, The Mill Pond, Evening, in 1929.

TOWER, MERIEL THERESA (1911-97)
Textile Designer / Painter. Born in Windsor in November 1911. The daughter of Canon Henry Tower (b.1862), C.V.O., and Kate Theresa Escombe (1867-1940). Her father, who originated from Sussex, was an Oxford scholar and a clergyman. Her mother, who originated from Durban, South Africa, was first married to a man named Gedge. Meriel had at least two siblings, Cicely and Ernest. At the time of Meriel's birth, the family was living at Holy Trinity Rectory and remained in Windsor until at least the time of her mother's death. Meriel was educated at the St Paul's Girls' School. Studied in London at the Westminster School of Art between 1929 and 1931, and the Chelsea School of Art between 1931 and 1934 under Boris Heroys.

Meriel became a freelance textile designer and a painter of landscapes, portraits and other subjects in watercolours and chalk. She was on the technical staff of Campbell Fabrics between 1936 and 1939. From 1946 she worked as a teacher at the Upton School, Windsor. Exhibited her work, including at the Royal Academy (1963-65), the Society of Women Artists (1950), at the Crafts Centre of Great Britain, with the Arts and Crafts Exhibition Society, with the Society of Industrial

Artists Textile Group and the Women's International Art Club. Exhibited works included: Allotments (watercolour), Scotsgrove Mill in the Rain and Seated Girl (chalk). Elected L.S.I.A. (Licentiate Society of Industrial Artists). Some of her block-printed fabrics were in the permanent collections of the Victoria & Albert Museum, London and the Leicester Art School Circulation Departments. Latterly, Meriel was based in Datchet. She died in Oxfordshire in December 1997, aged 86. SEE: British Textile Designers Today (Lewis), British Designers: Their Work, Series I (Lewis), Designers in Britain, 1947 (published for the Society of Industrial Artists) and Decorative Art 1950-51 (The Studio Publications).

TOWNSHEND, CAROLINE CHARLOTTE (1878-1944)

Stained Glass Designer. Born in St Pancras, London. The daughter of architect Chambrey Corker Townshend (d.1897), a pupil of George E. Street and friend of architect / designer John Dando Sedding. Her mother, Emily Gibson (d.1934), was one of the earliest students at what became Girton College, Cambridge. Emily was a leading member of the Fabian Society (which Caroline also joined) and a supporter of the Women's Suffrage movement. Caroline was one of at least four children (Brian, Geoffrey, Caroline and Rachel). Raised in London. She was educated for five years at St Andrews in Scotland, followed by two years at the Slade School, London. In 1900 she became one of Christopher Whall's (1849-1924) pupils and attended his classes in stained glass at the London County Council Central School of Arts and Crafts until 1903. Whall was one of the leading figures in stained glass at that time.

Townshend's first commission was a stained glass window for Chulmleigh Church, Devon (1903). As with a number of her female contemporaries (including Lilian Pocock and Margaret Rope), for much of her career (1903-26) Townshend worked in collaboration with the stained glass firm of Lowndes & Drury, where influential stained glass designer Mary Lowndes was based. In 1906 Townshend became one of their first tenants, renting a studio in their then newly built Glass House in Fulham. In 1912 she met Joan Howson (1885-1964), a pupil of the Liverpool City School of Art. Townshend took her on as an apprentice at her Glass House studio and, after the First World War, went into partnership with Howson. Townshend was largely responsible for designing their stained glass windows whilst Howson was largely responsible for their execution. Howson also specialised in the repair of medieval glass.

In 1914, the Bishop of Rockhampton, Australia invited Townshend to design five windows for St Paul's Cathedral in Queensland. The windows were executed and installed in 1914 and 1921, and were one of her most important earlier commissions. In 1916 Townshend compiled a paper on the stained glass work of Hugh Arnold, who was killed in the war. The paper was read at the March 1916 meeting of the Art Workers' Guild. In 1916 Townshend and Howson moved from the Glass House to Deodar Road, Putney, where fellow stained glass designer Margaret Rope was based. The new studio was so successful that they were able to employ three craftsmen to assist on commissions. One of the more important of those later commissions was the repair of the fourteenth-century windows of New College, Oxford, begun in 1933.

During the Second World War, the Deodar Road studio was closed, and the two women joined Margaret Rope in caring for evacuated children in Wales. Townshend died in Wales in 1944. After the war, Howson returned to Putney and opened the studio again. She continued to work in stained glass until the 1950s. Other commissions carried out by Townshend during her successful career included a three-light window for Greenhithe Parish Church, Kent (1905), St Crispin, Patron of Cobblers for the Cripples' Cobbling School (1906), two windows for Cowbit Church, Lincolnshire (1906 & 1916), William Blake for All Saints' Chapel, St Chad's Church, Gateshead (1908) and a stained glass panel made for her friend George Bernard Shaw (1910). Townshend was also a Member of the Society's Arts Group which was founded in 1907 by Holbrook Jackson and Alfred Orage. Townshend exhibited four designs at the Royal Academy (1927-34), including for Summertown Church, Oxford and for St John's, Boscombe, Wiltshire. Townshend left her small estate to Howson.

TRAQUAIR, PHOEBE ANNA (1852-1936)

Craftswoman / Painter. The daughter of a doctor, Phoebe Anna Moss was born in Co. Dublin. She trained at the Dublin School of Art in her early years before travelling abroad. She became a skilled craftswoman and artist, proficient in illumination, painting, calligraphy, bookbinding, metalwork, enamelling, mural painting and embroidery. In June 1873 she married Dr Ramsay H. Traquair, M.D., F.R.S., LL.D. (c.1840-1912) in Co. Dublin, and moved to Edinburgh, where he had been appointed Director of the Natural History Department of the Royal Scottish

Museum. Her artistic talents, encouraged by Ruskin and continued after her marriage, lead to her becoming a Member of the Royal Society of Painters in Watercolours and of the Edinburgh Arts and Crafts' Club. Her technical skills in bookbinding were acquired through classes of the Social Union. At least 20 of her bindings are currently known, one being for Women's Voices (1887), edited by Mrs William Sharp. Some of her bindings were illustrated in The Studio, Vol.18, 1899-1900, Winter Issue, Special Number, Modern Bookbindings and Their Designers.

Mrs Traquair was a key figure in the revival of manuscript illumination and lettering, and one of the first women of her generation to work in that field. Her work brought her into contact with the Guild of Women Binders. The short-lived but significant Guild was formed following a successful Exhibition of Women's Bindings held in London in 1897. The Guild was made up of some 67 women binders from the Chiswick Art Workers' Guild, the Edinburgh Arts and Crafts' Club, the Gentlewomen's Guild of Handicrafts, the Kirkby Lonsdale handcraft classes and the Royal School of Art Needlework as well as other individuals not directly associated with any specific class or workshop. A second exhibition was held in December 1898 to January 1899, to which Mrs Traquair contributed. One of her exhibits, a book cover designed and executed by her, was illustrated in The Studio, Vol.16, 1899, p.49.

Also an expert and talented embroideress, Mrs Traquair produced a number of significant works. In 1903 an ambitious four-panelled screen worked in silks was exhibited at the Seventh Arts and Crafts Exhibition. Representing the four stages of the spiritual life of man, the screen was begun in 1895 and completed only in 1902. The four panels were titled The Entrance (1895), The Stress (1897), The Despair (1899) and The Victory (1902). Her embroidered panel St George and the Dragon was shown at the 1905 exhibition of the Edinburgh Arts and Crafts' Club. Other embroideries were shown at the Scottish Society of Art Workers' exhibition (at its first, held in 1899) along with one of her illuminated missals.

Mrs Traquair similarly excelled in the design and execution of jewellery and enamelling. Some of her enamelled jewels, necklaces and pendants appeared at the 1905 Edinburgh Arts and Crafts' Club exhibition. Also shown on that occasion was a decorated casket designed and executed by her in her specially adapted studio and made for presentation to a Professor Butcher by his students when he resigned his Edinburgh chair. The casket was ivory bound with gold and set

with panels of translucent enamel, illustrating the story of Theseus and Ariadne. At the 1906 Arts and Crafts Exhibition, she showed an enamel triptych The Red Cross Knight and enamel pendants, two of which were illustrated in The Studio, Vol.37, 1906, p.133. Other examples of her jewellery had already appeared at the 1903 Arts and Crafts Exhibition. In 1907, some of her enamels appeared at the Scottish Arts and Crafts Exhibition.

During her career, Mrs Traquair exhibited elsewhere, locally, nationally and internationally. In the 1890s she showed works at the Queen's Rooms exhibition in Glasgow along with Frances Macdonald and others. At the Royal Scottish Academy she showed 19 works between 1893 and 1935 including a cross in brass and enamel designed by her, but with enamels by Lady Gibson, and a triptych titled Mother and Child. At the Royal Glasgow Institute, she showed a portion of a plaster decoration, created for the Sick Children's Hospital in Edinburgh, in 1895. In 1893 she contributed to the World's Columbian Exposition in Chicago, and in 1911 contributed to the Glasgow Exhibition.

Other works won Mrs Traquair medals in Paris, London and at the St Louis Exhibition. She was elected an Honorary Academician of the Royal Scottish Academy in 1920. Her mural decorations included not only for the Sick Children's Hospital (at the suggestion of Dr Patrick Geddes in 1884), but for the Catholic Apostolic Church, Edinburgh, for the Song School of St Mary's Episcopal Cathedral, for St Peter in Clayworth, Nottingham and for a private chapel at the New Forest for Lord Manners. Her decoration for the Catholic Apostolic Church in Broughton Street, Edinburgh, based on the parable of the ten virgins, was illustrated in The Studio, Vol.12, 1897. One of her largest schemes, it included the nave, chancel arch, roof, aisle, side chapel and gables. Mrs Traquair was still active in the late 1920s, by which time she was living at Colinton, Midlothian. With Ramsay, she had two sons and a daughter, Ramsay R. (c.1874-1952), Harry (c.1876-1954) and Hilda (1879-1964). Ramsay R. went on to become Professor of Architecture at the McGill University, Montreal, Canada, serving in the First World War with the 5th Royal Highlanders of Canada. Harry became a doctor, an eye specialist. Mrs Traquair worked with Ramsay on occasions, decorating some of his metalwork designs with enamels. Some of those were illustrated in the Art Journal, 1907, pp.236-237. Both Phoebe and Ramsay were buried at Colinton Parish Church. One of the most comprehensive articles on Mrs Traquair was given in the Art Journal, 1900, pp.143-148. An exhibition of her work was held at the Scottish National Portrait Gallery in 1993.

TREMEL, MAY (1882-1963)

Sculptor / Etcher / Painter. Born in Bradford, Yorkshire. The daughter of Ferdinand Tremel, a merchant, and Alice Mary. Her father originated from Bradford, her mother from Hull. Had a sister, Dorothy, who was two years younger, also born in Bradford. Raised in Bradford. Subsequently went to London to study at the Goldsmiths' College, followed by the Royal College of Art. Also spent time studying in Frankfurt. As a student Tremel won a bronze medal in the National Competition of Schools of Art. Subsequently based in Sydenham and Barnes (Gt. London) and in Sevenoaks, Kent. Exhibited at the Royal Academy (1907-36), the Walker Art Gallery, Liverpool, the Royal Institute of Painters in Watercolours, the Society of Women Artists (1924-31) and various provincial galleries. Further afield, she exhibited in Vienna, Nelson and Auckland, New Zealand and Kosice, Czechoslovakia. Exhibited works included: Sunset at Combe Martin, Above Bolton Abbey, Robin Hood's Bay (etching), Early morning on the Thames, Hammersmith (etching) and Low Tide, Padstow Harbour (etching). Produced mainly landscape etchings but also portrait busts, including one of her father which was exhibited at the Royal Academy in 1907. Tremel died in Tonbridge, Kent, aged 80.

TREVELYAN, AUDREY - SEE CLARKE, EFFIE BRUCE

TRIBE, BARBARA (1913-2000)

Sculptor / Painter. Born in Edgecliff, Sydney, New South Wales, Australia. Her parents were English. She began studying aged only 15 at the Sydney Technical College. There, she worked under G. Rayner Hoff, A.R.C.A., R.S., A.R.B.S., from 1928 to 1933. Awarded a Diploma with Honours with a bronze medal for sculpture in 1933. Elected an Associate of the Sydney Technical College. She excelled enough to become Hoff's assistant, working on the Anzac War Memorial for Sydney's Hyde Park. In 1935 she was awarded the New South Wales Travelling Scholarship, which enabled her to visit England and the Royal Academy schools. Tribe was possibly the first woman to win the scholarship. She studied at the Kennington City & Guilds School of Art, London under Edgar Silver Frith, A.R.B.S., between 1936 and 1937. She then attended the Regent Street Polytechnic School of Art under Harold Brownsword,

F.R.B.S. She remained in Britain thereafter. Initially based in London. But from around 1946 until her death in 2000 she was based at a studio in Paul, Penzance in Cornwall.

Tribe produced mainly portrait works, animals and statuettes in various materials including clay, wood, stoneware, alabaster, terracotta, marble and bronze. Also produced watercolours later in her career. During the Second World War, she worked for the Inspectorate of Ancient Monuments, recording interiors of important London buildings under threat of bombing. Executed a number of portrait sculptures of members of the Royal Australian Air Force, some of which are in galleries in Australia. Several of those were exhibited at the Royal Academy, including Squadron Leader R.H. Gibbes, D.S.O., D.F.C. & Bar, R.A.A.F. (bust, bronze) in 1944 and Flight-Lieut. Charles Leister, R.A.A.F. (bust) in 1946. Elected an Associate of the Royal Society of British Sculptors in 1945 and a Fellow in 1957.

In 1947 she married potter John A. Singleman. They lived permanently in Cornwall. Tribe acted as a teacher of modelling and sculpture at the Penzance School of Art from around 1948. She joined the St Ives Society of Artists and began exhibiting with them in 1948. Elected a Member of the Society from 1948 until her death. She contributed to the 1953 Football and Fine Arts Competition. Elected to the Society of Portrait Sculptors in 1953. Stylistically, she was influenced by Primitive Art and by Barbara Hepworth, who also lived and worked in Cornwall. Tribe exhibited elsewhere, including at the Royal Glasgow Institute (1949-51), the Royal Academy (8 works, 1940-57), the Royal Scottish Academy (1950) and the Society of Women Artists (24 works, 1949-64). Also, with the Royal Society of British Artists, the United Artists, the Women's International Art Club, the London Group, the Newlyn Society of Artists and in Sydney. Elected an Associate of the Society of Women Artists (1957-60) and a Member (1961-66). Exhibited works also included: Old Cornish Woman (baked clay), Eve (marble), Fragment (terracotta) and Sleeping Kid (stoneware).

Other significant works by Tribe included portrait studies of Winston Churchill, Gracie Fields, Sybil Mullen Glover and Bryan Pearce. She also executed a bronze head of Rowena Cade, founder and builder of the Minack Theatre at Porthcurno, Cornwall, currently kept at the theatre. Some of her works were reproduced in British Sculpture (1944-46) by Eric Newton (Tiranti). John Singleman died in 1961. Later in her career, Tribe took up printmaking, drawing and painting in watercolours and gouache. She was buried in Paul Cemetery, Penzance. Works in the collections of Stoke, Spode Potteries Museum, the R.A.F. Museum, Hendon, Vienna, Adelaide, Bathurst, Melbourne, the Australia War Memorial Museum, Canberra and the Roxy Theatre, Sydney. Exhibitions of her work were held at Stoke-on-Trent in 1979 and at the Mall Galleries, London in 1991. In 1998 Tribe was awarded the Jean Masson Davidson Medal for outstanding achievement in portrait sculpture. SEE: Patricia R. McDonald, Barbara Tribe - Sculptor, Sydney, 2000.

TROTTER, ALYS FANE (1862-1961)

Artist / Craftswoman. Born in Dublin, Ireland. The daughter of Maurice Keatinge, Registrar of Court of Probate, Dublin. Alys moved to England and studied at the Slade School, London under Professor Alphonse Legros. She remained in England thereafter, dying in Salisbury, Wiltshire in late 1961, aged 99. In 1886 she married Alexander Pelham Trotter (1857-1947) in Paddington, London. He was a student of Cambridge University and became a partner in the firm of Messrs Goolden and Trotter, dynamo manufacturers, of Halifax. He was also sometime President of the Physical Society, President of the Illuminating Engineering Society and Electrical Adviser to the Board of Trade (1899-1917). They had one daughter, Gundred Eleanor Trotter (Mrs Beck) in around 1889. The family lived in London initially, but later moved to Salisbury. Alys became best known for her painted boxes, an example of which was given in The Studio, Vol.51, November 1910, p.150. She began her work in decorative boxes sometime around 1895. Several examples were shown at an exhibition held at the Walker's Gallery in 1910. She followed the eighteenth-century style in which the work was prepared with colour ground in varnish and without oil throughout, except where oil gilding was used as a substratum for the varnish. That resulted in a translucency. Many coats of clear varnish were laid on, each layer ground with pumice and polished with tripoli. Some of her boxes took up to two years to complete, with up to 20 layers of varnish.

TUCKFIELD, DENISE - SEE WREN, D.

TUCKMAN, GHISHA - SEE KOENIG, G.

TUELY, DIANA M. - SEE LOW, D.M.

TUFF, DAISY - SEE BOXSIUS, D.

TURNER, KATHLEEN MARY (b.1886)

Embroideress / Needleworker. Born in Sutton, Surrey. The daughter of Thomas H. Turner, a carpet agent, and Ellen. Had at least one sibling, Gladys. Raised in London. Studied at the Camberwell School of Art. Taught at the School in the late 1900s and 1910s. Then moved to the Girls' Trade School for Dressmaking in London to teach. Subsequently moved to the Manchester Municipal School of Art, working as a needlework instructor. In around 1921 she began teaching at the Royal College of Art, London in a similar role, following on from Mrs Christie. She also held classes for teachers in the latest methods in needlework education. Elected an Associate of the Royal College of Art. Particularly influenced needlework in the north-west. Helped to inspire a revival in needlework in the 1910s and 1920s. A black silk costume with silk embroidery and yellow silk lining, designed and executed by Kathleen Turner, was illustrated in The Studio, Vol.83, January 1922, p.47. She occasionally exhibited her work, including at the 1910 Arts and Crafts Exhibition Society exhibition.

TURNER, MARGARET - SEE FELLS, M.

TURNER, WINIFRED (1903-83)

Sculptor. Born in Kensington, London in March 1903. The daughter of sculptor Alfred Turner, R.A. (1874-1940) and Charlotte Ann Gavin. Had at least one sister, Jessie, who was three years older. The girls were raised in London. Winifred inherited her father's artistic talent and became a sculptor. She studied under her father, but also at the London County Council Central School of Arts and Crafts between 1921 and 1924, and at the Royal Academy schools between 1924 and 1927. She was a Landseer prizeman. Also won other awards, including bronze and silver medals. Based in London throughout much of her early career, using a studio in Fulham Road for part of the time. Around the time of her father's death in 1940, she moved to Etchingham, Sussex. In early 1942 she married Thomas Humphrey Paget (1893-1974) in Chelsea, London. He was a successful coin and medal designer. Winifred worked into the 1960s at least, and died in Sussex in late 1983, aged 80.

Winifred enjoyed an extensive and successful career which covered at least five decades (the 1920s to the 1960s). Produced mainly figures and portrait works using various materials including bronze, terracotta and concrete. Exhibited her work, including at the Royal Glasgow Institute (1931-55), the Royal Academy (36 works, 1924-62), the Society of Women Artists (1939-40) and the Walker Art Gallery, Liverpool. Exhibited works included: Diana (statuette, terracotta), The Descent From the Cross (relief, terracotta), Rosalind (head, concrete) and Bronze Youth. Her bronze statue Thought, a seated figure, was purchased by the Chantrey Bequest in 1933. Elected an Associate of the Royal Society of British Sculptors (1930-43) and a Fellow (1943-69). Turner was also on the Society's Council (1942-44). A major exhibition of the work of Alfred and Winifred Turner was held at the Ashmolean Museum, Oxford in 1988. Her Crouching Youth was purchased by the Victoria & Albert Museum, London. Winifred was noted in Mary Chamot, Dennis Farr, Martin Butlin, The Modern British Paintings, Drawings and Sculpture, London, 1964. Winifred's works commanded up to £200 each. One of her pupils was Ferelyth Wills.

TURVEY, ROSALIND MARY (1901-76)

Illustrator. Born in St Albans, Hertfordshire in September 1901. The daughter of William Turvey, an engineering instrument maker, and Eleanor. One of at least four children (Violet, Lily, Rosalind and Wilfred). Raised in Hayes, Middlesex, but later spent time in London. Died in Surrey, aged 75. Studied at the Kingston School of Art and at the London County Council Central School of Arts and Crafts. Produced illustrations in watercolours and in pen & ink. Illustrated a number of children's books. Contributed to publications including Tatler, Courier and the Christian Science Monitor. Listed as still active into the 1950s.

TWELVES, MARIAN (1843-1929)

Spinster / Embroideress / Lace Maker. Born in Rotherhithe, Surrey. The daughter of William Twelves, a commercial clerk. Little is known of her childhood or early adult life, although she is thought to have been an accomplished embroideress, and is listed as a private teacher for a time. In her late 30s, she became housekeeper to Albert Fleming, a young solicitor based in Broxbourne, Hertfordshire. Fleming was a devotee of John Ruskin and began to write to him in 1873, by which time Ruskin had moved to Brantwood near Coniston in the Lake District. In

1883 Fleming decided to move to the region, taking Miss Twelves with him to look after his new home, Neaum Crag at Skelwith Bridge, during his winter absences. Inspired by Ruskin, Fleming and Marian Twelves founded the Langdale Linen Industry in 1883, a traditional Westmorland hand spinning workshop. Based at Elterwater in an old cottage, the workshop ran strictly to Ruskin's teachings, rejecting all modern methods in textile production, and promoting individual creativity.

Although Fleming provided the original idea and guidelines, it was Miss Twelves who taught herself to spin, who set up the workshop, and who ran it for the first six years. The Industry produced textiles and embroideries of an exceptional standard which regularly won prizes at the annual Home Arts and Industries Association exhibition in London, and at other national and international as well as local exhibitions. Following a dispute with Fleming, however, Miss Twelves left Elterwater in 1889 and moved to Keswick to work in conjunction with the then equally successful Keswick School of Industrial Arts. Run by two more Ruskin devotees, and along similar lines to the Langdale Linen Industry, the Keswick School helped to establish another branch of the Linen Industry which was known informally as the Ruskin Linen Industry. The Elterwater branch was taken over by one of Miss Twelves's original pupils, Elizabeth Pepper, and ran successfully until the 1920s.

The Keswick School's linen industry was just as successful as its sister branch at Elterwater, and exhibited at the 1890 Arts and Crafts exhibition. But it survived only until 1894. In that year, Miss Twelves moved to a cottage in the centre of Keswick and established a third branch which worked more closely under Ruskin's Guild of St George, to which she belonged. Although local women trained by Miss Twelves and Mrs Pepper established other smaller branches of the industry in Morland, Silverdale, Hawkshead and Troutbeck, the Keswick branch, now formally known as the Ruskin Linen Industry, was by far the most successful, winning widespread acclaim for its textiles.

Marian Twelves was also the creator of a form of textile decoration similar to Greek lace which she named Ruskin lace. The lace was eventually practised at every branch of the industry and is still made today by a small number of dedicated women. The Ruskin Linen Industry also ran commercially until the 1920s. In 1929 Miss Twelves died in Keswick, poverty-stricken and penniless. But for over 40 years she had brought the opportunity for creativity to many women across South Lakeland, also offering them the opportunity to make extra money whilst reviving the lost regional craft of spinning. Some of the industry's textiles were a clear demonstration that, given the right conditions, everyone was able to create. Examples of textile work by the various branches of the industry, including more adventurous pieces such as a child's decorated gown and a pair of embroidered linen slippers, can be seen at the Ruskin Museum in Coniston. Ruskin linens were also used in the late nineteenth-century revival of artistic bookbinding. But they proved less durable than the leathers normally used. Papers relating to the industry are currently kept in the Cumbria Record Office, WDS73 and WDS0116.

TYLDESLEY, ALICE - SEE KENDALL, A.

TYTLER, MARY S.F. - SEE WATTS, M.S.F.

U

UNDERWOOD, ANN (b.1876)

Painter. Born in East Grinstead, Sussex in January 1876. The daughter of George W. Underwood. Educated in Brighton. Studied portrait painting under Hubert von Herkomer. Herkomer ran a successful school of art at Bushey, Hertfordshire. Underwood produced miniature and portrait paintings. She exhibited her work, including at the Royal Academy (1907-38), the Society of Women Artists (1923-25), the British Empire Exhibition and various other London and provincial galleries. Also exhibited at the Royal Society of British Artists, including in 1912 when she showed several miniatures. Exhibited works included: The Artist's Sister, Ivy Burnett, The Gift, The Brown Dress and Leslie Baldwin. Underwood had a studio in East Grinstead. Elected a Member of the Royal Society of British Artists (1910-25). Also elected a Member of the Royal Society of Miniature Painters (1916).

UNDERWOOD, EDITH MARGARET (1864-c.1932)

Illuminator. Records suggest that Underwood was born in Camden Town, London, and that she was the daughter of painter and stained glass artist Alfred Bell and Jane. Her father originated from Dorset, her mother from Darlington. She was one of at least seven children (John, Emma, Edith, Alfrida, Rosalind, Florence and Guy). Edith studied art in London, and became an expert calligrapher and illuminator, working

mainly on vellum. She spent much of her life and career in London. In 1885 she married dental surgeon Arthur Swayne Underwood (1854-1916) in London. They had at least one son, Arthur, born in around 1887. Edith exhibited her work occasionally, including at the Society of Women Artists (14 works, 1897-1910). Exhibited works included: St John's Gospel, Exhortation to Prayer, War Hymn and Love and the Rose (Walter Scott), all illuminations on vellum. Edith also executed illuminated Christmas cards, produced a frontispiece on vellum for an edition of Spenser, title pages for altar books and a letter from The King to His People, also illuminated on vellum. Edith possibly died in Fareham, Hampshire. Works illustrated in The Studio, Vol.20, 1900, p.105.

UNWIN, MARY LOUISA HERMIONE (1866-1955)

Sculptor. Born in Keighley, Yorkshire. Spent much of her life and career living at Hall Royd in Shipley, Yorkshire. The daughter of Stephen Philip Unwin, a wool merchant, and Lucy. Her father originated from Coggleshall, Essex, her mother from Cheshire. One of at least five children (Philip, Mary, Edith, Lucy and Maurice). Her mother died young, leaving her father to raise the five young children. Mary was still living with her father when she was in her 40s. Possibly studied in Yorkshire. Produced mainly portrait works. Exhibited occasionally, including two works at the Royal Academy, Child's Head: a Study in 1892 and Owen, Son of H.A. Hering, Esq. (medallion, bronze) in 1899. Died in Leeds. Unwin was the author of A Manual of Clay Modelling, London, Longmans Green & Co., 1896. The manual was advertised in The Studio magazine in 1896.

URQUHART, ANNIE MACKENZIE (b.1881)

Decorative Artist / Black & White Artist. Born in Glasgow. The daughter of Angus and Jane Urquhart. Her father was a native of the Black Isle, Ross-shire. One of at least five children (Jeanie (or Jane), Annie, Angus, Robert and Farquhar). Studied at the Glasgow School of Art under Francis Newbery and Jean Delville of Brussels, and in Paris. Part of a significant wave of women artists to establish successful careers at the turn of the last century, encouraged by Newbery. She was still active into the 1930s. Spent much of her life living and working in Glasgow. But in the 1920s and 1930s, she spent some time living at Golders Green, London. Produced watercolour paintings and black &

white drawings. Also produced coloured pen drawings done on vegetable parchment, using a pen & ink outline first, then stipple colour on top with an almost dry brush. She had a distinctive edge to her work, often depicting children in costume.

Urquhart exhibited her work, including at the Royal Academy (1928), the Royal Scottish Academy (1908-22), the Royal Glasgow Institute (1904-11), in Edinburgh, Liverpool and elsewhere. Exhibited with the Glasgow School of Art at its exhibitions of work by past and present students. In 1909, for example, she showed Gossips and The Pied Piper. Other exhibited works included: The Goblin Wood, Dreams, The Daisy Chain (black & white), The Apple Tree (watercolour) and The Little Pink Girl. Some of her drawings were illustrated in The Studio, Vol.47, June 1909, pp.60-63.

URQUHART, EDITH MARY (1875-1945)

Painter. Records indicate that Edith Urquhart was born in Edinburgh, Scotland, but spent much of her life in England. Her father was the Rev. Edward William Urquhart, a clerk in holy orders. Her mother was Caroline. Edith had at least one sibling, Florence. In the early 1890s, the family was based at Bovey Tracey in Devon. Edward died in Middlesex in 1916. Edith studied art at Cheltenham, in Newlyn under Stanhope Forbes, and in London at the Heatherley's School and the Chelsea Polytechnic. She also painted in Brittany under Mrs Linden, at Pont-Aven and elsewhere. She became a painter of portraits and market sketches in oils, of landscapes in oils and watercolours and of gardens in watercolours. Also executed portraits in pastels. Based for much of her career at King's Road, Chelsea, but maintained ties with Scotland. She was one of the original members of the Scottish Society of Women Artists. Exhibited her work, including at the Royal Scottish Academy (1942), with the Scottish Society of Women Artists, the Society of Scottish Artists, the Royal Society of Portrait Painters, at the Grosvenor Gallery and the Colnaghi Gallery. Exhibited 34 works with the Society of Women Artists between 1924 and 1940, including Pink Caravan, The Coster's Baby, Prickly Pears, Granada and Tea in Kensington Gardens. Elected an Associate of the Society of Women Artists (1927-41). Also a Member of the Queen's Club, Edinburgh. Edith died at King's Road, Chelsea in January 1945.

V

VALLIS, MURIEL GRACE (1902-88)

Artist / Embroideress. Born in Frome, Somerset in October 1902. The daughter of Henry C. Porter (d.1910) and Ethel Catherine. Her father, an accountant and auctioneer, originated from Frome, as did her mother. She had at least one elder sibling, Henry Maurice. Raised in Frome. Educated at the Girls' High School, Trowbridge, Wiltshire. Studied at the Bristol Municipal School of Art. Studied for a Board of Education Drawing Certificate, a Secondary Teachers' Drawing Certificate (Oxford) and a City & Guilds of London Institute examination in embroidery. Worked as art mistress at the Brunts School, Mansfield. Also acted as assistant mistress at the School of Arts and Crafts, Accrington, Lancashire. Vallis exhibited her work occasionally, including at the Royal West of England Academy. Based in Trowbridge for much of her adult life and career. In 1928 she married Henry D.H. Vallis (1900-70) in Frome. He died in Trowbridge. Muriel also died in Trowbridge, aged 86.

VANS AGNEW, CATHERINE (1840-72)

Sculptor. Born in Wigtownshire, Scotland. The daughter of Col. Patrick Vans Agnew and Catherine Fraser. One of the youngest of a large family. Worked in London for a short time, until around 1871. In January 1872 she died in Rome, and was buried there. Produced portrait works. Exhibited two works at the Royal Academy, The Countess Moroni in 1867 and David Morier (bust) in 1868. Exhibited one work, D.B. Morier (bust), at the Society of Women Artists in 1869.

VANSTON, LILLA MARY (1870-1959)

Sculptor. Based in Dublin, Ireland. Possibly Miss Lilla Coffey. Lived at Willow Bank, Bushy Park Road, Dublin. Produced statuettes, medallions and portrait sketches. As Mrs Vanston, exhibited 11 works at the Royal Hibernian Academy between 1903 and 1921. Those included: Vanity, Miss Emily Coffey, Girl Resting (portrait sketch), Lord Ashbourne (sketch model, plaster) and Miss Elizabeth Young (statuette). Miss Lilla Coffey exhibited four works at the Royal Hibernian Academy between 1898 and 1901, including a portrait work of Miss Emily Coffey and Oidhe Chlainne Lir (The Fate of the Children of Lir). Miss Lilla Coffey was also based at Dublin.

VASCONCELLOS, JOSEPHINA ALYS HERMES DE (1904-2005)

Sculptor. Also sometimes Josefina or Fifina. One of twentieth-century Britain's most talented and productive female sculptors. Stylistically, highly individual and still defies categorisation. She was born at Moseley-on-Thames, Surrey in October 1904. The daughter of Brazilian Consulate Hippolyto H. De Vasconcellos (1882-1936) and Freda Coleman (1882-1971). Her father was Brazilian, her mother English. Encouraged by her father in art. She spent most of her life in England. Was educated in Southampton and in Bournemouth. Then studied at the Regent Street Polytechnic under Harold Brownsword, at the Royal Academy schools in London, at the Florence Academy under Andreotti, and in Bourdelle's studio in Paris. She worked in bronze, wood, stone, plaster, alabaster, lead, terracotta, perspex, aluminium and acrylic resin. Produced mainly figures and portrait works.

In 1930 Josephina was runner-up for the Prix de Rome. In the same year, she married artist and Anglican lay priest Delmar Hugh Harmood Banner. The marriage was not successful in some respects, due to his hidden homosexuality. However, they never separated. Life with an Anglican did see her Christian faith strengthen, and affected her work as her career progressed. The couple lived in London and Sussex for a time. But they settled permanently at The Bield at Little Langdale in the Lake District. There, they adopted two boys. Josephina worked in a studio next to the house, while Banner produced landscape paintings.

With Banner, in 1967 Josephina helped to found Outpost Emmaus, a centre for disadvantaged boys set in the Duddon Valley. This led to an M.B.E. for her. She was always highly productive as a sculptor, and worked almost until her death, aged 100. Works included Prince of Peace which measured 8ft in height. She completed many commissions throughout her long career. For example, her Reconciliation can be found in Coventry Cathedral, while her Mary and Child is in St Paul's Cathedral, London. Some works went abroad. During her lifetime, Josephina was the only living sculptor to have a statue in St Paul's. She was also possibly the world's oldest living sculptor, and was commissioned at the age of 97 by Richard Branson to produce Reconciliation.

Many of her works can be found in the Lake District at, for example, Holy Trinity Church, Kendal, St John's Church, Keswick, St Mary's Church, Maryport, Rydal Hall Gardens, St Bees Priory and Carlisle Cathedral. Cartmel Priory has four of her works: The Young Martyr, They Fled by Night, The True Vine and St Michael the Archangel. Josephina exhibited extensively throughout her career, including at the Royal Glasgow Institute (1926-59), the Royal Academy (1926-66), the Royal Scottish Academy (1938-54), the Society of Women Artists (1951-61), the Walker Art Gallery, Liverpool, at the Leicester Galleries and with the National Society. Also, at the Paris Salon and the Royal Society of Painters in Watercolours (1947). Exhibited works included: Andre Andersson (aluminium), The Hands of Godfrey Mowatt (bronze), Clouds in May (head) and Swan Fountain (bronze). She was elected a Member of the Society of Women Artists (1953-55), and a Member of the Art Workers' Guild (1971). Also elected an Associate and a Fellow of the Royal Society of British Sculptors.

Josephina also organised, or helped to organise, exhibitions for others. For example, with Kate Parbury and the Rev. Noel Parry Gore, she organised an exhibition of Christian Sculpture at St John's Wood Church. Also a founder member of the Society of Portrait Sculptors and an Associate (1940). She executed a number of important portrait works including studies of Roger Bannister, Dr Greta Graff, the Rev. E.W.S. Packard and General Sir William Platt. Purchasers of her work included the National Gallery of Brazil, Rio de Janeiro, the Glasgow Art Gallery, the Graves Art Gallery, Sheffield, the Southampton Art Gallery and Aldershot, for whom she executed a National Memorial. Her work was reproduced in The Studio, the Times, Country Life, the Illustrated London News, Sphere, The Listener and Northern Review. She was the subject of an illustrated article in The Studio, Vol.151, January 1956, pp.8-11. Also the subject of two books: Linda Clifford, Sculptor: Josephina De Vasconcellos (2000) and Margaret Lewis, Josefina De Vasconcellos: Her Life and Art, Flambard Press, 2002. Also the subject of a 30-minute documentary film, Out of Nature by the Mercury Film Co. Josephina died in a nursing home in Blackpool and was buried at Holy Trinity churchyard, Chapel Stile, Cumbria.

VENNING, DOROTHY MARY (b.1885)

Sculptor / Painter. Also sometimes Mary Dorothy. Born in Camberwell, London in January 1885. The daughter of Francis Wilson Venning, a schoolmaster, and Mary Ann. One of at least three children. Had two brothers, Francis Joseph and Harold. Educated at the Mary Datchelor School, Camberwell. Studied at the Bishop Otter College, Chichester. Produced sculptures in bronze and paintings, including portraits and miniatures. Based mainly in London during her career. Exhibited her work, including at the Royal Academy (12 works, 1916-36). Exhibited works included: A Young Girl (head, bronze), A Quakeress, Charlie (bust) and Eve (statuette).

VILLIERS-STUART, CONSTANCE MARY (1876-1966)

Painter / Illustrator. Born at Lunesdale, Lancashire. The daughter and possibly only child of Joshua Fielden and Frances. Her father, who originated from Warrington, Lancashire, was a J.P. who lived on private means. Her mother originated from Ardwick, Manchester. Constance was raised mainly in Norfolk, at King's Lynn. Studied in Paris and Rome. Remained in Norfolk for much of the rest of her life. Became an illustrator in watercolours and a painter of landscapes and architectural subjects. Awarded a silver medal by the Royal Society of Arts. Elected a Fellow of the Royal Horticultural Society. Elected a Member of the British International Association of Journalists, a Member of the Institute of Journalists and a Member of the Norwich Art Circle. Also a Member of the Bath Club, the Sesame Club and the Imperial Club. Illustrated a number of books, including her own Gardens of the Great Mughals (1913), and Spanish Gardens (1929). Contributed to various publications including Burlington Magazine (including The Last of the Rajput Court Painters), Country Life (on Spanish Mediterranean gardens) and Edinburgh Review (on nationality in gardens). Contributed two views of Greece to Fortnightly Review. In 1908 Constance married Lieut.-Col. Patrick Villiers-Stuart, D.S.O. in London. The couple lived at Beachamwell Hall, King's Lynn, Norfolk. He died in Norfolk in May 1949. Constance died in Norfolk in February 1966, aged 89. They had at least one daughter, Patricia (1910-98).

VIRTUE, ETHEL FRANCES (1863-1958)

Designer / Metalworker. Born at St Pancras, London. The daughter of George Henry Virtue (1827-66) and Maria (or Marian). Her father, who originated from Middlesex, was a publisher. Her mother originated from Northamptonshire. The youngest of at least five children (Helen, Herbert, Florence, Jessie and Ethel). Herbert subsequently became a publisher too. The family lived in Bassett Road, London for many years, and four of the siblings were still living with their widowed mother into their 30s and 40s. Helen (1856-1937) and Ethel are listed as living on private income at that time, so evidently did not need to work. However, both sisters became

involved in the decorative arts. Helen never married and became a craftswoman. She exhibited her own work at the Society of Women Artists (1898-1909, specifies only 'handicrafts').

Ethel also never married. She became more involved in her chosen field. It remains unclear if either Helen or Edith studied at a formal school of art, but probably studied in London. Ethel became a proficient and expert designer and maker of decorative jewellery for a period of at least 18 years. Her work appeared in some of the larger arts exhibitions held across the country. For example, she contributed jewellery to the 1901 Glasgow International Exhibition. One of her exhibits on that occasion was a silver clasp which was illustrated in The Studio, Vol.23, 1901, p.243. Also exhibited with the Women's International Art Club (certainly in 1908, 1909 and 1910). Exhibited at the 1908 New Gallery summer exhibition along with May Morris, Kate Button, Ethel Agnew and others. Exhibited almost annually at the Society of Women Artists between 1898 and 1916, showing up to three items each time. Her work was noted in an article Metalwork and Jewellery by R.E.D. Sketchley in the Art Journal in 1907, pp.165-178. She was still living in Bassett Road in 1916. She died in London, aged 95.

VIVIAN, ELIZABETH BALY (1846-1934)

Painter. Known as Lizzie. Born in Warwick in June 1846. The daughter of William Farquhar, an inventor and chronometermaker, and Hannah Sarah. Her father originated from Aberdeen, her mother from Worcestershire. Raised in Middlesex. The eldest of at least four children (Elizabeth, William, Ann and John). By at least 1871 Elizabeth was in Kensington, London sharing a house with her sister Ann (Annie), who was then a teacher of singing, and was working as a professional painter of portraits in oils and miniatures. She subsequently gave up painting miniatures. Shortly after in 1871, Elizabeth married portrait painter Comley Vivian (1847-1908) in Kensington. He originated from Bath, Somerset.

Elizabeth is presumed by Graves to have studied under her uncle, Frederick Cruikshank. But it is feasible that she also studied under Vivian. She spent most of her married life in London, latterly living with her eldest son Harold in Middlesex. She died in Brentford, Middlesex in late 1934, aged 88. Somewhat astonishingly, Elizabeth managed to conduct a lengthy and successful career as a painter whilst having nine children, four sons and five daughters. The Vivian children (Harold, Beatrice, Ida, Edith, Violet, Percival,

Madeline, Archibald and Valentine) were all born in London between 1872 and 1886, and were raised in London. Edith and Violet were twins.

Elizabeth exhibited (somewhat sporadically) over six decades, from the 1860s into the late 1910s, at least. Exhibited at the Royal Society of Painters in Miniature and at the Royal Academy (18 works, 1867-1918). She also copied old masters at the National Gallery and the Tate Gallery. Exhibited works included: Isaac Henderson, Esq., Lady Ida, Madame Constance Elizabeth d'Azevedo and In the Olden Time. Executed portraits of her children, and in 1917 exhibited a tribute to her late husband, In Memoriam Comley Vivian. Elected a Member of the Royal Society of Miniature Painters (1898) and a Member of the North British Academy (1911). Her miniature of the late King Edward VII was reproduced in 1925. Her son Harold became an art student. Comley Vivian exhibited at the Royal Academy (1877-92).

VYSE, AGNES FRANCES ELEANOR (1873-1967)

Designer / Metalworker. Born in Holloway, Middlesex. Raised in Croydon, Surrey. The daughter of John Vyse, a leather merchant, and Sarah Margaret. One of at least five children (Agnes, Alice, John, Nora and Eric). Active as a designer and metalworker in the first two decades of the twentieth century. One of her most prestigious projects involved 15 repoussé copper panels executed for Zanzibar Cathedral. Vyse designed the panels and jointly executed them with Henry Ross. Three of the panels, The Brazen Serpent, Melchizedek and Jonah, were illustrated in the Art Journal in 1907, p.53. The panels were based on the Old Testament and were set into a teak frame designed by an architect. Vyse exhibited some of her work at the Society of Women Artists (1911-14), and was elected an Associate of the Society (1914-15). She was also elected Honorary Secretary of the Clarion Guild of Handicraft. The Guild, formed in 1902, held annual exhibitions from 1902, and was supported by a number of leading artist / designers of the day, including Walter Crane. The Guild aimed to help craftsmen and craftswomen to sell their work. In 1921 Vyse married Frederick H. Cockle in Sussex. She died in Sussex.

W

WADE, CONSTANCE EDITH - SEE DUNN, C.E.

WADHAM, MILLICENT (1881-post-1919)

Sculptor / Artist. Born in Darlington. The daughter of Arthur Wadham and Sarah. Her father, a publisher and proprietor of engineering journals, originated from Barnstaple, Devon. Her mother originated from Bradford, Yorkshire. One of at least three children (Robert, May and Millicent). Initially raised in Camberwell, London, then Hornsey, Middlesex. Probably studied in London. Worked as a sculptor and artist from at least the age of 19. Lived with her widowed father at Stroud Green, Hornsey whilst working as a sculptor and artist, but also had a studio at Camden Road, London. Produced statuettes, busts and groups in bronze and occasionally drawings. Exhibited her work, including at the Royal Scottish Academy (1911), the Royal Glasgow Institute (1910), the Royal Academy (1909-19) and the Society of Women Artists (1902-14). Exhibited works included: Baby Bunting (bust, bronze), Joy (group, bronze), Wonder (statuette), Sketch of Miss Gertrude Elliot as Peggy in Mice and Men and The Crab (statuette, bronze).

WADSWORTH, GERTRUDE (b.c.1862)

Jewellery Designer / Metalworker. Born in Nottinghamshire. Based at Pembroke Studios, West Kensington, London in the early 1900s. Active until at least 1906. Exhibited three examples of her work at the Society of Women Artists in 1900. Exhibited at the 1904 Leicester Arts and Crafts Exhibition. Other exhibitors on that occasion included Ann Macbeth, Alice Shepherd and Jessie King. Also showed jewellery at the 1905 / 06 permanent Exhibition of Artistic Handicrafts held at the Lyceum Club. Showed jewellery at the Second Exhibition of Arts and Crafts held at the Lyceum Club in 1905. One of her exhibits on that occasion was a necklace in silver and opals which was illustrated in The Studio, Vol.36, January 1906, p.356. Also contributed to the October 1906 Society of Artists at Work exhibition held at the Grafton Galleries. The Society was organised by Mrs Charles Muller to promote the sale of handicrafts.

WAGER, RHODA (1875-1953)

Artist / Metalworker / Embroideress. Born in Middlesex. The daughter of George Wager and Jane Annabella. Her father, a dress corset designer, originated from Essex. Her mother originated from London. Rhoda was the fifth of at least eight children (Alfred, Amy, Ellen, Arthur, Rhoda, Christopher, Fred and Dorothy). Her brother Arthur became a dress corset cutter. Part of her childhood was spent in Little Bowden, Leicestershire. By at least the early 1890s the family was based in Gloucestershire. Rhoda studied at the nearby Bristol School of Art. Then moved to Glasgow to study at the Glasgow School of Art which was then under the strong influence of the Newberys. Wager also spent some time teaching at a girls' school. She became an expert designer and maker of decorative enamel and metalwork and an embroideress.

Rhoda was elected a Member of the Glasgow Society of Lady Artists' Club, with whom she exhibited some of her jewellery. In the early 1900s, she also had some connections with artistic metalworkers Arthur and Georgina Gaskin. In 1913 she moved to Fiji, living on her brother's sugar plantation. But by 1918 she was living in Sydney, Australia. In 1920 she married widower Percival George, a marine surveyor. She continued to design and produce decorative jewellery in Australia, and details of her time there can be found in Anne Schofield's entry in The Australian Dictionary of Biography (1990). Schofield states that Wager became a Member of the Society of Arts and Crafts of New South Wales, also joining the Melbourne and Brisbane Societies, exhibiting her work there. Her studio proved so successful that she was able to employ an assistant, Walter Clarence Chapman, and in 1928 was joined by her niece, Dorothy Wager. Rhoda retired in 1946. Schofield notes that Wager produced around 12,000 pieces of jewellery over a career which spanned approximately 25 years, all recorded in her sketchbooks. In 1951 Wager moved to Queensland. She died in Australia. One of her embroidered sideboard cloths was illustrated in colour in The Studio, Vol.50, 1910, p.125.

WALDRAM, BEATRICE ANNE MARY (1874-1955)

Ornamental Designer / Pottery Worker / Illuminator. Born in Stoke Newington, Middlesex in November 1874. The daughter of civil engineer John Waldram (b.1837) and Louisa Jane Malyon (or Maylon). One of at least seven children (four girls and three boys). Raised in Edmonton, Middlesex. One of her sisters, Louisa, was a musician. One of her brothers studied civil engineering, another horticulture. Beatrice was educated at the Drapers High School, Tottenham. She then studied at the Clapton School of Art where she was a gold and silver medallist in the

National Competition of Schools of Art. In the 1898 National Competition, she exhibited designs for wallpaper and friezes.

By the early 1900s, Beatrice was based in Islington, as a boarder in a shared house, and was working as a designer. She subsequently moved to a shared house in Great Russell Street, London, working as a designer and illuminator. Later, she had a studio at Downshire Hill, Hampstead, and worked from The White Cottage, Mill Hill, Hertfordshire where she died, aged 80. She was also a lecturer on art at the Montessori Training College in Hampstead. One of her pots was purchased by Princess Mary, and some of her pottery beads were purchased by the Queen. She was the author of Pottery For Beginners (Fountain Press). Whilst based at Great Russell Street, she exhibited four works at the Society of Women Artists between 1905 and 1908, three works written and illuminated by her and a book cover. Later in her life, in 1932, when she was still active as a designer, she travelled to India and Yokohama. On her death, she left part of her small estate to her personal manager, Colin Waldram, probably a relative.

WALFORD, BETTINE CHRISTIAN (b.1905)

Artist in Line & Wash / Watercolours / Pastels / Pencil / Pen & Ink. Born in London in January 1905. The daughter of Hugh S. Walford, a solicitor, and Mary Swan. Her father originated from London, her mother from Cheltenham. Had at least one sibling, John Henry (b.1901). Bettine studied art in London at John Hassall's School of Art, the Chelsea Polytechnic, the St Martin's School of Art and the Grosvenor School of Art. Studied under William Thomas Wood, R.W.S., and John McNab. Based in London for much of her career. Produced works of various subjects including buildings, landscapes and townscapes. Exhibited at the Royal Academy (1929-50), the Society of Women Artists (1930-49), the Royal Society of Painters in Watercolours, the Royal Institute of Painters in Watercolours, the Royal Society of British Artists, the New English Art Club, the Paris Salon, the Pastel Society, the National Society, the Women's International Art Club and the Goupil Gallery. Also, with the Artists of Chelsea, at the Walker Art Gallery, Liverpool and at the public galleries of Bradford, Brighton, Derby, Huddersfield and Hull. Held a one-woman show at the French Gallery, Berkeley Square in 1935. Held a one-woman show at the Kensington Gallery in 1951. Exhibited works included: Scaffolding, Shipyard, Wivenhoe, Interior - Fisherman's Workshed (line & wash) and New Waterloo Bridge Under Construction. Two of her watercolours were purchased by the British Museum in 1938. In 1932 Bettine married Henry H.W. Woodcock (1897-1959) in Chelsea.

WALGATE, MARION (b.1888)

Sculptor. Studied at the Gray's School of Art, Aberdeen. Also studied at the Royal College of Art, London. Elected an Associate of the Royal College of Art. Initially based in London. Later based in Cape Town, South Africa. Active from the 1910s to the 1930s at least. Produced plaques, busts and reliefs in copper and bronze. Exhibited at the Royal Academy (1913-32) and in Aberdeen. Exhibited works included: Miss Mary Haylock (bust), Miss Doris Bowman (plaque, copper), Val Myer, Esq. (plaque) and Diana (relief, bronze). Better known for her portrait sculptures of Dr Charles Murray, Archbishop Carter, Sir L. Starr Jamieson and Sir George Cary. Purchasers of her work included The Rhodes National South African Memorial Committee, the Teachers' Association, Prince Arthur of Connaught and the Princess Alice Home of Recovery for Children.

WALKER, AGATHA (1888-1980)

Sculptor / Painter / Pottery Artist. Particularly active in the 1920s and 1930s. Born in Old Walsingham, Norfolk in February 1888. Based for much of her career in Thame, Oxfordshire and, from around the later 1930s, at Wimborne, Dorset. Died in Dorset in December 1980, aged 92. Best known for her small statuettes executed in wax, plaster or bronze. Her statuettes were usually around 12" in height. When modelled in plaster, they were usually covered in a fine coating of wax, then coloured. This gave a translucency to the flesh. She specialised in portrait works of the well known, often modelling directly from life, creating an important historical record of notable people, films and plays. However, her works had to be kept under glass because of their delicacy. She often put movement into her work, with poses caught in mid-flow, and was particularly good at representing drapery.

Agatha was also known for her wax models, producing a series of Tanagra-like figures. Known for figures taken from The Beggar's Opera. She executed tiny carvings in ivory, which were less than half an inch long. Her portrait works included studies of Gwen Ffrongcon-Davies as Etain in The Immortal Hour and Edith Evans as Florence Nightingale in The Lady With the Lamp. In 1930 / 31 Agatha held an exhibition of work at the Fine Arts Society. Exhibited works

included studies of Gwen Ffrongcon-Davies as Lady Herbert in The Lady With the Lamp, Miss Jean Forbes-Robertson as Peter Pan (Studio Films) and Edith Evans as Mistress Page and Dorothy Green as Mistress Ford, both in The Merry Wives of Windsor (also Studio Films). Walker exhibited elsewhere, including at the Royal Academy (1927-34), the Royal Scottish Academy (1936), the Society of Women Artists (1937-38), the Royal West of England Academy, the Walker Art Gallery, Liverpool and in Cardiff. Other exhibited works included studies of Anne Boleyn (statuette), Queen Elizabeth (coloured statuette) and Nell Gwynne. During her career, Walker also designed a considerable number of war memorials and figures for the decoration of graves and gardens in bronze and lead. In her pastels and oil paintings, she hinted at the influence of the French pastellists. In March 1931 Walker was the subject of an illustrated article in The Studio, Vol.101, pp.212-215. Works in the Victoria & Albert Museum, London.

WALKER, CASSANDRA ANNIE (b.1875)

Designer / Decorative Artist. Also sometimes Cassandia. Born at Gateacre, Lancashire. The daughter of Rowland Ramsden Walker (1835-1919), an accountant, and Emily Ann Wallington Worthington (c.1842-1927). Her father originated from Wakefield, her mother from Middlesex. One of at least six children (William, Juliet, Marion, Cassandra, Ellen and May). Raised in Much Woolton and Little Woolton, Lancashire. Studied at the School of Architecture and Applied Arts at University College, Liverpool in the late 1890s. In 1898 she took a distinction for ornamental design at an exhibition of work by students of the School of Architecture and Applied Arts. She joined the Birkenhead Pottery as a designer. The Pottery was founded in 1894 by Harold Rathbone and produced Della Robbia wares. There, Walker assisted Rathbone from at least 1895. The Pottery survived only until 1906, despite signs that it was beginning to flourish after 1900, and despite the support of a number of eminent artists and designers including Lord Leighton, George F. Watts, Holman Hunt and Walter Crane. Some of its decorative wares were purchased by the Queen, the Prince of Wales and the Marchioness of Lorne.

Walker was not the only decorative artist employed by Rathbone, nor the only female. Gwendoline Buckler, Lizzie Williams and Hannah Jones all exhibited under the Della Robbia title, as did Cassandra. She exhibited Della Robbia ceramics from at least 1895, at the Second Manchester Arts and Crafts Exhibition.

There, she and Rathbone filled two cases with wares. In 1897 a Della Robbia plaque designed by Walker was shown at that year's (thirteenth) Home Arts and Industries Association Exhibition, as part of a larger display of Della Robbia. Other pieces were also designed by Walker on that occasion. The plaque was illustrated in The Studio, Vol.11, July 1897, p.116. The Pottery had already exhibited at the 1896 Home Arts and Industries Association exhibition, including a decorative jar designed by Gwendoline Buckler, which won her a Gold Cross and which was illustrated in The Studio, Vol.8, July 1896, p.98. Rathbone took a large stand at that particular exhibition, also showing a high relief panel designed by Conrad Dressler.

In 1898 Walker exhibited a Della Robbia coloured panel, Pandora, at the Walker Art Gallery, Liverpool Spring Exhibition of Arts and Crafts. The panel was also illustrated in The Studio, Vol.13, April 1898, p.190. In the same year, the Art Journal, p.28, illustrated a panel in Della Robbia ware, for an overmantel designed by Ellen M. Rope, which suggests that Rathbone also worked with outside designers too. In 1900 Walker again contributed to the Home Arts and Industries Association exhibition, showing a decorative panel The Apple-Gatherer. Rathbone showed several large vases on that occasion, one designed by Robert Anning Bell. In 1904 an overmantel of beaten copper by Mr R.P. Roberts, with painted low-relief Della Robbia panels designed and executed by Walker, and painted a bluish-green, was exhibited at Messrs Waring. Cassandra's sister Ellen became a Professor of Music. Another sister, Marion, is listed as a school art teacher in 1901. In 1901, both Marion and Cassandra are living with their parents in Toxteth Park. But both effectively disappear after that date. A Della Robbia dish by Walker, dated 1903, is currently in the collection of the Victoria & Albert Museum, London.

WALKER, HILDA ANNETTA (1877-1960)

Painter / Sculptor. Born in Mirfield, Yorkshire. The daughter of John Ely Walker and Mary Elizabeth. Her father, who originated from Batley in Yorkshire, was a manufacturer of blankets and rugs as well as being a J.P. Her mother also originated from Yorkshire. Hilda was the second of at least seven children (Edith, Hilda, James, Ronald, Kathleen, Dora and Eric). Her siblings were also born in Mirfield. The family lived at Knowle House in Mirfield, where Hilda was still living into the 1930s. She also worked at Wychcombe Studios in London, subsequently using a studio at Cranley Gardens in Kensington,

London. For a while, she lived at The Outpost in Mirfield and in Leeds. She died in June 1960, having lived latterly at Hebden near Skipton, Yorkshire.

Hilda may have studied in London. She became a watercolour painter of flowers, landscapes and other subjects, but worked more prolifically as a sculptor of figures and portraits in bronze and marble. She exhibited her work more in her later career. Exhibited at the Royal Academy (1921), the Royal Institute of Painters in Watercolours, in Liverpool, elsewhere in London and the provinces, and at the Paris Salon. Exhibited 15 works at the Society of Women Artists (1920-58). She exhibited at the Society in 1920 and 1921 but did not show again until 1950-58. Exhibited works included: Peter Pan (bronze), Ophelia (marble), The Seer (bronze), Sleep (bronze) and The Late Viscount Simon, K.C.V.O., K.C.S.I., M.C. (bronze). Elected an Associate of the Society of Women Artists (1951-58). A Member of the Forum Club. Some of her bronzes were reproduced. Hilda worked and exhibited almost until her death.

WALKER, KATE WINIFRED (1867-1949)

Painter / Sculptor. Born in Leicester. The daughter of Viccars Collyer (1836-1923) and Elizabeth Hills (1837-1923). Both originated from Brigstock, Northamptonshire. Her mother's sister, Sarah Tailley, was a writer. Her father worked as a requisitions dealer in the 1870s, then became a provisions merchant and confectioner employing some 34 men and seven boys. By the 1890s, however, he had become a nurseryman and seedsman. Kate was one of at least five children, all raised in Leicester. Her three brothers, Joseph, Herbert and William, also became nurserymen. However, Herbert Hood Collyer (b.c.1864) subsequently became a landscape painter. Her sister Maude became a teacher. Kate had a private education. She then became a student at the Birmingham School of Art. Produced some sculptures, but was mainly a painter of portraits in miniature.

Kate began to exhibit her work in around 1891, by which time she had moved back to the family home in Leicester, and continued to exhibit until at least 1943. Her career spanned some six decades. In the late 1890s, she spent a short time in London, at Cliveden Place. However, in 1900 she married architect Benjamin Walker, A.R.I.B.A., in Leicester. They lived mainly in Erdington, Birmingham thereafter. The couple had at least one son. Kate died in Birmingham, aged 81. She exhibited her work at the Royal Academy (37 works, 1891-1943), the Royal

Scottish Academy (1894) and the Royal Glasgow Institute (1899). Also, at the Royal Society of Miniature Painters, with the Royal Birmingham Society of Artists, at the Walker Art Gallery, Liverpool and at the Paris Salon. Exhibited works included: Sir William Gilstrap, Bart., Lady Henry Chamberlain, The Hon. Eleanor Rolls, Daughter of Lord Llangattock, Miss Dorothy Satchwell and Joan. Some of her works were on ivory. She was elected an Associate of the Royal Society of Miniature Painters (1909). A portrait photograph of Kate was given in The Year's Art for 1896. The annual journal included a number of portrait photographs of women artists in that particular volume. Her portrait of Lady Henry Chamberlain was reproduced in The Queen.

WALKER, KATHLEEN MELLINA (1901-post-1957)

Painter / Etcher / Engraver / Illustrator. Was Kathleen Robertson. Born in Wargrave, Berkshire. Educated at Westgate-on-Sea and Ramsgate, Kent. Studied at the Royal College of Art, London between 1920 and 1923 under Sir William Rothenstein and Sir Frank Short. Elected an Associate of the Royal College of Art in 1923. Awarded a British Institute Scholarship in etching and engraving in 1923. The recipient of the Royal College of Art Travelling Scholarship in 1924. Produced paintings in oils, watercolours and tempera, illustrations, etchings and engravings. In 1925 she married Ralph Hamilton Walker, housemaster at Rugby School. They had two daughters. Kathleen became art teacher at Bilton Grange School, Rugby from 1940. Spent much of her career in Rugby, and later in Sussex. Exhibited her work, including at the Royal Academy (1948-57), the Society of Women Artists (1952), the New English Art Club, at Bradfield Art Gallery and in the provinces. Exhibited works included: The Window Sill (oil), Jane at School and Susan (coloured pencils). Her illustrations appeared in Detectives in the Hills (Faber & Faber) and in the American Institute of Architecture magazine.

WALKER, WINEFRIDE ELEANOR CONSTANCE FLORENCE MARIA ROMAINE (1899-1952)

Sculptor. Born in London. The daughter of William Henry Romaine Walker (1854-1940) and Giunetta Catarina Maria. Her father, an architect based in Brighton and London, originated from Bury, Lancashire. He worked on extensions to the Tate Gallery, among other projects. Her mother was born in London. Winefride appears to have been the only child of older parents, both of whom were in their 40s when she was born. Raised in London and Brighton. Studied at the Royal College of Art, London, where she was awarded a diploma. Elected an Associate of the Royal College of Art in 1922. Became a sculptor of figures and animals in bronze. Had a studio in London. Exhibited her work, including at the Royal Academy (1924-32) and the Walker Art Gallery, Liverpool (from 1924). Exhibited works included: The Dinner-hour (statuette, bronze), Miss Sylvia Hobday (portrait statuette), Ballarines Espanoles (group) and Newsboy (statuette). Elected a Member of the Three Arts Club. Died in Chelsea, aged 52.

WALKER, WINIFRED ETHEL (1882-1965)

Flower Painter. Born in Hampstead, London. The daughter of James Walker (1851-1932) and Louisa Parker (1853-1922). Her father, a schoolmaster, originated from Bath, Somerset. Her mother also originated from Bath, and was a schoolmistress. Winifred was one of at least five children (Katherine, Robert, Frederick, Winifred and Charles). Her siblings were also born in Hampstead, and all were raised there. All the children were well educated. Katherine became a schoolmistress, Robert became a clerk, Frederick a draughtsman, Winifred an artist and Charles a manufacturer. As a child, Winifred was educated at the St Martin's School in London. She then studied at the Camden School of Art, where she won the King's Prize for Modelled Design and was awarded an Art Masters' Certificate. She also spent time studying in Ghent, where she was awarded the Medaille de Vermeuil. She became a botanical artist in oils and watercolours, and was still active into the 1950s at the age of around 70. She spent much of her career in London, but also spent time in Westcliff-on-Sea, Southend and in Worthing, Sussex. She travelled extensively to paint. She died in Bognor Regis, Sussex in October 1965, aged 83.

Winifred Walker enjoyed an extensive and successful career as a flower painter, and was particularly well known as a painter of plants of the Holy Bible, native flowers of California and Madeira, and flowers from Shakespeare's plays. Arguably the most prestigious aspect of her career, however, was her role as flower portrait painter to the Royal Horticultural Society. She was elected a Fellow of the Society in 1912. During her career, she was awarded more than 30 bronze, silver and silver-gilt medals by the Society. She won other medals for her work in London and Paris, and a gold medal in Philadelphia for her flower paintings. Also elected a Fellow of the Linnean Society, and a

Member of the British Watercolour Society (1924). For a time, she was artist to the University of California. She exhibited her work elsewhere, including at the Royal Academy (1919-28), the Society of Women Artists (1920-39), the Royal Institute of Painters in Watercolours, the Paris Salon and in Blackpool. In 1929, at the Chelsea Flower Show, she exhibited some of her flower studies completed during a recent tour of Canada and America. Exhibited works included: The Pewter Pot, From the Old-World Garden, From Japan, Delphiniums and Shakespeare's Flowers.

Walker's works were frequently reproduced, particularly in Colour magazine. For example, in its January 1926 issue (p.23) Colour offered a colour reproduction of her Rhododendrons. In November 1928 they illustrated her watercolour of Anemonies; in January 1929, p.28, her The Abol Rose was illustrated, and in March 1929 two of her oil paintings were reproduced in colour. For its May 1919 edition, Colour used her watercolour California as its front cover, and used her oil painting of flowers for its front cover of the February 1930 edition. In November 1930 Colour magazine advertised limited signed artist's proofs of Walker's flowers at one and a half guineas each, from her Rivercourt Road Studio in London. Queen Alexandra was a patron. In 1907 Winifred married Ernest Fryett, an auctioneer who originated from Brixton. They had a son, James, in 1909.

WALLACE, MARGARET ADELINE (1907-71)

Painter / Draughtsman. Born in Millbrook, Cornwall. The daughter of Dudley Corynden Boger, an Army Major, and Amy Eustace. Her mother was a miniature painter who exhibited at the Royal Academy (1904-05). Margaret had at least one sibling, Robert. Raised in Chester. Studied at the St John's Wood School of Art, London, and in Paris. Produced works in oils, watercolours and black & white. Exhibited her work, including at the Royal Institute of Painters in Watercolours, the Royal Society of British Artists, the United Society of Artists and the Society of Women Artists (1948-50). Exhibited works included: Condemned (watercolour), Potting Shed (watercolour), The White Cottage (watercolour) and Country House Kitchen (watercolour). In 1934 Margaret married Carew V. Wallace in Westminster, London. Later in her career, she was based in Windsor. She died in Wycombe, Buckinghamshire, aged 64.

WALLACE, OTTILIE H. - SEE MacLAREN, O.H.

WALLER, MARGARET MARY (1916-c.93)

Painter / Decorative Artist. Born in the West Riding of Yorkshire in November 1916. The daughter of painter Arthur Bassett Waller and Alice Emily Weston. Her father was born in Bolton, Lancashire in 1882, the son of a confectioner and baker. He became an artist and Principal of the Oswestry School of Art. Her parents married in Liverpool in 1913. Records suggest, but do not absolutely confirm, that her father died in the West Riding of Yorkshire in 1930, aged 48. Margaret was educated at the Friary Convent School in Venice and at the Belvedere School, Liverpool. She remained in Liverpool, studying at the Liverpool School of Art between 1934 and 1937. She then went to the Royal Academy schools, London between 1937 and 1939, studying under Sir Walter Russell, R.A., Walter T. Monnington, R.A., and Ernest Jackson. Awarded an Art Teachers' Diploma. Produced portrait and landscape paintings in oils and watercolours. She was also an artist in tempera, and a designer of decorative panels of sacred subjects in gold leaf. She was based in Liverpool at the start of her career, but also worked at the Mayfield Studio on the island of Sark in the Channel Islands. Exhibited her work, including at the Royal Academy (1951-53), the Society of Women Artists (1949-54) and the Walker Art Gallery, Liverpool. Exhibited works included: Wintry Sunday, Elizabeth's Garden (oil), Old Harbour, Newlyn (oil) and Percuil River From St Mawes (oil). Elected a Member of the Sandon Studios Society, Liverpool.

WALLER, MARY LEMON (1852-1931)

Painter. Born in Bideford, Devon. The daughter of the Rev. Hugh Fowler and Mary Ann Weekes. Her father became Headmaster of the King's School in Gloucester. Mary had at least one sibling, Margaret Lois Fowler who never married. In the early 1870s, Mary went to London to study at the Royal Academy schools, lodging in Bloomsbury with other female students including Clara Fell and Flora Davis. She was based in London thereafter, working principally as a portrait painter in oils and watercolours, including of children. Also produced the occasional landscape. She was based at Circus Road for much of her career. In 1874, before she had begun to exhibit her work seriously, Mary married artist and Royal Academy exhibitor Samuel Edmund Waller in Gloucester. They had at least one son, Maurice Lyndham Waller who was born in London in 1875. He became a Commissioner of Prisons and was later knighted for his services.

Despite her change in circumstances, Mary's career blossomed. She exhibited her work, including at the New Gallery, the Royal Academy (49 works, 1877-1917), the Royal Hibernian Academy (1890), the Royal Scottish Academy (1905), the Royal Society of Portrait Painters and the Society of Women Artists (18 works, 1886-1905). Exhibited works included: A Bacchante (watercolour), The Rose, The Card Dealer - Rossetti and Forbidden Fruit. Elected a Member of the Royal Society of Portrait Painters and a Member of the Albemarle Club. Also elected an Associate of the Society of Women Artists (1886) and a Member (1888-1911). Mary executed a number of portraits of distinguished sitters including The Hon. Victoria Bruce, Prince Marescotti Ruspoli, Countess Fitzwilliam, The Hon. Kitty Farrer and Sir Richard Levinge, Bt. Mary died in London in March 1931, aged 69, having worked consistently for over 40 years. She outlived her husband.

WALLIS, KATHERINE ELIZABETH (1861-1957)

Sculptor. Born in Peterborough, Ontario, Canada. Her mother's surname was Forbes. Katherine came from a family of Irish origin. She spent a number of years in Britain. Studied in Edinburgh, and at the Royal College of Art, London. She won a bronze medal and a scholarship. She also studied in Paris. Wallis spent much of her life travelling, moving around, dying in California in December 1957. Whilst in England, she was based at Oakley Street and Clarendon Road, London. Produced statuettes, reliefs, medallions and busts. Worked in bronze, marble and stone. Subjects included animals and portrait works. Exhibited her work whilst in Britain, including in Leeds, at the Royal Academy (1897-1914) and the Royal Glasgow Institute (1911). Exhibited works included: Head of a Child (medallion), A Little Canadian Fiddler (medallion), Mignonne (bust, marble), African Lynx (statuette, bronze) and The Goodlie Compagnie of Solitude (relief, bronze). She served as a nurse during the First World War.

WALSH, EDITH - SEE NORRIS, E.

WALSHE, CHRISTINA ANNE S. (1889-post-1934)

Artist / Journalist / Theatre Designer. Born in Cambridge. The daughter of William Henry Walshe, M.A., a Classics tutor and schoolmaster,

and Agnes. Her father originated from Malvern, Worcestershire, her mother from Gloucestershire. One of at least eight children, four boys and four girls. As a child, she spent time living in Great Malvern, Worcestershire and in Edgbaston, Warwickshire. Studied at the Birmingham School of Art. Became an accomplished decorative designer in stage and house, a director of the Glastonbury Players Ltd and Secretary to the Workers' Theatre (1924-26). She also worked as a journalist and a designer of costumes and scenery. She executed watercolour paintings and drawings, mainly for recreation. Based in London during her career. Worked on numerous productions during her career. For example, she executed costumes and scenery for The Immortal Hour, Queen of Cornwall, Olsectis and Bethlehem, all by composer Rutland Boughton (1878-1960). Also, Prince Ferelon by Nicolas Gatty and Franciscan Plays by Housman. She became close to Rutland Boughton, and executed a pencil sketch of him in 1911. Exhibited some of her work at a Theatre Art Exhibition held at South Kensington. Possibly the same Christina A.S. Walshe who married Thomas H. Richardson in Surrey in 1941.

WALTERS, AMELIA JANE (1843-1930)

Sculptor / Painter. Born in St Luke's, Finsbury, Middlesex. The daughter of Gregory Seale Walters (d.1876) and Johanna Huth (d.1896). Her father was a merchant. Her mother originated from Islington. One of at least five children (Frederick, Louisa, Thomas, Amelia and Edmund), with possibly more (records are inconclusive). Raised in London, and spent most of her life and career in the city. Probably studied in London, but details of her early life are sketchy. She certainly worked as a sculptor of portrait busts in terracotta and a painter of landscapes and other subjects. Exhibited her work rarely, but did show one work, The Trampling Surf on the Rocks and the Hard Sea-Sand, at the Royal Society of British Artists in 1892. Also exhibited six works at the Royal Academy between 1880 and 1892, including Undine, A Nor'-wester, Portrait (bust, terracotta) and A Bright Gleam From the West. She spent virtually all her adult life living with her brother Edmund, who became a clerk in holy orders. Neither ever married. On the 1911 national census, Amelia describes herself as an 'artist retired'.

WALTON, VIOLET (1901-93)

Designer / Embroideress / Painter / Illuminator. Born in Bootle near Liverpool in November 1901. The daughter of Albert Walton and

Susanna Elizabeth Shaw. Her father was a hairdresser and fancy goods dealer. Violet was educated at the Merchant Taylors' Girls' School at Great Crosby, Liverpool. Then studied at the Liverpool School of Art. Awarded a New Board of Education Art Teachers' Certificate and a London City & Guilds Certificate in crafts and embroidery. Produced designs, embroideries, paintings in oils and watercolours, sketches and illuminations. Worked as a temporary art mistress at the Grammar School, Ashton-in-Makerfield in 1925, and at the Liverpool School of Art in 1926. Exhibited at the Walker Art Gallery, Liverpool (1924-26). Based in Southport and Liverpool during her career. Died in Merseyside, aged 91.

WARD, NORA - SEE ENGLAND, N.

WARDLE, ELIZABETH (1834-1902)

Founder of the Leek Embroidery Society in Staffordshire in 1879. Also the Society's organiser. Elizabeth Wardle was the wife of Thomas Wardle (1831-1909). He was born in Macclesfield, the son of Joshua Wardle, a noted silk dyer in Macclesfield. Thomas married Elizabeth in 1857 in Leek. She was the daughter of Hugh Wardle (1802-60), a druggist, chemist and yeoman, and Elizabeth Young (1802-71). George Wardle, Thomas's brother, was William Morris's business manager for around 20 years. Thomas and Elizabeth had 14 children, nine of whom survived into adulthood (Mary, Gilbert, Arthur, Bernard, Frederick, Lydia, Margaret, Thomas and Elizabeth). Several of their daughters became involved in embroidery, like their mother. Thomas Wardle ran the Thomas Wardle silk firm in Leek, and was a founder member and President of the Silk Association of Great Britain and Ireland. He was knighted for his services to the silk industry in 1897. He printed designs for, among others, Walter Crane, and provided a deal of technical knowledge to the firm of Morris & Co.

Elizabeth Wardle was an expert needlewoman and executed embroideries from at least 1864, some of which were ambitious in scale and made for local churches. In 1879 she was inspired to found a more structured embroidery society in Leek, where local women were offered the opportunity to earn a small income or to undertake classes. Like other handcraft ventures of the late nineteenth-century, such as those founded in the Lake District, Leek never intended to offer women the means to become financially independent. Rather, they worked in their own homes in their spare time to earn additional income. Wardle provided the Leek Embroidery

Society with raw materials, including spun silks, sewing silks, embroidery silks, woven silks, brocades, chenilles and all manner of trimmings. Wardle's manufacturing industry also meant that the Leek Society had dye houses available. Some items were not available locally, however. Gold thread, for example, was imported from China, and some woollen cloths were purchased in Yorkshire. The Society was closely linked to the Leek School of Art Embroidery which Elizabeth founded in around 1881.

The Leek embroiderers specialised in working on printed or brocaded cloths, and in a variety of applique work also done on printed cloths. The Leek workers developed their own method of working on such cloths until part or all of the woven or printed design was obscured. They also concentrated on colour, influenced by Thomas Wardle's lifetime of studying colour and dyes. Embroideries executed included hangings, curtains, screens, mantel borders, cushions, bags, bedspreads and table centres. Ecclesiastical work, however, always took priority, and the Society executed numerous altar cloths for churches across the country. Those included Chester Cathedral, Lichfield Cathedral, Harborne Parish Church, Birmingham, All Saints' Church, Leek and St Edward's Church, Leek. Other church textiles executed by the Society included stoles, hangings, banners, litany falls, pulpit cloths, chalice veils and palls. Elizabeth took charge of some of the design work. Other designs were contributed by highly respected figures, including John Dando Sedding, Richard Norman Shaw and Gerald Horsley. Most were ambitious and time-consuming in relation to church textiles. The altar cloth for St Edward's Parish Church, for example, measured more than eight feet in length, and was made of silk plush worked all over, with panels of embroidery upon printed tussore silk inserted in the silk plush. The cloth cost £45, £30 of which was for workmanship.

The Leek Society exhibited its embroideries at a variety of national arts exhibitions, including those of the prestigious Arts and Crafts Exhibition Society. Leek submitted embroideries to their 1893 (fourth) exhibition, taking their rightful place alongside, among others, the Royal School of Art Needlework. At the same exhibition were four large frames of printed fabrics by Thomas Wardle, including a silk designed by Leon Solon. Walter Crane exhibited a printed silk design executed by Wardle. Other works were shown at the Second (1894) and Third (1895) Manchester Arts and Crafts Exhibitions. At the latter, Leek showed an altar cloth designed by Horsley which was highly praised. In 1906 Leek textiles were included in the Barrow-in-Furness Ecclesiastical Art Exhibition. In the early 1890s, one of John Dando Sedding's designs, worked by Leek, was sent to London for exhibition. The border of the piece, oblong in shape, was embroidered with the words of Matthew Arnold: Art Still Has Truth, Take Refuge There.

Such were Elizabeth Wardle's talents that she instigated a replica of the Bayeux Tapestry which was eventually acquired by the Museum of Reading. The replica was the work of 35 women of Leek; all supervised by Mrs Wardle. Her talents and successes were widely acknowledged in her lifetime, and the Leek Society was the subject of an article in The Studio, Vol.1, July 1893, pp.136-140 by Kineton Parkes. Parkes offered several illustrations including of the purple altar cloth made for St Edward's Church, the green altar cloth for All Saints' Church designed by Norman Shaw, two litany desk hangings, and a white memorial altar cloth made for Cheddleton Parish Church, Staffordshire. The last of those was designed by Horsley with figures of Mary of Bethany, Mary Virgin and Mary Magdalene embroidered in light colours on a white brocade ground, pink, white and blue flowers and leaves in various greens. The final cost, according to Parkes, was £100.

Leek continued to produce embroideries until around 1921, later run under the guidance of Lydia Wardle, one of Elizabeth's daughters. Elizabeth Wardle was clearly an exceptional woman who, like Marian Twelves of the Langdale Linen Industry, created and ran a significant textile venture which survived for several decades. Though comparatively small, such ventures produced highly important works, and played a significant role in providing working-class women with some form of additional income as well as the opportunity for a degree of creative expression.

WARDLEY, JOAN (1899-1978)

Painter / Decorative Artist. Born in London in November 1899. The daughter of Alfred Herbert Blundell (1869-1944), a solicitor, and Amelia Woodward Richardson (1875-1962). One of at least five children (Joan, John, George, Michael and Alfred), all born between 1899 and 1908. Raised in Kensington, London. Studied at the Royal Academy schools, London. Remained in London after completing her studies, based at Cheyne Court for a time. Became a painter of flowers. Also painted furniture and executed wall decoration. Exhibited her work occasionally. Showed Flowers at the Royal Academy in 1927. In 1923 she married Donald Jouie Wardley

(1893-1950) in Kensington. He originated from Derbyshire and served in the First World War. At the time of his death, the couple were based in Berkshire. Joan Wardley died in Rugby, aged 78.

WARNE, DORIS MAY - SEE GERRARD, D.M.

WARNER, LOUISA - SEE AUMONIER, L.

WARREN, EMILY MARY BIBBENS (1869-post-1951)

Painter / Illustrator. Born in Exeter, Devon. The daughter of Matthew H. Warren, an oil merchant who originated from Devon, and Mary who originated from Fulham. Raised in Exeter and London. One of at least four daughters. The eldest, Elizabeth Janet, was born in Canada and became an art mistress in London. Louisa Anne was born in Newfoundland and became an artist. Ada Matilda was born in Battersea, London and became an art mistress in London. Emily also became an artist, based in London and, latterly, Surrey. Emily spent some time in Canada too. All the girls were still living with their widowed mother, all unmarried, when they were in their 40s and 50s. Emily studied at the Royal College of Art, London. She became a painter of landscapes and architectural subjects and occasionally illustrated books. Emily had ties with artist and art critic John Ruskin, and executed a painting of his bedroom at Brantwood, his Lakeland home. Some of her works were exhibited in the Lake District, at the annual Coniston Institute exhibition held between 1900 and 1919. In 1903 her Fritillaries, owned by Ruskin, was shown at Coniston. That particular exhibition was dedicated to Ruskin and to local artist Arthur Severn, but also to those who had come under his personal influence as artists, including Warren. She exhibited her work elsewhere, including at the Royal Institute of Painters in Watercolours, the Royal Society of British Artists, the Walker Art Gallery, Liverpool and the Society of Women Artists (47 works, 1900-39). Other exhibited works included: Christchurch Cathedral, Oxford, Houses of Parliament, The Library, Seaforth Hall, Liverpool and The Angel Choir, Lincoln Cathedral. Elected an Associate of the Royal Society of British Artists and an Associate of the Society of Women Artists (1916-51). Illustrated Homes and Haunts of Ruskin.

WATERHOUSE, ELIZABETH (1834-1918)

Founder and organiser of the Yattendon, Berkshire metalwork class. The class, which had close ties with the Home Arts and Industries Association, ran successfully for more than 10 years, in the 1890s and early 1900s. Like Mary Ann Bassett's Leighton Buzzard class, and the Rawnsleys' Keswick School of Industrial Arts, Yattendon began as a small amateur venture aimed at providing locals with the opportunity to develop their creativity, and to earn additional income. In the case of Yattendon, other members of the Waterhouse family became involved, and it too caused a stir nationally as well as locally, far surpassing its original aims.

Elizabeth Waterhouse was the wife of celebrated architect Alfred Waterhouse (1830-1905). He was born in Liverpool, and during his career was responsible for the Manchester Town Hall among other notable buildings. Elizabeth was the daughter of John Hodgkin (1800-75), a London barrister, and Elizabeth (1818-1904). Her father originated from London, her mother from Ireland. She was one of at least four children born into a Quaker family. Elizabeth married Waterhouse in 1860 in Brighton. Initially, they lived in Rusholme, Lancashire, not far from Manchester, for whom, in 1868, Waterhouse began work on a magnificent Town Hall. Shortly after, they moved to Fox Hill in Sonning, Berkshire, and by at least the late 1880s the couple had moved to Yattendon Court in Yattendon, Berkshire. They remained there until their deaths, with Waterhouse designing houses in the county. They had at least six children (Paul, Mary, Frances, Amyas, Florence and Alfred). Paul became an architect and Amyas a General Practitioner. Florence remained at home with her elderly parents, joined for a time by Amyas, his wife Florence and their two young daughters. Money was evidently not lacking, with a number of servants employed at Yattendon Court.

Sometime in around 1890, Elizabeth Waterhouse set up a metalwork and repoussé class in Yattendon. The class ran in conjunction with the then-thriving Home Arts and Industries Association, which had been founded back in 1884. The Association had very specific aims, to establish classes in handcrafts across the country, to reject machines in favour of handwork, to revive interest in lost crafts, and to provide working men and women with the opportunity for individual creativity. Exactly what skills Elizabeth had in metalwork and repoussé remains unclear, but she probably followed the example of other similar classes and brought in a suitably trained teacher. However, she did provide most of the designs used by the metalworkers, seeking inspiration from aspects of nature such as birds, flowers, fruit, trees and animals. Some members of the class created their own designs on occasion, and at least three other members of the Waterhouse family - Paul, Amyas and Florence (Elizabeth's daughter) - supplied other designs.

Yattendon, like Leighton Buzzard, Compton and other handcraft classes, quickly established itself as a centre of excellent craftsmanship, and was soon selling its wares across the country. Locally, Yattendon metalwork was displayed and sold in the village shop. More significantly, the class exhibited regularly at the annual Home Arts exhibition, held in London. Initially, the class produced largely domestic items such as ewers, vases, trays, goblets, ashtrays, jugs, dishes and sconces, all with attractive repoussé decoration. Unlike the Newlyn metalwork class, which used very specific and easily recognisable design traits such as fish, boats and seagulls, Yattendon did not develop any specific design style which marked them out. However, they did create highly detailed decoration on most pieces, making them visually appealing if not particularly unique. As time went on, the class moved into more complex pieces, producing, for example, decorated copper screens, decorative plaques, fenders and mirror frames as well as fittings for furniture.

During the late 1890s and early 1900s, Yattendon drew the attention of The Studio magazine, which reported on the Home Arts exhibitions for a number of years. Because of that, a fairly obscure village handcraft class became relatively well known across England, and the workers themselves began to win some individual recognition and praise. Those involved included George Frost, Harry Smith, Alexander Aldridge, Michael Reynolds, George and Robert Loader, John Maher, Tom Green, John Fisher, Fred Crook and Charles and George Allum. In total, more than 17 men were associated with the Yattendon class, but apparently few or no women. On a number of occasions, The Studio offered photographs of metalwork executed by the class, most of which was shown at the Home Arts exhibitions. For example, in 1895 The Studio, Vol.5, August, p.170, illustrated a mirror frame designed by Mrs Waterhouse and executed by John Maher. In 1896 The Studio, Vol.8, July, pp.91-92, offered four photographs of work by the class, including one of the interior of the village shop complete with a display of goods. Further photographs were given every year until at least 1902.

Indications are that the Yattendon class also ventured into woodcarving, with equal success. At the 1897 Home Arts exhibition the class showed a carved settle designed by someone named Macey and executed by the class. The settle was illustrated in The Studio, Vol.11, July

1897, p.114. In 1900 the class showed a washstand in oak and pewter which was also illustrated in The Studio, Vol.20, July 1900, p.82, designed by Paul Waterhouse. The class continued to thrive into the early 1900s, but the death of Alfred Waterhouse in 1905 must have affected both Elizabeth and the class to some degree. Also by 1905, Elizabeth would have been around 71 years of age. If any carvers or metalworkers remained active after that date, they would have been additionally affected by the onset of the First World War in 1914, and then by Elizabeth's death in 1918.

WATES, FLORENCE ANNE (1868-1947)

Etcher. Born in Devonport, Devon. Raised in Devon. Studied at the Bath School of Art, Somerset. Remained in Bath thereafter, dying there aged 79. Known principally for her etchings of London, Bath, Wells, Glastonbury, Polperro, Bradford-on-Avon and elsewhere. Her etching of Waterloo Bridge was published by the Russell Art Co. The Bath Municipal Library purchased her Demolition. Exhibited her work locally in Bath and in Newcastle.

WATHERSTON, MARJORY VIOLET - SEE GEARE, M.V.

WATKINS, FRANCES J.G. - SEE MILLIGAN, F.J.G.

WATKINSON, HILDA M. - SEE MACK, H.M.

WATSON, AGNES (active early 1900s)

Bookbinder / Book Decorator. Based in Glasgow. Noted in Sarah Treverbian Prideaux's volume Modern Bookbindings Their Design and Decoration, London, Archibald Constable & Co., 1906. Prideaux notes that Miss Watson was one of a number of women noted in a paper 'recently' written by Mr Lewis F. Day. Others mentioned by Day included Jessie M. King, Jane F. Hamilton and Alice Gairdner. Watson exhibited some of her work in the Scottish Section of the 1902 Turin Exhibition. Also exhibited decorative book covers at the 1903 annual Glasgow School of Art Club Exhibition, some of which were illustrated in The Studio, Vol.30, 1903, p.110.

WATSON, CAROLINE (1760-1814)

Engraver. Born in London. Instructed by her father, Irish mezzotint engraver James Watson (d.1790). Like her father, she became a leading London engraver. She specialised in stipple engraving, and was particularly noted for her

works after Hoppner, Romney and Reynolds. Noted in Mrs E.F. Ellet's volume Women Artists in All Ages and Countries, London, Bentley, 1859. Ellet notes Watson to have engraved subjects in mezzotint and in the 'dotted manner'. Also that Watson was greatly admired. Subsequently noted in Walter Shaw Sparrow's volume Women Painters of the World, London, Hodder & Stoughton, 1905. Sparrow illustrates her Portrait of Sarah, Countess of Kinnoull from a stipple engraving after a miniature by Samuel Shelley. Sparrow also notes Watson to have been made engraver to Queen Caroline in 1785. Watson provided seven plates, stipple engraved, for William Hayley's The Life of George Romney, Chichester, T. Payne, 1809. Some of her works can be found in the National Gallery of Ireland.

WATSON, CONSTANCE STELLA (1899-1985)

Etcher / Sculptor / Potter. Born in Teignmouth, Devon. Her mother was Susannah. One of at least three children. Studied in London, at the Goldsmiths' College and the Royal Academy schools. Awarded a silver medal by the Royal Academy in 1925. Produced pottery groups, bronze figures and etchings. Worked mainly in London during her career. Died in Surrey, aged 86. She travelled to New Zealand. Exhibited her work at the Royal Academy, the Society of Women Artists (1925-29) and the National Gallery, Wellington. Exhibited works included: Courage (model for pottery group), The Enchanted Prince (bronze), Isis and Osiris (bronze bookends) and The Fairy Note (sketch for garden figure in bronze). Some of her works were illustrated in Eve and Woman. Purchasers of her work included the Aberystwyth Museum. Elected a Member of the Imperial Arts Club. Signed her work 'Stella'.

WATSON, FRANCES - SEE SUNDERLAND, F.

WATSON, MARY SPENCER (1913-2006)

Sculptor. Born in Kensington, London. Died at Langton Matravers, Dorset, aged 92. The daughter of painter George Spencer Watson, R.A (1869-1934) and Hilda Mary Gardiner (d.1952). Her father studied at the Royal Academy schools, and became a member and committee member of the distinguished Art Workers' Guild. In 1923 the family moved to Dunshay Manor at Langton Matravers, Swanage, Dorset. Mary remained there for much of the rest of her life. However, she also spent time working at Glebe Place,

London. In 1930 she studied at the Bournemouth School of Art part-time. The following year she applied to the Royal Academy schools but was rejected. So, in 1931 she spent the year at the Slade School, London. She was then accepted at the Royal Academy schools, and studied there between 1932 and 1936, winning prizes and medals. She also spent some time in 1936 at the London County Council Central School of Arts and Crafts, studying under Alfred Turner and John Skeaping. In 1938 she spent several months in Paris under Ossip Zadkine.

At her Dorset and London studios, Watson produced animal, figure and plant sculptures in stone, wood, terracotta, plaster, bronze and alabaster, and worked as an architectural sculptor. She used local Purbeck stone in her work. In 1937 Mary held her first one-woman exhibition at the Mansard Gallery at Heal's in Tottenham Court Road. Architect Sir Edward Maufe commissioned two large gilded angels in limewood for Guildford Cathedral. Architect Sir Frederick Gibberd commissioned Magic Beast for a primary school at Longbridge, and Cheiron Teaching the Young Hero for Harlow town centre.

Watson exhibited her work, including at the Society of Women Artists (1950), the Royal Academy (1945-56), the Women's International Art Club, the National Society of Painters, Sculptors and Gravers, at the Berkeley Galleries, at the galleries of Foyle's and Heal's, and the Crafts Centre. Exhibited locally at the Dorset County Museum. Exhibited works included: Elijah (statuette, terracotta), Ram's Head (alabaster), Musician (carving in Purbeck stone) and Christos (statuette, wood). An exhibition of her work was held in Salisbury in 2004. During the Second World War, Mary worked on her mother's farm at Dunshay and taught sculpture in the local schools. She was still active into her 90s. Also a dance and mime artist.

WATT, M. LINNIE (c.1846-1916)

Painter / Ceramics Artist. Based in London for much of her career, but spent time in Dinan, France later on. If records are correct, Watt died in Holloway Sanitorium, aged 70, her address at that time being Kensington Gardens Square. Watt has proved elusive in research, despite her highly successful and productive career. She studied at the Lambeth School of Art, and was trained by John Sparkes. She became an exhibiting artist, and a decorator for Doulton's of Lambeth in the latter decades of the nineteenth century. Her pottery designs included rustic scenes and figures, but particularly of children. She was

known as a rapid sketcher, and often sketched in the countryside. Initially, she produced designs for others to copy, but gradually began to paint them herself.

Although working for Doulton's, Watt found the time to exhibit her work extensively, including at the Royal Academy (12 works, 1877-1901), the Royal Society of British Artists (34 works, 1875-89), the Royal Scottish Academy (1877), the Royal Glasgow Institute (17 works, 1876-1907) and the Society of Women Artists (96 works, 1871-95). Also exhibited at the Liverpool Academy, at the French Gallery, at Crystal Palace and at the Dore Gallery (including in 1909). Exhibited at the Dudley Gallery, including in 1878 at the Fourteenth General Exhibition of Watercolours. Watt showed works there including Sea Breeze. Contributed to the annual exhibition of china painting at the Howell & James galleries in Regent Street, London. During her career, she exhibited sketches, watercolours, landscapes, figures and flowers as well as decorated china. Exhibited works also included: Chalk Cliffs, Broadstairs (watercolour), A Dyer's Shop, Siena, Hanging Out the Clothes and Going to Market (on china). Elected an Associate of the Society of Women Artists (1880-81) and a Member (1882-98).

WATTS, EVELINE MERYL (1910-92)

Painter / Modeller / Woodcut Artist. Known as Meryl. Born in Lewisham, London in April 1910. The daughter of Charles Isaac Watts, a paper merchant and cardboard box maker, and Eveline Keates. Raised in London. Educated at the Blackheath High School. Studied at the Blackheath School of Art under John Platt, James Woodford, Charles Paine, William Clause and Reginald Brill. Remained in London initially, but was also later based at Borth-y-Gest, Porthmadog, Wales, and in Northumberland. Died in Northumberland in early 1992, aged 81. Produced works in oils, watercolours, chalk and gouache. Also produced colour woodcuts and worked as a modeller. Concentrated on flowers, animals, birds, buildings and landscapes.

Watts exhibited her work over at least five decades, including at the Royal Academy (1934-40), the Society of Women Artists (76 works, 1937-70), at the New York World's Fair, in an Exhibition of British Art 1735-1935, in Vienna and Prague, in many of the world's capital cities with the British Council and with various London societies. Exhibited works included: Crocus (colour woodcut), Pelican (colour woodcut), Red Roofs, Portmeirion (colour woodcut), Sailing Preparations (chalk and watercolour) and Village

Mosaic (oil). Elected an Associate of the Society of Women Artists (1950) and a Member (1951-87). Works reproduced in the Art Review. Works purchased by the Contemporary Art Society, the British Council, the Ministry of Education and various galleries abroad including in Prague and Baghdad. In late 1977, aged around 67, Watts married Joseph Stanley Allen (1898-1997) in Northumberland. Allen had been married previously and had a distinguished career in architecture. He was Head of the Leeds School of Architecture and Professor and Head of the Department of Town and Country Planning at Newcastle University. He outlived Meryl by some five years, also dying in Northumberland, aged 99.

WATTS, MARY SETON FRASER (1849-1938)

Craftswoman / Designer / Architectural Ceramicist. The second wife of respected artist George Frederick Watts (1817-1904). Also the founder of the Compton Industry near Guildford, Surrey. Mary S.F. Tytler was born in Bombay, India in November 1849. Almost immediately after her birth, she was sent to Britain, living in Scotland for a time with her grandparents and other relatives. She subsequently studied at the Slade School, London and at the South Kensington schools. At some point, she met G.F. Watts, who was considerably older by some 32 years. Watts had already experienced a brief and unsuccessful marriage to actress Ellen Terry. They had married in London in 1864 when Terry was only 16 years of age. Her father, Benjamin Terry, was an artist, and another artist, Val Princep, acted as witness to the ceremony. The disastrous union was later satirised by Virginia Woolf in her play Freshwater. Thereafter, Watts remained unattached until he married Mary Tytler in 1886 in Epsom, Surrey. Watts, who originated from London, was a Cambridge (Hon. LL.D.) and Oxford (Hon. D.C.L.) scholar. The son of a wealthy gentleman, he was able to pursue art as a career, and became a Royal Academy exhibitor (from 1837) as well as a Royal Academician. Watts and Mary had a London home, Little Holland House in Kensington. But in around 1891 they also moved into a large country house, Limnerslease, in the village of Compton, Surrey, built by Ernest George. Around that time, they met orphan Lilian Mackintosh (Mrs Michael Chapman) whom they adopted.

By at least 1895, Mary Watts had founded a recreative evening class in pottery, intending to offer the villagers of Compton the opportunity to learn the art of terracotta. This quickly developed into what became known as the Compton Industry or the Terra Cotta Home Arts industry. The industry's workshops and studio were based at Limnerslease. Local clay from the area was used, and the traditional method of throwing on the wheel was adopted for small pieces, whilst larger pieces were cast in a mould. The terracotta was fired in a small kiln in the garden at Limnerslease. How much experience Mary Watts had in the art of terracotta remains unclear. But she took full charge of the class, taking the initiative where both shape and design were concerned, declining to employ outside help as other amateur handcraft classes and industries of the period elected to do. Initially, various basic decorative items were made and sold at Compton, including flower pots, garden vases, well heads and sundials. However, within a short time, and under Mary's direct influence, the industry began to experiment in other aspects of design such as decorative plaques, clay caskets, memorial pottery and building decoration. It is feasible that, as an artist, G.F. Watts also had some creative input at Compton.

Compton terracotta wares were exhibited regularly at the Home Arts and Industries Association exhibitions from at least 1896 until after 1907. In 1896 the industry showed several terracotta designs intended for a chapel then being built near Limnerslease along with other items in terracotta. Art and design journals in that year praised the quality of the industry's work, but also its self-reliance in using locally sourced materials, local villagers and its own designs. In 1897 Compton showed a series of terracotta slabs of Celtic design intended for the same local chapel at that year's Home Arts exhibition. The slabs were intended to fill the spandrel of an arch. Church decoration became an important aspect of Compton's work, with other similar panels exhibited at the 1902 Home Arts exhibition and illustrated in The Studio, Vol.26, July 1902, p.129.

The Compton industry continued to grow and develop over the following years, attracting a number of commissions, employing some four or five permanent workers at the same time as continuing its evening classes for those with employment elsewhere. One of its more significant commissions was the above mentioned local mortuary chapel which was designed by architect George Redmayne. Compton was awarded the task of producing the terracotta decoration, which included an altar modelled in small panels, each by a different member of the industry, to the designs of Mrs Watts, and a reredos containing a copy of a G.F. Watts painting The All-Pervading. The ironwork was provided by the local blacksmith, the oak doors by local carvers. Redmayne supervised all the work, and the chapel was completed in around 1898. The domed building was the subject of an article in The Studio, Vol.14, September 1898, pp.235-240, A Mortuary Chapel Designed by Mrs G.F. Watts. Her designs were described as eclectic, incorporating such things as birds, the tree of life, Celtic pattern, angels, butterflies, fish, cherubs and stars. The chapel was intended for local use. The industry completed commissions for other chapels and buildings including two candelabra for Adelaide Cathedral which were exhibited at the 1904 Home Arts exhibition along with a scene for a church floor representing The Evolution of Man. Some of Mrs Watts's terracotta designs were sold through Liberty & Co. and illustrated in the Art Journal, 1905, p.118. Other design work executed by Mrs Watts included a Pelican rug created for the firm of Messrs Alexander Morton & Co. of Carlisle. The rug was exhibited at the 1903 exhibition of the Cumberland and Westmorland Society of Arts and Crafts held at Tullie House, Carlisle.

In July 1904, G.F. Watts died, leaving Mary the substantial sum of £84,000. Mary remained at Limnerslease until her death in November 1938. The Compton industry continued to run successfully after his death and was still active in 1907. On her husband's death, Mary Watts designed a cinerary casket which was illustrated in the form of a drawing by Winifred Cooper in The Studio, Vol.32, September 1904. She also designed a memorial tablet to Watts which was to be placed in Postman's Park, St Botolph's, Aldersgate. On a more ambitious scale, she was instrumental in building a gallery at Compton to house a large collection of her husband's paintings. Known as the Watts Memorial Gallery, it was opened in around 1906 and was the subject of an article in the Art Journal, 1906, pp.321-324.

Mary Watts was evidently an industrious, talented and determined woman, if then considered an amateur. She was also a writer, publishing The Word in the Pattern (London, W.H. Ward), with illustrations and text, in around 1899. In 1912 her George Frederick Watts: The Annals of an Artist's Life (three volumes) was published. The Art Journal noted that Mrs Watts was not only a supporter of the Home Arts and Industries Association but a founder member. Founded in 1884, the Association aimed to offer the opportunity for creative expression to men and women of all social classes, and to offer a suitable pastime outside working hours. It was intended that classes in various handcrafts would be established across the country, and many of those thrived successfully for a number of years.

It would appear that moving to Compton presented Mary Watts with the ideal location and opportunity to start such a handcraft class, and Compton followed the general trend of creating a thriving and artistically rewarding industry which far surpassed its original purpose.

Outside the Home Arts, the Compton class contributed to the 1906 'Artists at Work' exhibition held in London. Mrs Watts also supplied designs for decorative bookbindings to bookbinder E. Gertrude Farran of Norfolk Street, London that were shown at the 1906 and 1910 Arts and Crafts Exhibition Society exhibitions. Both Mary and George Watts moved in prominent artistic circles of the day. In 1901 art student Vanessa Stephen is listed as visiting Limnerslease, possibly the young Vanessa Bell. Aside from all her other commitments, Mary Watts acted as President of Miss Farmer's club for girls employed as artists' models, which was reorganised in 1911 at 46 Markham Square, Chelsea. Mrs Watts was supported in her role by Mrs Lewis F. Day, Miss Una Taylor and others. Although G.F. Watts has remained the subject of books and exhibitions, Mary's achievements remain largely neglected.

WEAR, MAUD MARIAN (1873-1955)

Painter. Born in London. The daughter of Frederick Erasmus Wear (b.1846), a wine merchant's clerk and later a newspaper correspondent, and Alice (b.1851). Her father originated from Huddersfield, Yorkshire, her mother from New Cross, London. The third of at least four children (Kate, Edith, Maud and Blanche). Raised in Hackney, London. Educated privately. By at least 1891 she was living in Eastbourne, Sussex where she was a student. She returned to London to study at the Royal Academy schools between 1896 and 1901, living with her parents. Won a silver medal at the Royal Academy for painting the draped figure. Became a painter in oils and watercolours and a miniaturist. Produced mainly portraits and figures, but other subjects too.

Wear exhibited her work, including at the Royal Academy (45 works, 1900-49), the International Society of Sculptors, Painters & Gravers, the New English Art Club, the Glasgow Art Gallery, the Walker Art Gallery, Liverpool, the Paris Salon and in Leeds and Oldham. Exhibited works included: Mrs F.E. Wear, A Peasant Girl, The Red Shawl, Much Study is a Weariness of the Flesh and The Mother of Aubrey Beardsley (miniature). Taught at the London County Council Central School of Arts and Crafts. One of her pupils was Winifred Wild who also became a successful miniature painter, and a stained glass designer. Works illustrated in The Studio and Colour. For example, her The Little Schoolgirl appeared on the front cover of Colour, February 1929. Her portrait of Mrs Lambert was illustrated in Royal Academy Pictures. She moved a number of times during her career, living in London, Wiltshire, Dorset, Kent, Sussex and Gloucestershire. Worked until shortly before her death. Died in Hove, Sussex, aged 80.

WEBB, JOSEPHINE (1853-1924)

Painter. Born in Dublin, Ireland. One of a large family of Quakers. Her father was Thomas Webb. He ran a boot and shoe manufacturers and gents outfitters on Sackville Street Upper which was known as Thomas Webb & Fisher. Her mother was Mary. Two of the Webb daughters ran a wool shop next door to their father's business. Josephine was educated at the Alexandra College. Then studied at the Queen's Institute. At the latter, she won two silver medals for drawing in 1875. She showed early talent. Several of the family were artistic, but Josephine was the only one to become a professional artist. In the late 1870s, she visited Paris, studying at the Academie Julian at the same time as Sarah Purser. Had a studio in Dublin for much of her career. Produced portraits, flowers and landscapes. Also produced line & wash drawings, possibly influenced by Ralph Caldecott, and did charcoal drawings with a wash colour. She worked rapidly and directly. Exhibited her work, including at the Royal Hibernian Academy (30 works, 1880-1921), with the Watercolour Society of Ireland (including in 1902) and with the Dublin Arts Club. Exhibited at the Sketching Club exhibition of 1900. Also in 1900, she held a small exhibition in her studio of watercolours of French and Irish scenery. Held a one-woman exhibition in Dublin in 1913. Exhibited works included: Sir John Barrington, D.L., Lord Mayor, To Let for Building, The Wayfarer, The Dodder, near Templeogue Bridge and Marigolds. Known to have been sketched by John Butler Yeats.

WEBB, KATHARINE - SEE ADAMS, K.

WEBB, MARJORIE - SEE LANCE, M.

WEBB, MILLIE CECILIA (1888-1957)

Sculptor / Miniature Painter. Also known as Cecilia. Born in Stamford, Lincolnshire in April 1888. The daughter of architect Morpeth Webb (1861-1930) and Florence Sophia Cousins (1864-1949). The eldest of at least three children. Her sister Mahala (b.1887, known as Dora) became a

painter and sculptor. Her brother John Adams Webb (b.1892) became a land surveyor. As a child, she lived in Lincolnshire, but the family subsequently lived in Melton Mowbray, Leicestershire. She remained there for the rest of her life, living at the family home in Burton Road with Dora until her death in January 1957. Her mother was a teacher of painting at an art school. This undoubtedly influenced both Dora and Cecilia to study art. Cecilia is listed as a miniature painter on the 1911 national census, but became better known as a sculptor. Worked in plaster, clay and bronze, producing groups, figures and heads. Exhibited her work principally through the 1930s to the 1950s. Showed at the Royal Scottish Academy (1948-52), the Royal Academy (1944-53), the Royal Glasgow Institute (1946-55), the Society of Women Artists (1949-56) and the Paris Salon. Also exhibited at the Nottingham Castle Museum in the 1930s and with the Nottingham Society of Artists. Exhibited works included: Security (statuette group, plaster), Who Said Sugar (group, bronze), Little Lamb Who Made Thee? (statuette group, bronze), Miss Phoebe (baked clay) and Me and My Dog (baked clay). Cecilia left her £1600 estate to Dora, who survived her by some 16 years.

WELCH, LILIAN MARGERY - SEE DRING, L.M.

WELD, EULALIA H. - SEE SWINSTEAD, E.H.

WELLINGTON, IRENE (1904-84)

Calligrapher / Illuminator. Born at Lydd, Kent in October 1904. The daughter of Charles Edward Bass, a farmer, and Julia Elizabeth, both of whom originated from Lydd. The youngest of at least six children (Dorothy, Walter, Helen, Henrietta, Rhoderic and Irene). Raised in Lydd. Educated at the Ashford County School, Kent. Studied at the Maidstone College of Art, Kent, and at the Royal College of Art, London under Edward Johnston. Elected an Associate of the Royal College of Art. Became an expert calligrapher and illuminator carrying out numerous commissions. Those included the Oxfordshire and Buckinghamshire Light Infantry Roll of Honour for the Second World War. Also, an illuminated address for President Auriol as well as work for the British Council and H.M. Queen Juliana. Examples of her work can be found in the permanent collections of Christ Church Cathedral, Oxford and Winchester College.

From 1932 until at least 1943, Wellington taught at the Edinburgh College of Art. From 1944 until at least 1959, she taught at the London County

Council Central School of Arts and Crafts. In 1929 she was elected to the Society of Scribes and Illuminators. An example of her work, a poem by Kathleen Raine, was given in an article about the Society written by fellow member Claire Evans for The Studio, Vol.138, July 1949, pp.1-5. Wellington took part in celebrating 25 years of the Society in November 1945. In 1974 she was elected a Member of the Art Workers' Guild. One of her pupils was Ann Hechle (b.1939) who also became a Member of the Society of Scribes and Illuminators. Another was Joan Pilsbury (b.1926). Irene exhibited her work at the exhibitions of the Arts and Crafts Exhibition Society. Also, with the Society of Scottish Artists and the Society of Scribes and Illuminators. Examples of her work were also illustrated in the Studio Year Book and the King Penguin Book of Scripts by Alfred Fairbank. In 1944 Irene married Hubert L. Wellington at Henley, Oxfordshire. She died in Surrey in September 1984, aged 79.

WELLS, LILIAN G. - SEE PARKER, L.G.

WELLS, MADELINE RACHEL (1874-1959)
Decorative Artist / Painter. Also sometimes Madeleine. Born in India, the daughter of William Henn Holmes of the Indian Civil Service. Educated at home. Studied at the Westminster School of Art under Mouat Loudon, and at the London School of Art under Frank Brangwyn. Awarded the Brangwyn Medal at the latter. Studied lithography at the Central School of Arts and Crafts, London under Ernest Jackson. Became a successful decorative artist and painter. Worked in oils, watercolours, tempera and pastels. Subjects included portraits, landscapes, figures, animals and still life. Also produced watercolours on silk. Based in London, at the St Albans Studios, Kensington and at Palace Gardens Terrace. Painted on her travels, including in Spain, France and Vienna.

Exhibited her work, including at the Royal Society of British Artists. In 1917, for example, she showed Backgammon Players. Brangwyn was then President of the Society. Also exhibited with the Society of Painters in Tempera, the Society of Graphic Art, the Royal Institute of Oil Painters and the Society of Women Artists (69 works, 1919-60). Also, the Royal Institute of Painters in Watercolours, the Societe Nationale des Beaux-Arts, the Paris Salon (1948), the Walker Art Gallery, Liverpool, the Royal Academy (1931-43) and in Bournemouth, Derby and Hull. Other exhibited works included: Music (tempera), The Magic Hunt (tempera), Atlantis (tempera) and Grande Palace. Decorative works included: Visit of the Magi and John the Baptist, decorations for the Church of St Elizabeth, Marloes Road, London. Also, a frieze of the seasons for St Mary's Hall, Putney.

Her works were reproduced a number of times in Colour and The Studio. For example, her Judith was illustrated in Colour, June 1919. Other works appeared in the same journal in October 1922, p.63, in June-July 1924, p.6 (The Boating Party), in February 1926, p.6 (oil in colour), and in February 1929, p.9 & p.13 (a portrait and Wild Duck). Later, in June 1931, one of her portraits in oils was illustrated in Colour. Works acquired by the Rotherham Art Gallery and Lady Hamilton. Wells was elected an Associate of the Societe Nationale des Beaux-Arts in 1913. Elected a Member of the Royal Society of British Artists, a Member of the Society of Graphic Art, a Member of the Society of Women Artists (1922-59) and a Member of the Society of Painters in Tempera. In 1903, Wells married architect and artist Robert Douglas Wells at Chelsea Holy Trinity. Born in 1875, the son of an architect, Robert Wells was also a student at the London School of Art. He too was elected a Member of the Royal Society of British Artists as well as a Fellow of the Royal Institute of British Architects. The couple remained largely in London. Madeline died first, in Kensington in December 1959, aged 86.

WEST, CICELY (1897-1977)
Illuminator. Was Victoria Cicely, known as Cicely. Born in Northwood, Middlesex. The daughter of Joseph Walter West (1860-1933) and Ada Caroline Wise (1861-1952). Her father originated from Hull, but spent most of his life in Middlesex. He was a painter, illustrator and lithographer, and occasionally collaborated with Cicely. He was also a Member of the Royal Society of Painters in Watercolours. Cicely was one of at least four daughters (Iris, Marjorie, Sylvia and Cicely), all raised in Middlesex. She was educated at the St Paul's School, London. Then studied at the London County Council Central School of Arts and Crafts. Worked in a specialised field as an illuminator and a worker in script with raised gold. She lived with her parents in Middlesex until their deaths. Still active after her father's death. Cicely died in London in December 1977, aged 80. Her work varied, and included a Presentation Address for the City of Winchester to H.R.H. the Prince of Wales. Also, an arts club gift book, diplomas for the Royal Institute of British Architects, and an illuminated manuscript of Virgil's Georgics executed in collaboration with her father. Other commissions were carried out for Cambridge University.

Exhibited her work occasionally, including at the Society of Women Artists (1925), at various arts and crafts exhibitions, in Paris and at Wembley. Her script of Idylls of the King was reproduced in an illustrated catalogue for the Wembley exhibition. Elected a Member of the Society of Scribes and Illuminators.

WEST, NAN (b.1904)

Painter / Decorator / Illustrator. Was Katharine Ann, known as Nan. Born in London in October 1904. The daughter of Herbert Edgar West (b.1870) and Mary Theresa Gielgud (b.1874). Her father was a stockbroker. One of at least two children (also Herbert). Raised in London. Studied in London at the Byam Shaw School of Art and at the Slade School. Produced watercolour landscapes, some of which, including Pitti Palace, Florence and Lavenham, were exhibited at the Goupil Gallery in 1930 / 31. Also exhibited at the New English Art Club. Produced mural decorations. Reflected a sense of humour in her work on occasions. Exhibited some of her sketches for wall decoration in social as well as private rooms at the Mansard Annexe in 1931. In 1933 she married David W. Robertson in Rochford, Essex. Based in London prior to her marriage.

WESTRUP, ETHEL KATE (1885-1928)

Painter / Ceramicist. Known as Kate. Born in Hornsey, London. The daughter of Robert John Westrup, a flour factor, and Fanny. One of at least eight children (George, Philip, Nellie, Margaret, Mabel, Ethel, Willie and Emily). Raised in Hornsey. In her 20s, she was based at Fernhill Manor, New Milton, Hampshire with her mother and her sisters Emily and Nellie. She later lived in Cornwall, where she died, aged only 43. Presumed to have had some training in art. A naturally gifted artist. Produced oil paintings and drawings, mainly animal subjects. Sometime after 1911, she moved to Lamorna, Cornwall with Emily (1870-1960). Neither ever married. In the early 1920s, Kate founded the Lamorna Pottery with jewellery designer Ella Naper (1886-1972). Both made their own pots, but shared a workshop and ran the business as a co-operative. Kate used animal designs in her pottery. Lamorna wares were sold through various outlets, including galleries and exhibitions. Some were sold through the Collectors' Gallery in Manchester, some in Liverpool and some through the Newlyn Art Gallery. The pottery closed when Kate died in 1928.

Emily Westrup continued to live at Lamorna. She wrote stories and nursery rhymes for children and occasionally illustrated children's books. Nellie Westrup also illustrated children's books. Kate exhibited her paintings at the Royal Academy (1910) and the Society of Women Artists (1922-25). Exhibited works included: The Pups, Ploughing Our Potatoes, Reuben Among the Daisies and Goats and Gorse. Elected an Associate of the Society of Women Artists (1923-29). Kate also exhibited red chalk drawings of dogs at the Old Dudley Art Society's spring exhibition at the Alpine Club in 1912. Some of her works appeared in Punch (1914) and in The Rosebud Annual (1908).

WHALL, VERONICA (1887-1967)

Stained Glass Artist / Painter. Born at Stourbridge near Dorking, Surrey in April 1887. The daughter of renown stained glass artist Christopher Whitworth Whall (1849-1924) and portrait painter Florence Chaplin (1850-1936). Whall and Chaplin married in 1884. They had five children, Christopher, Veronica, Hew Bernard, Etheldreda and Louis. Hew, known as Bernard, initially became an actor. Veronica was raised in Dorking initially, then moved to Hammersmith, London. She remained there for much of her life and career. In London, her father became a teacher in stained glass at the L.C.C. Central School of Arts and Crafts, also teaching at the Royal College of Art from 1898.

Veronica studied at the Central School of Arts and Crafts from a young age, designing a figure of St Catherine at the age of 13 which was used in one of the stained glass windows made by her father for Gloucester Cathedral's Lady Chapel. The scheme of windows for the Cathedral was begun by her father in 1897 and is one of his finest commissions. Veronica also studied at her father's studio at Ravenscourt Park, learning about stained glass work. She acted as a model for some of Whall's figures, and later as his secretary. She also helped her brother Bernard to run the Stonebridge Press, a small private printing press. Became a highly competent designer of stained glass, also producing watercolour paintings and black & white sketches.

One of Veronica's earliest windows, designed with her father, was made for the Chapel at Greenwich Girls' School, Connecticut, U.S.A. (1913). In 1922 she and her father founded the firm of Whall & Whall Ltd, appointing Edward Woore, Whall's former pupil, as manager and co-designer for a short time. Veronica was director of the firm. They carried out a number of important commissions including St Christopher (1924), a stained glass window for Sproughton Church, Suffolk, and a window for St Catherine's

Church, Irchester, Northamptonshire (1924). Christopher Whall died in December 1924 and Veronica took over the firm with her brother, Christopher John Whall. The firm continued to thrive, with commissions including a window for Gloucester Cathedral dedicated to their father (1925-26) and windows for Carlisle Cathedral, Leicester Cathedral and for churches as far away as Australia and New Zealand.

The firm's later commissions included for St Peter's Church, Swinton, Manchester (1932, site of an earlier window designed by Christopher and Veronica Whall with Edward Woore, 1912), and for St Mary's Church, Osterley, Middlesex (1948). The firm also completed the scheme begun by Christopher Whall senior for Gloucester Cathedral. Veronica also worked on King Arthur's Great Halls, Tintagel, Cornwall, built in the 1930s by Frederick Thomas Glasscock as the home of the Order of the Fellowship of the Knights of the Round Table of King Arthur. Inside, the Hall contains 73 stained glass windows by Veronica Whall, executed between 1930 and 1933.

Veronica was a highly competent book illustrator and mural decorator too. During her career, she was elected a Member of the Arts and Crafts Exhibition Society. She exhibited at the Society's exhibitions, including in 1910 with her father. Exhibited elsewhere, including Brussels, Ghent, Liverpool and at Wembley. Exhibited at the 1914 Exposition des Arts Decoratifs in Paris. Exhibited at the Royal Academy between 1911 and 1945. Exhibits included designs for an east window in the Memorial Chapel at Brickenden, for a window at Barnwood Church, Gloucester and for a window at Denbigh Church. One of her exhibits was a design executed with F.R. Gadsby, also of the Ravenscourt Park studio, exhibited in 1941.

Veronica was the subject of an article in Stained Glass (Journal of the Stained Glass Association of America), Vol.XX, No.1, Spring / Summer 1935, pp.10-14, titled Glass, Lead and Light. More recently, works were included in an exhibition Women Stained Glass Artists of the Arts and Crafts Movement, William Morris Gallery, London, 1985-86. Various watercolours and black & white sketches were reproduced during her career. Some of her cartoons and designs were acquired for the permanent collections of the Victoria & Albert Museum, London and at Brussels. In 1953 Veronica retired, closing Whall & Whall Ltd. With her brother Christopher, she moved to a cottage in Great Staughton, Cambridgeshire. She died there, aged 80. Her mother's sister was sculptor Alice Mary Chaplin.

WHALLEY, MINNIE (active 1910s-1920s)
Painter / Metalworker / Embroideress. Born in Gloucestershire. Educated at Cheltenham and the Clifton High School. Studied at the Gloucester School of Art, the London County Council Central School of Arts and Crafts, and in Geneva. Produced paintings in oils, watercolours and tempera, including landscapes and still life. Also produced embroideries and works in pewter. Became art mistress at Dundee, at the Truro High School, Cornwall and at Penzance, Cornwall. She became associated with artistic activities in St Ives, Cornwall. Exhibited at the Royal West of England Academy (13 works, 1919-28). Exhibited works included: Moorland, Zennor, Old St Ives and Pink Roses.

WHEELER, ELLEN KATHLEEN (1884-1977)
Sculptor. Born in Reading, Berkshire. The daughter of Frederick Wheeler and Susan Ellen. Her father was a manager of the potteries. One of at least eight children (Ellen, Agnes, Marjorie, Lucy, Beatrice, Susan, Enid and Frederick). Raised in Berkshire. Studied under Esther Moore and Frank Calderon, and at the Slade School, London. Produced groups and statuettes in bronze. Exhibited her work, including at the Royal Scottish Academy (1911), the Royal Academy (1906-11) and the Salon des Artistes Francais. Exhibited works included: Death and Sleep (bronze), An Undine (statuette, bronze) and Equestrian Portrait Group (bronze). In 1914 she emigrated to America, where she had a studio. Specialised in animals, including a series of leading thoroughbreds of America. Until she left England, she lived with her parents at Tilehurst, Berkshire.

WHEELER, MURIEL (1888-1979)
Sculptor / Painter. Born in Shrewsbury. The daughter of Arthur Ward Bourne, a canal district supervisor, and Martha (or Pattie). Her parents originated from Newcastle. She had at least one sibling, Eva (b.c.1883). Raised in Shrewsbury, Shropshire and Wolverhampton. Educated privately. Studied under Edouard Lanteri (of the Royal College of Art), and Robert Jackson Emerson, F.R.B.S., who had a studio in Wolverhampton. Became a painter in oils and watercolours of still life, portraits, figures and landscapes. Also produced sculptures, mainly statuettes, heads, masks and panels in bronze, lead, terracotta and pewter.

Wheeler exhibited her work from at least 1919 until at least 1973. Exhibited at the Royal Glasgow Institute (1933-44), the Royal Academy

(60 works, 1919-69), with the Society of Portrait Sculptors, the Royal Birmingham Society of Artists and at various smaller galleries including Leeds. At the Society of Women Artists, she showed 108 works between 1928 and 1973. Exhibited sculptures included: The Source (three-quarter figure), Chariot of Aphrodite (lead panel), Infant Jesus and Madonna (statuette group, terracotta) and The Viscountess Sandon (head). Her paintings included: The Artist's Husband (oil on gesso), Reclining Nude (oil) and Lilies (watercolour). Executed several notable portrait works, including of Dame Adeline Genee Isitt, D.B.E., Hon. D. Mus. (Lon.), C.D., M.I. et A., B.M.I., P.R.A.D. Elected an Associate of the Society of Women Artists (1934-38), a Member (1939-76) and an Honorary Retired Member (1977-79). Acted as Vice President of the Society (1947-48) and President (1968-76). Elected a Member of the Society of Portrait Sculptors (founded 1953). Elected an Associate of the Royal Society of British Sculptors in 1942, and a Fellow in 1945. Also acted on the Society's Council (1946-48). A Member of the Soroptimist Club, London.

Wheeler worked mainly in London during her career, using studios at Chelsea, Gunter Grove, Tregunter Road and Cathcart Road. Latterly based in Mayfield, Sussex. She died in Sussex, aged 91, in December 1979. Her Mother and Child was purchased by the Newport Art Gallery. Some of her works were reproduced in Homes & Gardens, the Builder and the Architects' Journal. Her Carol Rosemary, shown at the second exhibition of the Society of Portrait Sculptors in 1955, was illustrated in The Studio, Vol.149, April 1955, p.142. In 1918 Muriel married sculptor Charles Thomas Wheeler (1892-1974) in Wolverhampton. He was the son of a journalist, and originated from Staffordshire. He was also buried there. As an art student, he was based in Wolverhampton and studied under Lanteri at the Royal College of Art. He was President of the Royal Society of British Sculptors (1944-49). They had at least two children, Neil in 1919 and Rosemary in 1927. Rosemary became an artist in oils, and exhibited her work at the Royal Academy (1951-63), the Society of Women Artists (1950-62) and elsewhere.

WHEELER, NORA CONSTANCE (1892-1967)

Artist / Illustrator. Born in Thrapston, Northamptonshire in May 1892. The daughter of William Essex (1858-1949) and Ada Mary Butcher (1858-1951). Her father was a master baker. Nora had at least one sibling, George.

Raised in Thrapston. She was educated at a private school in Kettering. Studied at the Hastings School of Art under Philip William Cole, E. Leslie Badham and Vincent H. Lines. Produced paintings in watercolours, including landscapes, and book illustrations. In 1916 she married Charles Edward Wheeler (1888-1950) in Thrapston. Born in Epping, he was in the 1st Royal Sussex Regiment but was also a clergyman. The couple had at least one son. They lived in St Leonards-on-Sea, Sussex. Nora exhibited her work occasionally, but mainly later in her career. Exhibited at the Society of Women Artists (1955-64) and abroad. Exhibited works included: Ramsgate, Come to the Fair and Fishing Boats, Chioggia. She produced illustrations for, for example, a book by C.A. John Hendry. Her work was in the permanent collection of The Nawab Salar Jung Collection. Nora died in Sussex, aged 74.

WHEELHOUSE, MARY VERMUYDEN (1868-1947)

Painter / Illustrator. Born in Leeds, Yorkshire. The daughter of Claudius G. Wheelhouse and Agnes Caroline. Her father, a surgeon, originated from Yorkshire, her mother from Lancashire. Had at least two siblings, Ethel and Caroline. Raised in Leeds, but later based in Filey, Scarborough and London at the Pomona Studios. Died in London. Studied in Paris for three years. Otherwise self-taught. Active as a painter from at least the late 1890s until at least 1933.

Her first success as an illustrator was with friend Christine Whyte. Together, they won a competition in The Bookman. They submitted a fairy story, The Adventures of Merrywink, with illustrations by Mary, which was published in 1906. Her second illustrated book was Les Maitres Sonneurs by George Sand for George Bell & Sons. Mary went on to illustrate a considerable number of books for Bell & Sons, including the stories of Mrs Ewing brought out in their Queen's Treasures Series. Other books illustrated by her, over a period of more than 15 years, included Mrs Ewing, Flat Iron For a Farthing (Bell, 1908), Elizabeth Gaskell, Cousin Phillis (Bell, 1908), Mary Baldwin, Holly House and Ridges Row (1908), Johann C. von Schmidt, Easter Eggs (1908), E.V. Lucas, Slowcoach (1910), Mary E. Phillips, Tommy Tregennis (1914), Amy Steadman, The Story of Florence Nightingale (1915) and Mrs Molesworth, Carrots (Bell, 1920). Mary exhibited her work, including at the Society of Women Artists (1901) and the Royal Academy (1896 & 1933). Exhibited works included: A Little Red Head, A Yorkshire Wold,

Twilight and The Towers and Roofs of Asolo. Exhibited some of her book illustrations at the Women's International Art Club exhibition for 1910, held at the Grafton Galleries.

WHELPTON, BARBARA FANNY - SEE CROCKER, B.F.

WHILE, MARY ETHEL (1878-1954)

Sculptor. Known as Ethel. Born in Mitcham, Surrey. The daughter of James Henry Collingwood, an architect and Civil Servant at the Office of Works Examiners, and Mary E. Oswin. Her parents originated from Lincoln. One of at least six children (James, William, Francis, Florence, Alice and Mary). The family was affluent enough to employ servants. Mary was educated at the Wimbledon High School. Studied at the Goldsmiths' College of Art, London. Became a sculptor of statuettes, busts and heads. Worked mainly in bronze. Exhibited at the Royal Glasgow Institute (1918), the Royal Academy (12 works, 1912-31), in Bristol and at the Society of Women Artists (1924). Exhibited works included: Ennui (sculpture), Music (statuette, bronze), The Little Schoolgirl (bronze) and May Collingwood (bust). In 1904 she married Harry (also Henry) Samuel While (1871-1936) in Deptford. He originated from West Bromwich and is initially listed as a gas engineer. However, he also worked as a sculptor, and exhibited his work at the Royal Glasgow Institute (1914) and the Royal Academy (1911-22). The couple lived and worked in London for much of the time, but also spent time in Kent and Middlesex. They occasionally collaborated. One of Mary's works, The Scroll of Honour, was illustrated in Academy Architecture and Academy Pictures. Harry While died in Middlesex in October 1936, aged 65. Mary died in Middlesex in September 1954, aged 75.

WHITE, BEATRICE MARY
(active 1910s-1920s)

Painter / Chinese Lacquer Worker. An oil and watercolour painter who also produced decorative lacquered goods of all descriptions. Exhibited at the Paris Salon, the Walker Art Gallery, Liverpool and the Society of Women Artists (1920-27). Exhibited at the Mendoza Galleries in 1919. Exhibited works included: On the Road to Fawley and Mist and Heat. Works reproduced in various arts journals and periodicals in England and abroad. Elected an Associate of the Society of Women Artists (1926-29). Based in London, in Chelsea and at The Old Well House Studio, Betchworth, Surrey. In 1923 she advertised tuition at The Old Well House in The Studio magazine.

WHITE, CLARE MAY EMERSON
(1903-97)

Painter / Designer / Writer. Born in Sidmouth, Devon. The daughter of Arthur Thomas White, a bank clerk, and May Isabel. Her father originated from Kent, her mother from Deptford. Had at least one sister, Margaret. Raised in Sidmouth. Educated in Tavistock and Dartmouth. Her mother died whilst Clare was still a child. Her father encouraged her in her art and education. She studied domestic science at Limpley Stoke. Then went to a finishing school at Lausanne, Switzerland where she studied history of art. She subsequently went to the Torquay School of Art between 1920 and 1923, working from life models. Influenced by Japanese design early in her career. Won a bronze medal at the Royal Drawing Society exhibition in London for a design for a tea cosy. Spent part of 1923 living in Paris before travelling Europe. Became a decorative artist and designer. Her watercolours were often brightly coloured, with a black outline, sometimes revealing a sense of humour.

White exhibited her work, including at the Society of Women Artists (1932-51), the Royal Academy (1934), the Paris Salon and at various London societies and galleries. Exhibited works included: In the Shadow of the Cathedral, Old Poultry Cross, Salisbury, Music and Flowers and Porte St Denis, Paris. In 1935 she designed scenery for a production at Paignton's Palace Theatre, designing other scenery during her career. Spent the Second World War in Paris, where she took a degree in economics. She was fluent in five languages. In 1949, having spent time living in Paignton, Devon, she moved to St Ives, Cornwall. There, she became a Member of the St Ives Arts Club, writing plays and designing posters and scenery. She was the first woman President of the Arts Club. Also joined the St Ives Society of Artists, serving on its committee, writing reviews for the local newspapers. Elected a Member of the Society from 1949 to 1957, and from 1969 to 1982. Exhibited her work with the Society, including in its touring exhibitions. Held at least one exhibition of her work at the Piazza Studios in St Ives. The Salthouse Gallery, St Ives held three shows of her work in the 1980s. After her death, in Cornwall at the age of 93, her work was shown at the Rotherham Art Gallery and at the Walker's Gallery.

WHITE, ELEANOR JOAN - SEE ELLIS, E.J.

WHITE, ERICA MILDRED (1904-91)

Sculptor / Painter. Born in Ealing, Middlesex in June 1904. The daughter of Frederick Charles White (b.1859), a solicitor, and Mildred Sarah Hutchings (b.1874). Her father originated from Somerset, her mother from Surrey. Had at least two elder brothers, Cyril (b.1895) and Geoffrey (b.1896). Raised in Middlesex. Educated at the St George's School, Harpenden, Hertfordshire. Studied at the Slade School, London, winning a two-year sculpture scholarship and a painting prize. Then moved to the London County Council Central School of Arts and Crafts where she won the British Institute Scholarship in sculpture. Subsequently went to the Royal Academy schools where she won bronze and silver medals as well as the Feodora Gleichen Memorial Award. Also awarded a London University Diploma in Fine Arts. Became a sculptor of busts, heads and figures in clay, bronze and stone, and a painter of portraits in oils and pastels. Based in London, Hampstead and The Triangle Studio, Kingsdown, Kent. Latterly based in East Sussex where she died aged 86. Exhibited her work, including at the Royal Academy (1925-59), the Royal Glasgow Institute (1925), the Society of Women Artists (1950-51), the Brighton Fine Art Galleries and in Bournemouth. Exhibited works included: The Black Hat (pastel), The Ugly Duckling (bust), Sheba's Daughter (oil) and The Imp (head, bronze). One of her more important works was a head of the late Rt Rev. A.F. Winnington Ingram, P.C., K.C.V.O., D.D., LL.D., Bishop of London, 1901-39.

WHITE, GERTRUDE (1859-1920)

Woodcarver. Was Annie Gertrude, known as Gertrude. Carved the chancel, clergy and choir stalls, designed by Messrs C.H. and N.A. Rew of Berkhampstead and presented to the Parish Church of St Mary, Hemel Hempstead, Hertfordshire by the Misses Anne and Helen Varney. Worked in oak, the carvings were redolent of the rich and elaborate Gothic style. Sections of the stalls were illustrated in the Art Workers' Quarterly, July 1905, pp.116-117.

Gertrude White was born in Hemel Hempstead and died there in March 1920, aged 61. The daughter of William White (d.1890) and Mary Anne (d.1899). Her father was a draper and silk merchant. Gertrude was one of at least eight children (William, Mary, Charles, Jessie, Gertrude, Barnard, Katherine and Allan), all raised in Hemel Hempstead. She lived with her parents, then with her widowed mother. After her mother's death, she lived with her sisters Jessie and Katherine, still in Hemel Hempstead. Both Gertrude and Jessie were woodcarvers, whilst Katherine was a music teacher, all working from home. Sometime after 1901 Jessie became Principal of a girls' school, South Hill in Heath Lane, Hemel Hempstead, and Gertrude lived with her at the school. Both still worked as woodcarvers, both then in their 50s. Probably taught locally.

WHITE, GWENDOLINE BEATRICE (1901-86)

Painter / Illustrator. Known as Gwen. Born in Exeter, Devon. The daughter of Sebastian Moreton White (b.1869) and Ethel Lena (b.1876). Her father, who originated from Winchester, was a motor engineer. Her mother originated from Exeter. The second of at least four children (Muriel, Gwendoline, Francis and Viola). Her siblings were also born in Exeter, and all were raised there. Gwendoline was educated at The Maynard School, Exeter. Then studied at the Bournemouth School of Art under H.E. Crocket, Leslie Moffat Ward (teacher of pictorial design) and Geoffrey Alan Baker (Principal at Bournemouth). Also studied at the Royal College of Art, London under Professors Randolph Schwabe (of the London Group), Malcolm Osborne (Professor of Engraving) and Ernest William Tristram (Professor of Design). Elected an Associate of the Royal College of Art. White became a painter in watercolours and tempera, and a book illustrator. Subjects included landscapes and portraits.

White exhibited her work, including at the Royal Academy (1929-51, 1959-69), and at the galleries of Liverpool, Derby, Bournemouth, Darlington, Gateshead, Kettering, Norwich, Dudley, Worcester, Birmingham, Poole and elsewhere. Exhibited works included: Poole Quay (tempera), The Visitor (tempera), Cinnabar Moths (tempera) and The Late Sir J. Voce Moore. Produced illustrations for a number of her own publications including Ancient and Modern Dolls (A&C Black, 1928), The Toys' Adventures at the Zoo (A&C Black, 1929), Ladybird, Ladybird (Murray, 1938), A Book of Toys (King Penguin, 1946), Eight Little Frogs (National Magazine Co., 1947), Dolls of the World (1962), Perspective for Artists, Architects and Designers (1968) and Antique Toys and Their Background (1971). Illustrated books by other authors including Rhoda Power, Ten Minute Tales and Dialogue Stories (1943) and Enid Blyton, Tales of Green Hedges (1946). White designed children's programmes and annuals for the BBC, and designed catalogues for the National Book League. Elected a Member of the National Book League. Taught book illustration and perspective part-time at the Farnham and St Albans Schools of Art. In 1934 Gwen married painter and stained glass designer Charles Rupert Moore (d.1982) in Dorset. He originated from Doncaster and was also an Associate of the Royal College of Art (1928). They had three sons. Gwen lived in various places during her life and career, including London, Radlett in Hertfordshire, Middlesex and Buckinghamshire. She died in Hertfordshire in November 1986, aged 84.

WHITE, GWENDOLINE MABEL (1903-73)

Writer / Illuminator / Wood Engraver / Painter. Born in Bridgnorth, Shropshire. The daughter of Arthur Edmund Jones, a baker and confectioner, and Sarah Ann Allbutt. Her father originated from Bridgnorth, her mother from Staffordshire. One of at least four children (Edmund, Gwendoline, Edna and Grace). All were raised in Bridgnorth. Gwendoline studied at the Royal College of Art, London. Elected an Associate of the Royal College of Art in 1925. Also studied at the Kidderminster School of Art. Produced paintings and wood engravings, and worked as an illuminator. Worked in various materials including tempera. Various subjects including landscapes and still life. In 1930 she married Adam Seaton White (b.1893) in Richmond, Surrey. He originated from Bangor and was a painter, sculptor and craftsman. He was also Principal of the Cheltenham School of Art, Gloucestershire. The couple lived mainly in Cheltenham, where Gwendoline died, aged 70. Both exhibited with the Cheltenham Group. Gwendoline also exhibited at the Royal Academy (1938) and with the New English Art Club. Exhibited works included: Pool at Cowley, Gloucestershire and Flower-Piece (tempera).

WHITE, HESTER MABEL (1871-1949)

Sculptor / Decorative Artist. Known as Mabel. Born in Stonehouse near Stroud in Gloucestershire. The daughter of William White, Vicar of Stonehouse, and Hester. One of at least five children (William, Gertrude, Arthur, Hester Mabel and Edith). All were raised in Stonehouse. William became a Cambridge scholar and a solicitor. Edith became a teacher. Mabel studied sculpture in London under Oscar Waldmann. Based in London thereafter, but also in Oxford. Died in Middlesex. She lived with Edith in Clarendon Road, Notting Hill for a time. Produced statuettes, busts, medallions and decorative panels in marble, bronze, plaster, copper, silver, sandstone, pewter and wood. Worked consistently for over 50 years, exhibiting her work from at least 1898 until at least 1948, immediately prior to her death. Exhibited her work, including at the Royal Academy (1898-1948), the Royal Hibernian Academy (1909) and the Royal Glasgow Institute (1908-11). Exhibited works included: The First Snowdrop (statuette, marble), A Nereid (statuette, bronze), The Thoughts of Childhood (bust, marble) and The Sleep of Brunnhilde (panel, copper). Noted in M.H. Spielmann, British Sculpture and Sculptors of To-day, London, Cassell & Co. Ltd, 1901.

WHITE, JESSIE MABEL P. - SEE DEARMER, J.M.P.

WHITE, MABEL REDINGTON (1888-1974)

Painter / Book Illustrator. Born in Woodford, Essex. The daughter of Frederick George Peacock and Mary Ann. Her father, a hide and leather broker, originated from Middlesex. Her mother originated from Hertfordshire. Had at least one sibling, Philip Redington Peacock. Educated at Neuville House. Studied at the Hornsey School of Art, at the King's College and at the Royal Academy schools, London. Became a painter of portraits and decorative pieces in oils and watercolours, and a book illustrator. Exhibited her work, including at the Royal Academy (1916-47), the Paris Salon, the Society of Women Artists (1911-31) and the Royal Institute of Oil Painters. Also, with the International Society of Sculptors, Painters & Gravers, at the Walker Art Gallery, Liverpool and the Royal Institute of Painters in Watercolours. Exhibited works included: The Artist's Grandfather, The Connoisseur, Woman's World and Divided Attention (watercolour). Her Summer Holidays was illustrated in Colour. One of her designs, for a miniature ceiling painting, was illustrated in The Studio. In 1917, Mabel married portrait painter Clarence Alfred Burke White (1885-1971). He was born in Fulham, the son of a commercial clerk. He studied at the Royal Academy schools at the same time as Mabel. They had at least one son and one daughter. They spent time living in Chiswick, but were later based in Essex. Clarence White died in Essex, as did Mabel, both aged 86.

WHITE, MARY SMEATON LOW (1842-1928)

Sculptor. Born in Dunfermline, Fife in Scotland. The daughter of G.L. White and Jessie. One of at least four daughters (Mary, Blanche, Ida and

Jessie). Raised in Aberdour. Studied sculpture, probably in Scotland. Produced portrait medallions, models, busts and decorative items such as ornamental brackets. Exhibited her work, including at the Royal Scottish Academy (22 works, 1865-77) and the Royal Hibernian Academy (1868). Exhibited works included: Ivy Urchin (model for an ornamental bracket), Fern Fay (model for an ornamental bracket), The Venerable Archdeacon of Westmorland (medallion) and The Rev. James George, Gateshead-on-Tyne (bust). In 1880 Mary married Alexander Sandison, a congregational minister, in London. They had at least one child, Alexander. They lived in Middlesex, London and, latterly, Surrey. Mary died in Surrey, aged 86. She apparently gave up her career after her marriage. Jessie White (b.1850) became a landscape painter, exhibiting her work at the Royal Scottish Academy in 1871. Blanche White (b.1845) also became a painter, of flowers, and exhibited her work at the Royal Scottish Academy in 1870.

WHITE, OLIVE LUBECK (1874-1963)

Sculptor. Born in Kensington, London. The daughter of Frederick White, a manufacturer and later Company Chairman, and Emily. One of at least seven children (Margaret, Geoffrey, Frederick, Emily, Olive, Sylvia and Gladys). Raised in London. Studied sculpture under Edouard Lanteri at the Royal College of Art, London between 1903 and 1906. Produced groups and portrait works. Exhibited one work at the Royal Academy in 1903, The Soul's Uprising (group, R. Browning). In 1908 she married the Rev. Frederick Meyrick Jones (1867-1950) in Chelsea. Born in Blackheath, London, he was a Cambridge scholar. By at least 1911 the couple were living in Holt, Norfolk. Olive appears to have largely given up sculpture at that point. Aged 89, she died in Dorset, as did her husband. An album compiled by Olive as a student was recently sold, and contained photographs of women sculpture students at the Modelling School of the Royal College of Art, along with a photograph of her portrait bust of Gladys White.

WHITHAM, SYLVIA FRANCES (b.1878)

Painter / Wood Engraver / Etcher / Craftswoman / Bookbinder. Born in Kensington, London in October 1878. The daughter of Arthur Milman (b.1829) and Frances. Her father, a barrister and later Registrar of London University, originated from Reading, Berkshire, her mother from Middlesex. One of at least four daughters (Ida Mary, Sylvia Frances, Enid Alice and Maud), all

born between 1876 and 1887. Her father was some 20 years older than her mother, though her mother died young, leaving Arthur Milman with four girls living at home, and all in their 20s, when he was in his 70s. The family had money, and employed four servants. Sylvia and her sisters were raised in Kensington and she remained there into her 20s whilst studying at the Royal Academy schools. Later, she was based in Chelsea, and latterly at Combe Martin, Devon. She ventured into various areas of art and the decorative arts. Produced etchings, engravings, bookbindings, other craftwork and paintings of landscapes, still life and portraits. Exhibited her work, including at the Royal Academy (1906-09), the New English Art Club (from 1910), at Colnaghi's on Bond Street, and at various provincial galleries. Exhibited works included: Campanula and Larkspur, Chelsea, A Girl Reading, The Coming Storm and Arthur Milman, M.A., LL.D. Elected an Associate of the British Watercolour Society in 1923. A Member of the National Club, the Labour Club and The Penn Club (1917). Sylvia married John Mills Whitham. Still active as an artist into the 1930s.

WICKES, ANNIE MARY (1868-1941)

Illustrator / Decorative and Portrait Painter. Also sometimes Anne. Born in Bengal, India. The daughter of Thomas Haines Wickes, Engineer in Chief of the north-west provinces, and Mary Boyd. Had at least one sibling, George. Educated at the South Hampstead High School and privately. Based in London and Middlesex for much of her life and career, dying in Hampstead, aged 72. Studied at the Slade School, London and at the British Museum. Won prizes for life, landscape and composition painting. Exhibited her work, including at the Royal Academy (1915-22), the International Society of Sculptors, Painters & Gravers, the National Portrait Society, the Royal Society of Portrait Painters, the Royal Institute of Oil Painters, the Royal Society of British Artists and the Paris Salon. Also, with the Royal Scottish Academy (1920), the Society of Scottish Artists, the New English Art Club (1888-95) and the Decorative Arts and Crafts Exhibition (1922-23). Held one-woman shows at Colnaghi's. Exhibited works included: Lilac, Tadpole Hunting Time, The Artist's Mother (chalk drawing) and Cecily Draws My Portrait (chalk drawing). Works reproduced in Colour.

WICKHAM, HELEN FLORENCE (1884-1982)

Pottery Worker. Born in Batcombe, Somerset. The daughter of Henry Thomas Wickham and

Rosalind Ellen. Her father, who was considerably older than her mother, died in 1886 at the age of 66. Helen was then still only two years of age. She was an only child and lived with her widowed mother for some years. She was educated privately. Raised in Middlesex and London, remaining there for most of her life, dying in London, aged 98. Indications are that Helen studied at the Slade School, London since she contributed to the School's exhibition of 1909. She became known chiefly for her pottery statuettes. Used a studio at Westbere Road, Hampstead for a time. Exhibited her work, including at the Society of Women Artists (1918-29), at Wembley and in Liverpool. Also exhibited in Paris, winning a bronze medal at the Paris International Exhibition of 1925. Exhibited works included: Minuet, The Secret, Young April and Sir Martin Harvey in 'The Only Way'. The Manchester Museum acquired her pottery figure Mischief.

WILD, WINIFRED EVELINE (1887-1970)
Painter / Decorative Artist / Stained Glass Designer. Born in Chalfont St Giles, Buckinghamshire. The daughter of Frederick Wild, an electrical engineer, and Eveline. She had at least one younger sibling, Gladys. Raised in London. Educated at private school and at the Bedford Park High School. Studied at the London County Council Central School of Arts and Crafts under Ernest Jackson, Noel Rooke, Carl Parsons and Maud Wear. Spent much of her life and career thereafter in Bournemouth. Died in Dorset. Produced portrait, landscape, figure and flower paintings in oils and watercolours, and miniatures. Also, decorative panels, and various designs including for stained glass. Exhibited her work, including at the Royal Academy (1919-65), the Paris Salon, the Royal Society of Portrait Painters, the Royal Institute of Oil Painters, the Society of Miniaturists, in Liverpool and at the Society of Women Artists (48 works, 1950-69). Exhibited works included: Design For R.A.F. (watercolour), The Annunciation (oil panel), The Blue Beret (oil) and Winchester Cathedral (oil). Elected an Associate of the Society of Women Artists (1957-59) and a Member (1960-72). Also a Member of the Green Bus Group and of the Bournemouth Arts Club. Sometimes listed as W. Eveline. Works in the collection of the Bournemouth Art Gallery.

WILDE, HELEN MARY - SEE COATON, H.M.

WILDE, WENDELA - SEE BOREEL, W.

WILKES, GRACE - SEE DIGBY, G.

WILKINS, AMY A. - SEE SANDHEIM, A.A.

WILKINSON, MISS L.M.
Bookbinder / Book Decorator. A pupil of Douglas Cockerell. Helped to supervise the mending of some of the ancient Sessions Books for the Middlesex County Council in the early 1900s. Another of Cockerell's pupils, Miss M. Ewan, took over from Miss Wilkinson. Miss Wilkinson was noted in Sarah Treverbian Prideaux's volume Modern Bookbindings Their Design and Decoration, London, Archibald Constable & Co., 1906. She exhibited some of her own work at the Goupil Gallery in 1898.

WILKINSON, STELLA ANDRIA - SEE BURFORD, S.A.

WILLATT, EVELYN E.E.M. - SEE GIBBS, E.E.E.M.

WILLETT, DOROTHY E. - SEE GOW, D.E.

WILLIAMS, MADGE (1903-86)
Painter / Illustrator. Born in Bristol. The daughter of David Charles Williams, a clergyman, and Marion. Had at least two siblings, George and Barbara. Spent much of her early life at The Rectory at Halesworth, Suffolk. Died in Suffolk. Barbara Williams studied music. Madge studied art in London. Became a successful commercial artist. Produced countless designs for postcards, usually based on comic studies of children or fairyland. Also illustrated for children's annuals. For around 30 years she worked for J. Salmon, producing postcard designs and greetings cards. Also worked for the Art and Humour Company, E.T.W. Dennis, Inter Art, Raphael Tuck and Valentine. Worked on the Madge Williams Fairy Series.

WILLIS, ETHEL MARY (1874-1945)
Painter / Engraver. Born in Paddington, London in October 1874. The daughter of Thomas Willis, an art collector, grocer and tea dealer in the city, and Mary Jane. Had a younger sister, Eleanor Elizabeth Willis. Raised in London, worked there for most of her life, and died there in May 1945. Lived mainly with her parents at the family home in Park Road, Chiswick, and remained in the house until her death. As a child, she was

educated at the Notting Hill High School. Studied at the Royal College of Art and the Slade School, London, at the Academie Delecluse in Paris and with Madame Debillemont Chardon in Paris. Awarded a School of Art Scholarship and a National Award. Awarded an Art Masters' Certificate. Became a painter of miniatures, portraits, landscapes and flowers in oils and watercolours, and a drypoint engraver. Taught miniature and pastel painting at the London County Council Central School of Arts and Crafts from 1904. Prior to that, taught miniature painting at the Halford House School of Art in Richmond. Also carried out private tuition in miniature painting, advertising in the leading arts journals, including in 1908.

Willis exhibited her work, including at the Royal Academy (1900-36), the Royal Glasgow Institute (1921), the Society of Women Artists (51 works, 1907-39) and the Paris Salon. Also, with the Royal Society of Miniature Painters, the Society of Miniaturists, at the New Gallery, the Walker Art Gallery, Liverpool, in Toronto and with the Royal Institute of Painters in Watercolours. Exhibited works included: Violet, A Cardinal (miniature), A Neopolitan Fisherman (miniature), The Princesses Elizabeth and Margaret Rose (1935) and Bluebell Vista, Kew. Elected an Associate of the Royal Society of Miniature Painters in 1914. Elected an Associate of the Society of Women Artists (1935-39) and a Member (1940). A Member of the Society of Miniaturists. Also a Member of the Faculty of Arts and of the British Empire Society of Arts Club. Her miniature of Field Marshal Earl Roberts, V.C., K.G., was purchased by J.J. Kinsey from the Walker Art Gallery, Liverpool in 1914 and presented by him to the National Gallery, New Zealand. Princess Victoria purchased one of her miniatures from the Royal Institute of Painters in Watercolours in 1920. Her Summer's Bounty (miniature) was purchased from the Toronto National Exhibition of 1926 for the permanent collection of Toronto. Also executed a portrait of Sir Harry F. Hepburn, Sheriff of London, which was bequeathed to the Corporation of London. Also, a portrait of His Majesty King George and of Sir Douglas Haig. Works reproduced in Salon Pictures.

WILLOUGHBY, VERA (1873-post-1939)
Painter / Illustrator / Decorative Artist. Was Edith Vera Christie, known as Vera. Born in Norwood, Surrey. The daughter of James R. Christie and Emily. Her father, who originated from Woolwich, was the son of a Professor of Mathematics, and was himself a tutor of

mathematics. Her mother was born in the West Indies. Vera had at least five siblings, Alice, Laura and Robert who were born in Woolwich, Douglas who was born in London, and Emily who was born in Hampshire. Vera studied art in London from at least 1891. Became a watercolour painter of various subjects, a book decorator and illustrator and a designer of posters, book covers and theatre costumes. She designed advertisements, including one for perfume. Worked for the London Press Exchange.

Vera was initially based in London. In late 1905 she married Lewis Willoughby, a wealthy Canadian who was seven years her junior. She continued to work long after her marriage. They had at least one child, Vera, in 1908. Soon after the marriage, which took place in Fulham, the couple moved to The Church House, Slindon near Arundel in West Sussex. Vera exhibited her work over a period of more than 40 years. For example, she showed two works at the Royal Academy, Study of a Head in 1894 and Heloise in 1898. Exhibited with the Women's International Art Club, including in 1909. In October 1920 held an exhibition of her work at the Dorien Leigh Galleries, Bruton Street, London. In 1936 she exhibited at the Basilica Gallery, London, including some of her illustrations.

Vera illustrated and / or decorated a considerable number of books over at least three decades, from the 1910s to the late 1930s, some for Peter Davies Ltd. For example, The Humours of History (c.1914), Benjamin Disraeli, Popanilla and Other Tales (wrapper designs), F.A. Vane, Memoirs of a Lady of Quality (1925), George Farquhar, The Recruiting Officer (1926), Laurence Sterne, A Sentimental Journey (1927), J.M. Edmonds (transl.), Some Greek Love Poems (1929), L. Frank, Carl and Anna and Breath (1931) and E.E. Frisk (ed.), Lovely Laughter (1932). Worked on at least five of her own volumes, A Vision of Greece (1925), Horati Carminum Libri IV (1926), The Four Gospels (1927, Peter Davies Ltd), Sappho Revocate (1928) and The Poems of Catallus (1929). For A Vision of Greece, she completed the text, the illustrations and all the decoration. One of her illustrations for The Four Gospels was given in The Studio, Vol.94, 1927, p.322. Other works illustrated in Colour. For example, a poster design in May 1915, p.129 and Eros, September 1920. She was the subject of an article in The Studio, Vol.94, 1927, pp.322-326 by Robert Swann, which states that Vera Willoughby also produced watercolours on wood. She contributed to The Bystander. May have returned to London later in her career. Her death remains difficult to trace. The subject of a book, Vera Willoughby,

Illustrator of Books, J.&E. Bumpus, 1929, by James Laver.

WILLS, FERELYTH ALISON (1916-2005)

Sculptor. Born in London in August 1916. The daughter of W.N. Howard. Educated at The Hall School, Weybridge and at the St Leonard's School, St Andrews, Fife. Studied at the London County Council Central School of Arts and Crafts under John Skeaping, Thomas Humphrey Paget and Winifred Turner between 1935 and 1939. Produced sculptures in wood, stone, metal and concrete. Also an artist in pastels and brush & ink. In 1943 she married Stanley B. Wills in Weston-super-Mare. Later based in Petersfield, Hampshire. They had at least two daughters. Ferelyth died in Chichester, Sussex, aged 89. Still active into the 1970s. Exhibited her work, including at the Royal Academy (1951), the Society of Women Artists (1971), at the Crafts Centre of Great Britain, with the Arts and Crafts Society and with the Petersfield Arts and Crafts Society. Works included: Squirrels (walnut). Elected a Member of the Arts and Crafts Society, of the Crafts Centre of Great Britain and of the Petersfield Arts and Crafts Society. Works reproduced in The Field.

WILSON, HILDA M.L. - SEE PEMBERTON, H.M.L.

WILSON, MARGARET EVANGELINE (1890-1977)

Painter / Artist in Silverpoint. Born in Boscombe, Hampshire in April 1890. The daughter of Sidney Hartwell Beard and Martha Elizabeth. Her father had independent means. Had at least one sibling, Elizabeth Catherine. Raised in Paignton, Devon. Studied at the Westminster School of Art and the Central School of Arts and Crafts, London. Also, at the Grande Charmier, Paris, the Royal Academy of Florence, and the Slade School and Royal Academy schools, London. Produced landscape, flower, portrait and miniature paintings in oils, and portraits in silverpoint. Taught art at the Chiswick Council School for Girls. Based in Grange-over-Sands and in Heysham, London and Bletchingley, Surrey during her career. Died in Hendon, Middlesex, aged 87.

Wilson exhibited her work, including at the Royal Academy (1916-41), the Royal Glasgow Institute (1938-45), the Royal Scottish Academy (1918) and the Society of Women Artists (1917-36). Also, at the Walker Art Gallery, Liverpool, the Paris Salon, the Royal Society of Portrait Painters and the Royal Institute of Oil Painters.

Exhibited works included: Viola le Good, Memories, Unfathomed Depths From Welsh Mountains and Roses and Alabaster. Won an Honourable Mention at the Paris Salon of 1927 for her Le Demi Solde. Some of her more prestigious sitters included Lord Arthur Hill, the Hon. Mrs Nelson Ward and Lady Muir Mackenzie. Her Strand on the Green was illustrated in The Studio, Vol.137, 1949. Some of her portraits in silverpoint were acquired by the Victoria and Albert Museum, London. Some of her portraits of children in silverpoint were acquired by the British Museum. In 1914 she married Robert Wilson in Paddington, London.

WILSON, MARION HENDERSON (1869-1956)

Artist / Craftswoman. One of Scotland's leading craftswomen in the late nineteenth and early twentieth centuries. Born in Glasgow. The daughter of Thomas Wilson and Isabella. One of at least four daughters (Isabella, Charlotte, Clementina and Marion), all born between 1863 and 1869. Raised in Glasgow. Remained there throughout much of her career, still at the family home with all her unmarried sisters in 1911, when they were in their 40s. Later based at Albert Road, Glasgow. Attended the Glasgow School of Art between 1884 and 1896. Trained chiefly in metalwork. Worked in various materials including brass, copper, steel and block tin. A highly creative worker, she designed and produced all manner of mostly domestic items such as decorative screens, overmantels, table and wall clocks, jardinieres, mirror and picture frames, plaques, door plates, switch plates, vases, electric bell-pushes and sconces. Used various motifs in her designs including cherubs, ships, peacocks, owls, roses and figures. She developed a technique of smoking the metal surface of an object in the flame of a candle, then polishing the raised parts to enhance the chief design.

Wilson was one of a number of women, including the Macdonald sisters and De Courcy Lewthwaite Dewar, to produce decorative metalwork in Scotland during that period. She also produced watercolour paintings and sculptures. Exhibited her work locally, including in 1898 / 99 when she showed a large plaque in hammered brass at the Glasgow School of Art Club annual exhibition, held at the Glasgow Fine Art Institute. The Club was made up of past and present students of the Glasgow School of Art. The plaque was illustrated in The Studio, Vol.15, January 1899, p.281. Exhibited at the Glasgow Exhibition of 1911. Also exhibited at the Royal Glasgow Institute (18 works, 1893-1912).

Exhibited works included: Summer (sculpture), Wild Roses (copper panel), An Italian Peasant (watercolour), Flora (sculpture) and Music (copper panel). Four of her works were illustrated in The Studio, Vol.47, July 1909, pp.136 & 138, including Spring and The Fairy Ship in beaten brass along with a clock with a ship design. Another of her works, Summer, a repoussé panel for an overmantel, was illustrated in The Studio, Vol.56, September 1912, p.317. Works in the Kelvingrove Art Gallery and Museum, Scotland.

WINDLEY, MAUDE ROSINNA (1876-1962)

Sculptor. Born in Barkby, Leicestershire. The daughter of Thomas Windley, a newspaper proprietor and alderman, and Julia. One of at least eight children (Lucy, Gertrude, Ethel, Sybil, Maude, Eliza, Thomas and Edith). Raised in Leicestershire. Possibly studied in London. Based in Chelsea early in her career. Returned to Leicestershire, where she died. Acted as art teacher at the Municipal School of Art, Leicester. Produced portrait medallions and busts in bronze. Exhibited at the Royal Academy (1906-35). Exhibited works included: Thomas R. Windley, Esq. (medallion), T.Y. Baker, Esq., R.N. (medallion), Sir Edwin Pears (portrait medallion) and Helen Mary Fletcher (bust).

WINDMULLER, RUTH - SEE DUCKWORTH, R.

WINNICOTT, ALICE BUXTON (1891-1969)

Painter / Pottery Worker / Modeller / Illustrator / Designer. Born in Claverdon, Warwickshire. The daughter of John William Taylor, M.D., F.R.C.S., Professor of Gynaecology, Birmingham and Birmingham University, and Florence. Her father died in 1906 whilst Alice was still a child. One of at least four children (Mary, Alice, John and Pauline). Raised in Edgbaston. Educated at the King Edward VI High School, Birmingham, and at Newnham College, Cambridge. Studied at several schools of art. She was taught privately at a French Impressionist school. Also, at Richmond under P. Conway and others; at Kingston under A. Collister; at Wimbledon under N. Babb; at St John's Wood under P. Maillard, and at the London County Council Central School of Arts and Crafts. At Wimbledon, she studied pottery techniques. Received her M.A. in 1915. Subsequently based in Pilgrim's Lane, Hampstead. Died in Pembrokeshire, aged 78.

Winnicott produced oil paintings, worked in clay for pottery and modelling, produced carpet designs and executed illustrations for scientific books and papers. Worked as the principal designer for the Claverdon Pottery (1935-46). Also designed for the Upchurch Pottery. Some of her designs for Upchurch wares were illustrated in The Studio, Vol.112, November 1936, p.277 in an article The English Pottery Industry. She exhibited her work, including at the Royal Academy (1936), the Royal Cambrian Academy, the South Wales Art Society and the Society of Women Artists (1933-37). Also exhibited in Eastbourne and Plymouth. Exhibited pottery and carpets at Heal's, Fortnum & Mason, the Royal Horticultural Society and elsewhere. Winnicott was the founder and President of the New Kingston Group (1930-31) and exhibited with the group. Elected a long distance Member of the South Wales Art Society. Produced a large carpet for Burlington House. Other works acquired by the Tate Gallery. Some of her carpet and pottery designs were illustrated in other arts journals, including in Decoration and The Flat Book. Signed her work A. Bourne Claverdon. In 1923 she married Dr Donald Woods Winnicott, M.A., F.R.C.P. in Frensham, Surrey.

WINSER, MARGARET (1868-1944)

Sculptor / Modeller. Born in Rolvenden, Kent. The daughter of Albert Winser, a grocer and draper, and Mary. One of a large family, of possibly 13 or more children. One of her brothers, Sidney, became a civil engineer. In the early 1900s, Winser shared digs with artist Janet Brennand at Parson's Green, London, which would indicate that Winser possibly studied in London. Brennand (later Marsh), who originated from Blandford, Dorset, worked as an art teacher in London and exhibited her work at the Royal Academy (1905-24). Winser subsequently left London and returned to Kent, living at Tenterden for much of the time. She died in Kent. She produced portrait medallions, busts and reliefs, working in bronze and other materials. Exhibited her work occasionally, including at the Royal Glasgow Institute (1929) and the Royal Academy (1904-29). Exhibited works included: Dame Ellen Terry, C.B.E. (bronze), Christmas (medal), Mourners: Portion of Memorial Relief and Dancing Children (medallion).

WITHERS, THE HON. AUGUSTA JOANNA ELIZABETH INNES (1791-1876)

Botanical and Bird Artist. Possibly was Miss Baker. Born in Cheltenham, Gloucestershire. In 1822 she married Theodore Gibson Withers (1782-1869) in London. He was an accountant who originated from Middlesex. The couple had at least two children, Theodore in 1823 and Augusta in 1825. They lived mainly in London, including in St John's Wood, Kensington and Chelsea, and very latterly at Albany Street, Regent's Park. Both died in London, Theodore aged 87, Augusta aged 85. Augusta became an expert and widely praised botanical and bird artist, known for her fine, detailed and accurate work. Her works are still available as prints today.

Augusta contributed to various publications, including Benjamin Maund's The Botanist (c.1840), John Lindley's Pomological Magazine and Curtis's Botanical Magazine. She illustrated Robert Thompson's The Gardener's Assistant (1859). Collaborated with Sarah Drake on James Bateman's Orchidaceae of Mexico and Guatemala. Active for at least six decades, from the 1820s to the 1870s. Exhibited her work, including at the Royal Academy (1829-46), the Royal Society of British Artists (68 works, 1832-65), the New Watercolour Society and the Society of Women Artists (43 works, 1857-75). Exhibited works included: A Study of Roses, Feather-Legged Bantams, Gooseberries and Currants and Apples From Nature. Mrs Withers was one of the earliest exhibitors with, and members of, the Society of Women Artists. Elected a Member (1857-79). Between 1833 and 1840 she is listed as Flower Painter in Ordinary to the Queen Dowager. Also listed as Painter in Ordinary to Her Majesty, and to the Horticultural Society.

WITTS, EMILY - SEE GRIFFITH, E.

WOOD, CAMILLE BERENICE (1888-1964)
Glass Painter / Decorator in Cut Paper. Known as Berenice. Born in Chelsea, London. The daughter of artist Davidson Knowles and Elise. Had at least one sibling, Veronica. Educated at the St Agnes College, Ealing. Studied at the Regent Street Polytechnic, London. Exhibited her work, including with the National Society of Artists, with the United Artists, at the Chinese and Russian Exhibition, with the Artists of Chelsea and the Society of Women Artists (1962). Elected a Member of the National Society of Artists. Works reproduced in The Queen and Sunday Dispatch. Based in London and died there, aged 75. In 1909 she married artist William Thomas Wood (b.1877) in London. He was elected to the Art Workers' Guild in 1919. They had at least one son and one daughter, Eliza.

WOODCOCK, BETTINE C. - SEE WALFORD, B.C.

WOODHOUSE, FRANCES C. - SEE ROGERS, F.C.

WOODRUFF, GLADYS - SEE DAWSON, GLADYS

WOODWARD, ALICE BOLINGBROKE (1862-1951)
Artist / Illustrator. Born in London in October 1862. The daughter of Henry Woodward, F.R.S., and Ellen Sophia. Her father, who originated from Norwich, was the Keeper of the Department of Geology at the British Museum. Her mother originated from Essex. Alice was raised in London. One of at least seven children (Henry, Ellen, Gertrude, Alice, Catharine, Martin and Mary), all born within a nine-year period. All the Woodward children were well educated and proved successful. Henry became a wood engraver; Ellen became an artist / metalworker; Gertrude became a scientific artist; Alice became an artist / illustrator; Catharine became a teacher of physical education; Martin became a biologist and Mary became an artist and art teacher. Ellen, Alice, Catharine and Mary were still living at home in Notting Hill with their parents when they were aged between 43 and 51 and their parents were aged 74 and 78. The children were educated at home by a governess.

Alice subsequently studied in London at the Royal College of Art and the Westminster School of Art, and at the Academie Julian in Paris for a few months. She is still listed as an art student in 1891. With her sisters, Alice drew from an early age, sketching at the British Museum where her father worked. It is said that Ruskin gave them a drawing lesson. Whilst still young, Alice made scientific drawings for her father and his friends, earning a small sum which contributed towards her art tuition. She studied for a time under Professor Fred Brown. Some of her drawings were published early on in the Daily Graphic. Through Joseph Pennell, at Westminster, she won commissions from Macmillan and Dent, and produced work for the Daily Chronicle. She used a studio in Chelsea initially, but subsequently worked from the family home. During the First World War, Alice worked on drawing maps for the Naval Intelligence Bureau. Latterly, she lived at Bushey, Hertfordshire, where she continued to draw and paint into the 1930s and 1940s. She died in Hertfordshire in July 1951, at that time living at The Mulberry Bush, Bushey.

Alice spent much of her career as a book illustrator, producing work for several major publishers including Blackie, Dent, John Lane and Macmillan over a period of more than 35 years. One of her first commissions was Banbury Cross and Other Nursery Rhymes for Dent in 1895 (with 62 illustrations). Also, Eric, Prince of Lorlonia (Countess of Jersey) for Macmillan in 1895. Numerous others followed, including To Tell the King the Sky is Falling (Sheila E. Braine, Blackie, 1896, 85 illustrations and decorations), Red Apple and Silver Bells (Hamish Hendry, Blackie, 1897, 152 illustrations) and Adventures in Toyland (Edith Hall King, Blackie, 1897, 78 illustrations and decorations). By 1903, she had illustrated at least 14 books for children and continued to work at a prolific rate. Later book projects included History of Little Goody Two Shoes (Macmillan, 1924) and Myths and Legends of the Australian Aborigines (1930).

Both during and after her career, Woodward's work received attention. One of her illustrations for To Tell the King the Sky is Falling was given in R.E.D. Sketchley's volume English Book Illustrators of To-day, London, Kegan Paul, 1903. Sketchley also notes of Woodward that 'when most successful she can draw a pleasing child with lines almost as few as those used by any modern artist' (p104), and that she 'has a quick appreciation of unconscious humour in attitude and expression'. The same illustration appeared in The Studio, Vol.9, 1896, p.216. In 1905, in his Humorists of the Pencil (London, Hurst & Blackett Ltd), J.A. Hammerton notes that Woodward was one of only a few women to produce humorous works. Also noted in later publications such as Mahony, Latimer & Folmsbee, Illustrators of Children's Books 1744-1945, Boston, The Horn Book Inc., 1947.

Woodward also contributed to periodicals and journals during her career, including The Illustrated London News, The Quarto and Strand Magazine. Also noted for her bookplates. One of those was given in Norna Labouchere's Ladies' Book-Plates, London, George Bell, 1895. Another was given in an article Modern Bookplates and Their Designers in The Studio, Vol.18, 1899-1900, p.32. Alice was noted as 'an artist of more robust and original quality, already acknowledged in the front rank of women designers, and gifted, perhaps, with a finer sense of composition in draughtsmanship than any of her peers'. Alice occasionally exhibited her work, particularly during the early years of her career, including at the Royal Academy (1890-1900), the Royal Society of British Artists (1886-90), the New English Art Club (1893) and the Royal Glasgow Institute (1891). Exhibited illustrations, watercolours, designs, landscapes, portraits and decorative works. Exhibited works included: Dial

Yard, Norwich, A Song Without Words, Moonlight: Decorative Illustration of a Poem (watercolour), Design for a Dance Programme and Illustration to The Hundredth Princess. Also contributed to the 1896 exhibition of the Arts and Crafts Exhibition Society, and showed at the Royal Institute of Painters in Watercolours, the Royal Scottish Society of Painters in Watercolours and in Manchester and Liverpool.

Mary Louisa Woodward (1868-1948) also became a successful exhibiting artist, producing miniatures, portraits, flowers, figures and interiors. She too used a studio in Chelsea before returning to work at the family home. She exhibited more extensively than Alice, including at the Royal Academy (1901-14), the Royal Society of British Artists (1890-93), the Royal Scottish Academy (1903-06), the Royal Hibernian Academy (1894-1907) and the Royal Glasgow Institute (1905-06). Also, at the Society of Women Artists (38 works, 1892-1907), the Royal Society of Miniature Painters and the Royal Institute of Painters in Watercolours. Exhibited works included: Martin F. Woodward, Esq., God's Acre, Cottage Interior, A Baby Girl and Miss Alice Warne. Mary died in Hertfordshire.

Ellen Caroline Woodward (1860-1943) became equally successful, as a painter, decorative artist and metalworker who also exhibited her work. She too later returned to work at the family home after using a studio in Chelsea, and having also spent some time at St Leonards-on-Sea in the 1890s. She produced jewellery, decorative gesso panels and other decorative work. Exhibited her work, including at the Royal Academy (1895), the Royal Society of British Artists (1890) and the New English Art Club (1894). Also exhibited a gesso panel at the 1906 Lyceum Club exhibition held by its members. Exhibited jewellery at the 1905 / 06 Second Exhibition of Arts and Crafts, also at the Lyceum Club. Exhibited jewellery at the '91 Art Club Exhibition held at the Alpine Club in 1905. Exhibited jewellery at the 1905 / 06 permanent exhibition of Artistic Handicrafts at the Lyceum Club. Jointly exhibited with E.M. Rope at the 1906 Autumn Exhibition at Liverpool's Walker Art Gallery, showing a cabinet in silver and bronze. Also exhibited at the Women's International Art Club exhibition for 1910 at the Grafton Galleries. Showed a small number of works at the Society of Women Artists (1902-10), including a gesso panel St Anthony. Ellen was a member of the Church Crafts League, and is listed in papers belonging to the League as one of its metalworkers. She also sat on the League's Committee. A Miss Woodward, possibly Ellen, exhibited at the United Arts Club exhibition in 1909, also held at the Grafton Galleries. Ellen died at Bushey, Hertfordshire.

WOODWARD, ELLEN C. - SEE WOODWARD, ALICE

WOODWARD, MARY L. - SEE WOODWARD, ALICE

WOOLLATT, LOUISA EMILY ELLEN (1908-76)

Designer / Embroideress. Known as Louie. Born in Oxford in December 1908. The daughter of Edwin Henry Judd-Morris (1884-1968), a bootmaker, and Louisa Florence Green (b.1885). Both parents originated from Oxford, where Louisa was raised. Educated privately. Studied at the Oxford School of Art and at the Royal College of Art, London under Sir William Rothenstein, Professor Ernest W. Tristram, Edward Johnston and Reco Capey. Awarded a design, embroidery and weaving scholarship. Elected an Associate of the Royal College of Art. Produced embroideries and embroidery designs, and wrote on embroidery. For example, her Sampler Book of Decorative Needlework was published in 1937, and her An Introduction to Embroidery Stitches was published in 1948. Elected to the Worshipful Company of Broderers in 1932. Won the Embroiderers' Guild Challenge Cup in 1945 and 1947. Early in her career, she worked at the Bradford College of Art and at the Halifax, Exeter and Newton Abbot Schools of Art. From 1949 she was crafts mistress at the Torquay School of Art. Exhibited her work, including at the Society of Women Artists (1935), with the Arts and Crafts Society, the Embroiderers' Guild, the Arts Council and abroad. Exhibited works included: Creation, Cinderella and Summer. Some of her embroideries were reproduced in The Studio, Embroidery, Embroideress and Good Housekeeping. Still active into the 1950s. In 1937 she married artist Leighton Hall Woollatt (1905-74) in Berkshire. He was a painter, mural decorator, sculptor, etcher, lithographer and draughtsman. The son of an art director and designer, he also studied at the Royal Academy schools. They had at least one daughter. The couple lived in various locations, including Torquay and Exeter. Louisa died in Exeter, aged 67.

WOOLMER, ELEANOR MARY - SEE GRIBBLE, E.M.

WOOLRICH, ELLEN GERTRUDE & SOFITA HOPLEY (1875-1958) & (1877-1960)

Bookbinders / Book Decorators. The daughters of Francis Woolrich (b.1846) who was born in Mexico to an English father and a Mexican mother, but lived in America. Ellen and Sofita were born in California. There were at least three other Woolrich children, Mary (b.1869) who was born in England; George (b.1871) who was born in Mexico, and John Francis (b.1880) who was born in California. Ellen (also Nelly), Sofita and John moved from America to England sometime between 1900 and 1902. John worked as an artist and illustrator, but appears to have left England sometime after 1911. All three lived together, including at Duke Street, Manchester Square in London, and evidently had money to travel abroad. Ellen and Sofita remained in London until their deaths, working for some considerable time as bookbinders and book decorators, showing their work at some of the major arts exhibitions of the day.

Bindings executed by the sisters are sometimes signed jointly, suggesting that they worked together, though Ellen appears to have taken a more prominent role. In her volume Women Bookbinders 1880-1920 (Oak Knoll Press / The British Library, 1996), Marianne Tidcombe suggests that the Woolrich girls were taught bookbinding by Douglas Cockerell. Cockerell taught a number of women, both at the L.C.C. Central School of Arts and Crafts and at his own studio. Tidcombe notes the high standard of work produced by the sisters, which also indicates the input of someone of Cockerell's standing. The sisters also moved in prominent artistic circles, and were particularly close to Jessie Bayes, also a decorative bookbinder.

The Woolrich sisters began to exhibit their work in England in around 1903, when Ellen contributed several bindings to the Arts and Crafts Exhibition Society's seventh exhibition, including a copy of Stevenson's Child's Garden of Verses, described as having some 'fine' tooling on Morocco. In 1904 some of their work was exhibited in Antwerp. It remains difficult to determine exactly which sister exhibited work, or if both did, since most exhibits are labelled simply 'Miss Woolrich'. In 1906, Ellen contributed to the Arts and Crafts Exhibition Society's eighth exhibition, showing, among other items, a pattern book with a cover designed and executed by her in leather and illustrated in

The Studio, Vol.37, March 1906, p.143. In the same year, Miss Woolrich (possibly Ellen) contributed to the Artists at Work exhibition held at the Grafton Galleries in October by the Society of Artists. The Society was organised by Mrs Charles Muller to promote the sale of handicrafts. Around 120 craftsmen and craftswomen contributed on that occasion. Contributions by 'Miss Woolrich' on that occasion included a decorative cover for A Book of Nursery Rhymes which was illustrated with other examples of her work in The Studio, Vol.39, December 1906, pp.246-247.

Also in 1906, The Studio carried advertisements for the Woolrich girls, offering teaching in artistic bookbinding, the cleaning and repairing of old books, and tuition in writing and illumination. A binding by 'Miss Woolrich' was illustrated in Sarah T. Prideaux's volume Modern Bookbindings Their Design and Decoration, London, Archibald Constable & Co., 1906. The sisters continued to work over the following decade at least, with both contributing to an Exhibition of Works of Art by Women Artists held at Waring & Gillow in May 1916. The Exhibition aimed to raise funds for women artists suffering due to war. It was visited by the Queen and Princess Mary. The Queen purchased works by the Woolrich sisters and others. In the same year, the sisters contributed to the Arts and Crafts Exhibition Society's eleventh exhibition, indicating a continued affinity with the Arts and Crafts movement. In 1929 Ellen Woolrich married Edward G. Hudson in Kensington. She was then around 54 years of age. She died in London in June 1958, aged 83. A widow on her death, she left her small estate to Sofita. Sofita died in London in September 1960, also aged 83.

WOON, ANNIE KATHLEEN (c.1862-1922)

Sculptor / Painter / Etcher. The daughter of Joseph Dillon Woon and Mary. Her mother originated from Yorkshire. One of at least four children (Charles, Rosa, Annie and May). All were born in Chelsea, London, but were raised mainly in Edinburgh. Dates of Annie's birth vary from 1856 to 1866. On her death, however, she is listed as aged 60, which would indicate 1862. Sometime between 1903 and 1905 the family left Edinburgh and returned to Chelsea. Charles Woon became a timber merchant. Rosa and Annie became artists, probably studying in Edinburgh. May became a clerk at the University of London. Rosa, a portrait painter, exhibited her work at the Royal Scottish Academy (1875-1900), the Royal Glasgow Institute (1875-82) and the Royal Academy (1873). Annie produced

paintings of flowers, portraits and figures, busts and bas-reliefs, aquatints and etchings. She exhibited at the Royal Scottish Academy (1878-1902), the Royal Glasgow Institute (1880-1903) and the Society of Women Artists (1905-08). Exhibited works included: Etching in Colour Aquatint of a Panel of Florentine Marble Inlay, Cynthia (bas-relief), On the Thames at Chelsea (etching) and Professor Copeland, Astronomer Royal for Scotland.

WORKMAN, EMILY D. - SEE CORRY, E.D.

WORTHINGTON, BEATRICE MAUDE (1883-1959)

Sculptor. The daughter of William Worthington (1841-1911) and Elizabeth Bradbury Neild (1842-1930). Her father was a veterinary surgeon who originated from Lancashire. Her mother originated from Styal, Cheshire. One of at least five children (three girls and two boys), all born and raised in Wigan, Lancashire. At the time of her father's death, in 1911, Beatrice was a student in London, studying sculpture under Professor Edouard Lanteri and living in a shared house in King's Road, Chelsea. She produced genre figures. In 1914 she travelled to Boston, Massachusetts. Died in Aylesbury, Buckinghamshire, aged 75. Apparently exhibited little.

WREN, DENISE TUCKFIELD (1891-1979)

Potter / Designer. Born in Albany, Western Australia. The daughter of Charles Tuckfield, an inventor, and Kate Hannah Woodman. Her parents originated from London, but spent several years living in Australia. Denise was one of seven children. The eldest four, Winifred, Denise, Dorothy and Phyllis, were all born in Australia. The youngest three, Charles, Marjorie and John, were born in East Moseley, after the family had returned to England, sometime in around 1900. Winifred (1889-1955) and Denise became art students in England, with at least four other siblings becoming students of various subjects. Denise was a design student at the Kingston upon Thames School of Art between 1907 and 1912. There, she came under the influence of Manx artist Archibald Knox (1864-1933). The School then had no kiln, so initially, she took her pots to be fired at a flower and chimney pot maker's and at a church-warden pipe maker's nearby.

Denise taught herself to throw on an old wheel adapted, and which she continued to use when she established her own pottery at 24 Kingston Market Place in 1912. Knox's teaching at

Kingston was considered too advanced, and in 1912 he resigned, taking his students, including Denise, with him. His silver and jewellery designs were salvaged and Winifred Tuckfield established the Knox Guild of Design and Crafts at Kingston Market Place, where his students could work. Denise established herself as a potter in the Guild rooms, with other members working at jewellery, spinning, weaving, embroidery and raffia work. Exhibitions were held in the Art Gallery above Kingston Library and at the Whitechapel Art Gallery.

In 1915 Denise married Henry Douglas Wren (1884-1947) in Kingston, Surrey. Wren, who originated from Middlesex, had begun his career as a shorthand writer and typist, but later turned to writing and pottery. The couple lived at Oxshott, Surrey where, in 1919, they built themselves a house and pottery workshop, Potter's Croft. They had at least one daughter, Rosemary in 1922. The interior of their home was decorated with furnishings, curtains and stained glass executed by the Knox Guild. Like her father, Denise had an experimental nature and devised a series of small kilns at Oxshott, adapted to her particular needs. The last of those was a salt-glazed kiln completed in 1963. The plans of her kilns were used by other potters. She not only made pottery at Oxshott, but took on pupils. Some of the earliest pieces produced there included plates, vases and candlesticks, coiled, thrown or press-moulded. Later in her career she produced pots for flower arrangements. In her latter years, she made models of elephants.

Denise exhibited her work, including at the British Empire Exhibition, Wembley in 1924 and 1925. Also showed some of her work at the Chelsea Flower Show. In 1925 she and Henry held an exhibition at the Central Hall, Westminster where the work of 30 other craftsmen and women was displayed. The exhibition ran annually until the late 1930s and became known as The Artist Craftsman. Some of Denise's textile designs were also sold through Liberty & Co., London. In 1927 she exhibited some of her work at the Society of Women Artists. A salt-glazed stoneware bottle measuring 8" in height by Denise was illustrated in The Studio, Vol.159, June 1960, p.200. In 1936 Potter's Croft advertised in the Rural Industries magazine, Winter, No.45, published quarterly by the Rural Industries Bureau. They advertised Oxshott throwing wheels and kiln designs for various fuels and other pottery equipment.

Denise was noted in Muriel Rose, Artist Potters in England, London, Faber & Faber, 1970 (first edition 1955). Rose illustrates a stoneware jar on three feet by Denise, some 5" high, with red body,

dated 1960. Rosemary Wren eventually took over the workshop, and with her mother launched a number of new pottery styles. In 1978 they moved to Devon, just before Denise died, aged 88. Winifred Tuckfield married Henry De Annand Brown-Morison in 1953, and died in Brighton some two years later.

SEE: Denise & Rosemary Wren, Pottery Making, London, Pitman, 1952.

WRIGHT, ALICE MAUD
(active 1910s-1920s)

Sculptor / Illustrator / Miniature Painter. Born in Hoxton. The daughter of Edward Cameron Wright. Educated privately. Studied under John Parker, R.W.S., and at the St Martin's School of Art under Walter Sickert. Also spent time in Paris. Awarded an Art Masters' Teaching Certificate. Produced plaques, illustrations and miniature paintings for manuscripts. Exhibited occasionally, including at the Royal Academy (1911-27) and the Royal Institute of Painters in Watercolours. Exhibited works included: John Finley (plaque), Magnificat, The Mirror and The Sentinel. Based in London.

WRIGHT, ETHEL M. (active early 1900s)

Embroideress / Designer. Based in Leeds, at Lynton Villa, Virginia Road. Active in the early 1900s. Between 1904 and 1909 she advertised in The Studio magazine, offering general house decoration, designs, stencils, friezes, embroideries, curtains, bedspreads and tablecloths. In 1900 she exhibited an embroidered cushion at the Leeds Arts and Crafts Exhibition. The cushion was illustrated in The Studio, Vol.21, January 1901, p.259 and described as 'exquisite'. In 1903 she exhibited at the Second Exhibition of embroidery held by the Worshipful Company of Broderers. Produced her own embroidery designs and executed them.

WRIGHT, GERTRUDE ELIZA (b.c.1881)

Sculptor. Born in Chorlton, Manchester. The daughter of Richard D'Aubrey Wright, a civil servant, and Eliza. Her father originated from London. Her mother died when she was still young. One of at least three daughters (Annie, Gertrude and Edith). Raised in Manchester, worked there and died there, aged 60. She remained living with her father into her 40s. Became a sculptor of groups, figures and reliefs in clay. Exhibited occasionally, including at the Royal Academy (1905-12) and at the Annual Exhibition of the Manchester Academy of Fine Arts (including in 1908 and 1909). Exhibited works included: Playmates (group) and Song (relief).

WRIGHT, PATIENCE (1725-c.1808)

Modeller. A largely forgotten name, but noted in Mrs Ellet's Women Artists in All Ages and Countries, London, Bentley, 1859. Ellet records that Patience Wright, or Patience Lovell as she was prior to her marriage, was born in Bordentown, New Jersey to Quaker parents. She showed an early talent for modelling, but was not encouraged as a child. So she made moulded figures from dough or local clay. In 1748 she married Joseph Wright of Bordentown. Whilst still in America she gained a reputation for accurate portraits in wax. Her husband died young, leaving her with three children to support. In 1772 she moved to London to work, mixing with the cultured classes. Considered a rival to Madame Tussaud. Produced a full-length likeness of Lord Chatham which was put in a glass case in Westminster Abbey. Also produced models of the King, the Queen, Lord Temple, Barry and Wilkes among others. Her wax portrait of Benjamin Franklin was reproduced by Wedgwood in jasper and basalt in around 1775. Also became known as 'Sibylla' and claimed to be able to foretell political events. Called in one magazine of 1775 'the Promethean modeller'. Her eldest daughter married an American named Platt. She inherited some of her mother's talents, and was well known in New York by 1787 for her modelling in wax. Mrs Wright lost favour with George III, so went to Paris in 1781. She returned to London in 1785.

WRIGHTSON, MARGARET (1877-1976)

Sculptor. Born at Norton Hall near Stockton-on-Tees. The daughter of Sir Thomas Wrightson, J.P., Chairman of Head Wrightson, M.P. for Stockton and, later, St Pancras, London. Whilst Margaret was still young, the family moved to Neasham Hall, Darlington. Had a younger sister, Jocelyn (1888-1979), who became a painter. Encouraged by her father, Margaret took up sculpture, studying at the Royal College of Art, London under Sir William B. Richmond and Edouard Lanteri as well as in Paris. Based in London for much of her career, using a studio in Bedford Gardens, Kensington for a time. She died in London. Produced portrait works, figures and animals. Worked in various materials including bronze, plaster, stone, marble, lead, silver, brass and, latterly, fibreglass. Her career eventually spanned seven decades, from the 1910s to the 1970s. Executed numerous important commissions during her lengthy career, including a statue of a Viking landing on the Northumbrian coast for Lord Runciman of Doxford Hall, Doxford which was later placed outside the headquarters of Northumberland County Council, Morpeth (in 1981). Other commissions included the Lamb Memorial for the Inner Temple Gardens, London, and a figure of St George as part of a war memorial at Cramlington, unveiled in 1922. During the war, she served as a driver with the Women's Auxiliary Ambulance Corps in France.

At the age of 86, Wrightson travelled to Paris to receive a medal of honour in the 1962 Salon exhibition. Elected a Fellow of the Royal Society of British Sculptors, a Member of the Society of Women Artists (1916-74), an Honorary Retired Member (1974-75), and a Member of the Darlington Society of Arts. Exhibited her work, including at the Society of Women Artists (1912-72), showing over 80 works there. Also, at the Royal Academy (1906-61). Exhibited works included a marble bust of Sir Thomas Wrightson, and another of Lady Wrightson. Also, The Spirit of Spring (statuette, bronze), a marble head of Lady Mary Stewart and a bronze statuette of a white bull terrier. Other works included: Spirit of the Garden, a fountain for Wynyard Park, Our Village Snob (bust, bronze), A Land Girl (statuette, bronze), The Village Shoemaker (bronze) and Penelope (stone).

WYATT, ETHEL W. - SEE CLAYTON, E.W.

WYATT, KATHERINE MONTAGU (1866-1946)

Painter / Illustrator. Born in Bloomsbury, London. The daughter of Thomas H. Wyatt, a civil servant in the War Office, and Julia. One of a large family of at least six children. Her brother Hugh became a solicitor. Another brother, James, became a medical student. Katherine studied art, possibly in London. Spent much of her career in London, but died in Surrey, aged 80. Assisted Rose Welby, Isabel Gloag, Susan Canton and others in running the Royal Female School of Art in London in the early 1900s (certainly in 1909). Produced landscape, figure, interior and building paintings. Also produced book illustrations, magazine covers and other decorative work. Illustrated (in colour), for example, M.R. Gloag, A Book of English Gardens, London, Methuen, 1906 (price 10s 6d). The book was reviewed in The Studio, Vol.39, December 1906, p.277. Wyatt exhibited her work, including at the Royal Academy (1889-1918), the Royal Society of British Artists (1890-94), the Society of Women

Artists (1892-95) and the Royal Society of Painters in Watercolours (certainly in 1903). Exhibited works included: The China Room, Holland House, The Tithe Barn, Abbotsbury, Just in the Grey of the Dawn and The Embroideress. Exhibited a study of Bosham Church, Sussex at the 1890 Exhibition of Studies, Sketches and Decorative Design held at the Royal Society of British Artists.

WYLLIE, GLADYS AMY
(active 1920s-1940s)

Embroideress. The daughter of Colonel R.J.H. Wyllie of the Bengal Staff Corps. Educated at West Hill, Eastbourne. Studied at the Edinburgh College of Art. Awarded a City & Guilds of London. Became an expert and gifted embroideress involved in secular and other work. Along with Mary Alison Wyllie, she organised the Modern Embroideries Society in its initial stages. By 1925 there were nine professional artists involved with the Society. Its chief aim was to encourage original design in embroidery along with good technique. In 1925 the Society held its third exhibition, to which Wyllie contributed. She also acted as Honorary Secretary of the Society.

For much of her career, Wyllie was based in Edinburgh, including at The Outlook Tower, Castle Hill. Later based at Blairgowrie, Perthshire. Her ecclesiastical work included vestments for Edinburgh Cathedral and embroideries for the Scottish Church in Jerusalem. Also produced a working design for a hood of a cape for the Archbishop of Capetown for St George's Cathedral, Capetown. Produced a design for a frontal for the Children's Chapel, St Mary's Cathedral, Edinburgh. Also, a design for an altar frontal for the Cathedral Church of St Michael and St George, Grahamstown, South Africa. Wyllie designed and executed numerous church banners, memorial embroideries and embroidered reredos.

Wyllie exhibited her work occasionally, including with the Society of Scottish Artists (including in 1927), the Society of Women Artists (1920-22), the Royal Scottish Academy (1933-41) and the Royal Scottish Watercolour Society. Elected a Member of the Society of Scottish Artists and a Member of its Council (1932-35). Some of her work was illustrated in The Studio magazine. For example, the magazine illustrated a centre panel for a pram cover, The Gooseman, designed and executed by Wyllie, in Vol.85, 1923, p.287. The cover was in applique with orange and black. It was exhibited at the Modern Embroideries Society exhibition in

Edinburgh along with a visitor's book with a design of two Egyptian figures and a reredos with angelic figures in olive and purple. In 1925, The Studio, Vol.89, p.344 illustrated details of a bedspread titled Autumn, revealing neat, meticulous and beautiful needlework of sound design. Her Eccles Panel was acquired by the Victoria & Albert Museum Circulating Department.

WYNN, SYLVIA S. - SEE KINGHAM, S.S.

Y

YEATS, LILY & ELIZABETH CORBET
(1866-1949) & (1868-1940)

Painters / Craftswomen. The daughters of Irish artist John Butler Yeats and Susan Pollexfen. Also, sisters to poet W.B. Yeats (1865-1939) and artist Jack B. Yeats (1871-1957). The family originated from Ireland, although Elizabeth was born in London. Initially, between 1886 and 1894, Lily Yeats worked as one of May Morris's embroidery assistants for the firm of Morris & Co. in London. The mere fact that she worked for such a prestigious firm indicates the exceptionally high standard of her needlework. She then returned to Ireland, and with Elizabeth Yeats and Evelyn Gleeson (1855-1944) founded a group of craft industries in 1902 in Dundrum, Co. Dublin. Known as the Dun Emer Industries, they were specifically designed to provide local women with additional income, and to create beautiful things. Crafts practised included embroidery (executed on Irish linen), weaving (of tapestries and rugs) and book printing, all done by hand. Later, bookbinding was added.

Lily Yeats took charge of the embroidery workshop, and in 1903 Dun Emer embroideries were shown at the Royal Dublin Society's Art Industries Exhibition. Held at Ball's Bridge, Dublin, the Exhibition also included the work of the Limerick Lace School, the Royal Irish School of Needlework and other local art industries. Dun Emer embroideries appeared again in 1904, by which time the Royal Dublin Society's exhibition was being held in a purpose-built hall paid for by the Society. Dun Emer also showed tapestry weavings and won all the awards in that category. In October 1903 the Art Workers' Quarterly illustrated two of a set of 30 banners then being executed by Lily Yeats at Dun Emer for the new Roman Catholic Church at Loughrea, Co. Galway. On each banner was to be represented an Irish saint with the name beneath. Some of the banners were designed by Jack B. Yeats and some by Mrs Jack B. Yeats.

In late 1902, Elizabeth Yeats founded the Dun Emer Press which, in 1908, became the Cuala Press. W.B. Yeats took the role of editorial adviser. Additional advice on book printing was given by, among others, Emery Walker (1851-1933) who had associations with the Doves Press and the Kelmscott Press. The Dun Emer Press specialised in books by living Irish writers, some decorated by Elizabeth Yeats. In 1904, the Press printed Twenty-One Poems by Lionel Johnson, selected by W.B. Yeats. In the same year, the Press printed Stories of Red Hanrahan by W.B. Yeats. A small number of other books followed, including a selection of love poems by W.B. Yeats. Elizabeth also instigated a series titled Broadsides. Consisting of 84 monthly issues, the first was published in 1908 by Dun Emer. The Cuala Press printed the remainder, the last of which was dated 1915. Broadsides included the poems of, among others, James Stephens, John Masefield, Ernest Rhys and James Guthrie. Illustrations were contributed by Jack B. Yeats and others. The Press also produced hand-coloured prints and greetings cards as well as executing private commissions for books of varying sizes. Bookplates were also designed and printed.

In 1908 the Yeats sisters left the Dun Emer Industries and set up the Cuala Industries at Churchtown, Co. Dublin, later moving to Dublin. There, they continued with embroidery and printing. The Cuala Press ran until at least 1917. Evelyn Gleeson continued at Dun Emer, where she excelled as a designer and maker of rugs, carpets and tapestries. Gleeson was born in Knutsford, Cheshire, the daughter of Irish General Practitioner Edward Moloney Gleeson and Harriet, who originated from Bolton, Lancashire. In Ireland, her father founded the Athlone Woollen Mills to create employment. Evelyn studied painting and design in London, and studied in Paris. She also spent six months with textile designer Alexander Millar. She subsequently lectured on the designing of rugs and carpets, and co-founded the Dun Emer Industries.

Gleeson exhibited her work at some of the Home Arts and Industries Association Exhibitions in London, including in 1905. In 1904 she exhibited a hand-tufted carpet, with a blue background decorated with a Celtic design in red, at the Irish Arts and Crafts Society Exhibition in Dublin. In 1906 she showed tapestries at an exhibition organised by the Gaelic League, held in Dublin. In the same year, she showed a small panel of tapestry weaving at the Artists at Work Exhibition held at the Grafton Galleries, London. Elizabeth Yeats also studied painting, and published two manuals on the subject, also taking a short course at the Women's Printing Society in London. Elizabeth exhibited some of her watercolour landscapes at the Royal Hibernian Academy (1898-99). Lily, also a painter, exhibited one of her flower studies at the Royal Hibernian Academy in 1898, whilst living in London with Elizabeth.

YOUNG, HELEN JEAN (1914-95)

Painter / Decorative Artist / Illustrator. Known as Jean. The daughter of John Stuart Young (1883-1957) and Helen Grace Horwood (1878-1969). Educated at the Grove School, Hindhead. Studied at the Farnham School of Art under Otway McCannell in 1931. Then at the Regent Street Polytechnic, London under John Skeaping. Then studied at the Royal Academy schools, London under Sir W.W. Russell and Walter Monnington between 1933 and 1938. She was a Belle Arti, Florence medallist in 1938. Based in Middlesex for much of her career. Died there, aged 80.

Young worked as a decorative artist, a painter of animals and figures, an artist in black & white and an illustrator. Worked in oils, pencil, chalk and pen. Produced illustrations and decorations for The Poetry of Easter, The Poetry of Christmas and The Hound of Heaven, published by Mowbrays Ltd. Exhibited her work, including at the Royal Academy (1937-69), the Society of Women Artists (1939-49), the Royal Society of British Artists, the New English Art Club, the Women's International Art Club, the Leicester Galleries and the Leger Gallery. Exhibited works included: Telling the Bees (oil), Pulling Radishes (oil), The Watercress Gatherers and Sleeping Rhino (chalk, ink & pencil). Elected a Member of the Royal Society of British Artists, the Women's International Art Club and the New English Art Club. Elected an Associate of the Society of Women Artists (1939-49). In 1950 she exhibited The Nativity at the Women's International Art Club. The painting was illustrated in The Studio, Vol.139, March 1950, p.65 along with her The Carpet Beaters. Her works were often an unusual interpretation of her subjects, at times slightly bizarre, her figures almost caricatures.

YULE, MARY WINIFRED - SEE
HAYES, M.W.

Z

ZAMBACO, MADAME MARIA (1843-1914)

Sculptor. Born Maria Terpsithea Cassavetti. Her mother was Euphrosyne, a member of one of the leading Greek families in London. Her father was Demetrius John Cassavetti. He was a wealthy merchant who died in Paris when Maria was still young. In 1861 Maria married Demetrius Alexander Zambaco, a doctor to the Greek community in Paris. He specialised in the dermatological effects of syphilis. The marriage lasted five years. In 1866 Maria returned to London with her children and her fortune of some £80,000. Her mother introduced her to Pre-Raphaelite artist Edward Burne-Jones, with a view to her modelling for him. He depicted her in a study of Cupid and Psyche. She became his mistress and appeared in other drawings and paintings. With money and independence, Maria was able to take up art and became a portrait sculptor and medallist of some repute in the 1880s. She exhibited several works at the Royal Academy (1886-88) including Professor A. Legros (bust, terracotta), Study of a Head, Marie Stillman, John Marshall, F.R.S. and Medusa's Horror (bust, bronze). Her relationship with Burne-Jones petered out when he could not leave his wife. The affair is noted in Fiona MacCarthy, The Last Pre-Raphaelite, London, Faber, 2011. Maria died in London, aged 71.

ZIMMERN, MARIA - SEE PETRIE, M.

ZINKEISEN, DORIS CLARE (1898-1991)

Painter / Designer / Decorative Sculptor. The elder daughter of Victor Zinkeisen and Claire Bolton Charles. Her younger sister, Anna (1902-76), also became an artist. Both girls were born in Scotland, Doris at Gareloch, Dumbartonshire. The girls were particularly close and occasionally worked together. Doris was raised in London and worked there. Both girls drew from an early age and attended a local art school. Both then won scholarships to the Royal Academy schools, at which point Anna was still only 15 years of age. Like Anna, Doris had a full and diverse career as an artist. She produced costume designs for the stage and theatre. For example, she designed costumes for Charles B. Cochrane's This Year of Grace at the London Pavilion. Four of the costumes were illustrated in The Studio, Vol.96, September 1928, p.194. Also produced costumes

for Cochrane's One Damn Thing After Another, and for Playfair's The Way of the World. Cochrane had already praised and illustrated Doris's work in 1927 in an article Stage Decoration and Fantasy in The Studio, Vol.94, December 1927, pp.392-398. In 1938 the same magazine illustrated her backcloth for Happy Returns along with her model set for The Taming of the Shrew (Vol.116, September 1938, pp.154-155). Other designs by her included a costume worn by Dorothy Gish in Nell Gwynne, designs for the Goya Ballet produced by Massine in Charles B. Cochrane's Bon Ton, and costumes for Caesar Borgia & Lucretia Borgia. In around 1938 her volume Designing for the Stage was published with illustrations, part of a How-To-Do-It series.

Zinkeisen was also an accomplished portrait, figure, flower and landscape painter in oils and watercolours. She exhibited her work regularly, including at the Society of Women Artists (1928-40), the Royal Scottish Academy (1927-37), the Royal Hibernian Academy (1930), the Royal Glasgow Institute (1932-36) and the Royal Academy (1918-40). Also exhibited at the Royal Institute of Oil Painters, the Royal Society of British Artists, at Heal's (with Anna), at the Fine Art Society, in Liverpool, at Wembley, at the Paris Salon, and with the Royal Society of Portrait Painters. Exhibited works included: Elsa Lanchester, Squadron-Leader Leslie, D.S.C., The Lass of Mile End and Miss Vivien St George in Costume. Doris was elected a Member of the Society of Women Artists (1940-49). Elected a Member of the Royal Institute of Oil Painters (1928). Her portrait of Anna Zinkeisen was hung on the line at the Royal Academy. In 1954 Doris held an exhibition of her work at the Fine Art Society, showing flower pieces, scenes of social life at the races, in cafes, dancers dressing and actors on stage. One of those, Dressing Room, was illustrated in The Studio, Vol.148, September 1954, p.94. It was there noted that one of her 'recent' commissions was the decor of the Noel Coward musical show After the Ball.

At least eight of Doris's works are in the Imperial War Museum collection, including Human Laundry, Belsen, April 1945, Welfare Work in a Services Hospital (1945) and Miss S.A.W. Wade, R.R.C., Principal Matron, 101 British General Hospital. Other portrait works were illustrated in The Studio, Vol.119, March 1940, pp.82 & 85. In 1934 Anna and Doris began a commission for decorating the Queen Mary for Cunard. Anna did the ballroom and Doris the verandah grill. Doris designed a frieze with theatrical and circus themes, part of which was illustrated in The Studio, Vol.111, March 1936, p.142. Doris and Anna also contributed to the Art Competitions of the 1948 London Summer Games. Like Anna, during the war, Doris joined the St John's Ambulance Brigade and enrolled as an auxiliary nurse. In 1927 Doris married a naval officer, Grahame Johnstone. They had a son and twin daughters.

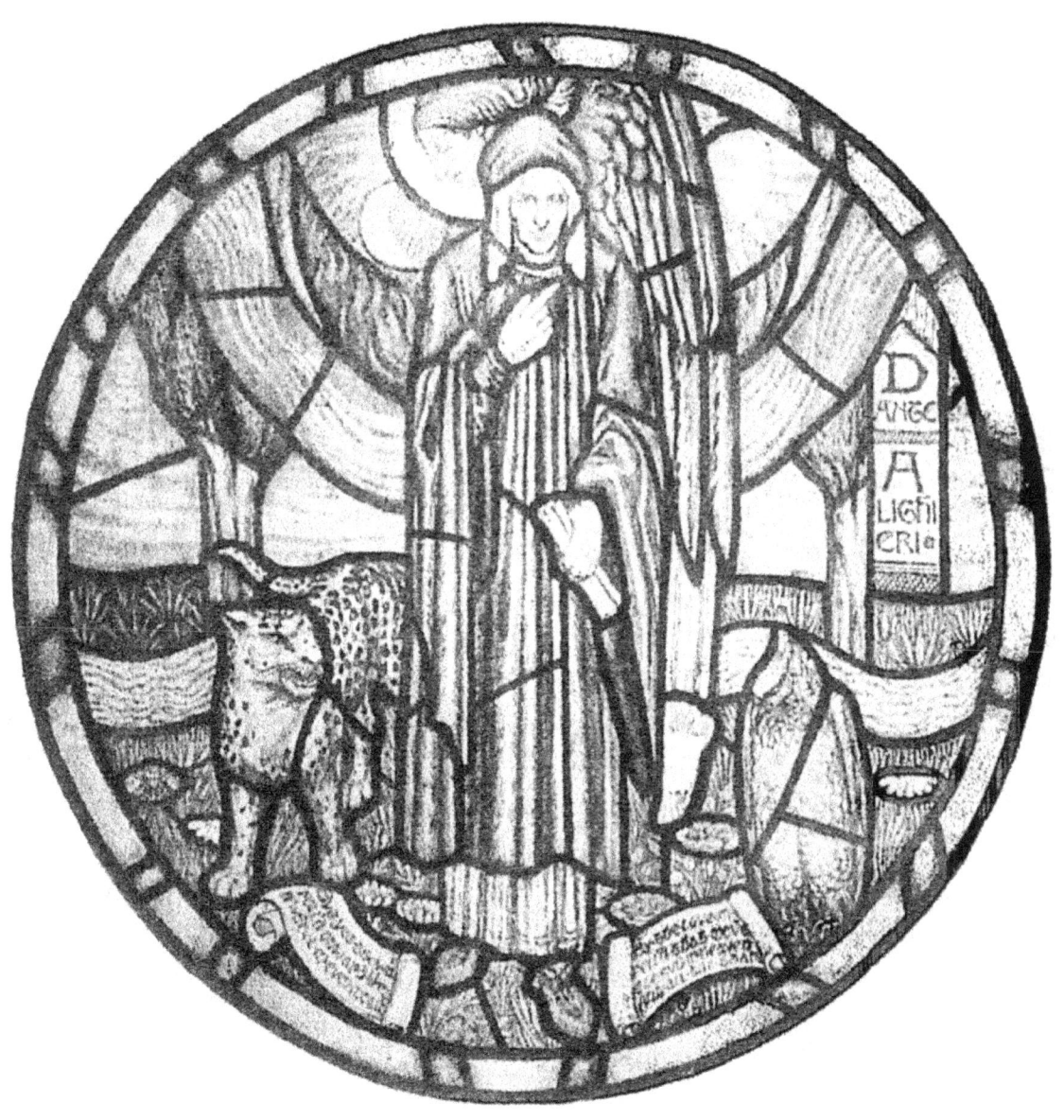

Cartoon for stained glass by Mabel Esplin

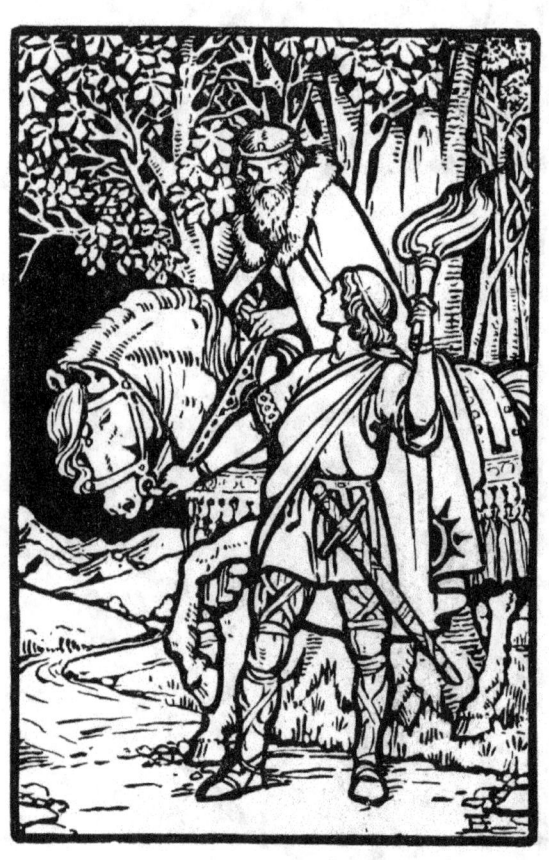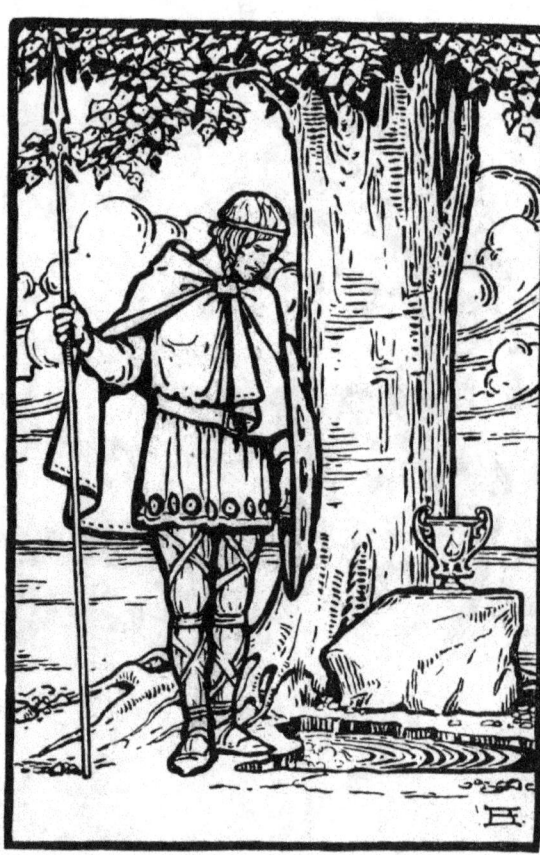

Illustrations by Beatrice Elvery (Glenavy) for Heroes of the Dawn (Maunsel & Co.)